EMPLOYEE COMPETITION

Covenants, Confidentiality, and Garden Leave

SECOND EDITION

EMPLOYEE COMPETITION

Covenants, Confidentiality, and
Garden Leave

SECOND EDITION

Edited By

PAUL GOULDING QC

UNIVERSITY PRESS

003154

OXFORD
UNIVERSITY PRESS

Great Clarendon Street, Oxford ox2 6DP

Oxford University Press is a department of the University of Oxford.
It furthers the University's objective of excellence in research, scholarship,
and education by publishing worldwide in

Oxford New York

Auckland Cape Town Dar es Salaam Hong Kong Karachi
Kuala Lumpur Madrid Melbourne Mexico City Nairobi
New Delhi Shanghai Taipei Toronto

With offices in

Argentina Austria Brazil Chile Czech Republic France Greece
Guatemala Hungary Italy Japan Poland Portugal Singapore
South Korea Switzerland Thailand Turkey Ukraine Vietnam

Oxford is a registered trade mark of Oxford University Press
in the UK and in certain other countries

Published in the United States
by Oxford University Press Inc., New York

British Library Cataloguing-in-Publication Data
Data available

Library of Congress Cataloging in Publication Data
Data available

Typeset by Glyph International, Bangalore, India

Printed in Great Britain on acid-free paper by
CPI Antony Rowe, Chippenham, Wiltshire

ISBN 978–0–19–958769–8

LIST OF CONTRIBUTORS

Editor

Paul Goulding QC
MA (Oxon), BCL (Oxon); Barrister, Blackstone Chambers

CONTRIBUTORS FROM BLACKSTONE CHAMBERS

Kieron Beal
MA (Cantab), LLM (Harvard)

Catherine Callaghan
BA, LLB (Victoria University of Wellington), LLM (Cantab)

Gerard Clarke
MA (Oxon)

Tom Croxford
MA (Cantab)

Nick De Marco
LLB (Lond)

Ivan Hare
LLB (Lond), BCL (Oxon), LLM (Harvard), MA (Cantab)

Robert Howe QC
MA (Cantab), BCL (Oxon)

Tristan Jones
MA (Cantab), MPA (Harvard)

Jane Mulcahy
BA (Lond)

Hanif Mussa
MA (Cantab)

Stephen Nathan QC
MA (Oxon)

Simon Pritchard
MChem (Oxon)

James Segan
BA (Oxon)

Diya Sen Gupta
MA (Cantab)

Mark Vinall
BA (Oxon)

Robert Weekes
MA (Cantab), LLM (NYU) (Fulbright scholar)

Sarah Wilkinson
MA, DPhil, BA (Oxon)

CONTRIBUTORS FROM OLSWANG

Dan Aherne
BA (Dunelm)

Luke Pardey
LLB (University of Technology, Sydney)

Sarah Sharma
LLB (Leic)

OTHER CONTRIBUTORS

Julian Parker
Stroz Friedberg Ltd

Aaron Stowell
Stroz Friedberg Ltd

Catherine Taylor
MA (Cantab)
(formerly a partner at Olswang)

FOREWORD

A simplistic consideration of the law of employee competition might suggest it can be understood by an analysis of the law of restraint of trade. That might have been true when the question in issue was whether a hairdresser could leave his or her salon and set up in competition on the other side of town. But these days the issues are likely to be much more sophisticated. Typically, a group of employees will together leave a high tech company and go as a team to work for a competitor, or set up on their own. How can the employer stop this? And how can they stop the employer stopping it?

As with most fields of human activity, the relevant legal principles cannot be analysed within the framework of a single legal category. The modern practitioner has to trespass into a range of legal fields, quite apart from the obvious starting point of contract. For example, the economic torts in particular are material where workers are induced to leave at the behest of a competitor; fiduciary obligations may arise where senior employees or directors take such a step; equitable principles relating to the protection of confidential information will come to the fore where the employer is in fear of losing business plans or formulae; and sometimes aspects of intellectual property may be relevant depending upon the nature of the information which employees may be hoping to take with them to use in the new set up.

In addition to these issues surrounding the substantive law, difficult questions may arise concerning the appropriate remedy and in particular, whether a claim for damages or a restitutionary claim exists in a particular context.

This book admirably analyses the relevant legal rules, but in addition, and of particular importance to the practitioner, it focuses on practical questions facing a prospective litigant: the importance of interlocutory relief; the nature of evidence required to maximise success; how to obtain freezing orders over assets; and where international disputes are concerned– and they are becoming increasingly common in a shrinking world – the proper forum for initiating proceedings.

One reason why this work provides such a valuable combination of scholarly and practical wisdom is that it combines the insights of specialist and highly expert barristers of Blackstone Chambers with the direct practical experience of solicitors at Olswang. These different perspectives are particularly valuable, for example, when dealing with the increasingly common problem, now given full consideration in this second edition, which arises when an employer suffers the loss of a team of employees who move en bloc to a rival or to set up in competition.

Another valuable dimension of this book is the draft documents, and in particular the model contractual terms. These are designed to assist a party to anticipate potential legal problems and to provide for them in advance, thereby avoiding costly and unnecessary litigation.

This second edition, like the first, is produced in user friendly form with flow charts and tables where appropriate. In addition, there is now a link to a Blackstone Chambers' website so that readers will be able to keep up with developments and not to have to wait with eager anticipation the third edition! The first edition of this book was a great success. I am confident that with each new edition it will grow in stature: a wise and scholarly work but providing solutions to everyday problems; valuable to academic and practitioner alike.

Sir Patrick Elias
Lord Justice of Appeal
Royal Courts of Justice
December 2010

PREFACE

Since the first edition of this book appeared four years ago, there has been a substantial number of important cases which have brought about significant developments in the law of employee competition.

One notable feature has been the increasing importance of the *international dimension* to litigation to enforce restrictive covenants and protect trade secrets. The challenges of cross-border litigation in this field are vividly illustrated by the cases of *Samengo-Turner v Marsh McLennan* in the Court of Appeal and *Duarte v Black & Decker* at first instance. The former case involved the interpretation of the Judgments Regulation on jurisdiction which gave rise to the grant of an anti-suit injunction to restrain New York proceedings on the ground that the employees had a right to be sued *only* in England as the place of their domicile, notwithstanding a New York exclusive jurisdiction clause. The latter case interpreted the Rome Convention on the law applicable to contractual obligations (since superseded by the Rome I Regulation) to the effect that English law of restraint of trade trumped Maryland law, despite this being the parties' chosen law, to determine the enforceability of a restrictive covenant in proceedings brought in England. This important trend is reflected in the creation of a new Chapter 7 in this second edition dedicated solely to the international dimension where these developments are examined in detail.

Shortly after the first edition of this book was published, the House of Lords re-fashioned the law of *economic torts* in the combined appeals under the name of *OBG v Allen*, one of which was *Mainstream Properties v Young*, an employee competition case. This decision brought about some much needed clarification of the law relating to inducement of breach of contract, an important element of claims against prospective employers who recruit employees from a competitor. This decision is explained at length in Chapter 2 on Duties.

Another area where employee duties have come under close scrutiny in recent years is in relation to *team moves*. Questions have arisen as to when employees are under a duty to disclose their knowledge of attempts to recruit them and their colleagues, whether springboard injunctions can be granted to deprive a competitor of an unfair headstart even when no misuse of confidential information is involved, and what disclosure orders can be obtained to discover the extent of a competitor's recruitment efforts (for example, *UBS v Vestra Wealth*, *Tullet Prebon v BGC*, *Vestergaard v Bestnet*, *Aon v JLT*). One contributor, at least, did his best to re-shape the nature and content of the *mutual duty of trust and confidence* in *RDF Media v Clements*, although whether that attempt has survived subsequent cases is open to question. These developments are discussed extensively in Chapters 2 (Duties), 9 (Pre-action Steps), and 10 (Injunctions).

As well as covering the major developments in law and practice in this field up to 1 October 2010, we have sought to maintain some of the distinctive approaches adopted in the first edition, such as the uniquely valuable checklists at the end of most chapters, and added novel features, such as the flow charts at the end of the International Dimension chapter and a new glossary of computer terms as part of Appendix 1 on Computer Forensic Investigations.

Speaking of teams, this edition has again been a collaborative effort between members of Blackstone Chambers (several of whom have appeared in a number of the recent leading cases), Olswang solicitors (who, as well as contributing substantively to key chapters, have meticulously updated checklists and shared their valuable know-how in the form of detailed sample clauses reproduced in the appendices), and Strotz Friedberg (formerly DGI Forensics, who have provided an updated guide to computer forensic investigations). I would also like to express my gratitude to those who contributed to the first edition but who due to other demands on their time have been unable to continue their involvement this time round, namely Kate Gallafent, Brian Kennelly, Tom de la Mare, Melanie Adams, Julia Palca, Paul Stevens, and Ed Wilding.

It can be difficult to keep abreast of the many cases and developments in this area. To assist in that effort, occasional papers from contributors, updating the contents of this book, will appear on the Blackstone Chambers website at http://www.blackstonechambers.com/practice_areas/employment.html.

The professionalism, efficiency and ongoing support of OUP has ensured the appearance of this expanded, second edition on time, and for that my special thanks go to Faye Judges, Briony Ryles, and also to Roxanne Selby whose idea this book was in the first place.

I am also very grateful to the Honourable Lord Justice Elias for writing a new Foreword to this second edition, who contributed so much to the law of employee competition when at the Bar, and who continues to do so from the Bench.

Paul Goulding QC
Blackstone Chambers
October 2010

CONTENTS

3. **Confidential Information and the Database Right**
Robert Howe QC, Diya Sen Gupta, Sarah Wilkinson,
Simon Pritchard, Dan Aherne, and Luke Pardey

Contents

10. Injunctions and Other Interm Remedies
Paul Goulding QC, Tom Croxford, Ivan Hare, Stephen Nathan QC, and Catherine Taylor

11. Damages and Other Remedies

Stephen Nathan QC and Catherine Taylor

APPENDICES

TABLE OF CASES

TABLE OF LEGISLATION

LIST OF ABBREVIATIONS

BHB	British Horseracing Board
CA 1998	Competition Act 1998
CAT	Competition Appeal Tribunal
CDPA 1988	Copyright Designs and Patents Act 1988
CJJA 1982	Civil Jurisdiction and Judgments Act 1982
CPA	Cameroon Postal Authority
CPR	Civil Procedure Rules
DPA 1998	Data Protection Act 1998
DTR5	chapter 5 of the Financial Services Authority's Disclosure and Transparency Rules
EA 2002	Enterprise Act 2002
EAT	Employment Appeal Tribunal
ECHR	European Convention on Human Rights
ECJ	European Court of Justice
ECtHR	European Court of Human Rights
ERA 1996	Employment Rights Act 1996
FAPL	Football Association Premier League
GCEU	General Court of the European Union
GMC	General Medical Council
HRA 1998	Human Rights Act 1998
LLP	limited liability partnership
LLPA 2000	Limited Liability Partnerships Act 2000
LTIP	Long-Term Incentive Plan
OFT	Office of Fair Trading
PIDA 1998	Public Interest Disclosure Act 1998
PPP	public private partnership
PTR	pre-trial review
TEU	Treaty on European Union
TFEU	Treaty on the Functioning of the European Union
TULR(C)A 1992	Trade Union and Labour Relations (Consolidation) Act 1992
TUPE	Transfer of Undertakings (Protection of Employment) Regulations 2006
UCTA 1977	Unfair Contract Terms Act 1977
VFM	value for money

1

INTRODUCTION

Paul Goulding QC and Ivan Hare

A. Aim

There has been a resurgence of employee competition disputes in recent years. These have presented lawyers with new challenges as well as engaging them in familiar battles. Clients are on the look-out for creative thinking, effective remedies, and workable solutions. On occasions, this is achieved through litigation; on others, by avoiding it. **1.01**

The new challenges have appeared in numerous guises. Some have a highly practical aspect, others a more legal content. Often, both are present. For example, take team moves. A desk of traders or brokers moves en masse from one bank to another. What are the legal issues involved? How can an employer discover what is going on? How can the team coordinate its move whilst acting lawfully? How can the new employer most effectively poach a team from a rival whilst limiting its exposure to injunctions and damages claims? **1.02**

New legal questions have recently come to the fore. When does an employee owe fiduciary duties? Is an employee or director under a duty to disclose his own misconduct? What is the impact of the Convention rights to privacy and freedom of expression on breach of confidence claims? How long can a period of garden leave be enforced? In what circumstances can an employer recover restitutionary or gain-based damages if he cannot prove actual loss from unlawful competition? **1.03**

Then there are the legal disciplines which appear on the margin of employee competition cases, unfamiliarity with which can unnerve the legal adviser. What about the international dimension? This is in play when, for example, a restrictive covenant in the contract of a US employee seconded to the United Kingdom is sought to be enforced throughout Europe. What is the proper law of the contract? In which forum should proceedings be commenced? How can an injunction be enforced in other jurisdictions? When are European and UK competition law principles relevant? Then there are the intellectual property issues which **1.04** sometimes rear their heads. Is there a claim to copyright or passing off or a trade mark infringement?

1.05   These legal questions need to be considered in the changed climate of court proceedings. The Civil Procedure Rules require parties to consider their pre-action steps carefully before rushing headlong into litigation. The ability of the court to fix speedy trials has also altered the legal landscape fundamentally. A trial can be fixed in a matter of weeks frequently rendering pointless a full-blown fight at the interim stage. Parties and their advisers are under a duty to examine alternative ways of resolving their disputes than through the courts, such as via mediation.

1.06   The scope of disputes about unlawful competition is not, of course, confined to employment. Restrictive covenants are often an essential element of an agreement between a vendor and a purchaser, whether of a business or shares in a company. Increasingly, partners leave one firm, and join another. This has been a notable feature affecting solicitors as the market for legal services has become more fluid. Does garden leave conflict with the rights of a partner? Is the enforceability of a restrictive covenant between partners to be tested as if it were akin to an employment, or to a vendor-purchaser, covenant, or by some different standard? Finally, what about joint venturers? If an investor funds a new business, does he have a legitimate interest which merits protection by an enforceable covenant? To this extent, the title of the book is inadequate since its scope is beyond competition concerning employees alone. Economy of words dictated the title, but wherever the phrase 'employee competition' is used below, it should be taken to encompass competition in these other spheres too, including vendor-purchaser, partnership, and other commercial arrangements.

1.07   The aim of this book is to cover the whole of this new terrain; to examine the legal issues in detail; and to provide practical guidance. For this reason, most chapters conclude with a checklist of points which we hope will be valuable for the hard-pressed adviser when there is not time for an in-depth analysis of the law. Likewise, the appendices contain advice on forensic investigations, drafting of covenants, sample clauses and court documentation, as well as other relevant materials.

1.08   It is undoubtedly the case that new issues will emerge in this field in the coming years, which will require treatment in future editions of this work. Pending the next edition, there is a companion website where a link may be found to occasional papers from the authors of this book relating to or updating the material which is found here. The website address is http://www.blackstonechambers.com/practice_areas/employment.html.

B. Structure of the book

1.09   The book consists of four parts: substantive law, pre-action steps, remedies, and the appendices.

Substantive law (Chapters 1 to 8)

1.10   Chapters 1 to 8 examine in detail the substantive law relevant to employee competition. This begins with a brief section on the doctrine of restraint of trade with which this chapter concludes. This doctrine underpins the whole of the book since it embodies the public policy considerations of freedom to work and freedom to contract which, whilst often in tension with one another, come into play when the court reaches decisions in individual cases.

Chapter 2 explores the duties owed by employees, directors, and others which are relevant to   **1.11**
unlawful competition. These duties are founded in contract, equity, and statute. The latter is
of recent importance in view of the codification of a director's duties in the Companies Act
2006. The central duty of good faith and fidelity is considered both as a fiduciary and a
contractual duty, and recent case law on the duty to disclose misconduct, as one incident of
this duty, is discussed. One particular manifestation of breach of this duty—diverting maturing
business opportunities—is examined in detail. The liability of third parties, such as the new
employer, for unlawful competition is considered in a section on the economic torts, a subject
of recent detailed examination by the Court of Appeal and House of Lords. Finally, there is
a separate section on team moves, looking at the legal and practical implications of a group
departure to a rival employer.

Chapter 3 deals with confidential information and the database right. The elements of the   **1.12**
duty of confidence are described and the impact of the Human Rights Act 1998 in this area
is explained. The difficult question of 'what is confidential information?' is discussed, with
particular reference to the role of express confidentiality clauses. The defences to, and remedies
for, a claim of breach of confidence are explained in detail. The little-known database right is
also explained, which is a valuable addition to an employer's armoury in situations where an
employee has removed part of a database, such as a client list. A claim for database right
infringement has certain advantages over common law confidential information claims
which are highlighted.

Garden leave is the subject of Chapter 4. This notion has become well established on the   **1.13**
battleground of employee competition yet is still of comparatively recent origin. This chapter
explores the emergence of garden leave against the background of the rule against specific
performance of contracts of personal service, which still has an important role to play (especially
in cases involving celebrities in the sports and entertainment worlds). The circumstances in
which a right to work arises, and the corresponding importance of garden leave clauses, is
then discussed. There are, broadly speaking, two ways in which an employee may be subjected to garden leave, namely through its imposition by an employer and through its
enforcement by the court. Both aspects are considered, in the course of which issues such as
the appropriate length of garden leave, and the parties' respective rights during the garden
leave period are explained.

Central to any book on employee competition is the enforceability of restrictive covenants.   **1.14**
This topic, which is tackled in Chapter 5, has had a new lease of life recently due, in part, to
the appearance of new forms of restrictive covenant (such as those found in employee benefit
arrangements) and recent case law. A seven-stage approach is adopted covering incorporating
and changing covenants, the nature of a restraint, repudiation, construction, legitimate
interests, reasonableness (including severance), and discretion. The subject of repudiation,
in particular, receives extensive treatment in the light of recent Court of Appeal dicta suggesting that *General Billposting v Atkinson* may no longer be good law. Particular difficulties
relating to covenants in the context of a TUPE transfer are also discussed.

Chapter 6 looks beyond the employment relationship to issues of unlawful competition in   **1.15**
other fields. This includes restrictions entered into between vendors and purchasers (such as
on the sale of a business or shares), between partners pursuant to a partnership or limited
liability partnership (LLP) agreement, and between business partners (for example as part of
a joint venture or shareholder agreement).

1.16   Chapter 7 is an entirely new chapter for the second edition of this work, and addresses the international dimension of employee competition. The creation of a stand-alone chapter dedicated to this topic reflects its increasing importance at the present time. The issues covered in this chapter include jurisdiction (where to sue), applicable law (what law governs the issues), and enforcement of judgments obtained overseas. The chapter discusses in detail important European measures including the Judgments Regulation and the Rome I and II Regulations, as well as important recent decisions such as *Samengo-Turner v Marsh & McLennan*[1] and *Duarte v Black & Decker*.[2]

1.17   Finally in this section, Chapter 8 provides an introduction to a number of related concepts, which arise from time to time in the context of employee competition disputes. These include competition law which inhabits some of the same ground as restraint of trade, and a basic understanding of which is useful and is provided here; sports cases, which have thrown up particular problems with regard to competition issues involving sportspeople, officials, and governing bodies; human rights concepts and institutions are explained; and, finally, an overview of intellectual property rights is provided, with an introduction to copyright, inventions and patents, registered trade marks, and passing off.

Pre-action steps (Chapter 9)

1.18   Bridging the sections on substantive law and remedies is Chapter 9, which provides a practical discussion of the pre-action steps which might prove useful and should always be considered. This chapter is written in three sections: from the perspective of the claimant employer, the defendant employee, and the defendant employer respectively. It explains the many tactical considerations that can have such a bearing on the outcome of disputes, and suggests steps that can and should be taken to maximize the chances of a successful outcome both through the courts and through negotiation. A further discussion of team moves, with the focus on the practical steps that might be taken to advance and to resist such moves, is also included.

Remedies (Chapters 10 to 12)

1.19   The final three chapters provide a comprehensive examination of the range of remedies available in employee competition cases.

1.20   Chapter 10 covers the remedy most frequently sought, namely interim injunctions. It explains the different types of injunction—prohibitory, springboard, and mandatory—and looks at the test applied by the courts in deciding whether to grant an interim injunction (*American Cyanamid* and its later refinements). The important requirement of an undertaking in damages is considered here, including which parties can benefit from it, when security may be necessary, and how damages are assessed when the undertaking is enforced. Other interim remedies are often sought in addition to, or in place of, more conventional interim injunctions, such as search, delivery up, disclosure, *Norwich Pharmacal* and freezing orders, and the relatively new remedy of an interim declaration. These are all discussed.

1.21   The increasingly important topic of damages is the focus of Chapter 11, together with other remedies. The principles of compensatory damages are explained, and the recent ground-breaking judicial recognition of the availability of restitutionary or gain-based damages for

---

[1]   [2008] ICR 18, CA.
[2]   [2007] EWHC 2720 (QB).

breach of contract is examined. The nature of an account of profits and equitable damages are discussed, in addition to more obscure yet important subjects such as exemplary damages, liquidated damages, and tracing as well as other remedies.

Finally, Chapter 12 provides an essential procedural guide to commencing and conducting   **1.22** High Court employee competition litigation. This will be of value to those less experienced in this arena, with an explanation of the rules on statements of case, making an application, disclosure, evidence, trial, judgments and orders, appeals, costs, and mediation and settlement. It will also be of use to the more experienced High Court litigator, for example in its detailed discussion of pre-action and third party disclosure, and the nature and form of Tomlin orders.

Appendices

The last section of the book consists of twelve appendices, which are designed to provide   **1.23** practical guidance and precedents for use in advising clients and conducting litigation.

Of particular and novel interest, Appendix 1 contains a guide to forensic investigations   **1.24** which can be an invaluable weapon in unearthing evidence of unlawful competition. This is written by a specialist in the field, with a great deal of experience in the conduct of such investigations. It is especially useful for those with only a rudimentary understanding of the world of technology, and contains helpful guidance on what can be done, as well as what should not be done, in order to retrieve and preserve evidence.

Appendix 6 contains a note of practical guidance on drafting restrictive covenants. This   **1.25** could have formed part of Chapter 5 but has been kept separate to enable easy reference, particularly for those involved in drafting such clauses.

Appendix 12 contains a table summarizing the leading employee competition cases. These   **1.26** are all discussed elsewhere in the book. The purpose of the table is to provide a resource which can be easily and quickly consulted in order to provide a feel for the sorts of periods for which restrictions are enforced by the courts in various contexts.

The remaining appendices contain sample materials of one form or another. These include   **1.27** sample employee duties, confidential information, and garden leave clauses and restrictive covenants (Appendices 2, 3, 4, 7, and 8), sample pre-action letters (Appendix 9), and sample pleadings and other documentation for court applications (Appendices 10 and 11). These are all produced subject to the usual but important health warning. They contain *sample* documentation. Their purpose is to provide ideas as to what might be useful. They should not be copied wholesale or without regard to the facts and circumstances of the individual case. But they will, hopefully, prove to be a useful resource.

C. Restraint of trade

Public policy

The doctrine of restraint of trade is one of a number of legal tools for giving effect to judicial   **1.28** perceptions of public policy. The doctrine is therefore part of the broader legislative and common law scheme which limits freedom of contract in order to prevent parties from enforcing agreements to achieve certain illegal ends (such as contracts to commit or conceal criminal offences, to sell public offices, or to interfere with the course of justice) or which contain terms which are considered unfair or unconscionable.[3]

1.29 The particular public policy which motivates the law on restraint of trade was defined in the following terms by Lord Macnaghten in *Nordenfelt v Maxim Nordenfelt Guns and Ammunition Co*:

> The public have an interest in every person's carrying on his trade freely: so has the individual. Interference with individual liberty of action in trading, and all restraints of trade of themselves, if there is nothing more, are contrary to public policy, and therefore void.[4]

1.30 In other words, the law seeks to give effect to two distinct interests: the autonomy interests of the individual employee to engage in economic activity of his own choosing and that of the public in general that the unit of production represented by the worker's efforts should be permitted to make a contribution to society.[5] However, set against this is the traditional judicial attachment to freedom of contract which seeks to uphold bargains freely entered into.

> As long as the restraint to which he subjects himself is no wider than is required for the adequate protection of the person in whose favour it is created, it is in his interests to be able to bind himself for the sake of the indirect advantages [such as employment or training under competent employers] he may obtain by so doing.[6]

1.31 When the doctrine was originally formulated in the Elizabethan era, all restraints of trade were considered contrary to public policy.[7] Gradually, this doctrine was relaxed so that partial restraints (as opposed to those extending throughout the country) might be enforceable.[8] The modern law operates as a common law presumption of unenforceability, save to the extent that the covenant is found to be reasonable.

1.32 Some commentators have described restraint of trade as the counter-point to the employee's obligations of fidelity to his employer which is more usually labelled the duty of trust and confidence. Among other things, the employee's duty of trust and confidence prevents him from improperly competing with his employer's business by, for example, working for a competitor in his spare time.[9] Thus the duty of trust and confidence requires the employee in some ways to identify his own goals with the economic aims of his employer whereas the

---

[3] *Chitty on Contracts* (30th edn, 2008), ch 16. The most comprehensive work on the subject is JD Heydon, *The Restraint of Trade Doctrine* (3rd edn, 2009). It is important to distinguish restraint of trade from the equitable doctrines which govern unfair or unconscionable bargains and which require the court to be satisfied that the defendant has behaved in a morally reprehensible way (*Panayiotou v Sony Music Entertainment (UK) Ltd* [1994] EMLR 229, 316–18 *per* Parker J).

[4] [1894] AC 535, HL, 565. In the *Nordenfelt* case itself, the House of Lords was prepared to enforce by injunction a covenant not to engage in the manufacture of guns or ammunitions for a period of twenty-five years. Given the nature of the business and the fact that customers were limited to domestic and foreign governments, it was not considered unreasonable for the purchaser of Mr Nordenfelt's patents and business to enforce the restriction.

[5] Simon Brown LJ referred to the latter as 'the public interest in competition and proper use of an employee's skills' in *J A Mont (UK) Ltd v Mills* [1993] ILR 172, CA.

[6] *Herbert Morris Ltd v Saxelby* [1916] 1 AC 688, HL, 707 *per* Lord Parker of Waddington. Lord Pearce referred to the distinction between restrictions which are 'directed towards the absorption of the parties' services and not their sterilization' in *Esso Petroleum Co Ltd v Harper's Garage (Stourport) Ltd* [1968] AC 269, HL, 328.

[7] *Colgate v Bacheler* Cro Eliz 872, 78 ER 1097, KB. Lord Hodson traced the doctrine back to Magna Carta in *Esso v Harper's*, n 6 above, 317.

[8] *Mitchel v Reynolds* (1711) 1 P Wms 181, 24 ER 347, Ch.

[9] *Hivac v Park Royal Scientific Instruments* [1946] Ch 169, CA. See further, D Brodie, *The Employment Contract: Legal Principles, Drafting, and Interpretation* (2nd edn, 2005), ch 7.

doctrine of restraint of trade vindicates the employee's right to assert his own distinct interests and engage in legitimate competition with his employer's business.[10] In reality, the contrast is not as neat as this suggests since the interests of both parties are being balanced within the doctrine of restraint of trade and in defining the mutual obligation of trust and confidence.[11] For example, it has been held that the duty of trust and confidence requires that 'each party must have regard to the interests of the other, but not that either must subjugate his interests to those of the other'.[12]

A further element of policy is the relationship between common law concepts of restraint of trade and domestic and European competition law. This relationship is discussed further at paragraphs 8.06 to 8.73 below. **1.33**

Defining the doctrine

As with all areas where the law is underpinned by public policy and subject to a test of reasonableness, there is substantial scope for uncertainty in the application of the doctrine. This uncertainty is exacerbated by the fact that the underlying public policy is likely to change over time.[13] Indeed, some judges have been reluctant to define the dividing line between contracts which are in restraint of trade and those which merely regulate the normal commercial relations between the parties and are therefore enforceable, preferring to rely on 'a broad and flexible rule of reason'.[14] Perhaps the most frequently cited definition is that provided by Lord Denning MR in *Petrofina (Great Britain) Ltd v Martin*: **1.34**

> Every member of the community is entitled to carry on any trade or business he chooses and in such manner as he thinks most desirable in his own interests, so long as he does nothing unlawful: with the consequence that any contract which interferes with the free exercise of his trade or business, by restricting him in the work he may do for others, or the arrangements which he may make with others, is a contract in restraint of trade. It is invalid unless it is reasonable as between the parties and not injurious to the public interest.[15]

Applying the doctrine

Once it is established that the doctrine applies, the test is a three-stage one: first, does the restraint protect a legitimate interest of the party protected; secondly, is it reasonable between the parties; and, thirdly, is it contrary to the public interest?[16] The burden is on the proponent of the restraint to demonstrate that it is in the interests of the parties, but on the party challenging it to show that it is contrary to the public interest.[17] **1.35**

In the context of employment, three interests have most frequently been recognized as legitimate: the protection of trade connections; the preservation of trade secrets and confidential information; and maintaining the stability of the workforce. However, the categories of **1.36**

---

[10] See MR Freedland, *The Personal Employment Contract* (2003), 171–86.
[11] Freedland, n 10 above, 172. As Freedland also points out, the legal techniques involved in implying obligations into contracts are very different from those which control the express terms within them.
[12] *Nottingham University v Fishel* [2000] ICR 1462, 1493C *per* Elias J; [2000] IRLR 471, 483.
[13] *Panayiotou v Sony*, n 3 above, 320.
[14] *Esso v Harper's*, n 6 above, 331 *per* Lord Wilberforce, 298 *per* Lord Reid, and 324 *per* Lord Pearce.
[15] [1966] Ch 146, CA, 169.
[16] *Esso v Harper's*, n 6 above, 300–1 *per* Lord Reid.
[17] *Herbert Morris v Saxelby*, n 6 above, 700 and 707–8 *per* Lord Parker.

legitimate interest that may be protected by reasonable restraints are not closed.[18] It is clearly established that the desire to restrict competition is in itself illegitimate.

1.37   Reasonableness is one of the most common concepts in legal analysis, but its meaning is heavily dependent on context. In some areas, it permits the employer or other decision-maker to enforce their decisions so long as they fall within a broad range of reasonable responses. In other areas, the judges get closer to substituting their own view of appropriate balance between the competing interests. The court is likely to take into account a number of factors, including the bargaining position of the parties, whether the contract was in standard form, whether the restraint exceeds the terms of the contract and the surrounding circumstances.[19]

1.38   The judges have offered some general guidance as to how the task should be approached. First, all aspects of the covenant should be analyzed to decide the full extent of the restriction. In the course of this enquiry, the court may well ask itself whether a covenant of narrower scope would have been sufficient to protect the employer's legitimate interests. The court will also not enforce a covenant which does not in fact offer any protection to the employer since if the covenant is not affording any benefit to the employer, its only effect is to restrain the employee. Both of these principles are illustrated by *Office Angels Ltd v Rainer-Thomas,* [20] in which an area restriction was held to be unjustified since a more limited non-solicitation or non-dealing clause would have offered adequate protection. The area restriction was also found to be inappropriate because most of the business' clients placed their orders by telephone and the location of the clients' offices was therefore irrelevant.

1.39   It is equally clear that the court will take account of the consideration for the promise, although it will not generally assess its adequacy.[21] This latter principle serves the pragmatic end that the court is not in a position to know which part of the overall consideration relates to the restraint in cases where the restriction is contained in the contract of employment which also includes a series of other employee obligations for which he may expect to be remunerated. However, there is also a more principled justification: since the law is, at least in part, concerned with vindicating the public interest, employers ought not to be able to purchase more protection than is reasonably necessary.[22]

1.40   The courts have also reiterated that they are concerned with the reasonableness of the restriction and do not wish to be drawn into an assessment of its proportionality as this might lead them down the road to examining the costs and benefits to the parties. In *Allied Dunbar (Frank Weisinger) Ltd v Weisinger,*[23] Millett J expressed the view that a focus on proportionality could too easily lead to the court assessing the adequacy of the consideration. However, judges have become more familiar with the concept of proportionality and have acknowledged its advantages over the less precise and sophisticated test of reasonableness in

---

[18] *Dawnay, Day & Co Ltd v D'Alphen* [1998] ICR 1068, CA, 1107–8 *per* Evans LJ.

[19] *Panayiotou v Sony*, n 3 above, 330–6.

[20] [1991] IRLR 214, CA.

[21] *Esso v Harper's*, n 6 above, 323 *per* Lord Pearce.

[22] *J A Mont v Mills*, n 5 above.

[23] [1988] IRLR 60. The *Weisinger* case should be treated with some caution because it did not concern the enforceability of the covenants against an ex-employee, but against the vendor of his business as a self-employed salesman of financial services and products.

the field of public law.[24] As such, it is likely that proportionality will have a broader role to play in assessing restraints of trade that the *Weisinger* case would suggest.

The temporal extent of the doctrine

Although frequently relied upon after the termination of an employment contract, the **1.41** doctrine of restraint of trade is not so confined. For example, in *Watson v Prager*,[25] the court held that the agreement entered into between the boxer Michael Watson and his manager Mickey Duff was subject to judicial supervision before termination. The agreement was held to differ from commonplace commercial contracts and hence to be subject to the requirement of reasonableness for two reasons. First, the parties were prevented by the British Boxing Board of Control from freely negotiating their own terms. Secondly, the agreement contained an inherent conflict between the defendant's duties as a manager to arrange a proper programme for his boxer and negotiate favourable terms for him, on the one hand, and Mr Duff's own financial interests as a promoter which might incline him to reduce the fighter's share of the purse (thereby increasing his own share), on the other. The contract failed the test of reasonableness because the manager was entitled to impose conditions on the boxer (including the share of the purse) unilaterally and because it contained an option for the manager to renew the contract for three years which was considered too long and therefore in restraint of trade.

Restraint of trade also applies to periods of garden leave. These are periods where the contract **1.42** remains in force, but where the employee is no longer actively working for the employer. During periods of garden leave, the employee is therefore prevented from working for another employer, but also from working for his own employer. This situation naturally gives rise to concerns about restraint of trade.[26] Courts have therefore recognized that there may be circumstances in which garden leave clauses are inserted in an attempt to circumvent the law on restraint of trade and that the courts may have to control their enforcement:

> [Garden leave] is a weapon in the hands of the employers to ensure that an ambitious and able executive will not give notice if he is going to be unable to work at all for anyone for a long period of notice. Any executive who gives notice and leaves his employment is very likely to take fresh employment with someone in the same line of business not through any desire to act unfairly or to cheat the former employer but to get the best advantage of his own personal expertise.[27]

If the garden leave clause is enforceable, the question arises whether the employer is entitled **1.43** to enforce all the restrictions which apply during the period of the contract of employment or only the more limited set which apply post-termination. The Court of Appeal has indicated that it is the former in *Symbian Ltd v Christensen*.[28] In this case, a clause prohibiting the

---

[24] *De Smith's Judicial Review* (6th edn, 2007), 11-077–085.
[25] [1991] 1 WLR 726.
[26] In cases where there is no contractual right to impose a period of garden leave, it may be found to be a repudiatory breach to do so thereby releasing the employee from the effect of the restraint (*William Hill Organisation Ltd v Tucker* [1999] ICR 291, CA). The circumstances are likely to arise where an employee requires continued performance or exposure to the market to maintain his skills.
[27] *Provident Financial Group v Hayward* [1989] IRLR 84, CA, 86 *per* Dillon LJ. In this case, Dillon LJ also stated that a garden leave clause would not be enforced by injunction where it prohibited an employee from working in a business which had nothing to do with that of his employer.
[28] [2001] IRLR 77, CA.

employee from taking any other employment 'during the term of this agreement' was fully applicable and could be enforced by means of an injunction to restrain the employee from working for a particular competitor during his period of garden leave. Although not directly addressed by the Court, the granting of injunctive relief on these facts suggests a distinction between the non-availability of such relief where it would compel the employee to work for the employer and its availability to police a period of enforced idleness.

1.44 Generally, the courts' approach to restraints of trade during the currency of the employment relationship is more flexible than that applied to post-termination restrictions. Whereas post-termination restrictions are either upheld or not, the courts have, for example, been prepared to grant an injunction for less than the full period of garden leave if the full period is considered to be unreasonable.[29] It may be that this more flexible approach is one which will eventually have an impact on post-termination restrictions too.

Conclusion

1.45 From this introduction to the law on restraint of trade, it is clear that this is an area of developing doctrine and one in which the courts are confronted with competing arguments of policy on a daily basis. The remainder of this book addresses how these conflicts are addressed in practice.

---

[29] *GFI Group Inc v Eaglestone* [1994] IRLR 119. See further, paras 4.55–4.59 and 4.221–4.223 below.

2

DUTIES

Tom Croxford, James Segan, Mark Vinall, Dan Aherne, and Luke Pardey

A. Sources of duties[1]

The duties to which an employee or director is subject are many and various. The sources **2.01** reflect the divisions between the courts of common law and equity and their later overlay by statutory obligations imposed to fill gaps or reflect changing social mores.

The common law imposed obligations on 'servants' that reflected their contradistinction to **2.02** their 'masters'. In contrast, equity imposed obligations on trustees, fiduciaries, agents, and others who were entrusted with property in certain categories of relationships. These, more onerous, duties reflected in part the social expectations of those judging the cases. Lord Atkin's hypothetical butler and cook[2] play an important part in defining the scope of the duties owed by a mere employee. The duties of such an employee are defined by explicit reference to the expectations of a master in relation to those servants.

The difficulty of distinguishing between the duties owed by fiduciaries and those owed **2.03** by mere employees has been a theme of recent decades, as the distinction between those

---

[1] See also Appendix 2, Sample Employee Duties Clauses below.
[2] *Bell v Lever Bros* [1932] AC 161, HL, 228.

who direct and those whose work has become less stark. The office of director of a company is one that no longer correlates precisely with the formerly rigid division between management and labour. Indeed, the title of director (as opposed to the office) is now given to vast numbers of people in many companies without regard to the special obligations owed by those appointed to such a position pursuant to statute.

2.04 At present, the statutory duties owed by employees are very limited indeed and mainly beyond the scope of this book. Those owed by directors are, however, now codified in the Companies Act 2006, the relevant provisions of which are considered in detail below. This chapter considers the three principal sources of duties—contract, equity, and statute—in turn.

Contract

Express

2.05 Appendix 2 to this book contains a sample outline of the express terms of an executive contract. Plainly, each such contract needs to be tailored to the employer and employee to ensure that it properly reflects their respective needs.

2.06 Employees are entitled to receive a written statement of particulars of employment.[3] Those written particulars must contain, amongst other matters, the bulk of the employee's entitlements to such matters as pay, holiday, notice, and working time. However, there is no need to provide any identification of the employee's duties, save in so far as that amounts to the flip side of the employee's entitlements, for example working time. There must be at least an identification of job title or a description of the role.[4]

2.07 Most employers in fact provide a written contract by way of compliance with the obligation to provide written particulars. Typically, that contract will define the principal duties owed by an employee, often by way of identification of functions and by partial restatement of the common law obligations. In particular, employment contracts tend to restate and identify the extent of duties of loyalty and the prohibition on the employee of undertaking work for competing employers.[5]

2.08 If the employer fails to provide written particulars of employment or a written contract of employment, that will not affect the employment status of the employee. A purely oral contract of employment is no less enforceable than a written contract of employment, despite breach of the Employment Rights Act 1996 (ERA 1996).[6]

2.09 The test of whether and when a contract of employment arises is the subject of normal contractual principles: offer, acceptance, and consideration. This point is not always at the forefront of the minds of the human resources professionals responsible for putting in place the contract of employment. Put at its most basic:

(1) The employer's offer must amount to an expression of willingness to contract on specific and identified terms (albeit that some of those terms may be identified by reference to an

---

[3] Employment Rights Act 1996 (ERA 1996), s 1(1).
[4] ibid s 1(4)(f).
[5] This is the approach taken in the draft at Appendix 2 below. We consider this to be good practice and effective, albeit that it should be noted that an unduly narrow formulation of these contractual duties can risk circumscribing the extent of any fiduciary obligations.
[6] ERA 1996, s 1.

extraneous document such as an employee handbook). That offer must be made with the intention that it will become binding as soon as it is accepted.

(2) Acceptance occurs when the employee unequivocally agrees to the full content of the offer prior to the offer being withdrawn. Such an acceptance of a written document is often by way of signature but need not be. In some cases, it may be seen to have occurred where the conduct of the employee is consistent only with such unequivocal agreement.

(3) Offer and acceptance are viewed objectively, without regard to the subjective views of the participants as to their own intentions. Thus, an employee who decides to start work but not to sign the contract in the hope that he will not be bound by the parts he does not like, is judged by his objectively viewed conduct in commencing work without protest pursuant to a written agreement, rather than his subjective but unstated hope of being bound by only part of that agreement.

(4) There must be consideration for the agreement unless the agreement is made by deed.[7] That is to say, there must be something of value (in the eyes of the law) given in return for the promise. In employment terms, the consideration is usually the employee offering to work and the employer offering to pay money.

In practice, most contracts of employment will arise prior to the employee's commence- **2.10**
ment of employment on acceptance of the offer. However, problems may arise where the contract of employment is not signed, as is sometimes the case, until on or after commencement. There may, in some circumstances, be held to be an offer subject to contract where there is an expectation that the contract will be formally recorded in writing at commencement. The alternative construction may be that there has been an offer and acceptance incorporating the employer's (unseen) standard terms.[8] Lastly, there may be a consensual variation of the original contract, the consideration for that being the employee continuing to work and the employer continuing to employ.

Far greater difficulty is caused where the written terms are provided after commencement **2.11**
but never signed: how does the employer later prove incorporation of terms? The question of whether the written terms form part of the contract may be critical to the interests of both parties in such circumstances. By way of example, restrictive covenants are rarely contained within the initial offer letter, but are more likely to be contained in the long form contract or employee handbook. In an extreme case, the purported variation may be so far-reaching as to amount in law to the termination of one contract of employment and the commencement of a new one, with concomitant consequences for the availability or otherwise of statutory and other remedies.[9]

---

[7] A restrictive covenant, however, even if contained in a deed, must be supported by consideration, albeit not necessarily evidenced within the deed: *Mitchel v Reynolds* (1711) 1 P Wms 181; *Davis v Mason* 5 TR 118; *Gravely v Barnard* (1874) 18 LR Eq 518.

[8] Incorporation of terms by express reference is commonplace, particularly in relation to terms set out in employee handbooks. If the contract is signed, those terms will be incorporated, but may, in relation to some of the terms, be subjected to the requirement of reasonableness under the Unfair Contract Terms Act 1977: *Brigden v American Express Bank Ltd* [2000] IRLR 94, but cf *Commerzbank AG v Keen* [2007] ICR 623, [2007] IRLR 132, CA. If the contract is not signed, the terms will only be incorporated if reasonable notice of them has been given by clear words of reference and the terms are not unduly onerous or unusual: *Circle Freight International v Mid East Gulf Exports* [1988] 2 Lloyd's Rep 427.

[9] See *Cumbria County Council v Ms E Dow and Others (No 2)* [2008] IRLR 109, EAT, in which the contractual question whether a new contract had been formed was determinative of a limitation issue for the purposes of equal pay claims.

2.12   Generally, a court will find that an employee commences work pursuant to a contract of employment, regardless of the state of the paperwork at that time. In that sense, a contract of employment is fully formed by the time of commencement of employment.

2.13   Thus, unless that contract contained, by implication or express reference, the terms provided on or after commencement, those terms will not be incorporated unless there can be shown to have been a variation of the contract.

2.14   Such a variation requires both acceptance by the employee and valuable consideration (in the sense set out above). Without a signature, proving acceptance may not be a straightforward matter, even in respect of a regularly amended document such as an employee handbook.[10] As importantly, it may be hard for the employer to show that there was consideration for the variation because the employee is already working for the employer under a fully formed contract.

2.15   As such, the employer will seek to prove that the contractual terms have been accepted by conduct. In accordance with the normal contractual principles set out above, the variation contained within the written terms can only be accepted by conduct if the conduct is, viewed objectively, intended to amount to acceptance of that variation. The key difficulty in showing such acceptance will normally be that the principal terms of concern to the employee, such as salary and working hours, will have been agreed prior to the employment commencing. The terms introduced by the lengthy written agreement are likely to be ones that the employee receives no immediate benefit from and which have no immediate practical effect on his work. In such circumstances, his silence whilst continuing to work is likely to be equivocal at best and thus insufficient to amount to acceptance. However, if there are any terms contained within the full written terms which have had a practical effect on the employee, perhaps in relation to holiday entitlement or hours of work, such an acceptance may more readily be inferred from his use of that holiday entitlement or his working to those hours.

2.16   Thus, if all of the core terms of the contract are contained in the offer letter and the written terms contain little new apart from negative or contingent obligations, the mere fact that the employee continued to work after having been given a copy of the terms may be insufficient because he may continue to work in compliance with the unvaried contract of employment rather than the newly provided terms.[11]

2.17   This analysis, whilst in accordance with strict contractual theory, has not always been followed to its logical conclusion by the courts. Indeed, in the case of *Credit Suisse v Armstrong*,[12] the Court of Appeal accepted at an interim stage that it was arguable that senior executives had accepted a variation of their contract by conduct by doing no more than acknowledging in writing receipt of a staff handbook containing revised terms. The receipt stated that if the defendants did not complain within a month they would be taken to have accepted the terms as revised. None of them made any such complaint.

---

[10] See, by way of example, *SG & R Valuation Service Co v Boudrais and Others* [2008] IRLR 770, paras 16 and 17, in which Cranston J doubted that the express incorporation into a contract of employment of an employee manual could 'be read as incorporating the manual as it exists from time to time', and in any event found that there was a requirement for signature of the amended version on the facts of that case.

[11] See, in a different context, *Jayaar Impex Ltd v Toaken Group Ltd* [1996] 2 Lloyd's Rep 437.

[12] [1996] ICR 882, CA.

It seems to have been important to the court in that case that the defendants were 'men of **2.18** experience and sophistication who are used to looking at complex documents'.[13] Indeed, this is the only apparent reason for the court's decision.

The court made reference to *Jones v Associated Tunnelling Co Ltd*[14] and *Re Leyland Daf*[15] in **2.19** support of the proposition that silence or inaction was insufficient to amount to acceptance. It also had cited to it *Aparau v Iceland Frozen Foods plc*[16] but made no reference to that case in its judgment. In each of those cases, the contract was held not to have been effectively varied, it being too much to expect an employee in such circumstances to consider the detail and forcefully object.

Further, as was stated in *Solectron v Roper*:[17] **2.20**

> . . . where the employer purports unilaterally to change terms of the contract which do not immediately impinge on the employee at all—and changes in redundancy terms will be an example because they do not impinge until an employee is in fact made redundant—then the fact that the employee continues to work knowing that the employer is asserting that that is the term for compensation on redundancies, does not mean that the employee can be taken to have accepted that variation in the contract.

However, in the *Credit Suisse* case, the Court of Appeal plainly considered that, where senior **2.21** executives signed for receipt of a document that expressly identified an alteration in their terms, they would probably be bound by those terms if they continued working without protest. This highlights the fact that acceptance by conduct is mainly a question of fact rather than law.

In practice, as stated above, the simplest way to prove acceptance is to prove that the employee **2.22** has taken some benefit from the written terms that was not provided by the prior written or oral agreement.

Implied

The implied terms in a contract of employment are also to be identified by the application of **2.23** traditional contractual principles. As the Privy Council held in *Attorney General of Belize and others v Belize Telecom Ltd*,[18] 'in every case in which it is said that some provision ought to be implied in an instrument, the question for the court is whether such a provision would spell out in express words what the instrument, read against the relevant background, would reasonably be understood to mean'.[19] Thus, as in any contract, the parties may be taken to have agreed a term that:

(1) amounts to the unexpressed common intention of the parties when viewed objectively—put in another way, if an officious bystander were to have asked the parties at the time of contracting whether a particular term was agreed, they would both have said 'Oh, of course';[20] or

---

[13] ibid 889.
[14] [1981] IRLR 477.
[15] Reported under *Powdrill v Watson* [1995] ICR 1100, HL.
[16] [1996] IRLR 119; appealed to Court of Appeal on other grounds [2000] ICR 341.
[17] [2004] IRLR 4.
[18] [2009] 1 WLR 1988.
[19] ibid 1994B–C *per* Lord Hoffmann.
[20] *Shirlaw v Southern Foundries* [1939] 2 KB 206, 227.

(2) was necessary to give business efficacy to the contract—by this is meant that the term must be implied to give the transaction such business efficacy as the parties must have intended.[21]

2.24 Further, a term may be implied because it was the reasonable, notorious, and certain custom of the market.[22] The limits on such implication are marked. If a practice is adopted because a party does so as a matter of policy rather than out of a sense of legal obligation, then it will not confer contractual rights.[23]

2.25 The use of custom and practice to vary terms rather than create them is conceptually difficult in relation to a term which is of only contingent or future relevance to an employee.[24] In such cases, the custom and practice relied upon is not certain (since the term varies), not reasonable (since it depends upon the will of the employer), and not notorious (since there is no consistent application of the term). It was, however, accepted in the *Solectron* case that a custom can apply even though a term has never affected an employee.[25] Indeed, there may be employees who join an organization and may be bound by an established customary term, even if they do not know of it at the time of recruitment.[26]

2.26 The most important implied terms in employment contracts, however, are implied not in fact[27] or by custom but rather by law. These terms are the characteristic terms of a contract of employment to which all such contracts are subject. These terms are the duty of trust and confidence and the duty of good faith and fidelity.

2.27 It has been suggested that these duties may be excluded from a contract of employment.[28] However, they are of such significance to the nature of a modern contract of employment that the courts would be extremely reluctant to construe an express term as having such an effect unless very clearly worded.

2.28 Indeed, it is possible to argue that since the implied duties of trust and confidence and good faith and fidelity are characteristic of a contract of employment, their exclusion would be likely to render the contract no longer one of employment at all. It is hard to imagine a contract of employment where the employer does not owe the employee a duty of trust and confidence. Similarly, a contract of employment where the employee owed no duty of good faith and fidelity to the employer would afford a startling degree of liberty to the employee.

Equity

2.29 In addition to duties imposed by contract, the employer and/or employee may owe duties imposed by the rules of equity. Those duties are owed because the Courts of Equity have

---

[21] *Luxor v Cooper* [1941] AC 108, HL, 137.
[22] *Devonald v Rosser & Sons* [1916] 2 KB 728, CA, 743. In that case the employers contended that they could close their works where there was a lack of orders without making any payment to the employees. It was said that there was an established practice to that effect. The Court of Appeal rejected the argument, stating that: 'It is neither reasonable nor certain because it is precarious depending on the will of the master.'
[23] *Young v Canadian Northern Railway Co* [1931] AC 32, HL.
[24] eg *Solectron v Roper* [2004] IRLR 4.
[25] eg terms arising from a custom fixing retiring age, such as in *Duke v Reliance Systems* [1992] ICR 549, [1982] IRLR 347, or establishing redundancy terms, such as in *Quinn v Calder Industrial Materials Ltd* [1996] IRLR 126.
[26] *Sagar v H Ridehalgh & Son Ltd* [1931] 1 Ch 310.
[27] ie by reason of the unexpressed intention of the parties or due to business necessity.
[28] *Mahmud v BCCI* [1998] AC 20, HL, 45.

traditionally imposed them. As stated above, such duties are owed by all company directors and by many others who hold property on behalf of another.

Given that the basis for the imposition of a fiduciary duty is a holding of property on behalf **2.30** of another, it is easy to see why company directors are fiduciaries: they have de facto control of the assets of the company and thus, in one sense, hold those assets on the company's behalf and, indirectly, on the shareholders' behalf.

However, the same is also true of some employees, albeit to a lesser extent. Employees may **2.31** in some circumstances hold confidential information, and be, in a very real sense, the primary custodian of the employer's goodwill. Despite this, the courts have shown a reluctance to impose fiduciary duties on such employees.

The differing paths that the law might have taken in this regard can be seen from the judgment **2.32** in *Robb v Green* [29] in which each of three judges considered that the employee who stole the trade secrets of his employer was equally liable at common law and equity for his misdeeds.

As we shall see below, the category of employees who will be subjected to fiduciary duties is **2.33** of uncertain, yet apparently narrow, ambit.

Statute

The statutory duties of directors have now been codified, in the Companies Act 2006. That **2.34** Act amends, restates, or codifies almost every aspect of company law.

Critically for our purposes, the Companies Act 2006 for the first time seeks to codify and **2.35** amend the duties of directors of companies, including the duties owed by shadow directors. The relevant provisions of the Companies Act 2006 are considered in detail below.

What the Companies Act 2006 does not purport to do is to codify the fiduciary duties owed by **2.36** those who are not directors or shadow directors of companies. For these individuals, the current law still applies. As importantly, there is an express preservation of the old jurisprudence on fiduciary duties to interpret the codified duties.

B. Who owes duties?

Employees

Contractual duties

As set out above, an employee owes contractual duties, both express and implied, under his **2.37** contract of employment. The implied duties in every contract of employment include a duty of good faith and a duty of trust and confidence. Although these contractual duties are properly distinct from fiduciary duties, the boundary has sometimes become blurred.

Neary v Dean of Westminster [30] provides an example of this trend. This was a decision of Lord **2.38** Jauncey of Tullichettle, exercising an unusual jurisdiction as a special commissioner appointed by the Queen as Visitor to Westminster Abbey. In the *Neary* case, an organist at Westminster Abbey had earned 'fixing fees' from external promoters in respect of events involving

---

[29] [1895] 2 QB 315.
[30] [1999] IRLR 288.

members of the choir of Westminster Abbey, and had retained surpluses accruing from such events. Despite there being no allegation that the organist had acted dishonestly, Lord Jauncey held that Westminster Abbey had been entitled summarily to dismiss him, because his conduct had fatally undermined the trust and confidence between the parties. This reasoning was based on the finding that the duty of trust and confidence was a 'fiduciary duty', and therefore included a duty not to make a secret profit. The case has been subsequently criticized on that very basis,[31] but continues to be cited with apparent general approval by the higher courts.[32]

Fiduciary duties

2.39   The employment relationship is not *of itself* a fiduciary one.[33] Although there are certain recognized categories of 'fiduciary relationships' (for instance solicitor-client), employer-employee is not such a relationship. In this regard, English law differs from that of Australia, in which the High Court of Australia has held that 'employee and employer' is one of the standard categories:

> The accepted fiduciary relationships are sometimes referred to as relationships of trust and confidence or confidential relations (cf. Phipps v. Boardman [1967] 2 AC 46, at p 127), viz., trustee and beneficiary, agent and principal, solicitor and client, employee and employer, director and company, and partners.[34]

2.40   In English law, however, it is not merely those fiduciaries who are in a recognized relationship who will owe fiduciary duties. Rather, it is possible for a fiduciary duty to emerge in a variety of other situations when one person places trust and reliance on another person to handle his affairs. Not every fiduciary will therefore owe the same duties, and it is possible for a fiduciary duty to exist even when there is no recognized fiduciary relationship.[35]

2.41   It is therefore unsurprising that for many years litigants on both sides of the fence have been seeking to argue that although the employment relationship is not per se a fiduciary one, there are fiduciary duties arising on the facts of their particular case. Recently, there has been increasing judicial recognition for the notion that fiduciary or fiduciary-style duties may arise *out of* the employment relationship,[36] in the particular circumstances of a given case.

2.42   The authoritative analysis of this question was provided by Elias J in the case of *Nottingham University v Fishel*.[37] In that case, the defendant scientist had been performing extensive private work, for which he had received payment, and for which the university's consent had not been obtained. It is important to note that that work involved other scientists under Dr Fishel's supervision. The claimant university claimed damages for both breach of contract and breach of fiduciary duty. Since there was no recoverable loss, the university's breach of contract claim failed.[38] The case therefore turned on whether Dr Fishel owed and had breached fiduciary duties.

---

[31] *Nottingham University v Fishel* [2000] ICR 1462, 1493 *per* Elias J.

[32] See eg *Dunn v AAH Ltd* [2010] IRLR 709, paras 5–6 *per* Rix LJ.

[33] *Bell v Lever Bros* [1932] AC 161, *per* Lord Atkin, 227–9; cf *A-G v Blake* [1998] Ch 439, 453.

[34] *Hospital Products Ltd v US Surgical Corp* (1984) 156 CLR 41, 96–7 *per* Mason J.

[35] *Henderson v Merrett* [1995] 2 AC 145, HL, 206 *per* Lord Browne-Wilkinson.

[36] *Normalec v Britton* [1983] FSR 318.

[37] [2000] ICR 1462, [2000] IRLR 471.

[38] Judgment was given before the House of Lords decision in *A-G v Blake* [2001] 1 AC 268, HL, and the judge felt that, in any event, it was not a suitable case for an award of restitutionary damages.

Elias J therefore embarked on a careful examination of the question of when an employee **2.43** owes such fiduciary duties. After a detailed analysis of the case law, Elias J recognized that although an employee does not automatically (or even generally) owe fiduciary duties, such duties may be imposed because of the particular contractual obligations he has accepted:[39]

> . . . the essence of the employment relationship is not typically fiduciary at all. Its purpose is not to place the employee in a position where he is obliged to pursue his employer's interests at the expense of his own. The relationship is a contractual one and the powers imposed on the employee are conferred by the employer himself. The employee's freedom of action is regulated by the contract, the scope of his powers is determined by the terms (express or implied) of the contract, and as a consequence the employer can exercise (or at least he can place himself in a position where he has the opportunity to exercise) considerable control over the employee's decision making powers. This is not to say that fiduciary duties cannot arise out of the employment relationship itself. But they arise not as a result of the mere fact that there is an employment relationship. Rather they result from the fact that within a particular contractual relationship there are specific contractual obligations which the employee has undertaken which have placed him in a situation where equity imposes these rigorous duties in addition to the contractual obligations. Where this occurs, the scope of the fiduciary obligations both arises out of, and is circumscribed by, the contractual terms; it is circumscribed because equity cannot alter the terms of the contract validly undertaken.

Applying this statement of the law to the facts of the case, Elias J held that Dr Fishel was not **2.44** subject to fiduciary duties in relation to the work which he personally undertook in his own right. The reason for this was that he was not, by reason of his contract, obliged to secure such work for the university and he could not have been obliged, by his contract, to undertake the work abroad that he did. As such, he was not obliged to act in accordance with the 'no conflict' rules considered below. Similarly, he made no secret profit because the pay he was receiving for the work was not for work he was doing as an employee of the university.

However, he was responsible, under his contract of employment, for the other embryologists **2.45** who had also done private work abroad. As Elias J stated, 'it was his duty to direct the other embryologists what to do and where to do it. By accepting work for them from which he was directly benefiting, he was in my view, clearly putting himself where there was a potential conflict between his specific duty to the university to direct the embryologists to work in the interest of the university and his own financial interest in directing them abroad'.[40] In this regard, Elias J noted that Dr Fishel had in fact used his position within the university to secure the services of those embryologists abroad.

Elias J therefore found that: (a) because of this conflict between a specific *contractual* duty **2.46** and personal interest, Dr Fishel owed and had breached a *fiduciary* duty to have no such conflict; and (b) because of the profit he made out of abuse of his *contractual* position, he owed a *fiduciary* obligation to account for the profits made by that abuse.

The *Fishel* case has achieved authoritative status in the decade or so since it was decided. In **2.47** particular, in *Helmet Integrated Systems Ltd v Tunnard*,[41] the Court of Appeal approved the analysis of Elias J, describing it as 'the clearest analysis of the distinction between the duty of fidelity which every employee owes and a fiduciary duty which requires an employee to act solely in the interest of his employer and not in his own interest, still less the interests of

---

[39] [2000] ICR 1462, 1491.
[40] ibid 1498.
[41] [2007] IRLR 126.

anyone else'.[42] The Court of Appeal reiterated and emphasized that the attribution of the label 'fiduciary' to a particular employee in itself says nothing—the only issue of substance is the ambit of the particular fiduciary duties which that employee owes.[43] It is critical to focus on the normal (contractual) duties of the employee, so as to determine whether in all the circumstances (such as seniority, degree of independence, and trust conferred) the imposition of a fiduciary obligation is warranted; there is thus a 'need to identify particular duties as the source of a fiduciary obligation'.[44]

2.48 The facts of the *Helmet* case provide a telling example of these principles in operation. A salesman at a manufacturer of protective equipment, Mr Tunnard, hit upon an idea for a new modular helmet for use by fire fighters, amongst others. He took steps, in his own time, to advance the idea, including applying for a government grant and having discussions with a competitor. Mr Tunnard then gave notice of resignation, incorporated a new company, sold a part-shareholding to the competitor, and developed and marketed the helmet in competition with his former employer. The Court of Appeal rejected the notion that such activity, including the failure to disclose during employment, was in breach of fiduciary duty, because having regard to Mr Tunnard's contractual duties as a salesman, there was no reason to impose any fiduciary obligation in respect of the development of a helmet:

> Mr Tunnard was employed as a salesman, not as a designer. It was never in the contemplation of either HISL, nor of Mr Tunnard, that he would develop a helmet. When he entered into his contract of employment with HISL he was entitled to believe that he could, subject to his obligations as to notice, leave when he wished and work in competition to HISL. He was further entitled to take preparatory steps prior to leaving in order to assess the viability of any competitive activity once he had left or whether it was sensible for him to leave at all.

The question whether an employee owes fiduciary duties, and if so which duties, is therefore highly fact-specific. Examples of the application of the *Fishel* approach in particular cases include *PMC Holdings Ltd v Smith*,[45] *Hydra plc v Anastasi*,[46] *Crowson Fabrics Ltd v Rider*,[47] *Cobbetts LLP v Hodge*,[48] and *Fish v Dresdner Kleinwort Benson*.[49] The fact-specific approach now adopted by the courts in light of *Fishel* is attractive not only because of its recognition of the long-standing rule that an employee is not per se a fiduciary, but also because it permits the coherent explanation of three previous authorities which were for some time felt to have caused confusion in this area.

2.49 The first of these authorities is *Agip (Africa) Ltd v Jackson*,[50] in which Millett J found that an employee of the claimant company owed a fiduciary duty to it by reason of the fact that, although not a director, he was a 'senior and responsible officer' who, when 'entrusted with possession of . . . signed payment orders', 'took advantage of possession of them to divert the money'.[51] Putting it in the terms of the *Fishel* analysis, the employee's contractual obligation to put the money in the bank had been put in conflict with his personal interest in stealing

---

[42] ibid para 36 *per* Moses LJ.
[43] ibid paras 36–8 *per* Moses LJ.
[44] ibid para 39 *per* Moses LJ.
[45] [2002] EWHC 1575 (QB).
[46] [2005] EWHC 1559 (QB).
[47] [2008] IRLR 288.
[48] [2009] EWHC 786 (Ch); (2009) 153(17) SJLB 29.
[49] [2009] IRLR 1035.
[50] [1990] Ch 265.
[51] ibid 290 *per* Millett J.

the money, giving rise to a fiduciary duty. In addition, he had abused his position to make a secret profit.

Millett J made plain that it will almost invariably be the case that an embezzlement of **2.50** company funds involves a breach of fiduciary duty. The basis for this seems to be that to divert company funds one needs to have been given practical possession of company funds. This is therefore likely to give rise to fiduciary duties in relation to such funds. On this analysis, whilst a company accountant will not generally owe fiduciary duties, if that accountant uses his position to divert the company's funds, he will owe fiduciary duties in relation to that diversion of funds (though not generally).

However, this latter proposition reveals a tension between the approaches adopted by **2.51** Millett J in that case and, more importantly in his similar analysis adopted later in *Bristol & West v Mothew,*[52] in which he stated: 'A fiduciary is someone who has undertaken to act for or on behalf of another in a particular matter in circumstances which give rise to a relationship of trust and confidence.' This broad formulation is the classical doctrine in relation to professional agents and yet the *Fishel* formulation seeks to narrow this dramatically in relation to employees. On this basis Lord Millett might be expected to find that an employee owed fiduciary duties in a broader category of circumstances than those identified by Elias J in *Fishel*.

In this context, one might see a parallel with the modern view of the consequences of the **2.52** receipt of a bribe. In *Daraydan v Solland,*[53] Lawrence Collins J viewed the recipient of a bribe as the constructive trustee of the bribe merely in consequence of receipt of it rather than by reason of the owing of a prior fiduciary duty, thereby preferring the decision of the Privy Council in *A-G for Hong Kong v Reid*[54] over the venerable decision of the Court of Appeal in *Lister v Stubbs.*[55]

The second authority is *Normalec v Britton,*[56] in which Walton J held that a commission- **2.53** based light bulb salesman owed fiduciary duties in relation to the confidential information he held as to clients and their needs. He held that the case was 'an exceptionally plain' one. It does not appear to have been argued that the salesman was not a fiduciary and, further, the judgment seems to have been *ex tempore.* The judgment reflects the views expressed around ninety years earlier in *Robb v Green*[57] to the effect that, where an employee is entrusted with confidential information, he is a trustee of that information and owes fiduciary duties in relation to it. This case, in so far as explicable at all, may best be explained by reference to the substantial autonomy of a commission-based salesman of this type and the trust reposed in him in relation to his use of the confidential information.

The third of those authorities is *Reading v The King,*[58] in which the Crown sought to retain **2.54** moneys it had confiscated from Reading. Reading, a sergeant in the army serving in Egypt during the Second World War, had worn his uniform whilst off-duty to sit in a drug-filled lorry during its transport to prevent it being searched. He had received some £20,000.

---

[52] [1993] Ch 1, 18.
[53] *Daraydan Holdings v Solland International* [2005] Ch 119.
[54] [1994] 1 AC 324, HL.
[55] (1890) 45 Ch D 1.
[56] [1983] FSR 318.
[57] [1895] 2 QB 315, CA.
[58] [1949] 2 KB 232, CA.

The Court of Appeal held that receipt of the sums in such circumstances rendered Reading a fiduciary on behalf of the Crown because he had received the sums by reason of his wearing his army uniform. Asquith LJ, giving the judgment of the Court, held that whilst Reading was a servant rather than a true fiduciary, he became in a 'fiduciary relation' in relation to moneys obtained by the wearing of his army uniform and the facilities attached to the wearing of that uniform (the ability to give a lorry safe conduct through Cairo), which at all times remained the property of the Crown.

2.55 In doing so, Asquith LJ identified the following basis for imposing such a 'fiduciary relation':

> A consideration of the authorities suggests that for the present purpose a 'fiduciary relation' exists (*a*) whenever the plaintiff entrusts to the defendant property, including intangible property as, for instance, confidential information, and relies on the defendant to deal with such property for the benefit of the plaintiff or for purposes authorized by him, and not otherwise and (*b*) whenever the plaintiff entrusts to the defendant a job to be performed, for instance, the negotiation of a contract on his behalf or for his benefit, and relies on the defendant to procure for the plaintiff the best terms available.

2.56 These propositions were given the express approval of the House of Lords on appeal.[59] This is not the easiest case to reconcile with more recent authority, and in particular the views of Elias J in the *Fishel* case, but the key seems to lie in the first instance decision of Denning J.[60] In that decision, Denning J stated that it was not enough that the employee had made money from the opportunities provided to him by his employment, but rather the employment needed to be the sole cause of his receipt of money. This high threshold of breach of trust in the authors' opinion renders the *Reading* case explicable in terms of the *Fishel* analysis.

2.57 In the authors' view, the following propositions can be advanced in relation to the use or misuse of tangible assets of the employer:

(1) Where an employee is made responsible for particular employees and uses those employees for his own benefit, he will owe fiduciary duties in relation to that behaviour.

(2) Where an employee is entrusted with money of the company or diverts company money to his own benefit, he will owe fiduciary duties in relation to it, even if a junior employee.[61]

(3) Where an employee receives a bribe, he will owe fiduciary duties in relation to that receipt of a bribe.

(4) Where an employee is entrusted with specific tangible property of the employer, he will also be held to owe fiduciary duties in relation to that property.

2.58 In relation to an employee's use or misuse of less tangible assets of his employer, the following propositions can be stated:

(1) Where an employee is specifically entrusted with a particular task by his employer and required to bring it to conclusion without significant managerial intervention, he will owe fiduciary duties in relation to the performance of that task.

(2) It is at least arguable that where an employee is possessed of confidential information, fiduciary duties will also attach. However, it is only such information that can properly be described as a trade secret (to which the equitable doctrine of confidentiality attaches) that fiduciary duties will be brought into play.

---

[59] *Reading v A-G* [1951] AC 507, HL.
[60] [1948] 2 KB 268.
[61] See *Tullett Prebon plc v BGC Brokers LP* [2010] IRLR 648, para 66 *per* Jack J, but see n 316 below.

(3) There is no authority for the proposition that the misappropriation of goodwill will, in and of itself, give rise to fiduciary duties on the part of a mere employee.

Directors

Barring one unusual exception set out below, all directors owe fiduciary duties. **2.59**

The unusual exception to which we refer is the case of *In Plus Group Ltd v Pyke*.[62] In this **2.60** case, Pyke had been excluded from management for some six months prior to engaging in competitive activity. In those circumstances, he was treated as if he had already resigned as a director, despite not having done so formally. Referring extensively to these peculiar facts, the judges of the Court of Appeal held that Pyke was accordingly not subject to the rigorous obligations owed by a fiduciary. This case is anomalous and for all practical purposes can be confined to its specific facts, as the Court of Appeal has itself subsequently empha-sized.[63] In general terms, as set out below, the means by which a fiduciary brings an end to his duties is to bring the fiduciary relationship to an end. A director achieves this by resigning.

In addition to fiduciary duties, directors owe concurrent tortious and contractual obliga- **2.61** tions to act with reasonable skill and care in the performance of their duties. These duties give rise to a remedy in damages only, rather than equitable remedies, but they are nevertheless extremely important. By way of example, since the first edition of this book was published, the High Court and Court of Appeal have disagreed as to whether it is arguable that a company may sue its own former directors for negligence and breach of other duties where those directors caused the company to participate in conduct which is contrary to EU competition law.[64]

Furthermore, directors may also incur personal liability for acts of the company: (a) under **2.62** certain provisions of company legislation which are not within the scope of this work; and/or (b) where the director himself commits a tort, where he assumes personal liability in relation to the tortious act, and where he procures and induces the company to carry out the tort.[65]

It should be noted that section 1157 of the Companies Act 2006 gives the court power to **2.63** excuse a director from all or part of any liability for any breach of duty if he has acted honestly and reasonably [66] and that having regard to all the circumstances of the case he ought fairly to be excused. This extends to relief from any liability to account for profits.[67]

Others

Consultants

Consultants may be agents (as to which see below), may be employees, or may be neither. As **2.64** such, the position of a consultant is best assimilated to one or other of those two categories

---

[62] [2002] EWCA Civ 370, [2003] BCC 332, CA.

[63] *Foster Bryant Surveying Ltd v Bryant* [2007] IRLR 425, CA, para 81 *per* Rix LJ.

[64] *Safeway Stores Ltd v Twigger* [2010] EWHC 11 (Comm), [2010] 3 All ER 577 (High Court); [2010] EWCA Civ 1472 (Court of Appeal).

[65] *MCA Recordings v Charly* [2003] BCLC 93; *Standard Chartered Bank v Pakistan National Shipping Corp* [2003] 1 AC 959, HL. For a detailed and authoritative consideration of the rules of attribution in respect of directors, see *Stone & Rolls Ltd (in liquidation) v Moore Stephens (a firm)* [2009] 1 AC 1391 and the authorities discussed therein.

[66] This is to be viewed objectively: *Coleman Taymar v Oakes* [2001] 2 BCLC 749.

[67] ibid para 82.

depending on the facts of the particular case. If a consultant is neither, he may still hold confidential material giving rise to some fiduciary duties.

Agents[68]

2.65 Agents, like employees, may owe both contractual and fiduciary duties.

2.66 The contractual duties of agents depend on the particular situation and the particular agreement made by the parties, and may thus vary enormously. Some agents are employees and undertake the usual contractual obligations of an employee, but others are not. Certain types of agent may owe no contractual duty to do anything at all. It is possible to be an agent without having any contract at all with the principal. The question of whether an agent is entitled to deal on behalf of the principal's competitors depends on the construction of the particular agreement between the agent and his principal.

2.67 Agents generally owe fiduciary duties, although it has been said that the 'facts and circumstances must be carefully examined to see whether in fact a purported agent and even a confidential agent is in a fiduciary relationship to his principal. It does not necessarily follow that he is in such a position. . .'.[69]

2.68 The nature and extent of the agent's fiduciary duties will depend on the nature and extent of his role, and of his power over the principal's affairs. Not all of an agent's actions will be done in a fiduciary capacity (for example where he simply carries out a specific instruction). As stated by Frankfurter J in *SEC v Chenery Corp*:[70] 'To say that a man is a fiduciary only begins analysis; it gives direction to further inquiry. To whom is he a fiduciary? What obligations does he owe as a fiduciary? In what respect has he failed to discharge those obligations? And what are the consequences of his deviation from duty?'

Partners[71]

2.69 A partner owes his partners a duty of good faith. This is no doubt a species of fiduciary duty, but has aspects which are specific to the partnership context. In particular, certain aspects of the duty are codified in the Partnership Act 1890. These include:

(1) A duty to 'render true accounts and full information of all things affecting the partnership'.[72] This includes a duty to inform the partnership of opportunities and other material information without being asked.

(2) A duty to account to the firm for 'any benefit derived by him without the consent of the other partners from any transaction concerning the partnership, or from any use by him of the partnership property name or business connexion'[73] and for all profits made without the consent of the other partners in 'any business of the same nature as and competing with that of the firm'.[74] Consent can only be given after the partner has made full disclosure of his interest.

---

[68] For a detailed treatment of the duties of agents, see *Bowstead & Reynolds on Agency* (19th edn, 2010) ch 6.

[69] *Phipps v Boardman* [1967] 2 AC 46, 127 *per* Lord Upjohn.

[70] 318 US 80 (1943) 85–6 quoted by Lord Mustill in *Re Goldcorp Exchange Ltd* [1995] 1 AC 74, 98.

[71] See further Chapter 6 below.

[72] Partnership Act 1890, s 28.

[73] ibid s 29.

[74] ibid s 30.

These duties are limited to the partner's conduct in the area of business in which the firm **2.70** operates. A partner may use property or information belonging to the firm in other areas, provided that it is not of value to the firm and he does not use it in competition with the firm's business (as will be seen, the duties of a partner are thus less onerous than those of a company director). Similarly the duties do not restrict a partner's ability to dispose of his partnership share, or to serve notice of dissolution of the partnership.

A partner also has a duty to act honestly, both in dealings with his partners and with third **2.71** persons.[75]

C. Good faith and fidelity

Good faith as a fiduciary duty

Overarching obligation

It has been said that the distinguishing obligation of a fiduciary is the obligation of loyalty.[76] **2.72** The classic statement is that a fiduciary is expected 'to act in the interests of the other—to act selflessly and with undivided loyalty'.[77] This core obligation to act selflessly is what distinguishes a fiduciary from a person who merely owes contractual obligations. The employee is entitled to pursue his own self-interest save where prevented from doing so by his contract.

This is reflected in the remedies traditionally awarded. Whereas equity will generally require **2.73** any profits to be disgorged as the means of best protecting the interests of the beneficiary of a fiduciary obligation, the common law will generally only award the victim of a breach of contract what he or she expected to gain from the arrangement.[78]

The core liability of the fiduciary to act loyally has three particular incidents in the context of **2.74** a senior employee or director:

(1) The fiduciary must account to his company for the entirety of its property and the profits made from his position as a fiduciary ('the no profit rule').
(2) The fiduciary must not allow his own interest and the interest of the company to conflict ('the no conflict rule').
(3) The fiduciary must disclose his own misconduct ('the disclosure rule').

We shall examine these rules in turn.

No profit rule

As set out above, one of the classic fiduciary duties is the duty not to make unauthorized **2.75** personal gain from one's position as a fiduciary. This rule against 'secret profits' has been held,

---

[75] *Carmichael v Evans* [1904] 1 Ch 486.

[76] *Bristol & West v Mothew* [1998] Ch 1, CA, 18 *per* Millet LJ.

[77] P Finn, *Fiduciary Obligations* (1977).

[78] Note, however, the developing law permitting gain-based damages for breach of contract: *A-G v Blake* [2001] 1 AC 268 for an account of profits for breach of contract; *Experience Hendrix v PPX Enterprises* [2003] FSR 46 for damages based upon a notional licence, but cf *World Wide Fund for Nature v World Wrestling Federation* [2008] 1 WLR 445. Although concerning competition law infringements rather than breach of contract, see also *Devenish Nutrition Ltd v Sanofi-Aventis SA* [2009] Ch 390. Note also the long-standing option of claiming reliance-based loss (wasted expenditure) rather than the expectation losses. See further Chapter 11 below.

in the leading case of *Regal (Hastings) v Gulliver*,[79] to be a subset of the rule against conflicts of interest.

2.76 It is not necessary, in order for a director or other fiduciary to breach this rule, that the employer should suffer any loss. Rather, as Lord Russell of Killowen observed in the *Regal* case: 'The liability arises from the mere fact of a profit having, in the stated circumstances, been made.'[80]

2.77 The rule was best summarized by Lord Upjohn in *Boardman v Phipps*[81] (which was not an employment case): 'The relevant rule for the decision of this case is the fundamental rule of equity that a person in a fiduciary capacity must not make a profit out of his trust, which is part of the wider rule that a trustee must not place himself in a position where his duty and his interest may conflict.'[82]

2.78 This rule is applied strictly,[83] and is subject only to the exception that a director may invest in business related to the business of the company, and make profits himself, so long as he does so with the informed consent of the shareholders in general meeting. Such permission may be sought in advance, or subsequent to the making of the profit.[84] Where the no profit rule has been breached, the court has an equitable discretion to make an 'offset' against the profit, so as to allow a reasonable amount for services rendered in generating the profit.[85]

2.79 The precise application of the no profit rule, as the Court of Appeal clarified in *O'Donnell v Shanahan*,[86] will vary according to the type of fiduciary to which it is applied. Where the fiduciary is in a 'general' fiduciary position (such as a directorship) no profit can be made from information gleaned by virtue of that position even if the information is used for a purpose entirely outside the directorship. However, where the fiduciary's duties are 'circumscribed by contract', for instance in a partnership, the same rule does not apply. In that situation, a partner's fiduciary obligations do 'not require him . . . to account to the firm for any profits made by the use of [partnership] information for a purpose that was beyond the scope of the business of the partnership'.[87] The same reasoning is likely also to apply to employee fiduciaries, where the 'fiduciary relationship must accommodate itself to the terms of the contract'.[88]

No conflict rule

The general principle

2.80 As noted above, the overarching fiduciary duty to act in the principal's best interests finds its application in a number of particular obligations. One of the most important of these is the fiduciary's duty to avoid any conflict between his duties to the principal and his own interests. The imperative need to avoid such conflicts has long been acknowledged to be 'an inflexible rule of a Court of Equity'.[89] Indeed, it goes 'back to the eighteenth century'.[90]

---

[79] [1967] 2 AC 134.
[80] ibid 145.
[81] [1967] 2 AC 36, HL.
[82] ibid 123 *per* Lord Upjohn.
[83] *Keech v Sandford* Sel Cas Ch 61, 62 *per* Lord King LC.
[84] *Regal Hastings v Gulliver* [1967] 2 AC 134, HL, 150 *per* Lord Russell.
[85] *Cobbetts LLP v Hodge* [2009] EWHC 786 (Ch), paras 113–155 and the authorities cited therein.
[86] [2009] BCC 822, paras 52–72 *per* Rimer LJ.
[87] ibid, para 68 *per* Rimer LJ.
[88] *Fish v Dresdner Kleinwort Benson* [2009] IRLR 1035, para 31 *per* Jack J.
[89] *Bray v Ford* [1896] AC 44, HL, 51 *per* Lord Herschell.
[90] *CMS Dolphin Ltd v Simonet* [2001] 2 BCLC 704, para 84 *per* Lawrence Collins J.

The no conflict rule is 'allied to but separate from' the no profit rule.[91] The main policy   **2.81**
consideration underpinning the rule is that a trustee must not be subjected to any temptation
to act in his own interest rather than the interests of the beneficiaries of the trust. In the words
of Lord Herschell, 'human nature being what it is, there is danger, in such circumstances, of
the person holding a fiduciary position being swayed by interest rather than by duty, and
thus prejudicing those whom he was bound to protect'.[92]

The no conflict rule 'retains its vigour in all jurisdictions where the principles of equity are   **2.82**
applied', although 'the precise scope of it must be moulded according to the nature of the
relationship'.[93] Some fiduciaries may be in a fiduciary position as regards certain aspects of
their activities but not others. In such circumstances, each transaction must be separately
considered to ascertain whether it falls within the sphere of the fiduciary duties, such that the
no conflict rule must be complied with.

Specific aspects of the no conflict rule

The inflexibility of the no conflict rule arises from its focus on the *appearance* of conflict and   **2.83**
the *risk* of detriment to the principal. That focus gives rise to, and is illustrated by, the following
key principles.

First, the central question which determines whether the rule is engaged is whether 'the   **2.84**
reasonable man looking at the relevant facts and circumstances of the particular case would
think there was a real sensible possibility of conflict'.[94] The question as to whether there is
such a possibility may be 'a matter of considerable difficulty'.[95] Any such finding is a question
of fact which appellate courts will be reluctant to disturb.[96]

Secondly, a fiduciary can be in breach of the no conflict rule where the principal has suffered   **2.85**
no loss or other detriment and even where his conduct has, in fact, been to the principal's
benefit.[97]

Thirdly, the fairness or otherwise of the transaction in which the fiduciary has a personal   **2.86**
interest is irrelevant.[98] In Lord Blackburn's words, 'in such cases we do not inquire whether
it was a good bargain or a bad bargain, before we set it aside . . . The mere fact [of the undisclosed conflict] authorises [the principal] to set aside the contract if he chooses to do so'.[99]
Nor is it relevant whether any gain by the fiduciary could ever have been obtained by his
principal. This has been the law 'since at least as early as *Keech v Sandford*'.[100]

---

[91] *Quarter Master UK Ltd v Pyke* [2004] EWHC 1815, [2005] 1 BCLC 245, para 55 *per* Paul Morgan QC
(sitting as a Deputy Judge of the High Court).
[92] *Bray v Ford* [1896] AC 44, HL, 51; *Costa Rica Rly Co v Forwood* [1901] 1 Ch 746, 761 *per* Vaughan
Williams LJ.
[93] *New Zealand Netherlands Society 'Oranje' v Kuys* [1973] 1 WLR 1126, HL, 1129–30 *per* Lord
Wilberforce.
[94] *Boardman v Phipps* [1967] 2 AC 46, HL, 124 *per* Lord Upjohn.
[95] *Re Thomson* [1930] 1 Ch 203, 216 *per* Clauson J; *Bhullar v Bhullar* [2003] EWCA Civ 424, [2003] BCC
711, para 30 *per* Jonathan Parker LJ.
[96] *Lapthorne v Eurofi Ltd* [2001] EWCA Civ 993, [2001] UKCLR 996, para 52 *per* Arden LJ.
[97] *Aberdeen Rly Co v Blaikie Bros* (1854) 1 Macq 461, 472 *per* Lord Cranworth LC; *Regal (Hastings) Ltd v
Gulliver* [1967] 2 AC 134, HL, 153 *per* Lord Macmillan.
[98] *Aberdeen Rly Co v Blaikie Bros* (1854) 1 Macq 461; *Wright v Morgan* [1926] AC 788, HL, 798 *per*
Viscount Dunedin.
[99] *McPherson v Watt* (1877–78) LR 3 App Cas 254, 272.
[100] *Wrexham Associated Football Club Ltd (in administration) v Crucialmove Ltd* [2006] EWCA Civ 237,
para 40 *per* Sir Peter Gibson, referring to *Keech v Sandford* (1726) Sel Cas Ch 61.

2.87 Fourthly, the honesty or otherwise of the fiduciary is irrelevant. A breach of the no conflict rule 'may be attended with perfect good faith'.[101] The rule 'might be departed from in many cases, without any breach of morality, without any wrong being inflicted, and without any consciousness of wrong-doing'.[102] This is not 'a licence for the rule to be departed from when it can be seen that no breach of morality or wrongdoing would ensue'; on the contrary, it means that the rule applies *irrespective* of considerations of morality.[103]

2.88 Fifthly, the rule cannot be circumvented by the fiduciary arranging a transaction through a third party if there is an understanding or agreement between them whereby the latter is in fact acting on behalf of the former.[104] This exemplifies equity's concern with substance rather than form.

2.89 Sixthly, the courts have emphatically rejected attempts to limit the rule to situations where there has been some improper dealing with property belonging to the principal. Thus, where a fiduciary has exploited a commercial opportunity for his own benefit, it is not necessary to consider whether the principal had a beneficial interest in the opportunity, which would be 'too formalistic and restrictive an approach'.[105]

2.90 In short, the courts' approach has been consistent and strict: a fiduciary who fails to avoid a conflict of interest has no defence based on his own good faith or the absence of loss (or even the presence of a gain) to his principal. The only scenario in which a conflict of interest can exist without a breach of fiduciary duty is where there has been prior authorization of the conflict by the principal.

Authorization of conflicts of interest

2.91 It is open to the principal expressly to authorize the fiduciary to act in a way which would otherwise be a breach of fiduciary duty. To achieve this, the principal may bring the fiduciary relationship to an end, or may alter the fiduciary's non-fiduciary duties in respect of a particular transaction in order that there is no conflict between those non-fiduciary duties and the fiduciary's personal interest.[106] For example, where a director of company, A, has a personal connection with the owner of its trading partner company, B, company A will either remove the director from his position or eradicate the conflict while retaining him, whether by ending the trading relationship with company B or putting in place procedures which ensure that he is not involved in managing that relationship. However, if there is full and accurate disclosure of the nature and extent of any conflict by the director and there is actual consent to such conflict then that will serve to modify the fiduciary duty.[107]

2.92 This exception to the otherwise inflexible no conflict rule respects the autonomy of the principal to forego the full rigour of equity's protection where he perceives some advantage in so doing.[108] However, the rules governing what will constitute a valid authorization

---

[101] *Bray v Ford* [1896] AC 44, HL, 48 *per* Lord Watson.

[102] ibid 52, *per* Lord Herschell; *Re Baumler (UK) Ltd* [2004] EWHC 7673, para 183(ii).

[103] *Re Drexel Burnham Lambert UK Pension Plan* [1995] 1 WLR 32, 37 *per* Lindsay J.

[104] *McPherson v Watt* (1877–78) LR 3 App Cas 254, 263 *per* Lord Cairns LC, 266 *per* Lord Hagan, 272 *per* Lord Blackburn; *Re Postlethwaite* (1888) 37 WR 200, CA.

[105] *Bhullar v Bhullar* [2003] EWCA Civ 424, [2003] 2 BCLC 241, CA, para 28 *per* Jonathan Parker LJ.

[106] *Movitex Ltd v Bulfield* [1988] BCLC 104, 118 *per* Vinelott J.

[107] *Gwembe Valley Development Co v Koshy* [2004] 1 BCLC 131. See also the procedures for the authorization of an interest in contracts set out in the Companies Act 2006, ss 182–7.

[108] *Imperial Mercantile Credit Association v Coleman* (1871) 6 Ch App 558, 568–70 *per* Lord Hatherley LC; *Boulting v Association of Cinematograph Television and Allied Technicians* [1963] 2 QB 606, 637 *per* Upjohn LJ.

further illustrate the strictness of the requirements imposed on a fiduciary and the lengths to which he must go to avoid liability.

First, the principal's consent must be fully informed. Valid consent can only be given after the **2.93** fiduciary has made 'full and frank disclosure of all material facts'.[109] There must be clear evidence of disclosure of the nature of the fiduciary's interest in the transaction, not merely the existence of the transaction.[110] The amount of detail required 'must depend in each case upon the nature of the contract or arrangement proposed and the context in which it arises', but the principal must in every case be 'fully informed of the real state of things'.[111] In the example given above, the director would be required, at the very least, to inform company A of (1) the nature of his relationship with the owner of company B, (2) the nature of company A's relationship with company B, and (3) the extent of his involvement in managing that relationship.

Secondly, the materiality of information is determined not by whether it would have been **2.94** decisive but merely by whether it may have affected the principal's consent. As Dyson LJ put it, 'there must be disclosure of everything that would or might influence the principal in his decision whether to proceed with the transaction at all, or to proceed with the transaction on the terms being offered by the other contracting party'.[112]

Thirdly, and as a consequence, it is no defence to a claim for breach of fiduciary duty for the **2.95** fiduciary to argue that the principal would have acted in the same way even if the information had been disclosed. 'Once the Court has determined that the non-disclosed facts were material, speculation as to what course the [principal], on disclosure, would have taken is not relevant.'[113] However, if it can be shown that disclosure would not have prompted the principal to abstain from the relevant transaction, the principal will not be able to recover equitable compensation for losses resulting from that transaction, since those losses will not have been caused by the fiduciary's breach of duty.[114]

Application of the no conflict rule to directors

The no conflict rule is particularly important in relation to directors. Every director, by virtue **2.96** of his holding office as such, owes fiduciary duties to the company.[115] Where (as is not uncommon) an individual sits on the boards of two or more companies, the possibility of the rule being engaged is enhanced.[116] This is because the rule applies not only where a director's personal interest conflicts or may conflict with his fiduciary duties to the company, but also where a director has an 'outside' duty which so conflicts or may so conflict.[117]

---

[109] *New Zealand Netherlands Society 'Oranje' v Kuys* [1973] 1 WLR 1126, PC, 1132 *per* Lord Wilberforce.

[110] *Dunne v English* (1874) LR 18 Eq 524, 533–5 *per* Sir George Jessel MR; *Movitex Ltd v Bulfield* [1988] BCLC 104, 121 *per* Vinelott J.

[111] *Gray v New Augarita Porcupines Mines Ltd* [1952] 3 DLR 1, 14 *per* Lord Radcliffe.

[112] *Johnson v EBS Pensioner Trustees Ltd* [2002] EWCA Civ 164, [2002] Lloyd's Rep PN 309, para 70.

[113] *Brickenden v London Loan and Savings Co* [1934] 3 DLR 465, 469 *per* Lord Thankerton.

[114] *Swindle v Harrison* [1997] 4 All ER 705, 735 *per* Mummery LJ.

[115] On the legal nature of the office of director, see *Gore-Browne on Companies* (44th edn, loose leaf) para 27.2.

[116] It has at times been considered the case that a director may, in the absence of contractual restraints or disclosing confidential information, become a director of another company in a competing business—see the decision of Chitty J in *London & Mashonaland Exploration Co Ltd v New Mashonaland Exploration Co Ltd* [1891] WN 165, approved by Lord Blanesburgh in *Bell v Lever Bros* [1932] AC 161, 195. Note the trenchant criticisms of this decision by Sedley LJ in *In Plus Group v Pyke* [2003] BCC 332, referring to the criticisms made by the authors of leading company law textbooks.

[117] See eg *Transvaal Lands Co v New Belgium (Transvaal) Land & Development Co* [1914] 2 Ch 488, CA, 503 *per* Swinfen Eady LJ; *Quarter Master UK Ltd v Pyke* [2004] EWHC 1815, [2005] 1 BCLC 245, para 55 *per* Paul Morgan QC (sitting as a Deputy Judge of the High Court).

2.97 Sections 175, 177, and 182 of the Companies Act 2006 give statutory form to the no conflict rule as it affects directors, with the bite of making breach of the rule, in so far as it applies to actual rather than proposed contracts, a criminal offence in addition to the consequences of breach of the fiduciary duty. Those sections are discussed in detail below.

Disclosure rule

2.98 The third incident of the duty of a fiduciary to act in the best interests of his employer or the company is a duty to disclose his own wrongdoing. The English courts have recently been creating a whole new suite of claims for wronged former employers. The duty to disclose one's own wrongdoing is a major weapon in such an employer's armoury. Since this is a complex and still-developing area of the law, it is necessary to trace the history of the evolution of the rule in some detail.

The contractual duty of disclosure

2.99 The question of whether there is a fiduciary duty to disclose misconduct is unavoidably interlinked with the question of whether there is a similar contractual duty. This is due to the decision of the House of Lords in *Bell v Lever Brothers Ltd*,[118] which has been for many years the starting point in any analysis of this question. *Bell v Lever Bros* is a notoriously difficult decision to follow and to apply, but since the defendants were both employees and directors (albeit of parent and subsidiary respectively), in theory both contractual *and* fiduciary duties could have been in play, albeit that the case seems to have been advanced only on the basis of breach of contractual obligations.

2.100 The facts of the case were not especially complex. Bell and his colleague were employees of Lever Bros, but were also directors of a subsidiary of Lever Bros for which they worked. They made secret profits in dealings in the cocoa market, and concealed those dealings. Thereafter, they entered into an agreement pursuant to which their employment was terminated and directorships vacated on payment of several years' salary.

2.101 The subsidiary claimed an account of the secret profits by reason of breach of fiduciary duty, and Lever Bros claimed repayment of the sums under the agreement for the termination of employment on the grounds that it was entered into either by reason of fraud or under a unilateral mistake of fact by Lever Bros, namely that it was not entitled to terminate the employment without payment. Bell and his colleague admitted liability to account for the secret profits to the subsidiary, but denied liability to Lever Bros in relation to the termination sums.

2.102 The case was originally heard by a jury.[119] The jury found: (a) that Lever Bros would have been entitled to terminate Mr Bell and his colleague's contracts of employment because of the transactions; (b) that it would have done so had it known about them at the time; but also (c) that the employees did not have the transactions in mind when entering into the termination agreements. The third of these findings negatived the possibility of a fraud on Lever Bros. On the basis of those findings, Wright J decided that the termination agreements should be set aside on grounds of mutual mistake. He held that all parties entered into those agreements under the common mistake that the contracts of service were binding, in the sense that they could not at that moment have been got rid of without the employees' consent.

---

[118] [1932] AC 161, HL.
[119] *Bell v Lever Bros* [1931] 1 KB 557.

The Court of Appeal (Scrutton, Lawrence, and Greer LJJ) took the same view as the trial **2.103** judge on mistake. They also held, although it was not pleaded, that his judgment could be supported on the ground that the employees during the termination negotiation were under a duty to disclose the offending transactions of fifteen months before; and that they were not excused from disclosure by reason of the fact that, as the jury had found, the transactions had passed from their minds.

When the case arrived in the House of Lords, therefore, whilst the principal issue was still **2.104** that of mistake, there was a further basis on which Lever Bros sought to maintain its claim, namely that Bell and his colleague had been under a duty to disclose the transactions. By a three to two majority, the House of Lords dismissed Lever Bros' claim based on mistake. The three law lords in the majority—Lords Blanesburgh, Atkin, and Thankerton—each also addressed the question whether Bell and his colleague owed a duty to disclose their wrong-doing to Lever Bros or the subsidiary:

(1) Lord Atkin held that there was no *contractual* duty of disclosure:

> It is said that there is a contractual duty of the servant to disclose his past faults. I agree that the duty in the servant to protect his master's property may involve the duty to report a fellow servant whom he knows to be wrongfully dealing with that property. The servant owes a duty not to steal, but, having stolen, is there superadded a duty to confess that he has stolen? I am satisfied that to imply such a duty would be a departure from the well established usage of mankind and would be to create obligations entirely outside the normal contemplation of the parties concerned.[120]

(2) Lord Thankerton held that in the absence of fraud, neither a servant nor a director of a company is legally bound forthwith to disclose any breach of the obligations arising out of the relationship so as to give the master or the company the opportunity of dismissal.[121]

(3) Lord Blanesburgh agreed with the answer given on this issue by the other two judges who were in the majority.

It is notable from their Lordships' opinions that the majority addressed the possibility of a **2.105** duty of disclosure almost exclusively as a contractual question. The question of whether there was a fiduciary duty to disclose was given little reasoned consideration:

(1) Lord Thankerton, on the basis of the single authority of *Healey v Rubastic*,[122] held that Mr Bell and his colleague owed no duty to disclose their secret profits, whether as employees *or* as directors.[123] Lord Thankerton did not make clear whether he intended this observation to apply in relation to fiduciary as well as contractual duties.

(2) Lord Blanesburgh did not address the question in his speech.

(3) Lord Atkin did not find it necessary to consider whether there was a fiduciary duty to disclose, because he held that Mr Bell was not in a fiduciary relationship with Lever (as opposed to the subsidiary).[124] He somewhat confusingly included 'special fiduciary relationships' within his list of contracts of the utmost good faith.[125]

---

[120] [1932] AC 161, 228.
[121] ibid 231–2.
[122] [1917] 1 KB 946.
[123] *Bell v Lever Bros* [1932] AC 161, HL, 231–2.
[124] ibid 228.
[125] ibid 227.

2.106   There was therefore a significant lacuna in the reasoning of the House of Lords in *Bell v Lever Bros*. Although the decision would appear to be authority for the proposition that a director or other fiduciary does not owe a duty to disclose his own misconduct short of fraud, and has sometimes been taken to be such, in truth their Lordships did not examine the position as regards the fiduciary duties owed by Bell in any depth. As such, less assistance can be derived from this decision by way of binding precedent than was at one time supposed. The case could have been (and perhaps would now) be put on the basis of: (a) the directors' *contractual* duty to disclose the wrongdoing of the *other*; and (b) the directors' duty *as directors* to disclose their *own* wrongdoing. However, that was not how it was argued.

2.107   The Court of Appeal recognized as much in *Sybron Corp v Rochem Ltd*.[126] In the *Sybron* case, the relevant issue for present purposes was whether a senior employee who conspired with other employees to set up and carry on a new business, Rochem, in competition with and so as to injure the business of Sybron, owed a duty to disclose these matters to Sybron. The decision in *Bell v Lever Bros*, of course, would seem to have stood in the way of such a duty.

2.108   However, the Court of Appeal effectively circumvented the decision in *Bell v Lever Bros*, finding that whilst the senior employee in question was under no duty to disclose his own misconduct, he was under a contractual duty to report the misconduct of the *other* employees of Sybron who were involved in Rochem. Stephenson LJ found support for this approach in an earlier decision of the Court of Appeal in the case of *Swain v West (Butchers) Ltd*.[127] This led him to express the following general principle, which he considered followed from the *Swain* case and was consistent with *Bell v Lever Bros*:

> . . . there is no general duty to report a fellow-servant's misconduct or breach of contract; whether there is such a duty depends on the contract and on the terms of employment of the particular servant. He may be so placed in the hierarchy as to have a duty to report either the misconduct of his superior, as in *Swain*, or the misconduct of his inferiors, as in this case.[128]

2.109   In arriving at this conclusion, the Court of Appeal engaged in a detailed examination of *Bell v Lever Bros* and regarded their decision as entirely consistent with that authority. The position as regards a contractual duty of disclosure would therefore appear, at this stage, to be fairly settled: an employee owes no duty to disclose his own misconduct, but in certain circumstances may owe a duty to disclose that of *other* employees.

2.110   The nature of those certain circumstances was clarified by Laddie J in *RGB Resources plc v Rastogi*.[129] Laddie J broke down the duty discussed in *Sybron* into: (a) 'a general obligation to whistleblow';[130] and (b) 'a duty to investigate'.[131] As to the former, the judge held that there was no general rule that an employee must be given a supervisory function before he had a duty to report other employees' misconduct. Rather, the existence of that duty was dependent upon a multitude of factors, including the terms of the contract of employment, the employee's seniority, the nature of the wrongdoing and its potential adverse effect on the company.[132]

---

[126]   [1984] Ch 112.
[127]   [1936] 3 All ER 261.
[128]   [1984] Ch 112, 126.
[129]   [2002] EWHC 2782 (Ch). See the case note by Lewis (2004) 33 ILJ 278 and the case note by Wynn-Evans on *Tesco v Pook* and *Item Software* (2005) 34 ILJ 178.
[130]   ibid paras 37–46.
[131]   ibid paras 47–9.
[132]   ibid para 40.

As to the latter, Laddie J recognized that it could not be assumed that there was a universal obligation to investigate whether there had been wrongdoing in the company. Although similar factors would apply, such an obligation would be likely to arise in fewer cases than those in which there was an obligation to report wrongdoing already known to the employee.[133]

The fiduciary duty of disclosure

It will be noted that *Sybron v Rochem*, like *Bell v Lever Bros*, left open the question of whether **2.111** there was a fiduciary, as opposed to contractual, duty to disclose misconduct. This point was argued in the Court of Appeal in *Horcal Ltd v Gatland*,[134] in which the claimant company sought to set aside a director's termination agreement on the ground that he had committed a breach of duty which he should have disclosed before concluding the agreement. The court found that there was no misconduct which might otherwise have to be disclosed, and therefore it was unnecessary for a concluded view to be expressed on this point. However, Goff LJ went on to observe, albeit *obiter*, that the argument that a director was under a duty to disclose any breach of duty on his part before entering a termination agreement could lead to an 'extravagant consequence' that a director might have to make a 'confession' as a prerequisite to entering a termination agreement.[135]

Goff LJ's observation did not prevent the Court of Appeal some years later from accepting, **2.112** albeit obiter, in *Van Gestel v Cann*,[136] the submission that a director does indeed have a positive duty to disclose his own wrongdoing. This decision did not attract attention at the time, and does not appear to have been treated as authoritative on this topic.

In recent years, however, the Courts have definitively established a fiduciary duty to disclose **2.113** one's own wrongdoing. The first edition of this work included a discussion of three first instance authorities which began this process, *Tesco Stores Ltd v Pook*,[137] *Dilmun v Sutton*,[138] and *British Midland Tool Ltd v Midland International Tooling Ltd*.[139] In the last of those cases, Hart J formulated the duty of disclosure very widely indeed:

> A director's duty to act so as to promote the best interests of his company prima facie includes a duty to inform the company of any activity, actual or threatened, which damages those interests. The fact that the activity is contemplated by himself is, on the authority of *Balston's* case, a circumstance which may excuse him from the latter aspect of the duty. But where the activity involves both himself and others, there is nothing in the authorities which excuses him from it.[140]

However, detailed consideration of those early first instance cases is now unnecessary in light **2.114** of two authoritative decisions of the Court of Appeal, *Item Software (UK) Ltd v Fassihi*[141] and *Helmet Integrated Systems Ltd v Tunnard*.[142] Those cases can be taken in turn.

In the *Fassihi* case, the Court of Appeal was faced squarely with the question of whether **2.115** a director owed a duty to disclose his *own* misconduct. Fassihi was a former director of the

---

[133] ibid para 47.
[134] [1984] IRLR 288, CA.
[135] ibid para 16.
[136] [1987] CL 454, CA.
[137] [2004] IRLR 618.
[138] [2004] 1 BCLC 468.
[139] [2003] 2 BCLC 523.
[140] ibid para 89.
[141] [2005] ICR 450, [2004] IRLR 928, CA.
[142] [2007] IRLR 126.

claimant company. During negotiations for the renewal of a distribution agreement, Fassihi had encouraged Item Software to take up a tough stance in ongoing negotiations, at the same time as writing to the client in question suggesting that he would set up his own company to take over the agreement. The claimant claimed that the defendant had breached his duty as a director and as an employee to act in good faith in its best interests by failing to disclose his breach of duty.

2.116 The Court of Appeal agreed, holding that a director does owe a fiduciary duty to disclose his own breach of duty, but that this duty is merely a manifestation of the more general duty to act in good faith in the best interests of the company. Arden LJ, with whom the other two members of the court agreed on the disclosure issue, framed her judgment in terms of the director's *fiduciary* duty:

> For my part, I do not consider that it is correct to infer from the cases to which I have referred that a fiduciary owes a separate and independent duty to disclose his own misconduct to his principal or more generally information of relevance and concern to it. So to hold would lead to a proliferation of duties and arguments about their breadth. I prefer to base my conclusion in this case on the fundamental duty to which a director is subject, that is the duty to act in what he in good faith considers to be the best interests of his company. This duty of loyalty is the 'time-honoured' rule: per Goulding J in *Mutual Life Insurance Co of New York v Rank Organisation Ltd* [1985] BCLC 11, 21. The duty is expressed in these very general terms, but that is one of its strengths: it focuses on principle not on the particular words which judges or the legislature have used in any particular case or context. It is dynamic and capable of application in cases where it has not previously been applied but the principle or rationale of the rule applies.[143]

2.117 Crucially, the court disposed of the case on this basis alone, and drew a distinction between fiduciaries and ordinary employees.[144] The court did not make a finding as to whether Fassihi would have owed the same duty of disclosure in contract as an employee.[145] However, after a detailed analysis of *Bell v Lever Bros*, the court did observe that the majority in that case did *not* decide that there could never be a contractual duty on the part of an employee to disclose his own misconduct. Rather, the House of Lords had merely held that on the particular facts of the case before it, there was no such duty. This latter part of the Court of Appeal's analysis is not entirely easy to reconcile with Lord Atkin's wine butler.

2.118 The limitations of the *Fassihi* duty of disclosure were exposed in the *Helmet Integrated Systems* case, which is summarized at paragraphs 2.47 to 2.48 above. As set out above, in that case the Court of Appeal held that an employee salesman who owed certain fiduciary duties was nevertheless under no duty to disclose the fact that he was involved in setting up a competitor company, preparing to leave in order to join that company, and developing a competitor product to be sold by that company. The key passage of the Court of Appeal's reasoning was as follows:

> I have accepted that Mr Tunnard's activities would have amounted to 'competitor activity' if undertaken by a competitor and I have accepted that he owed an obligation as a fiduciary not to misuse information about such activity for his own benefit or for the benefit of someone other than HISL. But it does not follow that he was under any obligation, be it fiduciary or otherwise, to inform HISL of his own activities or such activities undertaken on his own behalf.

---

[143] *Item Software*, para 41.
[144] ibid para 60.
[145] Despite the judge at first instance having so found.

There seem to me two fundamental reasons why Mr Tunnard was under no obligation to report his own activities. Firstly, the words of the job specification do not restrict Mr Tunnard's freedom to prepare for competition on leaving. Secondly, he was under no relevant fiduciary obligation to HISL.[146]

The key to the Court of Appeal's reasoning, as set out above, was that Mr Tunnard's normal **2.119** duties did not include the development of helmets or protective equipment at all; he was 'employed as a salesman, not as a designer', and thus it was 'never in . . . contemplation . . . that he would develop a helmet'.[147] There was therefore no duty of disclosure in respect of the development of such a helmet, notwithstanding the *Fassihi* case. Mr Tunnard's status as an employee but not a director appears to have been the key distinguishing feature, with Moses LJ summarizing the effect of the *Fassihi* case as being only that 'there is no overriding rule that an employee can never be under an obligation to report his own misconduct'.[148]

The net effect of the decisions in *Fassihi* and *Helmet Integrated Systems* would appear to be that: **2.120**

(1) a fiduciary, and in particular a director, will owe a duty to disclose his own misconduct whenever he in good faith considers that misconduct prejudices the best interests of his employer or the company in question;
(2) there is no overriding rule that this duty cannot apply in the case of an employee fiduciary, indeed the position in that regard is 'clear';[149] but
(3) in respect of mere employees, there is only a *contractual* duty to report on *other* employees, and even then only when in all the circumstances such a duty can be inferred from the nature of the employment.

These are relatively clear rules which are capable of straightforward application in a particular **2.121** case. The rules derive from and reflect the essential difference in standards of conduct which the law requires of fiduciaries on the one hand and employees on the other. However, the coherence of the scheme is disturbed by the existence of a contractual duty upon employees to report others' misconduct. Indeed, the Court of Appeal in *Fassihi* noted that, following the *Sybron* case, it would be arguable that no logical distinction can be drawn between a rule that an employee should disclose his own wrongdoing and a rule that he should disclose the wrongdoing of his fellow employees, even if that involves disclosing his own wrongdoing too.[150] If that were correct, then the distinction between fiduciaries and mere employees would fall away altogether.

It is suggested that, in the longer term, this may be the direction which the law takes. The **2.122** Court of Appeal in *Fassihi* held that the duty of disclosure was an incident of the duty of 'fidelity'. Whilst the court seemed to intend this to refer only to the fiduciary duty of a director, it is to be remembered that there is also an implied contractual duty of fidelity in every contract of employment, as is discussed below. Following *Bell v Lever Bros*, and even accounting for the gloss put upon it in *Fassihi*, that contractual duty does *not* in general require the disclosure of an employee's own wrongdoing.

---

[146] *Helmet Integrated Systems Ltd v Tunnard* [2007] IRLR 126, paras 46–7 *per* Moses LJ.
[147] ibid para 48 *per* Moses LJ.
[148] ibid para 41 *per* Moses LJ.
[149] *Hanco ATM Systems Ltd v Cashbox ATM Systems Ltd* [2007] EWHC 1599 (Ch), para 65 *per* Peter Smith J.
[150] *Item Software*, para 60.

2.123 If one accepts the proposition that *Bell v Lever Bros* is correctly decided and that *Fassihi* does not purport to undermine the *ratio* of *Bell v Lever Bros*, the decision in *Fassihi* is arguably consistent only with the proposition that the contractual and fiduciary duties of fidelity have significantly different contents.

Disclosing wider matters of interest to the employer

2.124 Employees may know of many matters that do not amount to serious misconduct by the employee/director or one of his fellow employees, but which would be of interest to the employer. The fiduciary duty of good faith is expressed in *Fassihi* in very broad and classical terms, which arguably include such matters.

2.125 It is important to note that the duty is a subjective one, focusing on the good faith decision of the employee. Thus a failure to disclose that is due to not considering the information important, or mere forgetfulness, cannot amount to breach of fiduciary duty albeit that it might amount to a breach of the obligation to exercise reasonable skill and care in the exercise of one's functions.[151]

2.126 However, the situation more commonly arises in relation to knowledge of another employee being unsettled, unhappy, or attending interviews with a competitor. The situation would be fortified in relation to a proposed 'team move'[152] where the senior member of the team is likely to owe some fiduciary duties and is likely to have knowledge that a team is being recruited from amongst his colleagues. In such circumstances, the fiduciary is under an obligation to disclose all of his knowledge and, indeed, under an obligation to use his best endeavours to persuade each such member of the team to remain with his current employer.[153] If he wishes to compete in conjunction with others, he must resign his office 'as soon as his intention has been irrevocably formed and he has launched himself in the actual taking of preparatory steps'.[154]

Exceptions

General power of resignation

2.127 The first exception to the fiduciary duty concerns resignation. A director (or other fiduciary) is able to resign at any time. Subject to any continuing obligations to account for trust property and to abide by obligations of confidentiality, the fiduciary obligations, and, in particular, the obligation of good faith, are then at an end. Further, and more importantly, the director is under no obligation to exercise that power in the best interests of the company. The director may resign at any point, regardless of how inconvenient or damaging his resignation may be to the company.[155] Accordingly, the wide *Fassihi* duty of disclosure must be at an end: (a) at the moment of resignation as a director; or (b) at the effective point at which the fiduciary obligations cease.

2.128 Furthermore, the scope of a fiduciary's obligations may alter during a notice period, even before resignation has formally taken effect. In *Foster Bryant Surveying Ltd v Bryant*,[156] the

---

[151] *Fulham Football Club v Tigana* [2004] EWHC 2585 (QB).
[152] As to team moves see further paras 2.260–2.287 and 9.41–9.45, 9.140–9.145, and 9.163–9.175 below.
[153] *British Midland Tool v Midland International Tooling* [2003] 2 BCLC 523.
[154] ibid para 89.
[155] *CMS Dolphin v Simonet* [2001] 2 BCLC 704.
[156] [2007] IRLR 425, CA.

Court of Appeal was faced with a claim against a director who had been effectively forced to resign, but who accepted a proposal during his notice period from the company's principal client that he should work for it essentially as an employee, although through a company of his own, after his resignation took effect. The company brought proceedings against the director alleging that by agreeing to the client's proposal before his resignation had taken effect, he had breached his fiduciary duty. The Court of Appeal upheld the judge's rejection of this claim, finding that the acceptance of the offer was 'no different from (at worst) setting in train preparations for potential competition after his resignation had become fully effective and he had ceased any relationship or employment with the company'.[157]

The Court of Appeal so held on the assumption that there was no diminution in the director's fiduciary duties during his notice period. However, Rix LJ then went on to doubt whether that assumption was in fact justified, holding: **2.129**

> As for the extent of his fiduciary duties, it seems to me that the judge's realistic findings as to the position within the company after Mr Bryant's resignation makes it very arguable that, so long as he remained honest and neither exploited nor took any property of the company, his duties extended no further than that. To demand more while he is excluded from his role as a director appears to me to be unrealistic and inequitable.[158]

In a situation in which a director is serving his notice period but is effectively excluded from the company, therefore, there may be a diminution in his fiduciary duties even before resignation has formally taken effect.

Looking for a new job

A second possible exception to the fiduciary duty of disclosure concerns situations in which a director or senior employee is: (a) unhappy or unsettled; or (b) attending interviews with a competitor. In both situations, it will be in the employer's best interests to know how the fiduciary is feeling and what he is doing, especially where the fiduciary has a short notice period, will be hard to replace, or will be engaging in competitive activity. In principle, following the *Fassihi* case, the fiduciary should therefore disclose his own likely departure to his employer. However, perhaps because of the unwieldy nature of such an obligation, the case law has evolved an exception of uncertain scope in this area. **2.130**

The problem arose, albeit tangentially, in *Searle v Celltech*.[159] The issue in that case was whether a former employee, who was subject to no covenants, could use his knowledge of his former employer's workforce to assist his new employer in soliciting those employees. In the course of deciding that, in that case, such information was not confidential and thus no interim injunction would lie, Cumming Bruce LJ stated, 'in the absence of restrictive covenants, there is nothing in the general law to prevent a number of employees in concert deciding to leave their employer and set themselves up in competition with him'.[160] **2.131**

This obiter statement, which had no apparent bearing on the result of the case, suggested that there was no duty to disclose. The relevant individual, a Dr Carey, was titled the Director of Research, but there is no suggestion that he was a statutory director. **2.132**

---

[157] ibid para 87 *per* Rix LJ. This is to be contrasted with the position in which a director receives and discusses an approach to recruit him during his employment, in which case he may be under a duty to disclose this fact: see eg *Kynixa Ltd v Hynes* [2008] EWHC 1495 (QB), para 262 *per* Wyn Williams J.

[158] ibid para 93 *per* Rix LJ.

[159] [1982] FSR 92.

[160] ibid 101.

2.133   The issue of disclosure of intention to leave then arose more directly in *Tithebarn v Hubbard*,[161] in which the Employment Appeal Tribunal (EAT) considered a case where it had been found that a senior employee (albeit not a director) had told a more junior employee that he was proposing to set up in competition with the employer and offered that employee a job in the future. On the assumption that it was a mere discussion for the future with an invitation that in due course the junior employee might care to join him, the EAT held that it did not, as a matter of fact, amount to a breach of contract.

2.134   To similar effect, in *Balston v Headline Filters*,[162] Falconer J held that as a matter of public policy and with regard to restraint of trade principles, a director need not disclose his personal intention to compete.

2.135   Subsequently, however, in *British Midland Tool Ltd v Midland International Tooling Ltd*,[163] the *Balston* case was distinguished by Hart J on the basis that it was limited to where the director was intending to compete on his own, without any involvement with other employees or directors of the employer. Somewhat surprisingly, given the result, Cumming Bruce LJ's obiter statement in the *Searle* case (see para 2.131 above) was briefly considered by Hart J and not disapproved.[164] Hart J's decision on this point appears to have been materially influenced by his finding that the senior management employees were held to have been in breach of their contractual duty of fidelity by '(at best) passive[ly] standing by while [the competitor] poached the workforce'.[165]

2.136   In *Shepherds Investments Ltd v Walters*,[166] it was argued that the *Balston* and *British Midland Tool* cases were inconsistent and that the *Balston* case should be preferred. Etherton J considered that, contrary to the *Balston* case, public policy and restraint of trade principles had no role in circumscribing the obligations of disclosure and that in so far as inconsistent, the *British Midland Tool* case should be preferred. As such, 'a director would be under a duty to alert his fellow board members to a nascent commercial threat to the future prospects of the company, and that duty would be all the greater (and certainly no less) when he himself was planning to be part of the threat'.[167] Etherton J did not, however, go beyond the proposition from the *British Midland Tool* case that it is the formation of irrevocable intent that forms the point at which the fiduciary duty (absent immediate resignation) would be breached. In *Cook v MSHK Ltd*,[168] the Court of Appeal assumed, without deciding, that a fiduciary had a duty to make disclosure to his employer or resign once he had formed a 'settled intention' to compete with his employer.[169]

2.137   There is an argument that *mere* employees may be entitled to have preliminary discussions with other employees for whom they have no responsibility and over whom they exert no control or influence to discuss a future outside the business. If those individuals then resign as soon as their plan is irrevocably formed (and avoid misuse of confidential information,

---

[161]   [1991] UKEAT 532/89/0711.
[162]   [1990] FSR 385.
[163]   [2003] 2 BCLC 523.
[164]   ibid paras 94–5.
[165]   ibid para 90.
[166]   [2007] IRLR 110.
[167]   Approving Hart J in *British Midland Tool v Midland International Tooling* [2003] 2 BCLC 523, para 81.
[168]   [2009] IRLR 838.
[169]   ibid paras 69–70 *per* Rimer LJ.

solicitation of clients, exclusive suppliers, or other employees) and are careful to avoid misleading their employers, whether as to the reasons for their departure or as to their intentions, they may commit no breach of their duty of fidelity. However, any more senior employee will be at serious risk of breach by a failure to alert their employer to a nascent commercial threat.[170]

In summary, given the conflicting first instance decisions and the running of the current **2.138** judicial tide against directors, the working assumption must be that directors and senior employees ought to disclose: (a) any action at all, if taken by others, that will lead to competitive activity; and (b) any action of their own, as soon as the irrevocable intention to compete is formed (unless they resign immediately).

Good faith as a contractual duty

Introduction

It is a characteristic term of every contract of employment that the employee owes a duty of **2.139** good faith and fidelity to the employer. The duty is of long standing, and was described in *Robb v Green*[171] as follows: 'I think that it is a necessary implication which must be engrafted on [a contract of service] that the servant undertakes to serve his master with good faith and fidelity.'[172]

Fact sensitivity

The practical scope of the duty of good faith is not easy to define but will vary according to **2.140** the nature of the contract. A contract of employment is not a contract of the *utmost* good faith. The obligation of the employee is not to subsume himself to the interests of the employer but rather to serve his employer in accordance with the terms of the contract.[173] The precise contours of the duty of good faith must therefore be ascertained according to the particular circumstances of a given employment relationship:

> It has been said on many occasions that an employee owes a duty of fidelity to his employer. As a general proposition that is indisputable. The practical difficulty in any given case is to find exactly how far that rather vague duty of fidelity extends. Prima facie it seems to me on considering the authorities and the arguments that it must be a question on the facts of each particular case.[174]
>
> . . . whether a particular act on the part of the servant is in breach of the contractual obligation [of good faith] the court has to determine, and the extent of the obligation, put in general terms, to show the good faith may vary very much indeed according to the particular nature of the contract.[175]

Related duties

Although the implied duty of good faith will inevitably overlap with any fiduciary duty **2.141** which the employee may owe to the employer, the two duties are by no means identical.

---

[170] But cf *Lonmar Global Risks v West* [2010] EWHC 2878 (QB) in which Hickinbottom J held that employees owed no general contractual duty of disclosure of the misconduct of others or the competitive intentions of third parties, still less the fact that they had invited other employees to join their nascent business venture.

[171] [1895] 2 QB 315.

[172] ibid 320 *per* Kay LJ.

[173] *Bell v Lever Bros* [1932] AC 161, HL.

[174] *Hivac v Park Royal* [1946] Ch 169, 174 *per* Lord Greene MR.

[175] *Vokes Ltd v Heather* [1945] 62 RPC 135, 141 *per* Lord Denning MR.

Importantly, the implied duty of good faith does not include, in the usual case, any prohibition as such on being in a position where self-interest may conflict with an employee's duty as employee.[176]

2.142 Furthermore, the implied obligation of trust and confidence is of little assistance in determining the scope of the obligation of good faith. Indeed, in *Mahmud v BCCI* the House of Lords held that 'the implied term [of trust and confidence] adds little to the employee's implied obligations to serve his employer loyally and not to act contrary to his employer's interests'.[177]

Particular incidents of the duty

2.143 The implied duty of good faith is thus distinct from the duty of trust and confidence, such that the particular requirements fall to be determined on the facts of each employment relationship. In particular, the other express terms of the contract may affect the scope and effect of the duty of good faith and fidelity. Notwithstanding this fact sensitivity, it is possible to observe some particular incidents of the duty which are of general application.

Competition during employment

2.144 The first and most common incident of the contractual duty of good faith is that it will almost invariably be breached where an employee is engaged in competition with his employer in time during which he is contracted to work for his employer.[178] The more senior the employee, the more likely that such competition will be a breach.

2.145 A fundamental requirement of this rule is that the competition be actual competition, as opposed to merely contemplated. The case of *Marshall v Industrial Systems and Control Ltd*[179] provides a useful illustration of this rule in action. In that case, the managing director of the respondent company placed a tender for a contract on the respondent company's behalf, at the same time as tendering for the same business in his personal capacity. The EAT found that the company acted properly in summarily dismissing him, because he was engaged in an actual attempt to 'deprive the company, of which he was managing director, of their best client'.[180]

2.146 This is to be contrasted with *Laughton and Hawley v Bapp Industrial Supplies Ltd,*[181] in which two employees wrote to suppliers indicating that they were intending to leave and set up in competition and seeking details of the suppliers' products. The employees were dismissed. There seems to have been no suggestion that the identity of the suppliers was confidential or in any sense protected. As such, this mere indication to suppliers as to an intention to compete was not a breach of the contractual duty of good faith.

2.147 Save in exceptional cases, this general rule against actual competition extends even to competitive activity undertaken during an employee's spare time.[182] It does not extend, however, to 'moonlighting' in other jobs which are *not* competitive with the business of the main

---

[176] *British Midland Tool v Midland International* [2003] 2 BCLC 523, para 94 *per* Hart J.
[177] [1998] AC 20, 46; [1997] ICR 606, 621 *per* Lord Steyn.
[178] *Thomas Marshall v Guinle* [1992] IRLR 294; *Nova Plastics Ltd v Froggatt* [1982] IRLR 146.
[179] [1992] IRLR 294.
[180] ibid para 16.
[181] [1986] ICR 634.
[182] *Hivac Ltd v Park Royal Scientific Instruments Ltd* [1946] Ch 169.

employer, since such work does not generally create a significant conflict of interest or otherwise cause harm to the employer.[183]

Rather, if an employer wishes to prevent his employee from working in *any* other job, he **2.148** must make express provision in the contract of employment. It appears that the courts will generally uphold such an express clause, notwithstanding the obvious restriction which it places upon an employee's freedom of contract.[184]

It should be noted that there is still, arguably, a rather anomalous exception relating to multiple **2.149** directorships, in that it has been held, in the *Mashonaland* case, that a person may act as a director of two competing companies without being in breach of his fiduciary duty to either.[185] As is noted above,[186] the *Mashonaland* case is a venerable authority, but has also been subjected to serious recent disapproval.[187] Until it is explicitly overruled, care is required in this area.

Preparing for competitive activity

Whereas actual competition during employment is unlawful, an employee may, in an **2.150** appropriate case, be able lawfully to prepare for future competitive activity which will be engaged in *after* his employment has ended. There is an obvious difficulty in drawing the line between permissible preparatory activity and impermissible actual competition, which can be illustrated by a comparison of two leading cases from the 1990s.

Balston Ltd v Headline Filters Ltd[188] concerned Mr Head, a director and employee who, after **2.151** deciding to resign, both: (a) agreed to take a lease on business premises, before having even given notice to his employer; and (b) once he had given notice, bought a company off the shelf. Both steps were taken with a view to future competition with the company, but both were found by Falconer J to fall into the category of *permissible* preparatory activity. Neither of these steps was held to amount to a breach of Head's duty of good faith as an employee, because neither constituted actual competition. However Head was in breach of his duty of good faith, whilst employed, in actively competing with his employer and approaching an employee of his employer to (indirectly) solicit her to join his new company.

In contrast, in *Lancashire Fires Ltd v SA Lyons & Co Ltd*,[189] preparatory steps were found to **2.152** breach the duty of good faith. In the *Lancashire Fires* case, the employee in question had, with a view to setting up his own business in competition with Lancashire Fires, bought equipment, rented premises, and misused confidential information. Moreover, and critically, he had entered an agreement with a potential client of the claimant to supply them with products once he had commenced trading and obtained finance from them to assist in the setting up of his new business and the refining of the processes necessary to manufacture product for that client. The Court held that the employee was not simply seeking employment with a competitor or taking preliminary steps to set up on his own,

---

[183] *Lancashire Fires v SA Lyons & Co Ltd* [1997] IRLR 113.
[184] *Symbian v Christensen* [2001] IRLR 77, in which the Court of Appeal upheld an injunction enforcing an express clause preventing the employee from engaging in *any other* employment during the term of his contract (albeit the injunction was expressed in narrower terms than the express clause), including during a period of garden leave in so far as such an injunction protected a legitimate interest of the claimant.
[185] *London & Mashonaland Exploration Co Ltd v New Mashonaland Exploration Co Ltd* [1891] WN 165.
[186] See para 2.96 above and accompanying footnotes.
[187] *In Plus Group Ltd v Pyke* [2002] 2 BCLC 201; cf *Bristol and West BS v Mothew* [1998] Ch 1, 18.
[188] [1990] FSR 385.
[189] [1997] IRLR 113, CA.

but rather his conduct placed him well on the wrong side of the line. The Court concluded: 'Indeed any employee with technical knowledge and experience can expect to have his spare time activities in the field in which his employers operate carefully scrutinised.'[190]

2.153 The key distinguishing feature between the *Balston* and *Lancashire Fires* cases seems to be that, in the latter case, the employee's position included the development of new projects and the refinement of processes, which were the very things he was undertaking whilst still employed, in conjunction with a potential client, for the benefit of his new undertaking.

2.154 The formation of a company or partnership for the purposes of future competition will always risk breaching the duty of good faith. In *Ward Evans Financial Services Ltd v Fox*, the Court of Appeal held that an employee's ability to serve his employer faithfully can in principle be impaired where he sets up a company for the purposes of future competition, even if that company does not trade until his current employment contract is terminated.[191] In contrast, in *Saatchi v Saatchi* it was held that an agreement that set up a partnership, but which expressly did not come into being until all parties were freed from their existing obligations, was not in breach of the duty.[192]

2.155 Ultimately, the key factor in drawing the line will remain whether, on the facts of a particular case, the allegedly preparatory activity impaired the employee's ability to serve his employer faithfully. In *Shepherds Investments Ltd v Walters*,[193] Etherton J held that 'the touchstone for what, on the one hand, is permissible, and what, on the other hand, is impermissible . . . is what . . . in the case of an employee, will be in breach of the obligation of fidelity'.[194]

2.156 This is a highly fact-specific test, as evidenced by Etherton J's later comments in the same case:

> It is obvious, for example, that merely making a decision to set up a competing business at some point in the future and discussing such an idea with friends and family would not of themselves be in conflict with the best interests of the company and the employer. The consulting of lawyers and other professionals may, depending on all the circumstances, equally be consistent with a director's fiduciary duties and the employee's obligation of loyalty. At the other end of the spectrum, it is plain that soliciting customers of the company and the employer or the actual carrying on of trade by a competing business would be in breach of the duties of the director and the obligations of the employee. It is the wide range of activity and decision making between the two ends of the spectrum which will be fact sensitive in every case.[195]

2.157 In the important case of *Helmet Integrated Systems v Tunnard*,[196] discussed elsewhere in this chapter, the Court of Appeal considered much of the line of authority discussed above and rejected the notion that the mere fact that a particular activity was 'preparatory' was in any way decisive of the issue of breach of duty:

> The battle between employer and former employee, who has entered into competition with his former employer, is often concerned with where the line is to be drawn between legitimate preparation for future competition and competitive activity undertaken before

---

[190] ibid 131.
[191] [2002] IRLR 120; cf *ABK Ltd v Foxwell* [2002] EWHC 9, Ch.
[192] 13 February 1995, Jonathan Parker J.
[193] [2007] IRLR 110.
[194] ibid para 108.
[195] ibid para 108.
[196] [2007] IRLR 126, CA. See paras 2.47–2.48 and 2.118–2.119 above.

the employee has left. This case has proved no exception. But in deciding on which side of the line Mr Tunnard's activities fall, it is important not to be beguiled into thinking that the mere fact that activities are preparatory to future competition will conclude the issue in a former employee's favour. The authorities establish that no such clear line can be drawn between that which is legitimate and that which breaches an employee's obligations.[197]

The Court of Appeal went on to make clear that the first issue was always the scope of **2.158** the duties owed by the employee—the invocation of the word 'preparatory' was not a short cut:

> ... it is insufficient merely to cloak activities with legitimacy by describing them as preparatory. The first task ... is to identify the nature of the employee's obligations. Once they have been identified, the court is then in a proper position to discern whether the activities of an employee undertaken in pursuance of a plan to be fulfilled on his departure is in breach of his duty to his employer or not.[198]

This approach, which is sensitive to the particular duties owed by a particular employee, **2.159** made it possible for Mr Tunnard, on the facts of the *Helmet Integrated Systems* case, to have engaged in quite wide-ranging preparatory activity during his employment without breaching his duties. Since he was a salesman rather than a designer, and since his employer had failed to impose any express restriction upon him with regard to preparatory activity in respect of his new helmet design, he was entitled to prepare to a quite considerable extent:

> The reason why Mr Tunnard did not breach any fiduciary obligation was because his own preparatory activity could not legitimately be described as 'competitor activity' in the context of his employment as a salesman and his right to prepare for competition once he had left employment as a salesman. However, the mere fact that his activities were preparatory was not, in my judgment, a sufficient answer to HISL's claim. Mr Tunnard's activities may well be described as reasonable and necessary acts of preparation for departure (see the judgment at para 62). But that of itself does not determine whether they amounted to a breach either of an obligation of fidelity or an obligation as fiduciary. Many activities might be described as reasonable and necessary for the purposes of future competition but that does not assist in deciding whether they were in breach of either obligation. The true reason, as I see it, why Mr Tunnard's activities did not amount to a breach of any obligation to HISL lies in the fact that HISL had not restricted the freedom which Mr Tunnard had to prepare for future competition on his departure.[199]

So, it was the fact that Mr Tunnard's employer had not restricted his 'right to prepare for competition' which was decisive.

This reasoning was followed and applied in *Pennwell Publishing (UK) Ltd v Ornstein*,[200] in **2.160** which it was held that in the absence of an express contractual restriction, the scope of steps preparatory to competition could include:

> ... identifying business partners, setting up a company and locating suitable premises and equipment, including where necessary actually acquiring them before the date of his departure.[201]

---

[197] ibid para 28 *per* Moses LJ.
[198] ibid para 32 *per* Moses LJ.
[199] ibid para 51 *per* Moses LJ.
[200] [2007] IRLR 700.
[201] ibid para 53 *per* Mr Justin Fenwick QC sitting as a Deputy High Court Judge.

This is a broad formulation, and indicates that the approach to preparatory activity which was taken by the Court of Appeal in the *Helmet* case may lead to a broadening of the scope of legitimate activity, at least where no express restriction has been imposed.

Copying or memorizing confidential information

2.161 A second incident of the contractual duty of good faith relates to confidential information. As set out above, the starting point for the implied duty of good faith and fidelity is *Robb v Green*.[202] In that case, the defendant had copied from his employer's books a list of the employer's customers with their addresses, with the intention of using that list, when he had left the employer's service, in order to set up a rival business and to induce the employer's customers to transfer their custom to him. This was described by AL Smith LJ[203] as the worst breach possible. The mere fact that none of the information in the list was in and of itself confidential was of no importance. The list as a whole had real value.

2.162 In the case of *Bullivant v Ellis*[204] the Court of Appeal considered whether injunctions should be continued in relation to a former managing director of the claimant who had taken with him confidential information on his departure from the claimant, including photocopies of the claimant's card index system. Despite challenge, the Court held that it was important that the principle in *Robb v Green*, 'which let it be said, is one of no more than fair and honourable dealing, should be steadfastly maintained'.[205]

2.163 In applying the above test, the courts have held that all of the following examples of conduct *will* breach the contractual duty of good faith:

(1) copying or memorizing trade secrets or other confidential information;[206]
(2) entertaining business offers from customers;[207] and
(3) soliciting the employer's customers.[208]

Recruiting or soliciting other employees

2.164 A third incident of the contractual duty of good faith is that it will almost invariably be a breach of that duty for an employee to recruit, encourage, or solicit other employees to leave the employer's employment.[209] This is especially so where the solicitation is with a view to forming a competitor *collectively*.

2.165 As set out above,[210] there was previously thought to be an exception to this rule in respect of the situation in which two or more employees *together* consider their future and then leave in concert. In this situation, the Court of Appeal has stated as follows:

---

[202] [1895] 2 QB 315, CA affirming the more illuminating judgment of Hawkins J [1895] 2 QB 1.

[203] ibid 320.

[204] [1987] ICR 464.

[205] ibid 475.

[206] See Chapter 3 below.

[207] *Sanders v Parry* [1967] 1 WLR 753.

[208] *Wessex Dairies v Smith* [1935] 2 KB 80, but cf *Lonmar Global Risks v West* [2010] EWHC 2878 (QB), in which Hickinbottom J suggested to the contrary. It is to be noted that he made no reference to most of the other recent cases cited in this section and the decision on this aspect would seem to run contrary to the general trend of authority in this area including, in particular, the *Tullett Prebon* case and the *Vestra* case.

[209] *Sanders v Parry* [1967] 1 WLR 753; *Marshall v Industrial Systems and Control Ltd* [1992] IRLR 294; *Adamson v BSL Cleaning Services* [1995] IRLR 193; *Balston v Headline Filters* [1990] FSR 385.

[210] See 2.131 above.

The law has always looked with favour upon the efforts of employees to advance themselves, provided they do not steal or use the secrets of their former employer. In the absence of restrictive covenants, there is nothing to prevent a number of employees in concert deciding to leave their employer and set themselves up in competition with him.[211]

Given the decisions cited above, discussions between employees as to proposed concerted competitive activity will rarely if ever be acceptable, given the near-inevitable damage to the employer as a result of such concerted activity. It remains possible that a discussion between close friends at a similar level within the business as to the potential of working together in the future will give rise to no breach. In such circumstances, neither employee would be soliciting the other and neither would be encouraging the other to terminate their employment with the employer. However, as set out in the *British Midland Tool* case, once an irrevocable intention to compete is formed, resignation and disclosure of the intention is probably the only certain means of avoiding a breach. **2.166**

A stark example of the courts' disapproval of the participation of senior employees in 'planned poaching raids' on the staff of their employer is provided by the case of *UBS Wealth Management (UK) Ltd v Vestra Wealth LLP*.[212] A former senior employee of the claimant bank, Mr Scott, managed to poach fifty-two of its employees, handing in resignation letters on their behalf on the same day. Although Mr Scott asserted that he had contacted each of the fifty-two employees individually and that there had been no contact between them regarding their mass defection, Openshaw J, in so far as he was able on an interim application, rejected this suggestion: **2.167**

> It is difficult to see how else the defections could have been organised or coordinated on this scale. I accept the convention in the City is that employees who are considering taking up alternative employment are under no obligation to their existing employers to disclose ongoing negotiations unless and until a clear agreement is made with the prospective employer, usually by the signing of a new contract of employment. I cannot accept that employees, in particular senior managers, can keep silent when they know of planned poaching raids upon the company's existing staff or client base and when these are encouraged and facilitated from within the company itself, the more so when they are themselves party to these plots and plans. It seems to me that that would be an obvious breach of their duties of loyalty and fidelity to UBS. [213]

The Court went on to find that the relevant department had been 'seething with plotting and planning for the mass exodus of staff for many months',[214] and that there was a formidable case that this would have involved clear breaches of duty on the part of the senior employees involved: **2.168**

> . . . the claimants have put together a formidable case that there was an unlawful plan to poach both staff and clients from UBS, that that plan was formulated and actively managed by Mr. Scott, and it was at every stage assisted and encouraged by senior staff, including each of these defendants. This is not, as Mr. Sutcliffe QC for Mr. Scott and Vestra contends, lawful competition dressed up as an unlawful conspiracy. It is, in my judgment, far more likely to be an unlawful conspiracy dressed up as lawful competition.[215]

---

[211] *Searle v Celltech* [1982] FSR 92, CA, 101–2 *per* Cumming-Bruce LJ.
[212] [2008] IRLR 965.
[213] ibid para 24.
[214] ibid para 28.
[215] ibid para 35.

2.169   A further recent example of the disinclination of the Courts to sanction 'raids' is provided by *Tullett Prebon Plc v BGC Brokers LP,*[216] a very complicated case factually, but which contains a succinct summary of the law applicable to the position of a 'desk head' where a competitor seeks to recruit his desk. In short, the desk head cannot assist the exercise:

> Where it is sought to recruit a desk as a whole, or the greater part of the desk, it is very likely that the desk head will be approached first with the object of sounding him out as to the desk. . . . He is obliged to inform his employer that the rival company is seeking to recruit the desk. . . . in my view the duty of a desk head in this situation is plain.
>
> In addition the desk head must not do anything to assist the recruitment of his desk . . . Where a desk head decides that he is in favour of the recruitment of his desk and thereafter assists the recruitment in such small or large ways as may arise, he is in plain breach of his duty: he has crossed the line between observing his duty to his employer and acting in the interest of his employer's rival.[217]

Diverting business opportunities

2.170   A fourth incident of the duty of good faith is that the duty will usually be breached where an employee takes steps during employment to divert business opportunities to himself, whether that business is to be undertaken before or after termination. This topic is covered in detail in paragraphs 2.181 to 2.219 below in relation to both fiduciary duties and contractual duties.

Misusing confidential information

2.171   A fifth incident of the duty of good faith relates to the misuse of confidential information by employees and ex-employees, which is given detailed treatment elsewhere in this work.[218] The relevant point for present purposes is that the implied duty of good faith was at least partly the basis for the decision in *Faccenda Chicken v Fowler,*[219] still one of the leading authorities on the obligation of confidence in employment contracts.

Answering questions truthfully

2.172   A sixth and final incident of the duty of good faith is a duty to answer certain questions truthfully. It may seem self-evident that an employer is entitled to a truthful and honest answer to a straight question. However, as with most things in relation to employment, this cannot be stated as an absolute proposition. There are three potential exceptions.

2.173   First, an employee may be entitled to tell a 'white lie' to his employer in certain circumstances. By way of example, an employee who is attending a job interview whilst taking a half day's holiday for the purpose need not tell his employer the true reason for taking the half day's holiday even if asked. The employee has an absolute entitlement to look for alternative employment, even if his departure would harm the interests of the employer, so long as he is not in breach of any covenants or other obligations. It may be that if the interview is pursuant to what seems to the employee to be a recruitment campaign by a competitor that may involve fellow employees, he will have to disclose that attempted recruitment even if this tends to disclose the fact that he is interested in being recruited. This is a more likely result the more senior the employee is.

---

[216] [2010] IRLR 648.
[217] ibid paras 68–9 *per* Jack J.
[218] See Chapter 3 below.
[219] [1987] Ch 117.

Secondly and similarly, in most cases an employee will be entitled to refuse to answer **2.174** questions about his private life or life outside work. The authors consider it unlikely that an inaccurate or untruthful answer in relation to such illegitimate questions would necessarily be considered to be a breach of duty. It would depend on the precise facts, and, in particular, on the reason for the employee telling the lie.

Thirdly and finally, whilst untruthfulness may amount to a breach, such breach may not be **2.175** repudiatory where an employee tells a lie without any intention of harming the interests of his employer, or concealing his own wrongdoing. In the case of *Fulham Football Club v Tigana*,[220] the claimant football club (Fulham) placed the defendant manager (Tigana) on garden leave during the latter period of his contract. Fulham was concerned that Tigana had been acting in breach of his duties in a variety of respects and so asked a series of questions of Tigana both orally and in writing. Some of Tigana's answers to those questions were said to be inaccurate. It was alleged that Tigana had thereby breached his contractual duty of fidelity and his fiduciary duty of good faith as a director.

It was contended (and accepted) that Tigana owed a contractual duty, as an incident of the **2.176** duty of good faith, to answer questions honestly. It was also contended that Tigana owed a *wider* fiduciary duty to give full and frank answers to questions. The judge considered that the correct test was whether Tigana deliberately concealed matters which he believed Fulham wanted to know.[221]

The principal ground for the judgment in favour of Tigana was that he had in fact given **2.177** honest but inaccurate answers to questions, having forgotten various matters that would have been of interest to Fulham.[222]

However, Elias J held, as an alternative ground for his finding, that even if Tigana had **2.178** deliberately concealed information from Fulham, such a breach of the contractual duty would not have been repudiatory because it was not done with the intention of harming Fulham nor to conceal his own wrongdoing but rather to divert unjustified suspicion from Tigana. Further, such a breach of fiduciary duty would not have rendered it equitable to deprive Tigana of his contractual rights (principally in unvested share options).

On appeal,[223] it did not prove necessary for this alternative finding to be considered by the **2.179** Court of Appeal.

Termination of the duty

The contractual duty of good faith ends in principle only with the termination of employ- **2.180** ment. There are two exceptions to this rule. First, there is a continuing duty not to misuse trade secrets.[224] Secondly, where an employee is put on garden leave, that act might also terminate or diminish the duty of good faith, notwithstanding the fact that the contract of employment still subsists.[225]

---

[220] [2004] All ER (D) 212 (Nov); affirmed [2005] EWCA Civ 895.
[221] ibid para 99.
[222] ibid para 103.
[223] [2005] EWCA Civ 895.
[224] *Mont (UK) Ltd v Mills* [1993] IRLR 172.
[225] *Symbian v Christensen* (8 May 2000, Scott VC). This was touched upon in *Fulham Football Club (1987) Ltd v Tigana* [2004] All ER (D) 212 (Nov), but no view was expressed by the judge (para 16). See, further, below.

D. Diverting business opportunities

Introduction

2.181   The contractual duty of fidelity, and the no profit and no conflict rules which are applicable to fiduciaries, will generally prevent an employee or director from diverting a business opportunity, of which they become aware as a result of their employment, away from their employer for their own gain.

2.182   An authoritative statement of the relevant principle was given in the early twentieth century by the Privy Council in *Cook v Deeks*.[226] In that case, directors of the Toronto Construction Company had negotiated a construction contract with the Canadian Pacific Railway, ostensibly on behalf of the company, but then entered into the contract personally, for their own gain. The Privy Council held that this was not open to the directors in question:

> . . . men who assume complete control of a company's business must remember that they are not at liberty to sacrifice the interests which they are bound to protect, and, while ostensibly acting for the company, divert in their own favour business which should properly belong to the company they represent. [227]

Since the directors had not observed this requirement, they held the contract they had acquired on trust for the Toronto Construction Company. The contract 'belonged in equity to the company and ought to have been dealt with as an asset of the company'.[228]

2.183   The underlying principle is therefore clear. The principle is built, however, upon duties which do not ordinarily outlast the length of the employment relationship or directorship, namely the contractual duty of fidelity and the fiduciary duties of no profit and no conflict. What happens, therefore, if a director or employee resigns in order to take advantage of a business opportunity of which he has become aware during his employment?

2.184   It is this difficult question which has occupied the courts in a series of decisions discussed below. For the busy practitioner, the most useful summary of the relevant authority is contained in the now-leading Court of Appeal authority of *Foster Bryant Surveying Ltd v Bryant*.[229] However, given the difficulty of the issue, it is necessary to take the most prominent authorities in turn.

The development of the law

Regal (Hastings) v Gulliver

2.185   The starting point for the development of the modern law in this area is the House of Lords decision in *Regal (Hastings) v Gulliver*.[230] In that case, the claimant company formed a subsidiary for the purpose of a specific property transaction, but found itself unable to fund the transaction in its entirety. Five of its directors resolved that they would personally fund the shortfall, each obtaining shares in the subsidiary company on a personal basis.

---

[226]   [1916] 1 AC 554.
[227]   ibid 563.
[228]   ibid 564.
[229]   [2007] IRLR 425, CA.
[230]   [1967] 1 AC 134.

The shareholdings were later sold at a substantial profit. After the directors had ceased to be such, the company brought an action to recover that profit.

The House of Lords, in a strongly expressed and unanimous judgment, held that the claimant **2.186** company was indeed entitled to recover the profit, because directors as fiduciaries were not entitled to profit personally from business opportunities which came their way in the course of the discharge of their duties. Lord Russell of Killowen stated the basic rule as follows:

> The rule of equity which insists on those, who by use of a fiduciary position make a profit, being liable to account for that profit, in no way depends on fraud, or absence of bona fides; or upon such questions or considerations as whether the profit would or should otherwise have gone to the plaintiff, or whether the profiteer was under a duty to obtain the source of the profit for the plaintiff, or whether he took a risk or acted as he did for the benefit of the plaintiff, or whether the plaintiff has in fact been damaged or benefited by his action. The liability arises from the mere fact of a profit having, in the stated circumstances, been made. The profiteer, however honest and well-intentioned, cannot escape the risk of being called upon to account.[231]

The strictness of this rule was recognized and emphasized by the House of Lords. Indeed, **2.187** Lord Russell decided the case on the basis that there were only two questions, being (1) whether the defendants made a profit from the shareholdings and (2) whether the defendants acquired the shares *by reason and in course of their office of directors*.[232] Since those two requirements were satisfied, the former directors were required to disgorge the profits which they had made.

Industrial Development Consultants Ltd v Cooley

The difficult problem of how to apply the decision of the House of Lords in *Regal (Hastings)* **2.188** to a situation in which a director had deliberately resigned in order to free himself to take up a particular business opportunity arose for decision in *Industrial Development Consultants Ltd v Cooley*.[233]

Mr Cooley, the managing director of IDC Ltd, had been engaged, unsuccessfully, in nego- **2.189** tiating contracts with the Eastern Gas Board relating to a new depot. Some time thereafter, the deputy director of the Eastern Gas Board made an approach to Cooley in a private capacity regarding the new depot. Cooley procured his release as managing director by making false claims of ill health, and was shortly afterwards offered contracts by the Eastern Gas Board for substantially the same business for which IDC Ltd had been bidding in the first place.

It will immediately be observed that, unlike in the *Regal (Hastings)* case, any profit made by **2.190** Cooley was made only *after* he had resigned from his fiduciary position. However, Roskill J still found Cooley liable to account for those profits. On the question of the precise fiduciary duty which Cooley owed, the Court held that information received as a result of a private approach was nevertheless information in respect of which Cooley owed a fiduciary duty to the company:

> The defendant had one capacity and one capacity only in which he was carrying on business at that time. That capacity was as managing director of the plaintiffs. Information which came to him while he was managing director and which was of concern to the plaintiffs and was

---

[231] ibid 144G–145A *per* Lord Russell of Killowen.
[232] ibid 145E–F *per* Lord Russell of Killowen.
[233] [1972] 1 WLR 443.

relevant for the plaintiffs to know, was information which it was his duty to pass on to the plaintiffs because between himself and the plaintiffs a fiduciary relationship existed . . .[234]

2.191 By concealing this information from his employer, and setting in train a plan to resign and take personal advantage of the business opportunity, Cooley put himself in a position of conflict of interest:

> From the time he embarked upon his course of dealing with the Eastern Gas Board . . . he embarked upon a deliberate policy and course of conduct which put his personal interest as a potential contracting party with the Eastern Gas Board in direct conflict with his pre-existing and continuing duty as managing director of the plaintiffs. That is something which for over 200 years the courts have forbidden.[235]

On this basis, Mr Cooley was ordered to account to IDC Ltd for profits which he 'has made and will make . . . as a result of having allowed his interests and his duty to conflict'.[236]

Island Export Finance Ltd v Umunna

2.192 The next and important stage in the development of the law in relation to diverting business opportunities came in the case of *Island Export Finance Ltd v Umunna and anor.*[237]

2.193 In that case, the defendant was the former managing director of the claimant, a company which pursued business in West Africa. During his term of office, the defendant secured a contract for the claimant from the Cameroon Postal Authority (CPA) for the supply of post boxes. However, the claimant company thereafter ceased business in that area. The defendant subsequently resigned, due to dissatisfaction rather than any desire to appropriate the claimant's business. The defendant set up his own company, which subsequently secured a new contract with the CPA for the supply of post boxes. The claimant sued for the defendant's alleged breach of fiduciary duty.

2.194 In a detailed judgment, Hutchison J rejected the claimant's case. Notably, he held that the law as set out in the Canadian case of *Canadian Aero Service v O'Malley*[238] ('*Canaero*') was an accurate description of the then law in England. In particular, Hutchison J relied on the following excerpt of Laskin J's judgment in the *Canaero* case:

> . . . a . . . director is precluded from obtaining for himself, either secretly or without the approval of the company . . . any property or business advantage either belonging to the company or for which it has been negotiating . . . In my opinion, this ethic disqualifies a director or senior officer from usurping for himself or diverting to another person or company with whom or with which he is associated a maturing business opportunity which his company is actively pursuing; he is also precluded from so acting even after his resignation where his resignation may fairly be said to have been prompted or influenced by a wish to acquire for himself the opportunity sought by the company, [or] where it was his position with the company rather than a fresh initiative that led him to the opportunity which he later acquired.[239]

---

[234] ibid 451F–G *per* Roskill J.
[235] ibid 451H–452A *per* Roskill J.
[236] ibid 454C *per* Roskill J.
[237] [1986] BCLC 460.
[238] (1973) 40 DLR (3d) 371.
[239] ibid 382 *per* Laskin J.

Hutchison J accepted this statement of the law with the single exception that he felt it was **2.195** likely that Laskin J meant 'and' rather than 'or'[240] in the above passage, in that the use of this word was probably meant as indicating the element of causation necessary to make the resignation of a director a ground for liability, and not indicating a separate ground for making him so liable. Such a separate ground would be both unnecessarily widely stated, having regard to the facts of the *Canaero* case, and in conflict with English rules of public policy in relation to restraint of trade.

On the facts of the *Umunna* case, Hutchison J held, there had been no breach of fiduciary **2.196** duty, because the claimant company had not been seeking to develop any business in the area of the supply of post boxes at the time when the claimant resigned. He had not therefore appropriated, in the words of the *Canaero* case, 'any property or business advantage either belonging to the company or for which it has been negotiating'. It is plain from the judgment that Hutchison J was at pains to prevent directors falling victim to de facto restrictive covenants for which the parties had never contracted. This interpretation is supported by Hutchison J's comment that:

> It would . . . be surprising to find that directors alone, because of the fiduciary nature of their relationship with the company, were restrained from exploiting after they had ceased to be such, any opportunity of which they had acquired knowledge while directors. Directors, no less than employees, acquire a general fund of knowledge and expertise in the course of their work, and it is plainly in the public interest that they should be free to exploit it in a new position. (ibid at 482)

The key differences between *Umunna* and the *Cooley* case, therefore, were that (1) the defen- **2.197** dant in *Umunna* had not resigned in order to pursue the business opportunity with the CPA, indeed that came along afterwards, and (2) the claimant company in *Umunna* was no longer in business in the area in which the business opportunity arose. It is readily comprehensible that, in those circumstances, there was no breach of fiduciary duty by the defendant. The defendant had neither profited from an opportunity which had come his way during his employment, nor had he put himself in any position of conflict. He was simply using expertise which had been acquired during his employment so as to engage in legitimate competitive activity thereafter.

Framlington v Anderson

The exact nature of the 'business opportunities' which are protected by the rule against **2.198** diverting such opportunities arose for consideration in *Framlington v Anderson*.[241]

In the *Framlington* case, the claimant company was negotiating with Rathbone to sell to it a **2.199** part of its business, in private client stock broking, which was managed by three of Framlington's directors. Those directors were excluded from the negotiations, and were informed that the claimant company was not concerned with the terms of remuneration which they would be able to negotiate with their prospective new employer. The directors duly negotiated a handsome deal under which they were allotted £1.67 million in shares in Rathbone, in return for five years of their services. The claimant company, after completion of the deal, brought proceedings against the directors alleging that they had breached their fiduciary duties and their duty of fidelity in negotiating the allocation of shares.

---

[240] As marked in square brackets above.
[241] [1995] 1 BCLC 475.

2.200   The court rejected the claimant's claim, finding that the directors had not breached their duty. Critically for present purposes, the court held that the client goodwill attaching to the directors represented an asset of the directors, and was not therefore a business opportunity capable of being diverted:

> The shares were paid in consideration of an asset of the three managers which they were willing to bring to Rathbone—an asset which belonged to them and which, on leaving the Framlington group's employment they were free to exploit for themselves, namely the client goodwill which attached to them as the persons who had, over many years, managed their clients' investments. The consideration shares were the price which the three were willing to accept in return for binding themselves under five year service contracts to make that goodwill available to Rathbone and for restricting their freedom, after the termination of their service contracts, to exploit that client goodwill for themselves or for others.
>
> Nor is it suggested, or can be suggested, that the three managers diverted to themselves some kind of maturing business opportunity which should have been made available to the plaintiffs of the kind which featured in *Industrial Development Consultants Ltd v Cooley* [1972] 1 WLR 443 to which I was referred. The opportunity which the plaintiffs had of extracting a payment from Rathbone in consideration of a transfer by FIM to Rathbone of one of its assets, namely its client goodwill in the private client investment management business which the three managers had been managing, was one that Mr Loach, on behalf of the group, was free to exploit and did exploit.[242]

On that basis, the court rejected the claim that the directors were in any way conflicted or in breach of their duties in negotiating the package which they had negotiated. It will be noted that the approach of the Court was to regard the goodwill in question as an 'asset' of one party or another.

Brown v Bennett

2.201   This turn in the developing case law towards a more proprietary basis of liability for the diversion of business opportunities received further impetus with the decision of the Court of Appeal in *Brown v Bennett*.[243]

2.202   The case did not in itself concern the diversion of business opportunities, but in the course of his reasoning Morritt LJ did make reference to what he described as 'the corporate opportunity cases', commenting as follows:

> Those are cases in which a beneficial commercial opportunity comes the company's way and forms knowledge owned or possessed by the directors as agents for the company. Those directors then seek to use that knowledge or opportunity for themselves and are subsequently held to be constructive trustees of it and of its fruits for the company whence they took it.[244]

Having referred to *Cook v Deeks*,[245] Morritt LJ then said, 'it seems to me that in cases such as that there is a distribution or a disposal of the property of the company in breach of trust'.[246] The Court of Appeal thus took an essentially proprietary, rather than personal, approach to the issue of diverting business opportunities.

---

[242] ibid 496 *per* Blackburne J.
[243] [1999] 1 BCLC 649, [1999] BCC 525.
[244] ibid 532 *per* Morritt LJ.
[245] [1916] 1 AC 554.
[246] [1999] 1 BCLC 649, [1999] BCC 525 at 532 *per* Morritt LJ.

CMS Dolphin Ltd v Simonet

The trend towards regarding a 'maturing business opportunity' as a form of property was **2.203** furthered in *CMS Dolphin Ltd v Simonet*.[247] The defendant director, Simonet, after falling out with his business partner, had resigned. He had already taken steps to set up in competition, including incorporating a company for the purpose. Simonet proceeded to start up his new business, and in doing so poached all of the staff of the claimant business, many of its actual and potential clients, and their contracts with the claimant.

In a detailed and considered judgment, Lawrence Collins J considered the key authorities, **2.204** including *Regal (Hastings)*, *Cooley*, *Canaero*, and *Umunna*. He held that, whilst it was natural, on the particular facts of the *Regal (Hastings)* and *Cooley* cases, that the decisions had turned on breaches of the fiduciary 'no conflict' rule which had occurred whilst the relevant directors were *in office*, the 'underlying basis' of the rule against the diversion of business opportunities was in fact that such opportunities were the property of the employer:

> In my judgment the underlying basis of the liability of a director who exploits after his resig-
> nation a maturing business opportunity of the company is that the opportunity is to be treated
> as if it were the property of the company in relation to which the director had fiduciary duties.
> By seeking to exploit the opportunity after resignation he is appropriating for himself that
> property. He is just as accountable as a trustee who retires without properly accounting for the
> trust property. In the case of the director he becomes a constructive trustee of the fruits of his
> abuse of the company's property, which he has acquired in circumstances where he knowingly
> had a conflict of interest, and exploited it by resigning from the company.[248]

If such reasoning is accepted in full, there is no logical distinction between a 'maturing' **2.205** business opportunity, and an existing or already-exploited business opportunity. Lawrence Collins J accordingly held that Simonet's duties were not limited to 'maturing' business opportunities, but rather applied to 'actual contracts or maturing business opportunities'.[249] This was part of the *ratio* of the case because almost all of the opportunities diverted by Simonet were already being undertaken by CMS Dolphin pursuant to retainers. On the basis of the *Simonet* case, therefore, directors may be precluded from usurping even the *existing* contracts of their ex-employers (in addition to maturing business opportunities) after termination of their employment.

This is a substantial extension of the *Umunna* principle, and arguably creates precisely the de **2.206** facto restrictive covenants that Hutchison J was seeking to avoid in that case, when emphasizing that directors ought to be free to use their own skill and experience upon leaving an employer.

If, as a result of the *Simonet* case, the property rights of a company extend to what is almost **2.207** goodwill rather than real property, then this affirms a shift in the basis of liability from the personal basis of breach of the no conflict rule to a proprietary basis of breach of the no profit rule. It also requires a far broader definition of 'property' than appears ever to have been contemplated in the *Umunna* case.

Indeed, the logical consequence of the *Simonet* decision is that the director was prohibited **2.208** from soliciting the clients of his former company, despite the absence of a covenant, because

---

[247] [2001] BCLC 315.
[248] ibid para 96.
[249] ibid para 129.

those clients were the *property* of the former company. The *Simonet* decision therefore appears to create a form of implied non-compete covenant, which could affect any director. This type of implied covenant has potentially far-reaching consequences.[250] Since it is not clear what trust property is protected, or when the continuing fiduciary duty in relation to it is deemed to cease, the *Simonet* covenant would apply in an uncertain manner and for an uncertain length of time.

2.209   The decision of Lawrence Collins J was subsequently described by the Court of Appeal, in the case of *In Plus Group Ltd v Pyke*,[251] as 'a valuable recent analysis of the law'.[252]

Three 'no conflict' decisions

2.210   In the three years or so after *Simonet* was decided, there were three judgments, in *Bhullar v Bhullar*,[253] *Crown Dilmun v Sutton*,[254] and *Quarter Master UK Ltd v Pyke*,[255] in which fiduciaries diverted business opportunities away from the companies to which they owed fiduciary duties, whilst they were *still in office*. It was therefore unnecessary in each case for the court to deploy the *Simonet* proprietary reasoning, and the cases were instead decided on the basis of the no conflict rule.

2.211   Indeed, in the *Bhullar* case, the Court of Appeal considered many of the relevant authorities, including *Regal (Hastings)* and *Cooley*, and, without referring to *Simonet*, held that those authorities reflected the application of the no conflict rule:

> . . . the concept of a conflict between fiduciary duty and personal interest presupposes an existing fiduciary duty. But it does not follow that it is a prerequisite of the accountability of a fiduciary that there should have been some improper dealing with property 'belonging' to the party to whom the fiduciary duty is owed, that is to say with trust property. The relevant rule, which Lord Cranworth LC in *Aberdeen Railway Co v Blaikie Bros* described as being 'of universal application', and which Lord Herschell in *Bray v Ford* [1896] AC 44 at p.51, described as 'inflexible', is that (to use Lord Cranworth's formulation) no fiduciary 'shall be allowed to enter into engagements in which he has, or can have, a personal interest conflicting, or which may possibly conflict, with the interests of those whom he is bound to protect'.
>
> In a case such as the present, where a fiduciary has exploited a commercial opportunity for his own benefit, the relevant question, in my judgment, is not whether the party to whom the duty is owed (the company, in the instant case) had some kind of beneficial interest in the opportunity: in my judgment that would be too formalistic and restrictive an approach. Rather, the question is simply whether the fiduciary's exploitation of the opportunity is such as to attract the application of the rule.[256]

2.212   There therefore remained a tension in the case law as to whether the rule against diverting business opportunities was a reflection of (1) a proprietary interest in a business opportunity (per *Framlington*, *Brown*, and *Simonet*), or (2) the personal liability of a fiduciary in respect of the no profit and no conflict rules (per *Regal (Hastings)*, *Cooley*, *Umunna*, *Bhullar*, *Crown Dilmun*, and *Pyke*).

---

[250]   However, this is precisely the position that applies in relation to partnerships—*Trego v Hunt* [1896] AC 7.
[251]   [2003] BCC 332.
[252]   ibid para 71 *per* Brooke LJ.
[253]   [2003] 2 BCLC 241.
[254]   [2004] 1 BCLC 468
[255]   [2005] 1 BCLC 245.
[256]   [2003] 2 BCLC 241, paras 27–8 *per* Parker LJ.

Ultraframe (UK) Ltd v Fielding

In his titanic judgment in *Ultraframe (UK) Ltd v Fielding*,[257] Lewison J sought to bring some **2.213** clarity to this area of the law. After an exhaustive analysis of the authorities, he considered there to be three separate but interlinked duties applying to directors that might create very different results:[258]

(1) the no conflicts rule applies only until the termination of a directorship but cannot apply beyond, termination of the directorship being the principal means to bring such conflicts to an end;
(2) the no profits rule applies to profits obtained by reason of the directorship and thus may outlast the termination of the relationship; and
(3) the obligation to account for trust property applies only in relation to matters in which the company already has proprietary rights, so will not generally apply to maturing business opportunities, but will apply to contracts, as in the *Simonet* case.

This analysis is valuable, though it does not necessarily make the giving of advice much easier. As Lewison J noted, the law relating to the accountability of a director for profits derived from diversion of corporate opportunities is still developing. Permission to appeal was refused[259] by the Court of Appeal in the *Ultraframe* case on the facts, without any consideration of whether the legal issues gave rise to any grounds of appeal.

Foster Bryant Surveying Ltd v Bryant

The most recent analysis of this issue at the appellate level is that of the Court of Appeal in **2.214** *Foster Bryant Surveying Ltd v Bryant*.[260] The Court was at pains to stress that this was 'not a case . . . where Mr Bryant resigned in order to attempt to take work or clients from the company',[261] since the defendant director, Mr Bryant, had been forced out of the business. Instead, this was a case where Mr Bryant was approached, during his notice period, by the claimant company's main customer, which asked him to perform a role, essentially as an employee albeit through a service company, so as to give continuity of the relationship.

With regard to the claimant company's assertion that Mr Bryant had breached his fiduciary **2.215** duty by accepting the offer of employment, Rix LJ conducted a wide-ranging review of the authorities on the diversion of business opportunities, and cited[262] the following statement of the relevant principles, taken from *Hunter Kane Ltd v Watkins*:[263]

1. A director, while acting as such, has a fiduciary relationship with his company. That is, he has an obligation to deal towards it with loyalty, good faith and avoidance of the conflict of duty and self-interest.
2. A requirement to avoid a conflict of duty and self-interest means that a director is precluded from obtaining for himself, either secretly or without the informed approval of the company, any property or business advantage either belonging to the company or for

---

[257] [2005] EWHC 1638 (Ch), [2006] FSR 17.
[258] ibid para 1332.
[259] Other than in relation to costs, in respect of which the appeal was dismissed, *sub nom Northstar Systems Ltd v Fielding* [2006] EWCA Civ 1660.
[260] [2007] IRLR 425, CA.
[261] ibid para 1 *per* Rix LJ.
[262] ibid para 8 *per* Rix LJ.
[263] [2003] EWHC 186 (Ch), which in turn had sought to distil previous judgments including, in particular, *CMS Dolphin v Simonet*.

which it has been negotiating, especially where the director or officer is a participant in the negotiations.

3. A director's power to resign from office is not a fiduciary power. He is entitled to resign even if his resignation might have a disastrous effect on the business or reputation of the company.

4. A fiduciary relationship does not continue after the determination of the relationship which gives rise to it. After the relationship is determined the director is in general not under the continuing obligations which are a feature of the fiduciary relationship.

5. Acts done by the directors while the contract of employment subsists but which are preparatory to competition after it terminates are not necessarily in themselves a breach of the implied term as to loyalty and fidelity.

6. Directors, no less than employees, acquire a general fund of skill, knowledge and expertise in the course of their work, which [it] is plainly in the public interest that they should be free to exploit . . . in a new position. After ceasing the relationship by resignation or otherwise a director is in general (and subject of course to any terms of the contract of employment) not prohibited from using his general fund of skill and knowledge, the 'stock in trade' of the knowledge he has acquired while a director, even including things such as business contacts and personal connections made as a result of his directorship.

7. A director is however precluded from acting in breach of the requirement at 2 above, even after his resignation where the resignation may fairly be said to have been prompted or influenced by a wish to acquire for himself any maturing business opportunities sought by the company and where it was his position with the company rather than a fresh initiative that led him to the opportunity which he later acquired.

8. In considering whether an act of a director breaches the preceding principle the factors to take into account will include the factor of position or office held, the nature of the corporate opportunity, its ripeness, its specificness and the director's relation to it, the amount of knowledge possessed, the circumstances in which it was obtained and whether it was special or indeed even private, the factor of time in the continuation of the fiduciary duty where the alleged breach occurs after termination of the relationship with the company and the circumstances under which the breach was terminated, that is whether by retirement or resignation or discharge.

9. The underlying basis of the liability of a director who exploits after his resignation a maturing business opportunity of the company is that the opportunity is to be treated as if it were the property of the company in relation to which the director had fiduciary duties. By seeking to exploit the opportunity after resignation he is appropriating for himself that property. He is just as accountable as a trustee who retires without properly accounting for trust property.

10. It follows that a director will not be in breach of the principle set out at point 7 above where either the company's hope of obtaining the contract was not a 'maturing business opportunity' and it was not pursuing further orders or where the director's resignation was not prompted or influenced by a wish to acquire the business for himself.

11. As regards breach of confidence, although while the contract of employment subsists a director or other employee may not use confidential information to the detriment of his employer, after it ceases the director/employee may compete and may use know-how acquired in the course of his employment (as distinct from trade secrets—although the distinction is sometimes difficult to apply in practice).

2.216 This statement of the principles is not without its difficulties. For instance, the seventh, ninth, and tenth principles, taken together, contradict the reasoning of Lewison J in *Ultraframe* that a 'maturing business opportunity' could *not* be regarded as a proprietary interest and only a concluded contract could. Indeed, on these principles, a 'maturing business opportunity' would be considerably better protected than an actual concluded contract. However, the principles were described later in his judgment by Rix LJ as 'perceptive and useful'.[264]

The Court of Appeal, whilst citing the statement of principles set out above, was also keen to **2.217** stress the fact-sensitivity of the equitable principles which were in play. In particular, in respect of the question whether profiting from a business opportunity after resignation would constitute a breach of duty, Rix LJ described the spectrum of possible cases as follows:

> At one extreme (*In Plus Group Ltd v Pyke* [2002] 2 BCLC 201) the defendant is director in name only. At the other extreme, the director has planned his resignation having in mind the destruction of his company or at least the exploitation of its property in the form of business opportunities in which he is currently involved (*Industrial Development Consultants Ltd v Cooley* [1972] 1 WLR 443, *Canadian Aero Service Ltd v O'Malley* 40 DLR (3d) 371, *CMS Dolphin Ltd v Simonet* [2001] 2 BCLC 704 and *British Midland Tool Ltd v Midland International Tooling Ltd* [2003] 2 BCLC 523). In the middle are more nuanced cases which go both ways: in *Shepherds Investments Ltd v Walters* [2007] 2 BCLC 202 the combination of disloyalty, active promotion of the planned business, and exploitation of a business opportunity, all while the directors remained in office, brought liability; in *Island Export Finance Ltd v Umunna* [1986] BCLC 460, *Balston Ltd v Headline Filters Ltd* [1990] FSR 385 and *Framlington Group plc v Anderson* [1995] 1 BCLC 475, however, where the resignations were unaccompanied by disloyalty, there was no liability.[265]

In the authors' view, this statement of the range of factual scenarios is likely to provide a helpful starting point for the consideration of this issue in future cases.

The present state of the law

After a period of considerable flux, the law has now been clarified to the extent that it is **2.218** possible to identify three classes of case in which liability may be founded under the rules prohibiting the diversion of a business opportunity:

(1) In the first class of case, a fiduciary profits personally, whilst he is still in office, from a business opportunity of which he becomes aware as a result of his fiduciary position ('opportunity'). Such action will invariably be unlawful and will render him liable to account (see, for example, *Cook v Deeks*, *Regal (Hastings)*, and *Bhullar*).

(2) In the second class of case, a fiduciary profits personally from an opportunity, but only after having resigned in order to pursue that opportunity. Such action will usually also be unlawful, because it stems from a breach of duty whilst such duties were still owed, which breach was furthered by the resignation (see, for example, *Cooley* and *Simonet*).

(3) In the third class of case, a fiduciary profits personally from an opportunity, after having resigned for reasons unrelated to that opportunity. In such cases there will have been no breach of the no conflict rule (see *Umunna*), but it might still be possible to found liability on the basis that an actual or maturing contract was properly to be regarded as the property of the business (see *Brown*, *Simonet*, and *Ultraframe*).

It is in respect of the qualification to the third principle that there is most doubt. The possibility, expressed most clearly in the *Simonet* case, of regarding actual or potential contracts of a business as its property, which cannot be appropriated or solicited by a former fiduciary even

---

[264] [2007] IRLR 425 para 76 *per* Rix LJ.
[265] ibid para 77 *per* Rix LJ.

after his or her resignation, is an attractive one to employers, but one which stands in tension with the law's general desire to allow free competition, and which overlaps with the principles on restraint of trade and misuse of confidential information. The authors expect to see further developments in the near future.

Contractual liability

2.219 It is of course important to recall that, whilst the above discussion deals with the duty not to divert business opportunities as a fiduciary obligation, it may just as equally have a contractual basis, arising as an incident of an implied duty of good faith and fidelity. It may therefore have applicability to a far broader range of employment relationships.

2.220 In some situations, it will make little difference which of the two bases for grounding the duty is adopted. Where the duty arises from an implied contractual duty of good faith and fidelity, it will invariably have been breached in circumstances where an employee takes steps, while still in employment, to divert business opportunities to himself to be undertaken after termination (see, for example, *Sanders v Parry*[266]). Equally, as indicated by the *Cooley* case, where employees owe fiduciary duties to their employers, these duties subsist for as long as those employees are employed; they will therefore invariably be breached where the employee takes steps to divert business opportunities whilst still in employment.

2.221 The situation is somewhat different where it is alleged that a duty has been breached outside the employment relationship. Contractual duties can outlast the actual employment relationship where, for example, they are embodied in post-termination restrictive covenants.

E. Companies Act 2006

2.222 As stated above, the Companies Act 2006 has codified the law in relation to the duties of directors. As at the time of writing, there have not yet been any cases which suggest that any substantive change has been made to the previous law.[267]

2.223 For our purposes, the most important changes relate to the duties owed by directors and the means by which those duties can be enforced. The nature of the duties and their application is set out in clear terms in section 170. This makes clear that the duties are owed by all directors[268] and, in general, shadow directors:

> **170. Scope and nature of general duties**
>
> (1) The general duties specified in sections 171 to 177 are owed by a director of a company to the company.
> (2) A person who ceases to be a director continues to be subject—
>   (a) to the duty in section 175 (duty to avoid conflicts of interest) as regards the exploitation of any property, information or opportunity of which he became aware at a time when he was a director, and
>   (b) to the duty in section 176 (duty not to accept benefits from third parties) as regards things done or omitted by him before he ceased to be a director.

---

[266] [1967] 1 WLR 753.
[267] See eg *Thermascan v Norman* [2009] EWHC 3694 (Ch).
[268] Suggesting a limitation of the exception in *In Plus Group v Pyke* [2003] BCC 332.

To that extent those duties apply to a former director as to a director, subject to any necessary adaptations.

(3) The general duties are based on certain common law rules and equitable principles as they apply in relation to directors and have effect in place of those rules and principles as regards the duties owed to a company by a director.

(4) The general duties shall be interpreted and applied in the same way as common law rules or equitable principles, and regard shall be had to the corresponding common law rules and equitable principles in interpreting and applying the general duties.

(5) The general duties apply to shadow directors where, and to the extent that, the corresponding common law rules or equitable principles so apply.

2.224 The general duties are listed in sections 171 to 177. Perhaps the most significant implication of section 170 is that section 171(2) identifies the post-termination obligations of directors, putting on a statutory footing the decision in *CMS Dolphin v Simonet*.[269] This liability is based firmly upon the no conflicts rule rather than the no profits rule (as to which see above).

2.225 In addition, there is an obligation not to accept benefits (ie secret profits) from acts done prior to becoming a director. Uncontroversially, section 171 also provides that directors must act in accordance with the company's constitution[270] and only exercise powers for the purposes for which they are conferred.

2.226 Section 172 identifies the paramount duty of good faith as an obligation to promote the success of the company for the benefit of its members as a whole, whilst identifying, on a non-exhaustive basis, the matters which the director may take into account, greatly expanding on the toothless section 309 of the Companies Act 1985. This indicates, perhaps surprisingly, that the members as a whole will benefit from matters that are far outside the narrow, short- and long-term, exclusively commercial interests of many shareholders of many companies. In many instances, these obligations may give rise to complaints by shareholders that the wrong interests are being considered or ignored. By way of example, one can imagine single interest pressure groups becoming shareholders of plcs and then bringing derivative actions to force those companies to take far greater notice of environmental concerns:

172. Duty to promote the success of the company

(1) A director of a company must act in the way he considers, in good faith, would be most likely to promote the success of the company for the benefit of its members as a whole, and in doing so have regard (amongst other matters) to—
    (a) the likely consequences of any decision in the long term,
    (b) the interests of the company's employees,
    (c) the need to foster the company's business relationships with suppliers, customers and others,
    (d) the impact of the company's operations on the community and the environment,
    (e) the desirability of the company maintaining a reputation for high standards of business conduct, and
    (f) the need to act fairly as between members of the company.

(2) Where or to the extent that the purposes of the company consist of or include purposes other than the benefit of its members, subsection (1) has effect as if the reference to promoting the success of the company for the benefit of its members were to achieving those purposes.

---

[269] [2001] BCLC 704.
[270] The new word for the company's articles.

(3) The duty imposed by this section has effect subject to any enactment or rule of law requiring directors, in certain circumstances, to consider or act in the interests of creditors of the company.

2.227 Section 173 reinforces the obligation upon a director to exercise independent judgment rather than slavishly following a particular line. However, this would not be infringed by the director acting in accordance with constraints entered into by the company in relation to the exercise of a director's discretion or in a manner authorized by the company's constitution:

173. Duty to exercise independent judgment

(1) A director of a company must exercise independent judgment.
(2) This duty is not infringed by his acting—
    (a) in accordance with an agreement duly entered into by the company that restricts the future exercise of discretion by its directors, or
    (b) in a way authorised by the company's constitution.

2.228 The non-fiduciary duty owed by all directors to exercise reasonable skill and care is refor-mulated on codification, by section 174, as a duty to exercise reasonable care, skill, and diligence. The threshold is a combination of the objective expectations of a company of a director holding the position in question and the subjective knowledge, skill, and experience of the particular director:

174. Duty to exercise reasonable care, skill and diligence

(1) A director of a company must exercise reasonable care, skill and diligence.
(2) This means the care, skill and diligence that would be exercised by a reasonably diligent person with—
    (a) the general knowledge, skill and experience that may reasonably be expected of a person carrying out the functions carried out by the director in relation to the company, and
    (b) the general knowledge, skill and experience that the director has.

2.229 The no conflicts rule is set out in section 175 together with the means of authorizing such a conflict. The most significant feature is that a conflict can be authorized by the board of directors, subject to constitutional issues, rather than the current law requiring approval by the shareholders:

175. Duty to avoid conflicts of interest

(1) A director of a company must avoid a situation in which he has, or can have, a direct or indirect interest that conflicts, or possibly may conflict, with the interests of the company.
(2) This applies in particular to the exploitation of any property, information or opportunity (and it is immaterial whether the company could take advantage of the property, infor-mation or opportunity).
(3) This duty does not apply to a conflict of interest arising in relation to a transaction or arrangement with the company.
(4) This duty is not infringed—
    (a) if the situation cannot reasonably be regarded as likely to give rise to a conflict of interest; or
    (b) if the matter has been authorised by the directors.

(5) Authorisation may be given by the directors—

    (a) where the company is a private company and nothing in the company's constitution invalidates such authorisation, by the matter being proposed to and authorised by the directors; or

    (b) where the company is a public company and its constitution includes provision enabling the directors to authorise the matter, by the matter being proposed to and authorised by them in accordance with the constitution.

(6) The authorisation is effective only if—

    (a) any requirement as to the quorum at the meeting at which the matter is considered is met without counting the director in question or any other interested director, and

    (b) the matter was agreed to without their voting or would have been agreed to if their votes had not been counted.

(7) Any reference in this section to a conflict of interest includes a conflict of interest and duty and a conflict of duties.

The no profits rule is set out in section 176. This identifies the twofold nature of the no **2.230** profits rule, both as to benefits received by reason of being a director and benefits received by reason of doing things as a director:

176. Duty not to accept benefits from third parties

(1) A director of a company must not accept a benefit from a third party conferred by reason of—

    (a) his being a director, or

    (b) his doing (or not doing) anything as director.

(2) A 'third party' means a person other than the company, an associated body corporate or a person acting on behalf of the company or an associated body corporate.

(3) Benefits received by a director from a person by whom his services (as a director or otherwise) are provided to the company are not regarded as conferred by a third party.

(4) This duty is not infringed if the acceptance of the benefit cannot reasonably be regarded as likely to give rise to a conflict of interest.

(5) Any reference in this section to a conflict of interest includes a conflict of interest and duty and a conflict of duties.

Section 177 provides the means of declaring interests in proposed transactions or arrange- **2.231** ments. The extent to which this ties in with potential breaches of the no conflict and no profit rule remains to be determined by judicial consideration. It is notable that declaration under section 177 is not expressed to have any effect on breach of the no conflict and no profit rules. This is surprising given that in most cases, interest in a proposed transaction or arrangement would give rise to the potential for a breach of the no conflict rule which can only be avoided by authorization (rather than mere declaration) under the terms of section 175:

177. Duty to declare interest in proposed transaction or arrangement

(1) If a director of a company is in any way, directly or indirectly, interested in a proposed transaction or arrangement with the company, he must declare the nature and extent of that interest to the other directors.

(2) The declaration may (but need not) be made—

    (a) at a meeting of the directors, or

    (b) by notice to the directors in accordance with—

        (i) section 184 (notice in writing), or

        (ii) section 185 (general notice).

(3) If a declaration of interest under this section proves to be, or becomes, inaccurate or incomplete, a further declaration must be made.

(4) Any declaration required by this section must be made before the company enters into the transaction or arrangement.

(5) This section does not require a declaration of an interest of which the director is not aware or where the director is not aware of the transaction or arrangement in question. For this purpose a director is treated as being aware of matters of which he ought reasonably to be aware.

(6) A director need not declare an interest—

   (a) if it cannot reasonably be regarded as likely to give rise to a conflict of interest;

   (b) if, or to the extent that, the other directors are already aware of it (and for this purpose the other directors are treated as aware of anything of which they ought reasonably to be aware); or

   (c) if, or to the extent that, it concerns terms of his service contract that have been or are to be considered—

      (i) by a meeting of the directors, or

      (ii) by a committee of the directors appointed for the purpose under the company's constitution.

2.232 The effect of a breach of any of the new statutory duties is identified in section 178 as being the same as is currently the case. Section 179 provides explicitly that more than one of the duties may be engaged at any time.

F. Economic torts and the liabilities of third parties

Introduction

2.233 This chapter has so far focused on claims and remedies available against the employee who is competing with his employer or former employer. But in appropriate cases the employee is not the only potential target. It may also be possible to bring proceedings against the employee's new or prospective employer, for the tort of inducing the employee's breach of contract, conspiracy, or unlawful interference with business. These 'economic torts' have been substantially remodelled in recent decisions of the House of Lords. In addition to the economic torts discussed below, in confidential information cases third parties may be liable for breach of confidence. In cases of breach of fiduciary duty by an employee, a third party may be faced with a claim that he is liable to account in equity for either dishonestly assisting in the employee's breach, or knowing receipt of trust property.

Inducing breach of contract

2.234 It is a tort for a third party knowingly and intentionally to procure a breach of a contract (including breach of an (enforceable) negative covenant which is all that survives of a contract which has otherwise been fully performed).[271] The leading case on this tort is now the decision of the House of Lords in *OBG Ltd v Allan* ('*OBG*').[272] The ingredients of the tort following *OBG* have been summarized as follows:

---

[271] *Rickless v United Artists Corp* [1988] QB 40, 58–9.

[272] [2008] 1 AC 1, [2007] IRLR 608, HL. There were, in fact, three conjoined appeals: *OBG Ltd v Allan*, *Douglas v Hello! Ltd*, and *Mainstream Properties v Young*. We shall refer to them together as *OBG*.

first, there must be a contract, second, there must be a breach of that contract, thirdly, the conduct of the relevant defendant must have been such as to procure or induce that breach, fourthly, the relevant defendant must have known of the existence of the relevant term in the contract or turned a blind eye to the existence of such a term and, fifthly, the relevant defendant must have actually realised that the conduct, which was being induced or procured, would result in a breach of the term.[273]

In addition, the claimant must show that he has suffered damage as a result (or, if he is seeking an injunction, that he will suffer damage unless an injunction is granted).[274]

Breach of contract

There must be a breach of contract. *OBG* makes clear that liability for inducing breach is a **2.235** kind of secondary, or accessory, liability, and there can be 'no secondary liability without primary liability'.[275] If a restrictive covenant is unenforceable for being in unreasonable restraint of trade, it will not be tortious to induce a breach of it. The same is true if the contract is voidable.[276] Before *OBG*, the scope of the tort had been extended to include cases where there was interference with the performance of a contract but no breach (for example because one party was excused from performing by a *force majeure* clause),[277] but *OBG* makes clear that an actual breach is required. It appears that the tort may also apply to inducing a breach of statutory duty (at least where the breach is actionable by the claimant)[278] or of certain equitable obligations.[279]

Inducement

OBG decided that inducing breach of contract is a kind of accessory liability, and therefore **2.236** the threshold for liability should be the same as for accessory liability for another person's tort.[280] A person who procures another's wrongful act by 'inducement, incitement or persuasion' will be liable, but not if he merely facilitates the act.[281] This appears to be a significant narrowing of the test, as earlier cases had held that any active step which facilitated a breach of covenant was sufficient for liability.[282] There must, of course, be a causal connection between the inducement and the breach.

---

[273] *Aerostar Maintenance International Ltd v Wilson* [2010] EWHC 2032 (Ch), para 163 *per* Morgan J.

[274] See the cases cited in *Clerk & Lindsell on Torts* (20th edn, 2010) §24-51, and *Lonmar Global Risks v West* [2010] EWHC 2878 (QB) at para 221.

[275] *OBG*, para 44 *per* Lord Hoffmann. See also para 172 *per* Lord Nicholls.

[276] *Proform Sports Management Ltd v Proactive Sports Management Ltd* [2006] EWHC 2903 (Ch), [2007] 1 All ER 542 (contract with footballer Wayne Rooney voidable because he was a minor when it was entered into).

[277] *Torquay Hotel Co Ltd v Cousins* [1969] 2 Ch 106; *Merkur Island Shipping Corp v Laughton* [1983] 2 AC 570, 608.

[278] *Meade v Haringey LBC* [1979] 1 WLR 637; *Associated British Ports Ltd v TGWU* [1989] 1 WLR 939, CA, 951–2; 959; 964 (reversed on other grounds). In *OBG*, Lord Nicholls expressly left the point open (at para 189).

[279] *Prudential Assurance Co Ltd v Lorenz* (1971) KIR 88 (duty to account); cf *Metall und Rohstoff AG v Donaldson, Lufkin & Jenrette Inc* [1990] 1 QB 391, 481 (no tort of procuring a breach of trust because the equitable claim for dishonest assistance was adequate).

[280] *OBG*, para 36 *per* Lord Hoffmann, referring to the principles set out in cases such as *CBS Songs Ltd v Amstrad Consumer Electronics plc* [1988] AC 1013 and *Unilever plc v Chefaro Proprietaries Ltd* [1994] FSR 135.

[281] *CBS v Amstrad* above.

[282] *British Motor Trade Ltd v Salvadori* [1949] 1 All ER 208. See also *Calor Gas Ltd v Express Fuels (Scotland) Ltd* [2008] CSOH 13; 2008 SLT 123 at para 47 (OBG 'reaffirmed that a positive act of inducement or procurement is essential'), and contrast the view of the authors of *Clerk and Lindsell on Torts* (20th edn, 2010) §24-42 ('none of the speeches in [OBG] directly addressed the issue of whether inconsistent transactions should still be seen as a form of direct inducement of breach' and suggesting the issue still needs to be clarified).

The mental element

2.237　Where D induces X to break his contract with C, C will only have a cause of action against D if D has the required state of mind. This requires both (1) knowledge and (2) intention.

Knowledge

2.238　As Lord Hoffmann said in *OBG*, 'To be liable for inducing breach of contract, you must know that you are inducing a breach of contract. It is not enough that you know that you are procuring an act which, as a matter of law or construction of the contract, is a breach. You must actually realise that it will have this effect. Nor does it matter that you ought reasonably to have done so'.[283] Thus an honest but unreasonable belief that there is no breach of contract will be a defence, whether the mistake is one of fact or law.[284] On the other hand, 'blind-eye' knowledge (knowledge of the existence of the contract coupled with a conscious decision not to enquire whether the act will be in breach of it), or being 'indifferent' to whether there is a breach or not, is sufficient.[285]

2.239　Thus, in a post-termination restrictive covenant case, a recruiting employer who knows that the target employee is subject to covenants, and who could easily find out what they are, but does not do so, is likely to be found to have a sufficient degree of knowledge.

Intention

2.240　The defendant must intend to procure a breach of contract. It is not necessary for him also to intend to cause economic damage to the claimant[286] (contrast the torts of causing loss by unlawful means and unlawful means conspiracy, where an intention to cause loss to the claimant is essential). One can intend to do something either for its own sake or as a means to an end. As Lord Hoffmann said in *OBG*:

> It is necessary for this purpose to distinguish between ends, means and consequences. If someone knowingly causes a breach of contract, it does not normally matter that it is the means by which he intends to achieve some further end or even that he would rather have been able to achieve that end without causing a breach . . . Again, people seldom knowingly cause loss by unlawful means out of simple disinterested malice. It is usually to achieve the further end of securing an economic advantage to themselves . . . On the other hand, if the breach of contract is neither an end in itself nor a means to an end, but merely a foreseeable consequence, then in my opinion it cannot for this purpose be said to have been intended. That, I think, is what judges and writers mean when they say that the claimant must have been 'targeted' or 'aimed at'.[287]

2.241　The line between a 'means to an end' and a mere 'consequence' can be difficult to draw. This is illustrated by contrasting the judgments of the House of Lords in *Douglas v Hello!* with those of the strong Court of Appeal they reversed.[288] The case involved a claim for interference with business by unlawful means, one element of which is 'intention' to cause harm. Both the House of Lords and the Court of Appeal agreed that foresight that one's conduct will probably injure the claimant is not sufficient to establish intention. The Court of Appeal

---

[283] *OBG*, para 39.

[284] *British Industrial Plastics Ltd v Ferguson* [1940] 1 All ER 479; *Mainstream Properties Ltd v Young* (one of the appeals heard with *OBG*).

[285] *OBG*, para 40, quoting *Emerald Construction Co Ltd v Lowthian* [1966] 1 WLR 691 at 700–1 *per* Lord Denning MR.

[286] *OBG*, para 8.

[287] *OBG*, paras 42–3.

[288] *Douglas and others v Hello! Ltd and others (No 3)* [2006] QB 125, CA (the court consisted of three successive Masters of the Rolls: Lord Phillips MR, Clarke and Neuberger LJJ).

took the view that even foreseeing that the conduct would *inevitably* cause the claimant harm was not sufficient, but the House of Lords took a different view. Where the defendant knows that the conduct and the injury are 'inseparably linked', or the harm is 'the other side of the same coin' as the conduct, it seems that it will follow that the injury will be regarded as a means to the defendant's end rather than merely a foreseeable consequence.[289]

In the common case where the new employer first learns of the covenants when he is informed **2.242** of them by the covenantee, after the employee has started to work for him, it is likely to be very difficult for the covenantee to show that the new employer, in continuing to employ the employee, has the necessary intention (and indeed it is doubtful whether continuing to employ the employee amounts to 'inducement' in any event).

By contrast, an employer who is aware that an employee is bound by enforceable covenants **2.243** but recruits him anyway because the business needs him, should be liable. While the employer's dominant purpose is to satisfy the needs of his business, he has chosen to achieve this aim by inducing the employee to breach his covenant. Inducing the breach is the means of achieving the aim, not merely an unfortunate side effect of it.

The new employer will not be liable if he honestly believes that his actions will not result in **2.244** an infringement of the claimant's contractual rights, even if he is wrong and even if his belief is unreasonable. Thus in *Mainstream Properties v Young* (one of the appeals heard with *OBG*), the defendant, who exploited a business opportunity with two of the claimant's directors in reliance on (inaccurate) statements by them that the claimant had been offered the opportunity and declined, was not liable.

However, questions of the enforceability of restrictive covenants are often less than clear- **2.245** cut. There may be an issue about whether the covenant is excessively wide so as to be in unreasonable restraint of trade, or about whether the employee is no longer bound by the covenant because he has been constructively dismissed. In practice, employers will rarely receive unqualified advice that a covenant is unenforceable: the advice is more likely to be expressed in terms of probabilities and risks. What is the position of the employer who knows that a covenant may or may not be enforceable, but chooses to take the risk and induce an employee to act inconsistently with it? In *Tullett Prebon plc v BGC Brokers LP*,[290] the new employer (BGC) declined to waive privilege in the legal advice it received, and Jack J concluded that BGC 'had no honest belief' that there would be no breach, and had intended that 'the brokers should leave whether or not they had good grounds for claiming con- structive dismissal', and had therefore been 'indifferent' to whether or not there was a breach of contract. BGC was liable for inducing breach of contract.

Justification

There is also a potential defence of 'justification', which applies in particular where the **2.246** defendant acts in order to protect an equal or superior right of his own.[291]

---

[289] *OBG*, para 134 *per* Lord Hoffmann, para 167 *per* Lord Nicholls. Compare the criminal law of murder as set out in *R v Woollin* [1999] AC 82.

[290] [2010] IRLR 648, para 178. See also *Kallang Shipping SA Panama v Axa Assurances Senegal (The Kallang)* [2008] EWHC 2761 (Comm); [2009] 1 Lloyd's Rep 124, para 92.

[291] *Edwin Hill & Partners v First National Finance Corp plc* [1989] 1 WLR 225; *OBG*, para 193 *per* Lord Nicholls; *Meretz Investments NV v ACP Ltd* [2007] Ch 197, paras 393–6 *per* Lewison J, affirmed on this point at [2008] Ch 244, CA, para 142 *per* Arden LJ and para 179 *per* Toulson LJ.

Causing loss by unlawful means

2.247 The judgments of the House of Lords in *OBG* also clearly set out the elements of the tort of 'causing loss by unlawful means'. This had previously been regarded as the 'genus' of which inducing breach of contract was one 'species', but *OBG* emphasized that they are different torts, in particular because inducing breach of contract is a kind of accessory liability, whereas in cases of causing loss by unlawful means, 'there is no other wrong for which the defendant is liable as accessory'. Unlike inducing breach of contract, it can apply to interference with business where there is no contract, or no breach.

2.248 The archetypal case of causing loss by unlawful means is so-called 'three-party intimidation', as in the eighteenth century case of *Tarleton v M'Gawley*.[292] In that case, the defendant sought to prevent the natives of the West African coast from trading with others until they paid him a debt he claimed they owed him. When certain natives attempted to trade with the plaintiff's ship, the defendant fired a cannon at their canoe so that 'the natives . . . were deterred and hindered from trading' with the plaintiff.

2.249 The elements of the tort, as set out in *OBG*, are: (1) an interference with the actions of a third party in which the claimant has an economic interest; (2) using unlawful means; and (3) with an intention thereby to cause loss to the claimant. In addition, the claimant must show that he has suffered damage as a result (or, if he is seeking an injunction, that he will suffer damage unless an injunction is granted). 'Intention' involves the same concepts of ends, means, and consequences discussed above in relation to inducing breach of contract. In *Pirtek (UK) Ltd v Joinplace Ltd (t/a Pirtek Darlington)*,[293] Briggs J held that the claimant's loss could be the 'obverse of the coin' to the defendant's gain, even where the gain 'may not have been matched, pound for pound, by a corresponding loss' to the claimant.

2.250 Lawful competition frequently involves intentionally causing harm to another's business, as a means to an end of making profits for oneself. The critical concept is therefore unlawful means. The debate about what counts as 'unlawful' was resolved by the House of Lords in *OBG*. The majority held that 'unlawful means' for this purpose does not include all torts, crimes, and other wrongs, but, in the words of Lord Hoffmann 'subject to one qualification, acts against a third party count as unlawful means only if they are actionable by that third party. The qualification is that they will also be unlawful means if the only reason why they are not actionable is because the third party has suffered no loss'.[294] The majority also added a further qualification: the means used must affect the third party's 'freedom to deal with the claimant'.[295]

2.251 This restriction seeks to avoid creating a cause of action 'based on acts which are wrongful only in the irrelevant sense that a third party has a right to complain if he chooses to do so'.[296] Some examples of unlawful means include making threats, making fraudulent statements, and committing a trespass to goods.

---

[292] (1793) Peake 270; 170 ER 153.

[293] [2010] EWHC 1641 (Ch), para 85.

[294] *OBG*, para 49. Lord Nicholls dissented at para 162.

[295] *OBG*, para 51, citing *RCA Corp v Pollard* [1983] Ch 135 and *Oren v Red Box Toy Factory Ltd* [1999] FSR 785, where the allegedly unlawful means involved the infringement of intellectual property rights. See also *Future Investments SA v Fédération Internationale de Football Association* [2010] EWHC 1019 (Ch).

[296] At para 56.

Conspiracy

A conspiracy requires a 'combination' (ie an agreement or understanding) between two or **2.252**
more natural or legal persons with a common design. There will rarely be direct evidence of an
agreement, so the court will usually have to draw inferences from the parties' actions. It is not
normally sufficient proof of a combination that a person knows or suspects what others are
doing but does nothing to stop it, but a person in a position of authority over others may be
held to be participating in a combination with them if his omission to stop their activities is 'a
sufficient signal to them that they have [his] backing in what they are doing'.[297] In principle, a
person can be party to the combination without himself carrying out any of the acts done
pursuant to it. There will not normally be a combination between an employer and his employees
who simply carry out his business, or between a director and his company where the director
does no more than carry out his constitutional role in the governance of the company.[298]

There are two distinct forms of actionable conspiracy, described respectively as 'unlawful **2.253**
means' and 'lawful means' conspiracy. In *Kuwait Oil Tanker Co SAK v Al Bader*, Nourse LJ,
giving the judgment of the Court of Appeal, defined them as follows:

> A conspiracy to injure by lawful means is actionable where the claimant proves that he has
> suffered loss or damage as a result of action taken pursuant to a combination or agreement
> between the defendant and another person or persons to injure him, where the predominant
> purpose of the defendant is to injure the claimant. A conspiracy to injure by unlawful means
> is actionable where the claimant proves that he has suffered loss or damage as a result of
> unlawful action taken pursuant to a combination or agreement between the defendant and
> another person or persons to injure him by unlawful means, whether or not it is the pre-
> dominant purpose of the defendant to do so.[299]

It will be noted from this description that lawful means conspiracy is an anomalous tort, **2.254**
since, in the absence of a conspiracy, a bad motive will not render unlawful that which is
otherwise lawful.[300] As stated by Nourse LJ, a lawful means conspiracy requires a predominant purpose to injure the claimant, that is causing injury as an end in itself, rather than
merely as a means to some other end. Such an intention can rarely be proved.

On the other hand, where the conspiracy is to use 'unlawful means', there is no requirement **2.255**
for a predominant purpose to injure the claimant,[301] but only an *intention* to do so (in the
sense of intention discussed above in relation to inducing breach of contract and causing loss
by unlawful means).[302]

Confusingly, however, the definition of 'unlawful means' for the purpose of unlawful means **2.256**
conspiracy has been held to be different from, and wider than, the definition laid down in

---

[297] *Digicel (St Lucia) Ltd v Cable & Wireless plc* [2010] EWHC 774 (Ch), para 74 of Annex I to the
judgment.
[298] *MCA Records Inc v Charly Records Ltd (No 5)* [2001] EWCA Civ 1441; [2003] 1 BCLC 93; *Digicel
(St Lucia) Ltd v Cable & Wireless plc* [2010] EWHC 774 (Ch), para 78 of Annex I to the judgment.
[299] [2000] 2 All ER (Comm) 271, para 108.
[300] *Allen v Flood* [1898] AC 1; *Lonrho Ltd v Shell Petroleum Co Ltd (No 2)* [1982] AC 173, 188 *per* Lord
Diplock.
[301] *Lonrho plc v Fayed* [1992] 1 AC 448, HL.
[302] *Meretz Investments NV v ACP Ltd* [2008] Ch 244, CA; *Bank of Tokyo-Mitsubishi UFJ Ltd v Baskan Gida
Sanayi Ve Pazarlama AS* [2009] EWHC 1276 (Ch), para 826. As to the need for the claimant to prove loss, see
Lonmar Global Risks v West [2010] EWHC 2878 (QB) at para 223(v).

OBG for the tort of causing loss by unlawful means. In *Revenue and Customs Commissioners v Total Network SL*,[303] the House of Lords decided that unlawful means in conspiracy could include criminal conduct (whether at common law or by statute) which gave rise to no private law cause of action. The judgments make clear that unlawful means conspiracy is a free-standing tort, not a form of secondary liability which would merely duplicate liability that the conspirators would anyway have as joint tortfeasors.

2.257 It is, however, essential that the unlawful conduct is in fact the means whereby the relevant loss is inflicted upon the claimant (sometimes referred to as 'instrumentality', following the dissenting judgment of Lord Nicholls in *OBG*). As Lord Walker said in *Total Network*: 'It is not enough that there is an element of unlawfulness somewhere in the story.'[304]

2.258 In an annex to his mammoth judgment in *Digicel (St Lucia) Ltd v Cable & Wireless plc*, Morgan J reviewed the authorities and concluded that (a) it is unclear from *Total Network* whether *every* crime is 'unlawful' for this purpose, but he inclined to the view that it was, but (b) non-actionable breaches of non-criminal statutes (such as regulatory provisions relating to telecommunications) do not count as unlawful means.[305] On the other hand, it appears that a breach of contract or a breach of fiduciary duty can be unlawful means for this purpose.[306]

2.259 In *Meretz Investments NV v ACP Ltd*,[307] the Court of Appeal held that a defendant would not be liable for unlawful means conspiracy if he believed that he had a lawful right to act as he did. This was summarized by Briggs J in *Bank of Tokyo-Mitsubishi UFJ Ltd v Baskan Gida Sanayi Ve Pazarlama AS*[308] as 'the requirement that the defendant must have known that the relevant conduct was unlawful, and that the unlawful part of it would cause harm to the claimant', and it requires the court to engage in 'a painstaking analysis of the extent to which the particular defendant shared a common objective with the primary fraudsters, and the extent to which the achievement of that objective was to the particular defendant's knowledge to be achieved by unlawful means intended to injure the claimant'. Here, as in other contexts, 'knowledge' includes 'blind-eye' knowledge.[309]

G. Team moves[310]

Introduction

2.260 'Team move' is far from being a term of art but is used to refer to two or more employees leaving their employer together to join a competitor. In this section 'employer' is used to refer

---

[303] [2008] 1 AC 1174, overruling *Powell v Boladz* [1998] Lloyd's Rep Med 116.

[304] ibid paras 95–6 *per* Lord Walker, and paras 116 and 119 *per* Lord Mance.

[305] *Digicel (St Lucia) Ltd v Cable & Wireless plc* [2010] EWHC 774 (Ch), para 53–4 of Annex I to the judgment.

[306] *Aerostar Maintenance International Ltd v Wilson* [2010] EWHC 2032 (Ch), paras 169–72 *per* Morgan J following the 'general approach' of previous case law despite doubts about the undesirable overlap with dishonest assistance and inducing breach of contract. See also the discussion by the same judge in *Digicel*, above, Annex I, paras 63–8.

[307] [2008] Ch 244, CA.

[308] [2009] EWHC 1276 (Ch), paras 837–47, and see the critical analysis of *Meretz* and *Tokyo-Mitsubishi* by Morgan J in *Digicel*, above, Annex I, paras 94–118.

[309] *Tokyo-Mitsubishi*, above, paras 837–40, citing *Manifest Shipping Co Ltd v Uni-Polaris Insurance Co Ltd (The Star Sea)* [2003] 1 AC 469, HL, and *Attorney General of Zambia v Meer Care & Desai* [2008] EWCA Civ 1007.

[310] See, further, the discussion on team moves in paras 9.41–9.45, 9.140–9.145, and 9.163–9.175 below.

to the initial employer of the team and 'competitor' is used to refer to the putative new employer.

In practical terms, the modern cases tend to involve groups of client-facing salesmen, **2.261** particularly the various forms of brokers. However, the reported cases (which are relatively few in number) include geneticists,[311] cutting tool makers,[312] and life policy investors.[313]

The current state of the law

Until recent years, the obiter remarks of Cumming Bruce LJ in the case of *Searle v Celltech*[314] **2.262** had provided considerable comfort to those advising individuals seeking to leave in concert. In that case, as stated at paragraph 2.131 above, Cumming Bruce LJ asserted that there was 'nothing in the general law to prevent a number of employees in concert deciding to leave their employer and set themselves up in competition with him'.

For the reasons set out above at paragraphs 2.137 to 2.145, that sense of comfort appears to **2.263** have been misplaced. The fiduciary obligation of any director or senior employee is to act in the best interests of the company by nurturing and encouraging more junior employees under his control to remain with the employer and remain loyal to that employer. As soon as such an individual has a personal interest in that more junior employee leaving his current employer (so as to join the new venture or competitor), the senior employee/fiduciary has a conflict between duty and interest giving rise to a breach of the fiduciary duty.

Similarly, it will be hard indeed for a senior employee or director to argue that the employer **2.264** did not need to know that a more junior employee was interested in, or contemplating, moving to a competitor. Thus, he would be in breach of his fiduciary duty and contractual duty of fidelity in failing to disclose that.[315]

Further, as was made plain in the *British Midland Tool* case, the mere fact that there is a **2.265** competitor vigorously seeking to recruit employees may well be a matter that a senior employee or director needs to reveal, to enable the employer to take appropriate, effective, and targeted steps to maintain the stability of the workforce.

The *Tullett Prebon* case[316] concerned the recruitment of members of three desks of inter- **2.266** dealer brokers by BGC, one of its competitors. Because of the substantial value of the case, its size in terms of the number of defendants and the nature of the litigants, it highlights the many facets of the legal issues relevant to a team move. The focus shifts through the following areas which are relevant to many team moves:

(1) The validity of a contractual obligation to report an approach by a competitor. Jack J held that the obligation was valid and not in undue restraint of trade.[317]

---

[311] *Searle v Celltech* [1982] FSR 92.
[312] *British Midland Tool v Midland International Tooling* [2003] 2 BCLC 523.
[313] *Shepherds Investments v Walters* [2007] IRLR 110, [2006] All ER (D) 213 (Apr).
[314] See 2.131 above.
[315] Self-evidently, if the more senior employee is not planning to leave, he may well think it is not necessary to pass on the information because he can deal with it himself. But where the more senior employee is planning to leave, the duty will be engaged.
[316] *Tullett Prebon plc v BGC Brokers LP* [2010] IRLR 648. The appeal from this decision was heard in December 2010, but no judgment has been handed down at the time of writing.
[317] ibid at para 67.

(2) The obligations of fiduciaries and other senior employees to report the interest of a competitor in recruiting the desk.[318]

(3) The obligation of a fiduciary and other senior employees not to do anything that might assist in the recruitment of other employees by the competitor.[319] This prohibition is absolute and thus includes the provision of non-confidential information if that information is intended to assist the competitor.

(4) The scepticism with which claims of constructive dismissal by the departing employees should be treated.[320] As part of this, Jack J adopts and adapts the secondary reasoning as to breach of the trust and confidence obligation expounded in *RDF Media v Clements*.[321] In that case, as a secondary ground for finding that there had been no constructive dismissal of the defendant, the judge held that the mutual obligation of trust and confidence was attenuated by the objective circumstances of employer and employee. Given that the *Boston Deep Sea Fishing* principle applied, the duty of trust and confidence could be attenuated by matters unknown to the person alleged to be in breach of duty. In the *Tullett Prebon* case, Jack J held that the employee's own conduct would be relevant in considering whether the employer's conduct had in fact been sufficient, objectively judged, to seriously damage or destroy the employee's trust and confidence. He considered recruitment exercise to the detriment of their employer and working with their new employer to provoke conduct which might be relied on in support of a claim for constructive dismissal.

(5) The differing forms of evidence that may be available to the employer concerning the apparent breaches of duty and the importance of securing that evidence. In particular, much of the relevant discussions were undertaken by means of mobile phone text messages and Blackberry Messenger messages,[322] with the devices being 'lost' at times convenient to the defendants.

(6) The difficulties faced by a lawyer representing a departing fiduciary or senior employee. In the case, the solicitor was alleged to have become a party to the unlawful means conspiracy, albeit that no claim was brought against him personally. His personal position was brought into sharp relief because many of the documents concerning the recruitment of the employees were copied to him or concerned his role or were generated by him but were not privileged. The case highlights the need on the part of solicitors in these situations to: avoid conflicts of interest; recognize that notes of meetings and email discussions between employees and the competitor concerning recruitment (as opposed to defending anticipated or actual litigation) will not be privileged; and, avoid playing a role on the recruitment that is separate from the provision of legal advice and assistance to their client.

(7) The issues concerning inducing breach of contract and unlawful means conspiracy. These issues are dealt with at length in the preceding section. Jack J held that, to avoid liability for inducing employees falsely to claim constructive dismissal a defendant competitor would need to show not merely that it had taken advice in relation to

---

[318] ibid at para 68.
[319] ibid at para 69.
[320] ibid at para 86.
[321] [2008] IRLR 207.
[322] See Appendix 1 for details of why these sorts of communication are only recoverable from the devices themselves and, unlike emails, will not appear on an email server or server back-up which can be the subject of interrogation or a disclosure application.

constructive dismissal but that (a) it had formed the subjective view that the employees had a good case for constructive dismissal, and (b) it asked the employees to leave because the employees had good grounds for claiming constructive dismissal, or to put it an other way, it was not indifferent as to whether there was such good cause.[323]

(8) The central relevance of both garden leave and enforceable restrictive covenants in protecting the business of employer by way of injunctive relief and the corresponding difficulties in the use of springboard relief to obtain equivalent protection. Indeed, Jack J did not justify his grant of injunctive relief on the basis of the springboard doctrine but rather as a form of *quia timet* relief to prevent further unlawful tortious acts.[324] It is to be noted that there appears to be growing reluctance on the part of judges, particularly, in the Chancery Division, to grant any substantial springboard relief.[325]

2.267 In most of the reported cases, the focus is on senior employees and managers, each of whom will owe extensive duties. A more difficult issue arises in relation to more junior employees. As set out above, the more junior employees may not be under an obligation to report intended competition by employees at a similar level over whom they have no control. In *Kynixa v Hynes*,[326] Wyn Williams J held that, in the circumstances of that case an employee who was not a fiduciary was obliged to report competitive approaches by reason of her contractual duty of fidelity, stating: 'I simply do not see how one can be acting as a loyal employee when one knows that three senior employees (including oneself) may transfer their allegiance to a group of companies which includes a competitor and yet not only fail to divulge that knowledge but also say things which would have the effect of positively misleading the employer about that possibility.'[327] In the *Tullett Prebon* case, Jack J stated, without explanation, that this was a decision on the particular facts and not of direct relevance to whether the desk head was obliged to report an approach in relation to the desk.[328] In any event, attempts to solicit junior employees for a competitive activity by a more senior employee or director would amount to serious misconduct by such an employee and would thus ordinarily be reportable by the junior employee to their employer, given the *Sybron* decision.

2.268 Any solicitation of clients or suppliers (where that was not truly activity preparatory to competition) would also be reportable by an employee if he was aware of other employees having behaved in that way.

2.269 On this analysis, team moves will generally result in breaches of duties of fidelity and fiduciary duties of good faith unless:

(1) those leaving are recruited separately and individually by the new employer without the assistance of senior members of the moving team;

(2) the senior individuals within the team are unaware of the attempts to recruit their colleagues, or have revealed that to the employer; and

---

[323] ibid at para 178.
[324] ibid at para 250.
[325] See by way of example *Vestergaard Frandsen A/S v Bestnet Europe Ltd* [2010] FSR 29, in which Arnold J reviews the entire basis for the grant of springboard relief.
[326] [2008] EWHC 1495, [2008] All ER (D) 30.
[327] ibid para 283.
[328] [2010] IRLR 648, para 68.

(3) the senior individuals do not pass on, whilst still employed, details of the other individuals who should be approached or details of their salaries or other information that would be useful to the competitor to the detriment of the employer.

2.270 In *UBS v Vestra Wealth LLP*,[329] Openshaw J took a markedly different approach to springboard injunctions from that adopted by Arnold J in *Vestergaard* and Jack J at trial in *Tullett Prebon*. His judgment arose from a contested application for springboard injunctions until a speedy trial could be heard in circumstances where a former employee of UBS, Mr Scott, walked into their offices to hand in letters of resignation on behalf of fifty-two members of staff. A further twenty-three resigned during the course of the following weeks and months. Mr Scott contended that he had not commenced recruitment of staff or clients until after his restraints had ceased. Further, he contended that he had recruited each member of staff independently, without any encouragement by any other member of staff.

2.271 At an interim hearing, Openshaw J found that such recruitment was inherently unlikely and that many or most of them must have been acting in concert. As such, they must have been in breach of duty to have been so plotting behind UBS' back.

2.272 He also found that a particular feature was the use of 'bridgeheading' pursuant to which more junior employees would arrive first, because they would be free from their notice period and covenants at an earlier stage. They would service the clients pending the arrival of the more senior individuals. In short, he found that there was likely to have been an unlawful conspiracy dressed up as lawful competition.

2.273 For that reason he granted a springboard injunction preventing further solicitation of clients or staff pending a speedy trial. It is worthy of note that he held expressly that springboard relief was available to prevent the continuation of an unfair advantage created by breach of any duty rather than simply a breach of the duty of confidentiality.

2.274 It may well be that this is an example of the greater willingness of a judge to grant short springboard relief pending a speedy trial where it is the only means of holding the ring. Indeed, that is the rationale for the entire doctrine, as posited by Arnold J in *Vestergaard*.

Issues for the employer

2.275 It will be seen from this analysis that the employer has considerable potential to bring a claim. This neglects the more obvious point that an effectively managed, well-motivated, and properly incentivized workforce is less vulnerable to being poached.

2.276 The greatest vulnerability to poaching occurs immediately after bonuses are paid. This is particularly so where the bonuses have been large in the past but are anticipated to be smaller in the future. This risk is reduced where the bonus is to be paid in tranches that vest over time.

2.277 The greatest vulnerability is to a competitor who knows the employer's workforce and has a senior ex-employee able to recruit its workforce. Thus, a competitor that has acquired one of the employer's senior employees is a far greater risk than one with no knowledge of the employer's business.

---

[329] [2008] IRLR 965.

The obvious sources of protection are effective non-poaching clauses in the contracts of **2.278** senior executives and effective restrictive covenants in the contracts of all employees together with a contractual obligation to report all approaches by a competitor. Plainly, these covenants will only be effective if the contracts containing them are not terminated by the employee's acceptance of the employer's repudiatory breach.

Once the employer is aware of the threat, the focus must remain on the retention of the **2.279** employees. As such, the employer needs information as to the nature and extent of the threat. In our view, talking to the employees suspected to be part of the team is the most effective immediate means to identify that threat.

As stated above, we consider that those in a fiduciary position will generally be required to **2.280** answer questions truthfully and accurately, save perhaps in relation to their own personal intentions, in relation to which they may be entitled not to answer.

Thus, questions should be directed to what that individual knows about any competitor's **2.281** attempts to recruit other employees of the employer and what the individual believes to be the case.

If, but probably only if, suitable grounds for suspicion of breach of duty have been raised, **2.282** analysis of emails, telephone records, electronic diaries, and suchlike should be considered. The risk of breaching the obligations of trust and confidence is always real and, given the effects on the enforceability of covenants, critical.

The other reason for great care prior to thorough investigation of extraneous material is that **2.283** the interests of the business are likely to be best served by securing the loyalty of the employees rather than conducting disciplinary investigations arising out of suspected disloyalty.

Once resignations commence, further questions can and should be asked as to the intentions **2.284** of the resigning employees and their detailed knowledge of others. Further, the resignations may entitle an employer to have a greater level of suspicion and therefore conduct more intrusive or effective analysis of suspected breaches of duty in relation to the solicitation of clients, suppliers, and employees.

Usually, assuming there are effective garden leave provisions, it will be appropriate to place **2.285** departing employees on garden leave whilst such investigations are carried out. Consideration can then be given to whether any form of injunctive relief, during the garden leave period, is appropriate.

Despite being an uncommon approach to such matters, early mediation often offers the best **2.286** opportunities to all parties. Once the employees have firmly decided to leave, there is little chance of changing their minds. However, at such an early stage, positive outcomes can be obtained for both parties that could not be achieved in court, such as orderly transfers of clients for a negotiated price combined with non-poaching agreements in relation to the remaining staff. This is likely to offer a better overall outcome for employer, competitor, and employees than injunctions, trials, and the loss of clients to third parties as a result of the chaos.

Issues for the competitor

There is, as set out above, no barrier to a competitor poaching a team from the employer, if that **2.287** is done without the use of members of the team, directly or indirectly, as recruiting sergeants.

2.288 For this reason, it has become increasingly common to use headhunters to assist in the process of recruitment to demonstrate the lawful and appropriate nature of the recruitment.

2.289 Similarly, making the members of the team aware of their responsibilities at an early stage in the recruitment process reduces the risk of a leak as to the plan or of the plan becoming unlawful.

2.290 It should be noted that the more information the members of the team have about the recruitment of others, the more likely it is that continued secrecy will give rise to a breach of duty. In essence, using the other members of the team as a lure to draw proposed new members of the team to the competitor is likely to result in the plan becoming known to the employer or in a breach of duty by employees.

2.291 The second critical issue is for the competitor to be aware of the liabilities it may incur. Most importantly, if the team would have been lured even if there had been no breaches of the duty of fidelity, damages are likely to be small.

2.292 Further, any document showing the incentivization of senior employees on the basis of how many junior employees join the competitor will be a disclosable document. Any such incentivization is self-evidently an inducement to that employee to breach their duties to the employer and would place any senior employee in a position of conflict of duty and interest.

2.293 Whilst vulnerable to the charge of being a paper trail to conceal breaches, documentation demonstrating the planning of the recruitment of the team and the means by which it was achieved can do much to dispel the suspicion of wrongdoing in the minds of both the employer and, more importantly, the judge hearing any interim injunction applications.

2.294 Separate legal representation of the team members is generally essential, not least because there may be issues of conflict that arise at high speed and which can wrong-foot any lawyer dealing with the case. In addition, if the competitor's lawyer has meetings with and gives advice to members of the team this may not always attract legal professional privilege or that privilege may swiftly be lost by the loss of confidentiality caused by the failure to recruit a putative team member.

2.295 If the competitor becomes aware of breaches by any member of the team, the competitor will need to avoid and be seen to avoid condoning or taking the benefit of such breaches. At that stage, the competitor becomes vulnerable to proceedings against it, brought on the basis of the economic torts of interference with contractual relations or conspiracy.

2.296 In addition, the competitor should seek to identify the risks inherent in the covenants which bind the team members and to identify any weaknesses within them. It should also ensure that the team members' lawyers are considering whether any members of the team have been constructively dismissed such that they can be freed from those covenants. In such a situation, the summary resignation will always carry a substantial risk of being met with immediate applications for injunctive relief, which generally stand a good chance of being granted, save in a very clear case, until a speedy trial.

2.297 The competitor must remain aware of the risk of search orders. The competitor may have no corporate knowledge of theft of confidential information or illegitimate solicitation but where such matters occur, the only effective remedy for the employer may be a search order of the competitor's premises. As such, the competitor must remain proactive to ensure that no confidential information or databases are uploaded onto its computer systems after recruitment.

The competitor should also give particular thought to the exit routes from litigation gen- **2.298** erated by the recruitment exercise. If litigation is commenced, interim injunctive relief is the norm pending a speedy trial. Thus, there will be immense disruption, substantial cost, and significant uncertainty. Preparation for this period is necessary. If the facts are sufficiently strong, it may be appropriate to have undertaken some work prior to the move to prepare to resist any application for interim relief pending a speedy trial. Otherwise, settlement strategies and budgets should be prepared in advance. Often, direct negotiations with the previous employer (covering compensation, client relationships and covenants) are the simplest and swiftest means of resolving matters at an early stage. Despite being little used in practice, disputes of this nature are ideally suited to early mediation.

H. Checklist

This checklist deals, first, with drafting issues relating to employee/director duties, and, **2.299** secondly, other topics discussed above.

Drafting issues

Consider the status of the employee

What is the current and likely future status of the individual? If they will be a mere employee, **2.300** the employer may decide simply to comply with the requirements of section 1 of the Employment Rights Act 1996 (ERA 1996) in relation to setting out either the job title and/or a brief description of the work for which the employee is employed and otherwise rely on the implied term of fidelity (possibly in conjunction with express restrictive covenants and confidentiality provisions as appropriate) to protect its interests. Short form express provisions are usually included however.

If the individual is a senior employee or a director (whether statutory, de facto, or shadow **2.301** director) it is prudent to include a detailed express duties provision, as well as restrictions that operate during employment and, if appropriate, after its termination.

Employee

A mere employee will owe express and implied contractual duties under the contract of **2.302** employment, including the implied duty of good faith and a duty of trust and confidence. They may also owe fiduciary duties, including in relation to their use (or misuse) of company funds/assets (including the use of employees for his own benefit) and undisclosed receipt of a bribe, arising from their specific contractual obligations.

Ensure compliance with the requirements of section 1 of ERA 1996. This will include setting **2.303** out in the contract the title of the job the employee is employed to do and/or a brief description of the work for which he is employed (for example in a job description attached to the contract).

Consider also the inclusion of the following 'short form' express provisions: **2.304**

• a requirement to carry out such duties as may be required by the company from time to time;

- an obligation to comply with all regulations, policies, and reasonable requests made, and instructions given by the company;
- a requirement for the employee to spend the whole of their time, attention, and ability carrying out their duties with due care and attention;
- an obligation to serve the company to the best of their ability and using their best endeavours to promote the interest of the company (and any relevant group company); and
- a requirement not, without the prior written consent of the company, to be in any way employed by, engaged, concerned, or interested in any other business.

2.305 Will the employee be in practical possession of company funds and/or other assets? If so, consider specifying that the employee must deal appropriately with those funds/assets in accordance with the prevailing company rules and policies. See paragraphs 2.39 to 2.58 above.

2.306 Will the employee be aware of or involved in generating new business opportunities for the company? If so, consider the inclusion of an obligation promptly to disclose to the board or a nominated manager any actual, potential, or maturing business opportunities enjoyed by the company. See paragraphs 2.181 to 2.221 above.

2.307 Does the company operate in an industry where 'team moves' are a real risk? If so, as well as appropriately drafted restrictive covenants, consider including an express duty requiring the employee to report intended competition by employees at any level and any attempts to solicit them for competitive activity. See paragraphs 2.260 to 2.298 above.

2.308 Does the company wish to ensure that the individual works only for the company and cannot 'moonlight' or carry out public duties in their spare time? If so, ensure that their duties provision includes an obligation to devote their whole time and attention and ability to carrying out their duties under the contract. If such a provision is not included, the individual can 'moonlight' in any job that is not competitive during their non-working time. If necessary, pre-approved exceptions to a whole time and attention requirement can be agreed by the company on an ad hoc basis. See paragraphs 2.144 to 2.149 above.

Senior employees and directors

2.309 All the considerations applicable to employees above apply equally to senior employees and directors, so review paragraphs 2.302 to 2.308 above.

2.310 In addition, it will generally be appropriate to set out detailed duties provisions to incorporate common law fiduciary duties as express contractual provisions. Therefore, consider the issues set out below.

2.311 If the employee is a statutory director, his employment will usually be conditional upon his also serving as a director. In addition, where the company is part of a group, the individual may also be required to serve as a statutory director of various group companies. If so, include an obligation to serve as a director of the company and any relevant group company (as a defined term) as notified by the board of the employing company from time to time.

2.312 The company will generally wish to ensure that it has as much flexibility as possible in relation to the duties it can require the senior employee/director to undertake and may also require the ability to instruct the individual to carry out work for other group companies. The senior employee/director will often wish to argue to the contrary, to define the scope of their role more narrowly. Consider, however, the inclusion of a wide obligation on the individual to carry out such duties and exercise such powers in relation to the company (or any group company) as may be assigned to them or vested in them by the board. Note, however, the impact of the implied duty of trust and confidence—the company must ensure that it has proper grounds for exercising this power in relation to the senior employee/director.

It is wise to include a re-statement of the fiduciary duty of good faith, by including a wide **2.313** general obligation to use best endeavours to promote and to at all times act in the best interest of the company and any group company.

In relation to disclosure obligations, consider a requirement to ensure that the Board is made **2.314** aware as soon as practicable of any activity, actual or threatened, which might affect the interest of the company and/or any group company. This broadly reflects the fiduciary duty to act so as to promote the best interest of the company (of which the duty of disclosure forms part) as set out by Hart J in the *British Midland Tool* case (see para 2.113 above). Such a provision also seeks to catch maturing business opportunities misconduct and likely staff resignations within its scope.

However, depending on the nature of the company's business and the commercial con- **2.315** siderations involved in the service contract negotiation, it may also be appropriate to include an express provision requiring disclosure of any actual, potential, or maturing business opportunities enjoyed (or that may be enjoyed) by the company or any group company, a requirement on the senior employee/director to disclose his own misconduct or the miscon- duct of any agent, employee, officer, or worker of the company of which he is, or ought reasonably to be, aware and a requirement to disclose the intention of any such person to resign from their employment or engagement with the company or any group company (although usually for practical purposes this latter obligation is limited to apply only in respect of those agents, employees, officers, or workers who report directly or indirectly to the executive).

It is usual to set out an express obligation on the executive to render his services in a pro- **2.316** fessional and competent manner. Depending on the work being undertaken by the senior employee/director, it may be appropriate to include a more onerous requirement to render their services in an expert and diligent manner and to the best of their ability.

Is effective team working a key aspect of the individual's role? If so, include an obligation to **2.317** render services in willing cooperation with others. Such a provision is also very helpful for the company when policing any handover by the executive to any new incumbent of the executive's role.

The company will wish to ensure that the senior employee/director is obliged to comply with **2.318** the company's codes, policies, and procedures and so a provision to this effect should be included.

Ensure that the director is obliged at all times to comply with the directions of the board or **2.319** of anyone duly authorized by it.

Will the employee be required to travel for the proper performance of his duties? If so, **2.320** include a provision requiring him to undertake such travel within and, if appropriate, outside of the United Kingdom as may be required. If extensive travel is a key aspect of the role, it is wise to state this expressly. Note the requirements of section 1(4)(k) of ERA 1996, which apply where the employee is required to work outside the United Kingdom for a period of more than one month.

2.321 Is the company (or any relevant group company) operating in a regulated sector or a member of a professional organization or association? If so, include a provision requiring the executive (so far as he is reasonably able to do so) to seek to ensure that the company and each group company complies in all material respects with the rules, procedures, policies, and codes of such a regulatory body/professional organization or association of which it is a member.

2.322 If relevant, include a requirement to comply with relevant rules and regulations (including company policies) with respect to dealings in company securities and the misuse and control of price-sensitive or inside information.

2.323 The board will generally wish to ensure that any director (and many senior employees) provide relevant information to it when required. Including an express provision to this effect is therefore prudent.

2.324 Particularly if the executive has moved from a competitor, it is wise to include a warranty whereby the executive confirms that he is not bound by any restrictive covenants or court orders, etc that affect his ability to perform his duties for the company and/or any group company.

Restrictions during employment

2.325 Senior employees and directors may be bound by their fiduciary duties in relation to competitive activity. However, it is prudent to include express restrictions on the employee. Such restrictions often include a saving whereby the board can give its prior written consent to the executive undertaking any 'outside' activity. If the company gives consent, it is wise to include a provision enabling the company to rescind that consent at a later date, and which requires the employee/director, if appropriate, to divest themselves of their interest in any such business.

2.326 The obligation can be modified, in the light of commercial considerations and depending on the relative bargaining strengths of the company and the executive, to cover:

- having any 'material interest' (appropriately defined) in any competing business;
- having any 'material interest' in a company that impairs or might reasonably be expected to impair the executive's ability to act at all times in the best interests of the company;
- having any 'material interest' that requires or might reasonably be considered to require the executive to use and/or disclose any confidential information.

2.327 Does the company wish to impose any practical day-to-day restrictions, such as capital expenditure limits, restrictions on entering into contracts, restrictions on employing or engaging other staff? If so, include them within the scope of an express duties clause.

2.328 Is the company happy for the executive to make preparations to compete with it? Assuming it is not, include an express provision dealing with this (this is particularly prudent in light of the decision of the Court of Appeal in *Helmet Integrated Systems*—see paras 2.157 to 2.159 above).

Presumably the company will wish to protect its relationship with clients, customers, and **2.329** suppliers. If so, include an express provision requiring the executive not to induce any such person to cease conducting business, or to reduce the amount of business, or adversely to vary the terms upon which business is conducted with the company, or to exclude the company from new business opportunities.

In addition, it is often wise to include a provision prohibiting the director from informing **2.330** clients, customers, and suppliers of the fact that he may resign or has resigned or that he has accepted employment whether to join or be associated with any competitor.

Impact of the Companies Act 2006

If the executive is a statutory director, consider including an express provision that he will at **2.331** all times comply with his duties as a director, as set out in Part 10, Chapter 2 of the Companies Act 2006.

In addition, given the disclosure obligations set out in Part 10, Chapter 2, it may be prudent **2.332** to include an express obligation on the director requiring him to declare to the board any interest that he may have (directly or indirectly) in any proposed transaction or arrangement with the company (or any group company) as soon as practicable and in any event before any such transaction or arrangement is entered into. Such a contractual notification provision goes beyond the notification required under the Act (as under section 177(6) of the Companies Act 2006 a director need not declare an interest in certain circumstances) and thus gives the company additional protection.

Economic torts and the liabilities of third parties

Inducing breach of contract

Has there been a breach of contract? If, for example, a covenant is unenforceable for being in **2.333** unreasonable restraint of trade, it will not be tortious to induce a breach of it.

Has the third party induced or procured the breach? Mere facilitation of the breach will be **2.334** insufficient (see para 2.236 above).

Did the third party know: **2.335**

(a) of the existence of the contract concerned; and
(b) that the induced or procured act would be in breach of that contract?

Knowledge must be actual and it does not matter that the third party ought reasonably to have known that a breach would occur if he honestly believed that there would be no breach. Although, in some circumstances knowledge may be inferred if, for example, the third party simply turns a 'blind eye' or is 'indifferent' to whether or not there will be a breach (see para 2.238 above).

Did the third party have the requisite intention to interfere with the performance of the **2.336** contract? Foresight that a breach may occur will be insufficient. Following the decisions in *OBG* and *Douglas v Hello!*, what is required is either:

• an intention to procure a breach of contract as an end in itself; or
• an intention to procure a breach of contract as a means of achieving a separate end (see paras 2.240 to 2.246 above).

2.337   Did the third party act in order to protect an equal or superior right of his own? If so, his conduct may be justifiable (see para 2.246 above).

Causing loss by unlawful means

2.338   Has there been interference with the actions of a third party in which the claimant has an economic interest?

2.339   Has that interference been achieved through unlawful means? In *OBG*, Lord Hoffman described 'unlawful means' in these circumstances as not including all torts, crimes, and other wrongs, but only acts against a third party that are themselves actionable by that third party (or would be actionable had the third party suffered loss) (see paras 2.247 to 2.251 above). The means used must also affect the third party's freedom to deal with the claimant.

2.340   Finally, was the interference undertaken with an intention to cause the claimant loss? The test for intention in these circumstances is the same as for inducement to breach contract— that is, was the intention to cause the claimant loss an end in itself or a means to an end? If the claimant's loss was a mere consequence, intention will not be established (see paras 2.247 to 2.251 above).

Lawful means conspiracy

2.341   Is there an agreement or understanding between two or more natural or legal persons with a common design to injure another person, where the predominant purpose of the defendants is to injure the claimant (see paras 2.252 to 2.254 above)?

Unlawful means conspiracy

2.342   Is there an agreement or understanding between two or more natural or legal persons with a common design involving the use of unlawful means with the intention (but not necessarily the predominate purpose) of injuring the claimant (see paras 2.255 to 2.259 above)?

2.343   Here, 'unlawful means' is wider than in the context of causing loss by unlawful means and includes criminal conduct that gives rise to no private cause of action provided that the unlawful conduct is in fact the means whereby the relevant loss is inflicted upon the claimant.

2.344   Did the defendant know the relevant conduct was unlawful, and that the unlawful part of it would cause harm to the claimant?

Team moves

2.345   Are two or more employees leaving their employer together to join a competitor? If one of the employees is a director or senior employee, they will be bound by their fiduciary obligation to act in the best interests of the company by nurturing and encouraging more junior employees under their control to remain with the employer and to remain loyal to that employer. As soon as they have a personal interest in the more junior employee leaving, the senior employee/director has a conflict and will be in breach of his fiduciary duty unless he resigns or discloses the intention (see paras 2.262 to 2.265 above).

2.346   If the individual is a more junior employee, they may not be under an obligation to report intended competition by employees at a similar level over whom they have no control, unless their contract includes an express duty to that effect. Such employees may, however, be under an obligation to report attempts to solicit by more senior employees as serious misconduct. Further, in some circumstances a failure to report intended competition may be in breach of a junior employee's duty of fidelity, particularly if they have positively misled their employer (see para 2.267 above).

Is the employee aware of other employees having solicited clients or suppliers? If so, such **2.347** solicitation would also be reportable by an employee (see para 2.268 above).

Have those leaving been recruited separately and individually by the new employer, with- **2.348** out the assistance of senior members of the moving team? If not, there will probably have been a breach of duty of fidelity and fiduciary duties of good faith by the senior members of the team.

Are the senior individuals within the team aware of the attempts to recruit their colleagues? **2.349** If they were so aware and have not revealed that fact to the employer, they will be in breach of their fiduciary duties.

Have the senior individuals passed on (whilst still employed) details of the other individuals **2.350** who should be approached, or details of their salaries or other information that would be useful to the competitor to the detriment of the employer? If so, they will be in breach of their fiduciary/good faith duties (see para 2.269 above).

Is there an express contractual obligation to reveal the fact of an approach by a competitor? **2.351** Such obligation may be enforceable (see para 2.266(1) above).

If you are the employer, consider the issues set out in paragraphs 2.275 to 2.286 above. **2.352**

If you are the competitor, consider the issues set out in paragraphs 2.287 to 2.298 above. **2.353**

If you are a lawyer advising the competitor or the relevant employees, take care to avoid **2.354** conflicts of interest, be aware of what will and will not be subject to legal professional privilege, and avoid playing a role in the recruitment process that is more than the provision of legal advice and assistance (see para 2.266(6) above).

3

CONFIDENTIAL INFORMATION AND THE DATABASE RIGHT

Robert Howe QC, Diya Sen Gupta, Sarah Wilkinson,
Simon Pritchard, Dan Aherne, and Luke Pardey

A. The duty of confidence: an overview[1]

Origins

Breach of confidence is one of the longest-standing equitable causes of action. As was pointed **3.01** out by Megarry J in the leading case of *Coco v Clark*:[2]

---

[1] See also Appendix 3, Sample Confidential Information Clauses below.
[2] [1969] RPC 41, 46.

The equitable jurisdiction in cases of breach of confidence is ancient; confidence is the cousin of trust. The Statute of Uses, 1535, is framed in terms of 'use, confidence or trust'; and a couplet, attributed to Sir Thomas More, Lord Chancellor avers that;

'Three things are to be helpt in Conscience; Fraud, Accident and things of Confidence'. (See 1 Rolle's Abridgement 374).

3.02 It is also, in practice, one of the most rapidly evolving and important causes of action, not only for employers but for anyone who has valuable secrets to protect—as demonstrated by the number of House of Lords decisions concerning actions for breach of confidence in high profile cases such as *Campbell v Mirror Group Newspapers Ltd*[3] (claim by the model, Naomi Campbell, concerning the publication of articles and photographs about her drug addiction), and *Cream Holdings Ltd v Bannerjee*[4] (claim by an employer against former employees to restrain the publication of confidential information) or by the series of High Court, Court of Appeal decisions, and one of the House of Lords in the long-running saga that is *Douglas v Hello! Ltd* (action by the actors Michael Douglas and Catherine Zeta-Jones over the publication of unauthorized photographs of their wedding).[5]

The nature of the right

3.03 The modern roots of the duty of confidence lie in a series of nineteenth-century cases, the most well known of which is *Prince Albert v Strange*.[6] That case, which concerned a claim by Prince Albert to restrain the publication of some private etchings which had fallen into the hands of the defendant through a third party, authoritatively established that the right could arise independently of any direct contractual relationship between the claimant and the defendant.

3.04 It is clear that the duty originates from the court's equitable, as opposed to common law, jurisdiction, and it has been described as an 'equitable wrong',[7] although others describe it as a 'tort'.[8] However, the equitable flavour is well demonstrated by the continuing concentration in recent authorities upon the role of the conscience of the recipient/holder of alleged confidential information.[9] This is of more than purely historical interest, however, as the remedies available for breach of confidence include, in addition to injunctive relief, equitable remedies such as (at the option of the claimant) either damages

---

[3] [2004] 2 AC 457.

[4] [2005] 1 AC 253.

[5] *Douglas v Hello! Ltd (No 1)* [2001] QB 967; *(No 2)* [2003] EWCA Civ 139, [2003] EMLR 29; *(No 3)* [2003] EWHC 55, [2003] 1 All ER 1087 (note); *(No 4)* [2002] EWHC 201; *(No 5)* [2003] EWCA Civ 332, [2003] EMLR 30; *(No 6)* [2005] EWCA Civ 595, [2006] QB 125; *(No 7)* [2003] EWHC 1781, [2003] EWHC 1781; *(No 8)* [2003] EWHC 2629, [2004] EMLR 2; *(No 9)* [2004] EWHC 63, [2004] EMLR 14. Appeal from *(No 3)* reported *sub nom OBG Ltd v Allen* [2007] UKHL 21; [2008] 1 AC 1 (CA reversed).

[6] (1849) 1 H&T 1. See also for a further indication of the nineteenth-century origins of the form of action *Morrison v Moat* (1851) 9 Hare 241 (confidentiality in a medical formula).

[7] *A-G v Blake* [2001] AC 268, 285 *per* Lord Nicholls. The classic statement is that of Lord Denning in *Seager v Copydex* [1967] 1 WLR 923, where he said: 'The law on this subject does not depend upon any implied contract. It depends upon the broad principle of equity that he who has received information in confidence shall not take unfair advantage of it.' See also Lord Phillips MR in *Douglas v Hello!* [2005] EWCA Civ 595, para 96; [2005] 4 All ER 128 and Peter Smith J in *Crowson Fabrics Ltd v Rider* [2008] IRLR 288, para 99.

[8] *Campbell v Mirror Group Newspapers Ltd* [2004] 2 AC 457, 465, para 15 *per* Lord Nicholls.

[9] See *Campbell v Mirror Group Newspapers Ltd* [2004] 2 AC 457, 464–5 *per* Lord Nicholls where he summarizes that a duty of confidence will be imposed 'wherever a person receives information he knows or ought to know is fairly and reasonably to be regarded as confidential'.

or an account of profits;[10] and in extreme cases proprietary consequences may flow from a breach of confidence. Equally, where proposed uses of confidential information do not trouble the consciences of reasonable men no action may lie (either because there is no contravening use or because there is a defence to a claim). Perhaps the best illustration of this is the case of *R v Department of Health, ex p Source Informatics*,[11] where Simon Brown LJ concluded:

> To my mind the one clear and consistent theme emerging from all these authorities is this: the confidant is placed under a duty of good faith to the confider and the touchstone by which to judge the scope of his duty and whether or not it has been fulfilled or breached is his own conscience, no more no less.

Together these features go well beyond that of an ordinary tort and show characteristics of **3.05** an equitable or proprietary wrong. Such equitable duties may be fleshed out as well as supplemented by contractual obligations, such that there are concurrent equitable and contractual duties. Thus the nature of the right or the particular aspect of it may also affect the extent to which it can survive, and be still enforced against an employee, following a wrongful dismissal.[12] The remedies for breach of confidence are addressed further at paragraphs 3.149 to 3.163 below.

What is becoming increasingly clear, however, is that the flexibility of breach of confidence **3.06** as a form of action is in fact taking it off in a number of discrete directions. Crudely put there are three broad types of breach of confidence case: (a) classic 'commercial' confidentiality cases, where the focus of the dispute is upon the protection of information of commercial value; (b) 'privacy' breach of confidence cases, the new emergent strain of breach of confidence as energized by the impetus given by Article 8 of the European Convention on Human Rights (ECHR) and the Human Rights Act 1998; and (c) 'state confidences', for instances as arising from public service or in a public context.[13]

This chapter is primarily concerned with 'commercial confidentiality' cases. Privacy cases **3.07** and state confidence cases may be relevant and will be drawn upon, particularly in so far as they illuminate the flexibility of this action, the various remedies to which it may give rise, and the defences available to a confidence claim. Further, the privacy aspect is often critical for employment arrangements where the employee assists in or is exposed to an employer's private life (for example as a personal assistant). But privacy and state confidence cases should be treated with caution as they have different points of emphasis. Privacy cases focus in particular upon the increasingly distinct notion of the 'reasonable expectation of privacy', a notion which gives rise to defences peculiar to private confidence claims. State confidence cases start from a different focal point, namely the public interest not private interests.[14] Accordingly, unless otherwise indicated, references to 'confidentiality' are to be taken as references to commercially confidential information.

---

[10] *A-G v Blake* [2001] AC 268, 285.

[11] [2001] QB 424, para 31. This case, and others involving anonymization or redaction, may be best viewed as cases where there is no detriment in use of the anonymized information. However, the conclusion that no detriment has been caused is one reached by an objective analysis of how conscience should operate in such circumstances.

[12] See paras 3.80–3.83 below.

[13] As typified, eg, by *A-G v Guardian Newspapers Ltd (No 2)* [1990] 1 AC 109 or *London Regional Transport v Mayor of London* [2003] EMLR 88.

[14] See Lord Keith in the *A-G v Guardian Newspapers Ltd (No 2)* [1990] 1 AC 109 (the '*Spycatcher*' case), 256–8, citing *Commonwealth of Australia v John Fairfax* (1980) 147 CLR 39 with approval.

Elements of the cause of action

3.08   In *Coco v Clark*,[15] Megarry J identified three elements to a claim for breach of confidence:

(1) The information itself must have 'the necessary quality of confidence about it'.
(2) That information must have been imparted in circumstances importing an obligation of confidence.
(3) There must be an unauthorized use (or threatened use) of that information to the detriment of the party communicating it.

3.09   This is still recognized as the 'classic exposition'[16] of the elements of the cause of action; although the second limb has been modified in some respects. It certainly remains the classic exposition for commercial confidentiality cases.[17]

First element: the necessary quality of confidence

3.10   The test of whether information has the 'necessary quality of confidence' is in reality a twofold one. It refers both to the inherent quality of the information and to the general inaccessibility of such information. In general terms much private information is capable of having the required quality of confidence. This can include such obvious matters as (in a privacy confidentiality context) marital affairs,[18] private conversations about personal relationships,[19] but also (in a commercial confidentiality context) secret processes,[20] ideas for gadgets,[21] and TV and game show formats;[22] potentially sensitive business information such as customer lists[23] and pricing information;[24] and equally information about commercial intentions.[25] The obligation of confidence may subsist even where a witness is giving evidence in court (although the court may make orders restricting the use made of that evidence or waiving confidentiality between the parties for the purposes of the case).[26] The dividing

---

[15] See n 2 above, 47–8.

[16] *Campbell v Mirror Group Newspapers Ltd* [2004] 2 AC 457, 464, para 13 *per* Lord Nicholls.

[17] See also *Saltman Engineering Co Ltd v Campbell Engineering Co Ltd* (1948) 65 RPC 203, CA, 210, 213 for Lord Greene MR's formulation of the elements of the cause of action; and *Electro Cad Australia Pty Ltd v Mejai RCS SDN BHD* [1999] FSR 291, 304.

[18] *Duke of Argyll v Duchess of Argyll* [1967] 1 Ch 302.

[19] *Stephens v Avery* [1998] Ch 449 (disclosure to a friend of a lesbian affair restrained); although cf *A v B plc* [2003] QB 195 (married footballer's right to confidence concerning various affairs outweighed by right to the freedom of expression by other party, and the freedom of the press), and *Terry (previously 'LNS') v Persons Unknown* [2010] EMLR 16 (lack of evidence of confidential information relating to extra-marital affair preventing interim injunction). See also *Lord Browne of Madingly v Associated Newspapers Ltd* [2008] QB 103 (mere fact that information communicated during relationship of confidence such as sexual relationship did not render it confidential information).

[20] *Lancashire Fires Ltd v SA Lyons & Co Ltd* [1996] FSR 629, CA, [1997] IRLR 113; cf *AT Poeton (Gloucester Plating) v Horton* [2000] ICR 1208, CA.

[21] *Seager v Copydex Ltd* [1967] 1 WLR 923, CA.

[22] *Talbot v General Television Corp Pty* [1981] RPC 1 (Australia, Supreme Court of Victoria); *Fraser v Thames TV* [1983] 2 All ER 101; and see, more recently, the Indian High Court case of *Gupta v Dasgupta* [2003] FSR 337.

[23] See *Lock International v Beswick* [1989] 1 WLR 1268, 1281 *per* Hoffmann J; or *Lansing Linde v Kerr* [1991] 1 WLR 251, CA, 260 *per* Staughton LJ.

[24] *Poly Lina v Finch* [1995] FSR 751. See also *JN Dairies Ltd v Johal Dairies Ltd* [2009] EWHC 1331 (Ch) (information in invoices as to quantities purchased and prices paid was confidential; appeal dismissed at [2010] EWCA Civ 348), but cf *Crowson Fabrics Ltd v Rider* [2008] IRLR 288, para 102 (sales figures and profit margins would have been carried in the employee's heads and was not confidential).

[25] *ABK Ltd v Foxwell & Baddow Hall* [2002] EWHC 9 (Ch), para 57.

[26] *Porton Capital Technology Funds v 3M UK Holdings Ltd* [2010] EWHC 114 (Comm).

line is, in principle, between information capable of separate identification and protection (so long as it remains confidential) and information that can more accurately be described as forming part of the inalienable general (or trivial) knowledge, experience, and acquired skill of the party receiving and using such information. Where information is partly private and partly public and the recipient adds ideas of his own, however, the courts are unlikely to restrain the recipient but may require him to pay a reasonable sum.[27] The question of whether various types of information have the 'necessary quality of confidence' in an employment context is particularly difficult. It has been subject to extensive consideration by the courts, particularly in the leading case of *Faccenda Chicken v Fowler*[28] and subsequent decisions in which that case has been considered and applied. This is discussed in paragraphs 3.26 to 3.64 below.

If the information in question is capable of being treated as confidential, it still remains to be **3.11** seen whether that information in fact retains that quality or has become too well known to deserve continuing protection. The requirement that the information should have the 'necessary quality of confidence' means only, as Lindsay J emphasized in *Douglas v Hello!*[29] that 'it must not be something that is public property and public knowledge'. In *Spycatcher* Bingham LJ (as he then was) identified this as the 'basic attribute of inaccessibility'.[30] But such inaccessibility need not be absolute; 'relative confidence' is distinctly possible.[31] Precisely what degree of publication is required to put material in the public domain is a question of fact and degree. As one judge succinctly put it:

> Clearly a claim that disclosure of some information would be a breach of confidence is not defeated simply by proving that there are other people in the world who know the information.[32]

As the Court of Appeal emphasized in *Douglas v Hello! Ltd (No 8)*, information would be **3.12** confidential if it was available to one person (or a group of people) and not generally available to others, provided that the person or group of people who had possession of the information did not intend that it should be available to others.[33]

Second element: circumstances importing an obligation of confidence

This second limb has been modified to some extent by the House of Lords decision in *Campbell* **3.13** *v Mirror Group Newspapers Ltd.*[34] Lord Nicholls pointed out[35] that 'this cause of action has now firmly shaken off the limiting constraint of the need for an initial confidential relationship' and that in doing so it had 'changed its nature'. He summarized the position as follows:

> Now the law imposes a 'duty of confidence' whenever a person receives information he knows or ought to know is fairly and reasonably to be regarded as confidential. Even this formulation

---

[27] See *Vestergaard Frandsen A/S v Bestnet Europe Ltd* [2010] FSR 2, para 39 *per* Arnold J.

[28] [1987] Ch 117, CA.

[29] [2003] 3 All ER 996, para 182; not disturbed on appeal [2005] EWCA 595.

[30] *A-G v Guardian Newspapers Ltd (No 2)* [1990] 1 AC 109, 215.

[31] See also *Green Corns Ltd v Claverley Group Ltd* [2005] EWHC 958, [2005] EMLR 748, paras 78–9.

[32] *Franchi v Franchi* [1967] RPC 149, paras 152–3 *per* Cross J; see also *A-G v Guardian Newspapers Ltd (No 2)* [1990] 1 AC 109, 282, where Lord Goff asked whether 'the information in question is so generally accessible that, in all the circumstances, it cannot be regarded as confidential'; and *A-G v Greater Manchester Newspapers Ltd* [2001] TLR 668, paras 33–4 (library materials or information on a website may not be in the 'public domain' so long as they remain obscure).

[33] [2005] EWCA Civ 595, [2005] EMLR 609. See also *In re BBC, In re A-G's Reference (No 3 of 1999)* [2010] 1 AC 145, para 18 *per* Lord Hope.

[34] [2005] EWCA Civ 595, [2005] EMLR 609.

[35] At paras 14–15.

is awkward. The continuing use of the phrase 'duty of confidence' and the description of the information as 'confidential' is not altogether comfortable. Information about an individual's private life would not, in ordinary usage, be called 'confidential'. The more natural description today is that such information is private. The essence of the tort is better encapsulated now as misuse of private information.

3.14 The focus is therefore now not so much exclusively on the circumstances in which the information is received, but rather also upon the nature of the information itself, and whether the person receiving the information knew or ought to have known that it was fairly and reasonably to be regarded as confidential. This approach has been restated with approval by the Court of Appeal in *Napier and another v Pressdram Ltd*.[36] It is an objective test.[37] Such an approach, in which certain types of information are taken (in descending scale) to be inherently understood to be or held as confidential, or presumptively so, very much ties in with the categorization of types of confidential information visible in commercial confidentiality cases since the *Faccenda Chicken* case, discussed in paragraphs 3.31ff below.

3.15 This new formulation is in fact not very dissimilar to the test originally proposed by Megarry J in *Coco v Clark*, where he suggested[38] that if the circumstances were such that 'any reasonable man standing in the shoes of the recipient of the information would have realised that upon reasonable grounds the information was being given to him in confidence', that would be sufficient to 'impose upon him the equitable obligation of confidence'.

3.16 From this twin-tracked approach of analysing both: (a) relationship/connections between confider and confidant; and (b) the nature of the information, it can be seen that obligations of confidence can arise in many circumstances. Certain types of formal relationship—for instance, of employer and employee, doctor and patient,[39] professional advisers, company and officer,[40] joint venturers sharing know-how,[41] government and security service personnel—implicitly give rise by their very nature to expectations of respect for confidence; parties may also agree or refine duties of confidence by contract. But even as between complete strangers the very nature of the information may demand that it should be treated as confidential in the hands of the person who comes into possession of it.[42] Equally, the nature of the relationship between parties and their mutual knowledge as to their position and expectations may cause the imposition of duties of confidence upon documents or information mistakenly disclosed.[43] Such principles have potentially wide significance when competitors

---

[36] [2009] EWCA Civ 443, [2010] 1 WLR 934, para 42 *per* Toulson LJ.

[37] *Author of a Blog v Times Newspapers Ltd* [2009] EWHC 1358 (QB), [2009] EMLR 22, para 8 *per* Eady J.

[38] [1969] RPC 41, 48.

[39] eg *W v Egdell* [1990] Ch 359, CA (although this decision is an example of the doctor/patient confidence being overridden by the public interest in ensuring that those treating a dangerous patient were warned of a consultant psychiatrist's concerns, following an examination of the patient).

[40] Typically, in such cases, the imposition of a duty of confidence is but a particular aspect of the wider fiduciary obligations in play in such circumstances.

[41] *Pell Frishman Engineering Ltd v Bow Valley Iran Ltd* [2009] UKPC 45.

[42] eg the person holding a private diary lost in a public place, an example suggested by Lord Goff in the *Spycatcher* case, [1990] 1 AC 109, 281. See also *Mars UK Ltd v Teknowledge Ltd* [2000] FSR 138. But a journalist who knew of a blogger's wish to remain anonymous was not bound to keep his identity confidential if he had deduced it from his research, see *Author of a Blog v Times Newspapers Ltd* [2009] EWHC 1358 (QB), [2009] EMLR 22.

[43] The best example of this is of legally privileged material mistakenly disclosed. See eg *IBM Corp v Phoenix International Computers Ltd* [1995] 1 All ER 413, and *English & American Insurance Co Ltd v Herbert Smith & Co* [1988] FSR 232.

come to be in possession of information about rivals and may prejudice the extent to which they can affect 'Nelsonian blindness' as to the information in question (for example information brought by a defecting employee, or leaked by an aggrieved former employee).

Further, in an employment context, one factor which the courts will often take into account **3.17** (if the evidence is presented) is whether and what steps the employer took to impress on the employee the confidentiality of the information.[44] The circumstances in which the information is acquired are therefore likely to continue to be relevant in an employment context, particularly for those 'weaker' forms of confidential information. Conversely, if the information is learned as a result of the alleged confider's open disclosure, this will undermine any action.[45] This topic is addressed further at paragraphs 3.57ff below.

Third element: disclosure to the detriment of the claimant

Whilst Megarry J in his formulation of the test proposed that detriment was a necessary **3.18** element of the wrong, he did so only tentatively, and made clear that he could conceive of cases where a claimant might have substantial motives for seeking to restrain a breach of confidence, and yet suffer nothing which could fairly be called detriment to him (the example which he gave was information which might gravely injure some relation or friend whom the claimant wished to protect). He noted that the point did not arise for decision in that case as detriment plainly existed.[46]

This aspect has not been much explored in subsequent cases, no doubt because it is unlikely **3.19** that the claimant would bring a claim unless he perceived that disclosure might harm him; and because in most cases if the information is confidential, the detriment caused by its disclosure is usually obvious.[47] It is suggested that detriment of a more than *de minimis* kind is a requirement,[48] and that detriment will usually readily be assumed where disclosure or unauthorized use of confidential information is threatened. The one area where considerations of detriment may continue to play a role is in those cases where it is proposed that the confidential information should be somehow anonymized (in the case of personal confidences)[49] or redacted (in the case of commercial confidences).[50] This is essentially a process that seeks to minimize or remove the detriment caused by disclosure.

Impact of the Human Rights Act 1998

All confidentiality cases decided before the introduction of the Human Rights Act 1998 **3.20** must now be read subject to the possible effect of the Act. As Lord Phillips pointed out in

---

[44] This was one of the factors specifically mentioned by Neill LJ in *Faccenda Chicken v Fowler* [1987] Ch 117, CA, 138. He considered that 'the attitude of the employer towards the information provides evidence which may assist in determining whether or not the information can properly be regarded as a trade secret'.

[45] As Megarry J put it in *Coco v Clark* [1969] RPC 41, 47–8: 'However secret and confidential the information, there can be no binding obligation of confidence if that information is blurted out in public or is communicated in other circumstances which negative any duty of holding it confidential.'

[46] ibid 48.

[47] But see *Crowson Fabrics Ltd v Rider* [2008] IRLR 288, para 104 *per* Peter Smith J, where the fact that the claimant could not identify any serious loss of business or customers reinforced the conclusion that the alleged confidential information was not in fact confidential.

[48] ie that 'equity ought not to be invoked merely to protect trivial tittle-tattle, however confidential', *Coco v Clark* [1969] RPC 41, 47 *per* Megarry J.

[49] See *R v Department of Health, ex p Source Informatics* [2001] QB 424.

[50] See *London Regional Transport v Mayor of London* [2003] EMLR 88 (the London Underground case).

Campbell v Frisbee,[51] the courts 'are in the process of adapting the law of confidentiality in the light of the [Act] in order to reflect the conflicting Convention rights of respect for private and family life and freedom of expression'. Although the Act may have less relevance in the context of most typical employment relationships (because the right to family and private life does not usually arise where the information is of a business nature) it will be significant where: (a) the employment is of a domestic type (as was the case in *Campbell v Frisbee*);[52] or, more frequently, (b) wherever a party seeks injunctive relief to restrain publication or disclosure by another of its confidential information. As Sedley LJ explained in the *London Underground* case, wherever the Court is asked to intervene in such a way using its coercive powers to control or interfere with a party's free expression, it must act compatibly with Article 10 of the ECHR.[53] Indeed, Lord Woolf observed in *A v B plc* that 'even where there is no public interest in a particular publication interference with freedom of expression has to be justified'.[54] This means that wherever interim injunctive relief is sought to prevent dissemination of confidential information, the Human Rights Act 1998 will be in play. Of course, the application of these principles will be particularly heightened in a journalistic context, for the reasons given by the House of Lords in *Campbell v Mirror Group Newspapers Ltd*.[55]

3.21 Further, section 12(3) and (4) of the Human Rights Act 1998 are of particular relevance to interim applications to restrain the dissemination of confidential information. They provide that:

> (3) No such relief [which might affect the exercise of the Convention right to freedom of expression] is to be granted so as to restrain publication before trial unless the court is satisfied that the applicant is likely to establish that publication should not be allowed.
> (4) The court must have particular regard to the importance of the Convention right to freedom of expression and, where the proceedings relate to material which the respondent claims, or which appears to the court, to be journalistic, literary or artistic material (or to conduct connected with such material), to—
>> (a) the extent to which—
>>> (i) the material has, or is about to, become available to the public; or
>>> (ii) it is, or would be, in the public interest for the material to be published;
>> (b) any relevant privacy code.

3.22 Whilst these provisions of the 1998 Act are primarily concerned with and directed at the freedom of the press, and largely tend to codify the requirements of Strasbourg case law which adopts a strict approach towards any prior restraint of the press, such provisions are potentially of more general application. Certainly, they are not limited to cases involving the press. As a result, wherever the employee seeks: (a) to contest the existence of any confidential information, or (b) to justify the disclosure and thus publication on grounds of public interest, as in *Cream Holdings v Banerjee*,[56] the Court will need to consider these provisions.

3.23 *Cream Holdings v Banerjee* is the leading case on the application of section 12(3) and (4) of the Human Rights Act 1998.[57] The claimants were attempting to restrain publication

---

[51] [2003] ICR 141, para 33.
[52] ibid.
[53] The *London Underground* case (n 50 above) para 61.
[54] [2002] EWCA Civ 337, [2003] QB 195, 206.
[55] *Campbell v Mirror Group Newspapers Ltd* [2004] 2 AC 457. See also *Murray v Express Newspapers plc* [2009] Ch 481, para 24 *per* Sir Anthony Clarke MR.
[56] [2005] 1 AC 253.
[57] Applied in *Lord Browne of Madingly v Associated Newspapers Ltd* [2007] EWCA Civ 295, [2008] QB 103.

of confidential information concerning alleged financial irregularities, which the first defendant, a former employee, had supplied to the second defendant, a local newspaper. The first instance judge granted the injunction, and the Court of Appeal upheld it; but the House of Lords discharged it. Their Lordships concluded that the disclosures were matters of serious public interest and therefore the right of freedom of expression was engaged; and that section 12(3) required the court not to restrain disclosure unless it was satisfied that 'the applicant's prospects of success at the trial are sufficiently favourable to justify such an order being made in the particular circumstances of the case'.[58] The reasoning of Lord Nicholls is worth citing in full:

> 16. Against this background I turn to consider whether, as the 'Echo' submits, 'likely' in section 12(3) bears the meaning of 'more likely than not' or 'probably'. This would be a higher threshold than that prescribed by the American Cyanamid case. That would be consistent with the underlying parliamentary intention of emphasising the importance of freedom of expression. But in common with the views expressed in the Court of Appeal in the present case, I do not think 'likely' can bear this meaning in section 12(3). Section 12(3) applies the 'likely' criterion to all cases of interim prior restraint. It is of general application. So Parliament was painting with a broad brush and setting a general standard. A threshold of 'more likely than not' in every case would not be workable in practice. It would not be workable in practice because in certain common form situations it would produce results Parliament cannot have intended. It would preclude the court from granting an interim injunction in some circumstances where it is plain injunctive relief should be granted as a temporary measure.
>
> 17. Take a case such as the present: an application is made to the court for an interlocutory injunction to restrain publication of allegedly confidential or private information until trial. The judge needs an opportunity to read and consider the evidence and submissions of both parties. Until then the judge will often not be in a position to decide whether on balance of probability the applicant will succeed in obtaining a permanent injunction at the trial. In the nature of things this will take time, however speedily the proceedings are arranged and conducted. The courts are remarkably adept at hearing urgent applications very speedily, but inevitably there will often be a lapse of some time in resolving such an application, whether measured in hours or longer in a complex case.
>
> 18. What is to happen meanwhile? Confidentiality, once breached, is lost for ever. Parliament cannot have intended that, whatever the circumstances, section 12(3) would preclude a judge from making a restraining order for the period needed for him to form a view on whether on balance of probability the claim would succeed at trial. That would be absurd. In the present case the 'Echo' agreed not to publish any further article pending the hearing of Cream's application for interim relief. But it would be absurd if, had the 'Echo' not done so, the court would have been powerless to preserve the confidentiality of the information until Cream's application had been heard. Similarly, if a judge refuses to grant an interlocutory injunction preserving confidentiality until trial the court ought not to be powerless to grant interim relief pending the hearing of an interlocutory appeal against the judge's order.
>
> 19. The matter goes further than these procedural difficulties. Cases may arise where the adverse consequences of disclosure of information would be extremely serious, such as a grave risk of personal injury to a particular person. Threats may have been made against a person accused or convicted of a crime or a person who gave evidence at a trial. Disclosure of his current whereabouts might have extremely serious consequences. Despite the potential seriousness of the adverse consequences of disclosure, the applicant's claim to confidentiality may be weak. The applicant's case may depend, for instance, on a disputed question of fact on which the applicant has an arguable but distinctly poor case. It would be extraordinary if in such a

---

[58] At para 22 *per* Lord Nicholls.

case the court were compelled to apply a 'probability of success' test and therefore, regardless of the seriousness of the possible adverse consequences, refuse to restrain publication until the disputed issue of fact can be resolved at the trial.

20. These considerations indicate that 'likely' in section 12(3) cannot have been intended to mean 'more likely than not' in all situations. That, as a test of universal application, would set the degree of likelihood too high. In some cases application of that test would achieve the antithesis of a fair trial. Some flexibility is essential. The intention of Parliament must be taken to be that 'likely' should have an extended meaning which sets as a normal prerequisite to the grant of an injunction before trial a likelihood of success at the trial higher than the common-place American Cyanamid standard of 'real prospect' but permits the court to dispense with this higher standard where particular circumstances make this necessary.

3.24 Thus, a claimant would ordinarily, but not always, be required by the court to satisfy it that he or she would be more likely than not to succeed at trial. The most obvious reach of these types of Human Rights Act arguments into commercial confidentiality cases is in fields such as employee moles and/or whistle-blowing cases,[59] and campaigning cases.[60] In *Attorney General v Random House Group Ltd*, however, it was held that the dicta in *Cream Holdings* are of no guidance where, in an application for an interim injunction, no trial is likely to take place.[61]

3.25 It is therefore always necessary to have in mind, when considering a claim for breach of confidence in an employment context, the possibility (and in an injunctive context, the probability) that the Convention right to freedom of expression may be engaged and, in personal services contracts, the right to respect for privacy.[62] This may significantly affect the prospects of success and, in particular, how the court approaches any balancing exercise with which it is faced[63] and the chances of getting (or successfully resisting) an interim injunction. This problem may be particularly acute if it is being suggested (or may be suggested) by the defendant that there is a potential public interest in disclosure of the information in question. This is addressed further in paragraphs 3.84 to 3.148 below.

B. What is confidential information?

The spectrum of confidence and the different means to obtain protection

3.26 Given the constituent definitional ingredients in confidential information,[64] it is plain that the term in truth embraces a wide spectrum of types of valuable information, whose relative value, duration of value or shelf-life, character and importance vary enormously. Some information may be of tremendous value but for a short period (for example market data or 'inside' information before a key deal), other information may be of similar value for longer periods (for example high quality data exclusively available to one player in a competitive field), some information may be of moderate value for a modest period (for example the state of negotiations on a particular proposed deal). Consideration of confidentiality in a commercial context necessarily brings with it three questions: (a) how can it be practically

---

[59] See eg *Mersey Care NHS Trust v Ackroyd (No 2)* [2006] EMLR 12, affirmed by the Court of Appeal [2008] EMLR 1.

[60] *Imutran v Uncaged Campaigns* [2001] 2 All ER 385.

[61] [2010] EMLR 9, para 40 *per* Tugendhat J.

[62] See *Browne* para 23 (n 57 above) for the order in which issues under the Human Rights Act should be considered in a confidentiality case.

[63] See *Douglas v Hello! Ltd (No 8)* [2005] EMLR 609.

[64] See paras 3.10–3.12 above.

protected or kept confidential; (b) for how long is it likely to be confidential or useful; and (c) if confidence is breached, what value does it have in the hands of a competitor?

The existence of this spectrum or varying nature of confidential information goes hand in **3.27** hand with the three legal means by which employers attempt in practice to protect commercially confidential information, namely: (a) reliance upon implied or equitable duties of confidence; (b) express confidentiality clauses or covenants, which may be concurrent with employment and/or operative post-termination; and (c) other post-termination covenants not expressed in terms of confidentiality.

Implied duties of confidence arise in two interrelated ways. First, respecting obligations of **3.28** confidence is part of the implied duty of good faith found in every contract of employment.[65] An employee is therefore bound to respect his employer's confidential information and to restrict his use of it to causes designed to assist his employer for so long as he remains an employee. Secondly, some information is by its very critical nature so obviously confidential that however it comes into a party's hands, and whenever it does so, it must be treated as imparted in circumstances of confidence. In a commercial confidentiality context these are called 'trade secrets'. The knowledge of, say, a mainframe administrator access code does not cease to be a vital secret to a business simply because the IT technician changes employer. Were he to use that information or impart it to another, it would constitute an obvious wrong because no one could honestly use such information for their own competing purposes with a clear conscience.

However, as we shall see, the delimitation of these 'trade secrets' is a controversial business. **3.29** As such, employers and employees are wise to avoid debate by endeavouring to agree in advance either: (a) what categories or types of information are to be treated as confidential; and/or (b) where precise categorization is impossible or overly rigid, what criteria will be used to identify confidential information. During the currency of employment such covenants can operate to provide certainty between the parties. However, post-termination covenants have the potential to operate much like restrictive covenants, and to engage the restraint of trade doctrine, if unduly widely drafted.

Lastly, given the burden of clear clarification and categorization (explained below), employers **3.30** may conclude for post-termination periods that it is more sensible, clearer, and more easily policed to formulate other restrictions designed to achieve the same or similar ends, such as non-compete clauses, non-solicitation clauses, potentially in conjunction with garden leave obligations.[66] Such alternative tools are particularly apposite to provide protection against the misuse of lower level, more ephemeral forms of confidential information that may have (for market reasons) some limited 'shelf-life' or tapering value.

Attempts at defining classes of confidential information

Following the Court of Appeal's decision in *Faccenda Chicken v Fowler*,[67] as subsequently **3.31** interpreted in cases such as *Lansing Linde v Kerr*,[68] *PSM International v Whitehouse*,[69]

---

[65] See Chapter 2 above for a discussion of this general duty which, in its many facets, operates to prevent many forms of competition by a current employee.
[66] See *Thomas v Farr plc* [2007] ICR 932, para 42 *per* Toulson LJ.
[67] [1987] Ch 117, CA.
[68] [1991] 1 WLR 251, CA.
[69] [1992] IRLR 279, CA.

Lancashire Fires Ltd v SA Lyons & Co Ltd,[70] and *AT Poeton (Gloucester Plating) Ltd v Horton*,[71] the broad principles regarding the various classes of confidential information (so far as relevant to the typical High Court employment case) are fairly easy to describe. However, they can be difficult to apply in practice, except in clear cases.

3.32 The essential problem with which the courts have had to grapple is the distinction between 'know-how', which an employee will inevitably acquire in the course of his employment and which he ought to be able to take away with him when his employment terminates and deploy for himself or a competitor, even if this is highly damaging to his former employer; and genuinely secret information which it would be unfair to allow the former employee to use.

3.33 In *Faccenda Chicken v Fowler* the Court of Appeal accepted the trial judge's (Goulding J's) division of information to which an employee might typically have access into three classes:

> **Class 1:** Trivial or public information which is not confidential at all, and which an employee is free to disclose or use.

> **Class 2:** Information which the employee must treat as confidential (either because he is expressly told that it is confidential or because from its character it obviously is so) but which once learned necessarily remains in the servant's head and becomes part of his own skill and knowledge applied in the course of his master's business. It might well be a breach of the employee's duties if he were to disclose this information whilst employed, but there is generally no restriction on him using or disclosing such information after termination of the employment.

> **Class 3:** Specific trade secrets so confidential that, even though they may necessarily have been learned by heart and even though the employee may have left the service, they cannot lawfully be used for anyone's benefit but the employer's.[72]

3.34 It is important to appreciate at the outset that these categories were described in a case in which there was no express confidentiality covenant (whether pre- or post-termination). As such Class 2 is something of a residual category, precisely because Class 1 information may be used post-termination without any restriction and Class 3 information may never be used post-termination (unless there arises some defence, such as subsequent publication, iniquity, etc). The question the *Faccenda* case does not explore is the extent (often, duration being the critical question) to which Class 2 information may be legitimately protected after termination of employment. For the reasons explained below, it may be better to see Class 2 information as falling into two categories, namely (for want of better terms) Class 2A and Class 2B, the difference between the two categories being that the latter is capable of protection by an appropriately drafted post-termination restraint.[73] This distinction is directly connected to the countervailing public interest underpinning the desirability of an employee being free to work.

---

[70] [1997] IRLR 113, CA.

[71] [2000] ICR 1208, CA.

[72] Generally, in decisions on this area, Class 3 is described by the shorthand 'trade secrets'. However, in *AT Poeton (Gloucester Plating) Ltd v Horton* [2000] ICR 1208, Morritt LJ suggested that the information then under consideration in that case was 'capable of being a trade secret', but he did not think that it attained 'that degree of confidentiality as to fall within class 3' (ibid 1218), which implies that some trade secrets might fall within Class 2. It is suggested that this is just an instance of mislabelling.

[73] See, further, below.

Distinguishing between the classes of information

These three classes of information are described in only fairly vague and general terms, and **3.35** in practice it can be very difficult to determine into which class any particular information or type of information might fall. The particular focus of debate, not surprisingly, has been the distinction between Class 2 and Class 3 information.

In the *Faccenda Chicken* case itself, the Court of Appeal suggested that in order to determine **3.36** whether any particular item of information comes within Class 3 it is necessary to consider 'all the circumstances of the case' including, but not limited to, the nature of the employment, the nature of the information, whether the employer impressed on the employee the confidentiality of the information, and whether such information may be easily isolated from other information which the employee is free to use or disclose.

This is a general test which provides some guidance but not much certainty. As a result, sub- **3.37** sequent to the *Faccenda Chicken* case, various additional tests for distinguishing between Class 2 and Class 3 information have been proposed.

'Objective' versus 'subjective' knowledge

In *SBJ Stephenson Ltd v Mandy*,[74] Bell J suggested that the correct test is to distinguish **3.38** between 'objective' and 'subjective' knowledge. This distinction derives from a passage in Lord Shaw's speech in *Herbert Morris Ltd v Saxelby*:[75]

> Trade secrets, the names of customers, all such things which in sound philosophical language are denominated objective knowledge—these may not be given away by a servant; they are his master's property, and there is no rule of public interest which prevents a transfer of them against the master's will being restrained. On the other hand, a man's aptitudes, his skill, his dexterity, his manual or mental ability—all those things which in sound philosophical language are not objective, but subjective—they may and they ought not to be relinquished by a servant; they are not his master's property; they are his own property; they are himself. There is no public interest which compels the rendering of those things dormant or sterile or unavailing; on the contrary, the right to use and expand his powers is advantageous to every citizen, and maybe highly so for the country at large.

This is a helpful suggestion, at least so far as it identifies the nature of the problem: trying to **3.39** distinguish between knowledge which might be regarded as forming part of the employee's general stock of accumulated know-how, as opposed to specific details which should be regarded as belonging to his employer.[76] However, it is not entirely satisfactory as a test in its own right, in that the implication of the passage appears to be that the employee is only free to use non-specific skills which he has acquired. This is unlikely to be correct in the context of a modern business. An employee may well acquire detailed knowledge both of his industry in general, and of his employer's business in particular, during the course of his employment. Such knowledge would probably not fall within the 'subjective knowledge' category as

---

[74] [2000] IRLR 233.

[75] [1916] 1 AC 688, 714, approved, along with *Faccenda Chicken v Fowler* (n 44 above), in *Berkeley Administration Inc v McClelland* [1990] FSR 505, 524.

[76] For further attempts to distinguish between ordinary stock of knowledge, skill, and experience on the one hand and confidential information on the other, see *Systems Reliability v Smith* [1990] IRLR 377, paras 63–66 *per* Harman J, and *Baker v Gibbons* [1972] 1 WLR 693, 700 *per* Pennycuick VC.

described by Lord Shaw. However, it is unlikely that much of it could properly be categorized as trade secrets falling within Class 3.

The 'honesty' test

3.40   Another test which has been proposed for the purposes of distinguishing between Class 2 and Class 3 information is what might be called the 'honesty test'—see, for example, *FSS Travel v Johnson*.[77] This test derives from a passage in the judgment of Cross J in *Printers & Finishers Ltd v Holloway*:[78]

> If the information in question can fairly be regarded as a separate part of the employee's stock of knowledge which a man of ordinary honesty and intelligence would recognise to be the property of his old employer and not his own to do as he likes with, then the court, if it thinks that there is a danger in the information being used or disclosed by the ex-employee to the detriment of the old employer, will do what it can to prevent that result by granting an injunction.

3.41   Whilst this is no doubt useful as a touchstone, it is considerably less specific even than the general list of factors which were put forward in the *Faccenda Chicken* case itself. In addition, the test is largely circular: in most cases where this issue arises, the question of what can properly be regarded to be a genuine trade secret (ie what information is 'the property of [the employee's] old employer') is the very issue which has to be decided.

The 'harm' test

3.42   Staughton LJ in *Lansing Linde v Kerr*[79] put the test in another way—he proposed a 'harm' principle:[80]

> It appears to me that the problem is one of definition: what are trade secrets, and how do they differ (if at all) from confidential information? Mr. Poulton suggested that *a trade secret is information which, if disclosed to a competitor, would be liable to cause real (or significant) harm to the owner of the secret. I would add first, that it must be information used in a trade or business, and secondly that the owner must limit the dissemination of it or at least not encourage or permit widespread publication.*
>
> *That is my preferred view of the meaning of trade secret in this context.* It can thus include not only secret formulae for the manufacture of products but also, in an appropriate case, the names of customers and the goods which they buy. But some may say that not all such information is a trade secret in ordinary parlance. If that view be adopted, the class of information which can justify a restriction is wider, and extends to some confidential information which would not ordinarily be called a trade secret.

3.43   The difficulty with this test is that it is probably over-inclusive. As has been mentioned above, there are many things which an employee may learn during the course of his employment, which form part of his stock of general knowledge or his detailed knowledge of his particular industry, and which when used for his own benefit or that of a new employer may cause significant harm to the former employer. It is in the nature of a market economy that an employer cannot expect indefinite protection from competition by former employees, even if they are taking advantage of knowledge and training which they have acquired from their former employer. It does not follow from the mere fact that the employer is harmed by the deployment of such information, and that he labelled it as 'confidential' during the

---

[77] [1998] IRLR 382, CA.
[78] [1965] 1 WLR 1, 5, cited with approval in *FSS Travel*, ibid para 34.
[79] [1991] 1 WLR 251, CA.
[80] ibid 260, emphasis added.

employment, that it can necessarily be regarded as sufficiently vital and sensitive to constitute a 'trade secret'.[81]

That said, Staughton LJ is undoubtedly right in principle in pointing out that trade **3.44** secrets are not confined to technical information (secret formulae or processes being the classic example),[82] but can include other commercially sensitive information such as names of customers and the goods which they buy. Many businesses by their nature do not have 'secret formulae'; their equivalent is highly sensitive commercial information about customers, business plans, pricing, and the like. In the same case, Butler-Sloss LJ expressed a similar view:[83]

> The starting point is *Herbert Morris Ltd v Saxelby* [1916] 1 A.C. 688. But we have moved into the age of multi-national businesses and worldwide business interests. Information may be held by very senior executives which, in the hands of competitors, might cause significant harm to the companies employing them. 'Trade secrets' has, in my view, to be interpreted in the wider context of highly confidential information of a non-technical or non-scientific nature, which may come within the ambit of information the employer is entitled to have protected, albeit for a limited period.

Subject to problems of definition (as to which, see the next section) there is no reason in **3.45** principle why such information should not be capable of protection as a trade secret.

Summary

Perhaps the safest conclusion to draw from the above cases is that designation of particular **3.46** types of information as Class 3 'trade secrets' does not depend upon satisfaction of any one special criterion; there is no 'magic ingredient'. Instead, identification of a trade secret is really a multi-factored and contextual inquiry that looks at factors such as: (a) the nature of the information; (b) how it was obtained or derived, and by whom; (c) how it has been protected; (d) what worth has been ascribed to it by the parties (subjectively) and what worth it has (objectively); (e) what value it has in the hands of a competitor; (f) whether the employee can realistically or practically be expected to abstain from using such information consciously or unconsciously, and if so for how long; (g) the 'ascertainability' of the information and the resources required to ascertain it; (h) the seniority and/or nature of the employee; (i) the proximity of the information to any core of secret processes or know-how; and (j) the extent of the 'severability' of the information in question, ie to what extent would requiring an ex-employee to abstain from using the trade secret in question impede that employee from continuing to pursue his or her livelihood. It is worthy of note that privacy confidences, where deserving of protection, may fall to be treated as if they were Class 3 trade secrets, and like commercial trade secrets they may in principle be capable of commercialization, in that the management of the publicity of one's private affairs may be part of an individual's trade or profession, essentially commoditizing an individual's private life.[84]

---

[81] See *Cranleigh Precision Engineering Ltd v Bryant* [1965] 1 WLR 1293, 1311 discussed in *Vestergaard* (n 27 above), paras 52–63 *per* Arnold J, and also *Under Water Welders & Repairers Ltd v Street & Longthorne* (1968) RPC 498 distinguished in *United Sterling Corp Ltd v Felton and Mannion* [1973] FSR 409.
[82] See eg *United Indigo Chemical Co Ltd v Robinson* (1931) 49 RPC 178, 187; *Bjorlow (Great Britain) Ltd v Minter* (1954) 71 RPC 321, 323.
[83] [1991] 1 WLR 251, 270.
[84] See *Douglas v Hello! Ltd (No 8)* [2005] EMLR 609, 645.

3.47   In *Lancashire Fires Ltd v SA Lyons & Co Ltd*,[85] Sir Thomas Bingham MR (giving the judgment of the Court) succinctly summarized the issue as follows:

> It is plain that if an employer is to succeed in protecting information as confidential, he must succeed in showing that it does not form part of an employee's own stock of knowledge, skill and experience. The distinction between information in Goulding J.'s class 2 and information in his class 3 may often on the facts be very hard to draw, but ultimately the court must judge whether an ex-employee has illegitimately used the confidential information which forms part of the stock-in-trade of his former employer either for his own benefit or to the detriment of the former employer, or whether he has simply used his own professional expertise, gained in whole or in part during his former employment.

3.48   In that case, one of the main issues on appeal was whether certain information (concerning manufacturing processes used by the employer) fell within Class 2 or Class 3. The Court of Appeal differed from the trial judge on this point, holding that certain information was indeed Class 3 and that therefore the defendant had acted in breach of confidence by making use of that information after he left employment. In reaching this view, the Court first reviewed the authorities, and then elaborated upon the various factors identified in the *Faccenda Chicken* case which were relevant in deciding whether information constituted a trade secret falling within Class 3, as follows:[86]

(1) The nature of the employment: 'the nearer an employee is to the inner counsels of the employer, the more likely he is to gain access to truly confidential information'.[87]

(2) The nature of the information itself: 'to be capable of protection, information must be defined with some degree of precision: and an employer will have great difficulty in obtaining protection for his business methods and practices'.[88]

(3) The steps (if any) taken by the employer to impress on the employee the confidentiality of the information:
   (a) if an employer impresses the confidentiality of certain information on his employee, that is an indication of the employer's belief that the information is confidential, a fact which is 'not irrelevant';[89]
   (b) but 'much will depend on the circumstances. These may be such as to show that information is or is being treated as, confidential; and it would be unrealistic to expect a small and informal organisation to adopt the same business disciplines as a larger and more bureaucratic concern'.[90]

(4) The ease or difficulty of isolating the information in question from other information which the employee is free to use or disclose: 'It is plain that if an employer is to succeed in protecting information as confidential, he must succeed in showing that it does not form part of an employee's own stock of knowledge, skill and experience.'[91]

---

[85]   [1996] FSR 629, 668–9; [1997] IRLR 113, para 18.

[86]   ibid.

[87]   ibid.

[88]   ibid.

[89]   ibid (referring to *Thomas Marshall (Exports) Ltd v Guinle* [1979] Ch 227, 248).

[90]   *Lancashire Fires* case (n 20 above). See also *Saltman Engineering Co Ltd v Campbell Engineering Co Ltd* (1948) 65 RPC 203, CA; *Yates Circuit Foil Co v Electrofoils Ltd* [1976] FSR 345; and *Thomas Marshall (Exports Ltd) v Guinle* [1979] 1 Ch 227 for a discussion of the 'implied' duty of confidentiality.

[91]   *Lancashire Fires* case (n 20 above). See also *First Global v Locums Ltd v Cosias* [2005] IRLR 873, paras 55–6.

It is suggested that, whilst each case will inevitably depend on its own facts, this is an **3.49** authoritative judgment which provides useful guidance to determine whether informa- tion can be regarded as falling within Class 3. *Lancashire Fires Ltd v SA Lyons & Co Ltd* [92] concerned a company manufacturing and supplying ceramic materials for artificial log fires. The owner's brother left the claimant company to form a competing interest, and stockpiled equipment, acquired premises, and diverted potential business from the claim- ant to his defendant company. Applying the above criteria, Sir Thomas Bingham MR considered that the defendant was doing more than simply taking preliminary steps to establishing its own business or pursuing a related activity at leisure, especially given his advanced technical knowledge of the claimant's business, and consequently was in breach of his duty of fidelity.[93]

However, what is clear is that it is the policy of the courts (particularly the Court of Appeal) **3.50** to analyse Class 3 narrowly. Given the temporally unlimited protection conferred on Class 3 information and the fact that such obligations arise as a matter of implication, this is unsurprising. Indeed, this category's ultimate significance lies (as a matter of practical real- ity) in the fact that it is that type of information in respect of which an employer: (a) can obtain relief (typically injunctive but also by way of damages) against former employees for use of such Class 3 information *after* termination of employment but *without a covenant*; and/or (b) can safely impose a temporally unlimited (or long-term) post-termination covenant.

Given these special features, in *AT Poeton (Gloucester Plating) Ltd v Horton*,[94] the Court of **3.51** Appeal held that courts should not be astute to find Class 3 trade secrets tucked away in a much wider and unjustified claim, particularly since such claims were easy to make but expensive and time-consuming to refute, and the parties had the option to obtain clarity by agreeing appropriate post-termination confidence obligations in detailed terms. Moreover, junior employees should not be exposed to such a risk except in clear cases. The *Poeton* case therefore constitutes a strong call for parties to agree express covenants regulat- ing confidential information. However, the solution proposed in the *Poeton* case brings with it two consequential problems: (a) the potential for sufficiently encompassing, but sufficiently precise, drafting; and (b) the extent to which post-termination obligations of confidence may legitimately be imposed.

The confidential information must be capable of being precisely defined

It has often been said that if an employer cannot define with precision the confidential **3.52** information which he wishes to protect, then that in itself may disentitle him to relief. The court will not make orders restraining use of 'confidential information' in general terms—it

---

[92] [1996] FSR 629.
[93] ibid paras 49–50.
[94] [2000] ICR 1208; see also the application of the *Poeton* case in *Dranez Anstalt v Hayek* [2002] 1 BCLC 693 overturned by the Court of Appeal [2003] FSR 32; and, for a similar approach, see *Cray Valley Ltd v Deltech Europe Ltd* [2003] EWHC 728 (Ch); and *Fibrenetix Storage Ltd v Davies* [2004] EWHC 1359. The *Poeton* case culminates a trend started by the decision of Laddie J in *Ocular Sciences Ltd v Aspect Vision Care Ltd* [1997] RPC 289 (yet another case where wide claims to Class 3 trade secrets were made in the absence of an express contractual restraint).

will only restrain the use of specified, identifiable information. As Balcombe LJ said in *Lawrence David v Ashton*:[95]

> I have always understood it to be a cardinal rule that an injunction must be capable of being framed with sufficient precision so as to enable a person enjoined to know what it is he is to be prevented from doing. After all, he is at risk of being committed for contempt if he breaks an order of the court. The inability of the plaintiffs to define, with any degree of precision, what they sought to call confidential information or trade secrets militates against an injunction of this nature. That is indeed a long recognised practice.

3.53   Similar statements can be found in a number of other cases, including *Lock plc v Beswick*;[96] *Ixora Trading v Jones*;[97] *Speed Seal Products v Paddington*;[98] *Mainmet Holdings v Austin*;[99] and most forcefully of all, by Laddie J in *Ocular Sciences Ltd v Aspect Vision Care Ltd (No 2)*, where it was held that an extravagant and obviously over-wide claim to Class 3 confidentiality might in fact be an abuse, particularly if only vague particulars were given (or if the particulars in fact given were premised upon unduly wide claims).[100] Equally, in *FSS Travel v Johnson*[101] (a case in which the employer was attempting to justify a restrictive covenant on the ground that it was necessary to protect trade secrets), the Court of Appeal dismissed the claim on the ground (amongst others) that the employer had 'failed to adduce sufficiently cogent relevant evidence to identify and establish a separate body of objective knowledge qualifying for protection as a trade secret by means of a restrictive covenant'.[102] Mummery LJ added that 'it is not sufficient for the employer to assert a claim that he is entitled to an accumulated mass of knowledge which he regards as confidential'.

3.54   Given the difficulties which the Court of Appeal has itself encountered when attempting to define what constitutes protectable 'confidential information' and the Class into which it falls, this may appear harsh. The three other great practical problems for an employer are that often: (a) it may be impossible to predict in advance (for pre- or post-termination obligations) what information may become particularly critical or valuable; (b) the employer, confronted with a dishonest employee who has stolen materials, does not know precisely what information the employee may have taken, such that it is capable of definition with precision. He is therefore driven to seek an order (particularly search orders, delivery up orders, or the like) in broad and general terms in order to ensure that all stolen information is captured; and (c) it may be a hugely onerous task to provide sufficient particulars of the confidential information, accurately identifying what is and is not confidential.[103] This is particularly so because of the notion of relative confidence. Particular dilemmas arise in the context of cases where applications for springboard relief might be necessary, given the need to act speedily in order to obtain injunctive relief.

---

[95]   [1989] ICR 123, CA, 132; [1991] 1 All ER 385, CA, 395.
[96]   [1989] 1 WLR 1268, 1280 (Hoffman J).
[97]   [1990] FSR 251 (Mummery J).
[98]   [1984] FSR 77 (Harman J); [1985] 1 WLR 1327, CA, 1332.
[99]   [1991] FSR 538, 544 (Lionel Swift QC).
[100]   [1997] RPC 289. For further examples, see also *Printers & Finishers Ltd v Holloway* [1965] 1 WLR 1, 6 *per* Cross J; *John Zink Co Ltd v Wilkinson* [1973] RPC 717, CA, 727 *per* Stamp LJ; *John Zink Co Ltd v Lloyds Bank* [1975] RPC 385, 392 *per* Templeman J.
[101]   [1998] IRLR 382, CA.
[102]   At para 37.
[103]   A problem identified but not solved in the *Ocular Sciences* case [1997] RPC 289, 360.

However, in the light of the authorities referred to above, which clearly establish the prime **3.55** importance of precisely defining the nature of the confidential information, those acting for employers need to exercise great care to ensure (so far as possible) that the claim defines the nature of the information which the employer wishes to protect with sufficient precision. Similarly, those acting for an employee should be cautious of offering undertakings concerning disclosure of confidential information, without a clear definition of precisely what information is intended to be covered by the undertaking. That said, the requirement for particularity in confidential information cases cannot be pushed too far: the purpose of requiring an employer to be specific about his claim for breach of confidence is to prevent the abuse which can arise from over-generalised and speculative claims, not to impose an unrealistic burden on the claimant.[104]

One area in which the court has departed somewhat from this strict approach is in relation **3.56** to what might be called 'John Doe Injunctions' or (a label more likely to stick) 'Harry Potter Injunctions'. An owner of confidential information may be able to demonstrate that its confidential information has been stolen or, but for injunctive relief, would be taken and disseminated. It had previously been thought, until the case of *Bloomsbury Publishing Group Ltd v News Group Newspapers Ltd,*[105] that it was a requirement that at least one defendant for a claim for breach of confidence needed to be identified. In fact the court found that it had jurisdiction to grant an order against people generically described with sufficient accuracy, in that case 'the person or persons who have offered the publisher of [a newspaper] a copy of the book "Harry Potter and the Order of the Phoenix" by J.K. Rowling'. Whilst such a principle has not yet had any application in an employment context, its importance is obvious, particularly for an employer dealing with an unknown mole.

Relevance of efforts by the employer to make clear the information was confidential

As noted above, whether the employer had taken steps to 'impress on the employee the con- **3.57** fidentiality of the information' was one of the factors specifically mentioned by Neill LJ in *Faccenda Chicken v Fowler*[106] as being relevant in determining the status of the information. He considered (citing with approval a finding to similar effect by Morton J in *E Worsley & Co Ltd v Cooper*)[107] that 'the attitude of the employer towards the information provides evidence which may assist in determining whether or not the information can properly be regarded as a trade secret'.

This has also been treated as a relevant factor in cases such as *Lansing Linde v Kerr,*[108] *Poly* **3.58** *Lina Ltd v Finch*[109] (where the judge referred to and relied on the fact that the information was designated as confidential in the employee handbook, and the fact that the minutes in question were marked 'confidential'), and *Brooks v Olyslager Oms (UK) Ltd*[110] (in which the Court of Appeal rejected a claim that financial information about the employer constituted

---

[104] *Goldenfry Foods Ltd v Austin et al* (Leeds District Registry, Ch D, 23 October 2009), *per* HHJ Langan.
[105] [2003] 1 WLR 1633.
[106] [1987] Ch 117, CA, 138.
[107] [1939] 1 All ER 290, 307.
[108] [1991] 1 WLR 251, CA; see the passage from Staughton LJ's judgment quoted at para 3.42 above.
[109] [1995] FSR 751.
[110] [1998] IRLR 590, CA.

'Class 3' information, in part because there was no evidence that the employer had ever impressed the confidentiality on the employee).

3.59 However, although these decisions show that the employer's attitude to the information can be evidentially important, it is ultimately only one factor to be taken into account, and is certainly not decisive. For example, the size and resources of the employer may be relevant. As the Court of Appeal pointed out in *Lancashire Fires Ltd v SA Lyons & Co Ltd*,[111] when holding that certain information constituted a trade secret even though there were few indications that the employer had taken steps to impress the confidentiality on the employee, 'it would be unrealistic to expect a small and informal organisation to adopt the same business disciplines as a larger and more bureaucratic concern'.[112] The Court added:

> We do not accept that it is incumbent on an employer to point out to his employee the precise limits of that which he seeks to protect as confidential, particularly where, as here, what is new is an integral part of a process. The limits are not easy to draw even with the assistance of expert witnesses.[113]

3.60 Against this, there are clearly limits to how far the courts are prepared to go in making allowances for the employer in this area. In *AT Poeton (Gloucester Plating) Ltd v Horton*,[114] Morritt LJ distinguished the *Lancashire Fires* case on this point, and rejected a claim to confidentiality in certain information by the employer on the ground that 'the claim to confidentiality was much wider than was justified'.[115] He held that in its reference to 'precise limits' in the *Lancashire Fires* case, the Court of Appeal 'made it clear that it was not dealing with the case in which extravagant claims are made in which the confidential nature of the small part is to be inferred'.[116] By parity of reasoning, it is unlikely that blanket claims to confidentiality of very broad classes of information (for example included in a handbook or a contract of employment) will be given much weight.

Rights of third parties

3.61 Where a third party, such as a subsequent employer, receives confidential information from an informant (in breach of that informant's own duty of confidence to the original confider), a duty of confidence may be owed by that third party to the confider seeking to protect such confidential information. This third party duty of confidence is owed where the third party has received the confidential information in the knowledge that the informant has breached his existing duty of confidence to the original confider.[117]

3.62 This principle has its grounding in equity, and accordingly the same broad principles apply to matters concerning wrongful knowledge of a third party in respect of a breach of confidence as to knowing assistance in a breach of trust. To be held liable, the third party must have been more than simply careless or naive in the course of receiving such information; rather, the third party must have been in some way aware that the information was confidential, or

---

[111] [1996] FSR 629, [1997] IRLR 113.
[112] ibid 668–9.
[113] ibid 674.
[114] [2000] ICR 1208.
[115] ibid para 24.
[116] ibid.
[117] See *Murray v Yorkshire Fund Managers Ltd* [1998] 1 WLR 951, CA, 957; *Thomas v Pearce* [2000] FSR 718, 720–1; *ABK Ltd v Foxwell* [2002] EWHC 9 (Ch), paras 81–9.

conducted themselves in such a manner as to be wilfully ignorant of the likelihood that the information obtained was imparted in breach of a duty of confidence. The leading authorities rely upon the judgment of Lord Nicholls in *Royal Brunei Airlines v Tan*,[118] which establishes an objective standard of dishonesty in assessing a party's conduct (ie not acting as an honest person would in the circumstances), to be equated with 'conscious impropriety'. Thus, an honest person does not act in such a manner as to deprive a beneficiary of trust assets, nor do they deliberately close their eyes or ears to the possibility that they are acting with such an effect.

However, there may be cases where third parties receiving confidential information may be **3.63** entitled to use information, or even under a duty to do so, especially where the public interest may be concerned,[119] although such exceptions are to be viewed as limited exceptions only and when circumstances permit.

Moreover, in circumstances where a group has held confidential information as a group asset, **3.64** a member's discontinuation in the group accordingly terminates any 'proprietary' rights held by the former member in relation to such confidential information, and the knowledge may be imparted to third parties outside of the group only with the group's consent.[120]

C. Express confidentiality clauses

General

There is considerable debate as to whether, and if so to what extent, an employer can extend **3.65** or enhance the protection of information which he designates as confidential by using an express covenant to that effect. The debate has also at times been obscured by the confusion of two related, but distinct, issues.

The first is the question of the extent to which an employer can use an express confidenti- **3.66** ality clause to protect a wider class of information than would be covered by the implied term (or duty) of confidence in *Faccenda Chicken v Fowler*.[121] The second is the question of the extent to which an employer can justify a typical restrictive covenant (such as a non-compete, non-dealing, or non-solicitation covenant) as being necessary to protect him against misuse of sensitive commercial information (ie wider than Class 3) by a departing employee.

As for the first question, it is tolerably clear that an employer cannot use an express covenant **3.67** to deem confidential what is on any view either part of the employee's skill and general knowledge or otherwise not confidential.[122] At best such a covenant might have some use in resolving a 'borderline dispute' for information on the cusp of Class 1 and Class 2, but beyond that the clause is likely to be unenforceable.[123]

---

[118] [1995] 2 AC 378, 389.

[119] See the *Spycatcher* case (n 14 above) for a discussion of third-party rights and duties generally, at 154–6, 173, 183, 214–18, 237–8, 244, 260–1, 268, 272, 281–2, and 285.

[120] See *Murray v Yorkshire Fund Managers Ltd* (n 117 above) 959 for Nourse LJ's discussion of group rights.

[121] [1987] Ch 117, CA.

[122] See *Ixora Trading Inc v Jones* [1990] FSR 251, especially 258–9 *per* Mummery J.

[123] Naturally, the point is only of real significance post-termination as during the currency of employment wider duties of loyalty, including duties of non-competition, will probably come into play.

3.68   The real area of controversy is as to the effectiveness of post-termination confidentiality covenants for information falling into Class 2. In *Faccenda Chicken v Fowler* the Court of Appeal, disagreeing with Goulding J on this point, appeared to doubt that an employer could ever protect confidential information other than trade secrets (ie Class 3 information), following termination of employment, by means of an express covenant, holding:

> The restrictive covenant cases demonstrate that a covenant will not be upheld on the basis of the status of the information which might be disclosed by the former employee if he is not restrained, unless it can be regarded as a trade secret or the equivalent of a trade secret: see, for example, *Herbert Morris Ltd. v. Saxelby* [1916] 1 A.C. 688, 710 per Lord Parker of Waddington and *Littlewoods Organisation Ltd. v. Harris* [1977] 1 W.L.R. 1472, 1484 per Megaw L.J.

> We must therefore express our respectful disagreement with the passage in Goulding J.'s judgment at [1984] I.C.R. 589, 599E, where he suggested that an employer can protect the use of information in his second category, even though it does not include either a trade secret or its equivalent, by means of a restrictive covenant. As Lord Parker of Waddington made clear in *Herbert Morris Ltd. v. Saxelby* [1916] 1 A.C. 688, 709, in a passage to which Mr. Dehn drew our attention, a restrictive covenant will not be enforced unless the protection sought is reasonably necessary to protect a trade secret or to prevent some personal influence over customers being abused in order to entice them away. In our view the circumstances in which a restrictive covenant would be appropriate and could be successfully invoked emerge very clearly from the words used by Cross J. in *Printers & Finishers Ltd. v. Holloway* [1965] 1 W.L.R. 1, 6 (in a passage quoted later in his judgment by Goulding J. [1984] I.C.R. 589, 601):

> 'If the managing director is right in thinking that there are features in the plaintiffs' process which can fairly be regarded as trade secrets and which their employees will inevitably carry away with them in their heads, then the proper way for the plaintiffs to protect themselves would be by exacting covenants from their employees restricting their field of activity after they have left their employment, not by asking the court to extend the general equitable doctrine to prevent breaking confidence beyond all reasonable bounds.' [124]

3.69   This apparent conclusion has, however, been questioned in subsequent cases. In *Balston v Headline Filters*,[125] Scott J doubted that 'the Court of Appeal could have intended to exclude all information in Goulding J's second category from possible protection by a restrictive covenant'.[126] He pointed out that an express restrictive covenant would not be needed to protect Class 3 trade secrets, as the implied term would do that; and that therefore Neill LJ must have been 'contemplating the protection by an express restrictive covenant of confidential information in respect of which an obligation against use or disclosure after the determination of the employment could not be implied'.

3.70   Similarly, in *Systems Reliability Holdings v Smith*,[127] Harman J agreed with Scott J's comments, and considered that the passage in the Court of Appeal's judgment in *Faccenda Chicken v Fowler* was obiter and therefore not binding on him.[128] He held that an express confidentiality covenant made in a sale of business agreement was reasonable, and therefore binding on the defendant in the circumstances of that case; albeit he limited the term of the injunction enforcing that clause to the same period as a separate non-compete covenant

---

[124] [1987] Ch 117, 137.
[125] [1987] FSR 330.
[126] ibid 347.
[127] [1990] IRLR 377.
[128] ibid para 65.

(about seventeen months from the sale of the business). Bell J in *SBJ Stephenson Ltd v Mandy*[129] and Morritt LJ in the *Poeton* case[130] also adopted a similar approach.

In *Lansing Linde v Kerr*[131] the matter was treated as one of definition: Staughton and **3.71** Butler-Sloss LJJ pointed out that 'trade secrets' could cover a wider class of information than technical formulae and the like, and there was no reason in principle why these could not be protected by express covenant, if appropriate.

It is suggested that the answer to this apparent confusion lies in the tendency in the judgments, **3.72** when this issue is discussed, not to distinguish between two distinct types of covenant, namely an express restrictive covenant to restrain competition or solicitation, as opposed to an express restrictive covenant to restrain disclosure of confidential information.

It is well established that the legitimate business interests which an employer may be entitled **3.73** to protect by an appropriately drafted non-competition or non-solicitation covenant include customer connections and goodwill, and trade secrets with which the employee has become acquainted during his employment. In the passage in *Faccenda Chicken v Fowler* referred to above, Neill LJ was referring to this type of restrictive covenant—as was pointed out by the Court of Appeal in the *Lancashire Fires* case.[132] Neill LJ was not considering the separate question of whether the parties could, in an appropriate case, agree as a matter of contract that certain information which would not fall within 'Class 3' should not subsequently be used or disclosed.

It is also suggested, in accordance with the ordinary principles of freedom of contract, that **3.74** there is no reason in principle why the parties cannot validly agree that the employee should not subsequently use or disclose specified classes of information (subject to questions of illegality or public policy), so long as such agreement is not somehow legally invalid. Examples of such enforceable agreements are to be found in *Campbell v Frisbee*,[133] *Archer v Williams*,[134] or *HRH Prince of Wales v Associated Newspapers Ltd*,[135] in all of which the employee entered into an express agreement that all information concerning the employer's personal and professional life was confidential and that s/he would not subsequently use or disclose it. Equally, in *A-G v Parry*[136] the Court accepted it to be well arguable that an express non-disclosure clause could provide a special foundation for a claim for breach of confidence, citing dicta of Lord Donaldson MR in the case of *A-G v Barker* to the effect that:

> It is, in my judgment, very important to notice that this is not a case such as *Spycatcher* where the Attorney-General is relying on a duty of confidentiality. His claim is based upon a breach of contract, the consideration for the covenant by Mr Barker (that he would not publish matter true or false concerning his experiences in the royal household) being the agreement by those concerned to take him on the staff of the royal household and to pay him wages or a salary. It is not in principle in any way different from the case of someone who enters into a

---

[129] [2000] IRLR 233, para 32.
[130] [2000] ICR 1208, 1218. Morritt LJ's assumption was that Class 2 information, which had not been protected by a post-termination confidentiality covenant, could and should have been, had the employer wished to obtain relief of the type sought.
[131] [1991] ICR 428, 437 *per* Staughton LJ, and 448 *per* Butler-Sloss LJ.
[132] [1996] FSR 629, 666–7.
[133] [2003] ICR 141.
[134] *Archer v Williams* [2003] EMLR 869.
[135] [2008] Ch 57.
[136] [2003] EMLR 223.

contract with a newspaper whereby the person concerned undertakes in consideration of a money payment, not to give their story to anyone else for publication. The newspaper in those circumstances would be likely to publish, but they would not be obliged to publish. That is an exact analogy here: the royal household would be entitled to authorise publication if they wished but equally are fully entitled under the contract to refuse to allow it.[137]

3.75 Further, and quite separately, an express confidentiality covenant may be of evidential significance in determining what information falls within Class 3, as it may demonstrate what the parties considered to be truly confidential.

3.76 However, an express confidentiality covenant, like any other restrictive covenant, or any other contractual provision which may inhibit a person from pursing their livelihood, is subject to the doctrine of restraint of trade (and, indeed, the more general requirements of competition law). It cannot be used as a 'back door' method to restrain legitimate competition from an ex-employee who is seeking to use the skills and know-how he has acquired during his employment. This is not a particular concern in personal employment of the types found in *Campbell v Frisbee*[138] or *HRH Prince of Wales v Associated Newspapers Ltd.*[139] The employees in those cases would not (on the face of it) need to use information about their employers' personal or professional lives in order to pursue their trade or career.[140] However, in other contexts, a wide-ranging restraint on the use of information acquired during employment may be highly objectionable, as it may in practice seriously inhibit or altogether prevent the employee from carrying on his profession. In these circumstances, if the employer has a legitimate interest in protecting trade secrets or customer connections, in many cases he should do so by an appropriately limited and tailored non-competition or non-solicitation covenant,[141] and not by means of an indefinite post-termination express confidentiality clause; nor (for that matter) by attempting to rely on the alleged implied obligations of confidence. The point was made forcefully by Scott J in *Balston v Headline Filters*[142] when rejecting the claim for breach of confidence in a case in which the claimant relied upon a very generally worded post-termination confidentiality obligation which contained little more by way of express obligation than that which would in any event be implied in law (as part of the mutual obligations of trust and confidence or duty of good faith).

3.77 This is illustrated by *Jones v Ricoh UK Ltd,*[143] in which Roth J summarily dismissed that part of the claimant's claim based on alleged breach of an express confidentiality clause, on the ground that the clause was plainly contrary to Article 101 TFEU and accordingly void and unenforceable.[144]

3.78 Post-termination confidentiality covenants must, on any view, be analyzed against the doctrine of the restraint of trade.[145] Their potential to inhibit competition is obvious. As such, the truth of the position appears to be that: (a) true trade secrets make for easy cases, as their

---

[137] ibid 259. Nourse LJ pointed out in argument and in his judgment that such an obligation, on its facts, could not possibly lead to any illegality or restraint of trade.

[138] [2003] ICR 141.

[139] [2008] Ch 57.

[140] See *A-G v Barker* [1990] 3 All ER 257, where a similar point was made.

[141] See also *Townends Grove Ltd v Cobb* [2004] EWHC 3432, para 27 *per* M Briggs QC.

[142] [1987] FSR 330, 351–2.

[143] [2010] EWHC 1743 (Ch).

[144] See para 48. He also held that it was therefore not necessary to consider separately the domestic law of restraint of trade (para 49).

[145] See eg *Intelsec Systems v Grech-Chini* [2000] 1 WLR 1190, 1205–6.

very nature (highly valuable, severable, or discrete) justifies protection for as long as they remain secret; but (b) attempts to protect Class 2 'mere confidential information' raise real questions of legitimate interest and proportionality; (c) badly drafted post-termination confidentiality clauses fail to distinguish between trade secrets and other forms of confidential information and purport to grant indefinite post-termination protection to both types of information, when for the latter some time-limited and tailored relief is more appropriate; (d) in many circumstances, other forms of post-termination restrictive covenant will be more appropriate for reasons of certainty, ease of enforcement, or policing; but (e) that said there may be categories of Class 2 confidential information that cannot be effectively protected through, for example, non-competition, non-solicitation, or non-dealing covenants. For these types of confidential information some form of post-termination confidentiality covenant may be appropriate, so long as it is tightly drafted both by reference to content and duration.

What this reveals is that the *Faccenda* case's Class 2 in fact comprises two categories:　　**3.79**

(1) 'Class 2A' information which may be protected during the currency of any employment relationship but which because it forms part of the so-called 'knowledge, skill or experience' of employees may not be protected by an express post-termination confidentiality covenant, but which may be accorded some modest amount of indirect protection by means of a well-framed restrictive covenant (eg non-competition, non-solicitation, or non-dealing). As explained further below, it is because such information tends to be *endemic, inherent, routine*, and *unavoidable* in any particular employment context that it presents very real problems from a restraint of trade perspective. To give an extreme example, suppose a carpenter develops a particularly efficient novel, speedy way of making a carpentry joint for a particular problem, which he keeps secret. His apprentice learns it. That apprentice could be prevented from disclosing the technique to a competitor, but if he set up in competition he could hardly be expected to 'unlearn' what has become second-nature to him.

(2) 'Class 2B' information which may also be protected for a reasonable period with an appropriately drafted post-termination clause. To give an example of such a clause: suppose an employee works as a consultant on a limited number of projects in competition with a modest number of competitors. Certain amounts of information about the projects are confidential, for example the designs the employer is advancing, the materials suggested for the pricing on the units ordered, the profit margin, and the status of negotiations for a new contract. These are unlikely to be 'trade secrets' but might be protected by an accurately drafted post-termination confidentiality covenant precluding the employee from revealing any such details for, say, four months, a period in which they will (so the evidence shows) have lost much of their market sensitivity. There is no reason why such a clause could not be combined with a non-dealing clause (for the customer concerned) of modest duration, so as to prevent conscious or unconscious use of the information.

The effect of dismissal on obligations of confidence

In accordance with the well-known principle in *General Billposting v Atkinson*,[146] where　**3.80** an employee is wrongfully dismissed, the employer, as the repudiating party, cannot enforce

---

[146] [1909] AC 118.

any post-termination restrictive covenants contained in the employment contract.[147] The question arises as to whether the same applies to any continuing obligations of confidence owed by the employee.

3.81 This point was considered by the Court of Appeal in *Campbell v Frisbee*.[148] As mentioned above, the defendant was employed by the claimant, and had entered into a written confidentiality agreement not to disclose any information about the claimant's personal or professional life. The defendant employee claimed that she was no longer bound by any obligations of confidence (express or implied) because she had been constructively dismissed. The claimant applied for summary judgment in relation to that part of her claim relating to her private life. The master gave summary judgment, and Lightman J dismissed the defendant's appeal. The Court of Appeal, however, allowed the appeal. The Court held that although it was arguable that a duty of confidentiality expressly assumed under a contract carried more weight, when balanced against the restriction of the right of freedom of expression, than a duty of confidentiality not buttressed by express agreement, the effect of wrongful repudiation on contractual duties of confidence was not clearly established, and the issue was not suitable for summary determination. That said, the Court also gave a strong hint as to what the ultimate outcome might be likely to be when the matter was fully considered, suggesting that the defendant 'would be well advised to reflect carefully on [Lightman J]'s conclusions in relation to the merits of the issues debated before him'.[149]

3.82 This cautious decision leaves this area of the law in a state of some uncertainty. It is suggested, however, that as a matter of principle it cannot be the case that a wrongful dismissal relieves the employee of every continuing obligation of confidence. At best it should only deprive the employer of any additional protection it has obtained through contract alone (for example a valid post-termination covenant not relating to trade secrets but compatible with the law of restraint of trade). Any other conclusion would have very surprising results. For example, an employee who had access to his employer's most secret processes or formulae, but was entitled to treat himself as constructively dismissed over some unrelated dispute about pay, would then be free to sell his employer's most valuable secrets to the highest bidder—providing the employee (in effect) with an unjustified windfall, and capriciously punishing the employer with the loss of a valuable type of intellectual property.

3.83 The most logical conclusion, which is consistent with the principle in *General Billposting v Atkinson*, is that a wrongful dismissal discharges any express continuing confidentiality covenants, but leaves the implied equitable obligation of confidence (as described in *Faccenda Chicken v Fowler* and the subsequent decisions) unaffected.

D. Defences

Introduction

3.84 Under the modern law, all of the true defences to a claim of breach of confidence can be analyzed under the rubric of a defence of public interest. Precisely what forms of public interest

---

[147] See Chapter 5 below.
[148] [2003] ICR 141.
[149] ibid para 36.

may justify action that is otherwise a breach of confidence is not capable of complete categorization, though the case-by-case development of breach of confidence makes it possible to map out certain areas in which the shape of a defence is well established (such as, for instance, the public interest in the disclosure of an iniquity). This leads to the heart of the modern version of the law of confidence. Ultimately, it will entail a judgmental balance between the particular interests being protected by the claim for confidence (which interests may be proprietary or quasi-proprietary in the case of commercial confidences, personal or private and underpinned by Article 8 of the ECHR in privacy cases, or themselves premised upon public interest reasoning in state confidence cases), and the asserted public interest said to justify disclosure.

The increasingly critical principle mediating this particular balancing exercise is the principle **3.85** of proportionality. It may not be sufficient, when seeking to defend a breach of confidence claim, merely to establish that some form of public interest justifies breaching confidence. In appropriate circumstances, it may be necessary to go further and justify the particular form of action taken. For instance, a public interest defence based upon putative wrongdoing may justify disclosure of information to the relevant regulatory authorities, but not to a commercial rival.

Establishment of publication or other forms of loss of confidence is often spoken of as if it **3.86** were a defence. In truth, a party showing that material has been sufficiently widely published or disseminated so as to destroy any claim for breach of confidence is merely showing that there was no confidence capable or deserving of protection. It is a factor negating confidence, rather than a justification for breaching confidence.

Development of the public interest principle underlying defences

As explained above, the historic roots of the public interest defences to breach of confidence **3.87** lie in equity. It is no surprise therefore that the most widely-accepted initial formulation of any defence to a claim of breach of confidence is itself equitably formulated in the famous adage that 'there is no confidence as to the disclosure of iniquity', as Wood VC famously put it in *Gartside v Outram*.[150]

The problem with this formulation is its excessively narrow concentration upon the **3.88** conduct,[151] more particularly *mis*conduct of the claimant, as a justification for publication of material. Moreover, the further danger of such a focus upon misconduct is that it inevitably tends to concentrate upon: (a) 'all or nothing' claims to confidence; and (b) publication as the form of use of the putative confidential material. This is a black and white world which, whilst still useful as a crude compass to those working in the media, belies much of the subtlety of the modern approach.

It was under the creative hand of Lord Denning MR in the 1960s and 1970s that 'iniquity' **3.89** began its transformation into a generalized defence of just cause or just excuse. First, in *Initial Services v Putterill*[152] (a case where it was being argued that breach of the Restrictive Trade Practices Act 1956 was not a crime and could not therefore justify disclosing the

---

[150] (1856) 26 LJ Ch 113.
[151] See similarly *Weld-Blundell v Stephens* [1919] 1 KB 520, where the fact that a letter negligently disclosed contained libellous statements did not destroy the duty not to disclose confidential information.
[152] [1968] 1 QB 396.

existence of a cartel, then merely a registrable agreement) Lord Denning MR simply widened the defence of iniquity to encompass:

> ... crimes, frauds and misdeeds, both those actually committed as well as those in contemplation, provided always, and this is essential, that the disclosure is justified in the public interest. The reason is because no private obligations can dispense with that universal one which lies on every member of the society to discover every design which may be formed, contrary to the laws of the society, to destroy the public welfare.

3.90   Such a formulation did little to loosen the unhelpful shackling of justification for breach of confidence to establishment of actual or inchoate misconduct, an approach others continued to adopt.[153] Indeed, on one level the reasoning employed by the Court of Appeal was tortuous given its anchoring in contract-based reasoning[154] as a rather roundabout way to test whether or not implied duties of confidence should be extended to afford a basis upon which to suppress revelations of civil wrongdoing.[155] But *Initial Services v Putterill* did introduce for the first time wider notions of public interest rather than pure equity as the underpinning of a defence. Subsequently the wider approach clearly showed itself in Lord Denning's comments in the later case of *Fraser v Evans* where he pointed out that 'No person is permitted to divulge to the world information which he has received in confidence unless he has just cause or excuse for doing so' before going on to conclude (having cited the *Gartside* and *Initial Services* cases) that: 'I do not look upon the word "iniquity" as expressing a principle. It is merely an instance of just cause or excuse for breaking confidence. There are some things which may be required to be disclosed in the public interest, in which event no confidence can be prayed in aid to keep them secret.'[156]

3.91   This loosening led in turn to the beginning of the modern formulation of the principle behind defences to claims of breach of confidence in *Lion Laboratories v Evans*.[157] The case involved some former employees of Lion Laboratories who had, without permission, taken documents with them relating to Lion Laboratories' electronic breathalyser. The documents in question cast doubt upon the accuracy of the functioning of the equipment. The former employees handed over the documents (it is unclear whether they were sold or not) to a newspaper interested in such a story, which prepared to publish them (until restrained). The judge at first instance held that the documents should not have been disclosed to the press (given their highly technical contents), but could have been to the Home Office as a 'more appropriate initial forum for discussion of [the breathalyser's] merits or demerits'.

---

[153] See further *Hubbard v Vosper* [1972] 2 QB 84; *Church of Scientology of California v Kaufman* [1973] RPC 635; and *Beloff v Pressdram Ltd* [1973] 1 All ER 241, especially at 259–60 where the defence of public interest failed, no 'iniquity' or 'misdeed' having been established.

[154] The essence of the argument was that any contract to keep such matters secret would be illegal on the ground that it was contrary to the public interest; see also the Australian case *Corrs Pavey Whiting & Byrne v Collector of Customs* (1987) 74 ALR 428, analyzed by RG Toulson and CM Phipps, *Confidentiality* (2nd edn, 2006) section 6-013.

[155] See ibid section 6-012.

[156] [1969] 1 QB 349, 361 and 362 respectively. See also *Woodward v Hutchins* [1977] 1 WLR 760, a case in which the *Initial* and *Fraser* cases were cited by Lord Denning MR, a decision that is perhaps satisfactory in terms of expressed principle, but unsatisfactory in terms of reasoned application of law to facts. The crude reasoning of the court appeared to be that if you hired a press agent, the defendant, to improve your image, he should be at liberty to publish anything that in fact presented you in a true, unfavourable light.

[157] [1985] QB 526.

In the leading speech, allowing the appeal, Stephenson LJ presented the dispute as one **3.92**
between 'two competing public interests' with the first being the preservation of the rights of
organizations and individuals to keep information secret and the second being 'the countervailing interest of the public in being kept informed of matters which are of real public
concern', an interest expressed by reference to the approach of Article 10 of the ECHR (a fairly
novel development at that time). This was a radical departure. *Lion Laboratories v Evans* was
not an 'iniquity' case;[158] rather it was the first instance of a wider public interest (that of
debate and scrutiny of activities of public interest by the press) defeating an otherwise
reasonable claim to confidence.[159] The basis for this was because:

> The courts will restrain breaches of confidence . . . unless there is just cause or excuse for
> breaking confidence . . . The just cause or excuse with which this case is concerned is the public
> interest in admittedly confidential information. There is confidential information which the
> public have a right to receive and others, particularly the press, now extended to the media,
> may have a right and even a duty, to publish, even if the information has been unlawfully
> obtained in flagrant breach of confidence and irrespective of the motive of the informer.[160]

The reasoning of the Court of Appeal stands in stark contrast to the reasoning of the majority
of a differently constituted Court of Appeal just three years earlier in the similar case of
Schering Chemicals Ltd v Falkman Ltd.[161]

The reasoning in *Lion Laboratories v Evans* has effectively been adopted by the House of **3.93**
Lords in the *Spycatcher* case, where Lord Goff stated:

> . . . although the basis of the law's protection of confidence is that there is a public interest
> that confidences should be preserved and protected by the law, nevertheless that public
> interest may be outweighed by some other countervailing public interest which favours
> disclosure. This limitation may apply, as the learned judge pointed out, to all types of confi-
> dential information. It is this limiting principle which may require a court to carry out a
> balancing operation, weighing the public interest in maintaining confidence against a coun-
> tervailing public interest favouring disclosure.
>
> Embraced within this limiting principle is, of course, the so called defence of iniquity. In
> origin, this principle was narrowly stated, on the basis that a man cannot be made 'the confi-
> dant of a crime or a fraud': see *Gartside v. Outram* (1857) 26 L.J.Ch. 113, 114, per Sir William
> Page Wood V.-C. But it is now clear that the principle extends to matters of which disclosure
> is required in the public interest: see *Beloff v. Pressdram Ltd.* [1973] 1 All E.R. 241, 260, per
> Ungoed-Thomas J., and *Lion Laboratories Ltd. v. Evans* [1985] Q.B. 526, 550, per Griffiths
> L.J. It does not however follow that the public interest will in such cases require disclosure to
> the media, or to the public by the media. There are cases in which a more limited disclosure is
> all that is required: see *Francome v. Mirror Group Newspapers Ltd.* [1984] 1 WLR 892. A classic
> example of a case where limited disclosure is required is a case of alleged iniquity in the Security
> Service. Here there are a number of avenues for proper complaint; these are set out in the
> judgment of Sir John Donaldson M.R. . . . Like my noble and learned friend, Lord Griffiths,

---

[158] Indeed, Stephenson LJ said ibid 538 'we cannot say that the Defendants must be restrained because what
they want to publish does not show misconduct by the plaintiffs'.

[159] Whilst Lord Denning MR's dicta in *Fraser v Evans* may have provided the germ of the reasoning for
this new wide approach, *Fraser v Evans* was on its facts an 'iniquity case' and it remained the position that,
until *Lion Laboratories v Evans* no one had succeeded in a defence outside the iniquity area: see ibid 537 *per*
Stephenson LJ.

[160] ibid 536 *per* Stephenson LJ, also 550 *per* Griffiths LJ.

[161] [1981] 2 All ER 321 *per* Shaw and Templeman LJJ, Lord Denning MR dissenting, where the only
distinguishing feature seems to have been that the TV company in fact paid for the information in question. See also
X v Y [1988] 2 All ER 648, where Rose J attempted to reconcile these authorities.

I find it very difficult to envisage a case of this kind in which it will be in the public interest for allegations of such iniquity to be published in the media. In any event, a mere allegation of iniquity is not of itself sufficient to justify disclosure in the public interest. Such an allegation will only do so if, following such investigations as are reasonably open to the recipient, and having regard to all the circumstances of the case, the allegation in question can reasonably be regarded as being a credible allegation from an apparently reliable source.[162]

3.94   Lord Griffiths put it somewhat differently as follows:

The courts have, however, always refused to uphold the right to confidence when to do so would be to cover up wrongdoing. In *Gartside v. Outram* (1857) 26 L.J. Ch. 113, it was said that there could be no confidence in iniquity. This approach has been developed in the modern authorities to include cases in which it is in the public interest that the confidential information should be disclosed: see *Initial Services Ltd. v. Putterill* [1968] 1 Q.B. 396, *Beloff v. Pressdram Ltd.* [1973] 1 A.E.R. 241 and *Lion Laboratories Ltd. v. Evans* [1985] Q.B. 526. This involves the judge in balancing the public interest in upholding the right to confidence, which is based on the moral principles of loyalty and fair dealing, against some other public interest that will be served by the publication of the confidential material. Even if the balance comes down in favour of publication, it does not follow that publication should be to the world through the media. In certain circumstances the public interest may be better served by a limited form of publication perhaps to the police or some other authority who can follow up a suspicion that wrongdoing may lurk beneath the cloak of confidence. Those authorities will be under a duty not to abuse the confidential information and to use it only for the purpose of their inquiry. If it turns out that the suspicions are without foundation, the confidence can then still be protected: see *Francome v. Mirror Group Newspapers Ltd.* [1984] 1 W.L.R. 892. On the other hand, the circumstances may be such that the balance will come down in favour of allowing publication by the media, see *Lion Laboratories Ltd. v. Evans* [1985] Q.B. 526. Judges are used to carrying out this type of balancing exercise and I doubt if it is wise to try to formulate rules to guide the use of this discretion that will have to be exercised in widely differing and as yet unforeseen circumstances. I have no doubt, however, that in the case of a private claim to confidence, if the three elements of quality of confidence, obligation of confidence and detriment or potential detriment are established, the burden will lie upon the defendant to establish that some other overriding public interest should displace the plaintiff's right to have his confidential information protected.[163]

3.95   These dicta from the *Spycatcher* case essentially complete the transmutation of the general defence of iniquity into one of disclosure in the public interest or with just cause. Furthermore, the *Spycatcher* and *Lion Laboratories* cases remain the leading cases on the public interest nature of defences, notwithstanding the passage of the Human Rights Act 1998. Indeed, the effect of subsequent cases, such as *Douglas v Hello!* and others, has not been to alter this basic template, but rather to: (a) expand the categories of public interest that might be recognized as founding legitimate action and (it might be argued) providing a principled basis for some areas where a defence has been contemplated on somewhat nebulous grounds; and (b) to provide further detail as to how the balancing exercise works in

---

[162] [1981] 2 All ER 321 *per* Shaw and Templeman LJJ, Lord Denning MR dissenting, where the only distinguishing feature seems to have been that the TV company in fact paid for the information in question. See also *X v Y* [1988] 2 All ER 648 where Rose J attempted to reconcile these authorities.

[163] [1981] 2 All ER 321 *per* Shaw and Templeman LJJ, Lord Denning MR dissenting, where the only distinguishing feature seems to have been that the TV company in fact paid for the information in question. See also *X v Y* [1988] 2 All ER 648 where Rose J attempted to reconcile these authorities.

principle, most obviously by reference to the principle of proportionality (discussed below). Accordingly, modern authority continues to cite both cases with approval.[164]

However, it should not be thought that the shift of focus from iniquity to public interest **3.96** renders equitable considerations irrelevant. Even if public interest factors may be insufficient to establish a defence, it is possible that relevant inequitable and/or iniquitous conduct might disentitle a claimant from equitable relief (typically injunctive) on the basis that equity only assists those with clean hands.

The most entertaining application of this principle is undoubtedly *McNicol v Sportsman's* **3.97** *Book Stores*,[165] a case that would nowadays no doubt be decided on the grounds of misleading advertising. The plaintiff had devised a 'failsafe' way of predicting horse-racing results using the phases of the moon which he sold under confidence. He sought to stop the defendant publishing it. The judge, Maugham J, refused, essentially on the grounds that he felt that the court should not assist someone make money out of claptrap, stating: 'the poor people all over this country who are deceived into paying two guineas for this system are getting something which is perfectly worthless'.

'Clean hands' reasoning also informed Megaw LJ's analysis in *Hubbard v Vosper*[166] when he **3.98** noted that there was evidence before the court that the plaintiffs sought to enforce secrecy on scientologists by improper methods, and agreed with the defendant that 'there is here evidence that the plaintiffs are or have been protecting their secrets by deplorable means . . . and, that being so, they do not come with clean hands to this court in asking this court to protect those secrets by the equitable remedy of an injunction'.

The emphasis on reasonableness and proportionality

Ever since the expanded just cause approach has been adopted the court has been careful to **3.99** emphasize the importance of any defendant acting reasonably in their proposed actions or use of the confidential material. This goes beyond and is distinct from Megarry J's use in *Coco v Clark* of the 'reasonable man' concept in assessing whether or not material is confidential at all.[167] It is equally distinct from, but more closely related to, any inquiry as to the *scope* of confidence owed. For instance, it may be the case that the evidence demonstrates that the reasonable, conscientious confidant would feel constrained from disclosing the material to a third party, but may be free to use it themselves. This is a recurring phenomenon in the context of commercial regulatory relationships between bodies producing complex products requiring marketing approvals (such as pharmaceuticals, pesticides, etc) and their regulator. If a package of test material is presented to the regulator, surely that body must be free to use that material, even if highly confidential, for its regulatory purposes, so long as such is not disclosed to, say, a third party competitor?[168] Such was the analysis adopted in the Australian

---

[164] As in eg *London Regional Transport v Mayor of London* [2003] EMLR 88; *Jockey Club v Buffham* [2003] QB 462, para 49 *per* Gray J; *McKennitt v Ash* [2005] EWHC 3003 (QB), [2006] EMLR 178, para 95 *per* Eady J, upheld on appeal [2006] EWCA Civ 1714, [2008] QB 73; *Mosley v News Group Newspapers Ltd* [2008] EWHC 1777 (QB), [2008] EMLR 20, para 13 *per* Eady J.

[165] (1930) McG CC 116.

[166] [1972] 2 QB 84. It also informed the approach of Goff J (as he then was) in *Church of Scientology v Kaufman* [1973] RPC 627. The potential for overlap with narrow 'iniquity' cases is obvious.

[167] [1969] RPC 41, 48.

[168] For a further discussion of third-party rights in equity with regard to confidential information, see *PSM International v Whitehouse* [1992] IRLR 279, CA, paras 37–8.

case of *Smith Kline & French v Community Services*[169] and continues to inform the regimes for the UK licensing of pesticides and pharmaceuticals.[170] But, again, in such circumstances, such analysis reveals that there is no putative breach of confidence, as the relevant obligation did not cover the conduct in question.

3.100 The use of the concept of reasonableness in the context of defences of just cause is akin to its use in the doctrine of restraint of trade. It is a limiting principle that tests what is done in the name of the just cause to ensure that it matches the interest said to be being pursued. Unsurprisingly, it first developed in the context of iniquity arguments. In *Initial Services Ltd v Putterill* Lord Denning commented that:

> The disclosure must, I should think, be to one who has a proper interest to receive the information. Thus it would be proper to disclose a crime to the police; or a breach of the Restrictive Trade Practices Act to the registrar. There may be cases where the misdeed is of such a character that the public interest may demand, or at least excuse, publication on a broader field, even to the press.[171]

3.101 This thinking continues to have a very strong impact in iniquity or whistle-blowing cases, as is demonstrated by the cases of *Francome v Mirror Group Newspapers Ltd*[172] and *Re A Company's Application*[173] and is discussed further below. But, subsequent cases show that in fact there is a wider principle at stake. First, in the case of *W v Edgell*,[174] Bingham LJ put the matter as follows:

> Where a man has committed multiple killings under the disability of serious mental illness, decisions which may lead directly or indirectly to his release from hospital should not be made unless a reasonable authority is properly able to make an informed judgment that the risk of repetition is so small as to be acceptable. A consultant psychiatrist who becomes aware, even in the course of a confidential relationship, of information which leads him, in the exercise of what the court considers to be a sound professional judgement, to fear that such decisions may be made on the basis of inadequate information and with a real risk of consequent danger to the public is entitled to take such steps as are reasonable in all the circumstances to communicate the grounds of his concern to the responsible authorities.

3.102 What this passage again demonstrates is that as the notion of public interest expanded to encompass the (higher) public interest in preventing possible future harm to others, a reasonableness test was used in order to keep in check what was done with the undoubtedly confidential information, in this case highly sensitive medical matters. Similar signs of such use of the concept of reasonableness appear in the case of *Hellewell v Chief Constable of Derbyshire*.[175] The case concerned the permissible use that could be made of a mugshot taken by Derbyshire police of Mr Hellewell, a recidivist thief and troublemaker. Laws J set those boundaries as follows:

---

[169] (1991) 99 ALR 679; see also eg *Hellewell v Chief Constable of Derbyshire* [1995] 1 WLR 804, where the reasonable use implicitly permitted was the prevention of crime: see 810 *per* Laws J. However, the *Hellewell* case illustrates how this form of reasoning spills over into the public interest defence.

[170] *R v Licensing Authority, ex p Smith Kline French* [1990] 1 AC 64. See also *FSA v Amro International SA* [2010] EWCA Civ 123 regarding the FSA's power to disclose confidential information to a foreign regulator.

[171] [1968] 1 QB 396, 405–6.

[172] [1984] 1 WLR 892.

[173] [1989] Ch 477.

[174] [1990] 1 Ch 359, 424.

[175] [1995] 1 WLR 804, 810 *per* Laws J. See also Bingham LJ in *A-G v Guardian Newspapers Ltd (No 2)* [1990] 1 AC 109, 222.

In my judgment, the use which the police may make of a photograph such as this is limited by their obligations to the photograph's subject as follows. They may make reasonable use of it for the purpose of the prevention and detection of crime, the investigation of alleged offences and the apprehension of suspects or persons unlawfully at large. They may do so whether or not the photograph is of any person they seek to arrest or of a suspected accomplice or of anyone else. The key is that they must have these and only these purposes in mind and must, as I have said, make no more than reasonable use of the picture in seeking to accomplish them.

I recognise, of course, that the term 'reasonable', as in so many areas of the law, is fluid and its application will depend on the circumstances of a particular case. I recognise also that it is as impossible as it is undesirable to lay down anything like a lexicon of the kinds of facts that will amount to reasonable use of such a picture by the police.

However, where the use in question is decided upon by the honest judgment of professional police officers, that will, of itself, go a long way to establish its reasonableness. Provided these bounds of principle are not transgressed, there will be an obvious and vital public interest in the use made of such photographs which the courts will uphold. It is perhaps confusing to put the matter on the basis that, in the celebrated dictum, 'there is no confidence in iniquity'; some little difficulty has been caused in the past by the question whether the iniquity must be proved or it is enough that it is the result only of reasonable suspicion.

Others have put the concern in different ways. Some commentators and judges are con- **3.103**
cerned that the recourse to widely based principles of public interest represents too wide and too uncertain encroachment upon the right to keep information confidential. Simon Brown LJ was very much alive to this concern in the *Source Informatics* case. Having derived his governing test for putative breach by asking whether the confidant's conscience would (or should) be troubled by disclosure of the confidence, Simon Brown LJ also recognized:[176]

> ... the importance of confining any public interest defence in this area of the law within strict limits—lest, as Gummow J put it at first instance in *Smith Kline & French Laboratories (Australia) Ltd v Secretary to the Dept of Community Services and Health,* [1990] FSR 617 at 663, it becomes 'not so much a rule of law as an invitation to judicial idiosyncrasy by deciding each case on an *ad hoc* basis as to whether, on the facts overall, it is better to respect or to override the obligation of confidence.

Ultimately, though, Simon Brown LJ used this as an additional justification for not drawing the scope of the obligation of confidence too widely in the first place (such that use of redacted material would entail no breach of confidence).[177]

Three cases post-dating the Human Rights Act 1998 have generalized this approach, whilst **3.104**
explaining the principle that underlies it. The first is *Imutran Ltd v Uncaged Campaigns Ltd*.[178] The case concerned an anti-vivisection campaign by Uncaged Campaigns against Imutran, a company involved in the research of xenotransplantation. Uncaged Campaigns and one of its chief campaigners had received a huge number of technical and highly confidential documents in both hard copy and CD Rom format from an anonymous source. Such materials consisted of detailed technical material (testing results, laboratory reports, etc), internal minutes and documents reviewing current practice, results, and so forth. The defendants

---

[176] *R v Department of Health, ex p Source Informatics* [2001] QB 424, para 52.
[177] At first instance in *London Regional Transport v The Mayor* [2003] EMLR 88 Sullivan J assumed, for the sake of argument, the LRT submission that *Source Informatics* set a test of 'exceptional circumstances' for the establishment of any public interest defence. This is almost certainly wrong and would seem to have difficulty surviving the Court of Appeal's judgment, though Walker LJ left the point open.
[178] [2001] 2 All ER 385, [2002] FSR 2.

sought to publish these documents (and an article based upon them) on Uncaged Campaign's website. Imutran applied for an injunction to prevent further and continued publication of its documents. Uncaged Campaigns argued, very forcefully, for its right of wider disclosure, basing its case, amongst other things, upon Article 10 of the ECHR and its right of campaigning or political free speech. However, the Vice-Chancellor, Sir Andrew Morritt, concluded that Imutran was entitled to a measure of injunctive relief, namely an order preventing further publication of the material to the public as a whole. Uncaged Campaigns should continue, however, to be free to send the material to relevant regulators (there being one such to ensure that animal testing was ethically and lawfully conducted) and to the RSPCA. His reasoning was as follows:

> 20. I turn then to the claim for breach of confidence. I have been referred to the well known line of cases . . . Each of them demonstrates that the public interest in disclosure may outweigh the right of the plaintiff to protect his confidences. They demonstrate that the court will also consider how much disclosure the public interest requires; the fact that some disclosure may be required does not mean that disclosure to the whole world should be permitted. . . .

> 24. . . . The circumstances as they existed in September 2000 and now do not justify the width of disclosure the defendants seek. On July 17, 2000 the House of Lords set up its ad hoc Select Committee to enquire into the very matters which concerned the defendants. Since the defendants put Imutran's documents on the internet the Home Secretary and the Council of RSPCA have called for reports from the Chief Inspector and Dr Jennings respectively. In so far as GLPMA and UKXIRA are concerned the documents obtained by the defendants have been available to them too. There is no impediment sought or in place such as to inhibit any regulatory authority from investigating all the matters of which the defendants expressed concern in Diaries of Despair.

> 25. Fifthly, when considering what is necessary in a democratic society and when paying particular regard to the importance of the right to freedom of expression it is relevant to consider which is the democratically selected responsible body or bodies and who would be the informed audience. In this case Parliament has considered the issue of animal experimentation as recently as 1986. It has laid down a licensing and inspection system and a forum for and source of continuing consideration and advice in the Animal Procedures Committee. The members of that committee are themselves bound to consider the protection of animals against avoidable suffering and unnecessary use in scientific procedures (section 20(2)). Two thirds of them must be medically qualified (section 19(3)(a)) and their annual report to the Home Secretary must be laid before Parliament (section 20(5)). In addition there is the RSPCA, GLPMA and UKXIRA all of whom have an interest in investigating one or more of the matters which concern the defendants.

> 26. Of course, the defendants' right to freedom of expression is an element in their democratic right to campaign for the abolition of all animal xenotransplantation or other experimentation. But they may continue to do that whether the injunction sought by Imutran is granted or not. The issue is whether they should be free to do so with Imutran's confidential and secret documents. Many of those documents are of a specialist and technical nature suitable for consideration by specialists in the field but not by the public generally. Given the provisos to the injunction sought there would be no restriction on the ability of the defendants to communicate the information to those specialists connected with the regulatory bodies denoted by Parliament as having responsibility in the field. I do not accept in these circumstances the defendants' assertion that the relationship between Imutran and the Inspectors appointed by the Home Secretary is too close for the latter to do their job properly. If that was ever so, and there is no evidence to that effect, it is unlikely to continue given the current interest of the House of Lords Select Committee and the Home Secretary's instruction of the Chief Inspector.

This approach, although it does not use such term, is the very apogee of proportionality-based **3.105** reasoning. It focuses upon both the rights of Imutran to maintain the continued confidentiality of research that (it being an interim relief case) may well have been highly commercially valuable and perfectly valid in many respects, as well as the right of Uncaged Campaigns to campaign. That right could be perfectly adequately safeguarded, whilst salvaging the underlying confidential information from total destruction through publication, by directing the campaign to where it was required, namely the regulator, the relevant prosecuting authorities (here, the RSPCA) and to Parliament. There was no need for the highly technical material to be published on the internet (other than to sabotage Imutran's research and development) as it would be incomprehensible to the public. Indeed (although this does not clearly appear from the report), Uncaged Campaigns would probably be free to 'gist' or summarize what it had learned in a way that respected the underlying, confidential technical information. The contrast in result between this case and that of *Lion Laboratories v Evans* is easy to explain. In the *Lion Laboratories* case the Court of Appeal clearly felt that the core issue, namely that breathalyser evidence may well be unreliable, was one that the motoring public at large had a right to know, particularly as it potentially impacted upon them and/or their reaction to any motoring prosecution based on such evidence. This core issue was sufficiently non-technical to warrant communication.[179]

The second case is that of *London Regional Transport v The Mayor*.[180] The case concerned an **3.106** attempt by the Mayor of London, Ken Livingstone, to publish a report, the Deloittes report, that was highly critical of the supposed value for money (VFM) offered by the proposed public private partnership (PPP) on the London Underground, to which he was strongly opposed. The Deloittes report had been prepared with access to a number of commercially confidential documents available only from the 'Deal Room' maintained by London Regional Transport (which was running the proposed PPP). The Mayor proposed publishing the Deloittes report in redacted form, so as to remove quotes from the confidential information. The point remained, however, that the very existence of the report was premised upon the prior use of such material, and the Mayor and his team (including Deloittes) had signed contractual undertakings strictly limiting what they could do with the Deal Room information.

In what has become a very widely cited speech Sedley LJ dealt with the matter as follows: **3.107**

55. Article 10 of the European Convention on Human Rights is not just about freedom of expression. It is also about the right to receive and impart information, a right which (to borrow Lord Steyn's metaphor in *R v Home Secretary, ex p Simms* [2000] AC 115, 126) is the lifeblood of a democracy. The Deloittes report is on one view a set of contested opinions about the bidding process; but on another it is an expert and adverse evaluation of it, the very fact of which is of public importance. Whether or not undertakings of confidentiality had been signed, both domestic law and Art. 10(2) would recognise the propriety of suppressing wanton or self-interested disclosure of confidential information; but both correspondingly recognise the legitimacy of disclosure, undertakings notwithstanding, if the public interest in the free flow of information and ideas will be served by it.

56. The difficulty in the latter case, as Miss Appleby's argument has understandably stressed, is to know by what instrument this balance is to be struck. Is it to be, in Coke's

---

179 [1985] 1 QB 526, 539–40 *per* Stephenson LJ.
180 [2003] EMLR 4.

phrase (4 Inst. 41), the golden and straight metwand of the law or the incertain and crooked cord of discretion? The contribution which Art. 10 and the jurisprudence of the European Court of Human Rights can make towards an answer is, in my view, real.

57. It lies in the methodical concept of proportionality. Proportionality is not a word found in the text of the Convention: it is the tool—the metwand—which the Court has adopted (from 19th-century German jurisprudence) for deciding a variety of Convention issues including, for the purposes of the qualifications to Arts. 8 to 11, what is and is not necessary in a democratic society. It replaces an elastic concept with which political scientists are more at home than lawyers with a structured inquiry: Does the measure meet a recognised and pressing social need? Does it negate the primary right or restrict it more than is necessary? Are the reasons given for it logical? These tests of what is acceptable by way of restriction of basic rights in a democratic society reappear, with variations of phrasing and emphasis, in the jurisprudence of (among others) the Privy Council, the Constitutional Court of South Africa, the Supreme Court of Zimbabwe and the Supreme Court of Canada in its Charter jurisdiction . . .

58. It seems to me, with great respect, that this now well established approach furnishes a more certain guide for people and their lawyers than the test of the reasonable recipient's conscience. While the latter has the imprimatur of high authority, I can understand how difficult it is to give useful advice on the basis of it. One recipient may lose sleep a lot more readily than another over whether to make a disclosure, without either of them having to be considered unreasonable. If the test is whether the recipient ought to be losing sleep, the imaginary individual will be for practical purposes a judicial stalking-horse and the judgment more nearly an exercise of discretion and correspondingly less predictable. So for my part I find it more helpful today to postulate a recipient who, being reasonable, runs through the proportionality checklist in order to anticipate what a court is likely to decide, and who adjusts his or her conscience and conduct accordingly.

59. It may not be in every dispute that this formula is able to be adopted. The argument about the extent of horizontal application (or cascade effect as I would rather call it) of Convention rights under the Human Rights Act is not resolved. But there are two distinct reasons why both sides have rightly argued from the Convention in the present case.

60. One is that all four parties are public authorities within the meaning of s.6—LRT as a statutory body providing public passenger services, LUL probably by virtue of s.6(3)(b). This status may not matter in the case of the defendants (since private individuals will in principle enjoy the same protection), but it certainly matters in the case of the claimants, since s.6 makes it unlawful for them to act incompatibly with the Convention rights. That, as it seems to me and as Miss Appleby QC has accepted in argument, means that they may neither contract out of the Act nor use their powers to stifle the Convention rights of others . . .

61. Secondly, while it does not necessarily follow from the court's own status as a public authority (s.6(3)(a)) that all its judgments have without more to be Convention-compliant (the issue is a complex one), it does in my view follow that where it is deciding whether or not to grant an injunction its judgment must respect both the relevant Convention rights and their qualifications. S.12 of the Act would explicitly have this effect in Art. 10 cases if it were not already the case by virtue of the earlier provisions of the Act and the existing doctrines of the common law.

3.108 The third case is that of *HRH Prince of Wales v Associated Newspapers Ltd.*[181] The case concerned published extracts of the Prince of Wales' handwritten travel journals recording his views and impressions of overseas visits which were circulated to certain individuals in an envelope marked 'private and confidential'. An employee who was subject to an undertaking of confidence acquired a copy of the journals and supplied them to the defendant newspaper.

---

[181] [2008] Ch 57, CA.

The Court of Appeal upheld the first instance determination that there had been a breach of confidence and held that when performing the balancing exercise it was relevant to consider the public interest in maintaining duties of confidence:

> 68. For these reasons, the test to be applied when considering whether it is necessary to restrict freedom of expression in order to prevent disclosure of information received in confidence is not simply whether the information is a matter of public interest but whether, in all the circumstances, it is in the public interest that the duty of confidence should be breached. The court will need to consider whether, having regard to the nature of the information and all the relevant circumstances, it is legitimate for the owner of the information to seek to keep it confidential or whether it is in the public interest that the information should be made public.
>
> 69. In applying the test of proportionality, the nature of the relationship that gives rise to the duty of confidentiality may be important. Different views have been expressed as to whether the fact that there is an express contractual obligation of confidence affects the weight to be attached to the duty of confidentiality. In *Campbell v Frisbee* [2003] ICR 141, para 22, this court drew attention to this conflict of view, and commented:
>
> We consider that it is arguable that a duty of confidentiality that has been expressly assumed under contract carries more weight, when balanced against the restriction of the right of freedom of expression, than a duty of confidentiality that is not buttressed by express agreement . . .
>
> We adhere to this view. But the extent to which a contract adds to the weight of duty of confidence arising out of a confidential relationship will depend upon the facts of the individual case.

This approach effectively replaces the emerging notions of reasonableness with the systematic **3.109** recourse to the principle of proportionality. Moreover, it is a mistake to think that such an approach is confined to cases involving public authorities as claimants/defendants. First, as Sedley LJ pointed out in the *London Underground* case, in any case where injunctive relief is sought (as it frequently is) the court will be bound, as a public authority, not to use its compulsive powers to restrain free speech in a disproportionate fashion. Secondly, in just about every situation possible to conceive Article 10 of the ECHR will be engaged. The right to free speech covers the freedom to impart and receive information, which may include not only political free speech of the kind at issue in the *London Underground* case, but also 'commercial free speech'.[182] Moreover, it may well be arguable that confidential information, as protected by the law of confidence, is a form of property right covered by Article 1 of Protocol 1 to the ECHR.[183] If either right is engaged, any limitation or interference (ie an injunction or award of damages) must be justified as proportionate. It is perhaps for this reason, and for the fact that Sedley LJ was correct in his supposition that proportionality offered a more certain, consistent, and predictable limiting principle, that this approach has been widely cited with approval.[184] Moreover, the vindication of other Convention rights, for example the right to life (as in some informant cases), free speech (as in the journalistic sources cases),

---

[182] See eg *Casado Coca v Spain* (1994) 18 EHRR 1, para 35.

[183] The point has not been decided in terms, but analogy to cases such as *van Marle v Netherlands* (1986) 8 EHRR 483 (business goodwill an A1P1 property right) suggests there is a case to be made. For a domestic analysis of the strengths and weaknesses of the proprietary angle to confidential claims, see N Palmer, 'Information as Property' in L Clarke (ed), *Confidentiality and the Law* (1990).

[184] See eg *Mersey Care NHS Trust v Ackroyd (No 2)* [2006] EWHC 107, [2006] EMLR 12 (a public authority case) and *Jockey Club v Buffam* [2003] QB 462, paras 48, 57 *per* Gray J (a case involving no public authority).

or fair hearing may all be relevant to assess the strength of the claim to confidentiality or the public interest defence cited against it.

3.110   Concentration on proportionality is necessary to test not just to whom material is disclosed (as was the focal issue in the cases cited above), but also to test precisely what material should be disclosed. One particularly graphic illustration of this is the treatment of photographs. Whilst photographs may serve to convey a story no words can tell, they can also heighten the embarrassment and distress caused by a particular revelation (as well as having a tendency to cross from public interest into public titillation). As such the courts have on occasion accepted that the publication of photographs may be unwarranted where the force of the public interest aspect of a story can be conveyed in words alone.[185]

3.111   Of course, as in any balancing exercise the weight attributable to certain factors will vary strongly according to context. One obvious example is the varying approach taken by the Court to the relevance of or weight to be attached to express contractual confidentiality clauses. Debate rages as to whether such clauses strengthen a claim for an injunction, a claim for breach of confidence, or are irrelevant. The cases show that such clauses were of little or no relevance or use in the *London Underground* case[186] because of the modest and fair use proposed (in particular the redactions offered) and the strong public interest in informed political debate. Conversely, it is easy to see why express confidentiality clauses may be accorded more weight where the corresponding public interest (as in celebrity hypocrisy cases) is so much weaker, a factor which explains why the Court of Appeal left the issue (as to the weight to be attached) open for trial in *Campbell v Frisbee*[187] and in the later case of *A-G v Parry* (the case of the Mirror reporter who insinuated himself to be employed in the Royal Household).[188] It is still easier to see why express covenants have real weight where the individual in question is not a public figure, as in *Archer v Williams*.[189] In purely commercial contexts it is therefore safe to conclude that, in the absence of true iniquity, real weight should be attached to express confidentiality clauses. The true position would appear to be that in a commercial context, in the absence of an argument that the clause in question is illegal as contrary to the public interest (as was effectively the reasoning of the Court of Appeal in the *Lion Laboratories* case), an argument that is only likely to have merit in cases of true iniquity and strong public interest, such clauses are likely to be fully enforceable.[190] This is consistent with the reasoning of the Court of Appeal in *HRH Prince of Wales*, which held that there is a public interest in maintaining duties of confidence.[191]

3.112   However, considerations of proportionality have their limit. It is now plain that reasonableness of action or proportionality cannot be used to create some form of procedural right,

---

[185]   See *Theakston v Mirror Group Newspapers Ltd* [2002] EMLR 398, paras 64, 70–1 *per* Ouseley J, an approach followed by the Court of Appeal in *A v B plc* [2003] QB 195; see also *Douglas v Hello!* [2004] EMLR 609, and *Mosley v News Group Newspapers Ltd* [2008] EWHC 1777 (QB) [2008] EMLR 20, paras 16–23 *per* Eady J.

[186]   *London Regional Transport v Mayor of London* [2003] EMLR 88.

[187]   *Campbell v Frisbee* [2003] ICR 141.

[188]   [2004] EMLR 223, following the earlier case of *A-G v Barker* [1990] 3 All ER 257.

[189]   *Archer v Williams* [2003] EMLR 869.

[190]   Where the party asserting a duty of confidence is a public body, the individual's free speech rights (if asserted in a case with proper merit) are likely to lead the court, in order to discharge its duties under HRA 1998, s 6, both to construe any contractual restraints narrowly, where possible and, if necessary, to develop the common law as to (un)enforceability of contracts so as to reach a Convention-compliant solution.

[191]   See para 3.108 above.

such as an opportunity to comment that might be required by the law of qualified privilege, before the material is used in an otherwise unobjectionable fashion. Thus in *Tillery Valley Foods v Channel Four Television*, the claimant, faced with a television company which wished to broadcast a documentary highlighting unhygienic practices in a food processing plant (the footage of which it claimed to be confidential having been covertly filmed), failed in its attempts to obtain a right of reply and thus access to the materials upon which the unfavourable report would be based.[192]

As such, it can be seen that in structural terms the main impact of the Human Rights Act 1998 to defences to claims of breach of confidence has been to bring to the fore the principle of proportionality as a means to: (a) test the reasonableness or nature and width of what it is proposed to do or has been done with the confidential information; (b) assist judges in striking the balance between private and public interest; and (c) add predictable principle to the public interest defence which had, hitherto, been both infrequently successful and uncertain. **3.113**

Two other Acts of Parliament that should not be forgotten when thinking about defences to breach of confidence, even in a commercial confidential information context, are the Data Protection Act 1998 (DPA 1998) and the Public Interest Disclosure Act 1998 (PIDA 1998). The former Act is relevant precisely because it is designed to add flesh to the bare bones of principle provided by Article 8 of the ECHR. As such it is a strong guide to the weight to be attached to personal information (in all of its different categories) and, more pertinently for present purposes the structured and carefully tailored approach that is taken towards justification for the use of such information. The principles it embodies (for example of consent, strict necessity of the form of use, control over dissemination, dissemination only where required to the relevant parties and only then as required, etc) are of wider relevance when considering public interest tests. As for PIDA 1998, it provides a clear route-map to the types of justified disclosure (notwithstanding any claim for confidence) that are felt to be so strongly in the public interest that they deserve the conferral of added employment protection.[193] It follows, almost axiomatically, that any party justifying their action by reference to one of the types of disclosure listed in the Public Interest Disclosure Act will have a strong prima facie case of public interest, which will be strengthened yet further if a proportionate approach to disclosure or use in line with the DPA principles is adopted. **3.114**

Difference between the 'public interest' and 'what the public is interested in'

Throughout the shift to grounding the defences to breach of confidence in the public interest the courts have been astute to emphasize that 'there is a wide difference between what is interesting to the public and what it is in the public interest to make known', as Lord Wilberforce so clearly put it.[194] Indeed, this was the first point Stephenson LJ was so concerned to note in his formulation of the public interest defence, observing himself that 'The public are interested in many private matters which are no real concern of theirs and **3.115**

---

[192] *Tillery Valley Foods v Channel Four Television* [2004] EWHC 1075.

[193] The relevant provisions are now to be found in the Employment Rights Act 1996 (ERA 1996), Pt IVA. ERA 1996, s 43 concerns contractual duties of confidentiality and provides: '(1) Any provision in an agreement to which this section applies is void in so far as it purports to preclude the worker from making a protected disclosure.'

[194] *British Steel Corp v Granada Television Ltd* [1981] AC 1096, 1168.

which the public have no pressing need to know'.[195] This distinction was revisited by the Court of Appeal in *HRH The Prince of Wales* where the Court held that the test to be applied when considering whether it was necessary to restrict freedom of expression in order to prevent disclosure of information received in confidence was not simply whether the information was a matter of public interest but whether in all the circumstances it was in the public interest that the duty of confidence should be breached; and that such a question was to be determined by applying the principles of proportionality.[196] In today's society the risk of confusing the two often appears most acute in press stories concerning celebrities.[197]

3.116   The decision in *Northern Rock plc v The Financial Times Ltd*[198] is a further illustration of the courts carrying out this balancing exercise, in a more commercial context. The applicant bank sought an injunction to restrain the further publication of detailed information contained in a document sent from a financial institution to other financial institutions and made available to the public through the defendant's website. The court granted an injunction, finding that there was a real possibility that the publication of extracts which had yet to be published by the mass media might do more harm than had already been caused by the publication on the defendant's website and therefore the court granted an injunction in respect of the information that was yet to be published by the mass media. The court accepted that in some cases there is a public interest in publishing material because without publication there is a risk of members of the public being deceived, or being kept from information which they are entitled to know in a democratic society. However, the court also stated that there is a competing interest in protecting some information (in that case, financial information) from premature publication. The court considered that the detailed commercial information in issue in *Northern Rock* was of the type that was to be protected by law (even though it had already been published on the defendant's website) and there was no public interest in its disclosure.

Burden and standard of proof

3.117   It is clear that, in line with ordinary principles, any party wishing to establish a public interest defence in a case of either commercial or privacy confidentiality bears the burden of proof. Such was amply demonstrated by the *Spycatcher* litigation.[199] However, the *Spycatcher* case made it equally clear that in state confidence cases the public body bore the burden of proof at every stage of analysis, such that it had 'not only to show that the information is confidential but also to show that it is in the public interest that it should not be published'.[200] In commercial and privacy confidentiality cases the fact that the defendant bears the burden to make out any defence may, in appropriate cases, make the proper analysis of cessation or expiry of confidence highly material. If showing that material was, and has not ceased to be, confidential is an essential prerequisite of any claim, then a claimant bears the burden; if cessation/expiry of confidence is a true defence, then the defendant has it.

---

[195] *Lion Laboratories v Evans* [1985] QB 526, 537. See also *Express Newspapers plc v News (UK) plc* [1991] FSR 36, 45 *per* Browne-Wilkinson VC; and *McKennitt v Ash* [2005] EWHC 3003 (QB), [2006] EMLR 178, para 95 *per* Eady J.
[196] See para 3.108 above.
[197]
[198] [2007] EWHC 2677 (QB).
[199] *A-G v Guardian Newspapers Ltd (No 2)* [1990] 1 AC 109, 283. See also the passage from Lord Griffiths' speech cited at para 3.94 above.
[200] *A-G v Guardian Newspapers Ltd (No 2)* [1990] 1 AC 109, 283.

As for the standard of proof required, this is likely to depend upon the particular public interest **3.118** defence asserted and upon the steps taken. Again, proportionality is likely to be a useful guiding concept, as the greater the publication and intrusion caused by the breach of confidence, the greater the justification for such interference that the court should require. Thus, a party that justifies publication to the public at large of confidential information by reference to iniquity may be required to prove the truth of the iniquity alleged not just, say, that the publisher had good reason to suspect it.[201] Where, however, a party acts in a more limited fashion and discloses information only, say, to a relevant regulator or to a lead investor in the company in question, reasonable grounds for suspicion may suffice.[202] It may be the case that certain types of case lie between these poles, such that certain allegations may be made (because of their seriousness and the public interest in their investigation) on the basis of a reasonably investigated case. Indeed, Lord Goff hinted at this in the *Spycatcher* case when he held that 'a mere allegation of iniquity is not itself sufficient to justify disclosure in the public interest. Such an allegation will only do so if, following such investigations as are reasonably open to the recipient, the allegation in question can reasonably be regarded as being a credible allegation from an apparently reliable source'.[203]

In cases involving disclosure to and publication by the press there are obvious parallels to be **3.119** drawn with the *Reynolds* approach to qualified privilege in a defamation context; the public interest thinking is clearly transposable. However, it is unlikely that such reasoning is trans-posable to many fields outside journalistic free speech. Unfortunately, since so many cases in this field are interlocutory in nature and fail to grapple clearly with this subject, the law presently remains unclear. Bingham LJ expressed the problems to be resolved clearly in the *Spycatcher* case as follows:

> . . . the duty of confidence is not overridden or ousted by the mere making of allegations, however wild and unsubstantiated, of misconduct, however grave. When this case was last before this court, Sir John Donaldson said . . . 'mere allegations of iniquity can never override confidentiality. They must be proved and the burden of proof will lie upon the newspapers.' With the first of those sentences I respectfully agree, but I venture to wonder if the second does not go somewhat too far. This is a field in which, in practical terms, newspapers could rarely, if ever, 'prove' the truth of their allegations. Public interest immunity considerations would deny them the ordinary right to inspect documents and call witnesses. But there could arise cases (leaving the present case entirely on one side) where there was a real public interest in disclosure of an iniquity in this field. It would not be satisfactory if the law were to acknowl-edge a right of disclosure but subject its exercise to a condition which could never in practice be met. I would prefer to hold that merely to allege iniquity is not of itself enough to oust or override the duty of confidentiality; the prospective publisher should have attempted to verify the truth of the allegation so far as he reasonably could; and the allegation should have such appearance of truth as it would be reasonable in all the circumstances to expect.[204]

Types of public interest

Iniquity

The evolution of the iniquity defence into the public interest defence is considered above. **3.120** Iniquity is 'nowadays regarded as no more than one aspect of the broader defence of public

---

[201] As in *Church of Scientology v Kaufman* [1973] RPC 635.
[202] An approach supported by *W v Egdell* [1990] Ch 359.
[203] *A-G v Guardian Newspapers Ltd (No 2)* [1990] 1 AC 109, 283.
[204] ibid 222–3.

interest or just cause'.[205] What has been held to be an iniquity warranting some form of disclosure is wide-ranging, embracing both criminal and civil wrongs. It can include: 'matters carried out or contemplated in breach of the country's security, or in breach of the law, including statutory duty, fraud, or otherwise destructive of the country or its people, including matters medically dangerous to the public; and doubtless other misdeeds of similar gravity';[206] anti-competitive behaviour (as in *Initial Services v Putterill*); misleading trading (again, as in *Initial Services v Putterill*); breaches of regulatory rules;[207] allegedly dangerous practices;[208] a past history of paedophilia (where there was a pressing need for such disclosure by the police);[209] and where there is good reason to doubt the propriety of the financial affairs of a public official.[210] Ultimately, there is no closed category of types of iniquity or misconduct capable of trumping confidence—the guiding principle is, surely, whether the actual conduct or suspected conduct is so serious or of such a nature that there is a public interest that it be known for a particular purpose or investigated by the relevant authorities.

3.121 Iniquity in the lower form of 'hypocrisy' or inconsistency with a carefully cultivated image is something frequently alleged as forming a public interest basis for disclosure of confidential information in a celebrity context.[211] It has been emphasized that the allegedly iniquitous conduct required to trigger the public interest defence is necessarily of a 'very high degree of misbehaviour'. 'Relatively trivial matters, even though falling short of the highest standards people might set for themselves, will not suffice.'[212] As a result, the submission that the claimant in that case (a professional musician) could not seek to restrain the publication of allegations which were said to show she had failed (in entirely human, non-criminal means) to live up to the 'moral compass' she had set herself and published was not accepted and relief (including damages) for their publication was granted. This relatively substantial curtailment of the so-called 'hypocrisy defence', so beloved of the tabloid media, is also of obvious relevance to those employees wishing to whistle-blow about their employer's activities. It suggests that such employees will have to show more than mere inconsistency or failure to adhere to the values the company publicly proclaims.

3.122 What is clear, from the case of *Harrods Ltd v Times Newspapers Ltd*,[213] is that a party seeking to assert a defence of iniquity may rely upon subsequent conduct (almost as a form of similar fact evidence) to prove a generalized iniquitous allegation. As a result, *The Times* was able to obtain discovery of the comings and goings of Harrods personnel after the time period covered by their published allegations (founded on confidential leaked material) to attempt to establish some form of systematic malpractice by Harrods in its employment practices.

---

[205] *Maccaba v Lichtenstein* [2005] EMLR 110, para 7 *per* Gray J. His conclusions were also obviously influenced by the limited nature of disclosure, namely to his Rabbi alone. See also Bingham LJ in *A-G v Guardian Newspapers Ltd (No 2)* [1990] 1 AC 109, 222.

[206] *Beloff v Pressdram Ltd* [1973] 1 All ER 241, 260.

[207] As in *Francome v Mirror Group Newspapers Ltd* [1984] 1 WLR 892 (Jockey Club rules); *Re A Company's Application* [1989] 3 WLR 265 (FIMBRA rules).

[208] As in *Hubbard v Vosper* [1972] 2 QB 84.

[209] *R v Chief Constable for North Wales Police, ex p AB* [1998] 3 WLR 57.

[210] *Long Beach Ltd v Global Witness Ltd* [2007] EWHC 1980 (QB).

[211] See the cases running from *Woodward v Hutchins* [1977] 2 All ER 751; *Campbell v Frisbee* [2003] EMLR 76; to *Theakston v Mirror Group Newspapers Ltd* [2002] EMLR 398; *A v B plc* [2003] QB 195, especially 208; *Campbell v Mirror Group Newspapers Ltd* [2004] 2 AC 457.

[212] The *McKennitt* case [2006] EMLR 178, para 97 (upheld on appeal [2008] QB 73). As a result, the earlier case of *Woodward v Hutchins* [1977] 1 WLR 760 must be considered to be of dubious continued relevance.

[213] [2006] EMLR 320.

Warren J was careful to emphasize that such arguments could not be used to support fishing expeditions. The initial pleaded allegations of iniquity or wrongdoing required sufficient evidence before they could be advanced in pleadings. The order for disclosure was overturned by the Court of Appeal because Harrods made an undertaking that it would not contest the existence of the relevant malpractice at trial (without making any admissions); however, the Court of Appeal stated that it was 'not persuaded that the judge [at first instance] was wrong to make the order that he did on the case that was presented to him'.[214] An extension to the principle articulated in *Harrods* is that a party seeking to rely on an iniquity defence is not precluded from refining the way the public interest defence is put after the event, ie a party might retrospectively defend publication by placing reliance on the public interest defence irrespective of the party's motivation at the time of publication.[215]

In whistle-blowing cases the courts have long focused considerable attention upon whether **3.123** the alleged iniquity justified general publication or simply disclosure to the relevant authorities. Such concern can be seen, for instance, in *Francome v Mirror Group Newspapers Ltd*.[216] Unidentified persons had secretly taped (by phone tap) the telephone of a leading jockey, John Francome, and disclosed the tapes to a newspaper which considered they demonstrated wrongdoing in the form of breaches of racing rules. The newspaper approached Mr Francome to verify their authenticity; he responded by seeking an interim injunction (and a speedy trial) restraining the use of the tapes obtained from the taps. The Court of Appeal granted an injunction preventing publication of the tapes, but inserted a proviso allowing (in effect) the newspaper to disclose them to the relevant prosecuting authorities as a way to allow the public interest to be protected pending trial. A similar approach can be discerned in *Re A Company's Application*, where Scott J refused to grant an injunction to restrain an ex-employee (allegedly, a vindictive and disgruntled one) from making reports about his former employer to its regulator.[217]

The protection offered to whistle-blowing employees is now to a degree enhanced by **3.124** PIDA 1998, which substantially amends the Employment Rights Act 1996 (ERA 1996). As a result, employees who make 'qualifying disclosures' to certain specified persons or institutions (including the employer or other responsible person, as well as investigatory authorities and prescribed persons) are protected against unfair dismissal. Qualifying disclosures consist of any disclosure which in the reasonable belief of the employee in question tends to show: (a) the actual or likely commission of a criminal offence; (b) failure to comply with a legal obligation; (c) the occurrence of a miscarriage of justice; (d) the actual or likely endangering of anyone's health and safety; (e) the actual or likely damage of the environment; and (f) the deliberate concealment of any of the above.[218] The disclosure must, however, be made in good faith and not for personal gain. Special provisions exist for 'exceptionally serious failures'.[219]

Quite apart from the enhanced employment rights that PIDA 1998 confers, its structure and **3.125** policy are significant, providing further evidence that an employee wishing to whistle-blow

---

[214] [2006] EWCA Civ 294, paras 33 and 34 *per* Chadwick LJ.
[215] *Mosley v News Group Newspapers Ltd* [2008] EWHC 1777 (QB), [2008] EMLR 20, para 112.
[216] [1984] 1 WLR 892.
[217] [1989] 1 Ch 477.
[218] See ERA 1996, s 43B.
[219] ibid s 43H.

without accusation of breach of confidence should seek to do so in a controlled fashion to someone competent to or charged with preventing the kind of misconduct in question. The House of Lords has considered the interaction between the law of confidence and PIDA 1998 in *Cream Holdings Ltd v Banerjee*,[220] Lord Nicholls holding that:[221]

> The graduated protection afforded to whistleblowers by sections 43A to 43L of the Employment Rights Act 1996, inserted by the Public Interest Disclosure Act 1998, section 1, does not militate against [the appraisal that the disclosures were matters of serious public interest]. Authorities such as the Inland Revenue owe duties of confidentiality regarding the affairs of those with whom they are dealing. The 'whistleblower' provisions were intended to give additional protection to employees, not to cut down the circumstances where the public interest may justify private information being published at large.

3.126 However, this leaves one large question unanswered. Where the disclosing ex-employee or mole is not solely motivated by public interest but also (or exclusively) by money, does this in any way alter the balance to be struck? It is often said that this sort of factor is irrelevant, just as bad faith or malice on the part of a source may be irrelevant to a newspaper's freedom to publish.[222] Yet clearly, Parliament thinks it of some significance otherwise PIDA 1998 would have extended protection to those receiving payment for making qualifying disclosures.[223] In truth, the answer may lie in the fact that publication cases are often tripartite, involving as they do the confider, the confidant, and the publisher. The strength of the claimant's position against confidant and publisher is not necessarily identical. In some borderline cases the particular facts may justify a finding of breach of confidence against an employee (for example an employee of the Royal Household, as in *A-G v Parry*) which cannot be defended because of the weight attributed to an express confidentiality clause and, arguably, the effect that trading secrets for money (and nothing else) should have on one's conscience; but at the same time a newspaper might, by reason of its distinct position, still be able to defend an injunction on public interest grounds.

Disclosure required by law

3.127 General duties of confidence must give way to statutory obligations to disclose material irrespective of potentially confidential status. Thus in *Tournier v National Provincial & Union Bank*,[224] Bankes LJ pointed out that obligations of disclosure under the Bankers Books Evidence Act 1879 would override any obligations of confidence.[225] More mundanely, and routinely, obligations of confidence constitute no bar to duties of disclosure,[226] nor do they generally justify a witness in refusing to answer questions or to produce documents if ordered to do so.[227]

---

[220] [2005] 1 AC 253.

[221] ibid para 24.

[222] *Lion Laboratories v Evans* [1969] 1 QB 349, 536; and see generally *Re A Company's Application* [1989] 3 WLR 265; *Mosley v News Group Newspapers Ltd* [2008] EWHC 1777, para 112.

[223] ERA 1996, s 43G(1)(c) provides that a qualifying disclosure is made in accordance with that section if the employee does not make the disclosure for purposes of personal gain.

[224] [1924] 1 KB 461, 473.

[225] For a general analysis of the *Tournier* case and banking confidentiality more generally, see M Gill, 'Banking Confidentiality' in L Clarke (ed), *Confidentiality and the Law* (1990).

[226] See *Alfred Crompton Amusement Machines Ltd v Customs & Excise Commissioners (No 1)* [1974] AC 405; *D v NSPCC* [1978] AC 171; *Science Research Council v Nassé* [1980] AC 1028; *British Steel Corp v Granada Television Ltd* [1981] AC 1096; and for the post CPR position, see the notes in the White Book (2010) at 31.3.36.

[227] See *British Steel Corp v Granada Television Ltd* [1981] AC 1096 and *Macmillan Inc v Bishopgate Investment Trust plc* [1993] 1 WLR 1372.

Of course, in striking the balance between the interests of the parties in such circumstances, the court will invariably strive to ensure that any invasion to confidence is proportionate, by ensuring that the applicant for disclosure has as full a measure of ordinary disclosure as is consistent with the adequate protection of the secret. In the *Warner-Lambert* case Buckley LJ put the matter as follows:[228]

> . . . the court must in each case decide what measure of disclosure should be made, and to whom, and upon what terms, having regard to the particular circumstances of the case, bearing in mind that, if a case for disclosure is made out, the applicant should have as full a degree of appropriate disclosure as will be consistent with adequate protection of any trade secret of the respondent.

These objectives can be achieved by giving disclosure subject to conditions (for example lawyer only or named client only disclosure, marked returnable copies, etc), hearing matters in private, by imposing reporting restrictions, by refusing to allow documents to be disclosed from the court file, and so forth.[229] Frequently problems of this kind are soluble by undertakings. Precisely similar considerations apply when disclosure obligations bite upon documents held by a party that contain the trade secrets or confidential information of a third party.[230]

3.128 One particularly problematic area, ever since the *British Steel* case, has been orders designed to obtain identification of a source. Here special principles derived from Article 10 of the ECHR and the importance of a free and critical press may be at play.[231]

Health

3.129 There are effectively two classes of case falling within this rubric. First there are those cases where disclosures of confidential information are required in the interests of the confider. Typically, this is an issue that arises where questions of capacity are in play, for instance with children, the mentally ill, and so forth. A good example of this is the case of *R(A) v GMC*,[232] which provides a graphic illustration of the problems that may arise. The case concerned an eminent paediatrician, C, who had formerly had care of Miss A, a child who had been extremely ill with what was suspected to be ME. Doctor C remained extremely concerned about her well-being, notwithstanding that she had passed to the care of another doctor, selected by her parents, who had advocated a largely passive treatment regime which allowed her to remain at home. The parents requested that C dissociate himself from the case. Notwithstanding this he continued to use what he knew about the case (which was undoubtedly

---

[228] See *Warner-Lambert Co v Glaxo Laboratories* [1975] RPC 354, 358. See also *Roussel Uclaf v Imperial Chemical Industries plc* [1990] RPC 45.

[229] The CPR contains ample machinery by which to achieve this. See eg CPR, r 31.22(1) (implied undertaking for disclosure documents), r 31.22(2) (orders possible to restrict use of a document referred to in open court), r 32.13 (equivalent provisions for witness statements), and r 39.2(3) (hearings in private). See *Lilly ICOS v Pfizer Ltd* [2002] 1 WLR 2253 and, most recently, *Harrods Ltd v Times Newspapers Ltd* [2006] EMLR 320.

[230] See the judgment of Moore-Bick J in *Premier Profiles Ltd v Tioxide Europe Ltd* [2003] FSR 380 for a review of the authorities and a fairly standard solution.

[231] *Goodwin v UK* (1996) 22 EHRR 123; *Camelot Group plc v Centaur Ltd* [1999] QB 124; *Ashworth Hospital Authority v Mirror Group Newspapers Ltd* [2002] All ER (D) 234; *Interbrew v Financial Times* [2002] All ER (D) 106; and *Mersey Care NHS Trust v Ackroyd (No 2)* [2006] EWHC 107, [2006] EMLR 12. One route through this particular morass may be to seek a 'Harry Potter injunction' against an unknown mole as that neither requires (immediate) disclosure of the source nor leaves a potentially unfair/wrongful leak unplugged: see *Bloomsbury Publishing Group Ltd v News Group Newspapers Ltd* [2003] 1 WLR 1633 and also *LNS v Persons Unknown* [2010] EWHC 119 (QB), [2010] EMLR 16.

[232] [2004] EWHC 880; [2004] ACD 54.

confidential) to continue to register his concerns both with his employer (the responsible health authority) and with other health professionals. A's parents complained to the General Medical Council (GMC) which brought proceedings for serious professional misconduct ranging over these and other issues. When they were dismissed, A's parents sought judicial review. One of the central questions was whether C was entitled to act in the way that he had done upon the confidential information. Charles J carefully considered the relevant legal regime, in particular the Children Act 1989, and cited the *London Underground* balancing test of Sedley LJ, before concluding that given the limited, responsible nature of the disclosure and the importance of child protection issues, Doctor C was right to be concerned and to use what he knew about A's case to report his concerns to the relevant authorities.

3.130 The other type of health case arises where the disclosure in question is sought to be justified in order to protect the health of others. *W v Edgell*[233] illustrates this category of case quite graphically. Edgell was a doctor who had been instructed to produce a psychiatrist's report on W for deployment before a Mental Health Review Tribunal. His report was most unfavourable such that W's solicitors decided not to deploy it. When the doctor discovered this, such was his concern (given his conclusions as to W's mental imbalance and the danger to society he posed) that he sent his report to the relevant treating hospital of his own motion. The hospital passed it to the Secretary of State who in turn put it before the Tribunal. W sought an injunction to restrain the use of such report and sought damages. Scott J dismissed the application and was upheld by the Court of Appeal, both concluding that such disclosure was justified on public safety grounds. However, the case was an extreme one on its facts (given W's record of extreme violence). It is also important to note how much weight the Court attributed to the GMC 'Blue Book', essentially a distillation of the received professional ethics, as a guide to what was effectively the objective conscientious choice.

3.131 A further example of a case in which this was argued was the case of *X v Y*.[234] The claimant X authority was seeking an injunction to prevent Y newspaper from engaging in any further publication of information it had obtained from unknown employees of X from confidential records. In particular, Y, which had already run stories about the fact that two doctors working at X hospital were HIV positive, wished to publish their identities. It argued that such was justified in the public interest. Rose J granted the injunction, holding that the public interest in preserving such medical confidence, and thereby preserving the anonymity of two HIV sufferers (even if they were doctors), outweighed that in disclosure, particularly as disclosure would merely add to fear (and act as a deterrent to going to hospital) and non-disclosure would not in any way impede debate.[235] *X v Y* illustrates, if anything, that *W v Edgell* was an extreme case and that the weight ordinarily attached to medical confidence is high. Once again 'context is everything'.

Prevention of public harm, Convention rights, and miscellaneous interests

3.132 In truth the iniquity defence and the second category of health case can be viewed as representative of wider, general notions of public interest in play, namely that duties of confidence may need to be trumped where the maintenance of the confidence threatens to cause some form of public harm. The most obvious cases are where there is a risk of crime, or injury to

---

[233] [1990] 2 WLR 471.
[234] [1988] 2 All ER 648.
[235] ibid 661.

life and limb, whether through mental illness as in *W v Edgell*[236] or through, say, negligent breach of health and safety legislation (a category of disclosure recognized as in the public interest by PIDA 1998).

The public interests in such disclosures are readily cognizable. Moreover, it can be helpful to **3.133** reassess or reappraise such public interests in terms of Convention rights protected by the Human Rights Act 1998. Thus, to give an easy example, the health cases like *W v Edgell* can be seen as part and parcel of the discharge by the courts of the positive obligation of the state to take positive steps to safeguard the right to life;[237] or, say, a whistle-blowing case concerning malpractice at a care home can be seen similarly as ensuring that individuals do not suffer inhuman or degrading treatment. Equally, the procedural rules, and the balance they strike, seek to ensure a fair balance between the protection of confidential information and the right to a fair hearing.

The Convention right or public interest that most frequently asserts itself is the right to free **3.134** speech. Given the relatively low weight accorded to commercial free speech, such as advertising or general communications aimed at customers or the public,[238] this right is typically most relevant in three contexts. First, it is relevant where the assertion of duties of confidence is likely to stifle political free speech (the most weighty form of free speech). Here the exacting application of the public interest defence to protect political discourse is well illustrated by the *London Underground* case considered in detail above. Where the publication of the information in question will truly (and it is a claim often lightly made) stimulate important public debate the court is likely to require very strong reasons to restrain publication, not least because of its duties under section 12 of the Human Rights Act 1998 (considered above). Secondly, the right is relevant where the breach of confidence by an employee or other confidant in the form of a 'leak' is cited as a ground for obtaining *Norwich Pharmacal* relief to disclose the identity of that source. Despite the invariable sanctity applied by journalists to their sources, the courts do not adopt a similar approach and, as the contrasting facts of *Goodwin v UK*[239] and *Camelot v Centaur*[240] illustrate, the courts will be astute to distinguish between the true journalistic scoop and the leak designed to do no more than cause commercial damage (as in *Camelot v Centaur* where the information in question was due to be published a matter of days later, and the source appeared to have been motivated by ill-will). Thirdly, there are the 'correcting the record' or 'hypocrisy' cases already considered above in the context of the iniquity defence, where a prerequisite to the successful invocation of the free speech defences seems to be either the substantial surrender by the confider of substantial areas of their private life or the conscious creation (most powerfully, using the press) of a public image that proves to be false.[241]

But the public interests cognizable by the law of confidence go beyond those protected by the **3.135** Convention (though these are undoubtedly accorded the greatest countervailing weight) to

---

[236] [1990] 2 WLR 471, 488.

[237] See *Z v UK* (2001) 34 EHRR 97 for an explanation of the positive obligations imposed by Art 2. Of course, more usually Art 2 is asserted as a basis for maintaining confidentiality, eg of sources, rather than breaching it: see eg *D v NSPCC* [1978] AC 171 (anonymity of source revealing child cruelty); or *R(A) v Lord Saville of Newdigate (Bloody Sunday Inquiry)* [2001] EWCA Civ 2048, [2002] 1 WLR 1249.

[238] See eg Lester and Pannick, *Human Rights Law and Practice* (3rd edn, 2009) para 4.10.16.

[239] (1996) 22 EHRR 123, ECtHR.

[240] [1999] QB 124, CA.

[241] See M Tugendhat, *Law of Privacy and the Media* (2002).

encompass other interests, such as, say, facilitating efficient and effective governance (often advanced as a basis for justifying inter-departmental use of information in the hands of government, along with implied consent); or environmental protection; or, in the world after the Freedom of Information Act 2000, the generally recognized public interest in public access to information.

3.136   Of course the weight attributed to each such public interest will vary greatly according to context; moreover, the categories of public interest are inherently open-ended, the categories of disclosure mentioned above being simply the best established. In principle any sufficiently weighty public interest may be advanced (particularly by a public body with regulatory power) to justify interfering with confidentiality, so long as the action taken is proportionate. A good example of this is provided by the compromise struck by UK and EC legislators when dealing with data packages for pharmaceuticals and pesticides. Undoubtedly, such packages are expensive to prepare and are highly commercially valuable. However, requiring their replication by generic manufacturers leads to an unwarranted duplication of animal testing. The legislative solution is to give protection to such data packages but for a limited duration of ten years.[242] Such period is not a representation of the time it takes for the confidential information in such packages to ebb away, but is rather a compromise between the competing interests.

Protection of the confidant's legitimate interests

3.137   It is sometimes forgotten that in an employment context the employee's legitimate interests (dressed in the guise of the doctrine of restraint of trade) can be asserted to found a public interest defence. The English doctrine of restraint of trade is premised, at least in part, upon notions of personal autonomy and individual liberty. Public policy dictates that an individual should be free to pursue their chosen career.

3.138   Until the decision of the House of Lords in *R (Countryside Alliance) v A-G*[243] it might have been thought that these matters also engaged Article 8 of the ECHR which has a strong emphasis on personal autonomy and self-determination (see for example *Sidabras v Lithuania*[244]). The *Sidabras* case concerned a former KGB officer who was, by reason of that former service, banned from participating in a wide range of professions. The European Court of Human Rights (ECtHR) found that Article 8 was engaged as a result. However, in the *Countryside Alliance* case Lord Bingham described the *Sidabras* case as turning upon 'very extreme . . . facts' and all of the speeches reasoned that the purpose of Article 8 was to protect individuals from unjustified intrusion by state agents into the private sphere within which those individuals might reasonably expect to be left alone to pursue their personal affairs and live as they chose. Hunting was, by its nature, an activity conducted in public with social aspects involving the wider community. Accordingly, their Lordships were not persuaded that any analogy could be drawn with the Strasbourg jurisprudence. In a typical case, or even a serious one such as the *Countryside Alliance* case where some of the claimants lost the only form of livelihood or profession they had ever known, Article 8 would have no application. Accordingly, it would appear that Article 8 has no application to protect

---

[242] See *R v Licensing Authority, ex p Smith Kline French* [1990] 1 AC 64; *R v MAFF, ex p Portman Agrochemicals* [1994] 3 CMLR 18.
[243] [2008] 1 AC 719.
[244] *Sidabras and Dziautas v Lithuania* (2004) 42 EHRR 104.

employee interests in working in a particular form of employment, and common law principles will have to suffice.

That the employee's legitimate interests act as a defence, rather than precluding a confidence **3.139** from arising in the first place, is evident from the fact that some types of information will be treated as confidential during the currency of an employment relationship, namely (to use *Faccenda*[245] terminology) Class 2 information (or at least what we have called Class 2A material, ie that not in principle capable of protection by an express post-termination covenant),[246] which as a matter of policy the law will not protect after termination precisely because of the inevitably restrictive effect it would have. In the balance that must be struck between the employer's interests and those of the employee to continue to work in their chosen profession, the latter weighs more heavily. The description of information forming part of the employee's 'experience, knowledge and skill' is a convenient label for those types of information which, for these policy reasons, the law will not directly protect by means of confidentiality obligations. But it is not an entirely accurate label; were the information in question merely part of the 'experience, knowledge and skill' of an employee (for example how to make a particular kind of carpentry joint more efficiently) and no more, the law of confidentiality would have no bite (or it would be Class 1 information). It is precisely because the confidential information in Class 2 is 'intermingled' with the pursuit of the profession that the dilemma arises.

Thus, one of the characteristics of true trade secrets is that they are, in loose terminology, **3.140** 'severable'. An individual can know a true trade secret, for instance the construction and properties of a new product under development (such as the composition of a new chemical yet to be put on the market), and yet still go to work for a competitor in the paint market. Hence, indefinite protection may be justified. Some other types of information (those Class 2 pieces of information deserving of protection), pricing margins, business leads, and so forth, may call for a more measured or proportionate response, precisely because the effect of untrammelled relief is to exclude the ex-employee from any further work in the sector. In many markets some types of information will necessarily be confidential, for example pricing margins, and yet *endemic, inherent, routine*, and *unavoidable*. Were the law to grant full protection to such information then, subject to shelf-life considerations (see below), effective relief would be very substantial and might potentially preclude the employee from working for a competitor at all for a very substantial time, an unjustifiable result particularly in the context of relatively low weight or low value confidential information. It is to address this problem that the restrictive covenant has been developed; and, for obvious reasons, there is a direct parallel between the common law notion of reasonableness and the more modern proportionality test set out in the *London Underground* case.

It is precisely because the test of proportionality or reasonableness is one of balancing of **3.141** interests that relief in a restrictive covenant should not necessarily be granted for the duration of the shelf-life of the confidential information (though of course it is safe to do so if the information is substantially or wholly 'severable' such that the employee remains largely unimpeded in the pursuit of their new employment); to grant such relief for such duration uncritically may not be to balance interests but simply to accord priority to confidential information and fail to attribute any weight to the legitimate interests and freedoms of the employee.

---

[245] See paras 3.26–3.64 above.
[246] See para 3.79 above.

Decay or loss of confidentiality

3.142 Whilst on one view (it is submitted the better), the contention that information has lost its confidential status through decay or the passage of time, such that it has passed its 'shelf-life', is an essential element in showing that the material is confidential and thus worthy of protection, frequently defendants in fact run allegations of decay or loss of confidentiality as if they were defences. Such disputes tend to focus on particular types of information, typically ephemeral market-sensitive information such as pricing levels, pricing margins, costs, business leads or business opportunities, customer names and/or lists, customer requirements, and contacts. Because the nature or weight of confidence and its duration is so very context-sensitive it is difficult to set out any general rules.

3.143 For instance, in some markets customers may be well known and the subject of regular competition (for example a market in which competitive tendering is used, such as in many areas of public service provision). In others (for example a market in which discretion in service provision is important, for instance security services such as safe installation, or provision of medical treatment), it may be a closely guarded secret and may remain so potentially indefinitely. In between there lie those cases where customer identities may remain confidential for a short period before they become, through a variety of means, market knowledge. In fact, given the features of most markets the situation of indefinite or even substantial confidentiality of customer identity is likely to be distinctly atypical.

3.144 For these reasons, Bell J's conclusions in *SBJ Stephenson Ltd v Mandy*[247] that the inclusion of customer names as protected confidential information for the purpose of a twelve-month express (but generally worded) confidentiality clause did not unduly extend the scope of post-termination restraint so as to render it unenforceable, is to be treated with considerable circumspection (particularly given the duration and effect of such restraint). Such information is undoubtedly *capable*, in the right circumstances, of being confidential, no more. The conclusion is perhaps more understandable in the light of the judge's finding that there was also a valid twelve-month non-solicitation covenant of wide breadth. Much more usual in a commercial context (as opposed to a professional context) is the situation where a particular business opportunity with a particular customer is confidential (such as where A has a habit of dealing with B alone and has recently told B it has a substantial order to place). The two should not be confused. Indeed, were customer identities routinely confidential, parties would not be in the habit of inserting post-termination non-solicitation clauses so as to protect customer connection as opposed to pure confidential information restriction (though of course a non-solicitation clause can in fact perform both functions). Thus, unsurprisingly, in *Dranez Anstalt v Hayek*,[248] Evans-Lombe J was unwilling to find that names of customers were so confidential as to amount to a trade secret (there being no operative post-termination restraints of any kind), his reasoning being that such names (even if memorized) formed part of the 'knowledge, skill and experience' the employee had acquired. This seems a proper conclusion on the facts of that case, but again not safely generalizable. Fortunately for the judge, unlike Bell J in *SBJ Stephenson v Mandy*, he did not have to grapple with the more difficult question as to whether customer names were Class 2A or Class 2B and thus potentially capable of being protected by an express covenant.

---

[247] [2000] IRLR 233, paras 35–36, 45–47.
[248] [2002] 1 BCLC 693, para 51.

In many cases familiarity with customer names is likely to be so endemic, inherent, routine, and unavoidable in any particular employment as to be incapable of protection. In *Meridian VAT Reclaim UK Ltd v Lowendal Group*,[249] where the court was faced with an interlocutory dispute as to the enforceability of an express covenant precluding a potential bidder for the company from using customer identity and other information received during the due diligence process, the judge simply concluded that there was an issue as to the enforceability of such covenant that needed to go to trial and granted relief in the interim.

3.145 Any party wishing to contend that information has ceased to be confidential (or conversely that it remains confidential) will need to deploy carefully structured evidence as to: (a) practice in keeping or not keeping the information confidential; (b) market practice in general; (c) how any information that is initially confidential enters the public domain (for example by customers or agents disclosing details to competitors, a particular problem with price levels, but not, obviously, margin information); and (d) general ephemerality (for example evidence showing that prices are fluid or unstable, such that sensitive information is unlikely to remain pertinent for long in any event). In general terms the best pointers as to what sort of evidence needs to be prepared are contained in the cases concerning springboard relief, precisely because in order to invoke the jurisdiction to grant such relief a party must show: (a) that any confidence in question has either expired or has been destroyed as a result of misconduct (for example publication or use); but (b) a quantifiable unfair advantage has been obtained. Such process of inquiry necessarily focuses acutely upon the nature of the confidential information, for how long it lasts in ordinary circumstances, for how long it has in fact lasted, and how long it would take a competitor using legitimate means to either reassemble the information (for example when assembling a customer list from scratch) or for how long the information would remain confidential before it became general market data or its inherent ephemerality rendered it of no account. Cases such as *Bullivant v Ellis*,[250] *Universal Thermosensors v Hibben*,[251] and *Sun Valley v Vincent*[252] offer useful guidance as to the areas of inquiry that should be undertaken and the types of evidence that should be adduced.

Consent

3.146 Consent is of course a defence to any claim of breach of confidence. Perhaps cases recognizing this most clearly, and where the defence may most frequently arise, are the medical confidence cases. Thus, in *C v C* a request by both a petitioner and a respondent to a divorce case to the respondent's doctor that he should disclose the respondents medical records, showing an intimate history of venereal disease, could not be resisted on the grounds of the sanctity of medical records, given the clear and effective patient consent.[253]

3.147 Of course, consent can give rise to a host of problems, for instance: (a) whether there is implied consent arising from the facts and circumstances of a particular relationship, for example does a patient give implied consent for a doctor to share information with other doctors? Or does the passage of information to one employee justify sharing such information with others, something as to which few contractual confidential clauses make express

---

[249] [2002] EWHC 1066.
[250] [1987] ICR 464, [1987] IRLR 491, CA.
[251] [1992] 1 WLR 840.
[252] [2000] FSR 825. See, further, paras 10.57–10.85 below on springboard injunctions.
[253] [1946] 1 All ER 542.

provision and perhaps more should? (b) whether the party purportedly giving consent has authority to grant such consent. To give an extreme case, one may ask whether a middle-ranking line manager of an employee can give consent to the disclosure by the junior employee of core business secrets of great market value. There is little case law testing this difficult issue in a confidentiality context. Given the equitable or conscience-based nature of the cause of action, a test of ostensible authority might seem commendable but the point is far from clear; and (c) to what extent the consent is otherwise effective, such as whether it is being given by someone who is mentally competent to give it (a recurrent issue in cases involving children, such as the famous *Gillick* litigation or the case of *R(A) v GMC* considered above, the mentally ill, or the physically unconscious).

3.148 One area in which consent, albeit somewhat as an undercurrent, is playing a modern role in a confidentiality context is in the zonal approach to confidentiality identified in *A v B* and widely adopted in celebrity privacy cases. The case of *A v B* concerned a well-known celebrity footballer who wished to keep details of an adulterous affair he had conducted out of the press. Lord Woolf MR used his judgment to set out a series of principles governing such cases, one of which was that if a party conducted themselves such as to put certain aspects of their private life that would otherwise and ordinarily be treated as confidential into the public domain or has fostered public discussion thereof, such areas of their life or 'zones' will no longer be deserving of protection: 'if you have courted public attention then you have less ground to object to the intrusion which follows'.[254] Whilst it is possible to analyze such cases as being ones concerned with whether or not there is confidential information, probably the better analysis is that in respect of these zones there is a form of implied consent to future publication.

E. Remedies

The range of remedies available

3.149 Given its equitable and (potentially) contractual roots, it is unsurprising that the range of remedies available to combat an actual or threatened breach of confidence is impressive. Remedies include damages (classic and, in appropriate cases, for injury to feelings), negative injunctions (of a classic or 'springboard' form), mandatory injunctions (to disclose sources or parties to whom information has been passed), accounts of profits, and, most ambitiously of all, proprietary claims.[255] The subject of injunctions, damages, and other remedies is covered in detail in Chapters 10 and 11 below. However, given the peculiar issues raised by breach of confidence, it may be helpful to set out here some of the principles specific to breach of confidence in short form.

Damages[256]

3.150 Like any tort action, the primary purpose of any action for damages for breach of confidence is to restore the claimant to the position in which he would have been but for the breach.[257]

---

[254] [2003] QB 195, 204–10.
[255] For a general analysis, see G Jones, 'Restitution of benefits obtained in breach of another's confidence' (1970) 86 LQR 463; P Birks, 'The remedies available for abuse of confidential information' (1990) LMCLQ 460.
[256] See J Beatson, 'Damages for Breach of Confidence' (1991) 107 LQR 209.
[257] See *Indata Equipment Supplies Ltd v ACL Ltd* [1998] FSR 248.

In so far as the claim for breach of confidence is conceived of as being purely equitable (which is far from clear), the jurisdiction to award damages exists either by virtue of section 50 of the Supreme Court Act 1981[258] or by reason of the jurisdiction to grant equitable damages.[259] Similarly, a contractual analysis typically leads to the same conclusion, precisely because the object of any express contractual obligation is negative, namely to ensure that confidential matters remain so.[260] There are no hard and fast rules (despite the attempts of some to argue for the same) as to how such analysis of loss is to be conducted. As Eveleigh J has explained in *Dowson Mason Ltd v Potter*:[261]

> In reply to that argument [to the effect that one must always attempt to value the stolen information] Mr. Thorley, on behalf of the plaintiffs, has referred the court to *General Tire & Rubber Co. v. Firestone Tyre & Rubber Co. Ltd.* [1975] 1 W.L.R. 819, 824, where Lord Wilberforce said:

> 'As in the case of any other tort (leaving aside cases where exemplary damages can be given) the object of damages is to compensate for loss or injury. The general rule at any rate in relation to "economic" torts is that the measure of damages is to be, so far as possible, that sum of money which will put the injured party in the same position as he would have been if he had not sustained the wrong.'

> Then Lord Wilberforce quoted Livingstone v. Rawyards Coal Co. (1880) 5 App. Cases. 25, 39, per Lord Blackburn.

> That principle enunciated by Lord Wilberforce is one which has been stated time and time again by judges in assessing damages; we apply it right across the board. In an ordinary accident case, in which the plaintiff claims for loss of wages, the court seeks to compensate him by putting him in the position in which he would have been if he had been able to continue at work uninjured; but in every case the court looks at the particular position of the plaintiff in order to discover what would have been the position if the wrong had not been done to him. So, where there is a claim for loss of wages, if it can be shown that the plaintiff would not have worked in any event, for example, if he had decided to retire or if his particular job would have ceased, that is a matter which is taken into account by the courts in assessing damages. Similarly, in a case such as the present, it seems to me that the particular position of the plaintiff has to be considered. Where we are dealing with someone who would have licensed the use of his confidential information, then almost invariably the measure of damages will be the price that he could have commanded for that information, and no question of loss of profits will arise, for the simple reason that he was always ready to allow someone else to manufacture at a price. If the plaintiff was a manufacturer who would have licensed another to use his secret then again he would, probably in all cases, be in the same position as the inventor who had sold it, because he would have exposed himself to competition and loss

---

[258] This largely re-enacts the Chancery Amendment Act 1858 ('Lord Cairns Act'), s 2 and provides that wherever the court has jurisdiction to entertain an application for an injunction, it may award damages in addition to or in substitution for an injunction. *Malone v Metropolitan Police Commissioner* [1979] 1 Ch 344, 360 *per* Megarry V-C suggests that where there is no case for an injunction, eg because the information has ceased to be confidential, no claim for damages will lie.

[259] Of course in employment cases this debate is largely otiose, since duties of confidence are implied into every contract of employment. But for the case for equitable damages, see RG Toulson and CM Phipps, *Confidentiality* (2nd edn, 2006) paras 9-030–032; compare and contrast Clerk & Lindsell, *Torts* (20th edn, 2010) paras 28-132–136.

[260] In *Faccenda Chicken v Fowler* [1987] Ch 117, in the Court of Appeal it was pointed out (ibid 135) that where an extant contractual obligation existed such should be the starting point of analysis. However, it does not detract from the fact that in the context of the breach of negative promise, the tortious measure and the contractual measure are basically the same. Relevant differences might exist, however, in concepts such as forseeability of loss.

[261] [1986] 1 WLR 1419, 1422.

of profits for a price, the price for which he had sold the secret. If, on the other hand, he was a manufacturer who would not have licensed its use, then he would not have been exposed to competition at the time when he was exposed because of the defendant's wrongdoing. This is the kind of analysis of the facts that one has to make in every case in which the court has to assess damages.

3.151 Given the range of types of confidential information in existence, and the different potential attitudes to disclosure (for example information never disclosed, information disclosed under licence, etc), the approach to the award of damages is necessarily highly contextual. Ways of measuring damage might include asking: what does the claimant ordinarily charge (or what would he have charged) for the provision of the information in question or what would a reasonable licence fee have been (if available from other sources)?[262] What profits have been lost as a result of the disclosure of information?[263] What damage has been caused by use of the information?[264]

3.152 It should, however, be pointed out that in many commercial contexts damages claims framed generally in terms of lost profits raise real problems of causation. The *Dowson* case is atypical in this respect, in that the effect of competition using stolen information could be mapped with sufficient certainty. Frequently this will not be so, particularly since a claimant will need to show that but for the breach of confidence he would have obtained the business in question.[265] Attempts to prove general loss to goodwill raise similar problems.[266] The practical result is that the courts will instead resort to attempting rough and ready valuation of the information by reference to actual or notional royalties, or by some calculation (where the information can be analysed in this way) of the costs of replacement or reverse engineering (most obviously where the information is a collection of data that could be replicated by experimentation). Damage is typically assessed by reference to the value of the information at the time of the actionable breach. Exceptionally, a later valuation date (typically trial, but potentially the date of use) may be accepted if to do otherwise would cause injustice.[267] However, it is worth bearing in mind that the overarching equitable consideration of 'conscience' may militate against the award of damages against an innocent party.[268] Conversely, when faced with unconscionable breaches the court will nevertheless strive to achieve relative justice between the parties.[269] The decision of the Privy Council in *Pell Frishman Engineering Ltd v Bow Valley Iran Ltd*[270] provides a useful and authoritative summary of the relevant principles. The Board held that the claimant's damages for breach of express confidentiality provisions and/or the implied equitable duty of confidence

---

[262] This is best illustrated by *Seager v Copydex* [1967] 1 WLR 923.

[263] The approach adopted in *Dowson Mason Ltd v Potter* [1986] 1 WLR 1419.

[264] In *Talbot v General Television Corp Pty* [1981] RPC 1, the court attempted to identify the extent to which a television treatment or concept had been diminished in value by reason of the breach that had occurred. This was also the approach of Lindsay J in *Douglas v Hello! Ltd (No 8)* [2003] EWHC 2629 (Ch) when assessing the loss of *OK* (rather than the Douglases). The majority of the House of Lords approved Lindsay J's assessment of loss in *OBG v Allan* [2007] 1 AC 1 at 50 and 94, overturning the Court of Appeal decision on liability in *Douglas v Hello! Ltd (No 6)* [2005] EWCA 595.

[265] See *Universal Thermosensors Ltd v Hibben* [1992] 1 WLR 840, 851.

[266] ibid 852.

[267] See *Johnson v Agnew* [1979] 1 All ER 883.

[268] See eg *Valeo Vision SA v Flexible Lamps* [1995] RPC 205 (no damages against an innocent recipient of confidential information who gave no value for it).

[269] See eg *Sanders v Parry* [1967] 1 WLR 53.

[270] [2009] UKPC 45.

should be assessed on the basis of what price the parties, acting reasonably, would have been prepared to negotiate in order for the claimant to allow the defendants to make use of that information. They also held that the Jersey Court of Appeal's approach to the assessment of damages, which had been based on the cost to the claimant of acquiring the confidential information in question, was incorrect in principle.

Two special heads of damage call for particular attention. First, on standard tort principles **3.153** one might expect exemplary damages to be available in the narrow circumstances where the defendant has cynically calculated that his profits may exceed the damages that would otherwise be available.[271] However, such conclusion might not follow if the foundation of the cause of action is in fact truly and purely equitable.[272] However, given the equitable roots of the cause of action it would seem more sensible to formulate a claim in such circumstances in terms of an account of profits.[273] Secondly, in appropriate cases, typically those involving private confidences, damages for injury to feeling (or aggravated damages) of a modest amount may be available.[274] Such damages should be at a level well below those awarded for serious physical or psychological injury. For instance, in *Archer v Williams*, Mary Archer obtained damages of £2,500 for the distress that she suffered as the result of reading revelations from her former PA, Miss Williams, in the *Daily Mirror* newspaper.[275] Likewise in the case of *McKennitt v Ash*,[276] the successful claimant recovered £5,000 in respect of the injury to feelings caused by a substantial book. (Of course, in such cases injunctive relief to prevent repeated or fresh revelations may be the prime relief, if not too late.)

Accounts and/or restitutionary damages

The right of a party to seek an account of profits for a pure breach of confidence is long- **3.154** standing and a reflection of the equitable origins of the action.[277] The remedy is particularly useful in circumstances where an action for damages offers little recompense and is a weak deterrent (for instance if the wronged party had no plans to exploit the information itself) but where the wrongdoer has profited substantially thereby.[278] The decision of the House of Lords in *A-G v Blake*[279] has probably added yet further vigour to such remedy, deciding as it does that an accounting remedy may be available for breach of contract even if the disclosure in

---

[271] See *Kuddus v Chief Constable of Leicestershire* [2002] 2 AC 122.

[272] See *Smith v Day* (1882) 21 Ch D 421, 428 (Brett LJ) (an *obiter dictum* supporting an exemplary award in equity); in *Douglas v Hello! Ltd (No 6)* [2003] EWHC 786, paras 272–3, Lindsay J was content to assume exemplary damages would be available in a case of 'outrageous' behaviour, without deciding the point; but cf the Australian decision in *Harris v Digital Pulse Pty* [2003] NSWCA 10. The position is extensively discussed in Law Commission, *Aggravated, Exemplary and Restitutionary Damages* (Law Com No 247, 1997).

[273] The course in fact suggested by Lord Scott in the *Kuddus* case (n 271 above), para 109.

[274] As in *Douglas v Hello! Ltd (No 8)* [2003] EWHC 2629 (Ch) (damages for distress); upheld on this point by the Court of Appeal in *Douglas v Hello! Ltd (No 3)* [2005] EWCA Civ 595.

[275] See *Archer v Williams* [2003] EMLR 869; *Cornelius v De Taranto* [2001] EMLR 329; *Campbell v Mirror Group Newspapers Ltd* [2004] 2 AC 457.

[276] [2006] EMLR 178 upheld on appeal [2008] QB 73.

[277] *Peter Pan Manufacturing Corp v Corsets Silhouette Ltd* [1964] 1 WLR; *Reading v A-G* [1951] AC 507; see the *Spycatcher* case, *A-G v Guardian Newspapers Ltd (No 2)* [1990] 1 AC 109.

[278] See the comments of Slade J in *My Kinda Town Ltd v Soll* [1983] RPC 15. The purpose of an account 'is to deprive the defendants of the profits which they have improperly made by wrongful acts committed in breach of the plaintiff's rights and to transfer such profits to the claimants'.

[279] [2001] AC 268.

question is of information no longer confidential.[280] One could almost term these 'springboard damages'. But the reasoning in *A-G v Blake* suggests that the claim for an account must be so much the stronger where until publication the information has in fact remained confidential.

3.155 Any party wishing to seek an account of profits must elect for such remedy rather than damages;[281] the time for election generally does not arise unless and until the wronged party is able to make an informed choice, provided that the election is not unreasonably delayed to the prejudice of the defendant.[282] As a result, in many cases where a claim for an account is likely to be a live remedy it may be sensible to seek initial trial on liability only.

3.156 Notwithstanding the above principles, claims for accounts rarely arise in a pure breach of confidence context. Instead, claims for an account involving confidential information have tended to be subsumed in a general accounting claim for a diversion of business opportunity by a fiduciary or a claim for some other form of breach of fiduciary duty in which the breach of confidence is an aspect of the fiduciary duties breached.[283]

3.157 The most obvious and compelling case for such a remedy is where a party has specifically promised not to disclose or publish information but does so for profit.[284] Such cases apart, the presence of conscious dishonesty, wilful or reckless breach of duty are factors likely to increase the court's willingness to award such a remedy. In the absence of dishonesty, and in particular when faced with lower level confidential information, the courts are likely to be reluctant to order an account.[285]

3.158 As to what proportion of profits may be recoverable, this is a potentially difficult question unless the case is a clear one where the profit in question could not have been made at all without the use of the confidential information.[286] In such cases the court will have to assess the extent to which the use of the confidential information in question enhanced profits (for instance by saving costs, improving efficiencies, and so on). The principle of proportionality may suggest that in complex cases such an exercise is simply unnecessarily complex and burdensome.[287] The alternative (also seen in other contexts, such as passing off) is to approach

---

[280] The prime significance of this decision is likely to be in the area of 'privacy' confidences. The reasoning in *A-G v Blake* may entitle employers to pursue former employees (PAs, hairdressers, advisers, etc) who use their former position not only to sell genuine secrets (a breach of confidence) but also to recycle or rehash stories already in the public domain.

[281] See *Sutherland Publishing Co Ltd v Caxton Publishing Co Ltd* [1936] Ch 323, 326.

[282] See *Island Records v Tring* [1996] 1 WLR 1256.

[283] The classic case being *Industrial Development Consultants v Cooley* [1972] 1 WLR 443, a case which has spawned much modern case law. *Normalec v Britton* [1983] FSR 318 is a classic example of mixed breach of fiduciary duty and confidence.

[284] It appears that the Court of Appeal in *Douglas v Hello! Ltd (No 8)* [2005] EWCA 595, [2005] EMLR 609 would have awarded an account, had any profits been made (see ibid paras 243–50). It is not clear whether that would be the position notwithstanding the fact that the Douglases had elected, as they plainly had, to seek damages. It may be that damages for injury to feeling (in contrast to damages for commercial loss) should be treated as distinct for the purpose of election.

[285] As in *Satnam Investments Ltd v Dunlop Heywood & Co Ltd* [1999] FSR 722. It is important to note that there was no claim for knowing assistance or knowing receipt, both pleas that are frequently open in true 'information theft' cases. But as the *Satnam* case illustrates, causation remains problematic. For a recent case where an account was held to be inappropriate see *Vercoe v Rutland Fund Management* [2010] EWHC 424 (Ch).

[286] See generally *Peter Pan Manufacturing Corp v Corsets Silhouette Ltd* [1964] 1 WLR, a case where there could have been no profit from the sale of the article in question (brassières) without a breach of confidence.

[287] See *Seager v Copydex* [1967] 1 WLR 923, especially 931–2 *per* Lord Denning MR where such practical considerations may have militated against the grant of an account.

an account in a fairly rough and ready manner, when in doubt favouring the injured party when justice so dictates (as when faced with dishonest breaches).[288] However, the courts can adopt a strict approach to the taking of an account, particularly where the confidential information is published for profit.[289]

There are some particular advantages in the taking of an account. It avoids having to prove **3.159** loss (which may be difficult, particularly if no exploitation of the confidential information was planned) and the party entitled is freed from any obligation to mitigate loss.

Proprietary claims

Most controversial of all is the extent to which a claimant can contend that by virtue of the **3.160** misuse of his confidential information he can assert some form of constructive trust over benefits, products, or funds resulting therefrom.[290] In the *Ocular Sciences* case,[291] Laddie J treated this as a question of fact and degree. Again, this type of claim is rarely considered purely through the lens of breach of confidence—instead, it tends once again to arise in the context of a wider claim of breach of fiduciary duty, typically involving the diversion of a business opportunity.

Negative injunctions

Given the difficulties with damages and accounting claims that arise in many breach of **3.161** confidence cases, as set out above, in most cases the prime remedies are negative injunctions to preclude further breach of confidence, and so-called 'springboard' injunctions designed to unravel the ongoing unfair competitive advantage obtained by historic use of confidential information.[292] These topics are considered in detail in Chapter 10 below. It is necessary here only to mention the width of discretionary relief that may be obtained in support of a claim for breach of confidence. It embraces not only classic negative injunctive relief but also: (a) springboard relief;[293] and (b) relief compelling the unravelling of relations, including contractual relations, entered into in breach of confidence. It had been thought that such relief was unobtainable as a result of comments of Sir Donald Nicholls VC in *Universal*

---

[288] See eg *Normalec Ltd v Britton* [1983] FSR 318, where the judge reached the general conclusion that the entire new business had been generated in breach of fiduciary duty and 'belonged' to the claimant. However, this was an interim injunction case, such that no final relief was granted, the effect of the injunction being the practical divestment of the unlawful or improper business. Cf *CMS Dolphin Ltd v Simonet* [2001] 2 BCLC 704, 746 for Lawrence Collins J's discussion of remedies for breach of director's duties in that case.

[289] In the *Spycatcher* litigation the newspapers ultimately had to account for the profit on the sales of the relevant editions containing excerpts from the Peter Wright book. No accounting allowance was made for the other parts of the newspaper (though this argument was always artificial—the problem is probably best approached through increased sales, seen against trend, as in the *Hello* case), nor for the fees paid to Peter Wright.

[290] In Canada the use of such remedial constructive trusts is typified by *LAC Minerals Ltd v International Corona Resources Ltd* [1990] FSR 441, (1989) 61 DLR (4th) 14.

[291] *Ocular Sciences Ltd v Aspect Vision Care Ltd* [1997] RPC 289.

[292] For a Scottish consideration of the basis for granting a negative interim injunction (interdict), see *Jack Allen (Sales & Service) Ltd v Smith* [1999] IRLR 19, paras 15, 17, 20, identifying 'harm' to the plaintiff (pursuer) as the primary basis upon which to grant injunctive relief.

[293] See *Vestergaard Frandsen A/S v Bestnet Europe Ltd* [2009] EWHC 1456 (Ch), where Arnold J 'laid to rest' any suggestion that the springboard doctrine meant that injunctions could be granted to restrain the continued misuse of confidential information once the information had ceased to be confidential.

Thermosensors Ltd v Hibben.[294] However, the Court of Appeal made it clear in the case of *PSM International v Whitehouse*[295] that this was not the case.

3.162   *PSM International v Whitehouse* concerned the defendant leaving his position as managing director of the claimant, and setting up a rival business designing and manufacturing goods intended to be supplied to the claimant's customers. Lloyd LJ noted that the previous decision in *Bullivant v Ellis*[296] had not considered, on appeal, the granting of an injunction against an individual to prevent performance of a concluded contract with a third party. However, he held that equitable relief was not limited to future contracts entered into by the defendant—'the arm of equity is not so short'—but could encompass a wider jurisdiction allowing the unravelling of previous contracts which had breached the defendant's duty of fidelity.[297] Consequently, the court was entitled to prevent contracts entered into in breach of the defendant's duty of confidence from being performed.

Mandatory injunctions

3.163   This topic is considered in Chapter 10 below.

F. Database protection

Introduction and overview

3.164   The *sui generis* database right[298] ('the Database Right') derives from the EC Database Directive[299] ('the Directive'). The Database Regulations[300] give the Directive effect in domestic law (both by amending the Copyright Designs and Patents Act 1988 (CDPA 1988) and by the free-standing provisions of the Regulations). This is a technical field which raises considerable complications at its fringes (such as in the application of its transitional provisions, or in the overlap with copyright per se). What follows is a discussion of the parts which might be of most interest to an employment lawyer dealing with problems of employee competition.

3.165   The Database Right is very broad. It may be exceptionally useful to an employer who is faced with an employee or employees who have taken parts of a computer database (for example classically, customer or supplier lists), not least because framing a case by reference to database rights moves the attention away from confidentiality (which may not exist, or may be exceptionally onerous to prove, particularly on a data item by data item basis) and moves into the value of the database as 'work done'.

3.166   There are, however, some possible disadvantages. The European Court of Justice's (ECJ's) decision in *William Hill v British Horseracing Board*[301] has created considerable confusion as to the precise ambit of the database right. Also, there is an argument that a claim which

---

[294] [1992] 1 WLR 840, 851.

[295] [1992] IRLR 279, CA.

[296] [1987] ICR 464, [1987] IRLR 491, CA.

[297] [1992] IRLR 279, 283.

[298] Called '*sui generis*' to distinguish it from the separate copyright in a database, for which certain additional requirements need to be satisfied (see CDPA 1988, s 3A). For a discussion of copyright and other intellectual property rights, see Chapter 7 below.

[299] Directive 96/9/EC.

[300] Copyright and Rights in Database Regulations 1997, SI 1997/3032.

[301] *William Hill v British Horseracing Board* [2004] ECR I-10415.

includes a claim for infringement of the database right should be brought in the Chancery Division (which may not always be desirable, because of listing or other procedural reasons). These points are discussed below.

What is a 'database' under the Regulations?

For the purposes of the Regulations, a database is 'a collection of independent works, data or other materials' which are: **3.167**

(1) 'arranged in a systematic or methodical way', and
(2) 'individually accessible by electronic or other means'.[302]

This is a broad definition, and is likely to cover most computer systems which contain lists of contacts, customer records, and the like. **3.168**

When does the Database Right arise?

Not every 'database' qualifies for the Database Right. A right subsists only if 'there has been substantial[303] investment in obtaining, verifying or presenting the contents of the database'.[304] On the face of it, 'investment' is also given an expanded meaning. It 'includes any investment, whether of financial, human or technical resources'. **3.169**

This apparently wide definition must be read, however, subject to the ECJ's interpretation of the Directive in the *William Hill* case.[305] Whilst not an employer/employee dispute, it is both the leading case on the Directive and of direct relevance to the employment context because the key passage upon which the judgment turns provides guidance as to what kind of tasks employees may be instructed to undertake in the expectation of the employer receiving protectable Database Rights as a result. The *William Hill* case concerned the use of information compiled by the British Horseracing Board (BHB) about races and riders. BHB had an elaborate system by which it compiled lists of entrants for horseraces, using a call centre manned by about thirty operators, and then put this information onto a database in order to produce a final list of runners, which would then be published the day before the race. The evidence was that BHB spent about £4 million a year on this exercise. William Hill obtained this information from various sources, and then published the lists of entrants for the races on its websites. BHB thought that William Hill ought to have permission to make use of this information, and sued William Hill for infringement of its Database Right. BHB succeeded at first instance;[306] but William Hill appealed, and the Court of Appeal referred a number of issues concerning the correct interpretation of the Directive to the ECJ.[307] **3.170**

---

[302] SI 1997/3032, reg 12(1).

[303] In *Football Datco Ltd v Britten Pools Ltd* [2010] RPC 17, the preliminary issue was to establish what rights, if any, subsisted in the annual fixture lists produced and published for the purposes of the English and Scottish Premier Leagues and football leagues. The claimants contended inter alia that the fixture lists were protected by the *sui generis* Database Right. Floyd J held that the claimant was involved primarily in creating the data and that the extra effort (if any) in obtaining, verifying, or presenting the data was trivial and not sufficient to attract the *sui generis* right.

[304] SI 1997/3032, reg 13(1).

[305] [2004] ECR I-10415. See also *Attheraces Ltd v British Horseracing Board Ltd* [2005] EWHC 3015, [2006] UKCLR 167.

[306] [2001] 2 CMLR 12.

[307] [2002] ECC 24.

3.171 The ECJ held that BHB did not have a Database Right in respect of the race information published by William Hill. It reasoned that the purpose of the Directive was to protect the investment in the obtaining, verification, or presentation of the contents of a database; and that this meant that the Directive applied to protect only investment in 'the creation of that database as such'.[308] The ECJ held that the expression 'investment in the verification of the contents of the database' must therefore be understood to refer to the resources used, with a view to ensuring the reliability of the information contained in that database, to the accuracy of the materials collected when the database was created and during its operation; and does not refer to the resources used for verificaton during the stage of creation of data or other materials which are subsequently collected in a database. Accordingly, whilst it was certainly the case that BHB spent a substantial amount of money *collecting* the data for incorporation in its database, this was not a relevant 'investment' for the purposes of establishing a Database Right.

3.172 This is not an easy distinction to follow or apply. However, in an employment context, an employer's database might typically consist of detailed customer contact information, in relation to which the employer has invested a substantial amount of time and energy not only collecting the details, but also in setting up the necessary hardware and software for the database, and thereafter ensuring that the details are kept up to date and amended from time to time. This appears to be different to the mechanical, non-creative task of gathering pre-existing information envisaged by the ECJ. In these circumstances, it is likely that at least a substantial part of the employer's investment will be a qualifying investment for the purposes of the Directive; and therefore that the database will attract the Database Right.[309]

Who owns the right?

3.173 The 'maker' of the database is the first owner of the right.[310] The 'maker' is usually[311] 'the person who takes the initiative in obtaining, verifying or presenting the contents of a database and assumes the risk of investing in that obtaining, verification or presentation shall be regarded as the maker of, and as having made, the database'.[312]

3.174 In a typical employer/employee relationship, this person would nearly always be the employer. However, the point is put beyond doubt by regulation 14(2), which provides that where a database is made by an employee in the course of his employment, 'his employer shall be regarded as the maker of the database', unless there is an agreement to the contrary. In *Pennwell Publishing (UK) Ltd v Ornstein*,[313] the database in issue was a contacts database contained in Outlook. As to the issue of ownership, Justin Fenwick QC (sitting as a Deputy Judge of the High Court) held that 'where an address list is contained on Outlook or some similar program which is part of the employer's email system and backed up by the employer, the database . . . will belong to the employer'.[314] Further, he said: 'Because this is not likely to

---

[308] [2004] ECR I-10415, para 30.
[309] For an application of these principles, see the *Football Datco* case, cited above.
[310] SI 1997/3032, reg 15.
[311] There are some exceptions concerning Crown databases: ibid reg 14(3)–(5).
[312] ibid reg 14(1).
[313] [2007] IRLR 700 (HC).
[314] ibid, para 127.

be appreciated by many employees, it is . . . highly desirable that employers should devise and publish an email policy . . .'[315]

The Regulations make no express provision for the ownership of a database made by an agent **3.175** concerning work done for a principal to belong to the principal, as noted by Bean J in *Cureton v Mark Insulations Ltd*.[316] Thus, in that case the database was owned by the agent and not the principal.

How is the Database Right infringed?

When it comes to infringement, the Regulation is again very broadly framed. A person **3.176** infringes the right if, without the consent of the owner, he 'extracts or re-utilises all or a substantial part of the contents of a database'.[317]

The definitions[318] give fairly generous meanings to these expressions: **3.177**

(1) 'Extraction' means 'the permanent or temporary transfer of' any of the contents of a database 'to another medium by any means or in any form'. This would very probably cover most means by which an employee might take parts of a database: downloading it, copying it to disc, sending it by email, or printing it out. In *Crowson Fabrics Ltd v Rider*,[319] the defendants sought to argue that they had made minimal use of the claimant's database and that this could not amount to 'substantial extraction'. Peter Smith J identified 'the act of transfer to [the defendants'] computer' as the extraction, rather than the subsequent use made of the data and said it did not help the defendants to argue about the (minimal) use made of the data if they extract substantial parts of the database.[320] The judge added in that case, the defendants 'do not take [the database] . . . for any reason other than to use it as they need from time to time'. In *Directmedia Publishing GmbH v Albert-Ludwigs-Universitat Freiburg*,[321] the ECJ held that it was not only acts of mechanical reproduction without adaptation that fell within 'extraction' and that the transfer of material from a protected database to another database following an on-screen consultation of the first database and individual assessment of the material contained therein is capable of constituting an 'extraction' within Article 7 of the Directive. Further, in *Apis-Hristovich v Lakorda*,[322] the ECJ held that the concept of 'extraction' within the meaning of Article 7 of the Directive is not restricted to acts of permanent transfer but also to those of temporary transfer. The ECJ also held that the objective pursued by the act of transfer is immaterial for the purpose of assessing whether there has been an extraction.

(2) 'Re-utilisation' means making the contents of a database 'available to the public by any means'. This is unlikely to be relevant to the type of case where a former employee wants to use the information for a new employer or a competing business of his own, but may be important where the employee is threatening to disclose the information to others.

---

[315] ibid, para 129.
[316] [2006] EWHC 2279 (QB).
[317] SI 1997/3032, reg 16(1).
[318] ibid reg 12(1).
[319] [2008] IRLR 288 (HC).
[320] ibid, para 120.
[321] [2009] 1 CMLR 7, [2009] RPC 10, ECJ.
[322] [2009] 3 CMLR 3, ECJ.

(3) 'Substantial', in relation to any investment, extraction, or re-utilization, means 'substantial in terms of quantity or quality or a combination of both'. This is a concept derived from copyright, and likely to be interpreted in a similar way. It is well established that the question of whether there has been 'substantial' copying is not determined simply by mechanically comparing the proportion of the work copied to the total of the work—the question is whether, having regard to both the nature and quantity of the copying, an important or significant part of the work has been used. For example, even a few bars of music may be a substantial part of a musical work if they are a recognizable reproduction of the essential part of the melody. It is also often said that 'what is worth copying is prima facie worth protecting'.[323]

3.178 In addition, even where the individual extraction is insubstantial, the Regulations also provide that repeated and systematic extraction or re-utilization of insubstantial parts of the contents of a database may amount to the extraction or re-utilization of a substantial part of those contents.[324]

3.179 The combined effect of these provisions is that in many employment cases, such as where an employee has downloaded a customer list, or details of pricing or tendering information, from his employer's computer system, the employer may well be entitled to sue for infringement of his Database Right. The database is broadly defined; the threshold for creation of the right is low (provided that the investment is of the right sort); and the infringement provisions are broad.

3.180 A recent example of a case in which there was held to be a clear breach of the Database Right is *First Conferences Services Ltd v Bracchi*.[325] The first defendant had emailed his personal email account attaching extracts from the claimant's database before resigning from the claimant and setting up in competition. Peter Smith J said that the evidence was that the claimant had spent a considerable expense and time in generating its database and that the first defendant had extracted information from the database including a large number of customer contacts and sales information. He said that the investment was of human or technical resources and concluded that this was a case of extraction and a breach of regulation 16(1) of the Regulations.

The position of third parties who acquire information (for example, from an employee)

3.181 It is also worth noting that in the *William Hill* case, William Hill argued that it had not infringed BHB's Database Right (even if it existed) because it had not directly accessed the database—it had obtained the information from third parties, who were in turn licensed by the BHB to supply details from the database. The ECJ rejected this argument, and held that the protection conferred by the Database Right also covered the use of data which, although

---

[323] *University of London Press Ltd v University Tutorial Press Ltd* [1916] 2 Ch 601, 610 *per* Petersen J, approved by both Lord Reid and Lord Pearce in *Ladbroke (Football) Ltd v William Hill (Football) Ltd* [1964] 1 WLR 273, 279, 293. Although note that this aphorism has been disapproved as being a 'misleading rhetorical device', in the context of infringement of copyright, by the Court of Appeal in *Baigent v Random House Group Ltd* [2007] EWCA Civ 247, [2007] FSR 24, para 97 *per* Lloyd LJ. It was held that, since the test of whether the copying is substantial is objective, the defendant's state of mind is irrelevant (except to the question of whether there should be additional damages).

[324] SI 1997/3032, reg 16(2).

[325] [2009] EWHC 2176 (Ch).

derived originally from a protected database, were obtained by the user from sources other than that database.

It follows that if an ex-employee infringes the Database Right, and provides information **3.182** from his former employer's database to the new employer, then there may also be room to argue that the new employer is also infringing the Database Right. Since the remedies available for infringement of the Database Right are the same as those for infringement of copyright,[326] lack of knowledge on the part of the new employer that he had infringed the former employer's Database Right might be a defence to a claim for damages,[327] but would not preclude a claim for account of profits, injunctions, and delivery up.

Advantages over common law 'confidential information' claims

Whilst not a panacea for all problems, the great strength of the *sui generis* Database Right is **3.183** that its key purpose is to protect business investment in data against *unfair use*. It does so:

(1) irrespective of considerations of confidentiality and duration of confidence;
(2) irrespective of considerations of originality;
(3) because it focuses on the existence or not of 'a substantial investment in obtaining, verifying or presenting the contents of the database';
(4) because infringement in this context is demonstrated by extraction or re-utilization of all or a substantial part thereof—naughty employees generally take the lot and decide what they need later;
(5) with the result that with appropriate steps in advance (by appropriately addressing the database's use in an employee's terms and conditions of employment, the intelligent design of database protocols, well-maintained record-keeping regarding data entry, regular update or amendment, and long-term investment in the database as a continuing asset) proof of the existence of such a right should be comparatively easy;
(6) so as to create a 'mixed intellectual property ("IP") right', almost halfway between copyright and confidence; but
(7) with the potential for the remedial flexibility of both (ie final remedies including damages, accounts, etc, interim remedies including delivery up and springboard injunctions).

Put together, these factors go some considerable way to mitigating the drawbacks of the **3.184** standard springboard template in information theft cases as:

(1) good record-keeping, coupled with well-drafted terms and conditions of employment and/or use of the relevant database should make proof of the relevant IP right comparatively simple; infringement in the form of copying will be as easy/difficult to prove as ever—the same case made on the same inferences will probably be advanced;
(2) arguments about confidentiality, duration of confidence, and the employee's ordinary skill and knowledge should also be side-stepped, saving cost in preparation and argument of the case, and enabling speedier preparation for court;

---

[326] See also *Ibcos Computers Ltd v Barclays Mercantile Highland Finance Ltd* [1994] FSR 275, holding that source code could be classed as confidential information.

[327] CDPA 1988, s 97(1): 'Where in an action for infringement of copyright it is shown at the time of the infringement the defendant did not know, and had no reason to believe, that copyright subsists in the work to which the action relates, the plaintiff is not entitled to damages against him, but without prejudice to any other remedy.'

(3) defences will be reigned back to narrower IP-type defences;

(4) remedies for the employer are broader—the rights and remedies of a copyright owner under sections 96 to 98 of CDPA 1988 apply to the owner of a database right;[328] and in copyright cases there is a prima facie right to a permanent injunction to restrain infringement.[329] Infringement of the database right may also entitle the owner to claim 'additional' (or flagrancy) damages under section 97 of the 1988 Act.[330]

3.185 These are potent advantages. But employers confronted with information theft, particularly those contemplating seeking interim and/or springboard relief, should not necessarily confine themselves to database rights, particularly given the interpretative difficulties presented by the *William Hill* case. Often the essential evil in information theft cases lies not in 'trade secrets stolen' but in 'work saved'. Quite apart from database rights both copyright (particularly apposite for electronic documents or files) and/or conversion (for physical copies) and/or passing off may offer appropriate procedural vehicles for a claim for relief, particularly as both such remedies: (a) may found claims for delivery up; and (b) in the case of breach of copyright or passing off, provide a potential entitlement to a claim for an account of profits (and thus a principled route to springboard relief which, ultimately, can be seen as relief designed to stop profits accruing in the first place).

Procedural issues: should a database claim be brought in the Chancery Division?

3.186 It appears that the answer to the above question is 'yes'. Schedule 1 to the Senior Court Act 1981 assigns to the Chancery Division all causes and matters relating to (amongst other things) 'patents, trademarks, registered designs, copyright or design right'. Furthermore, intellectual property proceedings are governed by their own dedicated provisions of the CPR, namely Part 63. Rule 63.13 provides that all intellectual property matters, as defined by the accompanying Practice Direction, are allocated exclusively to the Chancery Division, a Patents County Court or a county court where there is also a Chancery district registry. CPR 63PD18.1 defines (by list) those matters which constitute 'intellectual property rights'. The list includes, amongst other things '(9) database rights', '(12) technical trade secrets litigation'; and '(13) passing off'. Accordingly, any action making such claims must be brought in the Chancery Division.

3.187 In addition, the term 'technical trade secrets', although not defined, would appear to be intended to encompass confidentiality claims relating in whole or in part to matters such as chemical formulae, secret processes, industrial procedures, computer software or programming, and the like.

G. Checklist

Is there a duty of confidence?

3.188 Does the information have the necessary quality of confidence? Consider both the inherent quality of the information and the general accessibility of the information (see paras 3.10 to 3.12 above).

---

[328] SI 1997/3032, reg 23.
[329] See eg *PPL v Maitra* [1999] 1 WLR 870, CA.
[330] SI 1997/3032, reg 23.

Has the information retained that quality? If it is now in the public domain, it will no longer **3.189** have the necessary quality of confidence and no confidentiality duties will arise (see paras 3.11 to 3.12 above).

Was the information imparted in circumstances importing an obligation of confidence? Did **3.190** the person receiving the information know or should he have known that the information was fairly and reasonably to be regarded as confidential? Note that this is an objective test (see paras 3.13 to 3.17 above).

Did the employer take steps to impress on the employee the confidentiality of the informa- **3.191** tion? If so, what steps? These will be relevant factors considered by the court, particularly in the employment context (see paras 3.57 to 3.60 above).

Has there been disclosure to the detriment of the claimant? Detriment of a more than *de* **3.192** *minimis* kind is probably a requirement, but will usually be readily assumed (see paras 3.18 to 3.19 above).

Consider the potential impact of the Human Rights Act 1998. If the employment is of a **3.193** domestic type or, particularly, if an injunction restraining publication or disclosure is sought, convention rights of respect for private life and freedom of expression are likely to be engaged (see paras 3.20 to 3.25 above).

What is confidential information?

Consider the various 'classes' of confidential information set out in the Court of Appeal's **3.194** decision in *Faccenda Chicken v Fowler* and as interpreted by later cases (see paras 3.31 to 3.34 and paras 3.65 to 3.83 above).

Class 1: Is the information trivial or public information which is not confidential at all? If so, **3.195** an employee will be free to disclose or use it.

Class '2A': Is the information that which the employee must treat as confidential (either **3.196** because he was expressly told that it is confidential or because from its character it is obviously so)? Such information may be protected during the currency of the employment relationship but, because it forms part of the 'knowledge, skill or experience' of the employee, there will be no general restriction on him using or disclosing the information after the termination of his employment. Likewise, the information is, by its nature, unlikely to be capable of protection by an express post-termination confidentiality covenant. It may, however, benefit from some protection via a restrictive covenant (see para 3.79 above).

Class '2B': Information which is not a trade secret (and therefore not automatically pro- **3.197** tected following termination of the employment relationship) but may be protected for a reasonable period with an appropriately drafted post-termination confidentiality clause of limited duration. Such a provision could be combined with an appropriate non-dealing provision, so as to prevent conscious or unconscious use of the information (see para 3.79).

Class 3: Is the information a specific trade secret, so confidential that it cannot lawfully be **3.198** used for anyone's benefit but the employer's (see paras 3.35 to 3.51 above)?

Distinguishing between the classes of information

Consider whether the knowledge might be regarded as forming part of the employee's gen- **3.199** eral stock of accumulated know-how or whether the information constitutes specific details which should be regarded as belonging to his employer (see paras 3.35 to 3.41 above).

3.200   Is this information which, if disclosed to a competitor, would be liable to cause real (or significant) harm to the owner of the secret? If so, it may be classed as a trade secret (see paras 3.42 to 3.45 above).

3.201   Remember that identification of a trade secret is a multi-factored and contextual enquiry (see paras 3.46 to 3.51 above). Factors to consider include:

- the nature of the information;
- how it was obtained or derived, and by whom;
- how it has been protected;
- what worth has been ascribed to it by the parties (subjectively) and what worth it has (objectively);
- what value it has in the hands of a competitor;
- whether the employee can realistically or practically be expected to abstain from using such information consciously or unconsciously, and if so for how long;
- the 'ascertainability' of the information and the resources required to ascertain it;
- the seniority and/or nature of the employee;
- the proximity of the information to any core or secret processes or know-how; and
- the extent of the 'severability' of the information in question.

Can the confidential information be precisely defined?

3.202   Is the confidential information which the employer seeks to protect capable of being precisely defined? The court will only restrain the use of specified, identifiable information (see paras 3.52 to 3.56 above).

Liabilities of third parties

3.203   Has a third party, such as a subsequent employer, received confidential information from an informant (in breach of that informant's own duty of confidence to the original confider)? If so, a duty of confidence may be owed by that third party to the confider if the third party receives the confidential information in the knowledge that the informant had breached its existing duty of confidence (see paras 3.61 to 3.64 above).

Express confidentiality clauses

3.204   Is the express provision a valid agreement that the employee will not subsequently use or disclose specified classes of information? If so, and subject to questions of illegality or public policy, this should be an enforceable agreement (see paras 3.65 to 3.74 above).

3.205   Does the express covenant set out examples of confidential information? If so, the express provision will be of evidential significance in determining what information the parties considered to be truly confidential (see para 3.75 above).

3.206   Does the restriction on the use of confidential information in practice seriously inhibit or altogether prevent the employee from carrying on his profession? If so, such a wide-ranging restraint on the use of information may be objectionable on public policy grounds and, as such, is unlikely to be enforced. Such provisions will be analyzed against the doctrine of restraint of trade (see paras 3.76 to 3.79 above).

3.207   Does the contract also contain appropriately drafted post-termination restrictive covenants that do not directly relate to maintaining confidentiality (such as a non-dealing covenant)?

If so, it may be possible to protect certain types of confidential information in this way (see paras 3.76 to 3.79 above).

The effect of dismissal on obligations of confidence

Has the employee been wrongfully dismissed? If so, it is likely (but by no means certain) that **3.208** any contractual confidentiality provisions will fall away but the implied equitable obligation of confidence (as described in the *Faccenda* case) will be unaffected (see paras 3.80 to 3.83 above).

Defences to a claim of breach of confidence

Is there a possible overriding public interest in the duty of confidence being breached? If so, **3.209** there may be a defence to a claim relating to the disclosure, provided the disclosure has been made to the 'appropriate' person, such as the police, a regulator, or government department. The media will not, usually, be an appropriate person (see paras 3.84 to 3.116 above).

If so, the party wishing to establish a public interest defence (in the case of either a commer- **3.210** cial or privacy confidentiality claim) bears the burden of proof (see paras 3.117 to 3.119 above).

Is there a relevant type of public interest involved? Consider the following: **3.211**

- iniquity (see paras 3.120 to 3.126 above);
- whether the disclosure is required by law (see paras 3.127 to 3.128 above);
- health (see paras 3.129 to 3.131 above);
- prevention of public harm, Convention rights, and miscellaneous interests (see paras 3.132 to 3.136 above); and
- protection of the confidant's legitimate interest (see paras 3.137 to 3.141 above).

Is decay or loss of confidentiality an issue? If so, this is often run as a defence (see paras 3.142 **3.212** to 3.145 above).

Has there been consent (whether express or implied) to the disclosure of the confidential **3.213** information? If so, this will be a defence (see paras 3.146 to 3.148 above).

Remedies

Consider the following possible remedies: **3.214**

- classic damages (see paras 3.150 to 3.152 above);
- exemplary damages/account of profits (see para 3.153 above);
- damages for injury to feeling (or aggravated damages) if the case is one involving private confidences (see para 3.153 above);
- accounts and/or restitutionary damages (see paras 1.154 to 1.159 above);
- proprietary claims, such as a form of constructive trust over benefits, products or funds resulting from the misuse of the claimant's confidential information (see para 3.160 above);
- negative injunctions precluding further breach of confidence and so-called 'springboard' injunctions designed to unravel the ongoing unfair competitive advantage obtained by historic use of confidential information (see paras 3.161 to 3.162 above).

See, also, Chapters 9 and 10 below on remedies.

Database protection

3.215   Is there a collection of independent works, data, or other materials which: (1) are 'arranged in a systemic or methodical way' and (2) are 'individually accessible by electronic or other means'? If so, there will be a database for the purposes of the Database Regulations 1997 (see paras 3.164 to 3.168 above).

3.216   Has there been substantial investment in obtaining, verifying, or presenting the contents of the database? If so, a Database Right will probably exist (see paras 3.169 to 3.172 above).

3.217   Who is the person who took the initiative and assumed the risk of investing in obtaining, verifying, or presenting the contents of the database? That person will be regarded as the maker of, and as having made, the database. In a typical employer/employee relationship, the maker will nearly always be the employer (see paras 3.173 to 3.175 above).

3.218   Has a person extracted or re-utilized all or a substantial part of the contents of the database, without the consent of the owner? If so, the Database Right will have been infringed (see paras 3.176 to 3.180 above).

3.219   Has the alleged infringer used data which, although derived originally from a protected database, was obtained by the user from sources other than that database? If so, the protection conferred by the Database Right will nevertheless probably be engaged (see paras 3.181 to 3.182 above).

3.220   Consider the possible advantages of a Database Right claim over common law 'confidential information' claims (see paras 3.183 to 3.185 above).

3.221   Bring any Database Right claim in the Chancery Division (see paras 3.186 to 3.187 above).

4

GARDEN LEAVE

Paul Goulding QC, Jane Mulcahy, Dan Aherne, and Luke Pardey

A. Introduction[1]

Garden leave is a relatively recent phenomenon. It made its debut in the late 1980s. Whereas **4.01** the common law has honed the duties owed by an employee, and refined the principles applicable to restrictive covenants, over a great many years, the law on garden leave is still in its infancy. Some principles have become well established. Other issues remain unresolved. The background, emergence, and development of garden leave are examined in this chapter. This examination will seek to explain why garden leave has become so commonplace, how it operates in practice, and what factors the courts take into account in deciding whether to grant a garden leave injunction.

---

[1] See also Appendix 4, Sample Garden Leave Clauses and Appendix 5, Sample Particulars of Claim and Interim Injunction in Garden Leave Case below.

4.02 Frequently when an employee is offered a new job it is in the field in which he already works. The reason is obvious. The skills and experience which he has acquired through his current employment make him attractive to a rival employer. If the employee accepts the new job, one of two problems often confronts the current employer. The first occurs when the employee wants to start his new employment before his notice period has expired. He might walk out immediately, sometimes alleging constructive dismissal. Or he might give notice of resignation in accordance with his contract and initiate negotiations for an early leaving date. If there is no agreement on this, the employee may simply leave anyway before his notice period has expired in order to start in his new job. If the new employer is a competitor of the current employer, the latter will more often than not want to delay the employee's start date until the expiry of his notice period. For many years an application for an injunction to achieve this end had a major hurdle to surmount in the form of the rule against the specific performance of contracts of personal service.

4.03 The second problem materializes where the employee is content to work out his contractual notice. The difficulty here is that the employer may not want him to do so. If the employee is about to join a competitor, the employer may well want to keep the employee away from his confidential information, customers, and staff in the run up to his new job. But how can the employer deprive the employee of work without himself repudiating the employment contract and thereby releasing the employee from his continuing contractual obligations and enabling him to start his new job prematurely, the very thing the employer wants to prevent?

4.04 Garden leave emerged as a way of addressing these two problems. Exercising a contractual right to require an employee to stay at home, whilst at the same time paying his salary and providing him with his other contractual benefits—in other words, putting him on garden leave—goes a long way to overcoming the difficulties facing an employer described above.

4.05 However, garden leave is not a complete panacea. For a start, it is not always available, depending on the terms of the relevant employment contract. Even when it is available, its imposition has certain drawbacks as well as considerable benefits for an employer. There are also limits to garden leave, the precise parameters of which are still being worked out by the courts. Each of these issues will be discussed below.

4.06 This chapter will consider the following topics:

(1) the rule against specific performance of contracts of personal service—an understanding of this rule is essential to an understanding of garden leave, which emerged to counter the effect of the rule (in addition, the rule may still be applicable where garden leave is not, for one reason or another, available);

(2) the emergence of garden leave through a trilogy of cases in the late 1980s and early 1990s, and the concepts of garden leave, garden leave clauses, garden leave injunctions, and garden leave undertakings;

(3) the notion of a right to work and the importance of garden leave clauses in employment contracts;

(4) the practicalities involved in imposing garden leave, and what this entails;

(5) the steps necessary to enforce garden leave through the courts;

(6) a checklist of essential garden leave items.

In addition, sample garden leave clauses and sample court documents in a garden leave case (particulars of claim and interim injunction) are included in Appendices 4 and 5 respectively below.

B. The rule against specific performance of contracts of personal service

The rule stated

Most employment contracts contain a term or terms describing the employee's obligation to serve his employer. This obligation may be expressed in positive terms, or in negative terms, and sometimes both the positive and negative terms (or 'covenants' as they are sometimes called in the older cases) are included.   **4.07**

A positive covenant may include words to the effect that the employee shall 'devote the whole of his time, attention and abilities to carrying out his duties under the contract'. A negative covenant may provide that the employee shall 'not (unless otherwise previously agreed in writing by the company) undertake any other business or profession or be or become an employee or agent of any other person or persons'.[2]   **4.08**

The contract is also likely to provide that it is terminable by either party giving a specified period of notice of termination. If an employee purports to work for another employer before the expiry of his notice period, it might be thought that the court would restrain his actions by injunction. It is at that point that the rule against specific performance comes into play.   **4.09**

It is well established that the court will not, as a general rule, order specific performance of a contract of personal service (such as a contract of employment).[3] In relation to the contract of employment, this general rule is enshrined in statute, section 236 of the Trade Union and Labour Relations (Consolidation) Act 1992 providing: 'No court shall, whether by way of—(a) an order for specific performance . . . of a contract of employment, or (b) an injunction . . . restraining a breach or threatened breach of such a contract, compel an employee to do any work or attend at any place for the doing of any work.'   **4.10**

Section 236 reflects the common law general rule both in its direct (section 236(a)) and its indirect (section 236(b)) forms. Direct specific performance is straightforward. The court will not order an employer or employee specifically to perform an employment contract.   **4.11**

Indirect specific performance is a little more subtle and controversial. As section 236(b) provides, breach of a negative covenant in a contract of employment will not be restrained by injunction where the effect of the court's order would be to leave the employee with no alternatives except to perform the services or to remain idle.[4] The cases discussed   **4.12**

---

[2] This term is taken from the contract in question in the garden leave case of *Provident Group plc v Hayward* [1989] ICR 160, CA, discussed at paras 4.42–4.54 below.

[3] *Chitty on Contracts* (30th edn, 2008) paras 27-020–022; M Freedland, *The Personal Employment Contract* (2003) 368–76.

[4] Chitty (n 3 above) 27-065–069; A Burrows, *Remedies for Torts and Breach of Contract* (3rd edn, 2004) 529–34.

below, which form the background to the emergence of garden leave, are principally concerned with the rule against specific performance of contracts of personal service in its indirect form.

Early cases

Lumley v Wagner[5]

4.13   The starting point for this line of cases involves the opera singer Johanna Wagner. Ms Wagner contracted with Benjamin Lumley to sing for three months at his theatre, Her Majesty's in London, and 'not to use her talents at any other theatre, nor in any concert or reunion, public or private, without the written authorisation of Lumley' during the period of her engagement. When Frederick Gye persuaded Wagner to sing at the Royal Italian Opera, Covent Garden for a larger sum than stipulated in her agreement with Lumley, the latter applied for an injunction to restrain Wagner from singing at Covent Garden or any other theatre without Lumley's authorization during the existence of her agreement with Lumley. In *Lumley v Wagner*[6] the Lord Chancellor, Lord St Leonards, granted the injunction observing: 'It is true that I have not the means of compelling her to sing, but she has no cause of complaint if I compel her to abstain from the commission of an act which she has bound herself not to do, and thus possibly cause her to fulfil her engagement.'[7] The Lord Chancellor went on to declare that if he had only to deal with the affirmative covenant of Wagner that she would perform at Her Majesty's Theatre, without the negative covenant not to perform elsewhere during that period, he would not have granted any injunction.[8]

Whitwood Chemical Co v Hardman[9]

4.14   An obligation not to work for another may be implied from an express term to devote full time and attention to an employer. But this implied negative obligation will not necessarily be enforced by injunction. In *Whitwood Chemical Co v Hardman*[10] the defendant, a manufacturing chemist, agreed to work for the claimant as manager of its Normanton works for a period of five years, later extended to ten. Whilst the agreement contained a term that the defendant would give the whole of his time to the claimant's business, it contained no negative covenant that he would not work for others during this period. The defendant became actively engaged in forming a company with a view to carrying on a competing business during the unexpired term of his employment with the claimant. Kekewich J granted an injunction to restrain the defendant from giving less than the whole of his time to the claimant's business. He reasoned that he would be doing injustice to the ordinary construction of the English language if he failed to see in the positive covenant to devote his whole time to the claimant's business anything but a covenant that the defendant would not give his powers and his strength of body and mind to another business.[11] The Court of Appeal allowed the company's appeal and discharged the injunction. Lindley LJ emphasized

---

[5] 1 D M & G 604. See the illuminating article by AG Salmon, 'A Statue to a Leading Case' (1973) 117 Solicitors Journal 160.
[6] ibid.
[7] ibid 619.
[8] ibid 622.
[9] [1891] 2 Ch 416, CA.
[10] ibid.
[11] ibid 421.

the principle that the court does not decree specific performance of contracts for personal service and considered it immaterial whether that is brought about directly by decree of specific performance, or indirectly by injunction.[12] The difficulty for the claimant, according to Lindley LJ, was that it could not suggest anything which, when examined, did not amount to this, that the defendant must either be idle, or specifically perform the agreement into which he had entered.[13] Lindley LJ looked upon *Lumley v Wagner*[14] rather as an anomaly to be followed in cases like it, but an anomaly which it would be very dangerous to extend.[15] This reluctance to grant an injunction the effect of which was to compel an employee to remain idle or to continue to work for his current employer explains the refusal of injunctive relief in a number of cases at this time, notwithstanding that an employee is in breach of his contract of employment by working for another employer.[16] The current employer's remedy was said to be in damages alone.

Warner Bros v Nelson[17]

Another celebrity to buck the trend epitomized in cases like *Whitwood Chemical v Hardman*, **4.15** and find herself subjected to an injunction, was the film star Ms Nelson (better known as Bette Davis): *Warner Bros Pictures Inc v Nelson*.[18] The defendant agreed in 1934 to render her exclusive services as an actress to Warner Bros for fifty-two weeks (extendable, by the film company exercising its options, to 1942). She also agreed not, during the term of her contract, to 'render any services for or in any other phonographic, stage or motion picture production . . . of any other person . . . or engage in any other occupation without the written consent of the producer being first had and obtained'. In June 1936, the defendant declined to be further bound by the agreement, left the United States and, in September the same year, entered into an agreement in the United Kingdom with a third party.

Warner Bros sought an injunction to restrain her from breaching the first part of this negative **4.16** term whilst wisely desisting from seeking to restrain her from engaging in *any* other occupation. Branson J granted an injunction. The judge stated the conclusion to be drawn from the authorities to be that, where a contract of personal service contains negative covenants the enforcement of which will not amount either to a decree of specific performance of the positive covenants of the contract or to the giving of a decree under which the defendant must either remain idle or perform those positive covenants, the court will enforce those negative covenants.[19] It was in the application of this principle to the facts that the decision is perhaps surprising. Branson J noted that the defendant was stated to be a person of intelligence, capacity, and means, and no evidence was adduced to show that, if enjoined from doing the specified acts otherwise than for the claimant, she would not be able to employ herself both usefully and remuneratively in other spheres of activity, though not as remuneratively

---

[12] ibid 428.

[13] ibid 427.

[14] See n 5 above.

[15] [1891] 2 Ch 416, CA, 428.

[16] *Rely-A-Bell Burglar and Fire Alarm Co Ltd v Eisler* [1926] 1 Ch 609, following *Ehrman v Bartholomew* [1898] 1 Ch 671 and *Chapman v Westerby* [1913] WN 277. In each of these cases the term of the service agreement was lengthy, amounting to five, ten, and ten years respectively. In the *Rely-A-Bell* case approximately one year of the five-year term remained unexpired at the time of the hearing of the application for injunctive relief.

[17] [1937] 1 KB 209.

[18] ibid.

[19] ibid 217.

as in her special line.[20] 'She will not be driven, although she may be tempted, to perform the contract, and the fact that she may be so tempted is no objection to the grant of an injunction.'[21] The judge described the defendant as breaching her contract 'for no discoverable reason except that she wanted more money', perhaps a salutary reminder that such perceptions can and do influence the outcome of cases.

4.17　The court demonstrated the flexibility of its power in fashioning the scope and duration of the relief granted. Having stated the principle to be derived from the earlier cases,[22] Branson J added a further consideration: 'An injunction is a discretionary remedy, and the Court in granting it may limit it to what the Court considers reasonable in all the circumstances of the case.'[23] As to scope, the injunction granted was confined to forbidding the defendant from rendering services for any motion picture or stage production for anyone other than the claimants.[24] That part of the negative covenant restraining her from engaging in any occupation was not enforced (nor was it sought to be). As to duration, Branson J's approach was that 'the Court should make the period such as to give reasonable protection and no more to the plaintiffs against the ill effects to them of the defendant's breach of contract'.[25] Three years was the maximum duration of the injunction granted.[26] The concept of no more than reasonable protection to the claimant is reflected in later judicial pronouncements in garden leave cases.

Later cases

4.18　The approach taken in the early celebrity cases of *Lumley v Wagner*[27] and *Warner Bros v Nelson*[28] must now be reconsidered in the light of the detailed and critical scrutiny to which it was subjected in a number of cases from the 1960s to the present day involving celebrities, principally musicians and sportsmen.

Page One Records Ltd v Britton[29]

4.19　'The Troggs' pop group appointed Page One Records Ltd as their manager for a five-year term from 1966. They agreed during that period not to engage anyone else to act in that capacity, nor to do so themselves. One year later, the group purported to terminate the management agreement. The claimants, relying on *Lumley v Wagner*,[30] sought an interim injunction restraining the defendants from appointing anyone as manager other than themselves. Stamp J refused to grant an injunction: *Page One Records Ltd v Britton*.[31] The judge distinguished *Lumley v Wagner* on two grounds. First, there the only obligation on the part

---

[20] The defendant did not give any evidence herself, a factor which the Court of Appeal in *Warren v Mendy* [1989] 1 WLR 853, 865 (paras 4.24–4.30 below) considered to be of some significance.

[21] [1937] 1 KB 209, 219.

[22] See para 4.16 above.

[23] [1937] 1 KB 209, 217.

[24] ibid 219.

[25] ibid 221. The view of Hallett J in *Marco Productions Ltd v Pagola* [1945] 1 KB 111, that it is not necessary, in order to obtain an injunction, for a claimant to demonstrate that it may suffer damage as a result of a breach of the negative covenant, is unlikely to be followed today.

[26] [1937] 1 KB 209, 222.

[27] See n 5 above.

[28] See n 17 above.

[29] [1968] 1 WLR 157.

[30] See n 5 above.

[31] See n 29 above.

of the claimants seeking to enforce the negative stipulation was an obligation to pay remuneration, which could be enforced by the defendants; but here the obligations of the claimants, involving personal services, were obligations of trust and confidence which could not be enforced by the Troggs.[32] Secondly, Stamp J relied on the proposition, the converse of which he noted Branson J had stated in *Warner Bros v Nelson*, the proposition being: where a contract of personal service contains negative covenants the enforcement of which will amount either to a decree of specific performance of the positive covenants of the contract or to the giving of a decree under which the defendant must either remain idle or perform those positive covenants, the court will not enforce those negative covenants.[33] Stamp J observed that in the *Warner Bros* case Branson J felt able to find that the injunction sought would not force the defendant to perform her contract or remain idle. In contrast, on the evidence before him, Stamp J entertained no doubt that the Troggs would be compelled, if the injunction was granted on the terms sought, to continue to employ the claimants as their manager and agent. It was on this ground that he distinguished *Lumley v Wagner* and *Warner Bros v Nelson*, adding:

> . . . for it would be a bad thing to put pressure upon these four young men to continue to employ as a manager and agent in a fiduciary capacity one who, unlike the plaintiff in those cases (who had merely to pay the defendant money) has duties of a personal and fiduciary nature to perform and in whom the Troggs, for reasons good, bad or indifferent, have lost confidence and who may, for all I know, fail in its duty to them.[34]

Nichols v de Angelis[35]

The approach of Stamp J in *Page One Records Ltd v Britton* was preferred to that of Branson J in *Warner Bros v Nelson* by Oliver J, who conducted a comprehensive review of the authorities in *Nichols Advanced Vehicle Systems Inc v de Angelis and Team Lotus Ltd*.[36] That case concerned the young formula one racing driver, Elio de Angelis, who signed to drive for NAVS, as the claimants were known, and agreed not to drive for any other team during the term of his agreement with NAVS. When one of the most prestigious teams, Lotus, appeared to have lured away de Angelis, NAVS sought an interim injunction to enforce the negative stipulation contained in its agreement with the driver. **4.20**

Oliver J stated the principles which he considered to be deducible from the authorities, noting that although they are easy enough to state they are not always easy to apply.[37] The judge viewed *Warner Bros v Nelson*[38] as representing the high-water mark of the application of *Lumley v Wagner*.[39] Up to that point, no such injunction had been granted in a reported case in relation to anything but short-term engagements. In *Lumley v Wagner* the outstanding period of engagement was for twelve weeks, whereas in the *Warner Bros* case the injunction was granted for up to three years. Oliver J thought this appeared to be coming **4.21**

---

[32] [1968] 1 WLR 157, 165.

[33] ibid 166.

[34] ibid 166. See, also, *Zang Tumb Tuum Records Ltd v Johnson* (10 February 1988), where Whitford J considered *Warner Bros v Nelson* and *Page One Records Ltd v Britton* and concluded, like Stamp J, that it was not just a question of idleness or starvation, but rather whether the practical effect of the grant of an injunction would be to compel specific performance of a contract of personal service.

[35] 21 December 1979.

[36] ibid.

[37] ibid 23–4.

[38] See n 17 above.

[39] See n 5 above.

extremely close to specific performance.[40] Here the period was two years. The judge did not find *Warner Bros v Nelson* and *Page One Records Ltd v Britton* easy to reconcile but concluded the approach of Stamp J in his consideration in the latter case of what in substance amounts to specific performance to be the more realistic one. It did not seem to Oliver J to be realistic to say that nothing short of idleness and starvation is compulsive, and therefore no injunction which involves anything less than that can be said to infringe the principle that the court will not specifically enforce a contract of personal service.[41]

4.22   The judge concluded that there was a strong likelihood that, faced with the choice of either going out of Formula One racing altogether for the next year or two or going back to drive for the claimants, the defendant driver would feel compelled to the latter course. Accordingly, he declined to grant an injunction. He acknowledged a repugnance to permit a defendant to break with impunity, save for such damages as may be ultimately awarded, a clear contractual commitment into which he had freely entered but did not consider it to be the function of the court to punish what it may regard as shabby conduct.[42]

Lotus v Jaguar[43]

4.23   The boot was on the other foot for Lotus Cars when it sought an injunction to restrain Jaguar Cars from inducing the Lotus sales director, Putnam, from joining Jaguar as its UK sales and marketing director. Putnam's contract of employment with Lotus had eighteen months to run. One unusual feature of the case was that Lotus sought relief against Jaguar but not against Putnam personally, possibly in an attempt to circumvent the rule against specific performance that defeated the claimants in the *Nichols* case. Nourse J dismissed Lotus' application on the ground that the grant of an injunction against Jaguar would amount in substance and effect either to a decree of specific performance of the positive covenants of Putnam's contract of employment with Lotus or the giving of a decree under which Putnam must either remain idle or perform those positive covenants: *Lotus Cars Ltd v Jaguar Cars Ltd*.[44] In the course of his judgment, Nourse J referred with approval to Oliver J's judgment in the *Nichols* case and the latter's preference for the approach of Stamp J in *Page One Records Ltd v Britton*, as to what in substance amounts to specific performance, in preference to that of Branson J in *Warner Bros v Nelson*.

Warren v Mendy[45]

The facts in *Warren v Mendy*

4.24   The leading case in this area now is the decision of the Court of Appeal in *Warren v Mendy*.[46] The boxer Nigel Benn entered into a management agreement with the promoter and manager Frank Warren for a three-year term. One of Benn's obligations under the management agreement was not to enter into any agreement with any other manager without obtaining the prior written consent of Warren. Following a breakdown of the relationship between Benn and Warren, the boxer appointed Ambrose Mendy to advise him on all matters

---

[40]   See n 35 above 34–6.
[41]   See n 35 above 42–3.
[42]   See n 35 above 45.
[43]   1 July 1982.
[44]   ibid 7.
[45]   [1989] 1 WLR 853, CA.
[46]   ibid.

relating to his career. Warren obtained from Roch J a without notice injunction until trial restraining Mendy from inducing a breach by Benn of the management contract with Warren and from acting as Benn's manager or agent in relation to his boxing activities. The injunction was discharged by Pill J, a decision upheld by the Court of Appeal.

The issue in *Warren v Mendy*

The issue facing the court was summarized by Nourse LJ (giving the judgment of the court) **4.25** in the following terms:

> It is well settled that an injunction to restrain a breach of contract for personal services ought not to be granted where its effect will be to decree performance of the contract. Speaking generally, there is no comparable objection to the grant of an injunction restraining the performance of particular services for a third party, because, by not prohibiting the performance of other services, it does not bind the servant to his contract. But a difficulty can arise, usually in the entertainment or sporting worlds, where the services are inseparable from the exercise of some special skill or talent, whose continued display is essential to the psychological and material, and sometimes to the physical, well-being of the servant. The difficulty does not reside in any beguilement of the court into looking more tenderly on such who breach their contracts, glamorous though they often are. It is that the human necessity of maintaining the skill or talent may practically bind the servant to the contract, compelling him to perform it.[47]

Reconciling the earlier cases

Before embarking on a consideration of the authorities, Nourse LJ emphasized that an **4.26** injunction is a discretionary remedy, whose grant or refusal, especially at an interlocutory stage, depends on the infinitely variable facts of the individual case. Although statements of the principles on which the discretion ought to be exercised in some particular area are often authoritative, they are principles of practice rather than of law, whose application may be rendered inappropriate by the finest of factual variations between one case and another.[48]

Having reviewed the authorities,[49] the court concluded that, special considerations apart, **4.27** they were firmly with Oliver J in the *Nichols* case in preferring the approach of Stamp J in *Page One Records Ltd v Britton* to that of Branson J in *Warner Bros v Nelson*, both on grounds of realism and practicality and because that approach is more consistent with the earlier authorities. Any of those cases could be explained by the particular considerations which there arose, but the court agreed with Oliver J in thinking that the most significant feature of each of those in which an injunction was granted before *Warner Bros v Nelson* was that the term of the engagement was short, in none of them exceeding twenty weeks. Although it was impossible to state in general terms where the line between short- and long-term engagements ought to be drawn, it was obvious to the court that an injunction lasting for two years or more (the period applicable in *Warren v Mendy*) may practically compel performance of the contract.[50] The court very much doubted whether a want of mutuality alone would now

---

[47] [1989] 1 WLR 853, CA, 857. It will be remembered that Nourse J (as he then was) gave judgment in *Lotus Cars v Jaguar Cars* (n 43 above).

[48] [1989] 1 WLR 853, CA, 860.

[49] *Lumley v Wagner* (n 5 above); *Whitwood Chemical Co v Harman* (n 9 above); *Warner Bros v Nelson* (n 17 above); *Page One Records Ltd v Britton* (n 29 above); and *Nichols Advanced Vehicle Systems v De Angelis* (n 35 above). *Evening Standard Co Ltd v Henderson* [1987] ICR 588, CA, paras 4.34–4.41 below, was cited in argument but not referred to in the judgment.

[50] [1989] 1 WLR 853, CA, 865.

be decisive in a case of this kind.[51] But the presence of obligations involving mutual trust and confidence it thought may well be decisive, not merely because they are not mutually enforceable but because their enforcement, more especially where the servant's trust in the master may have been betrayed or his confidence in him has genuinely gone, will serve the better interests of neither party.[52]

Principles stated in *Warren v Mendy*

4.28 Consideration of the authorities led the Court of Appeal in *Warren v Mendy* to believe that the following general principles are applicable to the grant or refusal of an injunction to enforce performance of the servant's negative obligations in a contract for personal services inseparable from the exercise of some special skill or talent:[53]

(1) In such a case the court ought not to enforce the performance of the negative obligations if their enforcement will effectively compel the servant to perform his positive obligations under the contract.

(2) Compulsion is a question to be decided on the facts of each case, with a realistic regard for the probable reaction of an injunction on the psychological and material, and sometimes the physical, need of the servant to maintain the skill or talent.

(3) The longer the term for which an injunction is sought, the more readily will compulsion be inferred.

(4) Compulsion may be inferred where the injunction is sought not against the servant but against a third party if either the third party is the only other available master or if it is likely that the master will seek relief against anyone who attempts to replace him.

(5) An injunction will less readily be granted where there are obligations of mutual trust and confidence, more especially where the servant's trust in the master may have been betrayed or his confidence in him has genuinely gone.

4.29 The court emphasized that in stating these principles, it was not to be taken as intending to pay anything less than a full and proper regard to the sanctity of contract. To that end a judge would scrutinize most carefully, even sceptically, any claim by the servant that he is under the human necessity of maintaining the skill or talent and thus will be compelled to perform the contract, or that his trust in the master has been betrayed, or that his confidence in him has genuinely gone. But if, having done that, the judge is satisfied that the grant of an injunction will effectively compel performance of the contract, he ought to refuse it.[54]

4.30 The court made a final general observation in regard to damages which it is well to remember. Although it is often assumed that damages will not be an adequate alternative remedy to the grant of an injunction, the court in *Warren v Mendy* did not think that it can be assumed that they will always be an inadequate remedy now that damages are invariably assessed by a judge or master. The court suggested, for example, that in a case like *Warren v Mendy* it would be open to the court to refuse injunctive relief at the interim stage on an undertaking by the defendant to keep full and proper accounts of his receipts from acting on behalf of the servant and to pay a specified proportion of them into court or into a joint account. An arrangement

---

[51] ibid 866. cf Stamp J in *Page One Records Ltd v Britton* (n 29 above).

[52] [1989] 1 WLR 853, CA, 866.

[53] ibid 867. Nourse LJ explained that he used the expressions 'master' and 'servant' for ease of reference and not out of any regard for the reality of the relationship in many of these cases.

[54] ibid 867.

such as that would achieve the twin objectives of going some way to quantify the claimant's damages and preserving funds to meet any award which might later be made.[55]

Subsequent developments

Subaru Tecnica International Inc v Burns[56] was similar on its facts to the *Nichols* case, this time **4.31** involving a racing driver in the World Rally Championship who sought to leave Subaru and join Peugeot in breach of a negative covenant. It was argued for the claimant, in support of its application for an injunction to restrain this breach, that the general principle that a court should not enforce the performance of negative obligations in a contract for personal services, if the effect of so doing would be to compel performance of the positive obligations, applies only where the court is satisfied that the defendant's trust has been betrayed by the employer, or that his confidence in him has genuinely gone.[57] Nicholas Strauss QC (sitting as a Deputy High Court Judge) considered that if one were starting with a blank sheet of paper, without being constrained by earlier authorities, there might be much to be said for a general principle which enabled the court to grant an injunction which did have the effect of compelling performance, if satisfied that the relationship between the parties before the litigation was sufficiently sound to enable the contract satisfactorily to be performed, and that the litigation itself had not damaged it. Nevertheless he did not think the claimant's submission was consistent with any of the earlier authorities or with the statement of general principle in *Warren v Mendy* itself. The tenor of the judgments in the earlier cases is that there is a rule or settled practice of general application to all contracts for personal services involving a close relationship between the parties which applies, whatever may have been the circumstances giving rise to the dispute and even in cases in which there is no question of the employer having done anything wrong at all. It is the nature of the contractual relationship between the parties which calls for the application of the principle, irrespective of the details of the dispute.[58]

C. The emergence of garden leave

The concept of garden leave emerged in the late 1980s. It was given impetus by a trilogy of **4.32** cases between 1986 and 1993. Two of those cases were in the Court of Appeal, namely *Evening Standard Co Ltd v Henderson*[59] and *Provident Financial Group plc v Hayward*.[60] As will be seen below, in neither of these cases did the court grant a garden leave injunction in the sense in which it is understood today. However, the analysis undertaken in those two cases laid the foundation for the court's later enforcement of garden leave by injunction

---

[55] ibid 868. More recent support for the view that the adequacy of damages should not be ruled out was provided by Mackay J in *Aon Ltd v JLT Reinsurance Brokers Ltd* [2010] IRLR 600, who explained at para 26 that: 'It is not the same thing . . . to say damages may be difficult to prove as to say that damages are an inadequate remedy.' Cf *Tullett Prebon plc v BGC Brokers LP* [2010] IRLR 648, paras 223, 227.

[56] [2002] SLR 121.

[57] ibid para 82.

[58] ibid paras 83–4. There is no such rule or settled practice where the contract for personal services is more in the nature of a commercial arrangement between companies involving the employment of no named individuals, and where the services are not 'personal' in nature, notwithstanding the fiduciary obligations owed by one commercial entity to another: *Lauritzencool AB v Lady Navigation Inc* [2005] 1 WLR 3686, CA (time charter); *Regent International Hotels (UK) Ltd v Pageguide Ltd*, CA, The Times, 13 May 1985, Court of Appeal (Civil Division) Transcript No 164 of 1985 (hotel management contract).

[59] [1987] ICR 588, CA.

[60] [1989] ICR 160, CA.

which it first did, so far as reported cases are concerned, in the third case of the trilogy, *GFI Group Inc v Eaglestone*.[61] The grant of an injunction in aid of garden leave became more commonplace in a number of later cases in the 1990s and beyond.[62]

4.33 This trilogy of cases is examined below. It is important to do so not merely out of historical interest but because it will assist in understanding garden leave injunctions, as they have come to be known. This developing jurisprudence has given rise to a number of contentious issues, some of which remain unresolved, and which will be considered in detail after a discussion of the three early cases.

Evening Standard Co Ltd v Henderson[63]

The facts of *Evening Standard v Henderson*

4.34 Henderson was the production manager for the *Evening Standard* newspaper. His contract required one year's notice of termination. It also contained a provision that he would devote his entire services to his employer and not engage in outside work without his employer's prior permission. Robert Maxwell planned to start a rival newspaper to the *Evening Standard* and offered Henderson a job. Henderson gave two months' notice of termination instead of the twelve months' required by his contract. The *Evening Standard* sought until trial an injunction restraining the defendant from (a) working for the rival newspaper or otherwise acting in breach of his duty of good faith owed to the claimant, and (b) disclosing to a competitor confidential information belonging to the claimant. Evans J refused the application, and the claimant successfully appealed. The injunction sought was to last until the expiry of the defendant's contractual notice period which was a further ten months after the Court of Appeal hearing. In the present day, such injunctions would generally be sought and granted (if at all) only until speedy trial which can take place within two to three months of the interim hearing (if not sooner). Such an approach has been customary since the decision of the Court of Appeal in *Lawrence David Ltd v Ashton*[64] which post-dated *Evening Standard v Henderson*. It does not appear from the report of the latter case that consideration was given to ordering a speedy trial, which in any case would have taken longer to come on in the 1980s than it would today. The decision, therefore, appears to have proceeded on the basis that the interim injunction granted would probably remain in place for the unexpired ten months of the defendant's notice period. This is significant in view of the court's explanation in *Warren v Mendy* that the cases in which injunctions were granted to enforce negative covenants in contracts of personal service prior to *Warner Bros v Nelson* concerned short-term engagements no longer than about twenty weeks. In contrast, the injunction granted against Henderson was potentially to last more than twice that length of time.

The claimants' undertakings

4.35 Evans J's refusal to grant an injunction was based on the ground that its effect would be to compel Henderson during the remaining ten months of his contractual notice period either

---

[61] [1994] IRLR 119, [1994] FSR 535.

[62] eg *Euro Brokers Ltd v Rabey* [1995] IRLR 206; *William Hill Organisation Ltd v Tucker* [1999] ICR 291, CA; *Symbian Ltd v Christensen* [2001] IRLR 77, CA; *Crystal Palace FC (2000) Ltd v Bruce* [2002] SLR 81.

[63] [1987] ICR 588, CA. See P Goulding, 'Injunctions and Contracts of Employment: the Evening Standard Doctrine' (1990) 19 ILJ 98.

[64] [1989] ICR 123, CA.

not to work at all or to work nominally for the claimants.[65] In the Court of Appeal, Lawton LJ referred to what he described as a body of trite law which governs the sort of situation with which the claimants were faced, namely that you cannot get an injunction against an employee under a contract of service to enforce a negative covenant if the consequences of that injunction would be to put the employee in the position that he would either have to go on working for his former employers or starve or be idle. He referred to *Warner Bros v Nelson* but thought it was not clear what was meant in the authorities by being idle.[66] The claimants sought a way out of this problem by offering several undertakings. First, they undertook to pay the defendant his salary and other contractual benefits until such time as his notice, if it had been in proper form, would have run out. This reflected the fact that the claimants did not accept the defendant's repudiatory breach of contract (in purporting to leave without giving the full twelve months' contractual notice) as bringing the contract to an end, but rather kept the contract alive. In those circumstances, the claimants felt bound to perform the contract on their side.[67] Secondly, the claimants undertook not to seek to claim any damages against the defendant for the period when he was not working for them. The reason for this was that if they had been in a position to claim damages from him, their undertaking to pay his salary would have been of no value at all because they would have been able to say: 'As a result of your breach of contract and your not working for us, we have had to pay your salary. We claim it back by way of damages.'[68] Thirdly, the claimants offered[69] to have the defendant working for them as their production manager for the balance of his notice period. In fact, he had continued working in that capacity since his resignation up to the date of the appeal hearing.[70]

The Court of Appeal's decision

Applying the principles of the *American Cyanamid* case,[71] the court considered that there was **4.36** a serious issue to be tried as to the appropriate remedy for the defendant's seeming clear breach of contract. The question for the court was: what, in the circumstances of this case, was the balance of convenience? If the defendant left his employment straightaway and joined the rival newspaper shortly thereafter, the claimants would undoubtedly suffer damage which would be almost impossible to quantify. It followed, on the face of it, that the defendant ought not, pending trial, to be allowed to do what his contract was intended to stop him doing, namely working for somebody else during the period of his contract. But, against that had to be balanced what Lawton LJ had described as trite law:

> The injunction must not force the defendant to work for the plaintiffs and it must not reduce him, certainly to a condition of starvation or to a condition of idleness, whatever that may mean on the authorities on this topic. But all that, in my judgment, is overcome by the fact that the plaintiffs have made the offer they have. The defendant can go back to work for them. If he elects not to go back (and it will be a matter entirely for his election: there will be nothing in the judgment which forces an election on him) he can receive his salary and full contractual benefits under his contract until such time as his notice would have expired had it been for the proper period.[72]

---

[65] See the first ground of appeal, [1987] ICR 588, CA, 590.
[66] ibid 592.
[67] ibid 592–3.
[68] ibid 593.
[69] This is referred to by Lawton LJ as an 'offer' not an 'undertaking', although nothing seems to turn on the distinction since it appears to have been treated as tantamount to an undertaking.
[70] ibid 593.
[71] See paras 10.30–10.51 below for a discussion of the *American Cyanamid* principles.
[72] [1987] ICR 588, 594.

It followed that the balance of convenience favoured granting an injunction until trial.

Lessons of *Evening Standard v Henderson*

4.37 There are a number of points to note about the decision in *Evening Standard v Henderson*. First, it is not really a garden leave case. It did not involve the employer requiring the employee to stay away from work on garden leave. On the contrary, as appears from the third offer made by the claimants, they were content to allow the defendant to continue working in his normal role until trial. Whilst the injunction sought and obtained did restrain Henderson from working for a competitor until trial or the earlier expiry of his contractual notice period, he was free to return to work if he so wished. He was not put on garden leave.

4.38 Secondly, it is interesting to see how the decision was sought to be reconciled with the trite law, as Lawton LJ described it, namely the earlier authorities concerning the rule against specific performance.[73] Balcombe LJ, who was the other member of the two-judge court, was given a moment's pause by the Court of Appeal decision in *Whitwood Chemical Co v Hardman*.[74] However, that case was distinguishable from the present one, in his judgment, for two reasons: first, there was no negative restriction in the contract of employment there as there was here, and, secondly, the width of the injunction that was there sought. Having regard to the undertakings which the *Evening Standard* had offered, Balcombe LJ thought that the judge had been wrong to refuse the injunction. It is clear from this that Balcombe LJ considered that the undertaking to continue paying the defendant's salary and other contractual benefits was sufficient to overcome any concerns arising from the rule against specific performance. What is particularly noteworthy is that, had it been material, Balcombe LJ would have gone further. He was inclined to accept the alternative ground of the appeal raised by the claimants, namely that the evidence before the judge was not such as to indicate that there was no alternative employment at all, even in some other field, open to the defendant. To that extent, Balcombe LJ would have followed *Warner Bros v Nelson*.[75] It is, perhaps, significant that neither *Page One Records v Britton* nor the *Nichols* case, both of which cast some doubt on the correctness of the approach adopted in *Warner Bros v Nelson* (doubts echoed in the later Court of Appeal decision in *Warren v Mendy*) was cited in argument or referred to in the decision in *Evening Standard v Henderson*. Balcombe LJ's approach appears to mean that, as far as he was concerned, it was unnecessary for the claimants to undertake to pay the defendant's salary and other contractual benefits in order to obtain an injunction to stop him immediately joining a rival newspaper in breach of contract. In the light of this, it is arguable that an employer might still obtain an injunction today on a *Warner Bros v Nelson* basis to prevent an employee working for a rival during the continuance of his contract without undertaking to pay the employee's salary and other contractual benefits, albeit that would be an exceptional outcome.

4.39 Lawton LJ considered that the undertakings offered by the claimants were sufficient to overcome any concerns that the effect of the injunction would be to compel the defendant to work for the claimants on pain of idleness or starvation. Whether Henderson returned to work for the *Evening Standard* was 'a matter entirely for his election: there will be nothing in

---

[73] See paras 4.07–4.31 above.
[74] [1891] 2 Ch 416, CA.
[75] [1987] ICR 588, 595.

the judgment which forces an election on him'.[76] It is no doubt correct that Henderson would not starve as a result of the injunction having regard to the undertaking to pay his salary. But, if he was not to remain idle, he would surely have to continue working for the *Evening Standard* for ten months. It is not entirely easy to see why the injunction does not fall foul of the rule against specific performance in circumstances where the practical effect of the injunction is to compel the employee to return to work for his employer lest he remain idle for a period of ten months. The difference may be that Henderson did not have special skills or talent that required regular honing through work or publicity as in the case of a musician or boxer. Then again, the Court of Appeal was no doubt strongly influenced by the fact that Henderson appeared content to continue working for the *Evening Standard* in the meantime, as he had been doing. The real explanation may be that, in these circumstances, Henderson was not 'compelled' back to work by the injunction. Rather, he wanted to continue working. In such circumstances, the injunction had no effect on his current working arrangements; it simply prevented him joining a rival in breach of contract.

Thirdly, the underlying justification for the injunction appears to be that if he left prematurely, Henderson would be helping a rival of his employer before the expiry of his notice period. This is significant in view of the court's approach, developed in later garden leave cases, that an injunction will only be granted restraining an employee from joining a rival before his notice period expires if that is reasonably necessary to protect his employer's legitimate business interests.[77] Do those interests include not allowing an employee to assist a rival before his contract of employment ends? *Evening Standard v Henderson* suggests that this is indeed a legitimate interest. At the outset, the claimants argued that the defendant had acquired confidential information about the way the claimants produced their newspaper. When the matter was examined before Evans J it was clear that in law there was no confidential information which the defendant had acquired. What he had acquired was, as a result of doing his job, considerable expertise which would be valuable to a rival newspaper, but which could not in law be classified as confidential information.[78] However, it was obvious that the rival newspaper would very much like to get the services of an experienced production manager such as the defendant. 'If that newspaper could get his services when it started, it would benefit the new newspaper and injure the plaintiffs.'[79] **4.40**

Fourthly, it must be remembered that *Evening Standard v Henderson* involved an application for interim relief and was decided on the basis of *American Cyanamid* principles, namely a serious issue to be tried as to remedy and the balance of convenience pending trial. It seemed to Lawton LJ that as soon as possible there should be an examination in depth as to how the law stands in the kind of situation with which the court was confronted in this case. He stated the reason for this as follows: **4.41**

> There is a great temptation for employees, who have been bound by contract for a period to an employer, to break their contracts and go to other employers, usually for far higher salaries and, when they do (assuming that there is no question of confidential information), as the law stands at present, they can snap their fingers at their old employers because they can say: 'You cannot obtain an injunction against me which will have the effect of forcing me either to come

---

[76] [1987] ICR 588, 594.
[77] See paras 4.161 ff below.
[78] [1987] ICR 588, 592.
[79] ibid 591–2 *per* Lawton LJ.

back and work out my notice or starve, and it is no good your talking through your lawyers about paying damages because in the real word damages are impossible to quantify.' All the risk they are running in this kind of situation is that they will have to pay the costs of any legal proceedings.[80]

Lawton LJ concluded that it was time that some court examined the matter fully.[81] Although the emergence of garden leave has gone some way towards addressing Lawton LJ's concerns, there has not yet been the authoritative examination in depth for which Lawton LJ called all those years ago.

Provident Financial Group plc v Hayward[82]

4.42   The first reported case involving garden leave, and an application for an injunction in support of it, was *Provident Financial Group plc v Hayward*,[83] which was decided two years after *Evening Standard v Henderson*.[84] However, for the reasons discussed below, the court refused to grant an injunction and the defendant employee was, in effect, thereby released from his period of garden leave to join a competitor before the expiry of his notice period.

The facts of *Provident v Hayward*

4.43   Provident ran a chain of estate agents. Hayward, a chartered accountant, was employed as financial controller and subsequently financial director of the estate agency business. His contract was terminable on twelve months' written notice. It expressly provided that, during the continuance of his employment with Provident, he would devote the whole of his time, attention, and abilities to carrying out his duties under the contract and would not (unless otherwise previously agreed in writing by the company) undertake any other business or profession or be or become an employee or agent of any other person. A garden leave clause was also contained in the contract in these terms:

> . . . the company shall be under no obligation to vest in or assign to the executive any powers or duties or to provide any work for the executive, and the company may at any time or from time to time suspend the executive from the performance of his duties or exclude him from any premises of the company, but salary will not cease to be payable by reason only of that suspension or exclusion of the executive (unless and until his employment under this contract shall be terminated under any provision of this contract).[85]

4.44   Hayward gave notice of resignation to Provident on 1 July 1988 in order to take up employment with Asda Property Services as financial controller of their chain of estate agents' offices. Provident's and Asda's estate agency businesses were, at least to some degree, in competition with each other.[86] Provident agreed a six months' notice period (in substitution for the twelve months provided for in the contract) in return for Hayward entering into an express confidentiality covenant. His contract was, therefore, due to terminate on 31 December 1988. He worked his notice for a little over two months to 5 September 1988 until Provident

---

[80]   ibid 594.
[81]   ibid 595.
[82]   [1989] ICR 160, CA.
[83]   ibid.
[84]   See n 59 above. Judgment in *Provident v Hayward* was handed down one month before the Court of Appeal heard the appeal in *Warren v Mendy* (n 45 above).
[85]   [1989] ICR 160, CA, 163.
[86]   ibid 164.

required him to cease working at their premises. The reason for this was Provident's concern that Hayward might acquire further confidential information about Provident's business which it would or might be detrimental to them for him to have. The claimants undertook to pay the defendant's salary and provide his other benefits until the expiry of his notice period, provided he did not work for anyone else. In the first reported judicial recognition of garden leave, Dillon LJ observed: 'This expression is apparently known colloquially as "garden leave" and provisions to this effect are, we are told, commonly included in the current contracts of employment of senior executives.'[87]

A little over a month after being placed on garden leave, and with a little under three months of **4.45** his notice period remaining, the defendant informed the claimants that he proposed working for Asda within a matter of days. The claimants applied for an injunction which was refused. They appealed to the Court of Appeal. The first ground of appeal was that the judge erred in law in finding that the defendant could not be enjoined from breaking his contract because he would be 'idle' during the relevant period, despite the fact that he was being paid full salary and provided with all benefits by the claimants until the expiry of his notice period.[88] The argument essentially was that the employer's undertaking to pay the employee during garden leave did not answer the idleness objection referred to in the earlier indirect specific performance cases.

The Court of Appeal's decision

Dillon LJ acknowledged that it had been held that the court would not grant an injunction **4.46** which would prevent the employee working for anybody else at all, if the effect of granting such an injunction would be to compel him to go back to work for his previous employer. But they were all cases, he noted, in which no pay was being offered by the employer to the employee while the employee was away from the employer's business. 'The notion was that, without pay and enjoined from obtaining any work, the employee would be left to starve and the court could not force him back to work as the only alternative to starvation because that would be tantamount to specifically enforcing the contract of employment.'[89] Here, how-ever, there was no question of the defendant starving because he was offered his full pay up to the termination of his contract. Dillon LJ then considered *Evening Standard v Henderson* which he described as the only case, so far as he was aware 'in which that sort of situation arose'. But he concluded, correctly, that the case went off on a different aspect because the *Evening Standard* was prepared to continue to employ Henderson in his same job during the period of notice so that he was not going to be deprived of work and left on garden leave.[90]

But what of the concern, expressed in the earlier authorities, of the employee being idle as a **4.47** result of an injunction to restrain him working for another with the possible result that he is compelled back to work? Dillon LJ recognized that it was not enough that the employee had contracted in certain terms and would not starve if the terms were enforced against him while the employer continued to pay him in full. 'The employee has a concern to work and a concern to exercise his skills. That has been recognised in some circumstances concerned with artists and singers who depend on publicity, but it applies equally, I apprehend, to skilled workmen and even to chartered accountants.'[91]

---

[87] ibid 164.
[88] ibid 162.
[89] ibid 165–6.
[90] ibid 166.
[91] ibid 168.

4.48   It became, so it seemed to Dillon LJ, a question of considering what detriment the claimants would suffer if the negative covenant against working for another was not enforced by injunction. This approach appears less concerned with whether the employee would feel compelled by idleness to return to work than with whether the degree of harm to the employer from the employee's competitive employment justified the grant of an injunction.

4.49   Taylor LJ's approach was slightly different. Having questioned whether idleness and starvation were to be considered conjunctively or disjunctively (a question he left unanswered), he did not think the present case raised any such spectres. There would be no starvation on account of the undertaking to pay salary and other benefits. Even considering idleness per se as a separate matter, Taylor LJ thought it could hardly arise in this case. 'The defendant's skills as an accountant or financial director are unlikely to atrophy in a period of three months. Nor is he likely to suffer severe withdrawal symptoms for loss of job satisfaction over that period.'[92] It was, therefore, unnecessary for the court to grapple with the dilemma that might arise in circumstances where the employee felt compelled to work (because, for example, his skills might atrophy through idleness) and the employer exercised a contractual right to place the employee on garden leave. It is likely that this dilemma would now be resolved by the court striking a balance between the employer's need for protection, on the one hand, and the employee's need to exercise his skills, on the other, and limiting the duration of the injunction (and hence of enforced garden leave) accordingly.

4.50   In the event, the injunction was refused on the ground of the lack of harm to the claimants if the defendant joined the competitor before the expiry of his notice period. The three judges were agreed on this, each emphasizing the relatively short period of time until the defendant's employment terminated. For Dillon LJ 'there is no real prospect of serious or significant damage to the plaintiffs from the defendant working as financial controller in the administrative field that I have endeavoured to describe for Asda in the short period that remains until 31 December when he will be free to do so'.[93] Taylor LJ was 'not persuaded that any significant damage or detriment would result to the plaintiffs if the defendant, in the short period before 31 December 1988, works for Asda'.[94] As for Mann LJ: 'No serious damage is demonstrable in the space of the next six weeks.'[95] This emphasis is instructive. It is sometimes tempting to approach the question of the appropriate duration of a garden leave injunction by asking at what point the harm to the defendant employee is such that his enforced idleness should no longer be prolonged. In contrast, the Court of Appeal in *Provident v Hayward* put the spotlight on whether the harm to the employer from the employee's competition in breach of contract was serious enough to justify the grant of injunctive relief at all and, if so, for how long.

Lessons of *Provident v Hayward*

4.51   There are a number of other observations in the judgments of the court which are potentially significant for other cases. First, Dillon LJ suggested that there are limits to an employer's reliance on garden leave in order to protect itself from competition.

> The practice of long periods of 'garden leave' is obviously capable of abuse. It is a weapon in the hands of the employers to ensure that an ambitious and able executive will not give notice

---

[92] ibid 170.
[93] ibid 169.
[94] ibid 170.
[95] ibid.

if he is going to be unable to work at all for anyone for a long period of notice. Any executive who gives notice and leaves his employment is very likely to take fresh employment with someone in the same line of business not through any desire to act unfairly or to cheat the former employer but to get the best advantage of his own personal expertise.[96]

Secondly, the court acknowledged two types of interest which might justify the grant of an **4.52** injunction to restrain an employee working for a competitor during the continuance of his employment. It is not suggested that these two represent an exhaustive list of legitimate interests by any means. The first is the protection of confidential information. Here, Dillon LJ referred to Lord Denning MR's approach in *Littlewoods Organisation Ltd v Harris*,[97] namely that the difficulties in drawing the line between information which is and information which is not confidential, and in proving breach of a duty of confidence, may mean that the only practicable solution is to keep an employee from working for a competitor for a period of time. The second interest is in preventing an employee assisting a competitor whilst his employment continues. The court's approach to the question of whether this is a legitimate interest justifying the enforcement of garden leave is discussed in more detail below.[98] In *Provident v Hayward* Dillon LJ said:

> Of course, additionally, the defendant will, by his activities, be helping Asda which is in competition, to put its business on a sound administrative basis. He may thereby make it a better run business. Now, merely helping a competitor in that sort of way could not be restrained after the termination of the service agreement. On the other hand, for an employee to foster the profitability of a rival during the continuation of his employment could well, in appropriate circumstances, be restrained either under a clause in the contract like those in the defendant's contract, or as a breach of the duty of good faith.[99]

However, Dillon LJ did note that 'it is very common for employers to have somewhat exag- **4.53** gerated views of what will or may affect their businesses'.[100] According to Dillon LJ, the need to protect confidential information, or to prevent an employee from aiding a competitor, are matters to be considered not as questions of principle but as questions of discretion as to whether or not an injunction should be granted. He added words which have become a favourite of lawyers applying for injunctive relief on behalf of employers: 'I certainly would not wish to countenance the view that any employee can snap his fingers against his employers and disregard the notice provisions and obligations in his service agreement during his period of notice.'[101]

Thirdly, the court demonstrated the greater flexibility in its approach to the grant of an **4.54** injunction in aid of garden leave than is evident in relation to the enforcement of post-termination restrictive covenants. It was argued for the employee that the court could only grant an injunction in the precise terms of the relevant contractual covenant. This inflexible approach was rejected. The negative covenant in Hayward's contract was not to undertake any other business during the continuance of his employment. Dillon LJ observed: 'The lesser form of relief suggested, not to work during the continuance of the service agreement for specified rivals or rivals generally, if there were no express contract not to do so in

---

[96] ibid 165.
[97] [1977] 1 WLR 1472, 1479.
[98] See paras 4.208–4.211 below.
[99] [1989] ICR 160, CA 169.
[100] ibid 168.
[101] ibid 169.

the service agreement, could still be restrained as a breach of the employee's obligation of good faith.'[102] Taylor LJ considered that the court has power 'to narrow the scope of the contractual embargo'.[103]

GFI Group Inc v Eaglestone[104]

4.55 The first reported case in which an injunction was granted to restrain an employee from joining a competitor before the expiry of his notice period, which he was serving on garden leave, is *GFI Group Inc v Eaglestone*.[105] Nevertheless, the court declined to grant the injunction for the whole notice period, thereby demonstrating the flexibility of this remedy and proving a fertile source of argument for future cases.

The facts of *GFI v Eaglestone*

4.56 Eaglestone was a foreign exchange options broker. His employment was terminable on twenty weeks' notice, this period representing a negotiated compromise between the six months favoured by GFI and the three months proposed by Eaglestone at the commencement of his employment.[106] His contract of employment also contained a term that he would not, without the consent of GFI, during the continuance of the contract be interested in any other business.[107]

4.57 Eaglestone and two colleagues accepted offers of employment from a rival broker, Beresford Capital Market. Eaglestone's colleagues were entitled to terminate their employment on four weeks' notice, which they did, serving their notice before joining Beresford. GFI did not wish to have Eaglestone work out his notice and, in accordance with the approach taken in *Evening Standard v Henderson* and *Provident v Hayward*, they undertook to pay Eaglestone his salary and bonuses to the expiry of his notice period, and not to seek to claim back such sums as damages.[108]

The decision of Holland J

4.58 In exercising his discretion as to the grant of an injunction, Holland J placed some emphasis on the relationship which had been built up between Eaglestone and GFI's customers at GFI's expense. Beresford stood to benefit from this customer connection, built up through GFI's investment, should Eaglestone move immediately to Beresford. There was a real prospect of GFI sustaining loss in these circumstances, which would not readily be quantifiable.[109]

4.59 In considering the balance of convenience, the duration of the injunction exercised the judge. Given that Eaglestone's two colleagues had, by the time of the hearing before Holland J, already left GFI and started work for Beresford, the reality of the situation was that the

---

[102] ibid 167.
[103] ibid 170.
[104] [1994] IRLR 119, [1994] FSR 535.
[105] ibid.
[106] ibid para 12.
[107] ibid para 8.
[108] ibid paras 25–7. There is no indication in the report of the case that Eaglestone's contract contained a garden leave clause entitling GFI to require him to stay away from work, nor does this point appear to have given rise to any argument.
[109] ibid paras 29–35.

damage to GFI's customer connection to a certain extent had already been done. Bearing in mind the 'strong guidance from the authorities', as the judge saw it, that he should not grant more relief than was absolutely necessary to protect the situation,[110] Holland J with some reluctance granted an injunction for a period of thirteen weeks only, rather than the full twenty weeks of Eaglestone's notice period.[111] The recruitment of two colleagues on shorter notice periods thus benefited Eaglestone in the sense that he could start work for Beresford seven weeks earlier than would otherwise have been the case. Notwithstanding, and perhaps because of, the advantage gained by the employee, Holland J warned 'if there is a current impression that these periods in these contracts negotiated with these highly paid, highly skilled employees do not have the meaning that they purport to have, then the sooner that is corrected the better'.[112]

Some concepts defined

Against this background, and before looking in detail at some of the issues which have arisen in relation to garden leave, it may be helpful to define some of the concepts which are frequently used in this area. **4.60**

Garden leave

Strictly speaking, garden leave refers to the arrangement whereby an employer requires an employee to remain away from work and, generally, at home but not working whilst his contract of employment continues. But, life is never that simple. **4.61**

In principle, subject to the existence of an appropriate contractual term, garden leave may be imposed at any time during the continuance of the employment. It is more common, however, to put an employee on garden leave once notice of termination has been served, whether by the employer or the employee. The reason for this is that it is when an employee is heading for the exit door with the prospect that he will join a competitor, that the employer most wants to put distance between his business and the departing employee. **4.62**

There are also a number of add-ons which might strengthen the garden leave from an employer's point of view. For example, an employer might require an employee during garden leave to have no contact with customers, suppliers, or other employees. He might require the employee to return all company property, such as a laptop, mobile phone, or company documentation. He might instruct the employee to make himself available at home to be called on in order to deal with matters relating to his work and the employer's business. He might require the employee to resign any office held by him in the company, such as director. **4.63**

Garden leave is one way in which an employer can effectively put an employee in quarantine. But there are variations on this theme with a view to achieving the same end. For example, an employee might be given different responsibilities or allocated special projects to carry out. This arrangement would be designed to keep the employee away from matters relevant to his current job (and which might be of benefit to the prospective employer) whilst at the same time the employee provides some value for the money which the employer continues to pay him. **4.64**

---

[110] ibid para 38.
[111] ibid paras 40–1.
[112] ibid para 41.

4.65 Whether an employer is entitled as a matter of law to insist on any of these arrangements depends, in part, on what the contract provides. This is discussed further below. But these options reflect what in practice can, and often does, happen.

Garden leave clause

4.66 A garden leave clause is, at its simplest, an express term of the contract of employment which states that the employer is not required to provide the employee with work to do and may require the employee to stay away from work. There are, inevitably, degrees of sophistication of such clauses. Sample simple and long form garden leave clauses are set out in Appendix 4 below.

Garden leave injunction

4.67 A garden leave injunction is something of a misnomer. However, it is a term that has entered the legal lexicon in this context, and can refer to different forms of injunction which a court may grant in circumstances typically where an employee is on garden leave.

4.68 The most basic and common form of garden leave injunction is one which restrains the employee from working for another employer (whom it is better to identify by name) before the termination of his employment. It is preferable if this injunction can be based on an express negative covenant contained in the contract of employment that the employee will not, during the continuance of the contract, work for another. However, in the absence of such an express negative covenant, it may be possible to base such an injunction on the employee's implied duty of good faith.[113]

4.69 It will be apparent from this description that the injunction does not involve enforcement of any garden leave clause. However, the circumstances in which an employer seeks an injunction to restrain an employee from joining a competitor before the expiry of his notice period are, more often than not, those in which the employer puts the employee on garden leave. It might be more accurate, therefore, to describe this type of injunction as one in aid of garden leave.

4.70 However, where there is a garden leave clause of a more sophisticated variety, for example one which entitles the employer to insist on the employee having no contact with customers or colleagues, the court may grant an injunction to restrain breach of these ancillary provisions as part of the garden leave injunction.

Garden leave undertakings

4.71 Any garden leave injunction is conditional on the employer undertaking to the court, in addition to the claimant's usual cross-undertaking in damages, that the claimant will (a) continue to pay the employee his salary and provide his other contractual benefits; and (b) not seek to recover such sums by way of damages. These undertakings are discussed further below.[114]

D. Garden leave clauses

The right to work

4.72 The issue of idleness lies at the heart of the concept of garden leave. The starting point is the rule against indirect specific performance of contracts of personal service, which provides

---

[113] *Provident Financial Group plc v Hayward* [1989] ICR 160, CA, 167 *per* Dillon LJ.
[114] See paras 4.145 ff below.

that the court will not restrain breach of a negative covenant in a contract of employment by injunction where the effect of the court's order would be to leave the employee with no alternatives except to perform the services or to remain idle.[115] In *Evening Standard Ltd v Henderson*,[116] Lawton LJ summarized that 'trite law' as being that 'the injunction must not force the defendant to work for the plaintiffs and it must not reduce him, certainly, to a condition of starvation or to a condition of idleness, whatever that may mean on the authorities on this topic'.[117] However, the difficulty of what was actually meant by idleness in this context, as that term had been used in *Warner Brothers Pictures Inc v Nelson*,[118] was the example he gave of a problem which needed to be solved in this area of the law.

The Court of Appeal in *Provident Financial Group plc v Hayward*[119] was also concerned **4.73** with idleness but not with starvation. In that case there was no question of the employee starving because his employer had undertaken to pay the employee's salary and provide his other benefits until the expiry of the notice period, provided he did not work for anyone else. However, Dillon LJ took the view that the fact he might not starve was not a complete answer to whether the employer might place the employee on garden leave. 'The employee has a concern to work and a concern to exercise his skills. That has been recognised in some circumstances concerned with artists and singers who depend on publicity, but it applies equally, I apprehend, to skilled workmen and even to chartered accountants.'[120]

The full significance of the employee's concern to work and exercise his skills was not consid- **4.74** ered until the decision of the Court of Appeal in *William Hill Organisation Ltd v Tucker*.[121]

William Hill Organisation Ltd v Tucker

The facts in *William Hill v Tucker*

William Hill Index Ltd, a subsidiary of William Hill Organisation Ltd, was one of five **4.75** companies which offered spread betting. Tucker worked as a senior dealer for William Hill Index Ltd. Under his contract of employment Tucker was required to give six months' notice of termination. Tucker purported to resign on one month's notice to join City Index, one of William Hill's four spread betting rivals. William Hill replied that six months was required, that Tucker was not required to attend work, and that he would continue to receive his salary and other contractual benefits (including a bonus). It reminded him of his continuing duty of good faith as an employee.

William Hill applied for an injunction to restrain Tucker from joining a competitor until **4.76** the expiry of his notice period. The Judge (James Goudie QC, sitting as a Deputy High Court Judge) refused the application. He held that William Hill was under an obligation to provide work to Tucker which it did not do, entitling the employee to accept this repudiatory breach and bring the contract to an end. William Hill appealed to the Court of Appeal.

---

[115] See paras 4.07–4.31 above.
[116] [1987] ICR 588.
[117] ibid 594.
[118] [1937] 1 KB 209.
[119] [1989] ICR 160, CA. See paras 4.42–4.54 above.
[120] [1989] ICR 160, CA, 168.
[121] [1999] ICR 291, [1998] IRLR 31, CA.

4.77   The issue before the Court of Appeal was summarized by Morritt LJ (with whom Robert Walker and Stuart-Smith LJJ agreed), as follows:

> When an employee has given notice to determine his contract of employment, may his employer, whilst continuing to pay his remuneration, insist that he stay away from work for the duration of the notice period, colloquially known as sending him on garden leave? It is not disputed that he may do so if there is an express contractual power to that effect. The issue on this appeal is whether, in the absence of such a term, the employer was entitled to do so in the circumstances of this case.[122]

The approach of the Court of Appeal

4.78   Morritt LJ approached the matter in four stages. First, he dealt with what he described as the broad proposition upon which the judge had founded his decision, namely, that there was a duty on the part of the employer to provide a skilled employee with work and the opportunity to exercise his skills save where there is an express or implied right not to do so. He rejected that broad proposition, which was not supported by either party in the Court of Appeal.

4.79   Secondly, he identified the proper approach to be adopted. The issue of whether there is a 'right to work' is one of construction of the particular contract in the light of its surrounding circumstances. The crucial question is: what is the consideration moving from the employers under the contract of employment? Is it merely to pay a salary, or does the employer undertake some other additional obligation, such as to provide an opportunity for the employee to become better known, or to provide a reasonable amount of work? The answer will depend on the terms of the contract in the light of all the surrounding circumstances.

4.80   Thirdly, Morritt LJ identified certain situations in which the courts have recognized an obligation on the part of the employer to provide work. For example, such an obligation will arise in respect of actors who need to exercise their skills and gain publicity, or those engaged in specific projects such as employment on a particular voyage or in a specific and unique post, or where the remuneration depends on the employer providing the opportunity to earn it, for example where the remuneration is based on commission. However, he noted that the courts have been much more reluctant to find such an obligation in cases where the employee is engaged for an indefinite term and at a fixed wage or salary with no remarkable features, as, for example, in the case of a sales representative or domestic servant.

4.81   Fourthly, Morritt LJ acknowledged the change in social conditions in which the courts have increasingly recognized the importance to the employee of the work, not just the pay. He traced this back to a comment of Lord Denning MR in *Langston v AUEW*,[123] through to Dillon LJ in *Provident Financial Group v Hayward*,[124] although as Morritt LJ recognized the issue did not arise in that case given the existence of a garden leave clause in the contract. These changed social conditions must inform the legal approach to be adopted. But there are limits to this new approach. It was not suggested that there is an obligation to find work if there is none to be done, or none which can be done with profit to the employer. Nor is it said that the employer is bound to allocate work to the employee in preference to another employee if there is not enough for both of them. But, according to the decision in *William Hill*

---

[122]   [1999] ICR 291, 293.
[123]   [1974] ICR 180, CA; [1974] IRLR 15.
[124]   [1989] ICR 160, CA.

v Tucker, what the courts are now prepared to do is to find that there is a right to work in certain situations where previously there was none.

The critical issue, of course, is how does one distinguish between a situation where there is a **4.82** right to work from one where there is not. The *William Hill v Tucker* decision suggests that there are three factors which supported a right to work in that case.

(1) The post held by Tucker of senior dealer was a specific and unique post.
(2) The skills necessary to the proper discharge of his duties required frequent exercise.
(3) The contract provided for the hours and days of work, and imposed on the employee the obligation to work those hours necessary to carry out his duties. There was also an express right of suspension. This term would be unnecessary if an implied right to place an employee on garden leave existed. If the employer were entitled to keep his employees in idleness, the investment in his staff (a commitment referred to in the staff handbook) would be as illusory as the limited power of suspension would be unnecessary.[125]

Although the decision in *William Hill v Tucker* does not purport to identify a list of factors **4.83** which must exist for there to be a right to work, it is clear from the way in which the test was applied in that case that such a right is now more widespread than may have previously been supposed. Many employees in positions of seniority or importance are likely to be able to argue that their post is specific and unique. Equally, the need to exercise the skills necessary to the proper discharge of one's duties may arise across a whole range of skills and jobs. Furthermore, very many if not most written contracts nowadays identify specific hours and days of work, impose an obligation on the employee to carry out his duties in a full and professional manner, provide a limited power of suspension, and many staff handbooks contain some generalized reference to the employer's investment in staff.

The importance of a garden leave clause

The decision in the *William Hill* case emphasizes the importance of including an express **4.84** garden leave clause in contracts of employment. As Morritt LJ pointed out, if there is no right to work under the contract, then the employer is entitled to send his employee home on garden leave notwithstanding the absence of an express or implied power to do so because there is no contractual obligation to prevent him from doing so. However, if there is a right to work under the contract then, generally speaking, the employer needs a provision entitling him to send his employee on garden leave so as to absolve him from what would otherwise be a breach of contract.[126]

The criteria for a right to work in the *William Hill* case are likely to be satisfied in the case of **4.85** many senior employees such that there is a right to work under the contract. It follows that in the absence of an express garden leave clause it is in the very type of case where the employer most needs an injunction—because the employee is senior—that he will be least able to obtain one—because the imposition of garden leave without a garden leave clause will be likely to amount to a fundamental breach of the employee's right to work.[127] Furthermore, such a breach is likely to amount to a repudiatory breach, which, if accepted by the employee,

---

[125] [1999] ICR 291, 300–1.
[126] [1999] ICR 291, 301. In particular cases, however, the employee may forfeit his right to work because of his behaviour: see paras 4.87 to 4.99 below.
[127] Sample garden leave clauses are at Appendix 4 below.

will free the employee from both his notice period and cause the employer to lose the benefit of any enforceable post-termination restrictive covenants.[128]

4.86 It is important to remember that even where the contract contains an express garden leave clause, it does not follow that an injunction in its support will necessarily be granted.[129]

Placing an employee on garden leave without a garden leave clause

4.87 Two recent cases suggest that an employer may place an employee on garden leave notwithstanding the absence of a garden leave clause in the contract in circumstances where the employee is in breach of his duty of loyalty.

SG&R Valuation Service Co LLC v Boudrais[130]

4.88 Following the resignation of senior employees, who gave their required three months' notice, the employer discovered evidence of wrongdoing on their part including the misappropriation of confidential information, plans to divert business opportunities to a competitor, and solicitation of other employees to join that competitor. Having discovered the wrongdoing, the employer placed the employees on garden leave for the remainder of the notice period despite the fact that the contract did not contain a garden leave clause. The employees thereupon resigned, asserting a repudiation of their contracts by the imposition of garden leave, and sought to join the competitor with immediate effect. The employer applied for an interim injunction restraining the employees from working for the competitor until after expiry of their notice periods.

4.89 The issue which arose for determination was whether the employees could be compelled to spend their notice periods on garden leave in the absence of a garden leave clause in their contracts.

4.90 Cranston J began by outlining the approach adopted in the relevant authorities. They ask the question: under the contract of employment is there a right of an employee to work? If employees do not have that right to work, then they can be sent home and given no work, even though the contract continues. If they have the right to work, however, the subsequent question to ask is: in what, if any, circumstances does the employer have the right nonetheless to require them to stay away from work?[131]

4.91 The judge concluded that there was a right to work in this case, relying on three factors: first, the defendants' work was specialized requiring the regular exercise of significant skills; secondly, the defendants occupied high positions within the claimant; thirdly, they had a right to a bonus, and would be adversely affected by the inability to earn it.

4.92 Having decided there was a right to work, the judge then asked whether that meant that employers must always provide work and can never keep the employee away from it. He concluded that it did not: the right to work is not an unqualified right; it turns on whether the employee is ready and willing to work. Cranston J summarized the position as follows:

> Employees who have a right to work have that right subject to the qualification that they have not, as a result of some prior breach of contract or other duty, demonstrated in a serious way

---

[128] Under the well-established rule in *General Billposting Co Ltd v Atkinson* [1909] AC 118, HL. See paras 5.87 below.

[129] This issue is dealt with at paras 4.161 ff below.

[130] [2008] IRLR 770.

[131] ibid para 18.

that they are not ready or willing to work, or, to put it another way, that they have not rendered it impossible or reasonably impracticable for the employer to provide work. The breach of contract or other duty must constitute wrongdoing, by reason of which they will profit or potentially profit. In such circumstances, there is no obligation on the employer to provide work, although the contract of employment is ongoing.[132]

In this case, the employees exhibited behaviour which demonstrated that they were not ready **4.93** and willing to work in accordance with their contract of employment. There was, therefore, reasonable and proper cause for the employer to demand that they remain at home and it committed no breach of contract in doing so.

Standard Life Health Care Ltd v Gorman[133]

Cranston J's analysis in *Boudrais* was endorsed by the Court of Appeal in *Standard Life Health* **4.94** *Care Ltd v Gorman*. The defendants were agents who sold insurance for Standard Life, being paid on a commission basis. They resigned to join a competitor, Secure Health, an associated company of AXA. None of the defendants gave the required notice. Standard Life held the agents to their notice periods, suspended them without remuneration, and applied for an interim injunction restraining them from working for anybody other than Standard Life for the duration of their notice periods. A judge granted the injunction and the defendants appealed.

In the course of dismissing the defendants' appeal, Waller LJ, in his review of the authorities, **4.95** noted that in neither *William Hill* nor *Evening Standard* was it suggested that the employee was in breach of his duty of loyalty (other than by failing to give proper notice of termination). Waller LJ considered the question of whether obligations were interdependent to be important: there will be cases where it is necessary to analyse whether the obligation to pay, for example, and the obligation to provide work, is an interdependent obligation, ie one which only arises if the employee or the other party to the contract is fulfilling his obligations under the contract. Waller LJ explained: 'One is concerned first to interpret the contract and see where the obligations lie, and who has the obligations and at what stage, and in particular whether obligations are interdependent.'[134]

Waller LJ concluded that it was strongly arguable that the obligation in this case to provide **4.96** work had ceased to exist in circumstances where the agents had broken their duties of good faith. Even where the employer has decided not to accept that conduct as a repudiation, it was strongly arguable that the obligation to continue to supply work no longer continued. This was for two reasons: first, on the basis of Standard Life's express right to suspend in the event of a breach by the agent of the terms of the agreement; secondly, on the basis of Cranston J's analysis in *Boudrais*. As to the latter, Waller LJ said:

> It seems to me strongly arguable that in the circumstances of a case such as this, where the employer discovers that the employee has been in serious breach of duty and in breach of his duty of good faith, and then discovers that the employee is tied effectively to a rival already, and as here registered as an agent of a rival, then the employer has, even if he keeps the contract alive, no obligation to provide work; that obligation to provide work being interdependent with the obligation of the employee to act loyally.[135]

---

132 ibid para 24.
133 [2010] IRLR 233, CA.
134 ibid para 20.
135 ibid para 27.

4.97   Indeed, Standard Life was not required to undertake to pay the agents as a condition of the garden leave injunction since this was not required by the terms of the contract where the agent was suspended, and also having regard to the fact that the defendants were being paid by their new employer during this period.

4.98   Longmore and Jacob LJJ agreed with Waller LJ. Longmore LJ (with whom Jacob LJ also agreed) endorsed Cranston J's approach in *Boudrais* in the following passage:

> Quite apart from the arguments on suspension in the light of the particular clause in this case, it must in my view be at least arguable that Cranston J was right to conclude in the employment context . . . that an employee who has a right to work has that right subject to the qualification that he has not as a result of some prior breach of contract or other duty demonstrated in a serious way that he is not ready or willing to work, or that he has not rendered it impossible or reasonably impracticable for the employer to provide work.[136]

4.99   Employers would still be well advised to include an express garden leave clause in any service agreement but, in cases where such a clause is unavailable, the position of the employer is considerably strengthened by the decisions in *Boudrais* and *Gorman* in circumstances where the employee is guilty of misbehaviour.

The relationship between a garden leave clause and the notice period

4.100   It is not uncommon for an employer to put an employee on garden leave once notice of termination has been served. This is the critical period when the employer wants to distance the employee from the employer's affairs. However, it does not follow that an employer can put an employee on garden leave for the whole notice period. In practice, an employer may well wish the employee to work out the early part of his notice period before placing him on garden leave in order, for example, to effect a smooth handover of responsibilities.

4.101   An interesting issue arises in circumstances where an employer has placed an employee on garden leave for an intended period in excess of that which the court considers ought to be enforced by way of an injunction. Once the court-determined period has expired, is the employer required to allow the employee to return to work? Since the employer does not have the court's sanction to place the employee on garden leave for any further period, in principle it would seem to be a repudiatory breach of contract to prevent the employee from returning to work.[137] This would have significant implications for the enforceability of any post-termination restrictive covenants in the contract. This dilemma has not yet been explored by the courts but the solution may be to include a pay in lieu of notice provision in the contract, which would allow the employer lawfully to terminate the contract, albeit earlier than the period of notice would otherwise have expired.

The relationship between a garden leave clause and restrictive covenants

4.102   The relationship between a garden leave clause and restrictive covenants is dealt with at paragraphs 5.288 to 5.294 below.

---

[136]   ibid para 33.
[137]   This does not appear to have troubled Jack J in *Tullett Prebon plc v BGC Brokers LP* [2010] IRLR 648, where the conclusion of the twelve-month garden leave period that the court was willing to enforce fell within the duration of many of the departing employees' contracts of employment: see eg para 243.

E. Imposition of garden leave by the employer

Keeping the contract alive

In order to place an employee on garden leave it is necessary that the contract of employment **4.103**
is kept alive. Where an employee or employer gives contractual notice this will not cause any
difficulties: the contract will remain alive until the expiry of the contractual notice period.
Where an employee purports to resign and gives less than the contractual notice period or
threatens to work for another employer sooner, the employer is able to choose to affirm the
contract and keep it alive for the notice period: *Thomas Marshall v Guinle*.[138]

The importance of keeping the contract alive is highlighted by the case of *JA Mont (UK) Ltd v* **4.104**
Mills.[139] Mills was entitled to one year's notice. In February 1992 he entered into a written
severance agreement with his employer which provided that his employment was terminated
with effect from 29 February 1992. Under the terms of the severance agreement he was paid
compensation equivalent to a year's pay and was released from any further obligation to work
for Mont Ltd during that year. The payment was made on condition that he did not join
another company in the same industry as Mont Ltd within a year of leaving its employment.

Mills joined a competitor. Mont Ltd sought an injunction to enforce the restrictive covenant **4.105**
in the severance agreement. It accepted that on its face the covenant was too wide, but argued
that it ought to be construed in order to save it from being unenforceable in such a way that
Mont Ltd should be no worse off than it would have been had it chosen to keep the contract
of employment alive and placed Mills on garden leave. If that had been the case, Mills would
have been subject to an ongoing duty of good faith during that period.

Simon Brown LJ found Mont Ltd's arguments 'plausible, indeed attractive', but that ultimately **4.106**
they faced insuperable difficulties.[140] He noted that *Provident v Hayward*, so far from
blurring the distinction between, on the one hand, the position of employees after termination of their agreements and, on the other, employees still subject to their agreements and
still employed albeit on garden leave, in fact emphasized the distinction.[141]

It should be noted that Simon Brown LJ also rejected the argument that the claimants could, **4.107**
had they wished, have kept alive Mills' contract of employment for the twelve months of the
covenanted restraint. He held 'had the plaintiffs sought to put the defendant on 12 months'
"garden leave" or, indeed, simply provided him with inadequate work, he could have treated
that as constructive dismissal, and brought the contract to an end'.[142] He concluded that the
temptation to expand the court's powers by equating that particular post-employment case
with the 'garden leave' cases was to be resisted.

Trust and confidence

An issue which has arisen in a number of cases, but has never authoritatively been deter- **4.108**
mined, is whether it might be a breach of the mutual term of trust and confidence to place

---

[138] [1979] 1 Ch 227, 239, 242–3.
[139] [1993] IRLR 172, CA.
[140] ibid para 32.
[141] ibid para 37.
[142] ibid para 41.

an employee on garden leave. As noted in the previous paragraph, although the issue did not arise for determination in *JA Mont (UK) Ltd v Mills*,[143] Simon Brown LJ considered that were Mills to have been placed on garden leave for twelve months that would have amounted to a repudiatory breach of his contract such that he could have treated himself as having been constructively dismissed.[144]

4.109 In *TFS Derivatives Ltd v Morgan*,[145] the employee argued that a restrictive covenant should be rejected by the court because it would have been more appropriate for the employer to use a garden leave clause in order to obtain the protection which it sought. Cox J rejected this argument on the ground, amongst others, that it may be a breach of the implied term of trust and confidence to have placed an employee on a six months' enforced period of garden leave, even if pursuant to an express contractual term entitling the employer to do so.

4.110 It is suggested that the issue of whether placing an employee on garden leave might amount to a breach of the implied term of mutual trust and confidence will ultimately be likely to depend upon the justification provided by the employer for so doing. In circumstances where there are no legitimate interests to protect by use of a garden leave clause, or for the period sought to be imposed, it is more likely that an employee would be able to argue that its imposition was unreasonable and in breach of the implied term.

4.111 The continuing duty of mutual trust and confidence during a period of garden leave may also have repercussions for the terms which the employer may seek to impose during that period.[146]

When is an employee on garden leave?

4.112 The importance of establishing whether an employee has in fact been put on garden leave was made clear in *SBJ Stephenson Ltd v Mandy*.[147] Mandy was required to give six months' notice. However, he wrote to SBJ informing it that he wished to give notice to terminate his employment with immediate effect. SBJ replied, indicating that it would be seeking to enforce strictly the terms of his contract, including the requirement to give six months' notice, and reserved the right to place him on garden leave during that period. At a meeting a few days later, SBJ proposed that Mandy could be released sooner in return for his agreement to be bound by certain undertakings. According to Mandy, SBJ then placed him on garden leave. SBJ's understanding, however, was that it had been agreed that Mandy need not come into the office for a few days whilst he took legal advice on the proposals.

4.113 Shortly afterwards Mandy wrote to SBJ stating that by placing him on garden leave he had been prevented from carrying out his duties as divisional director. He said that he had taken legal advice and been informed that because there was no express clause in his service agreement which allowed SBJ to place him on garden leave SBJ had, following a recent court decision (being *William Hill v Tucker*) acted in repudiatory breach of his contract of employment. He purported to accept that breach, and claimed therefore no longer to be bound by the post-termination restraints set out in his service agreement.

---

[143] [1993] IRLR 172, CA.
[144] ibid para 41.
[145] [2005] IRLR 246.
[146] See paras 4.131 ff below.
[147] [2000] IRLR 233, [2000] FSR 286.

Bell J accepted the evidence of SBJ that Mandy had not in fact been placed on garden leave, **4.114** but that there had been agreement that he might remain away from work while he took legal advice with a view to resolving the basis upon which he would inevitably leave.[148] The result was that Mandy could not escape from his post-termination restraints on grounds of a repudiation by SBJ.

The effect of garden leave on the contract of employment

Where an employer places an employee on garden leave, the contract of employment may be **4.115** affected in three ways:

(1) The contract may itself expressly provide for different terms during the period of garden leave, for example, as to remuneration (see paras 4.145 ff below).
(2) The employer may choose to release the employee from particular duties which he would otherwise be required to perform under the contract of employment (see paras 4.136 ff below).
(3) Placing an employee on garden leave may affect the scope of those terms customarily implied into contracts of employment, notably the duty of good faith and fidelity.

The third issue, namely, the effect of garden leave on implied terms, first arose in connection **4.116** with the duty of good faith and fidelity in *Balston Ltd v Headline Filters Ltd*.[149]

Balston Ltd v Headline Filters Ltd

On 17 March 1986 Mr Head gave notice of resignation to Balston Ltd. Although he ought **4.117** ordinarily to have given three months' notice, by special arrangement it was agreed that his period of notice would expire on 11 July 1986 in order that he might retain the benefit of a share option scheme which required him still to be employed on 9 July 1986 in order to exercise his share options. On 16 April 1986 it was agreed that Head need no longer attend for work or otherwise perform any duties from 18 April for the remainder of his notice period (he was effectively on garden leave). On 2 May Head received a telephone call at home from a representative, Baker, of a long-standing customer of Balston. Baker was concerned that Balston had indicated that they would be increasing the price of their products very considerably. Head informed Baker that he was leaving Balston's employment, and that after the expiry of his notice period he would be prepared to supply those products to Balston's customer at the price previously offered by Balston. Following that call Head made active preparations for the company purchased by him on 25 April, Headline, to commence manufacture of the products as soon as possible after 14 July 1986.

Balston applied for an interim injunction to restrain Head and Headline from using certain **4.118** of its confidential information. In addition, Balston argued that Head should be restrained from taking the benefit of having set up Headline to compete with Balston and of having solicited the custom of Baker's company while employed by Balston on the grounds that this constituted a breach of Head's duty of fidelity to Balston. In particular, Balston argued that Head ought to have informed it of Baker's telephone call on 2 May 1986.

Scott J (as he then was) held that it was arguable that whilst Head had been released **4.119** from some of his duties of employment, the duty of fidelity survived. However, the

---

[148] [2000] IRLR 233, para 69.
[149] [1987] FSR 330 (Scott J), [1990] FSR 385 (Falconer J).

judge held that even if there had been past breaches of the duty of good faith during the period of garden leave, those did not sustain an interim injunction on their own account. Although he did not decide the point, he considered it 'highly questionable' whether an injunction, interlocutory or otherwise, could ever be justified on the grounds that the grant was necessary in order to deprive a contract breaker of the fruits of his breach of contract.

4.120 At trial, Falconer J held that Head continued to owe a duty of good faith during his period of garden leave.[150] However, whilst he found that there had been a breach of that duty by his entry into active competition for Baker's company's custom, he found that there had been no breach in not informing Balston of his telephone call on 2 May. The judge found that as at that stage his functions as an employee had ceased he was not under any duty to take any steps to further or advance Balston's business.[151] In other words, whilst the duty in principle survived, the scope of that duty depended upon the factual circumstances of the garden leave.[152]

Symbian v Christensen

4.121 Scott V-C returned to this issue as Vice-Chancellor in *Symbian v Christensen*.[153] Christensen's contract contained a garden leave clause entitling Symbian to suspend him from his duties and not require him to attend his place of work or provide him with any work during the period of notice, subject to Symbian providing the remuneration due to him during the relevant period. Christensen resigned in order to work for a competitor, Microsoft, and asked to be released sooner than this six-month notice period. Symbian sought an injunction restraining him from, amongst other matters, acting in breach of duties of good faith and fidelity owed to Symbian and implied into his contract of employment.

4.122 The Vice Chancellor was 'not impressed' by those implied duties being used as a platform for the grant of an injunction in such a case. He considered that a garden leave notice in effect puts an end to the relationship of employer and employee, involving obligations of good faith and fidelity both ways, although it does not put an end to the contractual relationship. This is because the garden leave notice not only requires the employee not to attend for work but forbids him to do so, just as it forbids him to take any part in the work of his employer or to enter upon his employer's premises. As such, the Vice-Chancellor considered that service of a garden leave notice fundamentally and irretrievably undermines the employment relationship between the parties. Nevertheless, the Vice-Chancellor granted an injunction restraining Christensen from being employed by Microsoft until the expiry of his six-month notice period based on the express restriction in his contract prohibiting him from working in any employment during the currency of the contract, which the Vice-Chancellor found continued to apply during the period of garden leave.

---

[150] [1990] FSR 385, 416.

[151] ibid 416.

[152] Similarly, Rix LJ's discussion in *Foster Bryant Surveying Ltd v Bryant* [2007] IRLR 425, CA, which refers to *Balston*, suggests that there is a public policy interest in allowing an outgoing employee to prepare to compete in the future and that, when considering an alleged breach of the duty of fidelity, the courts should adopt 'pragmatic solutions based on a common sense and merits based approach'. See, further, the discussion of *Foster Bryant* in paras 2.214–2.217 above.

[153] 8 May 2000.

Christensen sought permission to appeal. The Court of Appeal upheld the Vice-Chancellor's **4.123** order.[154] So far as the Vice-Chancellor's approach to the issue of fidelity was concerned, Morritt LJ noted that counsel for Christensen had 'confessed to some difficulty in seeking to justify that part of the Vice-Chancellor's judgment in his favour' but, as the court had heard no argument on the point from counsel for Symbian, it was not necessary to deal with the point and he said no more about it.[155]

It is suggested that the Vice-Chancellor's approach in the *Balston* case may be more readily **4.124** reconciled with that in *Symbian v Christensen* when the approach in the latter is limited to the facts of that particular case. Following the *Balston* case, the duty of fidelity or good faith may be attenuated during the period of garden leave depending on the factual circumstances. Thus, in the case of an employee who is required to provide some assistance with a handover of responsibilities during his period of garden leave, the scope of the duties of good faith and fidelity are likely to continue in a largely unchanged form. However, in the case of an employee who is not required to provide any services during the garden leave period, there is a very limited basis upon which to imply terms such as mutual trust and confidence or good faith, whether on the grounds of business efficacy or otherwise. Notably, in *Symbian v Christensen* there was no question of the employee being required to assist Symbian in any way during the period of his notice: rather, he was prevented from working in any way for the company, and prevented from entering the premises. In those circumstances, one can see how the duties of fidelity and good faith may have been attenuated nearly to vanishing point.[156]

RDF Media Group plc v Clements[157]

RDF Media v Clements lends support to the proposition that the nature and content of the **4.125** implied duty of trust and confidence is altered by a period of garden leave.

The claimant employer had purchased an independent television company of which **4.126** Clements had been the chairman and creative director. Clements' contract of employment with the claimant was terminable on six months' notice while the sale and purchase agreement contained restrictive covenants providing a three-year non-competition clause, which was reduced to two years if the claimant unlawfully dismissed him. Clements resigned from the claimant and indicated an intention to work for a competitor. The claimant refused to renegotiate the non-competition clause and placed Clements on garden leave.

In the days that followed, the claimant gave an interview to the press in which it referred to **4.127** Clements reneging on his contract and gave details of his 'dishonorable' conduct. Clements viewed these statements as defamatory and wrote to the claimant stating that he had been constructively dismissed. He then refused to accept further remuneration from the claimant during his notice period. The claimant responded by accepting Clements' letter as itself a repudiatory breach of contract.

One of the issues which fell to be determined was whether the claimant's statements to the **4.128** press amounted to a breach of the implied obligation of trust and confidence in circumstances where Clements was on garden leave at the time the statements were made.

---

[154] [2001] IRLR 77, CA.

[155] ibid para 47.

[156] This paragraph (in the previous edition of this book) was cited with approval in *RDF Media Group plc v Clements* [2008] IRLR 207, para 108.

[157] [2008] IRLR 207.

4.129   Bernard Livesey QC, sitting as a Deputy High Court Judge, held that the fact of garden leave was a relevant consideration in deciding whether there was a breach of this obligation. He explained:

> RDF argues that the effect of placing an employee on garden leave is to alter the nature and content of the implied obligation of trust and confidence. In my judgment that must be correct because whether there has or has not been a breach is a question of fact which must depend on the balance which is struck between the interests of the employer and those of the employee; where the balance is to be struck in any given case will depend on all the circumstances subsisting at the time in question and whether an employee is on gardening leave must be a relevant circumstance.[158]

4.130   The judge found that a campaign of vilification by the claimant in the press amounted to a breach of the obligation of trust and confidence, notwithstanding the fact that Clements was on garden leave. On the facts, however, Clements was unable to rely on this breach as he was himself already in repudiatory breach as a result of his prior transfer of loyalties to his prospective employer.[159]

The employer's rights during garden leave

Preventing the employee from working elsewhere

4.131   As the case of *Evening Standard v Henderson*[160] demonstrates, an employer may prevent an employee from joining a competitor whilst allowing him to continue to work for the employer during the notice period.

4.132   It is important to note that it does not necessarily follow from the mere fact that an employee has been placed on garden leave that he will be prevented from working for another employer. This issue arose in *Hutchings v Coinseed Ltd*.[161] Hutchings resigned from her employment with Coinseed. She wrote to Coinseed offering one month's notice and sought confirmation that Coinseed did not wish her to work the notice period. Coinseed replied confirming that it did not wish her to work her month's notice period but would pay her in lieu instead, which would be paid in the usual way at the end of the month. Her contract provided that Coinseed was entitled to pay her basic salary in lieu of notice, and that during any period of notice it was under no obligation to provide her with work and may, subject to continuing to pay her salary and providing her with other benefits due under her contract, require her to stay at home and do no work either for it or for anyone else.

4.133   Shortly after her resignation, Hutchings commenced work for a competitor. Upon discovering this, Coinseed refused to pay her salary for the period of notice. Hutchings claimed for these moneys. Coinseed argued that Hutchings had repudiated the contract by going to work for a competitor whilst still employed by them, on the modified basis set out in their correspondence. The Court of Appeal held that there had been no repudiation. It found that after the exchange of letters, there was no express obligation that Hutchings should not take another job. Equally, there was no implied obligation that she should not do so, given the fact that she had been released from further work for Coinseed.[162]

---

[158]   ibid para 106.
[159]   For a detailed discussion of this aspect of the case, see paras 5.118–5.124 below.
[160]   [1987] ICR 588, CA.
[161]   [1998] IRLR 190, CA.
[162]   ibid para 21.

However, this case would seem to be very much confined to its own facts. Although *Provident v* **4.134**
Hayward was referred to by the Court of Appeal in *Hutchings v Coinseed*, no consideration
appears to have been given to the suggestion in that case that to work for another employer
during a period of garden leave could amount to a breach of the duty of good faith.

Allocating different duties

An employer may wish the employee to continue to work during the period of notice, but to **4.135**
allocate to him different duties that do not, for example, involve customer contact. Whether
he can insist upon the employee undertaking such duties may depend upon whether there is
express provision for this in the contract. The simple sample garden leave clause at Appendix
4 below provides that the employer may, at its discretion, amend the employee's duties as part
of the garden leave arrangement. However, this does not mean that the employer's discretion
is unfettered. In line with the approach adopted in bonus cases,[163] the discretion would need
to be exercised rationally and not perversely, such that requiring the managing director to
work as a receptionist, for example, would almost certainly amount to a repudiatory breach
of his contract. An alternative analysis would be that in circumstances where the employee
continues to provide services to the employer, the duty of trust and confidence will continue in
full force, such that the allocation of duties inconsistent with the seniority of the employee
would amount to a breach of the implied term.

Requiring the employee to stay at home

The entitlement of an employer to require an employee to stay at home (albeit available on **4.136**
call) will be governed by the terms of the garden leave clause, where there is one. In the
absence of such a clause, following *William Hill v Tucker*[164] the imposition of garden leave is
likely to, although will not always necessarily, amount to a repudiation of the employment
contract.[165]

Before the recent development of garden leave, whether requiring an employee to stay at **4.137**
home during a period of notice amounts to a repudiatory breach of contract was considered
in *Spencer v Marchington*.[166] Spencer was employed by Marchington as general manager of
two branches of an employment agency. She was latterly engaged under a fixed-term contract
of one year from 1 June 1985 to 31 May 1986, which included a non-compete restrictive
covenant for a period of two years after termination. Spencer was to be remunerated at a rate
equivalent to 50 per cent of the profits made by the employment agencies during the trading
year to 31 May 1986. Marchington decided not to renew Spencer's contract when it expired.
This decision was communicated to Spencer by Marchington on 24 March 1986, just over
two months before the expiry of the fixed term contract. In view of Spencer's reaction to
being informed of that decision, Marchington decided that it would be better if Spencer
stopped work immediately and informed her that she need not work out her notice period.
Marchington confirmed that Spencer would be paid for her notice period at a rate of £1,000
per month, and the balance of moneys due would be given once the profits for the trading
year had been ascertained. Spencer subsequently opened her own employment agency, in

---

[163] eg *Clark v Nomura International plc* [2000] IRLR 766, CA, para 40.
[164] [1999] ICR 291, CA.
[165] Other than in those cases where the employee forfeits his right to work because of his own behaviour: see
paras 4.87 to 4.99 above.
[166] [1988] IRLR 392.

breach of the terms of the restrictive covenant in her contract. Spencer also claimed for an account of profits, in response to which Marchington counterclaimed for damages for breach of the restrictive covenant.

4.138 Spencer sought to defend the counterclaim on the basis not only that the restrictive covenant was unenforceable (as it was ultimately held to be), but that she had been constructively dismissed by her exclusion from the office on two grounds. First, she argued that being excluded from her appointment as general manager amounted to a fundamental and unwelcome change to her duties. Secondly, she argued that she was entitled to work in the business as general manager to ensure good profits because she was entitled to half of them. Thus, her exclusion from her appointment as general manager resulted in a unilateral reduction in pay.

4.139 The judge (John Mowbray QC sitting as a Deputy High Court Judge) accepted that Spencer was entitled to work in the business as a general manager to ensure good profits because she was entitled to half of them. He indicated that he was 'pretty clear' that excluding her from management at the start of her fixed term would have been a repudiation, although at the other end of the spectrum he would have been very surprised if an 'ordinary minor employee' at a wage being told not to work out a month's notice on dismissal involved a repudiation. However, he considered that asking Spencer to stay away from her desk from 24 March to 31 May was 'not quite important enough', even in the context of a twelve-month contract, to amount to a fundamental breach.

4.140 In the light of the decision in *William Hill v Tucker*, an employee in the position of Spencer might well now be able to argue that she had a right to work such that her exclusion from management in those circumstances was indeed a repudiation.

Contact with clients and other employees

4.141 An employer may wish to prevent his employee from having contact with his clients and/ or other employees during the period of notice. This is because the notice period provides the employer with the opportunity to consolidate the loyalty of his client base and workforce which are the very interests that placing the employee on garden leave are designed to protect. The sample long form garden leave clause at Appendix 4 below makes express provision for this at clause 1(c).

4.142 Difficult issues may arise in respect of social contacts. For example, an employee may wish to continue to meet other employees who might properly be regarded as friends above and beyond being mere colleagues. It is arguable that a blanket refusal to consider allowing an employee to attend, for example, an old friend's birthday party, would be so unreasonable as to constitute an irrational or perverse exercise of the requirement that he not contact other employees, alternatively a breach of the duty of trust and confidence, and thus a repudiation of the contract. In every case, it will depend upon the circumstances and the legitimate interest sought to be protected by the employer.

Return of property

4.143 An employer may wish an employee to return all documents and other materials belonging to the employer during the period of garden leave. The sample long form garden leave clause at Appendix 4 below makes express provision for this at clause 1(e).

4.144 An employer should be careful to ensure that he does not require the return of property which forms part of a contractual benefit to which the employee is entitled, such as to give rise to a breach of contract by the employer. For example, an employer should not require the return of a company car during the period of garden leave from an employee who is contractually entitled to its use. Similar issues may arise in respect of computers and PDAs.

The employer's duties during garden leave

Remuneration

In principle, any garden leave injunction will be conditional on the employer undertaking to the court, in addition to the claimant's usual cross-undertaking in damages, that the claimant will continue to pay his employee his salary and provide his other contractual benefits, and not seek to recover such sums by way of damages.[167]   **4.145**

Can an employer reduce the employee's contractual benefits which are payable during the period of garden leave? Many employment contracts which provide for participation in a bonus scheme now provide that the employee will not be entitled to any bonus if at the date of payment the employee is under notice to leave his employment. This type of provision would apply whether the employee continues in active employment or is placed on garden leave during that period. In principle an employer might go further and exclude an employee's entitlement to other benefits during the notice period, such as commission payments and entitlement to share options, as part of a garden leave clause.   **4.146**

The primary significance of the effect of such a provision would be its impact on the exercise of the court's discretion in deciding whether to grant an injunction in support of garden leave and for how long. Where an employee's remuneration is made up to a significant extent by commission or bonus payments, and the contract provides that he will not be entitled to those payments during his notice period, the court would be far less inclined to exercise its discretion to enforce a period of garden leave for any great length of time.   **4.147**

A more fundamental argument would be that such a clause fell foul of the Unfair Contract Terms Act 1977 and therefore could not be relied upon by the employer. This argument would face two hurdles. First, an employee would need to show that he had contracted with his employer as a 'consumer' within the meaning of sections 3 and 12 of the 1977 Act, alternatively on the employer's written standard terms of business. This proposition was supported by *Brigden v American Express Bank Ltd*,[168] in which Morland J held that contracts of employment are within the scope of section 3 of the 1977 Act. Secondly, an employee would need to show that the clause rendered a contractual performance substantially different from that which was reasonably expected of the employer or allowed it to render no performance at all of a relevant obligation to allow the employee to participate in a bonus/commission scheme, and did not satisfy the requirement of reasonableness in sections 3(2) and 11(1) of the 1977 Act.   **4.148**

Until recently, the principal difficulty with such an argument related to the second hurdle, based on the marked judicial reluctance to find that terms limiting the contractual payments to which an employee is entitled during his notice period fall within the scope of section 3(2)(b) of the Unfair Contract Terms Act 1977 as either entitling the employer to render a   **4.149**

---

[167] cf *Standard Life Health Care Ltd v Gorman* [2010] IRLR 233, where the terms of the contract did not require an agent to be paid whilst suspended (but where the court also had regard to the fact that the defendant agents were being paid by their new employer during their period of suspension).
[168] [2000] IRLR 94.

contractual performance substantially different from that which was reasonably expected of them or to render no performance in respect of any part of its contractual obligation. In *Brennan v Mills and Allen Ltd*,[169] His Honour Judge Peter Clark considered that a clause which provided that payment of commission was subject to the employee being in the employment of the company at the time of payment and not under notice, set out the employee's entitlement and limit of their rights and did not fall within section 3(2)(b). That approach was followed in *Peninsula Business Services Ltd v Sweeney*,[170] in which the EAT held that a clause providing that an employee had no claim whatsoever to any commission payments that would otherwise have been generated and paid, if he was not in employment on the date when they would normally have been paid did not fall within section 3(2)(b).

4.150 However, the whole issue was revisited by the Court of Appeal in *Commerzbank AG v Keen*.[171] Keen's contract provided that no bonus would be paid to him if on the date of the bonus he was not employed by the bank or if he was under notice to leave the bank's employment whether such notice was given or received by him. Keen was made redundant part-way through a performance year and not paid any bonus for that year. He claimed, amongst other matters, that the bank was not entitled to rely upon the provision purporting to exclude eligibility for a bonus when he was not employed by the bank as it fell within section 3(2) of the Unfair Contract Terms Act 1977 and did not satisfy the requirement of reasonableness.

4.151 Commerzbank applied for summary judgment on Keen's claim. In respect of his claim for a bonus for the performance year during which he had been dismissed, it argued, following the approach in *Peninsula v Sweeney*, that section 3(2)(b) of the 1977 Act did not apply. Morison J dismissed the bank's application.[172] He noted that 'the difference between a clause which excludes liability in respect of an accrued right on the one hand, and a clause which defines the ambit of a right on the other, is not easy to define'.[173] He considered that there was a respectable argument in that case for saying that the bonus was earned but was removed by the offending clause, in which case the clause might be struck down as being unreasonable under the 1977 Act. However, the Court of Appeal allowed the bank's appeal. It held that in relation to Keen's contractual terms as to remuneration he neither 'dealt as a consumer' with the Bank, nor were such terms the standard terms of the Bank's business. Accordingly, the 1977 Act did not apply.

4.152 Although there are no reported cases in which an employer has not given an undertaking to pay an employee's salary and other contractual benefits in order to obtain an injunction in support of a garden leave clause, in principle it might be open to an employer to argue that it would be unnecessary to do so. That argument could be founded on the approach of Balcombe LJ in *Evening Standard v Henderson*.[174] In that case Balcombe LJ considered that the undertaking to continue paying the defendant's contractual salary and other contractual benefits was sufficient to overcome any concerns arising from the rule against specific performance. However, he would have been inclined to go further and accept the alternative ground of appeal raised by the claimants, namely that the evidence before the judge was not

---

[169] Appeal Nos EAT/418/99, EAT/490/99, and EAT/549/99, Judgment 13 July 2000.
[170] [2004] IRLR 49.
[171] [2007] ICR 623, [2007] IRLR 132, CA.
[172] [2006] EWHC 785 (Comm).
[173] ibid para 30.
[174] [1987] ICR 588, CA.

such as to indicate that there was no alternative employment at all, even in some other field, open to the defendant. To that extent, Balcombe LJ would have followed *Warner Bros v Nelson*.[175] Such an outcome would be surprising given the subsequent development of the law on garden leave, but its possibility cannot be ruled out entirely.

Holiday

The requirement that the employer provide the employee with his contractual benefits during the period of garden leave will include his entitlement to holiday. **4.153**

The issue was considered in *Whittle Contractors Ltd v AR Smith*,[176] in which Smith brought a **4.154** claim for unpaid holiday pay. Smith's employment had terminated on 18 March 1994, but he had not been required to work from 26 January 1994. The employment tribunal decided that Smith was entitled to 4.66 days' holiday pay in respect of the period for which he had been employed in 1994. Whittle sought to appeal in reliance on the provision in Smith's contract of employment that holiday would be taken during the notice period, but if that was not convenient to the company, payment would be made in lieu. Whittle argued that as Smith had not actually worked since 26 January 1994, whilst he was on a paid leave of absence, he should be treated as having taken his holiday entitlement during the period of notice.

The EAT dismissed Whittle's appeal. It pointed out that if Smith had worked out his notice **4.155** period, and not actually taken holiday during that period, he would have been entitled to holiday pay in lieu. It rejected Whittle's submission that the position was different if the employee did not actually work out his notice period, and it was therefore as if he were already on holiday. It pointed out that the only reason that he was not actually working from 26 January was that he had a letter from the company saying that he would not be required to work from that date and would be paid in lieu. Payment in lieu included not only what he would have earned if he had actually worked during that period but also what he would have been entitled to as holiday pay in that period.

An employer can circumvent the result in *Whittle* through careful drafting. First, an employer **4.156** is entitled to provide that no contractual holiday entitlement over and above the holiday guaranteed by the Working Time Regulations accrues during a period of garden leave. Secondly, if the employee is not required to do any work during a period of garden leave, it is lawful to include a term which provides that any outstanding holiday as at the date of commencement of garden leave is deemed to be taken during that period: *Industrial and Commerce Maintenance Ltd v Briffa*.[177]

The employee's duties during garden leave

Duty of good faith

As discussed at paragraphs 4.117 to 4.124 above, although the implied duty of good faith **4.157** will ordinarily continue during a period of garden leave, it may be attenuated depending upon the circumstances. For this reason, it is advisable for any garden leave clause expressly to provide that the duty of good faith continues in full force and effect during the garden leave period (see clause 2 of each of the sample garden leave clauses at Appendix 4 below).

---

[175] [1937] 1 KB 209.
[176] EAT 842/94, Judgment 1 November 1994.
[177] UKEAT/0215/08/CEA, Judgment 22 July 2008.

Express duties

4.158 It is possible to provide for particular express duties to be owed by the employee during the period of garden leave. A common example of an express duty which is incorporated into a garden leave clause is that requiring the employee to give to the employer all such assistance and cooperation in effecting a smooth and orderly handover of his duties and responsibilities as the employer may reasonably require (see clause 3 of the sample long form garden leave clause at Appendix 4 below).

Directorships

4.159 Where an employee is a director of the company by whom he is employed, difficult issues may arise. Once the director is placed on garden leave, it is highly unlikely that the company would wish to allow the employee to continue to attend board meetings or take any management role. In order to avoid the risk that exclusion from management would constitute a repudiatory breach of contract, the employer should include a provision in the garden leave clause entitling it to require the employee to resign all offices upon placing him on garden leave (see clause 1(e) of sample long form garden leave clause at Appendix 4 below).

4.160 Care must be taken when drafting such a clause. A contractual term that purports merely to relieve a director of his duties when on garden leave is liable to be void in view of section 232 of the Companies Act 2006, which prohibits a director and company from contracting out of the director's liability. A term requiring resignation of office is strongly advisable. So as to secure a director's resignation, in the face of his own refusal to resign, it is advisable to include a power of attorney clause providing that each director is appointed attorney of the other to execute all documents which that director is obliged to execute. Where such a power of attorney clause is included, the contract should be executed as a deed.[178]

F. Enforcement of garden leave by the court

The general approach

4.161 A key purpose of a garden leave clause is that, if all else fails, an employer can enforce the period of garden leave through the courts in order to protect its business. This means applying for—and, more importantly, obtaining—an interim (and, occasionally, a final) injunction.

4.162 Before embarking on this (expensive) process it is necessary to remember three important matters. In the first place, a court will expect any garden leave clause to be justified on similar grounds as a restrictive covenant. That is to say, the claimant must have a legitimate interest to protect, and it must protect it reasonably, otherwise the court will decline to grant an injunction.[179] Secondly, the court shows greater flexibility in cutting down the terms of the contractual embargo when dealing with garden leave than it does with a restrictive covenant. So, even though an employer might obtain an injunction, it may be for less than the full notice period. The third point is crucial and underpins the two points already made: an

---

[178] Powers of Attorney Act 1971, s 1(1).

[179] The restraint of trade doctrine applies to restraints imposed during the subsistence of the contract: see *Symbian v Christensen* [2001] IRLR 77, CA, para 45, relying on *Esso Petroleum v Harper's Garage* [1968] AC 269, 328–9, and *Instone v Schroeder* [1974] 1 WLR 1308, 1315.

injunction is a discretionary remedy. That means that the court will need to be satisfied that it is 'just and convenient' before granting it.

The need for justification

In *Cantor Fitzgerald International v George*,[180] the Court of Appeal considered together both the application for permission to appeal and the substantive appeal brought by Cantor Fitzgerald International ('Cantor') against a first instance decision which allowed four of its brokers to leave for a rival firm. The brokers had indicated their intention to leave Cantor only six weeks after joining. Perhaps not surprisingly this had prompted a negative written reply by Cantor, which the judge at first instance held to constitute a repudiatory breach, so releasing the brokers from their contractual obligations. **4.163**

Cantor sought to overturn this on appeal, and the Court of Appeal indicated that it was by no means sure that it would have agreed with the judge that Cantor's letter constituted a repudiatory breach. Notwithstanding this, the appeal failed because the brokers in question were already working for a new employer by the time Cantor notified them that it was appealing the judge's decision.[181] **4.164**

The case is important for the statement of principle by Sir Thomas Bingham MR (with whom Peter Gibson and Schiemann LJJ agreed) as to the criteria for determining the appropriate period of garden leave: 'The learned judge, quite rightly, directed himself in terms of consideration of the period of restraint reasonably necessary to protect the plaintiff's legitimate interests . . . It is, I think, common ground that the period of restraint should be the minimum necessary for legitimate purposes and not the maximum.'[182] **4.165**

This emphasis on the need to justify a garden leave clause by reference to an employer's 'legitimate interests' is echoed and underlined in *William Hill Organisation Ltd v Tucker*.[183] As set out in more detail above,[184] Tucker planned to leave William Hill to join a rival spread betting organization. In response, William Hill attempted to keep him to his agreed notice period by placing him on garden leave. In the absence of an express garden leave clause, both the judge at first instance and the Court of Appeal considered that William Hill was unable to do so because Tucker, under his contract of employment, had a right to work and not just to pay. A second point raised was whether, if William Hill had the right to place Tucker on garden leave, the judge was correct in indicating that he would have granted an injunction for three months (rather than the full six months' notice period) on the basis that William Hill had a legitimate interest in preserving a stable workforce. Morritt LJ did not deal with the specifics of this, but emphasized as follows: **4.166**

> . . . there appears to be a trend towards increasing reliance on garden leave provisions in prefer-ence to conventional restrictive covenants, no doubt because hitherto the courts have treated

---

[180] 17 January 1996.

[181] There is a lesson here for anyone considering an appeal in a similar case. Sir Thomas Bingham MR stated: 'It does seem to me that in this situation it is incumbent upon a prospective appellant to give the earliest possible notice to the other side that it is sought or is likely to be sought to challenge a decision of this kind and, in particular, it is important to make early application to the Court of Appeal for an injunction or for the continuing of undertakings, as the case may be' (ibid 13).

[182] ibid 11–12.

[183] [1999] ICR 291, CA. See also *Symbian Ltd v Christensen*, 8 May 2000, 22–3; *TFS Derivatives Ltd v Morgan* [2004] IRLR 246.

[184] See paras 4.75ff above.

the former with greater flexibility than the latter . . . But the reported cases dealing with the court's approach to the grant of injunctions in this field show that if injunctive relief is sought, then it has to be justified on similar grounds to those necessary to the validity of an employee's covenant in restraint of trade. It seems to me that the court should be careful not to grant inter-locutory relief to enforce a garden leave clause to any greater extent than would be covered by a justifiable covenant in restraint of trade previously entered into by an employee.[185]

4.167 The possibility of an 'emerging trend' for employers to rely on garden leave in order to rein in employees for long periods of notice is a practice 'capable of abuse' as noted by Dillon LJ in *Provident Financial Group plc v Hayward*.[186]

4.168 The categories of legitimate interests considered as appropriate to found a basis for a valid garden leave clause are considered in more detail in paragraphs 4.191 to 4.217 below.

Flexibility

4.169 The court exercises greater flexibility when deciding whether, and to what extent, to enjoin a party on the basis of a garden leave clause than it does with a restrictive covenant. In the latter case, the court considers itself bound by the terms of the contract: either the restrictive covenant stands up, in which case an injunction reflecting the contractual prohibition may follow, or it falls, in which case no injunction is granted. However, with a garden leave clause the court displays more room for manoeuvre. As a result, any injunction obtained might be for a shorter period than that envisaged by the relevant terms of the contract.

4.170 The distinction between the approaches that the court will take was illustrated in the case of *JA Mont (UK) Ltd v Mills*.[187] The facts are set out at paragraphs 4.104 ff above. The case is important not so much for what the severance agreement said, but for what it did not say. On appeal, the company asked the Court of Appeal to treat the restrictive covenant, which was otherwise too wide to be enforceable, *as if* it was a garden leave clause in order for the court to take a more flexible approach to the terms of the injunction.

4.171 The Court of Appeal, however, was having none of it. There was no basis, according to Simon Brown LJ, for the company's reliance on *Provident v Hayward*[188] in order to make good its suggestion that the obligation in the severance agreement should be treated in the same way as a garden leave clause. Rather the *Provident* case *emphasized* the distinction between post-termination restrictions (such as that in Mills' severance agreement) and garden leave clauses (which apply while employment continues): 'the essence of the distinction is that because employees, by that very fact, owe a duty of good faith, the courts can, irrespective of the existence of any express contractual covenant, enjoin against its breach by preventing their employment by trade rivals. That is simply not the case once the contract of employment ends.'[189]

4.172 Simon Brown LJ quoted with approval the statement of Dillon LJ in *Provident v Hayward*:

[counsel] . . . persists that the negative term that is actually enforced must be expressed in the agreement; it is not possible to have a wide term in the agreement which the Court will

---

[185] [1999] ICR 291, CA, 301–2.
[186] [1989] ICR 160, 165.
[187] [1993] IRLR 172, CA.
[188] [1989] ICR 160, CA.
[189] [1993] IRLR 172, CA, para 37. This distinction was similarly emphasized in *Credit Suisse Asset Management Ltd v Armstrong* [1996] ICR 882, CA, 893–4. As to garden leave (at 893 *per* Neill LJ): 'It seems clear that the court has a wide discretion both as to the period of the injunction and as to its scope.'

whittle down so as to enforce as much of it as the Court thinks right. Of course that is correct when you have in the service agreement a contract restraining the employee after termination of his agreement from operating in a particular line of activity in a specified geographical area or over a prohibited period of restriction. If it is held that the area that has been chosen by the employer or the period of restriction are too wide or too long, the Court will reject the whole clause as void and will not enforce whatever maximum shorter or smaller field of restriction the Court thinks would have been permissible if the parties had made such an agreement.

But . . . the negative clause here not to work for anyone else during the term of the contract of service is a common form of clause which has often been held to be valid. The question is whether it should be enforced in particular circumstances by injunction. The lesser form of relief suggested, not to work during the continuance of the service agreement for specified rivals or rivals generally, if there were no express contract not to do so in the service agreement, could still be restrained as a breach of the employee's obligation of good faith.[190]

It was in these circumstances that it was possible to 'narrow the scope of the embargo', as stated by Taylor LJ in *Provident v Hayward*,[191] but not in the case of a post-termination restrictive covenant.

Discretion

Even if a garden leave provision is justified on its face (the claimant apparently having a legitimate interest to protect), and the court is in principle minded to grant an injunction (albeit tailored to the particular requirements of the case), no such injunction will follow if other factors militate against it. This is because an injunction is a discretionary remedy. So, for example, a court will not grant an injunction if *in fact* the claimant will not suffer damage as a result of the actions of its employee. Similarly, an injunction might be refused because of delay. The essentially discretionary nature of an injunction, and important factors informing the court's discretion, are considered in paragraphs 4.218 to 4.231 below.   **4.173**

Making the application

There are various issues for a claimant to consider when making an application for an interim injunction (over and above the legal and factual strengths and weaknesses of the case). For example, is the test to be applied to the possible grant of an injunction that of 'a serious issue to be tried' or is a more stringent consideration of the merits required because the interim application will effectively determine the case? Is it necessary to suggest that the court proceeds by undertakings (or a short-term injunction) in order for the matters in issue to be fully determined at a speedy trial rather than assessed at an interim hearing? In addition, a court must form a view as to the adequacy, or otherwise, of damages for each party. And what of factors going to the balance of convenience?   **4.174**

These matters, which inform the court's approach to all applications for interim injunctions, are dealt with in detail in Chapter 10 below. However, the following paragraphs deal with two particular examples within the context of garden leave: the application of the more stringent test required when an interim hearing is likely to dispose of the matter, and speedy trial.   **4.175**

---

[190] [1993] IRLR 172, CA, para 34.
[191] ibid para 35.

The more stringent test

4.176   In *Symbian Ltd v Christensen*[192] at first instance, the question of whether it was necessary for the claimant to demonstrate merits to a higher standard than the *American Cyanamid* 'serious issue to be tried' was dealt with by Scott V-C as follows:

> Whatever may be the directions . . . it is relatively unlikely, it seems to me, that a trial of this action can be staged before [the end of the notice period]. After that date a trial will be relatively pointless. This is, therefore, one of those cases where the answer given to the application for an interlocutory injunction is . . . likely to be an end of the proceedings.
>
> On an interlocutory application for an injunction, where there are no primary facts in dispute and, particularly, if a trial is unlikely for an injunction, [the court is] constrained to try to decide the answer to the issues that have been raised. It is not satisfactory simply to look for a modus vivendi to carry the parties over in a convenient fashion until all can be resolved at an eventual trial.[193]

Despite applying the higher threshold, the Vice-Chancellor granted an interim injunction in the circumstances of the case.

Speedy trial

4.177   An alternative to assessing the merits of the case on an interim application is for the court to approach the matter in accordance with *American Cyanamid* principles, but to order a speedy trial.

4.178   *Crystal Palace FC (2000) Ltd v Stephen Bruce*[194] is an example of this approach. Crystal Palace applied for a garden leave injunction after its then manager, Steve Bruce, was refused permission to talk to Birmingham City Football Club about its managerial vacancy and resigned in consequence (on the basis that trust and confidence had broken down). The case raised issues about whether or not Crystal Palace had been in repudiatory breach of Bruce's contract and various points about whether or not the club had any legitimate interest to protect. Where an employee has been constructively dismissed, the employer is not entitled to place him on garden leave. However, a court will rarely resolve a disputed assertion of constructive dismissal at an interim hearing (save in a very clear case), preferring to proceed on the basis that there is a serious issue to be tried on the point.[195] Bruce's attempt to resist the injunction rested, in part, on the fact that the court would have to apply the more stringent test involving an assessment of the merits of the claimant's case, which test (it was said) the claimant could not satisfy. However, Burton J instead ordered a speedy trial since it was possible to list such a trial beginning 10 December 2001, only a matter of a few weeks after the interim hearing on 22 November 2001. He stated:

> The Claimant . . . has put forward the proposition that there ought to be a speedy trial in this case . . . There was a time when there was criticism of the courts for being unable to operate as quickly as the parties would wish, but . . . it is no longer a difficulty to obtain a speedy hearing for those who genuinely need speedy justice, and the court has been able to offer a hearing date as early as December 10th . . .

---

[192]   8 May 2000.
[193]   ibid 16–17.
[194]   [2002] SLR 81.
[195]   See 5.155–5.159 for a discussion of the same point in relation to the enforcement of restrictive covenants by interim injunction in the face of a claim of constructive dismissal.

The background against which this discussion about a speedy trial has been carried on is the Court of Appeal decision in *Lawrence David Ltd v Ashton*[196] . . . where . . . Lord Justice Balcombe said . . . : 'A Defendant who has entered into a contractual restraint which is sought to be enforced should seriously consider, when the matter first comes before the court, offering an appropriate undertaking until the hearing of the action, provided that a speedy hearing of the action can then be fixed and the Plaintiff is likely to be able to pay any damages on his cross undertaking. It is only if a speedy trial should not be possible that it would then be necessary to have a contest on the interlocutory application . . .'[197]

He considered that a speedy trial was in the interests of both parties, with an interim injunction until the date the trial could be heard.

Evidence

Relevant issues

Before embarking on an application it is necessary for the claimant to adduce sufficient evidence to persuade the court that an interim injunction should be granted. For example, the claimant's evidence will need to address the following questions: **4.179**

(1) Is the defendant acting in such a way as to—at least potentially—be in breach of the contract of employment?
(2) Is there a legitimate interest to be protected?
(3) What is the minimum period necessary for the claimant to be protected?
(4) Is the claimant going to suffer damage, and can it show that the loss cannot be quantified?
(5) Is the claimant good for the cross-undertaking in damages?

Defendants should, of course, assemble such evidence as they can to counter the claimant's answers to these questions and to show, if they can, that the grant of an injunction will cause them to suffer undue damage which cannot be compensated by the claimant. **4.180**

The practicalities

It is important to assemble as much information as possible before applying for an injunction— indeed, even, where possible, before sending a letter before action (most garden leave injunctions being on notice applications which follow at least some correspondence between the parties). This sounds reasonably easy in theory. However, in practice the process of information collection is complicated by the need to apply to the court speedily in order to prevent too much damage being done—and to offset any concerns about delay. **4.181**

It is to be hoped that much of the evidence of potential wrongdoing can be obtained from within the claimant's business. For example, what do colleagues know about what is going on? A claimant should carefully consider whether information can be obtained from computers, including emails, mobile and other telephone records.[198] Indeed, the court has proved reluctant to make extensive orders for pre-action disclosure in order to bolster an employer's ability to plead its case. In *Aon Ltd v JLT Reinsurance Brokers Ltd*,[199] Mackay J **4.182**

---

[196] [1989] ICR 123, 135.
[197] [2002] SLR 81.
[198] The claimant must be careful to follow proper procedures so as not to fall foul of the raft of measures designed to regulate such investigations and to protect an employee's privacy. See Chapter 9 below for a more detailed consideration of practical steps that can be taken to gather evidence, and of the procedures that should be followed.
[199] [2010] IRLR 600.

discharged an order which provided for, inter alia, disclosure by affidavit of the departing employees' and the competitor employer's knowledge of the planning or preparation of the departures that had led to the litigation. The judge was of the view that the claimant already had sufficient material to plead its case and that there was no reason to subvert the normal process of disclosure followed under the adversarial system.[200]

4.183 Potential damage to the company is another crucial area which must be substantiated and explained to the court. An employer must show real or substantial actual or threatened harm to its legitimate interests in order for an injunction to be granted (*Provident Financial Group plc v Hayward*).[201] If, for example, a claimant is concerned about the misuse of confidential information, it will be necessary to show that the employee has had access to confidential information, is likely to be able to recall it, and is at risk of misusing it (intentionally or unintentionally), whilst it remains confidential. Or, with respect to trade connections, that he had recurrent contact with or knowledge of customers or suppliers, and is at risk of exploiting the influence he has thereby gained.

The course of proceedings

4.184 In relation to garden leave, it is almost always the case that the claimant makes an application to the court on notice to the employee only after the important steps of (a) sending an appropriate letter before action and (b) attempting to obtain undertakings, or other acceptable compromise. It may be that the defendant attends the first hearing, and makes submissions. Whether or not that is the case, the court will normally give directions for a hearing in the near future. The details of the process are dealt with in Chapters 10 and 12 below.

4.185 On some occasions, the grant or refusal of an interim injunction is appealed to the Court of Appeal. When the employer is the party appealing, on the basis that employees should have been enjoined but were not, it is incumbent upon the company to give notice of its intention to appeal and 'to make early application to the Court of Appeal for an injunction or for the continuing of undertakings, as the case may be'.[202] A failure to hold the ring pending the appeal could result in the employee obtaining employment elsewhere in the interim, which fact could be fatal to the employer's appeal.

4.186 Once the case reaches court, there will be various matters for the judge to consider: how should the garden leave clause be construed in the context of the contract; what legitimate interests does the employer seek to protect; and how should the court exercise its discretion? These matters are dealt with below.

Construction

4.187 As with all proceedings concerning the terms of a contract, the first step in any action to enforce garden leave is to satisfy the court that the clause (or clauses) in question support the potential imposition of an injunction. Admittedly this is not as crucial a step in relation to garden leave as with a restrictive covenant where the construction of the covenant is all important: a covenant will live or die by virtue of its interpretation by the court, there being no room for flexibility once the true meaning of the prohibition is ascertained (unlike with a garden leave injunction).

---

[200] ibid para 26. See, further, the discussion at 10.172 below.
[201] [1989] ICR 160.
[202] *Cantor Fitzgerald International v George* (17 January 1996). See n 181.

The issue of construction still has a place, however, in garden leave proceedings. Paradoxically, **4.188** it may be most important if—notwithstanding the cautionary tale in *William Hill Organisation Ltd v Tucker*[203]—the contract does *not* contain an express garden leave clause. As *William Hill v Tucker* illustrates, the main hope for a claimant in such a case, if he wishes to obtain an injunction to enforce part or all of the notice period, is to show that the contract as a whole does not confer on the employee a right to work, but only a right to remuneration.[204]

This was an issue which arose in *SBJ Stephenson v Mandy*.[205] As stated above,[206] Mandy, after **4.189** taking legal advice, wrote to the claimant stating that, in requiring him not to attend work he had placed him on garden leave and that this was a repudiatory breach of contract. He purported to accept that repudiation and asserted that, in the circumstances, he was not bound by the express restraints in his contract.

Bell J disagreed. He did not accept that Mandy had been placed on garden leave: he had **4.190** simply agreed to remain away from work while he took legal advice with a view to resolving the basis on which he would inevitably leave.[207] In any event, he did not construe Mandy's contract as giving him the right to work:

> My construction of Mandy's contract of employment is that clause 3 . . . merely defined his duties and obligations in office and that the words 'if any' . . . made it clear that there might not be any duties to perform . . . I would conclude that there was no obligation to permit Mandy to do his work, but only to pay his remuneration, so that SBJ was entitled to send him on garden leave during a period of notice.[208]

Legitimate business interests

The courts have made it clear that, in order for a garden leave injunction to be granted, the **4.191** employer must demonstrate a legitimate business interest that requires protection by that means. So, in *Cantor Fitzgerald International v George*,[209] Sir Thomas Bingham MR said that the judge at first instance in the case had been right to direct himself 'in terms of consideration of the period of restraint reasonably necessary to protect the plaintiff's legitimate interests'. Similarly, in *William Hill Organisation Ltd v Tucker*,[210] Morritt LJ emphasized that 'if injunctive relief is sought, then it has to be justified on similar grounds necessary to the validity of an employee's covenant in restraint of trade'.[211]

Although the categories of legitimate interest are not closed, the most common interests relied **4.192** on by employers are confidential information, client connection, and the stability of the workforce. The mere fact of assisting a competitor, whilst not considered an interest as such in relation to post-termination covenants, is arguably so in the context of garden leave. Finally, a company in administration has been held still to have legitimate interests which merit protection by a period of garden leave. These various categories are considered further below.

---

[203] [1999] ICR 291, CA.
[204] Alternatively, a claimant may, in appropriate circumstances, argue that the employee has forfeited his right to work as a result of his behaviour: see paras 4.87 to 4.99 above.
[205] [2000] IRLR 233.
[206] See paras 4.112–4.114 above.
[207] [2000] IRLR 233, para 69.
[208] ibid para 68.
[209] CA, 17 January 1996.
[210] [1999] ICR 291, CA.
[211] ibid 301–2.

Confidential information

4.193   The issue of an employer attempting to protect confidential information takes centre stage in the first 'proper' garden leave case of *Provident Financial Group plc v Hayward*.[212] Provident's subsidiary, Whitegates, employed Hayward as financial director of its estate agency business. On 1 July 1988 he tendered his resignation and it was mutually agreed that the period of notice would be six months, expiring on 31 December 1988. He stopped working on Whitegates' premises on 5 September 1988 and was placed on garden leave. However, on 13 October Hayward informed Whitegates that he intended to work for Asda as financial controller of its chain of estate agents' offices.

4.194   The importance of protecting the claimants' confidential information is reflected in the termination agreement reached between Whitegates and Hayward by which the latter warranted and undertook that, from 1 July 1988 for a period of two years he would not disclose, communicate, reveal, or transfer any confidential knowledge to any person including future employers.[213] It is no surprise, then, that the question of protecting such information was central to Provident's application for an injunction (which was refused) and to its appeal to the Court of Appeal.

4.195   The Court of Appeal set out the claimants' concerns over particular categories of information:

> The evidence set out the fears of the plaintiffs in the leading affidavit ... where [the managing director of Whitegates] refers to the defendant having confidential information relating to ... (a) corporate planning, the content of the three year profits forecasts ... (b) group strategy, the plans of Provident for the future of Whitegates; (c) profitability, the results, profits and losses of Whitegates' branches and various regional divisions; (d) developments, Whitegates' plans for the development of conveyancing, franchising and the future strategy in relation to its tied agreement with a certain insurance company.[214]

The problem for the claimants, however, was that the Court of Appeal did not see how any of this confidential information was relevant to Asda. It was this absence of detriment which led the Court of Appeal to dismiss the appeal.

4.196   The importance of protecting confidential information was also emphasized by the employer in *Symbian Ltd v Christensen*.[215] The Vice-Chancellor noted the requirement for a legitimate interest needing protection, and that 'it is common ground that Christensen is in possession of a great deal of information'.[216] However, he noted, too, that Symbian was not content to accept an injunction based on the express confidentiality clause in Christensen's contract:

> They point out with some justification the difficulty they would have in ever knowing whether there had been a breach. First there is the difficulty in drawing a clear line between what is protectable confidential information, and what is simply part of Christensen's expertise and know how. Second, there is the difficulty in being able to tell from things done by Microsoft [Christensen's proposed new employer] whether what is being done is the result of and indicates any divulging of confidential information.[217]

---

[212] [1989] ICR 160, CA.
[213] ibid 164. This would have covered the six months' notice period and eighteen months post-employment.
[214] [1989] ICR 160, CA, 168.
[215] 8 May 2000.
[216] ibid 24.
[217] ibid 24.

Customer connection

The protection of customer connection is at the heart of many garden leave cases, particularly **4.197**
those regarding employees in the financial services field.

One such case is *GFI Group Inc v Eaglestone*.[218] Eaglestone was employed by the claimant as **4.198**
a foreign exchange options broker, acting as a middleman between those wishing to deal in
options. He, together with two other brokers, was approached by another firm, Beresford
Capital Markets, who wanted to compete with the claimant. All three brokers subsequently
resigned, two giving four weeks' notice in line with their contracts and Eaglestone giving his
contractual notice of twenty weeks. Subsequently the claimant discovered that Eaglestone
was planning to work for Beresford before the twenty weeks were up. GFI applied for an
injunction.

In granting an injunction for a shorter period than the contractual notice (thirteen weeks) **4.199**
the court underlined that Eaglestone had paid out 'no less than £59,616 by way of entertainment expenses; that is, by way of payments aimed at nurturing his relationship with the
trader customers—that is, nurturing customer connection'.[219]

This was an important fact bearing upon the exercise of discretion according to Holland J: **4.200**

> . . . the defendant is an exceptionally highly paid employee of experience and standing who
> has had his personal relationships with the plaintiffs' customers carefully and expensively
> fostered at the plaintiffs' expense. I readily draw an inference that he and that relationship
> account for a significant amount of the goodwill that accrues to the plaintiffs, goodwill that
> was the product of expenditure exceeding £300,000 by the plaintiffs over the past year,
> expenditure that reflects the concept put before me of customer connection.[220]

Similarly in *Euro Brokers Ltd v Rabey*,[221] Rabey was employed by Euro Brokers as a money **4.201**
broker. His success in the job depended largely upon establishing and maintaining good
relations with customers and the company made generous provision for expenses to foster
customer relationships.

In February 1994 a rival firm began recruiting in London and this prompted Euro Brokers to **4.202**
review its employees' contracts. As a result, Rabey and Euro Brokers entered into a new contract
of employment on 28 February 1994. The contract was for one year and could be determined
by either party giving six months' notice in writing to expire on or after the fixed term.

On 6 June 1994 Rabey purported to resign with immediate effect. The employer made it **4.203**
clear that it required six months' notice. On discovering that Rabey intended to join the
rival firm which had prompted February's renegotiation, Euro Brokers placed him on garden
leave and, subsequently, sought an injunction to enforce that leave. The employer argued
that it needed the full six-month period to enable other employees to establish and cement
relations with Rabey's customers. Rabey argued that if he was kept out of the market for
more than three months he would lose his competitive edge and suffer damage.

Robert Reid QC (sitting as a Deputy High Court Judge) granted Euro Brokers an injunction **4.204**
until trial to enforce its right under the contract to require the defendant to remain on garden

---

[218] [1994] IRLR 119.
[219] ibid para 15.
[220] [1994] IRLR 119, para 20.
[221] [1995] IRLR 206.

leave for a period of six months following his resignation rather than the three offered. He cited *GFI v Eaglestone*[222] and, on the basis of that case, found that there was a customer connection of Euro Brokers which required protection:

> Although Rabey was not getting £300,000 a year's-worth of entertainment out of the company, he was getting over £10,000 a year plus the benefit of the various functions, such as Wimbledon and lunches with celebrity speakers and apparently other sporting events with which he entertained his clients at the expense of the company . . .

> . . . it does seem to me that there is a lavish and expensive customer connection which has been furthered at the expense of the plaintiff, that is something which is part of their goodwill and which they are entitled to protect. The protection of it requires in the instant case some form of injunctive relief.[223]

Stability of the workforce

4.205 The legitimate interest in maintaining a stable workforce was high on the agenda in the case of *Crystal Palace FC (2000) Ltd v Stephen Bruce*.[224]

4.206 Bruce purported to resign after Crystal Palace refused to allow him to talk to Birmingham City Football Club about a managerial vacancy. In response, Crystal Palace applied to the court for an injunction to hold Bruce to a nine-month period of garden leave. Bruce had already given various undertakings to the football club not to solicit or endeavour to entice away various employees, including the players at the club. But that was not sufficient to prevent Burton J granting an injunction (at least until speedy trial). Instead, he focused on the concern that—notwithstanding the undertakings given, and the fact that Bruce planned to take no active part in tempting away any employee—the mere fact of him leaving would be sufficient to de-stabilize the workforce: 'the relief that the Claimant seeks is one which seeks to palliate the risk of a senior manager leaving one company, joining its competitor the following day and then being followed to that competitor by key employees or employees who feel a loyalty towards that senior manager.'[225]

4.207 Burton J focused particularly on the position of the first team coach at the time, and on that of the club's players:

> Undertakings are given . . . not to solicit or procure any such players to leave Crystal Palace in breach of their contracts and not to procure any employer of the Defendant, such as Birmingham, to employ them, but that does not in any way cover the position of a player choosing not to renegotiate with Crystal Palace but to allow his contract to end and then join Birmingham, or any other club where Bruce might be, not at the solicitation or instance of Bruce but because they wish to follow him to the club where he has or may have gone.[226]

Assisting a competitor

4.208 Another point discussed in *Crystal Palace FC (2000) Ltd v Stephen Bruce*[227] was whether or not it was possible to enjoin an employee on the basis of a garden leave clause merely because they were leaving to join a competitor.

---

[222] [1994] IRLR 119.
[223] [1995] IRLR 206, paras 19, 21.
[224] [2002] SLR 81.
[225] ibid 84 (2nd col).
[226] ibid 85 (2nd col).
[227] [2002] SLR 81.

Crystal Palace argued that mere competition was enough, on the basis of Dillon LJ's judg- **4.209**
ment in *Provident Financial Group v Hayward*,[228] as recorded in the judgment of Burton J:

> Merely helping a competitor in that sort of way, that is, to put its business on a sound admini-
> strative basis, could not be restrained after the termination of the service agreement. On
> the other hand, for an employee to foster the profitability of a rival during the continuation
> of his employment could well, in appropriate circumstances, be restrained either under a
> clause in the contract like those in the Defendant's contact, or as a breach of the duty of
> good faith. I can well see that if the notice under a contract of employment is not for an
> excessive period after the employee is no longer required to work his notice, it may be said,
> forcibly and correctly for the employers, that the risk of his going to a rival and fostering
> the rival's business is one against which the employers are entitled to be protected because
> of the damage it will do them . . . [Counsel for Crystal Palace] submits that there could
> be . . . nothing plainer that the present case, where what is sought is the important and
> successful manager of one club going off immediately, notwithstanding a contract which
> obliges him to have a nine month notice period, to work for a direct competitor in the
> same position . . . [229]

This was not accepted by Bruce, as Burton J recorded.[230] Bruce argued that the comments **4.210**
of Dillon LJ were no longer good law, or should not be read to prevent mere competition,
in the light of Morritt LJ's determination in *William Hill Organisation Ltd v Tucker*[231] that
garden leave should be tested in the same way as a covenant in restraint of trade: since no
restrictive covenant would be upheld on the basis of mere competition, nor should a garden
leave clause be.

However, the point was not finally determined. Burton J was content that Crystal Palace's **4.211**
point was arguable and that was sufficient on an interim application.

Company in administration

An interesting example of a non-traditional legitimate interest (and further proof that the **4.212**
categories of interest are not closed) is the case of *Sendo Holdings plc v Brogan*.[232]

The claimant was the holding company of a group involved in the manufacture and distri- **4.213**
bution of mobile phones. It was placed in administration on 29 June 2005. The defendant,
Brogan, was the chief executive officer of the claimant.

On the date that Sendo Holdings was placed in administration, Brogan was given six months' **4.214**
notice of termination of employment by the administrators who invoked the garden leave
clause. He was required to stay away from work and not to contact Sendo's customers or
employees, to be bound by his duty of loyalty and to further the company's interests. The
administrators envisaged asking Brogan to do some work in due course.

By letter dated 9 July 2005, Brogan purported to terminate his employment summarily on **4.215**
the basis of alleged repudiatory breach of the implied term of trust and confidence. The
administrators affirmed the contract and, following Brogan's refusal to provide undertakings,
applied for an injunction to enforce the period of garden leave.

---

[228] [1989] ICR 160, CA, 169.
[229] [2002] SLR 81, 86 (1st col).
[230] ibid 86 (2nd col).
[231] [1999] ICR 291, 301–2.
[232] [2005] EWHC 2040 (QB).

4.216 Various issues were raised by the parties but the important one for present purposes was whether or not Sendo had a legitimate interest to protect. The claimant argued that the relevant interests were those of the company in administration. For example, it was always the intention of the administrators to ask for Brogan's assistance during the garden leave period. For his part, Brogan argued that there was no legitimate interest to protect because there was no business, no customers, and no employees (save a handful on temporary contracts).

4.217 Dobbs J decided for the claimant:

> I do not accept the Defendant's proposition that there is no business and thus no legitimate interest to protect. Whilst the company may not be trading it still has a duty to realise its position as a creditor and maximise value for its own creditors and ensure that the company is wound down in as efficient a manner as possible. It is said that Brogan could assist in this regard. Indeed, he has a duty to assist . . . I do find that the Claimant has a legitimate interest to protect for at least one if not more of the reasons set out above.[233]

Discretionary considerations

4.218 The court's exercise of its discretion is the final hurdle for a claimant attempting to obtain an injunction—and the potential saviour for a defendant. There are perhaps three questions for the parties and the court to consider: (a) What are the relevant parameters? For example, how long should an injunction last? (b) Is the employer likely to suffer damage (over and above hurt pride)? and (c) What harm is likely to be suffered by the employee, if any, and how does this affect the grant of the remedy?

The period of garden leave

4.219 The starting point is that the period of restraint should be the minimum necessary for legitimate purposes and not the maximum: *Cantor Fitzgerald International v George*.[234] Further, the court has a wide discretion both as to the period of the injunction to enforce garden leave and as to its scope: *Credit Suisse Asset Management Ltd v Armstrong*.[235]

4.220 In exercising that discretion, the court will be astute to recognize that the practice of long periods of garden leave is obviously capable of abuse: 'It is a weapon in the hands of the employers to ensure that an ambitious and able executive will not give notice if he is going to be unable to work at all for anyone for a long period of notice.'[236]

4.221 Some assistance as to how a court will determine the length of a garden leave injunction is found in *GFI Group Inc v Eaglestone*,[237] in which Holland J carefully set out his approach to the issue of whether, having concluded that there was a real prospect of the employer sustaining loss which was not readily quantifiable in damages, he should order garden leave for twenty weeks, that being the notice period provided in the contract, or for some lesser period.

4.222 He weighed in the balance the various factors for and against twenty weeks. On the one hand, the parties—who were of equal bargaining power—had agreed twenty weeks' notice. In addition, the period of notice was reached because the employer had initially wanted six

---

[233] ibid para 24.
[234] 17 January 1996, CA.
[235] [1996] ICR 882, 893 *per* Neill LJ.
[236] *Provident Group plc v Hayward* [1989] ICR 160, 165 *per* Dillon LJ.
[237] [1994] IRLR 119.

months, the employee had wanted three months, and twenty weeks was somewhere in the middle. What is more, both parties had proceeded on the basis that a significant period was required. On the other hand, there was no real indication that twenty weeks was in fact the period that was required in order to protect the employer from sustaining the damage identified. Further, the authorities strongly urged that the court should not grant more relief than absolutely necessary and two other brokers had already left to work for the same competitor having served out shorter notice periods of four weeks.

Ultimately, Holland J substituted a period of thirteen weeks for the twenty weeks requested **4.223** by the employer, swayed by the fact that other employees had already joined GFI's rival at an earlier date. However, he warned that otherwise he would have been strongly motivated to hold Eaglestone to his word in circumstances where, although in his business 'his word was his bond', he had suggested that the contract did not have the meaning it purported to have.[238]

It can be seen from the cases that it is very difficult to make any firm assertion about whether **4.224** a court will uphold a particular period of garden leave. Six months is, perhaps, a safe bet in some circumstances, but not in others. And longer periods can be upheld. Some indication of the outer limit of garden leave is given in *Credit Suisse Asset Management Ltd v Armstrong*.[239] In that case the relevant employees' contracts provided for three months', six months' and, in the case of six employees, twelve months' notice and (arguably) for six months' post-termination covenants. The employees argued that the covenants were unenforceable, as the employer had already obtained six months' protection by way of garden leave. The Court of Appeal upheld the judge's finding that the garden leave clause should not be enforced any further than the six months already served and that the covenants should be upheld.

However, whereas the judge had noted that he could see no reason why in appropriate cir- **4.225** cumstances a twelve-month garden leave period was not appropriate, Neill LJ appeared to go further, leaving open the possibility that: 'in an exceptional case where a long period of garden leave had already elapsed, perhaps substantially in excess of a year, without any curtailment by the court, the court would decline to grant any further protection based on a restrictive covenant.'[240]

In *Tullett Prebon plc v BGC Brokers LP*,[241] Jack J granted injunctions to enforce garden leave **4.226** provisions for a period of twelve months against a number of departing inter-dealer brokers.[242] The employer, *Tullett*, had sought a total period of relief lasting eighteen months, being comprised of a mixture, as necessary, of garden leave, enforcement of post-termination restrictive covenants, and springboard relief.[243]

---

[238] A similar exercise to that undertaken by Holland J was carried out by Robert Reid QC, sitting as a Deputy Judge, in *Euro Brokers Ltd v Rabey* [1995] IRLR 206. In the circumstances of that case the court granted an injunction for six months, as requested by the employer, rather than the three months preferred by the employee.

[239] [1996] ICR 882, CA.

[240] ibid 894.

[241] [2010] IRLR 648.

[242] ibid paras 234, 243, 244. In the case of some of the departing employees, the maximum available periods of garden leave expired before the end of the twelve months. In those cases, Jack J used enforceable restrictive covenants to 'top up' the period of restraint to a total of twelve months: see eg para 241.

[243] ibid para 213. In general, the employees' contracts contained six- or twelve-month notice periods followed by six months of restrictive covenants: see para 16.

Threatened damage to the employer

4.227　It is not sufficient that the employer has a legitimate interest to protect. It is central to the court's discretion that the employer has suffered, or is likely to suffer, detriment if an employee is not enjoined.

4.228　The lack of likely damage was the reason why no injunction was granted in *Provident Financial Group plc v Hayward*.[244] Although Hayward planned to leave Provident's estate agency business and work as financial controller of Asda's chain of estate agents' offices, the claimants would not suffer detriment if the garden leave clause was not enforced by injunction. The fact was that Hayward did not possess relevant confidential information and there was simply insufficient overlap between the two businesses:

> The defendant admits in his affidavit that he has one piece of highly confidential information . . . but it is not of the slightest interest to Asda and nor is there the slightest risk of his disclosing that piece of information which he has expressly undertaken not to disclose . . .
>
> As to other information, what the defendant is proposing to do, or is now doing with Asda, is that he is to be responsible as financial controller for the financial administration of Asda Property Services, reviewing and operating administrative and accounting systems and seeing what savings in costs can be effected. He has not had any part in the selling of houses for [Provident]. He has had no personal contact with customers as a salesman or a negotiator and he is not a surveyor or in any ordinary sense an estate agent. I find it very difficult to see how any confidential information that he has . . . can be relevant to Asda.
>
> . . . there is no real prospect of serious or significant damage to the plaintiffs from the defendant working as financial controller in the administrative field that I have endeavoured to describe for Asda . . . as a matter of discretion, in all the circumstances of this particular case, I would leave the plaintiffs to their remedy in damages and would not grant either form of the injunction which is sought.[245]

4.229　In contrast, in *GFI Group Inc v Eaglestone*,[246] Holland J stated: 'I am entirely satisfied that from the breach that I have identified, there is a real prospect of the plaintiffs sustaining loss, which loss will not readily be quantifiable in terms of damages.'

Harm to the employee

4.230　A factor counting against the grant of a garden leave injunction is where it would cause disproportionate harm to the employee. In *Euro Brokers v Rabey*,[247] the court considered whether the employee broker was likely to be harmed by a six months' injunction rather than three months. It decided that there was no evidence to suggest he would suffer pecuniary loss.[248] Further, there was no indication that he would otherwise be disadvantaged by the extra three months off:

> There is no evidence that his contract of employment with his respective new employers will go off if he cannot get into the market quickly. There is no evidence that his earnings are dependent on the cutting edge being finely honed . . . His new employers may not get quite as big a bargain as they anticipated when they agreed to take him on, but that is not the defendant's loss, and in my judgment there is no evidence that he would be unduly damaged

---

[244] [1989] ICR 160.
[245] ibid 168–9 *per* Dillon LJ.
[246] [1994] IRLR 119, para 35.
[247] [1995] IRLR 206.
[248] ibid para 22.

or damaged in any substantial way if he were kept out of the market for six months rather than three.[249]

The employee may contend that the effect of a garden leave injunction (restraining him from **4.231** working for a competitor before the expiry of his notice period) would be to compel him to work for his employer, an effect which the court should not countenance.[250] There is little recent authority on this point since the development of garden leave (other than the celebrity cases mainly involving sportsmen),[251] but in principle the argument is sound in a case where the employer would be willing to permit the employee to continue working. Whilst the court might look sceptically on an assertion by an employee that the injunction would have this effect, the risk of such an outcome would be a relevant factor which the court should take into account.

G. Checklist

Drafting

Would the employer's business be damaged, for example, because confidential information **4.232** would not be secure or because a competitor's business would be helped, if the employee in question were to join a competitor immediately following the termination of his contract with the current employer? If it would, then it would be sensible to include a garden leave clause in the employee's contract.

Is this employer only concerned that he might want to put the employee on garden leave **4.233** during the notice period, or are there any other commercial reasons why the employer might want to place the employee on garden leave even if the employee is not under notice? If there are any such reasons, then consider stating in the contract that the employer can place the employee on garden leave at any time, and not just during the course of the notice period. Be aware, however, that enforcing any such right in circumstances where an employee is not serving their notice period will often prove difficult, particularly, if the proposed period of garden leave is substantial. Remember, an employer in these circumstances will need to show that it has a legitimate interest to protect, and that it is protecting that interest reasonably.

How long is the employee's notice period? If it is short, and the employee is not particularly **4.234** senior, a short form garden leave clause may suffice (see Appendix 4 below).

What are the potential elements of garden leave that the employer might want to make use **4.235** of? For example:

- preventing the employee from working at all (see paras 4.131 to 4.134);
- requiring the employee to be available to carry out work on special projects (see para 4.135);
- requiring the employee to make himself available on call at home (see para 4.136);
- preventing the employee from attending the office (see paras 4.136 to 4.140);
- preventing the employee from contacting customers and suppliers (see paras 4.141 to 4.142);

---

[249] ibid para 23.
[250] See paras 4.07–4.31 above.
[251] ibid.

- preventing the employee from contacting fellow employees or consultants or agents of the employer (see paras 4.141 to 4.142);
- requiring the employee to return company property (see paras 4.143 to 4.144);
- requiring the employee to resign any offices (for example, as director or trustee) which he might hold as a result of his employment—note also that it would be advisable to include in the employee's contract a power of attorney empowering the company forcibly to remove the employee from any such office (see paras 4.159 to 4.160);
- providing that the employee is not entitled to the same remuneration package as when working (see paras 4.145 to 4.152); and/or
- requiring the employee to take accrued but untaken annual leave (see paras 4.153 to 4.156).

The garden leave clause should be designed to take each concern into account. Sample clauses are set out at Appendix 4 below.

4.236 Is the notice period longer than the maximum garden leave period necessary to protect the employer's business? For example, is the employee on a notice period of one year, while it is only necessary for the business to remove him from the market for six months? If it is, then the clause might provide either for a maximum garden leave period of less than the notice period, or it might contain a provision specifically allowing the employer to place the employee on garden leave for part only of the notice period. In those circumstances, it would be sensible for the contract also to contain a provision entitling the employer to terminate the employment early by making a payment in lieu of the outstanding notice period (see para 4.101 above).

Other related clauses

4.237 In order to ensure that an employee on garden leave does not damage his employer's business or work for a competitor, it is sensible to have the following clauses to enforce a garden leave provision:

- a clause requiring the duties of good faith and fidelity to subsist during the garden leave period; and
- a clause preventing the employee from working for others while employed.

(See para 4.115 above for the consequences of a lack of such clauses.)

Enforcing a garden leave provision

4.238 This section of the checklist assumes that (a) an employee has a contractual right to work and (b) the employer has attempted to place the employee on garden leave, or the employee has refused to go on garden leave and proposes to leave employment before the end of his notice period.

4.239 Is there a garden leave clause in the employee's contract of employment? If not, has the employee demonstrated in a serious way that he is not ready or willing to work, or rendered it impossible or reasonably impracticable for the employer to provide work? For example, has the employee breached his obligation to act loyally or in good faith? If so, the employer may be relieved of its obligation to provide work (see paras 4.87 to 4.99 above).

4.240 If the contract of employment contains a garden leave clause, the courts will look at the following matters in deciding whether it is enforceable:

- Is the contract still on foot, or has it been terminated? If terminated, the court will not grant a garden leave injunction and the employer should explore whether there are any relevant restrictive covenants (see paras 4.103 to 4.107 above).
- Does the employer have legitimate business interests to protect (see paras 4.191 to 4.217 above)? These might include protection of relationships with customers, protection of confidential information, or the stability of his workforce. Arguably protection against assisting a competitor may be a sufficient interest (see paras 4.208 to 4.211 above). If the employer cannot identify such an interest, no injunction will be granted.
- How long is the garden leave period for? If the period is too long, this might not negate the whole clause: the court might enforce garden leave for a shorter period than that expressed in the employment contract (see paras 4.169 to 4.172 above).
- Does the employee's job require him to keep his skills and market knowledge honed and perpetually up to date? If so, this is a factor which will be balanced with the employer's need for protection in deciding upon the length of any garden leave injunction (see paras 4.230 to 4.231 above).
- Might the employee suffer significant financial loss if some or all of the garden leave is enforced? If so, this will affect the grant of an injunction, or its length.

Is the employee going to join a competitor of the employer? If not, it is unlikely that a garden leave injunction would be granted (see paras 4.227 to 4.229 above). **4.241**

Even if the employee is to join a competitor, will it be in a role where his knowledge of the employer's business could give the new employer a significant competitive advantage? If not, a garden leave injunction is unlikely to be granted (see paras 4.227 to 4.229 above). **4.242**

Are there any other factors that might affect the garden leave injunction period? For example, have colleagues of the employee already joined the new employer so that imposing an injunction for the full garden leave period would not in fact achieve any meaningful protection for the original employer's business? If such factors exist, then this might reduce the period of any garden leave injunction (see paras 4.219 to 4.226 above). **4.243**

Will the employer suffer damage if the employee breaches his garden leave clause and can this be quantified? If no damage will be suffered, or if any loss can be quantified financially, an injunction is unlikely to be granted (see paras 4.227 to 4.229 above). **4.244**

Is the employer prepared to undertake to the court to continue to pay the employee his salary and provide other contractual benefits during the garden leave period and not to seek to recover such sums by way of damages? If not, or if not satisfied the employer has sufficient resources to meet the obligation, the court is most unlikely to grant any garden leave injunction (see paras 4.71 and 4.145 to 4.152 above). **4.245**

See also the checklist to Chapter 10 on injunctions.

5

RESTRICTIVE COVENANTS

Paul Goulding QC, Gerard Clarke, Tristan Jones, and Catherine Taylor

A. The general approach to restrictive covenants[1]

The value of restrictive covenants

5.01 A reasonable restrictive covenant is the most effective means available to an employer who wishes to restrict competition by a former employee. Time spent ensuring that reasonably drafted express covenants are incorporated in employment contracts is time well spent. The law reports are littered with examples of employers who had ample justification to restrict competition by a former employee but who inflicted defeat on themselves by their failure to make proper provision for this eventuality in the contract of employment.

5.02 The courts have time and again reminded employers that they will be reluctant to extend implied terms to protect those who could have achieved the desired result by the simple expedient of express terms. In *Balston Ltd v Headline Filters Ltd*,[2] Scott J reprimanded the claimant employers in these terms:

> Employers who want to impose fetters of this sort on their employees ought in my view to be expected to do so by express covenant. The reasonableness of the covenant can then be subjected to the rigorous attention to which all employee covenants in restraint of trade are subject. In the absence of an express covenant, the ability of an ex-employee to compete can be restricted by means of an implied term against use or disclosure of trade secrets. But the case must, in my view, be a clear one. An employee does not have the chance to reject an implied term. It is formulated and imposed on him subsequently to his initial entry into employment. To fetter his freedom to compete by means of an implied term can only be justified, in my view, by a very clear case.[3]

5.03 Steps should be taken not only to secure the inclusion of restrictive covenants in contractual documentation but also to ensure, wherever possible, that they are tailor-made for the particular employee, that they are regularly reviewed and that they are amended, when appropriate, to reflect changed circumstances.

The court's approach to enforcing restrictive covenants

5.04 In advising on the enforceability of restrictive covenants, it is helpful to have in mind a framework comprising the elements which a court will consider in reaching its decision. This chapter will endeavour to identify the principal elements of that framework.

5.05 The various steps in the court's approach become apparent from a detailed consideration of the case law on restrictive covenants. The challenge for the busy practitioner, however, is to identify those cases which will afford most assistance from amongst the huge number of restrictive covenant cases found in the law reports (which now include not only the official law reports but also the many law report services available online). In so far as the cases set out relevant principles to be applied, the litany is often repetitive. It must also be borne in mind that the enforceability of restrictive covenants depends on the many facts and circumstances of each individual case.

---

[1] See also Appendix 6, Drafting Restrictive Covenants: A Note and Appendix 7, Sample Restrictive Covenants (Employment) below.

[2] [1987] FSR 330.

[3] ibid 351–2.

The hard-pressed practitioner who is in need of an introduction to, or a refresher course on, **5.06** the approach of the court today to the enforcement of restrictive covenants would be well advised to read the decision of the Court of Appeal in *Office Angels Ltd v Rainer-Thomas & O'Connor.*[4] Indeed, the principles there set out in the judgment of Sir Christopher Slade were relied upon by Cox J in *TFS Derivatives Ltd v Morgan*[5] on the basis that there was no dispute between the parties that they were the relevant legal principles to be applied in order to answer the question whether the restrictive covenant in question was in unlawful restraint of trade. Whilst no single statement of relevant legal principles is likely to be exhaustive, the authority which the judgment of Sir Christopher Slade in *Office Angels v Rainer-Thomas* has acquired justifies setting them out here in full:

(1) If the Court is to uphold the validity of any covenant in restraint of trade, the covenantee must show that the covenant is both reasonable in the interests of the contracting parties and reasonable in the interests of the public: (see for example *Herbert Morris Ltd v Saxelby* [1916] AC 688 at p707 per Lord Parker of Waddington).

(2) A distinction is, however, to be drawn between (a) a covenant against competition entered into by a vendor with the purchaser of the goodwill of a business, which will be upheld as necessary to protect the subject-matter of the sale, provided that it is confined to the area within which competition on the part of the vendor would be likely to injure the purchaser in the enjoyment of the goodwill he has bought, and (b) a covenant between master and servant designed to prevent competition by the servant with the master after the termination of his contract of service: (see for example *Kores Manufacturing Co Ltd v Kolok Manufacturing Ltd* [1959] Ch 109 at p118 per Jenkins LJ).

(3) In the case of contracts between master and servant, covenants against competition are never as such upheld by the court. As Lord Parker put it in *Herbert Morris Ltd v Saxelby* (supra) at p709:

'I cannot find any case in which a covenant against competition by a servant or apprentice has, as such, ever been upheld by the Court. Wherever such covenants have been upheld it has been on the ground, not that the servant or apprentice would, by reason of his employment or training, obtain the skill and knowledge necessary to equip him as a possible competitor in the trade, but that he might obtain such personal knowledge of and influence over the customers of his employer, or such an acquaintance with his employer's trade secrets as would enable him, if competition were allowed, to take advantage of his employers' trade connection or utilise information confidentially obtained.'

On this appeal we are not concerned with trade secrets. The plaintiffs staff handbook contained special provisions (in clause 4.3) dealing with confidentiality, but no issue concerning confidentiality has been raised in this court.

(4) The subject-matter in respect of which an employer may legitimately claim protection from an employee by a covenant in restraint of trade was further identified by Lord Wilberforce in *Stenhouse Ltd v Phillips* [1974] AC 391 (at p400) as follows:

'The employers' claim for protection must be based upon the identification of some advantage or asset inherent in the business which can properly be regarded as, in a general sense, his property, and which it would be unjust to allow the employee to appropriate for his own purposes, even though he, the employee, may have contributed to its creation.'

(5) If, however, the Court is to uphold restrictions which a covenant imposes upon the freedom of action of the servant after he has left the service of the master, the master must satisfy the Court that the restrictions are no greater than are reasonably necessary for the

---

[4] [1991] IRLR 214, CA.

[5] [2005] IRLR 246. They were also expressly followed by the Court of Appeal in *Beckett Investment Group Ltd v Hall* [2007] ICR 1539, [2007] IRLR 793, para 21.

protection of the master in his business: (see *Mason v Provident Clothing & Supply Co Ltd* [1913] AC 724 at p742 per Lord Moulton). As Lord Parker stressed in *Herbert Morris Ltd v Saxelby* (supra) at p707, for any covenant in restraint of trade to be treated as reasonable in the interest of the parties 'it must afford *no more than* adequate protection to the benefit of the party in whose favour it is imposed' [Lord Parker's emphasis].[6]

5.07 *TFS Derivatives v Morgan* is the most recent exposition of the court's approach to the enforcement of restrictive covenants. It is particularly instructive since it was a decision reached, unusually, following a trial (which was expedited) rather than merely an interim application. This meant that the judge had to reach final conclusions on the enforceability of the covenants in question rather than determine the application in accordance with the *American Cyanamid* principles of whether there was a serious issue to be tried and where the balance of convenience lay.[7]

5.08 Having cited the relevant legal principles from Sir Christopher Slade's judgment, Cox J went on to identify a three-stage process to be undertaken in assessing the reasonableness of restrictive covenants in the interests of the parties. First, the court must decide what the covenant means when properly construed. Secondly, the court will consider whether the former employers have shown on the evidence that they have legitimate business interests requiring protection in relation to the employee's employment. Thirdly, the covenant must be shown to be no wider than is reasonably necessary for the protection of those interests. Reasonable necessity is to be assessed from the perspective of reasonable persons in the position of the parties as at the date of the contract, having regard to the contractual provisions as a whole and to the factual matrix to which the contract would then realistically have been expected to apply. The judge continued that, even if the covenant is found to be reasonable, the court will then finally decide whether, as a matter of discretion, the injunctive relief sought should in all the circumstances be granted, having regard, amongst other things, to its reasonableness as at the time of trial.[8]

5.09 In the light of the authorities, and taking a broad view, it is in fact possible to identify seven stages to the court's overall approach to the enforcement of restrictive covenants as follows:

(1) *Incorporation.* When considering whether a particular term is in unlawful restraint of trade it is, first, necessary to decide whether it was in fact a term of the contract between the employer and the employee. This can give rise to problems both at the commencement of the employment and at a later stage. At the commencement, difficulties can result where the terms of the contract are not all contained in one document, such as where restrictive covenants appear in a staff handbook to which reference may or may not be made in the offer letter or other contractual documentation. Confusion can also occur when the employer seeks to introduce covenants for the first time, or to change existing covenants, at a later stage during the employment. Unless the employee has signed a document accepting the new or changed covenants it may remain unclear

---

[6] [1991] IRLR 214, paras 21–5. Cited with approval in numerous subsequent cases. For a recent example, see *WRN Ltd v Ayris* [2008] IRLR 889, para 49. See also *Brake Brothers Ltd v Ungless* [2004] EWHC 2799 (QB), para 15 for a helpful summary of relevant principles.

[7] See Chapter 10 below.

[8] [2005] IRLR 246, paras 36–9. An approach followed by Sir Donald Rattee in *Dyson Technology Ltd v Strutt* [2005] EWHC 2814 (Ch), paras 49–50, and by Elizabeth Slade QC (sitting as a Judge of the High Court) in *Norbrook Laboratories (GB) Ltd v Adair* [2008] IRLR 878, paras 44–6.

whether he is bound by them. These problems are sometimes associated with the question of whether there is consideration for the covenants.

(2) *Restraint or not?* Sometimes it is not immediately clear whether the term in question amounts to a restraint of trade or not. This is rarely a problem in the case of direct restraints. However, the answer may be less obvious where the restraint is indirect. If, on analysis, the incorporated term does not amount to a restraint, then it is not subject to the restraint of trade doctrine and no question of reasonableness arises.

(3) *Repudiation.* If the employment contract has been terminated as a result of the employee's acceptance of the employer's repudiation, the orthodox view is that the employee is released from the restrictive covenants. This may occur, for example, where the employee has been wrongfully dismissed. This is sometimes referred to as the *General Billposting* rule, although the soundness of this so-called rule has recently been called into question. Clearly, if the employee is free of restrictive covenants because of the employer's repudiation, it is unnecessary to consider whether they are otherwise enforceable.

(4) *Construction.* Assuming a restrictive covenant is properly incorporated into the employment contract and survives its termination, the next stage is to decide what it means. This is relevant to the questions of reasonableness and whether the employee's actions (actual or threatened) amount to a breach of the covenant.

(5) *Legitimate interests.* Once the true meaning of the covenant has been ascertained, the court will consider whether the employer has demonstrated that he has legitimate business interests which merit protection by a restrictive covenant.

(6) *Reasonableness.* Assuming that legitimate business interests have been established, the next question is whether the restrictive covenant is reasonable. It must be shown to be no wider than reasonably necessary to protect those interests.

(7) *Discretion.* Finally, the court has a discretion whether to grant an injunction to enforce the covenant. The exercise of discretion can take account of a whole range of factors including the nature and extent of any actual or threatened breach.

It is suggested that these seven stages provide a useful framework within which to consider the court's approach to the enforcement of restrictive covenants in a little more detail. This approach will be adopted in the remainder of this chapter which will conclude with a section on restrictive covenants and TUPE, and a checklist of issues to be considered when approaching the topic of restrictive covenants. A note on drafting restrictive covenants is at Appendix 6 and sample employment restrictive covenants are set out in Appendix 7 below. **5.10**

Restrictive covenants in settlement agreements and consent orders

Before embarking on this detailed examination, reference should be made to the courts' particular approach to restrictions which appear in settlement agreements and consent orders. Given the public policy in favour of the settlement of disputes and the finality of litigation, the courts adapt their general approach to the enforcement of restrictions when found in such agreements and orders. **5.11**

In *WWF-World Wide Fund for Nature v World Wrestling Federation Entertainment Inc*,[9] which involved a trade mark dispute, the parties reached an agreement in settlement of their disputes and proceedings, which the defendant thereafter breached. The claimant commenced **5.12**

---

[9] [2002] EWCA Civ 196, [2002] FSR 33, CA.

proceedings for breach of the settlement agreement, which the defendant defended by alleging that it was void at common law and under EC law as being an unlawful restraint of trade. The Court of Appeal held that where the claimant had been party to settlement of a genuine dispute, designed to define the boundaries of his trading rights as against the defendant, he is entitled to expect it to be enforced. It is not for him to prove that it is reasonable. The presumption is that the restraints, having been agreed between the two parties most involved, represent a reasonable division of their interests. It is for the defendant, seeking to avoid the agreement, to show that there is something which justifies such a course, because the dispute was 'contrived', or because there was no reasonable basis for the rights claimed, or because it is otherwise contrary to the public interest.[10]

5.13 In *Gerrard Ltd v Read*,[11] the parties settled legal proceedings on the terms of a consent order. By one of the terms of the consent order, the defendant director and employee submitted to a nine months' confidentiality obligation in the nature of springboard relief.[12] He subsequently applied to the court to vary the period of the confidentiality restraint to six months, which corresponded with the period provided for in his employment contract. Two issues arose: first, whether the court had jurisdiction to vary the consent order; and, secondly, if so, whether the consent order should be varied.

5.14 Blackburne J held that the court had jurisdiction to vary a consent order, and that this extended to discharging a term which, as a matter of general law, is void and unenforceable, such as a term which is in unlawful restraint of trade, while leaving the remainder of the order in force.[13]

5.15 As to whether he should do so on the facts, the judge considered that, having agreed to a nine-month springboard restraint, which the court was willing to sanction when it made the consent order, there was considerable onus on the defendant to say why the court should now revisit that accord. This was not to suggest that, at the end of the day, it was other than for the claimant as restrainor to justify the restraint but simply to require the defendant as the person restrained to come forward with good reasons for saying why the court should re-open the matter. There is a public interest in holding a party to the terms of a consent order to which, with the benefit of independent legal advice, he had evidently been willing to be bound. The defendant failed in his application.[14]

B. Incorporating and changing restrictive covenants

5.16 Restrictive covenants are in general express terms agreed as part of a contract. The only exception to this rule is the restraint on use and disclosure of confidential information after employment has terminated which derives from an implied contractual term (even in the absence of an express term to that effect) and also from equity. Therefore, any covenant which seeks to protect, say, an employer's relationship with its customers or suppliers, or the stability of its workforce, must be contained in a contract. Examples of such contracts include

---

[10] ibid para 48.
[11] 21 December 2001.
[12] For springboard injunctions, see paras 10.57–10.85 below.
[13] *Gerrard Ltd v Read* (n 11 above) 17–18.
[14] ibid 27, 29.

an employment contract, a separate deed binding the employee,[15] a compromise agreement, and an employee incentive arrangement under which an employee is granted long-term incentive rewards with the employer, but any exercise of those awards is conditional upon the employee complying with various restrictive covenants.[16]

Incorporating restrictive covenants

In order to be legally binding on an employee, a restrictive covenant must form a contractual term, ie it must be incorporated into the employment contract. To do so, the usual elements, well known to contract law, must be satisfied: there must be offer, acceptance, consideration, and contractual intention.[17] **5.17**

By far the most straightforward way in which a restrictive covenant becomes a term of an employment contract is to ensure that it is incorporated when the contract is first formed. This is best achieved by an employer procuring an employee's signature to a written contract of employment which contains the restrictive covenant in full.[18] **5.18**

Sometimes, an employment contract is made up of more than one document. For example, a letter containing an offer of employment may refer to another document which is said to contain terms and conditions of employment, such as a staff handbook. If this is so, in order to achieve certainty as to the incorporation into the contract of the terms contained in the other document, the employer should make sure that the employee is provided with a copy of that other document and required to sign a statement that he accepts the terms contained in it as forming part of the terms and conditions of his employment. **5.19**

A number of problems can arise unnecessarily where the approach to the contractual documentation is not clear and complete before employment begins. For example, where an employee starts employment before signing the employment contract; or where the contract itself is executed but other contractual documentation is not provided until a later date; again, where contractual documentation (such as a staff handbook) is provided to but not signed for by the employee, or only made available for the employee to consult. **5.20**

Some of these problems are highlighted by the case of *Peninsula Business Services Ltd v Sweeney*,[19] albeit that the Employment Appeal Tribunal (EAT) (Rimer J presiding) adopted a robust approach to the employee's attempts to escape the written terms which he had signed. Peninsula offered Sweeney employment by letter dated 19 October 1998. The letter made clear that the offer was conditional upon Sweeney entering into Peninsula's standard contractual terms, including commission scheme rules. He was informed that, should he so wish, he could inspect the relevant documents, by arrangement, at the company's offices. Sweeney accepted the offer on 20 October and started work on 26 October. Soon afterwards, **5.21**

---

[15] For an example of restrictive covenants found in a separate deed (the covenants being those entered into on the sale of a business, in addition to separate covenants contained in an employment contract), see *Emersub v Wheatley* (14 July 1998), discussed in Chapter 6 below. See n 7 in Chapter 2 above in relation to consideration for restrictive covenants contained in a deed.

[16] Restrictive covenants are also contained in commercial agreements, for example Vendor–Purchaser Agreements and these are dealt with in Chapter 6. This section will refer to employment contracts, but the principles outlined could also apply to commercial agreements.

[17] See para 2.09 above for a brief summary of these requirements.

[18] An employee who is promoted without anything further being said about pre-existing restrictive covenants is likely to continue to be bound by them (*The Marley Tile Co Ltd v Johnson* [1982] IRLR 75, CA).

[19] [2004] IRLR 49.

he signed a document which contained the commission scheme rules. One of those rules provided that an employee was only entitled to commission if he was still in the company's employment on the payment date. Sweeney subsequently contended that he was not bound by this term since it was onerous and had not been specifically brought to his attention when he signed it.[20]

5.22 The employment tribunal upheld Sweeney's argument. It held, first, that the employment contract was concluded by Sweeney's acceptance on 20 October of the company's written offer without incorporation of the relevant commission rule precluding payment where the employee was not employed, and, further, that the commission rule was unduly onerous and had not been sufficiently brought to Sweeney's attention. The tribunal based this latter conclusion on a well-known dictum of Denning LJ in *Spurling (J) Ltd v Bradshaw*:[21] 'Some clauses which I have seen would need to be printed in red ink on the face of the document with a red hand pointing to it before the notice could be held to be sufficient.'[22] This dictum was later relied upon in the cases of *Thornton v Shoe Lane Parking*[23] and *Interfoto Picture Library Ltd v Stiletto Visual Programmes Ltd*.[24]

5.23 The EAT questioned whether any contract of employment had come into force when Sweeney started work on 26 October, since the offer letter made the employment contract conditional on Sweeney entering into the company's standard contractual terms, which he not by then done. Nevertheless, once the documentation of 28 October had been signed, both sides recognized that the employment was to be treated as having started on 26 October.[25]

5.24 In the EAT's judgment, what was referred to as the *Interfoto* principle did not, at any rate normally, apply to cases in which the term or condition in question is contained in a written agreement which a party has signed. It quoted Mellish LJ in *Parker v The South Eastern Rly Co*[26] who said: 'In an ordinary case, where an action is brought on a written agreement which is signed by the defendant, the agreement is proved by his signature, and, in the absence of fraud, it is wholly immaterial that he has not read the agreement and does not know its contents.'[27] According to the EAT, that statement reflects the usual rule which applies to written agreements, adding:

> It would make for wholly unacceptable commercial uncertainty if it were open to B, who has signed a written agreement, to say that he was not bound by one of the terms expressly contained in it because A had not first drawn his attention expressly to it. By signing, B is

---

[20] Sweeney also contended that the term was unreasonable contrary to the Unfair Contract Terms Act 1977, an argument which the employment tribunal accepted having regard to the term's 'penal and confiscatory nature'. The EAT disagreed, holding that the term was one which set out the employee's entitlement and the limits of his rights, and was, accordingly, not a term falling within UCTA 1977, s 3(2)(b) as claiming to entitle the employer to render a contractual performance substantially different from that which was reasonably expected of them or to render no performance at all in respect of any part of their contractual obligations: [2004] IRLR 49, paras 28–37. See also *Commerzbank AG v Keen* [2007] ICR 623, [2007] IRLR 132, CA on the application of UCTA 1977 to contracts of employment.

[21] [1956] 1 WLR 461, CA.

[22] ibid 466.

[23] [1971] 2 QB 163, CA.

[24] [1989] 1 QB 433, CA.

[25] [2004] IRLR 49, para 19.

[26] (1877) 2 CPD 416, CA.

[27] ibid 421.

treated as having agreed to that term (and all the others), however onerous it may be and whether he has read it or not.[28]

Where, however, the restrictive covenants were not actually contained in the documents **5.25** signed by the employee, but were simply referred to in them, and where there were also some 'extreme circumstances' surrounding the signing (where the signature was obtained under pressure of time, for example), there may be some scope for the application of the *Interfoto* principle.[29]

One of the lessons to be learned from the *Peninsula* case is that an employer can save itself a **5.26** lot of trouble by ensuring that all documentation containing contractual terms, including restrictive covenants, is signed by the employee before the employment commences.[30]

Changing restrictive covenants

From time to time, employers may seek to impose new restrictive covenants upon employees **5.27** or to vary the existing restrictive covenants. These changes, if they are to be effective, involve variations to the existing employment contract, and can be handled in one of two ways: variation by consent, or by terminating the existing contract and immediately offering a new contract including the new terms.

Variation by consent

Any variation of contract may be agreed between the parties. Consideration (normally some **5.28** benefit to the employee[31]) must be given in return for the covenants. There are three forms of agreed variation: express consent, implied consent, and amendments made pursuant to a reserved contractual power. Each of these will be examined below, but employers seeking to introduce new restrictive covenants would be wise to obtain express consent. The only time when express consent will not help the employer is if any covenants are to be introduced wholly or mainly as a result of a transfer of undertaking.

One final point of introduction—could an attempt to vary the contract of employment by **5.29** the introduction or amendment of restrictive covenants constitute grounds for constructive dismissal? If the employer acted in a sufficiently high-handed way so as to breach the term of mutual trust and confidence and if the restrictions were unreasonable so that the employer had no good reason to act in that way, the answer will be yes.[32] Accordingly, care should be taken. On a slightly different point see *Potter v North Cumbria Acute Hospitals NHS Trust*[33] for a recent discussion of what constitutes a variation of contract as opposed to a termination and re-engagement in the context of equal pay claims. Obviously an employer would usually

---

[28] [2004] IRLR 49, para 23.

[29] ibid paras 24–5 citing *Ocean Chemical Transport Inc v Exnor Craggs Ltd* [2000] 1 Lloyds LR 446, paras 48–9 *per* Evans LJ.

[30] See also *SG&R Valuation Service Co LLC v Boudrais* [2008] IRLR 770, paras 15–16, *Harlow v Artemis International Corp Ltd* [2008] EWHC 1126 (QB), paras 5–17 and paras 2.11–2.22 above.

[31] How much benefit is sufficient to form valid consideration? There is no right answer but £1 is risky, as is reliance on the employee continuing to work for the employer on otherwise unchanged terms as is the introduction of a variation by way of a deed unsupported by any consideration (see n 7 of Chapter 2 above). Ideally there should be some real monetary or other benefit (promotion for example) conferred on the employee, for the purposes of causing the employee to agree to the restrictive covenants. In such a case, the promotion should be conditional on the employee entering into the new contract.

[32] *Cantor Fitzgerald International v Bird* [2002] IRLR 867.

[33] [2009] IRLR 900, paras 41–98, in particular para 72.

prefer to vary the contract if at all possible, and what *Potter* demonstrates is that to be safe, it should agree with the employee that variation is the mechanism that applies when obtaining consent to the changes. However, it is arguable that changes to restrictive covenants would not be sufficiently fundamental to terminate the contract unless the employer expressly decides to do so,[34] and so the risk of this type of claim is reduced.

Express consent

5.30 While express consent may be either oral or in writing, given the importance of restrictive covenants an employer would be well advised to ensure that any consent is recorded in writing to avoid any evidential difficulties. Generally, it will be obvious whether or not the employee has expressly consented to the terms. Sometimes, the issue is more obscure. For example, in *Credit Suisse Asset Management Ltd v Armstrong*[35] employees were sent a staff handbook which contained new restrictive covenants, were advised to try to find time to read the book because it contained important contractual rights and obligations, and were given a month to raise queries or concerns failing which they were told they were to be treated as having fully accepted the terms in the handbook. The employees acknowledged receipt of the handbook and raised no queries about its terms. The Court of Appeal decided that there was a sufficient likelihood that the employer would persuade the court at full trial that the restrictions in the handbook were incorporated into the contract to justify an interim injunction to enforce the restrictions. The facts of this case are unusual, particularly in that the employees were told that if they did not query the new terms in the handbook they would be deemed to have accepted them. It is still safer for employers to rely on more specific express consent from employees.

Implied consent

5.31 In some circumstances, if an employer puts forward a change of a contractual term to an employee and the employee continues to work without protest, the courts may conclude that the employee has accepted the change. This general approach is unlikely to assist an employer who is seeking to introduce restrictive covenants into an employee's contract: it tends only to apply where the variation has immediate practical application (for example a change in the rate of pay), when the courts accept that if an employee continues to work after the variation (his pay packet having been reduced) he may well be taken to have impliedly agreed to the change if he has not said that he is working under protest (*Jones v Associated Tunnelling Co Ltd*).[36] Where the employer purports unilaterally to change terms of the contract which do not immediately impinge on the employee at all, the fact that the employee continues to work knowing that the employer is asserting that covenants will bind the employee in future does not mean that the employee can be taken to have accepted that variation. If the employee has not expressly accepted the change, the courts are likely to accept that his conduct is consistent with the original contract continuing so that the new terms are not incorporated.[37]

---

[34] See, for example, para 5.30 below and *Willow Oak Developments Ltd v Silverwood* [2006] ICR 1552, [2006] IRLR 607, CA.

[35] [1996] ICR 882; [1996] IRLR 450, CA. See also *Specialist Recruitment Group plc v Arthur* (24 February 2000).

[36] [1981] IRLR 477.

[37] *Solectron Scotland Ltd v Roper* [2004] IRLR 4 and *Aparau v Iceland Frozen Foods plc* [1996] IRLR 119 where, at para 15, Judge Hicks QC advocated 'great caution' in reaching the conclusion 'that an employee has, by merely continuing an employment without any overt change or overt acceptance of terms which the employer is seeking to impose, truly accepted those terms so as to vary the contract'.

In the recent case of *Khatri v Cooperatieve Centrale Raiffeisen-Boerenleenbank BA*,[38] the Court **5.32** of Appeal entered summary judgment against the bank employer in respect of a performance-related bonus. The bank had issued a variation letter containing a discretionary bonus replacing the performance-related bonus and restrictive covenants. The variation letter required a signature to evidence acceptance of its terms. The employee claimant did not sign or return it but just carried on working. Although the letter was meant to reflect a change to his employment in reality the only thing that changed was his reporting line. The Court of Appeal held, applying Elias J's 'only referable' test from *Solectron Scotland Ltd v Roper*,[39] that by simply carrying on working the employee could not be said to have accepted changes to his contract, changes which were wholly to his disadvantage both by removing his right to performance-related bonus and imposing restrictive covenants.

Reserved contractual power

In some contracts, an employer reserves a power to vary the contractual terms. These **5.33** provisions can assist an employer in making minor changes to the contract terms (perhaps changing the monthly pay date from one day in a calendar month to a later date). However, whether such clauses are able to assist an employer who wishes to impose restrictive covenants upon his employees is more debatable (*Wandsworth LBC v D'Silva*).[40] Courts will be wary of allowing any power which the employer has reserved to change a contract to be used so as significantly to change an employee's rights. Nonetheless an employer who wishes to explore this route should consider the recent case of *Bateman v Asda*,[41] where more significant changes were achieved by this method.

Dismissal and re-appointment

An employer who is unable to persuade employees to accept new restrictive covenants or rely **5.34** on a variation clause can, if the covenants are reasonable, seek to impose them by dismissing the relevant employees and re-appointing them on new terms. This may be done using the method of dismissal and re-appointment, provided that the process described below is followed.

Process

Employers cannot simply place covenants before an employee and require them to accept **5.35** them immediately. Individual consultation, and in some cases (such as where variations are to be imposed on twenty or more employees at the same establishment over a period of ninety days or less) collective consultation will be required.

Reason for change

If, after consultation, an individual does not agree to accept changes to his contract of **5.36** employment introducing restrictive covenants, it is open to the employer to give notice terminating the individual's current contract, and to offer each employee a new contract, to begin once the old contract has been terminated, including the new covenants. To do so,

---

[38] [2010] EWCA Civ 397; see also *Harlow v Artemis International Corp Ltd* [2008] EWHC 1126 (QB), paras 30–7.
[39] [2004] IRLR 4, para 30.
[40] [1998] IRLR 193.
[41] [2010] IRLR 270; note, however, that the decision of the EAT may have gone against the employer if evidence of the employees' understanding of the variation clause and in relation to trust and confidence had been raised in the employment tribunal.

there must be a sound business reason, which seems sensible to the employer, for incorporating restrictive covenants into the individual's contract (*RS Components Ltd v Irwin*).[42]

5.37 If the employer can show that:

(1) it has a genuine need for protection following which it seeks to introduce a covenant;
(2) the reason it is dismissing an employee for failing to accept the new covenant is not whimsical or capricious; and
(3) the employer genuinely believes that dismissal for refusing to accept the covenant is justified,

then the dismissal of the employee is a potentially fair reason for dismissal, on the basis of the catch-all reason in section 98(1)(b) of the Employment Rights Act 1996 of 'some other substantial reason'.

5.38 However, before finding that an employee was fairly dismissed for refusing to accept a covenant, the employment tribunal must review the reasonableness of the process which the employer adopts to introduce new covenants. Generally, an employer will need to satisfy the tribunal that it has conducted a fair procedure to demonstrate that any dismissal has been fair. It had been thought that refusal by an employee to sign up to a restraint which the court concluded was unreasonably wide could not amount to a potentially fair reason for the dismissal (*Forshaw v Archcraft Ltd*).[43] However, this decision has been disapproved, on the basis that the real question in deciding whether there was some other substantial reason to justify dismissal is whether the employer has a genuine belief that it has a real business need to introduce restrictive covenants. If the employer satisfies the court that this is the case, the court will not at this stage review the adequacy of the covenant, but will accept that dismissing an employee who refuses to accept the covenants could be potentially fair (*Willow Oak Developments Ltd v Silverwood*).[44] This means that the width of the covenant is not relevant to the decision whether the employer's reason for dismissal is a potentially fair one as falling within the 'some other substantial reason for dismissal' category.

5.39 If the employer has a genuine business need to introduce covenants any court reviewing the decision must then, under section 98(4) of the Employment Rights Act 1996, review whether the employer has acted reasonably or unreasonably in treating that reason as a sufficient one for dismissing the employee. The tribunal will consider two factors here: the reasonableness (or otherwise) of the proposed covenants, and whether the employer has adopted a reasonable procedure in seeking to impose them on the employee.

Individual consultation procedure

5.40 If fewer than twenty employees at an establishment are to be asked to accept new restrictive covenants, an employer must show that:

(1) it has a sound business reason for seeking to impose the covenants which is neither whimsical nor capricious;
(2) the procedure followed is fair; and
(3) the covenants are reasonable (or, perhaps, arguably reasonable).

---

[42] [1973] ICR 535, [1973] IRLR 239.
[43] [2006] ICR 70, [2005] IRLR 600.
[44] [2006] ICR 1552, CA; [2006] IRLR 607, CA.

It therefore makes sense for any employer wishing to impose new restrictive covenants on its employees to document its reasoning behind the commercial decision taken and to record why any alternative proposals have been rejected.

The employer must then, to comply with its obligations under section 98(4) of the **5.41** Employment Rights Act 1996, demonstrate that it has acted reasonably. In order to do so, the employer should provide the employee with a copy of the proposed covenants and give the employee sufficient time to consider the position and (if desired by the employee) take legal advice. The employer should not aggressively require the employee to sign the new covenants almost immediately, since any dismissal which follows the refusal may be found to be procedurally unfair (*Willow Oak Developments Ltd v Silverwood*).[45] If the individual, having had an opportunity to review the covenants, still refuses to accept them, or makes unreasonable suggestions as to alternative wording, the employer must consider his next step. He may have been persuaded by the employee's arguments that the covenants are unnecessary or he may accept that they should be modified. In the latter case, the employer should inform the employee, preferably in writing, of the modified drafting he is proposing. Alternatively, the employer may move to dismiss the employee for 'some other substantial reason' justifying dismissal.

Before dismissing the employee and offering re-employment on fresh terms incorporating the **5.42** covenants, the employer must ensure that it has adopted a fair procedure. With the repeal of the minimum statutory procedures, there are no requirements set out in legislation with which the employer must comply, in relation to this procedure. Therefore the first stage is for the employer to check that there is no contractual procedure relating to dismissals which applies in this situation. Assuming there is not, the employer should write to the employee setting out the circumstances which lead him to contemplate dismissing and re-engaging the employee and to invite the employee to attend a meeting to discuss the matter. The employee should be in possession of all relevant details before the meeting takes place and have a reasonable opportunity to consider them. These details include the proposed wording of the new covenants, the employer's explanation as to why it requires the change, and the fact that if the employee does not accept the change he may be dismissed and offered re-engagement on the new terms.

The employee may, if he wishes, be accompanied by a colleague or trade union representative **5.43** (see section 10 of the Employment Relations Act 1999 for details). After the meeting, the employer should inform the employee of its decision and notify the employee of his right to appeal, if applicable. If the employee wishes to appeal, there should be a further appeal meeting following which the employer must inform the employee of its final decision.

If this formal approach is to be adopted, the employee should, at or after the decision stage, **5.44** be given his full notice (or a payment in lieu of notice, if the employment contract allows for immediate termination upon the making of such a payment) before any new contract of employment is to take effect. If the employer simply announces that the change will be imposed immediately, this is likely to constitute a constructive dismissal should the employee resign in response.

All employees in the same category (for example in the same or a similar department, and of **5.45** similar grade) should be treated the same. If some employees are allowed to continue working

---

[45] ibid.

without being bound by the new covenants, or are allowed to agree to milder covenants than their peers, then the employees who are dismissed may successfully claim that they have been unfairly dismissed. This is because employers are expected to act consistently among employees, unless there is a sound and rational reason for not doing so (*The Post Office v Fennell*[46] and *Securicor Ltd v Smith*[47]).

Collective consultation

5.46 Section 188 of the Trade Union and Labour Relations (Consolidation) Act 1992 (TULR(C)A 1992) requires employers to consult with unions or employee representatives if they are proposing to dismiss as redundant twenty or more employees at one establishment within a period of ninety days or less. Less well known is that this clause will also apply where an employer seeks to change terms and conditions of the employment contracts of all or part of its workforce by giving notice to employees to terminate their engagement and re-engage them on new terms. This is by virtue of section 195(1) of TULR(C)A 1992, which defines references to 'dismissal as redundant' as being 'references to dismissal for a reason not related to the individual concerned or for a number of reasons all of which are not so related'. The collective consultation provisions would therefore apply to the imposition of restrictive covenants upon, say, a sales force of at least twenty employees.

Collective consultation procedure

5.47 If an employer is proposing to change restrictive covenants of at least twenty members of its workforce in a particular establishment, it should consult either with a union or with appropriate representatives. If such representatives do not exist, the employer should arrange for them to be elected, adopting the procedure set out in section 188A of TULR(C)A 1992. Once the representatives are in place, the consultation must begin in good time and in any event at least thirty days before the notices of dismissal are sent out if changes of contract are proposed for twenty to ninety-nine employees, and at least ninety days in advance if a hundred or more employees face the contractual changes.

5.48 The consultation must begin by the employer disclosing in writing:

(1) the reasons for its proposals;
(2) the number and descriptions of employees who will be affected;
(3) the total number of its employees of such description employed at the relevant establishment;
(4) the proposed method of selecting employees who are to be bound by the covenants;
(5) the proposed method of carrying out the dismissals (if change cannot be agreed), with due regard to any agreed procedure, including the period over which the dismissals are to take effect.

The consultation must include consultation about ways of avoiding the dismissals, reducing the number of the employees to be dismissed and mitigating the consequences of the dismissals, and is to be undertaken by the employer with a view to reaching agreement with the appropriate representatives.[48]

---

[46] [1981] IRLR 221, CA.
[47] [1989] IRLR 356, CA.
[48] See also *UK Coal Mining Ltd v National Union of Mineworkers (Northumberland Area) and another* [2008] IRLR 4 in relation to the extent of the duty to consult about the underlying reasons for the dismissals as part of the process.

If these consultations do not take place, the employer is at risk of facing a claim, brought **5.49** by a union, any employee representatives or, in the absence of any such representatives, by any of the affected employees themselves, for a protective award under section 189 of TULR(C)A1992. This award is in effect a penalty upon an employer who fails to carry out the consultation, in the absence of special circumstances meaning that he was unable to do so. A protective award is set at a maximum of ninety days' full pay. The statutory maximum week's pay levels do not apply.[49] The award may cover not only all those actually affected by the changes to contractual terms, but also all those whom the employer originally proposed would be affected. Because the awards are punitive rather than compensatory (*Susie Radin Ltd v GMB*[50] and *Sweetin v Coral Racing*[51]), the general rule is that an employment tribunal should first look at an award of ninety days' pay, and only reduce it if there are good reasons to do so. The focus is on the seriousness of the employer's default. Thus, for example, if an employer has at all times offered to consult with the union but its offers to do so have not been taken up, it is reasonable for an employment tribunal to award a twenty-day protective award to affected employees (*Unison v Leicestershire CC*).[52]

The employer will be obliged to notify the government of the dismissals where the collective **5.50** consultation obligations are triggered, pursuant to section 193 of TULR(C)A 1992. Finally, whilst undertaking collective consultation, the employer should not ignore its obligations in relation to individual consultation although the fact of the collective consultation, if done properly, will be taken into account when considering the fairness of the individual consultation.

Special case: changes following transfers of undertakings

Special problems arise where an employer seeks to introduce changes following the transfer **5.51** of a business which is subject to the Transfer of Undertakings (Protection of Employment) Regulations 2006 (TUPE). These, and other issues relating to restrictive covenants and TUPE, are considered at paragraphs 5.319 to 5.334 below.

Special case: compromise agreements

If an employer does not have suitable restrictive covenants in an employee's employment **5.52** contract, or if the existing covenants are thought to be unenforceable, the employer may seek to impose new or amended covenants on termination of the employment. Such terms might be included in a formal compromise agreement. There are two issues to be considered— enforceability of the covenants and tax issues.

Enforceability

Whether such a covenant is reasonable is generally construed by the court in accordance **5.53** with standard principles. An argument that as a matter of principle post-employment restrictions which are agreed at termination of employment are unacceptable was rejected many years ago (*Spink (Bournemouth) Ltd v Spink*).[53] In particular, the reasonableness of the covenant is to be judged at the time the compromise agreement is concluded (*Commercial*

---

[49] Employment Rights Act 1996, s 227, which is the section which limits some calculations of a week's pay to a statutory maximum, is not expressed to apply to TULR(C)A 1992, s 189.
[50] [2004] ICR 893, [2004] IRLR 400, CA.
[51] [2006] IRLR 252.
[52] [2006] EWCA Civ 825.
[53] [1936] Ch 444.

Plastics Ltd v Vincent).[54] Given that the covenant is going to take effect almost immediately, it is sensible for it to be drafted with a precise focus, perhaps naming specific clients and employees, or classes of clients and employees, who may be within the scope of the restraint. There have in the past been occasions where the courts have upheld covenants entered into in compromise agreements which are longer than would be acceptable if the covenant were in an employment agreement, on the basis that the employee is in a better bargaining position at the conclusion of his contract and is better able to assess the impact of terms which will immediately take effect. For example, in *Stenhouse Australia Ltd v Phillips*,[55] the Privy Council upheld a five-year covenant preventing solicitation of clients. However, it is doubtful that a non-solicitation covenant of this duration would be upheld today.

Tax Issues

5.54 HM Revenue & Customs generally regards restrictive covenants in compromise agreements as a matter for which the employee should expect to be compensated. Such compensation payments are taxable, even if made after the employment relationship has concluded, and attract National Insurance contributions (*RCI Europe v Woods (Inspector of Taxes)*).[56] If no specific sum is allocated as compensation for the covenants in the compromise agreement, HM Revenue & Customs is inclined to argue that the entire termination payment is consideration for the covenants, and is therefore fully taxable notwithstanding the provisions of sections 401 to 403 of the Income Tax (Earnings and Pensions) Act 2003 (£30,000 of termination payments may be tax free). It is therefore sensible for an appropriate, adequate amount of any payment made on termination of employment to be allocated expressly to the covenants. Generally, HM Revenue & Customs will not argue that clauses which are merely re-statements of covenants in the earlier employment agreement require separate compensation.

C. Is it a restraint?

The importance of the question

5.55 Having satisfied itself on the incorporation issue, namely whether the clause under consideration has been properly incorporated into the relevant contract so as prima facie to bind the parties, the next issue for the court is whether the clause in fact amounts to a restraint of trade. The answer is not always as straightforward as might first appear.

5.56 This question is important because the answer to it determines whether the restraint of trade doctrine applies. In other words, if the clause does amount to a restraint then it is unenforceable unless it reasonably protects the employer's legitimate business interests. If, however, on examination the clause does not purport to impose such a restraint, then it is unnecessary to subject it to the reasonableness test.

5.57 The issue is complicated by the fact that restraint of trade clauses take a number of forms. There are direct and indirect restraints. Direct restraints are the most common kind and are generally readily identifiable as clauses which are subject to the restraint of trade doctrine. Thus, a clause which purports to restrain an employee for a specified period of time following

---

[54] [1965] 1 QB 623.
[55] [1974] AC 391, [1974] 1 All ER 117, PC.
[56] [2003] All ER (D) 293.

the termination of employment from competing with his employer, or soliciting the latter's clients, or poaching his employees, is clearly a restraint of trade. It is prima facie unenforceable unless it satisfies the reasonableness test.

Indirect restraints, on the other hand, are not so obvious. This is apparent not only from the number of occasions on which the courts have been called on to decide the disputed question as to whether a particular clause does in fact amount to a restraint of trade. It also emerges from the fact that whilst the relevant principles may be easy to state, their application has proved more problematic. **5.58**

Neither can it be said that this particular issue is now settled. The reason is that restraint clauses continue to appear in novel forms that require consideration afresh of whether the clause in question is subject to the restraint of trade doctrine. Whilst the courts have considered the issue in relation to restraints linked to the receipt of pensions and insurance agents' commissions (see further below), they have not yet authoritatively done so in relation to other employment benefits such as share options, bonus clawbacks, or forgivable loans. **5.59**

A related question is the effect of the unenforceability of the restraint clause on the benefit to which it is linked. For example, if a pension is payable provided the employee does not compete with the employer, and the non-competition restraint is an unenforceable restraint of trade, is the pension still payable? What are the principles applicable in addressing this consequential issue? **5.60**

The test

Practical effect not form

The courts have developed a simple test in deciding whether the clause in question amounts to a restraint of trade: the court is concerned not with the form of the provision but with its substance and practical effect. It is uncontroversial that a court is concerned with the substance rather than the form of a particular contractual provision. Its task is to identify the true nature of the provision however the parties have chosen to express it. This is no less so as far as restraint clauses are concerned than it is in relation to other contractual terms. **5.61**

The point was made clearly by the Privy Council in *Stenhouse Australia Ltd v Phillips*.[57] Phillips was managing director of two companies that carried on business as insurance brokers. He resigned and set up business in competition. Clause 5 of his contract of employment provided that in the event that any client of the company should, within a period of five years following termination of employment, place insurance business so that Phillips received or became entitled to receive directly or indirectly any financial benefit from the placing of such business, then he agreed to pay to the company a one-half share of the gross commission he received in respect of the transaction. Clause 6 provided that he should not, for a period of three years following termination of employment, act as insurance broker for any client of the company. **5.62**

The case is of interest generally for its statement of the approach to the enforcement of restrictive covenants, and particularly where this concerns the interests of subsidiary companies within a group. However, it was also necessary for the Privy Council to consider whether **5.63**

---

[57] [1974] AC 391, PC.

clause 5 amounted to a restraint of trade. It concluded that it did. In so doing, it recognized that clause 5 was not on the face of it a restraint at all, but a provision for the payment of money: it was described by counsel for the company as a profit-sharing agreement. Lord Wilberforce stated: 'Whether a particular provision operates in restraint of trade is to be determined not by the form the stipulation wears but . . . by its effect in practice.'[58] This passage was subsequently cited with approval by Jonathan Sumption QC (sitting as a Deputy High Court Judge) who stated in *Marshall v NM Financial Management Ltd*: 'Whether a contractual provision is a restraint of trade depends on its substance and practical effect, not on its form.'[59]

Application of the test in practice

5.64 Whether the practical effect of a clause is to impose a restraint of trade requires careful analysis of the facts as illustrated by the court's approach in a number of cases.

Pension

5.65 The earliest case of importance on the point is *Wyatt v Kreglinger and Fernau*.[60] The defendant employer wrote to its employee, Wyatt, shortly before his retirement, informing him that it had decided to pay him a pension of £200 per annum. The letter added: 'You are at liberty to undertake any other employment or enter into any business, except in the wool trade.' The defendant paid this pension for nine years but, finding itself in straitened financial circumstances, wrote to the claimant informing him of the planned discontinuance of the pension. He commenced proceedings which the employer defended on the grounds, first, that there was no legally binding agreement to pay a pension and, secondly, if there was, it was void as being in restraint of trade. The Court of Appeal held, assuming a contractual obligation to pay a pension, it was in restraint of trade.

5.66 Scrutton LJ thought that:

> a stipulation by the employer that he will pay the plaintiff so much a year if the plaintiff does not enter into the wool trade for the rest of his life in any part of the country or world, appears to me to be a contract in restraint of trade which is unenforceable just as much as a contract by the employee not to trade in the wool trade for the rest of his life in any part of the world.[61]

Slesser LJ considered that: 'The public policy which has to be considered, the interest of the community, seems to be affected quite as much by an agreement that a person will give up a benefit which he would otherwise receive if he enters into a particular trade, as it is by a direct agreement by him not to enter into that trade.'[62]

5.67 *Wyatt v Kreglinger* concerned a gratuitous promise to pay a pension conditional on compliance with a restraint of trade clause. In *Bull v Pitney-Bowes Ltd*,[63] the defendant company required all its eligible employees to join their pension and life insurance scheme. A rule of the scheme provided for all of the employee's rights under the scheme to be cancelled if he

---

[58] [1974] AC 402.

[59] [1995] ICR 1042, 1047, [1996] IRLR 20, para 20. This decision was upheld by the Court of Appeal (see further below).

[60] [1933] 1 KB 793, CA. For an earlier illustration, see *Horwood v Millar's Timber and Trading Co Ltd* [1917] 1 KB 305, CA, albeit that was an exceptional case on its facts prompting Warrington LJ to say 'I am happy to think that it is very seldom that so oppressive a contract as this comes before these Courts' (ibid 313).

[61] [1933] 1 KB 793, CA, 807.

[62] ibid 809.

[63] [1967] 1 WLR 273.

engaged in activity in competition with the company. Following his voluntary retirement from the defendant's employment, the claimant, Bull, worked for a competitor of his former employer. He was duly notified that he would lose his rights to a deferred pension unless he discontinued his new employment. Thesiger J made declarations sought by the claimant employee that the relevant pension scheme rule was an unenforceable restraint of trade, following the decision in *Wyatt v Kreglinger*.[64] In doing so, he stated:

> So far as the individual is concerned, I appreciate the distinction relied upon by the defendants between (1) a covenant not to take up certain skilled work and (2) the discontinuance of a pension if one does choose to take up that work. The latter does not involve the breach of any promise; but from the point of view of the public and of the reason behind the rule at common law there is little, if any, distinction in principle. The relevant factor is the inducement not to take up work in which one is skilled.[65]

Profit-sharing

The facts in *Stenhouse Ltd v Phillips* are summarized in paragraph 5.62 above. Clause 5 required the employee to pay to his former employer half the gross commission he received from transactions with the employer's clients. Having stated the general principle that the court was concerned with the practical effect and not the form of the stipulation, Lord Wilberforce turned to consider the practical effect of clause 5:   **5.68**

> The clause in question here contains no direct covenant to abstain from any kind of competition or business, but the question to be answered is whether, in effect, it is likely to cause the employee to refuse business which otherwise he would take: or, looking at it another way, whether the existence of this provision would diminish his prospects of employment. Judged by this test, their Lordships have no doubt that the clause operates in restraint of trade.[66]

In support of this conclusion, their Lordships relied on a number of factors. First, the employee came under an obligation to pay even if business was obtained without his knowledge. Secondly, he had to pay 50 per cent of gross commission regardless of the financial benefit obtained by him. Thirdly, the clause operated potentially for more than five years. All these provisions were far more than 'profit-sharing' and contained 'in aggregate a substantial element of restraint of trade'.[67]

Repayment of training costs

Electronic Data Systems Ltd v Hubble[68] is perhaps of limited assistance since it concerned the refusal to grant summary judgment on the ground that the employee's defence was arguable. As a result, it involves no definitive determination of the restraint of trade issue. Nevertheless, it provides some insight into an unusual context in which this issue can arise, and into the Court of Appeal's approach to the question. Hubble worked for EDS, which specialized in the provision of computer services. He was required to undergo a training programme and to agree to sign a promissory note to repay training charges in the event that he resigned within thirty-six months from the date of commencement of phase II of the programme. The charges were specified on a diminishing scale ranging from £4,500 (within twenty-four   **5.69**

---

[64] Thesiger J declined to accept the 'very strong criticisms' which he noted (at 275) were made of the decision in *Wyatt v Kreglinger* expressed at the time in (1933) 49 LQR 465.
[65] [1967] 1 WLR 273, 282.
[66] [1974] AC 391, 402–3.
[67] ibid 403.
[68] CA, 20 November 1987.

months) to £1,125 (between thirty and thirty-six months). Hubble became discontented and resigned. EDS made a demand under the promissory note and commenced proceedings seeking summary judgment on its claim. The Deputy Master granted summary judgment and Hubble's appeal was dismissed by the judge. The Court of Appeal allowed his further appeal and granted Hubble leave to defend.

5.70   The ground on which leave to defend was given was that the presence of the promissory note acted as an unfair inhibition on the exercise of the employee's contractual right to leave the service of EDS by giving one month's notice, if he was dissatisfied with his present employment and wished to make use of his abilities elsewhere. Mustill LJ considered the general principles governing the relationship between the public interest in allowing an individual to make a contract, the corollary of which is inevitably a restriction on his freedom to act as he wishes, and the contrary public interest in not allowing the freedom to allow a contract to become a vehicle for oppression, as very clearly stated in *Macaulay v Schroeder Music Publishing Co Ltd*.[69] Mustill LJ referred in particular to the speech of Lord Diplock in that case who posed the relevant question to be answered as respects restraints during the continuance of a contract as whether the bargain was fair.[70] Counsel for both parties in *EDS v Hubble* accepted that this approach was relevant to the present case. The employee relied on a number of factors to justify him being released from this contractual promise. These included the argument that the promissory note was a powerful disincentive to any decision to make use of the one month's notice provision. Further, it was argued that it was to be inferred that the true motive of EDS in making this arrangement was not to get their money back, but to make sure that persons who by working in their organization had learned their ways and had developed skills did not go off to use their knowledge and skills in the employment of competitors. Mustill LJ (with whom Nicholls LJ agreed) concluded that it was arguable that the scheme was an unenforceable restraint of trade.

Commission

5.71   *Sadler v Imperial Life Assurance Co of Canada Ltd*[71] concerned the more common situation whereby in the event of termination of an insurance agent's service, commission would be paid to the agent in respect of insurance premiums paid under the relevant policies issued during the agent's appointment; but subject to the proviso that the agent's entitlement to such commission would cease if he entered into competing activities. As PJ Crawford QC (sitting as a Deputy High Court Judge) observed, there was thus 'a direct financial inducement for the agent not to enter into such activities but to restrict his post-termination employment to non-competing activities'.[72] The effect of the contractual provision was, in his judgment, that if the claimant was to recover post-termination commission he was in fact 'required to give up some freedom which he would otherwise have had, namely the freedom to take employment in whatever field he chose'.[73] The judge was unable to distinguish *Wyatt v Kreglinger* and *Bull v Pitney-Bowes*, the effect of which he held to be 'that a financial incentive to limit a former employee's activities amounts to a restraint of trade'.[74]

---

[69]   [1974] 1 WLR 1308.
[70]   ibid 1315–16.
[71]   [1988] IRLR 388.
[72]   ibid para 12.
[73]   ibid para 15.
[74]   ibid para 15.

Entitlement to renewal commission was conditional on the self-employed financial services **5.72** agent not competing for a period of one year after termination of the agency in *Marshall v NM Financial Management Ltd*.[75] Jonathan Sumption QC (sitting as a Deputy High Court Judge) did not think there could be any doubt that this condition was a restraint of trade. In his judgment it had been well established since *Wyatt v Kreglinger* 'that there is no relevant difference between a contract that a person will not carry on a particular trade and a contract that if he does not do so he will receive some benefit to which he would not otherwise be entitled'. The condition in question was 'a financial incentive to the agent not to carry on business in the specified fields'. It was therefore unlawful unless reasonable.[76] The company appealed only against the finding that the condition was severable, not against the finding that it was an unenforceable restraint of trade.[77] However, in the course of his judgment, Millett LJ addressed the question of whether the condition amounted to a restraint of trade in the following terms:

> It is settled law that there is no difference in this context between a contract by a person that he will not carry on a particular trade (which if valid would be enforceable against him) and a contract that if he does not do so he will receive a benefit to which he would not otherwise be entitled (which if valid would not prevent him from carrying on the trade but merely result in the loss of the benefit in question): see *Wyatt v Kreglinger and Fernau* [1933] 1 KB 793.[78]

A different result was reached in *Peninsula Business Services Ltd v Sweeney*.[79] Peninsula sold **5.73** employment advice packages and health and safety services. It employed Sweeney as a sales executive. He was entitled to commission on business done. Commission was payable at the end of the calendar month following payment by the customer of 25 per cent of the fee. The commission scheme rules provided that such commission was only payable if the salesman was still in the company's employment at the end of that month (this provision was known as section B). Following his resignation, Sweeney claimed entitlement to nearly £21,000 commission based on sales negotiated during his employment in respect of which the customer only paid 25 per cent of the fee after termination of his employment. An employment tribunal made a number of findings, one of which was that section B was void as being in unlawful restraint of trade in that in part it was designed to provide an economic disincentive or discouragement to the established salesmen from leaving their employment and working elsewhere. The employment tribunal relied on *Marshall v NM Financial Management* in reaching this conclusion.

The Employment Appeal Tribunal (EAT) (Rimer J presiding) disagreed. Rimer J summa- **5.74** rized the employment tribunal's point as being that because section B had the effect of imposing what they regarded as a penalty on resigning employees, it must have operated as a disincentive on them to resign and, therefore, to go and work for competitors whom they might, but for section B, have wished to work for. The EAT regarded the tribunal's conclusion that those circumstances turned section B into a contract in restraint of trade as wrong. Rimer J continued: 'We do not consider it seriously arguable that the commission penalty that Mr Sweeney suffered on resignation arose under a contractual term involving an unlawful

---

[75] [1995] ICR 1042, [1996] IRLR 20.
[76] [1995] ICR 1042, 1046.
[77] [1997] ICR 1065, [1997] IRLR 449.
[78] [1997] ICR 1065, 1071.
[79] [2004] IRLR 49.

restraint of trade. His employment contract did not impose any restraint on him as to whom he might work for, or what he might do, after leaving Peninsula.'[80]

Benefits linked to restraints

5.75 It is likely that the principles discussed above will be applied in due course to restraints which are increasingly to be found in employee benefit arrangements. For example, a bonus may be paid to an employee on the basis that it becomes repayable in the event that the employee joins a competitor. Similarly, a loan made by an employer to an employee may be forgiven provided the employee does not compete. Employees may be awarded deferred compensation in the form of, for example, share options or restricted stock which does not vest for a period of time. It is not unusual for scheme rules to provide that unvested options and stock will be forfeited in the event that the employee takes up competitive employment.

5.76 The courts have not yet authoritatively ruled on the enforceability of such schemes. When called on to do so, the courts will need to consider whether such provisions amount to a restraint of trade, and, if so, whether or not they go no further than reasonably necessary to protect legitimate business interests. As to the former question, the cases on indirect restraints discussed above lend support to the argument that benefits conditional on compliance with non-competition provisions are subject to restraint of trade principles.

5.77 As to whether such schemes are enforceable (assuming restraint of trade rules apply), it is necessary, first, to identify the relevant business interests and then to assess the reasonableness of the particular provisions. As to legitimate business interests, in addition to those typically relied upon (protection of confidential information, trade connections, and workforce stability), employee retention and incentivization, alignment of the interests of employees and shareholders, optimum tax treatment of employee remuneration, maximizing competitiveness, and promoting loyalty of award holders might all fall to be considered as potential legitimate business interests.

5.78 As far as reasonableness is concerned, a range of factors will be relevant. These may involve considerations additional to those which are typical in assessing the reasonableness of more orthodox covenants. For example, a standard post-employment non-competition covenant might be said to be unreasonable if its duration is greater than twelve months. In contrast, the vesting period for share options is typically three years or more. If the employee stands to forfeit his unvested share options in the event that he competes with the company during the (three-year) vesting period, is this restriction unreasonable on account of its duration? It might be argued that to require a grantee of share options to forebear from competition during such a vesting period, as a condition of the vesting of his share options, is not unreasonable given that, on the one hand, the company has an interest in maximizing its profits and, on the other hand, the grantee stands to benefit in terms of the price of his shares, reflecting the company's performance, following the exercise of his options.[81] Further, forfeiture which occurs following dismissal for cause or employee resignation might be considered more reasonable than forfeiture consequent on dismissal without cause (bad/good leaver provisions).

---

[80] ibid para 42. No reference is made in the EAT's decision to *EDS v Hubble* (see paras 5.69–5.70 above) and there is nothing to suggest it was cited during argument.

[81] In *Scheffel & Co PC v Fessler*, an Illinois court of appeals upheld a non-competition covenant in the context of a shareholder agreement where an accountant had been both a shareholder and officer of the company. The covenant lasted *as long as the retired shareholder received deferred compensation* from his former firm.

Again, the existence of a discretion on the part of the company to treat deferred benefits as vested in appropriate cases, which otherwise would be subject to forfeiture, might count in favour of the reasonableness of the overall scheme. Whether such arguments will prevail remains to be seen.

Consequences of a finding of unreasonable restraint of trade

Much attention is focused in practice on the question of whether a restrictive covenant is or is not an unreasonable restraint of trade. There is far less discussion about the consequences of a finding that a covenant is of the latter variety. This suggests that the consequences rarely give rise to difficulty. Two situations require separate consideration.   **5.79**

The first situation is the one that arises most frequently. An employer attempts to enforce a restrictive covenant. The court finds that the covenant is an unreasonable restraint of trade. The result is that the employer is unable to enforce the covenant. That is usually sufficient to dispose of the issue. In fact, whilst opinion has differed from time to time, the better view is that the restrictive covenant is unenforceable rather than illegal. This means that the parties may lawfully abide by the covenant if they so wish. However, a covenant in unreasonable restraint of trade will not be enforced by the court.[82]   **5.80**

The second situation is less straightforward. This occurs where it is argued that other contractual provisions are rendered unenforceable by reason of the unenforceability of the restraint to which those other provisions are linked. This issue has arisen in a number of the indirect restraint cases discussed above.   **5.81**

It will be recalled that in *Wyatt v Kreglinger* the defendant employers informed the employee that they would pay him a pension provided he did not work in the wool trade.[83] When they stopped paying the pension, the employee commenced proceedings seeking a declaration that the defendants were liable to pay him the pension. His action failed on the ground that the agreement (assuming it was an agreement) was in unreasonable restraint of trade, with the result that he was not entitled to his pension payment. As Greer LJ expressed it, the employee 'bound himself to something which was void in law, and in as much as the consideration was void the agreement would be altogether void'.[84]   **5.82**

The employee also commenced the proceedings in *Bull v Pitney-Bowes*.[85] He successfully sought declarations that the condition that he should not work in competition was in unreasonable restraint of trade and that he was entitled to receive his pension. The difference in outcome between this case and *Wyatt v Kreglinger* was due to the fact that in *Bull v Pitney-Bowes* the employee was required to join the employer's pension scheme during his employment. Accordingly, there was consideration for the pension apart from the employee's desisting from working in competition. In *Wyatt v Kreglinger*, on the other hand, the promise of a pension was made on retirement, the only stipulation being that the employee did not work in the wool trade. Assuming a binding agreement, there was no consideration other than the unenforceable restraint.   **5.83**

---

[82] *Chitty on Contracts* (30th edn, 2008) para 16-075.
[83] See paras 5.65–5.66 above.
[84] [1933] 1 KB 793, 808.
[85] See para 5.67 above.

5.84 In *Sadler v Imperial Life Assurance Co of Canada Ltd*,[86] the employer argued that if the proviso not to compete was unenforceable then it took the whole paragraph with it, including any obligation on the employer to pay post-termination commission. The judge concluded that:

> . . . the combined effect of the authorities was that a contract which contains an unenforceable provision nevertheless remains effective after the removal or severance of that provision if the following conditions are satisfied:
>
> 1. The unenforceable provision is capable of being removed without the necessity of adding to or modifying the wording of what remains.
> 2. The remaining terms continue to be supported by adequate consideration.
> 3. The removal of the unenforceable provision does not so change the character of the contract that it becomes 'not the sort of contract that the parties entered into at all'.[87]

The judge held that these three conditions were all satisfied on the facts of the case. First, the proviso was grammatically self-contained which could be removed without modification or addition. Secondly, there was ample other consideration to support the defendants' continuing obligation to pay post-termination commission. Thirdly, the fundamental nature of the provision for payment of post-termination commission remained unaltered by the removal of the unenforceable restraint of trade.

5.85 The same issue arose for consideration by the Court of Appeal in *Marshall v NM Financial Management Ltd*.[88] Millett LJ observed that although this question is described as one of severance, it is important to bear in mind that the court was not concerned to decide how much of an offending restriction should be struck down. In such a case the question is to what extent can the party who imposed the restriction enforce those parts of it which are not in unreasonable restraint of trade. The court here was concerned with a very different question, namely, whether the party who has been freed from an invalid restraint of trade can enforce the remainder of the contract without it.[89]

5.86 Millett LJ stated that it is obvious that, where the invalid restraint of trade provides the only consideration for the promise, the promisee cannot enforce it. This was the position in *Wyatt v Kreglinger*. At the other extreme, he noted, are cases where the invalid restraint is merely an incident of a larger transaction which could survive without difficulty the elimination of the invalid restraint, of which *Bull v Pitney-Bowes* was an illustration. But it is often and perhaps usually the case that the promise would not have been given but for the invalid restraint, yet this does not prevent the contract from being enforced without the invalid provision.[90] Adopting the formulation of Denning LJ in *Bennett v Bennett*,[91] Millett LJ stated: 'The contract will be upheld even if the consideration for the promise of the promisee includes an invalid restraint. It will be struck down in its entirety only if, in substance, and regardless of its form, it is an agreement for an invalid restraint.'[92] On the facts, in substance the consideration for the payment of renewal commission was not the acceptance by the claimant of the restraint, but his service in procuring business before his resignation.[93]

---

[86] See para 5.71 above.
[87] [1988] IRLR 388, para 19.
[88] See para 5.72 above.
[89] [1997] ICR 1065, 1069.
[90] ibid 1069–70.
[91] [1952] 1 KB 249, 261.
[92] [1997] ICR 1065, 1071.
[93] ibid 1072.

D. Repudiation

The importance of repudiation

The concept of repudiation is of central importance to the enforcement of restrictive covenants. **5.87** The reason for this is simple. The law, at least as it currently stands, is that repudiation of the employment contract by the employer, which is accepted by the employee, has the effect of releasing the employee from the restrictive covenants contained in the contract. This is sometimes referred to as the *General Billposting* rule after the House of Lords' decision which is the leading authority for the proposition.[94]

The *General Billposting* rule has obvious significance for employer and employee alike. As far **5.88** as the employer is concerned, however much time and effort has gone into the drafting of reasonable restrictive covenants, the benefit can be lost at a stroke by his repudiation of the employment contract. It is important to remember that it is not necessary for the employer to intend to repudiate. Rather repudiation can arise inadvertently. From the employee's point of view, the benefit of being freed from otherwise enforceable restrictive covenants as a result of the employer's repudiation may be considerable. Indeed, the employee may find himself with a windfall. As a result of his employer's actions, the employee may be able to recover damages for the employer's breach (so as to put the employee in the same position, so far as money can do so, as if the contract had been performed), whilst at the same time being released from the restrictive covenants. In this sense, the employee may be far better off than if there had been no repudiation by the employer.

Repudiation is not, of course, important only in relation to the enforcement of post- **5.89** termination restrictive covenants. It is relevant to other areas covered by this book. For example, an employer may lose the right to place an employee on garden leave as a result of his repudiation. Particular considerations apply, however, in relation to an employer's ability to protect his confidential information following his repudiation of the employ- ment contract. Given that confidential information is seen as a proprietary right of the employer, and that the duty of confidence is an equitable obligation quite apart from one founded in contract, an employer may be able to enforce his right to confidentiality notwithstanding his repudiation of the employment contract.[95]

As stated above, the *General Billposting* rule represents the law at least as it currently stands. **5.90** Doubt has been cast on whether the rule remains valid given developments in the law and commercial practice since the House of Lords' decision almost a century ago.[96] There are persuasive arguments in favour of a move away from the inflexibility of the *General Billposting* rule and it is to be hoped that the House of Lords has an opportunity to review the law in this area in the near future.

A striking illustration of the fundamental effect of repudiation on the attempt to enforce **5.91** restrictive covenants is provided by the case of *Cantor Fitzgerald International v Bird*.[97] Bird, Boucher, and Gill were all employed by Cantor Fitzgerald International (CFI) as brokers.

---

[94] [1909] AC 118, HL, discussed below.
[95] *Campbell v Frisbee* [2003] ICR 141, CA, discussed below.
[96] *Rock Refrigeration Ltd v Jones* [1997] ICR 938, CA *per* Phillips LJ, discussed below.
[97] [2002] IRLR 867.

CFI sought to introduce new remuneration arrangements for its employees. None of the three defendants was willing to accept the new arrangements. In the meantime, the defendants were approached to join Icap, a competitor of CFI. They accepted offers of employment with Icap. The employees' attempts to procure their early release from their CFI contracts having failed, each resigned and claimed constructive dismissal. The grounds for constructive dismissal were said to be the manner in which CFI sought to introduce the new remuneration arrangements which was said to amount to a breach of the implied duty of trust and confidence.

5.92 The employees' contracts contained restrictive covenants against soliciting or transacting business with any of CFI's clients with whom the employee had been actively involved during the previous twelve months. CFI commenced proceedings in which it sought injunctions to enforce these restrictive covenants. The employees' counterclaimed for damages for CFI's repudiation of the employment contracts.

5.93 As far as one of the employees was concerned, Boucher, the proposal to change his remuneration had been handled by a Mr Alcan, a senior managing director of CFI. Alcan had been enthusiastic but not aggressive in his advocacy of the new system. In contrast, the other two employees, Bird and Gill, had dealt with two other senior executives, Messrs La Vecchia and Amaitis. Their promotion of the new system was aggressive, accompanied by swearing and obscenities, and involved threats to pay nil bonuses under the current system. Their explanations of the new system were perfunctory and misleading, and consultation was inadequate. In short, the conduct of these executives towards the employees Bird and Gill was a breach of the duty of trust and confidence and, hence, a repudiation of the employment contract. This repudiation was accepted by the employees' resignation. As a result, in accordance with the *General Billposting* rule, the employees were no longer bound by their restrictive covenants. In contrast, Alcan's behaviour towards the employee Boucher did not overstep the line in the same way. His attempts to persuade Boucher of the merits of the new arrangements did not breach the duty of trust and confidence. As a result, Boucher was not constructively dismissed and remained bound by his restrictive covenant. An injunction was granted against Boucher enforcing the covenant.

5.94 The difference in outcome between *Bird* and *Gill*, on the one hand, and *Boucher*, on the other, is explicable entirely by the difference in the employer's conduct towards the employees. In the former case, the employer's conduct repudiated the employment contract as a result of which it lost the right to enforce the restrictive covenants. In the latter case, the employer's conduct was not repudiatory and the employee remained bound by the covenants.

5.95 In considering repudiation in this field, there are two distinct elements that require examination, (a) whether the employee has accepted a repudiatory breach by the employer; and (b) if so, what is the effect in law of that outcome. Each of these elements will be considered below in turn.

Repudiation and acceptance

5.96 Before the *General Billposting* rule can come into play, the employee must accept a repudiatory breach by the employer. There are two questions to be asked here:

(1) Is there a repudiation of the employment contract by the employer?
(2) If so, has the employee accepted the repudiation or affirmed the contract?

A recent line of cases has addressed whether, in answering these questions, it is relevant that   **5.97**
the employee may himself have committed a breach of contract prior to or at the same time
as the employer's alleged breach. This developing area of law is addressed below following the
discussion of these initial two questions.[98]

Is there a repudiation of the employment contract by the employer?

A repudiatory breach of contract by the employer can be a breach of an express or an implied   **5.98**
term of the contract.

However, whilst every breach entitles an employee to sue the employer for damages, not   **5.99**
every breach entitles an employee to resign and claim constructive dismissal.[99] It is only
breaches which are repudiatory that entitle an employee to take this course. Even then the
employee has a choice: he can continue with the contract (affirmation) and sue for damages
(if he wishes); or, he can terminate the contract in response to the repudiation, and sue for
damages (if he wishes). It is necessary, therefore, to consider what amounts to a repudiation
or repudiatory breach.

The meaning of repudiation

The classic definition of a repudiatory breach entitling an employee to resign was given by   **5.100**
Lord Denning MR in *Western Excavating (ECC) Ltd v Sharp*.[100] It still holds good today.
Lord Denning MR said:

> If the employer is guilty of conduct which is a significant breach going to the root of the
> contract of employment, or which shows that the employer no longer intends to be bound by
> one or more of the essential terms of the contract, then the employee is entitled to treat himself
> as discharged from any further performance. If he does so, then he terminates the contract by
> reason of the employer's conduct. He is constructively dismissed. The employee is entitled in
> those circumstances to leave at the instant without giving any notice at all or, alternatively, he
> may give notice and say he is leaving at the end of the notice. But the conduct must in either
> case be sufficiently serious to entitle him to leave at once. Moreover, he must make up his mind
> soon after the conduct of which he complains: for, if he continues for any length of time with-
> out leaving, he will lose his right to treat himself as discharged. He will be regarded as having
> elected to affirm the contract.[101]

This passage is important for a number of reasons, one of which is Lord Denning MR's
definition of a repudiatory breach by an employer as 'a significant breach going to the root of
the contract of employment, or which shows that the employer no longer intends to be
bound by one or more of the essential terms of the contract'.

Breach of the duty of trust and confidence

Many, if not most, of the cases in which an employee alleges constructive dismissal involve an   **5.101**
allegation that the employer has acted in breach of the duty of trust and confidence. This is a
relatively recent trend. It demonstrates the extent to which this implied term has become

---

[98] See paras 5.117–5.124 below.
[99] 'Constructive dismissal' is a term used in the context of the statutory right not to be unfairly dismissed.
It describes the situation in which an employee terminates the employment contract, with or without notice, in
circumstances in which he is entitled to terminate it without notice by reason of the employer's conduct:
Employment Rights Act 1996, s 95(1)(c). However, it is useful shorthand to describe termination at common
law in the same circumstances, as discussed in this section, whether or not an unfair dismissal claim is made.
[100] [1978] ICR 221, CA.
[101] ibid 226.

established in recent years. It is also testimony to the flexibility of the term, allowing an employee to complain of the cumulative effect of mistreatment under the trust and confidence rubric.

5.102 The implied term of trust and confidence may be stated as follows: 'The employer shall not without reasonable and proper cause conduct itself in a manner calculated or likely to destroy or seriously damage the relationship of trust and confidence between employer and employee.'[102] However, the obligation of trust and confidence does not prevail over express contractual terms.[103]

5.103 The test as to whether there has been a breach of the implied term is an objective one.[104] Neither the employer's intention nor the employee's perception is material, although the court may take account of the employee's reaction as an indication of the gravity of the employer's conduct.[105] The test is 'whether viewed objectively, the employer's conduct so impacted on the employee that the employee could properly conclude that the employer was repudiating the contract'.[106] It is therefore no answer for the employer to argue that his conduct fell within a range of reasonable responses. As Sedley LJ stated in *Buckland v Bournemouth University Higher Education Corp*:

> Take the simplest and commonest of fundamental breaches on an employer's part, a failure to pay wages. If the failure is due, as it not infrequently is, to a major customer defaulting on payment, not paying the staff's wages is arguably the most, indeed the only, reasonable response to the situation. But to hold that it is not a fundamental breach would drive a coach and four through the law of contract, of which this aspect of employment law is an integral part.[107]

5.104 Thus it was plainly a breach of contract to treat an employee as not being entitled to benefits resulting from his being a permanent employee when he was in fact a permanent employee. 'The good faith with which the erroneous belief was held does not alter the character of the failure.'[108]

5.105 Any breach of the implied term of trust and confidence will amount to a repudiation of the contract. This is because the very essence of a breach of the implied term is that it is 'calculated or likely to *destroy* or *seriously damage* the relationship'.[109]

5.106 Furthermore, an employer can breach the implied term of trust and confidence by one act alone or by a series of acts which cumulatively amount to a repudiatory breach of contract, even if the last in that series is not actually a breach of contract at all. As Dyson LJ explained in *Waltham Forest LBC v Omilaju*:[110]

> A final straw, not itself a breach of contract, may result in a breach of the implied term of trust and confidence. The quality that the final straw must have is that it should be an act in a series whose

---

[102] *Woods v WM Car Services (Peterborough) Ltd* [1981] ICR 666, 670 *per* Browne-Wilkinson J; *Lewis v Motorworld Garages Ltd* [1986] ICR 157; *Imperial Group Pension Trust Ltd v Imperial Tobacco Ltd* [1991] ICR 524; *Malik v BCCI* [1997] ICR 606, HL, 621 *per* Lord Steyn; *Transco plc v O'Brien* [2002] ICR 721, CA, paras 11–13 *per* Pill LJ; *Cantor Fitzgerald International v Bird* [2002] IRLR 867, paras 97–100 *per* McCombe J.

[103] *Fish v Dresdner Kleinwort Ltd* [2009] IRLR 1035.

[104] *Malik v BCCI* [1997] ICR 606, HL, 623 *per* Lord Steyn.

[105] *Tullett Prebon plc and others v BGC Brokers LP and others* [2010] IRLR 648, para 74.

[106] *Horkulak v Cantor Fitzgerald International* [2003] IRLR 756, para 34 *per* Newman J; *Waltham Forest LB v Omilaju* [2005] IRLR 35, CA, para 14 *per* Dyson LJ.

[107] [2010] ICR 908, [2010] IRLR 445, para 28.

[108] *Transco plc v O'Brien* [2002] ICR 721, CA, para 22 *per* Pill LJ.

[109] *Waltham Forest LB v Omilaju* [2005] IRLR 35, CA, para 14 *per* Dyson LJ (emphasis added).

[110] [2005] IRLR 35, CA.

cumulative effect is to amount to a breach of the implied term. I do not use the phrase 'an act in a series' in a precise or technical sense. The act does not have to be of the same character as the earlier acts. Its essential quality is that, when taken in conjunction with the earlier acts on which the employee relies, it amounts to a breach of the implied term of trust and confidence. It must contribute something to that breach, although what it adds may be relatively insignificant.[111]

In *Horkulak v Cantor Fitzgerald International*[112] at first instance, Newman J extracted from the speeches in the House of Lords in *Malik v BCCI*[113] and *Johnson v Unisys*[114] a number of points of particular relevance to the facts of that case (and to many in which the trust and confidence term arises in the context of restraint of trade), as follows: **5.107**

(i)   The notion of an employment contract giving rise to a 'master and servant' relationship is now obsolete (Lord Steyn, Mahmud 468).[115]

(ii) The obligation of mutual trust and confidence has emerged from the general duty of cooperation between contracting parties (see Professor Brodie: (1996) 25 ILJ 121).

(iii) The relationship remains defined by the respective role and responsibilities of the employer and the employee. The employer has the right to exercise authority and to instruct and direct, namely to 'manage his business as he sees fit' and the employee has a duty to comply with reasonable instructions and directions. The responsibility for the running of the business and the methods of achieving the legitimate aims of the business ultimately lie with the employer.

(iv) Given that the respective roles are, at their elemental level, as in (iii) above, the movement away from a master and servant relationship requires particular attention to the element of cooperation which underpins the character of the contract of employment. An employee's participation in the business cannot simply be regarded as the work of a servant for the benefit of the employer, but has to be recognised as '. . . one of the most important things in his or her life. It gives not only a livelihood but an occupation, an identity and a sense of self-esteem' (Lord Hoffmann *Johnson v Unisys* 286).[116]

(v)   In a master and servant relationship, the benefit for the servant was to be paid a wage. The 'cooperation' required of an employer, to which a contract of employment gives rise in modern times, cannot be met simply by remuneration, nor, in my judgment, can the level of it affect the principle which is now in play. I reject as fallacious the proposition, which has surfaced in argument from time to time, that where very substantial sums are paid by an employer, he acquires a right to treat employees according to a different standard of conduct from that which might otherwise be required.

(vi) In the instant case the thrust of some of the argument has been to the effect that huge salaries are paid in broking houses because employees may be subjected to stress, anxiety and summary treatment. As the expression goes, 'if you can't stand the heat of the kitchen, get out'. Obviously the court must recognise and pay regard to the character and nature of the business in question. But due regard will not exclude the application of the law as it has developed, for as Lord Steyn observed in *Johnson v Unisys Ltd* (paragraph 19, 283):

'. . . stress-related psychiatric and psychological problems of employees . . . [have] greatly increased.'

'These considerations are testimony to the need for implied terms in contracts of employment protecting employees from harsh and unacceptable employment practices.'

---

[111] ibid para 19.
[112] [2003] IRLR 756. The decision of Newman J was appealed only on the issue of quantum not liability.
[113] [1997] ICR 606, HL.
[114] [2001] ICR 480, HL.
[115] This is a reference to the *Malik v BCCI* report at [1997] IRLR 462 (see also [1997] ICR 606).
[116] This is a reference to the *Johnson v Unisys* report at [2001] IRLR 279 (see also [2001] ICR 480).

'Inevitably, the incidence of psychiatric injury due to excessive stress has increased. The need for protection of employees through their contractual rights, express and implied by law, is markedly greater than in the past'.

(vii)   The particular role and status of an employee will define the character and degree of cooperation to which the contract of employment gives rise. For example, a senior manager is likely to perform some of the employer's functions and will be seen by employees to be doing so, whilst also being subject to a more senior manager who is his employer.

(viii) A senior manager can cooperate in a business at a high level of involvement. In the performance of his contract he needs to cultivate and maintain the confidence of those employees over whom he exercises managerial control and he needs the support and cooperation of his 'employer', more senior management, to carry out his duties in this regard and generally. Since he has managerial duties, his judgment having been invoked cannot properly be subjected to instant and dismissive conclusions which accord no respect to his viewpoint. Cooperation at this level takes on characteristics akin to partnership. In this connection the so-called 'blood oath' agreement is not without relevance.

Other breaches

5.108   Employers may breach employment contracts in many ways other than by breaching the duty of trust and confidence. The essential test against which an alleged breach can always be measured is Lord Denning MR's in *Western Excavating v Sharp*.[117] A unilateral reduction in pay, and a change in job duties, have been held to amount to a breach.[118] Whether the breach is repudiatory depends on its seriousness in the circumstances. Thus, it has been held that a slight change in pay imposed on a reluctant employee by economic pressure exerted by the employer would entitle the employee to treat himself as discharged by the employer's breach.[119] Payment in lieu of notice may amount to a repudiation if there is no contractual term permitting this.[120] However, requiring an employee to stay away from work for the remaining two months of a twelve-month contract under which she was entitled to a share of profits was not a repudiation by the employer.[121]

5.109   The facts and circumstances of each case require careful examination, having regard to the principles referred to above, in deciding whether the employer has committed a repudiatory breach of contract.

Has the employee accepted the repudiation or affirmed the contract?

5.110   As Lord Denning MR said in *Western Excavating v Sharp*, the employee who is a victim of a repudiatory breach by the employer must make up his mind soon after the conduct of which he complains, otherwise he will lose the right to treat himself as discharged.[122]

5.111   An employee must accept the repudiation if he is to be discharged from performing his future contractual obligations by reason of the employer's breach. Acceptance should be clear and unequivocal. This is normally achieved by the employee resigning in writing.

---

[117] See n 100 above.
[118] Many of the cases are discussed in *Harvey on Industrial Relations and Employment Law*, Division DI.
[119] *Cantor Fitzgerald International v Callaghan* [1999] IRLR 234, CA, especially para 43 *per* Judge LJ.
[120] *Dixon v Stenor* [1973] ICR 157; cf *Rex Stewart Jeffries Parker Ginsberg Ltd v Parker* [1988] IRLR 483, CA.
[121] *Spencer v Marchington* [1988] IRLR 22.
[122] [1978] ICR 221, CA, 226.

It is advisable, albeit not essential, for the employee to state in his written resignation that he is resigning in response to the employer's breach(es) of the employment contract, and give some details of the alleged breach(es).

In *Cantor Fitzgerald International v Bird*,[123] which is discussed above, it was argued that the **5.112** employees had affirmed their contracts by delaying their resignations, and thereby lost their right to rely on the employer's repudiation. The employees had waited two months before resigning whilst indicating their discontent and giving clear signs of their intention to leave. McCombe J held that they had not affirmed their contracts. The judge set out the general position on affirmation by reference to a passage in *Chitty on Contracts*:

> Where the innocent party, being entitled to choose whether to treat the contract as continuing or to accept the repudiation and treat himself as discharged, elects to treat the contract as continuing, he is usually said to have 'affirmed' the contract. He will not be held to have elected to affirm the contract unless, first, he has knowledge of the facts giving rise to the breach, and, secondly, he has knowledge of his legal right to choose between the alternatives open to him. Affirmation may be express or implied. It will be implied if, with knowledge of the breach and of his right to choose, he does some unequivocal act from which it may be inferred that he intends to go on with the contract regardless of the breach or from which it may be inferred that he will not exercise his right to treat the contract as repudiated.[124]

McCombe J then referred with approval to a decision of the Employment Appeal Tribunal **5.113** in *Morse v Dorrington*,[125] in which Morison J cited the following passage from *Harvey on Employment Law*:

> There is no fixed time limit in which the employee must make up his mind. It depends upon all the circumstances including the employee's length of service, the nature of the breach and whether the employee has protested at the change. Mere protest will not, however, prevent an inference that the employee has waived the breach, although exceptionally a clear reservation of rights might do so. Where the employee is faced with giving up his job and being unemployed or waiving the breach, it's not surprising that the courts are sometimes reluctant to conclude that he lost his right to treat himself as discharged by the employer merely by working at the job for a few months.[126]

McCombe J concluded that affirmation 'is essentially the legal embodiment of the everyday **5.114** concept of "letting bygones be bygones"'.[127] This had not occurred on the facts of the case before him.

Breaches which do not cause the employee to resign

In a 'typical' restrictive covenant case, the employee's case will be that he is not bound by the **5.115** restrictive covenants because he resigned in consequence of the employer's repudiatory breach of contract. However, there may be circumstances in which an employee is released from restrictive covenants even if he did not resign in consequence of the breach.

In *Tullett Prebon plc and others v BGC Brokers LP and others*,[128] Jack J considered the position **5.116** of employees who resign and only subsequently discover that their employer was in repudiatory

---

123 [2002] IRLR 867. See paras 5.91–5.94 above.
124 Now (29th edn, 2004) para 24-003.
125 [1997] IRLR 488, 491.
126 [2002] IRLR 867, para 108.
127 ibid para 129.
128 [2010] IRLR 648.

breach of contract. The employee would have no claim for damages for constructive dismissal, as the breach did not cause him to resign.[129] However, in the same way as an employer who dismisses his employee can rely on grounds of which he was unaware at the time of dismissal, so too an employee can justify his departure by pointing to a repudiatory breach of contract which he only discovered afterwards. He may therefore be released from restrictive covenants even if he did not resign in response to the breach.[130]

The relevance of the employee's own breach

5.117 It is not uncommon for employment relationships to break down in a storm of allegations and counter-allegations. If the employee in such circumstances claims constructive dismissal on the basis of an alleged breach of contract by his employer, it is only natural that the employer would wish to point to the employee's own alleged breaches. Why, the employer might ask, should the employee gain all the advantages of proving constructive dismissal if his conduct was also open to criticism?

5.118 In *RDF Media Group v Clements*,[131] Mr Clements' employer, RDF, conducted what the judge described as a 'campaign of vilification' by criticizing him in briefings to the press. Mr Clements resigned, claiming that he was accepting RDF's repudiatory breach of the implied term of trust and confidence. It subsequently emerged that, prior to RDF's press briefings, Mr Clements had disclosed confidential information about RDF to one of its competitors. The court held that this conduct was itself a breach of the term of trust and confidence. RDF argued that Mr Clements could not rely on its alleged breach of the implied term of trust and confidence given that he had already breached it himself. Bernard Livesey QC (sitting as a Deputy High Court Judge) observed that:

> The question is not easy to resolve. I have been referred to some authority and ordinary contractual principles do not seem to provide a clear answer. The breach by Mr Clements preceded the breach by RDF; RDF was not at the time aware of the breach and so the contract continued in force, although RDF clearly did not affirm it. Had RDF known of Mr Clements' breach prior to its briefing of the Sunday Herald it would have accepted it as a repudiation of the contract and the representations to [the journalist] would not have been a breach of its implied obligation. Mr Casey argues that the proper analysis is that the contract did indeed continue, it was terminated by Mr Clements accepting RDF's repudiatory breach; the anterior breach by Mr Clements is not forgiven and forgotten, it remains but sounds only in damages. Where, as here, damages is not the essence of either party's claim for relief, I do not accept that such a result is either a satisfactory or equitable solution.[132]

5.119 The judge then outlined two ways in which the employee's breach could be relevant. First, and most striking, was the court's conclusion that where an employee is himself in repudiatory breach of a mutual obligation, he is not entitled to accept any repudiation of that obligation by his employer.[133] This conclusion was based on two House of Lords authorities concerning arbitration agreements.[134] Secondly, the judge held that the alternative way of looking at matters was this:

---

[129] ibid para 78.
[130] ibid paras 79–80.
[131] [2008] IRLR 207.
[132] ibid para 139.
[133] ibid para 140.
[134] *Bremer Vulcan Schiffbau Und Maschinenfabrik v South India Shipping Corp* [1981] AC 909, and *Paal Wilson v Partenreederei Hannah Blumenthal* [1983] 1 AC 854.

...if one looks objectively at the relationship between RDF and Mr Clements, that relationship had already been seriously damaged or destroyed by misconduct on his part which went to the root of the relationship. The point is one of causation as well as equity. As a matter of causation I would hold that the relationship was destroyed not by RDF but by Mr Clements as a result of his anterior breach of the mutual obligation. It would also be inequitable for Mr Clements if he were able to claim that RDF caused serious damage to the relationship where the relationship in question was already seriously damaged or destroyed by his own conduct.[135]

The *RDF* judgment has proved somewhat controversial. It was strongly endorsed by the **5.120** Employment Appeal Tribunal (Scotland) in *Aberdeen CC v McNeill*.[136] The employee claimed that he was constructively dismissed, relying on alleged breaches of the implied term of trust and confidence in disciplinary proceedings against him. The employer argued that, if there were any such breaches, the employee could not accept them because he had himself breached that term by, among other things, being drunk at work and sexually harassing another employee. The EAT accepted the employer's argument. However, in doing so it relied heavily on a principle of Scottish common law that: 'If a party to such a contract is in material breach of one of his obligations he cannot insist that the other party perform a reciprocal term.'[137]

In England and Wales, *RDF* has been less warmly embraced.[138] In *Tullett Prebon plc and* **5.121** *others v BGC Brokers LP and others*,[139] Jack J rejected the suggestion that where an employee is in repudiatory breach of his contract of employment he cannot accept a breach by his employer to bring the contract to end. Instead:

> The ordinary position is that, if there is a breach of a contract by one party which entitles the other to terminate the contract but he does not do so, then the contract both remains in being and may be terminated by the first party if the second party has himself committed a repudiatory breach of the contract.[140]

The court in *Tullett* also rejected the alternative suggestion in *RDF* that the employee's **5.122** conduct may have so damaged the mutual relationship of trust and confidence that the employer's conduct is of little effect. Jack J said:

> I accept that the relationship is a mutual one, but that means only that the employer is entitled to have trust and confidence in his employee, and the employee is entitled to have trust and confidence in his employer. If the one is damaged it does not follow that the other is damaged. Nor does damage to the one party's trust and confidence in the other entitle him to damage the other's trust and confidence in him.[141]

Instead, Jack J proposed a third way in which the employee's conduct may be relevant: **5.123**

> In my judgment the conduct of the employee may be relevant in this way. Whether the employer's conduct has sufficiently damaged the trust and confidence which the employee has in him objectively judged, is to be judged in all the circumstances. The circumstances will include the employee's own conduct to the extent that it is relevant to that question.[142]

---

[135] *RDF* para 141.
[136] [2010] IRLR 374.
[137] ibid para 87.
[138] See also *S G & R Valuation Service Co LLC v Boudrais* [2008] IRLR 770 paras 27–28, in which Cranston J doubted the *RDF* decision on this point.
[139] [2010] IRLR 648.
[140] ibid para 83.
[141] ibid para 84.
[142] ibid para 85.

5.124 The law on the relevance of an employee's conduct is therefore a developing area. In summary, the authorities currently suggest that if an employee has breached the implied term of trust and confidence, and if the employer has not affirmed the contract,[143] then:

(1) the employee will be unable to accept any subsequent breach of that term by the employer (the first principle in *RDF*); or

(2) as the employee has already destroyed the mutual trust and confidence, the employer's subsequent conduct will not constitute a breach of that term (the second principle in *RDF*); or

(3) the conduct of the employee will be taken into account in deciding whether the employer subsequently breaches the implied term of trust and confidence (the principle in *Tullett*).

The effect of repudiation

5.125 Employees do sometimes leave their present employment and join a competitor as a genuine response to their employer's breach(es) of the employment contract. Conversely, it is not infrequently the case that employees wishing to be released from their restrictive covenants contrive a claim of repudiation against their employer. The reason for this is what has come to be known as the *General Billposting* rule.

The *General Billposting* rule

5.126 By the *General Billposting* rule is meant the proposition that a repudiation of an employment contract by an employer, which is accepted by the employee in terminating the contract, has the effect that the employee is no longer bound by the restrictive covenants contained in the contract. This proposition is derived from the House of Lords' decision in *General Billposting Co Ltd v Atkinson*.[144]

5.127 Atkinson was employed as managing director and secretary of the company. His employment contract, which was entered into in 1901, was terminable by either party giving twelve months' notice in writing. Clause 9 of the contract purported to restrain Atkinson for a period of two years after termination from competing with the company within a radius of fifty miles, and further provided that if he did he would pay £250 as liquidated damages. The company dismissed Atkinson on 28 March 1906 without notice. He sued the company for wrongful dismissal and on 10 July 1906 recovered £350, being the amount of a year's salary and bonus calculated in the manner provided by the contract. In October 1906 Atkinson commenced business in competition with the company within the restricted area defined by clause 9 of the contract. That is to say, within three months of recovering damages for the company's breach of the employment contract, Atkinson commenced to act in breach of his restrictive covenant. In September 1907, the company commenced an action for damages for breach of clause 9.[145] The trial judge (Neville J) upheld the company's claim. The Court of Appeal allowed the employee's appeal, a decision affirmed by the House of Lords.

---

[143] For examples of an employer affirming a contract following an employee's breach, see *Cook v MSHK Ltd* [2009] IRLR 838, CA.

[144] [1909] AC 118, HL, affirming the decision of the Court of Appeal: [1908] 1 Ch 537, CA (Cozens-Hardy MR, Fletcher Moulton, and Buckley LJJ). See also *Measures Bros Ltd v Measures* [1910] 2 Ch 248, CA; *Konski v Peet* [1915] 1 Ch 530.

[145] The procedural history is summarized in the report of the Court of Appeal decision: [1908] 1 Ch 537, 538.

Three speeches only were given by the House of Lords. Lords Robertson and Collins gave **5.128**
short speeches, and the Earl of Halsbury agreed with Lord Collins. The latter considered the
true test applicable to the facts of the case to have been laid down by earlier authority: 'That
the true question is whether the acts and conduct of the party evince an intention no longer to
be bound by the contract.' Lord Collins continued: 'I think the Court of Appeal had ample
ground for drawing this inference from the conduct of the appellants here in dismissing the
respondent in deliberate disregard of the terms of the contract, and that the latter was thereupon justified in rescinding the contract and treating himself as absolved from the further
performance of it on his part.'[146]

Developments in the law after *General Billposting v Atkinson*

Lord Collins, in the passage from his speech in *General Billposting v Atkinson* cited in the **5.129**
preceding paragraph, refers to the innocent party 'rescinding' the contract. It was later pointed
out by Lord Porter in *Heymans v Darwins Ltd*[147] that the use of this term in this context may
not be correct:

> To say that the contract is rescinded or has come to an end or has ceased to exist may in indi-
> vidual cases convey the truth with sufficient accuracy, but the fuller expression that the injured
> party is thereby absolved from future performance of his obligations under the contract is a
> more exact description of the position. Strictly speaking, to say that on acceptance of the
> renunciation of a contract the contract is rescinded is incorrect.[148]

It is possible yet fruitless to expend much energy debating the correct terminology to describe **5.130**
the discharge of a contract. Terms such as 'repudiation', 'renunciation', 'rescission', and 'discharge'
have enormous capacity to confuse. In this chapter, in an attempt to achieve clarity and
consistency: 'repudiation' will be used to describe the conduct of the party (generally the
employer) who acts in fundamental breach of the contract; 'acceptance' will describe the act
of the innocent party (generally the employee) in accepting the repudiation so as to bring the
contract to an end; and 'termination' to describe the discharge of the contract by the innocent
party's acceptance of the repudiation. It is important to remember, however, that termination
of a contract in such circumstances does not extinguish accrued rights of the parties as at the
time of termination. As Lord Collins explained in *General Billposting v Atkinson* and Lord
Porter in *Heymans v Darwins*, the true effect is to absolve the innocent party from future
performance of his obligations under the contract (subject to what is discussed below).

Apart from acting as a corrective to terminological inexactitude, *Heymans v Darwins* is also **5.131**
a straw in the wind heralding a more questioning approach to the validity of the *General
Billposting* rule. The contract under consideration in *Heymans v Darwins* contained an arbitration clause providing for a reference to arbitration of any dispute relating to the contract.
The House of Lords held that the arbitration clause applied even if the dispute involved an
assertion that one or both parties had been discharged from further performance under the
contract as a result of one party's acceptance of the other's repudiation.[149]

---

[146] [1909] AC 118, 122.
[147] [1942] AC 356, HL.
[148] ibid 399.
[149] In *Hurst v Bryk* [1999] Ch 1, CA, Hobhouse LJ described arbitration clauses (such as that in *Heyman v
Darwins*), and jurisdiction clauses, as 'a special category of express ancillary contract which by necessary implication applies to the consequences of breach' (ibid 22). See also *Crowther v Brownsword*, unreported, 22 July
1999, CA, especially paras 25–6 *per* Mance LJ.

5.132   Of greater importance in the developing case law is *Photo Productions Ltd v Securicor Transport Ltd*.[150] The appellant provided security services. It entered into a contract with the respondent to provide a night patrol service at its factory. One of the appellant's employees lit a small fire in the factory that got out of control. The factory burnt down. The contract between the parties contained an exclusion clause excluding the appellant's liability in certain circumstances (which applied here). The Court of Appeal (Lord Denning MR presiding) followed the approach that where one party was in fundamental breach of the contract, which the other accepted so that the contract was at an end, the guilty party could not rely on an exclusion clause to escape from its liability for breach. The House of Lords disagreed. It held that the question of whether and to what extent an exclusion clause was to be applied to any breach of contract was a matter of construction of the contract.

5.133   The importance of this development for present purposes is that it emphasizes that, at least in relation to contracts where the parties bargain on equal terms, it is for the parties to decide the terms of the contract and for the court to construe it so as to ascertain the parties' intentions. This applies just as much to the circumstances where one party repudiates the contract as it does to other incidents of the relationship between the contracting parties.

Attempts to circumvent the *General Billposting* rule ('howsoever caused')

5.134   The *General Billposting* rule posed a problem for employers and a challenge for their lawyers. The problem has already been referred to: a repudiation of the employment contract by the employer, which might be unintentional, would be sufficient to deprive the employer of the protection afforded by restrictive covenants contained in the contract. The challenge for those advising employers was how to avoid this effect.

5.135   In rising to the challenge, and perhaps influenced by the approach adopted by the courts in allowing the parties to agree what should happen in the event of a repudiation (see *Photo Productions v Securicor*, discussed above), restrictive covenants were drafted so as to provide that they should apply even in the event of a repudiation by the employer. During the late 1980s and the 1990s it became increasingly common to encounter references to a period of restriction following termination 'howsoever caused', 'for whatever reason', 'however that comes about', and (when drafted by the most astute) 'whether lawful or not'. The courts had to decide whether these formulations circumvented the *General Billposting* rule.

5.136   In *Briggs v Oates*,[151] the termination of a solicitor's partnership during the currency of an employed solicitor's employment by the partnership was a breach of the contract that brought the employment to an end. The employment contract contained an area covenant whereby the solicitor agreed not to practice as a solicitor within a certain area for five years after the agreement 'shall have determined for whatever reason'. It was argued for the claimant that even if the reason for the determination were the wrongful dismissal of the defendant, the restrictive covenant would on its true construction still apply. Scott J rejected this submission. He noted that the breach of contract was accepted by the defendant as putting an end to the contract. 'In such a case outstanding contractual obligations of the injured party are in law discharged together with the contract.' The result did not, in his judgment, depend on the construction of the contract. However, the judge went on to consider the position if the above reason were wrong and if, on its true construction, the covenant did purport to

---

[150]   [1980] AC 827, HL.
[151]   [1990] ICR 473.

apply in the event of a wrongful dismissal. In that case, Scott J said (obiter) that he would regard the covenant as unreasonable: 'A contract under which an employee could be immediately and wrongfully dismissed but would nevertheless remain subject to an anti-competitive restraint seems to me to be grossly unreasonable. I would not be prepared to enforce the restraint in such a contract.'[152]

Scott J's approach was cited with approval by Lord Coulsfield in the Outer House of the Court of Session in *Living Design (Home Improvements) Ltd v Davidson*.[153] He was confronted by a restraint which purported to apply after the termination of employment 'however that comes about and whether lawful or not'. In Lord Coulsfield's view 'a restrictive covenant which is phrased so as to operate on the termination of the employment of an employee, however that comes about, and whether lawfully or not, is manifestly wholly unreasonable'.[154] In *PR Consultants Scotland Ltd v Mann*,[155] the Outer House of the Court of Session held that the words 'howsoever caused' qualifying the termination of employment were not apt to cover unlawful termination. There are many ways in which an employment contract can be lawfully terminated.[156]   **5.137**

In *Briggs v Oates* and *Living Design v Davidson*, it was the employer who sought to avail himself of the qualifying words so as to be able to enforce a restrictive covenant in the event of a wrongful dismissal. The tables were turned in *D v M*.[157] A non-solicitation covenant in that case purported to apply after termination 'for any reason whatsoever'; a non-competition covenant after termination 'irrespective of the cause or manner'. It was argued for the employee that a restrictive covenant that purported to apply in the event of a wrongful dismissal was unreasonable. In effect, it was contended that the words inserted with the aim of saving the covenant in the event of a repudiation by the employer served to defeat it even in the event of a lawful termination. Laws J agreed. He held that a restrictive covenant which on its face applies to the employer's benefit even where the termination has been induced by his own breach is necessarily unreasonable: 'Such a provision, if given effect, would constitute an evasion of the rule in *General Billposting*.'[158] In Laws J's view, the offending words could not be severed so as to save the covenant.[159]   **5.138**

Rock Refrigeration v Jones

Thus far, attempts by employers to circumvent the *General Billposting* rule by redrafting covenants and relying on construction arguments had not only failed but, rather, had backfired. Following *D v M* some restrictive covenants were now unenforceable that were not previously. However, a chink of light appeared at the end of this long tunnel in the form of the decision of the Court of Appeal in *Rock Refrigeration Ltd v Jones*.[160]   **5.139**

Jones was employed as industrial sales director of Rock Refrigeration. His contract of employment contained twelve-month post-termination restrictive covenants. These purported to   **5.140**

---

152 ibid 483–4.
153 [1994] IRLR 69.
154 ibid para 4.
155 [1996] IRLR 188.
156 ibid para 10 *per* Lord Caplan.
157 [1996] IRLR 192.
158 ibid para 23.
159 ibid paras 24–9.
160 [1997] ICR 938, [1996] IRLR 675, CA.

apply after termination of employment 'howsoever arising' and 'howsoever occasioned'. Jones resigned to join a competitor of his employer and the latter commenced proceedings to enforce the covenants. The trial judge (Sir Michael Davies), following *D v M*, held that the covenants were by their terms unreasonable restraints of trade, and therefore unenforceable, because they were expressed to take effect even where the contract was terminated by the employer's repudiatory breach.

5.141 The Court of Appeal allowed the appeal. It was the unanimous view of the three judges that the restrictive covenants were enforceable. *D v M* was overruled. Given the importance of the point at issue, and of the implications of the decision for future cases, it is necessary to examine the three judgments in a little detail.

5.142 Simon Brown LJ commenced his judgment by noting that the question raised on the appeal was one of some importance in the law relating to covenants in restraint of trade. He stated it thus: 'Is a restrictive covenant which is expressly provided to take effect upon the termination of a contract of employment "howsoever occasioned" necessarily unreasonable and thus unenforceable?'[161] Simon Brown LJ proceeded to answer this question by stating that the law applicable to covenants and restraint of trade had no relevance to the present situation. He continued:

> The most basic premise upon which the whole restraint of trade doctrine is founded is that, but for the doctrine's application, the covenant in question would otherwise operate to restrain the employee unduly. In other words the doctrine applies only where there exists an otherwise enforceable covenant. It renders unenforceable what otherwise would be enforceable.

> The whole point about the *General Billposting* principle is that, in cases of repudiatory breach by the employer, the employee is on that account released from his obligations under the contract and restrictive covenants, otherwise valid against him, accordingly cannot be enforced.[162]

> Thus: 'A covenant which in certain circumstances is discharged cannot be unenforceable under the restraint of trade doctrine merely because in the self-same circumstances it would be unreasonable to enforce it.'[163] It followed that it matters not whether covenants include or exclude phrases such as 'whether lawfully or not'. If they do, then to that extent they are merely 'writ in water, unenforceable under the *General Billposting* principle'.[164]

5.143 Morritt LJ similarly based his decision on an application of the *General Billposting* rule. This he stated as follows: 'It is not in doubt that if one party repudiates a contract and that repudiation is accepted by the other the latter is discharged from all further performance of primary obligations of the contract in question in addition to acquiring a right to damages for compensation for the breach.'[165] If the employment has been terminated by the wrongful act of the employer then, by definition, the employee must have accepted the repudiation and is no longer bound by its other terms.[166] Morritt LJ addressed the central question as follows:

> I do not see the question as depending on a point of construction. I would resolve it on the basis that the covenants, however expressed, cannot achieve the legally impossible. If the

---

[161] ibid 940.
[162] [1997] ICR 938, [1996] IRLR 675, CA, 946.
[163] ibid 946.
[164] ibid 946.
[165] ibid 948.
[166] ibid 950.

assumption of enforceability in the event of termination due to the employer's repudiation accepted by the employee is impossible then, even if as a matter of language the covenant applied in those assumed circumstances, the covenant cannot be unreasonable and therefore invalid as a whole on that account.[167]

As for the suggestion that the application of the *General Billposting* rule may enable an employee to retain for himself that which he should not when his employment had been terminated by his acceptance of his employer's repudiation, Morritt LJ doubted it. In his view, the employer's rights of property would remain unimpaired even if the employment terminated as a result of the employee's acceptance of his wrongful repudiation.[168]

It is the judgment of Phillips LJ that is, perhaps, most interesting and hints at a new way **5.144** forward. He agreed with the other two members of the court that the appeal should be allowed but explained that he did 'not find the route that leads to this conclusion as clear as the other members of the court'.[169] Phillips LJ reviewed the *General Billposting* rule and three recent decisions, namely *Briggs v Oates*, *Living Design v Davidson*, and *D v M*. He noted that counsel for the employee did not seek to contend that a restrictive covenant, however drafted, could survive the termination of the employment consequent upon the employer's repudiation. He explained:

> If a covenant otherwise reasonable, purports to remain binding in circumstances where the law will inevitably strike it down, I can see no justification for holding that it is, on that account, in unlawful restraint of trade. Thus, if [counsel] is correct to concede that the rule in *General Billposting* is of universal application, he cannot successfully support the decision of Sir Michael Davies. This is the short and simple route which leads to the conclusion that this appeal should be allowed.[170]

Phillips LJ then proceeded to discuss what he termed 'the alternative route'. In the course **5.145** of argument he had expressed reservations as to whether the *General Billposting* rule was consistent with more recent developments of the law of contract. He explained that when considering the case since the conclusion of argument, his reservations had grown. He declared: 'I have concluded that the rule in *General Billposting* accords neither with current legal principle nor with the requirements of business efficacy.'[171]

In discussing what he referred to as the problems with the *General Billposting* rule, Phillips LJ **5.146** stated that since 1909 (when *General Billposting v Atkinson* was decided) the law in relation to the discharge of contractual obligations by acceptance of a repudiation had been developed and clarified. He referred in this regard to *Heyman v Darwins* in which the House of Lords held that an arbitration clause remained binding after the acceptance of a repudiation.[172] He then cited from Lord Diplock's speech in *Photo Productions v Securicor*[173] in which he summarized the effect of accepting a repudiation as follows:

> (a) there is substituted by implication of law for the primary obligations of the party in default which remain unperformed a secondary obligation to pay money compensation to

---

[167] ibid 952.
[168] ibid 952–3.
[169] ibid 953.
[170] ibid 957.
[171] ibid 958.
[172] See paras 5.129–5.131 above.
[173] See para 5.132 above.

the other party for the loss sustained by him in consequence of their non-performance in the future and (b) the unperformed obligations of that other party are discharged.[174]

Phillips LJ saw no difficulty in applying these words to the reciprocal positive obligations that arise under a contract of employment: to provide services on the part of the employee, and to provide the consideration for those services on the part of the employer. But he considered that there were real difficulties in applying those words to the negative obligations that are placed on an employee by a restrictive covenant in relation to the period after his employment has ceased.[175]

5.147 Phillips LJ considered that the *General Billposting* rule posed practical problems for the employer who repudiates the contract: 'I do not accept that it is unreasonable for an employer to seek to impose restraints on his employee that will subsist, even should the employment come to an end as a consequence of a repudiation by the employer. On the contrary it seems to me commercially desirable that it should be possible to achieve this end.'[176] Phillips LJ continued in a passage of some potential importance for future developments in this area:

> In my judgment negative restraints agreed to apply after the termination of employment should not be equated with the primary obligations that are discharged when a contract of employment is terminated consequent upon repudiation . . . But for the *General Billposting* case I can see no principle of law which precludes the parties from validly agreeing to restraints that will subsist, even if the employment is brought to an end by repudiation. I think it at least arguable that, having regard to the subsequent development of this area of the law, not every restrictive covenant will be discharged upon a repudiatory termination of the employment.[177]

However, it was not necessary to resolve that issue. Assuming that the restrictive covenants survived the repudiatory termination, Phillips LJ held them to be reasonable: 'I do not consider that the remote possibility that the employer might terminate his employment in circumstances where it repudiated its obligation to comply with those terms rendered unreasonable covenants which purported to apply even if that contingency occurred.'[178]

5.148 Before leaving *Rock Refrigeration v Jones* it is worth taking a moment to consider the effect of the decision. Is Phillips LJ a lone voice crying in the wilderness for a review of the *General Billposting* rule? Did the other members of the court disavow his reservations as to the rule? The answer would appear to be no to both questions. For, as Phillips LJ explained, counsel's concession that the *General Billposting* rule was of universal application rendered unnecessary any examination by the court as to its continuing validity. This enabled Phillips LJ to advance the 'short and simple route', followed by the other two members of the court, to allowing the appeal. Indeed, Simon Brown LJ expressly recognized that his reasoning assumed the continuing validity of the *General Billposting* rule without him having reviewed it. As to his approach, he explained:

> All this, I should perhaps add, assumes (a) that all restrictive covenants necessarily become unenforceable upon the employee's acceptance of the employer's repudiatory breach—i.e.

---

[174] [1980] AC 827, 849.

[175] [1997] ICR 938, 958–9.

[176] [1997] ICR 938, 959.

[177] ibid 959–60. Another example of an ancillary or collateral obligation which survives termination consequent upon repudiation ('a discharge-proof provision') was the right to inspect records under an agency agreement: *Yasuda Fire & Marine Insurance Co of Europe Ltd v Orion Marine Insurance Underwriting Agency Ltd* [1995] QB 174, especially 187–91 *per* Colman J.

[178] [1997] ICR 938, 960.

that the *General Billposting* principle remains wholly unaffected by the *Photo Productions v Securicor* line of authority; and (b) that any wrongful termination of the contract by the employers will necessarily involve a repudiatory breach. Clearly the plot thickens . . . if either of those assumptions are unfounded.[179]

Developments in the law after *Rock Refrigeration v Jones*

The development regarding a possible departure from the *General Billposting* rule, found in **5.149** the judgment of Phillips LJ in *Rock Refrigeration v Jones* did not come to a halt with that case. Although the *General Billposting* rule has not since been authoritatively reconsidered, let alone set aside, further judicial dicta serve to reinforce Phillips LJ's assessment that it is ripe for fundamental review.

Indeed, Simon Brown LJ, one of the other two members of the court in *Rock Refrigeration v* **5.150** *Jones*, drew on Phillips LJ's analysis in the subsequent case of *Hurst v Bryk*.[180] Simon Brown LJ held that a partner's obligation to contribute to the future liabilities of a partnership was not one of those primary obligations from which a repudiatory breach discharges him. In reaching this conclusion, he drew heavily on the analysis of the House of Lords in *Heyman v Darwins*. He added:

> My approach to this issue, I may perhaps note, owes something to Phillips LJ's recent judgment in *Rock Refrigeration Ltd v Jones*, in which he envisages the continued enforceability of certain restrictive covenants following the repudiatory breach of an employment contract—a very different context, I recognise, but one nevertheless perhaps affording some help.[181]

Having stated his conclusion on the issue before him, Simon Brown LJ added: 'The doctrine **5.151** underlying the law of repudiatory breach is that a party shall not at one and the same time approbate and reprobate the contract. The law is not designed to achieve windfall profits for the innocent party; his undoubted right to damages is an ample safeguard against loss.'[182] This sentiment might, indeed, apply with some force in the field of restrictive covenants. It could be argued that Atkinson was fully compensated for his loss by the award of damages following his wrongful dismissal by General Billposting,[183] and that his release from the restrictive covenants was a windfall profit for him resulting from his employer's repudiation.

The Court of Appeal has more recently said that the law on the effect of an accepted repudia- **5.152** tion on contractual duties of confidence is unclear (*Campbell v Frisbee*).[184] Frisbee was engaged by the model Naomi Campbell to provide management services. Frisbee entered into a written confidentiality agreement to keep confidential, and not divulge to the media, information she acquired about Campbell in the course of her work. Following a breakdown in their relationship, Frisbee sold information about Campbell to the *News of the World*. Campbell sued Frisbee for breach of the written confidentiality agreement and the duty of confidence. Frisbee argued that she was released from her confidentiality obligations following her acceptance of Campbell's repudiatory breach of the contract for services (she contended in the

---

[179] ibid 947.
[180] [1999] Ch 1, CA, upheld by the House of Lords on other grounds: [2000] 2 WLR 740, HL.
[181] ibid 31.
[182] ibid 32.
[183] See para 5.126 above.
[184] [2003] ICR 141, CA.

alternative that disclosure was in the public interest). Campbell obtained summary judgment on part of her claim from the Deputy Master.

5.153 Lightman J dismissed Frisbee's appeal.[185] In the course of doing so, the judge reviewed a number of authorities including *General Billposting v Atkinson* and *Rock Refrigeration v Jones*. He concluded that, if it was necessary to decide the application by reference to the principles applicable in case of repudiation of a contract of employment by an employer, he would unhesitatingly hold (following the judgment of Morritt LJ in *Rock Refrigeration v Jones*)[186] that repudiation by Campbell and acceptance of that repudiation by Frisbee did not prejudice the rights of Campbell in respect of confidential information acquired by Frisbee in the course of her work.[187] 'There can be no conceivable justification for granting as a windfall to a wrongly dismissed employee a present of his employer's trade or other secrets or confidences.'[188] However, it was unnecessary to decide the case by reference to the *General Billposting* rule since it was not a case where the contractual relationship was under a contract of service between employer and employee: it was a contract for services between an independent contractor and a person engaging the services of that contractor. According to Lightman J, in the case of a contract for services, there could be no conceivable basis for the suggestion that a repudiatory breach by the client entitles the independent contractor to a release from obligations of confidentiality.[189]

5.154 The Court of Appeal allowed Frisbee's further appeal and gave her leave to defend the claim.[190] The judgment of the court was delivered by Lord Phillips MR who had called into question the *General Billposting* rule in *Rock Refrigeration v Jones*.[191] On the effect of repudiation in the circumstances of this case, Lord Phillips MR, having referred to *General Billposting v Atkinson* and *Rock Refrigeration v Jones*, said:

> We do not believe that the effect on duties of confidence assumed under contract when the contract in question is wrongfully repudiated is clearly established. While we do not consider that it is likely that Miss Frisbee will establish that Lightman J erred in his conclusions in a manner detrimental to her case, it cannot be said that she has no reasonable prospects of success on the issue. This issue of law was not one that was suitable for summary determination under CPR r24.[192]

Context in which the *General Billposting* rule may be relied upon

5.155 It is important to understand that the courts will approach an employee's reliance on the *General Billposting* rule differently according to whether the point is taken at an interim hearing or at a final trial.

5.156 At a final trial, the court can investigate all the facts relevant to the employee's claim that the employer repudiated the contract, and that the employee's acceptance released him from his restrictive covenants. The court will be in a position to reach a final determination on the repudiation question.

---

[185] [2002] EWHC 328 (Ch), [2002] EMLR 656. See L Clarke (2002) 31 ILJ 353.
[186] [1997] ICR 938, especially 952–3. See para 5.143 above.
[187] [2002] EWHC 328 (Ch), [2002] EMLR 656, para 21.
[188] ibid para 21.
[189] ibid para 22.
[190] [2003] ICR 141, CA. See L Clarke (2003) 32 ILJ 43.
[191] See paras 5.144–5.147 above.
[192] [2003] ICR 141, para 22.

Different considerations apply at the interim stage. When an employer applies for an interim **5.157** injunction pending trial, the employee may well advance his repudiation case at that stage. However, where the repudiation case depends on disputed facts (which will be so in the majority of cases), the court will be unable to resolve those disputed facts at the interim stage. The court will be inclined to find that there is a serious issue to be tried as to the repudiation question, and proceed to consider the balance of convenience. If an interim injunction is granted pending speedy trial, the repudiation issue can then be determined at the speedy trial.

Thus, in order to avail an employee at the interim stage, his repudiation case has to be either **5.158** unanswerable or very strong (relevant, in the latter case, where the judge at the interim hearing has regard to the respective merits of the parties' cases).[193] In *Lawrence David Ltd v Ashton*,[194] the employee claimed that a failure to give him proper notice of termination was a repudiation which had the effect of releasing him from his restrictive covenants. In considering this argument in the context of whether there was a serious issue to be tried for the purpose of granting an interim injunction, Balcombe LJ observed: 'This raises issues of fact, for example, the precise manner of his dismissal, how and when the employee left, and whether he has now been paid that to which he is entitled.' He noted *Dennis & Sons Ltd v Tunnard Bros & Moore*,[195] a first instance decision, which suggests that not every dismissal of an employee without notice may be repudiatory, before concluding that there was clearly a serious issue to be tried on the point.[196]

Thus, it will be a rare case in which a claim of repudiation will defeat the employer in **5.159** attempting to enforce a restrictive covenant at the interim stage. However, it is commonplace nowadays that a speedy trial is fixed to be heard within a matter of weeks of the court making an order for speedy trial. An employee's repudiation claim is one of the issues generally determined at a speedy trial, since it is relevant to the enforceability of covenants (whereas the issue of damages will probably be determined at a later date, if at all). This means that an employee's claim that the employer repudiated the employment contract can often be determined speedily in the context of a restrictive covenant case. Employers need to be alive to this possibility, and ready to defend their actions at short notice.

Conclusion on the effect of repudiation

This somewhat uncertain state of the authorities suggests that the present position may be **5.160** summarized as follows:

- The *General Billposting* rule remains good law for the time being, although its continuing validity is open to serious question for the reasons advanced by Phillips LJ in *Rock Refrigeration v Jones*. It is likely, however, to require a decision of the House of Lords if the rule is to be abrogated.[197]
- An employer probably does not lose his right to protect trade secrets and other confidential information as a result of his repudiation of the employment contract which is accepted by the employee, although this is not entirely free from doubt.

---

[193] See Chapter 10 below.
[194] [1989] ICR 123, CA.
[195] (1911) 56 SJ 162.
[196] [1989] ICR 123, 133.
[197] As to what mechanism might apply in place of the *General Billposting* rule, should it be departed from, see M Freedland, *The Personal Employment Contract* (2003) 390–2 and M Freedland (2003) 32 ILJ 48.

- An employee's claim that the employer repudiated the employment contract is unlikely to be resolved in the employee's favour at an interim hearing but is one of the issues that will generally be determined at a speedy trial.

E. Construction

What construction involves

5.161   Construction of a term of a contract simply means the process by which the court ascertains what the term means. The word 'interpretation' is used interchangeably with 'construction'. The court's aim is to discover the real meaning, or the true construction, or the proper interpretation, of the term.

5.162   In construing a restrictive covenant, the court is engaged in the same exercise as when it construes any other term of a contract. Hence, it is appropriate, first, to identify the proper approach to construction of contracts in general. However, particular issues have arisen from time to time in construing restrictive covenants which will be considered next.

5.163   There are numerous examples in the authorities of the construction of particular covenants. There are two clear dangers in dissecting these cases. The first lies in the tendency to believe that the meaning of a particular word or phrase adopted in one case will apply to the same word or phrase in another. This does not follow. The meaning of a word or phrase depends on its particular context which will differ from one contract to another. The second arises from the fact that it is almost always possible to find some dicta or approach in the decided cases to support a proposition which is sought to be advanced. There are passages that frequently favour both sides of an argument. Each case must be approached on its own merits with a healthy dose of common sense applied to the task of construction.

5.164   The focus of the discussion that follows, therefore, will be on principles of construction. Whilst a number of decided cases will be referred to in which these principles are identified, and whose particular findings illustrate the application of those principles, the temptation to extrapolate from these cases any fixed meaning of words or phrases, or any particular approach to be followed in all other cases, should be resisted.

General principles of construction

Common sense principles

5.165   The classic exposition of the correct approach to construction of contractual documents in general is now to be found in the speech of Lord Hoffmann in *Investors Compensation Scheme Ltd v West Bromwich Building Society*,[198] which was not a restraint of trade case. Lord Hoffmann explained that the approach adopted nowadays, subject to one important exception, is to assimilate the way in which contractual documents are interpreted by judges to the common sense principles by which any serious utterance would be interpreted in ordinary life.

---

[198] [1998] 1 WLR 896. Followed in *Chartbrook Ltd v Persimmon Homes Ltd* [2009] AC 1101, para 14 *per* Lord Hoffmann.

Almost all the old intellectual baggage of 'legal' interpretation has been discarded.[199] He summarized the principles as follows:

(1) Interpretation is the ascertainment of the meaning which the document would convey to a reasonable person having all the background knowledge which would reasonably have been available to the parties in the situation in which they were at the time of the contract.

(2) The background was famously referred to by Lord Wilberforce as the 'matrix of fact', but this phrase is, if anything, an understated description of what the background may include. Subject to the requirement that it should have been reasonably available to the parties and to the exception to be mentioned next, it includes absolutely anything which would have affected the way in which the language of the document would have been understood by a reasonable man.

(3) The law excludes from the admissible background the previous negotiations of the parties and their declarations of subjective intent. They are admissible only in an action for rectification. The law makes this distinction for reasons of practical policy and, in this respect only, legal interpretation differs from the way we would interpret utterances in ordinary life. The boundaries of this exception are in some respects unclear. But this is not the occasion on which to explore them.

(4) The meaning which a document (or any other utterance) would convey to a reasonable man is not the same thing as the meaning of its words. The meaning of words is a matter of dictionaries and grammars; the meaning of the document is what the parties using those words against the relevant background would reasonably have been understood to mean. The background may not merely enable the reasonable man to choose between the possible meanings of words which are ambiguous but even (as occasionally happens in ordinary life) to conclude that the parties must, for whatever reason, have used the wrong words or syntax: see *Mannai Investments Co Ltd v Eagle Star Life Assurance Co Ltd* [1997] AC 749.

(5) The 'rule' that words should be given their 'natural and ordinary meaning' reflects the common sense proposition that we do not easily accept that people have made linguistic mistakes, particularly in formal documents. On the other hand, if one would nevertheless conclude from the background that something must have gone wrong with the language, the law does not require judges to attribute to the parties an intention which they plainly could not have had. Lord Diplock made this point more vigorously when he said in *Antaios Compania Naviera SA v Salen Rederierna AB* [1985] AC 191, 201: 'if detailed semantic and syntactical analysis of words in a commercial contract is going to lead to a conclusion that flouts business commonsense, it must be made to yield to business commonsense'.[200]

These principles summarized by Lord Hoffmann apply fully to the construction or interpretation of restrictive covenants. Whilst rectification is rarely encountered in relation to such terms (see principle (3) above), there is no reason to believe that restrictive covenants are exempt from the approach outlined above.[201]   **5.166**

It is suggested that the above principles should form the starting point for an approach to the construction of restrictive covenants. Nevertheless, without detracting from the clarity and   **5.167**

---

[199] ibid 912.

[200] ibid 912–13.

[201] They were expressly followed, for example, in the restrictive covenant cases of *Beckett Investment Group Ltd v Hall* [2007] ICR 1539, [2007] IRLR 793, CA, paras 11, 15, and *Advantage Business Systems Ltd v Hopley* [2007] EWHC 1783 (QB), para 27.

conciseness of Lord Hoffmann's summary, it may be helpful to consider how the courts have dealt with the issue of construction in the particular context of restrictive covenants.

Defects of drafting

5.168   One of the problems frequently encountered in construing restrictive covenants is the result of defective drafting. This can manifest itself in a number of ways. First, the covenant may be insufficiently precise, for example, as to the business in which the employee is restricted from working. Secondly, the covenant may be worded so as to prevent the employee, on a literal reading, from working in a way that would not harm the employer's legitimate interests and hence is too wide. Thirdly, words or phrases may be too vague or uncertain, although it would appear to be a rare case where the court is willing to strike down a covenant on grounds of uncertainty of meaning.[202]

5.169   The courts have responded in a number of ways to these deficiencies. There are examples in the cases where the courts have been willing to read in limitations to the wording of the clause, or to eschew extravagant or fanciful constructions, so as to uphold the restraint. There are also occasions where the courts have felt unable to rescue the restraint from the failings of the draftsman.

5.170   One of the earliest indications of the court's willingness to overcome defects of drafting is found in the approach of Sir Nathaniel Lindley MR in *Haynes v Doman*.[203] He said:

> Agreements in restraint of trade, like other agreements, must be construed with reference to the object sought to be attained by them. In cases such as the one before us, the object is the protection of one of the parties against rivalry in trade. Such agreements cannot be properly held to apply to cases which, although covered by the words of the agreement, cannot be reasonably supposed ever to have been contemplated by the parties, and which on a rational view of the agreement are excluded from its operation by falling, in truth, outside, and not within, its real scope.[204]

5.171   This approach was followed by the Court of Appeal in *GW Plowman & Sons Ltd v Ash*[205] and *Home Counties Dairies Ltd v Skilton*.[206] In the latter case, an employee milkman agreed not, for a period of one year after termination of employment, to serve or sell milk or dairy produce to any customer of his employer (as defined in the agreement). The judge held that the covenant was unreasonable in that, covering as it did the sale and service of 'dairy produce', it prevented the employee from entering the employment of a grocer who sold such products as butter and cheese, and so went beyond the protection of the employer's goodwill. The Court of Appeal allowed the employer's appeal. Salmon LJ said:

> Although the words of clause 15 are no doubt wide enough, when read literally and in isolation, to be given a meaning which makes the clause void, nevertheless, if taken in the context of the whole agreement, it is clear that the clause is intended to restrict the employee's activities only when engaged in the same type of business as the employer's. The clause

---

[202] For an extreme example, see *Davies v Davies* (1887) 36 Ch D 359 (a restraint 'so far as the law allows'). See also *Gledhow Autoparts Ltd v Delaney* [1965] 1 WLR 1366. Cf *Dawnay, Day & Co Ltd v D'Alphen* [1998] ICR 1068, 1110 *per* Evans LJ: 'The meaning of the words themselves is not ambiguous or even uncertain: what can be said is that the definition may be difficult to apply in circumstances where a borderline case may arise.'

[203] [1899] 2 Ch 13.

[204] ibid 25.

[205] [1964] 1 WLR 568, CA, 572 *per* Harman LJ.

[206] [1970] 1 WLR 526, CA.

must be construed according to its manifest intention: so construed, it is, in my view, clearly enforceable.[207]

He added:

If a clause is valid in all ordinary circumstances which can have been contemplated by the parties, it is equally valid notwithstanding that it might cover circumstances which are so 'extravagant', 'fantastical', 'unlikely or improbable' that they must have been entirely outside the contemplation of the parties.[208]

In words which will be welcomed by any vexed draftsman, Cross LJ said:

It is in practice extremely difficult to frame restrictions which will adequately protect a trade connection and may not at the same time cover some cases where a breach will not injure the trade connection. If the court can see that the restriction has been carefully framed for a legitimate purpose, I do not think that it should hold it void as contrary to public policy in favour of an ex-employee who is in flagrant breach of it on such narrow grounds as those relied on in this case.[209]

This somewhat generous attitude to defective draftsmanship reached perhaps its high-water **5.172** mark in the majority judgments of the Court of Appeal in *Littlewoods Organisation Ltd v Harris*.[210] Harris was an executive director of Littlewoods which ran mail order and retail businesses. He covenanted not, for twelve months after termination of his employment, to enter into employment with the GUS group, a competitor of Littlewoods. When Harris resigned, to join the GUS group, Littlewoods sought to enforce the restrictive covenant to prevent him from doing so for twelve months. The principal issue for the Court of Appeal (whose judgments were delivered *ex tempore*) was whether Harris was in possession of confidential information so as to justify the non-competition covenant. Unlike the trial judge (Caulfield J), it held that he was. A further point was whether the covenant was too wide on the grounds that (a) it was, like the GUS group, worldwide whereas Littlewoods business was limited to the United Kingdom, and (b) it was not limited to the mail order business in which, at the time of his resignation, Harris exclusively worked.

Lord Denning MR referred to *Haynes v Doman*, *Plowman v Ash*, and *Home Counties Dairies* **5.173** *v Skilton* as cases in which the courts construed covenants in relation to the object to be attained. Lord Denning MR explained:

They limited them to that object. They refused to hold them to be bad because of unskilful drafting in which the draftsman inserted rather too wide words.

So that is one way of upholding a covenant which is intrinsically just and reasonable. It is by a process of interpretation so as to cut down wide words to words of more limited scope. But there is another way. This is where the words are so wide that on a strict construction they cover improbable and unlikely events. In such cases the courts should not apply the strict construction so far as to make the whole clause void or invalid or unenforceable. All that should be done is that, if that improbable and unlikely event takes place, the courts should decline to enforce it.[211]

---

[207] ibid 535.
[208] ibid 536.
[209] ibid 538.
[210] [1977] 1 WLR 1472, CA.
[211] ibid 1481–2. Cf *Dawnay Day & Co Ltd v D'Alphen* [1998] ICR 1068, in which Evans LJ said that 'the possibility of granting a limited injunction cannot rescue an invalid clause' (1108).

Applying this approach, Lord Denning MR held that the covenant should be limited to such part of the business of the GUS group as operates within the United Kingdom, and to the mail order side of the business.[212]

5.174   Megaw LJ acknowledged the dangers in going too far by way of construction so as to uphold an apparently unreasonable covenant. He recognized that if it were necessary, in order to render this restrictive covenant reasonable, to add to or vary the words used in the covenant, he would hold that the claim to enforce the covenant must fail. However, he felt able, like Lord Denning MR, to so construe the covenant as to limit its field of operation to GUS's mail order business in the United Kingdom 'without any necessity for alteration of the words'.[213]

5.175   If evidence were needed that there is a thin line between permissibly construing a covenant in such a limited way that it is reasonable and impermissibly rewriting a covenant, it is found in the fact that the third member of the Court considered that Lord Denning MR and Megaw LJ fell into the latter trap. Browne LJ relied upon the dicta of Chitty J in *Mills v Dunham* (which had already been cited by Megaw LJ), who said 'the court must take great care not to create a new agreement for the parties, nor carve out of an unreasonable agreement, something which would be reasonable, for the sake of upholding what would be otherwise void'.[214] Browne LJ concluded that to limit the ambit of the covenant by the process of construction in the manner favoured by the majority of the Court was to rewrite the clause so as to make enforceable that which would otherwise be unenforceable, which the court cannot do.[215]

5.176   Scott V-C distinguished *Home Counties Dairies v Skilton* in refusing to read in limiting words to the covenant in *Scully UK Ltd v Lee*.[216] The court rejected the employer's argument that the covenant (clause 17(c)) should be construed as limited to competing businesses and to relevant equipment because that was what the parties must have intended when it was signed. Scott V-C said:

> I of course accept that clause 17(c) must be construed in the context of the relevant commercial background and Scully's inferred purposes in imposing the restraints on its employee. The commercial background does not persuade me, however, that Scully was necessarily concerned only to restrain Mr Lee from involving himself in a competing business in the petrochemical industry. The best guide to Scully's intention is, after all, the contractual language itself. If the contractual language were to lead to some absurdity or to some plain improbability, I would be content to limit the language in order to accord with a more believable intention. But I can see nothing absurd or improbable in Scully intending the clause to have the wide effect consistent with the words used.[217]

5.177   An attempt to save a covenant by implying limiting words based on the reasoning in *Littlewoods v Harris* was equally unsuccessful in *JA Mont (UK) Ltd v Mills*.[218] Simon Brown LJ did not consider the covenant in *Mont v Mills* to be suffering, in Sir Nathaniel Lindley

---

[212]   [1977] 1 WLR 1472, CA, 1482.
[213]   ibid 1486–7.
[214]   [1891] 1 Ch 576, 580.
[215]   [1977] 1 WLR 1472, 1493.
[216]   [1998] IRLR 259, CA, para 48.
[217]   ibid para 45.
[218]   [1993] IRLR 172, CA.

MR's words in *Haynes v Doman* 'a mere want of accuracy in expression'. There was also a further consideration.

> If the Court here were to construe this covenant as the plaintiffs desire, what possible reason would employers ever have to impose restraints in appropriately limited terms? It would always be said that the covenants were basically 'just and honest', and designed solely to protect the employers' legitimate interests in the confidentiality of their trade secrets rather than to prevent competition as such. And it would be no easier to refute that assertion in other cases than it is here. Thus would be perpetuated the long-recognised vice of ex-employees being left subject to apparently excessive restraints and yet quite unable, short of expensive litigation and at peril of substantial damages claims, to determine precisely what their rights may be.[219]

Simon Brown LJ cited a passage from the speech of Lord Moulton in *Mason v Provident*   **5.178**
Clothing and Supply Co Ltd,[220] which due to its continuing relevance and powerful language merits setting out in full:

> It would in my opinion be *pessimi exempli* if, when an employer had exacted a covenant deliberately framed in unreasonably wide terms, the courts were to come to his assistance and, by applying their ingenuity and knowledge of the law, carve out of this void covenant the maximum of what he might validly have required. It must be remembered that the real sanction at the back of these covenants is the terror and expense of litigation, in which the servant is usually at a great disadvantage, in view of the longer purse of his master. It is sad to think that in this present case this appellant, whose employment is a comparatively humble one, should have had to go through four courts before he could free himself from such unreasonable restraints as this covenant imposes, and the hardship imposed by the exaction of unreasonable covenants by employers would be greatly increased if they could continue the practice with the expectation that, having exposed the servant to the anxiety and expense of litigation, the Court would in the end enable them to obtain everything which they could have obtained by acting reasonably.[221]

Simon Brown LJ recognized that this passage was directed at a covenant deliberately framed too widely, and at an argument that it might properly be whittled down rather than more narrowly construed. Nevertheless, as a matter of policy, it seemed to him that the Court should not too urgently strive to find within restrictive covenants ex facie too wide, implicit limitations such as alone could justify their imposition.[222]

Alternative meanings

Where the court is presented with two equally tenable meanings to a covenant, one of which would   **5.179**
lead to its enforceability, the other to it being struck down, which should the court choose?

In *Turner v Commonwealth & British Minerals Ltd*,[223] Waller LJ was of the view that if 'a   **5.180**
particular construction was to lead to the view that the clause was unenforceable, then an alternative view, which did not lead to the same result if legitimate, ought to be preferred'.[224]

Chadwick LJ addressed this issue in the course of giving valuable guidance on the issue of   **5.181**
construction in *Arbuthnot Fund Managers Ltd v Rawlings*.[225] The task of construction is one

---

[219] ibid para 26.
[220] [1913] AC 724, HL.
[221] ibid 745.
[222] [1993] IRLR 172, para 28.
[223] [2000] IRLR 114, CA.
[224] ibid para 14.
[225] [2003] EWCA Civ 518, CA.

which, in Chadwick LJ's judgment, the court ought to carry out on an application for interim relief (if there is one) if it can properly do so. 'Unless the court is satisfied that there are disputed facts which bear on the construction of the relevant contractual terms, and that those facts cannot be resolved without a trial, the court at the interlocutory stage is as well able to construe the relevant contractual terms as a court will be at trial.'[226]

5.182   In approaching this task, Chadwick LJ identified two factors to be borne in mind. First, in construing written documents the court should consider the circumstances at the time when they were made, and the position of the parties who entered into them. The second factor touches on the point alluded to by Waller LJ in the *Turner* case. According to Chadwick LJ 'it is not the function of the court to strive to give to the clause a meaning which enables it to have effect within the constraints of public policy if that is not the meaning which, as a matter of construction, the parties are to be taken to have intended that it should have'.[227] Rather:

> The court must steer a course between giving to the clause a meaning which is extravagantly wide; and giving to the clause a meaning which is artificially limited. The task of the court, in construing the contractual term is simply to ask itself: 'what did these parties intend by the bargain which they made in the circumstances in which they made it?'[228]

5.183   Cox J in *TFS Derivatives v Morgan* referred to this passage from Chadwick LJ's judgment in *Arbuthnot v Rawlings*. She suggested that a similar approach to construction was adopted by the Court of Appeal in the *Turner* case, referring to Waller LJ's dicta cited above.[229] It is, perhaps, far from clear that Chadwick and Waller LJJ adopted a similar approach where a covenant permitted of two constructions, one of which would lead to its enforceability, the other to its unenforceability. Nevertheless, Cox J concluded:

> . . . if, having examined the restrictive covenant in the context of the relevant factual matrix, the court concludes that there is an element of ambiguity and that there are two possible constructions of the covenant, one of which would lead to a conclusion that it was in unreasonable restraint of trade and unlawful, but the other would lead to the opposite result, then the court should adopt the latter construction on the basis that the parties are to be deemed to have intended their bargain to be lawful and not to offend against the public interest.[230]

Construction and breach

5.184   The proper construction of a restrictive covenant is of fundamental importance for a number of reasons. It is necessary to know the meaning of the covenant in order to be able to determine its enforceability. It is also essential to ascertain its true meaning in order to decide

---

[226]   ibid para 20.

[227]   ibid para 23. As Eady J put it in *Basic Solutions Ltd v Sands* [2008] EWHC 1388 (QB), para 22: 'It is not for the court to try to save an employer who has stipulated for unduly wide protection: see *J A Mont (UK) Ltd v Mills* [1993] IRLR 172.'

[228]   ibid para 24. Followed by Warren J in *BFS Group Ltd v Fox* [2008] All ER(D) 400.

[229]   [2005] IRLR 246, para 42.

[230]   ibid para 43. In the event, Cox J did not consider that there was any ambiguity in the covenant in question but, if there was, she would have been minded 'to adopt the approach advocated in the case of *Turner*' (ibid para 62). Cox J's approach involves the application of a well-established rule of construction, although she did not express any view as to the applicability of another rule of construction, namely the *contra proferentem* rule where there is ambiguity in a covenant put forward by an employer. See *Chitty on Contracts* (30th edn, 2008) paras 12-081 and 12-083–12-085. A similar approach to that of Cox J was adopted by HH Judge Seymour QC in *Advantage Business Systems Ltd v Hopley* [2007] EWHC 1783 (QB), para 30.

whether a breach of the covenant has occurred or is likely to occur. This last point is vividly illustrated by *Phoenix Partners Group LLP v Asoyag*.[231]

The defendant broker (Asoyag) agreed not, for a period of six months from the termination **5.185** of employment, to be engaged in any business 'which competes' with any business carried on by the claimant company (Phoenix) in which Asoyag had been actively engaged. Asoyag's activity at Phoenix was around 80 per cent in the EuroStoxx market. He moved to a competitor (GFI), to manage GFI's EuroStoxx desk. Phoenix was only able to broker a small number of EuroStoxx trades after Asoyag's resignation. Although it had been actively recruiting for another EuroStoxx broker to take Asoyag's place, it had not been successful.

An issue which would arise in the event of any trial of the action taking place was whether **5.186** any actual or potential breaches of the restrictive covenants have been established. As to this, the real contest between the parties was whether or not the part of the business of GFI in which Asoyag had contracted to be engaged could be said to compete with any part of the business carried on by Phoenix in which Asoyag was actually engaged during his employment with Phoenix.[232]

Sir Charles Gray (sitting as a Judge of the High Court) recognized that the validity of the **5.187** non-compete restriction must be judged by reference to the circumstances existing at the date of the contract. However, the question whether Mr Asoyag was acting or had acted in breach of the covenant had to be judged by reference to the dates when the acts relied on by Phoenix as constituting breaches took place.[233] The reality was that there had been no genuine trading by Phoenix in EuroStoxx for some time, and the judge saw no prospect of any such trading being resumed during the remaining portion of the three-month restraint period (a period of three months' garden leave having been set-off against the period of the restrictive covenant). Thus, there was no real prospect that Asoyag's broking on behalf of GFI in the EuroStoxx market would at trial be held to amount to competing with any part of the business carried on by Phoenix at the time of those trades on behalf of GFI.[234]

F. Legitimate interests

The requirement of a legitimate business interest

Once the meaning of a restrictive covenant has been ascertained, the next step is to identify **5.188** the interests of the employer which it seeks to protect. A restrictive covenant will only be enforceable if it protects a legitimate business interest of the employer. A covenant which merely seeks to protect an employer against competition by a former employee will not be enforced. This is sometimes referred to as 'a covenant in gross' or 'a covenant against competition *simpliciter*'. Protection against competition per se is not recognized as a legitimate business interest for the purpose of the enforceability of a restrictive covenant. Something more is required.

---

[231] [2010] IRLR 594.
[232] ibid paras 10, 18.
[233] ibid para 22.
[234] ibid paras 26, 28, 30.

5.189   This requirement was made clear as long ago as 1916 by Lord Parker of Waddington in *Herbert Morris Ltd v Saxelby*[235] when he said:

> In fact the reason, and the only reason, for upholding such a restraint on the part of an employee is that the employer has some proprietary right, whether in the nature of trade connection or in the nature of trade secrets, for the protection of which such a restraint is—having regard to the duties of the employee—reasonably necessary. Such a restraint has, so far as I know, never been upheld, if directed only to the prevention of competition or against the use of the personal skill and knowledge acquired by the employee in his employer's business.[236]

5.190   The point was reiterated in an oft-quoted passage from the speech of Lord Wilberforce in *Stenhouse Australia Ltd v Phillips*:[237]

> The accepted proposition that an employer is not entitled to protection from mere competition by a former employee means that the employee is entitled to use to the full any personal skill or experience even if this has been acquired in the service of his employer: it is this freedom to use to the full a man's improving ability and talents which lies at the root of the policy of the law regarding this type of restraint. Leaving aside the case of misuse of trade secrets or confidential information . . . the employer's claim for protection must be based upon the identification of some advantage or asset inherent in the business which can properly be regarded as, in a general sense, his property, and which it would be unjust to allow the employee to appropriate for his own purposes, even though he, the employee, may have contributed to its creation.[238]

The categories of interests are not closed

5.191   It has become customary to refer to three categories of legitimate business interests of an employer that merit protection by a restrictive covenant, namely:

(1) trade secrets and confidential information;
(2) customer connection; and
(3) stability of the workforce.

5.192   Lord Parker identified the first two of this trilogy as legitimate interests in *Herbert Morris v Saxelby*.[239] The fact that the list has grown since that time demonstrates a now well-established fact that the categories of legitimate interests are not closed. This was made plain by the Court of Appeal in *Dawnay Day & Co Ltd v D'Alphen*.[240] In that case, the interests of investors in a joint venture were sufficient to merit protection by an appropriate restrictive covenant. However, the same principle applies to the employment relationship. Whilst the three interests referred to above are well recognized, it should not be thought that anything outside of this categorization is unacceptable. As Evans LJ stated in the *Dawnay Day* case: 'The established categories are not rigid, and they are not exclusive. Rather, the covenant may be enforced when the covenantee has a legitimate interest, of whatever kind, to protect, and when the covenant is no wider than is necessary to protect that interest.'[241]

---

[235] [1916] AC 688, HL.
[236] ibid 710.
[237] [1974] AC 391, PC.
[238] ibid 400.
[239] See para 5.189 above.
[240] [1998] ICR 1068, [1997] IRLR 442, CA, discussed in Chapter 6 below.
[241] [1998] ICR 1068, 1106–7.

Trade secrets and confidential information

An employer may protect his trade secrets and confidential information by a reasonable **5.193** restrictive covenant. This is a well-recognized proprietary interest of the employer.

As far as express post-termination restraints are concerned, trade secrets and confidential infor- **5.194** mation may be protected simply by an express covenant against their use and disclosure after termination of employment. However, such a covenant is of limited usefulness for two reasons: first, the difficulty in defining confidential information, and, secondly, the difficulty in policing a covenant against misuse of confidential information. Accordingly, the employer's interest in protecting this part of its goodwill may justify a covenant against competition altogether. This was famously explained by Lord Denning MR in *Littlewoods Organisation Ltd v Harris*.[242]

Even where the employer has included a reasonably drafted non-competition covenant in **5.195** the employment contract, in purported protection of his trade secrets and confidential infor- mation, the court will generally still have to grapple with the thorny question of what amounts to trade secrets and confidential information. This issue arose in acute form in *FSS Travel and Leisure Systems Ltd v Johnson*.[243] Johnson was a computer programmer for FSS who were in the business of designing and marketing computer software for the travel indus- try. Johnson entered into a one-year non-compete covenant. Mummery LJ identified what he referred to as 'settled legal propositions affecting restrictive covenants' where trade secrets were sought to be protected. The full statement of these propositions repays careful consid- eration. For present purposes, the following three are of most relevance:

(3) Protection can be legitimately claimed for identifiable objective knowledge constituting the employer's trade secrets with which the employee has become acquainted during his employment.

(4) Protection cannot be legitimately claimed in respect of the skill, experience, know-how and general knowledge acquired by an employee as part of his job during his employment, even though that will equip him as a competitor, or potential employee of a competitor, of the employer.

(5) The critical question is whether the employer has trade secrets which can be fairly regarded as his property, as distinct from the skill, experience, know-how, and general knowledge which can fairly be regarded as the property of the employee to use without restraint for his own benefit or in the service of a competitor. This distinction necessitates examination of all the evidence relating to the nature of the employment, the character of the information, the restrictions imposed on its dissemination, the extent of use in the public domain and the damage likely to be caused by its use and disclosure in competition to the employer.[244]

In *Thomas v Farr plc*,[245] the employee relied on *FSS Travel* to defeat the enforcement of a non- **5.196** compete covenant on grounds of insufficient particularity of confidential information but to no avail. At a trial of the preliminary issue as to the enforceability of the covenant, the judge held that the employee had confidential information, which the employer had a legitimate interest to protect, within the following categories: business development, new geographical

---

[242] [1977] 1 WLR 1472, CA. See para 5.245 below. See also *Thomas v Farr plc* [2007] ICR 932, [2007] IRLR 419, para 48.
[243] [1998] IRLR 382, CA.
[244] ibid paras 31–3.
[245] [2007] ICR 932, [2007] IRLR 419, CA.

markets, acquisitions, and pricing and financial information. On appeal, the employee argued that the employer had failed to adduce sufficiently clear and cogent evidence to establish that he ever had, or was likely to have, any information which the employer could require to be treated as confidential after the termination of his employment, relying on the observations of Mummery LJ in *FSS Travel*.

5.197   Toulson LJ (with whom Scott Baker and Chadwick LJJ agreed) stated that in order to establish that the inclusion of a non-competition clause in an employment contract was reasonably necessary for the protection of the employer's interest in confidential information, the first matter which the employer obviously needs to establish is that at the time of the contract the nature of the proposed employment was such as would expose the employee to information of the kind capable of protection beyond the term of the contract (ie trade secrets or other information of equivalent confidentiality). The degree of the particularity of the evidence required to establish that matter must inevitably depend on the facts of the case.[246]

5.198   After quoting Aldous LJ in *Scully (UK) Ltd v Lee*[247] that 'the confidential information must be particularised sufficiently to enable the court to be satisfied that the plaintiff has a legitimate interest to protect. That requires an inquiry as to whether the plaintiff is in possession of confidential information which it is entitled to protect . . . Sufficient detail must be given to enable that to be decided but no more is necessary', Toulson continued:

> Provided that the employer overcomes that hurdle, it is no argument against a restrictive covenant that it may be very difficult for either the employer or the employee to know where exactly the line may lie between information which remains confidential after the end of the employment and the information which does not. The fact that the distinction can be very hard to draw may support the reasonableness of a non-competition clause. As was observed by Lord Denning MR in *Littlewoods Organisation Ltd v Harris* [1977] 1 WLR 1472, 1479, and by Waller LJ in *Turner v Commonwealth & British Minerals Ltd* [2000] IRLR 114, para 18, it is because there may be serious difficulties in identifying precisely what is or what is not confidential information that a non-competition clause may be the most satisfactory form of restraint, provided that it is reasonable in time and space.[248]

5.199   Toulson LJ added that if it had been the case that, as events turned out, Mr Thomas was unable to recall any truly confidential information after leaving Farr, that could afford a reason for the court not granting an injunction in support of the non-competition clause. It would not follow that the clause was unreasonably in restraint of trade at the time of his appointment.[249]

5.200   The difficulties in defining trade secrets and confidential information, and the various means of protecting them, are discussed in detail in Chapter 3 above. The extent to which this interest may be protected by post-termination restrictive covenants, and the reasonableness of such restraints, are discussed in paragraphs 5.233 to 5.253 below.

Customer connection

5.201   An employer may also protect his trade connections in an appropriate case. By 'trade connections' is meant the connections built up between an employee, on the one hand, and the

---

[246]   ibid para 41.
[247]   [1998] IRLR 259, para 23.
[248]   [2007] ICR 932, [2007] IRLR 419, para 42. Followed by Tugendhat J in *Extec Screens & Crushers Ltd v Rice* [2007] EWHC 1043 (QB), paras 82–8.
[249]   ibid, para 47.

employer's trade partners, on the other. 'Trade partners' generally means customers (a word used interchangeably with clients, depending on what is customary in the business in question), hence the phrase 'customer connection' to describe this interest. It can also mean potential customers in an appropriate case.[250] But it may also include suppliers and other trade partners, although such connections feature less frequently than those with customers in the case law.

The 'connection' referred to between an employee and customers has a number of aspects to it. It was referred to by Lord Parker in *Herbert Morris v Saxelby* as 'such personal knowledge of and influence over the customers of his employer . . . as would enable him, if competition were allowed, to take advantage of his employer's trade connection'.[251] Ultimately, what is sought to be guarded against is the ability of a former employee to take away customers from his employer. This ability of the employee, or threat as the employer would see it, arises in a number of ways.   **5.202**

Its most obvious manifestation is where an employee has dealt directly with a particular customer over a period of time. He has gained knowledge of the customer's business requirements, and the customer has come to rely on the employee to satisfy those requirements. To all intents and purposes, the employee is 'the business' as far as the customer is concerned.[252] Often, the relationship has been nurtured by the employee entertaining the customer at various functions, at his employer's expense, a feature which often carries weight with a court. Such a customer may be strongly inclined to follow that employee to a competitor, even without any encouragement to do so from the employee. This sort of customer connection would justify a non-dealing, as well as a non-solicitation, covenant.   **5.203**

However, a sales director may have less direct contact with customers, yet know their business requirements in detail by virtue of his position. He may be well placed to use his 'knowledge of' the customers (Lord Parker's words) to solicit their business on behalf of his new employer. Such knowledge may well justify a non-solicitation, though possibly not a non-dealing, covenant.   **5.204**

In certain limited circumstances, the protection of customer connection may justify a non-compete covenant. This might be so where the identity of customers is unknown or undocumented, such that non-solicitation and non-dealing covenants would be difficult to police, as in the case of a hairdresser. However, the courts have also been prepared to uphold a non-compete covenant for the purpose of protecting customer connection in less obvious fields such as City inter-dealer broking. The argument, in short, is that such is the nature of the business undertaken, with a desk of brokers regularly exchanging information about their trader clients, that it would be impossible to prove breach of a non-solicitation or non-dealing covenant, and that the only way to protect customer connection is to prevent an employee from joining a rival for a reasonable period of time.[253]   **5.205**

Because the employer is entitled to protect himself against the employee's exploitation of his knowledge of and influence over customers, the nature and longevity of that knowledge   **5.206**

---

[250] *International Consulting Services (UK) Ltd v Hart* [2000] IRLR 227; *Axiom Business Computers Ltd v Frederick* (Court of Session (Outer House), 20 November 2003).

[251] [1916] AC 688, 709.

[252] See eg *Scorer v Seymour-Johns* [1966] 1 WLR 1419, CA.

[253] *Dawnay Day & Co Ltd v D'Alphen* [1998] ICR 1068, 1095 *per* Robert Walker J; *TFS Derivatives Ltd v Morgan* [2005] IRLR 246, paras 15–17, 84 *per* Cox J.

and influence requires careful consideration. Factors such as whether the employee had contact with the customer, the nature and extent of that contact, when it last occurred, when the customer became, and when he ceased to be, a customer, are all relevant to the reasonableness of the covenant. This is considered in paragraphs 5.254 to 5.367 below.

Stability of the workforce

5.207 When an employee leaves to join a competitor, he will occasionally be interested in encouraging one or more of his former colleagues to join him. The former employer will see the employee as a threat to the stability of his workforce. This threat seems to have grown in recent years, especially in the banking and broking worlds where teams or 'desks' sometimes move en masse to a competitor.

5.208 It is now well established that an employer can, in principle, protect the stability of his workforce by a covenant restricting an employee from enticing away his former colleagues. This is often referred to as a 'non-poaching' covenant to distinguish it from a 'non-solicitation' covenant, which is used in the context of soliciting customers. Despite the different labelling, both covenants concern the prevention of soliciting, in one case employees, in the other customers. In addition, as far as the workforce is concerned, from time to time covenants are included in employment contracts which purport to prevent an employee from employing his former colleagues, even without any active poaching or solicitation on his part. Such covenants are of more doubtful validity.

5.209 For a period of time, the courts did not speak with one voice on this subject. Until the 1990s, *Kores Manufacturing Co Ltd v Kolok Manufacturing Co Ltd*[254] was the only reported case that touched the issue. However, that case concerned an agreement between rival employers not to employ former employees of each other, which was unenforceable. In *Hanover Insurance Brokers Ltd v Schapiro*,[255] Dillon LJ (with whom Nolan LJ agreed) expressed the view that staff were not an asset of the company 'like apples or pears or other stock in trade' and a covenant against poaching employees was unenforceable.[256] In *Ingham v ABC Contract Services Ltd*,[257] Leggatt LJ (with whom Russell LJ agreed) held that the claimant employers had a legitimate interest in maintaining a stable, trained workforce in what was acknowledged to be a highly competitive business. This was an interest which the claimants were entitled to protect against solicitation and enticement by their former employee. A non-poaching covenant was enforced in the context of a business sale agreement in *Alliance Group plc v Prestwich*.[258]

5.210 The enforceability of a non-poaching covenant in an employment contract was one of the issues that arose in *Dawnay Day & Co Ltd v D'Alphen*.[259] Counsel for the employees invited the court to follow the approach of Dillon and Nolan LJJ in *Hanover v Schapiro* rather than that of Leggatt and Russell LJJ in the *Ingham* case. The court declined the invitation. Evans LJ (with whom Ward and Nourse LJJ agreed) expressed his agreement with Leggatt LJ that

---

[254] [1959] 1 Ch 108, CA.
[255] [1994] IRLR 82, CA.
[256] ibid paras 15–16, 34.
[257] CA, 12 November 1993; Court of Appeal (Civil Division) Transcript No 1336 of 1993. The *Ingham* case was decided shortly before *Hanover v Shapiro* was reported and apparently without being referred to it.
[258] [1996] IRLR 25.
[259] [1998] ICR 1068, [1997] IRLR 442, CA, discussed in paras 6.98–6.102 below.

an employer's interest in maintaining a stable, trained workforce is one which he can properly protect within the limits of reasonableness. But it did not follow that this would always be the case.[260] Evans LJ explained:

> The clause can be regarded as objectionable because it restricts, not only the rights of the former employee to recruit staff for his new business, but also the opportunities of the remaining employees to learn about future employment possibilities for themselves. However, their ability and right to do so through making inquiries of their own, and through advertisements and other channels of communication in the normal way, is not restricted at all. The employer's need for protection arises because the ex-employee may seek to exploit the knowledge which he has gained of their particular qualifications, rates of remuneration and so on which the judge included in his general description of specific confidential information which the managers acquired.[261]

Introductory words identifying the legitimate interests

Occasionally a contractual term containing restrictive covenants has introductory words that identify the interests sought to be protected by the covenants that follow. This can be a liability as well as an asset. **5.211**

In *Office Angels Ltd v Rainer-Thomas*[262] the clause provided that: 'In the course of his or her employment by the company the employee has dealings with clients of the company and in order to safeguard the company's goodwill the employee agrees' and non-solicitation, non-dealing and area covenants followed. The claimant was an employment agency. During the hearing it sought to argue that the relevant covenant was imposed for the purpose of protecting not only its trade connection with its (employer) clients, but also its trade connection with its pool of temporary workers. Sir Christopher Slade approached this issue in the following way: **5.212**

> In a case where the wording of a covenant restricting competition by an employee after leaving his employer's service does not specifically state the interest of the employer which the covenant is intended to protect, the court is, in my judgment, entitled to look both at that wording and the surrounding circumstances for the purpose of ascertaining that interest, by reference to what would, objectively, appear to have been the intentions of the parties. However, in a second category of case where the employer, who proffers the covenant for the employee's acceptance, chooses specifically to state the interest of the employer which the covenant is intended to protect, the employer is not, in my opinion, entitled thereafter to seek to justify the covenant by reference to some separate and additional interest which has not been specified. An employee who is invited to enter into a covenant of this kind may wish to take legal advice as to its validity and effect before he accepts it. His legal advisers will, in my opinion, be entitled to give him such advice on the basis of the stated purpose of the covenant, if any such purpose is stated.[263]

Sir Christopher Slade considered the case before him fell within the second category.[264] The employer was likewise defeated by its own introductory words in *Countrywide Assured Financial Services Ltd v Smart*,[265] in which the point was expressed colloquially: 'if the employer nails his colours to the mast, he is stuck to those colours and that mast'.[266]

---

[260] [1998] ICR 1068, 1110–11.
[261] ibid 1111.
[262] [1991] IRLR 214, CA.
[263] ibid paras 38–9.
[264] ibid para 40.
[265] [2004] EWHC 1214 (Ch).
[266] ibid para 12.

5.213 However, such introductory words might also be prayed in aid in identifying the object of the covenant and defeating a fanciful construction that might otherwise render the covenant unenforceable. In *Arbuthnot Fund Managers Ltd v Rawlings*[267] the introductory words were: 'In order to protect the goodwill confidential information trade secrets and business connections of the company.' Chadwick LJ viewed those words as directing the reader to construe what comes afterwards with that object in view. 'Unless compelled by the language to do so, the court should not construe what comes afterwards so as to encompass activities which could never have been thought by the parties as likely to damage the goodwill or business connections which the clause (as a whole) is intended to protect.'[268] The introductory words also came to the employer's aid in construing the covenant in *TFS Derivatives Ltd v Morgan*.[269]

5.214 The lesson to be learned from these cases appears to be that, if introductory words are to be included identifying the employer's interests which are sought to be protected by the covenants that follow, then the interests identified should be comprehensive so as not to omit any interest which the employer might conceivably wish to rely upon to justify the covenant thereafter.

Covenants for the benefit of group companies

5.215 Where the employee works for a company which is part of a group of companies, this can give rise to particular problems of enforceability of restrictive covenants.

5.216 One such difficulty may arise where the covenant seeks to protect the business of the group rather than the particular company within the group for which the employee worked. This was the position in *Henry Leetham & Sons Ltd v Johnstone-White*.[270] An agreement was entered into between the defendant employee and a director of the claimant company who did so on behalf of the claimant company, which was the principal company of the group, and the subsidiary companies. The defendant agreed to serve the principal company or one of the subsidiary companies as he should be directed from time to time. In fact, the defendant was employed under this agreement by one of the subsidiary companies, the Cleveland Company. The agreement contained a covenant that the employee would not for five years after termination of employment work in the United Kingdom in relation to any goods dealt in by the principal or subsidiary companies. The attempt by the principal company to enforce the covenant failed since it was wider than necessary to protect the legitimate interests of the Cleveland Company for which the defendant alone worked. Farwell LJ stated:

> A man whose business is a corn miller's business, and who requires to protect that, cannot, if he has also a furniture business, require the covenantee [*sic*] who enters into his service as an employee in the corn business to enter into covenants restricting him from entering into competition with him in the furniture business also, because it is not required for the protection of the corn business in which the man is employed, however much it may be beneficial to the individual person the owner both of the corn business and of the furniture business.[271]

---

[267] [2003] EWCA Civ 518, CA.
[268] ibid para 22.
[269] [2005] IRLR 246, para 46.
[270] [1907] 1 Ch 322, CA.
[271] ibid 327.

The group arrangement was different, however, as was the outcome in *Stenhouse Australia* **5.217**
Ltd v Phillips.[272] The appellant company carried on business through subsidiaries as an insurance
broker. The respondent employee served under a contract of employment as managing director
of two of the subsidiary companies. When he left, the employee agreed, amongst other
things, for a period of five years not to solicit any client of the group with whom he had had
dealings or negotiations. It was submitted for the employee that the covenant was unreasonable in that the agreement was made with the appellant company, whereas the interests to be
protected were those of its subsidiaries. Lord Wilberforce considered that the facts were
distinguishable from those in the *Henry Leetham* case and did not support the employee's
argument 'technically attractive though it may appear'. He stated:

> The evidence is clear that the business of the Stenhouse Group was controlled and co-ordinated
> by the appellant company, and all funds generated by each of the companies were received by
> the appellant. The subsidiary companies were merely agencies or instrumentalities through
> which the appellant company directed its integrated business. Not only did the appellant
> company have a real interest in protecting the businesses of the subsidiaries, but the real inter-
> est of so doing was that of the appellant company. It is not necessary to resort to a conception
> of 'group enterprise' to support these proceedings. The case is, more simply, that of the appel-
> lant's business being to some extent handled for it by subsidiary companies.[273]

In *Dawnay Day & Co Ltd v D'Alphen*[274] at first instance, Robert Walker J observed that he **5.218**
thought he was referred to all the authorities in which groups of companies had been mentioned in the context of restraint of trade, although none was determinative of the outcome
in that case.[275]

The approach of the Privy Council in *Stenhouse* was followed by the Court of Appeal in **5.219**
Beckett Investment Management Group Ltd v Hall.[276] The defendant independent financial
advisers were employed by the holding company (BIMG) of a group whose subsidiary (BFS)
provided advice and services to clients. A twelve-month restrictive covenant prevented dealing
with a relevant client in relation to prohibited services which was defined as the provision of
advice in relation to pensions, life assurance, investments, and other advice of a type provided
by 'the company', which meant BIMG. At trial, the judge held that since BIMG did not
provide advice about anything to anybody but acted simply as a holding company, the non-
dealing covenant was of no practical utility whatsoever.

The Court of Appeal disagreed. Maurice Kay LJ (with whom Carnwath LJ and Sir Anthony **5.220**
Clarke MR agreed) started with the first of Lord Hoffmann's construction principles in the
Investors Compensations Scheme case that interpretation is the ascertainment of the meaning
which the document would convey to a reasonable person having all the background knowledge which would reasonably have been available to the parties *in the situation in which they
were at the time of the contract*. Both defendants had been employed within the Beckett
Group for some time, were familiar with the restructuring which was the catalyst for the new

---

272 [1974] AC 391, PC.
273 ibid, 404.
274 [1998] ICR 1068, [1997] IRLR 285.
275 [1998] ICR 1068, 1089–90. Robert Walker J referred to *Henry Leetham & Sons Ltd v Johnstone-White*
[1907] 1 Ch 322; *Littlewoods Organisation Ltd v Harris* [1977] 1 WLR 1472; *Business Seating (Renovations) Ltd
v Broad* [1989] ICR 729; *Stenhouse Australia Ltd v Phillips* [1974] AC 391, as well as authorities on groups of
companies as a single economic entity: *Adams v Cape Industries plc* [1990] Ch 433; *George Fischer (Great
Britain) Ltd v Multi Construction Ltd* [1995] 1 BCLC 260.
276 [2007] ICR 1539; [2007] IRLR 793, CA.

contracts and were well aware of what the respective roles of the holding company and the subsidiaries was going to be thereafter. In those circumstances, Maurice Kay LJ was reluctant to find for a construction which deprives a covenant of all practical utility in circumstances where all parties were familiar with the background to and aim of the clause.[277]

5.221 Taking this approach, he considered that the only sensible construction of the non-dealing covenant was a wider one which enables it to apply to advice of the kind in fact provided by BFS (the subsidiary). He did not feel inhibited by a 'purist approach to corporate personality'. The words of Lord Wilberforce in *Stenhouse*, namely that the 'subsidiary companies were merely agencies or instrumentalities through which the appellant company directed its integrated business' resonated in the present case.[278]

G. Reasonableness

The court's general approach to reasonableness

5.222 Reasonableness is a core principle of the law as to contracts in restraint of trade. The law takes as its starting point the proposition that contracts which restrain trade are unenforceable unless they are reasonable. This proposition was formulated by the House of Lords in *Nordenfelt v Maxim Nordenfelt & Co*.[279] Lord McNaghten expressed the concept thus:

> The public have an interest in every person's carrying on his trade freely: so has the individual. All interference with individual liberty of action in trading, and all restraints of trade of themselves, if there is nothing more, are contrary to public policy, and therefore void. That is the general rule. But there are exceptions: restraints of trade and interference with individual liberty of action may be justified by the special circumstances of a particular case. It is a sufficient justification, and indeed it is the only justification, if the restriction is reasonable—reasonable, that is, in reference to the interests of the parties concerned and reasonable in reference to the interests of the public, so framed and so guarded as to afford adequate protection to the party in whose favour it is imposed, while at the same time it is in no way injurious to the public. That, I think, is the fair result of all the authorities.[280]

5.223 The question of what is reasonable depends upon the relationship between the needs of the covenantee and the extent of the restriction which the covenant imposes. The restriction must be no more than is reasonably necessary to provide protection for the interest sought to be protected. As Lord Herschel observed in the *Nordenfelt* case, 'whether the covenant be general or particular the question of its validity is alike determined by the consideration whether it exceeds what is necessary for the protection of the covenantee'.[281]

5.224 The *Nordenfelt* case concerned a covenant entered into on the sale of a business,[282] but the test of reasonableness established by that case was quickly applied to restrictive contracts contained in contracts of employment (or, as they were known at the time, contracts between master and servant). The Court of Appeal considered an employment covenant in *Provident*

---

[277] ibid para 16.
[278] ibid paras 17–19.
[279] [1894] AC 535, HL.
[280] ibid 565.
[281] ibid 548.
[282] The courts typically adopt a more generous approach to upholding covenants in this context than they do in relation to employee covenants. See further Chapter 6 below.

Clothing Co v Mason.[283] Kennedy LJ addressed the reasonableness test, pointing out the balancing exercise required by that test:

> The other point with regard to the question of reasonableness is a point which is always one of some difficulty in such cases. The learned judge has got to draw the line between that which is reasonable and that which is unreasonable, having regard to the nature of the particular business and the position of the contracting parties on the one hand, and to the interests of the public and of freedom of trade on the other hand, which is always a somewhat difficult task. In this particular case, however, having regard to the nature of the plaintiffs' business, the question does not appear to me to present much difficulty, because the restriction involved certainly seems not to be wider than is reasonably necessary for the plaintiffs' protection.[284]

When the case reached the House of Lords as *Mason v Provident Clothing Co*,[285] the 'no more than necessary for protection' approach was upheld. Lord Shaw put forward a classic formulation of the principle:

5.225

> I have referred, my Lords, to the apparent antagonism between the right to bargain and the right to work. The extreme of the one destroys the other. But the public interest reconciles these two, and removes all antagonism by the establishment of a principle and a limit of general application. It may be that bargains have been entered into with the eyes open, which restrict the field of liberty and of labour, and the law answers the public interest by refusing to enforce such bargains in every case where the right to contract has been used so as to afford more than a reasonable protection to the covenantee. In every case in which it exceeds that protection, the public interest, which is always upon the side of liberty, including the liberty to exercise one's powers or to earn a livelihood, stands invaded, and can accordingly be invoked to justify the non-enforcement of the restraint.[286]

Soon afterwards, the House of Lords again made it clear that the test of reasonableness applied in the context of employment covenants in *Herbert Morris v Saxelby*.[287] Lord Parker of Waddington said:

5.226

> I think it clear that what is meant is that for a restraint to be reasonable in the interests of the parties it must afford *no more than* adequate protection to the party in whose favour it is imposed. So conceived the test appears to me to be valid both as regards the covenantor and covenantee, for though in one sense no doubt it is contrary to the interests of the covenantor to subject himself to any restraint, still it may be for his advantage to be able so to subject himself in cases where, if he could not do so, he would lose other advantages, such as the possibility of obtaining the best terms on the sale of an existing business or the possibility of obtaining employment or training under competent employers. As long as the restraint to which he subjects himself is no wider than is required for the adequate protection of the person in whose favour it is created, it is in his interest to be able to bind himself for the sake of the indirect advantages he may obtain by so doing. It was at one time thought that, in order to ascertain whether a restraint were reasonable in the interests of the covenantor, the Court ought to weigh the advantages accruing to the covenantor under the contract against the disadvantages imposed upon him by the restraint, but any such process has long since been rejected as impracticable. The Court no longer considers the adequacy of the consideration in any particular case. If it be reasonable that a covenantee should, for his own protection, ask for a restraint, it is in my opinion equally reasonable that the covenantor

---

[283] [1913] 1 KB 65, CA.
[284] ibid 77.
[285] [1913] AC 724, HL.
[286] ibid 739, see also 733 *per* Viscount Haldane LC.
[287] [1916] 1 AC 688, HL.

should be able to subject himself to this restraint. The test of reasonableness is the same in both cases.[288]

5.227 It is apparent from this passage that the court does not generally enquire into the relationship between the extent of the restraint and the consideration provided to support it. The Court of Appeal adopted a similar approach in *JA Mont v Mills*,[289] declining to regard as relevant to the issue of reasonableness a severance payment made to the employee in return for his agreement to a covenant. Payments made to support covenants could not save them where they were wider than necessary in *TSC Europe (UK) Ltd. v Massey*.[290] By contrast, the fact that employees were paid something extra for agreeing a covenant in a severance agreement was regarded as a legitimate factor in considering the interests of the parties by the Court of Appeal in *Turner v Commonwealth & British Minerals Ltd*.[291]

5.228 In *Herbert Morris v Saxelby*, the House of Lords also drew from the *Nordenfelt* case the concept that there are two distinct tests as to the validity of a covenant. The first is that the covenant be reasonable as between the parties. The second is that the covenant should be reasonable in the interests of the public. In other words, it should not be injurious to the public interest, which generally favours free trade.[292] This approach differed somewhat from the approach of Lord Shaw in the *Mason* case, in the passage cited above, which incorporated the question of public interest into the primary question of reasonableness as between the parties.

5.229 In practice, most restrictive covenant cases in the employment field turn on the issue of reasonableness as between the parties, but it remains in principle open to the court to strike down a covenant which it regards as contrary to the public interest. For an example of the court having regard to public interest considerations, see *Basic Solutions Ltd v Sands*,[293] in which Eady J at paragraph 37 regarded public interest as 'part of the background' in relation to a covenant in the context of supply of products intended to combat 'leaves on the line' in the railway network. Public interest there took priority over the protection of a party's legitimate interest in protecting trades secrets or confidential information. The public interest in competition was regarded as a decisive factor on the balance of convenience in *Thermascan Ltd v Norman*.[294]

5.230 As indicated by Lord Atkinson in *Herbert Morris v Saxelby*,[295] the burden of proof in this context lies on the party asserting that the covenant is contrary to the public interest, and it will not generally be easy to discharge this burden.[296] By contrast, when determining the reasonableness of a covenant as between the parties, the burden of proving reasonableness lies upon the covenantee (that is to say: the employer): *Herbert Morris Ltd v Saxelby*.[297] Cases in which the courts invoke public policy to strike down covenants tend to involve covenants which would be unreasonable as between the parties in any event. See, for example, *Sir WC*

---

[288] [1916] 1 AC 688, HL, 707.
[289] [1993] IRLR 172, CA. See also *Allied Dunbar v Weisinger* [1988] IRLR 60, paras 30–2.
[290] [1999] IRLR 22.
[291] [2000] IRLR 114, CA, para 19.
[292] [1916] 1 AC 688, 700, 707 HL.
[293] [2008] EWHC 1388 (QB).
[294] [2009] EWHC 3694 (QB), para 22.
[295] ibid at 700.
[296] *A-G of Australia v Adelaide Steamship Co* [1913] AC 781, 797.
[297] [1916] AC 688, HL, 707 *per* Lord Parker of Waddington.

Leng & Co Ltd v Andrews[298] where a lifetime ban on newspaper activity within twenty miles of Sheffield was regarded as unreasonable, and *Bull v Pitney-Bowes*[299] where a restriction on 'any activity or occupation which is in competition with or detrimental to the interests of the company' (with loss of pension rights in consequence of breach) was struck down.

The reasonableness of a restrictive covenant has to be determined by reference to the circum-stances of the parties as they were when the covenant was agreed. The covenant has to be reasonable from its inception. This well-established proposition was clearly stated by Diplock LJ in *Gledhow Autoparts Ltd v Delaney*.[300]   **5.231**

The relative equality or inequality of bargaining position between the parties may be a factor in the determination of reasonableness. The more junior the employee, the more difficult it may be to justify a restraint. Senior and well paid employees, who may have negotiated their contracts on an individual basis, may be more readily held to their bargains, subject always to overriding principles of reasonableness. See *M and S Drapers v Reynolds*[301] where Denning LJ observed: 'A managing director can look after himself. A traveller is not so well placed to do so. The law must protect him.' For a relatively recent example of this approach in practice, see *Hanover Insurance Brokers Ltd v Schapiro*[302] in which the Court of Appeal upheld twelve-month covenants restricting the activities of a company chairman.   **5.232**

Confidential information covenants

This topic is dealt with in Chapter 3 above.   **5.233**

Area covenants

Nature of area covenants

Whilst it is still said to be a fundamental principle that a party may not restrain competition per se, in practice this principle has been eroded by the use of covenants restricting the activities of a former employee in a certain geographical area ('area restraints') or by the use of limited 'non-competition' clauses, usually applied to particular business sectors ('non-compete covenants' or 'sectoral restraints').   **5.234**

An area restraint restricts an employee from undertaking specified activities within a particular geographical area. The court's approach to area restraints is cautious, given that these restraints are covenants against competition. This is illustrated by *Office Angels v Rainer-Thomas*[303] in which employees of an employment agency covenanted not to 'engage in or undertake the trade or business of any employment agency within a radius of 3,000 metres of the branch or branches of the company at which the employee was employed for a period of not less than four weeks during the period of six months prior to the date of such termination or, in the case of branch or branches in the Greater London area, then within a radius of 1,000 metres'. The Court of Appeal considered that this imposed too wide an area restraint, covering as it   **5.235**

---

[298] [1909] 1 Ch 763, CA.
[299] [1967] 1 WLR 273.
[300] [1965] 1 WLR 1366, CA, 1375.
[301] [1957] 1 WLR 9, CA. Hodson LJ said at 19: 'The managing director is not regarded in the same light as the traveller or canvasser.'
[302] [1994] IRLR 82, CA, para 21.
[303] [1991] IRLR 214, CA.

did an area of about 1.2 square miles, including most of the City of London. This was a case where some more limited and targeted form of restraint, such as a non-solicitation or non-dealing clause, would have been more appropriate.

Suitability of area covenants

5.236 Developments in modern business and communications mean that, in many cases, area restraints will be of little practical use, as the location from which business is transacted may be of no great importance. This was one of the factors which weighed against the covenant in the *Office Angels* case, as the business could be transacted for the most part by telephone, so the covenant had the effect of subjecting the employees to an onerous restriction on where they could work but at the same time failed properly to protect the employer. There was a lack of functional correspondence between the restricted area and the area in which customers were located. An area restraint was held to be inappropriate for a credit betting business in *SW Strange Ltd v Mann*.[304] The business was a credit, not a cash, business, customers' names and addresses were recorded, business was done mostly by telephone, and the employee's position was not such as would lead to his obtaining the goodwill of customers by rendering particular personal service to them.

5.237 In other cases, the international nature of the business may justify a continental or even worldwide restraint. This was recognized by the Court of Appeal in *Scully (UK) Ltd v Lee*.[305] The Court of Appeal had observed in *Commercial Plastics v Vincent*[306] that:

> The fact that the restriction is potentially world-wide in its operation is a remarkable feature prima facie needing justification, even when there is the limitation to competitors. In *Vandervell Products Ltd v McLeod*[307] (supra) Lord Evershed MR said: 'This is not a case of the sale of goodwill, but of a master and servant, and it must be rare, and, speaking from such experience as I have had, is indeed very rare to find an ex-servant restrained from exercising his trade in a competing business anywhere in the world, not only in England or Scotland, not only in Europe, but in all the five continents of the earth.'

This observation may, however, need to be qualified in the light of modern business trends. See also *Poly Lina Ltd v Finch*[308] and *Polymasc v Charles*,[309] upholding worldwide restraints. In *Lansing Linde Ltd v Kerr*,[310] the Court of Appeal doubted that a worldwide restriction on competition based upon confidential information would be upheld at trial, but the court's doubts appear to have been founded on the inadequacy of the evidence adduced to justify the restraint rather than upon principle.[311]

5.238 More limited area restraints may still have utility in relation to businesses with localized customer bases, and so are still found in the employment contracts of, for example, solicitors, localized sales staff, and even hairdressers. See, for example, *Marion White Ltd v Francis*,[312] in which the Court of Appeal upheld a restriction on undertaking hairdressing work within half a mile of the employer's premises.

---

[304] [1965] 1 All ER 1069.
[305] [1998] IRLR 259, CA, para 26.
[306] [1965] 1 QB 623, CA, 644.
[307] [1957] RPC 185, CA.
[308] [1995] FSR 1.
[309] [1999] FSR 711.
[310] [1991] ICR 428.
[311] ibid 439 *per* Staughton LJ, 445 *per* Beldam LJ, 448 *per* Butler-Sloss LJ.
[312] [1972] 1 WLR 1432, CA.

Where a business is highly localized, the restraint ought properly to reflect this. For this **5.239** reason, a restriction on a butcher trading within five miles of Cambridge was held to be unenforceable, where the employer's business drew its custom from within a mile of its premises (*Empire Meat Co v Patrick*).[313] To similar effect is *Spencer v Marchington*[314] where the restraint covered a radius of twenty-five miles from Banbury but the customers were concentrated within twenty miles, so that the covenant was too wide and unenforceable.

The court may also have regard to population density in the area covered by the restraint. **5.240** A rural area may justify a larger area of restraint (*Scorer v Seymour-Johns*).[315] Contrast the *Office Angels* case[316] where the restriction covered the densely populated (by rival employment agencies and job seekers) City of London. The reasonableness of an area restraint will be judged by reference to the nature of the business sought to be protected and the nature of the employment,[317] and by the limits of the restriction in time and space.

Nature of the business

As to the nature of the business, the court will consider whether it is the sort of business **5.241** which has localized custom, and whether (as in the *Office Angels* case)[318] the restraint offers effective protection. If the business is of a kind which tends customarily to be located in a particular area, such as the City of London or some other financial centre, this fact may tell against the enforceability of the clause, as an area restraint may go too far in precluding the employee from remaining employed within a particular business sector.

Temporal and spatial limits

As to temporal and spatial limits, it is fairly self-evident that the greater the duration of the **5.242** covenant and the wider its geographical extent, the more difficult it will be to justify as reasonable.[319] A shorter period of restriction may assist in justifying a wider geographical area of restraint, and, by the same token, where the area of restraint is small, a longer duration of restraint may be more readily defended.[320] *Greer v Sketchley Ltd*[321] provides an example of this relationship in action: the covenant was unenforceable because it covered the whole of the United Kingdom for a period of twelve months.

Lord Wilberforce explained the approach of the law to temporal limits in *Stenhouse (Australia)* **5.243** *Ltd v Phillips*:[322]

> The question is not how long the employee could be expected to enjoy, by virtue of his employment, a competitive edge over others seeking the clients' business. It is, rather, what is a reasonable time during which the employer is entitled to protection against solicitation of clients with whom the employee had contact and influence during employment and who were not bound to the employer by contract or by stability of association. This question, secondly, their

---

[313] [1939] 2 All ER 85, CA.
[314] [1988] IRLR 292.
[315] [1966] 3 All ER 347, CA, 350.
[316] [1991] IRLR 214, CA.
[317] *Gilford Motor Co v Horne* [1933] Ch 935, CA, 966.
[318] [1991] IRLR 214, CA.
[319] *Herbert Morris Ltd v Saxelby* [1916] 1 AC 688, HL, 715 *per* Lord Shaw.
[320] *Fitch v Dewes* [1921] 2 AC 158, HL, 163 *per* Lord Birkenhead.
[321] [1979] IRLR 445, CA.
[322] [1974] AC 391, PC. The case concerned a non-solicitation clause, but the observations on time limits are of general application.

Lordships do not consider can advantageously form the subject of direct evidence. It is for the judge, after informing himself as fully as he can of the facts and circumstances relating to the employer's business, the nature of the employer's interest to be protected, and the likely effect on this of solicitation, to decide whether the contractual period is reasonable or not. An opinion as to the reasonableness of elements of it, particularly of the time during which it is to run, can seldom be precise, and can only be formed on a broad and common sense view.[323]

5.244 It is impossible to state any general proposition as to what is or is not a reasonable period of restriction, as this will depend upon the circumstances of each case. For example, a two-year non-solicitation clause imposed on a salesman was upheld in *Spafax v Harrison*[324] but struck down in *Scully (UK) Ltd v Lee*.[325] Having said this, the modern trend appears to be towards shorter covenants, with durations of six months to one year being commonly encountered in practice. *Gilford Motor Co v Horne*[326] is unusual in upholding a covenant which was unlimited in time, but it is unlikely that such a covenant would be regarded as acceptable by a modern court. Field J regarded a two-year non-competition covenant as too long in *Duarte v The Black and Decker Corp*,[327] observing that counsel in that case had been able to find only three reported cases in which a two-year covenant was upheld, with the restriction being narrower than a ban on competition.

Non-competition covenants

Protection of trade secrets and confidential information

5.245 Despite the ostensible maintenance of the principle that an employer is not entitled to protect itself against competition, non-competition covenants are in frequent use in modern employment contracts. They are supported on the basis that lesser forms of restriction, such as confidentiality clauses and non-solicitation/dealing clauses, may be difficult to police effectively. The classic statement in this context was made by Lord Denning in *Littlewoods Organisation Ltd v Harris*:

> It is thus established that an employer can stipulate for protection against having his confidential information passed on to a rival in trade. But experience has shown that it is not satisfactory to have simply a covenant against disclosing confidential information. The reason is because it is so difficult to draw the line between information which is confidential and information which is not and it is very difficult to prove a breach when the information is of such a character that a servant can carry it away in his head. The difficulties are such that the only practicable solution is to take a covenant from the servant by which he is not to go to work for a rival in trade. Such a covenant may well be held to be reasonable if limited to a short period.[328]

5.246 This approach was re-affirmed by the Court of Appeal in *Turner v Commonwealth & British Materials Ltd*,[329] a case in which employees of a mining and exploration company covenanted,

---

[323] ibid 402.
[324] [1980] IRLR 442, CA.
[325] [1998] IRLR 259, CA.
[326] [1933] Ch 935, CA.
[327] [2007] EWHC 2720 (QB), para 109. The cases were *Plowman v Ash* [1964] 1 WLR 568 (a customer non-solicitation covenant), *Spafax Ltd v Harrison* [1980] IRLR 442, and *Dairy Crest v Piggott* [1989] ICR 92 (non-solicitation/non-dealing covenants). Field J added 'if a 2 years non-compete covenant is going to be upheld in English law, the scope of the balance of the covenant has got to be narrowly drawn'.
[328] [1977] 1 WLR 1472, CA, 1478.
[329] [2000] IRLR 114, CA.

as part of severance agreements, 'not to be involved whether directly or indirectly for a period of 12 months from termination date with any business which competes or is likely to compete with any business or project carried on by the company or any member of the group at the termination date in which business or project [the employee] was involved in the course of his employment by the company'. Waller LJ explained the basis for upholding this clause, as follows:

> 17. Thus a covenant restraining competition alone is unenforceable as between employer and employee. The seller of a business or partnership is in a different position because unless there is a covenant to restrain competition the vendor can win back the very goodwill that he has sold.

> 18. Thus to enforce the covenant at all the company would have to establish proprietary rights in the nature of trade connection or in the nature of trade secrets. I should emphasise that because those are the matters which they are legitimately entitled to protect it does not follow that clause 5.6 must be unreasonable because covenants restraining the use of confidential information or the canvassing of trade connections could be, and indeed in this case were, imposed. It has been recognised in many cases that because there are serious difficulties in identifying precisely what is or what is not confidential information, and who may or may not have been a customer during the period of an employee's service, a restraint against competing which is reasonable in time and space will not only be enforceable but the most satisfactory form of restraint.

Corporate Express v Day,[330] which concerned a non-solicitation of customers clause, plus a targeted non-compete clause, naming specific business rivals of the claimant company, followed the *Littlewoods v Harris* line. The clauses were upheld (although no injunction was granted on a discretionary basis). **5.247**

Another fairly wide-ranging non-competition clause was upheld by Cox J in *TFS Derivatives v Morgan*.[331] The employee, an equity derivatives broker, agreed that he would not 'for six months undertake, carry on or be employed, engaged or interested in any capacity in either any business which is competitive with or similar to a Relevant Business within the Territory, or any business an objective or anticipated result of which is to compete with a Relevant Business within the Territory'. Cox J severed the words 'or similar to' and upheld the clause as thus modified. The *TFS* case settled before it was heard by the Court of Appeal, and is a first instance decision only, but it has become commonly cited in cases in this field. **5.248**

For examples of non-competition clauses being upheld at trial, see *Thomas v Farr plc*[332] (twelve months, insurance broking), *Extec Screens & Crushers Ltd v Rice*[333] (eight months, sales of industrial equipment), and *Mantis Surgical Ltd v Tregenza*[334] (three months, sales of surgical equipment). **5.249**

It is important that the former employer's business actually competes with the business in which the former employee wishes now to be engaged. In *Pheonix Partners Group LLP v Asoyag*,[335] the former employer was no longer active in the field in which the new employer **5.250**

---

[330] [2004] EWHC 2943.
[331] [2005] IRLR 256.
[332] [2007] ICR 932, CA.
[333] [2007] EWHC 1043 (QB).
[334] [2007] EWHC 1545 (QB).
[335] [2010] IRLR 594.

carried on business, so the employee would not in fact be competing with the former employer, and the non-competition clause did not apply.

Protection of customer connection

5.251   Although restraints of this kind have conventionally been based on protection of confidential information, the *Turner*[336] and *TFS Derivatives*[337] cases demonstrate that non-competition clauses may validly be based upon other interests, such as trade connection. This represents a shift in position from the *Office Angels* case,[338] in which non-solicitation and non-dealing clauses were regarded as the preferred form of restriction to protect customer connection. However, each case depends on its own facts and there were particular reasons why trade connection required the protection of a non-competition covenant in the former cases.

Defining the type of business

5.252   Clauses such as this need to be precise in defining the type of business in which the employee may not be engaged during the operation of the restraint, and that business must be of the kind in which the employee was engaged by the employer. Failure to limit the restraint in this way will result in unenforceability. Examples of covenants which fell foul of this principle may be found in:

- *Routh v Jones*:[339] The restriction was too wide as it prevented a General Practitioner from working as a Consultant. *Commercial Plastics v Vincent*:[340] The restriction was on employment in PVC calendaring, but the employee had only been concerned with PVC calendared sheeting for adhesive tape, so the covenant was too wide. *Gledhow Autoparts Ltd v Delaney*:[341] The area restraint applied to persons who had never dealt with the employer and so was too wide.
- *Scully (UK) Ltd v Lee*:[342] The restriction was on engaging in 'any business involving or including the manufacture supply installing modification servicing advertising or otherwise dealing in overspill prevention or tank gauging equipment or without prejudice to the foregoing any other business which competes with any business carried on by the company at the date of this agreement'. This was unreasonable because the restriction was not limited to a business which was in competition with the employer. The employee had been concerned only with equipment used in the petrochemical industry, but the clause extended beyond such equipment.
- *Wincanton Ltd v Cranny*:[343] The restriction was on employment in 'any business of whatever kind within the UK which is wholly or partly in competition with any business carried on by the employer'. This restriction was unenforceable because it covered business activities in which the employee had not been engaged.
- *Norbrook Laboratories (GB) Ltd v Adair*,[344] in which the restriction extended to products which the employee had not sold, but which he might have been expected to sell within the last five years of the employment.

---

[336]   [2000] IRLR 114, CA.
[337]   [2005] IRLR 256, CA.
[338]   [1991] IRLR 214, CA.
[339]   [1947] 1 All ER 758, CA.
[340]   [1965] 1 QB 623, CA.
[341]   [1965] 1 WLR 1366, CA.
[342]   [1998] IRLR 259, CA.
[343]   [2000] IRLR 276, CA.
[344]   [2008] IRLR 878.

Reasonableness factors

The concept of reasonableness is a flexible one, and it is impossible to draw up an exhaustive **5.253** list of factors which will establish the reasonableness or unreasonableness of a specific covenant in a specific context, but the following factors will generally be relevant:

- What is the duration of the restraint?
- What is the geographical extent of the restraint?
- Is the business covered by the covenant clearly defined?
- In particular, does the restraint relate only to business in which (a) the employer was engaged at the time of termination of the employment, and (b) in which the employee had been engaged during the employment? In this context, it is advisable to specify in the covenant a period pre-termination of employment during which the employee must have been engaged in the business in question. Imposing a restriction in respect of an activity in which the employee had no recent involvement would often be regarded as unreasonable.
- Would a form of restraint less extensive than a non-compete clause afford the employer adequate protection?

Client non-solicitation covenants

A covenant to restrain an employee from soliciting business from a clearly defined class of **5.254** customers will potentially be a reasonable restraint. The restriction should be on solicitation in respect of a business of the same nature as that of the employer, as otherwise the employer has no legitimate interest in restricting solicitation.

Meaning of solicitation

The concept of 'solicitation' is not easy to define. A useful practical approach to this concept **5.255** may be suggested by the New Zealand case of *Sweeney v Astle*.[345] Does the conduct of the employee evidence a specific purpose and intention to obtain orders from the customers? Where it is the employee who initiates contact with a customer, and does something more than merely inform the customer of his departure from the former employment, the employee may be regarded as soliciting the customer. In *Taylor Stuart & Co v Croft*,[346] it was said to be acceptable for an employee to inform customers that he had left his former employment and to give his address, but not acceptable to inform them that he could be contacted at the given address. Care should be taken, however, not to confuse a non-solicitation clause with a non-dealing clause. Where the customer initiates contact, the employee may be entitled to respond, as in *Austin Knight (UK) Ltd v Hinds*.[347] In *Ward Evans Financial Services Ltd v Fox*,[348] the Court of Appeal considered the concepts of inducement and solicitation in relation to a clause designed to protect confidential information. The employees had agreed that they would not 'at any time before or after the termination date, induce or seek to induce by means involving the disclosure or use of confidential business information any customer to cease dealing with the company'. The court held that a breach of this clause required the employee to deploy the confidential information.

---

[345] [1923] NZLR 1198.
[346] CA, 7 May 1987.
[347] [1994] FSR 42.
[348] [2002] IRLR 120, CA, para 19 *per* Pill LJ.

The clause did not cover a situation in which the fact that the employee possesses the confidential information causes the customer to act.

Contact with the customers

5.256 The restriction can only relate to customers who were customers of the employer during the period of employment of the employee subject to the covenant. A restriction in respect of customers acquired after the cessation of the employment relationship is unreasonable (*Konski v Peet*).[349]

5.257 A problem may arise in respect of customers who have not had recent dealings with the employer. In principle, a covenant may apply in respect of such customers (*GW Plowman & Son Ltd v Ash*),[350] but the modern approach is to prefer some recent contact with the customers, as in the covenant upheld in *Business Seating (Renovations) Ltd v Broad*,[351] which was limited to customers who had dealt with the employing company during the twelve months before termination of the employment. The application of a covenant (in that case an area restraint) to persons who had no connection with the employer's business was fatal to the covenant in *Gledhow Autoparts Ltd v Delaney*.[352]

5.258 It used to be the case that the required contact was between customer and employer. The decision in *Business Seating v Broad* did not require that the covenanting employee should have had personal contact with the customers, and the Court of Appeal similarly imposed no such requirement in *Dentmaster (UK) Ltd v Kent*,[353] but it is now generally regarded as good practice for covenants to include such a requirement. Support for this approach may be derived from *Marley Tile Co Ltd v Johnson*,[354] particularly where, as in that case, the customer base is large and the employee cannot be expected to have known or dealt with more than a minority of the customers. For the same reason, the non-solicitation and non-dealing clauses in *Office Angels Ltd v Rainer-Thomas*[355] were held to be unreasonable. The fact that a covenant extended to all customers of the employer, including those with whom the employee had had no contact, was one of the reasons for the striking down of the covenant in *Austin Knight (UK) Ltd v Hinds*.[356] There the employee dealt with a relatively small number of customers, but the company's customer base was extensive. Similarly, in *WRN Ltd v Ayris*,[357] a covenant which applied to customers with whom the employee had not dealt was held to be too wide.

5.259 The extent to which actual customer contact will be required may also depend upon whether the employee was in a managerial position, or was merely a sales representative. The employee's managerial position, and corresponding knowledge of the customer base derived through sales reports and training duties, influenced the upholding of the covenant in *Spafax v Harrison*.[358]

---

[349] [1915] 1 Ch 530.
[350] [1964] 1 WLR 568, CA.
[351] [1989] ICR 729.
[352] [1965] 1 WLR 1366, CA.
[353] [1997] IRLR 636, CA.
[354] [1982] IRLR 75, CA.
[355] [1991] IRLR 214, CA.
[356] [1994] FSR 42, 58.
[357] [2008] IRLR 889.
[358] [1980] IRLR 442, CA.

Prospective customers

The extent to which a restriction may properly be applied to prospective customers is debatable. **5.260**
The possibility of applying a covenant to potential customers was raised in, but not determined by, *Gledhow Autoparts Ltd v Delaney*.³⁵⁹ On a strict view, mere prospects could be
placed in the same category as customers acquired after the employee leaves the employer's
service, and Millet J in *Business Seating (Renovations) Ltd v Broad*³⁶⁰ considered that a restriction on solicitation of customers of associate companies regarded as potential customers
would be unenforceable.

In some cases, however, the courts have been prepared to recognize restrictions in respect **5.261**
of prospects who are more than merely persons who have been identified as potential
customers, but are persons with whom the employer has had some dealings with a view
to establishing a business relationship. Covenants often use terms such as 'negotiations'
or 'material dealings' with prospective customers. In *International Consulting Services (UK)
Ltd v Hart*,³⁶¹ the High Court upheld a covenant restricting dealings with companies with
which the employer had negotiated in the twelve months before termination of the
employment. The court held that, in this context, 'negotiations' means more than a customer expressing an interest in employing the employer's services. The court took the
view that what is required is a discussion between the parties about the terms of a contract
which both parties have in view, and which is a real possibility. In *Axiom Business
Computers Ltd v Frederick*, an unreported case of 20 November 2003, the Outer House
of the Court of Session held that, given the nature of the employer's business, it had a
legitimate interest in protecting its connection with prospective customers with whom
negotiations had begun.

By contrast, the inclusion of potential customers with whom an employee had had dealings **5.262**
in the last two years of the employment was held to be unreasonable in *Norbrook Laboratories
(GB) Ltd v Adair*.³⁶² The reference to potential customers was severed from the covenant in
that case.

The fact that the employee initially brought customers to the employer when starting **5.263**
employment will not in itself preclude a non-solicitation covenant applying in respect
of those customers (*Hanover Insurance Brokers Ltd v Schapiro*),³⁶³ but this may be a factor
relevant to the length of the restriction imposed on the employee (*M and S Drapers v
Reynolds*).³⁶⁴

Furthermore, the fact that the customers may no longer wish to deal with the former **5.264**
employer is no basis for not upholding a restriction in respect of those customers. A situation in which the employee may exert influence over customers to follow the employee to
their new employment is precisely the situation which the restriction is intended to address
(*John Michael Design plc v Cooke*).³⁶⁵

---

³⁵⁹ [1965] 1 WLR 1366, CA, 1373 *per* Sellers LJ.
³⁶⁰ [1989] ICR 729.
³⁶¹ [2000] IRLR 227.
³⁶² [2008] IRLR 878.
³⁶³ [1994] IRLR 82, CA.
³⁶⁴ [1957] 1 WLR 9, CA.
³⁶⁵ [1987] ICR 445, CA.

Duration

5.265 As with other varieties of covenant, it is impossible to state any general rule as to the period of restriction on soliciting which will be acceptable in any given case. For examples of enforceable time periods in non-solicitation covenants, see *Spafax Ltd v Harrison*[366] (sales manager and salesman in motor spares, two years); *John Michael Design plc v Cooke*[367] (director and designer for shop fitting company, two years); *Rex Stewart Jeffries Parker Ginsberg Ltd v Parker*[368] (advertising director, eighteen months); *Dairy Crest Ltd v Pigott*[369] (milkman, two years), and *Business Seating (Renovations) Ltd v Broad*[370] (furniture salesman, one year). Contrast *Scully UK Ltd v Lee*,[371] in which a two-year non-solicitation clause imposed on a salesman of technical equipment was held to be too long.

Client non-dealing covenants

5.266 The practical weakness of non-solicitation clauses lies in the difficulty of defining solicitation and of proving that solicitation has occurred. For this reason, a non-dealing clause will often be used in combination with or instead of a non-solicitation clause. The use of a non-dealing clause will obviate the need for enquiry as to whether an employee has initiated contact with a customer or whether the employee's actions can be construed as solicitation.

5.267 In determining the reasonableness of a non-dealing clause, similar considerations will apply as in the case of non-solicitation covenants. The court will look at the duration of the restriction, and at the definition of the customers covered thereby. Modern covenants will tend to apply in respect of customers with whom the employer (and possibly the employee) has had dealings in a defined period before the termination of the employment.

Employee non-poaching covenants

5.268 The courts have come to recognize that an employer's investment in recruiting and training its workforce may give rise to a legitimate interest in maintaining the stability of that workforce.[372] This legitimate interest is the basis for covenants intended to restrain a former employee from poaching and (possibly) from employing former colleagues.

5.269 A suitably limited covenant to restrain an employee from soliciting former colleagues to leave the former employer may be upheld. The restriction ought ordinarily to be limited to employees of a particular level of seniority or to employees of a class in respect of whom the covenanting employee might be expected to exert some influence, such as members of a particular team or department of employees. The Court of Appeal in *Dawnay Day v D'Alphen*,[373] considered that the phrase 'senior employees' was sufficiently clear to render the covenant enforceable in that case, but in practice it is prudent to attempt a more precise definition if possible.

---

[366] [1980] IRLR 442, CA.
[367] [1987] ICR 445, CA.
[368] [1988] IRLR 483, CA.
[369] [1989] ICR 92, CA.
[370] [1989] ICR 729, CA.
[371] [1998] IRLR 259, CA.
[372] See paras 5.182–5.185 above.
[373] [1998] ICR 1068, CA.

In *Hydra plc v Anastasi*,[374] the non-poaching restriction was regarded as reasonable even **5.270** though it applied to all employees but this is explained by the fact that there were only twelve such employees. Ordinarily, a restriction applying across the workforce would be susceptible to challenge as being too wide.

The restriction need not be limited to enticement of employees to leave their employment in **5.271** breach of contract, but may apply also to enticement to employees to give proper notice and move elsewhere.

As in the case of non-solicitation of clients, there may be problems of definition and of proof **5.272** in relation to solicitation of employees. An employee who does no more than tell his or her former colleagues that he or she is taking new employment elsewhere is unlikely to be guilty of soliciting, but if the employee takes steps intended to encourage colleagues to move, this may breach a non-poaching clause.

Employee non-employment covenants

It might be thought that, if the court will uphold covenants which restrain dealings with **5.273** clients, even in the absence of solicitation of such clients by the covenanting employee, it ought, by parity of reasoning, to uphold covenants restraining an employee from employing former colleagues, but there is judicial reluctance to accept such an approach. Robert Walker J, in the first instance decision in *Dawnay Day v D'Alphen*,[375] regarded a non-employment clause as 'indefensible'. The clause was not relied upon by the employer and was not considered by the Court of Appeal.

In *Cantor Fitzgerald v Bird*,[376] the court refused to grant an injunction restraining the departing **5.274** employee 'from making any offer of employment to any broker employed in the claimant's rates division the terms of which take effect before the expiry of the fixed term (or as the case may be notice period) of the employee concerned'. This form of relief was considered too wide and unjustifiable. By contrast, in *TFS Derivatives v Morgan*,[377] the court upheld a non-employment clause as well as a non-poaching clause.

It may be possible to draw a principled distinction between clauses restricting dealing with **5.275** clients and clauses restricting employment of former colleagues. In the case of clients, even where there has not been solicitation, the employee in dealing with the clients may take advantage of knowledge of the former employer's confidential information and trade connection. In the case of former colleagues, the employee's ability unfairly to use influence over colleagues to the detriment of the former employer may be limited to the recruitment stage. Simply employing former colleagues will not, on this argument, involve the misuse of an advantage gained at the expense of the former employer.

The argument to the contrary is that the employee has acquired knowledge of the remunera- **5.276** tion, employment terms, and skills of colleagues gained during employment. Information of this type was regarded as relevant to the non-poaching covenant in *Dawnay Day v D'Alphen*[378] and was also put forward in support of the non-poaching and non-employment clauses in

---

[374] [2005] EWHC 1559.
[375] [1998] ICR 1068, 1096; [1997] IRLR 285, para 77.
[376] [2002] IRLR 867.
[377] [2005] IRLR 246.
[378] [1998] ICR 1068, CA.

TFS Derivatives v Morgan,[379] although in that case the court was not satisfied that the employee had more than a general knowledge of salaries, etc and it is not particularly clear from the decision why the non-employment clause was upheld.

5.277   In addition, non-employment clauses may be regarded as contrary to the public interest in permitting employees to change jobs (subject, of course, to any valid contractual restraints applying to the employees in question).

Miscellaneous post-termination restrictions

Association

5.278   Contracts of employment often include provisions prohibiting an employee from claiming to have any continuing association with the employer and its business after the cessation of employment. These provisions operate as a supplement to the general law restricting passing off.[380] Given that no one has the right falsely to represent that he or she has an association with another party's business, clauses of this kind should be unobjectionable.

Disparagement

5.279   Many employment contracts also contain restrictions on the employee making disparaging statements about the employer post-termination of employment. Clauses of this kind may be seen as supplementing the employer's rights under the general law as to defamation and malicious falsehood.

5.280   A complicating factor here is the employee's right to freedom of expression, which is guaranteed by Article 10 of the European Convention on Human Rights, to which the court, as a public authority under the Human Rights Act 1998, must give effect. The right has to be balanced against the rights of others, and specifically, in this context, against the rights of the employer, but it may be questioned whether the employee can validly be restrained by contract from making statements about the employer which are true. In the context of defamation, no injunction will be granted to restrain a statement which is alleged to be true.[381] It may be arguable, however, that, where an employee has contracted not to disparage the employer, the court is not bound to apply the defamation principle and allow the employee to make a disparaging statement merely because it is asserted (but not yet proven) to be true. It should be noted that any attempt to enforce a non-disparagement clause will be subject to section 12 of the Human Rights Act 1998.[382]

Ancillary clauses

Provisions permitting consent

5.281   Restrictive covenants sometimes include provision for the employer to consent to an employee undertaking a particular activity during the currency of the covenant. The reasonableness of such a provision is in practice only likely to be tested in circumstances where an employer withholds consent in relation to something which a former employee wishes to do. The fact that an employer could consent to the employee undertaking an action ought not

---

[379]   [2005] IRLR 246.
[380]   See Chapter 7 below.
[381]   *Holley v Smith* [1998] QB 726, CA.
[382]   See Chapter 3 above.

in principle to affect the reasonableness or unreasonableness of the covenant. If the restriction is too wide to be enforced, then it should not be upheld, regardless of a provision enabling the employer to consent to the employee's action. In any event, an employer can always consent to an employee doing something which would otherwise be restricted, and there is no need for an express provision to this effect.

In the little-known case of *Kerchiss v Kolora Printing Inks Ltd*,[383] a provision for the employer **5.282** to give consent (not to be unreasonably withheld) to an otherwise restricted activity was included by the court as one factor in support of the covenant. But it is difficult to reconcile this approach with the fundamental principles that a restriction must be reasonable if it is to be enforceable and that the reasonableness of the covenant should be judged as at the inception of the contract, rather than by reference to the reasonableness or unreasonableness of the employer's withholding of consent at the time of alleged breach. This approach has not featured in recent cases.

Provisions requiring notification

A contract may require an employee to notify the employer if the employee agrees to accept **5.283** a new job, and/or to notify the new employer of the restrictive covenants contained in the contract. It is not clear that such clauses qualify as restraints of trade, as they do not actually limit an employee's ability to take a new job. They are intended to assist the employer in knowing when it might need to enforce covenants, and in making a case against a new employer for inducement to breach of contract.

It is perhaps arguable that a clause requiring the employee to notify a new employer of restric- **5.284** tive covenants could limit an employee's freedom to work because the new employer might be persuaded by disclosure of restrictive covenants not to employ an individual subject thereto, but there is nothing in the clause itself which compels this result.

Even if such clauses could be regarded as restraints of trade, it is difficult to see why they **5.285** should be other than reasonable as adjuncts to restrictive covenants, confidential information clauses, notice periods, and garden leave clauses. Notification clauses simply require employees to be open about their plans and to inform new employers of obligations to which they may be subject.

Having said this, remedies for breach of such clauses are likely to be of limited practical utility. **5.286** It might be conceivable that a court would grant a mandatory injunction to compel an employee to inform the old employer of the identity of the new one, but in most cases the old employer obtains this information in any event without recourse to the court. As to damages, it is difficult to ascribe a monetary value to an employee's breach of a clause of this kind. The breach may put the employer to the expense of itself contacting the new employer, but it will ordinarily wish to do this in any event, in seeking to ensure that the new employer is aware of restrictions binding the employee.

Provisions permitting rewriting

The parties cannot by agreement alter the standard principles as to severance[384] or confer on **5.287** the court a power to rewrite the covenant as an alternative to declaring it to be unenforceable.

---

[383] [1960] RPC 235.
[384] See paras 5.264–5.276 below.

The basic prohibition on the court rewriting a covenant is made clear in *Mason v Provident Clothing and Supply Ltd*.[385] The application of this principle to a clause which purports to permit the court to substitute different periods or areas of restriction for those contained in the covenant is apparent from the decision of the Court of Session in *Living Design (Home Improvements) Ltd v Davidson*.[386] Clauses of this kind do not override the prohibition on judicial rewriting of contracts. If the covenant is unreasonable, and the unreasonable part of it cannot be severed applying ordinary severance principles, then the covenant cannot be enforced. The *Living Design* case, although a Scottish decision, has been generally followed and applied by the High Court in England and Wales. The Court of Session took a more positive view of 'saving' clauses in *Hinton & Higgs (UK) Ltd v Murphy*.[387] The court would have accepted a deletion of part of the covenant in accordance with the provision in the contract that 'in the event that any such restriction shall be void would be valid if some part thereof were deleted . . . such restrictions shall apply with such modifications as may be necessary to make them valid or effective'.[388] The court considered that in doing this it would not be rewriting the contract but giving effect to the parties' intentions.[389] The court's views on this point (which, in any event, were limited to deleting rather than altering words) were, however, obiter, as the covenant was held to be too wide in any event.

Interrelationship between garden leave and restrictive covenants

5.288   The subject of garden leave is dealt with in detail in Chapter 4 above. Where, as is frequently the case, a contract of employment includes a garden leave provision as well as restrictive covenants, an issue may arise as to whether both types of restriction are enforceable, and how they should inter-relate.

5.289   In *Credit Suisse Asset Management Ltd v Armstrong*,[390] employees argued that six-month post-termination restraints should not be enforced against them when they had already been subjected to six months of garden leave. The Court of Appeal rejected this argument, declining, in effect, to set off a period of garden leave against the period of a post-termination covenant. The court did, however, find that the existence of a garden leave clause might be a factor to be taken into account in determining the validity of a restrictive covenant as at the date of the contract. Neil LJ added:

> Terms which operate in restraint of trade raise questions of public policy. The opportunity for an individual to maintain and exercise his skills is a matter of general concern. I would therefore leave open the possibility that in an exceptional case where a long period of garden leave had already elapsed, perhaps substantially in excess of a year, without any curtailment by the court, the court would decline to grant any further protection based on a restrictive covenant.[391]

5.290   On the basis of this observation, and despite the rejection in the *Credit Suisse* case itself of the attempt to limit the effect of a covenant by reference to garden leave, it has become common-place for contracts to contain provisions reducing the extent of post-termination restriction

---

[385] [1913] AC 724, HL, 745.
[386] [1994] IRLR 69.
[387] [1989] IRLR 519.
[388] This is how the clause is set out in the report. There appears to be a 'but' missing after the word 'void'.
[389] ibid para 4.
[390] [1996] ICR 882, [1996] IRLR 450, CA.
[391] [1996] ICR 882, 894.

by reference to the period of garden leave served by the employee. This is the case even where the period of garden leave is less than a year. Thus the practice of employers has become more cautious than the decision in the *Credit Suisse* case would suggest. Notwithstanding this, there is not yet a reported decision in which a restrictive covenant has been held to be unenforceable because of the length of the period of garden leave served by the employee.

Given that, after the decision of the Court of Appeal in *William Hill Organisation Ltd v Tucker*,[392] garden leave clauses will themselves only be upheld to the extent that they are reasonable (applying the same approach as in the case of a post-termination restrictive covenant), if the court is asked to enforce a restrictive covenant in addition to a garden leave clause, or in circumstances where garden leave has already been served, the court may have regard to the overall reasonableness of the combined restraint. **5.291**

In *TFS Derivatives v Morgan*,[393] the employee advanced a novel argument, going much further than the point argued (unsuccessfully) in the *Credit Suisse* case, and contending that a restrictive covenant should be rejected by the court because it would have been more appropriate for the employer to use a garden leave clause in order to obtain the protection which it sought. **5.292**

Cox J declined to give general guidance on the relationship of garden leave clauses and non-competition clauses of the kind found in that case. However, she rejected the employee's argument: first, because garden leave would be more onerous than the covenant; secondly, because garden leave would not be appropriate in the case of summary dismissal[394] or in the event of an employee resigning without notice;[395] thirdly, because the use of a garden leave clause might breach the implied term of the employment contract as to trust and confidence;[396] and, fourthly, because the employee had been well paid to agree to the covenants (this met the point that an employer ought to pay an employee to stay out of the marketplace, as an employer does during garden leave). **5.293**

Although the court is not likely, therefore, to refuse to uphold a covenant on the basis that garden leave would have been the more appropriate form of protection, it remains possible for the court, applying its flexible approach to garden leave,[397] to decide that no garden leave injunction is appropriate where the employer can enforce a reasonable post-termination covenant against the employee. **5.294**

H. Severance

Severance principles

The court generally strives to uphold contracts, subject to overriding constraints of reasonableness and public policy. Where a restrictive covenant cannot be construed in such a **5.295**

---

[392] [1999] ICR 291, [1998] IRLR 313, CA.

[393] [2005] IRLR 246.

[394] Presumably Cox J meant by this a lawful summary dismissal, but see the discussion of wrongful dismissal and restrictive covenants at paras 5.83–5.143 above.

[395] This point is curious, since an employee who attempts to leave without notice may be compelled by a garden leave injunction (in effect) to remain employed during the contractual notice period or part thereof.

[396] Cox J did not elaborate further on the circumstances in which an express garden leave clause might breach the implied term.

[397] See Chapter 4 above.

manner as to make it reasonable and so enforceable, the court may nonetheless be able to save at least part of the covenant if it is capable of being severed. Lord Moulton explained the basis for severance in *Mason v Providential Clothing & Supply Co Ltd*:[398]

> My Lords, I do not doubt that the court may, and in some cases will, enforce a part of a covenant in restraint of trade, even though taken as a whole the covenant exceeds what is reasonable. But, in my opinion, that ought only to be done in cases where the part so enforceable is clearly severable, and even so only in cases where the excess is of trivial importance, or merely technical, and not a part of the main purport and substance of the clause.[399]

5.296   The court will not rewrite a badly written covenant, but, if it is possible to regard the covenant as containing distinct promises, the court may sever those promises which are unenforceable and leave intact those which are enforceable. As Lord Sterndale MR put it in *Attwood v Lamont*,[400] 'a contract can be severed if the severed parts are independent of one another and can be severed without the severance affecting the meaning of the part remaining'.[401] Younger LJ added:

> The learned judges of the Divisional Court, I think, took the view that such severance always was permissible when it could be effectively accomplished by the action of a blue pencil. I do not agree. The doctrine of severance has not, I think, gone further than to make it permissible in a case where the covenant is not really a single covenant but is in effect a combination of several distinct covenants. In that case and where the severance can be carried out without the addition or alteration of a word, it is permissible. But in that case only.[402]

5.297   These principles were elaborated upon by the High Court in *Sadler v Imperial Life Assurance Co of Canada Ltd*.[403] The court identified three conditions which must be fulfilled before a contract may be severed:

1. The unenforceable provision is capable of being removed without the necessity of adding to or modifying the wording of what remains.
2. The remaining terms continue to be supported by adequate consideration.
3. The removal of the unenforceable provision does not so change the character of the contract that it becomes 'not the sort of contract that the parties entered into at all.'[404]

5.298   The Court of Appeal followed this approach in *Marshall v NM Financial Management Ltd*.[405] At first instance[406] the judge added a fourth condition, namely the requirement that severance must be consistent with public policy. The Court of Appeal upheld the judge's decision, but did not discuss this additional requirement.

5.299   *Attwood v Lamont*[407] suggested that, when the court finds that restraints are severable, the court must go on to examine whether or not to treat the two restraints as separate by enforcing the valid and ignoring the invalid. The Court of Appeal rejected this approach (treating the relevant portion of *Attwood* as *obiter dicta*) in *T Lucas & Co v Mitchell*.[408] If the court finds

---

[398] [1913] AC 724, HL.
[399] ibid 745.
[400] [1920] 3 KB 571, CA.
[401] ibid 577.
[402] ibid 593.
[403] [1988] IRLR 388.
[404] ibid para 19.
[405] [1997] ICR 1065, [1997] IRLR 449, CA.
[406] [1996] IRLR 20.
[407] [1920] 3 KB 571, CA, 593.
[408] [1974] Ch 129, CA, 136 *per* Russell LJ.

that the restraints are separate and severable, no further step is required in order to render enforceable the valid portion of the covenant. Even when the part of a covenant which is unenforceable is not trivial, severance is permissible provided that the enforceable and unenforceable restrictions are, as a matter of construction, independent, so as to be separate and severable, with the result that the excision of the unenforceable restriction can be made without addition or modification.[409]

The test is not merely a linguistic or grammatical test. As Millet LJ said in the *Marshall* case: **5.300** 'This is a question of substance, not form.'[410] In order to sever a contract, the court will need to be satisfied that the parties intended to make distinct and separate promises.

The *Attwood* approach was reiterated by Kay LJ in *Beckett Investment Management Group* **5.301** *Ltd v Hall*.[411]

For this reason, covenants will often include a statement to the effect that each restriction is **5.302** intended to be a separate promise, separately enforceable. It will still be a matter for the court in each case, however, to determine the extent to which promises can be regarded as distinct and severable.

Similarly, employment contracts often include provision to the effect that, if a clause requires **5.303** some part of it to be deleted or requires some alteration in scope or duration in order to be enforceable, it should apply subject to the necessary amendments. The Court of Session considered a clause of this kind in *Living Design (Home Improvements) Ltd v Davidson*[412] and held that such a clause did not alter the court's power to sever a contract, which power can be exercised only where the conditions for severability were present. A clause of this kind did not empower the court to rewrite the covenant.[413]

Application of severance principles

Examples of clauses which were held not to be capable of severance include the clause in **5.304** *Attwood v Lamont*[414] which imposed restrictions in respect of 'the trade or business of a tailor, dressmaker, general draper, milliner, hatter, haberdasher, gentlemen's, ladies' or children's outfitter'. This was held to be intended to be a single promise, not a series of promises in respect of distinct types of trade. The clause could have been severed grammatically, but the court declined to sever the clause because of its view as to the intention underlying the clause.

In *Scully (UK) Ltd v Lee*,[415] the court declined to sever the words 'any other business which **5.305** competes with any business carried on by the company at the date of this agreement'.

By contrast, in *TFS Derivatives v Morgan*,[416] where the covenant applied to 'a business which **5.306** competes with or is similar to a Relevant Business', the court was prepared to sever the words

---

[409] See Scott V-C in *Scully (UK) Ltd v Lee* [1998] IRLR 259, CA, para 32.
[410] [1997] ICR 1065, 1071.
[411] [2007] ICR 1539, [2007] IRLR 793, CA. The suggestion by HH Judge Seymour QC, in *Advantage Business Systems Ltd v Hopley* [2007] EWHC 1783 at para 84, that *Beckett* does not follow the approach of *Attwood* appears incorrect, as the two Court of Appeal decisions are consistent with one another.
[412] [1994] IRLR 69.
[413] See further on this point, para 5.256 above.
[414] [1920] 3 KB 571, CA.
[415] [1998] IRLR 259, CA.
[416] [2005] IRLR 246.

'or is similar to', treating the covenant as containing distinct promises in respect of competition with the defined 'Relevant Business' and in respect of business which was similar to such Relevant Business. This conclusion is to be contrasted with the refusal to sever in *Wincanton v Cranny*[417] ('any business of whatever kind within the UK which is wholly or partly in competition with any business carried on by the employer') and *Scully (UK) Ltd v Lee*.[418]

5.307   The approach to severance in the *TFS* case was similar to that found in *Ronbar Enterprises Ltd v Green*,[419] although it should be noted that *Ronbar* was a vendor and purchaser case. The court in that case regarded it as permissible, as between the vendor and the purchaser of a business, to sever a clause so as, in effect, to limit its area of operation, by deleting reference to business similar to that of the claimant company. See also *Goldsoll v Goldman*,[420] another case of vendor and purchaser, in which the court severed a clause so as to reduce its geographical extent and so as to permit the vendor of an imitation jewellery business to deal in real but not imitation jewellery.

5.308   Returning to severance in the employment context, see *Business Seating (Renovations) Ltd v Broad*,[421] in which the covenant was expressed to apply in respect of customers of the employer but also in respect of customers of the employer's associated companies. The court treated the covenant as expressing distinct promises in respect of the employer's customers and those of its associated companies, and severed the latter promise as too wide to be enforceable.

5.309   Field J declined to sever a non-competition covenant in *Duarte v The Black and Decker Corp*.[422] The covenant required the employee not to compete with the employer, and also not to accept employment with companies listed in a schedule. Field J regarded this as one promise, not two distinct and several promises.

5.310   A non-dealing clause was upheld after severing a reference to potential customers in *Norbrook Laboratories (GB) Ltd v Adair*.[423]

I. Discretion

5.311   When an employer seeks to enforce a restrictive covenant by injunction, the court has a discretion to grant or to refuse an injunction, and may refuse an injunction even where the covenant is reasonable. Injunctions are equitable remedies, and all equitable remedies are discretionary. The court's discretion is exercisable both at the interim and at the final stages of court proceedings.[424]

5.312   The existence of the discretion allows the court to adopt a flexible approach to a covenant where, for example, the circumstances at trial are such as to render unreasonable the enforcement of a covenant which was reasonable when it was entered into. As Cox J held in *TFS Derivatives v Morgan*:[425] 'Even if the covenant is held to be reasonable, the court will then

---

[417] [2000] IRLR 276, CA.
[418] [1998] IRLR 259, CA.
[419] [1954] 1 WLR 815, CA.
[420] [1915] 1 Ch 292, CA.
[421] [1989] ICR 729.
[422] [2007] EWHC 2720 (QB), para 114.
[423] [2008] IRLR 878.
[424] See Chapter 9 below.
[425] [2005] IRLR 246.

finally decide whether, as a matter of discretion, the injunctive relief sought should in all the circumstances be granted, having regard, amongst other things, to its reasonableness as at the time of trial.'[426]

Discretionary considerations

The factors likely to affect the exercise of the court's discretion include: **5.313**

- the likely utility of the injunction: equity 'does nothing in vain', and the court will not grant an injunction if it would serve no useful purpose to do so;
- the presence or absence of evidence of a likely breach of the covenant;
- the amount of time remaining during which the covenant would be in force;
- any delay on the part of the employer in seeking to enforce the covenant, and, where there has been such delay, the reasons for it;
- the status quo;
- whether the grant of an injunction would result in the breach of contractual commitments already made to innocent third parties; and
- whether the damage caused by the breach of covenant can be compensated by readily calculated damages or other financial remedy, such as an account of profits.

Illustrations of the exercise of discretion

In *Corporate Express v Day*,[427] the court upheld as reasonable a non-solicitation of customers **5.314** clause and non-compete clause, naming specific business rivals of the claimant company, but went on to refuse injunctive relief on discretionary grounds. The reasons for this were: first, that the covenant had almost expired; and, secondly, that the injunction would cause the employee to lose her job with the new employer. This is an example of a familiar employee argument, usually brushed aside, but here having decisive impact, even though the argument could be made in many cases (for example in *Scully (UK) Ltd v Lee*[428] the employee's victory in the Court of Appeal was pyrrhic, as he had already lost his job by the time the appeal was heard).

In practice, however, it is comparatively rare for the court to exercise its discretion so as to **5.315** refuse an injunction in circumstances where the court has upheld the validity of a covenant. Lord Cairns LC, in *Doherty v Allman*,[429] took the view that an injunction to enforce a negative stipulation in a contract was practically obligatory:

> If parties, for valuable consideration, with their eyes open, contract that a particular thing shall not be done, all that a Court of Equity has to do is to say, by way of injunction, that which the parties have already said by way of covenant, that the thing shall not be done; and in such case the injunction does nothing more than give the sanction of the process of the Court to that which already is the contract between the parties. It is not then a question of the balance of convenience or inconvenience, or of the amount of damage or of injury—it is the specific performance, by the Court, of that negative bargain which the parties have made, with their eyes open, between themselves.[430]

---

[426] ibid para 39.
[427] [2004] EWHC 2943.
[428] [1998] IRLR 259, CA.
[429] (1878) 3 App Cas 709, HL.
[430] ibid 720.

5.316 This passage was explained by Colman J in *Insurance Company v Lloyd's Syndicate*,[431] a case concerning a breach of confidence in relation to an arbitration agreement:

> Lord Cairns was not in this passage withdrawing injunctions in support of express negative covenants from the category of discretionary remedies, he was merely emphasising the point that the court would not be deterred from making such an order by absence of proof of loss or damage to the applicant. In other words, proof of damage is not a threshold prerequisite for the remedy.

5.317 In *Dyson Technology v Strutt*,[432] Sir Donald Rattee applied the principles set out by Colman J in the context of employment covenants. The principles can be summarized thus:

(1) Express or implied negative covenants will in general be enforced by injunction without proof of damage by the plaintiff.
(2) The principle does not depend on whether the plaintiff is a person or a corporation. The ready availability of the remedy is not the consequence of equity's regard for the plaintiff's personal feelings but of equity's perception that it is unconscionable for the defendant to ignore his bargain.
(3) Although absence of damage to the plaintiff is not in general a bar to relief, there may be exceptional cases where the granting of an injunction would be so prejudicial to a defendant and cause him such hardship that it would be unconscionable for the plaintiff to be given injunctive relief if he could not prove damage. In such cases an injunction will be refused and the plaintiff will be awarded nominal damages.[433]

5.318 These decisions of the English High Court may be contrasted with the approach of the Outer House of the Court of Session in *Jack Allen v Smith*,[434] holding that an interim order enforcing a restrictive covenant in a contract of employment should not be granted unless the employer can also identify a perceived actual or potential harm arising from the alleged breach of contract, which harm is real and not fanciful, and which would justify interim restraint to avoid such harm being inflicted.

J. Restrictive covenants and TUPE

Introduction

5.319 At common law, a contract of employment is personal to the employee and therefore non-transferable.[435] This rule is, however, dramatically reversed wherever there is a 'relevant transfer' of an 'undertaking' within the meaning of the Transfer of Undertakings (Protection of Employment) Regulations 2006 (TUPE),[436] enacted like their predecessor regulations[437] to comply with the United Kingdom's obligations under the Acquired Rights Directive.[438]

---

[431] [1995] 1 Lloyd's Reports 272, 276–7.
[432] [2005] EWHC 2814, [2005] All ER (D) 355 (Nov).
[433] ibid para 70.
[434] [1999] IRLR 19.
[435] *North Wales Training and Enterprise Council Ltd (trading as Celtec) v Astley* [2006] ICR 992, para 2 *per* Lord Bingham.
[436] SI 2006/246.
[437] Transfer of Undertakings (Protection of Employment) Regulations 1981, SI 1981/1794. The commencement date for most of the key provisions of the 1981 TUPE Regulations was 1 May 1982.
[438] Council Directive 77/187/EEC.

In such circumstances, as is well known, the effect of TUPE is to preserve an employee's contract of employment, and the precise terms and conditions thereof, save for limited exceptions, so that they are enforceable as between the employee and the transferee in the same way as they were between the employee and the transferor.

It is beyond the scope of this work to give a detailed account of the types of entity that will **5.320** constitute an 'undertaking', or the circumstances in which there will be a 'relevant transfer'. Both of these questions have given rise to an enormous volume of case law, which is the subject of exhaustive treatment elsewhere.[439]

For present purposes, it is the interaction between restrictive covenants and TUPE which is **5.321** of relevance. As a matter of principle, where a TUPE transfer takes place, a restrictive covenant will transfer to the benefit of the transferee, as with other terms of a contract of employment. Such a covenant is a right or power under or in connection with a contract of employment, and therefore the new employer will be able to enforce it against the transferred employee.[440]

However, there are particular difficulties posed, and issues raised, when a transferee seeks **5.322** to take advantage of a restrictive covenant of which he enjoys the benefit because of TUPE. In such circumstances, the restrictive covenant will almost invariably have been drafted for very different circumstances than those in which it is sought to be enforced. The issues raised in such situations can be divided into: (a) construction issues, (b) incorporation issues, and (c) issues related to a refusal to transfer.

Construction issues

As noted above, a restrictive covenant is in principle just as enforceable by a transferee as by **5.323** a transferor. Applying this principle has not proved straightforward, however, as the case of *Morris Angel & Son Ltd v Hollande*[441] illustrates.

In the *Morris* case, the claimant sought to enforce a restrictive covenant against the defendant **5.324** which prevented the defendant, for a period of twelve months after the end of his employment, from entering into business with 'any person, firm or company who has at any time during the one year immediately preceding such cesser done business with the group'. The word 'group' was defined elsewhere in the contract, and referred to the defendant's original employer, with whom this covenant had been concluded. Subsequent to the agreement as to the covenant, the undertaking in question had transferred to the claimant. The question arose of whether TUPE had the effect of changing the entity, 'the group' to which the covenant referred. In other words, was the defendant prevented from doing business with customers of the transferor, or of the transferee?

In a relatively short decision, the Court of Appeal held that the correct answer was the **5.325** former. The true effect of TUPE (in its 1981 form) was to prevent the defendant from doing business with 'persons who in the previous year had done business with *the undertaking transferred*, of which the plaintiffs are deemed as a result of the transfer retrospectively to have

---

[439] McMullen, *Business Transfers and Employment Rights* (1998, Looseleaf); Wynn-Evans, *Blackstone's Guide to the New Transfer of Undertakings Legislation* (2006).
[440] Transfer of Undertakings (Protection of Employment) Regulations 2006, SI 2006/246, reg 4(2)(a).
[441] [1993] ICR 71, [1993] IRLR 169, CA.

been the owner'[442] (emphasis added). Dillon LJ justified this conclusion by observing that, if the covenant was found to transfer so as to prevent the defendant from soliciting customers of the *transferee*, that might transform the obligation 'into a quite different and possibly much wider obligation than the obligation which bound him before the transfer', which 'was not remotely in contemplation when the service agreement was entered into'.[443]

5.326 It would appear, therefore, that in the context of restrictive covenants, a good deal of purposive construction is permissible in order to meet the requirements of TUPE. Even where a covenant refers explicitly to the transferor, the *Morris* case is authority for the proposition that this can be treated as a reference to the transferee, or at least such part of the transferee as is composed of 'the undertaking transferred'.

5.327 A difficult question posed by this approach, which has not yet been answered by the courts, is what happens if the 'undertaking transferred' represents only *part* of the entity with reference to which the restrictive covenant is defined. If a group of companies, consisting of companies A and B, concludes a restrictive covenant with all of its employees which refers to the whole group, but then transfers *only* company A to a third party, is that third party entitled to enforce the covenant with reference to both companies A and B, or just company A? The *Morris* case would suggest the latter, and would appear to require that the third party's benefit from the covenant should be limited by reference to the 'undertaking transferred'.

Incorporation issues

5.328 A second issue relating to restrictive covenants arises from the fact that TUPE provides that *any* purported variation in an employee's terms and conditions will be void, if the sole or principal reason for the variation is (a) the transfer itself, or (b) a reason connected with the transfer which is not an 'economic, technical or organisational reason entailing changes in the workforce'.[444] The ECJ has clarified that this regulation renders unenforceable *any* waiver of an employee's existing rights, even if that waiver purports to occur in the context of a package which would otherwise have left the employee better off overall.[445]

5.329 The 1981 version of this provision was considered by the High Court and Court of Appeal in two cases involving Credit Suisse First Boston (Europe) Ltd ('CSFB'): *CSFB v Padiachy*[446] and *CSFB v Lister*.[447] Both cases arose from an agreement in November 1997 for CSFB's acquisition of Barclays de Zoete Wedd Services ('BZW'), an equities business. At the time of the acquisition, CSFB entered into separate contracts with various key employees offering them £2,000 and the prospect of a very generous retention payment in return for, amongst other things, various restrictive covenants. When employees tried to leave, CSFB sought to enforce the covenants.

---

[442] ibid 78 *per* Dillon LJ.
[443] ibid.
[444] TUPE, reg 4(4).
[445] Case 324/86 *Foreningen af Arbejdsledere i Danmark v Daddy's Dance Hall* [1988] ECR 739. However, a single change to an employee's terms and conditions which is unquestionably to his benefit will not be rendered unenforceable, even if concluded by reason of the transfer: *Power v Regent Security Services* [2008] ICR 442, CA.
[446] [1999] ICR 569; [1998] IRLR 504.
[447] [1999] ICR 794; [1998] IRLR 700.

However, both courts in the CSFB cases held that the covenants were unenforceable by **5.330** virtue of TUPE, because, quite simply, they represented a variation in the employees' terms and conditions by reason of the transfer from BZW to CSFB. This was so even though, on a fair view of the new arrangement as a whole, each employee was better off than under his previous contract. In both cases, the courts were bound to apply the decision of the ECJ in the *Daddy's Dance Hall*[448] case, so that it was irrelevant whether the employees' overall package at CSFB was better or not. The Court of Appeal in the *Lister* case observed that 'it is not for this court to consider whether the decision [in *Daddy's Dance Hall*] was wrong (whatever the consequences of it being right), but to construe the Directive and the Regulations in the light of it'.[449]

So, in both of the *CSFB* cases, the employee was not entitled to waive his rights under his **5.331** contract with his original employer. There was an open question in both of those cases as to whether as a result of the fact that the covenant was void, the employees were also disentitled from benefiting from the other aspects of the contract, namely the £2,000 consideration and the potential retention benefits. This issue has yet to be resolved.

Even though the courts were considering an earlier version of TUPE, it is thought that the **5.332** same decision would be reached if similar facts were presented before a court today. Regulation 4(4) of the current version of TUPE provides that any purported variation of the contract is void if the sole or principal reason for it is (a) the transfer itself, or (b) a reason connected with the transfer that is not an economic, technical, or organizational reason entailing changes in the workforce. While there may be economic reasons requiring the imposition of covenants, those reasons are unlikely to entail changes in the workforce, and, therefore, Regulation 4(4)(b) is unlikely to assist the new employer in this situation.

The only method for an employer who wishes to introduce restrictive covenants into con- **5.333** tracts of employment of those newly transferred to his employment, perhaps to harmonize terms and conditions across the workforce, is to terminate the existing employment agreements and re-employ the employees on new terms. This would involve the consultation procedures referred to earlier in paragraphs 5.27 to 5.49 above. Such an arrangement would have to be accompanied by a formal compromise agreement compliant with section 203 of the Employment Rights Act 1996 for each employee, under which the employee waives all rights to claim under TUPE.

Issues related to refusal to transfer

The third issue regarding the interaction between restrictive covenants and TUPE relates to **5.334** the situation in which an employee of the transferor refuses to be transferred to the transferee, and then upon ceasing to be employed by the transferor, sets up in competition with the transferee. Regulation 4 of TUPE is engaged in these circumstances, which provides, in so far as relevant, as follows:

> (7) [TUPE] . . . shall not operate to transfer the contract of employment and the rights, powers, duties and liabilities under or in connection with it of an employee who informs the transferor or the transferee that he objects to becoming employed by the transferee.

---

[448] Case 324/86 *Foreningen af Arbejdsledere i Danmark v Daddy's Dance Hall* [1988] ECR 739.
[449] [1999] ICR 794, 806; [1998] IRLR 700, para 33 *per* Clarke LJ.

(8) Subject to paragraphs (9) and (11), where an employee so objects, the relevant transfer shall operate so as to terminate his contract of employment with the transferor but he shall not be treated, for any purpose, as having been dismissed by the transferor.

5.335 The effect of this provision in the situation outlined above is that the employee's contract of employment with the transferor will terminate by operation of law at the date of the transfer, and that the employee will never therefore have a contract of employment with the transferee. It will not, therefore, be open to the transferee to enforce any restrictive covenant which the transferor enjoyed in the employee's contract of employment. Furthermore, since in most cases (save those where there is a transfer of only part of an undertaking) the transferor will no longer deal in the business of the undertaking which it has sold, it will no longer have a legitimate interest to protect, and so will not be able to enforce the restrictive covenant either.

5.336 The practical consequences of this situation are potentially far-reaching. Hypothetically, it would be possible for a group of senior executives to wait until shortly before a transfer of the undertaking in which they work, and then to resign in concert, in order to set up in competition with that undertaking, and (subject to any claims relating to their having hatched the plan before their employment terminated) to escape the effect of the restrictive covenants. The transferee may end up, in this scenario, having paid a price for a business which turns out no longer to be commercially justifiable.

5.337 There are two potential solutions to this problem. First, if the sale agreement has not yet been drafted, it would be possible for the sale to be made *conditional* upon certain named employees being transferred, ie not objecting. Secondly, the transferee may wish to seek from the transferor an assignment of the benefit of the restrictive covenants. Provided the formalities for an assignment are followed,[450] this would enable the transferee to seek relief from the court in order to restrain the employee's competitive activities. At any hearing, such an assignment may well be attacked as an ineffective assignment of a bare cause of action.[451] Such an attack would be unlikely to succeed, however, since the transferee would have a genuine (and indeed compelling) commercial interest in taking the assignment and enforcing it for his own benefit (*Trendtex Trading Corp v Crédit Suisse*).[452]

K. Checklist

5.338 This checklist is in two parts: first, it summarizes the principal issues relating to the enforcement of restrictive covenants; secondly, it sets out the main points which arise when changes to restrictive covenants are sought to be introduced.

Enforcing restrictive covenants

5.339 Are the restrictive covenants properly incorporated into a contract so that they bind the employee (see paras 5.16 to 5.26 above)? They might be included in:

- the contract of employment;
- a collective agreement which is incorporated into a contract of employment;

---

[450] Law of Property Act 1925, s 136.
[451] *Dawson v Great Northern and City Rly Co* [1905] 1 KB 260, CA, 271 *per* Stirling LJ.
[452] [1982] AC 679, [1981] 3 All ER 520, HL.

- a staff handbook;
- a specific confidentiality agreement.

Should any other contractual provision be regarded as a restraint (looking at substance, not **5.340** form (see paras 5.61 to 5.63 above)? This will happen when a provision has the practical effect of preventing an employee from leaving the employer or being involved in any competing business, for example:

- does the clause provide that the employee will lose certain benefits, such as membership of a pension scheme or entitlement to share options, if he takes certain steps following the termination of his employment (see paras 5.65 to 5.67 above)?
- does the clause require the employee to pay commission to the employer on business transacted after the termination of his employment (see para 5.68 above)?
- does the clause require the employee to forego commission he might otherwise have been entitled to if he joins a competing business (see paras 5.71 to 5.74 above)?

If the answer to any of these questions is yes, then the clause is likely to be subject to the doctrine of restraint of trade. If no, the restraint of trade doctrine will not apply. An undecided area is in relation to restraints which are linked to benefits such as share options, bonuses, or loans. In relation to these see paragraphs 5.75 to 5.78.

Is the covenant still binding upon the employee? Has the employee accepted a repudiatory **5.341** breach of contract by the employer as a constructive dismissal, and terminated the contract? If there has been a genuine constructive dismissal, then currently the employer will not be able to enforce any restrictive covenants (see paras 5.87 to 5.160 above).

Note: The House of Lords might in future contemplate revoking this rule, either generally, on the basis that an employee who has a right to damages for any breach of contract will receive a windfall profit if, as well as damages, he is freed from any post-termination obligations (see paras 5.139 to 5.148 above) or specifically with respect to confidentiality clauses in employment agreements (see paras 5.149 to 5.160 above).

What does the covenant mean? **5.342**

- Generally, it should be interpreted using common sense (see paras 5.165 to 5.167 above)?
- If the covenant is vague, can one construe it in such a way that it amounts to a legitimate restriction, without actually rewriting it (see paras 5.168 to 5.178 above)? If not, and if as a result the covenant is too broad, it will not be enforceable.
- Can the covenant bear more than one meaning? If so, and if any of the possible interpretations produces a legitimate covenant, that interpretation will be preferred (see paras 5.179 to 5.183 above).
- Once the restraint has been properly construed, has there actually been a breach, or threatened breach, of its terms? Only if so, can the court's remedies be called upon (see paras 5.184 to 5.187 above).

Has the employer produced evidence that it has a legitimate business interest which requires **5.343** protection (see paras 5.188 to 5.221 above)? Is it reasonable to expect the covenants in principle to give the employer that protection? If the answer to either question is no, the covenants are likely to be viewed as an unreasonable restraint of trade.

5.344 Is the covenant no wider than is necessary to protect the employer's legitimate business interests, judged at the date the contract is entered into (see generally paras 5.222 to 5.232 above)?

5.345 As for area covenants, reasonableness factors include (see paras 5.234 to 5.244 above):

- Is the area covered reasonable?
- Is the employee prevented from taking on roles other than that which he performed for the employer?
- Is the duration of the covenant reasonable?
- Would the employer's business interests be adequately protected by other less onerous covenants, such as one preventing solicitation of customers or misuse of confidential information?

5.346 As for non-competition covenants, reasonableness factors include (see paras 5.245 to 5.250 above):

- Is the duration of the covenant reasonable?
- Is the business with which the employee cannot compete narrowly defined?
- Is the territory covered by the covenant no wider than that covered by the employer's business?
- Would the employer's business interests be adequately protected by other less onerous covenants, such as one preventing solicitation of customers or misuse of confidential information?

5.347 As for customer non-solicitation and dealing covenants, reasonableness factors include (see paras 5.254 to 5.267 above):

- Does the covenant cover only customers or potential customers over whom the employee has influence, or about whom he has confidential information? Is that influence or confidential information recent?
- Is the duration of the covenant reasonable?

5.348 As for employee poaching or employment covenants, reasonableness factors include (see paras 5.268 to 5.277 above):

- Are the colleagues defined so as to include only those senior colleagues over whom the employee has influence or about whom he has confidential information? Is that influence or confidential information recent?
- Is the duration of the covenant reasonable?
- Are there public policy considerations which would prevent the enforcement of a covenant restraining the employee from employing former colleagues?

5.349 As for supplier and business partner non-solicitation and dealing covenants, reasonableness factors include:

- Does the covenant cover only suppliers or potential suppliers of core goods or services over whom the employee has real influence or about whom he has confidential information? Is that influence or confidential information recent?
- Is the duration of the covenant reasonable?

As to covenants relating to intermediaries:　　**5.350**

- Does the covenant cover only intermediaries over whom the employee has real influence or about whom he has confidential information? Is that influence or confidential information recent?
- Are there any public policy considerations which would make the covenant unenforceable?
- Is the duration of the covenant reasonable?

Is the period of any restrictive covenant reduced by any time which the employee is required　**5.351** to spend on garden leave? If yes, this will mean that a covenant which is otherwise reasonable will remain reasonable. If no, and if there is a garden leave clause elsewhere in the contract, there may be an argument that the covenants will last too long, protecting the employer not only during the garden leave period but also after employment has ended, and may therefore be unenforceable (see paras 5.288 to 5.294 above).

If any covenants appear on their face to be too wide, can they be severed from others, or can　**5.352** one delete ('blue pencil') certain words or phrases in the covenants so that they still read fluently, but so that the new wording provides only a reasonable restraint upon the departing employee? If yes, then the court may enforce the restrictive covenant with the offending words and phrases deleted (see paras 5.295 to 5.310 above).

Should the court exercise its discretion to grant an injunction (see paras 5.311 to 5.318 above)?　**5.353**

Introducing changes to covenants

This section looks at the issues first from the perspective of the employer and then from that　**5.354** of the employee.

Employer

Review existing contractual provisions. Are they adequate, and are they enforceable? If not:　**5.355**

- minute or record the reasons for the concerns, both as to the adequacy of the existing provisions and the sound reasons why change is needed to protect the business;
- draft new provisions which are likely to satisfy a sound business reason aimed at protecting the business.

If the new covenants are to be introduced to nineteen or fewer employees at the same estab-　**5.356** lishment over a ninety-day period, circulate the proposed new covenants to the employees, and invite them to agree to them. This must not be done aggressively, and the employees must be given sufficient time to consider their position (see para 5.41 above). It is sensible for the employer to meet the employees, either individually or in groups, to discuss the changes and the employees' concerns. There must be consideration for the covenants. Consideration may either be a monetary consideration (and it is sensible for such consideration to be adequate, and not just peppercorn), or the covenants may be introduced at a time when employees are to be given a pay rise or some other benefit such as share options, in which case the new remuneration arrangements could provide the consideration.

- If the employee accepts the new terms, or the parties agree modified covenants, seek to obtain evidence of this, preferably with the employee's signature.
- If the employee does not accept any changes, or proposes new changes which are unacceptable to the employer, continue as set out in the following paragraphs.

Note: If the reason for seeking to put new covenants in place is connected with the transfer of an undertaking (see paras 5.319 to 5.337 above), or if the employee's consent to the new terms is insufficient, the employer must follow the steps set out in the following paragraphs.

5.357 Where nineteen or fewer people are to be asked to accept new covenants, but any of them refuses to do so, the employer must follow a fair dismissal procedure (see paras 5.42 to 5.45 above).

5.358 The employer should write to the relevant individuals:

- informing them that the employer needs for sound and sensible business reasons to introduce new or amended restrictive covenants into the employment contracts with the employees;
- enclosing the proposed new terms;
- inviting them to a meeting to discuss the position (preferably not before two working days following receipt of the letter);
- informing them that if any employee does not reach agreement regarding new terms, the employee may be dismissed, and offered fresh employment on the new terms.

5.359 It is sensible, either with the letter described in the preceding paragraph or on some other occasion, for the employer to give the employee, orally or in writing, an explanation of the business needs which have motivated the employer to put forward new terms.

5.360 If the employee asks to be accompanied at the meeting by a colleague or a trade union representative, this should be allowed, and the meeting may need to be postponed by up to five working days following the date initially suggested by the employer if the proposed companion is unable to attend at the time initially put forward by the employer.

5.361 The employer must attend the meeting proposed. If the employee attends, the employer should explain his position and then ask the employee if he has any concerns and if so what they are. These should be discussed. If the employee has brought a companion, he must be allowed to address the meeting, and to confer with the employee during the meeting.

5.362 If the employee still does not accept the covenants, the employer should make his decision. That decision may be:

- not to impose any covenants at all, in which case he should write to the employee telling him of the decision;
- to require a modified form of the covenants, in which case he should, if he has not already done so, write to the employee enclosing the new form and inviting the employee to accept them; inviting comments (preferably in another meeting) and, if the employee does not then accept the new terms, moving on to the steps described in the following paragraphs. If any modifications are to be offered, the same terms should be offered to all employees in the same category; or
- to require the covenants in the same form already sent to the employee to apply to all employees of the particular employee's category, in which case, the employer must take the steps set out in the following paragraphs.

5.363 The employer should write to each employee informing the employee of the decision, giving him contractual notice to terminate his existing contract (or immediate notice and a payment in lieu of such notice, if the contract allows this), and offering him a new employment contract on the new terms. The employee must be told he has the right of appeal.

If employees accept the new contracts they will be bound by them in future. **5.364**

If an employee appeals against the decision, an appeal should be held, and the procedural **5.365** steps set out above apply to the appeal. If the appeal is rejected, the employee should be informed (preferably in writing) of the final decision.

Note: All employees in the same category must be treated the same: if some are allowed to continue working with new covenants, or with milder covenants than their peers, but other employees are not and are dismissed, such dismissals are likely to be unfair (see para 5.45 above).

If the covenants are to be introduced to twenty or more employees at the same establishment **5.366** over a ninety-day period the employer should follow the procedure described below. In addition, the employer is obliged to notify the government of the fact of consultation (see para 5.50 above).

Check whether an independent trade union is recognized to negotiate on behalf of the **5.367** employees. If it is not, arrange for the election of appropriate representatives (see para 5.47 above).

Begin consultation with the trade union or employee representatives about the changes **5.368** by providing the information set out in paragraph 5.48. This must begin in good time and at least:

- thirty days before any dismissal notices are sent out, if the provisions may affect twenty to ninety-nine employees at the same establishment;
- ninety days before any dismissal notices are sent out, if the provisions may affect one hundred or more employees at the same establishment.

Conduct consultation with a view to reaching agreement with the representatives: **5.369**

- If agreement is reached concerning the imposition of new covenants, record this in writing. It is sensible to send the new terms to all affected employees and to require them to sign them.
- If agreement is not reached, the individuals may be dismissed. It would be sensible to write to all the individuals informing them of the position and inviting them individually to agree to the new terms before dismissing them.

If the covenants are to be introduced into compromise or settlement agreements the employer **5.370** should:

- ensure the terms are valid; and
- allocate sufficient consideration to any new or amended covenants.

(See paras 5.11 to 5.15 and 5.52 to 5.53 above).

Employee

Where nineteen or fewer employees at the same establishment are being asked to accept new **5.371** restrictive covenants, if the employee is unhappy with the proposed covenants, in addition to trying to persuade the employer not to introduce them at all or to modify them, the employee should be alert to the following issues.

5.372 Is there a sound business reason for the introduction of each of the covenants (see para 5.36 above)?

5.373 Has the employer been courteous in relation to seeking the employee's consent to the covenants (rather than, for example, by being aggressive or rude or demanding an immediate signature) (see para 5.41 above)?

5.374 Has the employer written to the employee explaining his plans, inviting the employee to a meeting, and giving relevant details? Has the employer held a meeting, allowed a companion to attend on request, written to the employee setting out his decision, notified the employee of his right to appeal (if the employee has been dismissed), held any appeal and then informed the employee of the result of the appeal (see paras 5.41 to 5.43 above)?

5.375 Has the employee been given his proper notice period or, if not, does the contract allow the employee to be dismissed immediately upon payment in lieu of notice (see para 5.44 above)?

5.376 If the employee has been dismissed and offered new terms on re-engagement, are those terms the same as those offered to all employees of equivalent position (see para 5.45 above)?

5.377 Are there any other factors which would affect the reasonableness of the employer's decision (see, for example, para 5.39 above).

5.378 If the answer to any of these questions (at paras 5.372 to 5.377 above) is no, the employee may, if he has at least one year's service, have been unfairly dismissed.

5.379 If the employer asks the employee to attend a formal meeting to discuss the new covenants, the employee should consider whether or not he wants to be accompanied by a colleague or trade union official. The employee must make every effort to attend (but may postpone the meeting for up to five days to suit the convenience of any companion) (see para 5.43 above).

5.380 If twenty or more employees at the same establishment are being asked to accept new restrictive covenants, has the employer begun in good time to consult either a recognized trade union or elected employee representatives (see paras 5.47 to 5.48 above)? If not, then the trade union, employee representatives or, in the absence of either of these, any affected employee, can bring proceedings in the employment tribunal for a protective award (see para 5.49 above).

5.381 Has the employee recently joined the employer as a result of a transfer of undertaking? If so, are the employer's actions principally caused by the transfer itself (for example is it only the transferred employees who are being asked to accept new covenants)? If this is the case, then even if the employee accepts the new terms, they will not be binding on him (although query whether any consideration offered in return will be repayable) (see paras 5.319 to 5.337 above).

6

VENDOR–PURCHASER, PARTNERSHIP, AND OTHER COMMERCIAL AGREEMENTS

Paul Goulding QC, Robert Weekes, Dan Aherne, and Luke Pardey

A. Introduction[1]

Restrictive covenants are not only to be found in employment contracts. They are a valuable **6.01** means of protecting a party's interests in a variety of other situations. Those most commonly encountered are covenants taken by a purchaser from the vendor of a business or of shares, and covenants between partners. Recent case law demonstrates their popularity in other commercial arrangements such as those between investors in a joint venture business, and between franchisor and franchisee.

Whilst the framework of restraint of trade principles is similar in this commercial sphere to **6.02** that in the employment context, there are significant differences in the court's approach, notably to questions of legitimate interest and reasonableness. Restrictions in commercial agreements—and, in particular, their similarities to and differences from employment restrictions—will be examined in this chapter.

---

[1] See also Appendix 8, Sample Restrictive Covenants (Share and Business Sale and Partnership) below.

B. Vendor–purchaser agreements

Overview

Distinction between vendor–purchaser and employment covenants

6.03 It is axiomatic that no covenant which is in restraint of trade will be upheld unless it is both reasonable in the interests of the contracting parties and reasonable in the interests of the public.[2] However, a well-established distinction is drawn between the enforcement of restrictive covenants in the vendor–purchaser context and in the employment context.[3] Covenants in the latter context are the subject of closer and more critical judicial scrutiny than covenants in the former. As summarized by Sir Christopher Slade in *Office Angels Ltd v Rainer-Thomas*:

> A distinction is however to be drawn between (a) a covenant against competition entered into by a vendor with the purchaser of goodwill of a business, which will be upheld as necessary to protect the subject-matter of the sale, provided that it is confined to the area within which competition on the part of the vendor would be likely to injure the purchaser in the enjoyment of the goodwill he has bought, and (b) a covenant between master and servant designed to prevent competition by the servant with the master after the termination of his contract of service.[4]

Identity of the covenantor and the covenantee in vendor–purchaser covenants

6.04 In the business context, the covenantor is typically the vendor of the business (who may or may not be its sole proprietor) and the covenantee, the purchaser of that business. Although the goodwill of a company is strictly an asset of the company, rather than of a shareholder in that company, it is well established that covenants for the protection of the goodwill of a company may be given by and enforced against a person who sells some or all of his shares in that company.[5] In determining who is a legitimate covenantor where the goodwill belongs to a company, the court must look through the company (or lift the veil) to identify each shareholder who has been actively engaged in the company's business.[6]

6.05 However, the courts have also enforced covenants against covenantors who, at the time of giving the covenant, owned no goodwill at all. For example, in *Nordenfelt v Maxim Nordenfelt*,[7] the vendor had sold his ammunition business to the purchasing company, Nordenfelt, in 1886. He covenanted to act as the managing director of Nordenfelt for the following five years and not to compete with that business, so long as it carried on trading. However, in 1888 Nordenfelt merged with another company, Maxim, and a further company was incorporated to which the business and assets of Nordenfelt and Maxim were transferred. A term of the merger agreement was that Maxim would procure the original vendor to give a new covenant to Maxim-Nordenfelt, which restricted him from competing against it for a period

---

[2] *Herbert Morris Ltd v Saxelby* [1916] AC 688, 707.
[3] The principles discussed in this section are generally applicable whether the covenants are entered into between a vendor and purchaser of a business, or between the vendor and purchaser of shares in a company. Rather than repeat the terminology of 'business or share sale' on each occasion, the principles discussed in relation to a business sale may be taken to apply to a share sale, and vice versa.
[4] [1991] IRLR 214, CA, para 22.
[5] *Connors Bros Ltd v Connors* [1940] 4 All ER 179, PC, 191.
[6] *Dawnay, Day & Co v D'Alphen* [1998] ICR 1068, 1091 *per* Robert Walker J.
[7] *Nordenfelt v Maxim Nordenfelt Guns and Ammunition Co Ltd* [1894] AC 535.

of twenty-five years. The vendor in due course contended that the covenant was unreasonable because at the time of giving it there had been no sale of goodwill by him.[8] He had already parted with the goodwill to Nordenfelt. The House of Lords held that the vendor stood in the same position as if his new covenant had been given to Nordenfelt in consideration for the full price which that company had paid him for the stock and goodwill of his business.[9] This was because the new covenant was properly to be regarded as in lieu of and in substitution for the old, and the old covenant would have been kept alive if the new one had not been entered into.[10]

In *Connors Bros Ltd v Connors*, the Privy Council advanced this analysis one stage further. **6.06** Having referred to the *Nordenfelt* case, Viscount Maugham held on behalf of the board:

> This being accepted in the case of the sale of the business of a company and of a covenant entered into upon such a sale by a person who does not own the goodwill or any other assets of the company (which was the case of Nordenfelt) the same result may follow in a case where, instead of selling the undertaking, the shares or stock of the company or a large interest therein is being sold, and one or more of the directors or managers of the company, being interested in the sale, are willing, in order to enable the transaction to go through, or to obtain a better price, to enter into restrictive covenants with the purchaser. Every such case must depend on the surrounding facts and circumstances, and their Lordships do not propose to lay down a general rule, but there are many cases of that character in which, as it seems to them, the principles above referred to will apply, and where, in other words, the community is as interested in maintaining freedom of contract within reasonable limits as it is in maintaining freedom of trade.[11]

Meaning of goodwill

The goodwill of a business is easy to describe but difficult to define specifically.[12] It has notably **6.07** been held to include the connection with the customers together with the circumstances which, whether by habit or otherwise, tend to make that connection permanent;[13] the whole advantage of the reputation and connection of the firm, as gained by its work or investment;[14] the probability that customers will buy again from a business having done so previously or return to the premises of a business having been there previously;[15] and notably, whatever adds value to a business by reason of any or all of its situation, name, reputation, connection, introduction to old customers, and agreed absence of competition.[16] In connection with any business or business product, goodwill represents the value of the attraction of customers, which the name and reputation of that business or business product possesses.[17]

It should be recognized that the term 'goodwill' can be used in two quite different senses. **6.08** First, the general reputation of a business, once vividly described as 'some airy-fairy general reputation in the business or commercial community which is unrelated to the buying and selling or dealing with customers which is the essence of the business of any

---

[8] ibid 540 *per* Lord Herschell LC.
[9] ibid 541 *per* Lord Herschell LC, 551 *per* Lord Watson, 555 *per* Lord Watson, 560 *per* Lord Macnaghten.
[10] ibid 560 *per* Lord Macnaghten.
[11] *Connors Bros* (n 5 above) 191.
[12] *IRC v Muller & Co's Margarine Ltd* [1901] AC 217, HL, 223 *per* Lord Macnaghten.
[13] *Trego v Hunt* [1896] AC 7, HL, 17–18.
[14] ibid 24.
[15] *George Silverman Ltd v Silverman* (CA, 2 July 1969) 4.
[16] *Muller & Co's* case (n 12 above) 235 *per* Lord Lindley.
[17] *RJ Reuter Co Ltd v Ferd Mulhens* [1954] Ch 50, CA, 89 *per* Lord Evershed MR.

trading company'.[18] This is distinct from 'customer goodwill', the loss of which would result in a loss of business and which can therefore be measured in money terms.[19] Business sale covenants legitimately seek to protect the latter.

6.09 In this section we consider first, the conceptual basis for the distinction between business sale and employment covenants; secondly, the proper approach of the court to determining whether an express covenant falls within the business sale category or the employment category; thirdly, the test of reasonableness applied by the court where the covenant is held to be within the business sale category; and fourthly, the implication of restrictive covenants into contracts for the sale of goodwill, where no express restraint is agreed between vendor and purchaser.

Basis for the distinction between vendor–purchaser and employment covenants

6.10 Various justifications of policy and principle have been proposed for the distinction between covenants given in the business sale context and those in the employment context. The first is compelling. It is that business sale covenants can properly be regarded as facilitating trade, rather than fettering it.[20] As Lord Watson said in *Nordenfelt v Maxim Nordenfelt*, the object of allowing a trader to dispose of his lucrative business to a successor could not be achieved if the law 'reserved to the seller an absolute and indefeasible right to start a rival concern the day after he sold'.[21] If the goodwill of a business could immediately be attacked by its vendor, it would necessarily have a reduced price, even if it were saleable at all.[22] Accordingly, business sale covenants are typically attractive to both the vendor and the purchaser.[23] Without an enforceable covenant on the part of the vendor against competition, a purchaser cannot get what he is contracting to buy, nor can the vendor give what he is intending to sell.[24] Moreover, such covenants are in the general public interest because commercial activity would be deterred by any principle that the accumulated results of such activity could only be transferred under conditions which would make any buyer insecure.[25]

6.11 The second justification is also persuasive. It is that the distinction is an application of the established principle that a man should not be entitled to derogate from his own grant.[26] If the vendor were permitted to compete against the business he had sold, he would be derogating from his grant of the goodwill in that business to the purchaser. This principle is also the basis for implying covenants into contracts for the sale of goodwill which include no express restraint against competition.[27] In the employment context, the employee does not make any grant of the goodwill in his or her business to the employer and that employee is therefore entitled to compete for such goodwill, provided that by doing so, the proprietary rights of the employer are not infringed.

---

[18] *Lonrho plc v Al-Fayed (No 5)* [1993] 1 WLR 1495, CA, 1496 *per* Dillon LJ.

[19] ibid 1509 *per* Evans LJ.

[20] *Allied Dunbar (Frank Weisinger) Ltd v Weisinger* [1988] IRLR 60, para 20 *per* Millett J.

[21] *Nordenfelt* (n 7 above) 552.

[22] *Ronbar Enterprises Ltd v Green* [1954] 1 WLR 815, CA, 820–1 *per* Jenkins LJ; *Bridge v Deacons* [1984] AC 705, PC, 713 *per* Lord Fraser.

[23] In this respect it should be noted that the characteristic of being a 'purchaser' or a 'vendor' is not fixed or static. A purchaser itself may in due course become the vendor of that (or any other business) and vice versa, and each might therefore require the protection of similar restrictive covenants.

[24] *Attwood v Lamont* [1920] 3 KB 571, CA, 590 *per* Younger LJ; *Nordenfelt* (n 7 above) 548 *per* Lord Herschell LC.

[25] *Herbert Morris* (n 2 above) 713 *per* Lord Shaw.

[26] *Silverman* (n 15 above) 5 *per* Winn LJ.

[27] See paras 6.38–6.40 below.

The third justification is that a restrictive covenant is only valid in so far as it is reasonably **6.12** necessary to protect rights which are proprietary (or at least quasi-proprietary).[28] A restrictive covenant in the business sale context protects the property which is being sold. Goodwill is undoubtedly a form of property.[29] The right to such property is otherwise protected by the law of passing-off. The argument is that restrictive covenants in the employment context which are not concerned with the protection of the employer's proprietary rights (such as its customer connection or trade secrets), are deemed not to enable the employer to protect what he has, but rather to gain a special advantage he could not otherwise secure.[30] That is not the case with a business sale where property is being sold and covenants are sought to protect it.

The fourth justification is that covenants in the employment context are subject to an **6.13** inequality of bargaining power between the parties.[31] However, in the business sale context, the court has consistently taken the view that in arm's length commercial negotiations, the parties are the best judges of what is reasonable, of their own business interests, and of how the vendor of a business can best obtain the full value of what he has to sell.[32] This is perhaps also because the parties to a commercial sale agreement are better able to look after their interests by taking professional advice (or at least have the opportunity to do so) than an employee agreeing to a contract of employment.[33] Moreover, it is arguable that the parties are able themselves to regulate the proportionality of the various terms of a sale agreement (including any restrictive covenants) by simply adjusting the price.[34]

The fifth justification is that, as Robert Walker J held in *Dawnay Day & Co v D'Alphen*: 'the **6.14** fundamental reason for the stricter approach is that it is a stronger thing, requiring more cogent justification (both as between the parties and in the public interest) to prevent a working man or woman from earning his or her living as he or she chooses'.[35] As a matter of policy, the law deems the trade of the vendor to have been legitimately overridden on account of the first justification which is considered above; namely, the interests of both purchaser and vendor (and the public) in allowing the vendor to get the best price for the business and the purchaser to have the full benefit from it.[36]

Categorizing the covenants

It is important to note that the categories of employment cases and vendor–purchaser cases **6.15** are neither rigid nor closed nor even exclusive to each other.[37] A covenant may be enforced when the covenantee has a legitimate interest, of whatever kind, to protect, and when the

---

[28] eg *Dawnay, Day & Co* (n 6 above) 1108 *per* Evans LJ.
[29] eg *HP Bulmer Ltd v J Bollinger SA (No. 3)* [1977] 2 CMLR 625, CA, para 17 *per* Buckley LJ; *I N Newman Ltd v Richard T Adlem* [2005] EWCA Civ 741, [2006] FSR 16, CA, para 22 *per* Jacob LJ.
[30] *Attwood* (n 24 above) 590–1 *per* Younger LJ.
[31] *Dawnay, Day & Co* (n 6 above) 1091 *per* Robert Walker J.
[32] ibid 1080–1 *per* Robert Walker J; *Esso Petroleum Co Ltd v Harper's Garage (Stourport) Ltd* [1968] AC 269, HL, 300 *per* Lord Reid; *North Western Salt Co Ltd v Electrolytic Alkali Co Ltd* [1914] AC 461, HL, 471 *per* Viscount Haldane LC; *Buchanan v Alba Diagnostics Ltd* [2004] UKHL 5, [2004] SLT 255, HL, para 28 *per* Lord Hoffmann.
[33] *Silverman* (n 15 above) 9 *per* Fenton Atkinson LJ.
[34] *Allied Dunbar* (n 20 above) para 32 *per* Millett J.
[35] *Dawnay, Day & Co* (n 6 above) 1079.
[36] *Systems Reliability Holdings plc v Smith* [1990] IRLR 377, para 47 *per* Harman J.
[37] *TSC Europe (UK) Ltd v Massey* [1999] IRLR 22, para 27 *per* Judge Peter Whiteman QC; *Dawnay, Day & Co* (n 6 above) 1105–7 *per* Evans LJ.

covenant is no wider than is necessary to protect that interest.[38] Therefore, at least where covenants fall outside the two established categories, the proper approach for the court is not to attempt to place the agreement in any particular category, nor to apply the test of reasonableness of the category to which it is most analogous.[39] Rather, the court should ascertain the legitimate interests the covenantee was entitled to protect and consider whether those restraints are reasonable on the facts and in the circumstances of the particular case.[40] In performing this exercise the court should consider the substance of the particular transaction, rather than its form.[41] The latter proposition means that little, if any, weight should be placed on the form of the agreement in which the covenant is contained, namely whether it is in an employment contract or share sale or purchase agreement. The court may therefore conclude that the relevant transaction consists in several contracts which are entered into over a period of time.[42] This requirement to consider substance rather than form also means that the form in which the business, once sold, is carried on by the purchaser, has little relevance to the issue of the enforceability of the covenant.[43]

6.16 Applying the principle that the categories of employment cases and vendor–purchaser cases are not rigid, the court may find that the transaction fell into both categories. It may hold that the transaction was closer to the vendor–purchaser context than the employment one and gauge its assessment of reasonableness of the covenant accordingly. So in *Cyrus Energy Ltd v Stewart*, Lord Woolman sitting in the Outer House of the Court of Session held that:

> In my view, the authorities demonstrate that it is 'wrong and unnecessary' to classify relationships in too rigid a fashion (*Dawnay* at 1106D-F). The question must always be to consider the facts and circumstances of the individual case. Here, in my opinion, the transaction was closer to that end of the spectrum occupied by the sale of a business. Very few employees have a twenty five percent shareholding in the business by which they are employed, as well as holding a directorship and rights in the parent company. It seemed to me to be inapt to bracket the defenders with normal employees. There must have been good commercial reasons for them to decide to enter into the October 2006 transactions. According to their counsel, both businesses were viable at that stage. The defenders therefore had the opportunity to negotiate the terms of the contract. If they had not wished to place themselves under the obligations of the covenant, they should not have entered into the transaction. By doing so, I was inclined to give primacy to freedom of contract over freedom of trade.[44]

In finding that the interim interdict should be continued, the judge held that one of the 'crucial considerations' was that the covenant was made in circumstances closer to the sale of a business than to an employment contract.[45]

6.17 This flexible approach has been applied outside the business sale context. In *Kynixa Ltd v Hynes*,[46] the defendant employees had purchased shares in their employer, the claimant company. They entered into a shareholders agreement containing restrictive covenants. In considering

---

[38] ibid 1107 *per* Evans LJ. See also paras 6.97–6.110 below.
[39] *Bridge* (n 22 above) 714 *per* Lord Fraser.
[40] ibid 714; *Systems Reliability Holdings* (n 36 above) para 48 *per* Harman J; *Allied Dunbar* (n 20 above) para 22 *per* Millett J.
[41] ibid para 21 *per* Millett J; *TSC* (n 37 above) para 32.
[42] *Connors Bros* (n 5 above) 186 *per* Viscount Maugham.
[43] *Systems Reliability Holdings* (n 36 above) para 52 *per* Harman J.
[44] [2009] CSOH 53, para 25.
[45] ibid para 36.
[46] [2008] EWHC 1495 (QB).

whether the covenants were enforceable, Wyn Williams J took into account the fact that the defendants were both shareholders and employees.[47] In finding that the covenants were reasonable and enforceable, the judge considered the facts that the defendants were very senior employees and in the course of their employment, privy to confidential information belonging to the claimant.[48] The judge also considered factors specific to their position as shareholders. First, that they had a choice about whether or not to enter into the shareholders agreement and his finding that they chose to do so for potentially substantial gain.[49] This reasoning is consistent with one policy justification for the approach to business sale covenants, being that they are made between parties of equal bargaining power.[50] Secondly, that as shareholders they had a clear interest in the well-being of the claimant and in the taking of necessary steps to protect it from its competitors so far as that was legitimate.[51] This analysis is correct though its implications are striking—in effect, the defendants (as well as the claimant) had a legitimate interest in protecting the company (and their investment in it as shareholders) from themselves.

This balanced approach is highlighted in the decision in relation to the duration of the non-solicitation covenant. The defendant argued that the twelve-month period for such a covenant in the shareholder agreement was unreasonable. This was because one defendant had a six-month non-solicitation covenant in her contract of employment. The argument was a conventional one—if the parties thought six months was appropriate, why should a longer period in the shareholders agreement also be reasonable?[52] The judge rejected this argument. He held that the answer lay in the fact that the restraint applied to a person who was both an employee and a shareholder. It was not therefore appropriate to consider the defendant exclusively as an employee. Rather, the factors relevant to her status both as an employee and as a shareholder should be evaluated. Having regard to all these factors, the judge held that the duration of the covenant was reasonable and the covenant enforceable.[53] **6.18**

This approach of determining the substance of the underlying transaction is commonly required where the transaction involves both the sale of a business and the purchaser retaining the services of the vendor after that sale.[54] Covenants may there be given both in the share sale and purchase agreement and in the employment contract between purchaser and vendor. In such a case it is inappropriate to decide into which of the two categories the material covenants fall.[55] Similarly, it would be incorrect to look at the employment contract in isolation from the share sale and purchase agreement.[56] Rather, the court should consider the validity of any restrictive covenant in the context of the overall commercial bargain.[57] It has to consider and construe the covenant against the background of the whole transaction, so as to give it 'proper commercial validity'.[58] The court should be alert to the fact that some or all **6.19**

---

[47] ibid para 136 *per* Wyn Williams J.
[48] ibid para 170.
[49] ibid para 167.
[50] See para 6.13 above.
[51] ibid (n 46 above) para 170.
[52] ibid para 183.
[53] ibid paras 183–4.
[54] *TSC* (n 37 above) para 29 *per* Judge Peter Whiteman QC.
[55] *Dawnay, Day & Co* (n 6 above) 446.
[56] *TSC* (n 37 above) para 30 *per* Judge Whiteman QC; *Silverman* (n 15 above) 8 *per* Fenton Atkinson LJ, 10–11 *per* Phillimore LJ.
[57] *TSC* (n 37 above).
[58] *Silverman* (n 15 above) 10 *per* Phillimore LJ.

of the employees of the business which is sold may be crucial to the maintenance of the goodwill of that business.[59] The covenants in the contracts of employment of those employees, and in the share sale agreements of those employees who are shareholders, should therefore be considered together.

6.20   The case of *Alliance Paper Group plc v Prestwich*[60] concerned a transaction of this type. The claimant there applied for an injunction to enforce restrictive covenants contained in the service contract of the defendant managing director, who had been the major shareholder of the company sold to the claimant. The defendant had entered into his service contract together with a share sale agreement, which also contained restrictive covenants.[61] Judge Levy (sitting as a Deputy High Court Judge) held that the facts that the vendor was the managing director of the company at the time of its sale, he was negotiator of that sale, and it was his business which had been sold, required that the covenants in the service contract not only be viewed as those of an employee entering into a service contract, but also as those of a person who had negotiated sales of shares on his own behalf and on behalf of others, and who had benefited from those sales. The judge considered the reasonableness of each of those covenants against that background and held each to be valid and enforceable, whether according to the wider vendor test or the narrower employee test.[62]

6.21   *Allied Dunbar (Frank Weisinger) Ltd v Weisinger*[63] concerned a similar transaction. By a 'practice buyout agreement' including certain restrictive covenants, the vendor had sold his practice as a self-employed sales associate to the purchaser. At the same time, the vendor entered into a consultancy agreement with the purchaser. The restrictive covenants were contained in the practice buy-out agreement. However, they were expressed not to apply until the consultancy agreement was terminated and they therefore had the appearance of covenants in the employment context. Millett J held that, on their true construction, the covenants sought to protect the legitimate interest of the goodwill of the business sold, rather than the purchaser's present and future business as employer under the consultancy agreement. The fact that the covenants were contained in the buy-out agreement rather than the consultancy agreement was to be given very little weight. The substance of the transaction was that the consultancy agreement was a transitional arrangement in order to facilitate the transfer of the customer connection which the vendor had sold to the purchaser under the practice buy-out agreement.[64] In those circumstances, a covenant in the business sale context which provided for a deferred restraint of trade was reasonable and was, in fact, enforced.

6.22   An unusual example of the overlap between the employment case and the vendor–purchaser case is found in *Sendo Holdings plc (in Administration) v Brogan*.[65] The claimant was the holding company of a group of companies involved in the manufacture and distribution of mobile phones. The defendant had set up the group. He was its majority shareholder and driving force. He was also its CEO. The group was put in administration. The administrators sold some of the group's assets to Motorola. The sale agreement included a provision that the

---

[59]   eg *TSC* (n 37 above) para 49 *per* Judge Whiteman QC.
[60]   [1996] IRLR 25.
[61]   The parties also entered into a shareholder's agreement which was not held to be relevant to the application (ibid para 5).
[62]   ibid paras 15, 27.
[63]   [1988] IRLR 60.
[64]   ibid para 21.
[65]   [2005] EWHC 2040 (QB).

employment of the defendant should be terminated and he should be put on garden leave. The administrators complied with this provision. The defendant set up a new company. The claimant applied for an injunction requiring the defendant to comply with his employment contract. One of the issues before the court was whether the claimant had any legitimate interest to protect at all. In the conventional vendor–purchaser case, the claimant seeks to protect its business. But here there was no business, no customers, and no employees.[66] The defendant argued that the interest which the claimant sought to protect was not in fact its own interest at all—but that of Motorola. Thus any injunction would not prevent the defendant from competing with his employer but with a third party. Unlike the conventional vendor–purchaser case, the defendant had no contractual relationship with the purchaser. On the contrary, the group's assets had effectively been sold from under the defendant, the majority shareholder.

6.23 For the purposes of the application for continuation of an interim injunction, Dobbs J held that the claimant did have a legitimate interest to protect. Although it was not trading, it still had a duty to realize its position as a creditor and maximize value for its own creditors and ensure that the company was wound down in as efficient a manner as possible. The claimant contended that the defendant could assist in this regard.[67] It is questionable whether this proposition would have been upheld at trial. It is perhaps unlikely that the defendant would have been expected to—or allowed to—provide much assistance in circumstances where he had set up a business of his own. However, the more difficult issue was not determined at the interlocutory stage. This is whether the claimant's interest in complying with its contractual obligations to the purchaser, Motorola, was a legitimate interest and a proprietary or quasi-proprietary interest which the claimant was entitled to protect as against the defendant.[68]

6.24 The substantive approach to business sale transactions nevertheless has its limits. In *Emersub v Wheatley*,[69] a share sale transaction included (amongst other contractual documents) a contract of employment between the vendor and purchaser and a deed containing restrictive covenants given by the vendor relating to the sale of the shares. Wright J rejected the submission that, as the deed was intimately connected with the employment contract, in the event that the vendor was wrongfully dismissed, the principle in *General Billposting v Atkinson*[70] would disentitle the vendor from enforcing the restrictive covenants in the deed. The judge held that the contractual obligations were entirely separate and independent, had in fact been given by the vendor to different parties, and the vendor had received full consideration for giving the restrictive covenants in the form of payment for the sale of his shares. Therefore, what happened in relation to the employment of the purchaser was held to be irrelevant to the application of the covenants contained in the deed.

Reasonableness of covenants in vendor–purchaser agreements

6.25 It is necessarily difficult to define the level of scrutiny which the court will give to covenants which are held to fall in the business sale category or are otherwise held to be for the protection of a legitimate interest in the goodwill of a business. Notably, the courts would appear not to

---

[66] ibid para 24 (save for a handful of employees on temporary contracts).
[67] ibid para 24.
[68] ibid paras 21, 24.
[69] 14 July 1998.
[70] [1909] AC 118, HL.

have promulgated any rule analogous to the familiar *Wednesbury* principle in administrative law.[71] The courts have regularly held that the general principle is that the parties are deemed to be the best judges of what is reasonable.[72] However, this rule is not rigidly or inflexibly applied. As Gross J summarized the position in *Meridian VAT Reclaim UK Ltd v Lowendal Group*:

> In analysing those [legitimate] interests [which a party is seeking to protect] and the covenant or covenants in question, the context must be taken into consideration. It is a relevant feature that the context of the agreement or covenant under scrutiny is, for example, a commercial contract entered into between parties of equal bargaining power rather than, say, a contract between employer and employee. That said, the fact that the contract is a commercial contract freely entered into does not mean the restraint of trade doctrine is inapplicable. No simplistic answer can be obtained by categorisation of the contract. However, the application of the doctrine will likely be influenced by the context and nature of the contract in question. The restraint of trade doctrine is to be applied to factual situations, as Lord Wilberforce said, 'with a broad and flexible rule of reason': *Esso Petroleum v Harper's Garage* [1968] AC 269, 331. Were it otherwise, the doctrine would be capable of producing capricious or curious results.[73]

6.26 Certain obvious limitations apply. A bare covenant against competition, such as where a party undertakes in consideration for a sum of money paid to it not to carry on a particular branch of business, is unreasonable. It is trite law that any enforceable covenant which restricts competition must be ancillary to a main transaction, contract, or arrangement, and be reasonably necessary to render that transaction, contract, or arrangement effective.[74] However, in considering the substance rather than the form of the transaction, the court will construe any apparently bare covenant against the background of the entire commercial bargain of which that covenant forms part. Therefore, where a vendor entered into a deed containing a restrictive covenant, the sale of shares was not provided by that deed, and yet that deed was an essential element in the sale transaction (such that if the vendor had not been willing to enter into it, the transaction would not have been completed), the covenant was not in fact a bare restraint on competition and was supported by consideration.[75]

6.27 The *Office Angels* case established that real functional correspondence is required between the relevant covenant and any legitimate interest which is sought to be protected by that covenant.[76] Although the facts of that case concern employee covenants, the court did give some consideration to vendor covenants.[77] It is submitted that the same approach applies to both categories of covenant. Therefore, the court will only uphold a vendor covenant where there is real functional correspondence between it and any interest of the purchaser which is found by the court to be legitimate. Nevertheless, as Robert Walker J held in the *Dawnay, Day* case:

> . . . a rather less demanding approach is appropriate in a commercial case, even if the bargain that businessmen have struck does not make complete sense to a lawyer. Businessmen may recognise that the only way to reach agreement is to leave some unpredictable situation for

---

[71] *Associated Provincial Picture Houses v Wednesbury Corp* [1948] 1 KB 223, CA, 229–30 *per* Lord Greene MR.

[72] eg *Dawnay, Day v D'Alphen* [1998] ICR 1068, 1094 *per* Robert Walker J, 1109 *per* Evans LJ; *TSC Europe (UK) Ltd v Massey* [1999] IRLR 22, para 36 *per* Judge Peter Whiteman QC; *Emersub* (n 52 above); *George Silverman Ltd v Silverman* (CA, 2 July 1969) 9 *per* Fenton Atkinson LJ.

[73] [2002] EWHC 1066 (QB), para 24(2).

[74] *Vancouver Malt and Sake Brewing Co Ltd v Vancouver Breweries Ltd* [1934] AC 181, PC, 190–1 per Lord Macmillan.

[75] *Emersub* (n 69 above).

[76] *Office Angels v Rainer-Thomas* [1991] IRLR 214, CA, paras 59–60 *per* Sir Christopher Slade.

[77] See para 6.03 above.

future negotiation, or to concede some point which is unlikely to arise in practice, even if the concession is untidy or illogical.[78]

This functional correspondence requires that the covenant must be necessary in order to **6.28** protect the goodwill of the business sold by the vendor, and not that of the purchaser's own existing business. A covenant exacted only for the protection of a business with which the covenantor has never had any connection is no better and no more enforceable than a covenant against bare competition.[79] Similarly, a covenant which has no restriction whatsoever as to area, and where it is not reasonable for that covenant to have worldwide application, will be held to be unreasonable.[80] Likewise, if the vendor did not have any detailed knowledge of the business being sold nor was there any conceivable prospect of him competing with it, it is likely that the court would refuse to enforce such a covenant against that vendor.[81] (It is, however, difficult to conceive of the circumstances in which a purchaser would wish to enforce a covenant against such a vendor.)

Nevertheless, it is well established that in assessing the reasonableness of covenants in business **6.29** sale cases, the court will not be stringent in its consideration of whether the vendor restricted would in fact damage or significantly damage the goodwill of the business concerned. The principles applicable to business sale cases are not limited to those where the vendor was effectively sole proprietor or controlling proprietor of the business being sold. In such cases, it would generally follow that if the vendor were to compete with the business, the purchaser would not receive the whole of the profits of the business it was buying.[82] Yet, in *Systems Reliability Holdings v Smith*, Harman J held that covenants in restraint of trade should also be allowed and enforced when a number of vendors sell a business to a purchaser, notwithstanding the fact that some of those vendors have only small participations in the goodwill and the business which is being sold.[83]

In order to protect the goodwill of a business, it may be legitimate to require the vendor to **6.30** 'retire' completely for a period of time from any form of competing business.[84] It would be arguable that such a restriction may adversely affect the public interest in entirely denying the public the services of the vendor in the field in which he has previously carried on business. However, in a case concerned with goodwill, when the court is satisfied that the restraint is reasonable as between the parties, it has been held to be very difficult to prove that the public interest is affected.[85] Furthermore, it has even been stated *obiter* that, in assessing the reasonableness of a covenant in the context of a business sale, the court should not consider any interest other than that of the covenantee.[86] It is doubtful whether this proposition remains correct. It is axiomatic that the court should only uphold any covenant (whether of the employee or vendor categories) where that covenant is deemed to be in the public interest. The difficulty of proving any harm to the public interest in the enforcement of a covenant is

---

[78] *Dawnay, Day* (n 56 above) 1094 *per* Robert Walker J.
[79] *British Reinforced Engineering Co Ltd v Schleff* [1921] 2 Ch 563, 572–6 *per* Younger LJ.
[80] *Vancouver Malt* (n 74 above) 191 *per* Lord Macmillan.
[81] *Systems Reliability Holdings* (n 36 above) para 55 *per* Harman J.
[82] ibid para 50 *per* Harman J. It should be noted that the judge in that case apparently equated the goodwill in the business (which is typically a legitimate interest protected by vendor covenants) to the profits of that business (which is not).
[83] ibid para 54 *per* Harman J.
[84] *Allied Dunbar (Frank Weisinger) Ltd v Weisinger* [1988] IRLR 60, para 23 *per* Millett J.
[85] *Connors Bros Ltd v Connors* [1940] 4 All ER 179, 195; *Dawnay, Day* (n 56 above) 1110 *per* Evans LJ.
[86] *Silverman* (n 15 above) 6 *per* Winn LJ.

simply a matter of evidence. The public interest argument succeeded in *Dranez Anstalt v Hayek*, a case where the merits were clear and exceptional. It is considered in greater detail below.[87]

6.31 It is apparent that the court will regard the scope of an area covenant relatively uncritically. It is established that, in relation to the trade of a large manufacturer or merchant, it is not necessary to prove that the business which the covenant is intended to protect has been carried on in every part of the area mentioned in the covenant. As a matter of practicality, it is evident that the goodwill of a substantial business could not be adequately protected if the restrictive covenant had to be limited to the towns where actual sales could be proved, and therefore that the vendor would be free to operate a competing business in all the adjoining places.[88] In the *Allied Dunbar* case, Millett J rejected the submission that a restrictive covenant which effectively required the vendor not to compete in the financial services industry in the United Kingdom was unreasonable in scope because an alternative covenant not to deal with existing clients and with new clients introduced by them would have sufficed. The judge held that, to his knowledge, such an argument had never succeeded.[89] Moreover, the Privy Council has held that where a covenant applying to the sale of goodwill is concerned, if a restriction as to area is considered to be reasonable, that covenant will seldom be held unreasonable because it has no limit as to time.[90] It is unlikely that this proposition still holds sway. Any covenant expressed to be without limit of time can be expected to receive close scrutiny by the court.

6.32 However, it is correct that the degree of such scrutiny would be less in respect of a vendor covenant than an employee covenant. This is illustrated by reference to the reported authorities in this area. Amongst the more recent of these, the following vendor covenants have been upheld: a covenant precluding a vendor from engaging in any competing electrical engineering business, anywhere in the world, for a period of four years;[91] a covenant enjoining the vendor of his practice as a financial services salesman effectively from selling financial products in the United Kingdom for a period of two years;[92] a covenant prohibiting the vendor from carrying on a competing computer business for a period of seventeen months;[93] and a covenant enjoining the vendor from carrying on a competing paper merchandizing business, within a sixty-mile radius of Manchester Town Hall, for a period of seventeen months.[94] However, amongst the older authorities the following have been enforced by injunction: a covenant precluding a vendor from engaging in the business of manufacturing guns and ammunition, without limit of space, for a period of twenty-five years;[95] and a covenant precluding the vendor from engaging in the sardine business in Canada without limit of time.[96]

---

[87] [2002] EWCA Civ 1729, [2003] FSR 32, para 25 *per* Chadwick LJ. There the covenant operated to restrict a pioneer in the field of medical science from developing the ventilator he had invented and patented and those restrictions exceeded those already applicable under the Patents Act 1977. See paras 6.103 to 6.107 below.

[88] *Connors Bros* (n 5 above) 194 *per* Viscount Maugham.

[89] *Allied Dunbar* (n 20 above) para 28 *per* Lord Millett.

[90] *Connors Bros* (n 5 above) 195 *per* Viscount Maugham.

[91] *Emersub* (n 69 above) 4, 15 *per* Wright J.

[92] *Allied Dunbar* (n 20 above) paras 27–32 *per* Millett J.

[93] *Systems Reliability Holdings* (n 36 above) paras 36, 70 *per* Harman J. No geographical limit on the covenant is identified in the decision.

[94] *Alliance Paper* (n 60 above) paras 8, 26, 27 *per* Judge Levy.

[95] *Nordenfelt v Maxim Nordenfelt Guns and Ammunition Co Ltd* [1894] AC 535, 550 *per* Lord Herschell.

[96] *Connors Bros* (n 5 above) 190–6 *per* Viscount Maugham.

Five further factors can generally be excluded from the assessment of the reasonableness of a **6.33**
covenant in the business sale context. First, the honesty and cooperation of the defendant
vendor is immaterial.[97] So, a non-compete covenant is not rendered unreasonable because
the vendor has also entered into a non-dealing covenant, which depends on the honest cooperation of the vendor, and where there is no reason to doubt the honesty of the vendor in
seeking to abide by that covenant. In addition to the practical difficulty of determining the
extent of those characteristics at the time of the vendor giving the covenant, it would be self-
evidently unfair for the purchaser to be required to rely on those characteristics continuing
for any agreed period of time. As Millett J held:

> The purchaser of a business who is paying £386,000 for the goodwill is entitled to protect his
> investment by a suitably worded covenant which does not depend for its effectiveness on the
> vendor's honesty and co-operation. At the very least, if he obtains the vendor's agreement to
> the inclusion of a covenant which avoids these dangers, it hardly lies in the vendor's mouth to
> argue that he should have been content with less.[98]

Secondly, the financial need of the vendor is irrelevant. Although the receipt of a sum of **6.34**
money can generally be shown to be advantageous to a commercial party, as a matter of
policy, its liberty to trade is not an asset which it is permitted to sell, save within the limitations
imposed by the doctrine of restraint of trade.[99]

Thirdly, and by the same token, the price paid by the purchaser is not generally relevant. The **6.35**
fundamental question for the court is not whether the restriction sought to be imposed is
justified by the agreed price, but whether it is reasonably necessary to protect the identified
interest of the covenantee (the purchaser). Thus, the court will not generally concern itself
with evaluating what the restriction may be worth as opposed to what may in the circumstances be reasonably necessary.[100] Accordingly, the amount of the price will not generally
justify any finding as to whether or not there is a serious issue to be tried for the purposes of
an application for an interim injunction. The issue as to whether price may potentially be a
factor considered at trial has been left open.[101]

Fourthly, the fact that the same covenant might be unenforceable against some individuals **6.36**
but enforceable against others is immaterial. An identical covenant may be enforced against
those persons who have a sufficient knowledge of the business and interest in its goodwill as
to make that covenant reasonable.[102] The fact that the covenant would be unreasonable (and
therefore unenforceable) against other vendors is irrelevant.

Fifthly, there is the possibility of divergence between the scope of protection provided by a **6.37**
restrictive covenant contained in an employment contract and that contained in a share sale
or purchase agreement. In *Emersub v Wheatley*, Wright J considered the submission that,
where restrictive covenants in a service contract were similar in nature to those contained in
a deed relating to the sale of shares, save that the covenants in the service contract were of
shorter duration, the purchaser had no real need for protection from competition for the

---

[97] *Allied Dunbar* (n 20 above) para 28 *per* Millett J.
[98] ibid para 28.
[99] *Vancouver Malt* (n 74 above) 192 *per* Lord Macmillan.
[100] *Blockfoil Group v Flay* (18 December 2001, QBD), para 36 *per* Robin Purchas QC (sitting as a Deputy
High Court Judge).
[101] ibid para 36.
[102] *Systems Reliability Holdings* (n 36 above) para 56 *per* Harman J.

longer period required by the covenants in the deed.[103] The judge rejected that submission on the grounds that the purchaser could be deemed to have taken into account the fact that covenants contained in the contract for the sale of a business may be considerably more extensive (and still be enforceable), than those contained in a contract of employment. Moreover, the purchaser was deemed to have taken into account the fact that the vendor's employment might have come to an end prematurely for a variety of reasons.

Implied covenants in the vendor–purchaser context

6.38 It is well established that where the goodwill of a business is sold, without any express agreement by the parties as to the restraint of the vendor from further competition, he may lawfully set up a rival business.[104] However, he is not entitled to canvass customers of his previous business, and may be restrained by injunction from soliciting any person who was a customer of that previous business (prior to the sale) to continue to deal with the vendor or not to deal with the purchaser.[105]

6.39 This restriction is implied by law either, on the ground that the vendor is not entitled to depreciate or destroy that which he has sold, or, on the basis of an implied contract between vendor and purchaser to abstain from any act intended to deprive the purchaser of that which has been sold to him and to restore it to the vendor.[106]

6.40 Further restrictions are implied on the sale of goodwill, in the absence of any express provision dealing with the matter. The purchaser is precluded from carrying on business under the name of his former business,[107] from representing himself to be the successor to his former business, and from representing that he is carrying on a continuation of that business, or that his former business has any interest in his new business.[108] He is nevertheless entitled to represent to the public that he was formerly connected with the business which he has sold.[109]

C. Partnerships

Introduction

Partnerships and restraint of trade

6.41 Partnership law is a major subject in its own right. A detailed treatment is beyond the scope of this book.[110] However, it does merit some separate consideration in a work on restraint of trade. This is because the court's approach to the enforceability of restrictive covenants contained in a partnership agreement is often different from that adopted where the restriction

---

[103] *Emersub* (n 69 above).

[104] See eg *I N Newman Ltd v Richard T Adlem* [2005] EWCA Civ 741, [2006] FSR 16, CA, para 23 *per* Jacob LJ.

[105] *Trego* (n 13 above) 20–21 *per* Lord Herschell.

[106] ibid 21 *per* Lord Herschell; 25 *per* Lord Macnaghten.

[107] *Levy v Walker* (1879) 10 Ch D 436, CA, 448 *per* James LJ.

[108] *Hookham v Pottage* (1872) 8 Ch App 91, CA, 95 *per* Sir WM James LJ; *Trego* (n 13 above) 21 *per* Lord Herschell.

[109] *Hookham* (n 108 above) 95 *per* Sir WM James LJ.

[110] The leading textbook is *Lindley & Banks on Partnership* (19th edn, 2010). A useful, practical guide is J Davies, C Greenwood, and F Payne, *Employment, Partnership and Discrimination Law for Professional Partnerships* (2005).

is found in a contract of employment. The reason for this is that an outgoing partner who sells his interest in the partnership is more like the vendor of a business than an employee.

Unsurprisingly, the issue is not straightforward. The approach taken by the court, in a case **6.42** involving a partnership, will depend on many factors. These include the status of the partner in question (whether he is an equity or a salaried partner), whether he is held out as a partner, and whether he has an interest in the partnership which he sells when he ceases to be a partner.

Sources of partnership law

Partnership law has two sources, the common law and statute. Many of the rules and prin- **6.43** ciples applicable to partnerships have been developed by the courts through case law. However, it should not be forgotten that the Partnership Act 1890 provides a detailed set of provisions of direct and continuing importance to partnerships. Whilst its contents may not be of central importance in relation to restrictions on competition by partners, its potential relevance should not be overlooked in any such dispute.

Types of partnership

Partnership is defined by section 1(1) of the Partnership Act 1890 as 'the relation which **6.44** subsists between persons carrying on business in common with a view of profit'. There are two main types of partnership which the practitioner is likely to encounter. First, there is the general partnership, which is a longstanding and familiar type of partnership. The characteristics of 'an ordinary English partnership' have been identified as follows:

(1) the partnership is not a legal entity;
(2) the partners carry on the business of the partnership in common with a view of profit;
(3) each does so both as principal and (see section 5 of the 1890 Act) as agent for each other, binding the firm and his partners in all matters within his authority;
(4) every partner is liable jointly with the other partners for all the debts and other obligations of the firm (see section 9 of the 1890 Act); and
(5) the partners own the business, having a beneficial interest in the form of an undivided share in the partnership assets including any profits of the business.[111]

Secondly, a recent addition to the partnership family is the limited liability partnership or LLP, **6.45** a creation of the Limited Liability Partnerships Act 2000 (LLPA 2000). An LLP is a body corporate and not a partnership as defined by section 1 of the Partnership Act 1890. It has 'members' rather than 'partners', and they are agents for the LLP rather than for each other.[112]

LLPA 2000 provides that the mutual rights and duties of members of an LLP, and the mutual **6.46** rights and duties of an LLP and its members, will be governed by agreement between its members, or between the LLP and its members or, in the absence of agreement, by relevant regulations.[113] Section 4(4) of LLPA 2000 provides that a member of an LLP will not be regarded for any purpose as employed by the LLP unless, if he and the other members were partners in a partnership, he would be regarded for that purpose as an employee of the partnership.[114]

---

[111] *Memec v IRC* [1998] STC 754, 764 *per* Peter Gibson LJ.
[112] For a discussion of the nature of LLPs, see *Lindley & Banks* (n 110 above) paras 2-39–2-44.
[113] See Limited Liability Partnerships Regulations 2001, SI 2001/1090; Limited Liability Partnerships (No 2) Regulations 2002; and Limited Liability Partnerships (Amendment) Regulations 2005.
[114] See *Kovats v TFO Management LLP* [2009] ICR 1140, EAT.

6.47 Although there is as yet no relevant case law confirming the position, the combined effect of these provisions is likely to be that the enforceability of restrictions concerning members and former members of an LLP will be approached by the courts in a manner similar to that for partners in a partnership. Thus, in terms of the enforceability of restrictions in partnership and LLP agreements, it remains necessary to examine all the facts and circumstances concerning the nature of the relationship of the individuals, whether partners or members, in order to determine the approach a court will take.

Categories of partner

6.48 Those individuals involved in a partnership business may be divided broadly into two groups, namely partners and employees. However, partners may be further subdivided. This subdivision is sometimes described as first-tier and second-tier. The former comprises equity partners, who enjoy full partnership rights such as those described above. Profit sharing members of an LLP are, broadly speaking, in a comparable position, for present purposes, to equity partners in a partnership.[115]

6.49 Second-tier partners include salaried or fixed-share partners. The status of a salaried partner, in a firm of solicitors, is somewhere between an assistant or associate solicitor and a full or equity partner. Appointment as a salaried partner generally indicates an aspiration that the solicitor is on track towards full partnership. A salaried partner's rights are likely to be defined in writing. They may or may not include an interest in the partnership assets, including its goodwill. Thus a salaried partner may bear some of the hallmarks of an equity partner. Alternatively, a salaried partner may simply be an employee of the partnership. A fixed-share partner may be seen as closer to the position of an equity partner than is a salaried partner, but it is more important to have regard to substance than form or label. The enforceability of a restrictive covenant will be affected by the precise rights and obligations of the salaried or fixed-share partner. There is no substitute for examining these rights and obligations with care in approaching the question of the enforceability of restrictions against such a partner.

6.50 In *Briggs v Oates*,[116] the defendant was articled, called as a solicitor, became an assistant solicitor and then a salaried partner with a firm of solicitors. A written agreement set out the solicitor's rights and obligations as a salaried partner. It was intended that he would, following his appointment, be held out to the public as a partner. Nonetheless, the terms of the agreement made it clear, in Scott J's opinion, that, as between the firm and the solicitor, the defendant was not a partner but remained an employee. The agreement gave him no share of the profits and imposed on him no liability for losses. He was to be remunerated by a combination of salary and commission on bills delivered.[117] He was an employee despite some of the goodwill of the firm coming to attach to him personally.[118]

---

[115] For a discussion of the comparable status of profit sharing members of an LLP and partners in a partnership, see *Re Rogers (deceased)* [2006] 2 All ER 792.

[116] [1990] ICR 473.

[117] ibid 475.

[118] ibid 475. The salaried partner was subject to an area covenant for five years within a radius of five miles of the firm's offices. However, Scott J found that the dissolution of the partnership constituted a breach of the contract of employment of the salaried partner and brought it to an end.

Duty of good faith

Each partner owes a duty of good faith to every other partner, and the relationship between   **6.51**
partners is a fiduciary one: 'If fiduciary relation means anything I cannot conceive a stronger
case of fiduciary relation than that which exists between partners.'[119]

Garden leave

Garden leave is dealt with in Chapter 4 above. The principles discussed there generally apply   **6.52**
to partnerships. There is little authority on the imposition of garden leave on a partner.
However, there is no reason in principle to think that a garden leave provision contained in
a partnership agreement, properly applied, is any less lawful than in the context of an employment contract.

In *Voaden v Voaden*,[120] the parties were existing and former partners in a firm of surveyors.   **6.53**
After the defendant gave notice of retirement from the partnership, the continuing partners
agreed that the defendant could leave before expiry of his full notice period. However, the
defendant then started practising in competition with the claimants who contended that
they would not have agreed to shorten his notice period had they known this was his intention.
The claimants sought an injunction to restrain the defendant from competing for the duration of his notice period. They recognized that, if the defendant was to be restricted over that
period, then he had to be remunerated as if he were a continuing partner.

There was no garden leave clause in the partnership deed, but in considering its provisions,   **6.54**
Lindsay J said:

> Before I leave the Deed altogether I pause to consider what the Partnership Board might do
> in relation to the work to be done by an equity partner who shall have given the required one
> year's notice during that year. The management of the partnership is by the Deed entrusted
> in the first place to the Partnership Board and, given the size and diversity of the plaintiff's
> practice, the term 'management' must, in my view, include the ability in the board, within
> broad limits, to assign particular types of work and places of work to particular partners in the
> best interests of the firm, as the board reasonably and honestly perceives those interests to be.
> I say 'within broad limits' as there could, no doubt, be cases where, for example, the assign-
> ment by the board infringed a partner's rights as such or where the assignment was such that
> no reasonable board truly acting in the best interests of the firm could bona fide have assigned
> as it did.

Lindsay J referred to the discussion during the course of argument of garden leave cases   **6.55**
'under which an employer requires an employee during the period of his notice not to attend
the employer's premises and excludes him from access to the employer's business and affairs,
although still on full pay'. He continued:

> I can see that to seek fully to impose such conditions on an equity partner under this Partnership
> Deed could offend the provisions of the Deed. But I do not take [counsel for the defendant]
> to deny that it could have been open to the Partnership Board closely to regulate the defen-
> dant's activities during the period of his notice. I see no problem in the board requiring him,
> for example, not to mention his intending retirement to any clients other than in the terms
> and in cases agreed with the board and not to mention to clients his intention to practice on

---

[119] *Helmore v Smith* (1886) 35 Ch D 436, 444 *per* Bacon V-C. On the duty of good faith between partners
generally, see *Lindley & Banks* (n 110 above) ch 16.
[120] 21 February 1997.

his own account and to work out his notice under the supervision of some delegated partner so as to introduce continuing partners to the clients with whom he had been dealing and so as to ensure as smooth a transition as practicable, without there being any poaching for his next practice.

6.56   Notwithstanding any power that the continuing partners may have to regulate the conduct of an outgoing partner during his notice period (as suggested by Lindsay J in *Voaden v Voaden*), it is important to include a garden leave clause in a partnership agreement, and many now do so. It should make clear provision as to the circumstances in which a partner may be put on garden leave (generally after service of notice of retirement), who may make that decision, and what is to happen with regard to the partner's rights, especially as to remuneration, during the garden leave period. It is advisable to make clear that garden leave shall not affect the partner's entitlement to share in the profits of the practice.

Implied restriction after retirement

6.57   An outgoing equity partner, who has sold his share of the partnership assets to the continuing partners, may set up in competition and act for clients of the partnership provided he is not subject to any express restrictive covenant not to do so. What he may not do, however, is solicit the clients of the partnership to transfer their business to him.

6.58   Authority for this somewhat surprising proposition is found in the decision of the House of Lords in *Trego v Hunt*.[121] Their Lordships held that where the goodwill of a business is sold (without further provision), the vendor may set up a rival business, but he is not entitled to canvass the customers of the old firm, and may be restrained by injunction from soliciting any person who was a customer of the old firm prior to the sale to continue to deal with the vendor, or not to deal with the purchaser.

Express restrictions after retirement

6.59   The enforceability of restrictive covenants against partners, after they have ceased to be partners, involves consideration of the general principles affecting the enforceability of post-termination restrictions (which are discussed in Chapter 5 above) and of factors peculiar to the nature of partnerships. In particular, the sale by an outgoing partner of his share in the partnership, and the mutuality of the covenant which affects and benefits all partners, are two important considerations which weigh in favour of the enforceability of such restraints.

6.60   The leading authorities on the topic are discussed below. Whilst each case turns on its own facts and circumstances, one of the benefits of examining these cases is that it is helpful for the practitioner, when advising, to be able to see how the courts assess the various factors when deciding on the enforceability of a particular covenant.

6.61   In general terms, the courts are more inclined to enforce a restrictive covenant against an equity partner who has sold his share of the partnership on his retirement. This applies in the case of both area and non-solicitation/dealing covenants. Such a partner is treated as akin to the vendor of a business. In contrast, a salaried partner who does not own, and consequently who does not on retirement sell, any share in the partnership will be treated as being in much

---

[121] [1896] AC 7, HL.

the same position as an employee when it comes to the enforceability of restrictive covenants. The position of equity and salaried partners is considered in turn below.

Equity partners

Area covenants are amongst the more onerous forms of restrictive covenant in that they prevent **6.62** an outgoing partner from practising for a period of time within a defined geographical area.[122] These will be considered first, before turning to non-solicitation/dealing covenants.

Area covenants

In *Whitehill v Bradford*,[123] four doctors entered into a partnership agreement which prohibited **6.63** a retiring partner for twenty-one years from practising medicine within ten miles of Atherstone parish church. One of the doctors left the partnership and the remaining partners exercised their option to acquire his share of the practice. When the retiring doctor declared his intention to practise within the prohibited area, the Court of Appeal enforced the covenant. Lord Evershed MR emphasized that this was not a case of master and servant. It was a case in which the remaining partners were entitled to have themselves protected against the competition of an outgoing partner.[124] They were 'all of them grown and educated men and they were also separately advised'.[125] The court held that a limit of five miles was insufficient to protect the practice, and that as it was difficult to fix any limit between five and ten miles which would be sufficient, the prohibited area was not more than was reasonably required for the protection of the practice.[126] Twenty-one years was a long time and might well be equivalent to a life banishment from the area concerned. But the defendant was a relatively mobile person and the whole of the rest of the United Kingdom was open for the application by him of his professional skill.[127]

Ronbar Enterprises Ltd v Green[128] concerned a partnership between a company and the defen- **6.64** dant to publish a sports and entertainment newspaper. The agreement provided for the purchase by one partner of the share of the other partner, whereupon the partner whose share was purchased agreed for five years from such date not to be engaged 'in any business similar to or competing with the business of the partnership'. The restrictive covenant was considered to be unreasonable in that it restrained the defendant from carrying on a similar business to the partnership business in any part of the world. However, the words 'similar to' were severed and the resulting covenant against carrying on a competing business for five years anywhere in the world was prima facie valid.[129] The court appeared to proceed on the basis that the agreement was akin to one between a vendor and purchaser of a business, and the approach to enforcement of restrictions in such cases was to be followed here.[130]

---

[122] As discussed in Chapter 5 above, non-competition covenants are a variation on this theme in that they prevent an individual from competing with the covenantee, often without geographical limit. However, non-competition covenants have come under far less scrutiny by the courts in the context of partnerships than area covenants, and so the latter are the focus of discussion here.

[123] [1952] Ch 236, CA.

[124] ibid 250.

[125] ibid 246.

[126] cf *Lyne-Pirkis v Jones* [1969] 1 WLR 1293, CA.

[127] [1952] Ch 236, CA, 251.

[128] [1954] 1 WLR 815, CA.

[129] It was an application for interim relief only (ibid 821 *per* Jenkins LJ).

[130] See eg ibid 823 *per* Harman J.

6.65 In *Espley v Williams*,[131] the claimant and defendant entered into a partnership agreement to run an estate agency in Christchurch. The agreement provided that the goodwill of the partnership business belonged to the claimant alone, the defendant not acquiring any interest in it. This reflected the fact that the claimant alone put money into the business. The defendant covenanted for two years after termination of the partnership not to practise as an estate agent within a radius of two miles of the partnership premises. Effectively this covered the whole of Christchurch where there were another twenty-three estate agencies. After leaving the partnership, the defendant joined another estate agency within the prohibited area. Henry LJ cited the well-known passage in the speech of Lord Wilberforce in *Stenhouse Australia Ltd v Phillips*[132] to the effect that an employer's claim for protection must be based upon the identification of some advantage or asset inherent in the business which can be regarded as his property. It seemed to Henry LJ (with whom Aldous LJ agreed) that the advantage or asset here was the goodwill of the partnership to which the defendant had contributed. The goodwill was described as 'the attractive force which brings in custom'. The defendant was half of the attractive force of two people who were there. That being so, the judge had been quite entitled to find that this was not a covenant against competition, but that this goodwill amounted to a legitimate interest that the claimant was entitled to protect to make sure that half of the attractive force did not move down the road to open up shop in a competitor's close by.[133] Henry LJ rejected the argument that a non-solicitation covenant provided adequate protection, such that an area covenant went beyond what was necessary to protect the claimant's interests. The reason for this he thought was clear, namely that in practice such covenants are very difficult to enforce.[134]

6.66 In *Naish v Thorp Wright & Puxon*,[135] the claimant was a partner in a veterinary practice. The partnership agreement made provision for payment of the share of the goodwill to an outgoing partner. It also contained an area covenant against practising as a vet for a period of eight years after determination of the partnership within a distance of fourteen miles from the partnership premises.

6.67 At a time of difficulty with his professional and personal relationships, the claimant sought advice from solicitors and counsel as to (amongst other things) the enforceability of this restriction. Subsequently, he sued his legal advisers for damages for professional negligence relating to the advice which he received. The trial of the action required the judge to consider the enforceability of the restrictive covenant in the context of the legal advice which the defendant lawyers had given to the claimant. The usefulness of the decision is in the detailed consideration which the judge gave in his judgment to the factors relevant to the enforceability of the covenant.[136]

---

131 [1997] 1 EGLR 9, CA.
132 [1974] AC 391, PC, 400.
133 [1997] 1 EGLR 9, CA, 10.
134 See also *Dawnay, Day* (n 6 above); and *TFS Derivatives v Morgan* discussed at para 5.180 above.
135 21 May 1998.
136 The judge, HH Judge Robert Taylor (sitting as a Deputy Judge of the High Court), conducted a valuable review of a number of authorities: *Bridge v Deacons* [1984] 1 AC 705, PC; *Whitehill v Bradford* [1952] 1 Ch 236, CA; *Lyne-Pirkis v Jones* [1969] 1 WLR 1293, CA; *Connors Bros v Connors* [1940] 4 All ER 179, PC. He explained (transcript, 61) that he had incorporated many of the submissions of counsel for the defendants, Mr Patrick Elias QC (as he then was), in his own findings and conclusions.

The judge thought that the arguments for and against the enforceability of the restrictive **6.68** covenant were finely balanced. However, his ultimate conclusion was that it would probably be upheld and enforced by a court. His reasons, in summary, were these:[137]

(1) The covenant was part of an agreement whereby two intelligent, educated, and mature men entered into a professional partnership. It was not a contract of employment.

(2) The agreement provided that upon one partner serving notice of termination on the other the latter must effectively buy out the former by paying him a substantial sum representing his share of the goodwill. It was therefore in this respect closely analogous to a contract for the sale of a business.

(3) The covenant applied equally to both parties so that there was mutuality between them over it.

(4) At the time of entering into the agreement both parties were familiar with the nature and extent of the practice and with the general area in which the practice was being carried on.

(5) The precise terms of the covenant were arrived at as a result of discussions between the parties in which the terms of the restrictions were progressively cut down.

(6) The claimant took legal advice about the agreement before entering into it.

(7) At the time when the agreement was entered into, both parties had lengthy working lives ahead of them. It must have been within their reasonable contemplation that the circumstances in existence at the time when the agreement came to be terminated could vary widely and in particular the extent of the practice could well be very different from what it was when the agreement was entered into.

(8) There was nothing in the agreement injurious to the public interest. To paraphrase *Bridge v Deacons*, there is a clear public interest in facilitating the assumption by an established veterinary practice of a younger man as a partner.

(9) The duration of the covenant, namely eight years, was not unreasonably long, although it was a long time and was the factor which had given the judge most anxiety. The parties were the best judges of what was appropriate at the time. The practice was being carried on in a rural area where the population was comparatively static and no doubt had long memories. It might take the remaining partner many years to recover financially from having to pay the outgoing partner a very substantial sum by way of goodwill and while he was doing so he was reasonably entitled to protection from competition from the outgoing partner.

(10) The geographical extent of the covenant, namely fourteen miles from the partnership premises, was not unreasonably large. The practice was being carried on in a sparsely populated area with widely scattered farmsteads. At the time when the agreement was entered into the practice had clients at up to fourteen miles distance from the partnership premises so that a smaller geographical extent would have excluded a number of these clients.

(11) The ambit of the covenant was not unreasonable. It was argued for the claimant that the covenant should have been limited to soliciting or providing services for clients of the former partnership. The judge concluded, however, first, that the parties themselves were the best judges of whether an area clause or a non-solicitation clause was

---

[137] See n 136 above, transcript 61–6.

most appropriate and, secondly, that non-solicitation clauses are more difficult to police and consequently area clauses may legitimately be used to protect goodwill.[138]

6.69 Of all the factors which the judge considered, it was the provision for the payment of goodwill which in his view was the most crucial: 'Without such a provision the restraints . . . might be more difficult to justify.'[139]

Non-solicitation/dealing covenants: Bridge v Deacons[140]

6.70 The decision of the Privy Council in *Bridge v Deacons (A Firm)* remains a leading authority on the enforcement of restrictive covenants between equity partners in a solicitors' firm. It contains statements of general application to this area of law. However, it is important to remember that it involved only a covenant against acting for the firm's clients. It did not concern area covenants in partnership agreements. Furthermore, as with all cases which are discussed in this book, it is important to remember that, ultimately, the decision turns on its own particular facts. Having said that, it is an instructive illustration of the approach of the courts to the enforceability of partnership restrictions and is required reading for anyone advising in this field.

6.71 Deacons was one of the oldest and largest firms of solicitors in Hong Kong. Bridge joined as an assistant solicitor in 1967, became a salaried partner in 1973, and a full capital partner in 1974 at the age of 31.[141] He remained as a full capital partner until his retirement from the firm in 1982.

6.72 The restrictive covenant in the partnership agreement prevented Bridge from acting as a solicitor in Hong Kong for a period of five years after retirement for those who had been clients of the firm in the three years before he retired. In full, the relevant clause, 28(a), provided as follows:

> Except on dissolution, no partner ceasing to be a partner for any reason whatsoever shall for a period of five years thereafter act as a solicitor, notary, trade mark or patent agent or in any similar capacity in the Colony of Hong Kong whether as principal, clerk or assistant for any person, firm or company who was at the time of his ceasing to be a partner or had during the period of three years prior thereto been a client of the partnership provided however that this clause shall not apply to a partner acting in any such capacity in the course of employment with government or any public body or with any company or organisation which is not itself engaged in professional practice in any of the above fields.

6.73 After Bridge ceased to be a partner, the firm obtained an injunction to enforce this restrictive covenant, a decision that was upheld by the Hong Kong Court of Appeal and the Privy Council. Lord Fraser of Tullybelton delivered the judgment of the Privy Council. He started with the 'well established law that covenants in restraint of trade are unenforceable unless they can be shown to be reasonable in the interests of the parties and in the public interest'.[142] He cited the classic statement of the law from the speech of Lord Macnaghten in the *Nordenfelt* case.[143] He considered the two types of agreement in which such restrictions are customarily

---

138 Citing *Espley v Williams* [1997] 1 EGLR 9.

139 See n 136 above, transcript, 66. Cf *Dallas MacMillan & Sinclair v Simpson* (1989) SLT 454 (area covenant restraining retiring partner from practising within twenty miles from centre of Glasgow—which covered half of Scotland's law firms—held to be unenforceable).

140 [1984] 1 AC 705, PC.

141 Full capital partner may be treated, for present purposes, as equivalent to an equity partner.

142 [1984] 1 AC 705, 713.

143 [1894] 1 AC 535, 565.

found, namely vendor/purchaser and employee/employer agreements, referring in that connection to the speech of Lord Shaw of Dunfermline in *Herbert Morris v Saxelby*.[144] The agreement in the present case, being one between partners, did not conform exactly to either of these types of agreement, although it had some resemblance to both. In their Lordships' opinion a decision on whether the restrictions in this partnership agreement were enforceable or not could not be reached by attempting to place the agreement in any particular category, or by seeking for the category to which it was most closely analogous. The proper approach was that adopted by Lord Reid in *Esso Petroleum Co Ltd v Harper's Garage (Stourton) Ltd*, where he said: 'I think it better to ascertain what were the legitimate interests of the appellants which they were entitled to protect and then to see whether these restraints were more than adequate for that purpose.'[145] What were Deacons' legitimate interests depended largely on the nature of their business, and on the position of Bridge in the firm.

Deacons was divided into a number of departments which were largely separate from each other. Bridge became the partner in charge of the intellectual and industrial property law department. This department accounted for about 4.5 per cent of the total billed by the firm, and about 10 per cent of the firm's files were marked for Bridge's attention. Thus, he had no connection or dealings with over 90 per cent of the firm's clients, and, after leaving, he had no advantage over any other solicitor in seeking to attract their business. It was submitted for Bridge that, in these circumstances, the firm was not entitled to protection against Bridge acting for clients of the firm for whom he had never acted while he was a partner. The firm was only entitled to protect such part of its goodwill as would be threatened by Bridge if he were to set up in practice on his own account, and that part consisted only of the business which he was advantageously placed to attract because it came from clients for whom he had acted and to whom he was known.[146] **6.74**

This submission was rejected. In their Lordships' view it was necessary to recall that the firm's partners were the owners of the firm's whole assets, including its most valuable asset, goodwill. Bridge had owned a share of the assets while he was a partner, but he transferred his share to the continuing partners when he ceased to be a partner.[147] Thereafter, the continuing partners owned the whole of the assets. The question was whether it was reasonable, as between the parties, for the firm to obtain protection against appropriation by Bridge of any part of the goodwill, notwithstanding the 'departmentalization' of the practice.[148] **6.75**

Their Lordships considered that it was reasonable, provided (which was not suggested here) that the protection did not extend beyond the firm's practice. On this question the mutuality of the contract was a most important consideration. The contract applied equally to all the partners. None of them could tell whether he might find himself in a position of being a retiring partner subject to the restriction, or of a continuing partner with an interest to enforce the restriction.[149] **6.76**

---

[144] [1916] 1 AC 688, 713–14.
[145] [1968] AC 269, 301.
[146] [1984] 1 AC 705, 714–16.
[147] This was no less the case because the value placed on the goodwill when joining and leaving was nominal. There were good reasons for this (ibid 717–19).
[148] ibid 716.
[149] ibid.

6.77 In relation to other aspects of the reasonableness of the restrictive covenant, their Lordships made the following findings. The five-year period of restriction, and the three-year backward limitation on clients, were matters which were hardly susceptible of proof by scientific evidence. The inclusion of persons who had been clients within the previous three years was reasonable, having regard to the intermittent nature of a solicitor's employment by any particular client; there must be many regular clients of a solicitor's firm who do not have occasion to employ the firm even as often as once every three years.

6.78 The five-year duration was reasonable. There was no reported case where a restriction which was otherwise reasonable had been held to be unreasonable solely because of its duration. Their Lordships also had in mind that some weight should be given to the fact that the restriction was found in a partnership agreement which had evidently been carefully drafted and which must be taken to represent the views of experienced solicitors who would be well aware that an unduly severe restriction would be unenforceable. It was to be assumed that they considered the five-year period to be reasonable and their Lordships were not prepared to differ from that view.[150]

Salaried partners

6.79 In *Clarke v Newland*,[151] a salaried partner in a medical practice was restrained by injunction, after ceasing to be a salaried partner, from practising as a general medical practitioner in the practice area for a period of three years. However, it was common ground that the area and the period of restraint were reasonable and unobjectionable. The point at issue was the scope of the word 'practise'.[152]

6.80 In *Kao, Lee & Yip v Edwards*,[153] the defendant solicitor entered into a 'Salaried Partnership Agreement' with the claimant firm of solicitors which had five equity partners at that time. The defendant was described in the agreement as a salaried partner. He was entitled to a monthly salary, was not required to contribute any capital to the practice, nor was he entitled to a share of profits. The defendant was, however, held out to the outside world, and to staff members of the firm itself, as a partner. This was the first salaried partnership agreement entered into by the firm, and was regarded as a half-way house between the status of a solicitor and a full equity partner. In so far as it was relevant to place the contract into any particular category, in the court's judgment, it was plainly an employment contract.

6.81 The defendant agreed that upon termination of the partnership deed he would not, for a period of five years, solicit legal business from, or do any work or act normally done by solicitors for, anyone who had been a client of the practice within a period of three years preceding the termination. The defendant was put in charge of the litigation department. By reason of his position and the way he was presented by the equity partners to the outside world, he was able to develop strong professional links with clients of the firm who believed that they were dealing with a partner who had a stake in the firm.

6.82 In an action to enforce the restrictive covenant, it was found that the restriction was modelled on that in *Bridge v Deacons* except that the covenant in that case was restricted

---

[150] ibid 717. Cf *Kao, Lee & Yip v Koo Hoi-yan* [1995] 1 HKLR 248, HKCA.
[151] [1991] 1 All ER 397, CA.
[152] ibid 402.
[153] [1994] 1 HKLR 232, HKCA.

to Hong Kong. *Bridge v Deacons* was distinguished from the present case on two grounds. First, the defendant's position here, unlike Bridge, was, despite his 'salaried partner' status, akin to that of an employee of the firm. Accordingly, public policy leaned more heavily in his favour. Secondly, in *Bridge v Deacons* the restrictive covenant was in an agreement which bound all the partners including Bridge. By the agreement, he was admitted to full capital partnership and had a share in all the assets of the partnership including its goodwill. A covenant aimed at protecting clients' connections, an aspect of goodwill, was as much for his benefit as for that of the other partners. This aspect of mutuality as between the contracting parties was wholly absent in this case. For these reasons, *Bridge v Deacons* was distinguishable from the present case and the court was not bound to reach the same decision.

The restrictive covenant was tested according to the conventional criteria of legitimate interests **6.83** and reasonableness. The only legitimate interest was client connection, which formed part of the goodwill of the practice. The question was whether the covenant was wider than reasonably necessary to protect that interest. It was. In particular, it was geographically too wide in not being confined to Hong Kong. Five years was also 'far too long' for the protection of the claimants' legitimate interests.

A covenant which prohibited a chartered accountant who was a salaried partner for three **6.84** years from working for clients of the claimant firm irrespective of whether he had any contact or knowledge of that client or his affairs was unreasonable (*Taylor Stuart & Co v Croft*).[154] However, that part was severable, and the remainder against solicitation of those clients was reasonable.[155]

Solicitors

A special case?

Some of the leading authorities relating to the enforceability of restrictive covenants in part- **6.85** nership agreements involve solicitors. A number of these have been discussed above. Some concern equity partners, for example *Bridge v Deacons*.[156] Others concern salaried partners, for example *Kao, Lee & Yip v Edwards*.[157] Many of the cases concerning solicitors, however, deal with the enforceability of restrictive covenants contained in the employment contracts of solicitors who are not partners. The question has sometimes been discussed in these authorities of whether solicitors are a special case. Do the normal rules of restraint of trade apply to them or are they subject to a different regime on account of the professional services they provide, and the rules of the Law Society? These questions are discussed below.

The view that solicitors are a special case in this respect was espoused by Lord Denning MR **6.86** in *Oswald Hickson Collier & Co v Carter-Ruck*.[158] He considered that, as the relationship between a solicitor and his client is a fiduciary relationship, it would be contrary to public policy that he should be precluded from acting for a client when that client wanted him to

---

[154] 7 May 1997.

[155] *Per* Stanley Burnton QC (sitting as a Deputy High Court Judge), relying on *Plowman v Ash* [1964] 1 WLR 568 and *Lucas & Co Ltd v Mitchell* [1974] Ch 129. See also the discussion concerning the penalty/liquidated damages clause for breach of this restrictive covenant in Chapter 11 below.

[156] See n 22 above.

[157] See n 150 above.

[158] *(Note)* [1984] AC 720, CA.

act for him.[159] However, a different division of the Court of Appeal, and the Privy Council, subsequently declined to follow that approach.[160]

6.87   Harman J sought to breathe new life into the argument that solicitors are a special case (but in a different sense) in *Wallace Bogan & Co v Cove*.[161] Three solicitor employees resigned from the claimant firm and set up a new practice. There were no restrictive covenants in their employment contracts with the claimant. After leaving the claimant, the defendant solicitors wrote to clients of the claimant offering to act for them in the new firm. Harman J granted an interim injunction restraining the defendants from canvassing or soliciting the claimant firm's clients for twelve months. He held that there was a serious issue to be tried, namely whether there is to be implied into a contract of service between a solicitor and a firm of solicitors employing him an obligation after the contract is terminated not to canvass or solicit active customers of the employing firm with whom it had dealt for a period of time.[162] In the judge's view, solicitors are regarded by the law as having a more onerous obligation imposed upon them because of the special position which they occupy in relation to the client.[163]

6.88   The Court of Appeal allowed the appeal, discharged the injunction, and dismissed the action. Leggatt LJ stated that in canvassing clients the solicitor was taking advantage of a professional connection with clients. But that connection is no different in principle from the trade connection that, for instance, a milk rounds man may acquire with his employer's customers. Clients and customers alike represent the employers' goodwill which the employers are entitled to protect by an express covenant in reasonable restraint of trade, but which is not protected for them by an implied term if they do not bother to exact an express covenant.[164] 'There is in my judgment no warrant for treating solicitors in this context differently from any other professional or tradesperson. In the eye of the law all are equal.'[165]

6.89   It was argued in *Allan Janes LLP v Johal*[166] that a non-dealing covenant would preclude a solicitor from doing work for a client who, without any solicitation on the solicitor's part, had elected to choose her as his solicitor. Such a restriction was said to be in breach of a fundamental principle, enshrined in the Solicitors' Practice Rules, that a solicitor shall not do anything in the course of practising that compromises or impairs 'a person's freedom to instruct the solicitor of his or her choice'.[167] The argument was rejected. The rule does not purport to deal with the case where there is a restrictive covenant. The aspiration of the Law Society is a matter between the Society and its members but is not ultimately a matter which determines whether the court should find a restriction to be unreasonable from the point of view of the interests of the public.[168]

---

[159] ibid 723.
[160] *Edwards v Worboys (Note)* [1984] AC 737, CA; *Bridge v Deacons* [1984] 1 AC 705, PC, 719–20.
[161] [1997] IRLR 453, CA.
[162] ibid para 5.
[163] ibid para 7. Bristow J held that it was not possible to regard a restrictive covenant contained in a medical partnership agreement which might lead to a doctor being prevented by law from giving patients the care, which he was obliged under the National Health Service to give them, as other than contrary to the basic concept of the NHS and so contrary to public policy and unenforceable (*Hensman v Traill* (1980) 124 SJ 776). This decision was overruled by the Court of Appeal in *Kerr v Morris* [1987] 1 Ch 90, CA.
[164] [1997] IRLR 453, para 12.
[165] ibid para 15 *per* Leggatt LJ.
[166] [2006] ICR 742; [2006] IRLR 599.
[167] ibid para 52.
[168] ibid paras 58–9.

Enforcing restrictive covenants against employed solicitors

Solicitors are not therefore a 'special case' in the sense that they are immune from the principles **6.90**
in this branch of the law applicable generally, merely on the grounds that they are solicitors.
But that does not mean that a clause which is unreasonable for milk rounds men would also
be unreasonable for a solicitor. This is because whether a restriction is reasonable or not is a
question of fact and is dependent on all the circumstances of the case.[169] Given that there are
particular characteristics relating to a solicitor's practice which are relevant for the purpose of
the enforceability of restrictive covenants, it is instructive to see how the courts have
approached this question in the case of solicitors who are not partners but are simply employees
of their firm.

Fitch v Dewes[170] is, perhaps, largely of historic interest nowadays although it is still occasionally **6.91**
referred to in more recent judgments. The contract of employment of a solicitor contained
an area covenant prohibiting him from being engaged in the business of a solicitor within a
radius of seven miles of Tamworth Town Hall. The House of Lords held that the covenant,
though unlimited in point of time, did not in the circumstances exceed what was reasonably
required for the protection of the covenantee and was not against the public interest. Lord
Birkenhead LC gave the leading speech in which he placed great emphasis on the fact that
this was a contract entered into between two competent and experienced solicitors each
being able to understand and safeguard his own interests.[171] In a dictum often quoted in later
cases, the Lord Chancellor expressed his opinion that it was in the public interest that a
proper restrictive agreement of this kind between an established solicitor, possibly an elderly
man, and a younger man should be allowed: 'It is in the public interest, because otherwise
solicitors carrying on their business without a partner would be extremely chary of admitting
competent young men to their offices and to the confidential knowledge to be derived from
frequenting those offices.'[172]

In *Hollis & Co v Stocks*,[173] the claimants were a small firm of solicitors practising from an **6.92**
office in Sutton-in-Ashfield, Nottinghamshire, where the defendant solicitor worked. His
contract of employment contained a covenant that he would not, for twelve months after
termination, work within ten miles of the firm's office. It was argued for the defendant that
the effect of this covenant was to prevent him from working in any capacity within the
restricted area. It was held that on its true construction the covenant was confined to work
'as a solicitor'.[174] The Court of Appeal also upheld the judge's conclusion that the ten-mile
radius was reasonable. This area did not bar the defendant from working within the cities of
the East Midlands, notably Nottingham and Derby, that are outside the ten-mile radius.[175]

Allan Janes LLP v Johal[176] provides a recent illustration of the court's consideration of the **6.93**
particular circumstances relevant to the enforceability of restrictive covenants entered into
by a solicitor who is not a partner. The claimant was a fairly small firm of solicitors practising

---

[169] [2006] IRLR 599, para 32.
[170] [1921] 2 AC 158, HL.
[171] ibid 162.
[172] ibid 165.
[173] [2000] IRLR 712, CA.
[174] ibid para 25.
[175] ibid paras 10, 28.
[176] [2006] ICR 742; [2006] IRLR 599.

in High Wycombe. The defendant solicitor's contract of employment contained an area covenant and a non-dealing covenant. Within a week of leaving the claimant firm, the defendant was practising as a solicitor within the restricted area and soliciting clients of the claimant. Bernard Livesey QC (sitting as a Deputy Judge of the High Court), following a trial of the action, granted an injunction enforcing the non-dealing but not the area covenant. Having reviewed a number of the leading authorities and identified the key principles on restraint of trade in employment generally,[177] the judge noted that it was common ground that the claimant had a legitimate interest to protect in the form of its goodwill and client connections.[178]

6.94   The area covenant prohibited the defendant for one year after termination from practising as or doing the work of a solicitor within a radius of six miles of the claimant's office. On its true construction, the words 'do the work of a solicitor' added something to the word 'practise'. They included visiting and advising a client (orally and in writing) within the prohibited area, even if the defendant's office was outside that area.[179] Having considered *Fitch v Dewes*[180] and *Hollis & Co v Stocks*,[181] in both of which area covenants were upheld, the judge concluded that they were decisions on their own facts. However, in the instant case, an area clause, not limited to clients of the claimant, was wider than necessary to protect the claimant's legitimate interests. Having regard to the size of the population within a radius of six miles of the claimant's offices, an area covenant would serve mainly to protect the claimant from competition for the business of a very large number of business persons who were not, or had well and truly ceased to be, clients of the firm. The claimant was not entitled to that sort of protection.[182]

6.95   The non-dealing covenant prohibited the defendant for one year after termination from acting as a solicitor for any person who was a client of the firm in the previous twelve months. This prohibition was further limited by reference to geographical area. The defendant argued that the covenant was unreasonable having regard to the fact that it was not limited to those clients with whom she had dealt, and that she had dealt directly with only 9 to 10 per cent and indirectly (by providing holiday cover) with a further 5 per cent of those clients for whom the firm did work in the last twelve months of her employment. The argument was sought to be bolstered by reference to those authorities in which non-solicitation covenants foundered because they applied to all of the employer's clients and not merely those with whom the ex-employee had dealt (*The Marley Tile Co Ltd v Johnson*[183] and *Austin Knight (UK) v Hinds*).[184]

6.96   The judge acknowledged that the fact that the restriction was not limited to those clients with whom the defendant had personal contact in the period of one year prior to termination was an important consideration which significantly widened the restriction and that attempts to justify this width required to be carefully considered. After due consideration it was his judgment that the width of the clause was not fatal to its reasonableness.[185] This had to be

---

[177]   ibid paras 20–9.
[178]   ibid para 34.
[179]   ibid paras 41–3, referring to *Edmundson v Render* [1905] 2 Ch 320.
[180]   [1921] 2 AC 158, HL.
[181]   [2000] IRLR 712, CA.
[182]   [2006] IRLR 599, para 47.
[183]   [1982] IRLR 75, especially paras 14–17.
[184]   [1994] FSR 52, 58.
[185]   [2006] IRLR 599, para 62.

judged at the time the covenant was entered into. It was within the contemplation of the parties at that time that in pursuance of the objective of developing the relationship of the claimant with the defendant with a view to the latter becoming a partner, she would be introduced widely to a large proportion of the firm's key clients. The judge added: 'Her very presence as a respected member of the firm in which the partners had trust endowed her with a special status on which she could rely vis-à-vis even those clients with whom she had no prior contact.'[186]

D. Other commercial agreements

Introduction

So far in this chapter the approach of the courts to the enforceability of restrictive covenants **6.97** in the context of vendor–purchaser and partnership agreements has been discussed. There remains a category of agreement which neither falls within these two classes, nor is it an employment contract. It is a commercial agreement in which the parties make their own contributions, whether in terms of finance or skills or in some other form, and also enter into restrictive covenants against competition in the future. Such an arrangement may be described in a number of ways and comprise a variety of agreements, for example joint venture, or investment, or shareholders' agreements. Until relatively recently, there was no authority which set out the correct approach to the enforceability of restraints against competition in the context of such agreements. This gap has now been filled.

Joint venture agreements

Dawnay, Day v D'Alphen[187]

The leading case on the enforceability of restrictive covenants in agreements between inves- **6.98** tors is *Dawnay, Day & Co Ltd v D'Alphen*.[188] Dawnay Day entered into a joint venture with three Eurobond brokers which was operated through a jointly owned company, Dawnay Securities, of which the three brokers were employees and directors. The shareholders' agreement contained three restrictive covenants given by the brokers, each stated to last for a period of two years from the date of the agreement: first, not to carry on a business which competes with the Eurobond broking business carried on from time to time by Dawnay Securities; secondly, not to solicit in competition with Dawnay Securities anyone who had engaged its services; and, thirdly, not to entice away from the company any director, officer, employee, or other servant. These restrictions were extended to a period of one year after the broker ceased to be an employee or director of Dawnay Securities. The covenants were stated to be given by the brokers in consideration for Dawnay Day contributing approximately £650,000 to the joint venture company by way of start-up capital. Dawnay Day gave equivalent undertakings to the brokers. The service agreements also contained restrictive covenants not to entice away a director or senior employee of Dawnay Securities.

The brokers gave notice of termination of their employment to join Cantor Fitzgerald **6.99** International. Dawnay Day sought to enforce the restrictive covenants contained in the

---

[186] ibid para 63.
[187] [1998] ICR 1068, [1997] IRLR 442, CA, [1997] IRLR 285 (Robert Walker J).
[188] ibid.

shareholders' agreement, and there was a trial of a preliminary issue as to the enforceability of these covenants. It was argued for the brokers that Dawnay Day had no legitimate interest in enforcing the covenants, given that it was no more than an investor in and creditor of the business which was owned and carried on by Dawnay Securities. Evans LJ formulated the question thus: 'Does a joint venturer (who is not a partner) have a sufficient interest to be permitted to enforce anti-competition and anti-solicitation covenants against his fellow joint venturer, when the business is to be developed and carried on by a jointly-owned company?'[189]

6.100 Evans LJ (with whom Ward and Nourse LJJ agreed) was clear that it was not the law that such covenants can never be upheld outside the established categories of vendor/purchaser and master/servant cases. In support of this proposition, he relied on dicta from two well-known cases. First, in *Esso Petroleum Co Ltd v Harper's Garage (Stourport) Ltd*,[190] Lord Wilberforce said: 'The doctrine of restraint of trade is one to be applied to factual situations with a broad and flexible rule of reason.'[191] In the same case, Lord Reid said: 'I think it better to ascertain what were the legitimate interests of the appellants which they were entitled to protect and then to see whether those restraints were more than adequate for that purpose.'[192] In *Stenhouse Australia Ltd v Phillips*,[193] Lord Wilberforce said:

> Leaving aside the case of misuse of trade secrets or confidential information . . . the employer's claim for protection must be based upon the identification of some advantage or asset inherent in the business which can properly be regarded as, in a general sense, his property, and which it would be unjust to allow the employee to appropriate for his own purposes, even though he, the employee, may have contributed to its creation.[194]

6.101 Evans LJ concluded that the established categories are neither rigid nor exclusive. Rather, the covenant may be enforced when the covenantee has a legitimate interest (of whatever kind) to protect, and when the covenant is no wider than is necessary to protect that interest.[195] Dawnay Day's undertaking to make the capital contribution, and certainly the contribution after it was made, gave Dawnay Day a clear commercial interest in safeguarding itself against competition from the managers, individually or collectively, for the agreed periods.[196]

6.102 Evans LJ also rejected a submission for the brokers that the non-competition covenant was unreasonable on the ground that in restraining the carrying on of a business which competes with the business carried on *from time to time* by Dawnay Securities, this extended to business carried on for the first time after the brokers had ceased to be employees of Dawnay Securities. It was held that Dawnay Day was entitled to claim protection not only for those kinds of business which Dawnay Securities was carrying on when the brokers left, in the sense that their desks were actively dealing with clients, but also for other kinds which were in an advanced state of preparation. As for the duration of the covenants, whilst the period of one year was not argued to be unreasonable, Evans LJ noted that the Court should be slow to interfere with the parties' own assessment of what a reasonable period was. He approved the

---

[189] ibid 1104.
[190] [1968] AC 269, HL.
[191] ibid 331.
[192] ibid 301.
[193] [1974] AC 391, PC.
[194] ibid 400.
[195] [1998] ICR 1068, 1106–7.
[196] ibid 1108.

judge's finding below (Robert Walker J) that the covenant 'should be treated as part of a commercial bargain between business people of broadly equal bargaining power' and observed that there is ample authority that the parties are likely to have been the best judges of what was reasonable between them.[197]

Dranez Anstalt v Hayek[198]

Another illustration of the difficulties which can arise in relation to the enforceability of **6.103** restrictive covenants in agreements between investors is provided by *Dranez Anstalt v Hayek*. Zamir Hayek was a medical doctor who specialized in paediatrics. He invented, and patented, a ventilator (the HO ventilator) for the treatment of patients with breathing disorders. Together with two brothers, he exploited this invention through a number of companies into which ten outside investors invested US $5 million in return for 7.5 per cent of the share capital. The Hayek brothers signed a side letter addressed to the investors, which was collateral to the investment agreement, by which they agreed that they would only carry on the business of the design, manufacture, and sale of medical ventilators through these particular companies and would not compete in that business so long as the companies carried on that business. Subsequently, Zamir Hayek set up his own company to produce and sell a new ventilator (the RTX ventilator) which he had invented. The investors commenced proceedings for damages and an injunction for breach of the covenant contained in the side letter.

A number of points were dealt with in the judgments of Evans-Lombe J and the Court of **6.104** Appeal. Of interest for present purposes is the divergent approach taken by the courts to the question of whether the non-competition covenant was wider than reasonably necessary to protect the investors' legitimate interests. The defendants argued that the covenant was unreasonable in that it was unlimited in time (that is to say, it was to last as long as the claimants were conducting the relevant business). Evans-Lombe J accepted that in the usual restraint of trade cases, the imposition of a restriction for an indefinite period would ordinarily be fatal to the enforceability of a restrictive covenant. But he noted that it is well established that a less stringent approach is taken where the restrictive covenant appears in an agreement for the sale of a business.[199] It seemed to Evans-Lombe J that there is no valid distinction to be drawn between a covenant given by a vendor not to compete with a business being sold and a covenant given by the proprietors of a business to an intending investor in that business as a condition of making such an investment.[200] He concluded that it is not necessarily fatal to restrictive covenants given pursuant to commercial bargains that a covenant may not be given for a fixed period of time.[201]

The Court of Appeal disagreed.[202] Chadwick LJ (with whom Brooke LJ and Lord Woolf CJ **6.105** agreed) formulated the question which the judge had to address thus: whether, in the circumstances of this case, a covenant which sought to prevent Hayek, as the inventor of the

---

[197] [1998] ICR 1068, 1109–10.
[198] [2002] 1 BCLC 693 (Evans-Lombe J), [2003] FSR 32, CA.
[199] [2002] 1 BCLC 693, paras 106–7, citing *Nordenfelt v Maxim Nordenfelt Guns and Ammunition Co Ltd* [1894] AC 535, 552 *per* Lord Watson and *Allied Dunbar (Frank Weisinger) Ltd v Weisinger* [1988] IRLR 60.
[200] [2002] 1 BCLC 693, paras 108–9, relying on *Dawnay, Day v D'Alphen* (n 6 above).
[201] ibid paras 110–11.
[202] Without having the benefit of submissions on behalf of the claimants who were not represented and did not appear at the substantive appeal hearing.

HO ventilator, from competing in the business of manufacturing and selling ventilators, worldwide, for so long as the companies were conducting that business was reasonable having regard (a) to the respective interests of Hayek and the persons to whom the side letter was addressed and (b) to the interest of the public at large that Hayek should not be restricted from applying his inventive skills in a field of medical science in which he was expert and in the development of which there was an obvious public benefit.[203]

6.106 Chadwick LJ concluded that (in addressing the question of whether the restriction was reasonable in the public interest) the judge failed to relate the protection from competition, which the investors sought to obtain under the side letter, to the nature of the investment they were making. It was important, in Chadwick LJ's view, to keep in mind that the investors to whom the side letter was addressed were taking a relatively small stake (7.5 per cent) in a company, Dranez Holdings, to which the patent rights had been (or were about to be) transferred. The transfer of those rights was subject to existing licences to develop, manufacture, and sell the ventilator already granted to others. On a proper analysis this was not a case in which the investors were buying—or even investing in—the businesses producing the ventilator; they were investing in the patent rights which those businesses were licensed to exploit. In those circumstances, they were entitled to, and obtained, the protection from competition which registration of the patents provided. But it was not at all self-evident to Chadwick LJ that they were entitled to protect the businesses carried on from competition in so far as competition with those businesses did not involve infringement of the patents.[204]

6.107 *Dranez Anstalt v Hayek* also stands as one of those rare cases where the second limb of Lord Macnaghten's test in the *Nordenfelt* case was engaged, namely reasonableness in the interests of the public. Chadwick LJ's second criticism of the judge's approach was that he did not appear to have addressed the question of whether it could be in the interest of the public at large that Hayek be subject to greater restrictions in the application of his inventive skills than those which Parliament had thought right to impose under the Patents Act 1977.'In particular, it must be a wholly exceptional case in which the imposition of such restraints on a pioneer in a field of medical science—in the development of which there is, at least prima facie, such an obvious public benefit—can be justified.'[205] Chadwick LJ concluded that this was not such a case.

Franchise agreements

6.108 Franchise agreements have also provided scope for dispute about the enforceability of restrictive covenants. Cases have concerned the franchising of printing and copying services,[206] drainage services,[207] and even high class mobile lavatories for private functions.[208]

6.109 *Kall-Kwik Printing v Rush*[209] is a typical example. The franchise agreement contained a two-year, ten-mile area covenant following termination. The question arose as to how to classify a franchise

---

[203] [2003] FSR 32, para 21.

[204] ibid paras 23–4.

[205] [2003] FSR 32, para 25.

[206] *Prontaprint plc v Landon Litho Ltd* [1987] FSR 315; *Kall-Kwik Printing (UK) Ltd v Rush* [1996] FSR 114.

[207] *Dyno-Rod plc v Reeve* [1999] FSR 148.

[208] *Convenience Co Ltd v Roberts* [2001] FSR 625.

[209] [1996] FSR 114.

covenant: was it more analogous to a business sale or an employment covenant? His Honour Judge Roger Cooke (sitting as a Deputy Judge of the High Court) analyzed it in these terms:

> One way perhaps of looking at a franchise agreement is that this is a form of lease of goodwill for a term of years with an obligation on the tenant, as it were, to retransfer the subject matter of the lease at the end of the lease in whatever state it is. So to that extent there is an obligation to transfer goodwill in a particular form which is much more akin, I think, to the goodwill cases than to the servant cases.[210]

This approach was expressly approved by Neuberger J in *Dyno-Rod plc v Reeve*,[211] whose approach was, in turn, approved and followed by the Court of Appeal in *ChipsAway International Ltd v Kerr*[212] and by Briggs J in *Pirtek (UK) Ltd v Joinplace Ltd*.[213] As a result, a covenant in a franchise agreement has to satisfy a far less stringent test of reasonableness than is required in the employment cases.   **6.110**

E. Checklist

Vendor–purchaser agreements

Is the covenantor a person who is (or was) a shareholder and actively engaged in the business   **6.111** of the company? If so, that person will be a legitimate covenantor (see paras 6.04 to 6.06 above).

Did the sale agreement include the sale of the goodwill of the business (see paras 6.07 and   **6.112** 6.08 above)?

Is the covenant a business sale covenant, an employment covenant, or does it fall somewhere   **6.113** between both categories? A covenant in the business sale context will not be subject to such close scrutiny for various policy and principle reasons (see paras 6.10 to 6.14 above).

Does the covenant protect a legitimate interest of the covenantee and is the covenant no   **6.114** wider than is necessary to protect that interest? If so, what is the legitimate interest? Once the legitimate interest is identified, consider whether the restraints imposed are reasonable on the facts and in the circumstances of the particular case. Consider the following:

- little if any weight should be placed on the form of the agreement in which the covenant is contained;
- the relevant transaction may consist in several contracts which are entered into over a period of time;
- the form in which the business, once sold, is carried on by the purchaser has little relevance to the issue of enforceability of the covenant.

(See para 6.15 above.)

Does the purchaser retain the services of the vendor after the business sale, ie is there an   **6.115** 'earn-out' or interim consultancy? If so, covenants may be given in both the share or business

---

[210] ibid 119.
[211] [1999] FSR 148.
[212] [2009] EWCA Civ 320.
[213] [2010] EWHC 1641 (Ch). The decision in *Pirtek* considered the validity of a non-compete covenant both at common law and under the Competition Act 1998. As to the latter, see Chapter 8 below.

sale agreement and in the employment contract between the purchaser and the vendor. In those circumstances, it is incorrect to look at the employment contract in isolation from the share or business sale agreement. Instead, the validity of the restrictive covenant will be considered in the context of the overall commercial bargain.

6.116 Factors to consider when looking at the reasonableness of the covenant include the following:

- What was the covenantor's position in the company? If they were a sole proprietor/major shareholder/managing director it will generally follow that if they compete it will affect the value of the business transferred. However, whatever their position in the company they will usually be a legitimate covenantor if they were a shareholder (see paras 6.19 to 6.29 above).
- Did the individual play a part as a negotiator of the sale?
- Was it the covenantor's business (or relevant part of the business) that was sold?
- Did the covenantor negotiate the sale of shares on his own behalf? Did he negotiate on behalf of others (see para 6.20 above)?

6.117 Is the 'earn-out' a transitional arrangement in order to facilitate the transfer of the customer connection which the vendor has sold to the purchaser under the share sale/practice buy-out agreement? If so, the fact that covenants may be contained in the sale and purchase agreement rather than any consultancy agreement will be given little weight. The issue of whether a deferred restraint of trade is reasonable would depend on the circumstances of the case, in particular the legitimate interest of the purchaser to see that the value of his purchase is protected in the future (see para 6.21 above).

6.118 Has there been a repudiatory breach of contract, such as a wrongful dismissal of the vendor, during an earn-out period? If so, bear in mind that although restrictions in the employment/consultancy agreement will fall away as a result, restrictions in a related share sale agreement may continue to apply (see para 6.24 above).

6.119 Factors to consider in ascertaining the reasonableness of a restriction in the business sale context include:

- as a general principle, the parties are deemed to be the best judges of what is reasonable;
- a bare covenant against competition will be unreasonable;
- any enforceable covenant that restricts competition must be ancillary to a main transaction, contract, or arrangement;
- the court will consider the substance rather than the form of the underlying transaction;
- a covenant will be construed against the background of the entire commercial bargain of which that covenant formed part;
- real functional correspondence is required between the covenant and any interest of the purchaser which is found by the court to be legitimate, for example the covenant must be necessary in order to protect the goodwill of the business sold by the vendor and not of the purchaser's own existing business;
- a covenant which has no restriction whatsoever as to area and where it is not reasonable for that covenant to have worldwide application, will be held to be unreasonable;
- if the vendor was, for example, a bare shareholder and had no detailed knowledge of the business being sold or if there is no conceivable prospect of him competing with it, it is unlikely that a covenant would be enforced against that vendor;

- the fact that a vendor has only a small participation in the goodwill and the business that is being sold, does not preclude covenants being enforced against him.

(See paras 6.25 to 6.29 above.)

Note that a covenant requiring the vendor to retire completely for a period of time from **6.120** any form of competing business may be enforceable if that is necessary to protect fully the goodwill of the business sold (see para 6.30 above).

The scope of an area covenant will be regarded relatively uncritically (see para 6.31 above). **6.121**

The following factors can generally be excluded from the assessment of the reasonableness of **6.122** a covenant in the business sale context:

- the honesty and cooperation of the defendant vendor;
- the financial need of the vendor;
- the price paid by the purchaser for the business;
- the fact that the covenant might have been given by some people against whom it would be unreasonable to enforce it;
- any divergence between the scope of protection provided by a restrictive covenant contained in an employment contract and that contained in the share or business sale agreement.

(See paras 6.33 to 6.37 above.)

Does the business sale agreement contain express covenants at all? If not, a covenant restraining **6.123** the vendor from canvassing/soliciting customers of his previous business and not to induce them not to deal with the purchaser will be implied. However, the vendor may usually in such circumstances lawfully set up a rival business (see paras 6.38 to 6.39 above).

In addition, the following restrictions will be implied on the sale of goodwill (in the absence **6.124** of any express provision to the contrary or to similar effect):

- precluding the vendor from carrying on business under the name of his former business;
- precluding the vendor from representing himself to be the successor to his former business and from representing that he is carrying on a continuation of that business;
- precluding the vendor from representing that his former business has any interest in his new business.

(See para 6.40 above.)

The vendor is, however, in the absence of an express enforceable covenant to the contrary, **6.125** entitled to represent to the public that he was formerly connected with the business which he has sold (see para 6.40 above).

Partnership agreements

Ascertain the real status of the individual concerned. Are they: **6.126**

- an equity partner (ie enjoying a share in the partnership assets including any profits of the business);
- a 'salaried partner' who may or may not enjoy an interest in the partnership assets, including its goodwill—the true nature of a salaried partner's status will require close examination of all relevant circumstances;

- an employee of the partnership—some salaried partners may, in reality, be employees, particularly if they have no share of the profits and no risk of liability for losses, even if they are remunerated by a combination of salary and commission on bills delivered and if some of the goodwill of the firm attaches to them personally (see paras 6.48 to 6.50 above)?

6.127 The status of members of a limited liability partnership (LLP) is likely to be considered using the same approach (see paras 6.45 to 6.47 above). Accordingly, all matters referred to in this section of the checklist will generally apply equally to members of an LLP.

6.128 Each partner will owe a duty of good faith to every other partner and the relationship between the parties is a fiduciary one (see para 6.51 above).

Garden leave

6.129 Is there an express garden leave provision for retiring partners? If so, principles similar to those in the context of an employment contract are likely to apply in considering its enforceability. If there is no express agreement, the partnership may nevertheless have certain rights to restrict the retiring partner's activities during the notice period, for example to assign particular types of work and places of work to that partner in the best interests of the firm (see paras 6.52 to 6.55 above).

6.130 An express garden leave provision should address the following issues and specify clearly:

- the circumstances in which a partner may be put on garden leave (generally after service of notice of retirement);
- who may make that decision and when;
- what will happen with regard to the partner's rights, especially as to remuneration, during the garden leave period;
- that garden leave will not affect the partner's entitlement to share in the profits of the practice.

(See para 6.56 above).

Implied restrictions after retirement from partnership

6.131 Does the partnership deed contain any express restrictions applying after retirement? If not, certain restrictions will be implied, namely:

- against canvassing clients of the old firm;
- enabling the retiring partner to be restrained by injunction from soliciting any person who was a client of the old firm prior to the sale to continue to deal with the retiring partner, or not to deal with the continuing partners (see paras 6.57 to 6.58 above).

Express restrictions after retirement from partnership

6.132 The enforceability of restrictive covenants against partners, after they have ceased to be partners, will be considered against the general principles affecting the enforceability of post-termination restrictions. Note that:

- the courts are more inclined to enforce a restrictive covenant against an equity partner who has sold his share of the partnership on retirement, treating the partner as akin to the vendor of a business;

- a salaried partner who does not own, and consequently who does not on retirement sell, any share in the partnership is more likely to be treated as being in much the same position as an employee.

(See paras 6.59 to 6.61 above.)

The following provisions are in general more likely to be enforceable against equity (than salaried) partners: **6.133**

- area covenants, provided the prohibited area is not more than is reasonably required for the protection of the practice—however, the relative mobility of the retiring partner and consideration of whether the area covenant prevents him using his professional skill at all will be relevant factors (see para 6.63 above);
- an area covenant prohibiting competing business in any part of the world may be valid but probably only in conjunction with a temporal restriction and providing it is limited to actual competitive activity (see para 6.64 above);
- even if a non-solicitation covenant may provide adequate protection, an area covenant may be upheld instead because, in practice, non-solicitation covenants may be difficult to police and enforce (see para 6.65 above).

And the following will be relevant factors: **6.134**

- the covenant, being effective on retirement, will apply when the outgoing partner receives a substantial sum representing his share of the goodwill of the business—if so, it will be closely analogous to a contract for the sale of a business—this element is most crucial;
- the covenant is between two professional people (who may have received independent legal advice at the time of entering into the covenant) rather than being a contract of employment;
- the covenant will apply equally between all the partners and so there will be mutuality between them;
- whether at the time of entering into the agreement, both parties are familiar with the nature and extent of the practice and the general area in which the practice was being carried on;
- the extent to which there have been discussions and negotiations on the terms of the restrictions;
- whether the party took legal advice about the agreement before entering into it;
- the likely duration of the parties' working lives, as the extent of the practice could very well differ over time;
- whether or not the agreement is injurious to the public interest;
- whether there is a temporal restriction on the area covenant and, if so, whether it is unreasonably long (bearing in mind that the parties are probably the best judges of what was appropriate at the time) and the nature of the partnership's business;
- whether the geographical extent is unreasonably large or whether it is necessary in order to bring the majority of the clients of the partnership within its scope.

(See paras 6.66 to 6.69 above).

Factors relevant in relation to the enforceability of non-solicitation/dealing covenants (in particular, against solicitors) include: **6.135**

- whether there was a legitimate interest of the firm which they were entitled to protect and whether the restraints are no more than adequate for that purpose;

- the fact that the non-solicitation/dealing covenant applies to all clients of the firm will not necessarily be fatal to its enforceability if, in practice, the retiring partner dealt with or had a connection with only a small percentage of those clients (see paras 6.74 to 6.75 above);
- mutuality of the contract will be a most important consideration (see para 6.76 above);
- the length of the period of restriction and any backward limitation on clients are unlikely to be susceptible to proof by scientific evidence. They should take account of the intermittent nature of a solicitor's employment by any particular client (see para 6.77 above);
- the length of the period of restriction will be considered leniently, as it will have been considered by experienced solicitors as the parties to the agreement (see para 6.78 above).

6.136   With salaried partners, the crucial issue of mutuality as between the contracting parties may be absent and restrictive covenants are more likely to be judged more in line with employment cases. As such, the geographical extent of any area restrictions will be looked at closely, as will the duration of non-solicitation/dealing covenants (see paras 6.79 to 6.84 above).

Joint ventures and other commercial agreements

6.137   If there is no share or business sale and no partnership/LLP, is there a commercial agreement in which the parties make their own contributions, whether in terms of finance or skills or in some other form, and also enter into restrictive covenants against competition in the future? If so, the doctrine of restraint of trade will apply in relation to the restrictions contained in the agreement. In order to be enforceable, the covenant must identify a legitimate interest of the covenantee seeking to enforce the covenant, which they were entitled to protect, and the restraints must go no further than reasonably necessary in the circumstances to protect that interest (see paras 6.98 to 6.101 above).

6.138   Legitimate interests in such circumstances may include:

- a clear commercial interest in safeguarding the covenantee against competition from the covenantors (as managers of a business into which the covenantee had made a capital contribution) for an agreed period (see paras 6.98 to 6.101 above).
- protection not only of the type of business carried on by the organization at the time the covenantor leaves but also new kinds of business for which preparations were in an advanced state at the time of their departure (see para 6.102 above).

In assessing the reasonableness of such covenants, the courts will be slow to interfere with the parties' own assessment of what was a reasonable period of restraint, especially where parties are of broadly equal bargaining power (see para 6.102 above).

6.139   If the covenantee is an investor, the nature and size of the investment made will be relevant.

- What is the size of the investor's stake in the company?
- Is there other protection for the investment, such as a patent or other intellectual property registration (see paras 6.103 to 6.106 above)?

6.140   Consider the reasonableness of the covenant in the interests of the public (see para 6.107 above).

7

THE INTERNATIONAL DIMENSION

Catherine Taylor and Mark Vinall

A. Introduction

In a business environment which is increasingly global, employee competition issues may **7.01** need to be considered in an international context and this can raise complex issues for the practitioner.[1] Employees based in the United Kingdom may be employed by foreign companies, or have responsibility for business outside the United Kingdom, which the claimant employer may wish to protect. Alternatively, an employee based outside the United Kingdom may be responsible for UK-related business. The employment contract may or may not specify which country's law is to govern the relationship between employer and employee, or which country's courts are to determine disputes between them (and where it purports to do so it may not be effective). The practitioner will need to consider which court or courts have jurisdiction to hear the claim (jurisdiction), whether English law[2] is the applicable law (applicable law) and how readily any judgment will be enforced (enforcement).

The law in this area is complex and the possible different factual scenarios are numerous. **7.02** This chapter will consider (albeit briefly) the issues which arise in relation to jurisdiction, applicable law, and enforcement both in terms of the contractual relationship between employer and employee, and in the situation where a competitive employer has induced a breach of contract or committed a similar tort. For further detailed analysis, see *Civil Jurisdiction and Judgments* (5th edn), by Briggs and Rees, and *The Conflict of Laws* (14th edn), by Dicey, Morris, and Collins (and the supplement thereto, which deals with some fundamental changes which have taken place since the publication of the main work);

---

[1] An indication of increasing interest in the international dimension in this field is found in a new publication edited by Wendi Lazar and Gary Siniscalco on behalf of the International Labor and Employment Law Committee of the American Bar Association, *Restrictive Covenants and Trade Secrets in Employment Law: An International Survey*, published by BNA (2010), www.bnabooks.com.

[2] All references in this chapter to English law and courts are to the law and courts of England and Wales.

cross-references to the specific parts of these books will be made where appropriate to aid further research.[3]

7.03 Before the questions of jurisdiction and applicable law can be addressed, it is important to identify the nature of the particular legal relationship in question, and the parties to it. The legal relationship will determine the rules which apply, which in turn determine the jurisdiction and applicable law. Most often in this context the relationship will be governed by an individual contract of employment but it could also be a relationship governed by some other form of contract or indeed the rules of equity (for example, breach of confidence) or tort (for example, inducing breach of contract). This chapter will deal with jurisdiction over and the law applicable to individual contracts of employment between employer and employee (as discussed below, these concepts have been interpreted broadly).[4] If another kind of contractual relationship is in issue recourse should be had to the text books referred to in paragraph 7.02 above. We will, however, touch on the applicable law in relation to non-contractual relationships at paragraph 7.44 below. Further guidance to the rules applicable to legal relationships other than the individual employment contract can also be found at paragraph 7.58 in the context of the international recruiting employer.

7.04 Finally, in international situations it is always tempting to try to divine what a court in a country other than England might do. Because of the structure of the legislation and the fact that judgments of the European Court of Justice are binding on all member states in respect of some of that legislation, an accurate prediction seems more possible here than in some other areas of law. However, this chapter is solely concerned with how questions relating to jurisdiction, applicable law, and enforcement would be determined by the English court. Procedural matters, in particular, can be dealt with very differently in other countries. If the answers relating to another forum are required, advice from a lawyer in that jurisdiction should be obtained.

B. The rules applicable to the relationship between employer and employee

Jurisdiction—which court should hear the claim?

7.05 The first issue the parties will need to consider is which court should hear any dispute in relation to alleged breaches of an employment contract. An employer based in England is usually likely to wish to bring proceedings in the English courts, for convenience and because the system is familiar. This will not always, however, be possible or appropriate, especially where the employee is domiciled in another state. Bringing proceedings before a court that has no jurisdiction can be a costly error. An employer should therefore consider questions of jurisdiction at the outset. In certain circumstances the employer may have a choice of possible jurisdictions, and should consider the tactical benefits of each.

---

[3] See also Goulding and Vinall, 'The English approach to jurisdiction and choice of law in employment covenants not to compete' (2010) 31 Comparative Labor Law and Policy Journal 375; and Goulding, 'The Challenge of Cross-Border Litigation from an EU Perspective' in Lazar and Siniscalco (n 1 above).

[4] See eg *Samengo-Turner v J & H Marsh & McLennan (Services) Ltd* [2008] ICR 18, paras 29–31; *Duarte v Black & Decker Corp* [2007] EWHC 2720 (QB), [2008] 1 All ER (Comm) 401, paras 50–3; and *Benatti v WPP Holdings Italy SARL and others* [2007] 1 WLR 2316, paras 45–51. See also paras 7.09 and 7.42(1) below.

The rules which apply to determining the correct or most appropriate jurisdiction in which **7.06** to bring a claim start from a determination of whether the Judgments Regulation[5] will apply. The Judgments Regulation has direct effect in the United Kingdom pursuant to the European Communities Act 1972. It binds the United Kingdom and the other member states of the European Union[6] in relation to jurisdiction in 'civil and commercial matters' determining the allocation of jurisdiction between different member state forums. It applies in modified form to determine allocation of jurisdiction between the courts of England, Scotland, and Northern Ireland.[7] Where the question concerns the allocation of jurisdiction between England and one of Iceland, Norway, and Switzerland, it is governed by the Lugano Convention,[8] which has a similar structure to the Judgments Regulation but some differences of detail. The remainder of this section will therefore consider the rules where the Judgments Regulation applies and where it does not.[9]

The Judgments Regulation

The Judgments Regulation in the first place gives jurisdiction to a court in a member state if **7.07** the defendant enters an appearance.[10] So, if an employer were to commence proceedings relating to a breach in the United Kingdom and the employee enters an appearance (other than to dispute jurisdiction), then the UK court will have jurisdiction, irrespective of what other rules would have applied and the fact that the UK courts' right to hear the case is otherwise weak. 'Entering an appearance' in England is effected by acknowledging service of the claim or by filing a defence.[11] The employer could, therefore, take a risk and commence proceedings (subject to the procedure necessary to do so) in the hope that the defendant employee will not contest jurisdiction.

A challenge to the English court's jurisdiction is made by an application under CPR Part 11. **7.08** If the defendant employee contests jurisdiction, then whether the English court has jurisdiction to hear the employer's claim will next be determined by Articles 18 to 21 of the Judgments

---

[5] Council Regulation (EC) 44/2001 (also known as the 'Brussels I' Regulation). This superseded the Brussels Convention of 27 September 1968, as amended on various occasions, and given force of law in England by the Civil Jurisdiction and Judgments Act 1982 (as amended). So far as the UK is concerned, it came into force on 1 March 2002 and applies to proceedings instituted (ie issued: see Judgments Regulation, Art 30(1)) in the courts of England and Wales after that date.

[6] As from 1 July 2007, when the Danish opt-out ended, these are: Austria, Belgium, Bulgaria, Cyprus, Czech Republic, Denmark, Estonia, Finland, France, Germany, Greece, Hungary, Republic of Ireland, Italy, Latvia, Lithuania, Luxembourg, Malta, Netherlands, Poland, Portugal, Romania, Slovakia, Slovenia, Spain, Sweden, and the UK. The Brussels Convention continues to govern questions of jurisdiction between EU member states and Aruba and the French overseas departments.

[7] Civil Jurisdiction and Judgments Act 1982, Sch 4.

[8] There are two Lugano Conventions. The updated 2007 Convention is in force in relation to Norway (from 1 January 2010), but not yet in force in relation to Switzerland and Iceland, to which the 1988 Convention remains applicable at the time of writing. Switzerland is expected to ratify it with effect from 1 January 2011. The detail of these conventions will not be considered in this book and for their application see Briggs and Rees (para 7.02 above), ch 3.

[9] See Figures 7.1 and 7.2 at the end of the chapter, which provide a simple route through the legislation.

[10] Judgments Regulation, Art 24.

[11] A defendant who fails to tick the box on the acknowledgment of service form indicating that he intends to contest jurisdiction does not lose his right to challenge jurisdiction provided he makes an application under CPR Part 11 within the time limit provided for by the rules: *IBS Technologies (Pvt) Ltd v APM Technologies SA (No 1)* (Michael Briggs QC, unreported, 7 April 2003). A defendant who acknowledges service indicating an intention to contest jurisdiction but thereafter fails to make a timeous application under CPR Part 11 confers jurisdiction on the court under Art 24: *Maple Leaf Macro Volatility Fund v Rouvroy* [2009] 2 All ER (Comm) 287 (not considered on appeal [2009] EWCA Civ 1334).

Regulation, which contain specific provisions relating to 'jurisdiction over individual contracts of employment'.[12] Where an employer commences proceedings against an employee who is domiciled in a member state, these rules are relatively simple: the employer may bring proceedings only in the member state in which the employee is domiciled.[13] Further, this rule cannot be derogated from by a jurisdiction agreement unless the agreement is entered into after the dispute has arisen.[14]

7.09   In a multinational corporate group, an employee may have contractual relationships with group companies other than the company with whom he has a contract of employment strictly so called. Some groups are arranged so that the employees are employed by a service company, which supplies their services to the trading companies in the group. Covenants may be expressed to be given for the benefit of the whole group. In such a situation, the English courts have interpreted the concepts of 'individual contract of employment' and 'employer' broadly, so that, for example, a separate bonus agreement will be regarded as part of the contract of employment, and a group company suing to enforce a covenant will be regarded as an 'employer'.[15]

7.10   It is possible, but unusual, that the employee may wish to seize the initiative and commence proceedings. In that case, where the employer is domiciled (or deemed to be domiciled)[16] in a member state, the employee has the choice[17] of commencing proceedings (a) in the courts of the member state where the employer is domiciled; or (b) in another member state, in the courts of the place where the employee habitually carries out work or in the last place where he did so; or (c) in another member state if this is the place where the business which engaged him is or was situated and he does not or did not habitually carry out his work in any one country.[18] Employees suing their employers can also rely on jurisdiction agreements even if concluded before the dispute arose.[19] Although an employee claimant has a much wider choice of forum, that is not to say the results are always convenient for the employee. *Glaxosmithkline v Rouard*[20] involved an employee working in Morocco who alleged that a UK company and a French company were his joint employers. However, he was not permitted to sue them both in France as the ECJ construed the Judgments Regulation literally, even though an action against them both in France would have been possible in a non-employment case under the provisions of Article 6 of the Judgments Regulation that deal with co-defendants, and even though this meant he would have to bring proceedings in two separate

---

[12]   See *Samengo-Turner v J & H Marsh & McLennan (Services) Ltd* [2008] ICR 18, paras 29–31 and para 7.09 below as to the meaning of individual contracts of employment; see also *Benatti v WPP Holdings Italy SARL and others* [2007] 1 WLR 2316 (CA) paras 45–51 (whether an agreement was a consultancy or employment agreement).

[13]   Judgments Regulation, Art 20(1).

[14]   Judgments Regulation, Art 21.

[15]   *Samengo-Turner v J & H Marsh & McLennan (Services) Ltd* [2008] ICR 18, paras 29–33.

[16]   An employer domiciled in a non-member state is deemed to be domiciled in a member state if the dispute arises out of the operation of a branch, agency or establishment in a member state (Judgments Regulation, Art 18(2), and see Civil Jurisdiction and Judgments Order 2001, Sch 1, para 11(2)(c)).

[17]   Subject to the *lis alibi pendens* provisions of Art 27: if the employer starts proceedings against the employee in the employee's member state of domicile, that will deprive the employee of his choice of seeking declaratory relief in the courts of another member state: the employee's only option will be to counterclaim in the court where the proceedings have been commenced.

[18]   Judgments Regulation, Art 19.

[19]   Judgments Regulation, Art 21(2); 23.

[20]   Case C-462/06 [2008] ECR I-3965; [2008] ICR 1375, a decision described by Briggs and Rees at 2.105 as 'almost too crass to be credible'.

member states. Further, an employee choosing to take the initiative and commence proceedings should consider the possibility that the employer could bring a counterclaim in the proceedings to gain a tactical advantage.[21]

In relation to whether an individual is domiciled in a member state, this will be determined by **7.11** the laws of that member state. For UK purposes, the relevant definitions are set out in Schedule 1 to the Civil Jurisdiction and Judgments Order 2001. To establish domicile, an individual must reside in the United Kingdom and the nature and circumstances of his residence must indicate that he has a substantial connection with the United Kingdom.[22] Residence of over three months is deemed to satisfy the 'substantial connection' limb of the test unless the contrary is proved.[23]

On the basis that the Judgments Regulation applies, in summary: if an employer wishes to **7.12** commence proceedings in England, it will only be able to do so if the employee is based in England sufficiently to establish domicile. If that is the case, no permission of the UK court needs to be sought before the employee is served, irrespective of whether the employee is in England when served.[24] If the employee is domiciled in another member state, but proceedings have been commenced in the English court then the English court should decline jurisdiction (unless the employee enters an appearance and does not contest jurisdiction).

Samengo-Turner v Marsh & McLennan

A further variation arises where an English domiciled employee is sued in a court outside **7.13** England. The Judgments Regulation is an EU-wide scheme based on national courts trusting one another to apply its provisions correctly. Thus, if a French employer sues an English-domiciled employee in France, it is the responsibility of the French court to decline jurisdiction. However, the same responsibility will not necessarily be recognized by a court in a non-member state; the courts of non-member states are not bound by the Regulation and will have their own rules of jurisdiction which may be less favourable to employees. For example, proceedings against an English-domiciled employee might be brought in the United States on the basis of a jurisdiction agreement that is enforceable there.

That is what happened in *Samengo-Turner v J & H Marsh & McLennan (Services) Ltd*.[25] **7.14** Controversially, the English Court of Appeal concluded that the employees had a 'statutory right' under the Judgments Regulation to be sued in England, and granted the employees an anti-suit injunction to restrain the proceedings being brought against them in New York. This decision has been the subject of sustained academic criticism,[26] on the grounds that (a) the Judgments Regulation creates public law obligations binding on member states' courts, rather than private law rights and obligations for litigants which can be enforced by injunction, and (b) the Regulation does not apply to agreements to confer jurisdiction on a non-member state court so the court should not have found that Article 21 invalidated the New York jurisdiction clause.[27] However, the present position is that *Samengo-Turner*

---

[21] Judgments Regulation, Art 20(2).
[22] Civil Jurisdiction and Judgments Order, 2001, Sch 1, para 9(2); see also *Bank of Dubai Ltd v Fouad Haji Abbas* [1997] ILPR 308.
[23] Civil Jurisdiction and Judgments Order 2001, Sch 1, para 9(6).
[24] CPR, r 6.33.
[25] [2008] ICR 18 (CA).
[26] eg A Briggs [2007] LMCLQ 433; A Dickinson (2008) 57(2) ICLQ 465.
[27] Although note that the parties agreed that that if Judgments Regulation, Arts 18–21 were engaged the fact that the employer was not domiciled in a member state was irrelevant (see *General Insurance v Group Josi* [2001] QB 68): *Samengo-Turner v J & H Marsh & McLennan (Services) Ltd* [2008] ICR 18, para 25.

is binding below the level of the Supreme Court. Accordingly, a multinational employer will risk a successful anti-suit injunction if it sues an employee domiciled in England for breach of their employment contract in a jurisdiction other than England, notwithstanding a jurisdiction agreement which is valid under the law applicable to the employment contract.

The common law rules

7.15   If, however, the defendant employee is not domiciled in any member state, then Articles 18 to 21 are inapplicable and English common law rules of jurisdiction will apply (by virtue of Article 4 of the Judgments Regulation) (see paras 7.16 to 7.21 below) (although the rules relating to *lis alibi pendens* as set out in the Judgments Regulation will apply[28]).

7.16   In summary, jurisdiction pursuant to the common law rules depends on service of process and service may be made as of right upon a defendant who is present within the jurisdiction, even if not domiciled there.

7.17   In relation to service within the jurisdiction of a defendant who is physically present, it is beyond the scope of this book to describe what procedural steps must be taken to do this.[29] If the defendant employee wishes the UK court to decline to hear the case on the basis that some other forum is more appropriate, he can apply to the court for a stay of proceedings on the ground of *forum non conveniens*.[30]

7.18   If the defendant employee is not present in the United Kingdom, the claimant employer must obtain the permission of the court to serve the defendant out of the jurisdiction.

7.19   Permission is applied for under CPR, rule 6.36. The application is heard without any notice to the defendant employee and his opportunity to challenge it comes once service has been effected.[31] A high degree of frankness is required of the claimant employer in making the application. The test will then be whether:

(1)   the claimant employer can show a good arguable case that one of the grounds under paragraph 3.1 of Practice Direction 6B applies;
(2)   the claimant's claim raises a serious issue to be tried;
(3)   the court is satisfied that England and Wales is the proper place to bring the claim; and
(4)   it is not unjust to require the defendant to defend himself in England and Wales.[32]

---

[28]   Judgments Regulation, Art 27 provides that where proceedings involving the same cause of action between the same parties are brought in the courts of different member states, the court which is seised of the proceedings second must stay its proceedings (the *lis alibi pendens* rule). This applies even where jurisdiction would otherwise be determined in accordance with Judgments Regulation, Arts 18–21.

[29]   See CPR, Part 6 for the general rules relating to service of process.

[30]   The application will be made under CPR, Part 11. The main authority on *forum non conveniens* is *Spiliada Maritime Corp v Cansulex Ltd* [1987] AC 460. See also Briggs and Rees (para 7.02 above), chs 4 and 5.

[31]   CPR, Part 11.

[32]   For a recent example of the application of this test in an employee competition situation, albeit breach of the equitable duty of confidence, see *Fries and another v Colburn* [2009] EWHC 903 (Ch).

In relation to the grounds specified under paragraph 3.1 of Practice Direction 6B, the most **7.20** relevant grounds will be the following (although, of course, the whole of that paragraph should be considered in each case):

(1) the claim is for a remedy against a person domiciled in the jurisdiction—note, however, that in the context of a claim relating to a contract of employment, this will mean the employee is domiciled in the United Kingdom, a member state, and as such the Judgments Regulation will apply, so this ground may be less relevant;[33]

(2) the claim is for an injunction ordering the defendant to do or refrain from doing an act within the jurisdiction;[34]

(3) the defendant employee is a 'necessary or proper party' to an action brought against a co-defendant (the so-called 'anchor' defendant) on whom the claim form has been or will be served on some other jurisdictional basis[35]—so, for example, if another employee or the defendant employer could be served without permission in the United Kingdom, then the court may grant permission;

(4) a claim is made in respect of a contract where the contract:
   (a) was made within the jurisdiction,
   (b) was made by or through an agent trading or residing within the jurisdiction,
   (c) is governed by English law, or
   (d) contains a term to the effect that the court shall have jurisdiction to determine any claim in respect of the contract;[36]

(5) a claim is made in respect of a breach of contract committed within the jurisdiction;[37]

(6) a claim is made that no contract exists where, if the contract was found to exist, it would comply with the conditions relating to contracts set out above.[38]

As stated above, even if permission to serve out of the jurisdiction has been granted on the **7.21** basis of paragraphs 7.19 to 7.20 above, it may be challenged by the defendant employee pursuant to Part 11 of the CPR, either on the basis that the paragraph 3.1 criteria are not satisfied, or on the basis that England is not 'the proper place' to bring the claim under CPR, rule 6.37(3).[39]

Applicable law

The other key question which must be determined is what law will govern the terms of the **7.22** contract of employment.[40] This question raises multiple issues. This book deals with the English law principles relating to employee competition, but if the employee works outside England and Wales, could another law apply different principles to the interpretation and enforceability of the contract? Equally, if the employee is recruited outside the United Kingdom, by a foreign employer, will this have an effect? To what extent are employers able to circumvent

---

[33] PD6B para 3.1(1)—see also para 7.15 above.
[34] PD6B para 3.1(2). Note that the injunction must be a genuine part of the proceedings and not claimed merely to bring the claim within the rule, and there must be a reasonable prospect of it being granted (*The White Book* (2010) para 6.37.27).
[35] PD6B para 3.1(3).
[36] PD6B para 3.1(6).
[37] PD6B para 3.1(7).
[38] PD6B para 3.1(8).
[39] See Briggs and Rees (para 7.02 above), chs 4 and 5.
[40] See also Figure 7.3 at the end of this chapter, which addresses this question.

English principles of restraint of trade by including in their employees' contracts an express choice of the law of a foreign country which is more tolerant of extensive restrictive covenants?

7.23   The rules about choice of law for contractual obligations are now contained in a European Community Regulation known as 'Rome I'.[41] The Rome I Regulation recently replaced the Rome Convention,[42] which had been incorporated into English law by the Contracts (Applicable Law) Act 1990. Since the Rome I Regulation only applies to contracts concluded as from 17 December 2009,[43] practitioners will be dealing with both regimes for some time to come. Fortunately, at least so far as relevant to this book, the differences between them are relatively minor. Nonetheless, the first question for the parties should be: when was the contract of employment concluded?

7.24   Note that both the Rome Convention and the Rome I Regulation apply to determine the applicable law of a contract irrespective of whether the applicable law is that of a member state or other foreign state.[44]

'Chosen' applicable law

7.25   The general principle, enshrined in Article 3, is that a contract is governed by the law chosen by the parties, if the parties have made a choice which is express or otherwise demonstrated with reasonable certainty by the terms of the contract or the circumstances of the case.[45] Therefore, in principle, if the contract expressly states the choice of law, that law will be the governing law even if it is a law which is otherwise unconnected with the contract. If the contract does not include an express choice of law, as stated in Article 3, a choice of law may nonetheless be implied from the surrounding circumstances, for example the fact that previous contracts specified a choice of law, so as to leave the court in no doubt that the contract was to be governed by the law previously chosen, or that the contract refers to specific provisions of a system of law.[46]

7.26   In *Chunilal v Merrill Lynch International Inc*,[47] the employee was seconded to Hong Kong temporarily. When his employment terminated he argued that the contract he entered into on his secondment (which contained no express choice of law) was subject to English law rather than Hong Kong law as contended by his employer. In doing so he argued that the law of the contract could be demonstrated with reasonable certainty from the fact that the previous contract was accepted to be subject to English law and the terms of the contract itself. The judge rejected these arguments on the basis that the employment became international and Hong Kong centric on the commencement of the secondment, the contract which was entered into on secondment was a novation of the previous contract and that the terms were not conclusive to satisfy the reasonable certainty test.[48]

---

[41] Council Regulation (EC) 593/2008 of the European Parliament and of the Council of 17 June 2008 on the law applicable to contractual obligations (Rome I) [2008] OJ L 177/6.

[42] Convention on the Law Applicable to Contractual Obligations (1980) as amended [2005] OJ C 334.

[43] Rome I Regulation, Art 29.

[44] Rome Convention, Art 1(1); Rome I Regulation, Art 2.

[45] Rome Convention, Art 3; Rome I Regulation, Art 3.

[46] See Contracts (Applicable Law) Act 1990, s 3(3)(a), which refers to the report on the Rome Convention by Professor Mario Giuliano and Professor Paul Lagarde and *Base Metal Trading Ltd v Shamurin* [2003] EWHC 2419 (Comm) paras 29–30, where the report is cited in relation to the test of reasonable certainty.

[47] [2010] EWHC 1467 (Comm).

[48] ibid, para 18 (Burton J).

In contrast it has been suggested that a reference to a collective agreement in a contract of **7.27** employment, where the collective agreement is definitely governed by the law of one country, may lead to the law of that country being the choice of law for the employment contract.[49]

Another example of where reasonable certainty might be established is where the contract **7.28** states that arbitration or litigation should take place in a particular country. Such a reference may (but will not necessarily) lead to the law of that country being adopted as the law of the contract.[50] Also, if references to the legislation of one jurisdiction are made in the contract this may lead to the laws of that jurisdiction being implied to be the chosen law.[51]

Importantly for present purposes, however, there is an exception to the principle of freedom of **7.29** choice in the case of 'individual employment contracts',[52] which provides that an express choice of law cannot deprive the employee of the protection of those provisions of the system of law that would be applicable in the absence of choice which cannot be derogated from by agreement.[53] Another more generally applicable exception is that a court may refuse to apply the specified law if to do so would be 'manifestly incompatible' with the public policy of the court's own legal system.[54] These qualifications are dealt with further below at paragraphs 7.34 to 7.39.

No chosen applicable law

Where the parties have not chosen which law should govern a contract of employment, **7.30** Article 8(2)–(4) of the Rome I Regulation provides:[55]

> 2. To the extent that the law applicable to the individual employment contract has not been chosen by the parties, the contract shall be governed by the law of the country in which or, failing that, from which the employee habitually carries out his work in performance of the contract. The country where the work is habitually carried out shall not be deemed to have changed if he is temporarily employed in another country.

> 3. Where the law applicable cannot be determined pursuant to paragraph 2, the contract shall be governed by the law of the country where the place of business through which the employee was engaged is situated.

> 4. Where it appears from the circumstances as a whole that the contract is more closely connected with a country other than that indicated in paragraphs 2 or 3, the law of that other country shall apply.

So, where the contract is silent as to the choice of law and none can be implied with reasonable **7.31** certainty, if the employee is working outside the United Kingdom a great deal, there is a risk that if it is mainly in one other country, the law of that country will govern the contract. The first question in assessing this risk will be where or from where the employee habitually carries out his work (Rome I Regulation, Article 8(2); Rome Convention, Article 6(2)(b)). The European Court of Justice has held in the jurisdiction context that the phrase should be

---

[49] See Dicey, Morris, and Collins (para 7.02 above), para 33-068.
[50] Rome I Regulation, recital 12; *Compagnie Tunisienne de Navigation SA v Compagnie d'Armament Maritime SA* [1971] AC 572; *Egon Oldendorff v Libera Corp (No 2)* [1996] 1 Lloyd's Rep 380.
[51] *Keiner v Keiner* [1952] 1 All ER 643.
[52] Rome Convention, Art 6(1); Rome I Regulation, Art 8 (1). See n 4 above as to the meaning of 'individual contract of employment'.
[53] Referred to in the Rome Convention as 'mandatory provisions', but the meaning appears to be the same.
[54] Rome Convention, Art 16; Rome I Regulation, Art 21.
[55] The wording of Art 6 of the Rome Convention differs in various respects, but the changes generally reflect pre-existing case law developments (albeit the ECJ case law concerns the employment provisions of the Brussels Convention/Judgments Regulation, as to which see below).

understood to refer to the place where the employee has established the effective centre of his working activities and where, or from which, he in fact performs the essential part of his duties vis à vis his employer. In establishing where that place is, the fact that the employee spent two-thirds of his time in one place, had an office there, and returned to the office after business trips was relevant.[56]

7.32 If it is not possible to establish a choice of law based on the 'habitual' test described above, the court will consider where the place of business through which the employee was engaged is situated (Rome I Regulation, Article 8(3); Rome Convention, Article 6(2)(b)). In *Chunilal v Merrill Lynch International Incorporated*,[57] the court on the facts rejected the submission that the employee was engaged by a London entity rather than one based in New York.

7.33 Finally, a court may decide, under Article 8(4) of the Rome I Regulation (Rome Convention, Article 6(2)), that the system of law identified by the rules in Article 8(2) and (3) should not apply because it appears from the circumstances as a whole that the contract is more closely connected with another country.[58] Factors which will be taken into account when applying this test are the residence or centre of business operations of the employer, the residence or domicile of the employee, and the language and form of the contract of employment. In *Booth v Phillips*,[59] the claimant's husband accepted an offer of employment as chief engineer on a seagoing vessel by email sent to an individual who was acting on behalf of some of the defendants in Jordan. The claimant's husband subsequently died in an accident at work and one of the questions to be determined by the court was which law governed the contract. There was no express choice of law. As the claimant's husband was aboard a seagoing vessel, he did not habitually work in any one country. Therefore, the contract would be governed by the law of the country in which the place of business through which he was engaged was situated. Accordingly, this would be Jordan. However, the claimant sought to argue that there was a closer connection with England. The court rejected this argument on the basis that, in the first place, there was a connection with Jordan, in that the managers of the vessel were a Jordanian company and the owners, albeit a Liberian company, appeared to carry on business in Jordan. The claimant argued that there were other connecting factors with England, namely that the employee was based there, would be flown to and from there by the employer, the United Kingdom would be the base for leave purposes, and he would be paid in the United Kingdom. The court held that these were connecting factors but not strong enough to outweigh the connection with Jordan. The choice of law specified in the contract relating to the ship itself did not connect the contract of employment with England and the court refused to be swayed by the argument that an officious bystander would think the contract was governed by English law.

Qualifications to the choice of law rules

7.34 The rules described above are subject to a number of qualifications, the most important of which for employee competition purposes is that relating to public policy dealt with at

---

[56] *Rutten v Cross Medical Ltd* [1997] ICR 715 at 728G ff. See also *Pugilese v Finmeccanica SpA, Alenia Aerospazia division* [2003] ECR 1-3573, paras 19–26; and *Chunilal v Merrill Lynch International Inc* [2010] EWHC 1467 (Comm), paras 16 and 19.

[57] [2010] EWHC 1467 (Comm), paras 14, 17, and 20.

[58] See Case C-133/08 *Intercontainer Interfrigo SC (ICF) v Balkenende Oosthuizen BV* [2010] 3 WLR 24 (a case on Art 4 of the Rome Convention) as to the strength of the presumptions.

[59] [2004] 1 WLR 3292. See also *Base Metal Trading Ltd v Shamurin* [2003] EWHC 2419 (Comm) paras 31–4.

paragraph 7.38 below. However, the exceptions relating to mandatory rules of law may also be significant and for this reason they are also dealt with below.

Mandatory provisions

As stated above, in the case of 'individual employment contracts',[60] even if there is a choice of law agreed between the parties, mandatory provisions of law may prevail. An express choice of law cannot deprive the employee of the protection of those provisions of the system of law that would be applicable in the absence of choice which cannot be derogated from by agreement.[61] Article 8(2) to (4) of the Rome I Regulation (Article 6(2) of the Rome Convention) will apply to determine which state's mandatory rules will apply (see paras 7.30 to 7.33 above). **7.35**

In the context of employee competition the English court has held in *Duarte v Black &* **7.36** *Decker Corp* (albeit at first instance and *obiter*) that the English law relating to restraint of trade does not amount to 'mandatory rules' which provide protection to employees for the above purposes, because it is part of the general law of contract rather than being specific to employment.[62] However, that is not to say that the law of a country other than England relating to restrictive covenants could not fall into the category of mandatory rules. Accordingly, if an employee is working outside the United Kingdom and even if there is an agreed choice of English law the employee may seek to rely on local mandatory rules which render post-termination restrictions unenforceable under this exception (for example the requirement to make payment during their term, which is common in other European jurisdictions, but not in the United Kingdom or United States). So, if the employee works mainly in another country where the mandatory rules of law would render the post-termination restrictions void, the employer may not be able to rely on their terms.

The Convention and Regulation also make provision for the application of what the Regulation **7.37** calls 'overriding mandatory provisions'—provisions which, according to the relevant national law, are to apply irrespective of the law otherwise applicable to the contract.[63] The Convention and Regulation permit the application of such provisions of the law of the forum. So far as English law is concerned, it is unlikely that the law of restraint of trade would fall into this category—the English court would not feel obliged to apply its own law of restraint of trade to a case that was not otherwise governed by English law and had no factual connection with England.[64] The Regulation also permits the application of 'overriding mandatory provisions of the law of the country where the obligations arising out of the contract have to be or have been performed, in so far as those overriding mandatory provisions render the performance of the contract unlawful. In considering whether to give effect to those provisions, regard shall be had to their nature and purpose and to the consequences of their application or non-application'.[65]

---

[60] As to what may be an individual contract of employment in this context see *Samengo-Turner v J & H Marsh & McLennan (Services) Ltd* [2008] ICR 18, paras 29–31; and *Duarte v Black & Decker Corp* [2008] 1 All ER (Comm) 401, paras 50–3; cf *WPP Holdings Italy Srl v Benatti* [2007] 1 WLR 2316 and see paras 7.08–7.09 above and para 7.42(1) below.

[61] Rome Convention, Art 6(1); Rome I Regulation, Art 8(1).

[62] [2008] 1 All ER (Comm) 401, paras 54–5 ; see also paras 7.40–7.43 below.

[63] Rome Convention, Art 7; Rome I Regulation, Art 9.

[64] See the discussion of the status of the restraint of trade doctrine under other common law systems in *Apple Corps Ltd v Apple Computer Inc* [1992] FSR 431, and contrast *Duarte v Black & Decker Corp*, supra, at para 61 emphasizing the factual connection with England when applying the 'public policy' exception discussed at para 7.38 below.

[65] Rome I Regulation, Art 9(3). This possibility is a novelty in English law, as the UK had opted out of the equivalent provision of the Rome Convention, Art 7(1), which was in broader and more uncertain terms.

Public policy

7.38 Whether the applicable law has been chosen by the parties or decided by the terms of the legislation, a further important exception applies which is that a court may refuse to apply the specified law if to do so would be 'manifestly incompatible' with the public policy of the court's own legal system.[66] It has been held in England that the doctrine of restraint of trade is a matter of public policy, and that therefore the English court will not enforce, in England, restrictive covenants governed by foreign law which would not be enforceable under English law.[67]

7.39 Finally, whether there is an express or implied choice of law agreed between the parties, or no agreed choice of law, for postings to an EU member state consideration should also be given to the provisions of the Posting of Workers Directive.[68]

Duarte v Black & Decker Corp

7.40 The application of the Rome Convention to employee competition in breach of an individual contract of employment including an express choice of law, was considered in detail by Field J in *Duarte v Black & Decker Corp*.[69] Although this case is referred to in the discussion above, it merits further examination here both as a useful illustration and in particular in response to the question: 'To what extent are employers able to circumvent English principles of restraint of trade by including in their employees' contracts an express choice of the law of a foreign country which is more tolerant of extensive restrictive covenants?'.

7.41 The case involved a senior employee of Black & Decker Europe, an English company which was a subsidiary of a large corporation based in Maryland, USA. Mr Duarte was based in England and his contract of employment was governed by English law. However, he was also selected for Black & Decker's Long-Term Incentive Plan (LTIP) which operated on a world-wide basis. Participation in the LTIP was governed by a separate contract, which contained an express choice of Maryland law. It also included restrictive covenants (a) not to accept employment with ten named competitors of Black & Decker, and (b) not to hire any of Black & Decker's employees or to induce any to leave, for two years following termination of employment by resignation or for cause. Mr Duarte subsequently received an offer of employment (in England) from one of the listed competitors and issued proceedings in England for a declaration that the restrictive covenants were unenforceable as being in unreasonable restraint of trade.

7.42 The English court, therefore, had to decide whether the enforceability of the covenants was to be determined by reference to Maryland law (the law chosen by the parties) or English law (England being both the place where Mr Duarte worked and the forum). Field J concluded:

(1) Although the covenants were contained in the LTIP rather than the employment contract, they were nevertheless part of an 'individual employment contract' within the meaning of the Rome Convention. The employment provisions of the Convention could

---

[66] Rome Convention, Art 16; Rome I Regulation, Art 21.

[67] *Duarte v Black & Decker Corp* [2008] 1 All ER (Comm) 401, paras 56–63, and see paras 7.40–7.43 below.

[68] Directive 96/71/EC, which provides for posted workers to be subject to the law of their home state rather than the state to which they are posted, subject to 'a nucleus of mandatory rules for minimum protection to be observed in the host country'. See Case C-319/06 *Commission v Luxembourg* [2008] ECR I-4323 as to the definition of mandatory rules.

[69] [2008] 1 All ER (Comm) 401.

not be 'circumvented by hiving off certain aspects of an employment relationship into a side agreement which, standing alone, would not amount to an individual employment contract because neither party promises to work for the other.'[70]

(2) The doctrine of restraint of trade was not one of the 'mandatory rules' of English law the protection of which was preserved by Article 6(1) of the Rome Convention (Article 8(1) of the Rome I Regulation). In Field J's view, that article only applied to 'specific provisions such as those in the Employment Rights Act 1996 and the Factories Acts whose overriding purpose is to protect employees', and not to restraint of trade which was 'part of the general law of contract'. Accordingly Mr Duarte could not rely on Article 6 of the Rome Convention.

(3) However, it would be 'manifestly incompatible' with English public policy under Article 16 of the Rome Convention (Article 21 of the Rome I Regulation) for the court to enforce a foreign law restrictive covenant so as to restrain an employee from working for a new employer in England, if that restrictive covenant would be unenforceable under English law.

Duarte thus indicates that the 'public policy' exception makes it impossible for an employer **7.43** to use an express choice of foreign law to avoid the application of English law limitations on the enforceability of restrictive covenants (at least where the proposed restraint will operate in England). It leaves open for argument what the English court would do in a case with a weaker factual connection to England. Furthermore, it is only a first-instance decision.[71] An employer wishing to challenge it in the higher courts might argue that the European concept of 'public policy' does not necessarily include all those parts of contract law to which English lawyers give that label,[72] and that *Duarte* gives insufficient weight to the requirement that the application of the chosen law should be not only incompatible, but 'manifestly' incompatible, with the public policy of the forum.

Non-contractual relationships

Not all of the claims considered in this book are contractual. Employers may wish to bring **7.44** claims for torts, breach of fiduciary duty, or breach of confidence, among others. The law applicable to non-contractual obligations is now[73] subject to the 'Rome II' Regulation,[74] which in many respects represents a wholesale change from the pre-existing law.[75] A detailed discussion of its provisions is beyond the scope of this book, but the key elements are briefly discussed in the following paragraphs.

---

[70] At para 52, following the decision on the equivalent provisions of the Judgments Regulation in *Samengo-Turner v J & H Marsh & McLennan (Services) Ltd* [2008] ICR 18 (see para 7.09 above).

[71] Note also that the conclusions referred to at paras 7.42(2) and (3) are strictly *obiter* as Field J found that the restrictive covenants would not be enforceable under Maryland law in any case.

[72] See eg Case C-319/06 *Commission v Luxembourg* [2008] ECR I-4323, in which the ECJ made clear that member states could not define for themselves what counts as 'public policy' for the purpose of the Posting of Workers Directive.

[73] The interpretation of the temporal scope of Rome II (Arts 31 and 32) has proved controversial and is now subject to a reference to the ECJ in *Homawoo v GMF Assurance SA* [2010] EWHC 1941 (QB). See also *Bacon v Nacional Suiza Cia Seguros y Reseguros SA* [2010] EWHC 2017 (QB). It is, at least, safe to say that the Rome II Regulation *does not* apply to any events giving rise to damage which occurred before 20 August 2007, and *does* apply to events giving rise to damage which occurred on or after 11 January 2009. The position in relation to events occurring during the intervening period is regrettably uncertain.

[74] Regulation (EC) 864/2007 of the European Parliament and Council of 11 July 2007 on the law applicable to non-contractual obligations (Rome II) [2007] OJ L 199/40.

[75] Contained in the Private International Law (Miscellaneous Provisions) Act 1995 for tort, and in case law for other forms of non-contractual liability.

7.45 The provisions of the Rome II Regulation are binding on the courts of member states and are of universal application irrespective of whether the applicable law is that of a member state or not.[76]

7.46 For tort and delict cases, the starting point[77] is that the applicable law is the law of the country in which the damage occurs (irrespective of the country in which the event giving rise to the damage occurred and irrespective of the country or countries in which the indirect consequences of that event occur) unless the claimant and the defendant both have their habitual residence in some other country at the time the damage occurs in which case the law of that country shall apply. If it is clear from all the circumstances of the case that the tort/delict is manifestly more closely connected with some other country, then the law of that country shall apply. A manifestly closer connection with another country might be based in particular on a pre-existing relationship between the parties, such as a contract, that is closely connected with the tort/delict in question.

7.47 For unjust enrichment cases which concern a relationship existing between the parties that is closely connected with the unjust enrichment (for example a contract), the non-contractual obligation arising out of the unjust enrichment is governed by the law that governs that relationship. Otherwise, the applicable law is the law of a country where both parties have their habitual residence, or otherwise the law of the country where the unjust enrichment occurs. For all these rules, where it is clear from all the circumstances of the case that the non-contractual obligation arising out of the unjust enrichment is manifestly more closely connected with a different country, the law of that other country shall apply.[78]

7.48 Subject to certain exceptions, the parties are free to agree to submit non-contractual obligations to a law of their choice, by an agreement entered into after the event giving rise to the damage occurred, or 'where all the parties are pursuing a commercial activity, also by an agreement freely negotiated before the event giving rise to the damage occurred'.[79] It seems unlikely that employees (or at any rate most employees) will be regarded as 'pursuing a commercial activity'.

Enforcement

7.49 Assuming the employer establishes the jurisdiction of the English court and is successful in obtaining judgment against the defendant employer, how would he go about enforcing judgment in the relevant overseas jurisdiction? Equally, if judgment is obtained outside England and Wales, how would the English courts react to a request to enforce it?

7.50 The English court has made an order with worldwide effect to enforce a contractual confidentiality undertaking (*AG v Baker*)[80] and injunctions against a foreign defendant to stop it doing acts in England or abroad.[81] The enforceability of such a judgment in a foreign jurisdiction depends on the private international law of the country where enforcement is sought, and local law advice will be required.

---

[76] Rome II Regulation, Art 3.
[77] Rome II Regulation, Art 4.
[78] Rome II Regulation, Art 10.
[79] Rome II Regulation, Art 14.
[80] [1990] 3 All ER 257.
[81] *Board of Governors of the Hospital for Sick Children v Walt Disney Productions Inc* [1968] Ch 52.

Where such an order is granted by a foreign court, the question then is whether it will be **7.51** enforceable in England, so as to give the employer recourse to the English court should the defendant employee breach its terms. The rules applicable in this scenario will depend primarily on which court makes the judgment.

- If it is a court in another part of the United Kingdom, section 18 of the Civil Jurisdiction and Judgments Act 1982 provides for enforcement by registration.
- For a judgment of a court of any other member state,[82] then the Judgments Regulation will apply to determine the applicable rules. For the EFTA countries it is the Lugano Convention.
- If it is a US court, common law rules will apply.
- For certain other jurisdictions, statute may apply. So, for example, a judgment of the Singapore court will be subject to the Administration of Justice Act 1920 and that of an Australian court, will be subject to the Foreign Judgments (Reciprocal Enforcement) Act 1933.[83]

If the Judgments Regulation applies, the situation is very straightforward. Article 33 pro- **7.52** vides that a judgment given in a member state shall be recognized in the other member states without any special procedure being required. So, if a UK employer obtains a judgment in a court of a member state, but wishes also to enforce it in England, all the process requires is that the judgment is registered in the High Court.[84] Equally, a judgment of the English court should be enforced in other member states with similar ease.[85] In principle, this includes interim injunctions.[86] It should also be noted that Article 31 of the Judgments Regulation gives the English court jurisdiction to order 'provisional, including protective' measures even where the English court does not have jurisdiction over the substance.[87]

There are four qualifications to this principle contained in Article 34 of the Judgments **7.53** Regulation, two of which are directly relevant to an employee competition situation. They are as follows:

(1) Recognition manifestly contrary to public policy (Article 34(1)). In the employee competition context, a judgment enforcing an extremely wide restraint on an employee, which would be contrary to the public policy rules relating to restraint of trade, could be struck down on this basis.[88]
(2) Certain judgments in default of appearance (Article 34(2)). If a default judgment has been entered and the defendant was not served with proceedings or given sufficient time to prepare his defence and he did not fail to take up an opportunity to challenge the judgment, then recognition will be denied. This could include orders obtained on a without notice basis.

If, however, the judgment was not given by a member state, then the UK employer will need **7.54** to rely on the common law rules relating to enforcement (which may include specific statutes,

---

[82] See n 6 above in relation to the definition of member state.
[83] Although the statutory provisions relate primarily to the recognition of money judgments and so are of less relevance in the context of employee competition.
[84] Civil Jurisdiction and Judgments Order 2001, Sch 1, para 2, and see CPR, Part 74.
[85] Although local law advice should be taken to confirm this is the case.
[86] See Case 125/79 *Denilauler v SNC Couchet Frères* [1980] ECR 1553; Case C-99/96 *Mietz v Intership Yachting Sneek BV* [1999] ECR I-2277.
[87] Subject to certain limitations: see case C-391/95 *Van Uden Maritime BV v Firma Deco-Line* [1998] ECR I-7091.
[88] cf *Duarte v Black & Decker Corp* [2008] 1 All ER (Comm) 401.

depending on the country in which the relevant court is situated). For the purposes of this book it is only possible to outline briefly the English courts' approach to recognition of a non-member state judgment.

7.55 The common law rules which apply to the enforcement of a non-member state judgment in England require that a judgment must be for a debt or definite sum of money, be final and conclusive on the merits, and that it must be given by a court regarded by English law as competent to do so. An obvious difficulty with this test is that it will not allow the enforcement of an interim order for an injunction made by a non-member state court. Under section 25 of the Civil Jurisdiction and Judgments Act 1982 (CJJA 1982) as amended, the UK courts have power to grant interim relief (including injunctive relief) in aid of foreign legal proceedings, including foreign proceedings in a non-member state.

7.56 It is not clear whether an English court would grant such interlocutory relief. Under section 25(2) of CJJA 1982, the court may refuse to grant the interim injunction made by the court of a non-member state 'if, in the opinion of the court, the fact that the court has no jurisdiction apart from under [its statutory power to grant interim relief in aid of foreign legal proceedings] in relation to the subject matter of the proceedings in question makes it inexpedient for the court to grant it'.[89] Where the defendant is domiciled in the jurisdiction of the English court and the order would be of material benefit to the principal court, it seems unlikely that the English court would refuse to grant an injunction on the basis of this provision.

7.57 The test applied by the English court in relation to applications for injunctions in support of foreign proceedings is essentially the same as for all interim injunctions in the English court (ie the applicant must demonstrate an arguable case, which would be a matter of the relevant foreign law and the subject of expert evidence, that damages are an inadequate remedy and that the balance of convenience weighs in favour of making the order). In addition, the court is unlikely to grant an injunction if it would be contrary to public policy. So, for example, even if a restrictive covenant would be enforceable under the law of a particular US state, it is nonetheless unlikely to be enforced by an English court by way of interim relief if, under English law, it constitutes an unreasonable restraint of trade.[90]

C. The international dimension and the recruiting employer

7.58 Thus far, we have concentrated primarily on the rules which will apply to the relationship between claimant employer and defendant employee in an international situation, and by default the rules applicable to a relationship governed by an individual contract of employment. However, what is the position in relation to proceedings brought against a defendant employer who is not based in England, or where the recruitment takes place outside England?

---

[89] For discussion of the meaning of 'inexpedient', see *Credit Suisse Fides Trust SA v Cuoghi* [1998] QB 818 and *Motorola Credit Corp v Uzan (No 2)* [2004] 1 WLR 113.

[90] See paras 7.42–7.43 above.

Unfortunately for the practitioner, the rules which will apply will be different, because the cause of action against the defendant employer will be a non-contractual claim, so the applicable law will be determined in accordance with the Rome II Regulation.[91]   **7.59**

In relation to jurisdiction, the claim against the rival employer will not be a claim relating to an 'individual contract of employment' so Articles 18 to 21 of the Judgments Regulation will not apply. The starting point is therefore that a defendant rival employer who is domiciled in a member state must be sued in the courts of that member state (Article 2 of the Judgments Regulation), but it may also be possible to sue him (a) in the courts of the 'place where the harmful event occurred or may occur' under Article 5(3) of the Judgments Regulation, or (b) where the rival employer is sued along with the employee, in the courts of the employee's domicile under Article 6(1) of the Judgments Regulation. Where the defendant is not domiciled in a member state, the common law rules described above apply. One of the grounds in paragraph 3 of Practice Direction 6B is that: 'a claim is made in tort where (a) damage was sustained within the jurisdiction; or (b) the damage sustained resulted from an act committed within the jurisdiction'.[92] The ground relating to co-defendants[93] may also be relevant where the recruiting employer is being sued alongside an employee over whom the English court has jurisdiction on some other ground.   **7.60**

The domicile of the employer, which is likely to be a corporation is determined according to different rules from those applying to the domicile of an individual. Article 60 of the Judgments Regulation states that a company is domiciled at the place where it has its statutory seat, central administration, or principal place of business. 'Statutory seat' means the registered office, or, if there is none, the place of incorporation, or, if none, the place under the law of which formation took place.   **7.61**

---

[91]   See paras 7.44–7.48 above.
[92]   PD6B para 3.1(9).
[93]   PD6B para 3.1(3).

D. Flow charts

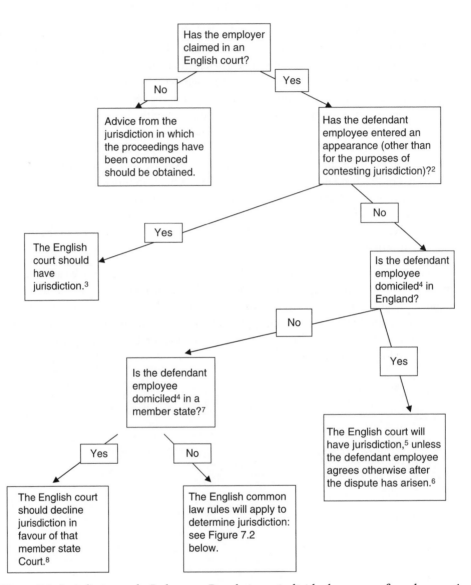

Figure 7.1 Jurisdiction—the Judgments Regulation—individual contract of employment[1]

[1] See n 4 above for the meaning of 'individual employment contract'.
[2] See para 7.07 as to what is meant by 'entering an appearance'.
[3] Judgments Regulation, Art 24 and see para 7.07 above.
[4] As to individual domicile for these purposes, see para 7.11 above.
[5] Judgments Regulation, Art 20(1) and see para 7.08 above.
[6] Judgments Regulation, Art 21 and see para 7.08 above.
[7] See n 6 above as to the definition of 'member state' for these purposes.
[8] See para 7.12 above.

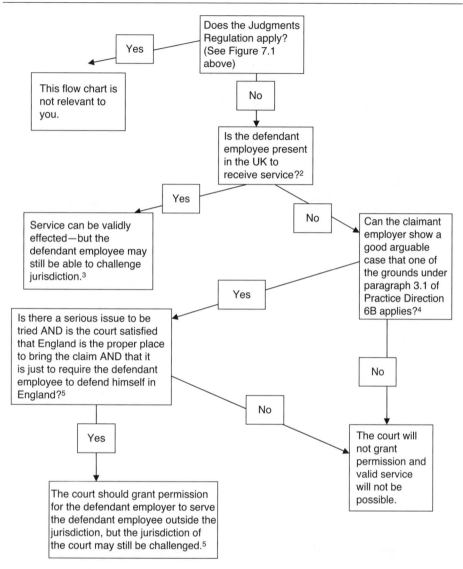

Figure 7.2 Jurisdiction—the common law rules—individual contract of employment[1]

[1] See n 4 above for the meaning of 'individual employment contract'.
[2] See paras 7.16 and 7.17 in relation to service in the jurisdiction.
[3] See para 7.17 above in relation to challenging jurisdiction.
[4] As to the grounds, see para 7.20.
[5] See para 7.21 above.

357

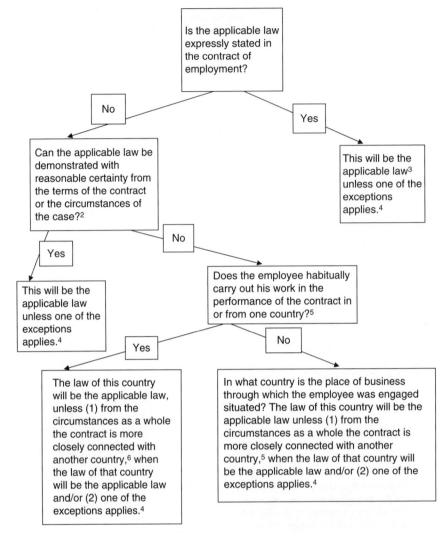

Figure 7.3 Applicable law of an individual contract of employment[1]

[1] See n 4 above for the meaning of 'individual employment contract'.

[2] See paras 7.25 to 7.29 above.

[3] See para 7.25 above.

[4] See the exceptions as a result of the application of the mandatory provisions (paras 7.35 to 7.37 above) and/or public policy (para 7.38 above), together with paras 7.40 to 7.43 on *Duarte v Black & Decker Corp* [2008] 1 All ER (Comm) 401.

[5] See paras 7.30 to 7.31 above.

[6] See paras 7.30 and 7.33 above.

8

COMPETITION, SPORT, HUMAN RIGHTS, AND INTELLECTUAL PROPERTY LAW

Kieron Beal, Nick De Marco, Hanif Mussa, and Sarah Sharma

A. Introduction

This chapter deals with a series of different but interrelated areas where problems of restraint **8.01** of trade or unfair competition regularly arise.

First, it is necessary in many employee and related competition cases to consider the poten- **8.02** tial impact of European Union (EU) and domestic competition law. These have assumed increasing importance in recent years, and an overview of the most relevant provisions and their application in this field, is provided below.

Secondly, one arena of activity where restraint of trade, under both domestic and EU law, has **8.03** assumed considerable significance is sport, particularly but not only in relation to the activities of sports governing bodies. The interpretation and application of the relevant legal principles in sports cases merit separate consideration, and an introduction to the subject is given in this chapter.

Thirdly, human rights jurisprudence is an integral part of the UK legal system, especially **8.04** since the Human Rights Act 1998 came into force, and employee competition is no excep- tion. Particular Convention rights feature more than others in this field, notably Article 8 rights to privacy, and Article 10 rights to freedom of expression. For this reason, a guide to the key sources and concepts of human rights law is set out below.

8.05 Finally, employee competition cases often trespass into the fields of intellectual property law, including copyright, patents, trade marks, and passing off. It is of great assistance for the practitioner to have, at least, a passing familiarity with the terminology and legal framework in these areas, and it is the aim of the concluding section of this chapter to provide that.

B. Competition law

Introduction

8.06 The basic prohibitions in EU competition law are set out in Articles 101 and 102 TFEU (formerly Articles 81 and 82 of the EC Treaty).[1] Article 101(1) TFEU prohibits, as incompatible with the internal market, all agreements between undertakings, decisions by associations of undertakings, and concerted practices which may affect trade between member states and which have as their object or effect the prevention, restriction, or distortion of competition within the internal market. This prohibition applies to agreements or concerted practices in particular which:[2]

- directly or indirectly fix purchase or selling prices or any other trading conditions;
- limit or control production, markets, technical development, or investment;
- share markets or sources of supply;
- apply dissimilar conditions to equivalent transactions with other trading parties, thereby placing them at a competitive disadvantage;
- make the conclusion of contracts subject to acceptance by other parties of supplementary obligations which, by their nature or according to commercial usage, have no connection with the subject of such contracts.

8.07 Article 102 TFEU provides that any abuse by one or more undertakings of a dominant position within the internal market or in a substantial part of it is prohibited as incompatible with the internal market in so far as it may affect trade between member states. This provision will not be considered in any detail below, since it is very unlikely to be engaged in restraint of trade cases.

8.08 Section 2 of the Competition Act 1998 (CA 1998) (the Chapter I prohibition) is in materially the same terms as Article 101(1) TFEU, and section 18 of CA 1998 (the Chapter II prohibition) is in materially the same terms as Article 102 TFEU, save for a threshold jurisdictional issue. While the EU competition provisions require that the anti-competitive conduct should produce an actual or potential effect on trade between member states or in a substantial part of the EU, the domestic competition provisions require an equivalent effect on trade in the United Kingdom or a substantial part of it.

8.09 The case law from the EU courts[3] is of direct relevance to the application of domestic competition law because section 60 of the CA 1998 requires consistency (so far as possible)

---

[1] The changes from Arts 81 and 82 EC to Arts 101 and 102 TFEU (the Treaty on the Functioning of the European Union) took effect with the entry into force of the Lisbon Treaty on 1 December 2009. Articles 81 and 82 EC were themselves formerly known, prior to the renumbering introduced by the Treaty of Amsterdam, as Arts 85 and 86 of the Treaty of Rome. Some of the earlier cases and decisions may accordingly refer to either Arts 81/85 and/or Arts 82/86 respectively.

[2] This non-exhaustive list is found in Art 101(1)(a)–(e) TFEU.

[3] Since the entry into force of the Treaty of Lisbon, the principal courts are the Court of Justice of the European Union (ECJ) and the General Court of the European Union (GCEU) (formerly the Court of First Instance or CFI).

between the domestic principles and the case law of the EU Courts. UK courts and regulators must also have regard to decisions of the EU Commission in this field.[4]

This part of Chapter 8 will examine:[5]   **8.10**

(1) the relevance of the prohibitions on anti-competitive behaviour to restrictive covenants;
(2) the interaction between competition law and the common law doctrine of restraint of trade;
(3) Article 101 TFEU and the Chapter I prohibition; and
(4) the potential application of Article 102 TFEU and the Chapter II prohibition.

The relevance of competition law to employers and employees

Before setting out the detail of these prohibitions and the grounds for exemption under them, it is necessary to consider the scope of their application in the area of restrictive covenants and other provisions or practices which restrict the ability of employees or consultants to move from one employer or firm to another.   **8.11**

As a general proposition, competition law does not apply to relations between an employer and an employee, since an employee is not treated as an economic undertaking distinct from the company or firm for which he or she works.[6] The European Court of Justice (ECJ) has recognized that the employment relationship between workers and the undertakings employing them is characterized by the fact that they perform the work in question for and under the direction of each of those undertakings. Generally, therefore, while employees are categorized as workers for the purposes of Article 45 TFEU (formerly Article 39 EC), their arrangements with employers fall outside the scope of Article 101 TFEU.[7]   **8.12**

Nonetheless, competition law may still be relevant in that: **8.13**

- individuals may in certain circumstances be classified as undertakings for the purposes of competition law.[8] Self-employed persons (such as consultants and the like) will be classified as an undertaking for the purposes of competition law if they carry on economic activity.[9] Any activity carried on by an individual (be it as a sole trader or as a partner) consisting in offering goods and services on a given market is an economic activity;[10]

---

[4] See also Case C-344/98 *Masterfoods* [2000] ECR I-11369, ECJ.

[5] Given the nature of this publication, the examination will necessarily be brief. For a more detailed treatment, reference should be made to P Roth QC (general editor), *Bellamy & Child, European Community Law of Competition* (6th edn, 2008), or R Whish, *Competition Law* (6th edn, 2008). For detailed accounts of the parallel investigatory powers available to the EU Commission in respect of suspected infringements of the EC competition rules, see C Kerse and N Khan, *EC Antitrust Procedure* (5th edn, 2005), and L Ortiz Blanco, *EC Competition Procedure* (2nd edn, 2006).

[6] Case C-22/98 *Jean Claude Becu* [1999] ECR I-5665, ECJ, paras 24–6. Similarly, agreements concluded in the context of collective bargaining between employers and employees and aimed at improving employment conditions are not, by reason of their nature and purpose, to be regarded as falling within the scope of Art 101(1) TFEU: Joined Cases C-180/98 to C-184/98 *Pavlov* [2000] ECR I-6451, ECJ, para 67.

[7] Case C-22/98 *Jean Claude Becu* [1999] ECR I-5665, ECJ, paras 24–6.

[8] The concept of an undertaking encompasses every entity engaged in an economic activity, regardless of the legal status of the entity and the way in which it is financed: Case C-67/96 *Albany* [1999] ECR I-5751, ECJ, para 77. See also the EU Commission decision in *Re UNITEL* [1978] 3 CMLR 306, where an opera singer was found to be an undertaking.

[9] *Pavlov* (n 6 above) paras 74 and 77. In Joined Cases T-217/03 and T-245/03 *FNCBV and others v Commission* [2006] ECR II-4987, the GCEU accepted that farmers would be undertakings for the purposes of competition law.

[10] Case 118/85 *Commission v Italy* [1987] ECR 2599, ECJ, para 7; and Case C-35/96 *Commission v Italy* [1998] ECR I-3851, ECJ, para 36.

- there is also some debate as to the extent to which employed professionals should be classified as an undertaking;[11]
- a person ceasing to be an employee who also either disposes of an interest in the undertaking or who thereafter carries on an independent economic activity in his own right may well be classified as an undertaking for these purposes.[12] Since competition law prevents restrictions on potential competition between undertakings, it catches both non-competition and non-solicitation clauses where a former employee sets up a business in potential competition with his ex-employer;
- it is arguable that the enforcement of a non-compete clause by a dominant undertaking may (in exceptional circumstances) offend Article 102 TFEU.[13]

8.14 The ECJ has ruled that collective agreements between bodies representing employers and employees, which on their face are caught by the competition rules, fall outside their scope because the social objectives of the TFEU and the Treaty on European Union (TEU) would be seriously undermined if such agreements were subject to Article 101(1) TFEU.[14] The same exclusion does not apply in the case of liberal professions, since their rules or agreements are not concluded in the context of collective bargaining between employers and employees.[15] Agreements concluded between employers and employees more generally which are outside the field of a collective bargaining agreement will not fall outside the scope of application of EU competition law.[16]

8.15 In addition, the doctrine of restraint of trade has been recognized as being a form of domestic competition law.[17] In the employment field, the competition rules are of particular importance in a commercial agreement or in conduct between undertakings which restricts the freedom of employees to work where and with whom they choose (for example, the kind of agreement at issue in *Kores Manufacturing Co Ltd v Kolok Manufacturing Co Ltd*).[18]

8.16 The competition rules also apply to the rules of professional associations and sports bodies which restrict the freedom of individuals or athletes to negotiate or contract with different undertakings, organizations, or clubs.[19]

---

[11] See the Opinion of AG Jacobs in *Pavlov* (n 6 above) at para 112: 'In principle employees who offer labour against remuneration fall outside the scope of Article 85(1). Employed professionals are, however, not typical "workers". Sometimes their "pay" is directly linked to the profits and losses of their employer and they do not really work "under the direction" of that employer. They therefore constitute one of the borderline categories envisaged in my Opinion in *Albany*. In the present cases it is however not necessary to take a final position on the issue because at the time of the decision under scrutiny all the LSV's members were self-employed medical specialists.'

[12] See Case 42/84 *Remia and others v Commission* [1985] ECR 2545, paras 17 to 20; and the Commission's decision in *Reuter/BASF* [1976] OJ L 254/40, [1976] 2 CMLR D44.

[13] There have been no reported cases of either Art 102 TFEU or the Chapter II prohibition being invoked in this way, but a potential argument that might be deployed is developed below.

[14] *Albany* (n 8 above).

[15] *Pavlov* (n 6 above), paras 67–70.

[16] ibid para 68.

[17] See *Days Medical Aids Ltd v Pihsiang Machinery Manufacturing Co* [2004] EWHC 44, [2004] 1 All ER (Comm) 991, para 265.

[18] [1959] Ch 108.

[19] Case C-519/04 P *Meca-Medina and Majcen* [2006] ECR I-6991, ECJ at paras 22–31. The distinction to be drawn is less about whether or not a rule is a 'sporting rule' and more about whether or not a particular rule has an effect on the pursuit of an economic activity. See also Case C-49/07 *Motosykletistiki Omospondia Ellados NPID (MOTOE) v Greece* [2008] ECR I-4863, ECJ, para 51.

The interaction between competition law and restraint of trade

Although the Commercial Court has held that the doctrine of restraint of trade is a form of **8.17** domestic competition law,[20] the principles and policy underlying the competition rules are very different from those of the restraint of trade doctrine. Although the terminology of both is similar, the different rules require different analyses.

First, while the restraint of trade doctrine is largely concerned with the effect of the restriction **8.18** between the parties, competition law is concerned with the object or effect of the restriction on competition in the market generally. The latter normally requires an economic analysis of the relevant product and geographical markets.

Secondly, the *effect* of an agreement may change with circumstances and thus fall within or **8.19** without Article 101(1) according to those circumstances. There is therefore a possibility that an agreement might initially be considered to be void as infringing Article 101 TFEU, but later be redeemed as circumstances change.[21] Conversely, an innocuous agreement might become pernicious if the factual and economic matrix changes. An example might be where, over time, the parties achieved a market share which provided the power to operate anti-competitively.

This, as Nicholls LJ noted in *Apple Corps Ltd v Apple Computer Inc*,[22] contrasts with the **8.20** common law of restraint of trade. The relevant time at which reasonableness of the agreement is to be considered under the restraint of trade doctrine is the time of entering into the contract which contains the restraint.[23] The court is concerned to see how an agreement is capable of operating viewed at the time the agreement is made, not to see how it has in fact operated viewed with the benefit of hindsight. The courts have refused to accept that supervening events (ie events subsequent to the start of the contract) can render an initially reasonable covenant unenforceable (and vice versa).[24] It would appear that the reason for this is that to hold otherwise would be to give rise to an unacceptable degree of legal uncertainty (*Gledhow Autoparts Ltd v Delaney*).[25]

In *Shell UK Ltd v Lostock Garage*,[26] Ormrod LJ expressed some concern about the pos- **8.21** sibility that a restrictive covenant might initially be enforceable but become voidable as being in restraint of trade through subsequent conduct post-dating the conclusion of the contract. In *Passmore v Morland plc*,[27] Chadwick LJ nonetheless accepted that this

---

[20] See *Days Medical Aids* (n 17 above), para 265.
[21] See *Passmore v Morland plc* [1999] 1 CMLR 1129, CA, paras 26–7; and Joined Cases T-125/97 and T-127/97 *Coca-Cola v Commission* [2000] ECR II-1733, GCEU, paras 81, 82, and 85. The fact that an agreement may benefit from a species of 'chameleon validity' in this way may cause problems for litigants in circumstances where an agreement was initially 'automatically void' pursuant to Art 101(2) TFEU but subsequently returns to life. The answer given by Chadwick LJ in *Passmore v Morland* (ibid), paras 28–34 was that the agreement would only be a nullity for as long as the prohibition in Art 101 was infringed. An agreement could accordingly return Lazarus-like to full binding effect as soon as the anti-competitive effect ceased. It is difficult to see how this reasoning could be applied to an agreement that is void because it has an anti-competitive object.
[22] [1991] 3 CMLR 49, CA, para 113.
[23] *Schroeder Music Publishing Co Ltd v Macaulay* [1974] 1 WLR 1308, 1309 *per* Lord Reid; *Watson v Prager* [1991] 1 WLR 726, 738 *per* Scott J.
[24] *Shell UK Ltd v Lostock Garage Ltd* [1976] 1 WLR 1187, CA, 1202 *per* Ormrod LJ.
[25] [1965] 1 WLR 1366, CA, 1377.
[26] [1976] 1 WLR 1187, CA.
[27] [1999] 1 CMLR 1129, CA, para 54.

concern at common law about 'a wholly novel doctrine' was now 'enshrined in Community competition law'.

8.22 Thirdly, unlike the restraint of trade doctrine, competition law is also enforced by public authorities: the EU Commission (in respect of multi-jurisdictional cases), the Office of Fair Trading (OFT), and the sectoral regulators.[28] Thus, conduct which may give rise to a claim for an injunction or damages under the CA 1998 may also be the subject of an investigation by the OFT. Court proceedings may be stayed pending any decision or orders of the OFT.

8.23 It may be preferable from a claimant's point of view to agree to such a stay, since the OFT's powers of investigation are stronger than the court's role in disclosure and the costs of the former will not be borne by the claimant. There is a novel procedure under section 47A of CA 1998, introduced in the Enterprise Act 2002 (EA 2002), which allows a damages claim to be brought in the Competition Appeal Tribunal (CAT) in reliance on a regulatory finding of infringement. In such a case, liability is largely undisputed and the principal issue is proving the loss alleged by the victim of the anti-competitive conduct (*BCL v Aventis SA*).[29]

8.24 Fourthly, a contract that offends Article 101(1) and is not exempt under Article 101(3) is 'automatically void' (see Article 101(2) TFEU). In contrast, a contract that is in restraint of trade is prima facie unenforceable if either party to the contract chooses not to abide by the contract and to invoke the doctrine.[30]

8.25 Fifthly, when an agreement infringes Article 101 TFEU, both parties to the agreement and third parties may bring actions for damages for loss arising from its operation.[31] In contrast, third parties may not bring a claim for damages in respect of a contract that is void as being in restraint of trade,[32] although they may obtain declaratory[33] or injunctive relief.[34]

8.26 The differences between the application of the competition law rules and the restraint of trade doctrine are also very significant in practice because of the supremacy of EU law rules. If there is a conflict of result, EU competition rules will prevail.

8.27 The ECJ held in *Walt Wilhelm*[35] (at paragraphs 4 to 7) that the parallel application of national and EU rules 'can only be allowed in so far as it does not prejudice the uniform application throughout the Common Market of the Community rules on cartels and the full effect of the measures adopted in implementation of those rules'. It stated that conflicts between EU

---

[28] There are Regulators for communications matters, gas, electricity, water and sewerage, railway, and air traffic services. The Regulators respectively are the Office of Communications (Ofcom); the Gas and Electricity Markets Authority (Ofgem); the Northern Ireland Authority for Energy Regulation (Ofreg NI); the Director General of Water Services (Ofwat); the Office of Rail Regulation (ORR); and the Civil Aviation Authority (CAA).

[29] [2005] CAT 4. See also *BCL Old Co Ltd v BASF SE* [2009] EWCA Civ 434, CA.

[30] *Esso Petroleum Co Ltd v Harper's Garage (Southport) Ltd* [1968] AC 269, HL, 297.

[31] See Case C-453/99 *Courage Ltd v Crehan* [2001] ECR I-6297, paras 25–7; and *Inntrepreneur Pub Co v Crehan* [2006] UKHL 38, [2006] 3 WLR 148.

[32] *Mogul Steamship Co Ltd v McGregor, Gow & Co* [1892] AC 25, HL at 39, 42–8.

[33] *Eastham v Newcastle United FC* [1964] Ch 413, 440 *per* Wilberforce J.

[34] *Nagle v Feilden* [1966] 2 QB 633, CA, 646 *per* Lord Denning MR.

[35] Case 14/68 *Walt Wilhelm* [1969] ECR 1, ECJ.

rules and national rules in the matter of the law on cartels must be resolved by applying the principle that EU law takes precedence.

In *BMW*,[36] Advocate General Tesauro took the view (although the issue was not ulti- **8.28**
mately resolved by the ECJ) that an exempt agreement under Article 101(3) TFEU could not be prohibited under national competition legislation (paragraphs 38 and 39) since 'the exemption granted to them cannot but prevent the national authorities from ignoring the positive assessment put on them by the Community authorities'. This applied whether the agreements were protected by individual exemption or an exempting regulation.

In *Bundeskartellamt v Volkswagen and VAG Leasing*,[37] Advocate General Tesauro addressed **8.29**
the separate question of a conflict between EU and national competition law 'not only where an exemption is granted . . . but also where the conduct at issue does not fall within the pro-hibition laid down in [then] Article 85(1)' (now Article 101(1)). In paragraphs 58 and 59 of his Opinion, Advocate General Tesauro considered, on the basis of the judgment in *Walt Wilhelm*, that where conduct was permitted by EU law as falling outside the scope of Article 101(1) it could not be prohibited under national competition rules.

In respect of the period after 1 May 2004, Article 3 of the Modernisation Regulation **8.30**
(Regulation 1/2003/EC)[38] under the heading 'relationship between Articles [101] and [102] of the Treaty and national competition laws' provides for the dual application of EU and domestic competition law by national courts in any situation where domestic competition law is to be applied. In this regard, Articles 3(2) and 3(3) state:

> 2. The application of national competition law may not lead to the prohibition of agree-ments, decisions by associations of undertakings or concerted practices which may affect trade between Member States but which do not restrict competition within the meaning of Article [101(1)] of the Treaty, or which fulfil the conditions of Article [101(3)] of the Treaty, or which are covered by a Regulation for the application of Article [101(3)] of the Treaty. Member States shall not under this Regulation be precluded from adopting and applying on their ter-ritory stricter national laws which prohibit or sanction unilateral conduct engaged in by undertakings.
>
> 3. Without prejudice to general principles and other provisions of Community law, paragraphs 1 and 2 do not apply when the competition authorities and the Courts of the Member States apply national merger control laws nor do they preclude the application of provisions of national law that predominantly pursue an objective different from that pursued by Articles [101] and [102] of the Treaty.

In the *Days Medical Aids* case,[39] Langley J held that the qualification in Article 3(3) was **8.31**
aimed at consumer protection laws relating to unfair contract terms and the like. The judge found that the common law doctrine of restraint of trade did not predominantly pursue different objectives to Articles 101 and 102. Langley J noted that there was a close relation-ship between the two sets of legal rules and referred in this regard to *WWF v World Wrestling*

---

[36] Case C-70/93 *BMW* [1995] ECR I-3439, ECJ.
[37] Case C-266/93 [1995] ECR I-3477, ECJ.
[38] Council Regulation (EC) No 1/2003 of 16 December 2002 on the implementation of the rules on com-petition laid down in Arts 81 and 82 of the Treaty ([2003] OJ L 1/1), as amended by Council Regulation (EC) No 411/2004 amending Regulation (EC) No 1/2003 ([2004] OJ L 68/1).
[39] See n 17 above.

Foundation[40] and *Apple Corps Ltd v Apple Computer Inc.*[41] He accordingly found that the common law doctrine of restraint of trade was a species of domestic competition law.[42]

8.32 The judge went on to find that, to the extent that there was a conflict between the application of the doctrine of restraint of trade and the application of Article 101 TFEU, the court was 'precluded by Community law from applying the restraint of trade doctrine'.[43] It follows that where an agreement falls within the potential scope of application of Article 101 TFEU,[44] but is either not prohibited by it,[45] or benefits from the application of the exemption conferred by Article 101(3) TFEU or a block exemption,[46] then the common law doctrine of restraint of trade cannot be applied. Langley J acknowledged that this may have significant repercussions in practice and warned that:

> It would, I suspect, come as something of a surprise to many practitioners if it were the case that the common law doctrine of restraint of trade even in the non-employment field had been emasculated let alone trumped by Community competition law.[47]

Article 101(1) TFEU and the Chapter I prohibition: general principles

Agreements, decisions, and practices

8.33 Some forms of concerted behaviour may be capable of classification under more than one of the descriptions 'agreement', 'decision', or 'concerted practice'. If parties cooperate so as to bring about a restriction of competition, little will turn on the precise form that the cooperation takes. The Commission, the General Court of the European Union (GCEU),[48] and ECJ have each given a broad definition to the concept of agreement. In *Tate & Lyle and Others v Commission*,[49] the GCEU applied earlier case law to the effect that an agreement to substitute interdependent conduct for competition would be made out when one only of the participants revealed its proposed pricing plans for the future, with the intention that the other participants would follow its lead. It was held that the requirement of independence did not deprive economic operators of the right to adapt intelligently to the existing and anticipated conduct of their competitors. Nonetheless it did strictly preclude any direct or indirect contact between such operators, where the object or effect was either to influence the conduct on the market of an actual or potential competitor or to disclose to such a competitor the course of conduct which they themselves had decided to adopt or contemplated adopting on the market.

8.34 In addition, the ECJ has held that evidence of anti-competitive behaviour may have to be established through inference and deduction. The court has gone so far as to indicate that in most cases, the existence of an anti-competitive practice or agreement must be inferred from

---

[40] [2002] EWCA Civ 196, paras 64, 66 *per* Carnwath LJ.

[41] See n 22 above, paras 109–13 *per* Nicholls LJ.

[42] See n 17 above, para 265.

[43] ibid para 266.

[44] Because, eg, it is an agreement that actually or potentially has an effect on trade between member states or in a substantial part of the EU.

[45] ibid para 263 and Art 3(2) of the Modernisation Regulation.

[46] ibid para 262 and Art 3(2) of the Modernisation Regulation.

[47] ibid para 254. See the *obiter* observation of Roth J in *Jones v Ricoh UK Ltd* [2010] EWHC 1743 (Ch), which indicates that the warning was justified.

[48] Formerly the Court of First Instance or CFI.

[49] Joined Cases T-202/98, T-204/98, and T-207/98 *Tate & Lyle and others v Commission* [2001] ECR II-2035, CFI, paras 54–61. The appeal by British Sugar in Case C-359/01 P *British Sugar plc v Commission* [2004] ECR I-4933, ECJ, did not address this point.

a number of coincidences and indicia which, taken together, may, in the absence of another plausible explanation, constitute evidence of an infringement of the competition rules.[50]

Thus the courts have not been unduly concerned about the rigid classification of con-   **8.35**
duct for the purposes of Article 101 TFEU, concentrating instead on the substance of any complaint.[51] Behaviour has been classified as amounting to both an agreement and a decision of an association of undertakings (the *Fire Insurance* decision),[52] and as constituting an agreement or at least a concerted practice (*Imperial Chemical Industries Ltd v Commission*).[53]

The Commission's decision in *Wood Pulp*[54] simply used the term 'restrictive practices'. The   **8.36**
GCEU has held that the Commission is entitled to describe a sustained process of collusion, some of which amounted to an agreement and some to a concerted practice, as 'an agreement and a concerted practice' without separately classifying the elements of each (*Rhone-Poulenc SA v Commission*).[55] However, the distinction can be of importance in determining who is liable for an infringement. The ECJ quashed the *Wood Pulp* decision[56] in so far as it found that price agreements concluded by the members of a trade association also constituted a decision by an association, since it was not shown that the association had played any separate role in the implementation of the agreements (*Ahlström Osakeyhtio v Commission*).[57]

Article 101 has been held not to apply to agreements between a principal and his agent.   **8.37**
Where the agent is a 'true' agent (through whom the principal contracts directly with customers) he forms part of the principal's undertaking (*Suiker Unie*).[58] The Commission has set out Guidelines on the issue,[59] which provide assistance in ascertaining whether an agreement is a 'true' agency agreement or not—the key factor being the commercial risk borne by the agent. This risk must be assessed on a case-by-case basis (*Daimler Chrysler v Commission*).[60]

Object or effect

The requirement for an 'object or effect' of restricting competition are alternative and not   **8.38**
cumulative.[61] The words are to be read disjunctively. In applying Article 101 TFEU to an agreement, the first step is to consider the object of the agreement in the light of its economic context in order to see whether its intended effect is appreciably to restrict competition.

---

[50]   Case C-407/08 P *Knauf Gips KG v Commission* [2010] ECR I-0000, ECJ, para 49. See also Joined Cases C-204/00 P, C-205/00 P, C-211/00 P, C-213/00 P, C-217/00 P, and C-219/00 P *Aalborg Portland and others v Commission* [2004] ECR I-123, paras 55–7.

[51]   See Case C-8/08 *T-Mobile and others v Raad van bestuur van de Nederlandse Mededingingsautoriteit* [2009] ECR I-4529, ECJ, para 24.

[52]   Commission Decision (EEC) 82/174 [1982] OJ L80/36, [1982] 2 CMLR 159.

[53]   Case 48/69 [1972] ECR 619.

[54]   Commission Decision (EEC) 85/202 [1985] OJ L85/1, [1985] 3 CMLR 474.

[55]   Joined Cases T-1/89, T-4/89, and T-15/89 [1991] ECR II-867, GCEU.

[56]   Commission Decision (EEC) 85/202 [1985] OJ L85/1, [1985] 3 CMLR 474.

[57]   Joined Cases 89/85, 104/85, 114/85, 116/85, 117/85 and 125/85–129/85 [1988] ECR 5193, [1980] 4 CMLR 901, ECJ.

[58]   Joined Cases 40–48/73, 50/73, 54–56/73, 111/73, 113/73, 114/73 *Cooperatieve vereniging Suiker Unie UA v Commission* [1975] ECR 1663, [1976] 1 CMLR 295, ECJ. See also Case C-73/95 P *Viho Europe BV v Commission* [1996] ECR I-5457, [1997] 4 CMLR 419, ECJ.

[59]   *Commission Guidelines on Vertical Restraints* [2000] OJ C291/1, [2000] 5 CMLR 1074.

[60]   Case T-325/01 *Daimler Chrysler v Commission* [2005] ECR II-3319, GCEU, paras 13 and 16.

[61]   Case C-8/08 *T-Mobile and others* [2009] ECR I-4529, ECJ, paras 28–30.

'Competition' means the competition which would exist in the absence of the agreement (*Société Technique Minière v Maschinenbau Ulm GmbH*).[62]

8.39　It is not necessary at this stage to consider what the effects of the agreement actually are (*Consten and Grundig v Commission*).[63] An agreement may therefore be caught by Article 101 before it has come into effect (see the *WEA-Filipacchi Music SA* Decision).[64] An agreement can be contrary to Article 101(1), whether or not the restrictive provision is complied with (*Trefileurope Sales v Commission*)[65] or enforced (*Dunlop Slazenger v Commission*),[66] or whether or not the attempt to restrict competition succeeds (*Compagnie Royale Asturienne des Mines SA and Rheinzink GmbH v Commission*).[67] The liability of a particular undertaking is established where it participates in a collaborative meeting with knowledge of its object, even if it did not proceed to implement any of the measures agreed at those meetings.[68]

8.40　If the analysis of the intended effects of the agreement does not disclose an appreciable restriction of competition, the actual effects of the agreement or practice should then be considered in order to see whether the agreement or practice in fact appreciably restricts competition (*Delimitis v Henninger Bräu AG*).[69]

8.41　The question of whether an agreement has the object of preventing, restricting, or distorting competition is a question of interpretation of the foreseeable effects of the agreement, not of the subjective intentions of the parties. Thus, the ECJ has held that it is not necessary to enquire which of the two contracting parties took the initiative in inserting any particular clause or to verify that the parties had a common intent at the time when the agreement was concluded; it is rather a question of examining the aims pursued by the agreement as such, in the light of the economic context in which the agreement is to be applied (*Compagnie Royale Asturienne des Mines SA and Rheinzink GmbH v Commission*).[70] Article 101 will apply whether or not the parties had a common purpose or one or more of them was apathetic or unwilling (*Trefileurope Sales v Commission*).[71]

---

[62] Case 56/65 [1966] ECR 235, [1966] 1 CMLR 357, ECJ; Case 99/79 *Lancôme SA v Etos BV* [1980] ECR 2511, [1981] 2 CMLR 164, ECJ; Cases T-374, 375, 384, and 388/94 *European Night Services v Commission* [1998] ECR II-3141, [1998] 5 CMLR 718, GCEU, para 136.

[63] Joined Cases 56, 58/64 [1966] ECR 299, [1966] CMLR 418; Case 123/83 *BNIC v Clair* [1985] ECR 391; Case 45/85 *Verband der Sachversicherer eV v Commission* [1987] ECR 405, [1988] 4 CMLR 264 (where the court said expressly that the same principles applied to decisions of associations of undertakings as to agreements). See also more recently Case C-510/06 P *Archer Daniels Midland Co v Commission* [2009] ECR I-1843, ECJ, para 140.

[64] Commission Decision (EEC) 72/480 [1972] OJ L308/52, [1973] CMLR D43 (*WEA-Filipacchi Music SA*); Commission Decision (EEC) 74/634 [1974] OJ L343/19, [1975] 1 CMLR D8 (*Franco-Japanese Ballbearings Agreement*); Commission Decision (EEC) 75/77 [1975] OJ L29/26, [1975] 1 CMLR D83 (*French and Taiwanese Mushroom Packers*); Commission Decision (EEC) 75/497 [1975] 2 CMLR D20 (*Virgin Aluminium Producers*).

[65] Case T-141/89 [1995] ECR II-791.

[66] Case T-43/92 [1994] ECR II-441, [1994] 5 CMLR 201, para 61.

[67] Joined Cases 29, 30/83 [1984] ECR 1679.

[68] See Joined Cases C-238/99 P, C-244/99 P, C-245/99 P, C-247/99 P, C–250/99 P to C–252/99 P, and C-254/99 P *Limburgse Vinyl Maatschappij and others v Commission* [2002] ECR I-8375, paras 508–10; Joined Cases C-189/02 P, C-202/02 P, C-205/02 P to C-208/02 P, and C-213/02 P *Dansk Rørindustri A/S and Others v Commission* [2005] ECR I-5425, ECJ, para 145. See also Case T-99/04 *AC-Treuhand AG v Commission* [2008] ECR II-1501, GCEU.

[69] Case C-234/89 [1991] ECR I-935, [1992] 5 CMLR 210.

[70] Joined Cases 29, 30/83 [1984] ECR 1679, 1703, 1704.

[71] Case T-141/89 [1995] ECR II-791.

In assessing the effects of an agreement upon competition, the agreement must be viewed in its **8.42** economic and legal context taking into account all relevant facts.[72] An agreement may have the object or effect of distorting competition, both where the parties are actual competitors and where they are potential competitors. The EU courts have stressed the importance of looking at the 'counterfactual' of what would have happened but for the agreement or practice.[73]

Prevention, restriction, or distortion of competition

An agreement may prevent, restrict, or distort competition within the meaning of Article **8.43** 101(1) TFEU not only as between the parties to the agreement but also as between one of them and third persons (*Etablissements Consten SARL and Grundig-Verkaufs-GmbH v EEC Commission*).[74] Article 101(1) thus applies both to agreements between actual or potential competitors, referred to as 'horizontal' agreements;[75] and to agreements between a supplier and an acquirer of goods or services, referred to as 'vertical' agreements.[76]

Article 101(1) is not infringed unless competition is 'appreciably' prevented, restricted, or **8.44** distorted. Similarly, Article 101(1) is not infringed where there would be no possibility of any appreciable competition even in the absence of the agreement. This may be the case, for example, where owing to extensive government regulation the scope for competition is minimal or non-existent (*Suiker Unie*).[77]

Article 101(1) applies to an agreement which prevents, restricts, or distorts competition in **8.45** the supply or acquisition of goods or services within the internal market, irrespective of the nationality or location of the parties (*Ahlström Osakeyhtiö v Commission*).[78]

An agreement which does not place restrictions on a party's commercial freedom ought not **8.46** to be regarded as one which prevents, restricts, or distorts competition on the grounds simply that it is onerous or commercially disadvantageous (*Bayer AG and Maschinenfabrik Hennecke GmbH v Heinz Sullhofer*).[79]

Restrictions necessary for the promotion of competition or to protect legitimate business interests

The EU courts have recognized that not every restriction on commercial freedoms will **8.47** amount to a restriction on competition for the purposes of Article 101 TFEU. This will be the case where the restrictions imposed by contract are ancillary to a contractual term

---

[72] Case C-399/93 *Oude Littikhuis and others* [1995] ECR I-4515, ECJ, para 10.

[73] Case T-328/03 *O2 (Germany) GmbH and Co v Commission* [2006] ECR II-1231, GCEU, paras 68–71.

[74] Joined Cases 56, 58/64 [1966] ECR 299, [1966] CMLR 418. See also Case 31/85 *ETA Fabriques d'Ebauches SA v DK Investment SA* [1985] ECR 3933, 3944, [1986] 2 CMLR 674, 684.

[75] Commission Notice: Guidelines on the applicability of Article 81 of the EC Treaty to horizontal cooperation agreements: [2001] OJ C3/2.

[76] See Commission Regulation (EU) No. 330/2010 of 20 April 2010 on the application of Article 101(3) of the Treaty on the Functioning of the European Union to categories of vertical agreements and concerted practices, OJ [2010] L 102/1. This 'Vertical Restraints Block Exemption' was formerly found in Commission Regulation 2790/2000 on the application of Article 81(3) of the Treaty to categories of vertical agreements and concerted practices, [1999] OJ L336/21; and the Commission Guidelines on Vertical Restraints [2010] OJ C130/1; and [2000] OJ C291/1.

[77] *Suiker Unie* (n 58 above) [1975] ECR 1663, 1923, 1924, [1976] 1 CMLR 295, 411.

[78] Joined Cases 89, 104, 114, 116, 117, 125–129/85 [1988] ECR 5193. See also Case C-306/96 *Javico v Yves St Laurent* [1998] ECR I-1983, ECJ.

[79] Case 65/86 [1988] ECR 5249.

imposed to protect a legitimate commercial interest. However, the case law has not always been consistent in its approach.[80]

8.48　The ECJ's practice has developed over time, so that it now examines the nature and scope of any putative restriction on competition in its full legal and economic context. In some cases, it has found that a restriction may fall outside the scope of application of Article 101(1) TFEU altogether. In others, it has considered that a restriction may be caught by the prohibition but benefit from an exemption under Article 101(3) where the overall pro-competitive benefit of an agreement or practice justifies it.[81]

8.49　The EU Courts and Commission have also considered whether legitimate commercial or business interests may be protected by means of restrictive covenants following the sale of a business from the perspective of EU competition law. Such covenants usually contain non-competition or non-solicitation clauses. It is these decisions that will probably have the greatest resonance for readers of this book. They are therefore covered in some detail.

8.50　In its decision in *Reuter/BASF*,[82] the Commission approved a non-competition clause found in an agreement governing the sale of a business. Dr Gottfried Reuter sold a group of undertakings which manufactured polyurethanes to BASF. The share transfer agreement prohibited Dr Reuter from carrying on certain activities in competition with BASF for a period of eight years. The Commission found that Dr Reuter was an undertaking for the purposes of Article 101(1). He engaged in economic activity through his firms and as a commercial adviser to third parties. The Commission noted that it was not normally necessary to protect the purchaser of a business when the material assets of a business were sold. However, in this case the sale included goodwill (including relations with customers) and know-how which were substantial parts of the assets transferred. In those circumstances, the Commission acknowledged that it was essential to prevent a vendor of a business re-acquiring his old customers directly or indirectly in the period immediately following the transfer. It was necessary to ensure that the vendor fully complied with his obligation to transfer the entirety of the relevant asset basis.

8.51　The Commission concluded that Article 101(1) would not, in principle, be infringed by a proportionate non-competition clause in such a context. However, the protection conferred had to be limited to the period required for the purchaser to take over undiminished the vendor's market position. Similar considerations also applied to restrictions on the use of know-how, which also had to be limited in time. The factors to take into account when assessing duration included the nature of the transferred know-how, the opportunities for its use and the knowledge of the purchaser. The geographical extent and subject matter of the

---

[80] Compare, eg, the approaches adopted in Case 56/65 *Société Technique Minière* [1966] ECR 235, [1966] 1 CMLR 357, ECJ; Case 56/64 *Grundig* [1966] ECR 299, ECJ at 342; Case 161/84 *Pronuptia de Paris GmbH, Frankfurt am Main v Pronuptia de Paris Irmgard Schillgalis* [1986] ECR 353; Case 258/78 *LC Nungesser KG v Commission* [1982] ECR 2015, 2069; and Case C-234/89 *Delimitis v Henninger Bräu AG* [1991] ECR I-935, [1992] 5 CMLR 210, ECJ.

[81] See eg the approach of the ECJ in Case C-309/99 *Wouters* [2002] ECR I-1577, ECJ where at para 97 the Court observed that not every agreement between undertakings which restricts the freedom of the parties necessarily falls within the prohibition laid down in Art 101(1), so that the rules governing the operation of the Netherlands legal profession did not fall within it. Contrast that with the judgment of the GCEU in Case T-112/99 *Métropole Télévision (M6) v Commission* [2001] ECR II-2459, at para 72, where the Court rejected the suggestion that any express 'rule of reason' fell to be applied at the Art 101(1) stage.

[82] OJ [1976] L254/40, [1976] 2 CMLR D44.

clauses ordinarily should reflect the markets in which the undertaking was active prior to the sale. On the facts, the Commission concluded that the clauses exceeded that needed to secure the legitimate protection of the transferred business.[83]

Subsequently, in *Mecaniver/PPG*,[84] the Commission followed a similar approach in relation **8.52** to a share sale agreement which contained a non-compete clause with a duration of three years. In this case, however, the Commission concluded that the clause was a 'legitimate means of ensuring the performance of the seller's obligation to transfer the full commercial value of the business'.[85] The period of protection and its geographical extent were not considered to be excessive. The Commission found that Article 101(1) was not infringed.

The approach adopted by the Commission in these cases was sanctioned by the ECJ in **8.53** *Remia BV and Verenigde Bedrijven Nutricia NV v Commission*.[86] The case concerned the validity of transfer agreements that contained non-competition clauses intended to protect the purchasers from competition from the vendor on the same market immediately after the transfers. The ECJ found that it was necessary to consider how competition would function without such clauses.[87] Since a business could not be effectively transferred if the vendor remained in competition with the business after the transfer, and since such transfers ultimately contributed to increasing the number of competitors in a market and therefore had beneficial effects on competition, the non-competition clauses did not contravene Article 101(1).[88] Nonetheless, in order to have that beneficial effect on competition, such clauses had to be necessary for the transfer of the undertaking concerned and their duration and scope had to be strictly limited to that purpose.[89]

Guidance as to the application of this case law may be derived from the GCEU's treatment **8.54** of ancillary restraints in *Métropole Télévision (M6)*.[90] If a restraint is a minor part of a major operation and is directly related and necessary to it, then that restraint may fall outside the scope of Article 101, if the main operation itself falls outside Article 101.

The ECJ has also held that Article 101 TFEU does not cut across legitimate interests held by **8.55** an undertaking in other areas, such as selective distribution systems,[91] exclusive copyright licences,[92] and plant breeders' rights.[93]

In England and Wales, these principles have been applied infrequently. Harman J in *Kall-Kwik* **8.56** *Printing UK Ltd v Bell*[94] was clearly reluctant to engage with the 'ingenious and elaborate' argument developed by the defendant's counsel based on Article 101 TFEU which the judge

---

[83] The Commission declined to consider whether or not an exemption should be granted under Art 101(3), since the agreement had not been notified to it under Regulation 17/62. The requirement for notification no longer applies.

[84] OJ [1985] L35/54.

[85] ibid para 15.

[86] Case 42/84 [1985] ECR 2545. Such cases are now dealt with under the EC Merger Regulation regime, Regulation 139/2004 [2004] OJ L24/1.

[87] ibid para 18.

[88] ibid para 19.

[89] ibid para 20.

[90] See Case T-112/99 *Métropole Télévision (M6) v Commission* [2001] ECR II-2459, paras 103–6.

[91] Case 26/76 *Metro SB-Grossmärkte v Commission* [1977] ECR 1875, ECJ.

[92] Case 262/81 *Coditel* [1982] ECR 3381, ECJ.

[93] Case 258/78 *Nungesser v Commission* [1982] ECR 2015, ECJ.

[94] [1994] FSR 674.

described as 'never . . . comprehensible in its effect'.[95] He concluded on the basis of the *Pronuptia* decision that a restrictive covenant found to be of reasonable ambit and extent did not fall within Article 101 TFEU at all. He nonetheless applied the doctrine of severance to dispose of any clauses in an agreement which would otherwise have been construed as anti-competitive.[96] He accordingly granted an interlocutory injunction to restrain the threatened breach of a restrictive covenant.

8.57 In *Pirtek (UK) Ltd v Joinplace Ltd*,[97] the defendants to a claim for damages and injunctive relief contended that a restrictive covenant contained in a franchise agreement relied upon by the claimant was void for infringing Article 101 TFEU. Briggs J noted that the relevant approach under section 2 of the CA 1998 would follow the approach adopted under Article 101 TFEU.[98] This in turn was similar, but not identical to, the approach followed at common law when assessing the validity of a restrictive covenant on competition following the termination of a franchise agreement.[99] The judge concluded that the level of know-how and assistance provided by the franchisor to the franchisee justified the relatively circumspect terms of the covenant in question,[100] so that the clause fell outside the scope of Article 101 TFEU. The judge reached a conclusion obiter that those aspects of the restrictive covenant which applied nationwide rather than merely in County Durham should be severed as going further than was necessary to protect the franchisor's legitimate commercial interests.

8.58 Finally, in *Robert Jones v Ricoh UK Ltd*,[101] the claimant sought damages for an alleged infringement of a confidentiality covenant in a trading agreement. The defendant applied for summary judgment in respect of the claim, on the basis that the clause in question fell foul of Article 101 TFEU and/or was in unreasonable restraint of trade. Roth J held that the covenant (which was of very wide range and scope) was a naked restriction on competition and fell within Article 101.[102] He found that the clause did not benefit from the Vertical Restraints Block Exemption and nor was he prepared to apply the provisions of Article 101(3) so as to grant an individual exemption for the clause.[103] The clause was accordingly void and unenforceable as a matter of EU competition law.[104]

Effect on trade between member states and the *de minimis* doctrine

8.59 An agreement, decision, or concerted practice must exercise an effect, direct or indirect, actual or potential, on the flow of trade between member states.[105] This is the case even if the actual effect of the agreement may well be to increase trade flows between member states.[106] The court has interpreted the test widely, so that even agreements between two undertakings

---

[95] ibid 680.

[96] Following *Chemidus Wavin Ltd v Société pour la Transformation et l'Exploitation des Résines Industrielles SA* [1977] FSR 181, CA.

[97] [2010] EWHC 1641 (Ch).

[98] ibid para 45.

[99] ibid para 50.

[100] ibid paras 57–60.

[101] [2010] EWHC 1743 (Ch), Roth J.

[102] ibid paras 42–4.

[103] ibid paras 45–7.

[104] ibid para 48. The judge declined to consider the alternative argument based on the common law of restraint of trade: see para 49.

[105] Case 56/65 *Société Technique Minière v Maschinenbau Ulm GmbH* [1966] ECR 234, ECJ.

[106] Cases 56 and 58/64 *Consten & Grundig* [1966] ECR 299, ECJ.

in a single member state do not fall outside it.[107] Similarly the threshold is met even if an actual effect on trade between member states is unlikely.[108]

Partly in response to the otherwise wide ambit of these provisions, the EU courts and the **8.60** Commission have developed a *de minimis* doctrine. The ECJ has held that an agreement falls outside the prohibition in Article 101(1) where it has only an insignificant effect on the markets, taking into account the weak position which the parties have in the product market in question (*Parker Pen v Commission*).[109] Article 101(1) does not apply to an agreement unless its effects, both upon competition and upon inter-state trade, are 'appreciable', ie not *de minimis*.[110] The *de minimis* doctrine will not be applied agreements containing 'hardcore' restrictions, including price and output fixing and market allocation.

Nonetheless, if an agreement affects competition, it is no defence for an individual participant **8.61** to say that his own position made no difference (*Ferrière Nord SpA v Commission*).[111] If market share is only slightly above the relevant threshold set out in the Notice on Agreements of Minor Importance, there is a heavier onus to show that the agreement in question has an appreciable effect on competition and trade (*European Night Services v Commission*).[112]

Article 101(2) and section 2(4) of the Competition Act 1998

Article 101(2) TFEU provides that agreements or decisions prohibited pursuant to Article **8.62** 101[113] are automatically void (*Robert Bosch GmbH*).[114] It has, however, been held that as a matter of EU law only those elements of an agreement which infringe Article 101 are void, unless it is impossible to sever them from the rest; the consequences for other provisions of the agreement are a matter for national law (*Société Technique Minière v Maschinenbau Ulm GmbH*).[115] Further, just as the prohibition under Article 101(1) is itself of transient application, in play only so long as an agreement offends the provision, so too the nullity under Article 101(2) can be transient. Thus, if circumstances change and the agreement in question ceases to offend Article 101(1), it will cease to be void under Article 101(2) (*Passmore v Morland plc*).[116]

Section 2(4) of CA 1998 similarly provides that 'any agreement or decision which is prohibited **8.63** by subsection (1) is void'.

---

[107] See Case 23/67 *Brasserie de Haecht v Wilkin (No 1)* [1967] ECR 407, ECJ; Case C-234/89 *Delimitis v Henninger Braü* [1991] ECR I-935 (foreclosure or compartmentalization of the national market may be suffi-cient to satisfy this threshold requirement).

[108] Case 161/84 *Pronuptia* [1986] ECR 353, ECJ.

[109] Case T-77/92 [1994] ECR II-549, GCEU.

[110] See Commission Notice on Agreements of Minor Importance which do not appreciably restrict compe-tition under Article 81(1) [2001] OJ C368/13; and Commission Notice on Guidelines on the effect on trade concept contained in Articles 81 and 82, [2004] OJ C101/81. See also Case 5/69 *Völk v Vervaecke* [1969] ECR 295, ECJ.

[111] Case T-143/89 [1995] ECR II-917, GCEU.

[112] Cases T-374, 375, 384, and 388/94 [1998] ECR II-3141, GCEU.

[113] Article 101(2) applies to an agreement or decision which is prohibited by Art 101(1) and not 'exempted' pursuant to Art 101(3). Article 101(2) does not provide that a concerted practice is void, presumably because concerted practices do not generally purport to give rise to legally binding obligations.

[114] Case 13/61 *Kiedinguerkoopbedrijf de Geus en Uitdenbogerd v Robert Bosch GmbH* [1962] ECR 45.

[115] Case 56/65 *Société Technique Minière v Maschinenbau Ulm GmbH* [1966] ECR 235, [1966] CMLR 357. See also Case 319/82 *Société de Vente de Ciments et Betons de l'Est SA v Kerpen and Kerpen GmbH & Co KG* [1983] ECR 4173, [1985] 1 CMLR 511, ECJ; Case 10/86 *VAG France SA v Etablissements Magne SA* [1986] ECR 4071, [1988] 4 CMLR 98, ECJ.

[116] [1999] 1 CMLR 1129, CA, paras 26–7 *per* Chadwick LJ.

Exemption

8.64   Article 101(3) TFEU provides that Article 101(1) may be declared inapplicable in the case of any agreement or category of agreements between undertakings, any decision or category of decisions by associations of undertakings, or any concerted practice or category of concerted practices which contributes to improving the production or distribution of goods or to promoting technical or economic progress while allowing consumers a fair share of the resulting benefit and which does not impose on the undertakings concerned restrictions which are not indispensable to the attainment of these objectives or afford such undertakings the possibility of eliminating competition in respect of a substantial part of the products in question.

8.65   Sections 6 to 11 of CA 1998 make provision for exemptions in similar terms to the relevant EU provisions.

8.66   Until 2004, an exemption under Article 101(3) could be granted either individually by a decision of the Commission; or in the form of a 'block exemption' in respect of a category of agreements, decisions, or concerted practices by Regulation. Nonetheless, under Article 9(1) of Regulation 17/62, only the Commission was able to grant an individual exemption. While national courts and national competition authorities could apply a Block Exemption Regulation, they could not grant individual exemptions for agreements. Furthermore, any agreement which had not been notified to the Commission could not benefit from an individual exemption under Article 101(3).[117]

8.67   Since 1 May 2004, however, and the entry into force of the Modernisation Regulation,[118] the power to grant exemptions has been de-centralized. The notification requirement has been swept away. Article 101(3) now operates as an 'exception' to Article 101(1). Exemption under Article 101(3) on an individual basis may now be obtained by a ruling from a national court or national competition authority on an individual basis. This change is intended, amongst other objectives, to free the Commission to pursue more serious cases of infringement of the competition rules as well as to encourage more private enforcement of the competition rules.[119] Thus, the Regulation seeks to replace the system of individual notification with a system where 'undertakings would have to make their own assessment of the compatibility of their restrictive practices with Community law, in the light of the legislation in force and the case law.'[120]

The potential application of Article 102 TFEU and the Chapter II prohibition

8.68   Article 102 TFEU prohibits an abuse by one or more undertakings of a dominant position within the internal market or a substantial part of it. The article contains a non-exhaustive list of abusive practices, such as imposing unfair purchase or selling prices or other trading conditions.

---

[117] This system of notification of agreements had the theoretical advantage of maintaining control over the enforcement of competition law in a unified body. But it created in practice a series of administrative delays for clearing or exempting pro-competitive agreements and an ever-increasing workload for Commission officials. This in turn led to considerable uncertainty in relation to large numbers of ordinary commercial agreements that appeared to fall potentially within the scope of the legislation but had little realistic prospect of ever being individually assessed by the Commission.

[118] See the reference at n 41 above.

[119] See the Commission White Paper on modernisation of the rules implementing Articles 81 and 82 of the EC Treaty, [1999] OJ C132/1, [1999] 5 CMLR 208; and the White Paper of 2 April 2008 on damages actions for breach of the EC antitrust rules (COM(2008)165 final).

[120] See para 77 of the modernisation White Paper, ibid.

The ECJ has recognized that the list of particular abuses found in Article 102 TFEU is not **8.69** exhaustive.[121] New types of abuse may (and no doubt will) emerge over time. In *Compagnie Maritime Belge*,[122] the court recognized that abuse may occur if an undertaking in a dominant position strengthens that position in such a way that the degree of dominance reached substantially fetters competition. In that case, the practice of operating 'fighting ships' in a liner conference, through selective price cuts timed deliberately to match those of a competitor, was held to be an abuse.

Furthermore, the General Court has held that Article 102 EC prohibits a dominant undertaking **8.70** from eliminating a competitor and thereby strengthening its position by using methods other than those which come within the scope of competition on the merits. Similarly, an intention to resort to practices falling outside the scope of competition on the merits cannot be said to be entirely irrelevant, since that intention can still be taken into account to support the conclusion that the undertaking concerned abused a dominant position, even if that conclusion should primarily be based on an objective finding that the abusive conduct actually took place (*Astra Zeneca v Commission*).[123] Whilst the fact that an undertaking is in a dominant position cannot deprive it of its entitlement to protect its own commercial interests when they are attacked,[124] it cannot use regulatory procedures in such a way as to prevent or make more difficult the entry of competitors on the market, in the absence of grounds relating to the defence of the legitimate interests of an undertaking engaged in competition on the merits or in the absence of objective justification.[125]

In *Atlantic Container Line*,[126] the General Court found that an abuse consisted of the outright **8.71** prohibition of individual service contracts in 1994 and 1995 and, where they were authorized with effect from 1996, the application of certain terms and conditions collectively agreed by the liner organization. The court found that the enforcement of such contractual terms (even if agreed with the parties themselves) resulted in a dominant undertaking weakening the competitive structure of the market to the detriment of consumers.

It is accordingly arguable that conduct by a dominant undertaking that consciously seeks to **8.72** drive a competitor from the market or exclude effective competition through non-price means might constitute an abuse in certain, exceptional circumstances. The Commission has, for example, indicated that a sporting organization might infringe Article 102 if it refused properly to certify, other than on legitimately objective grounds, a competing organiser or a market player meeting requisite quality and safety criteria.[127]

By parity of reasoning, on a given set of facts a decision by a dominant company to require **8.73** or enforce a non-competition clause or other form of restrictive covenant might be found to give rise to an arguable claim for infringement of Article 102 TFEU.

---

[121] Case C-333/94 P *Tetra Pak v Commission* [1996] ECR I-5951, ECJ, para 37.
[122] Joined Cases C-395 and 396/96 P *Compagnie Maritime Belge Transports v Commission* [2000] ECR I-1365, ECJ, paras 112 and 113.
[123] Case T-321/05 *Astra Zeneca v Commission* [2010] ECR II-0000, GCEU, paras 354 and 359.
[124] Case T-65/89 *BPB Industries and British Gypsum v Commission* [1993] ECR II-389, GCEU, para 69.
[125] Case T-321/05 *Astra Zeneca v Commission* [2010] ECR II-0000, GCEU, para 672.
[126] Joined Cases T-191, 212–214/98 *Atlantic Container Line and Others v Commission* [2003] ECR II-3275, para 1106.
[127] Commission Press Release IP/99/133 of 24 February 1999, [1999] 4 CMLR 596.

C. Sports cases

Introduction

8.74　The issues dealt with in this book may arise in a sporting context as in any other, with the principles to be applied broadly being the same; see, for example, the garden leave injunction granted in *Crystal Palace FC (2000) Ltd v Bruce*.[128]

8.75　However, the nature of professional sport means that the employment relationship can often contain some extraordinary features. For example, a professional football or rugby player is generally not free to walk out of his employment and join another club during the period of his contract, unless a 'transfer fee' is paid.[129] Such transfers of employment can only occur during specific periods, and are often strictly regulated, further restraining the freedom of the employee sportsman's ability to move between clubs as he chooses.

8.76　In addition, most sporting bodies have a framework of rules, commonly incorporated into the employee's contract of employment, that provide for the suspension of a sportsman from competing in competitions, and therefore carrying out his employment, for various disciplinary or doping offences. Whilst the principles governing the applicability and enforceability of these rules largely reflect those found within the disciplinary and regulatory framework of other professions, the frequency and scale of their application has led to a number of challenges to their legality on restraint of trade or competition law grounds.

8.77　The specific restraints that arise within sporting contexts, and their legality, are discussed in this section.

Restraint of trade

8.78　Restraint of trade issues can arise with a rather different emphasis in sports cases than in 'ordinary' employment cases because they will usually involve challenges to the enforceability of the rules of sports governing bodies which restrict participants' ability to earn a living from their sport.[130]

8.79　Examples of successful challenges of this kind include *Eastham v Newcastle United FC*[131] (football transfer rules and the 'retention' system), *Greig v Insole*[132] (rules banning participants in a breakaway series from playing test and county cricket), and *Stevenage Borough FC v Football League Ltd*[133] (qualifications for winner of Conference to be promoted to Football League—although the challenge failed on grounds of delay). An example of an unsuccessful challenge is *Gasser v Stinson* (athletics doping rules in restraint of trade but reasonable).[134]

---

[128] [2002] SLR 81. See ch 4 above.

[129] Although see, *Heart of Midlothian plc v Webster and Wigan AFC Ltd* (CAS/A/1298, 1299, 1300) for an examination of the compensation he must pay where he is able to leave during his contract after the so-called 'protected period' in football.

[130] Although, note that the court's power to grant declaratory relief in its supervisory jurisdiction over sporting bodies is not limited to cases of restraint of trade or unfairness. See *Mullins v McFarlane* [2006] EWHC 986 (QB).

[131] [1964] Ch 413.

[132] [1978] 1 WLR 302.

[133] *The Times*, 1 August 1996, affirmed 9 Admin LR 109, CA.

[134] 15 June 1988.

Once a rule is held to be in restraint of trade because it affects the claimant's ability to earn a living to a sufficient extent, the application of the reasonableness test requires consideration of the legitimacy of the governing body's aims and the proportionality of the means it has adopted to achieve them.

One area peculiar to sport which has raised arguments about restraint of trade concerns the rules regulating the transfers of players between different clubs. The regulation of player transfers, and the case law regarding the same, is most developed in football. **8.80**

Contrary to the situation within 'ordinary' employment law, the ability of a football player, for example (although there is now a very similar regulatory scheme in professional rugby), to leave his employment with one club and move to another is complicated by the fact that the previous employing club holds the player's registration (with the football authorities), without which the player is not entitled to play. Thus a player cannot simply walk out of one club and join another. Unless he does so in accordance with the rules, he will be prevented from playing for the new club. **8.81**

Previously, the situation in English law was worse for the player. Even if the player's contract had expired, and he was thus no longer playing for, or paid by, his former club, the player could be 'retained' by his previous club and could not transfer to another club without the consent of his previous club—which usually meant the payment of a fee. This situation was challenged by the player in *Eastham v Newcastle United FC*,[135] and the system was declared illegal and unenforceable as a restraint of trade. **8.82**

Later, the important decision of the ECJ in *Bosman*[136] (considered below) led to a further relaxation of the restrictions on professional footballers wishing to transfer between clubs within Europe. After *Bosman*, it is no longer possible for a club to demand the payment of a 'transfer fee' to transfer the registration of a player who is out of contract. **8.83**

Nevertheless, there remain restrictions on a player's ability to 'ply his trade' where he sees fit as a result of the transfer rules. For example, under the rules, a player can only move between clubs during a specified 'transfer window' (usually during the closed part of the season in the summer up until the end of August, and during the month of January). In addition, a player cannot approach another club to try and arrange a new contract for the period after his current contract ends, except in certain prescribed circumstances. **8.84**

This latter restriction was challenged in the *Ashley Cole* case. The former Arsenal player was disciplined by the Football Association Premier League (FAPL) for meeting Chelsea's then manager, José Mourinho, and Chief Executive, Peter Kenyon, on the basis that to do so was a breach of the FAPL's Rule K5 which states that a 'Contract player, either by himself or by any other Person on his behalf, shall not directly or indirectly make any such approach as is referred to in Rule K5 without having obtained the prior written consent of his Club'. **8.85**

An approach referred to in Rule K5 was 'an approach to a Club . . . with a view to negotiating a contract with such Club'. **8.86**

Mr Cole argued that Rule K5 was a restraint of trade, since the effect of the rule was to prevent a footballer from engaging in merely preliminary discussions regarding a possible move (such **8.87**

---

[135] [1964] Ch 413.
[136] Case C-415/93 *Bosman* [1995] ECR I-4921.

restraints are unusual in employment law) even to the extent of discussing potential employment in the period after the termination of his existing employment. The club, on the other hand, was free to discuss the future employment of the player without restriction.

8.88 The FAPL disciplinary commission, applying the *Nordenfelt* test,[137] agreed that Rule K5 was in restraint of trade but nevertheless found that it was reasonable. As regards the parties' interests, the FAPL disciplinary commission found that the restriction was not imposed unilaterally but was the result of a process of collective bargaining involving the Professional Footballers' Association.

8.89 As regards the public interest, the FAPL disciplinary commission found that 'we cannot escape the conclusion that if the restraint were removed, the number of transfers would increase and the balance between players' agents and the Premiership clubs would tilt significantly in favour of the agents (and their incomes). We consider that this is a potent consideration'.

8.90 The FAPL disciplinary commission was guided by authorities such as *McInnes v Onslow Fane*,[138] which indicate that a court should be slow to interfere with the manner in which a sporting body governs its own sport.

8.91 The FAPL Appeals Board, on Mr Cole's appeal, declined to follow the *McInnes v Onslow Fane* approach, since it considered that it applied to courts only (as an expression of non-expert judicial deference to the expert professional body) and not to the operation of discipline by the sporting authority itself. The Appeals Board upheld the finding that the restraint was reasonable since 'overall the Rule in fact works to the benefit of the great majority of players' and it was also in the public interest. A further appeal to the Court of Arbitration for Sport was rejected for lack of jurisdiction.

8.92 The aims involved in cases of this kind are generally very different from those involved in conventional employment cases, with governing bodies relying on considerations such as the need to preserve competitive balance in the competition, to maintain public interest in the sport, and to generate revenue for distribution to grass roots level. Sports governing bodies, whilst not public bodies for the purposes of judicial review, are subject to the same public law standard of review as public bodies are within the law of judicial review—see the detailed discussion in Lewis and Taylor's 2008 publication, *Sport: Law and Practice* (2nd edn) at paragraphs A2.8 and A4.1–A4.77 and also *Bradley v Jockey Club*:

> The function of the court is not to take the primary decision but to ensure that the primary decision maker has operated within lawful limits. It is a review function, very similar to that of the court of judicial review . . . the essential concern should be with the lawfulness of the decision taker: whether the procedure was fair, whether there was any error of law, whether any exercise of judgment or discretion fell within the limits open to the decision-maker, and so forth.[139]

8.93 These cases also highlight the ability of claimants to challenge restrictions other than the terms of contracts to which they are party, including individual decisions of governing bodies—see, for example, *Newport AFC v Football Association of Wales Ltd*.[140]

---

[137] See para 5.222 above.

[138] [1978] 1 WLR 1520.

[139] [2004] EWHC 2164 (QB), para 37 *per* Richards J, approved by the Court of Appeal [2005] EWCA Civ 1056. For an example of an independent sports' tribunal adopting this approach, see the decision of the FAPL Arbitral Panel (Sir Philip Otton, David Pannick QC, and Nicholas Randall) in *Sheffield United Football Club Ltd v FAPL* [2007] ISLR 77, paras 25–6.

[140] [1995] 2 All ER 87.

In a more conventional employment context, in *Leeds Rugby Ltd v Iestyn Harris*,[141] the alleged **8.94** restraint was an option in a compromise agreement entered into when Mr Harris left Leeds (the Release Contract) to switch from rugby league to rugby union and move to Cardiff RFC. The option provided that, should Mr Harris return to rugby league following a defined period playing rugby union, Leeds would have first option on re-employing him for a year. In fact, when Mr Harris returned to rugby league he went to play for Bradford Bulls instead.

Leeds brought an action for breach of contract against Mr Harris and for inducing breach of **8.95** contract against the Bradford Bulls. Mr Harris argued, amongst other things, that the option was an unreasonable restraint of trade.

Gray J found (at paragraph 49 of his judgment) that the option was 'a restraint on Mr Harris **8.96** because it prevents him, on leaving Cardiff prematurely, from playing rugby league for any club other than Leeds (as well incidentally as preventing him from playing rugby union for any other club). That is a restriction on the ability of Mr Harris to "ply his trade"'.

The judge found, however, that in the context of all of the relevant and interlocking agree- **8.97** ments that framed the original move from Leeds, the option had been reasonable both between the parties and in the public interest (paragraph 56). 'The Release Contract has only come into being because Mr Harris was determined to leave Leeds to play rugby union for Wales. At the time, Leeds had no alternative but to release him.'

Watson v Prager[142] provides a good example of the courts being prepared to intervene to find **8.98** a contract in a sporting context to be unenforceable because it amounted to a restraint of trade. The boxer, Michael Watson, had signed a boxer–manager agreement with the defendant. The agreement (like many professional sportsmen's agreements) was in the form prescribed by the relevant sports' governing body, the British Boxing Board of Control. The agreement was for a term of three years but gave the manager the option to extend it for a further three years if the boxer became a British, European, Commonwealth, or World champion. Watson became the Commonwealth middleweight champion in 1989, and the manager exercised the option to extend the contract's duration.

On the hearing of the preliminary issue as to whether the agreement was an unenforceable **8.99** restraint of trade, the court held that although it would not usually intervene in matters relating to the terms of a commercial contract or a contract of service freely entered into by the parties, the terms of the boxer–manager agreement were prescribed by the British Boxing Board of Control as the only terms a licensed boxer and licensed manager could enter into. It was not a normal commercial contract and public policy required judicial supervision to ensure the restrictions imposed were reasonable and not in undue restraint of trade. The agreement contained many restrictions on the boxer, and whilst a three-year contract with an option to renew on the boxer becoming a champion was reasonable, the option to renew for a period as long as a further three years was unreasonable.

The decision in *Watson v Prager* is interesting for various reasons. First, as many employment **8.100** contracts within professional sports are required to contain the standard terms of the governing body, there may be more justification for judicial intervention than in 'normal' employment

---

141 [2005] EWHC 1591 (QB), [2005] SLR 91.
142 [1991] 1 WLR 726.

contracts more freely negotiated. Secondly, the case has led to a suggestion that even in freely negotiated contracts, the courts may be prepared to intervene on restraint of trade grounds where the duration of the contract is for a particularly long period.[143]

8.101 In *Dwain Chambers v British Olympic Association*,[144] the effect of anti-doping rules on an athlete's ability to 'ply his trade' was considered by the courts. The athlete applied for an injunction challenging the legality of a BOC bye-law that made him ineligible for membership of the British Olympic team. He had previously been given a two-year suspension from participation in athletics for a doping offence but had returned to athletics. The BOC bye-law stated that any athlete who had been found guilty of doping was ineligible for selection for membership of the British Olympic team. But for this bye-law, Chambers qualified for a nomination by UK Athletics to the BOC for selection to be a member of the British Olympic team at the Olympic Games. Chambers argued that the bye-law was an unfair restraint of trade and thus illegal.

8.102 The court could not grant the relief (as it effectively disposed of Chambers' claim) unless it was satisfied to a high degree of assurance that Chambers could establish at trial that the bye-law fell outside the reasonable range of responses of the BOC and that he had been significantly restrained in his trade by the bye-law. The Olympic Games was an amateur event with no prize beyond the medals for the first three places, and it was not possible for the court to find that there had been a reviewable restraint of trade. There was no evidence that the bye-law had not been proportionate so as to give the degree of assurance sufficient to grant the relief sought.

D. Human rights concepts

8.103 In this jurisdiction, human rights are protected by the common law, by the European Convention on Human Rights (ECHR) incorporated into English law by the Human Rights Act 1998 (HRA 1998), and by the Charter of Fundamental Rights of the European Union (the Charter).[145] This section deals with the ECHR and the Charter.

The European Convention on Human Rights

8.104 In order to understand how the courts and tribunals enforce the rights protected under the ECHR in the context of employee competition cases, it is necessary first to consider the most important provisions of HRA 1998, namely sections 3, 4, and 6. Sections 3 and 4 of the HRA 1998 govern the relationship between legislation, including employment legislation, and the ECHR. Thus, section 3 requires that, so far as it is possible to do so, primary and secondary legislation must be read and given effect in a way that is compatible with Convention rights. This interpretive obligation applies to all concerned in interpreting a legislative provision, including courts and tribunals,[146] and its powerful nature was explained in the decision of the House of Lords in *Ghaidan v Godin-Mendoza*.[147] Section 4 of HRA

---

[143] See eg Lewis and Taylor, *Sport: Law and Practice* (2nd edn) para D1.22 and the footnote referring to the fact that this is the case in music industry cases, citing Beloff *et al*, *Sports Law* (1999), paras 4.77–9, and *Instone v Shroeder Music Publishing Ltd* [1974] 1 WLR 1308.

[144] [2008] EWHC 2028 (QB).

[145] OJ [2000] C364/01.

[146] See *Ghaidan v Godin Mendoza* [2004] 2 AC 557, para 106 *per* Lord Rodger.

[147] [2004] 2 AC 557, paras 25–33 *per* Lord Nicholls and paras 44–50 *per* Lord Steyn.

1998 complements section 3, and provides for the making of declarations of incompatibility where a domestic provision cannot be read or applied consistently with the ECHR. This power can only be exercised by those courts named in section 4(5) and does not extend to any statutory tribunal.

Section 6 of the HRA 1998 provides that it is unlawful for a public authority to act in a way which is incompatible with a Convention right. Accordingly, it imposes a free-standing duty on all public authorities to act compatibly with Convention rights. This would include public authorities carrying out functions in their capacity as employers. Section 6(3)(a) also specifies that a public authority includes any court or tribunal. Thus, a court or tribunal adjudicating an employment dispute between two private persons is required to conduct itself in a manner that is compatible with Convention rights. In order to comply with the duty under section 6, a court may be required to modify a common law cause of action such that it can be applied consistently with the Convention rights of the litigants, whether employer or employee. **8.105**

Turning to the substantive Convention rights protected under the HRA 1998, in confidential information and database cases, Article 8 of the ECHR may be engaged. Article 8(1) provides that everyone has a right to respect for his private and family life, his home, and his correspondence. Article 8(2) specifies the limited circumstances in which interference by a public authority with an individual's right under Article 8(1) may be justified. **8.106**

A key question is the extent to which 'private life' extends to business or professional activity. Statements by the European Court of Human Rights in *Nietmitz v Germany*,[148] *Amann v Switzerland*,[149] and *Rotaru v Romania*[150] all suggest that because an individual's private life may coalesce with or merge into professional or business activities, Article 8 'private life' protection also extends into these areas. **8.107**

This case law has been considered in *R v Worcester CC, ex p SW*[151] and in *R (D) v Secretary of State for Health*.[152] More recently, it has been analyzed by the House of Lords in *R (Wright) v Secretary of State for Health*.[153] **8.108**

Allegations of a breach of rights under Article 8 can arise in a number of contexts, although most commonly they concern the surveillance of employees. See for example, *McGowan v Scottish Water*,[154] where the EAT concluded that although an employee's right under Article 8 was engaged as a result of monitoring by private investigators engaged by a public authority employer, the interference was justified in all the circumstances, and the dismissal of the employee based on evidence obtained from such surveillance was upheld. **8.109**

Article 1 of the First Protocol to the ECHR provides that every natural and legal person is entitled to the peaceful enjoyment of his possessions and that no one shall be deprived of his possessions except in the public interest and subject to the conditions provided for by law and by the general principles of international law. **8.110**

---

[148] (1992) 16 EHRR 97, para 29.
[149] (2000) 30 EHRR 843, para 65.
[150] (2000) BHRC 449.
[151] [2000] HRLR 702, 717–19 *per* Newman J.
[152] [2006] EWCA Civ 989, para 35 *per* Laws LJ.
[153] [2009] 1 AC 739, paras 30–2 *per* Baroness Hale.
[154] [2005] IRLR 167.

8.111   Contractual rights are 'possessions' within the meaning of Article 1 (*Mellacher v Austria*;[155] *Wilson v First County Trust*[156]—as are the economic rights connected with running a business—*Tre Traktorer Akteiebolag v Sweden*;[157] *Wilson v First County Trust*;[158] *Capital Bank AD v Bulgaria*.)[159] Thus, the contractual right in a restrictive covenant as well as the economic interests which it seeks to safeguard may be possessions protected by Article 1 of the First Protocol.

8.112   Confidential information (especially client lists) and database content may also amount to 'possessions' protected by Article 1 of the First Protocol to the ECHR (*Van Marle v Netherlands*).[160] However, the protection of Article 1 does not apply unless and until it is possible to lay a claim to the possession concerned (*Ambruosi v Italy*).[161]

8.113   As a result of the application of the restraint of trade doctrine, a party may be deprived of the rights or possessions referred to above or there may be an interference with these rights. In those circumstances, the court (as a public authority under section 6 of HRA 1998) is obliged to justify the deprivation or interference. An interference or deprivation must be in the public interest and it must be proportionate (*Sprorrong and Lonroth v Sweden*).[162]

8.114   Article 1 recognizes that states are entitled, among other things, to control the use of possessions in accordance with the general interest, by enforcing such laws as they deem necessary for that purpose (*Parochial Church Council of the Parish of Aston Cantlow v Wallbank*).[163]

8.115   The scope of review of the object or purpose of a legal rule such as the restraint of trade doctrine is limited. National authorities have a wide margin of appreciation in implementing social and economic policies and their judgment as to what is in the public or general interest will be respected unless that judgment is 'manifestly without reasonable foundation' (*James v UK*).[164] National courts are bound, however, to review measures contested on this basis and, accordingly, to inquire into the facts with reference to which the relevant rule operates (*James v UK*).[165]

8.116   Any challenge in a restraint of trade case based on Article 1 of the First Protocol to the ECHR would be rendered even more difficult by the fact that ample procedural safeguards exist in the application of the restraint of trade doctrine. This is a relevant factor in assessing the proportionality of any interference (*Piron v France*).[166]

The Charter

8.117   With the entry into force of the Lisbon Treaty in December 2009, the Charter has been afforded enhanced legal status. Article 6(1) of the Treaty on European Union, as consolidated,

---

[155] (1989) 12 EHRR 391, paras 43–4.
[156] [2003] UKHL 40, paras 41–4, 106–9, 137, 168.
[157] (1989) 13 EHRR 309, para 53.
[158] [2003] UKHL 40, para 39, where Lord Nicholls observed *obiter* that '"Possessions" in art 1 is apt to embrace contractual rights as much as personal rights'.
[159] (2007) 44 EHRR 48, para 130.
[160] (1986) 8 EHRR 483, paras 41–2.
[161] (2002) 35 EHRR 125, para 20.
[162] (1982) 5 EHRR 35, paras 69, 73.
[163] [2003] UKHL 37, para 67 *per* Lord Hope.
[164] (1986) 8 EHRR 123, para 46.
[165] ibid para 52.
[166] (2002) 34 EHRR 14, para 43.

confirms that the Charter shall have 'the same legal value' as the EU Treaties. The United Kingdom has, however, negotiated a special exclusion in relation to the effect of the Charter. The Protocol on the Application of the Charter of Fundamental Rights of the European Union to Poland and to the United Kingdom ('the Protocol') provides in Article 1(1) that the Charter 'does not extend the ability of the Court of Justice of the European Union, or any court or tribunal of . . . the United Kingdom, to find that the laws, regulations or administration provisions, practices or action of . . . the United Kingdom are inconsistent with the fundamental rights, freedoms and principles that it reaffirms'. The precise legal effect of the Protocol is currently a matter of debate. It is to be noted, however, that many of the provisions of the Charter seek to reaffirm existing general principles of EU law and thus the rights recognized in the Charter may be enforceable by means other than reliance on the provisions of the Charter itself.

8.118 The field of application of the rights set out in the Charter is specified in Article 51(1), which provides that 'the provisions of this Charter are addressed to the institutions, bodies, offices and agencies of the Union with due regard for the principle of subsidiarity and to the Member States only when they are implementing Union law'. On the most expansive reading of the provision, the Charter simply applies as against member states within the sphere of competence of EU law. It may be, however, that a more restrictive meaning was intended and that Article 51(1) will be interpreted to mean that the Charter does not apply where, for example, member states are relying upon derogations provided for in specific fields of EU law.

8.119 Unlike the ECHR, the Charter makes specific provision for the freedom to choose an occupation and the right to engage in work. Article 15(1) of the Charter provides that 'everyone has the right to engage in work and to pursue a freely chosen or accepted occupation'. Article 15(2) provides that 'every citizen of the Union has the freedom to seek employment, to work, to exercise the right of establishment and to provide services in any Member State'. Pursuant to Article 52, these provisions are to be construed harmoniously with the legal sources from which they may draw inspiration, whether the EU Treaties (Article 52(2)), the ECHR (Article 52(3)), or the constitutional traditions common to the member states (Article 52(4)). Further, the imposition of restrictions on the exercise of these rights recognized in the Charter can be justified, although only where the conditions set out in Article 52(1) are met.

8.120 Should individuals be permitted to rely upon these rights recognized in the Charter in the domestic courts, it is possible to imagine an employee arguing that the particular terms of a restrictive covenant, although upheld under the restraint of trade doctrine, amount to an unjustified restriction on his right to work for whom he pleases under Article 15(1) of the Charter. The applicability of the rights recognized in the Charter would be clearest if the restriction in some way prevented the employee or ex-employee exercising his right to work or provide services in a different member state, and no derogation was relied upon.

E. Intellectual property

Introduction

8.121 The public policy requirements of the free movement of labour, on the one hand, and of the protection of intellectual property rights, on the other, are sometimes difficult to reconcile. The legal protection of intellectual property rights is derived from a desire to protect human creativity and endeavour. Where the fruit of that human endeavour belongs to an employer, the use of intellectual property rights to prevent a former employee from recreating the fruits of his employment for a third party competitor, has sometimes provided unexpected results. This section looks at how intellectual property rights might impact on employee competition, and how they might relate to restrictive covenants, confidential information, and garden leave. An in-depth examination of intellectual property law is beyond the scope of this book; this section therefore serves to highlight the main issues only.[167] Although intellectual property rights are often deployed together in litigation, we shall examine each right individually and consider particular or pertinent issues that arise in this context.

Copyright

The nature of copyright

8.122 Copyright protection arises in relation to original works that have been fixed, ie recorded in some form. Original works are those which have not been copied. To attract copyright protection, the work has to be 'fixed or recorded' although not necessarily by the person creating the work in the first place. The works in which copyright subsists fall into a number of categories and are described in section 1(1) of the Copyright Designs and Patents Act 1988 (CDPA 1988) as follows:

    (a) literary, dramatic, musical or artistic works;
    (b) sound recordings, films or broadcasts;
    (c) typographical arrangements for published traditions.

8.123 Pursuant to Section 11(2) of CDPA 1988 the copyright in a literary, dramatic, musical, or artistic work (if made by an employee in the course of his employment) will belong to the employer, subject to any contrary agreement between them. However, if the creator of the work is not employed[168] but contracted (such as a freelancer or consultant) then the first owner of the copyright (subject to agreement to the contrary) will be the creator. Assuming that an employer can show that the creator of the work was indeed an employee, then the next test to determine ownership will be whether they made the work in the course of their employment. This is not quite as straightforward as it may seem, and will turn on its facts.[169]

8.124 Copyright grants the exclusive right to prevent a third party from appropriating the skill and labour employed in the creation of that copyright work. Copyright infringement occurs where, without the licence of the copyright owner, a copy of the whole or a substantial part of the copyright work is made or if there is dealing in such a copy of the copyright work.[170] The test of whether a substantial part has been taken is a qualitative one, rather than a quantitative one. Accordingly, if a copyist takes the most important section from a long report (such as an executive summary) then qualitatively this may prove to be a substantial taking, even though quantitatively it may amount to a small portion of the overall report.

---

[167] For further texts on intellectual property, see: H Laddie, P Prescott, and M Vitoria, *The Modern Law of Copyright and Designs* (3rd edn, 2000); S Thorley *et al* (eds), *Terrell on the Law of Patents* (16th edn, 2006); and D Kitchin *et al* (eds), *Kerly's Law of Trade Marks and Trade Names* (14th edn, 2005).

[168] CDPA 1988, s 178.

[169] *Byrne v Statist* [1914] 1 KB 622.

[170] CDPA 1988, s 178.

Former employees and copyright infringement

Any allegation of copyright infringement against a former employee by an employer in relation to that employer's copyright work is likely to involve at least two legal concepts in copyright law. **8.125**

The first concerns how copying is proven. In determining whether copying has taken place, it is highly unusual for the copyright owner to be able to produce a witness who saw an act of copying taking place. As a result, a copyright owner must demonstrate details that have been reproduced or that are so similar that copying can be inferred or presumed from those similarities. It assists the copyright owner in his case if he can show that the plagiarist had the opportunity to copy. **8.126**

Once the presumption has been established, the burden then shifts to the defendant to show that he has independently created the work without copying. Often there are conflicts between the evidence presented by credible witnesses on both sides. In reconciling these conflicts of evidence, courts sometimes find that there has been subconscious copying. **8.127**

Where a former employee is accused of having committed the plagiarism, it is easy for the former employer to demonstrate that the former employee has at least knowledge of the relevant copyright works on which the employer is seeking to rely, where that employee is the creator of those works. **8.128**

The second concept which arises relates to what is referred to as the 'idea expression dichotomy'. Discredited more recently by the Court of Appeal as a US law concept that is not applicable to English law, it does, however, illustrate an important issue. Copyright is said to protect the expression and not the underlying idea. For example, copyright will protect the knitting pattern instructions for a jumper, but will not protect the design of a jumper made according to those knitting pattern instructions. The position is somewhat complex, however, since copyright goes beyond the mere protection of the form (for example the precise wording used in a novel) and extends to more ethereal parts of the work (such as the plot of the novel). As it is more difficult to prove that these ethereal elements have been taken, copyright owners are often hard pressed to raise a presumption of copying because the actual form of wording has not been replicated although there may be strong similarity with ideas. Again, in this context, at least an employer can show that a former employee had knowledge of the original work. **8.129**

The fact that a common link exists does not automatically result in infringement. This is best illustrated by the case of *Cantor Fitzgerald v Tradition*.[171] Cantor Fitzgerald as a bond broker, operated a sophisticated computer programming system which it had developed with a team of in-house computer programmers. The team had written the software code in its entirety. Tradition wished to replicate Cantor Fitzgerald's success, and employed the software team to write a similar trading system. Cantor Fitzgerald issued proceedings for copyright infringement in the Tradition trading system. After initial denials, Tradition admitted that approximately 2 per cent of the code in the Tradition system had been copied from the Cantor Fitzgerald system. It maintained, however, that the remainder of the code had been independently created without reference to the Cantor Fitzgerald system. Cantor Fitzgerald pursued the action in relation to the remaining code. Despite the fact that Cantor Fitzgerald's team had taken a copy of the Cantor Fitzgerald code with them, had copied the code into the Tradition system, **8.130**

---

[171] *Cantor Fitzgerald International (an unlimited company) v Tradition (UK) Ltd* [2001] EWCA Civ 942, CA, [2000] RPC 95.

and that Tradition had admitted that 2 per cent of their code had been copied, Pumfrey J held that the remaining code had not been copied. The remaining similarities in the system were explicable and were not derived from Cantor Fitzgerald's source code.

8.131 Any former employee seeking to replicate previous copyright works will always be subject to closer scrutiny than a third party who creates a work that looks similar to an original. The presumption of copying is much more easily made out, and therefore the burden on the former employee to demonstrate independent creation is that much greater.

Designs

8.132 UK design right shares many of the characteristics of copyright and is also governed by the provisions of the CDPA 1988. It is an unregistered right and protects the design of any aspect of the shape or configuration (whether internal or external) of the whole or part of an article.[172] As with copyright, the employer will be the owner of unregistered design right in designs created by employees during the course of their employment.[173]

8.133 UK registered designs are governed by the Registered Designs Act 1949. A registered design can protect the appearance of the whole or part of a product resulting from the features of, in particular, the lines, contours, colours, shape, texture, or materials of the product or its ornamentation.[174] Again, where a design is created by an employee in the course of their employment, the employer shall be treated as the original proprietor of the design (and shall have the right to apply for design protection).[175]

8.134 An important distinction between copyright and UK designs is that where a design is created in pursuance of a commission (ie the designer is not an employee), the person commissioning the design shall be treated as the original proprietor of the design.[176]

8.135 In addition to the two forms of UK design protection, European Community wide design protection (registered and unregistered) may protect designs created by employees. Where a design is developed by an employee in the execution of his duties or following instructions given by his employer, the Community design shall vest in the employer, unless otherwise agreed or specified under national law.[177]

Databases

The database right[178]

8.136 Compilations of data can be protected by copyright as literary works. In addition, the Copyright and Rights in Databases Regulations 1997 (the Database Regulations) introduced a new, separate database right. The Database Regulations define a database as 'a collection of independent works, data or other materials which are arranged in a systematic way and are individually accessible by electronic or other means'.[179]

---

[172] CDPA 1988, s 213.
[173] CDPA 1988, s 215.
[174] Registered Designs Act 1949, s 1(2).
[175] Registered Designs Act 1949, ss 2(1B) and 3(2).
[176] CDPA 1988, s 215(2) and Registered Designs Act 1949, s 2(1A).
[177] Council Regulation 6/2002/EC on Community Designs, Art 14(3).
[178] The Database Right is discussed more fully in Chapter 3 above, and so only a brief summary is provided here.
[179] Regulation 6.

Pursuant to Regulation 14(2) of the Database Regulations, an employer will be the owner of **8.137** a database made by an employee in the course of their employment, subject to any agreement to the contrary. The ownership of databases created by employees was considered in the case of *Pennwell Publishing (UK) Ltd and other v Ornstein*.[180] The case concerned a contact list held by an employee within Outlook on his employer's computer systems. The list had been built up by the employee and included contacts he had brought with him at the outset of his employment along with other contacts which he had developed during the course of and for the purposes of his employment. The court held that an address list contained in Outlook or a similar program which was part of the employer's email system and backed up by the employer was owned by the employer and may not be copied or removed by employees for use outside of their employment or after their employment comes to an end. As this was not likely to be appreciated by many employees the court suggested that it was highly desirable for employers to devise and publish an email policy covering this subject.

Inventions and patents

A patent is a monopoly right that allows its holder to exploit exclusively the invention delin- **8.138** eated by the claims of that patent. In order to infringe a patent there is no requirement of copying or knowledge of the patent. A patent will only be granted for an invention on the basis that it is new, not obvious, and has some industrial utility.

While an invention (prior to its disclosure) may amount to confidential information, its **8.139** ownership (as between employer and employee) is regulated by section 39 of the Patents Act 1977. Under section 39, an employer will own an invention made by an employee if:

(1) it was made in the course of the normal duties of the employee or in the course of duties falling outside his normal duties, but specifically assigned to him and the circumstances in either case were such that an invention might reasonably be expected to result from the carrying out of his duties; or
(2) the invention was made in the course of the duties of the employee and at the time of making the invention, because of the nature of his duties and the particular responsibilities arising from the nature of his duties, he had a special obligation to further the interest of the employer's undertaking.

Broadly, in terms of section 39, the first obligation (normal duties) relates to those employees **8.140** who are employed to 'invent'. The second (outside normal duties) relates to those, such as directors of a company, who have special obligations and responsibilities to that company because of the senior nature of their employment.

Inventions arising under any other circumstances will belong to the employee. Section 39 **8.141** provides that nothing in that section allows an employee to infringe the copyright or design right of an employer in order to work the invention.

The owner of an invention has the right to apply for a patent, and no one else may do so. If, **8.142** however, an employer or employee wrongfully applies for a patent for an invention, then proceedings may be brought pursuant to section 8 of the Patents Act 1977 contesting ownership of the patent, and seeking its transfer.

---

[180] [2007] IRLR 700.

8.143 An employee may make a claim for compensation from their employer in respect of an invention where a patent has been granted and either the invention or the patent is of 'outstanding benefit' to the employer. Section 40 of the Patents Act 1977 regulates claims for statutory compensation. 'Outstanding' means something out of the ordinary and not something one would normally expect to arise from the results of the duties that the employee is paid for.[181] The level of compensation awarded to the employee must amount to a fair share, having regard to all the circumstances of the benefit which the employer has derived or may be reasonably expected to derive from the patent.[182] In the first ever court award of compensation, the employees, a senior researcher and junior researcher, were awarded 2 per cent and 1 per cent respectively of the benefit of £50 million that was determined to have resulted from the patent.[183]

Registered trade marks and passing off

8.144 Trade mark law and passing off seek to ensure that the goods and services of a trader are not mistaken (deliberately or inadvertently) for another's goods or services.

Registered trade marks

8.145 A trade mark is often described as a 'badge of origin' indicating where goods or services originate from. Following the European Council Directive (First Council Directive to approximate the laws of the Member States relating to trade marks (89/104/EEC)), English registered trade mark law moved beyond this rigid concept to protect some of the other purposes that a trade mark seeks to fulfil. Pursuant to section 1 of the Trade Marks Act 1994 (which implemented the European Council Directive) a trade mark means any 'sign' which is capable of being represented graphically and which is capable of distinguishing goods or services of one undertaking from those of another undertaking. In particular, the trade mark may consist of words, designs, letters, sounds, colours, or the shape of goods or their packaging. These signs can be registered as a trade mark provided they are distinctive in their own right, or have become distinctive through use, and provided they do not conflict with earlier registrations.

8.146 A registered trade mark is infringed where a third party without permission uses, in the course of trade, a sign which is either identical or similar to the trade mark in relation to goods or services which are identical or similar. If the trade mark used is not identical for identical goods and services, infringement will only be made out if there is a likelihood of confusion on the part of the public.[184]

Passing off

8.147 Passing off is often limited to the 'classical trinity' whereby a successful claimant must prove as follows:

(1) He must establish goodwill or a reputation attached to the goods or services which he supplies in the minds of the purchasing public by association with the identifying 'get up'

---

[181] *GEC Avionics Ltd's Patent (Ellis' Application)* [1992] RPC 107.

[182] Patents Act 1977, s 41.

[183] *Kelly and Chiu v GE Healthcare Ltd* [2009] EWHC 181 (Pat).

[184] In addition a registered trade mark may be infringed pursuant to the Trade Marks Act 1994, s 10(3) if the trade mark has a sufficient reputation in the UK and the use takes unfair advantage of or is detrimental to the distinctive character or repute of that trade mark.

(whether it consists simply of a brand name or a trade description, or the individual features of labelling or packaging) under which his particular goods or services are offered to the public, such that the get up is recognized by the public as distinctive specifically of the claimant's goods or services.

(2) He must demonstrate a misrepresentation by the defendant to the public (whether or not intentional) leading or likely to lead the public to believe that the goods or services offered to them are the goods or services of the claimant.

(3) He must demonstrate that he suffers, or in a *quia timet* action that he is likely to suffer, by reason of the erroneous belief engendered by the defendant's misrepresentation that the source of the defendant's goods or services is the same as the source of those offered by the claimant.

This classical trinity of proving goodwill, confusion, and damage, however, does not fully embrace all of the situations where passing off may arise. The test applied by Lord Diplock in *Warnick v Townend*[185] identified five characteristics of passing off in order for there to be a valid cause of action: **8.148**

(1) a misrepresentation;

(2) made by a trader in the course of trade;

(3) to prospective customers of his or ultimate consumers of goods or services supplied by him;

(4) which is calculated to injure the business or goodwill of another (in the sense that this is a reasonably foreseeable consequence); and

(5) which causes actual damage to a business or goodwill of a trader by whom the action is brought or (in a *quia timet* action) will probably do so.

Conduct amounting to trade mark infringement and passing off

In certain industries, businesses are often synonymous with a core or key employee. When that employee leaves, it is sometimes the case that the former employer and remaining employees struggle to adapt to the new circumstances. In particular, it is not uncommon for the departing employee to wish to trade off his reputation as a leader in his field as part of his new trading name. However, by that stage the former employer's business may be synonymous with that name as a trade mark, and the goodwill associated with that name (ie as an origin of particular goods or services) has gone beyond the individual himself and properly belongs to that business. In these circumstances, the former employer's business may own a registered trade mark for the name of the goods or services with which the employee is synonymous. **8.149**

This is perhaps best illustrated by the case of *Emanuel v Continental Shelf 128 Ltd*.[186] Elizabeth Emanuel was a well-known designer of wedding apparel and began trading under the name of Elizabeth Emanuel in 1990. In 1996 together with another company, she formed Elizabeth Emanuel plc to which she transferred all the assets of her former business including its goodwill and an application to register the trade mark ELIZABETH EMANUEL, which was registered in 1997. Subsequently Elizabeth Emanuel left the company, while the company changed its name and then assigned its registered trade mark to a third party. That third party lodged a further application to register ELIZABETH EMANUEL as a trade mark. **8.150**

---

[185] [1980] RPC 31.
[186] [2006] All ER 444.

8.151 Elizabeth Emanuel filed a notice of opposition to the new trade mark application and also applied to revoke the existing registered trade mark. The basis of the opposition and revocation was that the trade mark corresponded to her name as the designer and the goods would be deceptive or liable to mislead the public as to their nature, quality, or origin. At first instance the opposition and revocation were dismissed. Subsequently, the matter was referred to the European Court on a number of questions. The European Court found that a trade mark corresponding to the name of the designer and first manufacturer of the goods might not, by reason of that particular feature alone, be refused registration on the ground that it would deceive the public. In particular, where the goodwill associated with that trade mark previously registered in a different graphical form had been assigned together with the business making the goods to which the mark related, the trade mark would not be refused on that basis alone.

8.152 Prima facie, therefore, the use by the employee of his name as a sign in the course of trade may amount to an infringement of that registration. However, section 11(2) of the Trade Marks Act 1994 provides that a registered trade mark is not infringed by 'the use by a person of his own name . . . provided the use is in accordance with honest practices in industrial or commercial matters'. What may constitute honest practices in industrial and commercial matters in this context has not been addressed. The former employer will seek to argue that the employee barred his right to use of the name at the point the business was set up and created. The employee will argue that he should not be barred from using his own name.

8.153 While there remains some uncertainty as to the result under registered trade mark infringement proceedings, the result is more certain in the context of passing off. In a passing off action, there is no own name defence, merely a question of whether there is a misrepresentation made by the former employee which is calculated to injure the business (in the sense that this injury is reasonably foreseeable). Unless the former employee seeks to distinguish himself and his new enterprise from his former employer, then it is likely that a successful passing off action will be made out, if confusion arises or, in a *quia timet* action, is likely to arise.

8.154 Similar considerations arise where former employees seek to represent that they are continuing the same business. In *Intelsec Systems Ltd v Grech-cini*,[187] the defendants were involved in the development and marketing of a video smoke detection system which had been produced by the claimant. The defendant former employees left their employer and set up a rival company in competition. The claimant issued proceedings seeking relief on the basis of passing off, infringement of copyright, and misuse of confidential information. They sought, amongst other things, an order that the employees disclose the names and addresses of all persons with whom they had had contact. On the application, the claimant produced evidence of the alleged passing off and contended that they needed an order to discover whether there had been other instances of passing off.

8.155 Mr Nicholas Warren QC (sitting as a Deputy Judge of the High Court) determined that there were different categories of customer that the employees had contacted. Where the contacts had been made during the course of employment on behalf of the employer, the defendants had to disclose those names and addresses (even if they were allowed to

---

[187] [2000] 1 WLR 1190, [1999] 4 All ER 11.

approach such contacts after the employment ceased). Similarly, if the employee had approached a contact of his own during his employment, there will be a prima facie breach of the duty of fidelity, and the employer was entitled to claim the contact as his own. The most important category related to those contacts made after termination of employment. Here the position was more difficult. However, an order was made for disclosure in order to rectify the misrepresentations arising out of the passing off. In the particular circumstances of the case, the evidence of passing off gave rise to a serious issue and the claimant was justifiably suspicious that there might be further examples of passing off. Accordingly, an order was made for disclosure of all the customers regardless of when and how the contact had originally been made (although certain restrictions of confidentiality were placed on their disclosure).[188]

A slightly more innocuous set of circumstances arises where employees wish to use work **8.156** done at a previous employer as an example of their own work by way of a reference. It is not uncommon for those particularly in the creative industries, such as graphic design, to exhibit examples of their previous work. However, this may amount to a registered trade mark infringement or passing off depending upon the circumstances. For example, a reference to work that an employee did at a previous employer, where that employer's name is used, will amount to use of that trade mark in the course of trade. As the trade mark will be identical and may be being used for identical goods or services for which it is registered, the owner of the trade mark may not need to prove confusion to make out an infringement. There is a defence to such infringement under section 10(6) of the Trade Marks Act 1994 which states that:

> . . . nothing . . . shall be construed as preventing the use of a registered trade mark by any person for the purpose of identifying goods or services as those of the proprietor of a licensee. But any such use otherwise than in accordance with honest practices in industrial or commercial matters shall be treated as infringing the registered trade mark if the use without due cause takes unfair advantage of, or is detrimental to, the distinctive character or repute of the trade mark.

If the employee seeks to trade off the former employer's trade mark, then clearly this will not **8.157** be used in accordance with honest practices. The precise ambit of lawful or unlawful use is often difficult to determine.

Passing off may prove to be a more effective cause of action for the employer. If the port- **8.158** folio references misrepresent the scope of the work undertaken by the employee, or misrepresent the employee's current business as having undertaken the previous work, then passing off may be made out. This is best illustrated by the case of *Bristol Conservatories v Conservatories Custom Built Ltd*,[189] where a former employee salesman for a conservatory company used his former employer's sales materials to sell conservatories for his new employer. These sales materials included projects that had been undertaken and completed by his former employer. There was no explicit reference, but the implicit reference was that the new employer had constructed the conservatories which were the subject of the photographs being shown to prospective customers. In the circumstances, passing off was made out.

---

[188] Distinguished in *Aon Ltd v JLT Reinsurance Brokers Ltd* [2010] IRLR 600 considered at para 10.172 below.
[189] [1989] PRC 455.

Remedies and procedure

8.159 Legal proceedings for infringement of intellectual property rights should be brought in the Chancery Division, and in the case of litigation concerning the infringement or validity of a patent before the Patents Court or the Patents County Court.

8.160 The remedies available to an intellectual property rights owner in respect of an infringement may include an interim and a final injunction, an account of profits, or an enquiry as to damages. An award of damages may be calculated by reference to the loss suffered by the intellectual property rights owner or by application of the 'willing licensee, willing licensor' test. In applying this latter test, the court settles an award on the basis of notional royalty, such royalty being determined on the assumption that the rights owner is a willing licensor and the infringer a willing licensee.

9

PRE-ACTION STEPS

Catherine Taylor

A. Introduction[1]

9.01 Very often, in employee competition situations, the tactics adopted by the parties at the early stages are as important as the legal principles which apply. This chapter will examine those tactical issues from the perspective of all the relevant parties: the claimant employer, who is struggling to retain key employees or who wishes to disrupt their arrival at their new employer as much as possible; the defendant employee(s), who are often thrust into highly stressful litigation; and the defendant employer who requires his new recruits to start work as soon as possible.

9.02 This chapter will, therefore, be less concerned with legislation and case law than other chapters, although, of course, it is based on principles derived from legislation and case law, as examined in the remainder of this book. In the first edition of this book four developments in the law in recent years were noted which have had a significant impact on the approach adopted to pre-action tactics. These continue to be relevant at the time of writing the second edition and are noted below.

9.03 First, the reforms to court procedure introduced in 1999 (the Civil Procedure Rules),[2] which specify the overriding objective of enabling the court to deal with cases justly. This means ensuring parties are on an equal footing, saving expense, ensuring there is proportionality in

---

[1] See also Appendix 9, Sample Pre-Action Letters below.
[2] See Chapter 12 below.

the way cases are dealt with and ensuring that they are dealt with expeditiously and fairly, and allotting an appropriate amount of resources. Some of these objectives seem directly at odds with the usual approach to employee competition litigation, but they need to be borne in mind. As a result, more applications to the court will be on notice to the other parties and progression to speedy trial is the norm. Further, the greater emphasis on pre-action steps means that tactics are even more important than before.

9.04 The second development is the ability of employers to place employees on garden leave. This is covered fully in Chapter 4 above, but obviously may provide further options for the claimant employer to protect its interests.

9.05 Thirdly, the duties of employees and directors have become more onerous over recent years, as is described in Chapter 2 above. This means that the tactics relating to team moves are now particularly fraught.

9.06 Fourthly, the potential liabilities of recruiting employers in terms of the torts of inducement of breach of contract, causing loss by unlawful means and conspiracy have undergone some fierce scrutiny in recent years, in particular, by the House of Lords in *OBG Ltd v Allan*.[3] For the recruiting employer what is now clear is that if economic loss is caused to a competitor as a result of their recruitment exercise, and it uses unlawful means in that exercise, such as inducing breach of contract, then even where there was no desire to harm the claimant employer, it will be liable. Equally in relation to the tort of inducing breach of contract, indifference on the part of the recruiting employer as to whether its exit plan will cause the recruits to breach their contracts will be sufficient to render the recruiting employer liable.[4] As the recruiting employer is often underwriting the losses of the employees, this may be of less significance economically, but where it may assist the claimant employer is in relation to obtaining injunctive relief.

9.07 Although there have also been numerous cases since the first edition which effect the subject matter of this chapter, one in particular requires mention, that is *Tullett Prebon plc v BGC Brokers LP*.[5] This case will be referred to throughout this chapter as it covers many of the tactical issues discussed, such as claiming constructive dismissal, express terms in a contract requiring disclosure and the use of indemnities, as well as a defendant employer's overall strategy in relation to team moves. Although only first instance, commentators have generally accepted that Jack J's judgment will have a significant influence in this area.

9.08 In addition to this legal background, there continues to be developments in communications technology, which means that the ability to retrieve evidence electronically continues to play a key role in these types of disputes. This potential for greater availability of evidence means that the seeking of pre-action or early disclosure should be more attractive although, as will be seen, overly wide requests are unlikely to succeed.[6] A claimant employer's options in terms of obtaining this evidence are examined in more detail in Appendix 1 to this book.

---

[3] [2008] AC 1. See, further, the discussion in Chapter 2 above.

[4] See paras 2.234–2.259 above and for a graphic illustration of the economic torts in the employee competition context see *Tullett Prebon plc v BGC Brokers LP* [2010] IRLR 648, paras 136–77.

[5] [2010] IRLR 648. The appeal from parts of this decision was heard in December 2010, but no judgment has been handed down at the time of writing.

[6] See para 9.80 below and generally paras 12.58–12.69 below.

Equally, from the defendant's perspective, it is probably more important to ensure that this type of evidence is not created in the first place, since even if a party manages to 'lose' the hardware containing the evidence this will not sit well with the court.[7]

Finally, though, it has to be remembered that employee competition situations, whilst always **9.09** very stressful for those involved, can often be exciting and exhilarating, especially for the leavers and for those involved in a large team move situation. A good example of this is found in *British Midland Tools v Midland International Tooling Ltd*,[8] where a team left an engineering company to set up in competition. Around the time the move was in progress, every time the managing director of British Midland Tools ventured on to the shop floor, he was greeted by those employees who were leaving, who whistled the theme tune from the film *The Great Escape*. Psychological warfare is a tactic we will not be covering (directly, at least) in this chapter.

B. The claimant employer

The contract of employment—a business asset

The claimant employer's most valuable pre-action step will be to ensure that it has an up- **9.10** to-date and well-drafted contract of employment in place which contains as appropriate all the key protections an employer can enjoy as described in Chapters 2, 3, 4, and 5 of this book.[9] Against that background, a claimant employer who fears poaching from competitors and who is not afraid of a contract which may be regarded as onerous should also consider the inclusion of the following:

(1) A term which requires the employee to produce a copy of his or her contract of employment (with remuneration terms perhaps blanked out), or its post-termination restrictions, to a new employer. This means that a new employer should be put on notice of the terms and conditions which affect the employee's ability to join him, thus improving the claimant employer's ability to claim inducement of breach of contract against the recruiting employer. If the new employer is not provided with the relevant terms by the defendant employee, then it may be possible to argue that there is a further breach of contract by the defendant employee.

(2) A term which requires the employee to disclose to his employer a direct or indirect approach to recruit him by a competitor. Bear in mind that a simple approach by a competitor will not involve an employee in any wrongdoing. Therefore, such an express provision will place a greater obligation on an employee than the common law position. This will be even more the case where the employee is junior. Nonetheless the court in *Tullett Prebon v BGC Brokers LP* held that such a provision was not in restraint of trade after review of the leading authorities on preparation to compete.[10] Such a provision is unlikely to be popular with the employee, but nonetheless again it can prove a useful restraint, particularly if a claimant employer wishes to pursue the disciplinary route described further below.

(3) A term which requires an employee to inform the claimant employer as soon as he or she becomes aware that another employee has been approached by or is proposing to leave

---

[7] *Tullett Prebon plc v BGC Brokers LP* [2010] IRLR 648, para 65.
[8] [2003] BCLC 523.
[9] See also Appendices 2, 3, 4, 6, and 7 for sample clauses and drafting notes.
[10] [2010] IRLR 648, para 67.

to join a competitor. This type of provision has not been specifically considered by the courts. However, the common law duty on a senior employee in this regard means that such a clause would only reinforce the senior employee's common law duty[11]and as such it should be uncontroversial. In relation to more junior employees such a provision may still be challenged on the basis it is in restraint of trade and the fact that more junior employees are not subject to the same common law duties. To assist in defeating such arguments the provision could be limited to those employees with whom the defendant employee works, rather than extending to the entire work force.

(4) Carefully drafted bonus or long-term incentive plan provisions which by delaying payment/receipt of benefit or providing for a clawback prolong the benefit of providing to the employee sometimes large amounts of remuneration. Such provisions may also fall foul of the principles of restraint of trade, although see *Sweeney v Peninsula Business Services Ltd*,[12] where the Employment Appeal Tribunal held that where an employee who left employment was deprived of commission already earned, this was not a restraint of trade because it did not impose a restraint on the identity of the new employer for whom the employee could work.[13] If such provisions involves a clawback of sums already paid or something similar, where an employee leaves in breach, the provision may also be regarded as a penalty, in relation to which see paragraphs 11.86 to 11.93 below.[14] As a general rule if an employer wishes to include this type of provision, it would be wise to make it clear that any bonus is paid in part for past services, but also to retain loyalty in the future.[15]

(5) Terms relating to data protection which inform the employee that the claimant employer will monitor and review an employee's communications and other actions on work equipment.[16]

(6) An express provision requiring an employee to return company property on the employer's request at any time during his or her employment. Although such a right would probably be implied (certainly at the end of the employment) it is helpful to have an express provision, not least as it means the employer can avoid arguments in relation to breaches of the implied term of trust and confidence where it demands the return of property. Consider also, if there is any possibility of an employee home working, including a right to audit in respect of home computer systems.

(7) A provision which makes it clear that the employee has received or has been given proper opportunity to take legal advice on post-termination restrictions and other similar provisions. This will assist in defeating arguments the employee may raise that he or she is not bound by the provisions because they were entered into under duress.

(8) An express choice of law and jurisdiction clause to ensure the claimant employer has as much control as possible over the law applicable to the contract and the jurisdiction in which any disputes will be considered.[17]

---

[11] See paras 2.98–2.138 and, for example, *Tullett Prebon plc v BGC Brokers LP* [2010] IRLR 648, para 68.

[12] [2004] IRLR 49.

[13] See also *Tullett Prebon plc v BGC Brokers LP* [2010] IRLR 648, paras 264–7, where a similar conclusion was reached.

[14] Note that the clawbacks were not regarded as penalties in *Tullett Prebon plc v BGC Brokers LP* [2010] IRLR 648, paras 268–70, even though they were triggered by, amongst other things, a breach of contract by the broker.

[15] See also *CMC Group plc v Michael Zhang* [2006] EWCA Civ 408.

[16] See paras 9.46–9.65 below.

[17] See Chapter 7 above.

In addition to ensuring that the contractual documentation contains the maximum **9.11** appropriate protection, a claimant employer should also review its contractual documentation regularly. In those industries where competition for employees is extremely high, a review every six months may be appropriate, although this will be ambitious. Further, the claimant employer should review its workforce regularly to ensure that all employees are signed up to appropriate documentation. Ideally, an employer will ensure that employees sign up to new contracts on promotion or even salary increase or other significant events as a matter of course.[18]

Other practical preventative steps

An employer should, if at all possible, institute procedures such that information which it **9.12** wishes to protect as confidential information is treated as such by employees. Documents containing confidential information should be labelled confidential and only be disseminated on a need to know basis. The fact that information is confidential should be stressed to employees. This is even more important as email makes the dissemination of information much easier than previously was the case. Whilst the fact that information is treated as confidential will not be conclusive, the fact that it is not treated as confidential will make it more difficult to enforce confidentiality provisions and restrictive covenants.[19]

Employee management of the most practical kind also plays a role. So, as already noted in **9.13** the introduction to this chapter, employees who owe fiduciary duties as directors, de facto directors or senior employees are subject to more onerous duties and give the claimant employer access to a wider range of remedies. Thus a practical point would be to expressly provide that those employees who are key to the employer are subject to fiduciary duties. Equally, if there is a key client, ensure that more than one employee has a strong relationship with it.

Departing employees—the danger signs

The managers of a claimant employer should always be alive to the fact that employees may **9.14** be preparing to compete. This responsibility goes all the way up to the top of the organization, as even the most senior employees may look to move on at some point. Common signs that an employee is looking to move on or that employees may be more vulnerable or likely to be approached by competitors are:

- A request for a copy of their contract of employment. An employee will have little reason to look at their employment contract during employment so a request to do so will usually indicate itchy feet.
- Email mistakes—all too often, an email wrongly addressed can give the game away.
- Dissatisfaction with working life generally or some specific aspect of working life. Moves often occur during times of economic downturn for that specific claimant employer when

---

[18] See *WRN Ltd v T M Aryis* [2008] IRLR 889, para 60 for an example of why this is a good policy.

[19] See eg *Faccenda Chicken v Fowler* [1987] Ch 117, CA, 138; paras 3.57–3.60 below; and *WRN Ltd v T M Aryis* [2008] IRLR 889, paras 81–5, where publication of confidential information on the claimant employer's website undermined its claims in respect of confidential information. The claimant employer can also consider 'seeding' databases with false data which can then be used to prove that an employee has lifted the employer's database—see *First Conference Ltd and others v R Bracchi and others* [2009] EWHC 2176 (Ch), paras 46–7 (and Appendix 1).

employees perceive that they will be paid better elsewhere. Equally in times of general economic buoyancy, competitor employers are generally more aggressive about offering lucrative deals to their competitors' key employees to secure the best team (and disrupt their competitors).

- The end of any earn-out or other 'tie in' period following the acquisition of a business— unless the claimant employer has anticipated the end of any incentive for the employee to stay and replaced it with a similar benefit—will be a time of particular vulnerability for the employer. The most frequent example of this is the period immediately after the payment of an annual bonus. If an employee is looking to leave they will have lined up another job and will be waiting for payment of the bonus to go. Other danger times are when a fixed-term contract expires.

- Where competitors are 're-tooling' or have spotted a business opportunity which is currently underdeveloped apart from by the claimant employer. A good example of re-tooling arose in the management consultancy world where the Big Four accountancy firms backed out of a management consultancy in the wake of the Enron saga in 2001/2002. However, by the mid-2000s they had decided to move back into this area, leading to more hiring.

- Times of uncertainty at an employer—if there are rumours of some kind of change to the business such as a takeover, sale, or float, or of a reorganization or redundancy programme, employees may be unsettled and so more open to an approach.

9.15 So, if a claimant employer becomes aware of vulnerability within an area of its workforce, what defensive steps are open to it?

(1) The claimant employer should respond strategically and speedily. Strategy is important in a situation where otherwise the natural reaction may be emotional. Speed is equally important, especially where the preferred remedy is some form of injunctive relief.

(2) The first step is probably to speak to the employee or team to try to establish whether the suspicions are well founded. If the claimant employer suspects a team move, approach the employees concerned or the most 'friendly' or possibly the most 'political' member of the team and sound them out. It is usually possible to detect whether an employee is looking around for alternative employment.

(3) If the employees deny any intention of moving, but the claimant employer still suspects to the contrary, the claimant employer may wish to look at their emails or, if they work on recorded telephone lines, listen to tapes. However, it may be difficult to show that it was proportionate under the terms of the DPA 1998 to take these steps at this stage and so risks will attach to such monitoring.[20]

(4) A claimant employer can pre-empt any move by offering enhanced remuneration and other incentives to the employees it believes to be on the point of resigning. Any such offers should be accompanied by a new contract of employment, including full protection.[21]

(5) Take steps to prepare for litigation. Most relief sought requires the claimant employer to move as quickly as possible. Therefore, the claimant employer should gather all the relevant contractual documentation, formulate a strategy based on the business aims,

---

[20] See, further, paras 9.48–9.51 and 9.54–9.59 below.
[21] See para 9.10 above.

send initial instructions to the lawyers, and try to establish who the new employer is likely to be and gauge their likely response.

More detail of how to deal with the issues which arise in specific situations is set out in the next few paragraphs.

How to deal with resignations

If an employee or employees resign there are a number of scenarios which may arise **9.16** depending on the contractual status of the employee, how key they are to the business, where they are going, and whether they are resigning alone or with others. What follows in this section is a consideration of the options open to the claimant employer by reference to whether the employee resigns lawfully or in breach, and their contractual status. It mainly concentrates on tactics depending on the contractual position. Additional factors will come into play where the employee is a fiduciary or acting in concert and these are dealt with at paragraphs 9.36 to 9.37 below.

Resignation on notice

No written contract

The worst case scenario for a claimant employer is that the employee resigns but has not **9.17** signed a contract of employment or equivalent. In this case, the terms of the contract will consist of any terms implied by law, relevant documents (and bear in mind that if the employee has not signed the latest version of the contract, the previous one may be binding still), the discussions between employer and employee, custom and practice in the industry, and the conduct of the parties. However, it is very unlikely that the employee will be bound by any post-termination restrictions. The employer is most likely to find itself relying on the following implied terms:

• during employment: duty of fidelity or fiduciary duties,[22] notice periods, and possibly garden leave;
• after employment: a limited duty of confidentiality.[23]

In relation to the notice period, this will be a minimum of one week after the first month of **9.18** employment. However, if no notice period has been agreed between the parties, the court may imply a period of notice longer than the statutory minimum, which will be what it considers to be reasonable notice assessed by reference to all the circumstances of the case (seniority, length of service, nature of employment, frequency of pay days, etc).[24]

If there is a good argument that a substantial notice period could be implied into the contract **9.19** the issue of garden leave should also be considered. Previously, absent an express garden leave provision, it was unlikely that a court would grant an injunction enforcing garden leave. However, two recent decisions[25] mean that garden leave should be considered where an employee has 'as a result of some prior breach of contract or other duty, demonstrated in a serious way that they are not ready or willing to work', or, to put it another way, where the

---

[22] See Chapter 2 above.
[23] See Chapter 3 above.
[24] *Hill v CA Parsons & Co Ltd* [1972] Ch 305, CA.
[25] *SG&R Valuation Service Co LLC v Boudrais* [2008] IRLR 770; *Standard Life Health Care Ltd v Gorman* [2010] IRLR 233. See, further, the discussion at paras 4.87–4.99 above.

employee has 'rendered it impossible or reasonably impracticable for the employer to provide work. The breach of contract or other duty must constitute wrongdoing, by reason of which they will profit or potentially profit'.[26] Thus, where the employee has been involved in misconduct, if it is of such a serious nature that the above test is satisfied, even if they offer to work their notice,[27] garden leave may be available notwithstanding the absence of an express provision.

9.20 Equally, wrongdoing during employment may give grounds for a springboard type injunction and the courts have recently been inclined to grant this relief particularly in the context of team moves where unlawful conduct is revealed—see *UBS Wealth Management (UK) Ltd v Vestra Wealth LLP*[28] and *Tullett Prebon plc v BGC Brokers LP.*[29]

9.21 In this scenario, the claimant employer therefore needs to consider options, as follows:

(1) Investigate whether the employee has committed any breaches during employment in preparing to compete or otherwise and consider whether:
  • they could form the basis of an action for damages or an injunction based on springboard relief;[30] and/or
  • if there is a sufficiently long implied notice period, whether garden leave is an option.[31]
(2) Consider whether any form of restraint based on the implied duty of confidentiality post-termination is feasible.
(3) Negotiate a deal with the employee whereby either in return for giving up arguments over the length of notice and garden leave or for a payment of money compensation, the employee agrees to protection by way of garden leave and/or post-termination restrictions.

Some contractual protection

9.22 If the claimant employer has some contractual protection, its choices are much wider, although it should still investigate whether the employee has committed any breaches of contract during employment, including any breaches of the express terms of the contract, and consider an action for damages or springboard relief based on these breaches.[32]

9.23 In addition, a claimant employer will need to decide what to do about the notice period. The options are:

  • Release the employee from it, but in such a way that the employer is not held to be in breach of it, so that there is no obligation to pay further moneys to the employee and so that the enforceability of any post-termination restrictions is not affected. This is obviously the cheapest option and is a good choice where the employer is confident about the enforceability of and protection afforded by the post-termination restrictions.

---

[26] *SG&R Valuation Service* (n 25 above), para 24 as endorsed by the Court of Appeal in *Standard Life Health Care Ltd v Gorman* [2010] IRLR 233.
[27] In the *Boudrais* case the defendant employees all offered to work their notice.
[28] [2008] IRLR 965.
[29] Interim injunction: [2009] EWHC 819 (QB). See further paras 10.77–10.85 below.
[30] See paras 10.57–10. 85 and Chapter 12 below.
[31] See paras 4.87–4.99 above.
[32] See paras 10.57–10.85 and Chapter 12 below.

- Place the employee on garden leave. As explained above at paragraph 9.19, an express term is no longer necessarily a prerequisite, although certain conditions will need to be satisfied if there is no express term (including employee misconduct). Once the right to place an employee on garden leave has been established, the claimant employer will also need to decide further tactical issues in relation to the garden leave itself. In the first place it will need to decide how long the employee should be on garden leave and at what pay. In relation to how long, if the notice period is over six months, the employer must be prepared for the fact that it may not be possible to keep the employee on garden leave for the whole period. However, the claimant employer does not need to inform the employee how long it predicts the employee will remain on garden leave (although a well-advised employee will put pressure on it to do so). In relation to the amount of pay, the claimant employer should review the drafting of the contract of employment carefully—does the payment to be made include bonus or commission? If not, should the employer pay it anyway? The risk of not doing so would be that if the employee were to receive significantly less remuneration (by reason of non-payment of discretionary elements) than he or she would receive if they were working, it is arguable that the garden leave clause may not be enforceable or that the court may be less inclined to exercise its discretion in favour of a garden leave injunction.[33]
- Finally, the claimant employer may have to allow the employee to work out some or all of the notice period due to the requirements of the business. In that case, the claimant employer may wish to consider some shortened period of garden leave. Alternatively, it should review the contract to see whether, within the business parameters, it would be possible to ring-fence the employee from valuable clients. If there is no express flexibility in the contract to allow this, the employer will need to proceed carefully to avoid breaching the implied term of trust and confidence.[34]

The claimant employer will also need to consider its approach to the post-termination restrictions, if any. There are a number of stages to this: **9.24**

- What are the real business interests that the claimant employer needs to protect? This will depend on the employee's seniority and their new role. The claimant employer needs to establish what its commercial priorities are in terms of what confidential information and which clients and employees it needs to protect. It also needs to establish if there are any other motivators, for example, business rivalry or the reaction of its other employees.
- The claimant employer then needs to consider whether the post-termination restrictions are both enforceable and cover the area of the business that it wishes to protect. If either of these matters is an issue, the claimant employer needs to be aware of this early on. Common issues are as follows. The claimant employer wishes to stop the employee working for the competitor altogether, but there is no non-compete covenant, or that which there is only prevents the employee from working for part of the competitor's business, not all of it. Solutions to this would be: rely on garden leave provision or consider whether springboard relief is possible. Again, there may only be a restraint on

---

[33] See paras 4.145–4.152 above. See also *Standard Life Health Care Ltd v Gorman* [2010] IRLR 233, paras 30–2, where a garden leave injunction was granted even though no undertaking to pay remuneration was offered. However, this was in the context of an agency agreement and the court was also aware that the employees were being indemnified by their new employer.

[34] Although see *Extec Screens and Crushers Ltd v Rice* [2007] EWHC 1043 (QB), where this type of protective act was not held to be grounds for constructive dismissal.

the solicitation of clients/employees and proving solicitation is likely to be extremely difficult. Solutions to this would be: use all efforts to cement relations with the existing clients/staff; consider the contracts of the clients/employees who are likely to be targeted and whether there are provisions in them which would slow their departure; consider springboard relief.

- Finally, it may be that, as a result, the claimant employer decides not to enforce some part of the post-termination restrictions. However, at the early stages, threats to enforce all of them may be appropriate, although there may be risks relating to costs if proceedings are commenced and not all of the threats are pursued.

9.25 See paragraphs 9.111 to 9.118 below, which outline some of the issues the defendant employee may raise in relation to the contractual position and in relation to which the employer may need to be prepared.

Resignation in breach

9.26 Not all employees will, however, offer the requisite notice. Some will just walk out, either because they believe (or are claiming) that they have been constructively dismissed or because their new employer is taking a very aggressive approach to the recruitment. This section will consider what other tactical considerations will apply in those circumstances.

No written contract

9.27 The tactical considerations where an employee walks out in breach but has no written contract will be similar to those discussed above at paragraphs 9.17 to 9.21.

9.28 Tactically, the claimant employer will need to decide whether to accept the employee's breach and so bring the contract to an end, or to allow it to continue. In the former case, the employer can cease paying the employee but will only be able to rely on the limited implied duty of confidentiality post-termination. In the latter case, the employer will have to keep paying the employee but may be able to argue that garden leave remains an option. The claimant employer therefore needs to consider how much it is prepared to pay to disrupt the employee's move as the latter option could be expensive both in terms of the remuneration payable to the employees and legal costs.

Some contractual protection

9.29 Where there is some contractual protection, as long as the notice period is of a useful length, the employer's better strategy is to refuse to accept the breach and either require the employee to return to work or confirm that they will be on garden leave.[35] Since in the most aggressive situations the employee will already have turned up at the future employer's offices, the claimant employer needs to act especially quickly to ascertain the employee's intentions and seek relief from the court if appropriate. If the employee is able to work for the competitor for a few days, it makes arguments about balance of convenience more difficult from the claimant employer's point of view.

Resignation and claim for constructive dismissal

9.30 What specific tactical issues arise in the situation where an employee resigns and claims constructive dismissal? In that situation, the claimant employer needs to bear in mind that

---

[35] See para 9.19 above in relation to how this will work where there is no express garden leave provision.

the task of enforcing the contract will be more difficult. In the first place, in the rare case where the constructive dismissal claim is obviously well founded, the court is unlikely to grant relief enforcing garden leave[36] or the post-termination restrictions.[37] In any case, the pre-action correspondence and the amount of evidence required to support any such application is likely to be increased and costs will go up accordingly. Finally, a court is likely to send matters off to a speedy trial because the factual issues surrounding the claim for constructive dismissal will only be able to be properly resolved after cross-examination of witnesses (although an order for speedy trial is now the norm in applications for interim injunctions).

Where constructive dismissal is alleged, the employer should try to discover whether the **9.31** employee was in repudiatory breach of the contract prior to the employer's alleged breach. If so, the claimant employer can argue that the defendant employee is unable to rely on its repudiatory breach to walk away from their contract—*RDF Media Group plc v Clements*.[38] However, this argument might not succeed given the later judicial doubt that has been cast on the decision in the *RDF* case.[39] Nonetheless the courts should take the employee's prior breach into account when considering the claim for constructive dismissal, which should assist the claimant employer.[40]

The usual actions of a claimant employer post resignation (trying to delay the resignation, **9.32** persuading an employee to stay, reminding them of their legal obligations) are unlikely in themselves to constitute constructive dismissal.[41] In fact a claimant employer would be well advised to try to persuade the employee to stay as this makes a constructive dismissal argument that bit more difficult to get off the ground.

Termination of employment by the claimant employer

Just because the claimant employer is dismissing the employee does not mean that it is **9.33** happy to release the employee concerned from their duties and restrictions.[42] Often, where an employee is dismissed for gross misconduct, the claimant employer is extremely concerned that the potentially 'unscrupulous' employee will end up at a competitor. Alternatively, the claimant employer may have had to dismiss an otherwise talented employee for reasons unconnected with their job performance. Finally, the employer may take a tactical decision to dismiss the defendant employee on the basis that he or she has breached their duties by organizing a team move or taking confidential information. In that situation, the claimant employer will be very concerned about the effect of the dismissal on the employee's post-termination obligations. Initially it would appear that where the claimant employer dismisses because of capability or redundancy, post-termination restraints may be less relevant. However, in the case of a capability dismissal, the employee will still have access to confidential information, clients, and employees, even if the use to which they are then put is ineffective. On redundancy, the same applies—although if a

---

[36] See para 4.178 above.
[37] See paras 5.139–5.141 above.
[38] [2008] IRLR 207.
[39] See paras 5.117–5.124 above.
[40] *Tullett Prebon* (n 4 above), paras 83–5.
[41] ibid eg paras 105–7; *Extec Screens and Crushers* (n 34 above), para 68.
[42] See eg *Foster Bryant Surveying Ltd v Bryant* [2007] IRLR 425, CA.

business area is being shut down altogether, the claimant employer may find it difficult to show any legitimate business interest to protect by the enforcement of post-termination restrictions.

9.34 The major concern for the claimant employer in this situation will be to ensure that it does nothing to affect the enforceability of the post-termination restrictions which apply to the affected employees. This can be very tricky in the situation where the employer is dismissing the employee for gross misconduct, as dismissal will normally be immediate with no notice period served. In addition to ensuring that there really are grounds for gross misconduct and that the dismissal is procedurally fair (although strictly from a contractual point of view this is irrelevant, it could become more relevant and so helpful to the defendant employee if there is a breach of either a contractual disciplinary procedure or the implied term of mutual trust and confidence), the employer also needs to decide whether it wishes the employee to go on garden leave. If it does, it should dismiss on contractual notice with a careful reservation of rights (albeit this will include paying the employee, which may be difficult for the employer to accept, depending on the reason for dismissal). Alternatively, the employer can terminate immediately and rely solely on the post-termination restrictions. Either way, again there is likely to be more correspondence and more evidence needed in support and, consequently, increased costs.

9.35 The main advantage of the situation where an employer terminates is that the employer controls the timing and it can minimize its costs as it ceases to be obliged to pay the employee on termination. It should put the employee(s) on notice of the stance it is taking in relation to the post-termination restrictions in the letter it sends notifying termination. It then needs to keep its intelligence alert to find out if an employee is joining a competitor and if so, which one.

Fiduciary duties

9.36 As already referred to above, these may give the claimant an additional weapon in its arsenal with which to enter into combat. Chapter 2 sets out fully the duties an employee may be subject to but the following questions will be useful in enabling the claimant employer to identify what the duties are and whether they will be useful.

- Does the employee owe fiduciary duties in addition to his or her contractual duties, because he or she is a director, de facto director or a senior employee with fiduciary duties in relation to some aspects of their job?
- If so, what are the extent of these duties, and is the employee in breach of them?
- Are the remedies available to the employer in respect of the breach of these duties of use to the defendant employer?[43]

9.37 One other point to bear in mind—if the employee resigns as a director or is dismissed or forced out, his fiduciary duties will be affected by, and could be extinguished by that act. In particular, in a dismissal situation the claimant employer should think carefully about whether it is practicable to keep the employee on as a director thus keeping alive his fiduciary duties.[44]

---

[43] See paras 11.94–11.129
[44] See eg *Foster Bryant Surveying* (n 42 above) and paras 2.127–2.129 above.

The new employer

As stated above, quite often the most difficult issue will be identifying which of the claimant **9.38**
employer's competitors is the new employer. The main means is usually market gossip.
This can often be verified by a phone call to the suspected new employer asking to speak
to the relevant employee. It is key in this situation that those on the business-side know to
inform the relevant individuals at the claimant employer as soon as they hear that the
employee has started work at a competitor employer. A failure to tell the legal department
or senior management can result in damaging delays which can be used against the claimant
employer.

As soon as the claimant employer is aware of the identity of the new employer, usually it **9.39**
should write to the new employer, putting it on notice of the restraints to which the employee
is subject and advising it not to induce any (further) breaches by the employee. This letter can
be written even when the identity of the new employer is uncertain. However, if the new
employer has been wrongly identified, this may make the claimant employer look stupid in
front of a competitor. It may also result in allegations of libel if the statements about the
employee who is leaving are not carefully reviewed. The content of the letter to the new
employer is dealt with below.

The claimant employer will also need to consider whether in the long term the new **9.40**
employer will be a party to any litigation. The claimant employer should consider carefully, first whether there is any evidence that satisfies the complex tests relating to the
economic torts,[45] and may well decide it has no case against the new employer. If it does
think there is a case, the risks of joining the new employer are that it may increase the
exposure under the cross-undertaking in damages.[46] The damage a defendant employee
may suffer is likely to be limited to loss of earnings. That suffered by a defendant employer
could include loss of profits or, indeed, some other corporate opportunity. Additionally,
if a claimant employer unsuccessfully sues a defendant employer, it may subsequently be
penalized in costs (in so far as proceedings get to the stage of costs being awarded). The
claimant employer should also bear in mind that a sophisticated defendant employer
will have indemnified the defendant employee(s) from the costs and damages associated
with any court order, so will feel the financial pain caused by any litigation even when it
is not joined as a defendant. Finally, where the proceedings require the claimant employer
to disclose confidential information, the defendant employer will have less access to it if
it is not a party to the proceedings. Arguments in favour of joining the defendant
employer are that if an economic tort can be shown to be a serious issue at the interim
stage then a court may be more open to granting an injunction particularly in team
move situations.[47] However, the key factor is likely to be the perceived psychological
edge that may be gained by doing so, and the fact that if a successful result is obtained it
will have much greater impact, including in terms of publicity, if the defendant employer
is a party.

---

[45] See paras 2. 234–2.259 above.
[46] See paras 10.87 ff below.
[47] *UBS Wealth Management (UK) Ltd v Vestra Wealth LLP* [2008] IRLR 965; *Tullett Prebon* (n 4 above), and
in terms of injunctive relief after trial: [2010] IRLR 648, paras 250–3.

Team moves[48]

9.41 The claimant employer's biggest nightmare is that a whole team of employees is looking to move together to a competitor. In that situation, some additional tactical points apply.

9.42 In the first place, investigation will be critical. It is human nature for a group to communicate about what is going on and, unless the group is extremely well advised from the beginning and, more importantly, has followed that advice, it will almost certainly have created some evidence on email or other electronic media or, if calls are recorded, on the telephone. It has even been known for employees in team moves to claim expenses for travel to team meetings which relate to the move. Therefore, investigations are of key importance.[49]

9.43 Further, the other weak spot of team moves involves the people. In particular, one or two people (usually the more senior employees) are likely to be organizing the team move. This will almost certainly mean that they are in breach of their duty of fidelity or fiduciary duties.[50] This can give the claimant employer a lever over them individually (and could give grounds for disciplinary action) (see paras 9.66 to 9.76 below). It could also form the basis for an application for springboard relief, especially as recently the courts appear to have been more open to granting injunctions based on unlawful recruitment utilizing senior employees as 'recruiting sergeants'.[51]

9.44 The other weakness in team moves is that the number of people involved means that it may be possible to turn one of the team, that is persuade one of the 'team' to stay and reveal what has gone on, particularly at the more junior level. Swift action is therefore required to approach all those who have been involved and try to 'turn' them. Care should be taken that in doing so the claimant employer does not induce a breach of contract with the new employer.[52]

9.45 For the latter reason, a mass walk out may be a preferred tactic of the team and their new employer. In that case, speedy recourse to the court is required.

Investigations

9.46 As should be clear from the preceding paragraphs in this chapter, evidence of what the defendant employee(s) have been doing or plan to do is central to any successful strategy. In addition to traditional paper-based evidence, further evidence can be easily generated via the electronic communications systems (computers, hardware of all kinds, mobile telephony) which are now a feature of most, if not all, workplaces.

9.47 Appendix 1 to this book deals with the detailed forensics which apply to searches of communications media used and other evidence produced by the defendant employees and the recruiting employer. This section will consider the legal and tactical issues relating to

---

[48] See also the discussion of team moves in paras 2.260–2. 298 above.

[49] See paras 9.46–9.80 and Appendix 1 below.

[50] In particular their duties of disclosure, see paras 2.98–2.138 above and paras 9.140–9.145 below.

[51] *UBS Wealth Management (UK) Ltd v Vestra Wealth LLP* [2008] IRLR 965; *Tullett Prebon* (n 4 above) *Brokers LP* [2009] EWHC 819 (QB), and in terms of injunctive relief after trial: [2010] IRLR 648, paras 250–3. Note the extent of the restraint granted in the *BGC* cases was also extremely useful; it stopped any recruitment not just unlawful recruitment and lasted for twelve months which was the time it took until the 'speedy trial' was completed and judgment delivered.

[52] *Tullett Prebon* (n 4 above), paras 184–96.

some of the forms of evidence considered in Appendix 1 as well as considering other forms of investigation such as surveillance, disciplinary processes, investigation into start-up businesses, and pre-action disclosure. Usually, these investigations will be most relevant where an employee is leaving as part of a team. However, although an employee who decides to move on to a new employer will not be in breach of their obligations per se by that decision if they attempt to take confidential information or clients the position may be somewhat different.

General points in relation to evidence collection

The claimant employer must consider the restraints on gathering evidence imposed by the **9.48** DPA 1998, the Regulation of Investigatory Powers Act 2000, the Telecommunications (Lawful Business Practice) (Interception of Communications) Regulations 2000, and the Human Rights Act 1998 (HRA 1998).[53] Some of these restraints fall away once proceedings are underway as the defendant employee will be on notice that evidence is being collected and investigation will be undertaken, although he may still be able to avail himself of his right to privacy (see paragraph 9.61 below). Further there are exemptions to the non-disclosure obligations under the DPA 1998 where the disclosure is required by law or is necessary for the purposes of or in connection with, any legal proceedings or for the purposes of obtaining legal advice or is otherwise necessary for the purposes of establishing, exercising, or defending legal rights.[54]

However, usually the crucial investigations take place before the employee is fully aware that **9.49** the employer is onto him and before legal proceedings are commenced. Indeed the employer often does not want the employee to know of his investigations in the hope that the employee will provide evidence of what the employer suspects is going on. At this stage the claimant employer is unfortunately subject to much more regulation and care should be taken not to breach those duties. There are a number of reasons for this:

(1) Investigation in breach of these provisions may in itself give rise to a claim for constructive dismissal, thus giving an added advantage to the defendant employee.

(2) Useful evidence may be rendered inadmissible if it is collected unlawfully, although the courts have, so far, taken a fairly robust view of this argument. So in the context of the HRA 1998, evidence obtained unlawfully has been admitted but only where it is clearly relevant to the issues (*Jones v University of Warwick*)[55] or justified on another basis.

(3) An unlawful investigation may mean the claimant employer is accused of coming to the court with unclean hands,[56] although there is no authority on this specific point.

(4) The employee could also avail himself of the remedies available to individuals under the data protection legislation itself.

---

[53] Detailed guidance in relation to the law regulating personal data referred to in this paragraph is beyond the scope of this book, and recourse should be had to specialist publications if that is what is required, but the following general guidance should be borne in mind.

[54] DPA 1998, s 35. Note the exemption is only in respect of disclosure—the investigation which produces the evidence, and the processing of it will all be subject to the obligations under the DPA 1998, although the justification of the employer's actions will be easier once legal proceedings are underway given the ongoing obligations in respect of evidence to which those who litigate are subject.

[55] [2003] 1 WLR 954, CA. See also *McGowan v Scottish Water* [2005] IRLR 167; and *Chairman of Governors of Amwell View School v Dogherty* [2007] IRLR 198.

[56] See para 10.20 below.

(5) Monitoring which does not comply with the legislation may constitute a criminal offence, although there is only limited scope in this context for criminal sanctions to apply.[57]

(6) Bear in mind that any evidence discovered in breach of an employer's duties may ultimately be disclosable in the proceedings, even if the claimant employer would prefer to keep it in the background, and not disclose the unlawful investigations it has undertaken to the employee.[58]

9.50 In practice, an employer is unlikely to be greatly concerned by this legislation in the heat of the moment, not least because it will always believe its investigation to be justified because it will consider its business to be at real risk of serious damage. The courts have not been overly enthusiastic about excluding evidence on the basis of breach of the various data protection legislation. Nonetheless, the claimant employer should avoid, if at all possible, investigations which are unlawful as it could give aggressive defendants a tactical advantage.

9.51 General points[59] to ensure an investigation is lawful are as follows:

(1) Most information which is gathered will contain personal data for the purposes of the DPA 1998, but this should not be automatically assumed if the investigation is challenged on the basis of this legislation. Recourse should be had to the case law and guidance issued by the Information Commissioner in this regard.[60]

(2) For all investigatory purposes an employer's life will be much easier if there is in place a wide-ranging policy which makes it clear that an employer will have access to anything the employee is doing at work and anything the employee creates or accesses on work equipment. This policy should specify for what specific business-related purposes this access will take place but should also state that access will also occur for the purposes of investigating wrongdoing by the employee and to investigate competitive activity. The employer should ensure that no employee can reasonably deny that they were aware of this policy.

(3) The employer should nonetheless tread carefully when investigating an employee where the investigation considers private property or communications of the employee. This will often be the case in employee competition cases. The employer should infringe privacy to the minimum extent that is consistent with its investigatory purposes and should have specific justification for its actions.

(4) Where the employee has not been informed of the fact that the specific monitoring will take place, this comes within the category of 'covert monitoring'. This also covers monitoring in a person's home or other place which they could expect to be private. According to the Information Commissioner, this type of monitoring will only be legal where the suspected wrongdoing is very serious—criminal offence or equivalent malpractice—and notifying the individual would prejudice the detection. The employer should ensure the investigation has been authorized by someone senior in the

---

[57] See eg *Tchenguiz and others v Immerman* [2010] EWCA Civ 908, paras 90–104.

[58] Legal professional privilege may apply if the monitoring is for the purposes of legal advice and/or litigation, but not if the monitoring activity is criminal or fraudulent: *Dubai Aluminium Co Ltd v Alawi* [1999] 1 WLR 1964; *Hughes v Carratu International plc* [2006] EWHC 1791 (QB); *Tchenguiz and others v Immerman* [2010] EWCA Civ 908, paras 138 and 159.

[59] For detailed guidance on all these issues see the Employment Practices Code, published by the Information Commissioner's Office (ICO) and section 3 in particular.

[60] *Durant v FSA* [2004] FSR 28, [2003] EWCA Civ 1746; ICO guidance note, 'Data Protection Technical Guidance: Determining what is personal data', 28 January 2009, available via the ICO's website.

organization, allow it to continue only as long as is strictly necessary for the purposes of the investigation, and if it is to be conducted by a third party, ensure that they comply with the data protection obligations of the employer. A similarly onerous approach will apply under the HRA 1998 (although see para 9.49 above in relation to the court's attitude to the admission of this type of evidence).

(5) If what the employer is doing could be challenged on the basis that it is in breach of the right to privacy or data protection legislation, the employer should document contemporaneously the justification for the investigation and the steps taken to minimize the infringement of the employee's rights. This documentation can then be produced in the employer's defence should a challenge be made.

The different types of investigation are considered below in light of these general points.　**9.52**

Paper and other physical evidence

If an employer suspects his employee is about to engage in unlawful competition , what is the　**9.53** best way for the employer to go about searching the employee's desk/office/locker with a view to obtaining any physical evidence of the employee's wrong doing?

(1) A first point to bear in mind is that actual paper documents must not only contain personal data, but must also be in a relevant filing system in order for DPA safeguards to apply. This may mean that an employer is not as regulated in this type of search as compared to electronic documents. Nonetheless, as stated above, the employer should ideally have in place a written policy, of which the employee is aware, making clear that such a search may take place.

(2) From a legal perspective, the least risky route would then be to do the search once the employee has been suspended from work and allowed to remove only what are clearly personal belongings. This may not be satisfactory if the employee has got wind of what is happening or where the most useful evidence is in the employee's personal belongings (for example, personal mobile phone, diary, etc).

(3) A covert search may well be in breach of the DPA 1998 unless the suspected wrongdoing is very serious—criminal offence or equivalent malpractice—and notifying the individual would prejudice the detection.

(4) In either case, further caution would need to be exercised in relation to anything which was clearly private, both from a data protection perspective and from a human rights point of view.[61]

Computers

The investigation of electronic communications (primarily email and internet, but also a　**9.54** review of more esoteric forms of data found on an employee's computer) is covered in Appendix 1, save for what will and will not be lawful in this context.

Most employers will already have certain monitoring systems in place—indeed in some　**9.55** industries the employee's expectation will be that anything done on their employer's equipment will be monitored or could be accessed. Notwithstanding this assumption, the underlying lawfulness of the monitoring should be checked,[62] ie that there is a policy in place

---

[61] See para 9.49 in relation to this.
[62] See the Employment Practices Code, section 3 published by the ICO. Note that constant monitoring to check for unlawful competition is unlikely to be lawful.

which informs the employee of the monitoring and that access to the data during the investigation can be justified. If there is no such policy then the conduct must be very serious and the employer should carefully document the reasons for its decision to go ahead (see para 9.51(4) above in relation to covert monitoring).

9.56 What if the analysis of the employee's data reveals wrongdoing via a private web mail account (for example Hotmail, Yahoo!) which has nonetheless left an imprint on the employer's system? Anything 'private' should be dealt with cautiously but if the obligations described above are complied with (and in particular, the employee is aware that what is done on the employer's system will not be private for these purposes) then the evidence should not be regarded as unlawfully obtained.

9.57 Similar (but not identical) constraints apply as a result of the Regulation of Investigatory Powers Act 2000 and the Telecommunications (Lawful Business Practice) (Interception of Communications) Regulations 2000.[63] See para 9.61 below for the application of the HRA 1998 to surveillance; the same principles will apply here.

Telephony

9.58 The monitoring of telephone lines is commonplace in certain industries for record keeping or quality control purposes. The points made above at paragraphs 9.54 to 9.57 apply to the use of these recordings for other purposes, such as detecting unlawful competition.

9.59 Mobile telephones and other mobile devices such as Blackberries provided by the employer should also be treated as computer systems described above. Texts can be retrieved which can often be illuminating although care needs to be taken if there are also private texts recoverable. Itemized bills which record the recipient and the time of the calls can also be useful.[64]

Surveillance

9.60 Changes in employee behaviour such as weekend working or more working from home can usually be picked up without the employer taking any more proactive steps than ensuring that all levels of management are astute to the movements of their staff. However, a suspicious claimant employer may also consider having the movements and other actions of an employee watched by a third party. This can take the form of physical surveillance (the employee is followed by a third party agent) or mechanical surveillance (phone taps and other listening devices). These are obviously extreme (and costly) tactics.

Physical surveillance

9.61 Before deciding to go ahead with physical surveillance, a realistic view of what can be achieved by doing so needs to be reached. Unless the claimant employer has a strong suspicion that a team of employees is meeting outside the office, with or without the competitor, little meaningful evidence is likely to be gathered by putting a defendant employee under physical surveillance. Any evidence gathered by these means might be excluded by a court if it is

---

[63] A useful starting point when considering these is the Employment Practices Code Supplementary Guidance published by the ICO.

[64] See *Tullett Prebon* (n 4 above), despite the fact a number of Blackberries which had been used during the relevant periods were lost, and with them potentially incriminating texts, a very useful picture of the pattern of calls was obtained by electronically merging the itemized records of calls and texts.

obtained unlawfully. This means that Article 8 of the European Convention on Human Rights (ECHR) (incorporated into domestic law by the HRA 1998)—the right to respect for private and family life—must not be breached (unless that breach can be justified as being for the prevention of disorder or crime, protection of health or morals, or for the protection of rights or freedoms of others) and the claimant employer must also comply with the provisions of DPA 1998. Thus, under HRA 1998, evidence concerning an employee obtained without their knowledge in a 'private' environment—their home, or a private social gathering, for example—may be unlawful.[65] If it is, the courts will only allow such evidence to be relied on in court if it is clearly relevant to do so (*Jones v University of Warwick*)[66] or justified on another basis. Also, overly intrusive surveillance, if the employee becomes aware of it, could be grounds for a claim of constructive dismissal.

In terms of DPA 1998, the points made in relation to covert monitoring are particularly relevant here. **9.62**

Mechanical surveillance

The claimant employer should always consider whether existing closed circuit cameras or recordings of telephone calls may produce evidence which is helpful (as long as that monitoring is legally compliant in the first place). The same points made above at paragraph 9.51 apply save that any arguments about whether this relates to personal data are likely to be limited. **9.63**

Additionally, the employer can consider installing other covert means of mechanical surveillance, for example cameras or sound recording equipment, or automatic recording of telephone communications and other electronic communications. **9.64**

The points made in relation to covert computer monitoring apply equally to covert mechanical recording. Thus, if an employee is recorded without their knowledge, this may be inadmissible as evidence (*Halford v UK*)[67] and, if the employee becomes aware of the recordings, could give rise to a claim for constructive dismissal. A claimant employer may decide to go ahead nonetheless, to give it the comfort that its suspicions about the employee's activities are well founded. However, it should consider that the fact of this surveillance and the results of it may be subject to the duty of disclosure in any future proceedings. **9.65**

Disciplinary processes

In the situation where a claimant employer suspects that a team of employees is leaving, one means of obtaining evidence of what they are planning and which can be used in the future in any litigation is to use disciplinary processes to put pressure on individuals in the group and to obtain information. **9.66**

If an employer has reasonable grounds to suspect that a senior employee is in breach of his obligations of fidelity or of his fiduciary duties due to their actions in organizing a team move, then there may be grounds for disciplinary action. Equally, if an employer believes a **9.67**

---

[65] But see *Wood v Commissioner of Police of the Metropolis* [2009] EWCA Civ 414, where it was held that Art 8 ECHR is not necessarily engaged.

[66] [2003] 1 WLR 954, CA. See also *McGowan v Scottish Water* [2005] IRLR 167; and *Chairman of Governors of Amwell View School* (n 55 above).

[67] [1999] IRLR 471.

more junior member of the team has breached his duties in relation to confidential information, this could also provide grounds for taking disciplinary action.

9.68 The advantage of interrogating employees under the auspices of a disciplinary process is that the claimant employer should have a better chance of defeating claims of breach of trust and confidence. It may also mean that if the claimant employer decides to dismiss the employee concerned, it should be a procedurally (at least) fair dismissal. Further, it will give the claimant employer grounds for commencing a search of emails and other investigations which may otherwise be in breach of DPA 1998. However, if the claimant employer undertakes disciplinary action against an employee without any grounds to do so, that in itself may be a breach of trust and confidence and so to the employee's advantage.

9.69 If the claimant employer does decide to undertake disciplinary action, the following points should be borne in mind.

9.70 The claimant employer should ensure that it abides by the employer's own disciplinary procedure, and should also have in mind the latest version of the ACAS code. Whilst a breach of the employer's obligations in this situation may not be fatal to the enforceability of post-termination restrictions, it could be and it will certainly help the employee's case generally. Also in any subsequent negotiation, a claim for statutory unfair dismissal will assist the employee tactically, albeit that as the employee will be mitigating his or her loss by joining a competitor employer, it will be more a tactical claim, rather than one of any great monetary value.

9.71 Should the employee be suspended? To be safe in doing so, there should be an express term allowing the employer to do so in the contract of employment and the suspension should be on full pay. If there is not and the employer suspends the employee, or does so without paying him, this may be grounds for constructive dismissal. The other disadvantages of suspension are that it tips the employee off as to the employer's suspicions and also means that the employee is out of sight. Particularly in team move situations, the employer may prefer to keep the employee close to hand. On the other hand, suspension can separate the employee from their work colleagues and clients and send a clear message, so it is certainly worth considering.

9.72 Bear in mind that the employee will have the right to be accompanied and will most often request to be accompanied by a 'partner in crime'. There is not much that can be done about this without risking the fairness of the process and giving the employee a specific claim in respect of that right.

9.73 The claimant employer should plan its questions carefully to maximize the information it obtains from the employees. Full and accurate notes should be taken of what is said (if possible, the claimant employer should obtain consent to the tape recording of the investigation meeting or have a shorthand writer available to capture all the information). The transcripts, if reliable, may be very useful in cross-examination in any subsequent trial, especially if the employees are being less than truthful. The claimant employer needs to bear in mind, however, that all of its statements will be recorded as well and ensure that its approach is appropriately measured.

9.74 Particularly where junior employees are concerned, the process can be used to put pressure on the defendant employee in what is, already, a very stressful situation. The claimant employer must be careful not to take this too far, however, to avoid the defendant employee claiming breach of the implied term of mutual trust and confidence and constructive dismissal.

See paragraphs 9.33 to 9.35 above for the considerations in relation to the decision to dismiss **9.75** the employee. If the decision is taken not to dismiss the employee as a result of the disciplinary action, consider whether any other sanctions could be used creatively. However, the claimant employer should bear in mind that any such steps which go beyond the employer's contractual rights will be risky.

Remember that the employee will usually have the right to appeal and can also drag out the **9.76** process, for example by raising a separate grievance in relation to the way in which the process has been conducted.

Other miscellaneous investigations

The claimant employer should consider investigating the following: **9.77**

(1) The employee's holiday and absence records—they may reveal an unusual pattern of absence, or one which is similar to that of other employees.
(2) Security records which track an employee's arrival in and departure from the office—this may show an unusual pattern of visits to the office.
(3) Review of the expense records of the defendant employee(s)—it has been known for employees to claim expenses relating to travel to group meetings to discuss leaving or for client visits which are clearly not for the benefit of the claimant employer.
(4) Examination of the company's photocopier records where the photocopier can only be activated using key codes or pass codes specific to each employee—an unusually large amount of photocopying may suggest removal of confidential information (although email removal is more common these days).
(5) Speaking to clients and customers to see if the defendant employee(s) have approached them in an unlawful way. However, generally, commercial considerations mean that the claimant employer is reluctant to involve clients at all. Circumstantial evidence of a reduction of activity with these clients or customers may, therefore, be more relevant.

The claimant employer needs to keep in mind that the constraints placed on it in relation to **9.78** data protection etc described earlier in this chapter will also apply here.

Where the claimant employer suspects that the employee may be going to compete via a **9.79** start-up, additionally the employer should check records at Companies House—to see if the defendant's name is connected with any corporate entity—and any other business records which may be relevant.

Pre-action court orders

It may be appropriate to apply for a court order, either before or shortly after commencement **9.80** of proceedings, in order to obtain evidence of unlawful competition. The most draconian of such orders, a search order, should only be used in the most serious of situations, as quite often the claimant employer may find itself in breach of the onerous obligations which apply to such orders and the costs incurred will be disproportionate. Other lesser forms of this relief may, however, be appropriate. These are dealt with in Chapters 10 and 12 below. In relation to team moves see, in particular, *Aon Ltd v JLT Reinsurance Brokers Ltd* [68]—the court has a wide discretion as to whether to grant disclosure orders at the interim stage and care should be taken when formulating pre-action orders or the application may end up back firing.[69]

Letters before action

9.81 If a claimant employer considers that it has sufficient evidence of breach or intent to breach by the defendant employee(s), it then needs to consider what steps to take (in addition to deciding how to deal with the termination of the employee(s)' employment). Writing to the defendant employee(s) and employer is usually the first step.

Who should correspond?

9.82 Generally, initial correspondence will be from the claimant employer direct to the employees concerned, especially if it involves placing the employee on garden leave or reminding them of their post-termination obligations where the employer only suspects that the employees intend to breach. Solicitors may well be involved on behalf of the claimant employer at this stage, but more likely behind the scenes.

9.83 In considering whether solicitors should go on the record, the claimant employer should consider the following factors. By solicitors coming on the record, this indicates that any pretence of a maintenance of trust and confidence in relation to the defendant employees is weakened. However, if the defendant employee is represented by solicitors, it will be more acceptable.

9.84 Solicitors are probably less prepared to make extravagant threats than the claimant employer would on their own behalf. Also, once solicitors are on the record, it will be more difficult to withdraw gracefully from the process should insufficient evidence come to light or should the claimant employer turn its attentions elsewhere. Solicitors' letters will definitely be a more intimidating threat to the defendant employee.

The addressees of the letters

9.85 The claimant employer will need to consider who should be sent the letters. The issues are as follows. The defendant employee will usually always be sent a letter, but in a team situation, should letters be sent to all those in the team who are moving? It may be decided not to send letters to more junior employees where:

- The claimant employer is trying to keep them on side, in the hope of persuading them to stay and/or provide evidence.
- The more junior employees may not have breached their obligations to the same degree or at all, in which case a letter will be less effective.
- Costs—sending letters to all the employees may increase costs significantly, especially if different employees instruct different lawyers.

Notwithstanding the above, the effect of letters to all employees in the team can be significant, causing consternation and, as a result, disruption to the team move.

---

[68] [2010] IRLR 600; cf *Hays Specialist Recruitment (Holdings) Ltd and another v Ions and another* [2008] IRLR 904.

[69] See also paras 10.167–10.178 and 12.58–12.69 below.

It will usually be sensible to write immediately to the defendant employer to, at the least, put **9.86** them on notice of the (actual or threatened) breaches and of the claimant employer's concerns about the involvement of the defendant employer. The claimant employer may decide not to do so where it is unsure about the identity of the defendant employer.

The claimant employer may also be tempted to copy some of these letter(s) to other parties, **9.87** for example various key people within the defendant employer. Caution should be exercised in this regard, as the contents of such letters before action are potentially libellous. Although any claim of defamation may be met by the defence of qualified privilege or justification, it is another tactic which can cause discomfort to the claimant employer.

Structure of the letters[70]

Whilst obviously it is not possible to prescribe the detailed contents of the letters here, as **9.88** this will vary depending on the factual context, there are common matters which should be dealt with as follows:

(1) The status of the defendant employee (resigned but still working/on garden leave, left, etc) and the identity of the employer which the employee is believed to be joining.
(2) The relevant contractual obligations of the defendant employee. These should be set out in some detail, if possible.
(3) The alleged breaches by the defendant employees or, where the letter is to the defendant employer, additionally, the alleged inducement of breach.
(4) The remedy the employer is seeking (undertakings, injunction, damages, disclosure, etc) and the repercussions if the addressee of the letter does not comply.
(5) A time limit for compliance.
(6) Encouragement to the employee to seek legal advice urgently (if the letter is to the employee directly).
(7) A general reservation of rights.

The threat

In drafting the letter before action, the claimant employer needs to think carefully about the **9.89** remedy it is seeking. The following factors should be taken into account.

Is injunctive relief appropriate? Assuming that the legal case stands up to scrutiny, it still may **9.90** not be appropriate where the harm has already occurred and cannot be remedied by the court, or where damages will be the appropriate remedy. Nor will it be appropriate where there has been too much delay. The letter before action can, of course, threaten another remedy, although the time limit is then likely to be different.

Is it appropriate to threaten the defendant employer at this stage or at all? It may only be **9.91** appropriate to put the defendant employer on notice of the defendant employee's contractual obligations at this stage if there is no evidence of an economic tort.[71] If there is evidence, then letters before action with suitable threats should be sent to the defendant employer as well.

Must the consequence of a failure to comply with the threatened remedy always lead to court **9.92** action? The claimant employer should be wary of threatening litigation and, in particular, an

---

[70] See the sample pre-action letters at Appendix 9 below.
[71] See paras 2. 234–2. 259 above.

injunction, if it does not intend to proceed with that course. Threats which are not pursued will eventually lead to a lack of credibility in respect of any further threats made by the employer.

9.93 The threat should be based on the legal remedies available to the employer. Thus in a springboard situation seeking restrictive covenants from the employees to fill a gap in the contractual documentation of the defendant will not sit well with the court.[72]

9.94 The time limit (for example for the defendant to give undertakings) that the claimant employer should include in the letter will depend on the relief sought. In the case of relief where short notice of the application is being given, a very short time limit will be appropriate of, say, twenty-four hours. In all applications for interim relief, the urgency of the matter will probably dictate a short time limit. In line with the overriding objective, a longer time limit may be appropriate where non-urgent remedies are sought. Also, where an unrepresented defendant employee is the addressee, a slightly longer time limit may be appropriate to ensure the employee is able to obtain legal advice.

9.95 In an interim application, the claimant employer also needs to consider the form of undertaking it will accept to resolve the matter. The options are as follows.

9.96 Where the claimant employer wishes to be as aggressive as possible about the relief sought and where it does not trust the defendant employees and employer, undertakings to the court should be sought. This, in effect, means that the parties agree a form of order for interim relief by consent and apply to the court for it to sanction that order pending speedy trial, an earlier interim hearing, or other agreement between the parties. It commits the parties to court proceedings, unless settlement is otherwise reached. This means that if the defendants are in breach of the order, the remedy of contempt of court will usually be available to the claimant employer. Equally, the claimant employer will be obligated under the cross-undertaking in damages.

9.97 In less aggressive situations, written undertakings in the form of the garden leave or post-termination restrictions should be sought. These are a re-affirmation of the legal obligations of the defendants. The remedy for breach will be the same as for breach of the original obligations, albeit that it will be more difficult for the defendants to put forward arguments relating to enforceability or to assert that they are not bound by the obligations. Such undertakings thus provide some comfort to the claimant employer and are more appropriate where the claimant employer is less sure of its intent to pursue litigation for whatever reason, indicating a less aggressive approach.

9.98 In an interim application, where an undertaking to the court is sought pending speedy trial or a later hearing, a cross-undertaking in damages must also be offered, either in the letter itself or in the draft order which is attached to the letter.

Enclosures

9.99 The claimant employer should, in line with the overriding objective,[73] enclose with the letter any relevant documentary evidence. This will certainly include the employee's contractual documentation (redacted as appropriate to hide remuneration details if it is going to the

---

[72] See *Crowson Fabrics Ltd v Rider* [2008] IRLR 288, para 64.
[73] CPR, r 1.1.

defendant employer) but could also include relevant emails and even statements taken from those involved (albeit it need not include the formal witness statement in support of the application at the initial stage, other than where the application is on short notice, where ideally it would).

Additionally, usually the letter will include the undertaking sought by the claimant employer. **9.100** This can either be in the simple form of a written undertaking or a court order.

Means of delivery

Where urgent interim relief is sought, it will be appropriate to send the letter to the defen- **9.101** dant employee(s) by means other than normal post. Courier, where a signed confirmation from the courier company can be provided to confirm that the letter has been delivered, may be sufficient but in very contentious and/or urgent situations, the claimant employer should consider the use of process servers who will be able to produce an affidavit of service.

Many defendant employees have personal fax numbers and/or email addresses. These could **9.102** be used, but should usually be used in addition to more traditional means of delivery and, in the case of an email, a telephone call to inform the defendant employee that the email has been sent. That said, there are no formal rules dictating how such correspondence should be delivered; the key issue should be to ensure that evidence of delivery and the timing of the delivery can be produced. Letters should be marked strictly private and confidential, especially those sent to the defendant employer, which may pass through other hands than those of the intended recipient.

Potential for settlement

Although the claimant employer will obviously be on the offensive in this matter, it should **9.103** always be open to a negotiated resolution. In fact, quite often, this will be the real intent behind the threat made, especially where only written undertakings are sought. Creative solutions such as profit sharing, future cooperation and a contribution to the costs incurred all have the massive advantage of saving cost and possibly minimizing the disruption to clients. Claimant employers should, however, be wary of pursuing threats purely for the purposes of settlement and with no intent of litigating, as the defendant employee and employer may simply call their bluff, leaving the claimant employer with no option but to back down quietly.

The claimant employer should also remain open to the option of alternative dispute resolu- **9.104** tion. Not only is this in accordance with the overriding objective, but it can lead to a cost-effective resolution. Mediation, in particular, should be considered, particularly where a defendant employer is involved and underwriting the dispute. However, often the competitive interests of the parties mean that the degree of cooperation required from the parties to make a mediation work will not be available.

The claimant employer should also consider the regime under Part 36 of the Civil Procedure **9.105** Rules. If the claimant makes a Part 36 offer to settle the claim which is accepted by the defendant(s), the claimant will receive his costs up until the date on which the defendant(s) serve notice of acceptance.[74] Further, if the claimant does better at any eventual trial than the Part 36 offer he made, the court may order additional interest on any damages awarded and

---

[74] CPR, 36. See further paras 12.157–12.170 below.

the costs awarded to the claimant on an indemnity basis. This can obviously put pressure on the defendants.

C. The defendant employee

The defendant employee's obligations

9.106 The first stage in assessing an employee's ability to move to a new employer involves considering what obligations the employee owes to his current employer.

Contract of employment

9.107 The most obvious set of obligations will be under the contract of employment. The following scenarios may apply:

No written contract

9.108 If there is no formal written contract of employment and the parties have proceeded on the basis of an oral understanding or exchange of brief letters or emails, there will, nonetheless, still be a contract of employment between the parties, albeit that it is based on whatever documents there are, what was discussed by the parties, and terms implied by law. Typically this will result in the following terms:

- Notice—the minimum notice will be one week to be given by the defendant employee, and one week per year of employment, subject to a maximum twelve weeks to be given by the claimant employer (in the absence of grounds for summary dismissal), as these are the notice periods applied by section 86 of the Employment Rights Act 1996. However, a longer period may be implied based on discussions between the parties, accepted practice at that particular employer, or custom and practice in the particular industry.[75]
- Garden leave—previously the position was that unless there was an express term in the contract the court would be unlikely to enforce a garden leave injunction. Now a court may enforce a garden leave injunction where there is a serious breach on the part of the employee—see paragraph 9.19 above.
- Implied duty of fidelity during employment.[76]
- Implied duty in relation to confidential information.[77]
- A court will not imply any further post-termination restrictions into the contract.[78]

A written contract but unsigned by the employee

9.109 The claimant employer will argue strongly that either the employee has accepted the terms of the contract by his or her conduct or that the unsigned contract is the best evidence of the terms of the contract between it and the employee. A court is likely to accept this in so far as there is no evidence to the contrary. An exception to this is in relation to restrictive covenants, where an unsigned contract may mean the restrictive covenants will not be enforced by the court.

---

[75] *Hill v CA Parsons & Co Ltd* [1972] Ch 305, CA.
[76] See Chapter 2 above.
[77] See Chapter 3 above.
[78] See eg *New ISG Ltd v B Vernon and others* [2008] ICR 319, [2008] IRLR 115, paras 15–19.

A written contract signed by the employee

In this case the employee will generally be bound by the express terms of the contract as well **9.110** as the implied terms set out above, unless one of the following applies.

Are the restrictions set out in a separate document which is said to be incorporated into the **9.111** contract of employment? If so, is it possible to challenge the incorporation and argue that the terms are not binding on the employee?[79]

Are the restrictions set out in a separate document, for example a long-term incentive scheme **9.112** or similar? It may be possible to challenge the restrictions on the basis that the parties to this type of arrangement will often not include the actual employer of the defendant employee[80] and/or on the basis of the law of that document which may not be UK law.[81]

Can the employee argue that he signed the contract of employment under duress? It will be **9.113** a difficult argument for the employee to maintain where he has continued to work under the terms of the new contract, as even if duress can be shown, it will only render the contract voidable and continued working may be held to be a ratification of its terms (*Hepworth Heating Ltd v Akers*).[82] However, where an employee did not receive legal advice on the enforceability or otherwise of the post-termination and other restrictions in his contract of employment, where there were complex provisions which the defendant employee did not properly understand, he may be able to argue that they are not binding on him (*R v HM A-G for England and Wales 2003*).[83]

Has there been any other variation of the relevant parts of the contract, for example of the **9.114** notice period or by the introduction of new restrictive covenants? If so, those parts of the contract may not be enforceable against the defendant employee unless the employee has consented to the variation either expressly or by implication and there is good consideration for the variation.[84]

Is there good consideration for the contract which contains the restrictions? This can be an **9.115** issue particularly where the employee signs up to new restrictions on leaving.[85]

Has there been a transfer of business or outsourcing which would come within the terms of **9.116** the Transfer of Undertakings (Protection of Employment) Regulations 2006 (TUPE)? If so, the protection provided by the post-termination restrictions contained in the contract may be reduced, limiting the scope of the restrictions to protecting the undertaking transferred (*Morris Angel & Son v Hollande*).[86]

Did the employee agree to the restrictions, whether as part of a new contract or otherwise in **9.117** connection with a transfer under TUPE? If so, the relevant provisions may not be enforceable by the employer against the employee as variations of contract where the reason for them

---

[79] For a recent example of this see *SG&R Valuation Service* (n 25 above), 15–17. See also paras 5.17 to 5.26 above.

[80] *Samengo-Turner v J & H Marsh & McLennan (Services) Ltd* [2008] ICR 18, [2008] IRLR 237, CA.

[81] *Samengo-Turner*; *Duarte v Black & Decker Corp* [2007] EWHC 2720 (QB), [2008] 1 All ER (Comm) 401.

[82] IDS Brief 36 (July 2003), EAT/846/02.

[83] [2003] EMLR 23.

[84] See paras 5. 27–5.53 above.

[85] *WRN Ltd v Aryis* [2008] IRLR 889, paras 43–6.

[86] [1993] ICR 71, [1993] IRLR 169, CA. See paras 5.323–5.327 above.

is the transfer (regulation 9 of TUPE 2006 and for pre-April 2006 transfers, *Wilson v St Helens BC*).[87] Further, an employee may be entitled to argue that post-termination restrictions are not enforceable, whilst remaining entitled to receive lucrative benefits under the same contract (*Credit Suisse First Boston (Europe) Ltd v Robert Lister*).[88] Finally, did the employee object to the transfer in accordance with regulation 4(7) of TUPE 2006? If so, the transferee employer may not be able to rely on the terms of the contract which would otherwise have transferred.[89]

9.118   The employee also needs to consider the financial impact of leaving to compete with his or her employer. Does the contract of employment or any ancillary documents contain bonus or share provisions which will be adversely affected (for example, a lapse of the benefits or a trigger of a clawback provision)? If so, and if the employee's negotiating position allows it, the defendant employee may wish to seek an indemnity from the new employer in respect of the sums he or she will lose.

Other obligations

9.119   In addition to the duties under a contract of employment discussed above, the employee may owe fiduciary duties. These are dealt with in detail in Chapter 2 above,[90] however, the employee should in particular be aware of the duties of disclosure of his own intentions and those employees for whom he is responsible.[91]

9.120   The defendant employee should also check any other agreements entered into in connection with his or her employment and in particular any share option or equivalent agreements as these may contain further contractual restraints on the employee.

Constructive dismissal

9.121   Whatever the contractual obligations applying to the employee, it may be possible to argue that the employee has been constructively dismissed as a result of the actions of the employer.[92] In that situation, the employee will not be bound by any obligations other than possibly those in respect of confidentiality (*Campbell v Frisbee*).[93] In order to free him or herself from the contract the employee does not need to leave *because* of the breach; the existence of a breach, together with his leaving, will be enough.[94] Tactically such a move may at first sight appear attractive to the defendant employee—it gives the defendant employee a better negotiating position and may, if it is a well-founded claim, defeat the legal case against him in its entirety. However, if the case put forward by the defendant employee is weak, the court is likely to regard it with scepticism.[95] The defendant employee (and those who are indemnifying him or her) would be wise also to consider the increased costs which will be generated if an argument for constructive dismissal is put forward. See also paragraphs 9.148 to 9.153 below in relation to the defendant employer and the economic torts.

---

[87]   [1999] 2 AC 52, [1998] IRLR 706, HL. See paras 5.328–5.333 above.

[88]   [1999] 1CR 794. See paras 5.328–5.333 above.

[89]   *New ISG Ltd v Vernon* [2008] ICR 18, [2008] IRLR 115.

[90]   See paras 2.37–2.138 above. The questions identified at para 9.36 are also useful to assist the employee in identifying what the issues may be.

[91]   See paras 2.98–2.126 above and in particular para 2.120.

[92]   See paras 5.100–5.124 in relation to the law relating to constructive dismissal.

[93]   [2003] ICR 141, CA. See paras 3.80–3.83 and 5.139–5.141 above.

[94]   *Tullett Prebon* (n 4 above), para 78.

[95]   ibid, para 86; *Extec Screens and Crushers Ltd v Rice* [2007] EWHC 1043 (QB).

Agreement with the new employer

One of the first things the defendant employee needs to consider is whether he or she will **9.122** tell the recruiting employer the terms of his or her current contract of employment. For obvious reasons, it will be better if the employee gives full disclosure of the terms of his contract and any restraints contained in it relatively early in the process. The only time that will not be the case is where the employee is concerned that it will be off-putting for the new employer.

The employee should then consider his or her contract of employment with the new employer **9.123** and the inclusion of the following provisions.

The contract of employment should state that although it is legally binding on the parties, **9.124** employment under it will only commence when the employee is legally free and able to join the new employer. Such a form of contract has been held to be lawful even when the date the defendant employee can join his new employer is months or even years ahead.[96] This can then be used to evidence the fact that the defendant employee had no intention of breaching those provisions (as to notice, or non-competition) in his contract of employment which are enforceable and binding on the employee. It is also useful for the defendant employer to evidence that it did not intend to induce breach. The employee should, however, understand that if he or she signs a contract in this form, it may bind him to actually join the new employer or face a breach of contract claim if he fails to do so. Therefore, if the discussions with the defendant employer are primarily being used as leverage in a negotiation with the claimant employer, a defendant employee should be careful about what commitment he or she makes to the defendant employer.

The defendant employee should seek an indemnity from the new employer in respect of any **9.125** losses he or she suffers as a result of his or her leaving. In the best case, this would cover any losses, for example bonus and/or share options and/or any clawbacks, claims for damages against the employee, and legal costs relating to any claim brought by the claimant employer. The new employer may attempt to resist the idea of an indemnity on the basis that it may be seen as evidence of inducement of breach or weaken any claim for constructive dismissal. In fact, such indemnities are commonly accepted as part and parcel of this type of transaction. Nonetheless the timing of the giving of an indemnity, for example very early on in the process, may not be helpful to the defendant employer. Also, an indemnity which goes beyond simply covering legal costs and damages may be more likely to be seen as evidence of inducement.[97]

An indemnity need not appear as a term of the employment agreement itself, but should **9.126** usually be in a separate document (although this is unlikely to defeat any disclosure obligation for long). The defendant employee will obviously require the indemnity to be in writing—this may be resisted by the employer on the basis that an oral agreement will be less incriminating. However, the existence of an oral agreement is likely to be disclosable under any cross-examination.[98] Alternatively, agreement in relation to the indemnity in respect of

---

[96] *Tullett Prebon* (n 4 above), para 142(b).
[97] See paras 9.158–9.159 below for a further discussion of indemnities from the defendant employer's point of view.
[98] See eg Jack J's comments in *Tullett Prebon* (n 4 above), para 193.

legal fees and damages could be reached between lawyers for the employee and new employer, who could then attempt to rely on the legal privilege relating to litigation matters, although this is unlikely to be a successful tactic.[99]

9.127 The defendant employee would, no doubt, also like to see wording dealing with some form of 'golden hello' or sign on bonus.[100] This is another way of dealing with deficits in the employee's bonus or share option position, but the same points made in relation to the indemnity above should be taken into account.

9.128 The employee should check that any post-termination restrictions are no more onerous than those in their existing contract, if arguments in relation to the latter are likely to be raised. Otherwise, if the new contract of employment is disclosed during the course of proceedings, the defendant employee's credibility in arguing that the restrictive covenants in the contract with the claimant employer are unenforceable may be affected, especially where the businesses of the old and new employer are similar.

9.129 Finally, the employee should try to negotiate post-termination restrictions that he or she considers are acceptable. As negative as it may seem at this stage, he will leave the defendant employer at some stage in the future. Relying on the assumption that the restrictions will be too wide to be enforceable is risky. Generally the claimant employer will have more resources to invest in disrupting the defendant employee's plans by litigation and may do so even when that litigation is based on unenforceable restrictions.

Dos and don'ts during employment

9.130 Chapter 2 sets out in detail the duties to which an employee is subject during employment. As a result of these obligations, there are a number of dos and don'ts the defendant employee should bear in mind, which apply if the employee wishes to avoid breaching his or her duties to the claimant employer, appearing to breach those duties, or enabling the claimant employer to discover their breach. They are a mixture of common sense rules and ways of avoiding the creation of unhelpful evidence.

Single employee leaving

9.131 The employee should consider whether they are bound under the express terms of the contract to disclose the approach of a competitor. If they do not, they risk being in breach of contract, which may be used tactically in any negotiations in relation to their departure.[101] Disclosure of an approach may in any case be beneficial as it may enable the employee to cement his or her position with his or her existing employer.

9.132 To state the obvious, the employee must continue to abide by his duties as an employee whilst still employed. So, for example, he should not disclose his employer's confidential information as part of the recruitment process, even though it may be tempting during the recruitment process to impress with talk of projects in development or details relating to employees who may follow.[102]

---

[99] ibid.

[100] Jack J held that payments of this type were lawful in *Tullett Prebon* (n 4 above), para 142(b).

[101] See para 9.10(2) above and *Tullett Prebon* (n 4 above), para 142(d).

[102] See eg *RDF Media Group plc v Clements* [2008] IRLR 207, para 137.

The employee should not take any documentation (in hard or electronic form) containing **9.133** company information, even if he or she does not consider it to be confidential. In the first place this could be categorized as theft of employer property. Secondly, even the printing of the information on the employer's paper or using the employer's equipment to email a file may be a breach of the employee's obligations to the employer, as it is use of the employer's property for the employee's own purposes. Further, the fact of the removal of the information will be used to create prejudice against the defendant employee in the court's eyes and in this situation the court is unlikely to be concerned with whether the information contained in the documents is actually confidential.[103] Any such information removal is likely to be detected. So, although it seems obvious, the employee should not email files of information to their home email address—this is one of the first things the employer might check.[104] The employee should not ask his or her secretary to print out client lists, etc as they may be questioned in this regard. Even printing out or photocopying documents to remove manually may be dangerous if the printing or photocopying can be traced back to the employee, especially if there are large volumes or the employee does not normally go near the photocopier. Finally, removing already existing original documents (in so far as they exist in the modern office) may be the least detectable way of information removal, but such documents will be subject to the disclosure obligation in any proceedings. Further, if the claimant employer seeks delivery up, or in more extreme situations, obtains a search order, their existence will be discovered earlier in the proceedings and, at best, adverse inferences drawn.

The employee should not speak to or communicate in writing with clients or employees **9.134** about his or her intention to leave prior to resigning. Even if the employee has no intention of soliciting clients or employees, again the fact of these conversations may be used to create prejudice. See also the dos and don'ts in relation to start-ups/team moves below.

Competitive start-up

Where the employee is setting up a new business to compete with the defendant employer, **9.135** the employee will wish to take certain steps to prepare to compete. Steps an employee may wish to take are looking for finance, premises, stationery and other equipment, setting up the legal entity, considering staff.[105] However, none of this should be done if it breaches the following rules.

There should be no diversion of opportunities which would otherwise be useful to the claimant **9.136** employer, for example, premises, new employees.

None of these activities should take place during work time or using work equipment, for **9.137** example email. In relation to the latter point, there is double jeopardy for the employee, as not only does he do something which is likely to be seen as a breach of the employee's employment duties, but also he provides the evidence of it.

If the employee is a director or otherwise owes fiduciary duties, he should be very cautious **9.138** about taking preparatory steps to compete before he has announced his intention to resign.[106]

---

[103] *JN Dairies Ltd v Johal Dairies Ltd* [2009] EWHC 1331 (Ch D); see also *WRN Ltd v Aryis* [2008] IRLR 889, paras 73–9.

[104] See Appendix 1 below.

[105] See Chapter 2 above, and in particular paras 2.150–2.160 in relation to an employee preparing to compete.

[106] See paras 2.72 ff and, in particular, 2.98–2.138 above.

9.139 The employee may also wish to create a business plan to obtain financing for the new business before he resigns. They should do so without using any confidential information of the employer (for example, employee and other costs, revenue streams from certain clients), and without evidencing any other breaches by the defendant employee. Otherwise a business plan can be extremely dangerous evidence against the employee (see *Walsh Automation (Europe) Ltd v Bridgeman*[107] where this guidance was not followed).

Team moves

9.140 Developments in case law mean that an individual's involvement in a team move is a risky business, especially if that employee owes fiduciary duties as a director, de facto director, senior employee, and/or enjoys responsibility for more junior employees.[108] The reality is that to avoid being in breach of those fiduciary duties and/or contract such a senior employee whilst being free to resign and join a competitor himself as a sole agent, must abide by the following rules if he knows he is likely to be joined by some colleagues:

(1) inform his employer of the competitor's approach as soon as a failure to do so would mean that he is no longer able to act in his employer's sole interest.[109] Arguably if the competitor says at the first meeting that it is intending to recruit colleagues irrespective of whether the employee to whom the approach is being made comes, the duty to disclose arises at that point;

(2) ring fence himself completely from the recruitment exercise relating to any colleagues. This obviously means no active recruitment by him of his colleagues to join the new employer, but also rules out background chats to reassure his colleagues that the move is a good idea and facilitate the move;

(3) report to his employer any actual approach to his colleagues as soon as he becomes aware of it;

(4) refrain from passing not only confidential information that would assist in the recruitment, but any information which would assist;[110]

(5) comply with his employer's instructions as to how to deal with the approach by the competitor, although presumably not to the extent that it would prevent the senior employee in this situation leaving.

9.141 In addition to these points for a senior employee, the following dos and don'ts apply to all employees.

9.142 An employee must consider carefully any express provisions in his or her contractual documentation requiring him or her to inform the employer of an approach by a competitor to him or her or another employee. A failure to inform the employer can be a breach of contract and put the employee on the back foot before anything has even happened. See paragraph 9.10 above in relation to these types of provisions. Absent such a provision, an employee who is not subject to fiduciary duties and subject only to the contractual duty of loyalty is *probably* not under a duty to disclose his own decision to leave along with other colleagues, but may

---

[107] [2002] All ER 79. See also *Tullett Prebon* (n 4 above), para 157, where details of employees retained in an employee's head after they have left are held not to be protectable confidential information, but cf para 69.

[108] See paras 2.37–2.71 above for the nuances of the duties attaching to the different types of fiduciary duty.

[109] See eg *Tullett Prebon* (n 4 above), para 68. See also paras 2.98–2.138 above for a full exposition of what this duty of disclosure entails.

[110] ibid, para 69.

be under a duty to disclose approaches to or the intentions of those other colleagues or at least not mislead the claimant employer about them.[111]

Human beings constantly communicate, but in team move situations, evidence of this communication can be extremely damaging. Any employee involved in a team move should not use company equipment (email, mobile, or other telephones) to communicate with other team members. Both email and telephone communications can be used in evidence. The fact of telephone calls, which can be evidenced by the call register, may also prove to be unhelpful evidence. Also destroying the evidence of these communications or conveniently losing the offending telephone or Blackberry is unlikely to stand the employee in good stead in the long term.[112]   **9.143**

The employees in a team move situation should also consider using headhunters to approach the   **9.144**
potential new employer on their own behalf and should expect to be approached by headhunters on behalf of the new employer. However, the fact that the headhunter is soliciting on behalf of the employee will not render legal what would otherwise be illegal acts by the employee.

Ultimately, though, even if an employee has been extremely careful evidentially, the   **9.145**
defendant employee and defendant employer are likely to be required at any trial to give evidence under oath as to their activities. Therefore, the employee's best tactic is, as far as possible, not to breach his terms and conditions and any other duties.

Response to letter before action

If a defendant employee receives a letter before action, his or her first step should be to   **9.146**
instruct lawyers, if he has not done so previously. If the employee has an indemnity from his new employer, in practice his response is likely to be dictated by the new employer. If the employee has no indemnity or is setting up a new business, he will have to make his own decisions. However, unless extremely wealthy, the best route will be to give the best undertakings the employee can offer to try to avoid litigation and the costs associated with it. Even if wealthy, the time and stress involved in any litigation means that the best route will often be to avoid it, if at all possible, especially where a new business is being established.

For further tactics on receipt of letters before action, see paragraphs 9.176 to 9.183 below.   **9.147**

D. The defendant employer

Potential liabilities

The economic torts

The defendant employer could potentially be liable for the various economic torts discussed   **9.148**
in detail in Chapter 2 above,[113] ie inducement of breach of contract, causing loss by unlawful means, and conspiracy.

---

[111] *Kynixa Ltd v Hynes, Preston & Smith* [2008] EWHC 1495 (QB), para 283; cf *Lonmar Global Risks Ltd v Barrie West and others* [2010] EWHC 2878. See also paras 2.120–2.123 and paras 2.166–2.169 above.

[112] *Tullett Prebon* (n 4 above), para 65 in relation to the loss of numerous Blackberries by the defendants. Nonetheless the claimants in this case were able to create a compelling picture of what had gone on during certain periods by reference to the call registers for the phones/Blackberries of various members of the teams which were merged electronically.

[113] See paras 2.234–2.259 above.

9.149 In employee competition situations the most likely tort to be committed by the defendant employer is inducement of breach of contract. This also usually forms the basis of the unlawful means necessary for the torts of causing loss by unlawful means and the most common type of conspiracy. This tort can occur whether it is one or several employees who are being recruited. The details of the tort are set out above in Chapter 2 but in reality if the contract of the defendant employee is more likely than not to be enforceable, then if the defendant employer recruits him in breach of its provisions, there is a risk that the tort will be made out. Equally if the defendant employee is likely to have committed some other breach of contract, such as assisting in recruitment in breach of his duty of fidelity or leaving when he is not entitled to, and the defendant employer is aware of and sanctions these plans, then again he is likely to have induced breach of contract. The defendant employer should consider this checklist when assessing its liability:[114]

- Is there or is there likely to be a breach of contract on the part of the defendant employee? This is the key point for the defendant employer to address—as to how to go about doing so, see paragraphs 9.155 to 9.157 below.
- Did the defendant employer induce or incite the breach in any way?
- Did he intend the employee to breach his contract or was he indifferent as to whether he did so, as long as he achieved his end?

If the answer to all these questions is yes, then the defendant employer will have induced breach of contract.

9.150 In relation to conspiracy by unlawful means[115] any legal advisor would be well advised to consider his or her own liability for this economic tort carefully, as well as that of their client, when acting for either the defendant employer or the defendant employee especially in a team move situation. The temptation to move beyond the role of detached advisor and become involved as a recruiter or in making the plan to claim constructive dismissal may be all too great. This is even more the case where the defendant employer is paying the fees of the lawyers for the defendant employees. [116]

9.151 Note also that an early plan to cause the recruited employee(s) to bring claims for constructive dismissal which have marginal merit with a view to securing an early departure date may well backfire. In addition to the extra costs generated by such a strategy, the defendant employer is at real risk of liability under the economic torts.[117]

9.152 Equally in a team move, using senior employees to provide information for and to assist with a mass recruitment is a sure road to liability for an economic tort. See paragraphs 9.163 ff below in relation to this.

9.153 Much of what follows is aimed at minimizing the liability of the defendant employer for economic torts but the reality is that they are a risk that must be assumed when aggressively recruiting, especially where team moves are concerned.

---

[114] See paras 2.235–2.247 for more detail in relation to this test.
[115] See paras 2.252–2.259 for detail on the recent developments in this area of the law.
[116] See *Tullett Prebon* (n 4 above), paras 170–6 for a discussion concerning the position of a lawyer for some of the employees. See para 9.162 below in relation to the issues of privilege that arise.
[117] ibid paras 179–82.

Indemnities

The other major potential liability for the employer will be payments under the indemnities **9.154**
to the employees. In certain industries these are now the norm. Points in relation to their
drafting are dealt with below at paragraph 9.159.

Analysis of the employees' obligations

From the previous sections, it will be seen that the defendant employer's legal liability whether **9.155**
under the economic torts or indemnities almost always turns on whether the defendant
employee(s) are in breach of contract. In order to establish what potential liabilities may
arise, the new employer should therefore obtain disclosure of the contracts of employment
and other obligations of the employees. Although by doing so, the defendant employer will
satisfy one of the constituent elements of the tort of inducement of breach of contract
(ie knowledge),[118] with sophisticated employers, ignorance of the contractual terms is
unlikely to carry much weight as a defence. Also, this disadvantage is outweighed by having
an accurate assessment of the legal and commercial risks attached to the recruitment. This is
obviously essential where an indemnity is being provided. The defendant employer will only
be able to assess risk based on the information provided by the defendant employee. Therefore,
it should consider making the defendant employee's new employment contract and/or
indemnity conditional on full disclosure of all obligations. See paragraph 9.159 below in
relation to more detail on the terms of the indemnity.

Early disclosure is also wise as an employee may be subject to an express term in his contract **9.156**
which obliges him to disclose an approach by a competitor.[119] A defendant employer should
be aware of this and that he may be inducing breach of contract if he swears the recruit to
secrecy.

An additional tricky issue for the defendant employer in this context is the fact that many of **9.157**
the employees' contractual provisions cannot be looked at in isolation, in particular the
restrictive covenants. The defendant employer may need information about the claimant
employer's business to assess properly the enforceability of the defendant employee's contractual terms. Can it require the defendant employee to disclose this information even
where such disclosure may be a breach of confidentiality by the defendant employee? If it
requires disclosure directly to it, it takes a risk that that would be inducement of breach of
contract and the defendant employee would be wise to refuse. Whilst the defendant employee
can disclose the information to their own legal advisors for the purposes of obtaining legal
advice and take advantage of the cloak of privilege,[120] no such protection will be available
where the defendant employee discloses the information directly to the defendant employer.
The safest route will either be for the defendant employer to rely on its own knowledge of the

---

[118] See paras 2.238–2.239 above.

[119] See para 9.10 above and *Tullett Prebon* (n 4 above), para 142(d).

[120] Although disclosure of confidential information to the employee's lawyers will strictly be in breach of
confidence, the legal privilege attaching to litigation means the fact that the information has been disclosed
need not be revealed. See *R v Derby Magistrates' Court, ex p B* [1996] AC 487 in relation to the scope of legal
privilege. Legal privilege will however cease to apply where the information relates to a criminal or fraudulent
enterprise: *Dubai Aluminium Co Ltd v Alawi* [1999] 1 WLR 1964; *Tchenguiz and others v Immerman* [2010]
EWCA Civ 908, para 138 (but see also paras 68–71, 259—legal privilege does not appear to have been raised
as a defence to the application to deliver up the documents, presumably because on the facts it had been waived).
In *Dubai Aluminium* Rix J held that this exception to the legal privilege rules did not extend to civil wrongs (in
that case trespass and conversion as a result of stealing documents from the claimant's dustbin).

industry or research into the industry without recourse to the defendant employee. Alternatively, the advice given to the defendant employee on the back of his full disclosure to his own solicitors can be shared with the defendant employer's lawyers, as long as none of the specific confidential information is referred to. The disclosure of the advice should not waive privilege attaching to the advice as common interest privilege applies—see paragraph 9.162 below.

Terms of the contracts and indemnities for the defendant employees

9.158   The defendant employer will obviously need to consider the terms of any new contract to be offered to the employees it is recruiting. The key point for the employer will be to minimize the risk of a claim of inducement of breach of contract. Although in *Tullett Prebon v BGC*,[121] the use of future conditional start dates (forward contracts), indemnities, and golden hellos were not of themselves held to be unlawful, they need to be drafted carefully.

9.159   In relation to any indemnity offered to the defendant employee, from the employer's perspective, the following should be considered:

- The indemnity should be conditional on full disclosure being given by the employee of his relevant contractual obligations and actions relevant to any possible claims that may be made against him by his current employer, subject always to his duties to his current employer.
- If possible, the indemnity should be limited to damages and costs arising from any litigation as a result of the employee leaving employment in accordance with what has been agreed with the new employer and should not cover any other claims the employee has in relation to their current employment generally (for example bonus or share options that may be lost on termination).
- The indemnity should give the employer complete control of the tactics and direction of any litigation, including the choice of lawyers and counsel and whether or not to settle. However, this needs to be framed carefully to avoid allegations of the employee being the defendant employer's 'puppet'.
- The indemnity should provide what will happen if the employee leaves the new employer's employment—will the indemnity continue? The employer may want the option to retain control of any litigation and it may be that the only way to do this is by continuing to foot the bill.

Tactics

Representation

9.160   Generally, the defendant employer and defendant employee(s) should have separate representation. This is to minimize the risk of accusations of inducement of breach of contract and in recognition that, whilst the interests of the defendant employer and the defendant employees are very closely aligned, there is potential for a conflict between those interests, for example where the employee has not disclosed all relevant facts to the new employer.

9.161   Do the individual defendant employees need separate representation? This will depend on whether there is any conflict between their positions. For example, where a senior employee

---

[121]   See n 4 above, para 142.

acts as 'recruiting sergeant' in relation to more junior employees a lawyer may not feel able to act for both groups of employees as the evidence of the more junior employees may be damaging to the case of the more senior employee. There is nothing to stop each individual employee being represented separately although it will increase costs.

Privilege

If, as is likely, the defendant employer and the employee are separately represented for proceedings, communications between them should be subject to common interest privilege (*Buttes Gas and Oil Co v Hanimer*).[122] Caution should be exercised, however, where the defendant employer's lawyers provide advice to the employee direct or vice versa. As the advice given is not being given to a client, it may not be privileged. Equally if a meeting is held between the defendant employer and defendant employee to discuss substantive issues at which one of their lawyers is present, again privilege may not attach. Another danger area is where a parent company of the defendant employer, which is not a party to any proceedings, is receiving copies of the advice—again no legal privilege may attach to it (*Three Rivers DC v Governor and Co of the Bank of England (No 5)*).[123] Finally, no privilege will attach to the negotiation of contracts by lawyers on behalf of the defendant employer and employee respectively, nor to arrangements made on behalf of their clients in relation to recruitment meetings or arrangements between the lawyers for the defendant employee and the defendant employer in relation to costs.[124]

9.162

Team moves

In a team recruitment situation, extra care needs to be taken. Typically, any team recruitment will only be discussed initially with the senior employee(s) in the group. Such senior employees will either be directors (whether actual or de facto) and as such fiduciaries or almost certainly owe duties in respect of their colleagues which are or are akin to fiduciary duties. Unfortunately for the defendant employer it is extremely difficult to have confidential discussions about a team move with such an employee without causing the senior employee or employees to breach their duties to the employer. The following are steps an employer can take to minimize the risk of any breach by the senior employee, or at least minimize the risk that evidence of a breach and inducement of it by the new employer will come to light.

9.163

Absent any express provision in the senior employees' contract which requires earlier disclosure,[125] the defendant employer should not instruct any defendant employee who is in a fiduciary position to keep confidential from the claimant employer the fact that an approach has been made and the basis of the approach. Preferably the discussions should be had on the basis that the senior employee's duties are acknowledged and that he must act as he sees fit to ensure that he continues to act in the sole interest of his employer. Certainly once the senior employee has formed a settled intention to leave, he should inform the claimant employer and be as open as possible with the claimant employer about who is at risk and

9.164

---

[122] [1981] QB 223.
[123] [2003] QB 1556, [2003] 3 WLR 667, CA.
[124] See *Tullett Prebon* (n 4 above), para 63(50)–(75) for an example of how this might impact on evidence.
[125] See para 9.10 above.

from which competitor. The defendant employee should also make it clear (if it be the case) that they believe other employees will follow them to a competitor.

9.165 One approach, therefore, is to tell the senior employee nothing about any planned recruitment of his colleagues and recruit him expressly on the basis that he comes alone. Obviously this should then be followed through and the senior employee should not, either before or after his resignation, be involved in the recruitment of other team members.[126] However, he should be encouraged to publish the fact of his resignation as widely as possible (subject always to the fact that (a) this may be a risky strategy where the employee owes fiduciary duties and (b) it will be a reasonable instruction of the claimant employer to require him to keep quiet the fact of his resignation until the claimant employer has had a proper opportunity to put its house in order).

9.166 The defendant employer should, in the meantime, take the following steps:

(1) Either directly or via a headhunter, approach the other team members separately. It should identify the other employees via information which is publicly available and document the fact that it has done so. The same approach should be taken to approaching the employees, ie it should not use home or mobile telephone numbers which could only have been provided by the senior employee. If using headhunters, written instructions should be given to them which support the case that the intention is to recruit people without reference to the senior person in the team and, if possible, each other. Ideally, suitable candidates from employers other than the claimant employer should also be recruited.

(2) Advertise for the other vacancies, but then see people from all employers, not just those from the claimant employer. Consider whether a media strategy would also assist, highlighting the defendant employer's desire to build up this part of the business.[127]

(3) Ensure that the proposed arrival of the senior employee is given as much publicity as possible. Whilst the claimant employer can order the senior defendant employee not to reveal the fact that they have resigned and are joining a competitor, that order cannot extend to the new employer. The new employer does, of course, take a risk that it will be embarrassed if the senior employee is persuaded to stay at his existing employer, or indeed join yet another competitor.

9.167 An alternative approach to this which has not been tested before the courts would be a bottom up approach—that is sign up the more junior employees first without the knowledge of the key senior employee and then present the senior employee with a fait accompli. At that point the senior employee would be obliged to inform his employer but he could do so and resign at the same time. The junior employees' contracts could be made conditional on the senior employee joining at either party's option. By this approach the risk of a breach of fiduciary duty would be minimized, but the practical efficacy of this approach must be doubted. It would require as a minimum significant funds for packages to tempt employees

---

[126] See eg *Lonmar Global Risks Ltd v Barrie West and others* [2010] EWHC 2878 and in particular para 185, where a senior employee was not found to have solicited his fellow employees in breach on the facts. Note , however, that he was also held not to owe any fiduciary duties (para 191: 'He was a somewhat lonesome salesman').

[127] See, however, *Lonmar Global Risks,* ibid, paras 115–120 where such a strategy did not prevent the court from deciding as a matter of fact that the defendant employer had targeted the more junior members of the team.

away without the comfort of the boss leading them, very skilful headhunters and employees who are able to keep their mouths shut. If the senior employee is a strong team manager, he or she might suspect something was afoot and scupper the whole plan by trying to find out what it is.

If the defendant employer, despite these obstacles, manages to sign up a group of colleagues, **9.168** it should also give consideration to the timing of the team's resignations and give instructions to the individual employees accordingly (if that is practical). The following guidelines are worth bearing in mind.

As stated above any employees with fiduciary duties should, to avoid breaching those duties, **9.169** resign sooner rather than later.[128]

More junior employees with less onerous contractual provisions (shorter notice and post- **9.170** termination restrictions) could be instructed to resign first. It may then be possible for the employees with more onerous provisions to argue that as the employees with less onerous provisions are able to start work more quickly, there is no point in enforcing their more onerous post-termination restrictions, as the enforcement of the provisions will not have the effect of protecting the legitimate business interests of the claimant employer (cf *GFI Group Inc v Eaglestone*).[129]

From a tactical perspective, will it be better if all the employees resign together or if they do **9.171** so in stages? The former has the advantage of surprise and also appearing as a fait accompli. It may also mean that the team sticks together, making it more difficult for the claimant employer to persuade employees to stay and reveal what has been happening. The disadvantage is that it is much more consistent with a coordinated team move and so in itself may be evidence of a breach by the employees coordinating the team move.[130] As a practical matter it will also be difficult to organize if a senior employee is not involved. Also the fact that employees resign together, will not with a sophisticated employer mean they are able to leave together—their contracts will have been drafted so that within a team the leaving dates are staggered.

A more gradual approach can be good where the employer is less likely to be suspicious if one **9.172** employee resigns and then other employees leave after becoming aware of this fact. This can be combined with advertisements for roles at the new employer and the use of headhunters. However, the likelihood of all employees moving is reduced—it gives the claimant employer opportunity to persuade members of the team to stay. Further a gradual approach may give the claimant employer the opportunity to apply for a springboard injunction, preventing the defendant employer from building on those resignations which have already taken place, particularly if those resignations which have already taken place are perceived to be unlawful.[131]

Should a defendant employer plot with the defendant employees to create a constructive **9.173** dismissal situation which applies to some or all of the employees? This is a very high risk strategy—taking advantage of the claimant employer's own acts which make constructive

---

[128] See paras 2.72 ff and, in particular, 2.98–2.138 above.
[129] [1994] IRLR 119. See paras 4.221–4.223 above.
[130] See *UBS Wealth Management (UK) Ltd v Vestra Wealth LLP* [2008] IRLR 965.
[131] ibid; *Tullett Prebon* (n 4 above) and after trial: [2010] IRLR 648, paras 250–3.

dismissal a viable option is one thing but actively instructing employees to create those arguments is another.[132]

9.174   One additional point has arisen out of *Tullett Prebon v BGC*. If the defendant employer does conduct the recruitment exercise unlawfully this may be grounds for those it has recruited arguing that they are no longer bound by their contracts with the defendant employer if, for example, their old employer 'turns' them and convinces them to stay.[133]

9.175   Ultimately team moves are not for the faint-hearted. The likelihood of the court granting a very effective springboard injunction at an early stage seems to be greater as a result of the decisions in *UBS Wealth Management (UK) Ltd v Vestra Wealth LLP*[134] and *Tullett Prebon plc v BGC Brokers LP*.[135] The defendant employer risks finding himself with a senior employee on an expensive package who is unable to work because of a court order, no team, and ongoing litigation with the costs and potential for damages associated with that. As a result, a careful cost benefit analysis should be undertaken although if that is done in writing care should be taken in relation to its contents as they will be disclosable.[136]

Response to the letter before action

9.176   On receipt of a letter before action the defendant employer will need to decide what response should be given by it and the defendant employee(s). Obviously, this will depend on many variables, but the main ones will be the commercial need to ensure that the defendant employee(s) are able to commence employment as soon as possible, the strength of the legal case against them, and any so-called 'smoking guns'. Quite often in these situations, the claimant employer will be unaware of the full extent of the activities of the defendant employee(s) and the defendant employer, whereas the latter is likely to be well aware of the issues which are unhelpful to their position and which should temper their approach to the litigation. Note, however, the obligations imposed on all parties in accordance with the overriding objective, including setting out details of their case in any pre-action correspondence.[137]

9.177   Depending on that assessment, the defendant employer needs to consider whether to offer no undertakings at all, only written undertakings, or whether to offer full undertakings to the court. The following considerations will apply.

9.178   No undertakings at all will be sensible where the defendant employer is very confident of its case or where it does not believe that the claimant employer will follow through with its threat to litigate the matter. Even then, the defendant employer should bear in mind the overriding objective, and case law which states that a defendant should give serious consideration to offering an appropriate undertaking until speedy trial (*Lawrence David Ltd v Ashton*).[138]

---

[132]   *Cantor Fitzgerald v Bird* [2002] IRLR 867; cf *Tullett Prebon Plc v BGC Brokers LP* [2010] IRLR 648.
[133]   ibid paras 199–206.
[134]   See n 47 above.
[135]   See n 4 above.
[136]   See eg the comments of Jack J in *Tullett Prebon* (n 4 above), paras 63(27) and (73).
[137]   See also Practice Direction—Pre-Action Conduct, paras 6, 7, and Annex A.
[138]   [1989] ICR 123, CA.

Written undertakings may be an appropriate means of assuaging the claimant employer's **9.179**
ardour for litigation or useful where the defendant employer does not believe that the
claimant employer will actually proceed to litigation. Note, however, that if such undertakings are provided, the defendant employee(s) and employer will not have the benefit of
any cross-undertaking in damages, unless one is negotiated. The other benefit of written
undertakings is that they can be confidential if such a term is negotiated as part of the
resolution.

Undertakings to the court may be appropriate if a matter is clearly going to be litigated, a **9.180**
speedy trial is likely to come on quickly and a cross-undertaking in damages may ultimately
be useful. The offer of undertakings can be used tactically by the defendant employer. So, for
example, where the claimant employer is seeking to enforce a non-compete covenant, and
arguably a provision restricting dealings with the claimant employer's customers would be
sufficient to protect the claimant employer's legitimate interests, an offer of such an undertaking can make it much more difficult for the claimant employer to justify the enforcement
of the non-compete covenant. This may result in undertakings to the court which are less
onerous to the defendant employee(s) and employer than would otherwise be the case.
However, a breach of undertakings given to the court in the form of a court order can give
rise to action for contempt of court, which may result in criminal liability for the parties in
breach.[139]

The defendant employer should also consider the use of the costs regime to assist resolution **9.181**
of an interim application. Part 36 of the CPR allows a defendant to make an offer under that
regime which includes the terms of undertakings which the defendant employer and
employee would be prepared to give. The defendant must, however, be prepared for the costs
bill which will be generated by the acceptance of such an offer. The pre-action costs of the
claimant employer in an interim application situation can be substantial. However, if the
claimant employer does not accept the offer and at trial fails to beat it, the defendant(s) will
generally receive their costs from the date twenty-one days after the offer was made. Bearing
in mind the truncated timetable which often applies in these types of situations, the defendants should consider such a tactic very soon after any interim order has been made or
undertakings agreed and then on an ongoing basis.[140]

The high costs involved make threats of an interim application particularly problematic for **9.182**
start-up businesses, as not only are they distracting but potentially a drain on the start-up's
initial funding, which it can well do without. If a defendant employer finds itself in that
situation, it should consider carefully the commercial considerations in not giving undertakings and if at all possible assuage the claimant employer. If it does not, at a minimum it
will have its own legal costs to bear, which can be significant.

For the same reasons, settlement will often be attractive to the defendant employer and often **9.183**
settlement negotiations will occur alongside the 'on the record' correspondence. Also, settle-
ments are often reached without any payments being exchanged, although the claimant
employer will, of course, look for one. This is because, at interim hearings of this type, a costs

---

[139] See paras 10.208–10.223 below.
[140] See also paras 9.103–9.105 above in relation to settlement, and 12.157–12.178 below in relation to Part
36 and settlement. For an example of a case where such an approach was taken, see *Tullett Prebon* (n 4 above)
(costs).

order will often be delayed until trial and so the defendants are able to take a more robust position on costs.[141] If, however, the claimant employer will not engage in without prejudice discussions, the defendant employer and employee should consider making an open offer of the undertakings they are prepared to give. By doing so and giving the claimant employer some of the protection he seeks, they may be able to make the claimant employer appear unreasonable before the court and so make the task of persuading the court to grant the full relief sought more difficult.

---

[141] See 12.155–12.156 below on the costs of interim applications.

10

INJUNCTIONS AND OTHER
INTERIM REMEDIES

Paul Goulding QC, Tom Croxford, Ivan Hare,
Stephen Nathan QC, and Catherine Taylor

A. Introduction[1]

Remedies in general

There is one key question which a legal adviser will frequently be asked by a client caught up **10.01** in a dispute about employee competition: what can be done? The employer wants to know what he can do to stop what he sees as unfair competition by a formerly loyal employee.[2] Conversely, the employee wants to know what steps might be taken against him if he takes up his new employment, or carries it on in a particular way. It is a timely reminder that however fascinating (to the lawyer) are the legal issues thrown up in this area of the law, it is the practical side to which answers must be found. The remaining three chapters of this book seek to go some way towards providing those answers.

---

[1] See also Appendix 10, Sample Witness Statement in Support of Application for Interim Injunction to Restrain Breach of Restrictive Covenant below.

[2] Or director, partner, joint venturer, or vendor, as the case may be.

10.02   This chapter considers injunctions and other interim remedies. Injunctions are the most common form of remedy in employee competition cases. They have certain obvious advantages. Interim injunctions can be obtained quickly, nascent competitive activities can be nipped in the bud, and they can provide tactical advantages in the settlement of disputes. In addition, there are special types of interim orders which can be very useful alongside or instead of the more usual type of injunction. These include search orders, delivery up orders, destruction and detention orders, disclosure orders, *Norwich Pharmacal* orders, freezing orders, and interim declarations.[3] They are all covered in this chapter.

10.03   Whilst many employee competition cases settle at or shortly after an application for an interim injunction, some cases continue through to trial. This might be the result of the speed with which trials can be heard nowadays. It might also reflect the fact that claimants are concerned to recover damages for losses suffered. This appears increasingly to be the case as evidenced by the number of recent cases on damages, and the increased creativity of the courts when it comes to damages and other final remedies. The following chapter considers these issues of damages, accounts of profits, tracing and other proprietary relief, and final declarations.

10.04   The final chapter of this book (Chapter 12) provides an overview of the practice and procedure of the High Court and County Court. It focuses on those rules and issues which most commonly arise in employee competition cases, and with which any practitioner in this field needs to be familiar.

Injunctions: the basics

10.05   Before embarking on a detailed examination of the principles applied by the courts in deciding whether or not to grant an injunction, some basic definitions are in order.

Jurisdiction to grant an injunction

10.06   The power of the High Court to award an injunction is based on section 37(1) of the Senior Courts Act 1981, which provides: 'The High Court may by order (whether interlocutory or final) grant an injunction or appoint a receiver in all cases in which it appears to the court to be just and convenient to do so.'[4]

10.07   The ultimate test, therefore, is whether an injunction is 'just and convenient'. This should always be borne in mind. It provides room for creativity. It is not necessary to show that the particular form of injunction has been granted before, but that it is 'just and convenient' on the facts of the particular case. This is subject to two qualifications. First, there must be an actionable wrong committed, or threatened,[5] before a court will intervene by way of injunction. Secondly, in exercising its discretion whether or not to grant an injunction, the court will generally act in accordance with principles which have been identified in previous cases. These are discussed below.

---

[3] These interim remedies are listed in CPR, r 25.1, and are discussed in the notes which are found after the rule.
[4] The Senior Courts Act 1981 (formerly the Supreme Court Act 1981 but re-titled by the Constitutional Reform Act 2005) is found in *The White Book*, Vol 2.
[5] Where an injunction is granted to prevent unlawful conduct that is threatened in the future, but has not yet taken place, it is known as a *quia timet* injunction.

Prohibitory, springboard, and mandatory injunctions

The Civil Procedure Rules (CPR) contain a Glossary which defines an injunction as 'a court **10.08** order prohibiting a person from doing something or requiring a person to do something'.[6]

A *prohibitory* injunction is a court order prohibiting a person from doing something. It is the **10.09** most common form of injunction in employee competition cases. It is granted, for example, to restrain an employee from breaching a restrictive covenant, or disclosing confidential information, or working for a competitor during garden leave.

A *springboard* injunction is a type of prohibitory injunction. It can be particularly useful in **10.10** the employee competition field. There is some controversy as to its ambit. In general terms, it prohibits competitive activity (of a defined nature appropriate to the circumstances of the case) so as to cancel out any unlawful springboard or head start gained as a result of the misuse of confidential information and, in light of recent authority, other unlawful conduct.

A *mandatory* injunction is a court order requiring a person to do something. In employee **10.11** competition cases mandatory orders tend to be ancillary to the primary order, such as orders to deliver up property. Each of these types of injunction is discussed in more detail below.

Interim and final injunctions

As section 37(1) of the Senior Courts Act 1981 states, injunctions can be 'interlocutory **10.12** or final'.[7]

An interlocutory or interim injunction is granted for an intervening period until the court **10.13** can determine whether a final injunction should be granted. 'Interlocutory' and 'interim' are interchangeable terms to describe this form of injunction ('interim' is generally used in this book). Thus, an interim injunction might be granted until a specified date, or until trial, and in each case 'until further order'.

A final injunction may be granted at trial after a final judgment by the court. A final **10.14** injunction may be limited or unlimited in time.

Since only a minority of employee competition cases continue after the interim stage, the **10.15** main part of this chapter will examine the court's approach to interim injunctions and other interim orders. Final injunctions will then be briefly discussed. The principles of contempt of court will then be considered, the penalties for which represent the ultimate deterrent to breach of an injunction (or undertaking given to the court) and other court orders. Finally, a checklist will identify in summary form the main issues to look out for in an employee competition case concerned with injunctions and other interim remedies.

Discretionary considerations

An injunction is a discretionary remedy. The exercise by the court of its discretion will depend **10.16** on the facts and circumstances of each individual case. However, there are certain factors which have been recognized as relevant to the exercise of the court's discretion, and which arise with some regularity in employee competition cases.

---

[6] *The White Book*, Vol 1, Section F.
[7] See para 9.06 above.

Overriding objective

10.17 The court must seek to give effect to the overriding objective stated in CPR, rule 1.1 when it 'exercises any power given to it by the Rules' or when it 'interprets the meaning of any rule'. The courts have called in aid the overriding objective in relation to managing applications for interim injunctions, in particular, the objective of dealing with the case in ways which are proportionate to the amount of money involved, the importance of the case, the complexity of the issues, and the financial position of each party.[8]

Delay

10.18 Delay in seeking an injunction is likely to count against an applicant for relief. This could be for a number of reasons. The delay might be relied on as evidence that the employer does not need an interim injunction otherwise it would have sought the court's intervention at an earlier date. Again, delay on the part of the employer in applying to the court may mean that the employee has taken on commitments (for example starting a new job) which it would be unjust to prevent him fulfilling.

Clarity

10.19 An injunction must be framed in clear and precise terms so that the defendant knows what he can and cannot do. This is of particular importance having regard to the fact that breach of an injunction is a contempt of court punishable by imprisonment.

Unclean hands

10.20 Even if the claimant employer has not repudiated the employment contract which, upon acceptance, discharges the defendant employee from his restrictive covenants,[9] any misconduct by the employer may count against the employer in the exercise of the court's discretion. However, it is not enough that the court disapproves of the employer or his behaviour. There must be some link between the misconduct and the relief sought. In addition, the refusal of relief on the basis of the employer's 'unclean hands' must be proportionate.

B. Interim injunctions

A typical scenario

10.21 A typical scenario in which an application is made for an interim injunction in an employee competition case is as follows. Evidence comes to light suggesting that the employee is acting, or is likely to act, in breach of a restriction in his employment contract (such as seeking to join a competitor before expiry of his notice period, or acting in breach of a post-termination restrictive covenant). The employer writes to the employee, setting out its concerns and asking for appropriate undertakings by a specified deadline. In the absence of a satisfactory response, the employer (or its solicitors) notifies the employee of its intention to apply to the court, and of the date and time of the application. The notice given must be three days ('on notice') or, in cases of urgency, it may be less ('informal notice'). The employer lodges at court and serves on the employee, a claim form, application notice (including draft order), and witness statement(s) in support. At the initial hearing, the court may grant an interim

---

[8] See the notes to CPR Part 25, esp at 25.1.3 of *The White Book* (2010); *A v B (A Company)* [2002] EWCA Civ 337, [2002] 2 All ER 545, CA; *Aon Ltd v JLT Reinsurance Brokers Ltd* [2010] IRLR 600, para 17.

[9] See Chapter 5 above.

injunction if the case is made out for urgent relief. The court is also likely to give directions for the full hearing of the application (such directions to include exchange of written evidence, skeleton arguments, and an expedited hearing).[10] This further hearing will most likely take place within seven to fourteen days after the initial hearing. At this further hearing, the court is likely to make an order for speedy trial. It may grant or continue interim injunctive relief pending trial. A speedy trial can take place within one to three months (depending on the urgency, shorter if absolutely necessary) following an order to that effect, with directions being given as to further interlocutory steps (such as disclosure, and exchange of witness statements). It is quite common for a defendant at this further hearing to give undertakings to abide by limited restrictions pending speedy trial (for reasons explained further below).

Of course, there are many variations to the above scenario, but it does represent the typical **10.22** progress of proceedings which has become fairly commonplace. In the light of this, it is critical to understand what approach the court takes in deciding whether or not to grant an interim injunction pending trial. This is discussed below.

It is important to emphasize at the outset that, in considering applications for interim **10.23** remedies, reference should be made to Part 25 of the CPR, the notes to Part 25, and Practice Direction 25A—Interim Injunctions. Part 25 contains the core rules on interim remedies, the notes to Part 25 summarize the key case law and applicable principles, and the practice direction gives practical guidance on the steps to take in making an application. These rules change from time to time and it is therefore important to consult these provisions in *The White Book* to ensure that the latest version is taken into account. It is also well to remember that important updates to Part 25 are found in Supplements to *The White Book* which should always be consulted. The procedure involved in making an application is considered in greater detail in Chapter 12 below on 'Practice and Procedure'.

Prohibitory injunctions

Generally, the court decides whether or not to grant an interim injunction in accordance **10.24** with what are known as the *American Cyanamid* principles. At one time, it was thought that the approach in restraint of trade cases was different, and that the *American Cyanamid* principles did not apply. In part, this was due to the fact that a restrictive covenant would have expired by the time the matter came on for trial, during a period when there were greater delays than at present in the court process.

It is now well settled that restraint of trade cases are not an exception to the *American* **10.25** *Cyanamid* approach. However, the precise approach may vary depending on whether a speedy trial can take place before the period of the restraint has wholly or substantially expired. The correct approach was laid down by the Court of Appeal in *Lawrence David Ltd v Ashton*.[11]

The *Lawrence David v Ashton* approach

In *Lawrence David v Ashton*, the employers applied for an injunction pending trial to prevent **10.26** the employee from joining a competitor in breach of a two-year non-competition covenant.

---

[10] The importance of the court dealing expeditiously with applications for interim relief was emphasized in *EE & Brian Smith (1928) Ltd v Hodson* [2007] EWCA Civ 1210, where a delay of four weeks in giving a judgment with reasons was described by the Court of Appeal as unacceptable: paras 28–30.

[11] [1989] ICR 123, CA.

The judge at first instance dismissed the application. The Court of Appeal allowed the appeal and granted the interim injunction.

10.27 The two-judge court (Balcombe and Fox LJJ) grappled with conflicting authority as to the correct approach to an application for an interim injunction in restraint of trade cases;[12] in particular, did the *American Cyanamid* principles apply? The court answered this question very clearly in the affirmative.

10.28 Balcombe LJ (with whom Fox LJ agreed) felt that it should be 'firmly stated that the principles of *American Cyanamid* apply as well in cases of interlocutory injunctions in restraint of trade as in other cases'.[13] He added:

> It is only if the action cannot be tried before the period of the restraint has expired, or has run a large part of its course, that the grant of the interlocutory injunction will effectively dispose of the action, thus bringing the case within the exception to the rule in *American Cyanamid*, such as was considered by the House of Lords in *NWL Ltd v Woods* [1979] ICR 867 (and I refer in particular to Lord Diplock's speech at p880) and also by this court in *Cayne v Global Natural Resources plc* [1984] 1 All ER 225. It is then that the judge may properly go on to consider the prospects of the employers' succeeding in the action.[14]

He concluded with words which have had, and continue to have, a profound impact in practice:

> I reiterate: there is no special rule relating to interlocutory injunctions in cases of restraint of trade. The normal rule in *American Cyanamid*, and the exceptions to that rule, apply. A defendant who has entered into a contractual restraint, which is sought to be enforced, should seriously consider, when the matter first comes before the court, offering an appropriate undertaking until the hearing of the action, provided that a speedy hearing of the action can then be fixed and the plaintiff is likely to be able to pay any damages on his cross-undertaking. It is only if a speedy trial should not be possible that it would then be necessary to have a contest on the interlocutory application. I do not believe that, in this comparatively limited type of case—limited in numbers, that is—the courts of first instance will not be able to arrange for a speedy hearing of the action, and thus avoid time being spent, usually unnecessarily, on contested interlocutory applications.[15]

10.29 There are a number of important points to note in this passage from Balcombe LJ's judgment. First, he refers both to the normal rule in *American Cyanamid*, and the exceptions to it. Both will be considered below. Secondly, he says that a defendant should consider giving undertakings until speedy trial. This comment has become very popular with employers and their advisers for obvious reasons. Unless a restrictive covenant is plainly bad, or there are other exceptional circumstances, this comment is frequently relied upon to exert pressure on a defendant to offer undertakings rather than resist an application for an interim injunction pending speedy trial. It gives a considerable tactical advantage to employers. Thirdly, Balcombe LJ suggests that there should only be a contested interim application if a speedy trial cannot be arranged. This would be a rarity nowadays. Whilst there is sometimes a

---

[12] Support for the view that *American Cyanamid* principles did not apply to restraint of trade cases was found in the judgments of Lord Denning MR in *Fellowes & Son v Fisher* [1976] QB 122, CA and (together with Lawton LJ) *Office Overload Ltd v Gunn* [1977] FSR 39, CA. The contrary view was followed in *Dairy Crest Ltd v Pigott* [1989] ICR 92, CA and by Nicholls LJ in *John Michael Design plc v Cooke* [1987] FSR 402, 405–6.
[13] [1989] ICR 123, 132.
[14] ibid 135.
[15] ibid 135.

difference between the Queen's Bench and the Chancery Divisions in terms of the delay in fixing trials, the courts can generally arrange speedy trials within such timeframe as the needs of the case require. The net effect of Balcombe LJ's comment, and the reduction in waiting times, means that there are fewer contested interim applications, and more cases proceeding towards speedy trial, than previously.

The *American Cyanamid* principles

The *American Cyanamid* principles refer to the approach which should generally be followed by the court in deciding interim injunction applications. The principles were identified by Lord Diplock (with whom their other Lordships agreed) in his speech in *American Cyanamid Co v Ethicon Ltd*.[16] They concern three matters: **10.30**

(1) serious issue to be tried;
(2) adequacy of damages; and
(3) balance of convenience.

Serious issue to be tried

Prior to the *American Cyanamid* case, it was thought that an applicant for an interim injunction had to show that he had a greater than 50 per cent chance (a prima facie case) of obtaining a final injunction at trial. This test was discarded by the House of Lords. A new threshold requirement was put in its place, namely a serious issue to be tried. Lord Diplock said: **10.31**

> The court no doubt must be satisfied that the claim is not frivolous or vexatious, in other words, that there is a serious question to be tried.

It is no part of the court's function at this stage of the litigation to try to resolve conflicts of evidence on affidavit as to facts on which the claims of either party may ultimately depend nor to decide difficult questions of law which call for detailed argument and mature considerations. These are matters to be dealt with at the trial . . . So unless the material available to the court at the hearing of the application for an interlocutory injunction fails to disclose that the plaintiff has any real prospect of succeeding in his claim for a permanent injunction at the trial, the court should go on to consider whether the balance of convenience lies in favour of granting or refusing the interlocutory relief which is sought.[17]

It is rare in a restraint of trade case for a court to conclude at the interim stage that there is no serious issue to be tried. Generally, such applications are decided on the balance of convenience. However, where a restrictive covenant is obviously flawed on grounds of lack of legitimate interest or unreasonableness, a court might conclude that there was no serious issue to be tried as to its enforceability. **10.32**

Adequacy of damages

If the claimant succeeds in demonstrating that there is a serious issue to be tried as to his entitlement to a final injunction, the court next turns to the adequacy of damages. Although Lord Diplock treated this as the first stage of the balance of convenience, nothing turns on its precise classification, and it has become customary to refer to this as a discrete, second stage in the *American Cyanamid* test. **10.33**

---

[16] [1975] AC 396, HL.
[17] ibid 407–8.

10.34 The adequacy of damages is first considered from the claimant's point of view. Lord Diplock said:

> As to that, the governing principle is that the court should first consider whether, if the plaintiff were to succeed at the trial in establishing his right to a permanent injunction, he would be adequately compensated by an award of damages for the loss he would have sustained as a result of the defendant's continuing to do what was sought to be enjoined between the time of the application and the time of the trial. If damages in the measure recoverable at common law would be adequate remedy and the defendant would be in a financial position to pay them, no interlocutory injunction should normally be granted, however strong the plaintiff's claim appeared to be at that stage.[18]

10.35 It is clear from this passage that if a defendant can demonstrate that a claimant would be adequately compensated in damages in the event that an injunction were granted at trial but not at the interim stage, then the application for an interim injunction should be dismissed. It is, however, very difficult for a defendant in an employee competition case to persuade a court that damages would be adequate for the employer. There are two principal reasons why it is frequently considered that damages are an inadequate remedy for the claimant. First, it may be impossible to quantify the employer's loss which is attributable to the employee's wrongdoing. If the employee solicits the employer's clients in breach of a restrictive covenant, the employer would face a number of evidential problems: how to prove that the loss of a client was due to the employee's solicitation rather than for other reasons? what is the knock-on effect on the employer's business of the employee's breach of covenant causing consequential loss to the employer? Secondly, an employee may be unable to pay any award of damages that is made due to his relative lack of resources. However, in an appropriate (and probably exceptional) case, a defendant may undertake to keep proper accounts of business transacted, and even to pay a proportion of revenue into court, pending trial. This may lead the court to conclude that damages would be an adequate remedy for the claimant, and accordingly to refuse to grant an interim injunction.[19] In *Phoenix Partners Group LLP v Asoyag*,[20] the judge was satisfied that the potential damage to the claimant employer, if an injunction to enforce a restrictive covenant were to be refused, would be limited and in any event capable of quantification.[21] The limited duration of the restraints was an important factor to be taken into consideration (three months only remaining following the set-off of three months on garden leave).

10.36 Assuming damages are not an adequate remedy for the claimant, the equivalent question is addressed from the defendant's point of view. As Lord Diplock put it:

> If, on the other hand, damages would not provide an adequate remedy for the plaintiff in the event of his succeeding at the trial, the court should then consider whether, on the contrary hypothesis that the defendant were to succeed at the trial in establishing his right to do that which was sought to be enjoined, he would be adequately compensated under the plaintiff's undertaking as to damages for the loss he would have sustained by being prevented from doing so between the time of the application and the time of the trial. If damages in the measure recoverable under such an undertaking would be an adequate remedy and the plaintiff would be in a financial position to pay them, there would be no reason upon this ground to refuse an interlocutory injunction.[22]

---

[18] [1975] AC 396, HL, 408.
[19] This was suggested by Nourse LJ in *Warren v Mendy* [1989] 1 WLR 853, 868.
[20] [2010] IRLR 594.
[21] ibid, para 44.
[22] ibid 408.

As far as the employee is concerned, if an interim injunction prevented him from starting a **10.37** new business, then similar difficulties would apply, as discussed above in relation to the employer, in terms of quantifying the loss resulting from a delay in doing business caused by an interim injunction until trial. By way of contrast, where the employee is prevented from starting work for a competitor, any loss of salary he may suffer in the meantime is likely to be readily quantifiable and of an amount which the claimant could pay pursuant to the undertaking in damages (provided the employee does not lose the job altogether).

In practice, interim injunction applications in employee competition cases frequently **10.38** proceed on the basis that damages are not an adequate remedy for either party.

Balance of convenience

If the court concludes that there is a serious issue to be tried but that damages are not an **10.39** adequate remedy for either party, it turns to consider the balance of convenience. This has a number of elements to it.

General Lord Diplock explained what he meant by the balance of convenience in the **10.40** following terms:

> It is where there is doubt as to the adequacy of the respective remedies in damages available to either party or to both, that the question of balance of convenience arises. It would be unwise to attempt even to list all the various matters which may need to be taken into consideration in deciding where the balance lies, let alone to suggest the relative weight to be attached to them. These will vary from case to case.[23]

What is meant by the balance of convenience has been expressed in a number of different **10.41** ways in later cases. In *Lansing Linde Ltd v Kerr*,[24] Staughton LJ said that once it was shown that there is a serious issue to be tried, the 'main question is then one of lesser evil: will it do less harm to grant an injunction which subsequently turns out to be unjustified, or to refuse one if it subsequently turns out that an injunction should have been granted'.[25] May LJ referred to it as the 'balance of the risk of doing an injustice' in *Cayne v Global Natural Resources plc*.[26]

Hoffmann J (as he then was) vividly expressed the dilemma facing the court in *Films Rover* **10.42** *Ltd v Cannon Film Sales Ltd*:[27]

> The principal dilemma about the grant of interlocutory injunctions, whether prohibitory or mandatory, is that there is by definition a risk that the court may make the 'wrong' decision in the sense of granting an injunction to a party who fails to establish his right at trial (or would fail if there was a trial) or alternatively, in failing to grant an injunction to a party who succeeds (or would succeed) at trial. A fundamental principle is therefore that the court should take whichever course appears to carry the lower risk of injustice if it should turn out to have been 'wrong' in the sense that I have described.[28]

The balance of convenience depends on all the facts and circumstances of each individual **10.43** case. By way of example, Browne LJ was firmly of the view that the balance of convenience

---

[23] ibid 408.
[24] [1991] 1 WLR 251, CA.
[25] ibid 256.
[26] [1984] 1 All ER 225, 237.
[27] [1987] 1 WLR 670.
[28] [1987] 1 WLR 680.

favoured the refusal of an interim injunction where the effect of enforcing a non-competition covenant until trial meant that the defendant solicitor would lose his new job and may find himself with no job at all (*Fellowes & Son v Fisher*[29]). The fact that the defendants were starting up a new business with no cash coming in and delay in commencing business could cause them disproportionate harm was an important factor weighing in the balance of convenience in *Lock International plc v Beswick*.[30] In contrast, in *Roger Bullivant Ltd v Ellis* May LJ stated that the fact that an injunction restraining a company from making unlawful use of confidential information may or will drive it into liquidation is of itself *nihil ad rem*, provided that the tests in *American Cyanamid v Ethicon* are satisfied.[31]

10.44   An interim injunction may be granted even though its effect is to prevent the defendant from fulfilling contracts into which he has entered with third parties. Such an injunction was granted where the defendant had entered into contracts with customers arguably using the claimant's confidential information in *PSM International plc v Whitehouse*.[32] Lloyd LJ agreed that the courts should be chary of granting an equitable remedy which would have the effect of interfering with the contractual rights of innocent third parties. But that equity has power to do so in an appropriate case, he did not doubt. The equitable jurisdiction was not confined to future contracts. 'The arm of equity is not so short.'[33]

Status quo

10.45   Preservation of the status quo is a legitimate consideration. Lord Diplock said:

> Where other factors appear to be evenly balanced it is a counsel of prudence to take such measures as are calculated to preserve the status quo. If the defendant is enjoined temporarily from doing something that he has not done before, the only effect of the interlocutory injunction in the event of his succeeding at the trial is to postpone the date at which he is able to embark upon a course of action which he has not previously found it necessary to undertake; whereas to interrupt him in the conduct of an established enterprise would cause much greater inconvenience to him since he would have to start again to establish it in the event of his succeeding at the trial.[34]

10.46   What is the relevant status quo is not always easy to identify. Is it, for example, the state of affairs before the employee embarked on the competitive activities, which the employer contends are unlawful? Is it the position immediately before proceedings are commenced, or before the application for an interim injunction is launched? Lord Diplock himself went some way towards answering these questions in *Garden Cottage Foods Ltd v Milk Marketing Board*.[35] In order to understand fully what he intended, it is necessary to set out the whole of the relevant passage.[36] Lord Diplock referred to the history of the trading relations between the relevant parties which, he said:

> ... make it difficult to identify what was the relevant status quo which it was said in *American Cyanamid Co v Ethicon Ltd* [1975] AC 396 it is a counsel of prudence to preserve *when other*

---

[29] See n 12 above, 139–40. See also *Series 5 Software Ltd v Clarke* [1996] 1 All ER 853; *Potters-Ballotini Ltd v Weston-Baker* [1977] RPC 202.

[30] [1989] 3 All ER 373, 379–80 *per* Hoffmann J.

[31] [1987] ICR 464, CA, 482.

[32] [1992] IRLR 279, CA.

[33] ibid para 37.

[34] [1975] AC 396, 408.

[35] [1984] 1 AC 130, HL.

[36] The last sentence of this passage is of considerable importance, despite its frequent omission in summaries of what Lord Diplock said.

factors are evenly balanced. The status quo is the existing state of affairs; but since states of affairs do not remain static this raises the query: existing when? In my opinion, the relevant status quo to which reference was made in *American Cyanamid* is the state of affairs existing during the period immediately preceding the issue of the writ claiming the permanent injunction or, if there be unreasonable delay between the issue of the writ and the motion for an interlocutory injunction, the period immediately preceding the motion. The duration of that period since the state of affairs last changed must be more than minimal, having regard to the total length of the relationship between the parties in respect of which the injunction is granted; otherwise the state of affairs before the last change would be the relevant status quo.[37]

In *Graham v Delderfield*,[38] Dillon LJ stated it must be service of the writ rather than its issue that fixes the status quo where there was no letter before action and there was delay after issue of the writ before service. The issue of the writ does not tell the defendants of its existence or indicate to them that a claim is being made against them. **10.47**

What this means is that the status quo is not fixed in one way for all cases. Rather, it means that state of affairs before the most significant recent change. Where an employer seeks an interim injunction to enforce a restrictive covenant, provided he applies soon after he learns of the employee acting (or threatening to act) in breach of the covenant, the status quo is likely to mean the period when the employee complied with the covenant.[39] **10.48**

Merits

Although the court should not conduct an in-depth examination of the merits of the case at the interim stage, the merits may have some part to play. Lord Diplock recognized that the party defeated at the interim stage may not be fully compensated for his loss in the intervening period until trial: **10.49**

> Save in the simplest cases, the decision to grant or to refuse an interlocutory injunction will cause to whichever party is unsuccessful on the application some disadvantages which his ultimate success at the trial may show he ought to have been spared and the disadvantages may be such that the recovery of damages to which he would then be entitled either in the action or under the plaintiff's undertaking would not be sufficient to compensate him fully for all of them.[40]

It is in these circumstances that the merits may have a part to play:

> The extent to which the disadvantages to each party would be incapable of being compensated in damages in the event of his succeeding at the trial is always a significant factor in assessing where the balance of convenience lies, and if the extent of the uncompensatable disadvantage to each party would not differ widely, it may not be improper to take into account in tipping the balance the relative strength of each party's case as revealed by the affidavit evidence adduced on the hearing of the application. This, however, should be done only where it is apparent upon the facts disclosed by evidence as to which there is no credible dispute that the strength of one party's case is disproportionate to that of the other party. The court is not justified in embarking upon anything resembling a trial of the action upon conflicting affidavits in order to evaluate the strength of either party's case.[41]

Precisely what Lord Diplock meant in relation to consideration of the merits at the interim stage has been much debated. In *Series 5 Software Ltd v Clarke*,[42] Laddie J conducted a **10.50**

---

[37] [1984] 1 AC 130, 140.
[38] [1992] FSR 313, CA, 317.
[39] *Unigate Dairies Ltd v Bruce, The Times*, 2 March 1988.
[40] [1975] AC 396, 408.
[41] [1984] 1 AC 130, HL, 408–9.
[42] See n 29 above.

detailed review of the pre-*American Cyanamid* position, and of the speeches in that case. He concluded that Lord Diplock did not intend to exclude consideration of the strength of the cases in most applications for interim relief. It appeared to Laddie J that what was intended is that the court should not attempt to resolve difficult issues of fact or law on an application for interim relief. If, on the other hand, the court is able to come to a view as to the strength of the parties' cases on the credible evidence, then it should do so. If it is apparent from the material that one party's case is much stronger than the other's then that is a matter the court should not ignore. After all, one of the purposes of the cross-undertaking in damages is to safeguard the defendant if this preliminary view of the strength of the claimant's case proves to be wrong.[43]

10.51 Laddie J summarized the matters which the court should bear in mind in deciding whether to grant interim relief as follows:

> (1) The grant of an interlocutory injunction is a matter of discretion and depends on all the facts of the case. (2) There are no fixed rules as to when an injunction should or should not be granted. The relief must be kept flexible. (3) Because of the practice adopted on the hearing of applications for interlocutory relief, the court should rarely attempt to resolve complex issues of disputed fact or law. (4) Major factors the court can bear in mind are (a) the extent to which damages are likely to be an adequate remedy for each party and the ability of the other party to pay, (b) the balance of convenience, (c) the maintenance of the status quo, and (d) any clear view the court may reach as to the relative strength of the parties' cases.[44]

Exceptions to the *American Cyanamid* principles

10.52 It will be recalled that Balcombe LJ said in *Lawrence David v Ashton* that the 'normal rule in *American Cyanamid*, and the exceptions to that rule, apply' in cases of restraint of trade.[45] One of those exceptions, relevant for present purposes, is where the case is unlikely to come to trial, either in good time or at all. This could arise where the restrictive covenant will expire, or will have run a large part of its course, by the time even a speedy trial can be heard. Alternatively, this might be so if, for example, the period of the restraint is short (such as three months), or the employee only breaches a longer covenant towards the end of the restricted period (or evidence of such breach only emerges towards the end of this period). In such circumstances, the court is entitled to have greater regard to the merits of the parties' cases than is permissible under an orthodox application of the *American Cyanamid* principles.

10.53 This was the position in a number of post-*American Cyanamid* cases: *NWL Ltd v Woods*,[46] *Cayne v Global Natural Resources plc*,[47] and *Lansing Linde Ltd v Kerr*.[48] In the latter case, the claimant sought an interim injunction to enforce a twelve-month, worldwide non-competition covenant. The application was made at a time when there was much greater delay in cases coming on for trial than is the case nowadays, and no trial was likely before the period of the restraint had almost expired. The judge refused to grant an injunction, his view as to the strength of the claim proving determinative, in the sense that he might well have granted

---

[43] ibid 865. See also *CMI-Centers for Medical Innovation GMBH v Phytopharm plc* [1999] FSR 235.
[44] [1996] 1 All ER 853, 865.
[45] [1989] ICR 123, 135.
[46] [1979] ICR 867, [1979] 1 WLR 1294, HL.
[47] [1984] 1 All ER 225, CA.
[48] [1991] 1 WLR 251, CA.

an injunction if he had thought the claim likely to succeed at trial.[49] The Court of Appeal dismissed the claimant's appeal.

Staughton LJ explained the importance of some evaluation of the merits in such a case.   **10.54**

> If it will not be possible to hold a trial before the period for which the plaintiff claims to be entitled to an injunction has expired, or substantially expired, it seems to me that justice requires some consideration as to whether the plaintiff would be likely to succeed at a trial. In those circumstances it is not enough to decide merely that there is a serious issue to be tried.[50]

Staughton LJ emphasized 'some assessment' because the courts constantly seek to discourage prolonged interim battles on written evidence. 'Where an assessment of the prospects of success is required, it is for the judge to control its extent.'[51] Beldam and Butler-Sloss LJJ agreed, the former considering some assessment of the merits in such circumstances to be an essential step in deciding whether to grant an interim injunction was 'just and convenient'.[52]

A recent illustration of the *Lansing Linde* approach is to be found in *Phoenix Partners Group*   **10.55**
LLP v Asoyag.[53] The employee broker's contract contained six-month restrictive covenants which, following a set-off of three months' garden leave, had three months to run when his employment terminated and he joined a competitor. Relying on *Lansing Linde*, the judge stated that since the period of injunction sought was less than three months in duration, so that there was no possibility of the trial taking place before the expiry of the covenants, some consideration needed to be given to the question whether the claimant would be likely to succeed in establishing an entitlement to injunctive relief at trial.[54] The judge refused the relief sought.

It should be remembered that section 12(3) of the Human Rights Act 1998 comes into play   **10.56**
where the grant of relief might affect the Convention right to freedom of expression. This is discussed in detail elsewhere in this book.[55]

Springboard injunctions

A springboard injunction can be particularly useful in employee competition cases.[56] In its   **10.57**
orthodox application, its purpose is to deprive a person of the springboard gained as a result of misuse of confidential information notwithstanding that the information is now in the public domain. However, there is some controversy about the precise ambit of the jurisdiction. For example, there is authority to support the proposition that springboard relief can be granted to cancel out the head start gained from other wrongdoing, such as a past breach of the duty of good faith, although this proposition is not universally accepted.

---

[49] ibid 259 *per* Staughton LJ.
[50] ibid 258.
[51] ibid 258.
[52] ibid 266.
[53] [2010] IRLR 594.
[54] ibid para 11.
[55] See Chapter 3 above.
[56] See P Goulding, 'Springboard Injunctions in Employment Law' (1995) 24 ILJ 152; D Ornstein, 'Extending springboard relief past breaches of confidence' (2009) 16(7) ELA Briefing 110.

Roxburgh J's classic statement in the *Terrapin* case

10.58   Any discussion of springboard relief properly starts with *Terrapin Ltd v Builders' Supply Co (Hayes) Ltd.*[57] The defendants manufactured prefabricated portable buildings to the claimants' design. After termination of their contract, the defendants sold buildings which incorporated the claimants' design, details of which had previously been disclosed by the claimants to the defendants in confidence. The defendants resisted the claimants' application for an injunction to restrain misuse of confidential information on the ground that the obligation of confidence was discharged by the claimants having sold the buildings and published brochures disclosing features of the buildings.[58]

10.59   Roxburgh J rejected the defendants' argument for the following reasons:

> As I understand it, the essence of this branch of the law, whatever the origin of it may be, is that a person who has obtained information in confidence is not allowed to use it as a springboard for activities detrimental to the person who made the confidential communication, and springboard it remains even when all the features have been published or can be ascertained by actual inspection by any member of the public.[59]

Roxburgh J explained that any member of the public dismantling the building would still have to prepare plans, conduct tests, and construct a prototype if he was to manufacture the product himself. He continued:

> Therefore, the possessor of the confidential information still has a long start over any member of the public. The design may be as important as the features. It is, in my view, inherent in the principle upon which the *Saltman* case rests that the possessor of such information must be placed under a special disability in the field of competition in order to ensure that he does not get an unfair start.[60]

Limited duration of springboard relief

10.60   Given that the springboard doctrine is predicated on depriving a wrongdoer of an unlawful head start, and that such advantage necessarily lasts for a limited period of time, it follows that any springboard injunction must likewise be limited in time. This was made clear by the Court of Appeal in *Roger Bullivant Ltd v Ellis.*[61]

10.61   Ellis was managing director of the claimants, who were specialist engineers, and was subject to a twelve-month restrictive covenant not to transact business with the claimants' clients. He left, taking with him many documents containing confidential technical and commercial

---

[57] The decision of the Court of Appeal in this case was reported first at [1960] RPC 128, CA. A footnote appearing in that report contained the classic statement made by Roxburgh J at first instance in that case which was subsequently approved by the Court of Appeal in *Seager v Copydex Ltd* [1967] RPC 367. As a result, the decision of Roxburgh J was later reported at [1967] RPC 349, 375, some eight years after his judgment was given. See the editorial note at [1967] RPC 375, 376.

[58] Junior counsel for the defendants was Douglas Falconer, who as Falconer J later granted the springboard injunction at first instance in *Bullivant v Ellis* [1987] ICR 464, CA. See paras 9.58–9.63 below.

[59] [1967] RPC 375, 391.

[60] ibid 392. The *Saltman* reference is to *Saltman Engineering Co Ltd v Campbell Engineering Co Ltd* (1948) 65 RPC 203, CA, in which Lord Greene MR enunciated the principles relevant to the definition of confidential information.

[61] [1987] ICR 464, [1987] IRLR 491, [1987] FSR 172, CA. The time-limited nature of the springboard had been considered in cases prior to *Bullivant v Ellis*: see *Potters-Ballotini Ltd v Weston-Baker* [1977] RPC 202, CA; *Fisher-Karpark Industries Ltd v Nichols* [1982] FSR 351. Lloyd LJ subsequently suggested the springboard principle as an alternative basis for the relief granted in *PSM International plc v Whitehouse* [1992] IRLR 279, para 28.

information belonging to the claimants, including a card index showing the names and addresses of the claimants' clients. There was a strong prima facie case that Ellis had used the confidential information in the card index in order to contact the claimants' clients for the benefit of the competing business which he had set up. Falconer J granted an interim injunction restraining the defendants from entering into or fulfilling contracts with any persons whose names and addresses appeared on the card index and who had been contacted by the defendants whilst the index or a copy of it was in their possession. This injunction was subsequently varied to exclude from its scope contracts in existence but unfulfilled at the date of the order.

The Court of Appeal allowed the defendants' appeal and discharged the springboard injunction. **10.62** However, it is important to bear in mind the chronology of the proceedings. Ellis left the claimants' employment in February 1985. An Anton Piller (search) order was executed some two months later. Falconer J granted the springboard injunction almost six months after the date when Ellis left with the claimants' confidential documents. The appeal was heard in May 1986, which was fifteen months after termination of the employment.

The question for the Court of Appeal was whether the springboard injunction ought to have **10.63** been granted at all and, if so, whether it ought to have been granted until trial or only for a more limited period.[62] Nourse LJ stated that Falconer J (the first instance judge) was fully entitled to conclude that the claimants had shown a strong prima facie case on the question of misuse of confidential information and that, on the evidence and submissions before him, the judge arrived at a decision with which it was impossible to interfere. However, no argument was addressed to the judge below to the effect that the springboard injunction ought not to have been granted until trial, but only for a period which would have ensured that the claimants did not enjoy the unfair advantage which the springboard had afforded them. This submission was, however, advanced for the defendants for the first time in the Court of Appeal.[63]

In accepting this submission, Nourse LJ said: **10.64**

> The purpose of Falconer J in granting the injunction was to prevent the defendants from taking unfair advantage of the springboard which he considered they must have built up by their misuse of the information in the card index. Granted, first, that such an advantage cannot last forever, secondly, that the law does not restrain lawful competition and, thirdly, that in restraining unlawful competition it seeks to protect the injured and not to punish the guilty, I cannot see that it is right for the terms of the injunction to extend beyond the period for which the advantage may reasonably be expected to continue.[64]

May LJ, to like effect, said that subject to the *American Cyanamid* principles:

> . . . interim injunctions can be granted to prevent defendants in such a situation from obtaining an unjust headstart in or a springboard for activities detrimental to the person who provided them with that confidential information . . . however, in relation to that type of information, as distinct from that concerning real trade secrets, the court should be concerned that it does not, in granting such an injunction, give the injured party more protection than he realistically needs and, in particular, discourage or prohibit what in the course of time becomes legitimate competition. I think in cases where 'springboard'

---

[62] [1987] ICR 464, 468 *per* Nourse LJ.
[63] ibid 475–6 *per* Nourse LJ.
[64] [1987] ICR 476.

interim injunctions in respect of confidential information are sought the judge should ask himself whether any injunction should be subject to a time limit other than the usual 'until trial or further order'.[65]

10.65 The court held that a time limit of one year ought to have been applied to the springboard injunction when first granted. This period, which had expired by the date of the appeal (hence the injunction was discharged), corresponded to the period of the restrictive covenant in Ellis' contract which may have had some bearing on the Court's determination of the appropriate period.

10.66 The perils of obtaining springboard-type relief are amply illustrated by the outcome in *Universal Thermosensors Ltd v Hibben*.[66] The defendant employees left their employment dishonestly taking with them customer lists and prices matrices belonging to their employer, the claimant, and set up a rival business. They approached, and obtained orders from, several customers whose names were contained in the claimant's lists, although they also compiled their own customer lists partly by legitimate means. Following execution of an Anton Piller (search) order, which retrieved the claimant's documents, the defendants consented to an order until speedy trial. The order restrained the defendants from soliciting or entering into or fulfilling any relevant contract with any person with whom the defendants had contact while various customer lists, including the claimant's, were in their possession. The consent order was similar in terms to that granted by Falconer J in *Bullivant v Ellis*.

10.67 Sir Donald Nicholls V-C held that the protection given to the claimant by this injunction by consent went beyond that required for the proper protection of its legitimate rights. Such an injunction, even for a limited period, could not be justified in the present case as affording the means of preventing the defendants from benefiting from the springboard effect of their use of the claimant's confidential information. Holding back the defendants' new business, even for a period of six or twelve months, would not have the effect simply of restoring the parties to the competitive position they each ought to occupy and that each would have occupied but for the defendants' misconduct. 'If it did, such a form of injunction would be fair and just.'[67] But the injunction would have a much more far-reaching effect. It would put the claimant in a better position than if there had been no breach of confidence. Given that the effect of the consent order was to close down the defendants' business, the claimant was ordered to pay £20,000 to the defendants on the cross-undertaking in damages.[68]

10.68 Jonathan Parker J examined the nature of springboard relief in *Sun Valley Foods Ltd v Vincent*.[69] That was another case of extensive removal by employees of the claimant's confidential documents and their misuse in the cause of a competing business. The claimant sought springboard relief. Jonathan Parker J, having reviewed the authorities, said:

---

[65] ibid 481.

[66] [1992] 1 WLR 840.

[67] ibid 855.

[68] ibid 858–9. In *Sun Valley Foods Ltd v Vincent* [2000] FSR 825, Jonathan Parker J described *Universal Thermosensors v Hibben* as not a 'springboard' case (834). This is correct in the narrow sense that springboard relief of six or twelve months was deemed by Nicholls V-C to be inappropriate. However, as Jonathan Parker J observed (834), Sir Donald Nicholls V-C regarded his approach in that case as being in accordance with the authorities, including *Bullivant v Ellis* [1992] 1 WLR 840, 856, which was a springboard case.

[69] [2000] FSR 825.

There is no room for doubt that the defendants have made unlawful use of material in which Sun Valley/Fields has a proprietary interest. But, as Nourse LJ explained in *Bullivant*, that in itself is not enough to found a claim for 'springboard' relief. Sun Valley also has to establish (a) that the defendants thereby gained an unfair competitive advantage over Sun Valley (to use the words of Roxburgh J, an 'unfair start') and (b) that as of today that advantage still exists and will continue to have effect unless the relief sought is granted.[70]

The judge concluded that any competitive advantage accruing to the defendants' new business from the unlawful copying of the claimant's specifications was of an ephemeral and short-term nature, and became exhausted at the latest by the expiry of a month after the unlawful copying took place.[71] Similarly, in *Moneygram International Ltd v Davar*,[72] Gray J considered that the past breaches of fiduciary duty were relatively trivial and that the proposed springboard injunction was disproportionate in the sense that it went well beyond what was reasonably required to protect the claimant against such limited headstart as may have been obtained.[73] Likewise, in *SG&R Valuation Service Co LLC v Boudrais*,[74] springboard relief was refused where the confidential information had been handed back or sterilized, and there was no evidence that it had been used.

These cases—*Universal Thermosensors*, *Sun Valley Foods*, *Moneygram*, and *Boudrais*—are a **10.69** timely reminder that the gravity of the defendant's misconduct is not a sure guide to whether and, if so, for how long springboard relief is appropriate. This point was emphasized by Flaux J in *Sectrack NV v Satamatics Ltd* in stating that logically, the seriousness of the breach and the egregiousness of the defendant's conduct cannot have any bearing on the period for which the springboard injunction should be granted—what matters is the effect of the breach of confidence upon the claimant in the sense of the extent to which the defendant has gained an illegitimate competitive advantage.[75]

Springboard relief is not confined to confidential information cases

The springboard authorities discussed above all involved the misuse of confidential informa- **10.70** tion. A question which arises intermittently in practice, but has yet to be authoritatively answered, is whether the court has jurisdiction to grant a springboard injunction where the wrongdoing involves a breach of contract but not the misuse of confidential information.

A typical example is where an employee breaches his contractual duty of good faith by soliciting **10.71** his employer's customers to transfer their custom to, or fellow employees to join him at, his new business or employer. In so acting whilst remaining in employment, the employee unlawfully gains a head start for the benefit of his new business or employer but may not have misused his employer's confidential information. There would appear to be little logic or

---

[70] ibid 834.

[71] ibid 835–6.

[72] [2003] EWHC 2368 (QB).

[73] ibid, paras 63, 68, 71.

[74] [2008] IRLR 770, paras 29–30. Cf *Foxtons Ltd v Hassell* [2010] EWHC 2199 (QB), in which a springboard injunction (against conducting business with persons identified by using the claimant's confidential information or property) of approximately three months' duration until speedy trial was granted, which was longer than the period of post-termination restrictive covenants, in circumstances where the full extent of the defendant's misuse of confidential information, and the extent, if any, to which it was continuing could not be known with certainty: para 19.

[75] [2007] EWHC 3003 (Comm), para 68. A springboard injunction of one year's duration was granted in *G Attwood Holdings Ltd v Woodward* [2009] EWHC 1083 (Ch), where a director had breached his fiduciary and contractual duty of good faith.

fairness in the court refusing to grant springboard relief to cancel out this head start, whilst coming to an employer's aid where the wrongdoing involves a misuse of confidential information.

10.72 Some doubt was cast on the court's willingness to intervene where a breach of confidence was not involved by Scott J in his judgment on the interim application in *Balston Ltd v Headline Filters Ltd*.[76] The judge considered it arguable that the defendant employee was in breach of his duty of fidelity whilst his employment continued. It was argued for the employer that the court should restrain the employee's competition so as to deprive him of the benefit of his contractual breaches committed during the continuance of his employment. Scott J disagreed:

> These past breaches of duty, if that is what they were, cannot in my judgment sustain an interlocutory injunction, on their own account. Whether an injunction, interlocutory or otherwise, can ever be justified on the ground that the grant is necessary in order to deprive a contract breaker of the fruits of his breach of contract, I regard as highly questionable. I do not decide the point, however, since I am clear that in this case the plaintiff's case for an interlocutory injunction must depend upon the misuse of confidential information case.[77]

10.73 The issue came squarely before Blackburne J in *Midas IT Services v Opus Portfolio Ltd*.[78] He expressed it thus:

> The question which has been debated before me is whether the so-called springboard injunction is limited to cases of misuse of confidential information . . . or . . . the injunction is but an illustration of a wider principle, namely the neutralising of any unfair advantage obtained by a person (or by those who have knowingly participated in his actions) as a result of a prior breach of duty by that person.[79]

Blackburne J expressed some difficulty with the approach of Scott J in *Balston v Headline Filters* referred to above. He referred to a mandatory injunction, such as to pull down a structure erected in breach of restrictive covenant. Such an order deprives the wrongdoer of the fruits of his breach of obligation. Blackburne J concluded, differing 'with diffidence' from Scott J, 'that in appropriate circumstances the court has power by injunction, interlocutory or otherwise, to deprive the person of the fruits of his breach of obligation'.[80]

10.74 This development in the springboard doctrine, which was approved by Blackburne J in *Midas*, was applied by Nelson J to the poaching of employees in *Siemens VAT v Technologies Ltd*.[81] In an extempore judgment followed a hearing on informal notice, the judge found that the claimant's evidence, on its face, showed a prima facie case that the defendants had sought to take the claimant's employees unlawfully, using confidential information (which included lists of employees, their telephone numbers, information as to their skills and

---

[76] [1987] FSR 330.

[77] ibid 341.

[78] 21 December 1999. See also *Renton Inspection and Technical Engineering v Renton* (CA, 25 October 1991); *CBT Systems UK Ltd v Campopiano* (26 June 1995) Carnwath J. In *Moneygram International Ltd v Davar* [2003] EWHC 2368 (QB), the defendant accepted, for the purposes of the application for interim relief, that the springboard principle was not confined to the field of confidence but was applicable where a headstart had been gained by past breaches of fiduciary duty: para 23. In the event, springboard relief was refused on proportionality grounds.

[79] *Midas IT Services* (n 78 above) 14.

[80] ibid 18.

[81] 19 March 2008 (unreported).

individual salaries).[82] Nelson J concluded that the authorities, and in particular *Midas*, make it entirely appropriate to consider that the general springboard principle can be applied, provided appropriate caution is exercised, to cases involving employees.[83] Appropriate caution involved ensuring that 'no proper restraint of trade or infringement of free and proper movement of labour is made'.[84] Importantly, there was evidence that the effects of the unlawful acts were continuing.[85] The Order prevented the defendant, until after the full hearing of the interim application, from (1) offering employment or entering into any contract of employment with any employee of whom the defendants became aware, or with whom the defendants held any discussion in relation to potential employment, at any time after it received any confidential information belonging to the claimant, and (2) inducing any employee of the claimant to terminate his contract of employment with the claimant.

A clear illustration of this extension of the springboard doctrine to cases not involving a misuse of confidential information is *UBS Wealth Management (UK) Ltd v Vestra Wealth LLP*.[86] Seventy-five employees resigned from the claimant in order to join a new competitor. Following an interim hearing, Openshaw J was firmly of the view that the claimants had put together a formidable case that there was an unlawful plan to poach both staff and clients from UBS, assisted by senior staff of UBS.[87] **10.75**

The judge noted the discussion in the authorities as to whether springboard relief is limited to cases where there is a misuse of confidential information.[88] It seemed to him that the law had developed in the twenty years since Scott J's dicta in *Balston*, and he saw no reason in principle by which it should be so limited. He stated his approach in the following terms: **10.76**

> In my judgment, springboard relief is not confined to cases where former employees threaten to abuse confidential information acquired during the currency of their employment. It is available to prevent any future or further serious economic loss to a previous employer caused by former staff members taking an unfair advantage, an 'unfair start', of any serious breaches of their contract of employment (or if they are acting in concert with others, of any breach by any of those others). That unfair advantage must still exist at the time that the injunction is sought, and it must be shown that it would continue unless restrained. I accept that injunctions are to protect against and to prevent future and further losses and must not be used merely to punish past breaches of contract.[89]

The defendants were restrained, until speedy trial, from soliciting or dealing with any UBS client (apart from those who had already expressed a wish to transfer their business from UBS) and from soliciting any UBS employee who had not yet resigned.

Applying the brakes to the springboard doctrine?

The more recent cases discussed above, namely *Midas*, *Siemens*, and *UBS*, suggest a willingness on the part of the courts to apply the springboard doctrine to novel situations, including those not involving misuse of confidential information but so as to deprive the wrongdoer **10.77**

---

[82] ibid para 11.
[83] ibid para 15.
[84] ibid para 17.
[85] ibid para 18.
[86] [2008] IRLR 965.
[87] ibid para 35.
[88] ibid para 3.
[89] ibid para 4.

from the benefits of his past misdeeds, where the justice of the case demands it. However, the trend has not all been in one direction. The most comprehensive review of springboard relief in recent times suggests that the courts should exercise considerable caution both as to whether to grant such an injunction at all and, if so, as to its form and duration.

10.78 In *Vestergaard Frandsen A/S v Bestnet Europe Ltd*,[90] Arnold J held that the defendants were liable for breach of confidence through misuse of the claimants' trade secrets. In a separate judgment he considered what remedies should be granted. In a valuable judgment, he considered, and attempted to disentangle, five closely related topics.[91] The first is the general principles applicable to the grant of injunctions to restrain misuse of confidential information, and in particular the circumstances in which an injunction may be refused on the ground that financial compensation is an adequate remedy. The second topic is the springboard doctrine. The third topic is information which has a limited degree of confidentiality as a result of limited inaccessibility. The fourth topic is whether, and if so in what circumstances, an injunction may be granted to prevent a defendant from continuing to benefit from a past misuse of confidential information. The fifth topic is whether, and if so in what circumstances, an injunction may be granted to prevent a defendant from continuing to manufacture and sell products which are derived from a misuse of confidential information, but do not themselves embody or disclose that information.

10.79 As for the *general principles*, Arnold J concluded that, in the absence of specific discretionary reasons for the refusal of an injunction, where the claimant has established that the defendant has acted in breach of an equitable obligation of confidence and that there is a sufficient risk of repetition, the claimant is generally entitled to an injunction save in exceptional circumstances.

10.80 In relation to the *springboard doctrine*, the judge embarked on a detailed review of the leading authorities from *Terrapin*[92] to *A-G v Times Newspapers*.[93] From this review of the authorities, Arnold J drew the following conclusions:

> (1) There never was any sound authority for the proposition that an injunction can be granted to restrain continued misuse of confidential information once the information has ceased to be confidential. *Terrapin* was not authority for that proposition. Nor was *Cranleigh*.[94] The Court of Appeal in *Speed Seal*[95] was in error in treating *Cranleigh* as authority for that proposition, but that was merely a decision not to strike out a claim before the facts had been found.
>
> (2) In any event, it is now clear from *Spycatcher*,[96] *Blake*[97] and *Times Newspapers*[98] that publication of the confidential information brings the obligation of confidence to an end. It matters not whether the information has been published by the confider, by a stranger or by the confidant

---

[90] [2009] EWHC 1456 (Ch).

[91] ibid para 28. It is to be noted that, in relation to injunctive relief, the judge 'received very little assistance from counsel at the hearing' and therefore 'what follows is the product of my own researches. I am conscious that I have not had the benefit of argument from the parties on many of the points discussed': ibid para 27.

[92] [1967] RPC 375; paras 10.58–10.59 above.

[93] [2001] 1 WLR 885.

[94] *Cranleigh Precision Engineering Ltd v Bryant* [1965] 1 WLR 1239, [1966] RPC 81 (the former report contains a slightly fuller statement of the facts while the latter includes a note of the arguments).

[95] *Speed Seal Products Ltd v Paddington* [1985] 1 WLR 1327, CA.

[96] *A-G v Guardian Newspapers Ltd (No 2)* [1990] 1 AC 109.

[97] *A-G v Blake* [1998] Ch 439, CA.

[98] *A-G v Times Newspapers Ltd* [2001] 1 WLR 885, CA.

himself. Accordingly, no injunction can be granted to restrain continued misuse of confidential information once the information has ceased to be confidential.

(3) If the springboard doctrine is understood to be that an injunction can be granted to restrain continued misuse of confidential information once the information has ceased to be confidential, then it should now be regarded as having been laid to rest.

(4) However, there are two other possible interpretations of the doctrine. The first is that information may have a limited degree of confidentiality even though it can be ascertained from public domain sources. The second is that an injunction may be granted to prevent the defendant from benefiting from a past misuse of confidential information even if it is no longer confidential.[99]

In terms of *relative confidentiality*, if the springboard doctrine is understood to be that information may possess a limited degree of confidentiality even though it can be ascertained by reverse engineering or by a process of compilation from public domain sources, Arnold J considered that it is soundly based.[100] **10.81**

As far as *benefiting from past misuse* is concerned, Arnold J reviewed the authorities and drew the following conclusions from them: **10.82**

(1) In general, the remedy for past misuse of confidential information is a financial one. Where appropriate, the claimant can claim a restitutionary remedy, namely an account of profits, which deprives the defendant of the benefit of his wrongdoing.

(2) As the law presently stands, it is not clear whether an injunction can be granted to prevent a defendant from benefiting from a past misuse of confidential information. Laddie J in *Ocular Sciences*[101] interpreted Lord Goff in *Spycatcher* as having concluded that the answer was no, but Arnold J was less confident of this. *Bullivant* and *Universal Thermosensors* suggest that the answer is yes, and Laddie J did not consider those cases.

(3) In Arnold J's view, it is significant that *Terrapin*, *Bullivant*, and *Universal Thermosensors* are all cases about interim injunctions. When an interim injunction is sought, the court's task is to hold the ring pending trial. It is not in a position to determine the parties' legal rights or to award either compensatory or restitutionary remedies. In these circumstances a limited injunction to prevent the defendant from benefiting from his (alleged) past misuse of confidential information may be the best way to preserve the status quo pending trial. If it turns out to have been wrongly granted, the court can require the claimant to compensate the defendant under the cross-undertaking in damages (as occurred in *Universal Thermosensors*).

(4) In any event, it seemed to Arnold J that the reasoning in both *Bullivant* and *Universal Thermosensors* indicates that considerable caution is required both as to whether to grant such an injunction at all and, if so, as to its form and duration. As Nicholls V-C pointed out in the latter case, the court must be careful to ensure that such an injunction does not put the claimant in a better position than if there had been no misuse. As the Court of Appeal pointed out in the former case, the duration of any such injunction should not extend beyond the period for which the defendant's illegitimate advantage may be expected to continue.[102]

Lastly, as to *derivative products*, if a permanent injunction is granted to restrain the manufacture and sale of a product which is derived from a past misuse of confidential information, but such acts do not amount to a continued misuse of that information, then the risk that **10.83**

---

[99] [2009] EWHC 1456 (Ch), para 76.
[100] [2009] EWHC 1456 (Ch), para 78.
[101] [1997] RPC 289.
[102] ibid para 93.

the claimant will end up in a better position than if there had been no misuse may become acute. Otherwise, the appropriate remedy in such a case is a financial one.[103]

10.84 *Vestergaard* was noted, but not considered in any detail, by Jack J in *Tullett Prebon plc v BGC Brokers LP*.[104] The claimant applied for an interim injunction following BGC's recruitment of a large number of Tullett's broker employees. The judge considered that, at that stage, there was a strong case for interim relief pending trial.[105] An interim injunction was granted preventing BGC from inviting an employee of Tullett to end his employment with Tullett *lawfully* and to join BGC when permissible. The injunction was sought by Tullett on a springboard basis.[106] This injunction remained in place between the interim hearing (April 2009) and fourteen days from the delivery of judgment following the trial (March 2010). Thus, its duration was approximately twelve months. In his judgment following trial, Jack J referred to the springboard doctrine but stated that the basis for the interim injunction was 'better put more simply' as follows:

> BGC was carrying on an unlawful course of conduct against Tullett and Tullett was entitled to an injunction to stop it. It is a kind of *quia timet* injunction. As BGC had shown an intention to recruit unlawfully it was not appropriate simply to injunct unlawful recruitment but all recruitment, because of the risk and likelihood of further unlawful means and the difficulty of detecting them.[107]

Thus, according to the judge, the rationale for the interim injunction was not the springboard principles but rather that the justice of the case required such wide-ranging relief having regard to the difficulty of policing a narrower injunction against *unlawful* recruitment pending trial. This demonstrates the flexibility of the equitable jurisdiction to grant injunctions and avoids some of the difficult issues regarding the nature and ambit of the springboard doctrine discussed by Arnold J in *Vestergaard*.

10.85 The flurry of cases in recent years demonstrates the utility of springboard relief, particularly but not only in the context of team moves. It is also plain that the law on this topic is far from settled, with some judges willing to extend the springboard doctrine (*Midas*, *Siemens*, *UBS*), some displaying a more cautious approach (*Vestergaard*), and others breaking free of such conceptual restraints where the justice and convenience of the case requires it (*Tullett*).

Mandatory injunctions

10.86 The court has power to grant an interim mandatory injunction (although such an order is relatively unusual in an employee competition case). The test for the grant of an interim mandatory injunction is different from that for a prohibitory injunction. Chadwick J proposed a four-step test in *Nottingham Building Society v Eurodynamic Systems plc*,[108] which Phillips LJ cited with approval in *Zockoll Group Ltd v Mercury Communications Ltd*[109] as follows:

---

[103] [2009] EWHC 1456 (Ch), para 96.
[104] [2010] EWHC 484 (QB).
[105] [2009] EWHC 819 (QB), para 10.
[106] ibid paras 13–16.
[107] [2010] EWHC 484 (QB), para 250.
[108] [1993] FSR 468, 474.
[109] [1998] FSR 354.

(1) The overriding consideration is which course is likely to involve the least risk of injustice if it turns out to be wrong.

(2) The court must keep in mind that an order which requires a party to take some positive step at an interlocutory stage may well carry a greater risk of injustice if it turns out to have been wrongly made than an order which merely prohibits action, thus preserving the status quo.

(3) It is legitimate to consider whether the court does feel a high degree of assurance that the claimant will be able to establish his right at trial.

(4) Even where the court is unable to feel such assurance, there may still be circumstances in which it is appropriate to grant a mandatory injunction at an interlocutory stage. Those circumstances will exist where the risk of injustice if the injunction is refused sufficiently outweigh the risk of injustice if granted.

Undertaking in damages

Preliminary

It has been the practice of the court in England for more than 150 years to require a litigant **10.87** who obtains an interim injunction pending trial or any other specified hearing to give an undertaking in damages to the respondent against whom the injunction has been obtained. Since the early 1980s, with the introduction of Mareva injunctions, the court has increasingly been concerned with the need to protect banks and other third parties to whom notice of the injunction has been given, and also with protecting the interests of those who may be affected by its terms, even if they are not directly parties to the action or are not even given any notice of it by the person who has obtained the injunction.

The position of each kind of party and how the present rules and practice of the court may **10.88** affect them are considered below. What they may need to do in order to ensure that they are adequately protected is also discussed.

It is important to appreciate that, unless the court otherwise orders, the order for an interim **10.89** injunction must contain an undertaking as to damages to be given by the applicant.[110] Thus, although the court has no power to compel the applicant to give one, the court will normally refuse the application if the applicant declines or is unable to give a satisfactory undertaking.[111] Nowadays, however, it is implicit that the applicant is offering an undertaking in damages.[112] The undertaking in damages is given to the court and therefore it is enforced by the court. It is not given to the respondent.

An applicant for an injunction made in the absence of the respondent is obliged to make **10.90** full and frank disclosure to the court of all things which it is relevant for the court to know in exercising its discretion on whether to grant the injunction.[113] These matters will include

---

[110] CPR 25APD 5.1(1).

[111] *Tucker v New Brunswick Trading Co of London* (1890) 44 Ch D 249, CA; *F Hoffman-La Roche & Co AG v Secretary of State for Trade and Industry* [1975] AC 295, HL; and *Lilly Icos LLC and others v 8pm Chemists Ltd and others* [2009] EWHC 1905 (Ch), [2010] FSR 4.

[112] *The Bank v A Ltd* (23 June 2000); *SmithKline Beecham plc v Apotex Europe Ltd (No 3)* [2005] EWHC 1655 (Ch), [2005] FSR 44.

[113] *Schmitten v Faulkes* [1893] WN 64; *R v Kensington Income Tax Commissioners, ex p de Polignac* [1917] 1 KB 486, CA, 514; *Siporex Trade SA v Comdel Commodities* [1986] 2 Lloyd's Rep 428, 437; and *Memory Corp plc v Sidhu* [2000] 1 WLR 1443, CA; see also the Chancery Guide 2005, para 5.16.

information as to the impact which the injunction may foreseeably have upon (a) the defendant(s) and (b) third parties, in particular (but not limited to) those upon whom the applicant intends to serve notice of the injunction, if it is granted. The failure to comply with this 'high duty' as it was described by Mummery LJ in *Memory Corp plc v Sidhu* is perhaps one of the most frequent reasons for an application to discharge an injunction.

Defendant who is a respondent to an application for an injunction

10.91 In modern times, when a claimant obtains an interim injunction against a defendant, it has always been the practice of the court to require the claimant to give an undertaking to pay for any damage which the defendant sustains by reason of the injunction and which the court considers that the claimant should pay. As Lord Diplock stated in *F Hoffman-La Roche & Co AG v Secretary of State for Trade and Industry*:

> The procedure has been evolved . . . of matching the injunction with an undertaking to pay any damage which it is just should be paid if it should turn out that the injunction was unjustified. Precisely because this procedure is so obviously just, it is almost universal: no interim injunction is given unless accompanied by the undertaking.[114]

10.92 This practice has now become a formal requirement under Practice Direction 25A, paragraph 5.1(1), of Part 25 of the CPR *unless the court orders otherwise*. This practice is reflected in the two standard form precedents for a freezing injunction and a search order[115] which are both annexed to the practice direction under Part 25 under the heading 'Undertakings given to the Court by the Applicant', but it applies to all injunctions. In addition, Chancery Practice Forms PF39CH and PF40CH contain two variations of the standard wording to be used for the undertaking in damages. It is perhaps unfortunate that the wording of each of these forms continues to be slightly different for no obvious reason; PF39CH says that it is an undertaking 'to pay any damages which the defendants . . . shall sustain which the Court considers the Claimant should pay', whilst the other form PF40CH says: 'If the Court later finds that this Order has caused loss to the Defendant . . . and decides that the Defendant . . . should be compensated for that loss, the Claimant will comply with any Order the Court may make.' The second form is to be preferred since, first this follows the draft order annexed to the practice direction[116] and, secondly, the intention always is that the defendant should be compensated for loss and is not to be limited by the word 'damages'.[117]

10.93 If an undertaking is given by the defendant in lieu of an injunction, before the introduction of the Civil Procedure Rules it used to be the position that the cross-undertaking in damages was implied unless the contrary was agreed and expressed at the time of the making of the order.[118] Although not referred to in the CPR themselves or Practice Direction 25A, this principle appears to be preserved and is included in paragraph 5.28 of the Chancery Guide 2009.

---

[114] See n 111 above, 356.

[115] There is some doubt as to whether or not a search order is an injunction, since it is made under CPR, r 25.1(1)(h) as opposed to r 25.1(1)(a). But it makes no difference since the standard form search order annexed to the practice direction now includes an undertaking as to loss; see Form SO, Miscellaneous Forms published as part of the White Book Service.

[116] See Form FI, Miscellaneous Forms, in the Civil Procedure Forms published as part of the White Book Service

[117] See *SmithKline Beecham plc v Apotex Europe Ltd (No 3)* [2005] EWHC 1655 (Ch), [2006] 1 WLR 872, para 43, and in the Court of Appeal [2006] EWCA Civ 658, [2007] Ch 71, CA, para 29.

[118] Practice Note [1904] WN 203.

Where, however, there are agreed undertakings on both sides, then there may be no reason for any such implication and an undertaking in damages may have to be expressly sought and given.[119] Because the CPR are silent on this subject, one can see scope for difficulty if the defendant has omitted, as part of the parties' bargain, to ask for a cross-undertaking in damages. The safest course for the defendant is, therefore, always to ask for the cross-undertaking in damages to be given by the claimant or to raise the matter with the judge at a hearing.

It will be noted from the wording of Practice Direction 25A that the court may, exceptionally, **10.94** not require an undertaking to be given ('unless the court otherwise orders'). In older times, it was suggested that one example for such an exception would be the case of clear fraud,[120] but one may doubt that these days there are any particular *categories* of exceptional case. Certainly, for a court to dispense with an undertaking in the Chancery or Queen's Bench Division, the circumstances will have to be very exceptional.[121]

In the case of the Crown, it is treated no differently from any other employer when it seeks **10.95** to obtain an injunction in support of the terms of an employment contract ('*jus privatum*') and it too will normally be required to give an undertaking in damages.[122]

Defendant who is not a respondent to the application for an injunction

There are occasions where a claimant applies for an interim injunction against defendant A, **10.96** but does not apply for it against defendant B. Although it is only defendant A who may be the subject of the interim injunction by way of prohibition, it may well be that the effect of the injunction will be to cause defendant B loss or expense which is not recoverable by an order for costs at the end of the trial.

The practice of the court prior to the introduction of the CPR was that an undertaking in **10.97** damages covered all defendants in the action, not just the defendant who was enjoined, and the wording of the undertaking did not distinguish between the defendants.[123] The new Practice Direction 25APD5.1(A), however, now requires the court to consider whether to require an undertaking also to 'pay any damages' sustained by any person other than the respondent, including another party to the proceedings or any other person who may suffer loss as a consequence of the order.[124]

Obviously, if the claimant who has obtained the injunction seeks to contend that a particular **10.98** defendant is not within the ambit of his undertaking, that defendant ought immediately to seek clarification of his position, if necessary by making an application to the court.

It should be noted that the two Practice Forms for injunctions, forms PF39CH and PF40CH, **10.99** also include within the wording of the applicant's undertaking that it covers loss suffered by 'the defendants or any other party served with or notified of this Order' and it seems to be assumed that, if the judge orders an undertaking to cover the possible loss of any such other party, the court will also direct that he is to be notified of the order. In most cases, it is likely that a defendant, who is not enjoined by the order, is nevertheless given notice of it by the claimant;

---

[119] *SmithKline Beecham* (n 117 above).
[120] *Ingram v Stiff* (1859) 33 cited in *Tucker v Silver* (1859) John 218, 220.
[121] *A-G v Albany Hotel Co* [1896] 2 Ch 696, CA, 700.
[122] *F Hoffmann-La Roche* (n 111 above).
[123] *Berkeley Administration Inc v McClelland* [1996] IL Pr 772 CA.
[124] This amendment was first published in the 2007 Supreme Court Practice.

and thus such a defendant clearly comes within the undertaking by that route. In all other cases, the position remains far from certain and continues to be unsatisfactory.[125] In the event of a defendant being left in doubt, he should make an application to the court for clarification and, if need be, a variation or discharge of the order if the claimant declines to extend the undertaking expressly to cover his possible expenses and/or losses. In the case of a third party, the court ought to be mindful to direct that he should be served with a copy of the order.

Defendant who is added after the undertaking has been given

10.100 In this case, the injunction is not directed at prohibiting the particular defendant from any conduct, but he is added as a co-defendant at some later stage. This may be done either on an application by the claimant or by a person with an appropriate interest in the litigation, including a person affected by the injunction.[126]

10.101 The court has expressed the view that a defendant in such a case *may* have the benefit of the undertaking in damages, but as Scott V-C observed in *Berkeley Administration Inc v McClelland*, he did 'not regard the correct answer as being clear from the decided cases . . . '.[127] For his part, Scott V-C thought that a defendant in such a case should be considered as being included, but he did not go on to say whether that was only prospectively in relation to loss suffered after the joinder or also retrospectively as well.

10.102 This makes the position very unclear. It is made all the more uncertain because it is normally accepted by the court that, if the person is added as a defendant on his own application, the claimant can elect to have his injunction discharged as an alternative to extending the undertaking in damages to the new defendant. It would be advisable, therefore, that any newly added defendant or a person applying to be added as a defendant should consider applying for an order that the injunction should be discharged *unless* the undertaking in damages is expressly extended to him, if he fears that he may have suffered, or will suffer, any expense or loss as a result of the injunction. In that way, his position can be made certain by the court as to any past expenses and losses as well as any future ones.

Person who has been served with the order or who is given notice of it

10.103 Since the early 1980s and the development of the Mareva injunction freezing a defendant's assets,[128] the court has become increasingly concerned to protect third parties on whom the order is served or to whom notice of it is given. In the case of a freezing injunction, the focus tended only to be upon banks and other financial entities which might be put to considerable expense in ensuring that their staff did not breach the terms of an injunction and in complying with any obligations of disclosure to the claimant. But it was also quickly recognized that persons such as banks or, in one instance, a port authority, needed to be protected in case of loss caused by the freezing injunction, such as loss of income directly caused by the order.[129] This is now reflected in Schedule B, paragraph 7, of the standard form freezing injunction set out in the appendix to Practice Direction 25A which provides a twofold protection for the third party consisting of:

---

[125] *SmithKline Beecham* (n 117 above) [2006] EWCA Civ 658, [2007] Ch 71, CA, paras 29–30.
[126] See CPR, r 19.2(2).
[127] *Berkeley Administration* (n 123 above). Roch and Potter LJJ agreed with him.
[128] This is now called a freezing injunction and we refer to that name for all such orders below.
[129] See eg *Searose v Seatrain* [1981] 1WLR 894; and *Clipper Maritime Co Ltd of Monrovia v Mineral-importexport* [1981] 1 WLR 1262.

(1) an undertaking that the applicant will 'pay the reasonable costs of anyone other than the Respondent which have been incurred as a result of this order . . .';

(2) an undertaking to compensate a person served with or given notice of the injunction 'if the court later finds that this order has caused such person loss and decides that such person shall be compensated for that loss'. The applicant is required to comply with any order made by the court in this regard.

This twofold form of undertaking corresponds with the obligation of the court which is now required by Practice Direction 25A, paragraph 5.1A to take account of any potential loss that may be suffered by other defendants or a third party as a result of the order and to decide whether or not to require an undertaking to cover such persons as well. **10.104**

Procedure form PF39CH follows closely the wording of the practice direction and says no more. The second procedure form, PF40CH, is slightly different in that it refers to compensation for 'loss' caused to 'any other party' served with or given notice of the order. The standard form of search order, annexed to Practice Direction 25A of the CPR, contains no comparable undertaking at all in respect of third-party costs or losses, even though one may reasonably contemplate or foresee that, in some situations, third parties (ie persons who are not defendants) may be put to cost and expense in complying with the order and may also suffer loss as a result of their complying with the order. **10.105**

Despite the variation in the forms , the courts are now more than ever alert to the question of expenses and loss caused by an injunction to persons who are not parties to an action. Initially this was predominantly the case in relation only to freezing orders.[130] The current practice, however, has moved on a long way and a court normally requires to be informed of the existence of the possibility of such expenses and losses as part of the applicant's obligation of frankness and full disclosure. Alternatively it is common to find that the draft form of order submitted by the applicant claimant as part of his application includes an appropriate form of wording covering such persons in relation to all injunctions, and not just freezing orders. **10.106**

A person served with, or who gets to know of, the injunction can first apply as an applicant under CPR Part 23 for a variation of the order by virtue of the court's own statutory obligation under Practice Direction 25A, paragraph 5.1A or (more formally) he can apply to be added as a defendant, if his interest in the litigation is a sufficient one. Rule 19.2(2) of the CPR provides that this is appropriate when it is 'desirable to add the new party so that the court can resolve all the matters in dispute in the proceedings' or when 'there is an issue involving the new party and an existing party which is connected to the matters in dispute in the proceedings'. Such a person would in most instances include the new employer of an employee following his being given notice of the injunction by the claimant. **10.107**

Secondly, such a person can also apply for the injunction to be varied, as took place, for example, in *Project Development Co Ltd SA v KMK Securities Ltd*.[131] Thirdly, such a person can apply for payment of his costs and losses caused by the injunction at the interim stage, as was done, for example, in *Imutran Ltd v Uncaged Campaigns Ltd*[132] (a breach of confidence case). **10.108**

---

[130] See *Z Ltd v A-Z and AA-LL* [1982] QB 558, CA, 586–7 *per* Kerr LJ.
[131] [1982] 1 WLR 1470.
[132] [2001] 2 All ER 385, [2002] FSR 2.

Other persons

10.109 Other persons may be affected by an injunction who are neither a defendant nor a respondent to the injunction, and who are neither served with nor given notice of it. This situation may occur when an employee, in alleged breach of a restrictive covenant, moves to a new employer or an employee commits an alleged breach of confidence and passes information to his new employer, and, for whatever reason, the original employer takes no active steps except against his employee.

10.110 First, as in the case of every undertaking to the court, the court may require a claimant to give an undertaking to cover the expenses and losses of a person within this category (such as the new employer); and the claimant then risks that, if he refuses to do so, the court will then refuse to grant an injunction or will discharge an injunction previously granted.[133] It follows that it cannot be imposed retrospectively. Secondly, much may depend on the precise wording of the court's order and the third party needs to be alert to check whether or not he is, in fact, properly covered by the undertaking.

10.111 It follows from the above that such a person, who wishes his position to be protected, will need to apply to the court for a discharge of its order unless the undertaking in damages is extended to cover his expenses and losses. At that stage, if the court is persuaded that it should protect the applicant's position, the claimant has the option to agree to extend his undertaking or to suffer the discharge of the injunction. It is, however, not always obvious or certain that the court will, in the exercise of its obligation under Practice Direction 25A, paragraph 5.1A, agree that the particular third party should have such protection: see, for example, the decision of Neuberger J in *Miller Brewing Co v Mersey Docks and Harbour Co*.[134]

10.112 Such a person, who is affected by the injunction, can also apply (if he is so minded) to be added as a defendant on the grounds set out in Part 19.2 of the CPR. If, for example, the new employer is funding the defence of the employee, he can also apply to be joined on that ground as well, since he may be exposed to a liability to pay the claimant's costs of the action by reason of his involvement in the litigation in that way.[135]

Security may be required

10.113 Where there is doubt about the adequacy of the protection given by the undertaking in damages, because, for instance, there is doubt about the sufficiency of the claimant employer's assets, the court may, as part of its discretionary exercise, require the undertaking to be supported by the provision of security, normally a bank guarantee or a payment into court.[136] If the defendant seeks security, the court first makes '*an intelligent assessment*' of the likely amount of the loss which the grant of the injunction may cause to the defendant. Then it is for the defendant to show that there is a sufficient level of risk of loss, such as to make it reasonable for the court to require security to be given by the claimant; one cannot be more

---

[133] *Allied Irish Bank v Ashford Hotels Ltd* [1997] 1 All ER 309, CA; *F Hoffman-La Roche* (n 111 above), 341, 361.

[134] [2003] EWHC 1606 (Ch); [2004] FSR 5, paras 44–8.

[135] See Senior Courts Act 1981, s 51(3).

[136] The practice is a long-standing one: see eg *Commodity Ocean Transport Corp v Basford Uniform Industries Ltd* [1987] 2 Lloyd's Rep 197, CA, 198, 199–200; and *East Molesey Local Board v Lambeth Waterworks Co* [1892] 3 Ch 289, 300. The Commercial Court Guide accurately reflects the principle upon which the High Court exercises its discretion to require security to be given in such circumstances: see Admiralty and Commercial Courts Guide supplementing CPR, Part 58, para F15.4.

specific since that decision can only be made against the particular circumstances of each different case.[137] Alternatively, a third party may be required to support the undertaking by an undertaking of his own, and the court can accept an undertaking from, for instance, a company director or majority shareholder.[138] It is usual to allow the applicant a reasonable period of time within which to provide such security if it is required.[139] The more serious or urgent the matter is in terms of its potential effect on the defendant, the shorter will be the period allowed for the provision of the security. If the applicant fails to provide the security as ordered, the injunction will normally be discharged and it is usual for the court's order to provide for an automatic discharge in that event.

It is widely accepted that, as part of the duty of full and frank disclosure to the court, the applicant for an injunction must disclose any financial difficulty which may affect his ability to pay damages if required by the court to do so. In the case of companies, this hurdle is usually overcome by giving evidence and exhibiting the company's recent annual accounts or other financial information. Similarly in the case of a foreign claimant without assets in the jurisdiction, the court will normally require that the undertaking in damages be supported by some form of security or an undertaking from a person within the jurisdiction.[140]   **10.114**

In order to get security for the cross-undertaking, the respondent to the injunction must first establish financial risk or exposure because of the applicant's poor finances. Secondly, he must satisfy the court that there is a real (as opposed to a fanciful) risk that the injunction may cause him loss and damage, even if that risk may be a slight one. Once he has got over these two hurdles, the fact that the court may be faced with considerable difficulty in assessing, at an early interim stage of the action, the amount of the potential damages (and thus fixing the amount required to be given as security) should not deter the court from making the best assessment that it can on the evidence before it. This will, in appropriate cases, include a discount for the likelihood of such damages being in fact suffered. This is in the same broad way that the court assesses the value of the loss of a chance.   **10.115**

The basis on which compensation is assessed

The primary task of the court is to compensate the beneficiary of the undertaking in damages if the injunction has caused him loss. The court, however, has, first of all, a discretion whether or not to enforce the undertaking and takes into account whether the conduct of the respondent in relation to the obtaining or continuing of the undertaking would make it inequitable to do so. Once the court has decided that it will enforce the undertaking, the measure of the damages which are awarded is not discretionary.[141]   **10.116**

Until recently the correct basis on which compensation is to be awarded was left undefined. It is now, however, clear that the damages are awarded in the form of equitable compensation   **10.117**

---

[137] *Harley Street Capital Ltd v Tchigirinski* [2005] EWHC 2471 (Ch), paras 17–19, applied and followed in *Sectrack NV v Satamatics Ltd and another* [2007] EWHC 3003 (Comm), para 99.

[138] An example of security being required is *Green Gas Power Ltd v Ashborder BV* [2005] EWHC 989 (Ch); where a shareholder was required to give security in support of the claimant company's undertaking in damages. In *Indicii Salus Ltd (In Receivership) v Chandrasekaran* [2007] EWHC 406 (Ch), Warren J considered the requirement for such security to be 'uncontroversial' in principle.

[139] *Southway Group Ltd v Wolff, The Times*, 21 May 1991.

[140] *Harman Pictures NV v Osborne* [1967] 1 WLR 723.

[141] *F Hoffman-La Roche* (n 111 above) 361; and *Lilly Icos* (n 111 above).

for the harm suffered[142] and not as if the court is awarding damages at common law (for example for a breach of contract[143]). The court will, therefore, apply a liberal method of assessment using the benefit of hindsight[144] in order to assess the loss sustained by the respondent/defendant by reason of the injunction (ie drawing the necessary distinction between such loss and the potentially different loss caused by the commencement or continuation of the litigation itself). This liberal method of assessment is used, for instance, in awarding equitable compensation for breach of fiduciary duty by a trustee assessed as at the date of the judgment; and in *Lilly Icos*, Arnold J held that this was the appropriate method for the assessment of compensation for loss caused by an interim injunction.[145]

10.118 It remains to be seen whether the court will continue to include aggravated damages as a separate possible head of compensation[146] and whether it will choose to include exemplary damages.[147] In principle, there seems no reason why equitable compensation should not include both these heads of compensation, as opposed to excluding them.

10.119 Two other aspects were considered by the Court of Appeal in *SmithKline Beecham*.[148] An undertaking does not entitle the person claiming compensation to include losses suffered by someone else who has been adversely affected by the injunction, such as another company in a group, other than himself. An undertaking is only intended to compensate those within its terms.[149] In addition, the Court of Appeal rejected a claim for restitution and held that restitutionary claims did not come within the wording of the undertaking given by the claimant. There was no 'performance interest' which could be created through the mechanism of an undertaking.

C. Other interim orders

Search orders

10.120 Employers are often suspicious about employees who leave to join competitors. In particular, employers often fear that their confidential information or property has been misappropriated. In some cases that suspicion is founded upon hard evidence which is often, but by no means always, the result of forensic examination of computer systems.[150] Where there is evidence

---

[142] *Les Laboratoires Servier v Apotex Inc* [2008] EWHC 2347 (Pat), [2009] FRS 3 and *Lilly Icos* (n 117 above).

[143] The suggestion for the application of principles as if awarding damages for breach of contract at common law emanated from a dictum of Lord Wilberforce in *F Hoffman-La Roche* (n 111 above) 361, but is no longer considered to be correct (although it may, in some cases, still be helpful in practice to use the analogy of contractual damages as a guide). See also the statutory form of the undertaking to be included in a freezing injunction annexed to CPR25APD, Schedule B (printed in Civil Procedure Forms, Miscellaneous Forms), which expressly refers to '*compensate for loss*'.

[144] ie excluding any common law rules about foreseeability which would be applied in the case of awards for contract or tort damages and awarding compensation up to the date of judgment.

[145] See n 117 above, paras 20–40.

[146] *Columbia Picture Industries Inc v Robinson* [1987] Ch 38.

[147] This was suggested as a possible head of compensation in *Digital Equipment Corp. v Darkcrest Limited* [1984] 512, 516.

[148] See n 117 above.

[149] A recent example of this is *Pirtek (UK) Ltd v Joinplace Ltd and others* [2010] EWHC 1641 (Ch), para 86.

[150] See Appendix 1 below for a guide to forensic investigations in this area.

of wrongdoing and evidence of serious risk of harm to the employer, as set out below, a search order may be an appropriate step to take to preserve the evidence and retrieve the property.

The search order is one of the nuclear weapons in the armoury of the litigator, having **10.121** been repeatedly described as 'truly draconian' by the courts. As such, its use is closely regulated by the courts and is reserved for the most serious cases of need. The preparation necessary to obtain an order is time consuming. Once obtained, the execution requires the presence of supervising solicitors and, often, independent forensic computing experts. The cost is invariably well into five figures and often into six prior to the first *inter partes* hearing in the case.

Nature of a search order

The search order is an order requiring a respondent to admit an applicant to premises for **10.122** the purpose of preserving evidence. It was given a secure statutory basis by section 7 of the Civil Procedure Act 1997 having been viewed as an order made pursuant to the inherent jurisdiction of the court (or perhaps pursuant to the general power contained in section 37 of the Supreme Court Act 1981 (since renamed the Senior Courts Act 1981)) prior to that date.

Section 7 permits an order to be granted to preserve relevant evidence or property which may **10.123** become the subject matter of the proceedings or in relation to which questions may arise. The order may direct any person to permit entry to any premises[151] where any person described in the order may (a) search or inspect anything described in the order; (b) make or obtain a copy, photograph, sample, or record of anything so described; (c) require to be provided with any information or article; and (d) retain for safekeeping anything described in the order.

Standard form of search order

An application is made pursuant to Part 25 of the CPR where specific provision is made **10.124** under rule 25.1(1)(h) and Practice Direction 25A—Interim Injunctions, which prescribes major modifications to the usual application procedure under Part 23.

It should be noted that frequent changes are made to the standard form order that may **10.125** be obtained from the Civil Procedure website. It should also be noted that there is an invariable time lag between a judgment which disapproves of parts of the standard form order and a revision to the standard form order. For this reason, a careful search of Lawtel (or equivalent) should be undertaken immediately prior to any application. Indeed, the standard form order at the time of writing has been described as a 'trap for the unwary'.[152]

For a salutary reminder of the perils of using an order that is not in the standard form and **10.126** failing to draw that to the attention of the judge, see the judgment of the Court of Appeal in *Memory Corp v Sidhu*.[153] The standard practice is now to provide a version of the proposed order for the judge, showing each and every variation from the standard form in redline or highlight, with the skeleton argument explaining and justifying each such variation.

---

[151] Including any vehicle—Civil Procedure Act 1997, s 7(8).
[152] *C v P* [2006] EWHC 1226 (Ch).
[153] [2000] 1 WLR 1443.

Conditions for the grant of a search order

10.127 The starting point in relation to the principles to be applied is to be found in the first Court of Appeal case dealing with what are now called search orders: *Anton Piller KG v Manufacturing Processes Ltd*.[154] In that case the rationale for Anton Piller orders (as they were previously known) was described by Lord Denning MR in these words:

> Let me say at once that no court in this land has any power to issue a search warrant to enter a man's house so as to see if there are papers or documents there which are of an incriminating nature, whether libels or infringements of copyright or anything else of the kind. No constable or bailiff can knock at the door and demand entry so as to inspect papers or documents. The householder can shut the door in his face and say 'Get out.' That was established in the leading case of Entick v. Carrington (1765) 2 Wils. K.B. 275. None of us would wish to whittle down that principle in the slightest. But the order sought in this case is not a search warrant. It does not authorise the plaintiffs' solicitors or anyone else to enter the defendants' premises against their will. It does not authorise the breaking down of any doors, nor the slipping in by a back door, nor getting in by an open door or window. It only authorises entry and inspection by permission of the defendants. The plaintiffs must get the defendants' permission. But it does do this: it brings pressure on the defendants to give permission. It does more. It actually orders them to give permission—with, I suppose, the result that if they do not give permission they are guilty of contempt of court. This may seem to be a search warrant in disguise. But it was fully considered in the House of Lords 150 years ago and held to be legitimate.[155]

10.128 Lord Denning MR then went on to consider the circumstances in which an Anton Piller order could properly be made. He said:

> It seems to me that such an order can be made by a judge ex parte, but it should only be made where it is essential that the plaintiff should have inspection so that justice can be done between the parties: and when, if the defendant were forewarned, there is a grave danger that vital evidence will be destroyed, that papers will be burnt or lost or hidden, or taken beyond the jurisdiction, and so the ends of justice be defeated: and when the inspection would do no real harm to the defendant or his case.[156]

> A little later on Lord Denning MR said of the practice: 'We are prepared, therefore, to sanction its continuance, but only in an extreme case where there is grave danger of property being smuggled away or of vital evidence being destroyed.'[157]

10.129 Most practically, Ormrod LJ said:

> There are three essential pre-conditions for the making of such an order, in my judgment. First, there must be an extremely strong prima facie case. Secondly, the damage, potential or actual, must be very serious for the applicant. Thirdly, there must be clear evidence that the defendants have in their possession incriminating documents or things, and that there is a real possibility that they may destroy such material before any application inter partes can be made.[158]

10.130 Finally, Shaw LJ said:

> The overriding consideration in the exercise of this salutary jurisdiction is that it is to be resorted to only in circumstances where the normal processes of the law would be rendered nugatory if some immediate and effective measure was not available. When such an order is

---

[154] [1976] Ch 55.
[155] ibid 60.
[156] ibid 61.
[157] ibid 61.
[158] ibid 62.

made, the party who has procured the court to make it must act with prudence and caution in pursuance of it.[159]

Despite the many amendments to the underlying statutory basis, rules of court, practice directions, and standard form orders, the above statements, and in particular the statement of Ormrod LJ, remain authoritative descriptions of the circumstances in which a court will consider granting an order. **10.131**

These conditions for the grant of a search order have more recently been stated by Warren J in *Indicii Salus Ltd v Chandrasekaran* as follows:[160] **10.132**

(1) there must be an extremely strong prima facie case;
(2) the damage, actual or potential, must be very serious for the applicant;
(3) there must be clear evidence that the defendants had in their possession incriminating documents or things;
(4) there is a real possibility that the defendants may destroy such material before an application on notice is made; and
(5) the harm likely to be caused to the respondent in his business affairs by the execution of the order must not be out of proportion to the legitimate object of the order.

Search orders in employee competition cases

The classic cases for Anton Piller orders were intellectual property cases, where there was illicit copying and distribution of copyrighted material. The approach taken in employment cases will often be different, as suggested by Hoffmann J (as he then was) in *Lock International plc v Beswick*: **10.133**

> *Anton Piller* orders are frequently sought in actions against former employees who have joined competitors or started competing businesses of their own. I have learned to approach such applications with a certain initial scepticism. There is a strong incentive for employers to launch a pre-emptive strike to crush the unhatched competition in the egg by causing severe strains on the financial and management resources of the defendants or even a withdrawal of their financial support. Whether the plaintiff has a good case or not, the execution of the *Anton Piller* order may leave the defendants without the will or the money to pursue the action to trial in order to enforce the cross-undertaking in damages. Some employers seem to regard competition from former employees as presumptive evidence of dishonesty. Many have great difficulty in understanding the distinction between genuine trade secrets and skill and knowledge which the employee may take away with him. In cases in which the plaintiff alleges misuse of trade secrets or confidential information concerning a manufacturing process, a lack of particularity about the precise nature of the trade secrets is usually a symptom of an attempt to prevent the employee from making legitimate use of the knowledge and skills gained in the plaintiff's service. That symptom is particularly evident in this case. Judges dealing with ex parte applications are usually also at a disadvantage in dealing with alleged confidential knowledge of technical processes described in technical language, such as the electric circuitry in this case. It may look like magic but turn out merely to embody a principle discovered by Faraday or Ampere. Even in cases in which the plaintiff has strong evidence that an employee has taken what is undoubtedly specific confidential information, such as a list of customers, the court must employ a graduated response. To borrow a useful concept from the jurisprudence of the European Community, there must be *proportionality* between the perceived threat to the plaintiff's rights and the remedy granted. The fact that there is overwhelming evidence that

---

[159] ibid 62.
[160] [2006] EWHC 521 (Ch).

the defendant has behaved wrongfully in his commercial relationships does not necessarily justify an *Anton Piller* order. People whose commercial morality allows them to take a list of the customers with whom they were in contact while employed will not necessarily disobey an order of the court requiring them to deliver it up. Not everyone who is misusing confidential information will destroy documents in the face of a court order requiring him to preserve them. In many cases it will therefore be sufficient to make an order for delivery up of the plaintiff's documents to his solicitor or, in cases in which the documents belong to the defendant but may provide evidence against him, an order that he preserve the documents pending further order, or allow the plaintiff's solicitor to make copies. The more intrusive orders allowing searches of premises or vehicles require a careful balancing of, on the one hand, the plaintiff's right to recover his property or to preserve important evidence against, on the other hand, violation of the privacy of a defendant who has had no opportunity to put his side of the case. It is not merely that the defendant may be innocent. The making of an intrusive order ex parte even against a guilty defendant is contrary to normal principles of justice and can only be done when there is a paramount need to prevent a denial of justice to the plaintiff. The absolute extremity of the court's powers is to permit a search of a defendant's dwelling house, with the humiliation and family distress which that frequently involves.[161]

10.134   This approach anticipates the Human Rights Act issues raised by search orders. Article 8 of the European Convention on Human Rights is engaged in relation to such matters, though the order may be justified under Article 8(2) as necessary to protect the rights of others.[162]

Application for a search order

10.135   Self-evidently, the application is made without notice. It may only be made in the High Court. Where the underlying claims include a claim for an account or intellectual property claims arising out of the misuse of databases, the application must be made in the Chancery Division.

10.136   The evidence for the application must be in affidavit form rather than the usual witness statement,[163] reflecting the additional importance of the application. The affidavits should contain primary evidence where possible rather than hearsay and thus there may be a number of them from those with knowledge of the different aspects of the evidence.

10.137   The evidence should address in turn the limbs of the test identified by Ormrod LJ in the *Anton Piller* case and deal with the concerns of Hoffmann J expressed in *Lock v Beswick*. It must disclose 'very fully' the reason for the order, including the probability that relevant material would disappear if the order were not made.[164] Bearing in mind the comments of Hoffmann J, careful consideration may need to be given to the evidence of disappearance, distinguishing that evidence from mere evidence of past wrongdoing in relation to confidential information.

10.138   In addition, the duty of full and frank disclosure must be complied with. This is an onerous duty[165] and requires an applicant to investigate the facts, rather than simply reciting those

---

[161] [1989] 1 WLR 1268, 1280. See also *Booker v McConnell plc v Plascow* [1985] RPC 425 *per* Dillon LJ.
[162] See generally *Chappell v UK* (1990) 12 EHRR 1; and *Niemitz v Germany* (1993) 16 EHRR 97. See also Lord Neuberger MR's reference in *Tchenguiz v Imerman* [2010] EWCA Civ 908, [2010] FLR 814, at para 118, to 'the safeguards of the Anton Piller (search order) jurisprudence . . . [being] not merely enshrined in our domestic law but . . . indeed essential if there is to be proper compliance with the Convention . . .'
[163] 25APD3.1.
[164] 25APD7.3(2).
[165] See *Indicii Salus Ltd v Chandrasekaran* [2008] EWCA Civ 67, para 8 *per* Longmore LJ.

facts known to him, and fairly present the evidence on which he relies.[166] This will include the identification of all likely means of defence and attacks on the evidence. A failure to comply with this duty may result in the order being set aside.[167]

Where, as is often the case, confidential information must be disclosed in the affidavit, **10.139** appropriate steps should be taken to ensure that that information will not become public as a result of that application. This will generally involve putting the confidential information in a sealed exhibit and seeking consequential orders to prevent the exhibit from going onto the court file.[168]

Execution of a search order

The order requires there to be a supervising solicitor to execute the search. He must be **10.140** experienced in the execution of search orders.[169]

As stated above, where the order is not in standard form, this must be disclosed to the judge **10.141** and justification must be provided. The now commonplace variant on the standard order is to provide for disk-imaging of computers.

This raises a series of special problems for those preparing for such a search. First, an inde- **10.142** pendent computer specialist is necessary to mirror the safeguards in relation to the supervising solicitor. Secondly, great care needs to be taken in relation to the privilege against self-incrimination and, to a lesser extent, legal professional privilege.

The privilege against self-incrimination

The privilege against self-incrimination is generally abrogated in relation to intellectual **10.143** property cases by section 72 of the Senior Courts Act 1981.[170] This will include many employment-related search orders.

As a disk imaging order will generally provide for a full forensic copy to be made of any **10.144** relevant hard drive or other electronic storage device there has previously been some debate as to whether privilege will continue to inhere in material brought to light by a search order but unconnected to the matter which gave rise to the order.

In the case of *C v P*,[171] the hard drive of the respondent to a search order had been imaged **10.145** and the court-appointed independent computer expert had found images of child pornography on the hard drive. As the possession of those images is illegal,[172] the respondent sought to claim the privilege against self-incrimination. At first instance Evans-Lombe J held that the respondent did not lose the entitlement to assert privilege by handing a disk to the supervising solicitor or computer expert,[173] but is not entitled to assert the privilege in relation to items already on the disk because there is no privilege against self-incrimination in relation to the production of a pre-existing document as opposed to the answering of questions.

---

[166] *Marc Rich v Krasner* (CA, 15 January 1999); and *The Gadget Shop v The Bug.com* [2001] FSR 383. See further Chapter 12 below.

[167] See eg *Elvee Ltd v Taylor* [2002] FSR 738, CA; cf *Brinks Mat v Elcombe* [1988] 1 WLR 1350.

[168] See also 25APD7.4(2).

[169] 25APD7.2.

[170] The privilege is also abrogated in relation to all fraud cases by the Fraud Act 2006, s 13.

[171] At first instance: [2006] EWHC 1226 (Ch) and on appeal to the Court of Appeal: [2008] Ch 1.

[172] Note that there is strict liability for possession of unlawful images of children.

[173] It was argued that because the documents were provided to someone who could be compelled to disclose them to law enforcement agencies, privilege was thereby lost.

The Court of Appeal upheld the decision at first instance in *C v P*,[174] but for different reasons. Where Evans-Lombe J sought to rely on the effect of the Human Rights Act 1998 affecting the scope of the privilege, the Court of Appeal held that even before the introduction of the Human Rights Act 1998 there was no privilege in such material. The Court of Appeal held that although the subject of the search order had been required to disclose the offending material to the supervising solicitor and computer expert because of the search order, there was no privilege in the material itself on account of the fact that it existed independently of the order.

10.146 The Court of Appeal has brought welcome clarity to the extent of the privilege in this area and confirmed that there is no bar to the reporting to the police of criminal activity which comes to light in the course of the execution of a search order.

Legal professional privilege

10.147 Disk-imaging orders also must deal with the issue of legal professional privilege. Plainly a disk may contain such material and a forensic copy may not be taken of only part of a disk. Such material must not be permitted to come into the hands of the applicant for such an order. In practice, such issues are normally dealt with by agreement between the respondent, the supervising solicitor, and the independent computer expert, with the relevant material being removed from the forensic copies of the hard drive prior to the image being searched for the applicant's confidential information or property.

Undertaking in damages

10.148 As with all without notice orders, an undertaking in damages is required.[175] In many employment cases, the search order will include the seizure of the tools of the employee's new business, including the computers and the software. As such, the potential liability on the undertaking in damages can be very great. The court will expect proof that the applicant will be able to meet any undertaking in damages and if that proof is in any way equivocal the court will expect some form of security by way of bank guarantee or otherwise. It is important that a claimant makes full material disclosure of its financial position relevant to the cross-undertaking in damages, as a failure to do so may result in the subsequent discharge of an order made without notice.[176]

10.149 If such security is not provided at the time of the application, its absence may provide the ground for the first application made by the respondent. Such an application would need to show that the risk of a claim against the undertaking in damages is significant and thus would be unlikely to succeed in circumstances where substantial quantities of improperly obtained or retained material have been identified on the execution of the search order.

Doorstep pillers

10.150 'Doorstep piller' orders were in vogue for a period when ingenious applicant counsel were seeking to obtain the benefits of an Anton Piller order but without the associated costs of a supervising solicitor by requiring immediate delivery up of documents to a solicitor standing on the respondent's doorstep.

---

[174] [2008] Ch 1.
[175] See paras 10.87 ff above.
[176] See *Sectrack NV v Satamatics Ltd* [2007] EWHC 3003 (Comm), para 96 *per* Flaux J.

These orders are no longer in vogue since the decision in *Adam Phones v Goldschmidt*,[177] in which the court held that there was little difference between such an order and an Anton Piller order and that, therefore, similar safeguards should often be put in place. This is now reflected in Practice Direction 25APD8 which requires applicants and the court to consider whether to require the presence of a supervising solicitor and the other safeguards on the execution of a doorstep piller. **10.151**

Such an order may still be worth considering where the evidence does not satisfy the high threshold for a search order. In particular, as was made clear by Hoffmann J in *Lock v Beswick*, the balancing act that must be undertaken prior to the grant of an order may more easily fall in favour of an applicant where the respondent's premises are not being searched and his privacy not being invaded. **10.152**

In general, such an order must permit legal advice to be taken.[178] In principle, there is nothing inherently objectionable to requiring a respondent in such circumstances to hand over particular items to the attendant supervising solicitor whilst legal advice is taken by the respondent. **10.153**

A further variant on this form of order was nicknamed by some practitioners the Challenge Anneka order.[179] This form of order required the near immediate delivery up of material to the offices of the applicant's solicitor, thereby avoiding the execution of the order at the premises of the respondent. Typically, on service of the order cash was handed to the respondent to ensure that he had sufficient money for a taxi fare to those offices. On one view, the provisions of 25APD8 would no longer apply because the order was not to be executed at the respondent's premises and there would be no need for a supervising solicitor. However, the only reason for seeking such an order would be to require the respondent to deliver up documentation without having time to consider, sift, or otherwise alter the documentation or take proper legal advice in relation to privilege. In such circumstances, aspects of the order are of a similar degree of intrusiveness to a doorstep piller and in many ways create a greater risk of the handing over of commercially confidential or privileged documentation to the applicant. As such, there seems little basis for a significant difference in the safeguards. **10.154**

Delivery up orders

In contrast to the doorstep piller and its variants, a normal delivery up order will require property and documents to be handed over within a reasonable period of time. **10.155**

The basis for such orders will generally be section 4 of the Torts (Interference with Goods) Act 1977, as identified in rule 25.1(1)(e) of the CPR. Section 4 provides that the court may make an order providing for the delivery up of any goods which are or may become the subject matter of proceedings or as to which any question may arise in proceedings. **10.156**

'Goods' are defined in section 14(1) of the 1977 Act as including all chattels personal other than things in action and money. As such, documents and other real property, belonging to the applicant will be encompassed within that definition but intangible property, such as **10.157**

---

[177] [2000] FSR 163.
[178] CPR 25APD 8 incorporating CPR 25APD 7.4(4)(a).
[179] This being a reference to a popular television programme in which Anneka Rice was challenged to travel around the country in a helicopter to meet impossible deadlines.

confidential information not embodied in one of the applicant's documents, will not be so included.[180]

10.158 Orders are often referred to as delivery up orders when they are, in fact, made under rule 25.1(1)(c)(i) for the detention, custody, or preservation of relevant property.

10.159 In addition, interim orders may be made in relation to confidential information or copies of databases under the provisions of the Copyright Designs and Patents Act 1988 or the Copyright and Rights in Databases Regulations 1997,[181] both of which provide for interim remedies of delivery up. These rights are considered in more detail in Chapter 3 above on confidential information.

10.160 Lastly, delivery up may be ordered as the interim version of a final remedy, thus falling within rule 25.1(1)(a) of the CPR. Such an order may be oppressive and may be drafted in such a way as to encompass all copies of a database that is critical to the employee respondent's new business and all documents derived from such infringing copies. However, even where obtained *ex parte*, there will generally be time to apply for the order to be set aside prior to compliance, rendering such orders considerably less draconian than the search order or its siblings.

10.161 The usual principles for the grant of mandatory injunctions will apply. These are contained in *Zockoll v Mercury Communications Ltd* applying *Nottingham Building Society v Euro-dynamic Systems plc* and are set out in paragraph 10.86 above.

Destruction orders

10.162 Orders requiring the respondent to destroy are rare other than in relation to confidential information. In such cases, the respondent may have stored the information on a computer or other electronic device. In such circumstances, the applicant may seek an interim order requiring the respondent not merely to stop using the confidential information but to destroy all electronic copies of the confidential information remaining on his computer.

10.163 Such an order is made under rule 25.1(1)(a) of the CPR and thus is subject to the *Zockoll* guidelines set out above. Notably, the destruction of information will contain a grave risk of injustice unless a copy is preserved of all such information, such a copy normally residing with the applicant's solicitor pending trial. Sometimes, the order will require the respondent to permit an independent computer expert to access the electronic device to confirm that the relevant confidential information has been securely and completely deleted.

10.164 Such an order is invasive of the respondent's privacy, albeit to a lesser degree than a full search order and albeit that compliance is never required on an *ex parte* basis. For this reason, it would be normal to provide full evidential justification for the need for such an order rather than some lesser order.

Detention, preservation, and inspection orders

10.165 Under rule 25.1(1)(c)(i) of the CPR an order may be made for the detention, preservation, and inspection of relevant property. Property is relevant if it is the subject of a claim or as to

---

[180] See eg *Ashworth Hospital Authority v Mirror Group Newspapers Ltd* [2001] 1 WLR 515, paras 55–7.
[181] SI 1997/3032.

which any question may arise on a claim.[182] This order is often at the heart of a search order, as can be seen from the standard form of that order. However, there is no reason in principle why such a detention, preservation, and inspection order should necessarily be an adjunct to a search order.

Indeed, as set out above, many forms of delivery up order are, in truth, detention, preservation, **10.166** and inspection orders, entitling the applicant to the preservation of property or evidence that may be only partly owned by him or in relation to which he may have no direct proprietary interest. The terms of such an order are not inherently objectionable, in that they will not extend far beyond the obligations inherent on any party to a claim in relation to the preservation of evidence.

Disclosure orders

Disclosure orders are typically made under rule 25.1(1)(g) of the CPR and are an order **10.167** directing a party to provide information about the location of relevant property or assets or to provide information about relevant property or assets. In terms, they are limited to cases where such property or assets are or may be the subject of a freezing injunction.

However, an order may also be made for the disclosure of documents at any time, both pre-action **10.168** and for early disclosure of documents under rule 31.12 or 31.16 of the CPR.

Further, the court probably has power to order a respondent to provide information pur- **10.169** suant to its general power to grant mandatory injunctions requiring the performance of obligations.

In *Intelsec Systems Ltd v Grech-Cini*,[183] it was held that where an employer brought a claim for **10.170** breach of confidence and passing off against former employees, the court had jurisdiction to make an order requiring the employee to disclose the names and addresses of business contacts irrespective of whether those contacts had been made before or after the termination of the employee's employment; but in the latter case only if it was necessary to rectify mis-representations arising out of passing off; and that any order made in respect of post-termination contacts must be proportionate and take into account the protection of the employee's own information.

This may include the power to make an order, on an interim basis, requiring an employee **10.171** who owes fiduciary duties to disclose details of his own misconduct,[184] and to require a mere employee (ie one not owing fiduciary duties) to disclose serious misconduct by others.[185] In each case, this would amount to requiring a respondent to comply with the duties to which they were already subject rather than imposing any fresh duty by way of court order. This power may be of particular importance in relation to team moves. It should be noted that the courts will generally avoid any injunction which would have the effect of specifically enforcing a contract of employment.[186] However, an employee cannot be said to be required to do work when required to reveal misconduct. As such, there can be no absolute bar to the

---

[182] CPR, r 25.1(2).
[183] [2000] 1 WLR 1190.
[184] See the discussion of *Item Software v Fassihi* [2005] ICR 450, CA in Chapter 2 above.
[185] See the discussion of *Sybron v Rochem* [1984] Ch 112 in Chapter 2 above.
[186] Note the effect of Trade Union and Labour Relations (Consolidation) Act 1992, s 236, which prevents any court from compelling an employee to do any work. See further Chapter 4 above.

granting of such an order, albeit that a court could be expected to show marked reluctance to compel performance of one of the primary obligations of an employee.

10.172 This marked reluctance to grant such orders was given concrete form in *Aon v JLT*.[187] In that case, Mackay J considered authorities, including the *Intelsec Systems* case, and concluded that whilst there was jurisdiction to make broad disclosure orders, they were 'on any view an exceptional and not a routine order which should not be made as a matter of course where prohibitory injunctions [preventing further breaches of contract, fiduciary duty and misuse of confidential information] are to be found'.[188] In that case, the following features were considered important:

- whether the claimant would be unable to plead his case without the order sought;
- whether the order was focused and proportionate or was tantamount to standard disclosure in an unpleaded case;
- whether the order would save costs;
- whether damages would not be an adequate remedy, by which is meant something more than that it would be difficult to prove the extent of damage;
- whether there are practical steps, short of an injunction, that the employer can take to protect against the recruitment of employees and the loss of clients;
- whether the disclosure provisions are necessary to permit policing of the prohibitory orders.

10.173 A disclosure order could be of critical importance when discovering the sources of confidential information, the uses to which such confidential information has been put, and the contacts that have been made using that confidential information. This is a form of order that is, in effect, the same as that for the provision of information under the search order jurisdiction.

10.174 The usual disclosure orders in relation to freezing orders and search orders are set out in the standard forms for each of those orders. In relation to freezing orders, disclosure is usually ordered in relation to all assets and their location, this being explicitly provided for by rule 25.1(1)(g) of the CPR.

10.175 In database cases and other theft of confidential information cases, provisions are often included requiring the respondent to identify the use to which confidential information has been put and, in particular, the identity of all clients contacted using the database or confidential information. Often such information will exist in documentary form and thus may be justified under provisions relating to disclosure under Part 31 of the CPR. Where such information is not readily in documentary form, it may be more difficult to shoehorn the request for information into one of the accepted categories of case for disclosure of information.

10.176 It should be noted that the court has, on occasions, stated in terms that 'an order should not be made which allows a plaintiff to interrogate a defendant so as to discover whether the plaintiff has a claim against the defendant'.[189] As such, the rules as to the provision of information in search order cases are truly ancillary to the primary provision in such orders, which is to detain and preserve relevant evidence. Similarly, in search order cases, the provision of information is to permit the policing of the order rather than proving the substantive underlying claim.

---

[187] [2010] IRLR 600.
[188] ibid para 24.
[189] *Den Norske Bank v Antonatos* [1999] QB 271, 290.

Thus, in general, interim orders should only be granted for the provision of information **10.177** where they are necessary for the policing of an order (as in the *Intelsec* case referred to above), or where the provision of information is claimed by way of a final injunction as a head of relief in the claim and thus where the interim relief can properly be viewed as an interim version of the final relief.

It should be noted that the disclosure provisions will bring into play the same issues of privilege **10.178** against self-incrimination that are raised in the search order cases. As such, unless the case is an intellectual property case which results in the statutory abrogation of privilege under section 72 of the Senior Courts Act 1981, or a theft case bringing about similar abrogation of privilege under section 31(1) of the Theft Act 1968 or section 5(2) of the Theft Act 1978, the privilege against self-incrimination may be claimed and this should be provided for in the order, particularly if sought on a without notice basis.

Norwich Pharmacal *orders*

The *Norwich Pharmacal* order is an order pursuant to which the respondent is required to **10.179** reveal the identity of wrongdoers where he has become mixed up in the wrongdoing. The order is made under the inherent jurisdiction of the court but has its closest link to CPR Part 31 applications (disclosure and inspection of documents). Indeed, it was formerly referred to as an action for discovery. Nevertheless, *Norwich Pharmacal* relief is regarded as substantive relief and therefore the principle that jurisdiction cannot be asserted over a party resident abroad purely for the purposes of the disclosure of documents does not apply in this context.[190]

The principles were initially refined in, and the order takes its name from, the case of **10.180** *Norwich Pharmacal v Customs & Excise Commissioners*.[191] In that case, the Commissioners of Customs & Excise had become innocently mixed up in the illicit importation of the chemicals manufactured abroad which Norwich Pharmacal alleged infringed their patent. The House of Lords held that the Commissioners were obliged to reveal the identity of the wrongdoer.

The *ratio* of the case is best expressed in the judgment of Lord Reid: **10.181**

> [The authorities] seem to me to point to a very reasonable principle that if through no fault of his own a person gets mixed up in the tortious acts of others so as to facilitate their wrong-doing he may incur no personal liability but he comes under a duty to assist the person who has been wronged by giving him full information and disclosing the identity of the wrongdoers. I do not think that it matters whether he became so mixed up by voluntary action on his part or because it was his duty to do what he did. It may be that if this causes him expense the person seeking the information ought to reimburse him. But justice requires that he should co-operate in righting the wrong if he unwittingly facilitated its perpetration.[192]

Since then, certain aspects have been clarified by other decisions. The power to make such **10.182** an order is not limited to cases of tortious wrongdoing. Rather any form of wrongdoing will suffice, including breaches of equitable and contractual obligations in relation to

---

[190] *Lockton Cos International v Persons Unknown* [2009] EWHC 3423 (QB).
[191] [1974] AC 133, HL.
[192] ibid, 175.

confidential information.[193] In *Mitsui v Nexen Petroleum UK Ltd*,[194] the court considered the past authorities and identified the three necessary conditions for the grant of relief as follows:

(1) a wrong must have been carried out, or arguably carried out, by an ultimate wrongdoer;
(2) there must be the need for an order to enable action to be brought against the ultimate wrongdoer; and
(3) the person against whom the order is sought must:
    (a) be mixed up in, so as to have facilitated, the wrongdoing, and
    (b) be able or likely to be able to provide the information necessary to enable the ultimate wrongdoer to be sued.

Even where all three conditions are satisfied the court retains a residual discretion whether, in all the circumstances, to grant an order.[195]

10.183 As is apparent from that summary, the jurisdiction is not limited to cases where the identity of the wrongdoer is unknown. Rather, it extends to cases where the applicant requires disclosure of crucial information in order to be able to bring its claim or where the applicant requires a missing piece of the jigsaw.[196] In particular, the information sought can extend beyond the identity of the wrongdoer to information showing that the alleged wrongdoer committed the wrong.

10.184 It was suggested by the court in *Mitsui v Nexen*[197] that a mere witness with no connection to the wrongdoing could be the respondent to a *Norwich Pharmacal* application if such a person was the only possible source of the information. This was certainly not the basis of the decision in the *Norwich Pharmacal* case in which Lord Reid stated in terms[198] that mere witnesses could not be made subject to such an application because it would be contrary to authority, principle, and public policy.

10.185 *Mitsui v Nexen* is not binding authority for any abrogation of the 'mere witness' rule, given the nature of the suggestion made by the court and the reason for the decision of the court. Even if the jurisdictional threshold is met, no order will be made unless it is necessary.[199] The test of necessity is strict, limiting *Norwich Pharmacal* relief to information which is vital to the applicant's assertion of rights against a wrongdoer or ability to protect himself or herself against further wrongdoing. That will be tested, principally, against whether there is some way to obtain the information other than by means of an order directed against a third party. This is because of the strong public interest in not subjecting non-parties to the court process unless it is necessary to do so. In *Nikitin v Richards Butler LLP*,[200] an application for *Norwich Pharmacal* relief was refused on the basis that the applicants already had enough information

---

[193] *Ashworth Hospital Authority v Mirror Group Newspapers Ltd* [2002] UKHL 29, [2003] FSR 17, HL affirming [2001] 1 WLR 515, CA; *Camelot v Centaur Communications Ltd* [1998] IRLR 80, CA.

[194] [2005] 3 All ER 511.

[195] *Sega Enterprises Ltd v Alca Electronics* [1982] FSR 516; applied in *Eli Lilly & Co Ltd v Neopharma Ltd* [2008] FSR 25 and *BNP Paribas v TH Global Ltd* [2009] EWHC 37 (Ch).

[196] *Axa Equity & Law Life Assurance Society v National Westminster Bank* [1998] CLC 1177, CA; *Aoot Kalmneft v Denton Wilde Sapte* [2002] 1 Lloyds Rep 417.

[197] [2005] 3 All ER 511, para 24.

[198] [1974] AC 133, 174. See also 178 *per* Lord Morris, 188 *per* Viscount Dilhorne, and 203 *per* Lord Kilbrandon, but cf 199 *per* Lord Cross.

[199] See *Mitsui v Nexen* (n 194 above).

[200] [2007] EWHC 173 (QB).

to bring claims if they wished to do so leading the judge to conclude that they were seeking disclosure not for the purposes of bringing an action but rather to defend connected but separate litigation.

Although the test is sometimes formulated in terms of court proceedings, for example as information necessary 'to a decision to sue or an ability to plead',[201] it is not a requirement that the applicant intends to or will bring court proceedings but rather merely that the information is necessary for the applicant to assert rights against a wrongdoer and/or protect himself or herself from further wrongdoing. Thus in *Ashworth Hospital Authority v MGN Ltd*,[202] the House of Lords upheld an order in favour of a secure mental hospital against a respondent newspaper for the identification of members of the hospital's staff who had disclosed confidential information patient records to the newspaper. The hospital sought the order so as to dismiss the offending employee and not necessarily for the purposes of any litigation.

10.186

There may be circumstances in which the applicant is concerned that the alleged wrongdoer will be notified in advance of the application to seek *Norwich Pharmacal* relief. As the case of *G v Wikimedia Foundation Inc*[203] made clear, it is possible for an applicant to apply for the court to prohibit disclosure of the fact of the making of the application in order to prevent the alleged wrongdoer being tipped off, although such prohibition would be expected to expire when the alleged wrongdoer had been served with an injunction or at the return date. Any applicant seeking a *Norwich Pharmacal* order will be required to meet the costs of the respondent. The respondent, if he is in doubt as to whether he needs to comply with the order, is entitled to put the matter before the court and have his costs for such a hearing met in addition.[204]

10.187

Freezing orders

Freezing orders are orders granted by the court to freeze the assets, and in particular the bank accounts, of respondents to the application. Prior to the introduction of the CPR, they were referred to as Mareva injunctions after one of the first cases which identified the scope of the relief.[205]

10.188

As with search orders, freezing orders are draconian in nature and granted only after careful consideration by the courts. The procedure is strictly prescribed in the CPR, in particular by rule 25.1(1)(f) and (g). Practice Direction 25APD contains the standard form order.

10.189

Freezing orders are usually, but not invariably, sought on a without notice basis prior to the commencement of proceedings. They will usually contain ancillary disclosure orders in relation to those assets. Unlike search orders, freezing orders are rarely sought in employment-related cases unless there is an allegation of fraud. The reason for this is that a freezing order has one aim, namely to prevent a defendant from dissipating his assets prior to judgment. However, it does not render the applicant a preferred creditor of the respondent—the applicant will have no greater claim over the assets frozen than any other creditor.[206] It should be noted that

10.190

---

[201] ibid para 24.
[202] [2002] 1 WLR 2033.
[203] [2010] EMLR 14.
[204] *Norwich Pharmacal* (n 191 above) 176 *per* Lord Reid.
[205] *Mareva Compania Naviera SA v International Bulk Carriers SA* [1975] 2 Lloyd's Rep 509.
[206] See eg *The Angel Bell* [1981] QB 65.

a freezing order may also be sought in support of a proprietary claim as well as in relation to a mere damages claim.

10.191   As with a search order, the application must be supported by evidence on affidavit, again highlighting the draconian nature of the relief. The evidence must show (a) a good arguable case in relation to a cause of action justiciable in the United Kingdom, (b) that the respondent has assets within the jurisdiction (whether money or property), (c) that there is a real risk of removal or dissipation of assets if the relief is not granted, and generally, (d) that the applicant will be good for any damage sustained in the event that the undertaking in damages is called upon.

10.192   The real risk of dissipation is generally the most significant issue. The case of *Z v A-Z*[207] made plain that it was not necessary to show that assets would be removed from the jurisdiction but rather that the defendant would make himself 'judgment proof' by whatever means. In most employment cases, even those of fraud, the employee is present within the jurisdiction with significant ties. In such cases, it will always be difficult to show that there is an intention on his part to make himself judgment proof. Indeed, as Kerr LJ made plain in *Z v A-Z*, the secure establishment of the respondent within the United Kingdom will be a strong factor against the grant of such an injunction.

10.193   The proper test is now set out in *The Niedersachsen*:[208] would 'the refusal of a [freezing order] . . . involve a real risk that a judgment or award in favour of the [applicants] . . . would remain unsatisfied'? This is an objective test that does not require the applicant to show that this is the respondent's purpose or intent.[209]

10.194   However, as is made plain by the standard form of order, the respondent is entitled to meet his ordinary living expenses and will not generally be prevented from engaging in his ordinary business, even if this puts at risk assets that would otherwise be available to satisfy a judgment. As such, in relation to employment claims it will be rare indeed that an order will be granted unless there is evidence of serious wrongdoing tantamount to dishonesty together with strong evidence that the respondent will either hide his assets or spirit them abroad unless the order is granted. Where a freezing order is granted it should be noted that mere notification of the order to the respondent's bank does not operate to create a duty of care between the applicant and the bank; the applicant must rely on the court ensuring the bank's compliance with the injunction and on the court's powers to punish the bank in default of compliance.[210]

10.195   As with all applications for injunctions on a without notice basis, there is a duty of full and frank disclosure which will apply both to the cause of action and also to the risk of dissipation. Further, any ancillary disclosure orders will give rise to similar issues of the privilege against self-incrimination as discussed above in relation to search orders.[211]

Interim declarations

10.196   Interim declarations are rarely sought in employee competition cases but the remedy was not available until relatively recently. The power to make an interim declaration is set out in

---

[207] [1982] QB 558.
[208] [1983] 1 WLR 1412.
[209] ibid and *Ketchum International v Group Public Relations* [1997] 1 WLR 4.
[210] *Customs & Excise Commissioners v Barclays Bank plc* [2007] 1 AC 181.
[211] See *Den Norske Bank v Antonatos* [1999] QB 271.

rule 25.1(1)(b) of the CPR. It is allied to the power to grant a final declaration identified in rule 40.20.

This power to make interim declarations in private law cases is of far more recent genesis than the power to grant final declarations. Indeed, as late as 1994, the courts declared that the interim declaration was 'unknown to English law'.[212] Interim declarations were introduced by the CPR pursuant to a recommendation to implement them in judicial review cases. However, on their introduction they were not limited to such cases and are available in all appropriate cases.

10.197

There must be a real issue raised between the parties, since the court will not decide hypothetical future questions: see the decision of the Court of Appeal in *Re Barnato*.[213] The principle has been recently re-affirmed by the Court of Appeal in *Horbury Building Systems Ltd v Hampden Insurance NV*[214] and in the Chancery Division in *A & P Birkenhead Properties Ltd v Northwestern Shiprepairers and Shipbuilders Ltd*.[215] The critical element is that there must be 'a dispute based on concrete facts': see *Well Barn Shoot Ltd v Shackleton*.[216]

10.198

The seeking of final declarations in employment cases is of long standing and is particularly used by individuals seeking judicial determination of their obligations under disputed restrictive covenants. Thus, in G*reer v Sketchley Ltd*,[217] the employee applied for a declaration that he would not be in breach of a twelve-month non-competition covenant. The trial of the action was expedited and the Court of Appeal held that the judge had taken the correct course to grant a declaration to the employee at the end of the trial that his intended action was not in breach of the covenant. An example of a case where the employer sought a declaration against its employee, when it was faced with a threatened course of conduct allegedly in breach of covenant, is *Commercial Plastics Ltd v Vincent*.[218]

10.199

It remains therefore to be seen how far the new power to grant an interim declaration will have practical value in employee competition cases.

10.200

D. Final injunctions

The default remedy for the court in relation to actionable wrongs is damages. The court may, in an appropriate case, grant an injunction. However, unlike damages, a permanent injunction is always a discretionary remedy.

10.201

As such, a defendant may always raise any of the equitable defences to the grant of an injunction. Those defences include laches (delay) and acquiescence. Acquiescence is particularly important where the claimant has stood by and watched the breach of covenants rather than taking any action to enforce them. Whilst such acquiescence may well indicate the lack of any need for the covenants, it will also be relevant in relation to a claim both for interim relief

10.202

---

[212] *Riverside Mental Health NHS Trust v Fox* [1994] 1 FLR 614.
[213] [1949] Ch 258, CA.
[214] [2004] EWCA 418, [2004] Build LR 431, CA.
[215] [2006] All ER (D) 402.
[216] [2003] EWCA Civ 002, [2003] All ER (D) 182, CA.
[217] [1979] IRLR 445, CA.
[218] [1964] 3 All ER 546.

and for a permanent injunction in the event that the claimant proves that the covenant is valid and otherwise enforceable.

10.203   The position remains as set out by AL Smith LJ in *Shelfer v City of London Electric Lighting Co*,[219] where he stated:

> Many judges have stated, and I emphatically agree with them, that a person by committing a wrongful act (whether it be a public company for public purposes or a private individual) is not thereby entitled to ask the court to sanction his doing so by purchasing his neighbour's rights, by assessing damages in that behalf, leaving his neighbour with the nuisance, or his lights dimmed, as the case may be. In such cases the well known rule is not to accede to the application, but to grant the injunction sought, for the plaintiff's legal right has been invaded, and he is prima facie entitled to an injunction. There are, however, cases in which this rule may be relaxed, and in which the damages may be awarded in substitution for an injunction as authorized by this section. In any instance in which a case for an injunction has been made out, if the plaintiff by his acts or laches has disentitled himself to an injunction the court may award damages in its place. So again, whether the case be for a mandatory injunction or to restrain a continuing nuisance, the appropriate remedy may be damages in lieu of an injunction, assuming a case for an injunction to be made out. In my opinion, it may be stated as a good working rule that—(1) If the injury to the plaintiff's legal rights is small, (2) and is one which is capable of being estimated in money, (3) and is one which can be adequately compensated by a small money payment, (4) and the case is one in which it would be oppressive to the defendant to grant an injunction:— then damages in substitution for an injunction may be given.
>
> There may also be cases in which, though the four above-mentioned requirements exist, the defendant by his conduct, as, for instance, hurrying up his buildings so as if possible to avoid an injunction, or otherwise acting with reckless disregard to the plaintiff's rights, has disentitled himself from asking that damages may be assessed in substitution for an injunction.[220]

10.204   A case demonstrating the effect of such acquiescence is *Shaw v Applegate*[221] in which a negative covenant (in relation to land) was breached by the defendant with the full knowledge of the claimant. The defendant spent significant sums and built up his business on the back of the failure to enforce the covenant. In those circumstances, a permanent injunction was refused.

10.205   In most employment cases relating to covenants, if the claimant has not sought an interim injunction in relation to covenants by the time of trial, the period of the covenant is likely to be close to expiring. As such, it may not be suitable to award a permanent injunction in relation to the covenant. However, in relation to misuse of confidential information, different considerations will apply, particularly given that the failure to obtain an interim injunction is unlikely to reflect acquiescence in the misuse of confidential information. As a matter of principle, the court will normally grant final injunctions in relation to an enforceable covenant without proof of actual damage unless, in an exceptional case, it would be unconscionable to do so because it would cause the defendant hardship or would be otherwise prejudicial.[222]

10.206   Most employment injunctions sought at trial are prohibitory injunctions, ie injunctions prohibiting the defendant from undertaking acts which would be in breach of covenant or

---

[219] [1895] 1 Ch 287.
[220] ibid 322–3.
[221] [1977] 1 WLR 970, CA.
[222] See *Dyson v Strutt* [2005] EWHC 2814, paras 70–6.

other obligations. There may be some circumstances where a mandatory injunction (ie one where the defendant is required to take positive action) is sought but even in such circumstances the mandatory injunction would not be a continuing mandatory injunction but rather one requiring a one-off act, such as the deletion of confidential information or the delivery up of goods.

As with all injunctions, the permanent injunction must be phrased such that the defendant **10.207** is well able to understand its precise scope and effect. In particular, any permanent injunction in relation to confidential information should identify with precision the information that is confidential and the extent of its protection.

E. Contempt of court

Introduction

The law of contempt arises from the court's inherent jurisdiction to protect the integrity of **10.208** its procedure and to enforce its own orders. There are a number of divisions, including civil and criminal contempts, contempts by publication, and contempts in the face of the court.[223] This section is concerned with civil contempts, ie 'conduct which involves a breach, or assisting in the breach, of a court order'[224] or an undertaking. Although civil, it would be misleading to regard this jurisdiction as being confined to private matters between the parties to litigation. Civil contempt in fact serves a dual role:

> . . . civil contempt . . . bears a two-fold character, implying as between the parties to the proceedings merely a right to exercise and a liability to submit to a form of civil execution, but as between the party in default and the state, a penal or disciplinary jurisdiction to be exercised by the court in the public interest.[225]

This dual role is reflected in the available sanctions: imprisonment, fines, or sequestration **10.209** of the contemnor's assets. It is established that committal or sequestration are also the appropriate remedies against a third party who is alleged to have aided or abetted the breach of an injunction or undertaking.[226] It also explains why the purpose of contempt proceedings is not to compensate the claimant, but rather to vindicate the authority of the court by punishing defiance of its orders and to ensure that those orders are obeyed.[227]

Safeguards

Since it involves what is effectively a penal sanction, judges are generally reluctant to invoke **10.210** the contempt jurisdiction unless they are satisfied: (a) that there has been a clear breach of the relevant order or undertaking, (b) that there is no alternative, and (c) that all procedural

---

[223] The leading work is D Eady and ATH Smith, *Arlidge, Eady and Smith on Contempt* (3rd edn, 2005) (hereinafter 'Arlidge'). Also useful, but less authoritative is CJ Miller, *Contempt of Court* (3rd edn, 2000).

[224] *A-G v Newspaper Publishing plc* [1988] Ch 333, 362.

[225] This statement from *Halsbury's Laws of England* (3rd edn, 1954) Vol 8 was quoted with approval by Edmund Davies LJ in *Jennison v Baker* [1972] 2 QB 52, 69–70. However, civil contempt is not itself a criminal offence (*Cobra Golf Inc v Rata* [1998] Ch 109) and (in contrast to criminal contempt) may be waived by the party for whose benefit an order was made (*Roberts v Albert Bridge Co* (1873) LR 8 Ch App 753).

[226] *Elliot v Klinger* [1967] 1 WLR 1165. Although the court may adopt the more lenient course of issuing an injunction against repetition of the contempt.

[227] *Crystalmews Ltd v Metterick* [2006] EWHC 3087 (Ch), para 8.

requirements have been complied with by the party seeking enforcement. Each of these limitations is now considered.

Establishing the breach

10.211   The court will not grant an order for committal in relation to an order or undertaking which is found to be ambiguous.[228] For this reason, it is essential that great care is taken in drawing up orders to remove the scope for later argument. In a case where there is some doubt about whether the defendant has complied with an undertaking to the court, it may be considered appropriate to apply for an order requiring him to state whether or not he had done so before moving to commit for contempt.[229]

Considering alternatives

10.212   The court will scrutinize applications for committal where there has only been a trivial or blameless breach of an order. In *Adam Phones Ltd v Goldschmidt*,[230] Jacob J held that resort to the contempt jurisdiction was a wholly disproportionate response and dismissed the application with costs awarded to the respondent.

10.213   Custodial sentences should be as short as is consistent with the circumstances of the case and consideration should always be given to suspending the sentence.[231] Although sequestration is the less draconian sanction available in contempt proceedings (since it does not involve the deprivation of individual liberty), it was still regarded as too drastic a course in *Edward Grey Ltd v Greys (Midlands) Ltd*.[232] In this case, the defendant gave an undertaking not to use a name, of which 'Greys' was the prominent word, in the Birmingham area. However, it did so and the court found it to be 'as clear a case of flagrant and deliberate flouting of this Court as could be imagined'. However, Wynn-Parry J refused to order sequestration (or even to impose a fine) in the light of the sincere apology which the defendant had offered and the effect such an order would have on the rest of its business and its customers.

Procedural requirements

10.214   Although the court has the power to dispense with service of the claim form or application notice where it considers it is just to do so,[233] personal service is generally insisted upon.[234] The court also insists on proof beyond reasonable doubt that the order which is said to have been breached was served on the alleged contemnor.[235] However, in a case of genuine urgency,

---

[228]   *R v City of London Magistrates' Court, ex p Green* [1997] 3 All ER 551. This case concerned an attempt to commit officers of the Serious Fraud Office for contempt of an order addressed to a company for the return of computers which the SFO had seized as part of an investigation. They were found not to be in contempt of the order, which was not addressed to them and which was ambiguous in its references to the downloading of information from the computers.

[229]   *Kangol Industries Ltd v Bray (Alfred) & Sons Ltd* [1953] 1 All ER 444.

[230]   [2000] FSR 163, [1999] 4 All ER 486. In this case, the defendant had sought to comply with the order and part of the reason for non-compliance was that there was no supervising solicitor and the order had been served on a Saturday morning when the defendant was unable to obtain legal advice.

[231]   The relevant sentencing principles are helpfully summarized in *Aspect Capital Ltd v Hugh Christensen* [2010] EWHC 744 (Ch), paras 47–54.

[232]   [1952] RPC 25.

[233]   RSC Ord 52, rr 3(4) and 4(3).

[234]   RSC Ord 52, rr 3(3) and 4(2) and CCR Ord 29, r 1(2). The rules on personal service under CPR, r 6.4 apply.

[235]   *Churchman v Joint Shop Stewards' Committee of the Workers of the Port of London* [1972] 1 WLR 1094, 1098.

the claimant may (with the permission of the court) communicate the terms of the injunction to the relevant person by telephone, fax, or email.[236] Proof of service is not required in relation to an undertaking since it is volunteered and hence the alleged contemnor is assumed to know of it.[237] There is authority for the proposition that the presence of the alleged contemnor at the hearing at which the order was made did not dispense with the requirement of personal service,[238] but it is doubtful that this is consistent with the modern procedure for service and aims of the CPR. In the case of mandatory orders, the contemnor must also be served with a copy of the order alleged to have been disobeyed.

The order must be endorsed with a penal notice. The penal notice must be prominently displayed on the front of the copy of the order and must contain a warning that disobedience to the order would be a contempt of court punishable by imprisonment or sequestration.[239] A prohibitory order may be enforced, however, if the court is satisfied that pending proper service in accordance with RSC Order 45, rule 7, the person against whom it is sought to be enforced had notice of it (by being present when the order was made, or by being notified of its terms by telephone, telegram, or otherwise).[240] Again, the court has power to dispense with service of a copy of the order if it thinks it just to do so.[241]   **10.215**

The criminal burden of proof also applies to establishing that there has been breach of the order or undertaking which reflects the fact that civil contempt is of a criminal character.[242] However, there is no obligation to demonstrate that the breach of the order or undertaking was committed with any particular state of mind, for example deliberately.[243] All that is required is that the conduct was intentional (in the sense of not being accidental) and that the contemnor was aware of the facts which rendered the conduct a breach of the order or undertaking.[244]   **10.216**

The alleged contemnor also has the option of approaching the court to request modification of, or release from, the terms of an order or undertaking.[245] However, there is no guarantee that such modification will be granted and the applicant would usually have to pay the costs of such proceedings.   **10.217**

Procedure generally

The procedure governing committals for contempt is contained in RSC Ord 52 (Schedule 1 to the CPR) (High Court) and CCR Order 29 (Schedule 2 to the CPR) (County Court) and the associated practice direction. The power to punish for contempt is generally exercised by the Divisional Court of the Queen's Bench Division as part of its inherent jurisdiction   **10.218**

---

[236] *Ex p Green* (n 228 above), 558. The court is generally less concerned with formal service in the case of prohibitory (rather then mandatory) injunctions.

[237] *Hussain v Hussain* [1986] 2 WLR 805.

[238] *Mander v Falcke* [1891] 3 Ch 488.

[239] RSC Ord 45, r 7(4).

[240] ibid r 7(6).

[241] ibid r 7(7). The court has the power under this provision to dispense with service retrospectively as well as prospectively (*Davy International Ltd v Tazzyman* [1997] 1 WLR 1256, CA).

[242] *Re Bramblevale Ltd* [1970] Ch 128, 137. RSC Ord 52PD1.4.

[243] *M v Home Office* [1994] 1 AC 377.

[244] The defendant's state of mind remains relevant to mitigation (*Re Mileage Conference Group of the Tyre Manufacturers' Conference Ltd's Agreement* [1966] 1 WLR 1137).

[245] *Cutler v Wandsworth Stadium Ltd* [1948] 1 KB 291.

over its own proceedings and those of inferior courts (RSC Ord 52, rule 1(2)). However, the county court does have the power to commit for breach of its orders and of undertakings given to it (CCR Ord 29(1) and (2)). An employment tribunal is 'an inferior court' for the purposes of RSC Ord 52 and the Divisional Court may therefore punish contempt of it.[246] In relation to an order obtained against a corporate body, committal is available against a director or other officer of the body. The corporate body itself cannot be committed, but may be fined or have its assets seized.[247]

10.219 A committal application should be made using the Part 8 claim form. However, if made in the course of existing High Court proceedings, an application may be commenced by application notice in those proceedings and a single judge of the Queen's Bench Division (a judge of another division of the High Court if the proceedings were assigned or transferred to another division) may make the order of committal.[248] The procedure governing applications in the Queen's Bench Division is contained on RSC Ord 52, rule 4.

10.220 The application must make sufficiently clear what the contemnor is said to have done in breach of the order or undertaking so that he may respond to the allegation. Thus, in a case involving alleged breach of an injunction restraining the defendant from making use of information acquired in the course of employment, the claimant must make absolutely clear and certain what information is said to have been disclosed and demonstrate that it had the necessary quality of confidentiality.[249]

10.221 Although the standard of proof is criminal, the proceedings themselves retain their civil character and hence the rules governing evidence are those in Part 32 of the CPR. Written evidence is given by affidavit.[250] The court may sit in private if, for example, a secret process, discovery, or invention is in issue.[251] Subject to any other statutory limits, the maximum sentence for contempt is two years.[252]

10.222 Appeals lie as of right to the Court of Appeal (Civil Division).[253] Since liberty is at stake, leave to adduce fresh evidence will be given where it is necessary to do so or expedient in the interests of justice without having to fulfil the more rigorous *Ladd v Marshall*[254] criteria.[255] The court has a discretion about whether to hear a contemnor who has not 'purged' his contempt. In the case of an individual who makes it clear that he will continue to defy the court's order whatever the outcome of the appeal, the court may refuse to hear the appeal.[256]

10.223 The court is plainly required to have regard to the rights of the alleged contemnor under Article 6 of the ECHR since the European Court of Human Rights operates an autonomous definition of 'criminal proceedings' and hence may apply the full range of procedural protections in contempt proceedings.

---

[246] *Peach Grey & Co (A Firm) v Sommers* [1995] 2 All ER 513.
[247] *R v Hammond & Co Ltd* [1914] 2 KB 866.
[248] RSC Ord 52, r 1(3).
[249] *PA Thomas & Co v Mould* [1968] 2 QB 913.
[250] RSC Ord 52PD3.1.
[251] RSC Ord 52, r 6.
[252] Contempt of Court Act 1981, s 14. The power to impose a fine is reserved in RSC Ord 52, r 9.
[253] Administration of Justice Act 1960, s 13 and the Senior Courts Act 1981, s 53.
[254] [1954] 1 WLR 1489.
[255] *Irtelli v Squatriti* [1992] 3 WLR 218.
[256] *X Ltd v Morgan-Grampian (Publishers) Ltd* [1990] 2 WLR 1000.

F. Checklist

Interim injunctions—general considerations

Is the defendant employee acting in breach of a restriction in his employment contract (such **10.224** as a restrictive covenant or garden leave provision), or is he threatening to do so? If so, then an interim injunction to restrain a breach of these restrictions is likely to be the most appropriate form of relief.

Will the claimant employer face any difficulties in persuading the court to exercise its **10.225** discretion? If any of the following apply, it may do so:

- delay;
- lack of clarity in relation to the terms of the injunction;
- unclean hands.

The court will also take into account the overriding objective set out in CPR, rule 1.1.

(See paras 10.17 to 10.20 above.)

Can the claimant employer show that the claim is not frivolous and vexatious; in other **10.226** words, that there is a serious question to be tried? Only if the answer is yes will an interim injunction be granted, although it is rare for a court to make such a finding (see paras 10.31 to 10.32 above).

Can the defendant employee show that damages are an adequate remedy for the claimant **10.227** employer? If the answer is yes, an interim injunction will not be granted (see paras 10.34 to 10.35 above). However, it will usually be fairly easy for a claimant employer to convince the court that damages are not an adequate remedy.

Can the claimant employer show that if the relief is granted, but subsequently the defendant **10.228** employee succeeds at trial, damages are an adequate remedy for the employee? If yes, this is a factor favouring the grant of an interim injunction (see paras 10.36 to 10.37 above).

Is there doubt as to the adequacy of the respective remedies in damages available to either **10.229** party or both? In that case, the court should consider the balance of convenience, ie will it do less harm to grant an injunction which subsequently turns out to be unjustified, or to refuse one if it subsequently turns out that an injunction should be granted (see paras 10.39 to 10.51 above).

Is the action likely to come to trial only after the restrictions sought to be enforced have expired? **10.230** Then slightly different principles will apply and, in particular, there may be some further assessment of the merits than would ordinarily be the case (see paras 10.52 to 10.55 above).

Springboard injunctions

Has there been: **10.231**

- a breach of the duty owed by the defendant employee in respect of confidential information (and possibly other breaches of contract or duty (see para 10.234 below)?
- some advantage gained by the defendant employee (or a connected party) as a result of that breach?

Only if the answer is yes to both questions may springboard relief be available (see paras 10.57 to 10.59 above).

10.232 Would the effect of granting the injunction put the claimant employer in a better position than if there had been no breach of confidence? If yes, then no relief will be granted (see paras 10.60 to 10.68 above).

10.233 Will the seriousness of the breach or the egregious nature of the defendant's conduct be taken into account when considering the length in time of the restraint granted? It should not be (see para 10.69 above).

10.234 Has the defendant employee committed some other breach (for example of fidelity or fiduciary duty) from which he has gained an advantage? If yes, it may be possible to obtain a springboard injunction to neutralize that advantage (see paras 10.70 to 10.85 above).

Undertaking in damages

10.235 Is the claimant employer prepared to offer an undertaking in damages in respect of the defendant to the application? (Usually) only if they are, will an injunction be granted (see paras 10.87 to 10.119 above).

Search orders

10.236 Where a claimant employer wishes to search the defendant's premises for relevant documents, can the claimant employer satisfy the following tests that:

- there is a strong prima facie case against the defendant employee;
- the damage, actual or potential, must be very serious for the claimant employer;
- there is clear evidence that the defendants have in their possession the incriminating documents or other property and there is a real possibility that they may destroy such material before any *inter-partes* application can be made?

Only if the answer is yes to all three questions might a search order be the appropriate relief (see paras 10.127 to 10.132 above).

10.237 What issues arise in relation to the evidence in support of such an application? The claimant employer must give full and frank disclosure in his evidence in support of the application (see paras 10.135 to 10.139 above).

10.238 Does the claimant employer wish to obtain an image of the computer disc of the defendant(s)? If so, he should be aware that this type of order is tricky to draft and to execute, due to the privilege against self-incrimination and legal privilege (see paras 10.140 to 10.147 above).

10.239 Could the claimant employer rely on some less draconian form of relief to protect confidential information or evidence? If so, he should consider:

- an order for delivery up (see paras 10.155 to 10.161 above);
- a destruction order (see paras 10.162 to 10.164 above);
- an order for detention, preservation, and inspection (see paras 10.165 to 10.166 above);
- a disclosure order (see paras 10.167 to 10.178 above).

10.240 Does the claimant employer suspect that an innocent third party is involved in the wrongdoing? If yes, the claimant employer should consider seeking a *Norwich Pharmacal* order against the third party, but only if the claimant employer is prepared to pay the third party's costs (see paras 10.179 to 10.187 above).

If seeking a *Norwich Pharmacal* order, is the claimant employer able to satisfy the following tests? That: **10.241**

- a wrong has been carried out by a wrongdoer;
- the order is necessary to enable action to be brought against the ultimate wrongdoer;
- the person against whom the order is sought is mixed up with the wrongdoing so as to have facilitated the wrongdoer and to be able or likely to be able to provide the information necessary to enable the ultimate wrongdoer to be sued;
- the person against whom the order is sought must be more than just a mere witness to the wrongdoing.

If so, the court may grant a *Norwich Pharmacal* order but retains a discretion as to whether to do so.

(See paras 10.179 to 10.187 above.)

Freezing order

Does the claimant employer have reason to suspect that the defendant employee is likely to dissipate his assets so as to avoid judgment? Then a freezing order may be appropriate, although it is unusual in the employment context (see paras 10.188 to 10.195 above). **10.242**

Interim declaration

Does a party (employer or employee) need a ruling on, for example, the enforceability of a covenant before trial, without seeking an injunction? If so, an interim declaration may be suitable, although this would be unusual in an employee competition case (see paras 10.196 to 10.200 above). **10.243**

Final injunction

At a final trial, does the claimant employer need to restrain the employee breaching his contractual restrictions? A final injunction may be appropriate, but could be denied if the claimant employer has delayed in seeking it or acquiesced in the employee's breaches (see paras 10.201 to 10.207 above). **10.244**

Contempt of court

Has there been a breach, or has a party assisted in the breach, of a court order or an undertaking? If so, the party may be guilty of contempt of court and sanctions of imprisonment, fines, or sequestration of the contemnor's assets may be available (see paras 10.208 to 10.209 above). **10.245**

Can the party alleging contempt of court show that: **10.246**

- there has been a clear breach of the relevant order or undertaking;
- there is no alternative; and
- that all procedural requirements have been complied with by the party seeking enforcement?

Only then will the penal sanction of contempt of court be made (see paras 10.210 to 10.223 above).

11

DAMAGES AND OTHER REMEDIES

Stephen Nathan QC and Catherine Taylor

A. Introduction

11.01 Apart from injunctions, which are dealt with in Chapter 10 above, the principal remedies which are available as a result of (1) a breach of a restrictive covenant, (2) a breach of a contractual duty of good faith, (3) a breach of fiduciary duty, and (4) a breach of confidence by an employee are as follows:

(1) and (2) breach of a restrictive covenant and breach of a contractual duty of good faith by an employee:
- damages,
- an account of profits (but only in exceptional circumstances),
- a declaration;

(3) and (4) breach of a fiduciary duty or a duty of confidentiality owed by an employee:
- an account of profits,
- damages,
- orders for delivery up or destruction of documents and other property,
- a declaration.

Damages, account of profits, and delivery up orders are considered in Sections B to H (paras 11.12 to 11.36) below. In Section I (paras 11.137 to 11.141) rules for following and tracing misapplied property and in Section J (paras 11.142 and 11.143), the remedy of declarations are discussed. Section K (paras 11.144 to 11.150) deals with the situation where a claimant employer has to make an election when he has claimed alternative remedies, and the timing of such an election. In Section L (paras 11.151 to 11.165), remedies available against third parties (a) in tort, (b) for assisting in a breach of fiduciary duty, and (c) for breach of confidence are addressed separately. Finally, in Section M (paras 11.156 to 11.173), the principles and rules governing an application for an interim payment are set out, since this is an important aspect of everyday litigation practice.

11.02 First, apart from interim orders[1], each of the remedies considered in this chapter arises, if at all, at the conclusion of a trial or upon a summary judgment. Some are alternative remedies, in respect of which a successful claimant may have to make an election at the appropriate time,[2] but it is important at the outset to emphasize that a prudent claimant must necessarily consider what remedies may be available to him and ought to include them all in the relief sought by the claim form against his employee (or ex-employee)[3] and any other person who is included as a defendant, even if they are properly to be considered as alternative and not cumulative remedies. The omission of that simple precaution may lead to a remedy being excluded from consideration by the court, and leave the claimant employer exposed to the risk that the court may refuse to allow a remedial amendment if the application to do so is left to a very late stage of the action.[4]

---

[1] Applications for such orders are governed by CPR, rr 23 and 25. Interim injunctions are considered in Chapter 10 above. Applications for interim declarations are discussed in Section J (11.142–11.143) below.

[2] The topic of election is considered in Section K (11.144–11.150) below.

[3] For convenience, in this chapter an ex-employee is included under the general word 'employee'.

[4] A vivid example of the vagaries—and the huge costs involved—of this in the context of restrictive covenants is *WWF—World Wide Fund for Nature v World Wrestling Federation Entertainment Inc* [2007] EWCA Civ 286, [2008] 1 WLR 445, in which the claimant had earlier informed the court that it was not proposing to seek restitutionary or gain-based damages and then changed its mind with a view to adding such a claim. In the

Secondly, it is important for the claimant employer to bear in mind that, whilst his common law remedy of damages and his right to an injunction may arise from contractual rights against his employee, equitable remedies, such as an account of profits for misuse of confidential information or breaches of fiduciary duties, do not necessarily depend upon contract. They arise from a separate cause of action based upon rights arising at common law in tort or in equity by virtue of rights 'akin to property' in the case of confidential information or the existence of a fiduciary relationship. These remedies are considered in Section G. The procedural significance is important; where the claimant employer finds himself unable to sue on the contract of employment (for example because he has wrongfully repudiated it and the court holds that the employee has accepted the repudiation), he may nevertheless be able to rely upon his equitable or other non-contractual rights in order to obtain a remedy. **11.03**

Thirdly, as seen in Chapter 10 above, one of the principal reasons why the courts in this jurisdiction have shown themselves to be willing to grant an interim injunction against an employee for breach of a restrictive covenant or a duty of good faith, etc or for misuse of confidential information, has been the recognition of the practical difficulty facing the claimant employer in quantifying the damage caused by reason of the employee's misconduct or by a third party's inducement of the employee's breach of duty, as was the case in *Fellowes & Son v Fisher*.[5] Although in many instances the action may come to an end with the grant or refusal of an interim order or a settlement, once a period of restraint on the employee has come to an end, the remedy of damages continues to be one of the primary remedies available to the claimant employer. On many occasions, there may well be sound reasons why the employer has not sought an interim injunction; he may learn of the employee's misconduct only after a considerable period of time, and thus make it too late for an injunction to be much of an effective remedy. He may have simply delayed too long in making his investigations or other steps so as to be held to be guilty of laches as happened in *Shaw v Applegate*.[6] He may be unable to give an effective cross-undertaking in damages or be unwilling to invest in the considerable legal costs involved in applying for an interim injunction and in the risk of liability attaching to him by reason of the cross-undertaking in damages which he is normally obliged to give if he obtains an interim injunction.[7] **11.04**

The fact that the employer does not seek an interim injunction does not hinder the enforcement of his rights, either at common law or in equity, save only to the extent that delay may give rise to circumstances where it is no longer possible, practicable, or alternatively reasonable for the court to grant an injunction and thus, for instance, the claimant may be left only with his remedy of damages. This is effectively what took place in *Wrotham Park Estate Co Ltd v Parkside Homes Ltd*,[8] where substantial damages were awarded, and in *Surrey CC v* **11.05**

---

absence of any prejudice, Peter Smith J allowed the amendment ([2006] EWHC (Ch) 184). This is to be contrasted with the earlier refusal of Jacob J in the same case ([2002] FSR 504) to allow an amendment by the claimant, WWF, to include a claim for an account of profits (which he had refused on the ground that such relief was not available for a breach of contract in the absence of exceptional circumstances). The Court of Appeal eventually decided in 2007 that the application to amend should have been refused by Peter Smith J on the grounds that it was an abuse of process.

[5] [1976] 1 QB 122. A more recent example of the relevant factors at work is *Alliance Paper Group plc v Prestwich* [1996] IRLR 25.

[6] [1977] 1 WLR 970 CA.

[7] This topic is considered separately in Chapter 10 above.

[8] [1974] 1 WLR 798. In that case, Brightman J considered it to be an unpardonable waste to make a mandatory injunction for the pulling down of housing, and instead awarded damages in substitution.

Bredero Homes Ltd,[9] where only nominal damages were awarded. In *Jaggard v Sawyer*[10] the court held that it would be oppressive to grant an injunction in circumstances where no interim injunction had been applied for and so it awarded damages in lieu. The *Wrotham* case, viewed as a contractual claim, later became central to the decision of the House of Lords in *A-G v Blake*,[11] in which the House decided that restitutionary or gain-based damages are available in contract claims in appropriate cases and the Court of Appeal in *WWF v World Wrestling Federation*[12] has resolved any doubts that such damages can be awarded, irrespective of whether or not an injunction has or could have been applied for. The relevant principles relating to restitutionary or gain-based damages are considered in paragraphs 11.38 to 11.62 below.

11.06   Fourthly, the field of restrictive covenants is one of the main areas in which the operation of the court's jurisdiction under section 2 of Lord Cairns' Act[13] plays an important continuing role. In its modern form, now contained in section 50 of the Senior Courts Act 1981, this jurisdiction gives the High Court[14] the power to award damages in place of, or in addition to, either an injunction or an order for specific performance.[15] This is an important power in cases where, for instance, the period of the employee's covenant is shortly to come to an end or where the court takes the view that the imposition of an injunction would be oppressive, even though the claimant is otherwise entitled to an injunction or specific performance. This may have a significant consequence in relation to claims for prospective or future damages. The principles upon which damages are to be awarded under Lord Cairns' Act are considered further in paragraphs 11.94 to 11.118 below. It should also be noted that the court has the power both to grant an injunction and to award damages as well. This is a very valuable power which is, it may be thought, too rarely employed.[16]

11.07   Fifthly, it should also be noted by way of introduction that a claim for damages or any other final remedy is barred only if the defendant can establish a defence of acquiescence; delay alone in bringing a claim is not normally sufficient, provided that it is brought within the relevant limitation period. A final remedy is only barred where, upon the facts of the particular case, the situation has become such that it would be dishonest or unconscionable for the claimant, or the person having the rights sought to be enforced, to continue to enforce it.[17] This was followed and applied by the Court of Appeal in *Gafford v Graham*[18] as regards the barring of a claim at common law. In that case, the Court of Appeal departed from part of

---

    [9] [1993] 1 WLR 1361, CA.
    [10] [1995] 1 WLR 269, CA.
    [11] [2001] 1 AC 268, HL.
    [12] [2007] EWCA Civ 286; [2008] 1 WLR 445.
    [13] Chancery Amendment Act 1858, s 2.
    [14] The County Court has the power to make an order which the High Court can make: County Courts Act 1984, s 38(1).
    [15] The history of this valuable power is set out in JA Jolowicz, 'Damages in Equity—A Study of Lord Cairns' Act' [1975] CLJ 224, DW Dobson 'Lord Cairn's Act: Dead or Alive?' Statute Law Rev (1985) 6(3):113, PM McDermott, 'Survival of Jurisdiction under the Chancery Amendment Act 1858 (Lord Cairn's Act)' CJQ Oct 1987, and S Watterson, 'An Account of Profits and Damages? The History of Orthodoxy' (2004) 24 OJLS 471. It is helpfully summarized in *Halsbury's Laws of England* (4th edn, Reissue 1991) Vol 24, para 834, n 3 and also in the judgment of Sir Thomas Bingham MR in *Jaggard v Sawyer* [1995] 1 WLR 269, CA.
    [16] The significance of this power can be seen, eg, in *Brazier v Bramwell Scaffolding Ltd* [2001] UKPC 59, a Privy Council case from New Zealand.
    [17] *Shaw v Applegate* [1977] 1 WLR 970 CA, 978 *per* Buckley LJ.
    [18] (1997) 77 P&CR 73 CA, 80 *per* Nourse LJ.

the earlier judgment in *Shaw v Applegate*[19] by expressing doubt as to whether there was any longer any distinction to be made between establishing a defence of acquiescence at common law and in equity. It is now considered that the same principles of acquiescence apply to both kinds of claim.

B. Compensatory damages for breach of contract

The primary remedy which is available to an employer against his employee who acts in breach of a restrictive covenant or in breach of his duty of good faith is for damages for breach of the term(s) of the contract of employment.[20] The general rule is that the court awards damages assessed as compensation to the employer for such net loss as the employer can establish that he has suffered as a result of the employee's breach of contract, after taking into account any steps which the employer has taken, or may have been obliged to take, by way of mitigation of his loss: 'The rule of common law is that where a party sustains a loss by reason of a breach of contract he is, so far as money can do so, to be placed in the same situation with respect to damages as if the contract had been performed.'[21]   **11.08**

Causation

Assuming that the claimant employer has established liability for the breach of the restrictive covenant or other contractual term, the largest hurdle which he faces is normally the need to prove, on a balance of probabilities, that the loss which he claims has been factually caused by the relevant misconduct of the employee. The wrongful act must be sufficiently closely linked to the loss claimed by the employer so that it can overcome the threshold test that, 'but for' the breach, the loss would not (on a balance of probabilities) have been suffered. This 'but for' requirement is common to both breaches of contracts and the law of tort. The court applies common sense in deciding whether a breach of duty was the cause of a loss or merely the occasion for it, in the sense of providing the opportunity for the loss to be incurred (see *Galoo Ltd v Bright Grahame Murray (A firm)*).[22] In the words of Lord Porter in *Monarch Steamship Co Ltd v Karlshamnes Oljefabriker*,[23] the breach of contract must be 'the effective cause'. Normally, the rule is that damages are assessed at the date of the breach of contract, but another date can be applied if that rule gives rise to an injustice.[24]   **11.09**

In the context of a claim for breach of a restrictive covenant, it may be necessary for the employer to establish, as part of the causal link between the employee's breach and his loss, that his clients or customers ceased to do business with him or that they did so sooner than they might otherwise have chosen to do. This was what happened in *Shepherds Investment Ltd v*   **11.10**

---

[19] See in particular the words of Goff LJ at 979 when he said 'I for my part think it is easier to establish a case of acquiescence where the right is equitable only . . .', with which both other judges concurred.

[20] This is necessarily an overview of a complex subject. The leading textbooks on the subject of damages include H McGregor (ed), *McGregor on Damages* (18th edn, 2009) and A Burrows, *Remedies for Torts and Breach of Contract* (3rd edn, 2004).

[21] *Robinson v Harman* [1848] 1 Exch 850, 855 *per* Parke B.

[22] [1994] 1 WLR 1360, CA.

[23] [1949] AC 196, HL, 212.

[24] *Johnson v Agnew* [1980] AC 367, HL, 400 *per* Lord Wilberforce and *South Australia Asset Management Corp v York Montague Ltd* [1997] 1 AC 191, HL, 221 *per* Lord Hoffmann.

Walters,[25] but in that case the claimant employer failed to establish the requisite causal link for lack of 'cogent evidence'. In *Nottingham University v Fishel*,[26] the university employed Dr Fishel as the full-time scientific director of the university's infertility unit from 1991 and, in due course, in 1997 he left to set up a rival clinic. From 1993 he had been appointed a Reader of the university. The university alleged that in breach of his contract of employment and also certain fiduciary duties, Dr Fishel had carried out work for external institutions without properly authorized consent. The university made three claims: (1) a claim for damages for loss of profits which it would have earned from his work, (2) a claim for an account of his profits on the footing that he was a fiduciary, and (3) a claim for restitutionary or gain-based damages equivalent to the profits which he had made from his breach of contract. As regards (1), the claim for compensatory damages, Elias J held[27] that the university had failed to demonstrate any loss caused by Dr Fishel's breaches of contract which he held to have taken place.

11.11   Sometimes, however, the 'but for' rule is necessarily relaxed. In the case where a loss may be said to have been caused by two different wrongdoers so that the wrongdoing of each of them amounts to a concurrent cause, it would offend common sense if neither of them was to be liable at all because the claimant could not prove the extent of their relative contributions to the cause of that loss. In such a case, each is held liable and can be sued alone. One example of this is *Crossley & Sons v Lightowler*,[28] in which there were several polluters of a river. The one who was sued was held liable and was not entitled to defend the claim by saying that, but for his acts, the river would nevertheless have been polluted. Significantly, the same reasoning can be applied where the loss suffered by an employer may have more than one possible cause: he need only show that the misconduct of the employee was *a cause* of his loss.

11.12   Thus, it can be seen that the threshold test can be lowered where, in the circumstances, it may be just to do so. This has happened in exceptional cases, and in particular (for present purposes) where a defendant has, by his misconduct, materially increased the risk of the loss taking place, but where the claimant cannot prove—and the defendant cannot disprove—that the breach of duty caused the loss. As Lord Nicholls in *Fairchild v Glenhaven Funeral Services Ltd*[29] held:

> Where justice so requires the threshold itself may be lowered. In this way the scope of a defendant's liability may be *extended*. The circumstances where this will be appropriate will be exceptional, because of the adverse consequences which the lowering of the threshold will have for a defendant. He will be held responsible for a loss the plaintiff might have suffered even if the defendant had not been involved at all.

How far it may be possible to rely on this statement of principle in the context of a breach of a restrictive covenant, a duty of good faith owed to the claimant or misuse of confidential information appears still to remain a matter for future decision. It will obviously require an exceptional set of circumstances, but what the circumstances will need to encompass remains open. What appears, however, to be clear both from cases such as *Fairchild v Glenhaven*

---

[25] [2006] EWHC 836 (Ch), [2007] IRLR 110.
[26] [2002] ICR 1462.
[27] ibid 1485.
[28] (1867) 2 Ch App 478.
[29] [2002] UKHL 22, [2003] 1 AC 32 HL, para 32.

Funeral Services Ltd[30] and *A-G v Blake*,[31] and the cases which have followed the *Blake* case,[32] is that we have reached a time when the boundaries of the remedies which are available in the case of contractual misconduct, whether by an employee or by a party to a commercial contract, have come under extensive review and modification when justice and fairness so require it, so that a claimant (and an objective observer) is not left feeling that the defendant 'has unjustly got away with it': *ubi judicia, ibi remedia*.

The standard of proof required of a claimant

The standard of proof of any facts in a civil case is the balance of probabilities. If that standard **11.13** is met, then the fact or series of facts is established. The standard, itself, however, necessarily needs to take account of the type of case or allegation which is being made, having regard (in particular) to the seriousness of the allegation being advanced. Thus, in a case of fraud, the standard is still called the balance of probabilities, but reflects the fact that the evidence needs to be all the stronger to satisfy the court that the standard has been met. Lord Nicholls succinctly set out the approach and the relevant adjustments in his speech in *Re H and ors (Minors)*:[33]

> The balance of probabilities means that a court is satisfied an event occurred if the court considers that, on the evidence, the occurrence of the event was more likely than not. When assessing the probabilities the court will have in mind as a factor, to whatever extent is appropriate in the particular case, that the more serious the allegation the less likely it is that the event occurred and hence, the stronger should be the evidence before the court concludes that the allegation is established on the balance of probability. Fraud is usually less likely than negligence . . . Built into the preponderance of probability standard is a generous degree of flexibility in respect of the seriousness of the allegation.[34]

This imports the need for the court to employ a fair degree of common sense.

Past and future loss

An important aspect of what needs to be proved at trial lies in the difference between **11.14** (a) losses which have been incurred prior to the date of assessment and (b) future unascertained losses arising from the breach of an employment contract. In relation to past facts, the standard of proof is the balance of probabilities. If that standard is met, the relevant facts are treated as true.

In relation to future events, including the possible future actions of third parties such as **11.15** customers of the employer, the claimant must establish such future facts with 'sufficient certainty' in order to recover his loss in full. Since that is frequently an impossible task, he may be able to recover damages on the basis of 'the loss of a chance' by the application of the principle in *Chaplin v Hicks*[35] so as to determine the chances of a particular event happening

---

[30] ibid.
[31] [2001] 1 AC 268, HL.
[32] Such as *WWF v World Wrestling Federation* [2007] EWCA Civ 286; [2008] 1 WLR 445.
[33] [1996] AC 563, HL, 586.
[34] This passage was relied on, eg, in *Ultraframe (UK) Ltd v Fielding* [2005] EWHC (Ch) 1638 *per* Lewison J (a case of directors allegedly 'stealing a business' for the benefit of another company). It was applied by the Court of Appeal in *Dodourian Group International Inc v Simms* [2009] EWCA Civ 169 (a case of alleged civil fraud).
[35] [1911] 3 KB 786, CA.

and to reflect those chances in the award of damages.[36] In *Allied Maples Group Ltd v Simmons and Simmons*,[37] following a preliminary trial of liability, the Court of Appeal reviewed the principal relevant authorities in the context of a claim brought against a firm of solicitors for negligent advice in drafting a commercial contract for the takeover of a group of department stores. The court held that alleged misconduct, consisting of past historical fact, falls to be judged on the balance of probabilities. Thus, if the fact is established on that standard, it is to be taken as true. Where a claim depends upon the claimant establishing that he would have acted in a certain way, he has to prove, upon the balance of probabilities, that he would have taken action to obtain the benefit or avoid the risk.[38]

11.16 But where the quantification of the claim depends upon future uncertain or hypothetical events (in this case the prospect of engaging in negotiations with the vendors, ie third parties, and successfully renegotiating with them a clause in the contract), the Court of Appeal held the claimant has to show that there was a real or substantial, rather than a speculative, chance that the third party would have acted so as to confer the requisite benefit or avoid the risk:

> . . . the plaintiff must prove as a matter of causation that he has a real or substantial chance as opposed to a speculative one. If he succeeds in doing so, the evaluation of the chance is part of the assessment of the quantum of damages, the range lying somewhere between something that just qualifies as real or substantial on the one hand and near certainty on the other. I do not think that it is helpful to lay down in percentage terms what the lower and upper ends of the bracket should be.[39]

(It should be noted that, although the members of the court agreed as to the principles to be applied, Millett LJ dissented on the facts since he considered that the chance of the claimant successfully renegotiating the contract with the third party was 'pure speculation'.)[40]

11.17 In *Industrial Developments Consultants Ltd v Cooley*,[41] a case better known for its statements of principle concerning the liability of a director as a fiduciary of a company, the court was concerned—in addition—with a contractual claim by the employer for breach of the defendant director's employment contract and a claim for the employer's loss of the opportunity to obtain a contract with a third party (Eastern Electricity Board), the opportunity for which had been concealed by the defendant and which in due course he obtained for his own company. Roskill J held that, by reason of the defendant's breach of his contract of employment, there had been a loss of the chance to obtain the contract with the Electricity Board, although the evidence from that third party was that the claimant's chance was, in the particular circumstances, slight. The judge, accordingly, assessed the claimant's chance at 10 per cent. This he regarded as sufficiently real or substantial so as to allow the claimant to go on to an assessment of the quantum of its loss.

---

[36] See *Mallett v McMonagle* [1970] AC 166, HL, 176 *per* Lord Diplock; and *Davies v Taylor* [1974] AC 207 HL, 212–13 *per* Lord Reid, 218–19 *per* Lord Dilhorne, and 219–20 *per* Lord Simon. Lord Reid's statement was applied by the Court of Appeal in *Allied Maples Group Ltd v Simmons and Simmons*: see n 37 below.

[37] [1995] 1 WLR 1602, CA. Further useful material can be found in *Hotson v East Berkshire AHA* [1987] AC 750, HL. (Note that this authority was referred to in the argument in the *Allied Maples* case, but not the judgments.)

[38] ibid 1610 *per* Stuart-Smith LJ.

[39] ibid 1614 *per* Stuart-Smith LJ.

[40] ibid 1625 *per* Millett LJ.

[41] [1972] 1 WLR 442.

In *SBJ Stephenson Ltd v Mandy*,[42] the defendant had been employed as a 'divisional director'   **11.18**
of a company carrying on business as an insurance broker and was subject to a restrictive
covenant concerning confidential information. He was held to have breached the terms of
the covenant by soliciting customers and to be liable in damages. The future losses after the
date of the trial were assessed on the basis of the loss of a chance. Bell J held that the employer
had lost a 'real or substantial chance' that a significant minority of customers would have
stayed for many years as customers of the employer but for the defendant's misconduct.
In *Sanders v Parry*,[43] an assistant solicitor agreed with an important client of his employer's
practice that he would set up a practice on his own and would then carry out that customer's
legal work. In doing so, he acted in breach of his obligations of good faith and fidelity during
his employment. Havers J assessed damages on the basis of the loss of the employer's chance
of retaining the client; it was possible that the defendant might have stayed on if he had been
offered a partnership or continued on as an assistant solicitor and the client might then have
agreed to continue giving his legal work to the practice. Havers J assessed the lost chance at
25 per cent of one year's net profits from the estimated fees which would have been earned
from the particular customer.

The fact that it may be difficult for the court to assess such damages does not mean that the court   **11.19**
cannot or does not do so, even if the result is necessarily an imprecise one. In *Chaplin v Hicks*[44]
part of Vaughan Williams LJ's *ratio decidendi* is a well-known statement of this principle:

> I do not agree with the contention that, if certainty is impossible of attainment, the damages
> for a breach of contract are unassessable . . . I only wish to deny with emphasis that, because
> precision cannot be arrived at, the jury has no function in the assessment of damages . . . it may
> be that the amount of their verdict will really be a matter of guesswork. But the fact that
> damages cannot be assessed with certainty does not relieve the wrongdoer of the necessity of
> paying damages for his breach of contract.[45]

The loss must not be too remote

Further, there is an additional hurdle which the claimant must cross, consisting of satisfying   **11.20**
the court that the damage which he has suffered is not too remote. The test for remoteness in
contract law starts with the 'rule' contained in *Hadley v Baxendale*.[46] This is set out in the
form of two limbs, which modern authority[47] shows are to be treated as overlapping tests and
not mutually exclusive ones, having regard to all the relevant circumstances and the common
knowledge of the parties:

> Where two parties have made a contract which one of them has broken, the damages which
> the other party ought to receive in respect of such breach of contract, should be such as may
> fairly and reasonably be considered, either as arising naturally, i.e. according to the usual
> course of things from such breach of contract itself, or such as may reasonably be supposed to
> have been in the contemplation of both parties, at the time they made the contract as the
> probable result of a breach of it.[48]

---

[42] [2000] FSR 286, [2000] IRLR 233.
[43] [1967] 1 WLR 753.
[44] [1911] 2 KB 786, CA.
[45] ibid 792.
[46] (1854) 9 Exch 341.
[47] See *The Heron II: Koufos v Czarnikow Ltd* [1969] AC 350, HL, 385 *per* Lord Reid; and *Jackson v Royal Bank of Scotland* [2005] UKHL 3, [2005] 2 All ER 71, paras 47–9 *per* Lord Walker.
[48] (1854) 9 Exch 341, 354–5.

11.21   In *Victoria Laundry (Windsor) Ltd v Newman Industries Ltd*,[49] the Court of Appeal modified the rule in *Hadley v Baxendale* by explaining that the contract-breaker is liable only to pay damages for such part of the loss actually resulting from the breach as is, at the time of the making of the contract, reasonably foreseeable as 'liable to result' from the breach. What is foreseeable at that time depends on the knowledge of both parties or at least the knowledge of the party who later commits the breach. The court imputes to everyone knowledge of the ordinary course of things (ie damage which may come within the first limb of the rule in *Hadley v Baxendale*). But there may be added to that imputed knowledge, the knowledge which the contract-breaker actually has in relation to special circumstances outside the ordinary course of things and which are of such a kind that a breach of contract would cause additional or further loss to the other party. If at the time of the conclusion of the contract the contract-breaker had considered the question of what loss might be suffered, a reasonable man in his position of knowledge would have appreciated that the loss in question would have resulted. It is not necessary for the claimant to prove that a reasonable man would have contemplated the particular loss; it is enough that he can foresee that it is likely to result: 'It is indeed enough if the loss (or some factor without which it would not have occurred) is a "serious possibility" or a "real danger". For short we have used the word "liable" to result. Possibly the colloquialism "on the cards" indicates the shade of meaning with some approach to accuracy.'[50]

11.22   In *Koufos v C Czarnikow Ltd (The Heron II)*,[51] the House of Lords effectively rejected the terminology of 'reasonably foreseeable' and the phrase 'liable to result' and some of the other phraseology of Asquith LJ, because it would include a most improbable or unlikely result and thus would go too far. Lord Reid set out the rule as being whether the loss in question is 'of a kind which the defendant, when he made the contract, ought to have realized was not unlikely to result from the breach . . . I use the words "not unlikely to result" as denoting a degree of probability considerably less than an even chance but nevertheless not very unusual and easily foreseeable'.[52]

11.23   The majority of the House thought that 'liable to result' was a convenient phrase, but one which did not have any sufficiently precise meaning and they preferred to employ the phrases 'a serious possibility' and 'a real danger'.[53] The use of phraseology incorporating the words 'reasonably foreseeable' was held to be more appropriate to the law of tort and it was felt that in contract it is 'better to use contemplate or contemplation'.[54] Nevertheless, as *McGregor on Damages* has noted,[55] the careful restatement of principle by Asquith LJ in the *Victoria Laundry* case has survived the strictures of the House of Lords in *The Heron II* and continues (with changes only of emphasis of language) to form the basis of the test of remoteness in contract. This is evident from the House of Lord's decision in *Jackson v Royal Bank of Scotland*,[56] in which the principal judgments were given by Lord Hope and Lord Walker. It is thus assumed that, if special circumstances are within the parties'

---

[49] [1949] 2 KB 528, CA.
[50] ibid 539–40 *per* Asquith LJ.
[51] [1969] 1 AC 350, HL.
[52] ibid 382–3.
[53] ibid 399 *per* Lord Morris, 415 *per* Lord Pearce, and 425 *per* Lord Upjohn.
[54] ibid 423 *per* Lord Upjohn.
[55] H McGregor (ed), *McGregor on Damages* (18th edn, 2009) para 6-163.
[56] [2005] UKHL 3, [2005] 2 All ER 71, HL.

contemplation, the defendant has also undertaken to bear *any* special loss which is referable to those circumstances.[57]

We think it worthwhile, however, to emphasize that it is the *type of loss*, and not the extent of the particular loss, which normally needs to be shown to have been within the parties' contemplation, as may be seen from two Court of Appeal decisions, *H Parsons (Livestock) Ltd v Uttley Ingham and Co Ltd*[58] and *Brown v KMR Services Ltd*.[59] Once it is shown or inferred that they have contemplated that kind of loss, that is sufficient; the court does not place a limitation on the size or amount of the loss. It is also not necessary for the parties to contemplate the precise manner in which the loss is caused. A helpful illustration, from which analogies to breaches of covenant can be drawn, is *Vacwell Engineering Co Ltd v BDH Chemicals Ltd*,[60] where a chemical was supplied in ampoules. A chemist dropped one ampoule into a sink containing water and this caused a very violent explosion resulting in the death of the chemist and extensive property damage. Rees J held that an explosion of a minor kind was within the parties' contemplation and it made no difference that the explosion and its consequences were far greater than the parties could reasonably have contemplated. **11.24**

A note of caution needs, however, to be made. In *Transfield Shipping Inc v Mercator Shipping Inc, The Achilleas*,[61] Lord Hoffmann and Lord Hope (in the minority) proposed an additional factor, namely that it is necessary to show that the defendant has *assumed responsibility* for the particular kind or type of loss which occurred; in other words that not only did the parties have such a loss within their contemplation, but also that they had in their mutual contemplation that the defendant was undertaking, within the scope of his obligations, a responsibility for a potential loss of that particular kind or type. (One example given was the case of a bank appreciating that a breach of contract on its part might cause loss of profits to its customer, but nevertheless neither party intended that the bank should be liable to pay compensation for such loss of profits.[62]) Lady Hale saw this as totally novel; and she and Lord Rodger adopted the (until now) conventional view of what needed to be established as regards remoteness. Lord Walker did not support the opinion of Lords Hoffmann and Hope.[63] **11.25**

The introduction of such an additional hurdle of proof could certainly give rise to evidential problems and, although it may be attractive, it seems unlikely for the time being at least that a further factual investigation into whether the parties both contemplated that the defendant was undertaking such responsibility will be necessary as part of the law on remoteness in contract claims, although it would always be open to a defendant to raise the issue.[64] (To this extent, therefore, the principles of remoteness of damage in contract will continue to remain slightly different from tort.[65]) **11.26**

---

[57] ibid para 26.

[58] [1978] QB 791, CA, 813 *per* Scarman LJ.

[59] [1995] 4 All ER 598, CA, 621–2, 642–3. See also *Transfield Shipping Inc v Mercator Shipping Inc, The Achilleas* [2008] UKHL 48, [2009] 1 AC 61 and *Chitty on Contracts* (30th edn, 2008) para 26-058.

[60] [1971] 1 QB 88.

[61] [2008] UKHL 48, [2009] 1 AC 61.

[62] *Mulvenna v Royal Bank of Scotland plc* [2003] EWCA Civ 1112; and *Banque Bruxelles Lambert SA v Eagle Star Insurance Co Ltd* [1997] AC 191.

[63] In the later case of *Sentinel International Ltd v Cordes* [2008] UKPC 60, para 50, Lord Walker appears to have come down firmly on the side of following the traditional view.

[64] A defendant would, for instance, certainly do so if there was a relevant clause excluding his responsibility.

[65] See *per* Lord Hoffmann in *South Australia Asset Management Corp v York Montague Ltd* [1997] 1 AC 191, 214.

11.27   In many instances of such breaches of contract by an employee, there is likely to be little argument about remoteness of the employer's loss, since most claims will probably involve the types or kinds of loss which are likely to have been within the parties' obvious contemplation without any need for more communication on the part of the employer. Nevertheless, in the context of employees' restrictive covenants, it would be a sensible precaution for the employer to have a carefully drawn covenant or a side letter (issued before or at the same time as the contract is made) which spells out, in a non-exclusive way, certain types of potential loss which could flow from breaches of the particular employee's covenants. In that way, at the date of the contract, they would clearly be placed within the parties' contemplation (ie within the second limb of the rule in *Hadley v Baxendale*) in the event of a subsequent breach of the covenant.

11.28   Certainly, in the case of senior or important members of staff, this will be a worthwhile precaution on the employer's part so as to avoid the risk that a court may hold, after the breach has taken place, that a particular type of loss claimed by the employer was not, after all, within the parties' contemplation at the time of making the contract. In all events, it is a counsel of prudence for the employer, when drafting any restrictive covenant, to review with his legal advisers what kind of loss might take place if there is a breach of it, and to consider (a) whether that does or does not come within the remoteness test set out above and (b) whether or not it needs to be mentioned specifically to *ensure* as far as possible that any such loss is going to be recoverable in the event of a breach.

11.29   Even if the claimant employer fails to show that a particular type of loss is excluded by the principle of remoteness, he may nevertheless be entitled to recover a sum representing a lesser loss of a particular kind which was clearly within the parties' contemplation at the time of contract. Thus, in *Cory v Thames Ironworks Co*[66] (a commercial case) the defendant was in breach of contract in failing to deliver a boat hull. The claimant was a coal merchant and it was within both parties' contemplation that the ordinary use of the hull would be for storing coal, but in fact (unknown to the defendant) the claimant wished to use it for a different, and much more profitable, purpose. The court held that the claimant could nevertheless recover the equivalent of the loss which was within the parties' contemplation, since there was no hardship or injustice in doing so. This principle has been often followed; for example it was applied by Thomas J in 1997 in *North Sea Energy Holdings NV v Petroleum Authority of Thailand*.[67] If, on the other hand, the actual loss suffered by the claimant (arising from a type of loss which was not contemplated) is *less* than a loss of the type which the court holds to have been contemplated by the parties, logically the claimant should also be able to recover, but that does not appear to be the case; the claimant cannot recover at all for that loss, since the type of loss was not within the parties' actual or reasonable contemplation. The principle in the *Cory* case would appear to be an exception which the court will continue to uphold, but at the same time confine. Otherwise it would be all too easy to circumvent altogether the restated rule in *Hadley v Baxendale*.

Quantum of recoverable losses

11.30   The quantum recovered by a claimant for breach of a restrictive covenant is the loss of net profits which the employer has thereby suffered. He must allow for the costs and expenses

---

[66] (1868) LR 3 (QB) 181.
[67] [1997] 2 Lloyds Rep 418 (Commercial Court).

which he would have had to incur, including (if appropriate in the particular case) a proportion of fixed overheads. A modern example of this is to be found in the judgment of Lawrence Collins J in *CMS Dolphin Ltd v Simonet*.[68] The claimant is entitled to claim the additional expenses which he has incurred as a result of the breach. He will also be able to recover the cost, for instance, of investigating a conspiracy between his employees: see *R+V Verischerung AG v Risk Insurance & Reinsurance Solutions SA*.[69]

Unreasonable acts by the employer

Unreasonable acts by the employer may amount to intervening conduct of a sufficient kind **11.31** that they break the chain of causation and bring an end to the period of the loss suffered by the employer. In *Galoo v Bright Grahame Murray*,[70] it was held that this falls to be judged by applying 'the court's common sense'. Thus, *reasonable* intervening steps by the claimant do not break the chain, as the court held in *Compania Naviera Maropan S/A v Bowaters Lloyd Pulp and Paper Mills Ltd*.[71]

Claimant's duty to mitigate

Furthermore, a claimant is obliged to try to mitigate his loss, if it is possible to do so. The **11.32** effect is that this duty may further restrict compensatory damages, or it may increase them if the attempted mitigation is unsuccessful. The basic principle is that the claimant is obliged to take such steps as are reasonable in the circumstances. Inaction altogether on his part may result in the exclusion of such damages as would have been avoided if reasonable steps had been taken by him by way of mitigation. The law imposes on a claimant the duty 'of taking all reasonable steps to mitigate the loss consequent on the breach and debars him from claiming any part of the damage which is due to his neglect to take such steps'.[72]

Such steps will obviously vary from case to case. If it is necessary, for example, to send infor- **11.33** mation to clients or customers or otherwise incur expense, such as advertising costs,[73] in order to allay their fears or concerns following a breach of covenant or misuse of confidential information, such steps would clearly be reasonable steps in mitigation and the costs and expense would be recoverable as additional special damage. By the same token, it would be unreasonable to require an employer to go in the opposite direction and take steps by way of mitigation which may adversely affect his trade or reputation, as was held in *James Finlay & Co Ltd v NV Kwik Hoo Tong Handel Maatschappij*.[74] Further, the claimant is not obliged to engage in complicated or difficult litigation (see *Pilkington v Wood*).[75] Further, the employer is not obliged to commence litigation against anyone else who may be liable apart from the

---

[68] [2001] 2 BCLC 704, paras 140, 141.
[69] [2006] EWHC 1705 (Comm).
[70] [1994] 1 WLR 1360, CA, 1375.
[71] [1955] 2 QB 68, CA.
[72] *British Westinghouse Electric and Manufacturing Co Ltd v Underground Electric Railways Co of London Ltd* [1912] AC 673, HL, 689 *per* Viscount Haldane LC.
[73] As in *Holden Ltd v Bostock & Co Ltd* [1902] TLR 317; *Riyad Bank v Ahli United Bank (UK) plc* [2005] EWHC 279 (Comm), [2005] 2 Lloyds Rep 409; *Ultraframe (UK) Ltd v Eurocell Building Plastics Ltd* [2006] EWHC (Ch) 1344.
[74] [1929] 1 KB 400, CA.
[75] [1953] Ch 770. See also *Williams v Glyn Owen & Co* [2003] EWCA Civ 750.

defendant whom he chooses to sue. It is said that this is a principle which, although part of the law on mitigation, is a principle in its own right.[76]

11.34   If a claimant takes an unreasonable step by way of mitigation, then he is barred from recovering that expense. It will not affect the quantum of his claim, except to the extent that he may, as a result, have omitted to take a different and reasonable step instead. However, it is important to note that the claimant is not disentitled from recovering his cost of taking steps by way of mitigation just because the defendant can suggest other measures which are less burdensome or less expensive in place of the measures actually taken by the claimant, as was held in *Banco de Portugal v Waterlow & Sons Ltd*.[77] If the steps taken are reasonable ones, the cost of them is recoverable. The subject, however, is not always an easy one to resolve and in the most recent decision of the House of Lords, Lord Hope appears to have advanced a small (but potentially significant) modification of Lord MacMillan's view in the *Waterlow* case: 'The wrongdoer is not entitled to demand of the injured party that he incur a loss, bear a burden or make unreasonable sacrifices in the mitigation of his damages. He is entitled to demand that, *where there are choices to be made, the least expensive route which will achieve mitigation must be selected.*'[78]

11.35   In its application, the test for assessing the reasonableness of steps taken by way of mitigation tends to be intensely fact sensitive and the employer needs to bear in mind, from the date of the breach, the facts which he may need to prove to demonstrate the reasonableness of what he has done in order to try to reduce his loss (if he can).

The relevance of the date of assessment and its impact on claims

11.36   There is a further aspect of claims for damages for breach of contract which may need to be borne in mind by the claimant employer. The position at common law used to be that the court would only assess loss resulting from causes of action which took place before the date of issue of the proceedings. This was modified in practice, as may be seen from *Bwllfa and Merthyr Dare Steam Collieries Ltd v Pontypridd Waterworks Co*,[79] and then ultimately in RSC Order 37, rule 6, with the result that, where there is a continuing breach of contract, the assessment of damages can take into account any facts up to the date of the assessment. There is, however, no longer a specific rule in the new Civil Procedure Rules which mirrors the former RSC Order 37, rule 6. But, nevertheless, there is no doubt that the principle (and practice) survives. It can be deployed even when the Court of Appeal or the House of Lords receives fresh evidence and then makes a fresh assessment, thereby enlarging (or reducing) the quantum of the damages awarded.

11.37   In the case where there is a doubt as to the nature of the breaches relied on, so that they may need to be looked at as separate causes of action and not as a continuing one, a claimant should consider whether or not he needs to issue separate proceedings in order to protect his position and then apply to consolidate the actions for the purpose of trial.[80] Where, however,

---

[76] *The Liverpool (No 2)* [1963] P 64, CA; and *Kommune v Depfa ACS Bank* [2010] EWHC 227. See also *Peters v East Midlands Strategic Health Authority* [2009] EWCA Civ 145, applying the same principle where a claimant chose to claim compensatory damages rather than to apply for statutory health benefits.

[77] [1932] AC 452, HL, 506 *per* Lord MacMillan.

[78] *Langdon v O'Connor* [2003] UKHL 64, [2004] 1 All ER 277, para 34 *per* Lord Hope (emphasis added).

[79] [1903] AC 426, HL, 431 *per* Lord Macnaghten.

[80] See CPR, r 3.1(2)(g).

there is a series of similar breaches (and not one continuing breach), equity may be able to give assistance to the claimant in two ways. First, the claimant may obtain an interim injunction to prevent further similar breaches of contract and thus prevent any further loss being thereafter incurred. Secondly, the court may decide to award damages in lieu of a final injunction under the power granted originally under section 2 of Lord Cairns' Act.[81] Such damages are intended to be 'just compensation' for future loss which would otherwise have been avoided had an injunction been granted.

C. Restitutionary or gain-based damages for breach of contract

General

Restitutionary or gain-based damages consist of an award of damages to a claimant, not by reference to any actual financial loss which he may be able to show that he has suffered (the 'compensatory principle'), but by reference to the gain or advantage obtained by the defendant (the 'restitutionary or gain-based principle'). The award of such damages reflects a modern recognition that an award of damages which is assessed only by reference to the financial loss which the claimant is able to prove at trial that he has suffered may not be a 'just' or 'adequate' remedy for a breach of contract. Under the restitutionary or gain-based principle, the defendant can thus be obliged to pay over by way of damages a sum equal, or calculated by reference, to the profit which he has made in circumstances where (a) the claimant has not suffered any actual loss, or (b) he is unable to establish that he has suffered a loss, or (c) the actual loss is disproportionately less than the profit made by the defendant.

11.38

Although, in the past, such damages have usually been referred to as 'restitutionary damages', in the landmark decision of the House of Lords in *A-G v Blake*,[82] Lord Nicholls (with whose speech the majority of the House agreed) indicated disapproval of this nomenclature as an 'unhappy expression',[83] since such damages are not actual restitution of something lost. Many practitioners, in consequence, now use the phrase 'gain-based damages' which more accurately corresponds with the nature of an award of damages of this kind.

11.39

Gain-based damages have long been known and understood in the common law in the context of the torts of trespass[84] and wrongful detention of goods. In *The Mediana*[85] the Earl of Halsbury LC posited the question:

11.40

> Supposing a person took away a chair out of my room and kept it for twelve months, could anyone say you had a right to diminish the damages by showing that I did not usually sit in that chair, or that there were plenty of other chairs in the room? . . . a jury may have very often a very difficult task to perform in ascertaining what should be the amount of damages of that sort.[86]

In the tort of conversion, a claimant had a choice. He could either recover damages based on the compensatory principle or he could recover the proceeds of the conversion from the defendant by recourse to a legal fiction by which the claimant 'waived the tort'.

---

[81] See para 11.06 above.
[82] [2001] 1 AC 268, HL.
[83] ibid 284.
[84] eg *Whitwham v Westminster Brymbo Coal and Coke Co* [1896] 2 Ch 538, CA.
[85] [1900] AC 113, HL.
[86] ibid 117.

11.41 In equity, a wrongdoer could be required to yield up all his gains and the normal remedy was an injunction and, incidental to the injunction, an order for an account of all profits made by the defendant by his wrongdoing. The wrongs included a breach of confidence.

11.42 In the case of breaches of contract, however, it had long been held that gain-based damages could not be recovered at common law at all—see, for example, *Teacher v Calder*,[87] *Tito v Waddell (No 2)*[88] (a decision of Megarry V-C), and more recently the Court of Appeal's decision in *Surrey CC v Bredero Homes Ltd*,[89] in which the claimant recovered only nominal damages. This position is reflected in Lord Hoffmann's speech in *Co-operative Insurance Society Ltd v Argyll (Holdings) Ltd*[90] where, in the context of a case concerning the alternative remedies of damages and specific performance and/or an injunction, he held that a remedy which enables a party to a contract to obtain more in money terms than the performance due to him, is unjust and so cannot be permitted.

11.43 During the 1980s and 1990s there was much academic criticism of this lacuna or anomaly.[91] The position was also considered by the Law Commission in its Report in 1997, 'Aggravated, Exemplary and Restitutionary Damages'. In *A-G v Blake*,[92] the House of Lords reviewed the existing law and held that, as an exception to the normal compensatory rule, the remedies of gain-based damages and an account of profits would henceforth be available in cases of breaches of contract (the latter remedy being available only in exceptional circumstances). Lord Nicholls, with whom Lord Goff and Lord Browne-Wilkinson agreed, held[93] that 'in a suitable case damages for breach of contract may be measured by the benefit gained by the wrongdoer from the breach. The defendant must make a reasonable payment in respect of the benefit he has gained'. In his judgment, Lord Nicholls then went on to focus upon the remedy of an account of profits, ie giving 100 per cent of the profits earned from the defendant's wrongdoing as opposed to a lesser sum.

A-G v Blake

11.44 The case of *Blake* was an unusual one in that the UK government sought to prevent a notorious Soviet spy and former member of the British security service from profiting from his memoirs in which he disclosed information obtained during his work for the government. The confidential information, which he had held, was by then in the public domain. Thus, he was not a fiduciary and, under normal principles, he was not liable to account for the profits of his literary endeavours. However, Blake was in breach of his contract of employment, which contained a covenant against disclosure of any official information. The House of Lords rejected a novel cause of action based in public law (which the Court of Appeal had

---

[87] [1899] AC 451, HL (Sc).

[88] [1977] Ch 106, 332.

[89] [1993] 1 WLR 1361, CA. It is worth noting that the court included Steyn LJ, who questioned altogether the desirability of allowing gain-based damages in contract claims. By 2000, now Lord Steyn, he was a member of the Committee of the House of Lords which decided *A-G v Blake*. He had by then been persuaded that his original stance was no longer tenable, and held that there could be exceptions to the 'normal compensatory rule' for damages in contract.

[90] [1997] 3 All ER 297, HL, 305.

[91] Some of these are referred to in the judgments of Lord Nicholls at [2001] AC 268, HL, 278, 283, 284; see also 291 *per* Lord Steyn. A more comprehensive list can be found in A Burrows, *Remedies for Torts and Breach of Contract* (3rd edn, 2004) 395–400.

[92] [2001] 1 AC 268, HL.

[93] ibid 283–4.

held to be available), and instead held that there was a common law remedy of an account of profits arising by reason of Blake's breach of contract.

The majority of the House left open the circumstances in which the new remedies would be **11.45** available. As regards the remedy of an account, the House was of the view that it would only be granted very exceptionally. Lord Steyn held[94] that 'exceptions to the general principle that there is no remedy for disgorgement of profits against a contract breaker are best hammered out on the anvil of concrete cases'. Lord Hobhouse dissented as to the juridical basis for granting gain-based damages and an account of profits. This needs further elaboration.

The majority of the House accepted that there was an unjustified lacuna in the case of a breach **11.46** of contract, if there continued to be no remedy based on the gains made by the wrongdoer: Lord Nicholls warned against the lawyer's ailment of a 'hardening of the categories'.[95] Lord Nicholls' decision relied, in part, upon the decision at first instance in *Wrotham Park Estate Co Ltd v Parkside Homes Ltd*.[96] This was a case concerning a restrictive covenant over land on which developers had built some new houses in breach of a covenant owed to the owners from whom the land had been purchased. For social and economic reasons the judge refused to grant a mandatory injunction to pull the houses down. There was no loss to the claimant since its land was not diminished in value at all, but the defendant developer had made a very considerable profit by its breach. Brightman J awarded the claimant damages equivalent to 5 per cent of the net profit made by the defendant on the footing that this was the reasonable price which he estimated would have been the appropriate amount required to be paid for a relaxation of the covenant. That decision, however, was specifically not followed in the subsequent decision of the Court of Appeal in 1995 in *Surrey CC v Bredero Homes Ltd*.[97] Lord Nicholls, however, held that the approach in the *Wrotham* case was to be preferred. He also referred to the inconsistency between tort and contract and held that such an inconsistency of approach hitherto was not justifiable.[98]

Having decided that damages calculated by reference to the profit of the wrongdoer might **11.47** be awarded for breach of contract, Lord Nicholls then tackled the claim for 100 per cent of the profit on the footing of an account of profits and concluded that, as a matter of principle, there was no reason to rule out that form of remedy in contract.[99] He concluded that, in the case of an account of profits, no fixed rules could be applied save that the remedy would only be appropriate where:

(1) the remedies of compensatory damages, specific performance, and injunction would be 'inadequate';
(2) all the circumstances have been considered, including the subject matter of the contract, the purpose of the provision which had been breached, the circumstances of the breach, the consequences of the breach, and the circumstances in which relief is being sought;
(3) the claimant has a legitimate interest in preventing the defendant's profit-making activity and hence in depriving him of his profit.

---

[94] ibid 291.
[95] ibid 284.
[96] [1974] 1 WLR 798.
[97] [1995] 1 WLR 269, CA.
[98] [2001] 1 AC 268, 278–9.
[99] ibid 284–5.

11.48 Lord Nicholls also added that, of itself, any *one* of the following facts would not be a sufficient ground for departing from the normal (compensatory) measure of damages for breach of contract:

- the fact that the breach was cynical and deliberate;
- the fact that the breach enabled the defendant to enter into a more profitable contract elsewhere;
- the fact that, by entering into a new contract, the defendant put it out of his power to perform his contract with the claimant.

11.49 For his part, Lord Steyn relied on the principle that, as a remedy for Blake's breach of contract, practical justice militated in favour of an order requiring the disgorgement of his profits (ie an account of profits) as an exceptional remedy in the circumstances, particularly since Blake's position was very close to that of a breach by a fiduciary, although as a matter of law he was no longer a fiduciary holding confidential information. It was not necessary to construct any remedy based on constructive trust in order to achieve that, as had been done in the US case of *Snepp v United States*.[100]

11.50 Lord Hobhouse dissented on the ground that, if Blake's employment covenant continued to be enforceable, compensatory damages were available on the same footing as in the *Wrotham* case[101] and the earlier way-leave cases,[102] with the court imposing on the parties a hypothetical price to be paid for a release from the covenant, regardless of whether or not the parties would ever have agreed to such a release in reality. This could be assessed by reference to the sum which would have to be expended on acquisition of the property or the right (for example the cost of a notional licence fee on the facts in the *Wrotham* case) or by reference to the cost of maintenance or of interest during the period of deprivation. Lord Hobhouse therefore rejected the much broader basis for non-compensatory damages for breach of contract which the majority of the House had decided should be available, particularly since this was not a commercial case and he was concerned that the commercial consequences might be very far-reaching and disruptive.

The new remedy of gain-based damages for a breach of contract after
A-G v Blake

11.51 Notwithstanding Lord Hobhouse's concerns, the courts have thus far found little difficulty in absorbing the new remedies of gain-based damages and an account of profits for breach of contract.[103] In *Esso Petroleum Co Ltd v Niad Ltd*,[104] Morritt V-C held[105] that Esso had a particular interest in its Pricewatch scheme promoting the daily prices of its petrol in comparison with the prices charged by its competitors; it had advertised the scheme to the public and it had made commitments to local trading standards authorities and the British Advertising Council about it. Compensatory damages were an inadequate remedy, since Esso had suffered no loss of profits which it could prove, resulting, for example, from a specific downturn in sales.

---

[100] 444 US 507.

[101] [1974] 1 WLR 798.

[102] These were late nineteenth and early twentieth century cases where wrongdoers had carried out work on or extracted material from neighbouring land without the owners' permission and were required to pay damages for trespass, quantified as being the notional cost for a licence to carry out the acts involved.

[103] As to account of profits for breach of contract, see paras 11.87 and 11.100–11.102 below.

[104] [2001] All ER (D) 324.

[105] ibid: see, in particular, paras 63–5.

The defendant's conduct had been a serious breach, which, despite complaint made on four occasions, the defendant had continued. The judge held that it was sufficient that the defendant's enrichment was unjust 'because it was obtained in breach of contract' and the fairness of a remedy of having to pay over to the claimant the extra benefit obtained by the defendant was the remedy 'that matches most closely the reality of the case'.

In *CMS Dolphin Ltd v Simonet*,[106] Lawrence Collins J held that, but for the fact that he **11.52** decided that the claimant was entitled to relief on an alternative basis, the two features consisting of (1) the characterization of the relevant contractual obligation as a fiduciary one, and (2) a finding that the claimant had a legitimate interest in preventing the profit-making activity of the defendant would have been sufficient to allow the court to grant the exceptional remedy of a gain-based remedy for breach of contract, and he went on to hold that 'this is such a case'. The fact, however, that the judge expressly relied upon the first factor, the existence of a fiduciary duty (albeit a duty which arose in contract), puts this case rather more into the category of cases where an account of profits (ie 100 per cent of them) or equitable damages in substitution would have been ordered anyway as part of the equitable remedies available in a case of a breach of fiduciary duty.

In 2003, in *Experience Hendrix LLC v PPX Enterprises Inc*,[107] the Court of Appeal was **11.53** concerned with a commercial case in which there had been substantial and repeated breaches of a settlement agreement reached following an earlier claim relating to the exploitation of recordings made by the late Jimi Hendrix. Relying on the *Blake* case, the claimant claimed, inter alia, either an account of profits or damages assessed on the basis of such sum as it could reasonably have demanded for relaxing the prohibitions in the settlement agreement. The Court of Appeal declined to order an account of profits, on the ground that the case was not sufficiently exceptional, but did make an order for damages to be assessed, based on the sum which could reasonably have been demanded for modification of the settlement agreement. The Court of Appeal held that the appropriate rate for this would, however, be significantly greater than the contractual royalty rate for other recordings, which had been earlier agreed upon as part of the original settlement; the court considered that the appropriate rate would probably be at least double.

In his judgment, Mance LJ pointed to the distinction that gain-based damages (ie based on the **11.54** *Wrotham*-type assessment) were *not* characterized as exceptional by Lord Nicholls in the *Blake* case, whereas the remedy of an account of profits was so described. Further, as regards an award of damages based on an evaluation of the profit made by the wrongdoer, the dissenting speech of Lord Hobhouse was to a similar effect.[108] Thus, he held, it is open to a court to make an award which is related, or limited, to any actual financial gain obtained by the wrongdoer by his breach of contract. Mance LJ[109] succinctly summarized the position as regards gain-based damages for breach of contract as being very similar to what happens in tort,[110] namely:

> . . . the law gives effect to the instinctive reaction that, whether or not the [claimant] would
> have been better off if the wrong had not been committed, the wrongdoer ought not to gain

---

[106] [2001] 2 BCLC 704, para 142.
[107] [2003] EWCA Civ 323, [2003] EMLR 25, CA.
[108] [2003] EWCA Civ 323, [2003] EMLR 25, CA, paras 24 and 25.
[109] ibid para 26.
[110] He referred to the House of Lords' decision in *Kuwait Airways Corp v Iraqi Airway Co* [2002] UKHL 19, [2002] 2 AC 883, HL, a case in which he had been the trial judge at first instance.

an advantage for free, and should make some reasonable recompense . . . The law can in such cases act either by ordering payment over of a percentage of any profit or, in some cases, by taking the cost which the wrongdoer would have had to incur to obtain (if feasible) equivalent benefit from another source.

11.55 Mance LJ held that the circumstances, although clearly within the guidelines given by Lord Nicholls in *A-G v Blake* with regard to the remedy of an account, were not sufficiently exceptional to justify an order for an account of profits; and so he refused to order an account, but instead awarded gain-based damages.[111] Gibson LJ helpfully set out three main reasons why he too was prepared to make an order for gain-based damages, ie damages measured by the benefits gained by the wrongdoer from his breach, as being that:

(1) there had been deliberate breaches of contract by the defendant for its own advantage or reward;
(2) the claimant would have difficulty in establishing financial loss caused by the breaches; and
(3) the claimant had a legitimate interest in preventing the defendant's profit-making activity carried on in breach of its contractual obligations.

It is suggested that the combination and relative significance of each of these three factors form, at least, a practical basis for assessing whether or not a claimant employer should be entitled to damages based upon the gain made by the defendant.

11.56 In 2007, the Court of Appeal in *WWF—World Wide Fund for Nature v World Wrestling Federation Entertainment Inc* held that gain-based damages (ie damages calculated on 'a Wrotham Park basis' as the notional cost of a licence or release to do the act complained of) are a form of compensatory damages and that the law had, therefore, been correctly stated in the *Experience Hendrix* case.[112] Thus, although the object is to deprive the defendant of his wrongful gain, the sum awarded is the court's reasonable assessment of the loss of value in the claimant's right. In the case of an employee's covenant, the covenantee (the employer) may lose all or part of the commercial value of his proprietary right consisting of the benefit of the employee's covenant; and a loss to this right, caused by the breach of the employee's covenant, may fall to be measured as if the parties had freely and reasonably negotiated for a release of the employee from his covenant immediately prior to the breach. In effect, there has been 'a transfer of value for which the wrongdoer must account'.[113]

11.57 Such an assessment can be made regardless of whether or not the claimant has made a claim for, and obtained an injunction to prevent, future breaches of contract. If the claimant has obtained such an injunction, then the assessment of that loss is limited to the period from the date of the first breach of contract by the defendant up to the date of the grant of the injunction.[114]

11.58 The Court of Appeal also held, as did the House of Lords in *A-G v Blake*, that there could in principle be a separate (alternative) remedy for an account of profits for breach of contract.

---

[111] ibid para 44.
[112] ibid paras 48–53.
[113] *Per* Arden LJ in *Devenish Nutrition Ltd v Sanofi-Aventis SA (France)* [2008] EWCA Civ 1086, [2009] Ch 390, para 38.
[114] ibid para 53.

Thus, as Peter Smith J succinctly put it at first instance: **11.59**

> The House of Lords in *Blake* has created (albeit *obiter*) a new concept of damages to apply
> when the traditional method of damages affords no adequate remedy to the innocent party:
> This concept in my view is the negotiation at arm's length of a notional transaction whereby the
> price that could have been obtained for a relaxation of the rights that were infringed can take
> place.[115]

The Court of Appeal upheld the judge's decision as a matter of principle that gain-based   **11.60**
damages are compensatory in nature. It did not, moreover, indicate that there was anything wrong with any of the principles that Peter Smith J gave for the assessment of such
damages. This is a useful list when it comes to considering the evidence to be deployed,
namely:[116]

(1) the overriding principle is that the damages are compensatory, and not punitive;
(2) the primary basis is to consider what sum would have been arrived at in negotiations
    between the parties, had each been making reasonable use of their respective bargaining
    positions without holding out for unreasonable amounts;
(3) the outcome of that hypothetical negotiation must be determined by reference to the
    parties' actual knowledge at the time when such negotiation would have taken place,
    normally at the date of the breach;
(4) the fact that the innocent party would never have agreed to any such sale, relaxation, or
    licence is irrelevant;
(5) the conduct of the wrongdoer as to the manner of his breach is irrelevant;[117]
(6) the decision to award damages on this basis is discretionary according to the circum-
    stances of the case, but the decision to do so should only be taken when damages
    would be 'an inadequate remedy' and without such an award the innocent party
    would obtain no just recompense for the breach by the wrongdoer in doing what he
    had agreed not to do;
(7) the decision can take into account all relevant circumstances, including delay by the
    claimant in advancing a claim or in prosecuting it, with the result, for example, that the
    wrongdoer has been led to think that no claim on this basis will be advanced. If he acts
    in reliance upon that, it may be a bar to the claim for damages on the gain-based principle.
    Alternatively, a part of the claim may be disallowed by reason of delay which has caused
    prejudice.

The judge went on to suggest that the evidence which could be deployed in support of each
side's hypothetical negotiations was wide-ranging, as if they were re-creating the circumstances notionally preparatory to a hypothetical bargaining.

In *Pell Frischmann Engineering Ltd v Bow Valley Iran Ltd*,[118] the Privy Council held that   **11.61**
the assessment of the notional 'licence fee' falls to be made as at the date of the breach.

---

[115] [2006] EWHC 184 (Ch).
[116] ibid para 174.
[117] In arriving at this principle, the judge expressly rejected the suggestion of Professor Burrows that one
pre-condition for this remedy is that the wrongdoer has acted cynically and deliberately calculated to make
gains: judgment paras 154, 168–70, 172. He thus appears not to have followed the guidelines relied on by
Gibson LJ in the *Experience Hendrix* case: see paras 11.53–11.55 above. The Court of Appeal in the *WWF* case
did not suggest that Peter Smith J was wrong in this approach.
[118] [2009] UKPC 45, para 49.

Although the Privy Council considered that post-valuation facts and events are normally irrelevant for the purpose of assessing the value of the right,[119] it is difficult in reality to see how they can be excluded since such events may usefully inform the court as to the true value of the rights involved in the notional negotiation. The counter-argument is that the court can only take into account what the parties would have contemplated at the time of their notional negotiation, and thus one should exclude from the exercise any exceptional profits which the parties would not have contemplated.

11.62 A recent example of this kind of award of damages in relation to misuse of confidential information in breach of a covenant in a commercial contract is *Vercoe and Others v Rutland Fund Management Ltd*.[120] The judge's methodology in assessing the damages is a useful illustration of the material (including expert evidence) which a claimant may need to put forward in order to make good his claim for an award of gain-based damages.

Three important features

11.63 Thus, it can be seen that the remedy of gain-based damages for breach of contract has as its starting point three important features:

(1) It must be shown that the ordinary rule of compensatory damages, based on the claimant having to prove a financial loss caused by the breach, would produce an unjust or inadequate result. In this sense, difficulty or inability in proving damages is obviously a critical starting point, but even where the claimant can show that he has suffered some financial loss, he may show that this provable loss is totally inadequate, by comparison with the profits which the defendant has made (or intended to make).

(2) The award must not be advanced as a form of punishment, but rather as 'just compensation' for the improper advantage obtained by the defendant by reason of his wrongdoing.

(3) The claimant must take great care in preparing his evidence in order:
    (a) to persuade the court that, in all the circumstances, it should make an award on this basis, and
    (b) to obtain the best notional 'price' which the court will fix as the arbiter of the hypothetical bargaining.

11.64 It is also worth noting that the principles suggested by Peter Smith J (see para 11.60 above) have the benefit, first, of allowing the defendant to have the value of his own input or contribution to the profit which has been made and, secondly, of avoiding the potential problem caused by the situation where the defendant acts in breach of contract but he fails to make any significant profit (for example, because he is a bad businessman). The wrongdoer has nevertheless gained an advantage from his wrongdoing, by saving expense, for which the court will require him to pay an appropriate, albeit hypothetical, 'price' or 'fee'. Thirdly, the judgment sidesteps (theoretically at least) the difficult evidential question as to the extent of the causal connection between the breach on the one hand and, on the other hand, the profit made as a result of the breach. Clearly there must be some causal connection, if the court is to take into account any element of profit as part of its calculation of the hypothetical price or fee, but the approach suggested by Peter Smith J means that one makes the assessment

---

[119] ibid para 50.
[120] [2010] EWHC 424 (Ch).

based on what the parties would have anticipated as the likely profits at the time of breach, and not necessarily the actual profits which have, in fact, been made (or not made).[121]

Conclusion

As Lord Steyn observed in *A-G v Blake* in his colourful metaphor, the factors to be taken into **11.65** account will need to be 'hammered out on the anvil of concrete cases'.[122] Inevitably, neither Peter Smith J's decision nor the Privy Council's decision in the *Pell Frischmann* case is going to be the last word in this complex area of development in remedies at common law.[123] Nevertheless, this series of recent decisions is likely to be a source of considerable encouragement to employers faced with employees who have consciously chosen to break the terms of their restrictive covenants or other contractual terms (for example the duty to act in good faith) in circumstances where the employer may find it hard to produce cogent evidence establishing an actual and substantial loss of profits that has been caused by the wrongdoing of the employee.

D. Contractual damages for breach of confidence

This section considers the remedy in damages which an employer may have against his **11.66** employee for a breach of contract consisting of the misuse of confidential information. This common law remedy is to be contrasted with the alternative cause of action in equity arising from a breach of a duty of confidence which comes into being 'whenever a person receives information he knows or ought to know is fairly and reasonably to be regarded as confidential'.[124] Equity provides, in part, remedies which are separate (for example account of profits) and, in part, coextensive with the common law (damages). We consider separately the equitable remedies for breach of confidence in paragraphs 11.94 to 11.143 below.

The availability of common law remedies and equitable ones may overlap and be alternatives **11.67** or they may be cumulative, the test being whether they give rise to a double recovery. Where they overlap, the claimant may be put to an election, normally at the time when he applies for judgment. This is considered separately in paragraphs 11.144 to 11.150 below. The normal and prudent course, however, is for the claimant to advance his various claims in the alternative, rather than to opt at the outset of the action for one or other form of remedy. As is well understood: 'There is nothing conclusive about the form in which the writ is issued, or about the claims made in the statement of claim. A plaintiff may at any time before judgment be permitted to amend.'[125]

Apart from an injunction, the normal remedy which is sought for a breach of a contractual **11.68** term of confidentiality is an award of damages. There is no need to rely on anything more

---

[121] We have used the word 'theoretically' because one may reasonably suppose that the prudent claimant will seek to say, in a case where the profits have turned out to be considerable, that any reasonable person would have expected such large profits. In the context of litigation, we cannot see any basis upon which the defendant could claim to be entitled to withhold disclosure of documents or information about his actual profits and what he calculated or expected them to be even if he did not achieve his expectation.

[122] [2001] AC 268, 291.

[123] The judgment is the subject of an appeal to the Court of Appeal as at the time of writing.

[124] See *Campbell v Mirror Group Newspapers Ltd* [2004] UKHL 22, [2004] 2 AC 457, HL, para 14 *per* Lord Nicholls; *A-G v Guardian Newspapers Ltd (No 2)* [1990] 1 AC 109, HL, especially 281–2 *per* Lord Goff.

[125] *United Australia Ltd v Barclays Bank Ltd* [1941] AC 1, HL, 19 *per* Lord Simon.

than the contract itself, if the claimant so chooses, as the Court of Appeal held in *Faccenda Chicken Ltd v Fowler*.[126] This is of obvious importance where there is an express obligation of confidentiality in the employment contract, as was the case in *Archer v Williams*.[127] In the absence of a breach of an express term of the employment contract, the claimant may be able to rely upon an implied term.

11.69 Having established the breach of contract, the claimant must establish, as with other compensatory damages, (a) his loss of relevant profits, (b) that the loss was caused by the particular breach of contract, and (c) that his loss is not too remote. As explained above, it may now be possible, in appropriate circumstances, to obtain the alternative of gain-based damages.

E. Exemplary damages

General

11.70 The present law is clear. In contrast to the law of tort, exemplary or punitive damages for breach of contract is not an available remedy in England and Wales as the law currently stands—see the 1909 case of *Addis v Gramophone Co Ltd*.[128] There are many examples in which the courts have, since then, continued to maintain that position. Thus, in *Kenny v Preen*[129] the Court of Appeal held that exemplary damages could not be awarded in a case of breach of contractual covenant by a landlord (there was no claim advanced by the claimant in tort). In *Malik v Bank of Credit and Commerce International SA*,[130] the Court of Appeal again held that there could be no claim for exemplary damages for a breach of contract. The court's decision on this point was not the subject of an appeal to the House of Lords, although other issues were. In *Hargreaves v Barron Industrial Services Ltd*,[131] the Court of Appeal noted that a claim for exemplary damages for breach of contract had been struck out at an earlier interim stage. In *Council of the City of Newcastle upon Tyne v Allen* and *Degnan v Redcar and Cleveland BC*,[132] a judgment in combined appeals concerning claims for exemplary damages under the Equal Pay Act 1970, the Employment Appeal Tribunal (Burton J, President) extensively reviewed, inter alia, the case law in contract and concluded that there could be no claim for exemplary damages for a breach of contract.

11.71 In tort cases, exemplary or punitive damages[133] are a category of remedy which the common law continues to permit, in spite of the varied criticisms made in, for example, *Rookes v Barnard*[134] and *Cassell & Co Ltd v Broome*.[135] They are damages over and above compensatory damages and are intended to be a form of punishment and deterrence. The judicial view *had* been that such damages are an anomaly, substantially frozen in time by reference to:

- the causes of action in which such damages had by that time been awarded; and
- the three types of conduct identified by Lord Devlin in *Rookes v Barnard* in 1964.

---

[126] [1987] Ch 117, CA, 135.
[127] [2003] EWHC 1670 (QB).
[128] [1909] AC 488, HL.
[129] [1963] 1 QB 499, CA, 513.
[130] [1995] IRLR 375, [1995] 3 All ER 545, CA.
[131] [2003] EWCA (Civ) 1038.
[132] [2005] ICR 1170, [2005] IRLR 504.
[133] We shall use the term 'exemplary damages'. Some other jurisdictions refer only to 'punitive damages'.
[134] [1964] AC 1129, HL.
[135] [1972] AC 1027, HL.

The first of these has been removed by the House of Lords in *Kuddus v Chief Constable of Leicestershire Constabulary*,[136] so that exemplary damages can now be awarded by the court in the case of any tort. But it continues to be the position in English law at present that the categories of conduct, which may attract such damages, are limited to those set out by Lord Devlin in *Rookes v Barnard*.

Lord Devlin's second category

For present purposes only the second of Lord Devlin's categories of conduct[137] is relevant. **11.72** This consists of 'the defendant's conduct [which] has been calculated by him to make a profit for himself which may well exceed the compensation payable to the plaintiff'. The view of the House of Lords is that ordinarily, in a contract case, the court is not concerned with the attitude of mind of the defendant, since it is argued that much commercial activity may depend upon the freedom of a party to a contract being able, upon payment of compensatory damages, to make a new bargain for himself with a third party and thereby make for himself a greater profit than under his first bargain. It is, therefore, not appropriate for the court to consider imposing any element of punishment or deterrence beyond ordinary compensatory damages and/or an injunction.

Time for review by the court?

It is suggested, however, that the position stated above may itself now require review by the **11.73** courts in the present day in which the requirement of adherence to principles of commercial morality plays an increasingly important role in modern commercial life. As Lord Mackay succinctly put it in *Kuddus v Chief Constable of Leicestershire Constabulary*,[138] 'the genius of the common law is its capacity to develop and it appears strange that the law on this particular topic [exemplary damages] should be frozen by reference to decisions that had been taken prior to and including *Rookes v Barnard* . . . the existence of the anomaly is itself illogical'. As we have seen from *A-G v Blake*,[139] the House of Lords (following an impetus initiated by the Court of Appeal in that case) demonstrated its ability to create a new remedy of gain-based damages in contract to cover those situations where the reasonable man would otherwise think that a defendant 'has got away with something'.

Prior to the *Kuddus* case[140] it was believed that the court's power to award exemplary damages **11.74** was limited to specific causes of action in tort. In that case, however, the House of Lords removed this restriction and held that, although restricted to tort, the remedy was not, as a matter of law, limited to a closed number of causes of action. Now that the field lies open in any cause of action in tort, one may legitimately question why the common law should any longer draw a distinction between contract and tort in the absence of sound reason, provided that the conduct itself comes within the second of Lord Devlin's categories in *Rookes v Barnard*. This becomes all the more significant if one bears in mind that the categories of cause of action in tort, for which exemplary damages were always available, include wrongful interference with contractual relations. One may ask why should an employee—who

---

[136] [2001] UKHL 29, [2002] 2 AC 122, HL.
[137] [1964] AC 1129, HL, 1226–7.
[138] [2001] UKHL 29, [2002] 2 AC 122, HL, para 33.
[139] [2001] 1 AC 268, HL.
[140] [2001] UKHL 29, [2002] 2 AC 122, HL.

cynically breaches an expressly agreed covenant in his employment contract—be exempted from any possible liability to pay exemplary damages, whilst a third party—such as his new employer who has encouraged and assisted him because of the great profits to be made and who may be thus guilty of wrongful interference with the former employer's contractual relations with his employee—is at risk of an award of such damages? Similarly, exemplary damages are an available remedy against both the employee and a co-conspirator in the tort of conspiracy.

11.75 Thus (by parity of reasoning with that of the House of Lords in *A-G v Blake*)[141] in a modern commercial world there appears now to be a lack of logic in the exclusion of breaches of contract from the categories of conduct in tort which may attract exemplary damages.

11.76 It is, however, to be borne in mind that England is almost unique within the EU in allowing exemplary damages, and this may prove to be a substantial stumbling block to any extension of the existing position at common law in this jurisdiction. On the other hand, given that the House of Lords in the *Kuddus* case saw no reason, as a matter of English domestic policy, to maintain the law's previous limitation of exemplary damages to specific tortious causes of action which was imposed by *Rookes v Barnard*, the same logic would suggest that EU policy ought not to be a cause for maintaining the exclusion of exemplary damages in cases of breach of contract, as least when it comes to really serious or dishonest breaches of covenant by employees, such as the cases where employees 'steal' part (or all) of their employer's business.

11.77 The Law Commission, in its 1997 report '*Aggravated, Exemplary and Restitutionary Damages*',[142] recommended against any extension of exemplary damages to the law of contract for the following reasons:

(1) historically exemplary damages have never been awarded for breach of contract;
(2) breaches of contract primarily concern pecuniary loss rather than non-pecuniary loss; in contrast most of the torts in which exemplary damages are awarded involve non-pecuniary loss;
(3) in contract the need for certainty of damages is perceived to be greater than in tort;
(4) in contract, the rights and duties of the parties are fixed by their mutual agreement whereas in tort the duties are imposed by law;
(5) the 'doctrine of efficient breach' dictates that the parties should have available the option of breaking the contract and paying compensatory damages, if they are able to find a more remunerative use for the subject-matter of the promise. To award exemplary damages would tend to discourage 'efficient breach'.

It is not without significance that the Law Commission also pointed out that, where there are concurrent causes of action in both contract and tort, the prudent litigant can claim under all the different heads, leaving it open to him to make an election as to the one(s) which he will pursue at the conclusion of the trial.

Conclusion on contractual position

11.78 More than a decade later,, each of these reasons given by the Law Commission may be thought no longer to hold much persuasive force, apart perhaps from (5) above. But even

---

[141] [2001] 1 AC 268, HL.
[142] Law Com No 247, 1997, paras 1.71–2.

that is doubtful in view of the majority decision of the House of Lords in *A-G v Blake*.[143] Given that the nature of exemplary damages is that they are a form of punishment/deterrence, it is inevitable that, whether in contract or in tort, they can only be imposed by the state and not by the parties themselves. To do otherwise would involve the introduction of an unlawful penalty clause.

11.79 Furthermore, if in similar circumstances, a party can claim both in tort (exemplary damages available) and in contract (exemplary damages not available), one begins to appreciate that the common law may have perpetuated yet another unjustifiable anomaly or pointless 'hardening of the categories' (to use Lord Nicholls' phrase).[144] This is particularly true of employment cases which may often be closer to 'tort situations' than businessmen's commercial bargains. Any risk of unfairness to a defendant would be prevented by virtue of the fact that, as in any breach of contract case, the determination and any award is made by a judge. Finally, it is also worthy of note that the Law Commission was not, in principle or as a matter of policy, opposed to an expansion of the availability of exemplary damages. On the contrary, its report recommended some, albeit limited, expansion.

11.80 On balance, the authors continue to think, therefore, that the time has come when, in an appropriate case, it would be helpful for the appellate courts to advance the debate and to review the validity of continuing this exclusion in cases of breach of contract, especially in the case of employee restrictive covenants.[145]

Breach of confidence and exemplary damages

11.81 There is, thus far, no instance in England and Wales where exemplary damages have been awarded for breach of confidence. It should, however, be noted that at first instance in *Douglas v Hello! Ltd (No 3)*,[146] Lindsay J said: 'I am content to assume, without deciding, that exemplary damages (or equity's equivalent) are available in respect of breach of confidence.' In New Zealand, exemplary damages can be awarded—see *Aquaculture Corp v New Zealand Green Mussel Co Ltd*[147] and *Cook v Evatt (No 2)*.[148]

F. Liquidated damages

General

11.82 The payment of liquidated damages is a remedy which arises from the agreement of the parties themselves to a contract to pay such damages. As part of their bargain, they agree that, upon breach of a specified kind, a specific or variable sum is to be paid or that particular property[149] is to be transferred as the agreed remedy for that breach. The courts will award the innocent party the agreed sum or remedy provided that it represents a genuine pre-estimate of

---

[143] One of Lord Hobhouse's principal reasons for dissenting appears to have been based upon the concept of 'efficient breach'. The majority of the Committee in the House of Lords, however, did not agree with him.

[144] *A-G v Blake* [2001] 1 AC 268, HL, 284.

[145] It could now only be done by the Supreme Court (or by legislation).

[146] [2003] EWHC (Ch) 786, [2003] 3 All ER 996, para 273.

[147] [1990] 3 NZLR 299.

[148] [1992] 1 NZLR 676.

[149] The principle of penalty clauses was extended to property transfers in *Jobson v Johnson* [1989] 1 WLR 1026, CA.

his loss. If the agreed sum is a penalty, then the term of the contract is, as a matter of public policy, not enforceable[150] and the courts award the normal measure of damages available at common law (provided this is pleaded).

11.83 We have included this topic in relation to restrictive covenants because such agreed damages clauses may often be agreed in employment contracts, particularly in the case of senior employees, where the employee wishes to protect his position against his employer in case he is dismissed. Where he is dismissed in accordance with the terms of the contract, no question of liquidated damages arises—he is simply paid the agreed sum.[151] Where, however, he is dismissed in breach of contract, the issue may become a significant point: is the clause a penalty or a liquidated damages clause?

11.84 There is, however, no special regime which applies only in relation to the innocent employee who is dismissed in breach of his contract of employment. The same principles of law can apply *mutatis mutandis* to the employer who wishes to protect himself from the consequences of a breach by the employee. The problem lies, therefore, not so much with the *principles of law* as in the *practicality* of devising a form of wording which is a lawful liquidated damages clause and which, in a particular employment situation, adequately protects the employer in at least a number of specified situations.

11.85 In the case of a money trader, for example, there may well be certain types of situations, in which both employer and employee can readily contemplate that a particular breach of covenant (if the covenant is a valid one) will cause significant loss of a particular kind to the employer. In such a case, apart from the problems of drafting, there is no reason why the parties should not make a pre-estimate of the likely loss which the court may uphold as a valid liquidated damages clause. This could provide a better 'solution', for both employer and employee, than the expense of hurried applications for injunctions and long drawn-out litigation and the long period of uncertainty as to the extent of the employee's actual liability. We think that it may also have the salutary advantage of focusing the employee's attention on the considerable outlay which he (or his new employer on his behalf) may have to make if his chosen route is to breach the terms of his employment covenants. A recent example of this approach by the employer is the case of *Tullett Prebon Group Ltd v El-Hajjali*,[152] in which the liquidated damages clause was upheld.

Liquidated damages or a penalty?

11.86 In order to determine whether a clause is a liquidated damages clause or a penalty, the law provides certain principles. Although the main underlying principle is that the law generally seeks to uphold and enforce the bargain which the parties have made for themselves ('*pacta sunt servanda*'), as Lord Browne-Wilkinson held in *Workers Trust Bank Ltd v Dojap Investments Ltd*,[153] 'in general a contractual provision which requires one party in the event of his breach of the contract to pay or forfeit a sum of money to the other party may be unlawful as being a penalty, unless such provision is a genuine[154] pre-estimate of the loss which the innocent

---

[150] See eg *Robophone Facilities Ltd v Blank* [1966] 1 WLR 1428, CA, 1446 *per* Diplock LJ.

[151] eg *Abrahams v Performing Rights Society* [1995] ICR 1028.

[152] [2008] IRLR 760.

[153] [1993] AC 573, PC, 578.

[154] Although the word 'genuine' is normally used, it conveys only the sense that the clause is intended by the party, for whose benefit it has been agreed, to be compensatory as opposed to a deterrent, *per* Buxton LJ in *Murray v Leisureplay plc* [2005] EWCA Civ 963, [2005] IRLR 946, CA, para 111.

party will incur by reason of the breach'. This principle was applied by the Court of Appeal in *Cine Bes Filmcilik Ve Yapimclick v United International Pictures*,[155] *Murray v Leisureplay plc*,[156] and again in *Euro Land Appointments v Claessens International Ltd*.[157]

In *Dunlop Pneumatic Tyre Co Ltd v New Garage and Motor Co Ltd*,[158] Lord Dunedin set out **11.87** what has become a classic statement of the relevant principles. In summary, first, the validity of the provision falls to be judged at the time of the making of the contract not its breach. Then:

(1) If the sum to be paid is 'extravagant and unconscionable in amount' in comparison with the greatest loss that could conceivably be proved, it will be a penalty.
(2) It will be a penalty if the breach consists only in not paying a sum of money, and the sum of money stipulated is a sum greater than the sum which ought to have been paid.
(3) There is a presumption of penalty when a single lump sum is made payable by way of compensation 'on the occurrence of one or more or all of several events, some of which may occasion serious and others but trivial damage'.
(4) It is no obstacle to the sum being a genuine pre-estimate of damage, that the consequences of the breach are such as to make precise pre-estimation almost an impossibility. Rather in such a situation, it is probable that the pre-estimated damages were 'the true bargain of the parties'.

It is a matter of construction of the contract for the court to determine whether the predomi- **11.88** nant contractual function of the term was to deter a party from breaking the contract or to compensate the innocent party for breach of it. In many instances, that may be deduced by the court by comparing the amount that would be payable on breach with the loss which may be sustained if breach occurs,[159] but it is important to bear in mind that the court necessarily is required to adjudicate on the question by reference to the time when the contract is made and not at the time of the breach. Any discrepancy is, therefore, not decisive. It is 'no more than a guide to the answer to the question whether the clause is penal'.[160]

The court, however, ought not to be astute to descry a term as a penalty clause. 'Great caution' **11.89** needs to be exercised before striking down a clause as penal.[161] In his advice to the Privy Council in *Philips Hong Kong Ltd v A-G of Hong Kong*, Lord Woolf held that it is, therefore, 'normally . . . insufficient . . . to identify situations where the application of the provision could result in a larger sum being recovered by the injured party than his actual loss'.[162] Where, however, it should be obvious that the 'liquidated damages' are totally out of proportion to certain of the losses which may be sustained in the event of a breach covered by the provision, then it is likely that the clause is a penalty. 'The alleged genuine pre-estimate of loss . . . [has] to relate to the overall net balance of losses payable on termination less the credits to which [the defendant] would have been entitled at common law.'[163] 'A contractual

---

[155] [2003] EWCA Civ 1669.
[156] [2005] EWCA Civ 963, [2005] IRLR 946, CA.
[157] [2006] EWCA 385, [2006] All ER (D) 79, CA.
[158] [1915] AC 79, HL, 86–8.
[159] *Lordsvale Finance plc v Bank of Zambia* [1996] QB 752, 762.
[160] *Murray v Leisureplay plc* [2005] EWCA 963, [2005] IRLR 946, CA, para 106 *per* Clarke LJ, referring to Lord Woolf's judgment in *Philips Hong Kong Ltd v A-G of Hong Kong* [1993] BLR 49, PC, 58–9.
[161] ibid para 114, *per* Buxton LJ.
[162] [1993] BLR 49, PC, 58–9.
[163] *Murray v Leisureplay* (n 154 above), para 39 *per* Arden LJ.

provision does not become a penalty simply because the clause in question results in overpayment in particular circumstances. The parties are allowed a generous margin.'[164] In *Tullett Prebon Group Ltd v Al-Hajjali*, the judge emphasized that, in most cases, it will only be when a clause can be shown to be extravagant or unconscionable in relation to the greatest conceivable loss that it will be found to be a penalty.[165]

11.90   The burden of proof lies on the person seeking to say that it is a penalty, and not the other way around.[166] Evidence on all relevant factors can be given by the parties:

> . . . the purpose of adducing that evidence is not so that the parties can demonstrate that they have agreed to opt out of the remedies regime provided by the common law but rather that the reasons they had for doing so constitute adequate justification for the discrepancy between the contractual measure of damages and that provided by the common law.[167]

11.91   In an employment contract, it may well be quite difficult to predict with any degree of precision what loss may actually be suffered, but that should not of itself be a reason for the court to hold that their pre-estimate of damages is to be held to be a penalty. Rather, now that the court has jurisdiction in contract cases to award damages on a gain-based principle where that is appropriate, the new approach (which recognizes the difficulty of reaching such precision) ought perhaps to allow the parties to have regard to the commercial price which they agree (with the benefit of legal advice) would have to be paid in order to obtain the employee's release from particular covenants. That would seem to be a more rational and businesslike approach, certainly in the case of senior employees who may well, for all practical purposes, be in an equal bargaining position with the employer.

11.92   The *Murray* case is itself a useful authority for the practitioner in that the Court of Appeal has helpfully set out, step by step, the route which the court could follow, in order to determine whether a provision in a director's employment contract is or is not a penalty. In the *Murray* case, the Court of Appeal reversed Colman J in holding that the clause was a penalty. In *Taylor Stuart & Co v Croft*,[168] the judge held a 'liquidated damages clause' to be a penalty because it quantified the maximum damage, which a firm of accountants might suffer when an employee solicited customers of the firm, rather than being a genuine pre-estimate of loss. He, however, started from the position that: 'The court should look favourably at a clause which seeks to estimate by a formula what is notoriously difficult, if not impossible, to quantify in individual cases.'[169] Another example of the step by step approach in action is *Tullett Prebon Group Ltd v Al-Hajjali*, in which the validity of the liquidated damages clause was upheld.[170]

11.93   A further significant question may arise as follows: what happens if the provision is held to be a penalty clause, but the claimant employer's actual loss is significantly greater than the contractual provision provides? This was left undecided by the courts in both *Cellulose*

---

[164]   ibid para 43.
[165]   [2008] IRLR 760, para 38.
[166]   *Robophone Facilities Ltd v Blank* [1966] 1 WLR 1428 (CA), 1447 *per* Diplock LJ; see also *Murray v Leisureplay* (n 154 above), para 106.
[167]   [2005] IRLR 946, CA, para 52.
[168]   9 April 1997 (Stanley Burnton QC sitting as Deputy High Court Judge).
[169]   ibid 17.
[170]   [2008] IRLR 760.

Acetate Silk Co Ltd v Widnes Foundry Ltd[171] and *Robophone Facilities Ltd v Blank*.[172] It was, however, decided by the Court of Appeal in *Jobson v Jobson*[173] that the employer, who has suffered the loss and for whose benefit the clause has been inserted, is limited overall to what he agreed to as the limit of the damages which he could recover under the clause. This would certainly accord with the public policy that the court holds a clause to be a penalty in order to protect the employee and not to advantage the employer so as to enable him to obtain more than he had originally negotiated in the contract. Much may, however, turn on the precise wording of the clause and it is, therefore, important for the employer to ensure that its wording accords with his precise intention.

G. An account of profits and equitable damages

Preliminary

An account of profits was, historically, a remedy to which equity had exclusive jurisdiction in aid **11.94** of a purely equitable right, such as the rights of a beneficiary of a trust or any person to whom another owes fiduciary duties. Equity also, inter alia, had the right to make an order for an account when it was ancillary to the grant of an injunction to prevent the breach of a common law right.[174] The distinction is principally of historical interest these days, since the Judicature Act 1873 permitted the High Court to make an order for an account to be taken in any case where an account could previously have been ordered, either in equity or at common law. This historical point, however, explains the considerable caution of the modern courts in extending the right to an account beyond those categories of causes of action where it had previously existed.

In the context of employer/employee relationships, the remedy of taking an account and **11.95** obtaining an order for payment of the amount found due is available as 'the standard remedy'[175] which a claimant obtains as a matter of course where:

(1) the court is satisfied that the defendant owed the claimant a fiduciary duty which he has breached; or
(2) the defendant is in breach of a duty of confidence which the law imposes upon him and which is owed to the claimant.

Following the decision of the House of Lords in *A-G v Blake*,[176] an account is also now available, but only in exceptional circumstances where:

(3) there has been a breach of contract and in respect of which the claimant employer has 'a legitimate interest in preventing the defendant's profit-making activity and, hence, in depriving him of his profit';[177] then an account may be the 'just response' where 'practical justice' requires it.[178]

---

[171] [1933] AC 20, HL.
[172] [1966] 1 WLR 1428, CA, 1446–8 *per* Diplock LJ.
[173] [1989] 1 WLR 1026, CA (Kerr LJ dissenting).
[174] Although no longer of any practical significance, historically one advantage of seeking an account in Equity in the Court of Chancery lay in the fact that the defendant was made to go on oath.
[175] The phrase is that of Lord Nicholls in *A-G v Blake* [2001] 1 AC 268, HL, 287.
[176] [2001] 1 AC 268, HL.
[177] ibid 285 *per* Lord Nicholls.
[178] ibid 285 *per* Lord Nicholls and 292 *per* Lord Steyn.

As an alternative to an account of profits, the court can award damages which Professor Edelman characterizes as 'disgorgement damages'. He argues[179] that such damages should be available in circumstances where the wrongdoer has acted deliberately to make a profit by breaching another's proprietary right. In the case of an employer, his right in the benefit of his employee's covenant is a proprietary right and the normal case, which we are examining in this work, is one where the employee deliberately sets out to breach his covenant with a view to making a greater profit for himself.

Procedure

11.96 An account and an inquiry as to damages are both very flexible and useful tools within the court's armoury. (It is the usual course in the Chancery Division for the court to direct an inquiry as to damages rather than to assess damages as part of the trial itself.) In the High Court the account or inquiry is conducted by a High Court Judge or a Master; in the county court it is conducted by a district judge.[180] When the court orders an account of profits or an inquiry as to damages, it will normally give detailed directions as to the manner in which the account is to be taken and verified or the inquiry is to be conducted.[181] In the process of carrying out the account, either party may object or raise queries, but a written notice is required to be given in each case.[182] The directions which the court gives may include, at any stage, a direction for a hearing (with evidence including expert evidence, if appropriate) to resolve issues which have arisen.

The first category—breach of fiduciary duties

11.97 A number of relationships come within the category of fiduciary ones, such as the relationship of a director to his company.[183] The expression 'fiduciary duty' is strictly confined to those duties which are fiduciary in nature, and, therefore, it is relevant to note that, in the context of remedies, it does not extend to the duty of skill and care or other contractual duties which may be owed.[184] It is also important to understand that:

> A fiduciary duty may co-exist with contractual duties and the existence of a basic contractual relationship has in many situations provided a foundation for the erection of a fiduciary relationship . . . the fiduciary relationship cannot be superimposed upon the contract in such a way as to alter the operation which the contract was intended to have.[185]

11.98 The position of an employee and the question of whether or not fiduciary duties arose such as would entitle the court to grant the remedy of an account, have been the subject of judicial consideration in, for example, *Nottingham University v Fishel*,[186] *PMC Holdings Ltd v*

---

[179] *Recent Developments in the law of Restitution*, Oxford Practitioners Lecture, 8 March 2010. See, in particular, *Livingstone v The Rawyards Coal Co* (1880) 5 App Cas 25, 31, 34, and 39 and *per* Lord Diplock in *Broome v Cassell & Co Ltd* [1972] AC 1027, 1129.

[180] CPR, 40APD.9.

[181] CPR, 40APD.1.

[182] CPR, 40APD.3.

[183] *Selangor United Rubber Estates Ltd v Cradock (No 3)* [1968] 1 WLR 1555, 1582.

[184] See eg Lord Browne-Wilkinson in *Henderson v Merrett Syndicates Ltd* [1995] 2 AC 145, HL, 206; and *A-G v Guardian Newspapers (No 2)* (n 124 above).

[185] *Hospital Products Ltd v US Surgical Corp* (1984) 156 CLR 41 *per* Mason J, whose statement was approved by the Privy Council in *Kelly v Cooper* [2003] AC 205, PC, 215.

[186] [2000] ICR 1461.

Smith,[187] and *Hydra plc v Anastasi*.[188] Part of an employee's work may give rise to a fiduciary duty, whilst other parts may not; it is a matter for detailed analysis.[189] However, the court has emphasized that 'a great deal of caution needs to be exercised' before holding that any particular employee also owes a fiduciary duty to his employer.[190]

An account of profits is provided as one equitable remedy for the breach of the fiduciary's **11.99** duty because the fiduciary employee is not permitted to allow his duty to the beneficiary (the employer) to conflict with his own private interests and he is not allowed to make a private gain from his position as a fiduciary. Although the rule is said to be a very strict or inflexible one, the court achieves some degree of flexibility by applying a varying standard when it comes to the determination as to whether or not there has been a conflict of interest, such as to require the fiduciary to account for the profit which he has made. The position is most succinctly stated in paragraph 33-002 of Goff and Jones, *The Law of Restitution* (7th edn, 2007), in terms of the 'intensity' of the fiduciary relationship. The more intense it is (for example the position of a company director), the more vigilant is the court in its oversight of the fiduciary; but 'in relationships where the fiduciary element is less intense, and where the fiduciary has acted honestly and in his beneficiary's best interests, the court may be more reluctant to find a potential conflict of interest'. As Lord Upjohn pointed out in *Phipps v Boardman*,[191] the court makes a three-stage inquiry consisting of:

(1) An examination of the question whether there is a fiduciary relationship in relation to the particular circumstances.
(2) A determination of the specific duties which have arisen by reason of that relationship and asking whether the defendant has committed any breach of those duties.
(3) If a breach is established, the defendant becomes accountable for any profit made by reason of that breach.

Also, once it has been established that the fiduciary has benefited from an abuse of his position, **11.100** he holds the benefit on a constructive trust.[192] For modern instances, the cases of *A-G for Hong Kong v Reid*[193] and *A-G v Guardian Newspapers Ltd (No 2)*[194] are useful examples. This extends to the case where, for example, a director or employee, owing a fiduciary duty, diverts to himself the benefit of a contract or other commercial opportunity which he came to know in the context of his fiduciary duties. A well-known example of this is the case of *Industrial Development Consultants Ltd v Cooley*,[195] where a director was held liable by Roskill J for diverting a contract for his own benefit in circumstances where he had got to know of the commercial opportunity by virtue of his position as managing director and it was his duty to pass that information on to his company's management. He was required to disgorge the profits which he had unjustly made. A fiduciary may also be liable for the profits made

---

[187] [2002] EWHC 1575 (QB).
[188] [2005] EWHC 1559 (QB).
[189] *New Zealand Netherlands Society Inc v Kuys* [1973] 1 WLR 1126, PC, 1130 *per* Lord Wilberforce. A modern example in the employment field is *Murad v Al-Saraj* [2005] EWCA Civ 959, CA.
[190] *ABK Ltd v Foxwell* [2002] EWHC 9.
[191] [1967] 2 AC 46, HL, 127.
[192] *Keech v Sandford* (1728) Cas temp King 61; (1726) Sel Cas t King (Macnaghten) 175.
[193] [1994] 1 AC 324, HL.
[194] [1990] 1 AC 109, HL.
[195] [1972] 1 WLR 443.

by a third party, depending on the circumstances and whether, in particular, he acted dishonestly.[196]

11.101 In the case of a fiduciary, there may be circumstances in which, although he is obliged to disgorge his profit, he is nevertheless allowed in equity to recover a reasonable remuneration for his work. Thus, in *Phipps v Boardman*,[197] the House of Lords ameliorated the strict rule by allowing the family solicitor (who was also a beneficiary) to be paid a generous *quantum meruit* for his work since he had acted honestly. In contrast, in *Guinness plc v Saunders*,[198] the House of Lords firmly rejected any basis for remuneration of, or an equitable allowance to, the director (Mr Ward), even though the court proceeded on the assumption that he had acted honestly at all times. This varying approach adopted by the court suggests that its approach is likely to be fact sensitive.

11.102 The liability of the fiduciary to account for his profit made from the abuse of his position is quite separate from, and irrelevant to, the fact that the beneficiary (the employer) may or may not have suffered any loss thereby. This is clearly important in those cases where the employer finds himself in difficulty in being able to proving a loss. He does not need to do so.

The second category—misuse of confidential information

11.103 In the case of misuse of confidential information, the fiduciary employee who breaches his duties is liable to account for his profits. A modern example is the case of *A-G v Guardian Newspapers Ltd (No 2)*,[199] in which a member of MI5 was held to be in breach of a fiduciary duty by seeking to publish confidential information acquired during his government service. A more prosaic example, of long standing, is the case of a milk rounds man who had copied a list of his employer's customers and used the list for a new business.[200] Information is treated as if it is akin to property, so that it is treated as if it is 'owned' by the beneficiary and 'belongs' to him. In *Phipps v Boardman*,[201] there was a difference of opinion,[202] with the House of Lords being divided over the question of whether it was property 'in the strict sense'. The point was expressly kept open by Lord Goff in *A-G v Guardian Newspapers Ltd (No 2)*,[203] whilst at first instance Sir Nicholas Browne-Wilkinson V-C had relied upon the right of confidence as a property right.[204] In *Douglas v Hello! Ltd (No 3)*,[205] however, the Court of Appeal has now held that confidential information does not fall to be treated as property that can be owned and transferred. In that case the court preferred to use the words of Lord Upjohn in *Phipps v Boardman* that 'in the end the real truth is that it is not property in any normal sense, but equity will restrain its transmission to another in breach of some confidential relationship'.[206] On appeal in the *Douglas* case, sub nom *OBG Ltd and others v Allan and others*,[207] the House of Lords held that it was sufficient that there was a right to an

---

[196] See eg *Regal (Hastings) Ltd v Gulliver* [1967] 2 AC 134n, [1942] All ER 378, HL.
[197] [1967] AC 46, HL.
[198] [1990] 2 AC 663, HL.
[199] [1990] 1 AC 109, HL. See also *Vercoe v Rutland Fund Management Ltd* [2010] EWHC 424 (Ch).
[200] *Robb v Green* [1895] 2 QB 315, CA.
[201] [1967] 2 AC 46, HL.
[202] ibid 102 *per* Lord Cohen, 107 *per* Lord Hodson, 115 *per* Lord Guest, and 127–8 *per* Lord Upjohn.
[203] [1990] 1 AC 109 HL, 281–2.
[204] [1987] 1 WLR 1248, 1264.
[205] [2006] QB 125, CA, paras 119, 126–36.
[206] [1967] 2 AC 46, HL, 127–8.
[207] [2008] 1 AC 1.

obligation of confidence held by Ok! magazine which could be enforced against third parties; the House did not find it necessary to address the question of whether this was, or was to be treated as, 'property'.

This approach accords with the earlier case of *Mustad & Son v Dosen*,[208] in which the House **11.104** of Lords had allowed a purchaser of confidential information to sue to protect it from disclosure on the footing that it was a property right.

For most purposes, however, it does not make any difference whether confidential informa- **11.105** tion is or is not to be treated as a form of property; the remedy of an account of profits in cases of breach of confidence has by now been firmly established. It would, however, make a substantial difference when it comes to an attempt by the claimant to trace as if the information was itself property.[209]

The liability for breach of confidence is not limited to fiduciaries. Apart from the principles **11.106** of a constructive trust based on a breach of fiduciary duty, it is now firmly established that there is a separate cause of action for breach of confidence.[210] Lord Denning MR, in *Seager v Copydex Ltd*,[211] held that the cause of action 'depends on the broad principle of equity that he who has received information in confidence shall not take unfair advantage of it. He must not make use of it to the prejudice of him who gave it without obtaining his consent'. The duty lies 'in the notion of an obligation of conscience arising from the circumstances in or through which the information was communicated or obtained'.[212] This is now recognized as grounding a wider cause of action which operates against 'a form of unconscionable conduct, akin to a breach of trust . . . Now the law imposes a "duty of confidence" whenever a person receives information he knows or ought to know is fairly and reasonably to be regarded as confidential'.[213] In reaching his statement of principle, Lord Nicholls relied upon the passage in the speech of Lord Goff in *A-G v Guardian Newspapers Ltd (No 2)* referred to above. The relevant authorities are helpfully gathered and reviewed in the Court of Appeal's judgment in *Douglas v Hello! Ltd*.[214]

The third category—an account of profits as a remedy for breach of contract

As we have seen in paragraphs 11.44 to 11.50 above, in *A-G v Blake*[215] the House of Lords **11.107** held[216] that, in exceptional circumstances, an account of profits could be ordered against a wrongdoer for breach of an employment contract. The remedy is discretionary where 'a just response to a breach of contract so requires'.[217] The decision of the majority of the House of

---

[208] [1964] 1 WLR 109n, HL.

[209] See eg the statement by Scott J at first instance in *A-G v Guardian Newspapers (No 2)* (n 124 above), 173.

[210] It is not within the scope of this work to consider in detail the separate development of the law in respect of individual privacy rights based on Art 8 of the European Convention on Human Rights, but see Chapter 8 above for an overview.

[211] [1967] 1 WLR 923, CA, 931.

[212] *Moorgate Tobacco Co Ltd v Philip Morris Ltd (No 2)* (1984) 156 CLR 414, 438; see also *A-G v Guardian Newspapers (No 2)* (n 124 above), 281 *per* Lord Goff.

[213] *Campbell v Mirror Group Newspapers Ltd* [2004] UKHL 22, [2004] 2 AC 457, HL, para 14 *per* Lord Nicholls. Note that Lord Nicholls, however, dissented on the principal issue before the House of Lords concerning the interaction between ECHR, Arts 8 and 10.

[214] [2005] EWCA Civ 595, paras 54–90.

[215] [2001] 1 AC 268, HL.

[216] Note: Lord Hobhouse dissented.

[217] ibid 284.

Lords was given by Lord Nicholls. He emphasized first that the remedy will *only* be available as a remedy when the remedies of damages, specific performance, and injunction do not provide an adequate remedy, but that otherwise no fixed rules can be laid down. It was held that the court will have regard to all the circumstances, including the subject matter of the contract, the purpose of the contractual provision which has been breached, the circumstances of the breach, the consequences of the breach, and the circumstances in which this form of relief is being sought. Beyond that, Lord Nicholls held, it would be difficult and unwise to be more specific.[218] He rejected two possible categories suggested by Lord Woolf in the Court of Appeal, namely (a) the case of a skimped performance (because an account of profits was not necessary) and (b) the case where the defendant has done the very thing he contracted not to do (because that was too wide a definition). Lord Nicholls did, however, agree with Lord Woolf that the presence of any *one* of three particular factors would not of itself be sufficient; the three factors are:

(1) the fact that the breach was cynical and deliberate;
(2) the fact that the breach enabled the defendant to enter into a more profitable contract elsewhere; and
(3) the fact that by entering into a new and more profitable contract the defendant put it out of his power to perform his contract with the claimant.

11.108 All three of these factors (or at least two of them) may, however, be present in many instances of a breach of a restrictive covenant. As Lord Steyn observed,[219] it will therefore depend very much on future decisions as to how this remedy comes to be developed (as much in the area of restrictive covenants as in other areas).

11.109 Certainly the facts in the *Blake* case were very unusual in that it was clearly in the public interest to deter a notorious Soviet spy, who had worked for the UK government security service, from profiting from the sale of his autobiography, even if the information which he was publishing was no longer secret. His position in contract was that the obligations of secrecy, which he had undertaken in his employment contract, were very close to fiduciary obligations.[220] In *Snepp v United States*,[221] the court had determined that, in a similar situation, the US government employee held his profits under a constructive trust and this was, in the considered view of Lord Steyn, 'instructive'.[222]

11.110 There is, however, a marked reluctance on the part of the courts to go down the route of awarding an account as a remedy, whether in contract or in tort, as suggested by the House of Lords in the *Blake* case, and as is well illustrated by *Forsythe-Grant v Allen*.[223] This case involved a tort claim in nuisance, in which the Court of Appeal not only concluded that the facts were not sufficiently exceptional, but also took care to emphasize that an account was very much to be regarded as an equitable remedy which required the claimant to show either an actual fiduciary obligation or a 'quasi-fiduciary' obligation,[224] such as that owed by the person who has received confidential information. The same

---

[218] ibid 285.
[219] ibid 291.
[220] ibid 287.
[221] 444 US 507.
[222] [2001] 1 AC 268, 292.
[223] [2008] EWCA Civ 50.
[224] ibid para 41 *per* Toulson LJ.

reluctance was also shown by the Court of Appeal—and the deployment of the hurdle of the requirement for exceptional circumstances—in *Devenish Nutrition Ltd v Sanofi-Aventis SA (France)*.[225]

Taking an account and the alternative remedy of damages

Taking an account of profits can be a long and difficult process. The starting point is that the **11.111** defendant is treated as if he has conducted the business and made profits on behalf of the claimant.[226] The court seeks to determine what profits have been made which have been caused by the relevant breach of duty, ie by the defendant's wrongful activity. The profits are not to be reduced because the defendant could have done the same thing, without wrongdoing.[227] Where, for instance, a misuse of confidential information relates only to a part of a business or a particular product, the inquiry is normally confined to the profits attributable to that part of the business.[228] The defendant is also entitled to have taken into account all the costs and expenses attributable in this way. If necessary, the court will make its own apportionment of the costs and expenses, since the objective is not to impose compensation which is punitive. The court should not engage in substantial rounding up, but the fact that the apportionment exercise may be a difficult one should not mean that the court cannot reach a just conclusion.[229] Ordinary accounting principles for apportioning costs and expenses of parts of a business can provide a useful guide to the court. For example, financing costs and capital expenditure appear clearly to be allowable items, as is tax paid by the defendant (unless he recovers it back by a reclaim or tax credit, in which case he must account for that repayment to the claimant).[230] In the *Celanese International* case, Laddie J considered that there was no onus of proof on either party as such, since the court is making an inquiry as to the correct position and so it is not tied to the alternative positions of, or by the arguments advanced by, the parties, since they may both be wrong.[231] It should, however, be noted that in *Normalec Ltd v Britton*,[232] Walton J's approach was rather less precise and indicated that, if the court harboured doubts, it may be appropriate to lean in favour of the claimant.[233]

At first instance in *A-G v Guardian Newspapers Ltd (No 2)*,[234] Scott J took the view that, in **11.112** the circumstances of an extract of *Spycatcher* published in an edition of the *Sunday Times*, the newspaper had benefited from an increased circulation. The judge held (at that stage) that the newspaper was required to account for the whole profit attributable to the increase in circulation. The judge, however, refused to make any apportionment of the profit so made, but his judgment on this point is brief and it is thus unclear what he exactly had in mind in this regard.

---

[225] [2008] EWCA Civ 1086.

[226] *Celanese International Corp v BP Chemicals Ltd* [1999] RPC 203, para 36. This was a breach of patent case.

[227] ibid paras 37–40.

[228] ibid paras 38, 44–54.

[229] ibid paras 76, 81.

[230] [1999] RPC 203, paras 101–9, 129–37.

[231] ibid para 74; see also *My Kinda Town Ltd v Soll* [1983] RPC 15, CA, 57.

[232] [1983] FSR 318.

[233] See also *My Kinda Town* (n 231 above) and *Ultraframe (UK) Ltd v Fielding* [2005] EWHC 1638 (Ch), paras 1533 ff.

[234] [1990] 1 AC 109, HL, 168–9.

Damages as an alternative

11.113   Being an equitable remedy, an account is a discretionary one. If there is a breach of fiduciary duty or a breach of confidence, the court will normally order an account, but it is not bound to do so. It may, instead, make an order for damages or an inquiry as to damages (see *Peter Pan Manufacturing Corp v Corsets Silhouette Ltd*).[235] In *Seager v Copydex Ltd (No 2)*,[236] the Court of Appeal refused to make an order for an account and instead ordered the defendant to pay to the claimant as damages the market value of the information which had been misused, on the footing that the damages were to be assessed in the same way as user or gain-based damages for conversion of the claimant's property. In other words, the court used a tortious basis for assessing damages, not a contractual one; see *per* Winn LJ in the *Seager (No 2)* case.[237]

11.114   The court in the *Seager (No 2)* case went on to hold as a general proposition that, once the user damages had been paid, the recipient was entitled to treat the information for all time as his own, and thus would be free to licence its use by others to the extended detriment of the person whose confidence has been breached. This ruling by the Court of Appeal may have gone too far and may not correctly represent the law relating to such damages. (The Court of Appeal in that case appears to have equated damages for breach of confidence with damages for the tort of conversion of a chattel, but breach of confidence is not an identical common law tort and one does not need to 'waive the tort' in order to become entitled to damages for breach of confidence, which is what the Court of Appeal appears to have had in mind.) There is, for instance, the possibility of an intermediate state of affairs, when confidential information has been misused in a commercial context for a period of time and the misuse is ended by an injunction. Damages may be awarded on the basis of the user or gain-based principle up to the date of the injunction, but thereafter any further use of the information would be unlawful (for that is the protection given by the grant of an injunction).

11.115   On the other hand, if the court chooses, either of its own decision or upon an election by the claimant, not to grant an injunction (as it may do under its jurisdiction under section 50 of the Senior Courts Act 1981),[238] then necessarily the court can make an assessment of the just amount or 'price' which falls to be paid by the defendant in lieu of an injunction over such period as the court considers to be fair and during which, in the case of confidential information, that information will continue to have a commercial value to the claimant. An example of the way to calculate the quantum of the damages in such a case is *Seager v Copydex Ltd (No 2)*.[239] (But it is suggested that the damages cover only the defendant's own misuse and not any misuse by others.)

11.116   As we have seen in the case of restitutionary or gain-based damages for breach of contract, a normal way of assessing damages in lieu of an injunction is for the court to determine what hypothetical licence fee would reasonably have been required to be paid for the right to act in the way that the wrongdoer has acted—see paragraphs 11.38 to 11.62 above and, in particular, the recent decision of Peter Smith J at first instance in *WWF—World Wide Fund*

---

[235] [1969] 1 WLR 96, CA.
[236] [1969] 1 WLR 809, CA.
[237] ibid 815.
[238] ie the current version of what was formerly s 2 of Lord Cairns' Act. See para 11.06 above.
[239] [1969] 1 WLR 96, CA.

for Nature v World Wrestling Federation Entertainment Inc with regard to the principles of assessment of the claimant's special damage which he set out.[240]

It appears to be open to the court always to make an award of damages in lieu of any equitable **11.117** remedy.[241] Thus, it is also open to the employer to pursue his claim against the employee both on the basis of compensatory damages and (in the alternative) damages for unjust enrichment, leaving it to a later stage to make his election as to which remedy to have. Election is considered separately in paragraphs 11.144 to 11.150 below. The *Seager (No 2)* case, however, indicates that the normal measure of damages in a case of breach of confidence is the same as in tort, ie the claimant is entitled to be placed in the same position he would have been in but for the tort. He must therefore, inter alia, establish causation and that the damage claimed is not too remote if he seeks to recover compensatory damages[242] as opposed to gain-based damages. The same approach was adopted by the Court of Appeal in *Douglas v Hello! Ltd (No 3)*.[243] See also the Court of Appeal's decision in *Indata Equipment Supplies Ltd v ACL Ltd*.[244] Thus, if the claimant employer seeks compensatory damages, he must prove (1) a loss (normally of profits) which (2) was of a kind which was foreseeable and (3) in respect of which the wrongful conduct of the defendant was *a cause*.[245]

It will depend very much on the facts of the case. Where damages are difficult or impossible **11.118** to assess on a compensatory basis, the claimant can normally claim damages based on the restitutionary or gain-based principle, for example see the judgment of Slade LJ in *Dowson & Mason Ltd v Potter*.[246] Significantly, if the same measure of damages is applied as in the tort of conversion (as was held in the *Seager (No 2)* case[247] where the court's award was based on the user or gain-based principle), then the court should pay little or no attention to intervening acts of third parties which a defendant may assert had the effect of reducing the value of the claim. Rather the defendant is required to pay the full price for the hypothetical licence, regardless of the acts of third parties; see in particular the House of Lords' decision in *Kuwait Airways Corp v Iraqi Airways Co*[248] (a tort case).

Misuse of confidential information

In the case of misuse of confidential information, the claimant has three alternative pos- **11.119** sibilities: (1) an account of profits, (2) damages on a compensatory basis, or (3) damages in lieu of an account, based upon the notional licence fee which could have been charged— see Lord Wilberforce's judgment in *General Tire & Rubber Co v Firestone Tyre Co Ltd*,[249] which was applied by the Court of Appeal in *Douglas v Hello! Ltd (No 3)*.[250] In the *Douglas* case, the Court of Appeal relied on the *General Tire* case in the context of a claim for breach of

---

[240] [2006] EWHC 184 (Ch); see also J McGhee (ed), *Snell's Equity* (31st edn, 2005) para 18-18.
[241] See eg *Saltman Engineering Co Ltd v Campbell Engineering Co Ltd* [1948] 65 RPC 203, CA, in which an inquiry as to damages was ordered.
[242] See *Universal Thermosensors Ltd v Hibben* [1992] 1 WLR 923, 851.
[243] [2005] EWCA Civ 595, [2006] QB 125, CA, paras 243–9.
[244] [1998] FSR 248, CA.
[245] See *Overseas Tankship (UK) Ltd v Mort Docks & Engineering Co Ltd (The Wagon Mound)* [1961] AC 388. For a review of the extensive case law and principle of remoteness of damage in tort, the reader may wish to consult H McGregor (ed), *McGregor on Damages* (18th edn, 2009) ch 6.
[246] [1986] 1 WLR 1419, 1426–8.
[247] [1969] 1 WLR 809, CA, 813, 815.
[248] [2002] 2 AC 883, HL.
[249] [1975] 1 WLR 819, 824–5.
[250] [2005] EWCA 595, [2006] QB 125, CA, para 244.

confidence and held that, in principle, the two alternative remedies of (a) an account or (b) damages in lieu are available for a breach of confidence. The damages can be assessed on the footing of the value of the information or the notional cost of a licence; alternatively they can be based on the claimant's loss of profits caused by the misuse of the information: see *Dowson & Mason Ltd v Potter*.[251] As stated above,[252] damages for breach of confidence are awarded on a tortious basis, ie to award such sum as will put the claimant into the position he would have been in but for the tort or breach of confidence or alternatively on again-based footing.

11.120 In *Seager v Copydex Ltd (No 2)*,[253] the Court of Appeal held that damages should be assessed on the basis of the market value of the information which had been misused or a capitalized value of a royalty which could have been sought, ie this is an example of the gain-based principle being applied.

Douglas v Hello! Ltd (No 3)—*a problem or not?*

11.121 In the *Douglas* case, the judge's decision (upheld by the Court of Appeal) was that the actor Michael Douglas and his actress wife Catherine Zeta-Jones had commercially valuable confidential information (comparable to a trade secret) about their wedding plans, which they were entitled to exploit, and for breach of which they were entitled to damages. Amidst much publicity, they had given an exclusive licence to Ok! magazine to publish certain approved photos of their wedding. A rival magazine Hello! had published different photographs obtained unlawfully by a freelance photographer who had infiltrated the wedding. The Court of Appeal accepted that damages for breach of confidence could be assessed in a number of different ways. In this instance, the Douglases had chosen to claim both damages for their hurt feelings (compensatory damages) and damages calculated on the footing of a notional licence fee (ie gain-based damages).

11.122 The Court of Appeal refused to interfere with the judge's finding that, *if* that had been the correct basis for an award of damages on the facts, the appropriate amount for such a notional licence would have been assessed at £125,000. But the Court of Appeal (agreeing with Lindsay J) held that the Douglases were not entitled to recover damages quantified by reference to the value of a notional licence fee. The Court of Appeal upheld the judge's ruling that the claimants could recover modest damages for hurt feelings caused by the breach of confidence (ie damages for interference with their right to privacy), and further compensatory damages of a modest sum representing their expenses of mitigation, but they could not recover damages on the gain-based principle because 'there are obvious problems with assessing the Douglases' damages on a notional fee basis'.[254] The most important problem identified by the court was that they had previously sold the exclusive right to exploit their confidential information to the third claimant, a magazine called Ok! for a substantial amount.[255] Thus, the court considered that they would not have been in a position to have granted any licence (even a notional one), and to award them any such sum now would involve the claimants in

---

[251] [1986] 1 WLR 1419, CA.
[252] See para 11.117 above.
[253] [1969] 1 WLR 809, CA.
[254] [2005] EWCA 595, [2006] QB 125, CA, para 246. Note: part of the Court of Appeal's judgment is the subject of an appeal to the House of Lords as at the time of writing.
[255] ibid paras 246–9.

being unjustly enriched.[256] The fact that the publishers of Ok! expropriated to themselves a right which they did not have and thereby unjustly—and substantially—enriched themselves by their wrongdoing appears to have been given little, if any, weight by the court on this point. Instead the court reasoned that this was not a case for payment of any sort of 'royalty' or licence fee, because, inter alia, (i) the defendant Hello! had made a loss, (ii) the Douglases would never have contemplated granting a licence to Hello! since they had already granted an exclusive licence to OK! magazine for authorized photographs, and (iii) they were not in a position to grant a further licence to Hello!. The Court of Appeal thus appears to have given little, if any, regard to Lord Nicholls' statement of principle in *A-G v Blake*:[257]

> ... the common law, pragmatic as ever, has long recognized that there are many commonplace situations where a strict application of this principle [compensatory damages] would not do justice between the parties. Then compensation for the wrong is measured by a different yardstick ... the price a reasonable person would pay for the right of user ... the reality is that the injured person's rights were invaded but, in financial terms, he suffered no loss ...

The other reasons given by the Court of Appeal also do not seem to accord with another underlying principle of gain-based damages, namely that they are assessed (in such a case) as being the notional value of a *hypothetical licence*, ignoring altogether:　　**11.123**

(1) the unwillingness of the claimant to contemplate granting a licence; and
(2) the unwillingness of the defendant to pay the notional value as assessed by the court.[258]

In addition, unless it is to be distinguished simply on the particular facts, this decision of the　**11.124** Court of Appeal seems to conflict with the principles for assessing gain-based damages identified by (a) Mance LJ in the earlier Court of Appeal decision in *Experience Hendrix LLC v PPX Enterprises Inc*[259] and (b) the later Court of Appeal decision in *WWF—World Wide Fund for Nature v World Wrestling Federation Entertainment Inc*,[260] in which the judgment in the *Experience Hendrix* case was expressly approved by the court.[261] It is also to be noted that, although there was an appeal to the House of Lords as between Hello! and Ok! magazines, the Douglases themselves did not appeal and thus the Court of Appeal's decision in the *Douglas* case stands.

A problem for the practitioner seems to stem, perhaps, from the fact that, first, the *Experience*　**11.125** *Hendrix* case was not cited to the Court of Appeal in the *Douglas* case, whilst, secondly, the judgment of Peter Smith J in the *WWF* case contains no reference to the Court of Appeal's decision in the *Douglas* case, although it would clearly have been relevant to his own decision.[262] As a result it seems as though, inadvertently, the principles applying now in the law of contract for the assessment of gain-based damages have diverged substantially from the principles which apply to the assessment of such damages in cases of breach of confidence (ie where damages fall to be assessed in accordance with principles of tort).

---

[256] ibid para 247. Why was it so unjust? This was simply asserted by the Court of Appeal without any explanation. The underlying principle of gain-based damages is to deprive the *defendant* of his unlawful gains.
[257] [2001] 1 AC 268, 278, 279.
[258] [2005] EWCA 595, [2006] QB 125, CA, paras 243–9.
[259] [2003] EWCA Civ 323, [2003] EMLR 25, CA.
[260] [2007] EWCA Civ 286.
[261] ibid, paras 48–53.
[262] Note: the Court of Appeal's decision in the *Douglas Case* was cited by counsel during the argument before Peter Smith J.

11.126   We must await the outcome of future judgments in order to see if there is to be unity of approach in tort, contract, and breach of confidence. The Court of Appeal's decision in the *Douglas* case appears, without any considered explanation, to have departed from the principle that damages in this area fall to assessed *solely* on the basis of a hypothetical situation.

11.127   In conclusion with regard to the decision in the *Douglas* case, it does seem remarkable that a photographic magazine should have been able to steal a march on its rivals and make use of material, which the court has held was protected by confidentiality, by having to make a payment of very low compensatory damages totaling just £14,500, for hurt feelings and recoverable mitigation expenses when at the same time the Court of Appeal recognized that, *if* a notional licence fee had been the correct basis for the award of damages, the judge's assessment of the value of a notional commercial licence of £125,000 should not be interfered with. The discrepancy between £14,500 and £125,000 is so very large that one might reasonably have expected the court to hold that (a) a strictly compensatory basis for damages has produced such an inadequate response that it would leave people thinking that 'the defendant has unfairly got away with something' and (b) one is inexorably led along the same logical line as the House of Lords applied in *A-G v Blake*,[263] to the effect that a gain-based award of damages should have been preferred in order to 'do justice between the parties'.[264] Perhaps the explanation lies, on the one hand, in the Court of Appeal's wish to keep damages recovered in England for hurt feelings to a very modest level and, on the other hand, an inherent reluctance to accept that a modern-day celebrity may be entitled to treat his private life as a commodity which he is entitled to treat as capable of commercial exploitation. If that is correct, then the *Douglas* case ought to have relatively little impact in the commercial field of employment law.

Exemplary damages

11.128   As we have seen, exemplary damages may be available as a further remedy for breach of confidence.[265] In England and Wales, the courts have gone so far as to assume that the remedy is available but there is, as yet, no actual High Court decision to that effect. In New Zealand, however, the High Court has held that exemplary or punitive damages are an available remedy 'whether the action is founded in law or equity'.[266]

Articles 8 and 10 of the European Convention on Human Rights— the tension between them

11.129   There is one type of situation which falls into a subcategory, namely where the employee seeks to disclose to the media information which is confidential about his employer's lifestyle or business affairs. Where the employer is an individual (and not a corporation), as part of his rights to confidentiality, he may be entitled to rely upon his right to privacy guaranteed to him under Article 8 of the European Convention on Human Rights (ECHR).

---

[263] [2001] 1 AC 268, HL.

[264] ibid 278 *per* Lord Nicholls.

[265] See, in particular, *Douglas v Hello! Ltd (No 3)* at first instance: [2003] EWHC (Ch) 786, [2003] 3 All ER 996, para 273 *per* Lindsay J.

[266] *Cook v Evatt (No 2)* [1992] 1 NZLR 676, 705 *per* Fisher J.

In contrast, regardless of whether the employer is an individual or a corporation, the employee **11.130** may seek to rely upon his rights to freedom of expression guaranteed to him under Article 10 of the ECHR, which includes the right to impart information and ideas without interference by public authority. By section 6 of the Human Rights Act 1998 it is unlawful for a court to act in any way or make an order which is incompatible with a Convention right and inevitably, therefore, the court must now consider what remedy (if any) is available, having regard to the employee's rights under Article 10. The interplay and balance between these two Convention rights, and the way in which Article 10 in particular may operate, have been the subject of extensive consideration in a recent employment decision, *Archer v Williams*,[267] and in a number of important media decisions in the Court of Appeal, *A v B plc*[268] and *Douglas v Hello! Ltd (No 3)*,[269] and in the House of Lords in *Reynolds v Times Newspapers Ltd*[270] and *Campbell v Mirror Group Newspapers Ltd*.[271] In each of these cases the question of damages was considered. In the *Campbell* case the House of Lords restored the original order for damages made by the trial judge, Morland J.

For present purposes, it is important to note that these decisions establish two points. First, **11.131** in an appropriate case, an employer (who is an individual) may recover general damages for hurt feelings resulting from the breach of confidence. Secondly, in England and Wales such damages are to be awarded only on a modest scale. In the case of Ms Campbell (a well-known fashion model who sued over a newspaper article and a photograph suggesting that there was evidence, including confidential material, that she had lied about not having been a drug-taker) and Lady Archer (who sued her secretary for disclosing her employer's confidential information) they were each awarded only £2,500. In the *Douglas* case, the two claimants were each awarded £3,750 for their hurt feelings over a magazine publishing secretly-shot photographs of their wedding when they had given the exclusive rights to another well-known celebrity magazine.

H. Delivery up and destruction orders

These orders have been referred to in Chapter 10 above. We include them in this chapter as **11.132** well in order to emphasize their importance in the court's armoury of available remedies. Such orders are granted for the purpose of giving full effect to a prohibitory injunction in the case of confidential information.

It is part of the court's inherent jurisdiction that it has power to make orders for delivery up **11.133** or destruction of documents or copy documents which have been obtained or made in breach of a duty of confidentiality or any material containing or made from information which is confidential to the claimant.

The remedy is a discretionary one, but is commonly granted in cases where the court has **11.134** doubts as to whether the defendant will comply with the injunction. The court decides whether to order delivery up (which the claimant and his solicitors control) or destruction verified by affidavit (which the defendant and his solicitors control); if the documents are

---

[267] [2003] EWHC 1670 (QB).
[268] [2002] EWCA Civ 337, [2003] QB 195, CA.
[269] [2005] EWCA Civ 595, [2006] QB 125, CA.
[270] [2001] 2 AC 127, HL.
[271] [2004] UKHL 22, [2004] 2 AC 457, HL. See also *Imerman v Tchenguiz and others* [2010] EWCA Civ 908.

owned by the defendant (as in the case of copy documents which may have additional information on them of commercial value to the claimant), the defendant is normally allowed to destroy them—see, for example, *Peter Pan Manufacturing Corp v Corsets Silhouette Ltd*,[272] where the defendant was ordered to destroy brassières manufactured as a result of the misuse of confidential information.[273] But if the court considers that the defendant is not to be trusted, delivery up may be the more prudent course for the claimant employer to ask for and for the court to adopt, as in *Alperton Rubber Co v Manning*.[274]

11.135   The power is derived from the previous jurisdiction of the Court of Chancery and thus the process is confirmed upon affidavit: the defendant must swear an affidavit that he is delivering up all documents, etc or that he has destroyed all documents covered by the order—see, for example, *Prince Albert v Strange*[275] and, more recently, *Imerman v Tchenguiz*.[276] As Russell J explained in *Mergenthaler Linotype Co v Intertype Ltd*:[277] 'The order is made and the relief is given with a view to assisting the plaintiff and ensuring to the plaintiff the fruits of success in the action.'

11.136   In *Saltman Engineering Co Ltd v Campbell Engineering Co Ltd*,[278] the Court of Appeal took the view that it should order the immediate delivery up of engineering drawings created by the defendant in breach of confidence, but decided that it would not exercise its power to make a mandatory order requiring destruction of manufacturing tools made by using the drawings; instead it exercised its jurisdiction under Lord Cairns' Act[279] to make an order for an inquiry as to damages in lieu, on the grounds that an order for destruction would result in the destruction or sterilization of tools which might serve a socially useful purpose.[280] An important element in the court's decision in any particular case may be the extent to which the confidential information played a part in the drawing, schedule, equipment, or product which has been made using the confidential information. Where the defendant is considered to have been dishonest (having fully appreciated his obligation of confidentiality) and the information played a considerable role, the court can exercise its power to order the destruction of machinery used to produce infringing articles as well as the articles themselves.[281]

I. Tracing

11.137   We include the right to trace in this chapter, since there may be some occasions when it will prove to be a useful tool to the claimant. Tracing is, strictly speaking, not a remedy but a method of proof. It is a mechanism by which the court enables a claimant to trace property

---

[272] [1969] 1 WLR 96, CA.

[273] As a further alternative, the court can order delivery up to a third party for destruction so as to prevent the claimant from seeing any additional information on the documents which is confidential to the defendant.

[274] (1917) 86 LJ Ch 377.

[275] (1849) 2 De G & Sm 652 and on appeal (1849) 1 Mac & G 25.

[276] [2010] EWCA Civ 908, and at first instance [2009] EWHC 2024 (QB). The form of the Order in that case was for delivery up (verified by affidavit) of all papers containing the claimant's confidential information (including papers held by Counsel and solicitors in respect of which privileged notes and information could be removed or obliterated).

[277] [1927] 43 RPC 381, CA, 382. This was applied, eg, in *Industrial Furnaces Ltd v Reaves* [1970] RPC 605, 626.

[278] [1964] 3 All ER 413, CA.

[279] Chancery Amendment Act 1858, s 2 (now Senior Courts Act 1981, s 50).

[280] [1964] 3 All ER 413n, CA, 415.

[281] eg *Reid & Sigrist Ltd v Moss and Mechanism Ltd* [1932] 49 RPC 461.

in which he has a legal or equitable interest. For present purposes, however, we are not concerned with tracing property at common law, since the common law rule was that, as soon as the property in which the claimant had a legal interest became mixed up with other property (for example money paid into a bank account), the right to trace ceased.

Under equitable rules of tracing, however, equity acts upon the conscience of the owner **11.138** of a legal interest. He is required to carry out the purposes for which the property was vested in him (by an express or implied trust) or which the law imposes upon him by reason of his unconscionable conduct (a constructive trust). A claimant with an equitable title to property[282] (such as property held under a constructive trust[283] or property which is subject to a fiduciary relationship before it has been misapplied) is entitled to follow or trace his equitable title in such property into the hands of a fiduciary or a third party or into other property which has been acquired in substitution for the original property. In such cases, the claimant is entitled to recover the property which he has unjustly lost and equity allows him to trace his equitable ownership into that property, subject to defences open to those who may have innocently acquired and retained property subject to a trust, such as bona fide purchase for value of the legal interest[284] or change of position.[285] Since equity acts upon the conscience of the trustee, a person cannot be a trustee if he is ignorant of the facts alleged to affect his conscience. A helpful summary of the law is set out in the judgment of Lawrence Collins J in *Commerzbank Actiengesellschaft v IMB Morgan plc.*[286]

It is, thus, clear that, if the employer can establish that his relationship with his employee is **11.139** a fiduciary one in respect of the particular matter in issue, the employer may be able to establish a constructive trust which enables him not only to obtain an account of profits, but also to trace into the property acquired by the employee with those profits. In the context of misuse of confidential information (in respect of which the courts have held that such information is 'not property in any normal sense'),[287] equity acts upon the conscience of the defendant. It should, therefore, be arguable that a claimant is entitled against an employee to trace the property made from the misuse of such confidential information so long as the court is able to establish sufficient facts to justify the imposition of a constructive trust on the employee, and against any third party to whom he has communicated that information and who then in turn has made use of it in circumstances which would give rise to accessory liability of a third party under a constructive trust.[288]

---

[282] *Re Diplock* [1948] Ch 465, CA; and *Westdeutsche Landesbank Girozentrale v Islington LBC* [1996] AC 669, HL.
[283] ie 'an institutional constructive trust', being one which arises by operation of law by reason of the circumstances which give rise to it.
[284] ibid 705–6 *per* Lord Browne-Wilkinson.
[285] *Foskett v McKeown* [2001] 1 AC 102, HL; there appears, however, still to be a debate about this: see eg J McGhee (ed), *Snell's Equity* (31st edn, 2005) paras 28–36.
[286] [2004] EWHC 2771, [2005] 1 Lloyd's Rep 298. See also *Governor and Co of the Bank of Ireland v Pexxnet Ltd* [2010] EWHC 1872 (Comm).
[287] *Phipps v Boardman* [1967] 2 AC 46, HL, 127–8 *per* Lord Upjohn; *Douglas v Hello! Ltd* [2005] EWCA 595, [2006] QB 125, CA, paras 126–30.
[288] See *Agip (Africa) Ltd v Jackson* [1990] Ch 265, 289 *per* Millett J, *Westdeutsche Landesbank Girozentrale* (n 282 above), 715 *per* Lord Browne-Wilkinson; *United Pan-Europe Communications NV v Deutsche Bank AG* [2002] 2 BCLC 461, which was applied in *Button v Phelps* [2006] EWHC 56 (Ch). See also the discussion in Goff and Jones, G Jones (ed), *The Law of Restitution* (7th edn, 2006) para 34-024.

11.140   Thus far, however, that has not happened in England, although in *A-G v Guardian Newspapers Ltd (No 2)*,[289] Lord Goff suggested that there could be such a form of constructive trust. (In that case, the House of Lords held that the *Sunday Times* was liable to account for its profits from its editions which contained extracts from the *Spycatcher* book written by a former member of the UK security services.)

11.141   In Canada, the Supreme Court has held that there can be a constructive trust in the case of a breach of confidence (see *LAC Minerals Ltd v International Corona Resources Ltd*),[290] but ten years later the court stressed that the imposition of such a trust was 'discretionary'[291] and fact dependant (see *Cadbury Schweppes Inc v FBI Foods Ltd*).[292]

J. Declarations

11.142   One well-known form of remedy is a declaration whereby the court declares what are the parties' respective rights in any particular issue. As with other equitable remedies it is discretionary. It is provided in rule 40.20 of the CPR that a declaration may be granted, whether or not any other remedy is sought by the claimant.

11.143   As a matter of practice, the court is very reluctant to grant a declaration without a trial (for example by consent of the parties) and the Court of Appeal has stressed that, in such circumstances the power should only be exercised when, in Scarman LJ's words in *Wallersteiner v Moir*, to deny it would 'impose injustice on the claimant'.[293] Since a declaration is a judicial act, it therefore requires evidence.[294] This principle of practice continues to be applied, as, for example, in *Patten v Burke Publishing Co Ltd*[295] and *Financial Services Authority v Rourke*.[296]

K. Alternative remedies—making an election

11.144   A claimant cannot have a double recovery. Thus, for instance, he cannot in principle recover damages and also have an account of profits. That would only be possible if he brings into the accounting the amount of damages recovered, otherwise he would be obtaining double compensation.

11.145   If and to the extent that the remedies overlap or are inconsistent, the claimant is, therefore, required by the court to make an election. As Lord Nicholls succinctly explained in *Tang Man Sit v Capacious Investments Ltd*:

> Faced with alternative and inconsistent remedies a plaintiff must choose, or elect, between them. He cannot have both . . . He is required to choose when, but not before, judgment is

---

[289] See n 124 above, 288.

[290] (1989) 61 DLR (4th) 14 SC.

[291] But it should be noted that such a form of constructive trust would seem to be a 'remedial constructive trust', where the remedy is tailored by the court to suit the remedy which it thinks should be imposed. Thus far, English law has not been prepared to recognize remedial constructive trusts: *Westdeutsche Landesbank Girozentrale* (n 282 above), 716 *per* Lord Browne-Wilkinson.

[292] (1999) 167 DLR (4th) 577 SC.

[293] [1974] 1 WLR 991, CA, 1030 *per* Scarman LJ.

[294] ibid 1029 *per* Buckley LJ.

[295] [1991] 1 WLR 541.

[296] The Times, 12 November 2001.

given in his favour and the judge is asked to make orders against the defendant . . . he must make up his mind when judgment is being entered against the defendant. The Court's orders are intended to be obeyed. In the nature of things, therefore, the court should not make orders which would afford a plaintiff both of two alternative remedies.[297]

This election can be deferred until the time, usually final judgment,[298] when the claimant can **11.146** make a reasonably informed assessment of which alternative may suit him best: 'There is, however, no reason of principle or convenience why that stage should be deemed to be reached until the plaintiff applies for judgment.'[299] The principles governing an election, however, rest in fairness and a litigant is therefore not required to make an election until he is in a position to be able to make a fully informed decision.

In *Tang Man Sit v Capacious Investments Ltd*,[300] the claimant had obtained a judgment for an **11.147** account as a result of a breach of trust. Subsequently, the Privy Council (a) allowed him to sue for damages for the loss which the breach had caused on the condition that he would give credit for the amount recovered upon the taking of the account and (b) ordered further disclosure to be given. Thus, the court recognized that, in that situation, the remedies of an account and damages can be effectively cumulative and not inconsistent or alternative remedies. This was applied, for example, in *Westminster CC v Porter*.[301] In contrast, in *Halifax Building Society v Thomas*,[302] the Court of Appeal held that the claimant had exercised an election upon which it could not go back.[303] In *Daraydan Holdings Ltd v Solland International Ltd*,[304] Lawrence Collins J observed that the Court of Appeal's decision in the *Halifax* case was 'controversial'.

It follows that, where the claimant is uncertain as to which remedy will bring him a better **11.148** result, he may need to make plain to the court that he is *not* making an election when, for example, after the delivery of the court's judgment the claimant asks the court to make an order that an account be taken. He is entitled to reserve his position and should expressly so state. Normally, however, once the claimant *accepts payment* as a result of one or other form of order, that act 'confirms and reinforces an election made between alternative remedies at the time judgment was entered'.[305]

The classic example where a claimant will want to make an election (if he can) is where **11.149** he has suffered no loss as a result of the misuse of his confidential information. In such a case he will almost certainly wish to apply for an account of profits made by the wrongdoer and, indeed, in extreme cases the court may even go as far as holding that the entirety of the employee's new company is held by him on a constructive trust for the employer so that an account would yield significantly more than the employer may have lost: see *Normalec Ltd v Britton*.[306]

---

[297] [1996] AC 514, PC, 521.
[298] ibid 521–2 *per* Lord Nicholls: 'That is the normal rule.'
[299] *United Australia Ltd v Barclays Bank Ltd* [1941] AC 1, 19 *per* Viscount Simon LC.
[300] [1996] AC 514, PC.
[301] [2002] EWHC 1589, [2003] Ch 436, paras 2–3.
[302] [1995] 4 All ER 673, CA.
[303] Note that G Jones, the editor of Goff and Jones, *The Law of Restitution* (7th edn, 2006) para 36-17, argues strongly that the *Halifax* case was wrongly decided.
[304] [2004] EWHC (Ch) 662, para 89.
[305] [1996] AC 514, HL, 526 *per* Lord Nicholls.
[306] [1983] FSR 318.

11.150 It should, however, be noted that the claimant may not always be allowed by the court to make an election if the alternative remedy is a discretionary one, as in the case of an account—a point emphasized by Lord Nicholls in *A-G v Blake*.[307]

L. Remedies against a third party

Remedies against a third party for inducing a breach of the employment contract

General

11.151 The principles governing liability for this tort are considered in Chapter 2 above and have been recently reviewed by the House of Lords in *OBG Ltd v Allan*.[308] Apart from an injunction, the available remedy is a claim for damages. Primarily, in tort, the court seeks to place the claimant in the same position as if the wrong had not been committed. In other words, the law primarily focuses upon compensatory damages to award 'that sum of money which will put the party injured, or who has suffered, in the same position as he would have been in if he had not sustained the wrong for which he is now getting his compensation or reparation'.[309]

11.152 In contrast to most torts, it is not necessary to prove any special damage, because damages are at large and the law presumes that, in the ordinary course of business, the act of procuring a breach of contract must inflict damage upon the claimant, *per* Nevile J in *Goldsoll v Goldman*.[310] Thus, for the purpose of establishing liability, the law infers (without need to prove special damage) what is the kind of loss for which the claimant is entitled to compensation.[311]

11.153 The courts have repeatedly confirmed that pecuniary losses to a business are to be inferred, leaving it to the claimant to establish the quantum of that loss in the particular circumstances. Normally, the first and principal element of loss is a loss of profit resulting from the breach which has been induced, as in *Goldsoll v Goldman*. Loss of profit can take many forms. In addition, recovery includes additional costs which may be incurred as a result of confidential information being divulged, as was the case in *Bent's Brewery Co Ltd v Luke*.[312] Such additional costs include the expense of setting up a system for detecting and then countering the misuse of confidential information, as in *British Motor Trade Association v Salvadori*.[313] Whether or not the particular loss, for which the claimant makes his claim to special damages, comes within the test of what is foreseeable is 'fact sensitive'. A recent example of the approach of the court in economic torts can be seen in *Douglas v Hello! Ltd (No 3)* in the Court of Appeal[314] and on appeal sub nom *OBG Ltd v Allan*.[315]

---

[307] See n 11 above, 279. See also *Vercoe v Rutland Fund Management Ltd* [2010] EWHC 424 (Ch) and Goff and Jones, *The Law of Restitution* (7th edn, 2006) para 34-021.

[308] See n 207 above.

[309] *Livingstone v The Rawyards Coal Co* [1879–80] 5 App Cas 25, HL, 39 *per* Lord Blackburne.

[310] [1914] 2 Ch 603. See also the Court of Appeal's decision in *Exchange Telegraph Co Ltd v Gregory & Co* [1896] 1 QB 147.

[311] See Lord Hoffmann's speech in *Banque Bruxelles Lambert SA v Eagle Star Insurance Co Ltd* [1997] AC 191, 210–12.

[312] [1945] 2 All ER 570.

[313] [1940] Ch 556.

[314] [2005] EWCA Civ 595, [2006] QB 125, CA, paras 238–42.

[315] See n 207 above.

Certainly, pecuniary loss resulting from management time spent on undoing or mitigating the loss can be recovered, as can be seen from both the *British Motor Trade Association* case and also *Lonrho plc v Fayed*.[316]   **11.154**

Loss of reputation resulting from a breach of confidential information is generally not a head of damage which is recoverable for this economic tort. The claimant must sue separately for defamation, if he can—see the Court of Appeal's judgment in relation to the tort of conspiracy in *Lonrho plc v Fayed (No 5)*,[317] but see also *Mahmud v Bank of Credit and Commerce International SA*, in which the House of Lords held that, where a breach of contract gave rise to a financial loss which is recoverable on ordinary principles, then such damages did not cease to be recoverable because they could also be recovered in an action for defamation.[318]   **11.155**

Can the claimant obtain restitutionary or gain-based damages?

As explained above, damages have repeatedly been said to be at large in the tort of inducing a breach of contract. As an alternative to compensatory damages, therefore, there seems no reason in principle why a claimant should not be entitled to ask the court to assess those damages on the footing of the gain or profit made by the defendant or the saving of cost which he has achieved. This would necessarily be an exception to the general rule of compensatory damages in those circumstances where the claimant cannot prove a specific pecuniary loss or where his loss is completely disproportionate to the substantially larger profit made by the tort feasor. In such circumstances, even though the interest harmed is not a right in property as in the case of, say, conversion of goods, the law ought, one may think, to use the analogy of conversion in order to find 'a means to award [the claimant] a sensibly calculated amount of money' (to adopt the words of Lord Nicholls in his speech in the House of Lords *A-G v Blake*),[319] based on the gain made by the wrongdoer and so that he is deprived of an appropriate part of the benefit which he has obtained by his wrong.[320] But the recent decisions in both *Forsythe-Grant v Allen*[321] and *Devenish Nutrition Ltd v Sanofi-Aventis SA (France)*[322] indicate that it may be very difficult to satisfy the court that the circumstances justify such an approach to the assessment of damages unless the claim relates to a proprietary tort.   **11.156**

Exemplary damages

The court can award exemplary damages in the case of inducing a breach of contract. This was always so before *Rookes v Barnard*,[323] but the position has been confirmed in *Kuddus v Chief Constable of Leicestershire*,[324] in which the House of Lords held that this remedy is available in the case of all torts.   **11.157**

---

[316] [1993] 1 WLR 1489, CA.
[317] [1993] 1 WLR 1489, CA. See also *Foaminol Laboratories Ltd v British Artid Plastics Ltd* [1941] 2 All ER 393, 399–400
[318] [1998] AC 20, HL.
[319] See n 11 above, 279.
[320] But cf *Phillips v Humfray* (1883) 24 Ch D 439, CA.
[321] [2008] EWCA Civ 50.
[322] [2008] EWCA Civ 1086. See also *Stoke on Trent CC v W & J Wass Ltd* [1998] 1 WLR 1406, CA.
[323] [1964] AC 1129, HL.
[324] [2002] 2 AC 122, HL.

11.158   It is an essential element that the claimant can establish that the circumstances of his claim to exemplary damages come within one of the three categories of conduct enunciated by Lord Devlin in *Rookes v Barnard*. As indicated above, in the context of restrictive covenants the only relevant category is likely to be the second category consisting of the case where the defendant:

> . . . with a cynical disregard for a plaintiff's rights has calculated that the money to be made out of his wrongdoing will probably exceed the damages at risk, it is necessary for the law to show that it cannot be broken with impunity. The category is not confined to money making in the strict sense. It extends to cases in which the defendant is seeking to gain at the expense of the plaintiff some object—perhaps some property which he covets—which he either could not obtain at all or not obtain except at a price greater than he wants to put down.[325]

11.159   The second category is illustrative and is 'not intended to be limited to the kind of mathematical calculations to be found on a balance sheet'.[326] *McGregor on Damages*[327] suggests that exemplary damages are 'largely' an indirect means of preventing the unjust enrichment of a wrongdoer. Consistently with this view, one may expect that in an appropriate case a court will consider whether the time has now come to hold that, in place of (a) compensatory damages and (b) exemplary damages, the claimant is entitled to damages calculated on a more easily accepted and calculated basis of gain-based damages. Certainly, that was the view of Lord Scott in *Kuddus v Chief Constable of Leicestershire*.[328]

Remedies against a third party for assisting in a breach of fiduciary duty

11.160   Where a third party assists in a breach of fiduciary duty it makes no difference whether the third party actually received any property held on a constructive trust. Once liability for giving assistance has been established, the third party is liable jointly and severally with the person who owed the fiduciary duty to account as if he is a trustee himself.[329] As Lord Nicholls held, giving the judgment of the Privy Council in *Royal Brunei Airlines Sdn Bdh v Tan*,[330] 'a liability to make good resulting loss attaches to a person who dishonestly procures or assists in a breach of trust or fiduciary obligation'.

11.161   Although the nature of the remedy is compensatory as regards the liability of the third party,[331] the same remedies are available to the claimant consisting of (a) an account of profits, or alternatively (b) equitable damages.

Remedies against a third party for breach of confidence

General

11.162   Once liability has been established against the third party for a breach of confidential information, the third party is liable to the same remedies as may be granted against the employee who held that information. Thus, for example, in *A-G v Guardian Newspapers Ltd (No 2)*,[332]

---

[325] [1964] AC 1129, HL, 1226–7.
[326] *Broome v Cassell & Co Ltd* [1972] AC 1027, HL, 1079 *per* Lord Hailsham.
[327] H McGregor (ed), *McGregor on Damages* (18th edn, 2009) para 11–050.
[328] [2001] UKHL 29, [2002] 2 AC 122, HL, para 109.
[329] See eg *Agip (Africa) Ltd v Jackson* [1990] Ch 265.
[330] [1995] AC 378, PC, 386, 392.
[331] *Twinsetra Ltd v Yardley* [2002] UKHL 12, [2002] 2 AC 164, para 107 *per* Lord Millett.
[332] See n 124 above.

the *Sunday Times* was held liable to account for its profits made from the misuse of the UK government's confidential information. As an alternative, the third party can be held liable to pay equitable damages in lieu of the remedy of an account. An example of this is *Saltman Engineering Co Ltd v Campbell Engineering Co Ltd.*[333] In addition, the remedies of an order for delivery up or destruction are available to a claimant in an appropriate case.

One can, however, see that a problem may arise where (1) a third party misuses confidential information confided by C to D, who has in turn communicated it to the third party and (2) D then compensates C for his original misuse in accordance with the court's order to pay damages. If the judgment of the Court of Appeal in *Seager v Copydex Ltd (No 2)*[334] is correct, the payment by D to C represents payment for the right to use the information as if he now owned it. Lord Denning MR (with whom the two other Lords Justice agreed) held:[335] 'Once a lump sum is assessed and paid, the confidential information would belong to the defendants in the same way as if they had bought and paid for it by an agreement of sale.' **11.163**

If, however, the correct analysis is that such damages are paid as gain-based damages (as if for a notional licence granted to the defendant), then 'ownership' in the information does not pass to the defendant at all. All he obtains by payment of such damages is no more than a personal right to make use of the information, provided that the court has taken into account in its assessment a 'just sum' representing future misuse by him after the date of the court's assessment, as well as damages for the defendant's past misuse up to that date. **11.164**

Exemplary damages

It should also be noted that it may be possible to obtain exemplary damages—see paragraph 11.74 above and the judgment at first instance of Lindsay J in *Douglas v Hello! Ltd (No 3)*.[336] **11.165**

M. Interim payment

The remedy of interim payments is an important one with regard to the subject matter of this book. The jurisdiction and the procedure for obtaining such orders are contained in section 32 of the Senior Courts Act 1981[337] and rules 25.6 and 25.7 of the CPR. The court has no inherent power of its own, apart from statute, to make an interim award.[338] **11.166**

An order for an interim payment is available when: **11.167**

(1) the defendant has admitted liability to pay damages or some other sum of money to the claimant;[339] or

(2) the claimant has obtained a judgment against the defendant for damages or a sum of money to be assessed (for example the taking of an account or the making of an inquiry as to damages remains to be carried out);[340] or

---

[333] [1948] 65 RPC 203, CA.

[334] [1969] 1 WLR 809, CA.

[335] ibid 813.

[336] See n 146 above, para 273.

[337] In the County Court, the statutory provision is County Courts Act 1984, s 50.

[338] *Moore v Assignment Courier Ltd* [1977] 1 WLR 638, CA.

[339] CPR, r 25.7(1)(a).

[340] ibid, r 25.7(1)(b).

(3) the court is satisfied that, if the claim went to trial, the claimant would obtain judgment for a substantial amount of money (other than costs) against the defendant from whom he is seeking an order for an interim payment.[341]

It should be noted that (3) above is an exception to the general rule that a defendant is entitled to have a trial and final judgment before he is held liable to pay over any money to a claimant. The authorities show that the restrictions contained in CPR r 25.7 must be strictly adhered to: see *R (Teleos plc) v Commissioners of Customs and Excise*.[342]

11.168 A claimant may make more than one application, but in each case (a) it cannot be made before the expiry of the period for acknowledging service, and (b) the application must be supported by evidence and must be served fourteen days before the hearing date.[343] The CPR provide for service of evidence in answer by the defendant and in reply by the claimant.[344]

11.169 The court is required not to make an interim order for payment of more than a reasonable proportion of the likely amount of the final judgment. The actual proportion is entirely within the discretion of the assessing tribunal, be it a High Court Master or a judge. The court can order one lump sum payment or instalments.[345]

11.170 The making of an order is a matter of discretion for the court (see the use of the word 'may' in CPR r 25.7(1)). Although the wording of the previous RSC Order 29, rule 11 included the clearer words 'if it thinks fit', it is recognized that the court continues to have the same wide discretion. There is no requirement for the claimant to show that he would suffer any prejudice if he did not get such a payment: see *Schott Kem Ltd v Bentley*,[346] a case where an order for an interim payment was made when the claimant was seeking an account of profits for misuse of confidential information. The order can also be made subject to conditions.[347] It has been suggested by Rimer J in *Casio Computer Co Ltd v Sayo*[348] that the court could impose a sanction that, if payment is not made, the defendant shall be debarred from defending, but this may be thought to be too harsh a sanction having regard to (a) the court's overriding objective to act justly and fairly[349] and (b) the defendant's right under Article 6(1) of the ECHR to access to the court.

11.171 It should, however, be noted that in the context of the former Rules of the Supreme Court (RSC Order 29, rules 10 and 11) the court indicated that an application for an interim payment should not be made at all, if the court would be required to consider complicated factual issues or difficult points of law requiring many hours to resolve. This procedural restraint remains in place under the new Civil Procedure Rules: see *Bovis Lend Lease Ltd (formerly Bovis Construction) Ltd v Braehead Glasgow Ltd*.[350]

---

[341] ibid, r 25.7(1)(c).
[342] [2005] EWCA Civ 200; The Times, 9 March 2005, CA, and Civil Procedure (The White Book) Vol 2, paras 15-96–15-105.
[343] CPR, r 25.6(1), (2), and (3).
[344] ibid r 25.6(4) and (5).
[345] ibid r 25.6(6) and 25.7(4).
[346] [1991] QB 61.
[347] CPR, r 3.1(4). See *The White Book* (2006) para 3.1.4.
[348] 28 January 2000.
[349] CPR, rr 1.1(1), 1.2.
[350] (2000) 71 Con LR 208.

The fact that an interim payment has been made, whether by order of the court or **11.172** voluntarily, is a fact which must not be disclosed to the trial judge until all questions of liability and the amount of money to be awarded have been decided, unless the defendant agrees to such disclosure.[351]

In addition, the court has power to adjust, vary, or discharge an interim payment order at any **11.173** time prior to or at the trial of an action. The court can also order all or part of it to be repaid.[352] These powers are obviously most likely to be used when, following a trial, the claim fails or the claimant recovers an amount less than the interim payment which he has received. The court can also order one defendant to reimburse another defendant who has made an interim payment where there is a claim for contribution, indemnity, or other remedy as between those defendants and the court would have been able to make an order for an interim payment against the first one.[353] Where the amount of a final judgment is less than the interim payment made by the defendant, the CPR now provide that the court can award interest on the amount which has been overpaid.[354]

N. Checklist

General

Where an employee has breached his restrictive covenants or duty of good faith, what are the **11.174** main remedies (other than an injunction) that will be available to the employer?

- damages (see paras 11.08 to 11.65 above);
- an account of profits (but only in exceptional circumstances) (see paras 11.107 to 11.110 above);
- a declaration (see paras 11.142 to 11.143 above).

Where an employee has breached a fiduciary duty or a duty of confidentiality, what are the **11.175** main remedies (other than an injunction) that will be available to the employer?

- an account of profits (see paras 11.97 to 11.106 above);
- damages (see paras 11.113 to 11.118 above);
- orders for delivery up or destruction of documents and other property (see paras 11.132 to 11.136 above);
- a declaration (see paras 11.142 to 11.143 above).

Where a defendant employer has induced a breach of contract, what are the main remedies **11.176** (other than an injunction) that will be available to the claimant employer against the defendant employer?

- compensatory damages calculated on a tortious basis;
- possibly restitutionary or gain-based damages;
- exemplary damages.

(See paras 11.164 to 11.165 above.)

---

[351] CPR, r 25.9.
[352] CPR, r 25.8(1).
[353] ibid r 25.8(2)(c) and (3).
[354] ibid r 25.8(4). This power is a new one introduced by the CPR.

Compensatory damages

11.177 What is the most obvious remedy for breach of restrictive covenants and a contractual duty of confidentiality (other than an injunction)? A claim for compensatory damages, that is a claim for compensation for the net loss that the employer can establish he has suffered as a result of the employee's breach of contract, after taking into account mitigation (see para 11.08 above).

11.178 What hurdles must the claimant employer overcome in terms of establishing entitlement to damages?

- causation—that on the balance of probabilities the loss which he claims has been factually caused by the relevant misconduct of the employee (see paras 11.09 to 11.12 above);
- the standard of proof required of the claimant employer—although the balance of probabilities is the standard applied, the more serious the allegations, the higher the standard (see para 11.13 above);
- the distinction between past and future loss—for the past: straightforward balance of probabilities; for the future: 'sufficient certainty' or claims for loss of a chance (see paras 11.14 to 11.19 above);
- the loss must not be too remote—ie it must be damages for such part of the loss actually resulting from the breach as is, at the time of the making of the contract, reasonably foreseeable as liable to result from the breach (see paras 11.20 to 11.29 above);
- quantum of recoverable losses—ie the net loss of profit suffered by the claimant employer (see para 11.30 above);
- unreasonable acts by the claimant employer—which may break the chain of causation (see para 11.31 above);
- the claimant employer's duty to mitigate (see paras 11.32 to 11.35 above);
- the relevance of the date of assessment and its impact on claims—any facts up to the date of assessment can be taken into account to reduce or enlarge the damages claimed (see paras 11.36 to 11.37 above).

Restitutionary or gain-based damages

11.179 When will the claimant employer wish to argue for gain-based damages?

- where the claimant employer has not suffered any actual loss;
- where it is unable to establish that it has suffered a loss; or
- where the actual loss is disproportionately less than the profit made by the defendant(s).

(See paras 11.38 to 11.43, but also paras 11.56 to 11.65 above for the latest statement of the test.)

11.180 When will a claim for gain-based damages be available as a remedy for breach of contract?

- where the remedies of compensation, damages, specific performance, and injunction would be inadequate;
- where all the circumstances have been considered, including the subject matter of the contract, the purpose of the provision which has been breached, the circumstances of the breach, the consequences of the breach, and the circumstances in which the relief is being sought;

- where the claimant employer has a legitimate interest in preventing the defendant's profit-making activity and hence depriving him of profit.

(See paras 11.44 to 11.62 above.)

What factors will help a claimant employer to assess whether a claim for gain-based damages is appropriate?   **11.181**

- Have there been deliberate breaches of contract by the defendant for its own advantage or reward? There should be.
- Would the claimant employer have difficulty establishing financial loss caused by the breaches? It should do.
- Does the claimant employer have a legitimate interest in preventing the defendant's profit-making activity carried on in breach of its contractual obligations? It should do.

(See para 11.55 above.)

Exemplary or punitive damages

Will the claimant be able to claim exemplary or punitive damages as a result of a breach of contract? No (see para 11.70 above).   **11.182**

Will the claimant employer be able to claim exemplary or punitive damages as a result of a tort? Yes, if the defendant's conduct has been calculated by him to make a profit for himself which may well exceed the compensation payable to the claimant employer (see paras 11.71 to 11.72, 11.128, and 11.157 to 11.159 above).   **11.183**

Can exemplary damages be awarded in respect of a breach of confidence? There have been no instances where they have been, but at first instance a court has considered that it may be possible (see paras 11.81 and 11.165 above).   **11.184**

Liquidated damages

How will the parties distinguish between an enforceable liquidated damages clause or an unenforceable penalty clause?   **11.185**

- Is the amount a genuine pre-estimate of the loss which the innocent party will incur by reason of the breach? It should be.
- Is it an extravagant and unconscionable amount to be paid by reference to the greatest loss which could conceivably be proved? It should not be.
- Are some of the events which will trigger the payment trivial and some of them serious? If so, it is more likely to be a penalty.
- Is it difficult to estimate the damages? This is not necessarily a problem, as the amount may then be a true bargain between the parties.

(See paras 11.82 to 11.93 above).

Account of profits and equitable damages

When will the remedy of an account of profits usually be available?   **11.186**

- in relation to a breach of fiduciary duty (see paras 11.97 to 11.102 above);

- where there is a breach of the duty of confidence (see paras 11.103 to 11.106 above);
- in similar (exceptional) circumstances to those where gain-based damages would be awarded (see paras 11.107 to 11.110 above).

11.187 How will the court go about taking an account of profits?

- the court will determine what profits have been made as a result of the relevant breach of duty;
- the defendant is entitled to have taken into account costs and expenses and the court may conduct this apportionment.

(See paras 11.111 to 11.112 above.)

11.188 Can the court choose to award damages instead? Yes, because an account of profits is a discretionary remedy, but if it does award damages instead, they will usually be calculated as if the wrong committed is a tort, ie by proving:

- a loss of profits;
- which was of a kind which was foreseeable; and
- in respect of which the wrongful conduct of the defendant was a cause;

unless it is a breach of confidence, when the damages may be calculated on the footing of a notional licence fee.

(See paras 11.113 to 11.127 above.)

11.189 What should a claimant do if there is more than one remedy available to it?

- consider pleading all of them, but be aware that there is no double recovery;
- wait until judgment and assess which remedy to elect, although being careful not to elect too soon, if it is uncertain.

(See paras 11.02 and 11.144 to 11.150 above.)

11.190 When might a claimant employer be able to persuade the court to make an order for interim damages?

- where the defendant has admitted liability; or
- when there is a judgment on liability, but damages have not yet been awarded; or
- when the court is satisfied that money would be awarded as part of any remedy and it would not require a consideration of complicated factual issues or difficult points of law.

(See paras 11.166 to 11.173 above.)

12

PRACTICE AND PROCEDURE

Catherine Callaghan and Robert Weekes

A. The Civil Procedure Rules

Background

The relevant procedural rules for employment proceedings in the High Court, county court, **12.01** or the Civil Division of the Court of Appeal are the Civil Procedure Rules (CPR), found in *Civil Procedure* (otherwise known as *The White Book*).

Structure and content

The CPR are divided into separate parts, each of which contains rules for different aspects of **12.02** civil procedure. Many of the parts are supplemented by practice directions, which provide guidance that should be followed (but unlike rules do not have binding effect) and which should yield to rules in the CPR where there is a clear conflict between them. Practice directions are also of considerable importance because they often provide an aid to interpretation of the rules themselves.

12.03 In addition to rules and practice directions, regard should also be had to any relevant pre-action protocols and court guides. Although there are currently no pre-action protocols specifically relevant to employment, the Practice Direction on Pre-Action Conduct applies to employee competition proceedings in the High Court (but will not apply to applications where notifying the other potential party in advance would defeat the purpose of the application, such as freezing orders).[1] Those litigating in the Chancery Division or Queen's Bench Division of the High Court should pay careful attention to the requirements of the Chancery Guide or the Queen's Bench Guide, which are both contained in Volume 2 of *The White Book*. These court guides largely consist of narrative explanations of rules and practice directions but they also contain valuable additional guidance on practice approved by judges, particularly concerning applications or preparation for hearings.

12.04 It is also important to be alive to the way in which the CPR are updated. It is advisable to consult the Cumulative Supplements published from time to time and *Civil Procedure News* (provided as part of *The White Book* subscription service), which is a monthly newsletter summarizing key developments. Recent amendments to the CPR can also be found online on the *White Book on Westlaw UK* and digitally on the *Civil Procedure CD*.

The overriding objective

12.05 The fundamental purpose of the CPR and of the underlying system of procedure is to enable the court to deal with cases justly; this concept is known as the 'overriding objective'. Rule 1.1(2) of the CPR explains that 'dealing with a case justly' includes, so far as is practicable:

(a) ensuring that the parties are on an equal footing;

(b) saving expense;

(c) dealing with the case in ways which are proportionate:
    (i) to the amount of money involved,
    (ii) to the importance of the case,
    (iii) to the complexity of the issues, and
    (iv) to the financial position of each party;

(d) ensuring that it is dealt with expeditiously and fairly; and

(e) allotting to it an appropriate share of the court's resources, while taking into account the need to allot resources to other cases.

12.06 The court must seek to give effect to the overriding objective when it exercises any power given to it by the CPR, or when it interprets any rule.[2] In addition, the court must further the overriding objective by actively managing cases.[3] The parties are also under an obligation to help the court to further the overriding objective.[4]

The main relevant rules

12.07 The main rules in the CPR which will be of particular relevance to parties litigating an employee competition case will be Part 7 (the Claim Form and Particulars of Claim), Part 15 (the Defence and Reply), Part 16 (Statements of Case), Part 23 (applications for court

---

[1] Practice Direction—Pre-Action Conduct, C1-001 to C1-011.
[2] CPR, r 1.2.
[3] ibid r 1.4.
[4] ibid r 1.3.

orders), Part 25 (interim remedies), Part 31 (disclosure and inspection of documents), Part 32 (evidence), Part 35 (experts and assessors), Part 36 (offers to settle), Parts 43 to 48 (costs), and Part 52 (appeals). Parts 7, 15, and 16 are dealt with together below under the heading 'Statements of case'.

B. Statements of case

General

Proceedings are commenced with a claim form, accompanied or followed by particulars of claim. In response, the defendant files a defence, and a claimant may then file a reply to a defence. These documents are described generically as statements of case.[5]   **12.08**

The claim form

A party wishing to commence legal proceedings to prevent employee competition will do so by filing a claim form in accordance with Part 7 of the CPR. The form which must be used is practice form N1.[6] Proceedings are started when the court issues the claim form.[7] The claim form is issued on the date entered on form N1 by the court.[8] This is usually done by a date stamp on the claim form itself.   **12.09**

The content of the claim form

The claim form must be headed with the title of the proceedings, which will state the claim number (this should be left blank on the claim form for the court to fill in), the court or division in which they are proceeding (for example the Queen's Bench Division of the High Court), the full name of each party, and his or her status in the proceedings (ie claimant or defendant).[9] The claim form must include the claimant's address at which he resides or carries on business, and should if possible include the defendant's address.[10] The claim form must contain a concise statement of the nature of the claim, and specify the remedy which the claimant seeks.[11] For example, where a former employee has set up business in competition with the employer, removed confidential documents, and acted in breach of restrictive covenants in his contract of employment, the claim form might state something along the following lines: **12.10**

> This is a claim to restrain the breach of restrictive covenants contained in the defendant's contract of employment. The claimant seeks the following relief:
> (i)   injunctive relief to prevent further breaches;
> (ii)   delivery up of documents;
> (iii) damages; and/or
> (iv) an account of profits.

---

[5] A 'statement of case' is defined in CPR, r 2.3(1) as meaning a claim form, particulars of claim where these are not included in a claim form, defence, Pt 20 claim, or reply to defence, and includes any further information given in relation to them voluntarily or by court order under CPR, r 18.1.

[6] 7APD.3, para 3.1.

[7] CPR, r 7.2(1).

[8] ibid r 7.2(2).

[9] 7APD.4, para 4.1. See also 16PD.2, para 2.6, which sets out what is meant by a full name in respect of each kind of claimant.

[10] 16PD.2, paras 2.2–2.5.

[11] CPR, r 16.2(1)(a) and (b).

12.11 In addition, where the claimant makes a claim for money, which is likely to be the case where an employee has caused financial loss to the employer, the claim form must contain a 'statement of value'.[12] In other words, the claimant must state the amount of money which he is claiming and state whether he expects to recover (a) not more than £5,000; (b) more than £5,000 but not more than £25,000; (c) more than £25,000, or whether he cannot say how much he expects to recover.[13] The amount which a claimant expects to recover will affect where the claimant will bring proceedings: proceedings (whether for damages or a specified sum) may not be brought in the High Court unless the value of the claim exceeds £25,000.[14] If the claim form is to be issued in the High Court, then the claim form must state that the claimant expects to recover more than £25,000.[15] In addition, where the claimant's only claim is for a specified sum, the claim form must contain a statement of the interest accrued on that sum.[16]

Service of the claim form

12.12 The rules governing service of the claim form have changed substantially since 1 October 2008 and no longer require service to be achieved within four months after the date of issue but instead require a claimant to complete a required step in relation to a chosen method of service within four months after the date of issue. For post, DX or next day delivery, the required step is posting, leaving with, delivering to, or collection by the relevant service provider. For fax, the required step is completing the fax transmission and for email, it is sending the email.[17] For service out of the jurisdiction, the rule remains that the claim form must be served within six months of the date of issue.[18] However, the claimant may apply for an extension of time for serving the claim form. Generally, the claimant should make an application to extend time within the four- (or six-) month period specified by rule 7.5 of the CPR.[19] An application for an extension must be made in accordance with Part 23 of the CPR and supported by evidence, and may be made without notice.[20]

Pre-claim applications

12.13 It is possible, in certain circumstances, to apply to the court for interim relief before a claim form has been issued and any such application should be made in accordance with the provisions of Part 23 of the CPR.[21] However, where an application for interim relief is made before the issue of a claim form, either the applicant must undertake to the court to issue a claim form immediately or the court will give directions for the commencement of the claim.[22] Where possible, the claim form should be served with the order for the injunction (if any).[23]

---

[12] CPR, r 16.2(1)(c). See also 16PD.2, para 2.1.

[13] CPR, r 16.3(2). When calculating how much he expects to recover, the claimant must disregard interest, costs, any possible defence of contributory negligence, or any set-off or counterclaim which may be made against him: see CPR, r 16.3(6). The statement of value in the claim form does not limit the power of the court to give judgment for the amount which it finds the claimant is entitled to: see CPR, r 16.3(7).

[14] See 7APD.2, para 2.1 and also para 2.4.

[15] CPR, r 16.3(5)(a).

[16] ibid r 16.2(1)(cc).

[17] ibid r 7.5(1).

[18] ibid r 7.5(2).

[19] ibid r 7.6(1) and (2). If the claimant applies outside that initial period, the court may make an order extending time only in limited circumstances: see CPR, r 7.6(3).

[20] ibid r 7.6(4). See also 7 APD.8, paras 8.1 and 8.2.

[21] See CPR, r 23.2(4) and 23APD.5. See also CPR, r 25.2 and 25APD.4, paras 4.1–4.4.

[22] 25APD.4, para 4.4(1).

[23] 25APD.4, para 4.4(2).

Particulars of claim

The particulars of claim are intended to set out the claimant's case and in particular, to set out **12.14** the facts necessary to establish the claimant's cause(s) of action. Particulars of claim can be included on the claim form itself.[24] The claimant can prepare the particulars of claim as a separate document and serve them with the claim form[25] or alternatively can serve them on the defendant within fourteen days after service of the claim form.[26]

Service of the particulars of claim

Particulars of claim must be served on the defendant no later than the latest time for serving **12.15** a claim form.[27] If the claimant chooses to serve the particulars of claim separately from the claim form, then he must remember to file at court a copy of the particulars.[28] Whichever way the particulars of claim are served, the claimant must also remember to provide the defendant with the requisite court forms for defending the claim, admitting the claim, and acknowledging service.[29]

The content of the particulars of claim

The content of the particulars of claim will depend on the nature of the claimant's cause of **12.16** action. For example, if the claimant is alleging a breach of express or implied terms of a contract (for example breach of a restrictive covenant or breach of the implied duty of fidelity), then at a minimum the claimant must set out the facts establishing (a) the existence of the contract, (b) the nature and scope of particular terms relied on, (c) the lawfulness of any restrictive covenants, (d) the alleged breach(es), and (e) the loss suffered by the claimant as a result of the breach(es). The claimant may refer in the particulars of claim to any point of law on which the claim is based, and may attach to the particulars any documents which are crucial to the claim (such as the contract of employment).[30] In addition, the particulars of claim must satisfy the minimum requirements set down by rule 16.4 of the CPR. Hence, the particulars must include:

(1) if served separately from the claim form, the name of the court in which the claim is proceeding, the claim number, the title of the proceedings, and the claimant's address for service;[31]

(2) a concise statement of the facts on which the claimant relies;[32]

(3) a statement that the claimant is seeking interest (if applicable), details of the basis on which the right to claim interest arises, and details of the interest calculation that comply with rule 16.4(2) of the CPR;[33]

(4) a statement that the claimant is seeking aggravated, exemplary, or provisional damages (if applicable), and the grounds for claiming them;[34]

---

[24] CPR, r 7.4(1)(a).
[25] ibid r 7.4(1)(a).
[26] ibid r 7.4(1)(b).
[27] ibid rr 7.4(2) and 7.5. See also 7APD.6 and 16PD.3, para 3.2.
[28] CPR, r 7.4(3).
[29] ibid r 7.8(1).
[30] CPR, note 16.4.1. See also 16PD.7, para 7.3.
[31] CPR, r 16.4(1)(e) and 16PD.3, para 3.8.
[32] CPR, r 16.4(1)(a).
[33] ibid r 16.4(1)(b).
[34] ibid r 16.4(1)(c) and (d).

(5) where the claim is based on a written agreement, a copy of the contract or documents constituting the agreement should be attached to the particulars of claim;[35]

(6) where the claim is based on an oral agreement, the particulars should set out the contractual words used and state by whom, to whom, when, and where they were spoken;[36]

(7) where the claim is based on an agreement by conduct, the particulars must specify the conduct relied on and state by whom, when, and where the acts constituting the conduct were done;[37]

(8) where the claimant wishes to rely on the following matters in support of his claim, the particulars must set out any allegation of fraud, the fact of any illegality, details of any misrepresentation, details of all breaches of trust, notice or knowledge of a fact, details of unsoundness of mind or undue influence, details of wilful default, and any facts relating to mitigation of loss or damage.[38]

Defence

12.17   If a defendant wishes to defend a claim brought against him, then he must file a defence.[39] The defendant has two options: he can either file a defence within fourteen days after service of the particulars of claim, or he can file an acknowledgment of service within fourteen days after service of the particulars of claim and then file a defence twenty-eight days after service of the particulars of claim.[40] The latter option is preferable to most defendants because it ensures that a defendant who files an acknowledgment of service has twice as long to prepare a defence as one who does not. In addition, the parties can agree to extend the period for filing a defence by up to twenty-eight days, provided the defendant notifies the court in writing of any agreement.[41] Failure to file a defence within the specified time limits could result in the claimant obtaining judgment in default.[42]

The content of the defence

12.18   The defendant can use form N9B or N9D for the defence.[43] The defence should be a comprehensive response to the particulars of claim, while also setting out the defendant's version of events. In respect of each allegation in the particulars of claim, the defendant must make an admission, a denial, or a requirement for proof.[44] Denials must be explicit; the defendant must state his reasons for denying an allegation and if he intends to put forward a different version of events from that given by the claimant, then he must state his own version.[45] If the defendant fails to deal with an allegation, he will be taken to admit that allegation in certain circumstances.[46] Similarly, if the defendant disputes the value of the claim, he must state why he disputes it and, if he is able, give his own statement of the value of the claim.[47]

---

[35]   16PD.7, para 7.3.
[36]   16PD.7, para 7.4.
[37]   16PD.7, para 7.5.
[38]   16PD.8, para 8.2.
[39]   CPR, r 15.2.
[40]   ibid rr 15.4(1) and 10.3(1).
[41]   ibid r 15.5(1) and (2).
[42]   ibid r 15.3 and Part 12.
[43]   15PD.1, para 1.3.
[44]   CPR, r 16.5(1).
[45]   ibid r 16.5(2) and 16PD.10, para 10.2.
[46]   CPR, r 16.5(3) to (5) and 16PD.10, para 10.3.
[47]   CPR, r 16.5(6).

The defence must include an address for service, to the extent that this has not already been provided.[48] As with the particulars of claim, a defence can refer to any point of law on which it is based, and attach any essential documents.[49]

Where the defendant wishes to make a counterclaim against the claimant or another party, **12.19** this should be done in accordance with the requirements of Part 20 of the CPR, and the defence and counterclaim should normally be contained in the one document, with the counterclaim following on from the defence.[50]

Service of the defence

The defence must be served on every other party to the proceedings.[51] However, the CPR are **12.20** vague about who must serve a copy of the defence. In practice, the court will serve the defence if the defendant provides a copy to the court but not otherwise. Hence, defendants would be advised either to serve copies direct on the claimant and other parties and inform the court they have done so, or, on filing the defence, supply sufficient copies for the court to serve pursuant to rule 6.21(4) of the CPR.

Reply

A claimant can file a reply to a defence if he wishes. A reply would normally only be necessary **12.21** where the claimant wishes to allege facts in answer to the defence which were not included in the particulars of claim. A claimant must file any reply when he files his allocation question- naire and serve it on all other parties at the same time.[52] A claimant who does not file a reply will not be taken to admit the matters raised in the defence.[53] A claimant who files a reply but fails to deal with a matter raised in the defence will be taken to require the matter to be proved.[54] The reply should not contradict the claim; if the claimant wishes to depart from the case set out in the particulars of claim, he should amend the particulars rather than serve a reply.[55]

C. Applications for interim relief[56]

General

Applications for interim relief are governed by Parts 23 and 25 of the CPR. Rule 25.1(1) of **12.22** the CPR lists a number of interim remedies that a court can grant. The main types of interim relief that will be sought in employment proceedings are as follows:

(1) interim injunctions;[57]
(2) orders for the detention, custody, preservation, or inspection of relevant property;[58]

---

[48] ibid r 16.5(8) and 16PD.10, paras 10.4–10.6.
[49] 16PD.13, para 13.3.
[50] CPR, r 15.7, Pt 20, and 15PD.3, para 3.1.
[51] CPR, r 15.6.
[52] CPR, r 15.8.
[53] ibid r 16.7(1).
[54] ibid r 16.7(2).
[55] ibid note 16.7.3.
[56] See also Chapter 10 above.
[57] CPR, r 25.1(1)(a).
[58] ibid r 25.1(1)(c)(i) and (ii).

(3) delivery up orders;[59]

(4) freezing injunctions;[60]

(5) search orders;[61]

(6) orders for pre-action disclosure and inspection;[62]

(7) orders for non-party disclosure and inspection.[63]

Importantly, the fact that a particular kind of interim remedy is not listed in rule 25.1(1) does not affect any power that the court may have to grant that remedy.[64] Further, the court may grant an interim remedy whether or not there has been a claim for a final remedy of that kind.[65]

12.23 The High Court has jurisdiction to grant any of the interim remedies listed above. The county court may make any order (whether final or interlocutory, conditional or absolute) which could be made by the High Court if the proceedings were in the High Court,[66] but the county court does not generally have power to grant search orders or freezing injunctions.[67] However, the High Court has power to hear an application for an injunction made in the course of or in anticipation of proceedings in a county court in circumstances where a county court does not have that power.[68]

12.24 Interim remedies are generally applied for and obtained at the interlocutory stage between commencement of proceedings and final judgment. However, an application for an interim remedy may be made at any time, including before proceedings are started and after judgment has been given.[69] This rule is subject to any rule, practice direction, or other enactment which provides otherwise, and a court may grant an interim remedy before a claim has been made only if the matter is urgent or it is otherwise necessary to do so in the interests of justice.[70] In addition, a defendant can only apply for interim relief after he has filed either an acknowledgement of service or a defence.[71]

Notice of an application

Whether or not to make an application on notice

12.25 When making an application for interim relief, one of the first decisions to be made is whether or not to make the application on notice to the respondent.[72] There are three possibilities under the CPR:

(1) with notice (formerly known as an '*inter partes*' application);

(2) without notice (formerly '*ex parte*');

(3) informal notice (formerly '*ex parte* on notice').

---

[59] ibid r 25.1(1)(e).

[60] ibid r 25.1(1)(f).

[61] ibid r 25.1(1)(h).

[62] ibid r 25.1(1)(i).

[63] ibid r 25.1(1)(j).

[64] ibid r 25.1(3).

[65] ibid r 25.1(4).

[66] County Courts Act 1984, s 38.

[67] County Court Remedies Regulations 1991. For the exceptions to this rule, see ibid reg 3.

[68] High Court and County Courts Jurisdiction Order 1991, art 3.

[69] CPR, r 25.2(1).

[70] ibid r 25.2(2)(a) and (b).

[71] ibid r 25.2(2)(c).

[72] The 'respondent' is defined in CPR, r 23.1 as (a) the person against whom the order is sought, and (b) such other person as the court may direct.

Generally, applications should be made on notice to the respondent. However, there will be **12.26** situations where, in order for interim relief to have any practical value, applications will need to be made in secret, without notice to the respondent. Applications for search orders and freezing injunctions are invariably made without notice for this reason. As explained below, in most other cases, applications should be made on three clear days' notice in writing to the respondent, unless urgency requires that only informal notice is given. Informal notice (ie less than three days) may give the respondent enough time to attend the hearing and make representations but usually not enough time to prepare reply evidence.

Applications with notice

Generally, under rule 23.4(1) of the CPR, a copy of the application notice must be served on **12.27** each respondent. Rule 23.7(1) further provides that where notice is given, a copy of the application notice must be served as soon as practicable after it is filed at court and must in any event be served at least three clear days before the court is to deal with the application (except where another time limit is specified in the CPR or a practice direction).[73]

Paragraph 4.2 of Practice Direction 23A provides that where an application notice should be **12.28** served but there is not sufficient time to do so, informal notification of the application should be given unless the circumstances of the application require secrecy. This is the source of the power in the CPR to give 'informal notice'. For example, this may be appropriate where an employee is about to start work with a competitor of the employer in breach of a non-compete covenant, or without having given proper notice of resignation, and a garden leave period is sought to be enforced. In such cases, the employer may need to act very quickly such that there is not enough time to give three days' notice, but there is no good reason not to give any notice.

Applications without notice

There are a number of provisions of the CPR that address the circumstances in which an **12.29** application may be made without notice. Rule 23.4(2) provides that an application may be made without notice if this is permitted by a rule, practice direction, or court order.[74] Rule 25.3(1) is an example of such a permission: it provides that the court may grant an interim remedy on an application made without notice if it appears to the court that there are 'good reasons for not giving notice'. There is generally a good reason not to give notice where giving such notice would defeat the purpose of making the application, such as applications for search orders or freezing orders. Further guidance is found in paragraph 3 of Practice Direction 23A, which provides that an application may be made without notice to the respondent only:

(1) where there is exceptional urgency;[75]
(2) where the overriding objective is best furthered by doing so;
(3) by consent of all parties;
(4) with the permission of the court;

---

[73] See also 23APD.4, para 4.1.

[74] A further example is CPR, r 34.17(b), which permits an application for an order or evidence to be obtained for proceedings in other jurisdictions to be made without notice.

[75] The Queen's Bench Guide (January 2007) paras 7.12.9–7.12.12 (Vol 2, para 1B-52) and the Chancery Guide (October 2009) paras 5.41–5.45 (Vol 2, para 1A-44) provide guidance on the practice where applications have to be made in circumstances of exceptional urgency.

(5) where a date has been fixed for the hearing but the party wishing to make an application at that hearing does not have sufficient time to serve an application notice and so makes the application orally at the hearing;

(6) where a court order, rule or practice direction permits.

12.30   If a party makes an application without notice, the evidence in support of the application must state the reasons why notice has not been given.[76] Normally, it will be inappropriate to make an application without notice if there has been pre-application correspondence between the parties and/or there has been delay on the part of the party making the application.[77]

Duty of full and frank disclosure

12.31   An applicant on a without notice application has a number of obligations. The first and most important is the well-established duty to make full and frank disclosure to the court of all relevant matters. This principle dates back to the cases of *Castelli v Cook*[78] and *Rex v Kensington Income Tax Commissioners, ex p de Polignac (Princess)*.[79] The duty encompasses a duty to disclose all material matters of fact, law, and procedure, and is imposed on both the applicant party and his legal representatives.[80] The duty of disclosure applies not only to material information known to the applicant but also to any additional information which he would have known if he had made reasonable and proper inquiries, and therefore the applicant is obliged to investigate the facts prior to making the application.[81] The applicant is also obliged to draw to the court's attention matters which are or may be adverse to the application; it is not sufficient to rely on general statements or merely to exhibit numerous documents within which may be contained adverse points.[82]

12.32   The burden is even more onerous where a telephone application is made to a judge who has no papers before him.[83] It remains counsel's role to inform the court of salient points even where the court has formed a clear view on the papers before it.[84] It may even be necessary to disclose the fact or content of without prejudice communications if it is clear that without doing so the court may be misled.[85]

---

[76] CPR, r 25.3(3).

[77] See eg *Jain v Trent Strategic Health Authority* [2009] 1 AC 853, HL (concerning an application made without notice in circumstances where the applicant had been preparing the application for some time, and could therefore have given notice to the respondent).

[78] (1849) 7 Hare 89, 94.

[79] [1917] 1 KB 486, 509.

[80] *Memory Corp plc v Sidhu (No 2)* [2000] 1 WLR 1443, 1454–5 *per* Robert Walker LJ and 1459–60 *per* Mummery LJ. The material facts are those which it is material for the judge to know in dealing with the application; materiality is to be decided by the court, not by the applicant or his legal advisers: see *Brink's Mat Ltd v Elcombe* [1988] 1 WLR 1350, 1356 *per* Ralph Gibson LJ. See also 25PD3.3.

[81] *Brink's Mat* (n 80 above) 1356 *per* Ralph Gibson LJ and 1358 *per* Balcombe LJ. See also *Siporex Trade SA v Comdel Commodities Ltd* [1986] 2 Lloyd's Rep 428, 437 *per* Bingham J (as he then was).

[82] *Siporex Trade* (n 81 above) 437 *per* Bingham J. See also *Sectrack NV v Satamatics Ltd* [2007] EWHC 3003 (Comm), paras 90–6 where counsel failed to take the judge to material information buried in pages of exhibits.

[83] *R (Lawer) v Restormel BC* [2007] EWHC 2299 (Admin), [2008] HLR 20, para 69. In that case, Munby J discharged an injunction in part because applicant counsel failed to draw the judge's attention to the legal as well as factual significance of a solicitor's attendance note.

[84] See eg *Pattihis and Healy (trading as Healy Solicitors) v Jackson and Mishcon de Reya* [2002] EWHC 2480, a case in which counsel made no submissions at the hearing, the judge having stated at the outset that it was plainly a suitable application for an order.

[85] *Linsen International Ltd v Humpuss Sea Transport Pte Ltd* [2010] EWHC 303 (Comm), paras 51–5.

Moreover, in addition to the duty to make full and frank disclosure, the applicant must **12.33** present a without notice application fairly. In other words, it is not enough to disclose material facts; he must also present fairly the facts which he does disclose.[86] In *Marc Rich & Co Holding GmbH v Krasner*,[87] Carnwath J stated: 'Full disclosure must be linked with fair presentation. The judge must be able to have complete confidence in the thoroughness and objectivity of those presenting the case for the applicant. Once that confidence is undermined he is lost.'

The reason for the requirement of full and fair disclosure is obvious: the court is being asked **12.34** to grant relief, which will often be draconian and cause injustice to the respondent, in the absence of the respondent. The court is wholly reliant on the information provided by the applicant. Unsurprisingly, therefore, the consequences of a breach of the duty are extremely serious. Where a material non-disclosure or misrepresentation is established at the subsequent *inter partes* hearing, the court will generally discharge the injunction or order (and may further penalize the applicant in costs).[88] According to Balcombe LJ in *Brink's Mat Ltd v Elcombe*, the rule that a without notice injunction will be discharged if it was obtained without full or fair disclosure has a twofold purpose: first, it will deprive the wrongdoer of an advantage improperly obtained; and secondly, it serves as a deterrent to remind applicants of their duty of full and fair disclosure.[89] Further, it is not necessary to show that the party alleged to be in breach intended to breach the duty: failure to observe the duty is sufficient to discharge the order.[90]

However, in order to avoid injustice and to recognize the practical realities of applications **12.35** which are required to be made in some haste, the court retains a discretion, notwithstanding proof of material non-disclosure, to continue the injunction or grant a fresh order on terms or adopt some other proportionate mechanism for dealing with the non-disclosure such as reducing the scope of the injunction or ordering indemnity costs.[91] In determining whether to exercise the discretion in favour of the applicant, the court will take into account all relevant circumstances, including the gravity of the breach, the degree of culpability of the applicant and his legal advisers, whether or not a refusal to continue the order would be proportionate or just, and whether or not the order would have been granted even if full disclosure had been made. In *Brink's Mat v Elcombe*,[92] the Court of Appeal overturned a decision to discharge an injunction in circumstances where the material non-disclosure

---

[86] *Bank Mellat v Nikpour* [1985] FSR 87, 92 *per* Slade LJ; *The Gadget Shop Ltd v The Bug.Com Ltd* [2001] FSR 26; *The Arena Corp Ltd v Schroeder* [2003] EWHC 1089, para 117.

[87] 18 December 1998 (upheld on appeal in *Marc Rich & Co Holding GmbH v Krasner*, Court of Appeal, 15 January 1999).

[88] For examples of cases where the court refused to make a finding of material non-disclosure or misrepresentation, see *Pattihis and Healy (trading as Healy Solicitors) v Jackson and Mishcon de Reya* [2002] EWHC 2480, paras 37–56; *Guerrero v Monterrico Metals plc* [2009] EWHC 2475 (QB), paras 18–22. For examples of cases where the court discharged injunctions or orders as a result of material non-disclosure, see *Behbehani v Salem* [1989] 1 WLR 723, CA; *Dubai Bank Ltd v Galadari* [1990] 1 Lloyd's Rep 120, CA; *The Giovanna* [1999] 1 Lloyd's Rep 867; *National Landlords Association v Stimpson* [2008] EWHC 2340 (QB); *Complete Retreats Liquidating Trust v Logue* [2010] EWHC 1864 (Ch); *Charles Russell LLP v Rehman* [2010] EWHC 202 (Ch).

[89] [1988] 1 WLR 1350, 1358.

[90] *Jain and another v Trent Strategic Health Authority* [2008] QB 246, para 82 (upheld in [2009] 1 AC 853).

[91] *Brink's Mat* (n 80 above), 1359; *Alphasteel Ltd (in liquidation) v Shirkhani* [2009] EWHC 2153 (Ch); *Ian Franses (Liquidator of Arab News Network Ltd) v Al Assad* [2007] EWHC 2442 (Ch), [2007] BPIR 1233.

[92] [1988] 1 WLR 1350. For other examples of cases in which the court continued the injunction or order despite material non-disclosure, see *Dadourian Group International Inc v Simms* [2007] EWHC 1673 (Ch); *Sectrack NV v Satamatics Ltd* [2007] EWHC 3003 (Comm); *Amadeo Hotels Ltd Partnership v Zaman* [2007] EWHC 295 (Comm); *Venus Wine and Spirit Merchants plc v Kejriwal* [2007] EWHC 1642 (QB).

was innocent and the injunction would have been granted if the additional information had been before the judge hearing the without notice application. However, more recently, in the case of *The Arena Corp Ltd v Schroeder*,[93] Alan Boyle QC (sitting as a Deputy Judge of the High Court) discharged a freezing order obtained by HM Customs & Excise because of the serious nature and extent of the breaches even where there was prima facie evidence of fraud by the defendant and therefore a strong case for the continuation of a freezing order until trial.[94]

12.36   The rule providing for discharge of injunctions for material non-disclosure is therefore a potentially powerful weapon in the hands of defendants and their legal advisers. However, defendants should be careful not to allege material non-disclosure unless there are good grounds for doing so. As Slade LJ noted in *Brink's Mat Ltd v Elcombe*:

> In one or two other recent cases coming before this court, I have suspected signs of a growing tendency on the part of some litigants against whom ex parte injunctions have been granted, or of their legal advisers, to rush to the *Rex v Kensington Income Tax Commissioners* [1917] KB 486 principle as a *tabula in naufragio*, alleging material non-disclosure on sometimes rather slender grounds, as representing substantially the only hope of obtaining the discharge of injunctions in cases where there is little hope of doing so on the substantial merits of the case or on the balance of convenience.[95]

Duty to make note of hearing

12.37   Secondly, it is also the duty of counsel and solicitors, on a without notice application, to make in the course of the hearing a full note of the hearing, or if this is not possible, to prepare a full note as soon as possible afterwards, and to provide a copy of that note with all expedition to all affected parties.[96] This is essential so that the parties affected may know what occurred, the basis on which the order was made, and in order for the respondent to be in a position to make an informed application for discharge of any injunction.[97] It is not appropriate for counsel or solicitors to rely on the existence of a transcript as this will not always be available.[98] It is particularly important for counsel to make a written note of his recollection of the hearing in circumstances where counsel's conduct was subject to, or likely to be subject to, controversy.[99] The duty to provide the respondent with a full note of the hearing arises whether or not the respondent requests it.[100] It is also normal practice for the party obtaining interim relief without notice to give undertakings to reduce the allegations made before the judge into a witness statement (if they have not already done so) to be served as soon as practicable on the respondent.[101]

---

[93]   [2003] EWHC 1089.

[94]   See also *Alma Communications v Feedback Communications Ltd* [2004] All ER (D) 118, where Laddie J found a profound breach of the duty of full and frank disclosure and refused to continue the injunction obtained at the without notice hearing.

[95]   [1988] 1 WLR 1350, 1359.

[96]   *Interoute Telecommunications (UK) Ltd v Fashion Gossip Ltd* (23 September 1999, Lightman J). See also *Thane Investments Ltd v Tomlinson* [2002] EWHC 2972, paras 18–19 and CPR, note 25.3.10.

[97]   *Interoute Telecommunications* (n 96 above).

[98]   *Cinpres Gas Injection Ltd v Melea Ltd* [2005] EWHC 3180, paras 21–2.

[99]   *Memory Corp plc v Sidhu (No 2)* [2000] 1 WLR 1443, 1459 *per* Mummery LJ.

[100]   *Thane Investments Ltd v Tomlinson* [2002] EWHC 2972, para 19.

[101]   See also *G and G v Wikimedia Foundation Inc* [2009] EWHC 3148 (QB), [2010] EMLR 14, para 28.

In *Thane Investments Ltd v Tomlinson*,[102] Neuberger J did not consider that the failure to provide a note of the hearing justified discharge of the injunction in that case.[103] In contrast, in *Cinpres Gas Injection Ltd v Melea Ltd*,[104] Pumfrey J set aside an injunction partly because of the failure to make a record of what was said at the without notice hearing and provide it to the respondent as soon as practicable. Failure to make such a note may also lead to an award of indemnity costs.[105] **12.38**

Service of order, application notice, and evidence

Thirdly, where the court has disposed of a without notice application and has made an order, whether granting or dismissing the application, the applicant is under a duty (unless the court orders otherwise) to serve the order, a copy of the application notice, and any evidence in support on any party or person against whom the order was either sought or obtained.[106] This rule reflects the general principle that applications have to be decided on the basis of evidence known to both parties. It also has very important implications for the content of applications or, more particularly, evidence in support. Applicants will need to bear in mind that everything they put before the court must also eventually be put before the respondent, whether or not the application is successful. Therefore, in breach of confidence cases, the applicant will have to balance the need to set out sufficient evidence to establish that the information in question has the necessary quality of confidence against the desire not to disclose further business secrets to the respondent. **12.39**

A respondent who was not served with a copy of the application notice may apply to have the order set aside or varied.[107] An application to set aside or vary an order made without notice must be made within seven days of service of the order.[108] The court can extend the time limit pursuant to rule 3.1(2)(a) of the CPR particularly where the provisions of rule 23.9 have not been complied with.[109] **12.40**

Documents required for application

In order to make an application for interim relief, the applicant will need to lodge at court the following documents: **12.41**

(1) an application notice in form N244;
(2) a claim form or draft claim form;
(3) supporting evidence (either in the form of a witness statement or affidavit); and
(4) a draft order.

---

[102] [2002] EWHC 2972.

[103] This decision was overturned on appeal but for different reasons: see *Thane Investments Ltd v Tomlinson (No 1)* [2003] EWCA Civ 1272. See also *Pattihis and Healy (trading as Healy Solicitors) v Jackson and Mishcon de Reya* [2002] EWHC 2480, paras 57–8, where Nelson J was not satisfied that late delivery of the note of the hearing was a proper ground for discharge of the order in that case.

[104] [2005] EWHC 3180.

[105] *Interoute Telecommunications* (n 96 above).

[106] CPR, r 23.9(1) and (2).

[107] ibid r 23.10(1).

[108] ibid r 23.10(2).

[109] See *Sarayiah v Suren* [2004] EWHC 1981, paras 67–78.

Application notice

12.42 Generally, an applicant must file an application notice in order to make an application for interim relief.[110] The notice should generally be in Practice Form N244.[111] The application notice must state the order being sought and briefly explain why the applicant is seeking the order.[112] For example, if the employer seeks to prevent the former employee from working for a competitor in breach of his contract and the return of client files belonging to it, the application notice might state in Part A of Practice Form N244 that the claimant intends to apply for an order (a) for injunctive relief pending trial in the terms of the attached draft order and (b) that the defendant forthwith deliver up to the claimant the documents listed in the attached draft order because the claimant believes that the defendant intends to breach or has breached restrictive covenants contained in his contract of employment and the defendant has documents in his possession, power, or control that belong to the claimant. It is also a good idea to cite in the application notice the relevant provision(s) of the CPR that entitle the applicant to seek, and the court to grant, the particular order. In addition, the application notice must state whether a hearing is sought or whether it can be dealt with on the papers.[113] If the applicant wishes the application to be dealt with by a judge, rather than a Master or district judge, this should be stated in the application notice.[114]

12.43 Question 10 of the application notice requires the applicant to state whether he wishes to rely on a witness statement, statement of case, or evidence set out in that part of Form N 244 in support of the application. For evidence in support of an application, see paragraphs 12.46 to 12.50 below.

12.44 In cases of real urgency, the court may dispense with the need to file an application notice.[115] However, it is generally advisable for any application for interim relief to be made by filing an application notice. In the Court of Appeal case of *Thane Investments Ltd v Tomlinson (No 1)*,[116] Peter Gibson LJ criticized the omission of an application notice in an application for a freezing order that was made by the defendants immediately following handing down of judgment in which the claimant's claim for wrongful dismissal failed and the defendants succeeded in their counterclaim.

Claim form

12.45 An application for interim relief may be made before the issue of the claim form.[117] However, the court may grant interim relief before a claim has been made only if the matter is urgent or it is otherwise necessary to do so in the interests of justice.[118] In such cases, the applicant must undertake to the court to issue a claim form immediately or the court will give directions for the commencement of a claim.[119] Where possible, the claim form should be served with the order for the injunction.[120] It has become common practice to serve the claim form

---

[110] CPR, r 23.3(1).
[111] See ibid note 23.0.18 and 23APD.2, para 2.1.
[112] CPR, r 23.6.
[113] 23APD.2, para 2.1.
[114] 23APD.2, para 2.6.
[115] CPR, r 23.3(2).
[116] [2003] EWCA Civ 1272, paras 21–8.
[117] CPR, r 25.2(1).
[118] ibid r 25.2(2)(b).
[119] ibid r 25.2(3) and 25APD.4, para 4.4(1).
[120] 25APD.4, para 4.4(2).

without particulars of claim, and to serve the latter within fourteen days of service of the claim form in accordance with rule 7.4(1)(b) of the CPR. This practice is useful where solicitors have not been able to take full instructions on a client's case, or there has been insufficient time to draft the particulars of claim, when the claim form is issued.

Supporting evidence

An application for interim relief must be supported by evidence, unless the court orders **12.46** otherwise.[121] The general rule is that evidence at hearings other than the trial (which includes hearings of applications for interim remedies) is to be by witness statement (rather than by affidavit) unless the court, a practice direction, or any other enactment requires otherwise.[122] However, applications for search orders and freezing injunctions must be supported by affidavit evidence.[123] In applications for other interim injunctions, the applicant has the choice to rely on evidence set out in (a) a witness statement, (b) his statement of case, or (c) Box 10 of the application notice itself, provided that the application notice or statement of case is verified by a statement of truth.[124]

The evidence in support must set out the facts relied on for the claim being made against the **12.47** respondent, including all material facts of which the court should be made aware.[125] For example, in an application for an interim injunction to restrain the potential breach of restrictive covenants, the evidence should identify the contract and the particular terms relied on, set out the facts constituting breach, and provide evidence of loss or potential loss flowing from the breach. Further, in restrictive covenant cases, the evidence will need to establish the legitimate interest that the covenant is seeking to protect and set out the facts relevant to its reasonableness. In breach of confidence cases, the evidence will need to set out the facts relied on as showing that the information has the necessary quality of confidence, subject always to the need to maintain the confidentiality of the information.[126] For example, in *Lawrence David Ltd v Ashton*,[127] the claimants failed to obtain an injunction to prevent disclosure of confidential information because they failed in their evidence to identify with sufficient particularity any trade secrets or confidential information requiring protection. In applications for search orders, the affidavit must disclose very fully the reason the order is being sought, including the probability that relevant material would disappear if the order were not made.[128]

If the application was made without notice, the evidence in support of the application must **12.48** provide reasons why no notice was given.[129] The evidence should also set out the ability of the applicant to pay damages to the respondent under the cross-undertaking.

---

[121] CPR, r 25.3(2).

[122] ibid r 32.6(1).

[123] 25APD.3, para 3.1. See the discussion of *Thane Investments Ltd v Tomlinson* [2003] EWCA Civ 1272 below.

[124] CPR, r 23.6 and Part 22. See also 25APD.3, para 3.2 and CPR, r 32.6(2).

[125] 25APD.3, para 3.3.

[126] As to means of safeguarding the confidentiality of this information whilst referring to it in evidence, see *Warner-Lambert Co v Glaxo Laboratories Ltd* [1975] RPC 354, CA. See also *Porton Capital Technology Funds (A Body Corporate) v 3M UK Holdings Ltd* [2010] EWHC 114 (Comm), in which the court ordered the creation of a 'confidentiality club'.

[127] [1989] ICR 123, [1989] IRLR 22, CA.

[128] 25APD.7, para 7.3(2). See the requirements for search orders generally at 25APD.7.

[129] CPR, r 25.3(3) and 25APD.3, para 3.4.

12.49 The failure to comply with the procedural requirements relating to evidence may result in discharge of the order. In *Thane Investments Ltd v Tomlinson (No 1)*,[130] the judge at first instance dismissed the claimant's claim for wrongful dismissal as a director of the defendant companies and upheld the defendants' Part 20 counterclaim for misfeasance in his conduct as a director. Immediately after judgment was handed down, the defendants applied for a freezing order against the claimant and another former director who had given evidence for the claimant (and who was not present or represented at the hearing to hand down judgment). In support of the application, the defendants presented the court with a claim form, a draft order, and a witness statement from the solicitor having conduct of the proceedings. The witness statement relied on the exhibited judgment which had just been handed down as containing all the material facts needed for satisfaction of the conditions for the granting of a freezing order. Although the application had been made without notice to the non-party director, the witness statement did not set out why notice was not given. Although the freezing order was initially granted, the Court of Appeal discharged the freezing order because of the defendants' failure to comply with the procedural rules relating to evidence. In particular, Peter Gibson LJ criticized the use of a witness statement when the practice direction required the use of affidavit evidence to support an application for a freezing order; he also criticized the failure to indicate why notice had not been given and the reliance on the judgment as evidence when that judgment did not provide any evidence of a real risk of dissipation of assets.[131]

12.50 It should be remembered that if the case proceeds to trial, the witness can be cross-examined about any discrepancies between the evidence given in support of the application and his or her oral evidence at trial or any subsequent witness statement.

Draft order

12.51 A draft of the order sought should be filed with the application notice and be brought to the hearing of the application. If the case is proceeding in the Royal Courts of Justice and the order is unusually long or complex, it should also be supplied on disk for use by the court office in a format compatible with the court's word processing software.[132]

12.52 Any order for an injunction must contain a cross-undertaking by the applicant to pay damages sustained by the respondent (or any other party served with or notified of the order).[133] If the application is made without notice, an order for an injunction must contain an undertaking by the applicant to serve on the respondent the application notice, evidence in support, and any order made as soon as practicable.[134] Any order for an injunction sought without notice must also specify a return date for a further hearing at which the court will consider whether to continue the relief.[135] If the order is sought before filing an application notice or claim form, the order must also contain an undertaking to file and pay the appropriate fee on the same or next working day.[136]

---

[130] [2003] EWCA Civ 1272. Applied in *Renewable Power & Light plc v Renewable Power & Light Services Inc* [2008] EWHC 1058 (Ch).

[131] ibid paras 21–7.

[132] 23APD.12, para 12.1. See also 25APD.2, para 2.4.

[133] 25APD.5, para 5.1(1).

[134] 25APD.5, para 5.1(2).

[135] 25APD.5, para 5.1(3).

[136] 25APD.5, para 5.1(4) and (5).

A draft order for an injunction must set out clearly what the respondent must do or not do.[137] **12.53** In *Lawrence David Ltd v Ashton*,[138] Balcombe LJ stated: 'I have always understood it to be a cardinal rule that any injunction must be capable of being framed with sufficient precision so as to enable a person injuncted to know what it is he is to be prevented from doing.'[139] A court will be unwilling to grant an order for an interim injunction where it would be practically impossible for the respondent to understand whether he has complied with the requirements of the order. For example, in the case of *Berry Birch & Noble Financial Planning Ltd v Berwick*,[140] Cox J refused to make an order for an injunction to restrain alleged breaches of confidentiality clauses where the terms of the draft order sought to restrain the defendants from using or disclosing 'Confidential Information', which was defined as including the claimant's 'business methods, finances, ideas, strategies, concepts, methodologies, processes, formulae, source codes and software programs'. Cox J stated that: 'Since it is unclear whether, for example, a particular idea, concept or methodology is confidential, it would be practically impossible for the defendants to understand whether they have complied with those paragraphs of the order.'[141]

Where a freezing injunction or search order is sought, precedent forms are annexed to the **12.54** Practice Direction 25A—Interim Injunctions, and may be modified in any particular case.[142]

Where to make the application

The application must be made to the particular court where the claim was started or, if the **12.55** claim has been transferred to another court since it was started, to the court to which the claim has been transferred.[143] If the application is made before a claim has been started, it must be made to the court where it is likely that the claim to which the application relates will be started, unless there is good reason to make the application to a different court.[144] Any such reason should be set out in the body of the application notice or in a covering letter to the court.

In Queen's Bench Division proceedings in the Royal Courts of Justice, an application for a **12.56** hearing by a Master should be issued in the Masters' Support Unit, Room E16 and an application for a hearing by a judge should be issued in the Listing Office, Room WG8.[145]

D. Disclosure

Introduction

Disclosure and inspection are a vital part of the litigation process as they enable the parties to **12.57** evaluate the strength of their respective cases. The duty to disclose documents only arises

---

[137] See 25APD.5, para 5.3.
[138] [1989] ICR 123, [1989] IRLR 22.
[139] [1989] ICR 123, 132.
[140] [2005] EWHC 1803.
[141] ibid para 20.
[142] 25APD.10.
[143] CPR, r 23.2(1) and (2).
[144] ibid r 23.2(4) and 23APD.5.
[145] Queen's Bench Guide (January 2007) para 7.12.2 at Vol 2, 1B-52.

where the court orders it, although the parties can proceed with disclosure and inspection on a consensual basis. Disclosure may take place:

- before the commencement of proceedings (pre-action disclosure);
- between parties to the proceedings;
- against a non-party to the proceedings.

Pre-action disclosure

12.58 Pre-action disclosure is potentially one of the most useful weapons in the High Court employment litigation arsenal. It may be used by a prospective claimant to determine whether or not it has a cause of action at all, and whether or not to issue proceedings. In addition, it may be a much cheaper alternative to an application for a search order. It may therefore prove useful to an employer who believes that a (former) employee has removed confidential information belonging to it or has set up in competition with the employer.

12.59 Section 33(2) of the Senior Courts Act 1981 empowers the court to order pre-action disclosure. Section 33(2) provides that the power which it confers shall be exercisable 'in such circumstances as may be specified in the rules'. The relevant rule is rule 31.16 of the CPR. Under that rule, any application for pre-action disclosure should be made in accordance with Part 23, and must be supported by evidence (usually a witness statement).[146] Rule 31.16(3) provides:

> The court may make an order under this rule only where—
> (a) the respondent is likely to be a party to subsequent proceedings;
> (b) the applicant is also likely to be a party to those proceedings;
> (c) if proceedings had started, the respondent's duty by way of standard disclosure, set out in rule 31.6, would extend to the documents or classes of documents of which the applicant seeks disclosure; and
> (d) disclosure before proceedings have started is desirable in order to—
>   (i) dispose fairly of the anticipated proceedings;
>   (ii) assist the dispute to be resolved without proceedings; or
>   (iii) save costs.

12.60 This rule sets out four jurisdictional thresholds that an applicant has to satisfy in order to obtain pre-action disclosure. Even if the applicant does that, the court still has a discretion regarding whether or not to grant pre-action disclosure.[147] It is therefore much harder to obtain pre-action disclosure than disclosure during the course of the proceedings. The principal authority dealing with this rule is the Court of Appeal decision of *Black v Sumitomo Corp*.[148] Rix LJ explained in that case that there are two separate questions which a court must consider on an application: first, whether the jurisdictional thresholds have been met, and secondly, whether it is appropriate in all the circumstances for the court to exercise its discretion in favour of granting pre-action disclosure, which will not be in every case but only where there is some aspect of the case which takes it out of the ordinary run.[149]

---

[146] CPR, r 31.16(2).
[147] See *Black v Sumitomo Corp* [2002] 1 WLR 1562, para 37 *per* Rix LJ.
[148] ibid.
[149] ibid para 85. *Black v Sumitomo* was followed recently in *Kneale v Barclays Bank plc (t/a Barclaycard)* [2010] EWHC 1900 (Comm), paras 19–20; and *Red Spider Technology Ltd v Omega Completion Technology Ltd* [2010] FSR 6, para 9.

As to the first two elements in rule 31.16(3) of the CPR, there is no longer any statutory **12.61** requirement that a claim is likely to be made.[150] Rix LJ found that for the purposes of rule 31.16(3)(a) and (b), the respondent or applicant is 'likely to be a party to proceedings' where it is established that he *may well* be a party *if* subsequent proceedings are issued.[151] This is a fairly low threshold. It is notable that Rix LJ did not define this jurisdictional threshold by reference to any degree of arguability of the applicant's possible claim. However, the Court of Appeal in the subsequent decision of *Rose v Lynx Express Ltd & Bridgepoint Capital (Nominees) Ltd*,[152] in which *Black v Sumitomo* was not cited, held that the substantive claim pursued in the proceedings should be properly arguable and have a real prospect of success. The *Rose* test was followed and applied by David Steel J in *Pineway Ltd v London Mining Co Ltd*[153] but its correctness was doubted by Patten J in *BSW Ltd v Balltex Ltd*[154] and Flaux J in *Kneale v Barclays Bank (t/a Barclaycard)*.[155] Flaux J held that because rule 31.16(3)(a) and (b) require the applicant to show that proceedings may well ensure, the applicant has to show some sort of prima facie case which is more than a merely speculative 'punt'.[156]

As to the standard disclosure requirement in rule 31.16(3)(c), Rix LJ approved Waller LJ's **12.62** observations in *Bermuda International Securities v KPMG*[157] that the court must be clear what the issues in the litigation are likely to be, ie what case the claimant is likely to be making and what defence is likely to be run, so as to ensure that the documents being asked for are ones which will adversely affect the case of one side or the other, or support the case of one side or the other.[158] This means applicants for pre-action disclosure should be precise in setting out their intended case and should specify the documents or class of documents to be disclosed: the more diffuse the allegations and the wider the disclosure sought, the more sceptical the court is likely to be.[159] In *Hutchinson 3G UK Ltd v O2 (UK) Ltd*,[160] David Steel J held that all the documents within a class or category must be subject to standard disclosure, and the applicant must show that it is more probable than not that the documents are within the scope of standard disclosure in regard to the issues that are likely to arise. Documents which are simply relevant as part of the background or which might merely lead to a train of inquiry are not disclosable in an application for pre-action disclosure.[161]

---

[150] See Senior Courts Act 1981, s 33(2) originally enacted as Administration of Justice Act 1970, s 31, which used to read: 'On the application . . . of a person who appears to the High Court to be likely to be a party to subsequent proceedings in that court *in which a claim* in respect of personal injuries to a person or in respect of a person's death *is likely to be made*, the High Court shall . . .'.

[151] See *Black v Sumitomo Corp* [2002] 1 WLR 1562, paras 71–2 *per* Rix LJ.

[152] [2004] EWCA Civ 447, para 4.

[153] [2010] EWHC 1143 (Comm), paras 21–2.

[154] [2006] EWHC 822 (Ch), paras 19–21.

[155] [2010] EWHC 1900 (Comm), paras 29–37.

[156] ibid para 38.

[157] [2001] Lloyd's Rep PN 392, para 26.

[158] *Black v Sumitomo*, n 147 above, para 76.

[159] See *Briggs & Forrester Electrical Ltd v Governors of Southfield School for Girls* [2005] EWHC 1734, para 17, citing the decision of Morison J in *Snowstar Shipping v Graig Shipping plc* [2003] EWHC 1367. In *Aon Ltd v JLT Reinsurance Brokers Ltd* [2010] IRLR 600, a team move case, Mackay J discharged an order for early disclosure made against all five respondents on the basis that, although it was precise and detailed, it was excessively wide and onerous, amounted to an obligation to give standard disclosure of all relevant documents, and was not necessary to enable the applicant to plead its case.

[160] [2008] EWHC 55 (Comm), paras 38 and 44. Approved in the context of post-termination breach of restrictive covenants in *Hays Specialist Recruitment (Holdings) Ltd v Ions* [2008] IRLR 904, para 30.

[161] *Hutchinson*, para 40. See also *Pineway Ltd v London Mining Co Ltd* [2010] EWHC 1143 (Comm), para 49; and *Hays Specialist Recruitment (Holdings) Ltd v Ions* [2008] IRLR 904, para 30.

12.63 As to the question of the desirability of ordering pre-action disclosure, Rix LJ held in paragraphs 79 to 81 of *Black v Sumitomo*[162] that paragraph (3)(d) of rule 31.16 involves a two-stage process: first, a jurisdictional threshold whereby the court is only permitted to consider the granting of pre-action disclosure where there is a real prospect in principle of such an order being fair to the parties if litigation is commenced, or of assisting the parties to avoid litigation, or of saving costs in any event; secondly, if there is such a real prospect, then the court should go on to consider the question of discretion, which has to be considered on all the facts and not merely in principle but in detail. Important considerations will include the nature of the injury or loss complained of, the relevance of any pre-action protocol or inquiries, and the opportunity which the complainant has to make his case without pre-action disclosure. This approach has been followed in the employee competition context in *Hays Specialist Recruitment (Holdings) Ltd v Ions.*[163]

12.64 Finally, applicants for pre-action disclosure should note that under rule 48.1(2) of the CPR, the applicant will generally pay the costs of the application for pre-action disclosure, and the costs of complying with any order for disclosure. However, the court may make a different order, having regard to all the circumstances, including the extent to which it was reasonable for the person against whom the order was sought to oppose the application, and whether the parties have complied with any pre-action protocols.[164] In *SES Contracting Ltd v UK Coal plc*,[165] the Court of Appeal overturned an order that the respondent to an application for pre-action disclosure pay the applicant's costs, holding that rule 48.1(2) implicitly recognizes that it will not usually be unreasonable for the respondent to require the applicant to satisfy the court he ought to be granted the relief which he seeks.

Disclosure during proceedings

12.65 'Disclosure' simply means stating that a document exists or has existed.[166] Usually, the object of disclosure is to enable a party to inspect the documents disclosed. A party has a right to inspect a disclosed document except where the document is no longer in the disclosing party's control,[167] the disclosing party has a right or duty to withhold inspection,[168] or inspection would be disproportionate.[169] A 'document' is defined broadly in Part 31 to mean anything in which information of any description is recorded, and therefore covers email and other electronic communications, databases, documents stored on servers and back-up systems, and deleted electronic documents.[170]

Standard disclosure

12.66 Unless the court orders otherwise, an order to give disclosure is an order to give 'standard disclosure'.[171] Standard disclosure requires a party to disclose only (a) documents on which

---

[162] [2002] 1 WLR 1562.

[163] [2008] IRLR 904, David Richards J granting the application for pre-action disclosure in a case concerning breach of confidence and breach of post-termination restrictive covenants.

[164] CPR, r 48.1(3).

[165] [2007] EWCA Civ 791; [2007] 5 Costs LR 758.

[166] CPR, r 31.2.

[167] ibid r 31.3(1)(a). The meaning of control is set out in r 31.8.

[168] ibid r 31.3(1)(b). A party has a right or duty to withhold inspection, for example where the document is legally privileged, or where disclosure would expose the disclosing party to a criminal offence or penalty.

[169] CPR, r 31.3(1)(c) and (2).

[170] ibid r 31.4 and 31PD.2A, para 2A.1.

[171] CPR, r 31.5(1).

he relies, (b) documents which adversely affect his own or another party's case or which support another party's case, and (c) documents he is required to disclose by a relevant practice direction.[172] This means parties are not obliged to disclose documents as part of standard disclosure which are relevant to the issues in the proceedings but which do not obviously support or undermine either side's case. This reflects a deliberate intention by the drafters of the CPR to curtail the disclosure process and get away from the traditional approach based on 'telling the story' or 'leading to a train of inquiry', as exemplified by the decision in *Compagnie Financière et Commerciale du Pacifique v Peruvian Guano Co.*[173]

When giving standard disclosure, a party is required to make a reasonable search for documents **12.67** other than those on which he relies.[174] The factors relevant in deciding the reasonableness of a search include: (a) the number of documents involved, (b) the nature and complexity of the proceedings, (c) the ease and expense of retrieval, and (d) the significance of any document which is likely to be located in the search.[175]

Standard disclosure is by list in the relevant practice form (form N265).[176] The list must indi- **12.68** cate those documents in respect of which a right to withhold inspection is claimed, and those documents which are no longer in the party's control and what has happened to them.[177] The list must include a disclosure statement in the terms set out in rule 31.10(6) of the CPR.[178]

Solicitors are under a duty to take positive steps to ensure that their clients understand the **12.69** nature and scope of the duty of disclosure, the importance of not destroying documents that might have to be disclosed, and the duty to search for and produce documents for inspection if they are required to do so.[179] It is not enough for solicitors to instruct their clients to preserve documents; steps should be taken to ensure that the documents are preserved.[180]

Specific disclosure

If a party believes that the disclosure of documents given by a disclosing party is inadequate, **12.70** or he seeks disclosure of a particular document or class of documents that the disclosing party refuses to disclose, then he may make an application to the court pursuant to rule 31.12 of the CPR for an order for specific disclosure or inspection.[181]

The application should be made in accordance with Part 23 and must be supported by evidence **12.71** (usually a witness statement).[182]

Non-party disclosure

Non-party (or third party) disclosure is potentially useful in employee competition proceed- **12.72** ings where the claimant employer seeks documents relating to the employee's misconduct

---

[172] ibid r 31.6.
[173] (1882) 11 QBD 55.
[174] CPR, r 31.7(1).
[175] ibid r 31.7(2). See also 31PD.2, para 2.
[176] CPR, r 31.10 and 31PD.3, para 3.1.
[177] CPR, r 31.10(4).
[178] See also the form of disclosure statement set out in the Annex to Practice Direction 31—Disclosure and Inspection.
[179] See *Rockwell Machine Tool Co Ltd v EP Barrus (Concessionaires) Ltd* [1968] 1 WLR 693, 694 *per* Megarry J.
[180] *Infabrics Ltd v Jaytex Ltd* [1985] FSR 75; see also CPR note 31.10.6.
[181] CPR, r 31.12(1) and 31PD.5, para 5.1.
[182] 31PD.5, para 5.2.

that are held by the employee's new or prospective employer, or even (although less likely) the employer's own clients.

12.73 The power of the court to order non-party disclosure is very similar to its power to order pre-action disclosure. The court's power to order disclosure against a non-party is found in section 34(2) of the Senior Courts Act 1981. As with section 33(2) in relation to pre-action disclosure, section 34(2) provides that the power shall be exercisable 'in such circumstances as may be specified in the rules'. The specified rule in question is rule 31.17 of the CPR, which is similar in structure to rule 31.16. As with pre-action disclosure applications, an application for non-party disclosure should be made in accordance with Part 23 and must be supported by evidence.[183] Rule 31.17(3) provides:

> The court may make an order under this rule only where—
> (a) the documents of which disclosure is sought are likely to support the case of the applicant or adversely affect the case of one of the other parties to the proceedings; and
> (b) disclosure is necessary in order to dispose fairly of the claim or to save costs.

12.74 Rule 31.17(3) involves a three-stage analysis: first, the court must consider whether the threshold condition in paragraph (3)(a) is met, namely whether the documents sought are likely to support the case of the applicant or adversely affect the case of another party to the proceedings; secondly, if so, the court must consider whether the threshold condition in paragraph (3)(b) is met, namely whether disclosure is necessary to dispose fairly of the claim or to save costs; and thirdly, the court must exercise its discretion regarding whether or not to make the order.[184]

12.75 In order to satisfy the first threshold condition, it is not necessary to show that the documents sought *will* support the applicant's case or that they *will* adversely affect the case of another party; it is sufficient that they are 'likely' to do so. Chadwick LJ, giving the judgment of the Court of Appeal in *Three Rivers DC v Governor of the Bank of England (No 4)*,[185] held at paragraph 32 of the judgment that the degree of probability required is modest, so that the word 'likely' in this context (as with pre-action disclosure) means no more than 'may well'.

12.76 The second threshold condition imposes a test of necessity (which is a higher threshold than that of desirability of disclosure, which applies to pre-action disclosure). Third-party disclosure ought not to be ordered by the court if it is not necessary to do so. If, for example, there is another way to obtain the information, or making an order at the particular stage in the proceedings would increase rather than save costs, then the court will not order non-party disclosure.[186]

12.77 At the third stage of exercising the discretion, wider considerations such as the public interest may come into play. The court will only reach this stage if the two conditions in (a) and (b) of rule 31.17(3) are met (see para 12.73 above).[187]

---

[183] CPR, r 31.17(2).
[184] *Frankson v Home Office* [2003] 1 WLR 1952 (CA), paras 10–13 *per* Scott Baker LJ. More recently, see *Flood v Times Newspapers Ltd* [2009] EWHC 411 (QB), [2009] EMLR 18, paras 22–5.
[185] [2003] 1 WLR 210. Third-party disclosure was not considered on appeal to the House of Lords.
[186] *Frankson v Home Office* [2003] 1 WLR 1952, CA, para 12 *per* Scott Baker LJ.
[187] ibid para 13.

E. Evidence

Witness evidence

There is a distinction between the way in which witnesses give evidence at a trial and the **12.78** way in which they give evidence at any other hearing. In general, any facts which need to be proved by the evidence of witnesses must, at a trial, be given by oral evidence and any witness evidence to be given at any other hearing must be in writing, usually in the form of a witness statement.[188] There are exceptions to this rule: for example, affidavits must be used instead of witness statements in any application for a search order or freezing order.[189]

Witness statements

A witness statement is a written statement signed by a person which contains the evidence **12.79** that that person would be allowed to give orally.[190] This means that witness statements should be restricted to admissible evidence, and should therefore exclude opinion, argument, and discussion of legal issues. On the other hand, as a result of the Civil Evidence Act 1995, hearsay evidence is now generally admissible in civil proceedings and can therefore be included in a witness statement. The witness statement must indicate which parts of it are hearsay evidence by stating which of the statements in it are made from the witness's own knowledge and which are matters of information or belief, and explain the source for any matters of information or belief.[191]

Witness statements must comply with the requirements of the Practice Direction attached **12.80** to Part 32.[192] This requires witness statements to be in the witness's own words and expressed in the first person.[193] Witness statements should also state the full name and residential or business address of the witness, a description of the position he holds and the name of his firm or employer (if the statement is written in his professional capacity), his occupation, and the fact that he is a party to the proceedings or an employee of such a party (if relevant). Witness statements should follow the formatting requirements of paragraphs 17 and 19 of Practice Direction 32. They should also contain a statement of truth, normally placed at the end of a statement before the date and signature.[194]

As part of its case management, the court will give directions for the service of witness **12.81** statements.[195] The court will normally direct that witness statements be exchanged after disclosure and will generally impose a deadline for service. The court can direct that parties should exchange witness statements simultaneously or sequentially, although the more usual course is simultaneous exchange.[196]

---

[188] CPR, rr 32.2(1) and 32.6.
[189] 32PD.1, para 1.4(2). For the required form of an affidavit, see 32PD.2 to 32PD.16.
[190] CPR, r 32.4(1).
[191] 32PD.18, para 18.2.
[192] CPR, r 32.8.
[193] 32PD.18, para 18.1.
[194] 32PD.20.
[195] CPR, r 32.4(2).
[196] ibid r 32.4(3).

12.82   Where a party has served written evidence for a hearing other than the trial, any other party can apply to the court for permission to cross-examine the witness giving the evidence.[197] This is potentially a very useful weapon in the hands of a party to an application for a search order or freezing injunction (or other types of interim relief). For example, in *Den Norske Bank ASA v Antonatos*,[198] the claimant bank obtained a search order and freezing order against the defendant (who was the manager of the bank's Greek shipping finance business), which required the defendant, inter alia, to provide details of his assets. Having received the defendant's affidavit, in which the defendant purported to confirm that he had given full disclosure of all assets affected by the freezing injunction, the claimant bank applied for and obtained permission to cross-examine him on his disclosure of assets. In *Kensington International Ltd v Republic of Congo*,[199] Morison J granted an application to cross-examine a non-party on his affidavit sworn pursuant to a search order because he was involved in attempts by Congo dishonestly to evade paying its judgment creditor and he had useful information to give under cross-examination which would aid execution.

12.83   Failure to attend for cross-examination in breach of an order to do so can have serious consequences. If the court gives permission to cross-examine a witness on his written evidence, and the witness fails to attend, his evidence may not be used unless the court gives permission.[200] In *Phillips v Symes*,[201] Waller LJ noted the harshness of this rule, stating:

> Where someone has purported to comply with either undertakings or orders to make disclosure by affidavit, we doubt whether it is right to place the deponent in the position that, unless he is prepared to be cross examined on his affidavits, they count for nothing at all. On the other hand, without cross examination, the court is entitled to attach little weight to them: see *Comet Products UK Ltd v Hawkex Plastics Ltd* [1971] 2 QB 67, CA.

Oral evidence at trial

12.84   If a party has served a witness statement and wishes to rely on the evidence of the witness who gave that statement, generally it must call that witness to give oral evidence at the trial.[202] Where the witness is called to give evidence, his witness statement stands as his evidence in chief.[203] This reduces trial time so that once the witness is sworn in and has confirmed the truth of his witness statement, then unless there are any supplementary questions, the trial will move straight to cross-examination. This contrasts with the position in the employment tribunal where often the tribunal requires witnesses to read their statements aloud.

12.85   The party relying on the witness's evidence will need to seek the court's permission to ask any supplementary questions at trial (for example to amplify the witness statement or address matters which are raised in the opposing party's witness statements), and the court will only give permission if it considers that there is a good reason not to confine the evidence of the witness to the contents of his statement.[204]

---

[197]   ibid r 32.7(1).
[198]   [1999] QB 271, CA.
[199]   [2006] EWHC 1848 (Comm); [2006] 2 CLC 588.
[200]   CPR, r 32.7(2).
[201]   [2003] EWCA Civ 1769.
[202]   CPR, rr 32.2(1)(a) and 32.5(1).
[203]   ibid r 32.5(2).
[204]   ibid r 32.5(3) and (4).

The opposing party can cross-examine a witness on any matter raised in his witness **12.86** statement.[205] Indeed, a witness can be cross-examined on any issue relevant to the case, or on any issue going to the witness's credibility, although whether the court permits any particular question to be put to a witness will be entirely within the court's discretion.[206] The court has the power to limit cross-examination, for example by limiting the issues to be explored on cross-examination or by limiting the time to be spent on cross-examination of a particular witness. The decision of a judge in this regard will usually only be overturned on appeal if it was outside the range of decisions at which a judge can legitimately arrive, or plainly wrong.[207] Parties will need to take this into account when considering whether to call particular witnesses to give oral evidence at trial.

If a witness cannot be present at the trial location, the court may allow witnesses to give **12.87** evidence by video link or other means.[208] This will assist parties who wish to rely on the evidence of witnesses located outside the United Kingdom and who find it difficult to travel to the court hearing the trial. A non-resident claimant's application to give evidence by video link at the trial of his action would not be refused on public policy grounds simply because the reason for the application was to avoid the risk of arrest and extradition on an unrelated matter[209] or to avoid a potential liability to capital gains tax.[210]

Expert evidence

The court's power to control expert evidence

In certain circumstances, parties to employee competition proceedings may wish to adduce **12.88** expert evidence. For example, expert evidence may be relevant in relation to the confidential quality of a particular idea, process, or invention, or the effect on an employee of being kept out of the market for a specified period of time. Parties are entitled to use experts to advise them on any specialist or technical matter at any stage of a dispute or legal proceedings, if they so wish (and at their own cost), but they must have the court's permission to call an expert or rely on the evidence of an expert for the purpose of court proceedings.[211] In *Gurney Consulting Engineers (A Firm) v Gleeds Health & Safety Ltd*,[212] the Court held that it is not necessary to seek permission to rely on an expert's report which had been served on behalf of a party who had ceased to be involved in the proceedings; providing permission had already been given to rely on it, another party could use the report.

Parties will generally apply for permission to adduce expert evidence in the allocation **12.89** questionnaires, which require parties to state whether they will be seeking to adduce expert evidence and if so, the expert's name and field of expertise, and whether the case is suitable for a single joint expert.[213]

---

[205] ibid r 32.11.
[206] ibid r 32.1.
[207] See *Watson v Chief Constable of Cleveland Police* [2001] EWCA Civ 1547, paras 21–4 *per* Sir Murray Stuart-Smith; and *Three Rivers DC v Bank of England* [2005] EWCA Civ 889, para 42 *per* Rix LJ; cf *Hayes v Transco plc* [2003] EWCA Civ 1261.
[208] CPR, rr 32.3 and 32PD.33 (Video Conferencing Guidance, contained in Annex 3 to the Practice Direction).
[209] *Polanski v Conde Nast Publications Ltd* [2005] 1 WLR 637, HL.
[210] *McGlinn v Waltham Contractors Ltd* [2006] EWHC 2322 (TCC), [2006] BLR 489.
[211] CPR r 35.4(1). See also r 35.2, which defines what is meant by an 'expert' for the purpose of Part 35.
[212] [2006] EWHC 43 (TCC).
[213] CPR r 35.4(2). For the form of allocation questionnaires, see Court Form N150.

12.90 The court has the power to control the evidence in the case, including expert evidence. It will do this by restricting the use of expert evidence to that which is reasonably required.[214] The court will seek to give directions at an early stage in the case in respect of expert evidence: in multi-track cases, this will generally be at the case management conference, and in fast-track cases, this will be done in the directions. The court may direct that no expert evidence is to be adduced at all (or only in relation to a particular issue), or may limit the number of expert witnesses which each party may call. Where possible, the court will direct that expert evidence to be given on a particular issue is to be given by a single joint expert.[215] The court may also limit the amount of the expert's fees and the expenses that a party who wishes to rely on an expert may recover from the other party.[216] Generally, the parties are jointly and severally liable for the payment of a single joint expert's fees and expenses.[217]

The expert's duty

12.91 Irrespective of any obligation an expert owes to the party who instructs him and who pays his fees, the expert owes an overriding duty to the court to assist the court on matters within his expertise.[218] This means that expert evidence should be the independent product of the expert, uninfluenced by the pressures of litigation. An expert should assist the court by providing objective, unbiased opinion on matters within his expertise, and should not assume the role of an advocate or give an opinion on issues of law. An expert should consider all material facts, including those which might detract from his opinion. An expert should make it clear when a question or issue falls outside his expertise and when he is not able to reach a definite opinion, for example because he lacks sufficient information. If, after producing a report, the expert changes his view on any material matter, that change of view should be communicated to the parties without delay and, where appropriate, the court.[219] Where the expert has a conflict of interest, this will not necessarily disqualify him as an expert if his opinion is independent, but the court is likely to decline to act on his evidence or to give permission for his evidence to be adduced. A party who wishes to call an expert with a potential conflict of interest should disclose details of that conflict at as early a stage in the proceedings as possible.[220] Annexed to the Practice Direction supplementing Part 35 is a protocol for the instruction of experts to give evidence in civil claims, and experts are expected to have regard to the guidance contained in this protocol.[221]

12.92 Where a single joint expert is used, each instructing party may give their own instructions to the expert.[222] Any instructions sent to the expert must also be sent to the other instructing parties.[223] Where each party uses their own expert, the material instructions given by that

---

[214] CPR, r 35.1 and 35PD.1.
[215] CPR, r 35.7(1) and 35PD.1.
[216] CPR, rr 35.4(4) and 35.8(4).
[217] ibid r 35.8(5).
[218] ibid r 35.3.
[219] 35PD.2, paras 2.1–2.5. These paragraphs of the Practice Direction are based on the judgment of Cresswell J in *National Justice Compania Naviera SA v Prudential Assurance Co Ltd ('the Ikarian Reefer')* [1993] 2 Lloyd's Rep 68, paras 81–2.
[220] *Toth v Jarman* [2006] EWCA Civ 1028, [2006] Lloyd's Rep Med 397, paras 100–2.
[221] See 35PD.1 and Protocol annexed to Practice Direction.
[222] CPR, r 35.8(1).
[223] ibid r 35.8(2).

party to their expert are not privileged from disclosure, and the expert is required to recite the substance of the material instructions in his report.[224]

Generally, expert evidence must be given in the form of a written report.[225] That report **12.93** must comply with the requirements set out in the Practice Direction—Experts and Assessors.[226] For example, the expert's report should be addressed to the court and not to the party or parties from whom the expert received his instructions. The expert's report must give details of the expert's qualifications and any material on which the expert has relied in making his report. The expert's report must set out the substance of all material instructions, whether written or oral, on the basis of which the report was written. The expert's report must make clear which facts in the report are within his own knowledge, and give a summary of the conclusions reached. The expert must give reasons for his opinion and set out any qualifications on his opinion. At the end of the report, there must be a statement that the expert understands his duty to the court and has complied with that duty. It must also be verified by a statement of truth in the form set out at paragraph 3.3 of the Practice Direction.[227]

Parties are entitled to put written questions to an expert about his report, whether he is a **12.94** single joint expert or an expert instructed by another party.[228] These questions should be put within twenty-eight days of receipt of the report, and where put direct to the expert, should be copied to the other party or parties.[229] The expert's answers to those questions are treated as part of the expert's report.[230]

The court can direct the experts (if more than one) to have a discussion to try to identify the **12.95** expert issues and, where possible, reach agreed opinion on those issues.[231] The court may also direct that following the discussion, the experts prepare a statement for the court showing the issues on which they agree and those issues on which they disagree, with a summary of their reasons for disagreeing.[232] Under Part 35, there are circumstances (albeit rare) in which a party, dissatisfied with the amended opinion of his expert after the experts' discussion, can obtain permission to rely on additional expert evidence.[233]

The court can direct an expert to give oral evidence at a trial or hearing, particularly in multi- **12.96** track cases where there remain issues in dispute between experts even after written questions and discussions between experts. Where an expert witness is called to give oral evidence, his report stands as his evidence in chief, and he may be cross-examined by the other party on any matter contained in the report or relevant to his status as an expert. In fast-track cases, the general rule is that the court will not direct an expert to attend the hearing or trial unless it is necessary to do so in the interests of justice.[234]

---

[224] ibid r 35.10(3) and (4).
[225] ibid r 35.5.
[226] ibid r 35.10(1).
[227] 35PD.3, paras 3.1–3.3. See also CPR, r 35.10(2) and (3).
[228] ibid r 35.6(1).
[229] 35PD.6, paras 6.1 and 6.2.
[230] CPR, r 35.6(3).
[231] ibid r 35.12(1).
[232] CPR, r.35.12(3).
[233] *Stallwood v David* [2006] EWHC 2600 (QB), [2007] 1 All ER 206.
[234] CPR, r.35.5(2).

F. Trial

12.97 As Mummery LJ held in *Alliance Paper Group plc v Prestwich*, disputed claims for the enforcement of restrictive covenants in employment contracts are typically resolved by the court in one of three ways:

1. [On an application for interim injunction] . . . If the court takes the view that the covenant is invalid, there is no serious issue to be tried and no question arises on the granting of an injunction or on assessing damages. If, on the other hand, the court takes the view that there is a serious question to be tried on the validity of the covenant, the balance of convenience usually favours the grant of an interim injunction. The grant of an injunction at that early stage prevents the employee from inflicting any serious damage on the employer and may be determinative of the whole case.

2. By consent an application for interim injunction is treated as the trial of an action. If that procedure is followed, pleadings are usually dispensed with and a direction made for cross-examination on [witness statements] as to the disputed facts. By this procedure the court is able to make a quick decision before the employee has had any opportunity to inflict damage on the employer . . .

3. An order for a speedy trial.[235]

12.98 The second of these options is appropriate where extensive disclosure and witness evidence is not required. It may be useful where the principal issue is one of construction of the covenant in question.[236] However, even in such a case it will rarely be suitable. The substantial majority of claims to enforce restrictive covenants give rise to disputed issues of fact both in relation to the work conducted by the employee whilst employed by the claimant employer (for example for the purposes of a non-solicitation covenant, the nature of the employee's work, and his knowledge of and contact with customers) and the post-termination work conducted by him (following the same example, whether the employee has solicited those customers). The third option is considered at paragraph 12.99 below. Moreover, each of the options requires consideration of the means and consequences of settlement of such claims, which is considered at paragraphs 12.171 to 12.199 below.

Speedy trial

12.99 Claims for the enforcement of restrictive covenants are singularly appropriate for speedy trial.[237] For two reasons, an order granting or refusing an interim injunction may otherwise effectively dispose of the case. First, the duration of the covenants (if they are to be enforceable) will be limited. If a trial is not expedited, the covenants may have expired. In such a case, any claim for injunctive relief would fall away and the damage that the covenants are intended to prevent would either have already occurred (if no interim injunction were granted) or have been entirely prevented (if an interim injunction were granted) before the enforceability of the covenant were finally determined. Secondly, if interim relief were granted, its terms may preclude the defendant employee not only from competing with the claimant employer, but also effectively from undertaking any employment or offering any services within his field

---

[235] The Times, 11 December 1997, CA.
[236] See eg *Greer v Sketchley Ltd* [1979] FSR 197, CA, 199.
[237] eg *Dairy Crest v Pigott* [1989] ICR 92, CA, 98; *Lawrence David Ltd v Ashton* [1989] ICR 123, CA, 134.

of expertise.[238] The court requires particularly cogent justification to prevent an individual from earning his living as he chooses.[239] It is therefore imperative that the court swiftly resolves at trial whether the employee has been wrongly prevented from doing so by the granting of the interim injunction. As Mummery LJ summarized in the *Alliance Paper* case:

> Restrictive covenant cases are urgent. The duration of the covenant is often short. The effect of an injunction on an employee pending trial may be to deprive him of his livelihood and the public of the benefit of his skill and experience. The refusal of an injunction may inflict irreparable harm on the employer. The speedy trial option is therefore often adopted in such cases.[240]

An order for a speedy trial may resolve an application for an interim injunction for the enforcement of restrictive covenants. Where there is a serious issue to be tried and damages are not a sufficient remedy, it may be unnecessary to engage in a detailed interlocutory hearing to consider where the balance of convenience lies. If a speedy trial is possible, the best solution will be to obtain undertakings from the defendants or (in the absence of such undertakings being offered) to impose injunctive orders and then move on to a speedy trial. This is because a proper trial is infinitely better than an imperfect interlocutory process which—in the absence of a speedy trial—would effectively dispose of the case.[241] As the Court of Appeal held in *Lawrence David Ltd v Ashton*: **12.100**

> A defendant who has entered into a contractual restraint, which is sought to be enforced, should seriously consider, when the matter first comes before the court, offering an appropriate undertaking until the hearing of the action, provided that a speedy hearing of the action can then be fixed and the plaintiff is likely to be able to pay any damages on his cross-undertaking. It is only if a speedy trial should not be possible that it would then be necessary to have a contest on the interlocutory application. I do not believe that, in this comparatively limited type of case—limited in numbers, that is—the courts of first instance will not be able to arrange for a speedy hearing of the action, and thus avoid time being spent, usually unnecessarily, on contested interlocutory applications.[242]

A speedy trial may also be appropriate where an application for interim relief is, or probably would be, unsuccessful. Notably, in an action for breach of confidence where there was an intense factual dispute between the parties (which the court was necessarily unable to resolve at an interim hearing) and the balance of convenience held to be heavily against the granting of interlocutory relief, Laddie J held that the case 'cried out for a speedy trial rather than an interlocutory injunction'.[243] Moreover, where a claimant persists with an unmeritorious application for an interim injunction and refuses to consent to the respondent's offer of a speedy trial, the claimant may legitimately be penalized by the award of costs against him in any event.[244] **12.101**

The court has jurisdiction to make an order for speedy trial in the exercise of its general power to fix the trial date [245] and also has a general power to expedite any hearing that has already **12.102**

---

[238] As a matter of practicality, the defendant employee may be unwilling or unable to find alternative employment for the period in which he is bound by the interim injunction.

[239] *Dawnay, Day & Co v D'Alphen* [1999] ICR 1068, 1079 *per* Robert Walker J.

[240] See n 235 above.

[241] See *Financial Dynamics Holdings Ltd v Miles*, QBD, 11 February 2002 *per* HHJ Macduff QC (sitting as a Deputy Judge of the High Court).

[242] [1989] ICR 123, CA, 135.

[243] *CMI-Centres for Medical Innovation GMBH v Von Keudell* [1999] FSR 235, para 69.

[244] *Bushbury Land Rover Ltd v Bushbury Ltd* [1997] FSR 709, 712.

[245] CPR, r 29.2(2).

been fixed.[246] It behoves a litigant who wishes to have his or her trial on quickly and therefore to leapfrog other litigants, to make a clear case for expedition to the court.[247] In *Ifone Ltd v Davies*, Laddie J addressed the considerations for the court in determining whether to order a speedy trial:[248]

> The court will not order a speedy trial unless it is convinced, first of all, that there are pressing reasons justifying such a course, that is to say reasons which show that the claimant or defendant, or whichever party is applying for the speedy trial, need unusually speedy resolution of the dispute to avoid injustice. In deciding what to do, the court must also bear in mind the needs of other litigants. At the end of the day it is being asked to put one case ahead of all other cases in the list and to give it preferential timetabling treatment.

12.103   Thus unparticularized references to commercial uncertainty pending the resolution of the dispute will be insufficient to justify expedition. The court must be satisfied that such uncertainty should be irremediable or of an extent necessary and appropriate to justify other cases being leapfrogged. A significant period of time may be required to prepare for a speedy trial. It must then be considered whether the uncertainty would actually be made any worse if trial were ordered on a conventional timetable.[249] These will often be very real considerations in an application for speedy trial in a case involving a former employee's restrictive covenants. Both the claimant and the business for which the former employee (whether or not a defendant to the claim) is now working may be adversely affected by the uncertainty as to whether the covenants will be enforced.

12.104   The court will also be reluctant to make such an order where the party applying for it has delayed (without satisfactory explanation) in making its application.[250] Evidently, such delay suggests that the party does not require the urgent resolution of the matter which it now seeks by way of speedy trial. Moreover, the court is unlikely to make such an order where the issues in the case are significantly lacking in particularity.[251] In those circumstances it would be difficult for the parties or the court to set an appropriate timetable for trial or even to estimate the likely duration of such a trial. The court may require a 'litigation plan', meaning a definition of (and preferably agreement of the parties to) the issues in dispute, the scope of disclosure required on each side, and the extent to which any evidence would be required, if at all.[252]

12.105   At the time of fixing a speedy trial, the court is likely to make directions as to the timetable towards trial. In the appropriate case, this timetable may be highly accelerated.[253] A claimant who secures interim injunctions pending speedy trial must carry out its obligations to work diligently towards achieving that speedy trial.[254] If the claimant fails to do so, the court may discharge the interim injunction (or refuse to continue it) with an award of indemnity costs

---

[246]   ibid r 3.1(2)(b).

[247]   *Intervet (UK) Ltd v Merial* [2009] EWHC 1065 (Pat), para 8 *per* Mann J.

[248]   [2005] EWHC 1504 (Ch) para 10; see also *Daltel Europe Ltd v Makki* [2004] EWHC 1631 Ch, paras 11–13 *per* Lloyd J.

[249]   *Intervet* (n 247 above), paras 6–8 *per* Mann J.

[250]   ibid, *Ifone* (n 248 above) para 11.

[251]   ibid, para 12; *Parsons v Granada plc* [2002] EWHC 2398, 2.

[252]   *Parsons* (n 251 above), 2–3.

[253]   eg in *Crowson Fabrics Ltd v Rider* [2008] IRLR 288, paras 2–3, the speedy trial was directed to commence five days after the hearing of the interim injunction application. The defence, disclosure, and witness statements were filed two days before trial.

[254]   *EDO Technology Ltd v Campaign to Smash EDO* [2006] EWHC 598, [2006] All ER (D) 338, para 68.

against that claimant for some or all of the costs of the proceedings up until the order for discharge.[255] It is also likely that on such discharge, the claimant would be liable on the cross-undertaking in damages. The Court of Appeal has even indicated that, where a speedy trial had been ordered, a defendant would be entitled to an undertaking from the claimant that it would proceed to get the matter to trial with expedition.[256] However, the giving of such an undertaking is unlikely to be necessary, given the current practice of the court in setting out a detailed timetable to trial in its order for a speedy trial.

In order to facilitate the swift hearing of a case in the High Court which is held appropriate **12.106** for a speedy trial, the court may be prepared to order that the case be transferred from the Chancery Division to the Queen's Bench Division and vice versa.[257] Given the difficulty in scheduling a speedy trial (for the court and frequently for the availability of counsel who have been instructed for the purposes of any interim injunction application) and the cost (in terms of personnel of the parties and their legal fees), a speedy trial will typically be limited to resolving the issues of liability and the granting of final injunctive relief. It should be noted that, in order to determine that issue of liability, the court will often have to decide a substantial factual dispute as to whether the employee was constructively dismissed by the employer and hence whether the covenant is enforceable having regard to the principle in *General Billposting v Atkinson*.[258]

Guidelines for trial preparation

Extensive guidance as to preparation for trial is provided by both the Queen's Bench Guide **12.107** and (in somewhat greater detail) the Chancery Guide.[259] The following is a summary of the principal features.

To ensure that court time is used efficiently there must be adequate preparation of cases **12.108** prior to the hearing, including the preparation and exchange of skeleton arguments and bundles of documents, and dealing out of court with queries which need not concern the court. The parties should also use their best endeavours to agree before any hearing what are the issues or main issues.[260] This obligation must be keenly observed in the context of a speedy trial where urgency typically limits the court to consideration only of those matters directly relevant to the issues of liability and the granting of final injunctive relief.

Realistic estimates of the length of time a hearing will take should be given.[261] The parties **12.109** must inform the court immediately of any material change in a time estimate and keep each other informed of any such change.[262] This is particularly necessary in preparing for a speedy trial, where the trial estimate is likely to be fixed in advance of disclosure and the

---

[255] ibid paras 68, 69. Nevertheless the discharge of the injunction does not permit the defendant to partici-pate with impunity in the activities which were enjoined by it. If the defendant does resort to such activities, the court may exercise its powers to act on an interim basis afresh (ibid para 71).

[256] *Johnson v Bloy (Holdings) Ltd* [1987] IRLR 499, CA, para 27.

[257] *Hughes v London Borough of Southwark* [1988] IRLR 55, paras 49–56 (post-judgment discussion).

[258] [1909] AC 118. See paras 5.87–5.160 above.

[259] *White Book* (2010) Vol 2, Sections 1B and 1A respectively.

[260] Chancery Guide (October 2009) para 7.2; Queen's Bench Guide (January 2007) paras 7.11.5–7.11.6.

[261] Chancery Guide (October 2009) para 7.3.

[262] ibid para 7.7.

exchange of witness evidence. Where estimates prove inaccurate, a hearing may be adjourned to a later date with the party responsible for that adjournment likely to be ordered to pay the costs thrown away.[263] The consequence for a blameworthy claimant who has secured an interim injunction pending trial may also be the discharge of that injunction.

12.110 Trial bundles must be prepared in sufficient time for their contents to be agreed with the other parties (so far as possible), references to the bundles to be used in skeleton arguments, and bundles to be delivered to court at the required time.[264] Detailed guidance for the preparation of bundles is set out in Practice Direction 39, and Appendix 6 to the Chancery Guide. Failure to follow that guidance may be penalized in costs.

12.111 The general rule is that for the purpose of all hearings before a judge (which include the trial of a claim for the enforcement of restrictive covenants), skeleton arguments should be prepared. The exceptions to this general rule are where the application does not warrant one (for example because the hearing is likely to be short) or where the application is so urgent that the preparation of a skeleton is impracticable or where an application is ineffective and the order is agreed by all parties.[265] The timing for delivery of skeleton arguments is as follows:

(1) for trials, not less than two clear days before the trial is due to come on for hearing or if earlier, one clear day before the trial judge is due to begin pre-reading. The same rules applies to applications by order in the Chancery Division;[266]

(2) for applications to a judge without notice, with the papers the judge is asked to read on the application;[267]

(3) for all other applications to a judge in the Chancery Division—including interim applications—as soon as possible and not later than 10am on the day preceding the hearing;[268] and

(4) for substantial applications in the Queen's Bench Division, not later than one day before the hearing.[269]

In most cases before a judge, a list of persons involved in the facts of the case, a chronology, and a list of issues will also be required.[270] In practice, such documents have greater utility if their contents are agreed between the parties or the areas of disagreement at least identified. Unless the court gives any other direction, the parties shall arrange between themselves for the delivery, exchange, or sequential service of skeleton arguments, lists of persons, lists of issues, and chronologies.[271]

12.112 Photocopies of authorities should generally be provided at the same time as the filing of the skeleton argument with the court. Excessive citation of authority should be avoided.

---

[263] ibid para 7.8.
[264] ibid para 7.11.
[265] ibid para 7.18.
[266] Chancery Guide (October 2009) para 7.20; Queen's Bench Guide (January 2007) para 7.11.11(1).
[267] Chancery Guide (October 2009) para 7.21.
[268] Chancery Guide (October 2009) para 7.22.
[269] Queen's Bench Guide (January 2007) para 7.11.11(2).
[270] Chancery Guide (October 2009) para 7.28; Queen's Bench Guide (January 2007) para 7.11.10.
[271] Chancery Guide (October 2009) para 7.29.

It should be limited to the expression of legal principle rather than the application of such principle to particular facts.[272] This is a difficult stricture to apply to claims for the enforcement of restrictive covenants. The enforceability of a covenant may turn on its factual scope (such as whether it endures for two years or six months). Recent authority concerning analogous covenants may indicate the trend of judicial opinion as to that issue of fact. It would be an error of law to say that because similar covenants have been upheld in previous cases, the instant covenants should be upheld or to search for 'tariffs' from the decided cases.[273] However, both claimants and defendants will look to such cases for guidance.

In cases estimated to take more than ten days and in other cases where the circumstances warrant it, the court may direct that a pre-trial review (PTR) be held.[274] The purpose of a PTR is for the court to review the state of preparation of the case, deal with any outstanding procedural matters, and set directions as to how the case is to be tried.[275] Accordingly, at the PTR, the court will typically set a timetable for trial and a list of issues, both of which may be agreed substantially or entirely between the parties in advance of the PTR. A further purpose of a PTR is to provide another opportunity for settlement of the case, prior to the full trial costs being incurred.[276] A PTR will normally be heard by a judge, and if a trial judge has been nominated and if possible, it will be heard by that judge.[277] The review must be attended by the trial advocates[278] and perhaps by the parties themselves or representatives of the parties who are authorized to settle the case.[279]   **12.113**

A PTR may be less appropriate in advance of a speedy trial than an ordinary trial (although that will by no means always be the case). At the return date for any application for interim injunctive relief or at the hearing of a successful application for speedy trial, the court will usually set directions up until the commencement of the speedy trial.[280] As addressed above, the issues to be tried will usually be limited to those of liability and final injunctive relief. The parties will typically be ordered to seek to agree and then file a list of issues without a PTR being convened for that purpose.[281] Moreover, the court will usually order that both parties apply to the court if, and as soon as, it comes to the notice of either of them that the trial date may have to be vacated. Therefore, in the event that either or both parties fail to comply with the directions set for trial, the position may be reviewed by the court on an application to vacate the trial date, rather than at a PTR.   **12.114**

---

[272] Chancery Guide (October 2009) para 7.35; Practice Note (citation of cases: restrictions and rules) [2001] 1 WLR 1001.

[273] *Allan Janes LLP v Johal* [2006] ICR 92, para 27 *per* Bernard Livesey QC (sitting as a Deputy High Court Judge); *Dairy Crest Ltd v Piggott* [1989] ICR 92, CA, 95 *per* Balcombe LJ.

[274] Chancery Guide (October 2009) para 3.20, Queen's Bench Guide (January 2007) para 7.6.1.

[275] Chancery Guide (October 2009) para 3.25; Queen's Bench Guide (January 2007) para 7.6.6.

[276] *The White Book* (2010) para 29.7.1.

[277] Chancery Guide (October 2009) para 3.21; Queen's Bench Guide (January 2007) para 7.6.1.

[278] Chancery Guide (October 2009) para 3.22; Queen's Bench Guide (January 2007) para 7.6.3; CPR, r 29.3(2).

[279] As suggested in *The White Book* (2010) para 29.7.1.

[280] The court will typically order that the filing of pre-trial checklists can be dispensed with. It should be noted that pursuant to CPR, r 29.7, the court will consider whether to hold a PTR or cancel a PTR which has already been fixed, on receipt of the parties' pre-trial checklists.

[281] Moreover, the parties can generally be expected to seek to agree the timetable for trial between themselves (subject to the court's approval).

G. Judgments and orders

General rules

12.115   The following general rules are applicable to judgments and orders.[282]

12.116   Every judgment or order will be drawn up by the court unless it is a consent order or the court orders otherwise.[283] In claims for the enforcement of restrictive covenants, the relevant orders will almost always be drawn up by the parties. This is in particular because the injunctive relief sought should generally be in a detailed draft order filed by the claimant in advance of the hearing of his application or of trial.

12.117   According to the extent of relief ordered (if any) that draft will be modified by the claimant prior to it being approved and sealed by the court. Where an order which is not made by consent is drawn up by the parties, the recitals should be kept to a minimum and the body of the order confined to setting out the decision of the court and the directions required to give effect to it.[284]

12.118   A judgment or order takes effect from the day when it is given or made or such later date as the court may specify.[285]

12.119   A person who is not a party but who is directly affected by a judgment or order (such as an employer of an employee against whom covenants are enforced by interim injunction) may apply to have the judgment or order set aside or varied.[286]

12.120   A party must comply with a judgment or order for the payment of an amount of money (including costs) within fourteen days of that judgment or order unless otherwise specified by the judgment or order or rule of the CPR, or the court has stayed the proceedings or judgment.[287]

12.121   The court may at any time correct an accidental slip or omission in a judgment or order.[288]

Tomlin orders

12.122   A Tomlin order stays proceedings by consent, on agreed terms of settlement set out in a schedule to the order, with liberty to apply for the purpose of carrying those terms into effect.[289] In the event of the terms of the order or schedule being breached, the innocent party is entitled to apply for an order restoring the claim (under the liberty to apply provision) and an order for injunctive relief or specific performance to secure compliance with the terms of

---

[282]   It is arguable that under the CPR 'judgment' means the final decision of the court on a claim and 'order' is any other decision: *The White Book* (2010) para 40.1.1. The preferable view is that the distinction between the two terms is archaic and has no relevance under the current procedural regime: ibid paras 40.1.1, 40.2.3. Further terminological confusion is caused by the use of the term 'judgment' not only to mean the decision of a judge, but also his reasons for that decision.

[283]   See CPR, r 40.3(1).

[284]   Chancery Guide (October 2009) para 9.11.

[285]   CPR, r 40.7(1).

[286]   ibid r 40.9.

[287]   ibid r 40.11.

[288]   ibid r 40.12.

[289]   Practice Note [1927] WN 290.

the schedule. The terms of settlement may be in the form of a separate settlement agreement made between the parties to the proceedings.

A Tomlin order has particular utility for the purposes of recording and giving effect to the settlement of disputes as to the enforcement of restrictive covenants. The principal advantages of this order are as follows. First, swift relief—an application to enforce the terms of the order and schedule can be sought without the necessity to issue fresh proceedings. However, in order to give effect to the schedule to the Tomlin order, the court must still make fresh orders. This is because the schedule to the Tomlin order is not part of the order itself; rather, it is a record of the compromise reached between the parties.[290] **12.123**

Secondly, remedial flexibility—as stated above, provided a Tomlin order is in the appropriate form with a qualified stay and with liberty to apply, and provided the application is strictly to enforce the terms embodied in the order and the schedule, and does not depart from the agreed terms, an order giving effect to the terms may be obtained under the liberty to apply in the original action. This is notwithstanding the facts that the compromise itself goes beyond the ambit of the original dispute and that the provision sought to be enforced is something which could not have been enforced in the original action and which, indeed, is an obligation which did not then exist but arose for the first time under the compromise.[291] The court only approves and orders the terms of the consent order, not the terms of the schedule to that order.[292] (Accordingly the court will not give guidance as to whether or not the terms in the schedule are enforceable.) Moreover, where the terms of settlement contained in the schedule to the Tomlin order take the form of a settlement agreement which is independent of, and not conditional upon, the Tomlin order being made, it is separately enforceable pursuant to an action for breach of contract.[293] It is trite law that the forbearance of one or both parties to sue the other can constitute good consideration, notwithstanding any dispute between them as to the facts of the case or the law.[294] **12.124**

The price of such remedial flexibility—and the consequence of the schedule being a separately enforceable contract—is that the court does not have a general power to vary the schedule to a Tomlin order. So the court cannot vary the parties' agreement because there has been a material or unforeseen change in circumstances after the order was made which might undermine or invalidate the basis of the agreement, unless there would be a power to do so as a matter of the law of contract. There is no general power to vary a settlement agreement. Incorporating that agreement into a schedule to a Tomlin order does not change the position.[295] **12.125**

Thirdly, confidentiality—the schedule to the Tomlin order is typically neither read nor discussed by the court. A non-party to the proceedings would be entitled to make an application to the court for disclosure of the order (including the schedule) from the court file.[296] **12.126**

---

[290] *Horizon Technologies International Ltd v Lucky Wealth Consultants Ltd* [1992] 1 WLR 24, PC, 30.

[291] *EF Phillips & Sons Ltd v Clarke* [1970] Ch 322, 325 *per* Goff J.

[292] *Noel v Becker* [1971] 1 WLR 355, CA, 356–7; *Community Care North East (a partnership) v Durham CC* [2010] EWHC 959 (QB), paras 25, 28 *per* Ramsey J.

[293] eg *Thakrar v Ciro Citterio Menswear plc (in administration)* [2002] EWHC 1975 *per* Morritt V-C; *Horizon Technologies* (n 290 above).

[294] *Chitty on Contracts* (30th edn, 2008) paras 3-051, 3-054.

[295] *Community Care North East* (n 292 above), paras 34, 35.

[296] CPR, r5.4C(1)(b). For an order that confidential settlement agreements contained in schedules to Tomlin orders should be disclosed to a party (a co-defendant) see: *L'Oreal SA v eBay International AG* [2008] FSR 37.

The court would then exercise its discretion as to whether to grant inspection taking into account all the circumstances of the case.[297] It is likely that any such application would be refused. The public policy in facilitating the settlement of disputes arguably includes the ability to settle disputes on confidential terms by way of a Tomlin order. The schedule to the Tomlin order need not have been approved by the court and therefore arguably ought not even to have been read by the court. However, confidentiality can be secured either by the settlement agreement being annexed to the order as a schedule and provision made in the order to the effect that a copy of the schedule 'not be obtained' by any party other than the parties or their advisers.[298] Alternatively and most conveniently, the settlement agreement might not be annexed to the order but simply identified in the recital to the order (for example referring to confidential terms of settlement being made in a letter of a certain date).

12.127 A subsidiary advantage of the Tomlin order is that a party might make an application to lift the stay ordered, for the purposes of continuing to litigate their claim against the party in breach. This advantage is largely illusory. An application to reinstate the claim would be unlikely to succeed, unless the innocent party were able to establish that their compromise of the proceedings was vitiated by mistake or fraud.[299] This is because the bargain between the parties, as embodied in the Tomlin order, is precisely that action would not be resorted to after making the order, save for the purpose of enforcing its terms.[300] As Foskett summarizes (with references to most cited authorities omitted):

> The importance of the words used in the usual form of *Tomlin* order is that a *conditional* stay of the proceedings is provided for, the action remaining alive for the purposes of enforcement . . . An operative stay prevents the action from moving forward any further, or resuming 'its active life', without an order of the court, such an order not being granted lightly and only in a 'proper case'. The Court of Appeal has drawn attention to the 'great difficulties' that would be faced by a party seeking the removal of a stay to an action 'stayed by consent following a compromise'.[301] Consistent with the analysis of the effect of a *Tomlin* order in *Hollingsworth v Humphrey*,[302] it is submitted that the 'great difficulties' would lie in suggesting that the compromise was itself in some way conditional and not conclusive of the action and/or that the stay could be removed for the purpose of proceeding with the original claim.[303]

However, a continuing attraction of Tomlin orders is apparently that parties are resistant to the reality of, or simply ill-informed as to, precisely those difficulties. A party commonly agrees to such orders on the basis that the (largely illusory) opportunity to revive the claim is a significant deterrent to the other from breaching the terms of the order. In the unlikely event that the compromise of the proceedings were rescinded, it would be rescinded in full. A misrepresentee cannot claim a remedy of partial rescission.[304]

---

[297] *Dian AO v Davis Frankel & Mead* [2004] EWHC 2662 (Comm), [2005] 1 WLR 2951, para 57 *per* Moore-Bick J (concerning affidavits and witness statements filed in support of an application for summary judgment, rather than an order).

[298] CPR, r 5.4C(4); see *McKennit v Ash* [2008] QB 73, 75 for an example of such an order, albeit in a different context to that of protecting the confidentiality of a Tomlin order.

[299] Where the compromise has been made the subject of a consent order, the consent order may also be set aside: *Dietz v Lennig Chemicals Ltd* [1969] 1 AC 170, HL, 184.

[300] *Hollingsworth v Humphrey* (CA, 10 December 1987) 8.

[301] Relying on *Rofa Sport Management AG v DHL International (UK) Ltd* [1989] 1 WLR 902, CA, 911.

[302] *Hollingsworth* (n 300 above) 8.

[303] D Foskett, *The Law and Practice of Compromise* (7th edn, 2010) para 9–28.

[304] *De Molestina v Ponton* [2002] 1 Lloyd's Rep 271, 286 *per* Colman J; *Chitty on Contracts* (30th edn, 2008) para 6–118.

A genuine deterrent is nevertheless that the innocent party could issue an application seeking **12.128** an inquiry for damages against the party in breach, arising out of its failure to comply with the terms of the Tomlin order. This would be in addition, or in the alternative, to an application that those parties be ordered to comply with the terms of the schedule. The Court of Appeal in the *Hollingsworth* case held that a party to a Tomlin order was required to issue separate proceedings for breach of contract.[305] However, in *The Bargain Pages Ltd v Midland Independent Newspapers Ltd*, the Vice-Chancellor distinguished the *Hollingsworth* dictum on the ground that it was given prior to the introduction of the CPR and ordered, in the original proceedings which were stayed by way of a Tomlin order, an inquiry as to damages for breach of that order.[306]

A further potent means of enforcement is the jurisdiction of the court to join non-parties to **12.129** the proceedings for the purposes of the enforcement of the Tomlin order. In *The Bargain Pages* case, the court considered, and declined on the facts of the case, an application by a party to a Tomlin order to join non-parties to proceedings for the purpose of enforcing that order against the non-parties. Notably, the court did not decline the application to join the non-parties on the ground that, because they were not parties to the order, the court had no jurisdiction to enforce the terms of the schedule against it. Rather, the court held that the non-parties had not agreed to the terms of the schedule and were therefore not obliged to perform its terms.[307]

This mechanism is particularly attractive for a former employer seeking to enforce the terms **12.130** of a Tomlin order made against his former employee for the enforcement of restrictive covenants contained in the employment contract. The former employer might have elected not to join the new employer of the employee to the original claim for injunctive relief, either for want of evidence that the new employer was inducing or procuring a breach of that employment contract, or, in order to limit the exposure of the former employer on the cross-undertaking in damages. However, where the new employer had agreed to the terms of the compromise and has subsequently assisted the employee in breaching the terms of that order, the former employer might be able to join the new employer of the employee to the proceedings and apply to enforce the Tomlin order against that new employer.

H. Appeals

Appeals against any order of a High Court judge are made to the Court of Appeal.[308] Appeals **12.131** from the order of a circuit judge making any decision other than a final decision are to a single judge of the High Court.[309] Appeals from the order of a circuit judge making a final decision in a multi-track case are to the Court of Appeal.[310] A final decision is a decision of a court that would finally determine (subject to any possible appeal or detailed assessment of costs) the entire proceedings whichever way the court decided the issues before it.[311] Accordingly, the

---

[305] *Hollingsworth* (n 300 above) 9.
[306] [2003] EWHC 1887, [2004] FSR 6, paras 38–46.
[307] ibid paras 4, 8, 37.
[308] Senior Courts Act 1981, s 16.
[309] Access to Justice Act 1999 (Destination of Appeals) Order 2000 (SI 2000/1071), art 2; PD52, para 2A.1, Table 1.
[310] ibid.
[311] PD52, para 2A.2.

grant or refusal of interim relief is not a final decision.[312] But a decision of a court is treated as a final decision where it is made at the conclusion of part of a hearing or trial which has been split into parts.[313] Therefore, an appeal from an order made by a circuit judge at a speedy trial, in a case allocated to the multi-track, would lie to the Court of Appeal.

Obstacles to appeal of interim orders

12.132 Two particular obstacles stand in the way of any appeal against the grant or refusal of an interim injunction to enforce restrictive covenants. The first is the limited power of review of the appellate courts in such cases. The decisions whether to grant an injunction and if so, on what terms, require the exercise of discretion by the first instance judge, which is generally reviewable only where he has made an error of law, fresh evidence has been made available, or circumstances have changed. The second is urgency. The Court of Appeal will not entertain an appeal if either the relevant covenant has almost run its course or the matter is about to be finally determined at trial.

12.133 First, the function of the appellate court on appeal against the grant or refusal of an interim injunction is limited to review on circumscribed grounds. As Lord Diplock held in *Hadmor Productions Ltd v Hamilton*:

> An interlocutory injunction is a discretionary relief and the discretion whether or not to grant it is vested in the High Court judge by whom the application for it is heard. Upon an appeal from the judge's grant or refusal of an interlocutory injunction the function of an appellate court, whether it be the Court of Appeal or your Lordships' House, is not to exercise an independent discretion of its own. It must defer to the judge's exercise of his discretion and must not interfere with it merely upon the ground that the members of the appellate court would have exercised the discretion differently. The function of the appellate court is initially one of review only. It may set aside the judge's exercise of his discretion on the ground that it was based upon a misunderstanding of the law or of the evidence before him or upon an inference that particular facts existed or did not exist, which, although it was one that might legitimately have been drawn upon the evidence that was before the judge, can be demonstrated to be wrong by further evidence that has become available by the time of the appeal; or upon the ground that there has been a change of circumstances after the judge made his order that would have justified his acceding to an application to vary it. Since reasons given by judges for granting or refusing interlocutory injunctions may sometimes be sketchy, there may also be occasional cases where even though no erroneous assumption of law or fact can be identified the judge's decision to grant or refuse the injunction is so aberrant that it must be set aside upon the ground that no reasonable judge regardful of his duty to act judicially could have reached it. It is only if and after the appellate court has reached the conclusion that the judge's exercise of his discretion must be set aside for one or other of these reasons, that it becomes entitled to exercise an original discretion of its own.[314]

12.134 This obstacle lies not only in the path of an appeal against the decision whether to grant an interlocutory injunction. It also applies to an appeal concerning the terms of such an injunction. In *A-G v Punch Ltd*, Lord Hoffmann emphasized that considerations of discretion and the balance of convenience are even more important when it comes to deciding upon the scope of the interlocutory injunction.[315]

---

[312] ibid.
[313] PD52, para 2A.3.
[314] [1983] 1 AC 191, HL, 220.
[315] [2003] 1 AC 1046, paras 75, 84.

Secondly, an employer who contends that an ex-employee is in breach of restrictive covenants **12.135** has not only to move swiftly to restrain the breach, but also, if unsuccessful at first instance, either to ensure that an appeal is brought on speedily or else abandoned in favour of a final trial.[316] In the case of *Wincanton Ltd v Cranny*, the Court of Appeal dismissed an appeal against the refusal of interlocutory relief on the ground that only three months of the twelve-month covenant were left to run. This was notwithstanding the facts that permission to appeal had been granted by the first instance judge, counsel for the appellant employer had written a letter to the court at the time of lodging his appeal notice requesting an expedited hearing, and the court concluded that the first instance judge had wrongly decided that the covenant in question was unenforceable. Where a covenant has almost run its course, the balance of convenience in respect of granting interim relief was held to lie fairly and squarely in the respondent's favour.[317] This was in particular because, if the court were to grant any interlocutory relief against further solicitation, it would not impose any restriction upon the respondent's continued dealing with the customers who had, by then, already been successfully solicited by the respondent.[318] As Sedley LJ stated: 'Clocks may be able to be turned back and films rewound, but genies cannot be put back in their bottles.'[319]

Similarly, in the case of *SBJ Stephenson v Mandy*,[320] the Court of Appeal refused to consider **12.136** the merits of an appeal against an interim injunction enforcing restrictive covenants in a contract of employment on the ground that the speedy trial was imminent. Nourse LJ said:

> I do not accept the proposition that a person who has had an interlocutory order wrongly made against him has an unqualified right two weeks before the trial to have it set aside, when, first, he is protected by a cross-undertaking as to damages whose value has not been doubted and, secondly, there is no evidence before the court that additional substantial harm will be suffered between now and trial.[321]

Appeal procedure

Appeals to the civil division of the Court of Appeal and to the High Court are governed by **12.137** Part 52 of the CPR.[322] Detailed requirements as to the conduct of and preparation for applications for permission to appeal and appeals themselves are set out in the Practice Direction to Part 52, which all parties to an appeal are required to follow.[323] The following are the principal features of this procedure.

Permission to appeal is required (subject to exceptions which do not apply to actions enforcing **12.138** restrictive covenants).[324] Permission to appeal may only be given where the court considers that the appeal would have a real prospect of success or there is some other compelling reason why the appeal should be heard.[325]

---

[316] *Wincanton Ltd v Cranny* [2000] IRLR 716, para 27.
[317] ibid para 23.
[318] ibid para 24; *Universal Thermosensors Ltd v Hibben* [1992] 1 WLR 840, 854.
[319] *Wincanton* (n 316 above) para 28.
[320] CA, 30 June 1999.
[321] ibid 3.
[322] CPR, r 52.1(1).
[323] ibid r 52.2.
[324] ibid r 52.3(1).
[325] ibid r 52.3(5).

12.139 An appellant's notice must be filed in all cases.[326] The application for permission must be made in that notice and filed twenty-one days after the date of the decision of the lower court that the appellant wishes to appeal (save where the lower court gives a direction for a longer or shorter period of time).[327] At the appeal hearing, a party may not rely on a matter not contained in his appeal notice unless the appeal court gives permission.[328] A party may nevertheless amend his appeal notice with permission of the court. Such an application would usually be heard at the hearing of the application for permission to appeal or of the appeal, unless that course would cause unnecessary delay or expense.[329]

12.140 A respondent may file and serve a respondent's notice.[330] He must do so if he seeks permission to appeal or if he wishes to ask the appeal court to uphold the order of the lower court for reasons different from or additional to those given by that court.[331] The respondent's notice must be filed within such period as directed by the lower court or within fourteen days after the date of (a) being served with the appellant's notice where permission to appeal was given by the lower court; (b) being notified that the appeal court has given the appellant permission to appeal; or (c) being notified that the application for permission to appeal and the appeal itself are to be heard together.[332]

12.141 The powers of the appeal court which are most likely to be exercised in a claim for enforcement of restrictive covenants are that of affirming, setting aside, or varying the order or judgment made by the lower court, and the making of a costs order.[333]

12.142 The appeal court will allow an appeal only where the decision of the lower court was wrong, or unjust because of a serious procedural or other irregularity in the proceedings in the lower court.[334] The grounds for appeal should set out clearly the reasons why it is claimed that the decision of the lower court was wrong or unjust and specify in respect of each ground whether the ground raises an appeal on a point of law or is an appeal against a finding of fact.[335] The appeal court may draw any inference of fact which it considers justified on the evidence.[336]

I. Costs

General costs rules

The court's discretion on costs

12.143 Prior to the CPR, the successful party was generally entitled to all his costs. The CPR have given the courts much greater flexibility to make costs orders that fairly reflect the realities of the case, while also setting out clear guidelines as to the matters to which the courts should have regard in deciding what orders to make. Part 44 of the CPR sets out the general rules on

---

[326] PD52, para 5.1.
[327] CPR, r 52.4(2).
[328] ibid r 52.11(5).
[329] PD 52, para 5.25.
[330] CPR, r 52.5(1).
[331] ibid r 52.5(2).
[332] ibid r 52.5(4), (5).
[333] ibid r 52.10(2)(a), (e).
[334] ibid r 52.11(3).
[335] PD 52, para 3.2.
[336] CPR, r 52.11(4).

costs and is always the starting point when considering costs. The main costs rule is contained in rule 44.3 of the CPR. The court has discretion as to whether costs are payable, and, if so, the amount of those costs and when they are to be paid.[337] The general rule is that the unsuccessful party pays the successful party's costs, but the court can make a different order, and often does.[338] In determining what order (if any) to make, the court must have regard to all the circumstances, including the conduct of all the parties, whether a party has succeeded on part of his case even if he has not been wholly successful, and any payment into court or admissible offer to settle made by a party which is drawn to the court's attention and which is not an offer to which costs consequences under Part 36 apply.[339] The conduct of the parties will include conduct before and during proceedings; whether it was reasonable to raise, pursue, or contest a particular allegation or issue; the manner in which a party pursued or defended the case; and whether a successful claimant exaggerated his claim.[340]

The court has enormous flexibility as to the kind of costs orders it can make. It can order **12.144** payment of a proportion (ie percentage) of a party's costs, a stated amount of a party's costs, costs from or until a particular date, costs incurred prior to proceedings,[341] costs relating to particular steps taken in the proceedings, costs relating to a distinct part of the proceedings (ie an issue-based order), and interest on costs.[342] The court can also order the payment of the costs 'of and incidental to' proceedings or applications, which include the reasonable costs of a party's experts (including in-house experts employed by a party) in investigating, formulating, and prosecuting the proceedings.[343]

In general, the task for the judge in making an award of costs under these rules is to deter- **12.145** mine (a) who succeeded in the action and (b) what order for costs justice requires. Having identified the successful party, the judge essentially has to determine whether to apply the general rule that costs follow the event, or to make an order that reflects the outcome of different issues.[344] The 'issues-based' approach enables a successful party to be deprived of its costs of a particular issue on which it failed, irrespective of whether that party acted unreasonably or improperly in raising the issue.[345] However, it is not necessary for the court to make an issues-based order to achieve a result that reflects the loss of particular issues; the court will generally make, and indeed is expressly encouraged by rule 44.3(7) to make, a percentage order. Hence, where a successful party loses on a number of issues, the judge could make an order requiring the unsuccessful party to pay (for example) 60 per cent of the winner's costs. Alternatively, the court could make a costs order that reflects the conduct of the parties, for example, an order to pay costs from the date on which a party conducted itself

---

[337] CPR, r 44.3(1).

[338] ibid r 44.3(2).

[339] ibid r 44.3(4).

[340] ibid r 44.3(5).

[341] This includes costs incurred as a result of a threatened application for interim injunctive relief, which the claimant withdraws outside the door of the court before the issue of proceedings: see *Associated Newspapers Ltd v Impac Ltd* [2002] FSR 18.

[342] CPR, r 44.3(6).

[343] *Admiral Management Services Ltd v Para-Protect Europe Ltd* [2002] 1 WLR 2722, paras 27–34. This is an inroad on the principle that payment for work done by employees of a litigant is not recoverable as an item of costs. Applied in *Sisu Capital Fund Ltd v Tucker (Costs)* [2005] EWHC 2321 (Ch), [2006] 1 All ER 167, paras 47–8; and *Floe Telecom Ltd (in Administration) v Office of Communications (Costs)* [2006] CAT 18, para 9.

[344] *AEI Rediffusion Music Ltd v Phonographic Performance Ltd* [1999] 1 WLR 1507, 1522–3 *per* Lord Woolf MR.

[345] *Summit Property Ltd v Pitmans* [2001] EWCA Civ 2020, para 16.

unreasonably (for example by rejecting a reasonable offer of settlement or by failing to respond to a clear indication of willingness to negotiate a reasonable settlement[346]).

12.146   In *Multiplex Constructions (UK) Ltd v Cleveland Bridge UK Ltd*,[347] Jackson J comprehensively reviewed a number of costs authorities and derived from them a number of helpful principles:

(1) In commercial litigation where each party has claims and asserts that a balance is owing in its own favour, the party which ends up receiving payment should generally be characterised as the overall winner of the entire action.

(2) In considering how to exercise its discretion the court should take as its starting point the general rule that the successful party is entitled to an order for costs.

(3) The judge must then consider what departures are required from that starting point, having regard to all the circumstances of the case.

(4) Where the circumstances of the case required an issue-based costs order, that is what the judge should make. However, the judge should hesitate before doing so, because of the practical difficulties which this causes and because of the steer given by rule 44.3(7).

(5) In many cases the judge can and should reflect the relative success of the parties on different issues by making a proportionate costs order.

(6) In considering the circumstances of the case the judge will have regard not only to any part 36 offers made but also to each party's approach to negotiations (insofar as admissible) and general conduct of the litigation.

(7) If one party makes an offer under part 36 or an admissible offer within rule 44.3(4)(c) which is nearly but not quite sufficient, and the other party rejects that offer outright without any attempt to negotiate, then it might be appropriate to penalise the other party in costs.

(8) In assessing a proportionate costs order the judge should consider what costs are referable to each issue and what costs are common to several issues. It will often be reasonable for the overall winner to recover not only the costs specific to the issues which he has won but also the common costs.[348]

Basis of assessment

12.147   The court can award costs on either a standard or indemnity basis. Where the amount of costs is to be assessed on the standard basis, the court will only allow costs which are proportionate to the matters in issue and will resolve any doubt which it may have as to whether costs were reasonably incurred or reasonable and proportionate in amount in favour of the paying party.[349] Where the court orders costs to be assessed on the indemnity basis, the court will resolve such doubts in favour of the receiving party.[350] From this it is apparent that the differences between the two bases of assessment are twofold: first, as to the onus which is on a party to establish that the costs were reasonable; and secondly, the requirement of proportionality does not exist in relation to an order made on the indemnity basis.[351] In practice, if

---

[346] *Lyreco UK Ltd v Martin* [2009] EWHC 2105 (QB), para 18.

[347] [2008] EWHC 2280 (TCC), [2009] 1 Costs LR 55.

[348] ibid, para 72. Upheld on appeal in *Cleveland Bridge UK Ltd v Multiplex Constructions (UK) Ltd* [2010] EWCA Civ 449, para 39. These principles were cited with approval in *Lyreco v Martin* (above note 346), para 10; *Fitzroy Robinson Ltd v Mentmore Towers Ltd (A company incorporated in Jersey)* [2010] EWHC 98 (TCC), para 9; and *BskyB Ltd v HP Enterprise Services UL Ltd* [2010] EWHC 862 (TCC), para 11.

[349] CPR, r 44.4(2).

[350] CPR, r 44.4(3).

[351] *Excelsior Commercial & Industrial Holdings Ltd v Salisbury Hammer Aspden & Johnson* [2002] EWCA Civ 879, para 15.

costs are awarded on a standard basis, the successful party will generally receive about two-thirds of their costs, whereas on the indemnity basis, they will generally receive all of their costs.

The CPR do not provide any guidance as to when it is appropriate to order indemnity costs. **12.148** The Court of Appeal in *Excelsior Commercial & Industrial Holdings Ltd v Salisbury Hammer Aspden & Johnson*[352] held that before an order for indemnity costs is made, there must be some conduct or circumstance which takes the case 'out of the norm'. The circumstances which take the case out of the norm include the pursuit of a hopeless claim, the use of litigation for ulterior commercial purposes, or the making of an unjustified personal attack by one party.[353] It is not, however, necessary to show lack of probity or conduct deserving of moral condemnation in order to get an order for indemnity costs.[354] In *Esure Services Ltd v Quarcoo*,[355] the Court of Appeal clarified what it meant by conduct outside the norm: the word 'norm' is not intended to reflect whether something occurs often and so might be seen as 'normal', but is intended to reflect something outside the ordinary and reasonable conduct of proceedings. If a claim is brought dishonestly and is maintained dishonestly, the court can mark its disapproval by making an order for indemnity costs.[356]

Procedure for assessing costs

The court can make a costs order at any stage in a case. In particular, the court may make a **12.149** costs order when it deals with an application, makes an order, or holds any hearing. Where the court orders a party to pay costs to another party, it may either make a summary assessment of the costs, or order a detailed assessment of costs.[357] Judges are encouraged to make a summary assessment wherever practicable, and the general rule is that the court should make a summary assessment of costs at the conclusion of a hearing which has lasted not more than one day.[358] A party who intends to claim costs by way of summary assessment must prepare a schedule of costs, preferably complying with form N260, and must file it at court and serve it on the party against whom the order is sought not less than twenty-four hours before the date fixed for the hearing.[359]

Detailed assessment is the procedure by which the amount of costs is determined by a cost **12.150** officer in accordance with Part 47 of the CPR. Generally, the court will order detailed assessment at the conclusion of a trial. The party in whose favour detailed assessment has been ordered (the receiving party) will then commence the procedure by serving a notice of commencement and a copy of their bill of costs within a specified time period. The paying party is then entitled to serve points of dispute. If the costs are disputed, there will then be a detailed assessment hearing to determine the amount of the costs.

Where a court orders detailed assessment, the court has power to order the paying party **12.151** to make an interim payment on account.[360] In *Mars UK Ltd v Teknowledge Ltd*,[361] which

---

[352] ibid.
[353] See *Noorani v Calver* [2009] EWHC 592 (QB), para 9.
[354] *Excelsior v Salisbury* (above n 351) paras 36–7.
[355] [2009] EWCA Civ 595.
[356] ibid, paras 24–5 *per* Waller LJ and para 31 *per* Longmore LJ.
[357] CPR, r 44.7.
[358] 44PD.7, paras 13.1 and 13.2.
[359] 44PD.7, para 13.5(1)–(4).
[360] CPR, r 44.3(8).
[361] [2000] FSR 138.

concerned an application for an interim payment made to the judge who conducted the trial, Jacob J held that the successful party ought to get his costs as soon as possible, and the court should normally order an amount to be paid on account.[362] Laddie J in *Dyson Ltd v Hoover Ltd*[363] held that there is no such presumption where the judge being invited to make an order for interim payment has not heard the full trial.[364] The court has a discretion and therefore will take into account all of the circumstances of the case before ordering an interim payment, including the likelihood of an appeal and the financial positions of the parties.[365] The Court of Appeal in *Blakemore v Cummings (Practice Note)*,[366] considering both *Mars* and *Dyson*, held that there is no legal presumption one way or the other that a successful party should be able to realize the benefit of a costs order in his favour by an order for interim payment. It is simply a factor, albeit one carrying significant weight, to be taken into account by a judge in the exercise of his wide discretion under rule 44.3(8).[367]

Costs against non-parties

12.152   The court has jurisdiction to order a non-party to proceedings to pay the costs of a successful party under section 51 of the Senior Courts Act 1981.[368] Guidance as to the exercise of the court's discretion to order payment of costs by a non-party was given by the Court of Appeal in *Symphony Group plc v Hodgson*.[369] The Court of Appeal noted that an order for payment of costs by a non-party will always be exceptional.[370] However, the court has been prepared to make such an order where:

(1)   the non-party controlled or directed the action for his own benefit, for example a director of an insolvent company who causes the company improperly to issue or defend proceedings;[371]

(2)   the non-party maintained or financed the action, provided that the funder had an interest in the outcome of the litigation and the funding provided was responsible for the litigation taking place;[372]

(3)   the person was a witness or expert witness in the action and gave evidence that was false or dishonest.[373]

12.153   The court will generally be unwilling to make such an order where the successful party had a cause of action against the non-party (for example for inducement of breach of contract) and could have joined him to the proceedings but did not do so, or where the successful party

---

[362]   ibid 153.

[363]   [2003] EWHC 624.

[364]   ibid para 30.

[365]   *Dyson* (n 363 above) paras 32–33.

[366]   [2010] 1 WLR 983.

[367]   ibid, para 23.

[368]   *Aiden Shipping Co Ltd v Interbulk Ltd* [1986] 2 AC 965, 975.

[369]   [1994] QB 179.

[370]   ibid 192 *per* Balcombe LJ.

[371]   See, eg, *R + V Versicherung AG v Risk Insurance & Reinsurance Solutions SA* [2005] EWHC 2586 (Comm); *Petromec Inc v Petroleo Brasileiro SA Petrobras* [2006] EWCA Civ 1038, para 10; *Dolphin Quays Developments Ltd v Mills* [2008] 1 WLR 1829; and *DNA Productions (Europe) Ltd v Manoukian* [2008] EWHC 2627 (Ch).

[372]   *SBJ Stephenson Ltd v Mandy (No 2)* [2000] FSR 651; *Hamilton v Al Fayed* [2002] EWCA Civ 665; *Princo Digital Disc GmbH v Phillips Electronics NV* [2003] EWHC 2589; *Thomson v Berkhampsted Collegiate School* [2009] EWHC 2374 (QB), [2009] 6 Costs LR 859.

[373]   *R + V Versicherung AG* (n 371 above); *Phillips v Symes* [2004] EWHC 2330 (Ch).

failed to warn the non-party at the earliest opportunity of the possibility that he may seek to apply for costs.[374] The availability of security for costs is also an important factor in the exercise of the discretion to order payment of non-party costs; the discretion may be exercised more readily in favour of the applicant if security is not available.[375]

The procedure for making an application for costs against a non-party is set out in CPR, **12.154** rule 48.2. An application for costs against a non-party should normally be made to, and determined by, the trial judge.[376] Rule 48 provides that where the court is considering whether to exercise its power under section 51 of the Senior Courts Act 1981 to make a costs order against a non-party, that person must be added as a party to the proceedings for the purposes of costs only, and he must be given a reasonable opportunity to attend the hearing at which the court will consider the matter.[377] What is intended is a summary procedure for the determination of the application, which may nonetheless provide for disclosure orders, cross-examination, and service of skeleton arguments.[378]

Costs on interim applications

Although the award of costs is always a matter for the court's discretion, in relation to interim **12.155** applications, the discretion tends to be exercised as follows. The court will generally make a summary assessment of the costs at the end of the application hearing if it lasted one day or less.[379] Where the hearing is without notice, costs will generally be reserved. At an interim hearing on notice, the main costs orders are:

(1) costs in the case (the costs of the application are awarded to the party who ultimately wins at trial);
(2) claimant's costs in the case (the claimant will recover his costs of the interim application if he wins at trial—irrespective of the final outcome the defendant will have to pay his own costs of the interim application);
(3) defendant's costs in the case (the reverse—the claimant pays his own interim costs whatever the final outcome and also the defendant's costs if the defendant wins at trial);
(4) costs reserved (the decision about costs will be deferred to the trial judge).[380]

However, there is nothing to prevent the court on an interlocutory application ordering the **12.156** unsuccessful party to pay the successful party's costs. Where, for example, the application for an interim injunction falls so far short of satisfying the criteria for the grant of interlocutory relief that the applicant should never have sought it, the court can penalize the applicant in costs, even if the applicant has good prospects of succeeding at trial.[381]

---

[374] See *Symphony Group plc v Hodgson* [1994] QB 179, 193. cf *R + V Versicherung AG* (n 371 above) paras 20–1.

[375] *Dolphin Quays v Mills* (n 371 above) para 62.

[376] *Symphony Group* (n 374 above) 193.

[377] CPR, r 48.2(1).

[378] *Thomson v Berkhamsted Collegiate School* (n 372 above) paras 13-15

[379] 44PD.7, para 13.2.

[380] See 44PD.2, para 8.5. The court would normally reserve costs if an interim injunction is granted or the defendant accedes to it reasonably promptly because there are no successful or unsuccessful parties for costs purposes: see *Desquenne et Giral UK Ltd v Richardson* [2001] FSR 1, paras 12–14. However, see *Fox Gregory Ltd v Spinks* [2006] EWCA Civ 1544.

[381] See *Bushbury Land Rover Ltd v Bushbury Ltd* (CA, 14 November 1996).

Part 36

General

12.157 Part 36 of the CPR sets out a procedure for either party to make a settlement offer to the other, and sets out the specific consequences of accepting or not accepting a settlement offer made in accordance with the rules in that Part. Part 36 offers can be a useful tactical weapon in the litigation armoury as a result of the costs consequences of making such offers. Its purpose is to encourage parties to settle litigation by providing incentives to do so. Part 36 does not prevent parties making an offer to settle in any way they choose, but if the offer does not comply with its provisions, then the costs consequences will not apply.[382] Part 36 of the CPR has been substantially amended with effect from 6 April 2007. The main change is that payments into court have been dispensed with; it is no longer necessary for offers of settlement to be accompanied by payments into court.[383] In addition, Part 36 has been divided into two sections: Section II applies to offers to settle made in the context of road traffic accidents, and Section I contains rules about offers to settle in all other cases.

12.158 A 'Part 36 offer' may be an offer made by either the claimant or the defendant to settle the claim. For example, it may be an offer to accept (or make) payment of, say, £50,000 and a permanent injunction preventing the defendant from disclosing the claimant's confidential information. A Part 36 offer may be made at any stage including before proceedings have begun, and in appeal proceedings.[384] Part 36 can apply to claims and counterclaims, and can relate to the whole claim, part of a claim, or an issue in the claim.[385] As an injunction is not a separate cause of action, a Part 36 offer made in relation to the whole claim will, if accepted, put an end to any claim for an injunction.

12.159 Part 36 offers are to be treated as 'without prejudice save as to costs' and therefore the fact of the offer and its amount must not be communicated to the trial judge until the case has been decided.[386] The restriction on communication does not apply to interlocutory proceedings before a judge who will not be the trial judge.

The form and content of a Part 36 offer or payment

12.160 A Part 36 offer must comply with the form and content requirements of rule 36.2 of the CPR. For example, it must be in writing and must state whether it relates to the whole of the claim or to part of it or to an issue that arises in it and if so which part or issue and state whether it takes into account any counterclaim.[387] It must specify a period of not less than twenty-one days within which the defendant will be liable for the claimant's costs if the offer is accepted ('the relevant period'), unless the offer is made less than twenty-one days before the start of the trial, in which case the 'relevant period' will be the period up to the end of the trial or such other period as the court has determined.[388]

---

[382] CPR, r 36.1(2).
[383] The history of and reasons for this amendment, which took effect from 6 April 2007, are set out in Michael J Cook, *Cook on Costs 2010* (Lexis Nexis, 2009) paras 14.1–14.3.
[384] CPR, r 36.3(2).
[385] ibid r 36.2(2).
[386] ibid r 36.13(1) and (2).
[387] ibid r 36.2(2).
[388] ibid r 36.2(2)(c), 36.2(3), and 36.3(1)(c).

Prior to 6 April 2007, a Part 36 offer could be withdrawn or reduced at any time before it was **12.161** accepted. Under the amended rule 36.3(5), a Part 36 offer may be withdrawn or its terms changed to be less advantageous to the offeree before expiry of the relevant period only if the court gives permission.[389] After expiry of the relevant period, the offeror does not require the court's permission to withdraw or reduce an offer which has not been accepted.[390] This is done by serving written notice of the withdrawal or change of terms on the offeree.[391]

Rule 36.4 provides that a Part 36 offer by a defendant to pay a sum of money in settlement **12.162** of a claim must be an offer to pay a single lump sum which is payable within fourteen days. An offer which does not comply with that requirement will only have Part 36 consequences if it is accepted by the offeree.[392] A Part 36 offer which offers to pay or accept a sum of money will be treated as inclusive of all interest for the period set out in rule 36.3(3).

Acceptance of Part 36 offers

A Part 36 offer is accepted by serving written notice of the acceptance on the offeror.[393] A Part 36 **12.163** offer can be accepted at any time unless the offeror serves notice of withdrawal on the offeree.[394] However, the court's permission is required to accept a Part 36 offer in certain circumstances, such as where the offer was made by some but not all of multiple defendants, or where the trial has started.[395] In *Sampla v Rushmoor Borough Council*,[396] Coulson J rejected the argument that there was an implied term that the offer could not be accepted once trial had started. The express words of rule 36.9(3) presuppose that, subject to the court's permission, an offer is capable of being accepted after the trial has started. The test for whether the court will exercise its discretion to allow the offer to be accepted after the trial has commenced is whether there has been a sufficient change of circumstances such that it would be just to refuse to allow the offeree to accept the offer.[397] Unless the parties agree, a Part 36 offer may not be accepted after the end of the trial but before judgment is handed down.[398]

Part 36 is a self-contained code and displaces the general law of offer and acceptance.[399] Part 36 **12.164** proceeds on the footing that the offer remains on the table and available for acceptance until the offeror chooses to withdraw it in accordance with the rules.[400] Hence, a Part 36 offer will remain open for acceptance even where the offeree has previously rejected it or has subsequently made a counter offer, which is contrary to the general position at common law.[401] Further, Part 36 permits an offeror to make more than one offer, all of which are at any

---

[389] In deciding whether to exercise the discretion to permit withdrawal of an offer, the court will consider whether there has been a sufficient change of circumstances since the offer was made to make it just that the defendant should have an opportunity of withdrawing it: see *Flynn v Scougal* [2004] EWCA Civ 873, para 39.

[390] CPR, r 36.3(6).

[391] ibid r 36.3(7).

[392] ibid r 36.4(2).

[393] ibid r 36.9(1).

[394] ibid r 36.9(2).

[395] ibid r 36.9(3).

[396] [2008] EWHC 2616 (TCC), paras 39–41.

[397] ibid para 46.

[398] CPR, r 36.9(5). This rule reflects the decision in *Hawley v Luminar Leisure plc* [2006] EWCA Civ 18, [2006] Lloyd's Rep 307, para 29.

[399] *Gibbon v Manchester CC; LG Blower Specialist Bricklayer Ltd v Reeves* [2010] EWCA Civ 726, paras 5–6.

[400] CPR, rr 36.9(2) and 36.3(5)–(7).

[401] *Gibbon v Manchester CC* (n 399 above) para 16. See also *Sampla v Rushmoor BC* (n 396 above), paras 27–38.

time available for acceptance; a later offer is not to be treated as superseding or revoking an earlier offer.[402] Moreover, there is no room for the concept of implied withdrawal: withdrawal of a Part 36 offer requires express notice in writing.[403]

The costs consequences

12.165 A Part 36 offer will have different costs consequences depending on: (a) whether the offer was accepted; (b) if so, at what time; and (c) if not, a comparison between the offer and the judgment obtained.

Acceptance of Part 36 offer or payment

12.166 If the Part 36 offer is made more than twenty-one days before trial and is accepted within the relevant period, then the claimant will be entitled to his costs of the proceedings up to the date on which notice of acceptance was served on the offeror.[404] Where a defendant's Part 36 offer relates to only part of the claim, and the claimant abandons the balance of the claim at the time of serving notice of acceptance within the relevant period, then the claimant is entitled to the costs of the proceedings up to the date of serving notice of acceptance, unless the court orders otherwise.[405] In either of these cases, costs will be assessed on the standard basis if the amount is not agreed.[406]

12.167 If, however, the offer was made less than twenty-one days before the start of trial, or it was accepted after the expiry of the relevant period, then unless the parties are agreed on liability for costs, the court will make an order as to costs.[407] Where the offer was accepted after the expiry of the relevant period, unless the court orders otherwise, the claimant will be entitled to the costs of the proceedings up to the date on which the relevant period expired and the offeree (whether claimant or defendant) will be liable for the offeror's costs for the period from the date of expiry of the relevant period to the date of acceptance.[408] This creates a powerful incentive for a party who wishes to accept an offer to do so within the relevant period to avoid costs liability for the subsequent period up to acceptance.

12.168 Rules 36.10(4) and (5) are silent as to the basis on which costs are to be assessed. There is no rebuttable presumption that the claimant is entitled to indemnity costs where a late offer has been accepted or there has been late acceptance of an offer, and it is wrong to draw an analogy with the costs rules in CPR 36.14, which set out the costs consequences following trial where the offer has not been accepted.[409]

12.169 The effect of accepting a Part 36 offer relating to the *whole* claim is to stay the claim upon the terms of the offer.[410] The effect of accepting a Part 36 offer relating to *part* of the claim is to stay that part of the claim upon the terms of the offer, and unless the claimant abandons the balance of the claim (in which case Rule 36.10(2) and (3) applies), liability for costs is

---

[402] *Gibbon v Manchester CC* (n 399 above) paras 29, 32.
[403] CPR, r 36.3(7).
[404] ibid r 36.10(1).
[405] ibid r 36.10(2).
[406] ibid r 36.10(3).
[407] ibid r 36.10(4).
[408] ibid r 36.10(5).
[409] *Fitzpatrick Contractors Ltd v Tyco Fire and Integrated Solutions (UK) Ltd (Formerly Wormald Ansul (UK) Ltd)* [2009] EWHC 274 (TCC), paras 17–29.
[410] CPR, r 36.11(1) and (2).

decided by the court, unless agreed.[411] Any stay does not affect the court's power to enforce the terms of a Part 36 offer or to deal with any question of costs relating to the proceedings.[412] Where an offer is or includes an offer to pay a single sum of money, that sum must be paid within fourteen days of the date of acceptance and if not so paid, judgment may be entered for the unpaid sum.[413] Where a Part 36 offer is accepted which is not an offer to pay a single sum of money, and it is alleged that the terms of the offer have not been honoured, then an application can be made to enforce the terms of the offer without needing to start a new claim.[414]

Non-acceptance of a Part 36 offer

Rule 36.14 sets out certain costs consequences where a Part 36 offer has been made but not accepted, and judgment has been given. The court retains a discretion to depart from those consequences where it would be unjust to follow them. **12.170**

Rule 36.14 now provides that: **12.171**

(1) This rule applies where upon judgment being entered—
   (a) a claimant fails to obtain a judgment more advantageous than a defendant's Part 36 offer; or
   (b) judgment against the defendant is at least as advantageous to the claimant as the proposals contained in a claimant's Part 36 offer.

The previous rules distinguished between Part 36 payments into court to settle money claims (where the costs consequences following judgment were triggered if a claimant 'failed to better' a Part 36 payment) and offers of terms and conditions on which to settle non-money claims (where it was necessary to consider whether a judgment was 'more advantageous' than an offer). Under the new rule, money claims and non-money claims are to be treated in the same way, requiring an analysis of whether the judgment is 'more advantageous' than the defendant's offer or 'at least as advantageous' as the claimant's offer. **12.172**

In *Carver v BAA plc,*[415] the Court of Appeal considered the meaning of 'advantageous' in the context of a personal injury case where the claimant beat the defendant's Part 36 offer to settle a money claim by only £51. The Court of Appeal considered that the change in wording of the rules signified a change of approach, and that in determining where the balance of advantage lay in a money claim, the court is entitled to take into account all of the circumstances of the case, including the emotional stress of the trial and the incurring of irrecoverable costs.[416] It therefore upheld the judge's decision to order the claimant to pay the defendant's costs. The principles set out in *Carver* are of general application and are not confined to personal injury cases.[417] The decision in *Carver* was strongly criticized by Lord Justice Jackson in his *Review of Civil Litigation Costs: Final Report*[418] as introducing an unwelcome degree of uncertainty into the Part 36 regime. The report recommended that the effect of *Carver* **12.173**

---

[411] ibid r 36.11(3).
[412] ibid r 36.11(5).
[413] ibid r 36.11(6) and (7).
[414] ibid r 36.11(8).
[415] [2009] 1 WLR 113, CA.
[416] ibid paras 21–33.
[417] *Multiplex Constructions (UK) Ltd v Cleveland Bridge UK Ltd (No 7)* [2008] EWHC 2280 (TCC), paras 70–1.
[418] TSO, 2010.

should be reversed judicially or by rule change, and that it should be made clear that in any purely monetary case, 'more advantageous' means better in financial terms by any amount, however small.[419] Subsequent High Court decisions have noted and agreed with those criticisms while considering themselves bound by *Carver*.[420] However, in *Gibbon v Manchester CC*,[421] the Court of Appeal held that in most cases obtaining judgment for an amount greater than the offer is likely to outweigh all other factors.[422]

12.174 Where the defendant does not accept the claimant's Part 36 offer and the claimant subsequently obtains a judgment which is at least as advantageous to him as his offer, then the court will, unless it is unjust to do so, order that the claimant is entitled to: (a) interest on the whole or part of any sum of money (excluding interest) awarded at a rate not exceeding 10 per cent above the base rate for some or all of the period starting with the date on which the relevant period expired; (b) his costs on the indemnity basis from the date on which the relevant period expired; and (c) interest on those costs at a rate not exceeding 10 per cent above base rate.[423] In *Huck v Robson*,[424] the Court of Appeal held that a claimant who beats his Part 36 offer at trial has a prima facie entitlement to indemnity costs and the crucial question for the court is whether it would be unjust to order indemnity costs.[425] The same applies with interest.[426]

12.175 On the other hand, where the claimant does not accept the defendant's Part 36 offer, and the claimant fails to obtain a judgment which is more advantageous than the offer, the court will, unless it is unjust to do so, order that the defendant is entitled to his costs from the date on which the relevant period expired and his interest on those costs.[427] Unlike rule 36.14(3), rule 36.14(2) makes no reference to indemnity costs. This means that in normal circumstances, costs should be awarded on the standard basis, unless the circumstances take the proceedings out of the norm and justify an order for indemnity costs, [428] for example if the claim is hopeless or speculative, if the Part 36 offer is particularly generous, if the defendant made multiple attempts to settle the case, or if the claimant unreasonably rejected the offers.[429]

12.176 What, then, is the tactical advantage for a defendant in making a Part 36 offer if, unlike a claimant, he does not get indemnity costs when he beats his offer at trial? The advantage is that the defendant can lose the case but still recover his costs incurred after the expiry of the period for accepting the offer. In other words, in relation to that period, it reverses the general position in rule 44.3 of the CPR that the winning party will get their costs. This creates an incentive for defendants to make Part 36 offers or payments at an early stage of the proceedings.

---

[419] ibid, para 2.9 of Chapter 41.
[420] See *Gibbon v Manchester CC* (n 399 above) paras 40 and 50; *Midland Packaging Ltd v HW Chartered Accountants (A Firm)* [2010] EWHC B16 (Mercantile), para 29.
[421] See n 399 above.
[422] ibid para 40 *per* Moore-Bick LJ and para 51 *per* Carnwath LJ.
[423] CPR, r 36.14(3).
[424] [2003] 1 WLR 1340, CA.
[425] ibid paras 76–7.
[426] *R v Bryn Alyn Community (Holdings) Ltd* [2003] EWCA Civ 383; applied in *Chantrey Vellacott v Convergence Group plc* (unreported, Chancery Division, 31 July 2007).
[427] CPR, r 36.14(2).
[428] See *Excelsior Commercial and Industrial Holdings Ltd v Salisbury Aspden & Johnson* [2002] EWCA Civ 879, para 19.
[429] *Noorani v Calver (No 2)* [2009] EWHC 592 (QB).

In deciding whether it would be unjust to make either of the orders under rules 36.14(2) and **12.177** (3), the court will take into account all the circumstances of the case, including the terms of any Part 36 offer, the stage in the proceedings when any Part 36 offer was made, including how long before the trial started the offer was made, the information available to the parties at the time when the Part 36 offer was made, and the conduct of the parties with regard to the giving or refusing to give information for the purposes of enabling the offer to be made or evaluated.[430]

The costs consequences set out in rule 36.14 do not apply to a Part 36 offer (a) that has been **12.178** withdrawn, (b) that has been changed so that its terms are less advantageous to the offeree, and the offeree has beaten the less advantageous offer, or (c) made less than twenty-one days before trial, unless the court has abridged the relevant period.[431] Likewise, the costs consequences set out in rule 36.14 do not apply where the claimant loses his claim or fails to do better than the terms of his own Part 36 offer, or conversely, where the claimant obtains a judgment more advantageous than a defendant's Part 36 offer. The ordinary costs consequences set out in Part 44 will apply instead. The court will be required under rule 44.3 to consider an offer to settle that does not have the costs consequences set out in Part 36 in deciding what order to make about costs.

J. Mediation and settlement

Advantages of settlement

Settlement is the predominant means of resolving claims for injunctive relief to enforce **12.179** restrictive covenants. As Lord Denning MR notably observed in *Fellowes & Son v Fisher*,[432] applications for interim injunctions to restrain breaches of restrictive covenants rarely come to be determined at trial. This is for several reasons which are set out below.

First, the grant of an injunction at an early stage prevents the employee from inflicting any **12.180** serious damage on the employer. Even if the injunction continues until speedy trial of the action, the period of the restrictive covenant might well have expired (or almost expired) by the time of the hearing. In those circumstances, there is little incentive for the claimant, having received the relief it principally sought, to pursue its claim and the granting of interim relief may therefore be determinative of the entire action.[433]

Secondly, the evidence adduced in respect of any application for or discharge of an interim **12.181** injunction and the reasoned judicial decision in respect of such an application or applications, frequently provides the parties with an early and useful indication as to the merits of their respective positions.[434]

Thirdly, if an injunction is not granted, the claimant might seek to limit its potential financial **12.182** loss by means of settlement. The less welcome alternative would be to bear such loss, which might in any event be irrecoverable, pending trial.

---

[430] CPR, r 36.14(4).
[431] ibid r 36.14(6).
[432] [1976] 1 QB 122, 129, 133–4.
[433] *Lawrence David Ltd v Ashton* [1989] ICR 123, 135 *per* Balcombe LJ, CA; *Alliance Paper Group plc v Prestwich* (CA, 11 December 1997).
[434] As Lord Denning MR said in the *Fellowes & Son* case: 'The parties accept the prima facie view of the court or settle the case' (n 432 above) 129.

12.183   Fourthly, there are the costs in terms of the claimant's resources, such as expenditure of management time, and legal fees in preparation for trial.[435] In the event that costs are awarded on the standard basis, a significant portion of the successful party's costs will be irrecoverable. Moreover, the legal costs of preparation for a speedy trial typically exceed those of preparation for trial without an expedited timetable.

12.184   Fifthly, the legal costs incurred and any award of damages may not be recoverable against a defendant employee, who often has relatively limited financial resources. Depending on the factual basis for the claim, the claimant may elect to join a third party with more extensive financial resources to the proceedings, such as a new employer of the defendant or a corporate recipient of the claimant's confidential information. However, the risk entailed in such a course of action would be that of the claim proving unsuccessful and of the costs of the third party in defending the claim being awarded against the claimant. A further risk of joining the third party as a defendant and obtaining interim injunctive relief against it, would be the further exposure of the claimant pursuant to a cross-undertaking in damages.[436]

12.185   Sixthly, there is the absence of any swift and final resolution to the dispute.[437] If a speedy trial is ordered, it is likely to be limited to issues of liability and the granting of final injunctive relief. The issue of damages is likely to be considered at a separate hearing.

12.186   Seventhly, unlike resolution at trial, the process of negotiation of settlement and its terms are likely to be confidential.[438] This has particular benefit in the context of claims to restrain misuse of confidential information (where the owner of the information might, on the basis of well-founded beliefs or otherwise, fear the leaking of the information which is the subject of the litigation). Likewise, where the employee alleges repudiatory breach of contract as a defence to the enforcement of restrictive covenants contained in his employment contract.[439] The matters alleged to constitute the breach might damage the commercial reputation of the employer and even affect the stability and morale of existing employees.

12.187   Eighthly, the avoidance of a negative determination as to the enforceability of a restrictive covenant. An employer may have several employees on the same or similar covenants as those whose enforceability is challenged. In the event of a judicial determination that those covenants were in fact unenforceable, those other employees would be likely to disregard those covenants and the employer may be deprived of the protection from competition which they were designed to provide.

12.188   Ninthly, there is the opportunity to obtain a solution wider than or different from that which could be achieved in litigation.[440] For example, the parties may agree to a period of restraint which is different from that provided in the covenant. Moreover, they might enter into a profit-sharing or instalment-payment arrangement with regard to business that was taken by

---

[435]   See Chancery Guide (October 2009) para 17.2(1).

[436]   Although the third party might apply for and receive the benefit of that cross-undertaking in damages in any event. See paras 10.73–10.103 above.

[437]   See Chancery Guide (October 2009) para 17.2(2).

[438]   See Chancery Guide (October 2009) para 17.2(3), where it is noted that: 'The settlement of disputes by ADR can . . . enable litigants to achieve settlement of their disputes while preserving their existing commercial relationships and market reputation'.

[439]   *General Billposting v Atkinson* [1909] AC 118, HL.

[440]   Chancery Guide (October 2009) para 17.2(4).

means of unlawful solicitation of clients, diversion of maturing business opportunities, or removal of confidential information.

Obligation to consider settlement

Consideration of the settlement of any dispute is now a positive procedural obligation. The **12.189** Chancery Guide provides that: 'Legal representatives in all cases should consider with their clients and the other parties concerned the possibility of attempting to resolve the dispute or particular issues by ADR[441] and they should ensure that their clients are fully informed as to the most cost effective means of resolving their dispute.'[442] The Queen's Bench Guide contains a similar direction.[443] The Court of Appeal has affirmed that this obligation applies to all members of the legal profession who conduct litigation.[444]

The court may itself provide assistance to the parties for the purposes of the settlement of **12.190** their dispute. The court is obliged to further the overriding objective by actively managing cases[445] and such case management includes 'encouraging the parties to use an alternative dispute resolution procedure if the court considers that appropriate and facilitating the use of such procedure'.[446] A party which considers that ADR might be an appropriate means of resolving their dispute or particular issues in it, may then apply to the court for directions at any stage.[447] An appropriate direction for the parties to pursue ADR appears at Appendix 7 to the Admiralty and Commercial Court Guide.[448]

An action may be stayed pending ADR. It is important to note that if an action is stayed and **12.191** unless the court orders otherwise, any interim injunction is automatically set aside.[449] However, the urgency entailed in preparing for a speedy trial is generally inconsistent with a stay for the purposes of pursuing settlement of the action. Moreover, maintaining the action on an active footing may allow pressure to be brought on any settlement negotiations.

Costs of settlement

The settlement of proceedings gives rise to two particular issues in relation to the appropri- **12.192** ate award of costs. The first concerns the absence of any settlement. If the successful party at trial refused to agree to ADR, the court may refuse him some or all of his costs. It will generally be inappropriate for a court to exercise this jurisdiction in respect of successful claims to enforce restrictive covenants. The second concerns the award of costs to be made where there is a partially-successful settlement. Namely, where the issues of liability are settled but the parties cannot agree which of them should bear the costs and/or the amount of those costs. This issue is directly relevant to actions for the enforcement of restrictive covenants.

---

[441] In *Halsey v Milton Keynes General NHS Trust* [2004] EWCA Civ 576, [2004] 1 WLR 3002, para 5, the court held: 'In practice . . . references to ADR are usually understood as being references to some form of mediation by a third party.'

[442] Chancery Guide (October 2009) para 17.4.

[443] Queen's Bench Guide (January 2007) para 6.6.1.

[444] *Halsey* (n 441 above) para 11.

[445] CPR, r 1.4(1).

[446] ibid r 1.4(2)(e).

[447] Chancery Guide (October 2009) para 17.5, Queen's Bench Guide (January 2007) para 6.6.2.

[448] *The White Book* (2010) Vol 2, para 2A-164.

[449] ibid r 25.10.

Costs of refusing to seek to settle

12.193   In *Halsey v Milton Keynes General NHS Trust*,[450] the Court of Appeal considered the costs consequences of a refusal by the successful party at trial to agree to mediation. The court recognized that its obligation, when deciding what order to make about costs, to consider all the circumstances of the case, including the conduct of the parties before and during the proceedings,[451] permitted the court to deprive a successful party of some or all its costs on the ground that it had refused to agree to ADR.[452] The court held that the factors relevant to the question of whether a party has unreasonably refused ADR will include (but are not limited to) (a) the nature of the dispute; (b) the merits of the case; (c) the extent to which other settlement methods have been attempted; (d) whether the costs of ADR would be disproportionately high; (e) whether any delay in setting up the ADR would have been prejudicial; and (f) whether the ADR had a reasonable prospect of success. No single factor will be decisive and the factors set out above are not an exhaustive checklist.[453] The burden lies on the unsuccessful party to show that a party has unreasonably refused ADR and therefore that the court should depart from the general rule that the unsuccessful party will pay the costs of the successful party.[454] This burden includes the unsuccessful party showing that there was a reasonable prospect that the mediation would have been successful.[455]

12.194   The principles set out in the *Halsey* case have been extended beyond an unreasonable refusal to engage in mediation. In *Carleton (Earl of Malmesbury) v Strutt & Parker*, Jack J held that those principles applied where a party agreed to mediation but then caused the mediation to fail by reason of his unreasonable position in the mediation.[456] However, mediation agreements usually provide that the mediation takes place on a without prejudice basis. The disclosure of without prejudice documents will not be ordered on an application for costs and the *Halsey* case has not changed that position.[457] Therefore, the cases in which it might be alleged (still less successfully alleged) that a party took an unreasonable position in a mediation are likely to be few and far between. Of more general application, in *Daniels v The Commissioner of Police for the Metropolis*, Dyson LJ applied the principles in *Halsey* where it was alleged that a defendant had unreasonably refused even to enter into negotiations to attempt to settle a case.[458]

12.195   It is unlikely that the court would find that a successful claimant for the enforcement of restrictive covenants had unreasonably refused to consider ADR. This is because first, a claimant may have no alternative but to seek injunctive relief on a without notice basis.[459] It would there plainly be impossible for the claimant to pursue settlement without putting the defendant on notice and potentially destroying the position that the application is intended to secure. It is also unlikely, if a without notice application is being contemplated, that the defendant would already have made any proposal to engage in ADR. The claimant cannot

---

[450]   [2004] EWCA Civ 576, [2004] 1 WLR 3002.
[451]   Pursuant to CPR, rr 44.3(2) and 44.3(5).
[452]   *Halsey* (n 450 above) paras 12–13.
[453]   ibid para 16.
[454]   Pursuant to CPR, r 44.3(2)(a).
[455]   *Halsey* (n 450 above) para 28.
[456]   [2008] EWHC 424, para 72.
[457]   *Reed Executive plc v Reed Business Information Ltd* [2004] 1 WLR 3026, CA, paras 14, 15, 28–30, 34 *per* Jacob LJ; *Aird v Prime Meridian Ltd* [2006] EWCA Civ 1866, para 5 *per* May LJ.
[458]   [2005] EWCA Civ 1312, paras 26–30 *per* Dyson LJ.
[459]   See para 12.29 above.

have refused a proposal which has not been made.[460] Secondly, it may be appropriate to seek injunctive relief on an informal (short) notice basis.[461] Such an application would likely be impossible if the claimant were first obliged to engage in the time-consuming pursuit of ADR. In any event, it may be perfectly reasonable to refuse a proposal of mediation at such an early stage. A premature mediation may waste time and lead to a hardening of positions on both sides which make any subsequent attempt of settlement doomed to fail[462] or at least more difficult. Thirdly, after the hearing of an application for interim relief, the delay entailed in pursuing (at least formal) ADR may jeopardize any speedy trial of the claim.

The Court of Appeal in the *Halsey* case also identified three circumstances where the subject matter of disputes rendered them intrinsically unsuitable for ADR. None is likely to be relevant in the employee competition context. First, where a binding precedent would be useful to the parties. But as addressed above, a principal attraction of settlement for an employer is that it avoids an adverse precedent—namely a court ruling that covenants also contained in the contracts of other employees are unenforceable. The defendant employee will typically be interested only in resolving his dispute and not in obtaining a precedent to the benefit of other employees or rival employers. **12.196**

The second situation is where injunctive relief is essential to protect the position of a party.[463] This is typically the case in an action for the enforcement of restrictive covenants. However, the fact that the relief claimed includes final injunctions should not render that claim incapable of resolution by mediation. The court frequently orders final injunctions with the consent of the parties.[464] **12.197**

The third situation is where allegations of fraud or other commercially disreputable conduct (such as claims of theft of confidential information) are made.[465] Such allegations are common in claims for the enforcement of restrictive covenants. But such disputes should be appropriate for mediation. An employee (and his new employer) would usually wish to avoid public allegations of misconduct. A claimant employer should be conscious of the higher evidential burden which it must discharge in order to prove allegations of fraud. **12.198**

In any event, these three factors do not detract from the obligation of all parties at least to consider settlement of the dispute and the means of doing so. As the Court of Appeal warned in the *Halsey* case: 'A party who refuses even to consider whether a case is suitable for ADR is always at risk of an adverse finding at the costs stage of litigation.'[466] **12.199**

Costs of successful settlement

The case of *Promar International Ltd v Clarke*[467] concerned the proper approach of the court where a claim for enforcement of restrictive covenants has been settled, save for the award of costs. The claimant employer claimed injunctive relief and damages for an alleged breach of a restrictive covenant contained in an employment contract. The claim was settled during **12.200**

---

[460] See *Vale of Glamorgan Council v Roberts* [2008] EWHC 2911 (Ch), para 8.
[461] See para 12.28 above.
[462] *Nigel Witham Ltd v Smith* [2008] EWHC 12 (TCC), paras 8, 9, 31–3 *per* HHJ Peter Coulson QC.
[463] *Halsey* (n 450 above) para 17.
[464] See paras 12.22 ff above.
[465] *Halsey* (n 450 above) para 17.
[466] ibid para 33. The court held this risk is particularly acute where the court has made an order requiring the parties to consider ADR.
[467] [2006] EWCA Civ 332.

the claimant's opening speech in the speedy trial, on the defendant employee's undertaking to comply with the terms of the covenant and the claimant agreeing not to pursue its claim for damages. The Court of Appeal there affirmed that *BCT Software Solutions v C Brewer and Sons Ltd*[468] is an authority of general applicability to cases which have settled or been resolved without a judgment being delivered, where the trial judge is then asked to adjudicate on the issue of costs.[469] (But note that the *BCT* case concerned a claim for infringement of copyright in computer software, rather than a claim to enforce restrictive covenants.)

12.201 The starting point is that a judge has jurisdiction to make an order for costs where all substantive issues have been disposed of by agreement, though he is not obliged to do so.[470] However, there is also no convention that the court should make no order as to costs in cases where it is difficult to fathom from the terms of a settlement who is the winner and who is the loser.[471]

12.202 In the *BCT* case, the Court of Appeal applied the following principles.

12.203 The first question for the court in every case is whether it is satisfied that it is in a position to make an order about costs at all. This is made clear by the opening words of rule 44.3(2) of the CPR, which provide that: 'If the court decides to make an order about costs'.[472] In addressing that question, the court must have regard to the need (if an order about costs is to be made) to have a proper basis of agreed or determined facts upon which to decide, in the light of the principles set out under the other provisions in part 44 of the CPR, what order should be made. The general rule, if the court decides to make an order about costs, is that the unsuccessful party will be ordered to pay the costs of the successful party.[473] But the court may make a different order.[474] Unless the court is satisfied that it has a proper basis of agreed or determined facts upon which to decide whether the case is one in which it should give effect to 'the general rule'—or should make 'a different order' (and, if so, what order)—it must accept that it is not in a position to make an order about costs at all. That is not an abdication of the court's function in relation to costs; it is a proper recognition that the course which the parties have adopted in the litigation has led to the position where the right way in which to discharge that function is to decide not to make an order about costs.[475]

12.204 There are straightforward cases in which it is reasonably clear from the terms of the settlement that there is a winner and a loser in the litigation. In such cases the parties will usually recognize the result and agree the award of costs. If there is no such agreement, the decision is not usually a difficult one for the judge to make.[476] There are, however, more complex cases in which it will be difficult for the judge to decide who is the winner and who is the loser without embarking on a course which comes close to conducting a trial of the action that the parties intended to avoid by their compromise.[477] This is particularly true in cases involving

---

[468] [2003] EWCA Civ 939.
[469] *Promar* (n 467 above) para 31.
[470] *Venture Finance plc v Mead* [2005] EWCA Civ 325, para 10.
[471] *Brawley v Marizynski (No 1)* [2002] EWCA Civ 756, [2003] 1 WLR 813, para 18.
[472] *BCT* (n 468 above) para 22 *per* Chadwick LJ.
[473] CPR, r 44.3(2)(a).
[474] ibid r 44.3(2)(b).
[475] *BCT* (n 468 above) para 23 *per* Chadwick LJ.
[476] ibid para 4 *per* Mummery LJ and para 25 *per* Chadwick LJ.
[477] ibid para 5 *per* Mummery LJ.

a large number of issues or claims for discretionary equitable relief.[478] Often the truth is that neither party has won or lost.[479]

In all but straightforward compromises (which are, in general, unlikely to involve the judge) **12.205** the judge is entitled to say to the parties: 'If you have not reached an agreement on costs, you have not settled your dispute. The action must go on, unless your compromise covers costs as well.'[480] The judge should be slow to embark on the determination of disputed facts solely in order to put himself in a position to make a decision about costs.[481] He may therefore make no order as to costs.[482]

The Court of Appeal is entitled to approach an appeal against a costs order, which has been **12.206** made as part of a compromise, with an even greater degree of reluctance than is usually the case when it is asked to interfere with the discretion of a trial judge.[483] It should only interfere with such a costs order if the appellant makes out a case of manifest injustice.[484]

In *Promar* the claimant sought an order for the majority of its costs of the action. The claimant **12.207** said that it had principally sought injunctive relief, such relief was effectively offered by the defendant (in the form of an undertaking), and the defendant did not do so until the commencement of the trial.[485] The Court of Appeal rejected the claimant's appeal holding that the concession of the damages claim by the claimant and the concession of the claim for injunctive relief by the defendant meant that there was no winner and no loser and that neither party was therefore exclusively responsible for the abortive trial.[486] Consequently, the existing award, which made no order as to costs, was not manifestly unjust.[487]

In *Pathway Resourcing Ltd v Kaul*,[488] Morgan J considered how the guidance in the *BCT* case **12.208** should be applied where the parties invite the court to determine the issue of costs; the parties have agreed to dispose of all other issues without a trial; but the court doubts the wisdom of deciding that issue. He held:

> It is clear that the judge should try to make the parties confront the reality, which is that they have not settled the whole case and should go away and try to do so. But what if they do not settle the question of costs? It seems to me implicit in BCT that the court will then have to try the issues sufficiently to determine their ability for costs.[489]

The judge went on to identify the principle to be applied. First, the extent to which the court would be prepared to look into previously unresolved substantive issues will depend on the circumstances of the particular case, not least the amount of costs at stake and the conduct of the parties. Secondly, the court should bear in mind the guidance in the *BCT* case about the lack of wisdom in deciding costs when the court does not know who is the winner and who is the loser. Thirdly, the court has the alternative of warning the parties they must settle

---

478 ibid para 7 *per* Mummery LJ.
479 ibid para 5 *per* Mummery LJ.
480 ibid para 6 *per* Mummery LJ and para 26 *per* Chadwick LJ.
481 ibid para 26 *per* Chadwick LJ.
482 ibid para 18 *per* Mummery LJ and para 24 *per* Chadwick LJ.
483 ibid para 8 *per* Mummery LJ.
484 ibid paras 9, 15 *per* Mummery LJ.
485 *Promar* (n 467 above) paras 14, 29.
486 ibid paras 37, 39.
487 ibid para 40.
488 [2008] EWHC 3078 (Ch).
489 ibid, para 39.

the issue of costs and the fallback of directing that the matter should go to a trial at which the issue will be determined in a proportionate way.[490] Having considered the circumstances of that case, the judge ordered that if the parties did not settle the issue of costs, the case should proceed to trial.[491]

12.209 The *BCT* guidance and its application in the *Promar* and *Pathway Resourcing* cases puts in a difficult position the claimant who, having incurred significant litigation costs, is offered an undertaking by the employee in terms which approximate to the restrictive covenant. It is commonly the position that the principal remedy sought by the claimant is injunctive relief to enforce the covenant. This is because, as addressed above, if an interim injunction has been granted at an early stage, the claimant may have limited the damage it has suffered by way of unlawful competition; and secondly, the defendant employee may be unable to meet any potential award for damages in any event (as in the case of the defendant in the *Promar* case).[492] Moreover, having been offered the relief it principally seeks, the claimant may well be reluctant to risk losing its claim at trial and, also, to incur the expense of that trial (which might also be irrecoverable). However, if he were to accept the undertaking offered and were unable to settle the issue of costs, he would be exposed to two significant risks. First, that the court might refuse to make any order as to costs, whether or not the claimant invited the court to determine issues of disputed fact or law for the purposes of its costs application.[493] Secondly, that the court might order the case to proceed to trial, with its attendant costs, uncertainty, and inconvenience. Given such risks, the merit for the claimant in negotiating a settlement of costs will often be obvious.

---

[490] ibid, para 41.
[491] ibid, paras 49, 50.
[492] *Promar* (n 467 above) para 14.
[493] See also *Pathway Resourcing* (n 488 above) para 42.

APPENDICES

APPENDIX 1

Computer Forensic Investigations

Julian Parker and Aaron Stowell of Stroz Friedberg Ltd

1.01 This appendix provides (1) an overview of potential sources of evidence in the workplace, (2) guidance on securing computer evidence, and (3) a brief guide to some commonly applied computer forensic techniques, all of which are relevant to investigations into competitive activities by employees and others.

Sources of evidence

1.02 Where there is wrongdoing in the workplace, such as unlawful competition, computer misuse, intellectual property misappropriation, or fraud, there is usually a range of potential sources of evidence. These include, but are not limited to, computer systems. Table 1 below lists some of the more productive sources of evidence in such situations.

Table 1 Sources of evidence

Evidential source, resource, method	Comments
Documents • Purchase orders • Invoices • Correspondence • Printed emails • Printed faxes, etc	Shredded documents may be reassembled. Do not ignore documents written in foreign languages, programming code, shorthand, and other material that may not be readily intelligible. Consider forensic tests to determine forgery, to recover latent fingerprints, and reveal indentations.
Backup tapes and journalled storage	Often overlooked, backup tapes, and journalling storage systems may retain evidence wiped from current systems.
Data storage devices • External hard disks • USB thumb drives • Media cards • CDs/DVDs • Iomega Zip diskettes • Floppy diskettes	These external, portable or removable storage devices can be used to misappropriate data, and to conceal correspondence and transactions. Forensic trace evidence of the use of removable storage devices may be located by analyzing the system registry, log files, link files, and Internet Explorer history on computer systems. Deleted files may be recovered from these removable storage devices if they can be located.
Email • Electronic mail • Deleted emails • Attachments orphaned in temporary folders • Web-based email accounts such as AOL Mail, Gmail, Hotmail, MobileMe Mail, Yahoo! Mail, etc	Electronic mail is an abundant source of evidence. Forensic analysis enables deleted emails and attachments to be identified and recovered. Attachments opened or previewed from email messages may remain in temporary folders on the computer after the email is deleted. Frequently email correspondence from many web-based email services can be recovered from the Internet cache of an employee's computer or as deleted files or fragments.

(Continued)

Table 1 *Continued*

Evidential source, resource, method	Comments
Multimedia • Digital cameras • Camcorders	JPEG and other photographic image files often depict key evidence. Remember also video formats (MPEG and AVI) and sound files (WAV).
Audio recordings • Voicemail • Answerphone • Tape recordings • Dictaphones • Cassettes, etc	Voicemail may be downloaded from the internal telecoms system or external service provider. Digital audio recordings may be stored on a central server or locally on computers. Evidential tapes should be write-protected, copied and transcribed. Expert processing is advisable.
Telephony • Mobile telephones • Itemized telephone bills • Telephone call logs • Interception	Contact details, last numbers dialled, incoming calls, SMS text and MMS messages, and email may be downloaded from mobile telephones (but consider legal issues relating to access). Call logs and billing data that is the property of the organization may be reviewed and analyzed to establish suspicious contacts or to confirm association between parties. Telephone interception or geo-location must comply with local law. Where interception is contemplated, expert assistance is advisable.
Computers • File Servers • Desktops and workstations • Laptops and notebooks • Blackberrys, Smartphones, PDAs, MIDs, etc • Mainframes	Expert forensic investigation is advisable for all systems which the employee may have accessed. Backup and synchronization files from PDAs and organizers may be located on laptops, notebooks, and desktop computer systems. These should be retrieved and examined. Most PDAs, etc. have built-in mobile telephones. See ground rules for processing computer evidence.
Fax machines, printers and photocopiers • Printouts • Call logs • Memory • Fax or print servers • Interception	Printouts will show header information, which makes the sender's identity traceable, but these can be forged by reprogramming the machine. Depending on the make and model of machine, fax transmissions or recent print or copy jobs may be stored in memory and retrieved. Some larger multifunction devices contain hard disks that can be analyzed to recover previous print jobs. A fax server may have replaced a traditional device in software, sending faxes directly to a recipient's computer. Print job artefacts may still exist on a print server. Interception must comply with local law. Where contemplated, expert assistance is advisable.
Office search • Contents of desks, drawers, cabinets • Whiteboards, desk jotter, calendar • Post-it notes, etc	Some of the quickest retrievals of 'smoking gun' documents have been from office searches. Operationally, the search will usually be conducted covertly—take care not to disrupt the search area and to replace everything as found. Original documents should be photocopied or photographed and returned *exactly* to the location in which they were discovered.

Table 1 *Continued*

Evidential source, resource, method	Comments
Audit trails • Event logs • Web log • Mail log • Router log • Firewall log • Access control	To trace the computers and operators involved in suspicious events or transactions on networks and systems. Audit trails are essential to resolve many computer crimes—careful consideration is required to assess the appropriate scope, coverage, and level of detail recorded. The period that audit trails are retained also requires consideration—from the investigator's perspective, the longer the better.
CCTV	To track people's whereabouts on any given day. Poor CCTV imagery has seriously hindered many investigations—consider a quality control audit and advances such as motion activated and low light recording.
Rubbish	May be recovered from waste paper baskets, commercial waste, and residential locations BUT must comply with local law otherwise search may be illegal and evidence retrieved inadmissible in some jurisdictions.
Typewriter ribbons	Typewriters are still used in some offices. Software has been developed that can read and interpret the strike marks on ribbons to recompose letters and other communications.
Transactional records	Transactional records (such as access or changes made to a database) may be downloaded and analyzed using data interrogation software.
Covert monitoring • Audio monitoring • Concealed video recording • Remote systems surveillance • Keystroke logging	Any covert surveillance must comply with local law. Video sequences should show an accurate time and date. Covert monitoring technology usually requires specialist implementation.
The Internet • Websites • News groups • Discussion groups • Subscriber databases • Libraries • Other research facilities	Google it! The quickest answers to many technical questions and other enquiries are often a mouse click away. Beware that access to a website may be recorded and the browser's identity established—if the investigation is covert, web searches should be conducted at an Internet café or from a non-attributable computer. Consider also subscriber databases, libraries, and other archives as sources of information.

1.03 Methods shown in Table 1 are legal in some countries but not others. Telephone interception and rubbish searches are particularly sensitive. The admissibility of any evidence obtained by these methods is likely to be contested. Whatever methods are contemplated should be assessed by the organization's external legal advisers and, if cleared, should be approved at senior level.

1.04 Mistaken or ill-advised evidence processing cannot usually be corrected at a later stage. The methods and procedures used to collate and process evidence may be subjected to intense scrutiny by a court.

What steps should be taken to secure computer systems?

1.05 Should the decision be made to suspend or dismiss an employee, suitable exit procedures must be in place to:

- preserve evidence;
- safeguard critical systems and processes from sabotage; and
- secure and account for company assets assigned to the departing employee.

1.06 Access to key systems and processes should be revoked. It is vital to secure systems against sabotage. It may be necessary, depending on the circumstances, for a suitably qualified incident response team to take all exposed systems offline temporarily, whilst they are audited and secured. To control this exercise it is necessary to prepare a comprehensive schedule of every system in use and its status. The action list should include the following:

- revoke the employee's remote access network and email facilities;
- consider initiating comprehensive backups for relevant systems, to assist recovery in the event of sabotage and to secure evidence of possible wrongdoing;
- secure and preserve the data on computers and networks used by the employee, together with any disks or data storage media and any paper-based evidence or other potentially relevant material;
- the accounts of the employee should be deactivated, and if the employee possesses a high level of access to technical systems, the administrative passwords should be changed on all systems and an audit conducted to identify any obvious vulnerabilities;
- telephone answering systems and voicemail should also be secured against tampering or the unauthorized re-recording of answer messages;
- the lockdown should include systems and websites hosted by third parties;
- do not allow the employee any unsupervised access to systems or processes. It may be appropriate to accompany them from the building and not to allow unaccompanied access;
- notify relevant departments, including those who staff or guard reception points and entrances to the premises;
- ensure a right of audit or inspection is included in employment contracts, so company property, information, and computer systems are returned on demand;
- if necessary, change locks.

1.07 Computing devices and the data on them should be secured so that the wrongdoers cannot hide, destroy, or tamper with evidence.

1.08 Dismissed employees have often returned computers and other data storage devices to their employer with data wiped clean using sophisticated evidence elimination software. While an inference to conceal or destroy evidence may be drawn in such circumstances, the underlying information is irrevocably lost. This re-emphasizes the absolute necessity of securing all equipment as soon as reasonably practicable.

1.09 It is vital that all company property—keys, mobile telephones, computers, data storage devices, access control devices, wireless access cards—and any proprietary information should be retrieved. Remember, keys can be duplicated and that it may be necessary to change the locks on certain doors.

1.10 The practice of 'home-working' and 'remote working' imposes additional risks and difficulties. If possible, the organization should stipulate a 'right of audit' to computer systems used by any employee for business purposes at home, as part of the standard employment contract. Without a contractual 'right of audit' the company may demand the return of its equipment but anything further, such as inspecting the employee's own computer, is likely to be strongly resisted.

1.11 Security guards, receptionists, and others who control access to the premises should be advised of any suspensions or dismissals, so that they may intercept those involved should they attempt to return to the building.

1.12 The dismissed employee may well remain in contact with friends and associates within the company, and may cajole or otherwise persuade them to destroy or conceal evidence. This reinforces the wisdom of securing evidence at an early stage.

Evidence of employee competition or removal of confidential information

1.13 Where an employee moves to a competitor or where the misappropriation of confidential information is suspected, it is advisable to search computer systems, electronic mail, mobile telephones, and other computing and data storage devices for evidence, which may comprise:

- negotiations and discussions with the new prospective employer, business associate, or recruiter;
- discussions with other employees about leaving;
- discussions with clients, customers, or suppliers about transferring their business to the new employer;
- draft business plans;
- written applications for funding from banks and others;
- the removal or transmission of customer lists, databases, trade secrets, confidential information, and other intellectual property.

1.14 The foundation of any successful computer forensic investigation is that it should comply with the applicable legal rules on access to systems and information. In most corporate investigations, the systems to be investigated are clearly the property of the company and there is no doubt regarding the right of access, either by the company or its agents. Difficulties arise when employees, or others, use their own computers or hardware in the conduct of their day-to-day business and a right of audit or inspection is not expressly stated in their employment contracts. Expert legal advice should be sought when conducting or contemplating a computer forensic investigation in such circumstances.

Computer forensic processing

Basic rule: do not alter original data

1.15 Computer forensic examination is a specialist task, and the correct initial response to secure the evidence is of key importance. Should a non-expert undertake the initial steps to secure computer evidence, two simple rules should be followed:

- If the computer is switched *on*, it should *not* be switched *off*.
- If the computer is switched *off*, it should *not* be switched *on*.

1.16 Prevent anyone from gaining unauthorized access to the machine, and summon expert assistance. These simple rules apply equally to other computing devices, including mobile telephones.

1.17 A fundamental principle applies whenever processing evidential data, in whatever format it is stored:

- Avoid inspecting the original data as this will cause alterations.

The value of computer-based evidence is often compromised within thirty minutes of being discovered, due to hasty and ill-advised inspection.

1.18 Examination of electronically-stored data should not be conducted directly; instead a copy of the data stored on the device should be made. The objective is to freeze the data by taking backups or copies without altering the source data in any way. It is essential not to contaminate the original evidence by introducing any accidental changes.

1.19 Potentially damaging changes to the original data include:

- deletion of evidential files;
- accidental writes to the evidential disk;
- installation of diagnostic software on the evidential disk;
- changes to dates and time stamps;
- relocation of evidential files or directories;
- creation of files or directories;

- recovering deleted files directly on the evidential disk;
- executing native software or applications, batch files, or macros on the evidential disk.

1.20 With regard to computers, under NO circumstances should you ever boot into an original evidential disk. The temptation to switch on the computer should be resisted. The simple act of booting into a computer causes radical changes to the constitution of the operating system and several hundred files may be altered as a result. This can cause the loss of important evidence, particularly in those areas of the disk where data is temporarily cached from memory. As an example, evidence in the *swap file*—a temporary cache used by Windows and other operating systems which records significant volumes of data from RAM—may be lost irrevocably if the computer is booted directly.

1.21 Conversely, when a computer is processed in accordance with proper investigative methods, evidence may be recovered that otherwise might be destroyed. Many users are unaware of the sheer amount of data that gets trapped locally on their computers, even if they had no intention of saving it. Forensic examination can recreate a precise history of Internet usage, including websites visited and even the search terms that have been entered in common Internet search engines. Likewise, email accessed via the Internet can be recovered—often a crucial factor in investigating the misuse of proprietary information or breaches of restrictive covenants.

1.22 The important point in securing such evidence is that a computer cannot be powered up and booted without the evidence on its disk *changing*. It is necessary, therefore, to copy the contents of the computer's evidential hard disk whilst preventing the native operating system installed on this disk from executing and this is achieved by processing the evidential hard disk in a controlled environment.

Disk imaging

1.23 Exact *copies* of the evidential data stream on the original computer are made using a process known as disk imaging whereby the data is copied to a disk or other storage media as an exact bit-stream replication. Disk imaging technology is non-invasive—it does not alter the constitution of the original evidential data in any way.

1.24 The advantage of this method of processing over a conventional backup is that unallocated data storage clusters and other areas of forensic interest on the original evidential disk, in which deleted data may reside, are copied. This data may then be recovered and analyzed.

1.25 It is necessary to distinguish between a standard computer backup and a forensic image copy. A conventional backup faithfully duplicates the contents of files and folders as they are stored in the directory tree structure of the system. However, a standard backup will *not* copy many areas on the evidential disk, which are only made accessible using forensic disk-imaging techniques, including:

- unallocated data storage clusters which may contain residual data from previous files;
- file slack space which may contain fragments of evidence from previous files;
- disk slack space which also may contain evidential data from a previous data partition;
- deleted files and directories.

1.26 The use of disk-imaging technologies is long established in both civil and criminal proceedings in the United Kingdom, the United States, and many other jurisdictions. The fact that the entirety of the data (extant and deleted) belonging to an individual is copied *indiscriminately* has inevitably led to legal arguments relating to the issues of privilege, commercial confidentiality, and self-incrimination. In practice, these arguments have usually been resolved through independent adjudication—typically, the forensic expert gives an undertaking not to disclose any information that may be privileged, confidential, or self-incriminating, and any material thought to fall within these categories is assessed by an independent solicitor or court appointee.

Continuity of evidence

1.27 Ensuring the continuity of evidence, also known as the chain of evidence, is fundamental. It is necessary to be able to account for computer evidence at all times, including its initial seizure and its subsequent custody. All actions pertaining to the exhibit should be recorded in statements and exhibit receipts should support any transit or transfer. Computer data is susceptible to tampering or inadvertent alteration and extra precautions must therefore be taken to ensure its evidential integrity (such as keeping any data storage media in a secure marked envelope, anti-static bag, or a law enforcement standard evidence bag).

Evidential integrity

1.28 It is necessary to establish and demonstrate the evidential integrity of the forensic disk image. How can we be sure that the forensic image is an exact copy of the original evidential disk in the employee's computer? Even a seemingly insignificant discrepancy between the original disk and the image copy of it may undermine the probity or credibility of the evidence. If required to do so, the computer forensic investigator should be able to demonstrate to a court that the image copy upon which their evidence is based is identical to the original disk.

1.29 As stated, the forensic imaging methodology is non-invasive and it is a guiding principle that any software developed for this purpose should not alter or change the data on the original evidential disk. As an additional safeguard, hardware write-blocking devices are used to prevent accidental changes being made to the evidential disk. There are a number of disk-imaging software packages available on the market, amongst the most widely used are Guidance Software's EnCase and Access Data's Forensic Tool Kit Imager. These products incorporate safeguards based on mathematical principles, which verify the integrity of each image produced.

1.30 There are limited circumstances under which it may not be possible to create a forensic image without introducing any alterations to the original media. For example, there are certain models of mobile telephones which current forensic techniques cannot preserve without first changing a small amount of data on the phone. A full forensic preservation should be an investigator's goal. If this is not possible, the preservation methodology should affect the original evidence as little as possible and document any changes.

Computer clocks

1.31 A common error when evidence from computer systems is processed is for the investigator to fail to make a note of the real date and time and compare this with the computer's clock. Any discrepancies in dates and times should be accounted for, so that the probable chronology of files and directories can be calculated.

1.32 Most forensic software audit trails will record the computer clock readings automatically. The common mistake, however, is for the investigator to fail to make a note of the real date and time when they inspect the system and its content.

1.33 Regarding the chronology of events, it is essential, therefore, that the investigator records:

- the computer clock date and time;
- the real date and time;
- the international time zone where the computer is located and the time zone to which it is set;
- whether the 'Daylight Saving Changes' function has been selected, which will automatically adjust the clock as necessary;
- the operating system clock date and time, which may vary with the computer clock date and time.

1.34 There are many potential pitfalls that may ensnare the investigator when analyzing computer evidence, many of which relate to *times* and *dates*. For example, it might be reported that 'Smith made a call at 9:56am'. It is necessary, here, to reserve judgment, and ask some key questions:

- Was this call ever *actually* made?
- How do we know it was *Smith* who made the call and not someone else?
- Which clock recorded 9:56am?
- Was this clock *accurate* when the record was produced?
- Which *time zone* was the clock set to?
- Was the call made in this time zone, or another?
- Where was Smith when the call was made?

There is a clear risk of assuming too much.

1.35 Microsoft Office documents retain information relating to significant events and dates, as shown in **Figure 1** below. Where backdating is suspected, the investigator will look for a discrepancy between the metadata shown and any dates or events detailed in the body of the document itself. The accuracy or inaccuracy of the computer's clock is critical in this respect.

Figure 1 Dates and times

1.36 Most users have no real understanding of the complexities of the machines they use, and what happens to the data they produce. This fact is crucial when investigating the backdating or forgery of documents, for example. Even when sophisticated users try to alter documents and anticipate the effect this will have on other surrounding data, it is almost impossible for them to do so correctly—the complex interaction between the operating system and other software processes nearly always causes an anomaly or a trail that indicates this attempted deceit. The metadata of falsified documents may look correct to the forger, but forensic examination will show it to be out of place in comparison to that of other, unaltered documents.

Deleted files

1.37 When the user of a computer deletes a file, the operating system marks the file as deleted and frees the disk space it occupied for reuse by a new file. The data remains *in situ* until a new file overwrites it. The deleted data may remain on the disk for a considerable period depending on the intensity and magnitude of computer use, the size of the computer's hard disk, and other technical variables. Deleted data may thus be recovered—often the entire file may be retrieved, or vestigial remnants of it may be located and exported. Deleted information may be recovered from a computer using a variety of specialist software tools.

What you see is what you get?

1.38 Many computer software packages proclaim that *what you see is what you get* (WYSIWYG). The concept is that information shown on screen reflects exactly the data as it is recorded on disk, in storage, or as printout. In forensic investigations, however, it should never be assumed that WYSIWYG applies, as often this is not the case.

1.39 Printed documents and correspondence observed on screen (for example through the Windows operating system interface) do not *necessarily* reflect all related information within the soft copy. This is a very important fact that is not widely appreciated by the legal profession.

1.40 By way of illustration, **Figure 2** shows correspondence between the fictitious Messrs Smith and Reeves as it is displayed through the Windows interface.

Figure 2 Document displayed in Windows

However, when the same document is viewed using a hexadecimal editor, a different version of the letter appears, revealing a paragraph that has been suppressed by Microsoft Word on screen but which has been retained within the soft copy document (**Figure 3**).

1.41 This phenomenon occurs when the 'fast save' component is utilized within Microsoft Word, a feature that is on by default. The Fast Save feature, however, is not utilized in Microsoft Word 2003 SP3 and upward. In litigation it is important to remember that printouts and information viewed on screen need not necessarily reflect the underlying data as it is stored on disk and forensic investigation has often proved this to be the case.

Metadata

1.42 One of the more oblique and unexpected routes by which sensitive information may leak is through *metadata*. This is a little understood risk that pertains to any individual or organization that transmits electronic documents, as it can result in the unwitting disclosure of data. Metadata has often proved to be of immense forensic value.

1.43 Microsoft Word files contain within their coding significant information (called metadata) about each document's origin, history, and provenance. Some of this metadata is not apparent through the Word software interface and can only be seen using specialist software.

1.44 Metadata also records the user and affiliation to which the software was originally registered, and the created, modified, saved, and printed times and dates of the file.

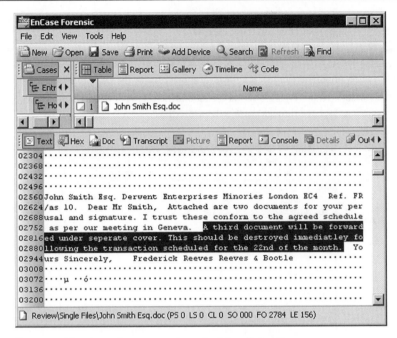

Figure 3 The same document viewed with a disk editor

1.45 Editorial amendments to documents may also be recorded. In this respect, the 'track changes' and 'fast save' options within Microsoft Word are particular risks to the unwary, and equally helpful to the forensic investigator.

1.46 For the security minded, metadata may be stripped from a wide range of data formats automatically using various tools. Many businesses, including law firms, use such tools to ensure their data is as 'clean' as possible when it leaves their control and carries little or no metadata with it.

Potential other sources of email and documents

1.47 There are several specialist forensic software packages to assist in the investigation of the different electronic mail systems currently in use within the corporate environment. It is possible to recover deleted electronic mail from certain archive formats, track conversations, and index sizeable mail archives for rapid text searches.

1.48 Webmail services such as Hotmail, Gmail, and Yahoo! are sometimes used by departing employees to illicitly export data from corporate computers because they believe these services bestow anonymity and are untraceable. Historically, use of these webmail services deposited readily accessible message artefacts on the computer hard disk, however, recent changes to the webmail services have reduced the amount and quality of artefacts left behind on the computer.

1.49 Both the Google Desktop Search and Windows Desktop Search applications (called Windows Search Service in Windows Vista and 7) index documents, web pages, chat applications, and both corporate and web-based email in order that the user can perform fast searches. The indexed information is copied to a cache that allows for easy viewing of the files' contents without having to open the original document.

1.50 Computer forensic techniques allow these indexes to be accessed, enabling the recovery of complete documents and emails even after removal from the user's computer. Google Desktop also indexes network storage locations and removable media, which is especially helpful as documents not residing on the local machine might appear in the Google Desktop cache. In addition, encrypted documents are indexed and cached when decrypted by the user, so whilst the file may exist in an encrypted state on the hard disk there may be a decrypted copy in the Google Desktop cache.

1.51   There have been numerous cases where 'anonymous' webmail services have been misused to transmit confidential data or to conspire. In various such instances the mail messages and the transmitted attachments have been recovered from the employee's workstation. Such evidence may have immense probative value.

Encrypted documents

1.52   Password protected Word documents and Excel spreadsheets regularly feature in investigations and the proven technical capability to decrypt these files is immensely valuable to investigators. While older versions of the Microsoft Office Suites employed weak methods of encryption, the newer 2007 package implements by default a secure 128 bit AES algorithm, making password cracking a lengthy process involving greater computing power.

1.53   One method of password cracking that has been known to greatly reduce the amount of time required to gain access to the encrypted file relies on the probability that the user has written down the password in unencrypted form elsewhere on the computer. A keyword list is compiled from all documents on the computer and is then run against the password protected file using password cracking software.

1.54   In various instances, encrypted business plans, marketing brochures, and other documents relevant to nascent or competitive ventures have been located by investigators and decrypted.

   Figure 4 shows a single word dictionary attack to open a password protected Microsoft Word 2007 file. Due to the increased strength of the encryption used, breaking some of the more complicated passwords can take in the region of three days, however many passwords are identified in around twenty minutes. This example shows *Passware Recovery Kit Standard*, a commercially available password recovery toolkit found at <http://www.lostpassword.com/kit-standard.htm>. The continual increase in processing power serves to constantly reduce the length of time taken to recover even complex passwords.

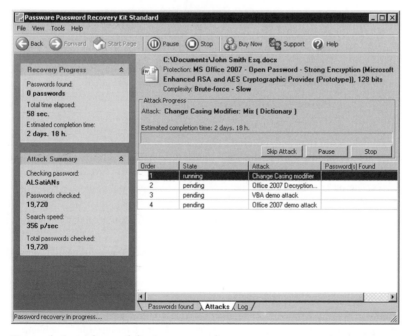

Figure 4 A single word dictionary attack

Intellectual property

1.55 Technology that facilitates the storage and sharing of intellectual property also makes it easier to steal. The range of highly portable devices by which information may be transferred between locations and systems has expanded in recent years. Capacities of these devices have rapidly increased whilst progressions in manufacturing processes have allowed the devices to become much smaller. A single DAT tape, the size of a small matchbox, can store the entire intellectual property of many small and medium-sized enterprises, while an LTO tape, half the size of a standard paperback book, can store 1.8 terabytes of compressed data. USB thumb drives in particular are readily available in a wide array of designs, some of which are highly concealed, for example, in wristbands, soft toys, and key fob designs as illustrated in **Figure 5**.

Figure 5 USB devices

1.56 The technologies to store and process data have also converged with a range of multi-functional devices now hitting the market. These and similar developments, such as solid-state memory for digital cameras, have caused some major revisions in the training of investigators in the search and seizure of computer evidence.

1.57 Other portable devices increasingly include many mobile telephones or Smartphones which not only have storage capability, but also have various connectivity options and in many cases, built in cameras.

1.58 Without resorting to spot checks and searches of people and their possessions and computers, it is extremely difficult to monitor or prevent the illicit use of external data storage devices. Due to their portability, these devices are easily mislaid or lost, which introduces another risk should the information stored on them be confidential or sensitive.

1.59 The information on thumb drives and other portable data storage devices and media may also be *copied* quickly and *surreptitiously*, which emphasizes the need for encryption or biometric access control when sensitive data is in transit.

1.60 Forensically, it is possible to determine the first time and date that a specific USB device such as a thumb drive or other device has been attached to a given computer. The firmware of the USB device can provide information that uniquely identifies the device. This information includes an iSerial-Number which in most instances is unique to the device.

1.61 For example, upon insertion of the USB device into a computer running Windows XP, Windows locates and loads the appropriate drivers for the USB storage device and updates a file named Setupapi.log. The log entries provide the unique instance ID which in most cases incorporates the USB device's iSerialNumber. Figure 6 shows three examples of the information on a computer running Windows XP logs for the three devices highlighted.

```
A--> CdRomRICOH_CD-R/RW_MP7083A
        - Device Description: CD-ROM Drive
        - Hardware ID: IDE\CdRomRICOH_CD-R/RW_MP7083A
        - Class GUID: {4D36E965-E325-11CE-BFC1-08002BE10318}
        - Service: cdrom
        - Driver: {4D36E965-E325-11CE-BFC1-08002BE10318}\0001
        - Manufacturer: (Standard CD-ROM drives)

I--> Disk&Ven_Generic&Prod_USB_SD_Reader&Rev_2.00
        - Device Description: Disk drive
        - Hardware ID: USBSTOR\DiskGeneric_USB_SD_Reade_2.00
        - Class GUID: {4D36E967-E325-11CE-BFC1-08002BE10318}
        - Service: disk
        - Parent Id Prefix: 7&fb9486&0
        - Driver: {4D36E967-E325-11CE-BFC1-08002BE10318}\0005
        - Manufacturer: (Standard disk drives)

J--> Disk&Ven_SanDisk&Prod_Cruzer_Mini&Rev_0.1
        - Device Description: Disk drive
        - Hardware ID: USBSTOR\DiskSanDisk_Cruzer_Mini_0.1
        - Class GUID: {4D36E967-E325-11CE-BFC1-08002BE10318}
        - Service: disk
        - Parent Id Prefix: 7&21e31e8b&0
        - Driver: {4D36E967-E325-11CE-BFC1-08002BE10318}\0007
        - Manufacturer: (Standard disk drives)
```

Figure 6 Section of Setupapi.log

1.62 The problem is that there can be rarely any indication of *which* files have been copied to (or from) these devices. Although the misappropriation of data using thumb drives in some instances is traceless, other indications may exist on the computer.

1.63 The misuse of write enabled CD drives can be easier to investigate as some of the software packages that enable the user to 'burn' data to a CD record audit trails, which, in some cases, provide comprehensive details of the files and folders that were copied, when, and from which location.

1.64 Those who remove data often leave telltale traces of their actions. **Figure** 7 shows a screenshot of the WinZip program where an internal history of previously created archive files is maintained. The archive file itself has since been moved to the user's USB thumb drive but its file name clearly indicates its purpose.

1.65 Finally, computer users in the workplace can only try to eliminate the data they can access—and they can't normally access backup tapes. If email or other documentation is missing from a user's computer, it may be available to be restored from a backup tape or other archive under the control of the IT department.

1.66 The importance of regular and up-to-date backups cannot be over-emphasized. Backups are the single most important defence against a range of potential disasters and have on many occasions proved to be a rich seam of evidence.

Figure 7 WinZip file creation history

Hand-held devices

1.67 The market is flooded with a variety of hand-held computing devices, Smartphones and similar devices. Many of these operate by the use of complicated operating systems which are capable of storing large quantities of forensic evidence.

1.68 Mobile phones are no longer simple communication devices, but are capable of many of the same tasks as full computer systems. These various devices should be considered as part of any investigation. Most Smartphones are capable of storing significant quantities of call history; SMS history; email content; photographs; contact lists, and calendar entries, as well as having the ability to install custom applications (apps) to allow the user to perform many additional tasks.

1.69 GPS enabled devices can be used to track the locations where the device has been, as well as saved or favourite locations. Frequently the GPS coordinates are saved with photographs taken using the device, providing not only the date and time that a photograph was taken, but also the specific location.

1.70 Many of these devices contain large built in storage as well as expandable storage slots enabling them to store significant quantities of data, often rivalling a standard desktop computer.

1.71 Where a mobile phone contract is in place, the investigation team may also find value in examining the itemized billing call history.

Conclusion

1.72 In short, computer forensic techniques can recover deleted documents and emails; retrieve hidden and encrypted data; demonstrate that information has been copied to external devices or email accounts; and detect fraud, forgery, and Internet misuse. Beyond this, forensic examination is also often used simply to establish facts: was a particular email sent? If so, was it opened, printed, and by whom?

1.73 By necessity this appendix has only been an overview of computer forensic techniques, but it does provide a flavour of what an investigation may reveal. The ubiquitousness of computers, PDAs, mobile telephones, and other computing devices in the modern working environment has meant that their forensic investigation has frequently proved its worth in litigation.

Glossary

- **Access control device**
  Many buildings have door access control devices activated by door fobs, or swipe cards. The fob or card ID is checked against an access control list to confirm that the card has the required permission to enter. Frequently the access to any door records the card ID and the date and time of access in a database.

- **Computing device**
  Any device that provides access to or can process electronic data. A computing device is the packaged whole of components (processing unit, memory, storage device, input device, graphics display, and operating system) that function together as a single unit. There are a number of different types of computing devices and common categories include computer, MID, PDA, mobile phones/SmartPhones and media player. Continued convergence between the functions offered by devices in different categories and the emergence of new types of device is blurring the fine lines between each category of device.

- **Computer**
  Computer is a broad term which covers a number of common form factors such as desktop, laptop, notebook/netbook and server.

- **DAT/LTO tape**
  DAT and LTO are two different physical formats of tape media that can be used to store data. Tape is a magnetic storage media that is accessed in a linear fashion, and can hold very large volumes of data given its physical size. DAT tapes are physically smaller, and can store less data than LTO tapes.

- **Data storage device**
  A storage device is a broad description to encompass any electronic device capable of storing digital information in a stable or non-volatile state. Extending the description outside the digital realm, pen and paper combined can be thought of as the most basic storage device. When applied to digital information the term storage device includes internal storage—built into the computing device, external—provided in a enclosure and connected via a specific port (such as USB, Firewire, ESata, or Ethernet), or as removable storage media. The types of storage device are broadly speaking magnetic—hard disk drives (HDD), floppy and zip diskettes or tape, semiconductor—flash memory either as a solid state drive (SSD), USB 'thumb drive' or media card), or optical—CDs, DVDs, or Blu-ray.

- **JPEG**
  A JPEG file is a picture file that has been saved using JPEG encoding. The Joint Photographic Experts Group (JPEG) format allows for large and detailed picture files to be compressed to significantly reduce the size of the file. It is because of this that JPEG files are frequently used on the Internet, and a common file type for digital cameras. The extension for a JPEG file could be either JPEG; JPE, or JPG. Other common picture formats include GIF; BMP; PNG, and TIFF.

- **Media card**
  Media card is a term used to collectively describe the digital storage used with devices such as digital cameras, PDA, mobile phones/SmartPhones, and other computing or electronic devices that provide the functionality for expandable storage. Common formats of media card include CompactFlash (CF), SmartMedia (SM), memory stick (MS), multimedia card (MMC), secure digital (SD), xD-Picture Card (xD), and many variations on these formats.

- **Media player**
  A device designed for the purpose of playing stored digital media (music, video, photos, or text). Media players are often able to deal with a wide variety of file formats such as MP3 for music, MPEG for video, and JPEG for photos. Common types of media player include Apple iPod, Microsoft Zune, Archos vision, and ebook readers such as Amazon Kindle. Many media player functions are offered by most other computing devices such as computers, MIDs, PDA, mobile Phones/SmartPhones.

- **Metadata**
  Metadata is often described as being 'data about data' and as such can be described as being data that provides information pertaining to the properties of the document. As an example the data of an object would be its description and details—'a bright red rubber ball'. The metadata may be more specific such as where the ball was stored, when, and by whom—'Steve put the ball in the cupboard on Wednesday'. The metadata may be more in-depth information about the ball, such as where it was

made, the specific formula or rubber used and the process—'made in France from vulcanized Kerala rubber, Patent number 766-349958295'. Thus, when referring to metadata for digital data it can be file system metadata such as when the document was created, last amended, or last accessed and where it is stored. It may also be internal or embedded metadata for a document (although this does not exist with all types of file formats) for example the original author, the user account that most recently amended the document, or when it was last printed.

- MID
  Mobile internet device, this is a term used to describe a fairly new type of device such as iPads and other tablets which are predominately used for Internet browsing and accessing email in a portable form factor. Most MIDs include media player functionality for listening to music, watching video, displaying photos, and as ebook readers or for games.

- MMS
  Multimedia messaging service or MMS. These are similar to an SMS, but are capable of including pictures as well as text.

- MPEG and AVI
  MPEG and AVI are moving picture files, commonly referred to as video clips. These will usually include both a visual and audible component, but may be either in isolation.

- PDA
  The term personal digital assistant or PDA, is used to describe any portable hand held device that is capable of storing and organizing a user's data, such as the Blackberry, or Palm devices. They frequently include mobile phone functionality as well, but this is not a requirement.

- Programming code
  Programming code or source code can be described as the human readable form of the various instructions and routines which constitute an application. There are a number of different programming languages that each have their own specific structure and syntax, and as such both function and appear different to each other. To the untrained eye, it may not be possible to understand what the programming code means, but to the correct expert, it can be read as a native language.

- SMS
  Short message service or SMS. These are commonly referred to as text message in the United Kingdom. Text messaging is extensively used on mobile phones.

- Storage media
  Is really a subset of storage device, limited to devices where the removable and interchangeable media is used with a specific device designed to read and write to that media. It covers optical media—CDs, DVDs, or Blu-ray, magnetic media—floppy and zip diskettes or tape and semiconductor media—which covers a wide range of media cards.

- Thumb drive
  A data storage device that uses semiconductor flash memory to store data. There are many different terms used to describe a USB thumb drive, such as USB flash drive, USB pen drive, USB memory stick. These highly portable devices are readily used to move data between computers.

- WAV
  A WAV file is a recording of a sound wave, commonly referred to as an audio clip. This may be used for capturing telephone conversations or dictation recordings. Other common audio clip formats include MP3, AIFF, and RAM.

- Wireless access card
  Wireless access cards are frequently provided to laptop computer users to allow internet connections via 3G or Wi-Fi protocols when away from the employer's office or in areas of an office or site that do not have cabled network connections. Often access to a corporate network by wireless connection is limited to only the specific access cards distributed by the company.

- Zip drive
  An Iomega Zip drive is the name given to a piece of hardware that operated with similar functionality to the common floppy disk drive with a compatible diskette, but with far greater capacity and improved performance and reliability.

Sample Employee Duties Clauses

Dan Aherne and Luke Pardey

1. Job description and duties

1.1 During the continuance of his employment and without prejudice to the Executive's implied duty of fidelity, the Executive will:

    1.1.1 serve the Company as [*Job Title*] [and as] [a statutory director of the Company] [and of such Group Companies as are notified to the Executive by [the Board] from time to time];

    1.1.2 carry out such duties and exercise such powers in relation to the Company [or any Group Company] as may from time to time be assigned to or vested in him by [the Board];

    1.1.3 [at all times comply with his duties as a director as set out in any relevant legislation, including (without limitation) Part 10, Chapter 2 Companies Act 2006;]

    1.1.4 [declare to [the Board] any interest that he may have (directly or indirectly) in any proposed transaction or arrangement with the Company [or any Group Company], as soon as practicable and in any event before any such transaction or arrangement is entered into;]

    1.1.5 well and faithfully serve the Company [and any Group Companies] to the best of his ability and carry out his duties in a proper and efficient manner;

    1.1.6 use his best endeavours to promote, and at all times act in the best interests of, the Company [and any Group Company];

    1.1.7 ensure that [the Board] is aware as soon as practicable of:

        1.1.7.1 any activity, actual or threatened, which might affect the interests of the Company [and/or any Group Company];

        1.1.7.2 any actual, potential, or maturing business opportunity enjoyed by the Company [or any Group Company];

        1.1.7.3 his own misconduct or the misconduct of any agent, employee, officer, or worker of the Company [or any Group Company] of which the Executive is, or ought reasonably to be, aware;

        1.1.7.4 any offer of engagement or approach made by a Competing Business to any agent, employee, officer, or worker of the Company [or any Group Company] of which the Executive is, or ought reasonably to be, aware;

        1.1.7.5 the intention (whether settled or not) of any agent, employee, officer, or worker of the Company [or any Group Company] who reports directly or indirectly to the Executive to resign from their employment or engagement with the Company [or any Group Company];

    1.1.8 render his services in a professional and competent manner and in willing cooperation with others;

    1.1.9 unless prevented by ill-health or other unavoidable cause, devote his whole time and attention and abilities to carrying out his duties under this Agreement;

    1.1.10 at all times comply with the directions of [the Board] or of anyone duly authorized by it [and with][,] the terms and provisions of the Company's codes, policies, and procedures as amended from time to time [and the codes, policies, and procedures of any Group Company so far as they are relevant to the Company and/or the work carried out by the Executive from time to time];

    1.1.11 undertake such travel within and outside of the United Kingdom as may be required for the proper performance of his duties;

1.1.12 (so far as he is reasonably able to do so) seek to ensure that the Company [and each Group Company] complies in all material respects with the rules, procedures, policies, and codes of any professional organization or association of which it is a member; [and]

1.1.13 [at all times comply with the provisions of clause [   ] of this Agreement with respect to dealings in Company Securities and the misuse and control of price sensitive or inside information].

2. Obligation to provide information to the board

2.1 The Executive will report to [the Board] or such person as [the Board] may from time to time determine and at all times keep [the Board] (or such other person) fully informed of his activities and will promptly provide such information and explanations as may be requested from time to time by [the Board] (or such other person).

2.2 The Executive will not at any time knowingly or willingly do or cause or permit to be done anything that is calculated or may tend to prejudice or injure the interests of the Company [or any Group Company] and if during his employment the Executive learns of any act or omission by any other person whether or not employed by the Company [or any Group Company] that is calculated or may tend to prejudice or injure the interests of the Company [or any Group Company] he will promptly report it to [the Board] giving all necessary particulars of it and will fully cooperate with the Company [or any Group Company] in any consequent action that it may take.

3. Warranty—no restriction on performance of duties

3.1 The Executive confirms, represents, and warrants that he is not bound by or subject to any agreement, arrangement, court order, obligation, or undertaking which in any way restricts or prohibits him entering into, or performing his duties under, this Agreement. [The Executive hereby indemnifies and holds harmless the Company against all claims, costs, damages, and expenses which the Company may incur in connection with any claim that the Executive was so bound or subject.]

4. Restrictions during employment

4.1 Other than in the proper and normal course of his duties, the Executive will not at any time during the continuance of his employment, without the prior written consent of [the Board]:

4.1.1 [have any Material Interest in any trade, business or occupation whatsoever other than the business of the Company [or any Group Company] except as disclosed in Schedule [1];]

4.1.2 [have any Material Interest in any Competing Business;]

4.1.3 [have any Material Interest in any person, firm, or company that impairs or might reasonably be considered by the Company [or any Group Company] to impair his ability to act at all times in the best interests of the Company [and any Group Company];]

4.1.4 [have any Material Interest in any person, firm, or company that requires or might reasonably be considered by the Company [or any Group Company] to require him to use and/or disclose any Confidential Information [*as defined in service agreement*] in order properly to discharge his duties or to further his interest in such person, firm, or company;]

4.1.5 incur on behalf of the Company [or any Group Company] any capital expenditure in excess of such sum as may be authorized from time to time by resolution of the Board;

4.1.6 enter into on behalf of the Company [or any Group Company] any commitment, contract, or arrangement which is otherwise than in the normal course of the Company's [or the relevant Group Company's] business or is outside the scope of his normal duties or authorizations or is of an unusual or onerous or long-term nature;

4.1.7 engage any person on terms which vary from those established from time to time by resolution of the Board;

4.1.8 employ or engage or attempt to employ or engage, induce, solicit, or entice away or attempt to induce, solicit, or entice away any agent, consultant, employee, officer, or worker of the Company [or any Group Company];

4.1.9 directly or indirectly make preparations to compete with any business carried on by the Company [or any Group Company]; [or]

4.1.10 [induce or attempt to induce any [client] [or] [customer] [or] [supplier] of the Company [or any Group Company] to cease conducting any business or to reduce the amount of business or adversely to vary the terms upon which any business is conducted with the Company [or any Group Company] or to exclude the Company [or any Group Company] from new business opportunities in relation to goods or services of a kind normally dealt in by the Company [or any Group Company][; or][.]]

4.1.11 [inform any agent, client, consultant, customer, employee, officer, supplier, or worker of the Company [or any Group Company] or any third-party agent who may be in the habit of dealing with the Company [or any Group Company] that he may resign or has resigned from the Company [or any Group Company] or that he has accepted employment with or is to join or be associated with any Competing Business.]

4.2 The [Company][Board] may at its absolute discretion at any time and from time to time upon written notice to the Executive require the Executive to take [immediately][as soon as practicable] all steps necessary fully and effectively to relinquish the whole or any part of any Material Interest disclosed in Schedule 1 or in respect of the holding of which the Board has at any time given its prior written consent under clause 4.1 [if the Company [or any group Company] [reasonably] considers that it is not in the best interests of the Company [or any Group Company] for the Executive to continue to hold that Material Interest].

5. Relevant definitions

'**Board**'   the board of directors of the Company from time to time or any committee of the Board to which powers have been properly delegated, including a remuneration committee;

'**Company Securities**'   means any shares or other securities issued by the Company [or any Group Company] from time to time;

'**Competing business**'   any business in [geographical area eg England and/or Scotland and/or Wales and/or Northern Ireland] that competes or is preparing to compete with any business carried on by the Company [or any Group Company];

'**Material Interest**'   any direct or indirect interest, whether as an agent, beneficiary, consultant, director, employee, partner, proprietor, shareholder (other than a minority shareholder holding not more than 3 per cent of any class of securities quoted or dealt in on a Recognized Investment Exchange), or otherwise;

'**Recognized Investment Exchange**'   a recognized investment exchange or an overseas investment exchange, each as defined by section 285 of the Financial Services and Markets Act 2000.

APPENDIX 3

Sample Confidential Information Clauses

Dan Aherne and Luke Pardey

1. Confidentiality

1.1 [The Executive recognizes that confidential information (which may include commercially sensitive information) is important to the business of the Company and will from time to time become known to the Executive. The Executive acknowledges that the following restraints [upon which the Executive has [had the opportunity to receive] [received] independent legal advice] are necessary for the reasonable protection of the Company, of its business, [the business of any Group Company] and its [or their] clients and their respective affairs.]

1.2 During the continuance of the Executive's employment (except in the proper performance of his duties) and after the Termination Date, the Executive will:

1.2.1 observe strict secrecy as to the affairs and dealings of the Company [and all Group Companies];

1.2.2 not, without the prior written consent of [the Board], make use of or divulge to any person any confidential information;

1.2.3 not cause or facilitate the publication or disclosure of any confidential information; and use his best endeavours to prevent the publication or disclosure of any confidential information.

1.3 The obligations contained in clause 1.2 will cease to apply to any confidential information upon it coming into the public domain, other than in circumstances where the confidential information comes into the public domain as a result of or in connection with a breach by the Executive of clause 1.2 or any other unauthorized conduct of the Executive.

2. Detailed definition of confidential information[1]

2.3 For the purposes of this Agreement, confidential information includes:

2.3.1 financial information relating to the Company [and any Group Company] including (but not limited to) management accounts, sales forecasts, dividend forecasts, profit and loss accounts and balance sheets, draft accounts, results, order schedules, profit margins, pricing strategies, and other information regarding the performance or future performance of the Company [or any Group Company];

2.3.2 client or customer lists and contact lists, details of the terms of business with, the fees and commissions charged to or by and the requirements of customers or clients, prospective customers or clients of, buyers from and suppliers to the Company [or any Group Company], price lists, discount structures, pricing statistics, market research reports;

2.3.3 any information relating to expansion plans, maturing business opportunities, business strategy, marketing plans, and presentations, tenders, projects, joint ventures or acquisitions and developments contemplated, offered, or undertaken by the Company [or any Group Company];

2.3.4 details of the employees, officers, and workers of and consultants to the Company [or any Group Company] [, their job skills and capabilities] and the remuneration and other benefits paid to them;

2.3.5 [copies or details of and information relating to know-how, research activities, inventions, creative briefs, ideas, computer programs (whether in source code or object code), secret processes, designs and formulae, or other intellectual property undertaken, commissioned, or produced by or on behalf of the Company [or any Group Company];]

---

[1] This definition should *always* be considered in detail to ensure irrelevant items are removed.

2.3.6 confidential reports or research commissioned by or provided to the Company [or any Group Company] and any trade secrets and confidential transactions of the Company [or any Group Company]; [and]

2.3.7 [[*Use for companies conducting business over the Internet*] key metric information such as details of website page hits, visitors, visits, orders per day, total order volumes, average order size, volumes of goods shipped or held in stock, customer acquisition costs, repeat rates, and word of mouth rates;] [and]

2.3.8 [[*Use for IP-heavy companies*] details of any marketing, development, pre-selling or other exploitation of any intellectual property, or other rights of the Company [or any Group Company], any proposed options or agreements to purchase, licence, or otherwise exploit any intellectual property of the Company [or any Group Company], any intellectual property which is under consideration for development by the Company [or any Group Company], any advertising, marketing, or promotional campaign which the Company [or any Group Company] is to conduct]; [and]

2.3.9 any information which the Executive [ought reasonably to know] [is aware] is confidential and any information which has been given to the Company [or any Group Company] in confidence by agents, buyers, clients, consultants, customers, suppliers, or other persons.

2.4 The list in clause 2.3 is indicative only and is not exhaustive.

3. Non-disclosure to media[2]

3.1 [Without prejudice to clause 1.2, the Executive undertakes that he will not while an employee of the Company [or any Group Company] nor after the Termination Date disclose, publish, or reveal to any unauthorized person any incident, conversation, or information concerning any director, employee, agent, or consultant of the Company [or any Group Company] or any of its [or their] [clients,] customers, guests, or visitors which comes to his knowledge during the continuance of his employment, or any incident, conversation, or information relating to his employment by the Company, unless duly authorized in advance in writing by [the Board] so to do, save as required by law. The Executive acknowledges and understands that this undertaking includes an agreement on his part not to publish, procure, facilitate, or encourage the publication of any such matter in any book, newspaper, periodical, or pamphlet or by broadcasting on television, cable, satellite, film, Internet, or any other medium now known or devised after the date of this Agreement or by communication to any third party including a representative of the media.]

4. Requirement not to make notes or memoranda

4.1 [The Executive will not at any time during the continuance of his employment with the Company make otherwise than for the benefit of the Company [(or any Group Company for which the Executive is directed to provide his services)] any notes or memoranda relating to any matter [within the scope of the [business of the Company [or such Group Company] or] concerning any of the dealings or affairs of the Company [or any Group Company].]

5. Saving for protected disclosures

5.1 Nothing in this Agreement precludes the Executive from making a protected disclosure as the same is defined in section 43A of the Employment Rights Act 1996.[3]

---

[2] This provision is helpful where disclosure to the media is an issue. Such wording is untested but may be helpful in establishing a breach of confidence claim. See eg *Archer v Williams* [2003] EWHC 1670 (QB).

[3] ERA 1996, s 43J(1) provides that 'any provision in an agreement ... is void in so far as it purports to preclude the worker from making a protected disclosure'.

APPENDIX 4

Sample Garden Leave Clauses[1]

Catherine Taylor

Simple clause

1. The Company shall be under no obligation to vest in or assign to you any powers or duties or to provide any work to you, and the Company may, at its discretion, [at any time, including] during any period of notice given by either party amend your duties and/or suspend you from the performance of your duties and/or exclude you from any premises of the Company and/or require you not to communicate with any clients or prospective clients of the Company or any of the Company's employees, agents or consultants [or suppliers] and/or require you to work from home ('Garden Leave Arrangement').

2. Salary will continue to be payable and contractual benefits (excluding bonus or commission) will continue to be provided during the course of any Garden Leave Arrangement. You shall throughout any period of Garden Leave Arrangement continue to act as an employee of the Company and shall comply with your obligations under this agreement including, but not limited to your duty of good faith.

Long form clause

1. The Company is under no obligation to vest in or assign to the Executive any powers or duties or to provide any work for the Executive and the Company may [at any time or] during [all or part of] any period of notice given by either party suspend the Executive and require him:
   (a) not to perform some or all of his duties and/or to carry out alternative duties of a broadly similar nature to some or all of the work he normally performs; and/or
   (b) to carry out special projects for the Company [or any Group Company]; and/or
   (c) to abstain from contacting any client, consultant, customer, supplier [*insert any other contact as appropriate*], adviser, agent, director, employee or worker of the Company [or of any Group Company]; and/or
   (d) not to enter any premises of the Company [or any Group Company]; and/or
   (e) to resign from any and all offices in the Company [and any Group Company][2] and/or to return to the Company all documents and other materials (including copies) belonging to the Company [and/or any Group Company] [except that the Executive will be entitled to retain until the termination of his employment or for as long as he continues as a director of the Company [and/or any Group Company] copies of board papers received by him in his capacity as a director of the Company [or any Group Company]].

2. Salary and Benefits [(excluding bonus, commission and entitlement to share options) [*insert any other provisions regarding reduced benefits, for example a reduction of holiday entitlement to the minimum specified under the Working Time Regulations*]] will not cease to be payable to the Executive by reason of any suspension, exclusion or requirement pursuant to Clause [1] and throughout any such period of suspension or exclusion or requirement the Executive:
   - will continue to be an employee of the Company;
   - will continue to be bound by the duty of fidelity and by the terms of this agreement;
   - must, unless otherwise agreed in writing, remain on call to perform such work as is required of him;

---

[1] These sample clauses should be read in conjunction with paras 4.131–4.159 and 4.333–4.339, which provide a commentary and guidance on the duties of an employer and employee during garden leave and a drafting checklist.

[2] Note that this requirement will only be truly effective if it is backed up by drafting elsewhere in the service agreement.

- may not directly or indirectly be employed by nor provide services to any third party;
- must not make any internal or external announcement regarding the Company or its business, or his suspension, exclusion or any requirement, unless it has previously been approved in writing by the Company;
- may not make any preparations to compete with the Company [or any Group Company]; and
- must take any outstanding holiday (including any holiday which accrues during the period of the suspension, exclusion, or requirement), provided that holiday periods are agreed with the Company in advance [in accordance with its standard policy].

3. The Executive agrees that during any period of notice given by either party he will give to the Company or such person nominated by it all such assistance and cooperation in effecting a smooth and orderly handover of his duties and responsibilities as the Company may reasonably require.

4. The Company may during any period of notice given by either party appoint a person to perform the Executive's duties jointly with him or, during any period of suspension pursuant to clause [1], to perform the Executive's duties in his place.

Related clause

* If the agreement is to allow for any garden leave period to be shorter than the notice period, the following Payment in Lieu of Notice clause should be included in the contract.

[ ] The Company may in its absolute discretion choose to terminate the Executive's employment at any time and make a payment equivalent to the Executive's salary [and the cost to the Company of the benefits [specifically granted to the Employee by this Agreement/set out at clause [ ]] (less tax, National Insurance contributions and any other deductions required by law) that would have been payable during the shorter of:

- the minimum period of notice to which the Executive would have been entitled [under clause [ ]]; and
- any unexpired period of notice.

APPENDIX 5

Sample Particulars of Claim and Interim Injunction in Garden Leave Case

Jane Mulcahy

A. Sample particulars of claim

IN THE HIGH COURT OF JUSTICE

QUEEN'S BENCH DIVISION

Claim No. HQ [   ]

BETWEEN

MADRICK LIMITED

Claimant

–and–

JOHN STEPHENS

Defendant

PARTICULARS OF CLAIM

The parties

1. The Claimant is the largest manufacturer of children's clothing in the United Kingdom, continental Europe, and throughout the world.
2. The Defendant is employed by the Claimant as Senior Vice President—North Europe and is based in London. He reports directly to Mr Bill Dinmont ('Mr Dinmont'), the President and Chief Executive Officer of the Claimant.

Terms of employment

3. The Defendant has been employed by the Claimant since 30 March 2003, latterly pursuant to a contract dated 1 November 2008 ('the Agreement').
4. The Agreement contains the following express terms:
    4.1. by clause 4.1, it is provided that the Defendant's normal working hours will be from 9am to 5.30pm from Monday to Friday together with such additional hours outside those hours or at weekends or during bank holidays as, in the opinion of the Claimant, are reasonably necessary for the performance of his duties;
    4.2. by clause 9.1, it is provided that the Defendant shall give six months' notice in order to terminate the Agreement;
    4.3. by clause 10.1, the Claimant shall be under no obligation to vest in or assign to the Defendant any powers or duties or to provide any work to the Defendant, and the Claimant may, at its discretion, at any time (including during any period of notice given by either party), amend the Defendant's duties and/or suspend the Defendant from the performance of his duties and/or exclude the Defendant from any premises of the Claimant and/or require the Defendant not to communicate with any clients or prospective clients of the Claimant or any of the Claimant's employees, agents or, consultants and/or require the Defendant to work from home ('the Garden Leave Arrangement');
    4.4. by clause 10.2, salary will continue to be payable and contractual benefits will continue to be provided during the period of any Garden Leave Arrangement. The Defendant shall throughout any period of Garden Leave Arrangement continue to act as an employee of the Company and shall comply with his obligations under the Agreement;

628

4.5. by clause 21.1, the Defendant is to devote his entire time, attention, and best talents and abilities during office hours and such other hours as may be required for the proper performance thereof exclusively to the performance of his duties. Further, he is not to accept any other employment or be interested in any other business activity in any capacity during his employment without the Claimant's prior written consent;

4.6. by clause 23, the Defendant is obliged to surrender to the Claimant all property, materials, documentation, and other information in any form belonging to the Claimant or to any of its associates, affiliates, or subsidiaries which the Defendant has in his possession or under his control at that time.

5. The Agreement is subject to the following implied terms:

5.1. the Defendant must serve the Claimant in good faith and with fidelity;

5.2. the Defendant must not without reasonable and proper cause act in a manner calculated or likely to destroy or seriously damage the trust and confidence inherent in the employment relationship.

Purported termination

6. By a letter dated 21 August 2010, handed to Mr Dinmont's assistant, Ms Selina Bell, on 22 August 2010, the Defendant purported to resign with one month's notice only.

7. By an undated letter given to the Defendant on 24 August 2010, the Claimant rejected the Defendant's attempt to resign with less than the contractual period of notice specified in clause 9.1 of the Agreement.

8. In a letter dated 26 August 2010, the Defendant re-iterated his intention to terminate his employment with effect from 21 September 2010. He stated that he intended to take up employment, as of 22 September 2010, with Tibble Clothing Ltd ('Tibble Clothing'), the Claimant's leading competitor in the United Kingdom.

9. In these circumstances, given the matters set out above, such statements amounted to anticipatory and repudiatory breach of the Agreement.

10. By letter dated 27 August 2010, the Claimant informed the Defendant that it would not release him from the Agreement prior to the end of the required six-month notice period (being 21 February 2011) and that it required him to remain at home on garden leave pursuant to clause 10.1 of the Agreement until that date. The Claimant thereby affirmed the Agreement.

11. By letter dated 28 August 2010, the Defendant once more stated his intention to terminate his employment under the Agreement with effect from 21 September 2010.

12. By a letter of the same date, the Claimant informed the Defendant that it would not accept such a termination and would apply to the Court for injunctive relief. The Claimant thereby re-affirmed the Agreement.

Relief sought

13. By a letter dated 29 August 2010, the Claimant through its solicitors requested undertakings from the Defendant to avoid urgent injunctive relief being sought to prevent the Defendant from commencing employment with Tibble Clothing.

14. These undertakings were provided by letter dated 31 August 2010 from the Defendant's solicitors and apply until 21 September 2010.

15. In these circumstances the Defendant threatens and intends to breach the Agreement with effect from 21 September 2010 by:

15.1. commencing employment with a competitor, prior to the expiry of his notice period, in breach of clauses 9.1, 10.2, and 21.1;

15.2. acting in breach of the implied terms referred to in paragraph 5 of these Particulars of Claim.

16. Unless restrained by the Court, the Defendant will be in breach of the Agreement and the Claimant will suffer loss and damage thereby. The Claimant will give full particulars of such loss and damage in due course.

17. In any event, the Claimant is entitled to and seeks delivery up of all property, materials, documentation, and other information in any form belonging to the Claimant or to any of its associates, affiliates, or subsidiaries which the Defendant has in his possession or under his control at that time.

18. The Claimant claims and is entitled to interest on any damages pursuant to section 35A of the Senior Courts Act 1981 at such rate and for such period as the Court thinks fit.

And the Claimant claims:

(1) An injunction restraining the Defendant from doing any of the following prior to 21 February 2011:
   (a) carrying on, being employed or otherwise engaged, concerned or interested in any capacity (whether for reward or otherwise) in, or providing any technical, commercial, or professional advice to, and in any way assisting Tibble Clothing Ltd or any other company owning, operating, or engaged in the business of children's clothing manufacture within the United Kingdom other than the Claimant or its associated companies;
   (b) otherwise acting in breach of his contractual duties of good faith and fidelity to the Claimant.
(2) Damages for breach of the Agreement.
(3) Delivery up of all property of the Claimant which is in the Defendant's control.

The Claimant believes that the facts stated in this Particulars of Claim are true.

....

Bill Dinmont   Date

President & Chief Executive Officer, Madrick Ltd.

B. Sample Interim Injunction

PENAL NOTICE

IF YOU THE WITHIN NAMED JOHN STEPHENS DISOBEY THIS ORDER YOU MAY BE HELD TO BE IN CONTEMPT OF COURT AND LIABLE TO IMPRISONMENT OR FINED OR YOUR ASSETS SEIZED.

ANY OTHER PERSON WHO KNOWS OF THIS ORDER AND DOES ANYTHING WHICH HELPS OR PERMITS THE DEFENDANT TO BREACH THE TERMS OF THIS ORDER MAY ALSO BE HELD TO BE IN CONTEMPT OF COURT AND MAY BE IMPRISONED, FINED, OR HAVE THEIR ASSETS SEIZED.

IN THE HIGH COURT OF JUSTICE

QUEEN'S BENCH DIVISION

Before the Honourable Mr Justice [   ]

Claim No. HQ [   ]

BETWEEN

MADRICK LIMITED

Claimant

–and–

JOHN STEPHENS

Defendant

ORDER FOR AN INJUNCTION

IMPORTANT

NOTICE TO THE RESPONDENT

(1) This Order prohibits you from doing the acts set out in this Order. You should read it all carefully. [You are advised to consult a Solicitor as soon as possible.] You have a right to ask the Court to vary or discharge this Order.
(2) If you disobey this Order you may be found guilty of Contempt of Court and you may be sent to prison or fined or your assets may be seized.

THE ORDER

This is an order for injunction made against John Stephens (the 'Defendant') by Mr Justice [   ] on the application of Madrick Limited (the 'Claimant'). The Judge read the witness statement listed in Schedule A and accepted the undertakings set out in Schedule B at the end of this Order.

IT IS ORDERED that:

THE INJUNCTION

1. Until the earliest of trial, further order or 22 February 2011, the Defendant must not by himself, his servants, agents, or otherwise howsoever:
   (a) carry on, be employed or otherwise engaged, concerned, or interested in any capacity (whether for reward or otherwise) in, or provide any technical, commercial, or professional advice to, and in any way assist Tibble Clothing Ltd or any other company owning, operating, or engaged in the business of children's clothing manufacture within the United Kingdom other than the Claimant or its associated companies;
   (b) otherwise act in breach of his contractual duties of good faith and fidelity to the Claimant.

COST OF THE APPLICATION

2. The costs of this Application are reserved [to the Judge hearing the trial of this action].

VARIATION OR DISCHARGE OF THIS ORDER

The Defendant may apply to the Court at any time to vary or discharge this Order, but must inform the Claimant's legal representatives in writing at least forty-eight hours prior to making such an application. If any evidence is to be relied upon in support of the application, the substance of it must be communicated in writing to the Claimant's solicitors in advance.

THE EFFECT OF THIS ORDER

1. A Defendant who is an individual who is ordered not to do something must not do it himself or in any other way. He must not do it through others acting on his behalf or on his instructions or with his encouragement.
2. [A Defendant which is a corporation and which is ordered not to do something must not do it itself or by its directors, officers, employees, or agents or in any other way.]

INTERPRETATION OF THIS ORDER

1. In this Order the words 'he', 'him', or 'his' include 'she' or 'her' and 'it' or 'its'.
2. Where there is more than one Defendant (unless otherwise stated) references to 'the Defendant' mean both or all of them.
3. An Order requiring 'the Defendant' to do or not to do anything applies to all Defendants.

COMMUNICATIONS WITH THE COURT

All communications to the Court about this Order should be sent to Room [   ], Royal Courts of Justice, Strand, London WC2A 2LL quoting the case number. The telephone number is [   ]. The offices are open between 10am and 4.30pm Monday to Friday.

SCHEDULE A

The Judge read the witness statement of Otto Douglas dated 1 September 2010 before making this Order.

SCHEDULE B

UNDERTAKINGS BY THE CLAIMANT

1. If the Court later finds that this Order has caused loss to the Defendant, and decides that the Defendant should be compensated for that loss, the Claimant will comply with any Order the Court may make.
2. The Claimant will continue to pay the Defendant his remuneration and benefits to which he is entitled pursuant to his contract of employment during the injunction period.

3. In the event that the Defendant does not undertake work pursuant to his contract of employment during the period of this injunction, the Claimant undertakes not to claim damages from the Defendant arising out of such a failure.

NAME AND ADDRESS OF CLAIMANT'S SOLICITORS

The Claimant's solicitors are: [Name, address and telephone numbers both in and out of office hours.]

APPENDIX 6

Drafting Restrictive Covenants: A Note

Catherine Taylor

This note should be read in conjunction with the sample clauses set out at Appendix 7 (Employment) and Appendix 8 (Business Sales).

1. In choosing which covenants to include in a contract of employment, an employer should identify the business interests the employer is trying to protect (see paragraphs 5.188 to 5.221 above). They could include:
   - protecting trade secrets and other confidential information;
   - retaining customer connections—this might include actual and potential customers;
   - maintaining key relationships with suppliers and business partners;
   - maintaining a stable workforce;

   but cannot include simple protection against competition, or the desire to prevent employees from using skills which they have learnt during their employment.

   Note: If the covenants are prefaced by a paragraph which sets out the business needs which the covenants are designed to protect, the employer will be stuck with those reasons. It may therefore be sensible not to include any such preface or to double check that it does accurately protect the interests which are sought to be protected (see paragraphs 5.211 to 5.214).

2. Identify the covenants which will give effect to the business needs. These may include:
   - area covenants;
   - non-competition covenants;
   - covenants preventing solicitation of customers;
   - covenants preventing dealing with customers;
   - covenants preventing poaching or employment of staff, including preventing a team move;
   - covenants preventing solicitation of or dealing with suppliers;
   - covenants preventing solicitation of or dealing with business partners;
   - covenants preventing solicitation of or dealing with intermediaries;
   - covenants preventing the employee from passing himself off as still having a connection with the employer following the termination of his employment.

3. The provisions should be no wider than is necessary to protect the employer's interest. See below in relation to points on this. Enforceability as a matter of law will be judged at the time they are entered into (see paragraph 5.231 above). Accordingly the safest route is to update them regularly.

4. In order to ensure the restrictive covenants are drafted as beneficially as possible instructions should be taken from someone within the employer's organization who is sufficiently senior and who has the depth of knowledge of the employer's business to ensure that the restrictions meet the business' need. In particular, this person should have full and detailed knowledge of the relevant area of the business where the employee works, including knowledge of its confidential information, customers, etc and they should also know the role of each employee or class of employee within that organization. Finally they should be senior enough to decide what aspects of the business need protection and what type of protection.

General provisions

5. An employer would be wise to ensure that covenants prevent an employee from doing certain acts both 'directly and indirectly' to protect against evidential difficulties should it appear that it was not the employee himself who breached a provision, but a third party under his direction.

6. Covenants should generally only restrain employees from doing the forbidden acts on behalf of a business which competes with the employer's business. This does not apply to covenants aimed at maintaining a stable workforce.

7. If the employer is part of a group of companies, it may want its covenants to protect other companies within the group. However, such a clause should be restricted to businesses, customers, staff, and so on with whom the employee has a connection (see paragraphs 5.215 to 5.221 above).

8. An employer may want to require an employee to notify his new employer of the covenants, so that if there is any breach in future it can contemplate suing the new employer for inducing the employee to breach the covenants (see paragraphs 5.283 to 5.286 above).

9. An employer may include a clause allowing it to alter any covenant if it is adjudged unreasonable. However, the courts are unlikely to give effect to such a clause (see paragraphs 5.287 above).

10. The employer may as a precaution want to include a clause reducing the period of any restrictive covenant by the period an employee has spent on garden leave. This is not obligatory, but it may be sensible (see paragraphs 5.288 to 5.294 above).

11. If an employee has received legal advice on the covenants as part of the negotiation this can be recorded in the contract to ensure it is not forgotten when they come to be enforced.

Specific covenants

12. Area and non-competition covenants (see paragraphs 5.234 to 5.253 above).

Identify the business need which requires a non-compete covenant, and why it cannot be dealt with by using a less onerous covenant such as one restraining solicitation of and/or dealing with customers. For example, is the identity of customers unknown or undocumented? Is the nature of the business such (for example where groups of salesmen or traders sit together at open plan desks) that it would be impossible to police whether an employee is breaching a covenant not to solicit customers (see paragraph 5.205 above) or is the employee in possession of genuine confidential information about the employer's business, which is more than just skill and know-how? If yes, then a non-compete covenant may be justified.

Detailed elements:
- **Period**: the covenant should last no more than is necessary for the employer to forge new connections with customers, or for the confidential information to become stale. It is common for these covenants to last for six to twelve months.
- **Restricted business**: the businesses with which the employee cannot compete must be narrowly defined to encompass only those businesses (whether belonging only to the employer or to other companies in the employer's group) in respect of which the employee can be said to have current customer connections or confidential information.
- **Area**: the area covered by the covenant must be no wider than that covered by the employer's business. Global covenants may be justified for international businesses, but for smaller more localized businesses, such as hairdressers or solicitors, the area covered should only be that over which the employer's business has a real reputation (see paragraphs 5.236 to 5.240 above).

13. Covenant preventing the solicitation of customers (see paragraphs 5.256 to 5.265 above).

Identify the business need which requires the covenant. This is generally the need to protect the employer's relationships with its customers.

Detailed elements:
- **Period**: the covenant should last for no longer than is necessary to allow the employer to forge new relationships with its customers so that the customer should not be vulnerable to a competitive approach from the employee. Generally these covenants are drafted to last for about one year, but longer periods have been upheld (see paragraph 5.265 above).
- **Customer**: the covenant should cover only customers or potential customers over whom the employee will have some influence, for example because (a) he has dealt with them; (b) those who report to him deal with them; and/or (c) he has confidential information about them. Generally, it is sensible for covenants in employment contracts to cover only those customers with whom the employee has dealt during a short period, say one year, before his employment ends.

Covenants covering all an employer's customers may, however, be valid where the employer's business is very small or where the employee is very senior and possesses confidential information regarding customers with whom he does not necessarily deal (see paragraphs 5.256 to 5.259 above).

14. Covenants preventing dealing with customers (see paragraphs 5.266 to 5.267 above).

Identify the business need which requires the covenant. This is generally the need to protect the employer's relationships with its customers.

Detailed elements:
- **Period**: the covenant should last for no longer than is necessary to allow the employer to forge new relationships with its customers so that the customer should not feel the need, unsolicited, to contact the employee to do business with him. Generally these covenants last for six to twelve months. They should never last for longer than a covenant preventing the employee from soliciting customers.
- **Customer**: the covenant should cover the same customers as identified in paragraph 13 above.

15. Covenants preventing poaching/employment of colleagues (see paragraphs 5.268 to 5.277 above).

Identify the business need which requires the covenant. This is generally the need to maintain the stability of the workforce.

Note: public policy considerations may mean that a covenant which prevents an employee from directly or indirectly employing colleagues, as opposed to merely soliciting them to join him, is unenforceable (see paragraphs 5.273 to 5.277 above).

Detailed elements:
- **Period**: the covenant should last for no longer than is necessary for the employee to lose his influence over his colleagues. Generally, these covenants last for six to twelve months.
- **Colleagues**: while the category of colleagues to be protected by this covenant is not limited to employees but can include, for example, consultants or non-executive directors, those affected must be senior (see paragraph 5.269 above) and generally should have had some dealings with the employee in the period of, say, one year before the termination of his employment.
- **Team moves**: the covenant can seek to prevent the employee from moving to a competitor if a colleague has already joined the competitor within a limited period. This type of covenant has yet to be tested by the courts.

Other covenants

16. Non-solicitation of suppliers or business partners.

Identify the business need which requires the covenant. For the covenant to be reasonable, the employer must have special relationships with suppliers or business partners which it wants to protect, for example, because it has exclusive or advantageous arrangements with them or confidential information relating to them.

Detailed elements:
- **Period**: the covenant should last for no longer than is necessary to allow the employer to forge new relationships with its suppliers or business partners. Generally these covenants last for six to twelve months.
- **Supplier/business partner**: the covenant should only cover those suppliers (a) with whom the employer has a special relationship (it should not cover suppliers of administrative or mundane goods or services); and (b) with whom the employee or someone reporting to him has an established and recent connection.

17. Covenants relating to intermediaries.

Identify the business need which requires the covenant. This may be that the employer's trade is introduced to it by intermediaries with whom it has spent considerable effort in forging relationships. These covenants are rare, and there is no case law in which they are reviewed. Great care should be taken in ensuring that a covenant of this nature does not offend against public policy: for example if the intermediary is professionally obliged (perhaps by being subject to the rules of the Financial

Services Authority) to give clients best advice, then this might be a relevant factor in assessing the reasonableness of a covenant preventing an employee from dealing with an intermediary.

Detailed elements:

- **Period**: the covenant should last for no longer than is necessary to allow the employer to forge new relationships with intermediaries. The covenants tend to last for six to twelve months.
- **Intermediaries**: the covenant should define the intermediaries who are affected by it with some precision, and should in any event only affect those intermediaries who introduce work to the employer and with whom the employee has an established and recent connection in the period of, say, one year before the employment ends.

18. Covenants preventing the employee from passing himself off as still connected with the employer following termination of his employment.

These covenants reinforce the general law of passing off and are likely to be enforceable.

Sample Restrictive Covenants (Employment)

Catherine Taylor

Note: These drafts relate only to post-termination restrictions. See Appendices 2 and 3 for sample clauses relating to (a) restrictions during employment and (b) confidentiality. Also, see Appendix 8 for sample restrictive covenants in Business and Share Sale Agreements.

A. Short clause

(Suitable for letter agreements)

1.1 You agree that you will not:

    (a) for the period of [three/six] months after the Termination Date engage as a director, principal, member of a limited liability partnership, partner or consultant, or accept employment or become a shareholder (other than a minority shareholder beneficially entitled to not more than 3 per cent of the issued share capital of a company) in a business or concern of whatever kind which is, [during the months prior to/at] the Termination Date, a competitor of any business owned or managed by the Company [or any Group Company] in which you were engaged or for which you were responsible during the twelve months prior to the Termination Date. For these purposes 'competitor' shall mean: [*list competitors*] [*define competitor*] and includes those preparing to compete with such business;

    (b) for the period of [six/twelve] months after the Termination Date for the purposes of any business in direct or indirect competition with the Company [or any Group Company], either on your own behalf or on behalf of any other person, firm, limited liability partnership, company, or other entity, directly or indirectly solicit or entice away, or try to solicit or entice away from the Company [or any Group Company], or deal with any Client [or Supplier], or induce or attempt to induce any Client [or Supplier] to cease conducting any business with the Company [or any Group Company], or to reduce the amount of business conducted with the Company [or any Group Company], or adversely to vary the terms upon which any business is conducted with the Company [or any Group Company];

    (c) for the period of [six/twelve] months after the Termination Date, either on your own behalf or for any other person, firm, limited liability partnership, company, or other entity, directly or indirectly solicit, interfere with, entice away, or try to entice away from the Company [or any Group Company] any Senior Employee;

1.2 [The post-termination period of the restrictions set out in clause [1.1] shall be reduced pro rata by any period during which you are required not to attend the Company's premises pursuant to clause [   ](garden leave).]

Definitions

'**Client**' shall mean any person, firm, limited liability partnership, company or other entity which at any time during the [twelve] months before the Termination Date was a client [or prospective client] of the Company [or any Group Company] and with whom or which you had material dealings during that period;

'**Group Company**' [any holding company of the Company and] any subsidiary of the Company [or of any such holding company] (where 'holding company' and 'subsidiary' have the meanings attributed to them in section 1159 Companies Act 2006 and for the avoidance of doubt are deemed to include limited liability partnerships);

'**Senior Employee**' shall mean any person employed by the Company [or any Group Company] at any time during the [three] months before the Termination Date [[earning in excess of [£40,000] per annum] [on grade [   ] or above] [working in a [senior] technical or managerial capacity]] and with whom you had material dealings during the [twelve] months before the Termination Date;

'**Supplier**' shall mean any person, firm, limited liability partnership, company or other entity who or which at any time during the [twelve] months before the Termination Date supplied goods or services (other than those of an administrative nature and utilities) to the Company [or any Group Company] and with whom you had material dealings;

'**Termination Date**' shall mean the date this employment agreement terminates, irrespective of the cause or manner.

B. Short clause for salesman

You agree that you will not for a period of [six/twelve] months following the termination of your employment on your own behalf or for any person, firm, limited liability partnership, company, or other organisation:

- solicit orders in [territory] for any goods or services which are the same as or similar to any goods or services which you have been promoting, selling or attempting to sell on behalf of the Company during the [six/twelve] months prior to the termination of your employment; and

- solicit business from any customer of the Company with whom you have dealt during the year prior to the termination of your employment in relation to goods or services which are the same as or similar to any goods or services which you have been promoting, selling or attempting to sell on behalf of the Company during the [six/twelve] months prior to the termination of your employment.

C. Short area covenant

You agree that you will not for a period of [six/twelve] months following the termination of your employment work [as a [job title]] for or own any interest (except shares quoted on a recognised stock exchange) in any business in [area] which competes with any business of the Company in which you have been involved during the year before the termination of your employment.

D. Detailed long clause

1. Protection of the company's interests

1.1 The Executive agrees with the Company that he will not directly or indirectly:

    1.1.1 for a period of [   ] months immediately following the Termination Date:

        1.1.1.1 carry on or set up or be interested in a Competing Business save that he may be interested: (1) in securities in a company whose shares or other securities are listed, traded and/or dealt in on [any market of a Recognised Investment Exchange][any securities exchange or market] provided that he does not hold (and is not interested, directly or indirectly) in shares or securities conferring more than 3 per cent of the votes that could be cast at a general meeting of that body corporate; or (2) in any class of securities not so listed, traded or dealt provided that he does not hold (and is not interested, directly or indirectly) in shares or securities conferring more than [20] per cent of the votes that could be cast at a general meeting of that body corporate;

1.1.1.2 act as a consultant, employee or officer or in any other capacity in a Competing Business;

1.1.1.3 either on his own account or on behalf of any Competing Business:
(a) supply or facilitate the supply of Restricted Goods or Services to; or
(b) deal with any Client;

1.1.1.4 [either on his own account or on behalf of any Competing Business deal with a Supplier;]

1.1.1.5 either on his own account or for any Person employ or otherwise engage or facilitate the employment or engagement of the services of any Key Employee whether or not any such Key Employee would in entering into the employment or engagement commit a breach of contract;

1.1.1.6 [either on his own account or for any Person deal with any Business Partner.]

1.1.2 for a period of [   ] months immediately following the Termination Date:

1.1.2.1 either on his own account or for any Person induce, solicit or entice or try to induce, solicit, or entice any Key Employee to cease working for or providing their services to the Company [or any Group Company] whether or not any such Key Employee would by entering into the proposed employment or engagement commit a breach of contract;

1.1.2.2 either on his own account or on behalf of any Competing Business directly or indirectly induce, solicit, or entice or endeavour to induce, solicit, or entice any Client to cease conducting any business with the Company [or any Group Company], or to reduce the amount of business conducted with the Company [or any Group Company], or adversely to vary the terms upon which any business is conducted with the Company [or any Group Company], or to exclude the Company [or any Group Company] from new business opportunities in relation to any Restricted Goods or Services;

1.1.2.3 [on behalf of any Competing Business directly or indirectly induce, solicit, or entice or try to induce, solicit, or entice any Supplier to cease conducting business with the Company [or any Group Company] or to reduce the amount of business conducted with the Company [or any Group Company] or adversely to vary the terms upon which any business is conducted with the Company [or any Group Company];]

1.1.2.4 [on behalf of any Competing Business directly or indirectly induce, solicit, or entice or try to induce, solicit, or entice any Business Partner to terminate its arrangements with the Company [or any Group Company], or to seek to vary those arrangements, irrespective of whether any such action would be in breach of the Business Partner's contractual arrangements with the Company [or Group Company];]

1.1.2.5 [become an employee of, or consultant to, or provide services to a Competing Business at the same time as or in the [   ] months after any Key Employee is or has been employed by, become a consultant of, or otherwise provided services to that Competing Business.]

1.1.3 at any time after the Termination Date or, if later, the date on which he ceases to be a director of the Company [or any Group Company] present himself or allow himself to be held out or presented as being in any way connected with or interested in the business of the Company [or any Group Company] (other than as a shareholder or consultant, if that is the case).

1.2 The Executive agrees that each of the restrictions set out in clause 1.1 constitutes entirely separate, severable, and independent restrictions on him. The Executive acknowledges that he [has received] [had the opportunity to receive] independent legal advice on the terms and effect of the provisions of this Agreement, including the restrictions above.

1.3 [The duration of each of the restrictions set out in clause 1.1 above will be reduced pro rata by any period during which the Company suspends the Executive from the performance of his duties pursuant to clause [   ] (garden leave).]

1.4 [While each of the restrictions in clause 1.1 is considered by the parties to be reasonable in all the circumstances it is agreed that if any one or more of such restrictions either taken by itself or them-selves together, is adjudged to go beyond what is reasonable in all the circumstances for the protection of the legitimate interests of the Company [or any Group Company] but would be adjudged reasonable if any particular restriction or restrictions were deleted or if any part or parts of its or their wording were deleted, restricted, or limited in a particular manner then the restrictions set out in clause 1.1 will apply with such deletions, restrictions, or limitations as the case may be.]

1.5 If the Executive accepts engagement (whether as a director, consultant, or in any other capacity) or employment with any third party during the period of any of the restrictions set out in clause 1.1 he will on or before such acceptance provide the third party with full details of these restrictions.

1.6 The Executive will not induce, procure, authorise, or encourage any other Person to do or procure to be done anything that if done by the Executive would be a breach of any of the provisions of clause 1.1.

1.7 [The restrictions entered into by the Executive in clause 1.1 are given to the Company for itself and as trustee for each and any Group Company and the Company hereby declares that to the extent that such restrictions relate to any Group Company the Company holds the benefit of them as trustee.]

1.8 The Executive agrees that if his employment is transferred to a Person other than the Company [or any Group Company] ('the new employer') pursuant to the Transfer of Undertakings (Protection of Employment) Regulations 2006, he will, if required, enter into an agreement with the new employer that will contain provisions that provide protection to the new employer similar to that provided to the Company [and any Group Company] in clause 1.1.

Definitions

In this Agreement the following words and expressions will have the following meanings, unless the context otherwise requires:

['**Business Partner**' any Person who has entered into a joint venture or partnership with the Company or any Group Company with whom the Executive had material dealings during the Relevant Period.]

'**Client**' any Person, (i) who or which at any time during the Relevant Period was [to the knowledge of the Executive] provided with goods or services by the Company [or any Group Company] or (ii) who or which was a Prospective Client or (iii) about whom or which the Executive has confidential information, and in each case with whom or which the Executive or any person who reported directly to him had [material] dealings at any time during the Relevant Period;

'**Competing Business**' any business in [*geographical area eg England, UK, Europe*] which competes or is preparing to compete with any business, carried on by the Company [or any Group Company] in which the Executive has been involved to a material extent during the Relevant Period;

['**Group Company**' [any holding company of the Company and] any subsidiary of the Company [or of any such holding company] (where 'holding company' and 'subsidiary' have the meanings attrib-uted to them in section 1159 of the Companies Act 2006 and for the avoidance of doubt are deemed to include limited liability partnerships);]

'**Key Employee**' any person who at the Termination Date or at any time during the Relevant Period is an officer or employee of [or consultant to] the Company [or any Group Company] [earning [£40,000] (including bonuses and commission, if any, but excluding any appropriate VAT) or more on an annualised basis] [who is a manager in the [creative/technical/production department[s] of the Company or any Group Company]] with whom the Executive in the course of his employment has had [material] dealings at any time during the Relevant Period;

'**Person**' Any person, firm, limited liability partnership, company, corporation, organisation, gov-ernmental or non-governmental body, or other entity;

'**Prospective Client**' any Person to whom or which during the Relevant Period the Company [or any Group Company] had submitted a tender, taken part in a pitch or made a presentation or with whom or which it was otherwise negotiating for the supply of goods or services;

'**Recognised Investment Exchange**' a recognised investment exchange (including an overseas recognised investment exchange), each as defined by section 285 of the Financial Services and Markets Act 2000;

'**Relevant Period**' the period of [twelve] months immediately preceding the Termination Date;

'**Restricted Goods or Services**' goods or services of a type provided by the Company [or any Group Company] at the Termination Date in relation to any business in which that Executive has been involved to a material extent during the Relevant Period;

'**Supplier**' any Person who or which at any time during the Relevant Period: (i) supplied goods or services (other than utilities and goods or services supplied for administrative purposes) to the Company [or any Group Company] or (ii) was negotiating with or had pitched to the Company [or any Group Company] to supply goods or services (other than utilities and goods or services supplied for administrative purposes) to the Company [or any Group Company], and in each case with whom or which the Executive or any person who reported directly to him had [material] dealings at any time during the Relevant Period;

'**Termination Date**' the date on which this Agreement terminates irrespective of the cause or manner.

E. Longer form covenant in relation to suppliers [and intermediaries]

1 The Executive agrees with the Company that he will not directly or indirectly for a period of [   ] months immediately following the Termination Date

1.1 try to procure the supply of goods or services from any Supplier on behalf of a Competing Business or interfere with or try to terminate or reduce the levels of such supplies to the Company [or any Group Company] where such supply, or, as appropriate, its termination or reduction may have an adverse effect on or cause loss to such company. [For these purposes any arrangement between the Company [or a Group Company] and a third party whereby that third party sources customers, or goods, or services for the Company on any Group Company shall also be deemed to constitute a supply of a service by such third party];

1.2 knowingly interfere with any arrangement(s) between the Company [or any Group Company] and any third party or parties whereby the Company [or the relevant Group Company] holds a licence or permission to carry on its business and/or benefits from discounts or other beneficial trading terms extended to it by a supplier of goods or services by virtue of such arrangement(s); and/or

1.3 knowingly or recklessly do or say anything which is or is calculated to be prejudicial to the interests of the Company or any Group Company, or its or their businesses, or which results or may result in the discontinuance of any contract or arrangement of benefit to the Company or any Group Company.

[relevant definitions as for previous sample long-form clause]

F. Detailed passing off clause

The Executive agrees that, save in the proper performance of his duties, he will not during his employment or after the Termination Date make use of any corporate or business brand, or domain name, or logo, or style which is identical or similar to or likely to be confused or associated with any corporate or business brand, or domain name, or logo, or style of the Company or any Group Company or which might suggest a connection with the same.

G. Clause requiring new employer not to induce a breach of the covenants

In consideration of the Company allowing [name] to join you on [date] [and agreeing not to pursue litigation against you for alleged prospective inducement of [name] to breach his contract of employment, you undertake that you will not induce or procure the breach by [name] of any of his/her obligations in clauses [   ] of his/her contract of employment [save for clauses [   ]].

H. Clause for compromise agreement confirming
restrictive covenants

Notwithstanding the termination of the Executive's employment, the Executive acknowledges and affirms that [he/she] remains bound by those provisions of [his/her] contract of employment dated [date] that are expressed to continue after termination of [his/her] employment [including, without limitation, clauses [   ] (confidentiality), [   ] (restrictions), [   ] (intellectual property) and [   ]].

Sample Restrictive Covenants
(Share and Business Sale and Partnership)

Dan Aherne and Luke Pardey

A. Share sale agreement provisions

1. Protection of the interests of the buyer[1]

1.01 The Sellers acknowledge that the Buyer is buying the Shares in accordance with the terms of this Agreement and that the Buyer is therefore entitled to protect the goodwill of [the Company] [each Group Company].[2] Accordingly, each of the Sellers[3] agrees that it shall not, directly or indirectly, alone or jointly with any other person, and whether as shareholder, partner, director, principal, consultant, or agent or in any other capacity:

    1.01.01 for a period of [   ] years[4] starting on the Completion Date,[5] carry on or be engaged, interested, or concerned in, or assist any business which within [*specify territories where the*

---

[1] These provisions are Buyer-friendly. They assume simultaneous exchange and completion and no earn-out. Competition law issues may be relevant to these restrictions if any are given by corporate entities. See Chapter 7 above.

[2] The restrictions protect the business as sold to the Buyer at Completion. If the Seller is to continue to have an interest in the business after Completion (via deferred consideration or an earn-out), consider whether the restrictive covenants ought to be renewed at that date. Eg there will have been staff turnover—ought the business to be protected from poaching of new Senior Employees who may have joined after Completion but during the earn-out period of whom the Seller would have gained knowledge solely through its continued participation in the Business? This can be done by inserting a new clause repeating the restrictions but substituting a reference to the date of payment of the further consideration for the words 'Completion Date' and 'Completion' in relation to time periods and in the definitions of Customers, Senior Employees, Suppliers, and Prospective Customers.

[3] Ensure that the correct party/parties are giving these covenants. These sample clauses envisage a number of individual sellers. Where a Seller is a corporate entity, it may also be appropriate to obtain the covenants from the parent company or alternatively, from specific individuals, eg managers in an MBO. Note that clause 1.05 contains a covenant by the Seller to ensure compliance by its Associates—however, this would not give the Buyer a remedy against the offending Associate.

[4] For the purposes of clauses 1.01.01 to 1.01.08, the non-compete period (including restrictions in relation to customers and suppliers) legitimately required for the protection of the goodwill is dependent on the circumstances, but the basic principle is that they will be unenforceable to the extent that they go beyond what is necessary to protect the Buyer's interests in relation to subject matter (ie should be limited to competition with the business as carried on at Completion); geographical field (ie should be limited to the territories in which the Company carried on business at Completion); and duration of the non-compete covenants. Longer periods will need to be justified by exceptional circumstances (eg nature of the business). Longer periods for the covenants against poaching employees may be permissible as they are deemed not to impose blanket prohibitions on the covenantors' ability to do business.

[5] Case law indicates that the Buyer is entitled to the protection of its goodwill but clearly this extends from the date on which the purchase takes place. Restrictions that are triggered at a later date may in the absence of further consideration (eg earn-out/bonus/deferred consideration) be unenforceable.

target carries on business at Completion] competes with the any business of [the Company] [any Group Company];

1.01.02 for a period of [   ] years starting on the Completion Date, and to the detriment of any business of [the Company] [any Group Company] carried on as at Completion, accept business from any [Customer][Client];[6,7]

1.01.03 for a period of [   ] years starting on the Completion Date, and to the detriment of any business of the [Company] [any Group Company] carried on as at Completion, accept business from any Prospective [Customer][Client];

1.01.04 for a period of [   ] years starting on the Completion Date, and to the detriment of any business of [the Company] [any Group Company] carried on as at Completion, solicit business from any [Customer][Client];

1.01.05 for a period of [   ] years starting on the Completion Date, and to the detriment of any business of [the Company] [any Group Company] carried on as at Completion, solicit business from any Prospective [Customer][Client];

1.01.06 for a period of [   ] years starting on the Completion Date, and to the detriment of any business of [the Company] [any Group Company] carried on as at Completion, induce or endeavour to induce any Supplier to cease to supply, or to restrict or adversely to vary the terms of supply to, that business;

1.01.07 for a period of [   ] years starting on the Completion Date, and to the detriment of any business of [the Company] [any Group Company] carried on as at Completion, employ or engage the services of any Senior Employee;[8]

1.01.08 for a period of [   ] years starting on the Completion Date induce or endeavour to induce, any Senior Employee to leave his position, whether or not that person would commit a breach of his contract by so leaving.

1.02 Nothing in clause [1.01] shall prohibit any Seller from holding any interest in any securities listed or dealt in on any market of a recognized investment exchange (as defined in section 285 of the Financial Services and Markets Act 2000) if that Seller and any Associate of that Seller are together interested in securities which amount to less than [3] per cent[9] of the issued securities of that class and which in all circumstances carry less than [3] per cent of the voting rights (if any) attaching to the issued securities of that class, and if neither that Seller nor any Associate of that Seller is involved in the management of the business of the issuer of the securities or any subsidiary undertaking of that issuer except by virtue of the exercise of any voting rights attaching to the securities.

1.03 No Seller shall disclose or use, nor cause or facilitate the unauthorized disclosure or use of, any confidential information or trade secrets relating to [the Company] [any Group Company] or any of its [or their] customers or suppliers, and each of the Sellers shall use their best endeavours to prevent the publication or disclosure of any such confidential information or trade secrets, as the case may be. This clause shall not prohibit disclosure of:

1.03.01 confidential information or trade secrets under a legal obligation involuntarily incurred, or if required by the law of any relevant jurisdiction or by any competent

---

6 Select the correct term here, and in clauses 1.01.03, 1.01.04, and 1.01.05. If the Company operates a retail business, these clauses may not be appropriate and if so, should not be included.

7 If including the restrictions in clauses 1.01.02 and 1.01.03, their duration should be no greater, and usually shorter than those for the non-solicitation covenants in clauses 1.01.04 and 1.01.05.

8 The inclusion of all grades of employees will likely render the scope of this subparagraph excessive (and therefore unenforceable). Limit to defined 'Key' or 'Senior' Employees. The Buyer will need to be able to show that such workers have the requisite access to confidential information, etc to render the protection/retention of them a legitimate and protectable business interest.

9 Under chapter 5 of the Financial Services Authority's Disclosure and Transparency Rules (DTR5), the first threshold for disclosure of direct or indirect holdings in certain (principally UK) companies admitted to AIM or the Main Market of the London Stock Exchange is 3 per cent of the voting rights. This is the historic suggested starting point for negotiating the threshold for the carve-out which in practice is often agreed at a higher level.

regulatory or governmental body or securities exchange in any relevant jurisdiction, provided that in any such case, the relevant Seller shall take all such steps as may be reasonable and practicable in the circumstances to consult with the Buyer before the relevant disclosure is made and shall take into account the Buyer's reasonable comments;

1.03.02　any confidential information or trade secret which is in or becomes part of the public domain without breach of this clause; or

1.03.03　confidential information or trade secrets to any Associate of any Seller, or to any professional advisers of a Seller or any Associate of any Seller for the purpose of obtaining professional advice.

1.04　No Seller shall at any time after the Completion Date use in any manner in the course of any business, or (so far as within its power) permit or encourage to be so used other than by [the Company] [a Group Company], the names [*insert details*], or any other trade or business name or any mark, sign, or logo used by [the Company] [any Group Company] or any confusingly similar name, mark, sign, or logo, or present itself or permit itself to be presented as in any way connected with [the Company] [any Group Company] or interested in the Shares.

1.05　Each of the Sellers shall ensure that none of its Associates takes or omits to take any action that, if taken or omitted by that Seller, would constitute a breach of clause 1.01, 1.03, or 1.04.

1.06　Since the Sellers have confidential information relating to the [Company] [Group Companies], and a detailed awareness of the [Company's] [Group Companies'] customer connections, and since the purchase price payable for the Shares has been calculated on the basis that each of the Sellers would assume the obligations set out in this clause [1], the parties acknowledge that each of those obligations is reasonable as to subject matter, area, and duration and is necessary to protect the Buyer's legitimate interest in the goodwill of the [Company] [Group Companies].

1.07　Without prejudice to any other remedy which may be available to the Buyer, the parties agree that the Buyer shall be entitled to seek injunctive or other equitable relief in relation to any breach of clauses 1.01, 1.03, 1.04, and 1.05, it being acknowledged that an award of damages might not be an adequate remedy in the event of such a breach.

1.08　While the restrictions in this clause [1] are considered by the parties to be reasonable in all the circumstances it is agreed that if any provision of this clause [1] is found by any court of competent jurisdiction to go beyond what is reasonable in all the circumstances for the protection of the goodwill of [the Company] [any Group Company] but would be adjudged reasonable if any part of the wording of the provision were deleted, restricted, or limited in a particular manner, the provision in question shall apply with such deletions, restrictions, or limitations as may be necessary to render it valid.

1.09　[Each of the Sellers and the Buyer acknowledge that they have entered into this Agreement on an arm's length basis and that they have taken independent legal advice in so doing.]

1.10　Each of the obligations assumed by the Sellers in this clause [1] is separate and severable and shall be construed and be enforceable independently of the others, and is assumed without prejudice to any other obligation of the Seller implied at law or in equity.

1.11　In this clause [1]:

1.11.01　'Associate' means in relation to any person, a person who is connected with that person within the meaning of section 839 of ICTA;

1.11.02　'Buyer' means the Buyer, any ultimate parent undertaking of the Buyer from time to time and all direct or indirect subsidiary undertakings from time to time of any such parent undertaking within the meaning of section 1162 of the Companies Act 2006;

1.11.03　'Completion' means completion of the sale and purchase of the Shares in accordance with this Agreement;

1.11.04　'Completion Date' means the date on which Completion takes place;

1.11.05 '[Customer][Client]'[10] means any person who was a [customer][client] of [the Company] [any Group Company] as it was carried on at Completion during the period of [   ] months[11] ending on the Completion Date;

1.11.06 'Prospective [Customer][Client]' means any person who was at any time during the period of [   ] months ending on the Completion Date negotiating with any of the Sellers or [the Company] [any Group Company] and reasonably likely to become a [customer][client] of [the Company] [any Group Company];[12]

1.11.07 'Sellers' means [   ];

1.11.08 'Senior Employee'[13] means any person employed or engaged by [the Company] [any Group Company] in a [director/managerial/senior] [sales] position [with remuneration in excess of £[   ] per annum (including bonuses and commission, if any, but excluding any appropriate VAT)] on the Completion Date or any other person who held such a position during the period of [   ] months[14] ending on the Completion Date;

1.11.09 'Shares' means [set out relevant definition of shares to be purchased];

1.11.10 'Supplier' means any supplier of goods or services to the Company during the period of [   ] months ending on the Completion Date.

B. Business sale agreement provisions

1. Protection of the interests of the buyer[15]

1.01 The Seller acknowledges that the Buyer is buying the Business [as a going concern] in accordance with the terms of this Agreement and that the Buyer is therefore entitled to protect the goodwill of the Business.[16] Accordingly, the Seller agrees that it shall not, directly or indirectly, alone or jointly with any other person, and whether as shareholder, partner, director, principal, consultant, or agent or in any other capacity:

1.01.01 for a period of [   ] years[17] starting on the Completion Date, carry on or be engaged, interested, or concerned in, or assist any business which within [*specify territories where the Business is carried on at Completion*] competes with the Business;

---

[10] Consider the appropriate term to use—eg professional services firms usually refer to 'clients' where other businesses use 'customer'. Be aware that if the target is a retail business a covenant attempting to restrict the poaching of retail customers will be unenforceable and should not be included. In other cases, a relatively small number of loyal, long-term customers may be apparent. In such cases it may be appropriate to list the customers of the target. If a list is included, ensure it includes any associated or connected person of such customers.

[11] A period of six, nine, or twelve months would be usual here, in the definition of 'Supplier' and in the definition of 'Prospective [Customer] [Client]'.

[12] A court may well view protecting any prospective customers as going too far—if prospective customers can be identified, enforceability is more likely to be ensured by targeting the clause only at them.

[13] It may be appropriate to refer instead to 'Key Employees' as the employees may be 'key' to the business even if not 'senior' by reference to status or salary.

[14] Usually no more than twelve months. Consider the nature of the Company's business.

[15] See n 1 Section A above.

[16] The restrictions protect the Business as sold to the Buyer at Completion. If the Seller is to continue to have an interest in the Business after Completion (via deferred consideration or an earn-out), consider whether the restrictive covenants ought to be renewed at that date. Eg there will have been staff turnover—ought the Business to be protected from poaching of new Senior Employees who may have joined after Completion but during the earn-out period of whom the Seller would have gained knowledge solely through its continued participation in the Business? This can be done by inserting a new clause repeating the restrictions but substituting a reference to the date of payment of the further consideration for the words 'Completion Date' and 'Completion' in relation to time periods and in the definitions of Customers, Senior Employees, Suppliers, and Prospective Customers.

[17] For the purposes of clauses 1.01.01 to 1.01.08, the non-compete period (including restrictions in relation to customers and suppliers) legitimately required for the protection of the Business is dependent on the circumstances, but the basic principle is that they will be unenforceable to the extent that they go beyond what is necessary to protect the Buyer's interests in relation to subject matter (ie must be limited to competition with the Business as carried on at Completion); geographical field (ie must be limited to the territories in which the Business was carried on at Completion); and duration of the non-compete covenants. Longer periods will need to be justified by

1.01.02 [for a period of [   ][18] years starting on the Completion Date, and to the detriment of the Business carried on as at Completion, accept business from any [Customer] [Client];][19, 20]

1.01.03 for a period of [   ] years starting on the Completion Date, and to the detriment of the Business carried on as at Completion, accept business from any Prospective [Customer] [Client];

1.01.04 for a period of [   ] years starting on the Completion Date, and to the detriment of the Business carried on as at Completion, solicit business from any [Customer][Client];

1.01.05 for a period of [   ] years starting on the Completion Date, and to the detriment of the Business carried on as at Completion, solicit business from any Prospective [Customer] [Client];

1.01.06 for a period of [   ] years starting on the Completion Date, and to the detriment of the Business carried on as at Completion, induce or endeavour to induce any Supplier to cease to supply, or to restrict or adversely to vary the terms of supply to, the Business;

1.01.07 [for a period of [   ] years starting on the Completion Date, and to the detriment of the Business carried on as at Completion, employ or engage the services of any Senior Employee;][21]

1.01.08 for a period of [   ] years starting on the Completion Date induce or endeavour to induce, any Senior Employee to leave his position, whether or not such person would commit a breach of his contract by so leaving.

1.02 Nothing in clause 1.01 shall prohibit the Seller from holding any interest in any securities listed or dealt in on any market of a recognized investment exchange (as defined in section 285 of the Financial Services and Markets Act 2000) if the Seller and any other member of its Group are together interested in securities which amount to less than [3] per cent[22] of the issued securities of that class and which in all circumstances carry less than [3] per cent of the voting rights (if any) attaching to the issued securities of that class, and if [neither] the Seller [nor any other member of its Group] is involved in the management of the business of the issuer of the securities or any subsidiary undertaking of that issuer except by virtue of the exercise of any voting rights attaching to the securities.

1.03 The Seller shall not disclose or use, nor cause or facilitate the unauthorized disclosure or use of, any Business Know-how or any other confidential information or trade secrets relating to the Business or any of its customers or suppliers, and shall use all reasonable endeavours to prevent the publication or disclosure of any such Business Know-how or other confidential information or trade secrets, as the case may be. This clause shall not prohibit disclosure of:

1.03.01 Business Know-how, confidential information, or trade secrets under a legal obligation involuntarily incurred, or if required by the law of any relevant jurisdiction or by any competent regulatory or governmental body or securities exchange in any relevant jurisdiction, provided that in any such case the Seller shall take all such steps as may be reasonable and practicable in the circumstances to consult with the Buyer before the relevant disclosure is made and shall take into account the Buyer's reasonable comments;

1.03.02 any Business Know-how, confidential information, or trade secret which is in or becomes part of the public domain without breach of this clause or clause 1.05; or

---

exceptional circumstances (eg nature of the business). Longer periods for the covenants against poaching employees may be permissible as they are deemed not to impose blanket prohibitions on the covenantors' ability to do business.

[18] Usually a maximum of two or three years here and in the other covenants.

[19] Select the correct term here, and in clause 1.01.03. If the Business is a retail business, this clause (and clauses 1.01.03, 1.01.04, and 1.01.05) may be inappropriate and if so, should not be included.

[20] See n 7 Section A above.

[21] See n 8 Section A above.

[22] See n 9 Section A above.

      1.03.03 Business Know-how, confidential information, or trade secrets to any other member of the Seller's Group, or to any professional advisers of the Seller or any other member of the Seller's Group for the purpose of obtaining professional advice.

1.04 The Seller shall not at any time after the Completion Date use in any manner in the course of any business, or (so far as within its power) permit or encourage to be so used other than by the Buyer, the names [*insert details*], or any other trade or business name or any mark, sign, or logo used by the Seller [or any member of its Group] in the course of or in relation to the Business, or any confusingly similar name, mark, sign, or logo, or present itself or permit itself to be presented as in any way connected with or interested in the Business.

1.05 The Seller shall ensure that no member of its Group from time to time takes or omits to take any action which, if taken or omitted by the Seller, would constitute a breach of clause [1.01], [1.03], or [1.04].

1.06 Since the Seller has confidential information relating to the Business, and a detailed awareness of the customer connections of the Business, and since the purchase price payable for the Assets has been calculated on the basis that the Seller would assume the obligations set out in this clause [1], the parties acknowledge that each of those obligations is reasonable as to subject matter, area, and duration and is necessary to protect the Buyer's legitimate interest in the Business.

1.07 Without prejudice to any other remedy which may be available to the Buyer, the parties agree that the Buyer shall be entitled to seek injunctive or other equitable relief in relation to any breach of clauses [1.01], [1.03], [1.04], and [1.05], it being acknowledged that an award of damages might not be an adequate remedy in the event of such a breach.

1.08 While the restrictions in this clause [1] are considered by the parties to be reasonable in all the circumstances it is agreed that if any provision of this clause [1] is found by any court of competent jurisdiction to go beyond what is reasonable in all the circumstances for the protection of the goodwill but would be adjudged reasonable if any part of the wording of the provision were deleted, restricted, or limited in a particular manner, the provision in question shall apply with such deletions, restrictions, or limitations as may be necessary to make it valid.

1.09 [Each of the Seller and Buyer acknowledges that it has entered into this Agreement on an arm's length basis and that it has taken independent legal advice in so doing.]

1.10 Each of the obligations assumed by the Seller in this clause [1] is separate and severable and shall be construed and be enforceable independently of the others, and is assumed without prejudice to any other obligation of the Seller implied at law or in equity.

1.11 In this clause 1:

      1.11.01 'Assets' means the assets and rights to be sold under this Agreement, as listed in [*insert details*];

      1.11.02 'Business' means the business of [*insert details*] carried on by the Seller [in the United Kingdom] at Completion [under the name and mark [*insert details*]];

      1.11.03 'Business Know-how' means all know-how, trade secrets, techniques, information, expertise, or proprietary knowledge used by the Seller [or any other member of its Group] at Completion in the course of or in relation to the Business;

      1.11.04 'Completion' means completion of the sale and purchase of the Business and the Assets under clause [*cross-refer to relevant clause*];

      1.11.05 'Completion Date' means the date on which Completion takes place;

      1.11.06 '[Customer][Client]'[23] means any person who was a [customer][client] of the Business as it was carried on at Completion during the period of [   ] months[24] ending on the Completion Date;

      1.11.07 'Group' means [   ];

      1.11.08 'Prospective [Customer][Client]' means any person who was at any time during the period of [   ] months ending on the Completion Date negotiating with any of the Seller or

---

[23] See n 10 Section A above.
[24] See n 11 Section A above.

any member of its Group and reasonably likely to become a [customer][client] of the Business as carried on at Completion;[25]

1.11.09 'Senior Employee'[26] means any person employed or engaged in the Business in a [director/managerial/senior] [sales] position [with remuneration in excess of £[   ] per annum (including bonuses and commission, if any, but excluding any appropriate VAT)] on the Completion Date or any other person who held such a position during the period of [   ] months[27] ending on the Completion Date;

1.11.10 'Seller' means [   ];

1.11.11 'Supplier' means any supplier of goods or services to the Seller for the purposes of the Business during the period of [   ] months ending on the Completion Date.

C. Partnership agreement provisions

1. Suspension and garden leave

1.01 The Management Committee may for such period and upon such terms as the Management Committee may in its absolute discretion determine, suspend from acting as a member of the Partnership any Partner:

1.01.01 who is a Bad Leaver, at any time prior to the date on which such Partner ceases to be Partner;[28]

1.01.02 pending the outcome of an investigation by the Management Committee into the conduct of any Partner.[29]

1.02 Without prejudice to the generality of the provisions of clause 1.01, the Management Committee may at any time decide that the terms applicable during any period of suspension may include one or more of the following directions, namely that the Suspended Partner will:

1.02.01 not enter any one or more of the Partnership premises;

1.02.02 not engage in any business or professional activity connected with the Partnership and/or Practice;

1.02.03 not hold himself out or permit himself to be held out as being in any way authorized to bind the Partnership and/or Practice;

1.02.04 not contact or have any communication with any clients or suppliers of the Partnership and/or Practice, any person who refers work to the Partnership and/or Practice, or any intermediary with whom the Partnership and/or Practice has had dealings as the Management Committee may, from time to time during the Suspension Period, specify;

1.02.05 not contact or have any communication with any Partners, employees, and consultants of the Partnership and/or Practice as the Management Committee may, from time to time during the Suspension Period, specify;

1.02.06 resign any directorships, trusteeships or appointments which he has accepted in the circumstances set out in clause [   ];[30]

1.02.07 be deemed not to be a Partner for the purposes of [Partners Meetings];

1.02.08 use his best endeavours (but consistent with the law, rules, and regulations applicable to professional conduct as a [   ]) to ensure that any person, firm, company, or entity [(other than his Relevant Excluded Clients)] who is or was at any time whilst he has been a Partner, a client of the Practice, remains a client of the Practice;

---

[25] See n 12 Section A above.

[26] See n 13 Section A above.

[27] See n 14 Section A above.

[28] Consider whether the duration of the suspension pursuant to this clause should be limited to, eg, six months to ensure that any post-retirement restrictions are not rendered of unreasonable duration.

[29] This provision does not include any unfettered right to suspend at any time, as this is most unlikely to be acceptable to the partners.

[30] Cross-refer to any provision in the agreement pursuant to which a partner may accept such appointments with, eg, clients of the Practice.

1.02.09 do all such things as the other Partners may from time to time reasonably require.

1.03 The Management Committee will notify the relevant Partner of the terms of any suspension pursuant to clause 1.01 as soon as practicable after making the decision to suspend.

1.04 During any Suspension Period the other Partners will be entitled to give such reasonable and truthful explanations for the Suspended Partner's absence from the Partnership premises and his unavailability to clients and other persons as they may in their absolute discretion think fit.

1.05 [If any question arises concerning the existence or exercise of the powers conferred by this clause [1] such question will forthwith be referred to mediation and arbitration under the provisions of clause [   ].[31]]

1.06 During the Suspension Period the Suspended Partner will be entitled only to payment of his [fixed share] [notional salary], provided that the Management Committee has absolute discretion, during or following such suspension, as to whether to pay the Suspended Partner any amounts in addition to his [fixed share] [notional salary].

1.07 Any Partner suspended under this clause [1] must not be employed by or provide services to any third party during the Suspension Period.

1.08 Except as set out in this clause [1], during any Suspension Period the Partner concerned will continue to be entitled to all other rights of a Partner.

2. Notification

2.01 Each Partner and Outgoing Partner must:

2.01.01 immediately inform the Management Committee in writing if he receives an offer of partnership, membership of a limited liability partnership (an LLP), employment, engagement, or agency with any other business;

2.01.02 ensure that the Management Committee is aware as soon as reasonably practicable of:

2.01.02.01 any actual, potential, or maturing business opportunity enjoyed by the Partnership and/or the Practice;

2.01.02.02 his own misconduct or the misconduct of any agent, employee, officer, Partner, or worker of the Partnership and/or the Practice, of which the Partner is, or ought reasonably to be, aware;

2.01.02.03 any offer of engagement or approach made by another business to any agent, employee, officer, Partner, or worker of the Partnership and/or the Practice of which the Partner is, or ought reasonably to be, aware;

2.01.02.04 the intention (whether settled or not) of any agent, employee, officer, Partner, or worker of the Partnership and/or the Practice who reports directly or indirectly to the Partner to resign from their employment, engagement, or position with the Partnership and/or the Practice.

3. Restrictions whilst a partner

3.01 Other than in the proper and normal course of his duties, the Partner will not at any time whilst a Partner or Outgoing Partner, without the prior written consent of [the Management Committee]:

3.01.01 [have any Material Interest in any trade, business, or occupation whatsoever other than the Partnership and/or Practice except as disclosed in Schedule [1];]

3.01.02 [have any Material Interest in any Competing Business;]

3.01.03 [have any Material Interest in any person, firm, or company that impairs or might reasonably be considered by the Partnership to impair his ability to act at all times in the best interests of the Partnership;]

3.01.04 [have any Material Interest in any person, firm, or company that requires or might reasonably be considered by the Partnership to require him to use and/or disclose any Confidential Information [*cross-refer to definition in partnership agreement*] in order

---

[31] Cross-refer to a provision regarding mediation/arbitration, if relevant.

properly to discharge his duties or to further his interest in such person, firm, or company;]

3.01.05 [incur on behalf of the Partnership any capital expenditure in excess of such sum as may be authorized from time to time by the Management Committee;][32]

3.01.06 [enter into on behalf of the Partnership any commitment, contract, or arrangement which is otherwise than in the normal course of the Practice or is outside the scope of his normal duties or authorizations or is of an unusual or onerous or long-term nature;][33]

3.01.07 [engage any person on terms which vary from those established from time to time by the Management Committee;][34]

3.01.08 employ or engage or attempt to employ or engage, induce, solicit, or entice away or attempt to induce, solicit, or entice away any agent, consultant, employee, officer, Partner, or worker of the Partnership;

3.01.09 directly or indirectly make preparations to compete with any business carried on by the Partnership and/or the Practice; [or]

3.01.10 [induce or attempt to induce any client [or supplier] of the Partnership and/or the Practice to cease conducting any business or to reduce the amount of business or adversely to vary the terms upon which any business is conducted with the Partnership and/or the Practice or to exclude the Partnership and/or the Practice from new business opportunities in relation to services of a kind normally dealt in by the Partnership and/or the Practice [; or][.]]

3.01.11 [inform any agent, client, consultant, customer, employee, officer, supplier, or worker of the Partnership and/or the Practice or any third-party agent who may be in the habit of dealing with the Partnership and/or the Practice that he may resign or has resigned from the Partnership or that he has accepted employment of partnership with or is to join or be associated with any competitor of the Partnership.]

3.02 The Management Committee may at its absolute discretion at any time and from time to time upon written notice to the Partner require the Partner to take [immediately][as soon as practicable] all steps necessary fully and effectively to relinquish the whole or any part of any Material Interest [disclosed in Schedule [1] or] in respect of the holding of which the Management Board has at any time given its prior written consent under clause [3.01] [if the Management Board [reasonably] considers that it is not in the best interests of the Partnership and/or the Practice for the Partner to continue to hold that Material Interest].

4. Restrictions after ceasing to be a partner

4.01 Each Partner hereby covenants that, if he ceases to be a Partner other than by reason of the dissolution of the Partnership, expulsion under clause [   ][35] (mental health) or clause [   ][36] (incapacity), he will:

4.01.01 not for a period of [   ][37] from his Termination Date carry on or be interested in or act as partner, member, employee, consultant, officer, or agent of any Competing Business in the Restricted Area;

4.01.02 not for a period of [   ][38] after his Termination Date directly or indirectly, [save in relation to Relevant Excluded Clients][39] whether as principal, director, consultant, or employee, solicit, or endeavour to solicit, instructions to provide [   ] services from any

---

[32] These types of administration issues may be dealt with here or elsewhere in the Agreement.

[33] See n 32 above.

[34] See n 32 above.

[35] Cross-refer to relevant provisions in the agreement.

[36] Cross-refer to relevant provisions in the agreement.

[37] A period of six, nine, or twelve months would be usual here.

[38] A period of up to two years would be usual here and in paragraphs 4.01.03, 4.01.04, and 4.01.07 below.

[39] If the Partner concerned brought a client 'following' with him to the Partnership, he will probably wish to negotiate a carve-out for those clients from any restrictions. See definitions (below) which are drafted on the basis that there will be an agreed list of such clients that will have effect for an agreed duration.

Client nor induce any Client to cease conducting business with or procuring [   ] services from the Practice or to reduce the amount of business conducted with the Practice, adversely to vary the terms upon which its business is conducted with the Practice or exclude the Practice from new business opportunities in relation to services of a kind normally dealt in by the Practice;

4.01.03   not, for a period of [   ] after his Termination Date directly or indirectly, [save [in relation to Relevant Excluded Clients] [or] [on behalf of the Practice],] whether as principal, director, consultant, or employee, accept instructions to provide [   ] services from, provide [   ] services to, or attempt to provide [   ] services to any Client;

4.01.04   not, for a period of [   ] after his Termination Date directly or indirectly, either for his own account or for any other person, solicit or entice away, or endeavour to solicit or entice away, from the Practice any Key Person;

4.01.05   not, for a period of [   ][40] after his Termination Date, become a partner in, member of or consultant to a [   ] practice or, for the purposes of providing [   ] services, a director or employee of or consultant to a company:

— at the same time as any other [Key Person] [Partner, Outgoing Partner or employee, former employee of or consultant or former consultant to the Partnership];[41] or

— which contains as a partner, director, employee, or consultant any [Key Person] [Partner, Outgoing Partner or employee, former employee of or consultant or former consultant to the Partnership];

4.01.06   not, directly or indirectly, during the period of [   ] after his Termination Date, as a partner in a firm or member of an LLP or director or employee of a company providing [   ] services, or as an internal [   ] adviser to any organization, offer employment to or employ any person who during the period of twelve months prior to his Termination Date was a Partner or a [   ] employed by the Partnership [and who during such period of twelve months worked in the same Key Group as the Outgoing Partner];[42]

4.01.07   use his best endeavours (but consistent with the law, rules, and regulations applicable to professional conduct as a [   ]) for a period of [   ] following his Termination Date to ensure that any person, firm, company, or entity [(other than his Relevant Excluded Clients)] who was at any time that he was a Partner a client of the Practice, remains a client of the Practice before and after his Termination Date;

4.01.08   not after his Termination Date present himself or allow himself to be held out or presented as being in any way connected with or interested in the Partnership and/or Practice; and

4.01.09   neither while a Partner nor after his Termination Date make, or authorize to be made on his behalf, any derogatory, disparaging, or pejorative statements about the Practice, the Partnership or its Partners, employees, agents, consultants, officers, or clients.

4.02   It is hereby declared that:

4.02.01   the provisions of each of clauses [   ] to [   ] respectively are intended to be read and construed independently of each other so that none of such separate provisions shall be dependent on any one or more of any of the other such provisions; and

4.02.02   the restrictions set out in clauses [   ] to [   ] respectively are reasonable in extent and duration and go no further than is reasonably necessary to protect the legitimate business interests of the Partnership and the Practice.

---

[40] A period of up to one year would be usual here and in paragraph 4.01.06.

[41] If the practice is large, seeking to restrict the partner from working with any former partner/employee etc may be unenforceable. Consider defining 'Key Person' (see definitions section) and so narrowing the application of the restriction.

[42] If the practice is large, seeking to restrict the partner from employing any former partner/employee may be unenforceable. Consider narrowing the application of the restriction by including the words in square brackets.

4.03 An Outgoing Partner shall not accept employment or any office or position of profit with any client with whom he has had dealings while a Partner [(other than any of his Relevant Excluded Clients)] for twelve months following the Termination Date.

4.04 Each Partner accepts and agrees that, if he is offered partnership, employment consultancy, or any other business activity while a Partner or in the [thirty-six months] following the Termination Date, he will inform the person, firm, company, or other entity making such an offer of the nature, duration, and extent of the restrictions and provisions specified in this clause [   ].

4.05 [Notwithstanding the provisions of clause [   ] [*provision for mediation/arbitration*],] each of the Partners accepts and agrees that injunctive relief may always be available to the continuing Partners should a Partner infringe any of the provisions of this clause [   ], and that damages may not be an adequate remedy for any such infringement.

5. Protective covenants in relation to confidential information of the practice

5.01 Each Partner hereby covenants that he shall while he remains a Partner and at all times after the Termination Date observe strict secrecy as to the affairs and dealings of the Practice, the Partnership, and its or their clients and (save in the ordinary course of the business of the Practice):

5.01.01 shall not, without the prior written consent of the Managing Partner/Management Committee, make use of or divulge to any person; and

5.01.02 while a Partner, shall use his best endeavours to prevent the publication or disclosure of:

— details of the work done by or on behalf of the Practice, as well as details of the requirements of clients of the Practice, including without limitation, the terms of business with them and the fees charged to them;

— details of any advice given to clients of the Practice (unless expressly authorized by the relevant client to reveal such advice);

— details of any advertising, marketing, or promotional campaign that the Practice is to conduct;

— any information relation to:

— expansion plans, business strategy, marketing plans, merger, affiliation or amalgamation plans, investment plans, and sales forecasts of the Practice;

— financial information, results, and forecasts of the Practice;

— details of the Partners, employees, consultants, and officers of the Practice, of the profit shares remuneration and other benefits paid to them and of their charge out rates;

— information relating to pitches, tenders or projects contemplated, offered or undertaken by the Practice;

— confidential reports or research commissioned by or provided to the Practice;

— any trade secrets of the Practice including know-how and confidential transactions;

— any source codes or other confidential information relating to any software used or licensed by the Practice; and

— any information which is designated confidential by the Practice, any information the disclosure of which would result in a breach of professional duties of client confidentiality or professional privilege and any confidential information which has been given to the Practice.

5.02 Any Partner shall not while he remains a Partner (save in the ordinary course of the Partnership's business), nor shall any Outgoing Partner at any time after the Termination Date, disclose, publish, or reveal to any unauthorized person any incident, conversation, information, or document concerning any Partner, employee, agent, consultant, or officer of the Practice or of any of its clients, guests, or visitors that is confidential or otherwise personal and private in nature, which has or will come to his knowledge while a Partner or any such incident, conversation, or information relating to the Practice unless duly authorized in writing by the [Managing Partner/Management

Committee] so to do. No Partner or Outgoing Partner will publish any such matter in any book, newspaper, periodical, or pamphlet or by broadcasting or transmission on television, cable, satellite, film, Internet or any other medium now known or devised after the date of this Agreement or by communication to any third party including a representative of the media.

5.03 The restrictions in clause [ ] and [ ] will not prevent an Outgoing Partner after the Termination Date from using, divulging, publishing, or disclosing any information which becomes available generally to the public other than by reason of a breach of this Agreement.

Relevant Definitions

'Bad Leaver' means an Outgoing Partner who leaves pursuant to clauses [ ] (struck off), [ ] (suspended), [ ] (enforced retirement), [ ] (expulsion), or who serves notice to retire pursuant to clause [*insert references to notice to retire provision*];

'Client' means any person, firm, company, or other entity who or which was at any time during the Relevant Period a client of the Practice or was negotiating to become a client of the Practice, or was in the habit of dealing with the Practice [and with whom or which the Partner [or any member of the [*insert details of the relevant group if required*] had [material] dealings during the Relevant Period]];

'Client Team' means a group comprising one or more Partners and one or more [senior] employees working in conjunction or cooperation [not necessarily in the same location] to provide or develop services for a particular actual client or prospective client of the Practice;]

'Competing Business' means the business carried on by the Practice[43] and in which the Partner was materially involved (during the Relevant Period);

['Key Group' means one of the operating groups into which the Practice is divided (currently [*specify*])];[44]

['Key Person' means any person who during the period of [twelve months] prior to the Outgoing Partner's Termination Date was either:

— a Partner in the same Key Group [or Client Team][45] as the Outgoing Partner; or

— a Partner with whom the Outgoing Partner had regular dealings; or

— an individual employed by the Partnership and working in the same [Key Group][46] or [Client Team] Sub-Group as the Outgoing Partner;]

'Management Committee' means the committee referred to in clause [*cross-refer to relevant provision in agreement*] or such other committee as the Partners may by Special Majority determine will manage the Partnership;

'Outgoing Partner' means a Partner who has ceased to be a Partner for any reason and the personal representatives or trustees in bankruptcy of such Partner as the case may be;

'Partner' means any person who is from time to time a Partner in the Partnership;

'Partnership' means the partnership existing between the Partners on the terms of this Agreement;

'Practice' means the business carried on by the Partners as [ ] in partnership on and from the Commencement Date on the terms and subject to the conditions of this Agreement;

'Recognized Investment Exchange' means a recognized exchange or an overseas investment exchange, each as defined by section 285 of the Financial Services and Markets Act 2000;

'Relevant Excluded Clients' means, in relation to any Partner, clients of his whose names appear on a list agreed, in accordance with clause [ ],[47] with that Partner upon his first joining the

---

[43] Consider whether the Partnership carries on any other business(es) and, if so, amend this definition and the restrictions as appropriate.

[44] Depending on the size of the partnership/practice, it may not be necessary to restrict non-solicitation only to members of the Key Group in this way and so this definition may not be needed.

[45] Depending on how the firm organizes its work, reference to either or both of Key Group and Client Team may be appropriate.

[46] Depending on the size of the partnership/practice and the teams involved, this definition may not be needed or may need to be further refined, eg to a sub-group, if it is not to risk being too wide to be enforceable.

[47] Cross-refer to relevant provision of the agreement.

Partnership. Once the period for which the list is specified to last has expired, the clients on that list will cease to be Relevant Excluded Clients;

'Relevant Period' means the period of [two years] ending with the Termination Date;

'Restricted Area' [*insert relevant details*];

'Suspended Partner' means a partner suspended pursuant to clause [1.01];

'Suspension Period' means any period of suspension pursuant to clause [1.01];

'Termination Date' means the date on which any Partner ceases to be a Partner pursuant to the provision of clause [   ][48] or by death.

---

[48] Cross-refer to relevant termination provision(s).

Sample Pre-Action Letters

Catherine Taylor

Set out below are letters relating to two scenarios: (1) where the defendant employee is alleging constructive dismissal and/or the claimant employer wishes to enforce garden leave; and (2) where the defendant employee has already left employment and the main issue is the post-termination restrictions.

Obviously there are many permutations on these scenarios, but these precedents should provide a useful starting point for most situations. There are three letters for each scenario—one to each of the defendant employee and the defendant employer from the claimant employer, and a response to the claimant employer from the defendant employee.

See also paras 9.81 to 9.105, 9.146 to 9.147, and 9.176 to 9.183.

1. From Claimant Employer to Defendant Employee where the Defendant Employee is alleging constructive dismissal and/or the Claimant Employer wishes to enforce garden leave

[On headed notepaper of solicitors to the Claimant Employer]

Strictly private and confidential—to be read by addressee only

[Name and address of Defendant Employee]

[Date]

[*By hand*] [*by fax*] [*by email*]

Dear [Sir] [Madam]

Claimant Employer v Defendant Employee(s) [and Defendant Employer]

We are instructed on behalf of [Claimant Employer] in relation to your [purported resignation and] commencement of employment with [Defendant Employer].

We note that you have recently commenced employment with [Defendant Employer]. However, [despite your assertion that you have been constructively dismissed by our client (to which we shall return)] you remain an employee of [Claimant Employer]. Accordingly, you owe our client a contractual duty of fidelity[1] until your employment lawfully terminates on [date]. You also remain bound by the contractual provisions of your contract of employment, set out in the [set out details] (the 'Contract of Employment'). We enclose [a copy] [copies] of [this] [these] document[s] for your information.

In so far as you are not already on notice, we put you on express notice of the following contractual and other obligations to which you are subject:

Termination date

The Contract of Employment contains provisions regarding the term of your employment at clause [   ]. This states that:

'[*set out terms*]'.

---

[1] Or a fiduciary duty if appropriate.

Accordingly, your employment will end on [date].

Your obligations

[*Set out the relevant terms and conditions of the Defendant Employee's contract and any other relevant obligations. Include those which apply during employment if you are relying on garden leave or believe the Defendant Employee had breached his or her obligations. Set out the post-termination obligations where the issue also relates to these*].

In addition, as mentioned above, you continue to be bound by the duty of fidelity implied into your contract of employment with our client [and your fiduciary duties as a result of your role as [*set out basis for fiduciary duties*]].

Recent events

[*Set out recent relevant events, for example, the rebuttal of a constructive dismissal claim and any evidence of breach by the employee.*]

You remain our client's employee and will remain so until [date]. Our client therefore requires you [to cease work for [Defendant Employer] immediately and] to remain on garden leave for the remainder of your employment with our client. During this time you should not attend any of our client's offices nor contact any of our client's customers, clients, employees, or suppliers without our client's express consent.

Further, we refer you to the restrictive covenants contained at clause [   ] of the Contract of Employment. Your employment with [Defendant Employer] even following the termination of your employment with our client in a competitive role would [also] constitute a clear breach of these covenants. To be absolutely clear, our client has not and will not release you from any of the terms of your Contract of Employment.

[*Contractual undertaking*]. [Our client therefore requires you to give undertakings in the form attached. [As you have already commenced employment with [Defendant Employer], without notice to our client in breach of your contractual obligations,] unless these undertakings are received by [time] on [date] our client [will][may] have no alternative but to apply to the Court for immediate relief.]

[*Undertakings to the Court*] [We enclose a draft order containing certain undertakings which our client requires you to give to the Court. Our client will very shortly serve on you an application and supporting documents seeking the relief set out in the draft order pending [a speedy trial][an interim hearing] of this matter. Please confirm by [time] on [date] that you will comply with the terms of the draft order pending [speedy trial][the hearing] by consenting to an order made by the court in that form to avoid the necessity of such a hearing taking place.]

We advise you to take legal advice on the contents of this letter as a matter of urgency.

In the meantime, all our client's past, present, and future rights are fully reserved.

[Yours faithfully]

2. From Claimant Employer to Defendant Employee where the Defendant Employee has already left employment

[On headed notepaper of solicitors to the Claimant Employer]

Strictly private and confidential—to be read by addressee only

[Name and address of Defendant Employee]

[Date]

[*By hand*] [*by fax*] [*by email*]

Dear [Sir] [Madam]

Claimant Employer v Defendant Employee(s) [and Defendant Employer]

We are instructed on behalf of [Claimant Employer] in relation to your resignation and commencement of employment with [Defendant Employer].

We write to remind you that you remain subject to certain obligations owed to our client as set out in your contract of employment [*set out details*] (the 'Contract of Employment'). We enclose [a copy] [copies] of [this] [these] document[s] for your information.

Your obligations

In so far as you are not already on notice, we put you on express notice of the following contractual and other obligations to which you are subject:

[*Set out the relevant terms and conditions of the Defendant Employee's contract and any other relevant obligations. Include those which apply during employment if you believe the Defendant Employee had breached his or her obligations whilst employed. Set out the post-termination obligations where the issue relates to these*].

Recent events

[*Set out recent relevant events, for example, the rebuttal of a constructive dismissal claim and any evidence of breach by the employee.*]

We refer you to the restrictive covenants contained at clause [   ] of the Contract of Employment. Your employment with [Defendant Employer] in a competitive role would constitute a clear breach of these covenants. To be absolutely clear, our client has not and will not release you from any of the terms of your Contract of Employment.

[*Contractual undertaking*]. [Our client therefore requires you to give undertakings in the form attached. As you have already commenced employment with [Defendant Employer], [without notice to our client in breach of your contractual obligations,] unless these undertakings are received by [time] on [date] our client [will][may] have no alternative but to apply to the Court for immediate relief.]

[*Undertakings to the Court*] [We enclose a draft order containing certain undertakings which our client requires you to give to the Court. Our client will very shortly serve on you an application and supporting documents seeking the relief set out in the draft order pending [a speedy trial][an interim hearing] of this matter. Please confirm by [time] on [date] that you will comply with the terms of the draft order pending [speedy trial][the hearing] by consenting to an order made by the court in that form to avoid the necessity of such a hearing taking place.]

We advise you to take legal advice on the contents of this letter as a matter of urgency.

In the meantime, all our client's past, present, and future rights are fully reserved.

[Yours faithfully]

3. From Claimant Employer to Defendant Employer where the Defendant Employee is alleging constructive dismissal and/or the Claimant Employer wishes to enforce garden leave

[On headed notepaper of solicitor to Claimant Employer]

Strictly private and confidential—to be read by addressee only

[Name and address of Defendant Employer]

For the attention of the [Head of Human Resources] [Managing Director] [Head of Department][2]

[Date]

---

[2] Consider who will be the most effective person to whom to send the letter.

[*By hand*] [*by fax*] [*by email*]

Dear [Sir] [Madam]

Claimant Employer v Defendant Employee(s) and Defendant Employer

We are instructed on behalf of [Claimant Employer] in relation to [Defendant Employee(s)].

Our client has very recently become aware that [Defendant Employee] [has started] [intends to start] employment with you. [Defendant Employee] is, despite his suggestion that he has been constructively dismissed by our client, still an employee of [Claimant Employer]. Accordingly, [Defendant Employee] owes our client a contractual duty of fidelity [3] until his employment lawfully terminates. He also remains bound by the contractual provisions of his contract of employment, set out in the [set out details] (the 'Contract of Employment'). We enclose [a copy] [copies] of [this] [these] provision[s] for your information.

In so far as you are not already on notice, we put you on express notice of the following contractual and other obligations to which [Defendant Employee] is subject:

Termination date

The Contract of Employment contains provisions regarding the term of [Defendant Employee's] employment at clause [   ]. This states that:

'[*set out terms*]'.

Accordingly, [Defendant Employee's] employment with our client would terminate on [date].

[Defendant Employee's] obligations

[*Set out the relevant terms and conditions of the Defendant Employee's contract and any other relevant obligations. Include those which apply during employment if you are relying on garden leave or believe the Defendant Employee has already breached those obligations. Set out the post-termination obligations where the issue relates to these.*]

In addition, as mentioned above, [Defendant Employee] continues to be bound by the duty of fidelity implied into his contract of employment with our client [and his fiduciary duties as a result of his role as [*set out basis for fiduciary duties*]].

Recent events

Against this background, [Defendant Employee] resigned on [date]. Our client wrote to [Defendant Employee] on [date] reminding him of his contractual obligations to our client, including his obligations which continue following the termination of his employment with our client.

[*Set out any further correspondence or relevant facts.*]

[Defendant Employee] remains our client's employee and will remain so until [date]. Our client therefore requires [Defendant Employee] to cease work for you immediately and to remain on garden leave for the remainder of his employment with our client. During this time, he should not attend any of our client offices, nor contact any of our client's customers, clients, employees, or suppliers without our client's express consent.

Further, we refer you to the restrictive covenants contained at clause [   ] of the Contract of Employment. Your employment of [Defendant Employee] even following the termination of his employment with our client in a competitive role would also constitute a clear breach of these restrictions. To be absolutely clear, our client has not and will not release [Defendant Employee] from any of the terms of his Contract of Employment.

---

[3] Or a fiduciary duty if appropriate and set out on what basis.

[Contractual undertakings

We enclose draft undertakings which we require you to sign. Should you fail to sign and return these to us by [time] on [date] our client [will] [may] have no choice but to apply to the Court for relief in the form of the undertakings.]

[Undertakings to the Court

We enclose a draft order containing certain undertakings which our client requires from you. Our client will very shortly serve on you an application and supporting documents seeking the relief set out in the draft order pending [a speedy trial][an interim hearing] of this matter. Please confirm by [time] on [date] that you will comply with the terms of the draft order pending [speedy trial] [the hearing] by consenting to an order made by the court in that form to avoid the necessity of such a hearing taking place.]

In the meantime, all our client's past, present, and future rights, including its right to pursue you for damages, are fully reserved.

[Yours faithfully]

4. From Claimant Employer to Defendant Employer where the Defendant Employee has already left employment

[On headed notepaper of solicitor to Claimant Employer]

Strictly private and confidential—to be read by addressee only

[Name and address of Defendant Employer]

For the attention of the [Head of Human Resources] [Managing Director] [Head of Department][4]

[Date]

[*By hand*] [*by fax*] [*by email*]

Dear [Sir] [Madam]

Claimant Employer v Defendant Employee(s) and Defendant Employer

We are instructed on behalf of [Claimant Employer] in relation to [Defendant Employee(s)].

Our client has very recently become aware that [Defendant Employee] [has started] [intends to start] employment with you. However, Defendant Employee remains subject to certain obligations to our client as set out in [his] [her] contract of employment [set out details] (the 'Contract of Employment'). We enclose [a copy] [copies] of [this] [these] provision[s] for your information.

[Defendant Employee's] obligations

In so far as you are not already on notice, we put you on express notice of the following contractual obligations to which [Defendant Employee] is subject:

[*Set out the relevant terms and conditions of the Defendant Employee's contract and any other relevant obligations. Include those which apply during employment if you believe the Defendant Employee has already breached those obligations. Set out the post-termination obligations where the issue relates to these.*]

Recent events

Against this background, [Defendant Employee] resigned on [date]. Our client wrote to [Defendant Employee] on [date] reminding him of his contractual obligations to our client, including his obligations which continue following the termination of his employment with our client.

[*Set out any further correspondence or relevant facts.*]

---

[4] Consider who will be the most effective person to whom to send the letter.

We refer you to the restrictive covenants contained at clause [   ] of the Contract of Employment. Your employment of [Defendant Employee] in a competitive role would constitute a clear breach of these restrictions. To be absolutely clear, our client has not and will not release [Defendant Employee] from any of the terms of his Contract of Employment.

[Contractual undertakings

We enclose draft undertakings which we require you to sign. Should you fail to sign and return these to us by [time] on [date] our client [will] [may] have no choice but to apply to the Court for relief in the form of the undertakings.]

[Undertakings to the Court

We enclose a draft order containing certain undertakings which our client requires from you. Our client will very shortly serve on you an application and supporting documents seeking the relief set out in the draft order pending [a speedy trial][an interim hearing] of this matter. Please confirm by [time] on [date] that you will comply with the terms of the draft order pending [speedy trial][the hearing] by consenting to an order made by the court in that form to avoid the necessity of such a hearing taking place.]

In the meantime, all our client's past, present, and future rights, including its right to pursue you for damages, are fully reserved.

[Yours faithfully]

5. From Defendant Employee to Claimant Employer where the Defendant Employee is alleging constructive dismissal and/or the Claimant Employer wishes to enforce garden leave

[On headed notepaper of the solicitors to the Defendant Employee]

Strictly private and confidential

[Name and address of Claimant Employer's solicitors]

[Date]

[By hand] [by fax] [by email]

Dear Sirs

Claimant Employer v Defendant Employee(s) [and Defendant Employer]

We are instructed on behalf of the defendant employee to respond to your letter dated [   ] received on [   ]. *[If appropriate make points about any delay in delivery, the inadequate time given to respond].*

Our client commenced employment on [   ]. *[Set out any relevant history of the employment including any grounds for alleging constructive dismissal.]* Accordingly, our client had no choice but to resign from his employment on [date] in response to your client's fundamental breach of contract. Our client is therefore free from all contractual obligations to your client and fully entitled to commence employment with his/her new employer [as he/she has done]. In any case, even if our client had not been constructively dismissed, you would not be entitled to place him on garden leave for the following reasons: *[set out reasons, for example no signed contract; no garden leave clause; length unreasonable].*

Further, the post-termination restrictions referred to in your letter are not enforceable against our client (in so far as they were enforceable on their terms, which is [not admitted] [denied]).

[No undertaking to be offered

Accordingly, our client is free to commence work and will defend vigorously any proceedings which are commenced against him/her. Kindly ensure that we are given proper notice of any application, that is service of the application and supporting evidence on three clear days' notice. [We are instructed to accept service.]]

[Compromise undertakings

Notwithstanding our client's position as set out above, we are instructed to offer limited contractual undertakings pending [a speedy trial] [an interim hearing] of this matter, subject to the [speedy trial] [hearing] taking place within a window of [date] to [date]. We have ascertained from the Listing Office that dates for a [   ] day trial are available within that window. The contractual undertakings are as follows: [*set out undertakings*].

[We also require a cross-undertaking in damages from your client in relation to the proposed undertakings above.]

If your client will not agree to the proposal above, kindly ensure that we are given proper notice of any application, that is service of the application and supporting evidence on three clear days' notice. [We are instructed to accept service.]]

In the meantime, all our client's rights are fully reserved.

[Yours faithfully]

6. From Defendant Employee to Claimant Employer where the Defendant Employee has already left employment

[On headed notepaper of the solicitors to the Defendant Employee]

Strictly private and confidential

[Name and address of Claimant Employer's solicitors]

[Date]

[*By hand*] [*by fax*] [*by email*]

Dear Sirs

Claimant Employer v Defendant Employee(s) [and Defendant Employer]

We are instructed on behalf of the defendant employee to respond to your letter dated [   ] received on [   ]. [*If appropriate make points about any delay in delivery, the inadequate time given to respond*].

Our client denies that he/she is bound by the terms of the post-termination restrictions for the following reasons: [*set out grounds of dispute including contract not signed; restrictions do not cover the competitive activity; temporal, geographical extent of the restrictions too wide*].

[No undertaking to be offered

Accordingly, our client is free to [commence][continue] to work for [Defendant Employer] and will defend vigorously any proceedings which are commenced against him/her. Kindly ensure that we are given proper notice of any application, that is service of the application and supporting evidence on three clear days' notice. [We are instructed to accept service.]]

[Compromise undertakings

Notwithstanding our client's position as set out above, we are instructed to offer limited contractual undertakings pending [a speedy trial][an interim hearing] of this matter, subject to the [speedy trial] [hearing] taking place within a window of [date] to [date]. We have ascertained from the Listing Office that dates for a [   ] day trial are available within that window. The contractual undertakings are as follows: [*set out undertakings*].]

[We also require a cross-undertaking in damages from your client in relation to the proposed undertakings above.]

If your client will not agree to the proposal above, kindly ensure that we are given proper notice of any application, that is service of the application and supporting evidence on three clear days' notice. [We are instructed to accept service.]]

In the meantime, all our client's rights are fully reserved.

[Yours faithfully]

Sample Witness Statement in Support of Application for Interim Injunction to Restrain Breach of Restrictive Covenant

Robert Weekes

IN THE HIGH COURT OF JUSTICE
QUEEN'S BENCH DIVISION

Claim No. [   ]

BETWEEN
FORMER EMPLOYER LIMITED
Claimant
– and –
FORMER EMPLOYEE
Defendant

WITNESS STATEMENT OF DIRECTOR OF FORMER EMPLOYER

I, [NAME], [POSITION], [ADDRESS OF FORMER EMPLOYER LIMITED] WILL SAY AS FOLLOWS:

1. I am a Director of the Claimant in this matter, [FORMER EMPLOYER LIMITED]. I am duly authorized by it to make this statement in support of its claim for interim injunctive relief under CPR, rule 25.1(1)(a), restraining the Defendant from breaching certain terms of his contract of employment with FORMER EMPLOYER LIMITED.

2. Except where I state otherwise, the matters contained in this witness statement are within my own knowledge. Where I make a statement based upon a matter of information or belief, I clearly indicate that this is the case and state the source of that information or belief.

3. Exhibit [x] to which I refer in this statement contains a paginated bundle of true copy documents which are relevant to this claim. References in this witness statement to page numbers are references to [x].

4. [SUMMARY OF CLAIM AGAINST FORMER EMPLOYEE].

5. [SUMMARY OF INTERIM INJUNCTIVE RELIEF SOUGHT].

6. [DESCRIPTION OF BUSINESS OF FORMER EMPLOYER LIMITED].

7. [DESCRIPTION OF EMPLOYMENT OF FORMER EMPLOYEE WHILST AN EMPLOYEE OF FORMER EMPLOYER LIMITED including date of commencement, positions held].

8. [RELEVANT PROVISIONS OF CONTRACT OF EMPLOYMENT OF FORMER EMPLOYEE including relevant covenants being set out in full].

9. [ANY RELEVANT PROVISIONS OF THE EMPLOYEE HANDBOOK].

10. [DESCRIPTION OF WORK ACTUALLY PERFORMED BY FORMER EMPLOYEE FOR FORMER EMPLOYER LIMITED including matters material to covenants (legitimate interests and reasonableness) eg the role of Former Employee in building up client relationships or his access to confidential information, geographical area in which Former Employer operated, types of products with which Former Employee dealt, and clients with whom Former Employee dealt etc].

11. [REMUNERATION received by Former Employee from Former Employer Limited during course of his employment].

12. [EVENTS LEADING UP TO TERMINATION OF EMPLOYMENT OF FORMER EMPLOYEE including any evidence that Former Employee intended to compete against Former Employer Limited contrary to restrictive covenants].

13. [TERMINATION OF EMPLOYMENT OF FORMER EMPLOYEE including any notification on behalf of Former Employer Limited that restrictive covenants would be enforced against Former Employee. In case of a without notice application, careful consideration should be given to, and full and frank disclosure given of, any matters which might in due course be relied upon by Former Employee as grounds for alleging constructive dismissal, or generally unenforceability of covenants].

14. [EVIDENCE OF CONDUCT OF FORMER EMPLOYEE WHICH IS CONTRARY TO THE RESTRICTIVE COVENANTS including explanation of circumstances in which Former Employer Limited came to discover such conduct].

15. [STATEMENT OF GROUNDS FOR BELIEF THAT FORMER EMPLOYEE IS ACTING IN BREACH OF RESTRICTIVE COVENANTS AND FOR BELIEF THAT, UNLESS RESTRAINED BY INJUNCTION, FORMER EMPLOYEE WILL CONTINUE TO DO SO].

16. [STATEMENT OF REASONS WHY BALANCE OF CONVENIENCE FAVOURS INJUNCTION BEING GRANTED].

17. [ANY CORRESPONDENCE BETWEEN FORMER EMPLOYER LIMITED AND FORMER EMPLOYEE RELATING TO ALLEGED CONDUCT IN BREACH OF RESTRICTIVE COVENANTS].

18. [STATEMENT OF WILLINGNESS TO PROVIDE A CROSS-UNDERTAKING IN DAMAGES including reference to relevant evidence supporting means of Former Employer Limited to meet such a cross-undertaking].

19. [WHERE WITHOUT NOTICE APPLICATION IS MADE, EXPLANATION OF REASONS FOR URGENCY including explanation of speed with which Former Employer Limited has reacted to discovery of conduct of Former Employee].

I believe that the facts stated in this witness statement are true.

Signed ....

Date ....

APPENDIX 11

Sample Prayer for Relief for Inclusion in Particulars of Claim

Stephen Nathan QC

And the Claimant claims:

(1) A Declaration that [the Defendant . . .];

(2) An Order that the Defendant be restrained by himself, his servants, agents, or otherwise howsoever directly or indirectly from doing or attempting to do the following acts or any of them: [   ];

(3) An Order that the Defendant do deliver up upon Affidavit to the Claimant, or to such other person as the Court may direct, the documents (including all copies thereof or extracts therefrom) and the other property in the Defendant's possession or power which are described in Schedule A; or alternatively directions for the disposal thereof by destruction as the Court may think fit;

(4) Damages (including damages calculated on the gain-based principle) OR [in the Chancery Division] an inquiry as to damages (including damages calculated on the gain-based principle) and payment of all sums found due upon the making of such inquiry;

(5) Alternatively at the Claimant's option an account of all profits made by the Defendant [by reason of . . .] and payment of all sums found due upon taking such account;

(6) Equitable compensation;

(7) Exemplary damages [where appropriate];

(8) *Interest pursuant to section 35A of the Senior Courts Act 1981 on the sum found due to the Claimant to be assessed;*

Tracing claim:

(9) A Declaration that [specify fund or asset] was received by the Defendant upon a constructive or resulting trust and that the Claimant is entitled to trace in equity all other assets acquired by, or derived from, or representing [such fund or traceable assets] ('the traceable assets');

(10) An Order that the Defendant give an account upon Affidavit and full disclosure of documents relating to the nature, location, and value of the traceable assets and as to what has become of them;

(11) An Order that the Defendant deliver up the [fund or asset] and the traceable assets to the Claimant (so far as they are in his power or control), and/or equitable compensation for their loss, and/or diminution in value with compound interest thereon.

APPENDIX 12

Summaries of Cases on Restrictive Covenants[1]

Catherine Taylor

Case name	Facts	Judgment
Nordenfelt v Maxim Nordenfelt Guns and Ammunition Co Ltd [1894] AC 535, HL	The owner of a gun manufacturing business sold it to a company and covenanted in the contract of sale not to engage in a similar business, except on behalf of the company, anywhere in the world for the next twenty-five years. This was alleged to be a valid covenant, despite its apparent generality.	**Twenty-five-year covenant enforced, despite generality of the terms of the covenant.** The covenant, although unrestricted as to space, was not, having regard to the nature of the business and the limited number of the customers, wider than was necessary for the protection of the company. In general, restraints of trade will be unlawful, but there are exceptions. Restraints of trade may be justified where the restriction is reasonable with 'reference to the parties concerned and to the public'.
Trego v Hunt [1896] AC 7, HL	A business was carried on in partnership, with the understanding that when the partnership split, one of the parties would gain the goodwill of the partnership.	**The partner that it had been understood would not gain the benefit of the goodwill could be restrained from canvassing the clients of the former partnership.** The partner with the benefit of the goodwill was able to bring an injunction on the other partner to stop him from using the goodwill of the defunct partnership.
Haynes v Doman [1899] 2 Ch 419	A hardware manufacturer covenanted with its employee that he should not divulge any of the company's secrets, the mode of conducting business, or any information regarding the company and, after the termination of employment, work for or serve any other person or firm carrying on the same type of business within a radius of 25 miles from the company's factory. The employee left the firm and later joined a competitor 3 miles from the original employer. The original employer brought an action for breach of the restrictive covenant.	**The court granted the injunction in favour of the company, as the restriction on divulging confidential information or, after employment, working for the same kind of business within a 25-mile radius of the company was deemed necessary for the business and not unreasonable even though it was unlimited as to time.** The court also approved the principle of severance.

(Continued)

[1] Case summaries are arranged chronologically and cover both employment and non-employment cases. Many thanks to Caroline Watkins and Luke Hill who assisted in the preparation of these summaries.

Continued

Case name	Facts	Judgment
Henry Leetham & Sons Ltd v Johnston-White [1907] 1Ch 322, CA	The employee worked for several companies within a group. The business's area included the United Kingdom and Ireland. The employee agreed not to, in the United Kingdom, enter the service of any competing firms within five years from the termination of his employment. The restrictions were to be made as if with each company, and could be enforced by any of the group companies. The business he actually worked for was limited geographically to the North of England. On termination he took up work with a competitor.	**The covenant was deemed to be with the individual company that employed the employee. This meant that the geographical extent of the covenant was too great to be enforceable.**
Sir WC Leng & Co Ltd v Andrews [1909] 1 Ch 763, CA	The employee was a minor employed as a junior reporter for a provincial newspaper. Within his contract was a term that he would not, on leaving his position, work for or in conjunction with any newspaper business within a 20-mile radius of the town where the paper was based for an unlimited period in the future. The employee later entered into employment with another newspaper company.	**The restriction was wider than was needed in order to protect the business interests of the original employer not least because of its unlimited duration. Furthermore, the contract would have been unenforceable in any event as the employee was underage.**
Mason v Providential Clothing & Supply Co Ltd [1913] AC 724, HL	A canvasser for the respondents appealed against a decision by the Court of Appeal to enforce a covenant to restrict him from working with competitors for three years within 25 miles of London.	**The House of Lords considered the restriction wider than anything that could be reasonably required for the protection of the respondents' business and reversed the decision.** Lord Moulton took the view that the offending clause was not severable from the rest of the contract but in any case severance should only occur when the excess was not a main part of the substance of the clause.
Konski v Peet [1915] 1 Ch 530	The claimant employed the defendant at his tailor's business as a saleswoman. The covenants in her contract included not to solicit the claimant's customers and not to advertise that she had recently been in the claimant's employment. She went into business with another of the claimant's former employees and the claimant alleged that she had solicited his customers directly and used his name.	**As the covenant had no provision as to how long the restriction would last and prevented Miss Peet from soliciting customers who had ever dealt with the claimant employer, whether during her employment or not, the restriction was too wide and the claim was dismissed (Neville J).** It would be unreasonable to include customers who had dealt with the employer before and subsequent to the employee's employment.

Case name	Facts	Judgment
Gilford Motor Co v Horne [1933] Ch 935, CA	A managing director for a motor parts company was restricted by a non-deal covenant, specifying that the employee could not deal with 'customers or those in the habit of dealing with the company'. After leaving the company amicably on agreement he set up his own business in the same trade. The decision of the first instance judge was that the term was found ambiguous and too wide.	**The restraint of trade covenant applied only to customers of the company during Mr Horne's employment, and the covenant was therefore not too wide. The restriction was enforced.** Lord Hanworth MR saw no reason why two references to customers in the covenant could not be used and did not find the term ambiguous. Injunction granted.
Empire Meat Co v Patrick [1939] 2 All ER 85, CA	A manager in a butcher's shop appealed against a decision to enforce the covenant he had entered into on the grounds that it was too wide. The covenant was to restrain him from carrying on any butcher's business within 5 miles of the shop.	**Where a business is highly localized, regard must be had to the proved facts as to the area from which the customers come. As the original court had not considered this properly the appeal was allowed.** As the shop only traded to customers within a 2-mile radius, the 5-mile radius stipulated in the covenant was too wide.
Routh v Jones [1947] 1 All ER 758, CA	The defendant employee was employed by a partnership as a medical assistant and was restricted by a covenant preventing him from practising in any department of medicine or filling any professional appointment within a radius of 10 miles within five years after his appointment at the practice. Evershed J had previously ruled against the enforcement of this covenant because he found a defect in both branches of the restriction which went further than was necessary for the protection of the parties' interests.	**The covenant was invalid as a restraint of trade clause. It prevented Mr Jones from practising in areas which would not have caused detriment to Routh's practice (eg consultancy, or appointment as a medical officer of health).** Lord Greene MR commented that the party seeking the injunction has the burden of proving that special circumstances exist to justify the injunction.
Ronbar Enterprise Ltd v Green [1954] 1 WLR 815, CA	The claimant and defendant had been partners in the publication of a weekly newspaper. When the claimant bought the defendant out he sought to enforce the covenant restricting the defendant from competing with the business for five years. Roxburgh J found the covenant too wide and the words 'similar to or' relating to competing businesses were severed to make the provision enforceable. The defendant appealed on the grounds that the area restriction was too wide.	**The appeal was dismissed on the grounds that striking out the words did limit the area restriction, although not geographically. However, the strike out did limit the restriction to only those businesses that were in competition with the claimant. The covenant was sufficiently limited by this exclusion so as not to be too wide.**

(Continued)

Continued

Case name	Facts	Judgment
M and S Drapers v Reynolds [1957] 1WLR 9, CA	The employee worked as a draper. He covenanted with the employer not to canvass or solicit orders as a draper for any of the clients listed on the employer's books in the three years prior to the termination of his employment for a period of five years after the termination of the employment. The employee left the employment and carried on as a draper dealing with clients of his former employer. The employer tried to enforce the covenant.	**Taking into account the position and standing of the employee, the term of five years was so long as to be unreasonable.** The fact that the restriction will prevent the employee, a salesman, from selling goods to persons who were part of his trade connection before his employment began, and in relation to whom his knowledge was not acquired in the service of or at the expense of his employers, is a factor weighing against the validity of the restriction.
Kerchiss v Colora Printing Inks Ltd [1960] RPC 235	An employee of a manufacturer of flexographic inks was restrained from being employed by a manufacturer of any type of ink for three years in a wide area without consent which was not to be unreasonably withheld. In return, the employer remunerated him during this time. The employer had a substantial amount of goodwill over the area covered by the covenant.	**The court considered that the covenant was reasonable in its terms to protect the business of the employer from injury to the goodwill by reason of the former employee using confidential information.** Despite the provisions in the covenant it was not void or unenforceable. The provision for obtaining the employer's consent was included as a factor in support of the reasonableness of the covenant.
Plowman (GW) & Son Ltd v Ash [1964] 1WLR 568, CA	A salesman covenanted with his employer not to canvass those who were clients of the employer during his employment for a period of two years after termination of the contract of employment. After termination, the employee took up employment with a local competitor and called on two of his previous customers. The original employer sought an injunction to prevent this.	**The injunction was granted as the two-year covenant was reasonably needed in order to protect the legitimate business interests of the employer.** There was an implied term that the covenant applied to the type of goods that the employer dealt with. Further, the salesman could ask potential customers if they had been clients of the original employee before engaging with them.
Commercial Plastics Ltd v Vincent [1965] 1QB 623	The claimant company was involved in the production of PVC. It had specific knowledge and expertise in the process of sheeting PVC onto adhesive tape. An employee covenanted not to seek employment with any competitor in the PVC calendaring field for one year after termination of employment.	**The one-year non-compete covenant failed on two grounds. First, there was no geographical limit so it would be construed as prohibiting employment by any competitor in the world. Secondly, the company's specific expertise was regarding the process of sheeting PVC onto adhesive tape not PVC in general.** The covenants were thus too general to be enforced.

Case name	Facts	Judgment
Printers & Finishers Ltd v Holloway [1965] 1WLR 1	A former flock printers' works manager went to work for a competitor. The claimant sought to enforce a restrictive covenant relating to disclosure of information contained in its documents, any secret information gained from visiting its factory and information derived from the defendant's knowledge.	**Cross J granted an injunction against the new employer not to use any information relating to specific processes obtained by the defendant on his visit to the secret factory.** He observed that if trade secrets are likely to be taken from the employer by being carried around in the employees' heads, the proper way of protecting the employers' interest is to impose a covenant.
Gledhow Autoparts v Delaney [1965] 1WLR 1366, CA	The defendant was a 'traveller' salesman for the claimant company, with a wide sales territory comprising fourteen or so counties. He was bound by a covenant for three years after leaving the claimant's service not to solicit 'in the same class of goods in the area in which he had been operating'. His former employers were granted an interlocutory injunction to enforce this. The defendant appealed on the ground that the covenant went beyond what was necessary to protect the employers' interests.	**The three-year non-solicit covenant was too wide because it included persons whom the employee had never called upon during his employment as a salesman. The appeal was allowed.** This category of people could never be the subject of proprietary interest for the claimant because they had never done business with them. The large area covenant would not have been too wide if it had been the sole restriction.
Bull v Pitney-Bowes Ltd [1966] All ER 384	The claimant had been employed by the defendant company for a number of years and had been obliged to join a pension scheme that was at the outset of the employment non-contributory. The pension was held as a trust fund. The claimant retired at 45 having complied with the scheme. He was therefore entitled to a deferred pension on his normal retirement date. The rules of the pension stated that any retired member who was employed in any activity in competition with or detrimental to the defendant company's interests, and who failed to discontinue the activity when so required, would be liable to forfeit all his rights under the scheme. On retirement the claimant entered employment with a competitor and the defendant company informed the claimant that if he failed to stop he would lose his rights.	**Although the relevant provision was not a covenant or promise it was held that restraint of trade would apply to the trust as the pension rights were conferred under an employment contract.**

(Continued)

Continued

Case name	Facts	Judgment
Home Counties Dairies Ltd v Skilton [1970] All ER 1227	The employee (a milkman of one year's service) covenanted with the employer not to enter into employment with any other dairyman whilst in employment and also for a period of twelve months after the termination of employment not to sell any dairy product to anyone who had been a customer in the final six months of the employment once the employment had terminated. After termination of employment the milkman went to work for a competitor on the same milk round as before. The employer sought an injunction to restrain breach and damages due to the breach.	**The twelve-month restraint was upheld as it was not deemed too wide or unreasonable to be enforceable.** Even though the clause did not expressly refer to only restraining the employee in his trade as a dairyman it could be construed in this way. The twelve-month time limit was also not unreasonable.
White (Marion) Ltd v Francis [1972] 1WLR 1432, CA	The employee was a hairdresser. Within her employment contract was a covenant for a period of twelve months not to be employed by a ladies hairdresser in a half mile radius of the original employer. The employee was dismissed and joined a competitor 150 yards away. The original employer applied for an injunction. This was not granted. The employer appealed.	**On appeal it was held that the covenant was valid as the personnel of a hairdresser were important for the goodwill of the business. Even if the employee now worked as a receptionist, she was still in contact with the clientele and thus she will affect goodwill. It is reasonable for a company to protect its goodwill.**
Stenhouse Ltd v Phillips [1974] AC 391	The employee of an insurance company acted as managing director of two subsidiary companies. On giving in his notice, he set up in competition with his former employer. In the process of negotiating his resignation he signed a number of covenants relating to competition with the company. These included a five-year non-solicit clause, provisions to pay half of any money earned by competitive actions to the company and that the employee should not act as an insurance broker for any of the company's clients for a three-year period.	**The five-year non-solicit clause was in restraint of trade, but reasonable and so thus enforceable. The clause entitling the company to half of the remuneration gained by the employee and the three-year period of not acting for a client of the company were deemed unenforceable due to unreasonableness.** The five-year non-solicit clause was held to be enforceable because the court found it was a narrow restraint which left open a wide field of unrestrained competitive activity. It also only extended to a comparatively small number of clients with whom the employee had dealt directly. Finally, the period was a reasonable period during which the employer required protection as determined by the judge. Although the clause forcing payment to the company was not in restraint of trade, when read with the three-year restraint of trade, both became unenforceable for unreasonableness.

Case name	Facts	Judgment
Littlewoods Organisation Ltd v Harris [1978] All ER 1026	Littlewoods operated, in competition with another company, a mail order service. The defendant worked for Littlewoods in this business. The employee covenanted not to work for a competitor company for a twelve-month period after termination of the employment. The employee gave notice and informed Littlewoods that he would be accepting a position with the competitor company. Littlewoods sought an injunction.	**Littlewoods were entitled to protect themselves by a twelve-month non-compete provision as the defendant had confidential information about the business that would be detrimental were the employee to use it for the competitor.** The court should construe where possible the covenant as valid and enforceable. So even though the clause could be read so as to apply to the competitor's worldwide business it should be construed as referring only to the UK business.
Spafax v Harrison and Taylor [1980] IRLR 442, CA	The defendants were a branch sales manager and a salesman for the claimant which sells parts to the motor trade. Their contracts contained a confidentiality covenant (the enforcement of which was later abandoned by the claimant in the case of Mr Harrison) and a non-solicitation/dealing covenant which was enforceable for two years. Both covenants were found reasonably necessary restrictions for the protection of the claimant's legitimate trade interests, because of the measure of damage that the defendants could do at first instance.	**Both the restriction on confidentiality and that relating to customers were binding. A two-year non-solicitation/ non-dealing clause was binding as the circumstances were such that the defendants could do extensive damage to the trade interests of the company without it.** Because Mr Harrison's duties as a branch manager took him outside his own sales territory, what might seem to be a wide covenant was in fact necessary to protect the trade interests of the company. Injunction granted.
Bridge v Deacons [1984] AC 705, PC	A partner in a law firm in Hong Kong signed, as part of his partnership agreement, a covenant not to act as a solicitor in the province of Hong Kong, for any person that had been a client of the firm at any time in the previous three years, for five years after the termination of the partnership agreement. The partner worked for the period immediately prior to his retirement within a specialist niche of the firm and had nothing to do with 90 per cent of the firm's clients. He retired from the firm. The firm sought an injunction against him.	**The court held that the five-year restraint was enforceable.** The court needed to consider the legitimate interests of that business. As a firm of solicitors, the partners knew what was a reasonable time period for this type of restraint of trade. The covenant was upheld as it legitimately sought to protect the business interests of the firm.

(Continued)

Continued

Case name	Facts	Judgment
John Michael Design plc v Cooke [1987] ICR 445, CA	A shop fitters' firm enforced a covenant on the defendants restraining them from competing for two years after termination by doing business with any clients from the previous four years. The defendants set up a firm of design consultants and secured the business of a client of the claimant (Hornes). Hornes stated that they would not be using the services of the claimant in any event. Swinton Thomas J granted the claimants an injunction but excluded Hornes from its scope.	**The decision was reversed and Hornes was included in the scope of the injunction, as the employer was entitled to protection in respect of all clients who might cease to do business with them.** O'Connor LJ pointed out that when clients were proposing to transfer allegiance from the claimant to the defendant, this was exactly the type of case which the covenant was intended to protect the employer from.
Allied Dunbar (Frank Weisinger) Ltd v Weisinger [1988] IRLR 60	The defendant was a self-employed sales associate of the claimant company. The defendant sold his business to the claimant company covenanting not to be involved in a similar activity for two years post-termination. After a third party approached the defendant to employ him, the claimant company sought an injunction to enforce the covenant.	**The test to be applied to the two-year non-compete clause was that between vendor and purchaser, not the more stringent test between employer and employee. The issue was whether the covenant was more than was reasonably necessary to protect the claimant's interest.** In this case the claimant company could legitimately protect the goodwill of the business it had purchased by enforcing the covenants.
Spencer v Marchington [1988] IRLR 292	An employment agent was dismissed from an agency in Banbury and took a job with a new agency in Leamington Spa. She took one member of staff with her and the agency's best customer moved its business to her new agency. The agency counterclaimed for unpaid wages by alleging that she had breached the restrictive covenant which prevented her from conducting business within 25 miles of Banbury and 10 miles of Leamington Spa.	**A radius of 25 miles was found to be too wide based on the current customer list which encompassed around a 20-mile radius.** Mowbray J held that legitimate interests to be protected include trade connection with existing customers. He based this judgment on the actual customer list and not the one estimated by the defendant company when drafting the covenant.
Rex Stewart Jeffries Parker Ginsberg Ltd v Parker [1988] IRLR 483, CA	The managing director of an advertising agency was made redundant with a week's notice and received six months' pay in lieu of the notice period in his contract. A covenant in his contract restrained him from soliciting customers who 'to (his) knowledge is or has been a customer during (his) period of employment' for a period of eighteen months. The judge held that the claimant had not breached the terms of Parker's contract and that the covenant could be amended by deleting the words 'is or' and reference to associated companies so that the covenant was not too wide to be enforceable.	**The appeal was dismissed. The claimants' payment in lieu of notice was deemed to have terminated the contract properly. The restraint period of eighteen months was not too long given the influence Mr Parker had and opportunities to develop relationships with customers as managing director.** The judge had been entitled to sever parts of the covenant so as to leave standing the restriction on solicitation of the claimant's customers up to the time of Mr Parker's termination of employment.

Case name	Facts	Judgment
Dairy Crest v Pigott [1989] ICR 92, CA	A milkman was restrained from dealing with or solicitation of the dairy claimant's customers for a period of two years. This was enforced by an interlocutory injunction granted by Warner J because he felt that he was bound by case law. The defendant had argued that the period of two years was too long.	The decision was upheld that two years was in fact a reasonable time restraint, although the judge had erred in thinking that he was bound by case law; it was a question for the judge on the facts.
Hinton & Higgs (UK) Ltd v Murphy [1989] IRLR 519	Two former employees of the claimant, a company involved in health and safety consultancy services, were subject to an eighteen-month restriction in their contract on working for clients of the claimant. The contracts also contained clauses permitting modification of the restrictions if they were found void. The employer sought to enforce the restrictions.	The eighteen-month non-dealing covenant could be amended by removing the provision which meant that any past clients of the company would be within the terms of the restriction, as it was provided elsewhere in the contract that the parties had made a different version of it which could be applied if the covenant was found void. However, as there were no territorial limitations and clients of companies in the same group were included in the restriction, it was too wide in any case.
Clarke v Newland [1991] All ER 397, CA	Two GPs went into partnership with a covenant in the agreement 'not to practice in the practice area within three years of termination'. The defendant breached this by setting up practice as a GP within 100 yards from the claimant's surgery. In the first hearing the judge held that the covenant was unreasonably wide and dismissed the injunction application.	The covenant should be construed in the context to which it applied (namely medical practice) rather than generally. The appeal was allowed and the injunction granted. The Court of Appeal held that on the facts (ie as the claimant had been in practice for over forty years as a GP and both had worked together for six years) the covenant referred to practising as a General Medical Practitioner rather than practising in general.
Lansing Linde Ltd v Kerr [1991] ICR 428	The employee's contract contained a number of restrictive covenants, among them an undertaking not to compete with the employer during his employment or for twelve months after termination which had worldwide effect (although it did not apply to geographical areas where the business did not compete with the claimant employer or its associated companies). The defendant employee became managing director of a company in direct competition with the claimant employer. The employer started an action seeking an interlocutory injunction restraining him from competing against them by working for the competitor for the twelve-month period.	As a trial could not take place immediately, the period of restraint would have substantially expired if an injunction were granted. The strength of the argument put by the company should be considered. On the basis that a worldwide restraint would probably not have been upheld at trial, the injunction was not granted.

(Continued)

Continued

Case name	Facts	Judgment
Office Angels Ltd v Rainer-Thomas [1991] IRLR 214, CA	A branch manager and a consultant of an employment agency in the City of London had covenants in their employment contracts preventing them for a six-month period after termination of their employment from 'engage(ing) in or undertake(ing) the trade or business of an employment agency within a radius of 1,000 metres of the branch at which they had been employed'. Before the Court of Appeal it had been contended that the wording was wide enough to preclude the appellants from seeking to recruit any job-seekers or employer-clients from within the kilometre circle.	**The terms of the covenant restricting engagement with an employment agency for a 1,000 metre radius in the City of London for six months were deemed too wide and ambiguous to be reasonable.** The wording of the covenant was wider than necessary. A restriction which precluded the defendants, albeit for only six months, from opening an employment agency anywhere in an area of about 1.2 square miles, including most of the City of London, was not appropriate or necessary for the protection of the claimant's connection with its clients. Also the area restriction was not an appropriate form of covenant as it would do little to protect the claimant's connection with their clients as orders were placed over the phone. Further, a non-dealing/non-solicitation of clients covenant would have provided adequate protection. Additionally, the covenant did not extend to the temporary workers the agency placed as they were not referred to in the introductory words of the covenant which referred only to clients.
Mont (JA) (UK) Ltd v Mills [1993] FSR 577, [1993] IRLR 172	The employer paid a year's emoluments in exchange for the employee not working for a competitor company for one year as part of a severance agreement. The employee took up employment with a competitor and the employer sought to enforce the covenant.	**At first instance the one-year non-compete covenant was upheld. On appeal the decision was overturned and the appeal allowed.** The court should not 'whittle down the scope' of the covenant to grant more limited relief nor ensure that the employee be restricted by the covenant even though the covenant is unreasonable as there was no attempt to focus on the protection actually needed. Nor could the fact that the employee had been paid a year's money convert the clause into a garden leave clause— once the employment had ended there was no duty of fidelity which was the basis for a garden leave clause.

Case name	Facts	Judgment
Morris Angel & Son Ltd v Hollande [1993] ICR 71, [1993] IRLR 169	The employer of the defendant transferred the business to the claimant under TUPE 1981. The claimant immediately dismissed the defendant and applied to enforce the restrictive covenant contained in the defendant's contract with his former employer which prevented him from doing business with customers of the company for twelve months. Judge Laurie QC held in the High Court that the restriction only applied to customers of the former employer and not the claimant. The defendant appealed.	**The appeal was allowed. Dillon LJ held that the effect of TUPE 1981, reg 5(1) was to transfer the benefit and burden of contracts of employment and could therefore be read as referring to the transferee as the owner of the undertaking once the transfer had been made.** It followed that Morris Angel & Son could enforce the covenant if Mr Hollande did business with any persons who had done business with the undertaking transferred in the previous year.
Ingham v ABC Contract Services Ltd (Unreported, 12 November 1993)	The defendant, a recruitment consultant whose covenants prevented him for one year from soliciting or dealing with the company's clients and soliciting any employees, appealed against the grant of an injunction.	**The competitive nature of the business of the employer proved that they had a legitimate interest to protect in relation to both restrictions. In particular they have a legitimate interest in maintaining a stable, trained work force in what is acknowledged to be a highly competitive business.**
Hanover Insurance Brokers Ltd v Schapiro [1994] IRLR 82	The claimant covenanted with its employees that they must not solicit any employees of the company or the company's customers or clients for a period of twelve months after the termination of employment. Four of the employees left and set up in competition.	**The clause restraining solicitation of employees was held to be too wide to be enforceable. The clause was so wide that employees, irrespective of expertise or seniority and including those who were employed by the company after the employees had left the company, would be covered.** The covenants restraining the solicitation of clients would be enforceable and the argument of the chairman that it was unenforceable as it covered clients that he had brought with him was not upheld (*MS Drapers v Reynolds* [1957] 1 WLR 9 CA distinguished).
Austin Knight (UK) Ltd v Hinds [1994] FSR 42	A recruitment consultant who was employed by a competitor after being made redundant by the claimant company was alleged to be bound by a restraint of trade clause which prevented her from dealing with any of the claimant's customers including those she had never dealt with in the course of her employment.	**The covenant was unreasonably wide because it was not limited to customers of the branch where Ms Hinds worked.** The result of adhering to the restriction would mean that she would have been unable to take any employment in that field. This was supported by a lack of evidence of Ms Hinds' misconduct regarding confidential information and enticing customers away from Austin Knight.

(Continued)

677

Continued

Case name	Facts	Judgment
Living Design (Home Improvements) Ltd v Davidson [1994] IRLR 69	A promotions manager was restricted by a covenant in her contract not to be engaged as a principal or an employee by any business in competition with the petitioners for six months. The covenant included the words 'however (the termination) comes about and whether lawful or not'. Part of the agreement contained a clause which permitted modification of the restrictions if they were found.	**The court held that it was wholly unreasonable to include the words 'however (the termination) comes about and whether lawful or not' in the restriction.** Lord Coulsfield found that the offending part of the clause could not be severed because it seemed to be part of the main import of the clause. The interests of Living Design were nevertheless protected by other restrictions which were enforceable in the contract.
Kao, Lee & Yipv Edwards [1994] HKLR 232, HKCA	A salaried partner in a law firm was represented to the client body as a partner. The five-year restriction on solicitation in his contract of employment was tested according to whether the legitimate interest (being client connection) was protected and whether the covenant was too wide.	**Although the employee had the apparent status of a salaried partner, which indicated that a wider covenant could be imposed on him than that on an employee because of his regular contact with clients, in fact that was not the case and he was really an employee. Therefore, the stricter test applicable to employer/employee covenants applied and *Bridge v Deacons* [1984] 1 AC 705 could be distinguished.** The restriction was also too wide as the geographical area stipulated in the covenant was worldwide rather than confined to Hong Kong.
Poly Lina Ltd v Finch [1995] FSR 1	The company manufactured bin liners and plastic goods. By way of a contract of employment the employer prohibited disclosure of confidential information in respect of the business; a prohibition on soliciting the employer's customers for one year following termination of employment; and a prohibition on competing with the employer for one year following termination of employment. On receiving six months' notice the employee commenced similar employment as a market controller for a competitor. The original employer commenced proceedings for breach of the covenants.	**The employee's knowledge of the claimant's products could reasonably be expected to cause commercial damage. Information in the employee's knowledge was confidential and amounted to trade secrets. The attempt by the employer to protect the commercial information from being disclosed to competitors was justified.** The one-year timescale and the breadth of the covenants were both reasonable and thus enforceable.

Case name	Facts	Judgment
Marshall v NM Financial Management Ltd [1996] IRLR 20	Mr Marshall was a self-employed agent of an insurance company. He was paid purely on commission. A clause in his contract provided that if he had worked for a five-year period prior to resigning and did not go on to be employed by a competitor within one year or has attained the age of 65, he would continue to be paid commission for contracts he had instigated during his employment. Mr Marshall (after twelve years' employment with NM Financial Services) joined a firm of independent financial advisers. He claimed entitlement to ongoing commission, arguing that the clause amounted to restraint of trade.	**The proviso restricting payment of post-termination commission amounted to an unreasonable restraint of trade and was thus unenforceable.** There is no relevant difference between a contract that a person will not carry on a particular trade and a contract that if he does not do so he will receive some benefit to which he would not otherwise be entitled. The principles in relation to severance set out in *Sadler v Imperial Life Assurance Co of Canada Ltd* [1988] IRLR 388 upheld.
Alliance Paper Group plc v Prestwich [1996] IRLR 25	Upon the sale of a company a director (who was also previously a majority shareholder) was retained with restrictive covenants that he was not to, in competition with the company for a twelve-month period after termination of his employment, solicit clients and that for the same period he could not approach any member of staff of the company who had been employed during the last six months of his employment. Within six months of the termination of his employment he had set up in competition with the company. A number of staff resigned shortly afterwards. The company applied for an injunction enforcing the covenant.	**The employee was in breach of valid one-year restrictive covenants. As a previous shareholder, he was viewed as both a vendor and a person who had entered into a service contract.** The covenant on solicitation of employees was enforceable notwithstanding the decision in *Hannover Insurance Brokers Ltd v Schapiro* [1994] IRLR 82.
Credit Suisse Asset Management v Armstrong [1996] ICR 882, [1996] IRLR 450, CA	The claimant provided fund management services to private clients. The ten defendants who had previously been fund managers were placed on garden leave for their varying periods of notice. The employers discovered that the defendants were seeking employment with a competitive firm once their employment terminated, and sought to enforce the six-month restrictive non-competition clauses in their contracts. The defendants argued that their periods of garden leave should be set off against the covenant period.	**The provision of garden leave did not allow the courts to rewrite the restrictive covenant so as to be enforceable for a lesser period than the parties originally agreed.** Neill LJ refused to set off any of the garden leave time against the covenants as there was no basis for this action. It was considered that in cases where a long period of garden leave has already elapsed the court may dispense with protection based on a restrictive covenant, however, this did not apply in this case.

(Continued)

Continued

Case name	Facts	Judgment
Espley v Williams [1997] 1 EGLR 9, CA	The parties who were two estate agents in Christchurch, New Zealand set up a partnership with restrictive covenants restricting competition in a specific area, solicitation of clients, and use of name. The employee breached the non-compete restriction after leaving the partnership but gave an undertaking to be bound by the non-solicitation and use of name clauses. The employer sought to protect the goodwill, all of which he was entitled to by the agreement, by seeking an injunction. The employee appealed and argued that the non-compete clause was a covenant against competition rather than to protect a legitimate interest.	**Goodwill is a legitimate interest that the claimant is entitled to protect. A non-solicitation covenant does not necessarily provide such adequate protection of interests that adding a non-compete covenant would push the restriction beyond what is necessary. Appeal dismissed.** The original judgment was upheld; Henry LJ adding that even though combining a non-solicitation and non-compete restrictive covenant is customary in that industry, the court could find that certain combinations of these covenants would be beyond what is necessary to protect the employer's interests.
Dentmaster (UK) Ltd v Kent [1997] IRLR 636, CA	The claimant company imposed a six-month non-solicitation covenant and a non-compete covenant on the defendant, who was a technician skilled in removing dents from car bodywork. After termination of his employment it was found that he had been working for a customer of the claimant. The claimant asked him (via solicitors) to sign an undertaking not to breach the covenants but he refused. An interlocutory injunction was refused on the grounds of the non-solicitation clause being too wide because it included customers that Mr Kent had not dealt with personally.	**There was no requirement that there had to be a backward temporal limit on the employer's dealings with the customers.** The Court of Appeal allowed the appeal and granted the injunction.
Taylor Stuart & Co v Croft (Unreported, 7 May 1997, CA)	The claimant, a chartered accountants' firm, was seeking damages for the defendant's breach of a covenant in restraint of trade. The defendant, a salaried partner, was restrained from working for any client for three years after his employment. The issues in the case included whether the covenant was enforceable; if not, whether it was severable and if the defendant had in fact breached the claim by inserting the words 'I can be contacted as above' in a letter to a client. Finally a separate clause set out damages that were to be paid were the covenant breached—was this clause enforceable?	**The covenant was too wide to be enforceable as a whole but could be severed. The defendant was found to have breached the covenant by giving his address for contact. This was deemed to be solicitation because it was an invitation to contact him.** It was considered acceptable for the employee to give his address but the terminology used in the letter was indicative of proposing future contact. The clause setting out damages was not enforceable as it was a penalty.

Case name	Facts	Judgment
Scully UK Ltd v Lee [1998] IRLR 259, CA	The employee was a sales manager and engineer for the employer. The employee resigned and took a position with another engineering company. The original employer thought that the new position would put the employee in breach of his covenants, and an injunction was sought accordingly. The employee had covenanted not to be involved with overspill prevention or tank gauging equipment or any other business which competes for a twelve-month period, within the United Kingdom with the original employer. There was also a non-solicitation clause that prevented business between the employee and any client of the employer with whom the employee had had dealings, for two years after termination of the employment.	**On appeal both the twelve-month non-compete and the two-year non-solicit were found to be unenforceable.** Although the employee had gained confidential information that might aid the new employer, the wording of the covenants was too wide to be limited to direct competitors and so was unreasonable and thus not enforceable. It was not possible to sever the unenforceable parts. The non-solicitation clause was unenforceable as the two-year period was unreasonably long.
Dawney Day & Co Ltd v D'Alphen [1998] ICR 1068	The employees were brokers in European bonds. The employer was a securities business set up as a joint venture between the employees and the claimant. The employees subsequently left the employer having given three months' notice. The employees had agreed in the initial joint venture agreement not to compete with the joint venture business and not to solicit staff and clients from the joint venture company for a period of one year. The employees contended that these clauses amounted to unlawful restraints of trade. At first instance the judge held the clauses were enforceable.	**The Court of Appeal held that a party to a joint venture had sufficient interest to be allowed to enforce a restraint of trade against a fellow party to the joint venture even when that party was neither the employer or the purchaser of the business.** The court upheld the restraints as they protected a legitimate interest and were only wide enough in scope to protect that interest. In particular, although the non-compete referred to 'the business of Eurobond broking as carried on by the company from time to time', this drafting was not too wide even though it covered business which was done after the employees had left employment. Also, the restraint on solicitation of employees was enforceable since an employer's interest in maintaining a trained stable workforce was a legitimate interest to protect. Nor was the term 'senior employee' too uncertain to be enforceable.
CSFB v Padiachy [1998] IRLR 504	The defendants were employed by a company that was transferred under TUPE 1981 to the claimant. In the subsequent renegotiation of their contracts a three-month non-competition covenant was added. The defendants gave their notice shortly afterwards and the claimants sought to enforce the non-competition clause.	**The High Court refused the application. As the non-competition clause was added in negotiations as a result of the transfer, it was void under TUPE 1981 even though the employee was better off as a whole under the renegotiated contract.**

(Continued)

Continued

Case name	Facts	Judgment
		It was also unlikely that in addition to the covenants already imposed by their former contracts in respect of non-solicitation and a garden leave provision, the court would enforce a further restriction.
CSFB v Lister [1998] IRLR 700	The claimant bank appealed against a decision of Moore-Bick J to refuse an injunction to restrain the respondent from working with a competitor after he was transferred to them under TUPE. One of the terms of the new contract was not to be employed by a competitor for a period of three months after termination of contract and the respondent was remunerated significantly in shares worth £625,000 for agreeing to this. The respondent had begun working for a competitor before the three months had expired.	**The Court of Appeal dismissed the appeal because TUPE preserved all of his rights under his contract of employment with his former employer and the restriction introduced by variation to that contract was invalid.** Any restriction on these rights could not be enforced as a matter of public policy, despite Mr Lister being remunerated for having agreed to the restriction in his contract negotiations.
Polymasc Pharmaceuticals plc v Charles [1999] FSR 711	The defendant employee worked in a highly technical field of biochemistry. The employer company held a family of patents over a particular type of technology. The employee left to work for another company involved with the same type of technology, despite having covenanted that he was obliged to safeguard the company's expertise and would not take up competing employment for one year after termination of employment. The employer made out that the employee was not to be trusted in terms of safeguarding the secrets and applied for injunctive relief.	**Evidence showed that the employee was not to be trusted, so the employer had a right to request an injunction. Competing business was deemed a reasonable term in this case as any number of businesses could use the company's technology. It could be strongly argued that the new employment would breach a valid restraint of trade clause.** Injunctive relief was granted but the scope of the limitation was narrowed so as to limit the hardship conferred by the injunction on the employee.
TSC Europe Ltd v Massey [1999] IRLR 22	The defendant employee started a call centre company and subsequently sold on the business. He remained with the business as a key employee. He signed covenants that he would not solicit employees from the company for a period of three years after the date of the sale agreement or a period of one year after the termination of his employment. He would continue to receive payments after termination unless termination was due to serious misconduct. The defendant employee terminated his employment, started a competing company and three of the original company's employees joined him in the new company. The original company ceased payments and brought an action for breach of contract.	**The enforceability of a covenant agreed as part of a transaction for a business purchase as well as an employment situation should be considered in the context of the entire commercial bargain.** The court ruled that the clause restricting solicitation was unenforceable as it was an unreasonable restraint of trade. Whilst the stability of the workforce was a legitimate interest to protect, it restrained solicitation of employees without reference to their importance to the business or technical knowledge or experience and it applied to any employee who joined the business during the prohibited period, including those whose employment began after the defendant ceased to be an employee.

Case name	Facts	Judgment
FSS Travel and Leisure Systems Ltd v Johnson [1999] FSR 505, [1998] IRLR 382, CA	The employee was a computer programmer. Following a promotion, he signed a new contract containing a covenant which prevented him from joining any competing company for a twelve-month period after termination of his employment. The employee terminated his employment and took up employment with a competitor. The employer sought to enforce the restrictive covenant.	**The court would not uphold a covenant that had the sole purpose of protecting an employer from a former employee; there must be distinct subject matter in need of protection for the covenant to be enforceable, for example a trade secret.** General know-how of the employee could not be covered by a restraint of trade clause. The clause failed as the employer was attempting to limit the application of the employee's know-how and skill.
Turner v Commonwealth & British Minerals Ltd [2000] IRLR 14, CA	The employees worked for a mining and exploration company operating in the Soviet Union, mainly in Tajikistan. At the end of the employment the employees entered into a severance agreement. In exchange for payments they agreed not to be involved with any business which competes or is likely to compete with any business or project of the employer with which the employee was involved in the course of his employment for a twelve-month period. After leaving the employment, the employees set up on their own, doing a similar business, but outside the sphere of influence of the employer. The employees then started to develop in an area of Tajikistan that had been part of the employer's activities, but that was no longer. Payments were stopped by the employer and the employees sued.	**When determining the reasonableness of a restraint of trade, the fact that a party was paid something extra for agreeing to the covenant does not mean that the employer no longer has to justify the restraint but is a legitimate factor to be taken into account.** Here the restraint was held not to be unreasonable, and was therefore enforceable.
International Consulting Services (UK) Ltd v Hart [2000] IRLR 227	The defendant was employed as a consultant in the business of providing consultancy services in the telecoms sector. His contract contained a twelve-month covenant restraining dealings with customers including dealings with companies or persons who were in negotiation for the supply of services. In the course of his employment he sought to obtain a prospective customer's business for his own company and resigned shortly afterwards. His dealings with the customer were discovered and the claimant began proceedings to enforce the covenant. The defendant argued that as the customer was prospective rather than actual the claimant had no legitimate interest.	**The covenant was not too wide despite including customers with whom the ICS had 'negotiations', rather than actual customers. In this context the term meant more than just expressing an interest in using the claimant's business. The claimants legitimately regarded the connection as part of the goodwill of the business.** Because of Mr Hart's 'central and influential' position as a senior consultant he might have had input into a proposal for negotiations even if he had not actually been in contact with the customer. The High Court found for the claimant.

(Continued)

Continued

Case name	Facts	Judgment
Hollis & Co v Mark Richard Stocks [2000] IRLR 712	A solicitor was restricted from working within a 10-mile radius of the firm's office. He appealed, stating that the covenant meant that he was unable to work at all, rather than just in the capacity of working as a solicitor, and the covenant was therefore too wide.	**The covenant was considered objectively as part of the contract to establish its width. Other terms detailing specific tasks defined the meaning of 'work'. Appeal dismissed.** Aldous LJ found that as the rest of the employment contract was titled and referred to working as a solicitor only, and the covenant itself contained details of the type of work undertaken, the interpretation of 'working' meant 'as a solicitor' as it passed the officious bystander test.
Ward Evans Financial Services Ltd v Fox [2002] IRLR 120, CA	The defendants began the process of setting up a company while employed by the claimant. Both worked their notice period and left before the new company gained PIA authorization. While Mr Fox was in the course of working his notice period he visited a customer in the course of dealing who asked him when he would be coming again, to which he responded that he was leaving Ward Evans. As a result of this conversation the customer transferred their business to his new firm. The restrictive covenants in the defendants' contracts prevented them from having a material interest in any competitor company and inducing customers to cease dealing with the claimant. The first claim was dismissed in the High Court on the grounds that the new company had not been formed by the time the defendants left the claimant company.	**The Court of Appeal allowed the appeal. The fact that Mr Fox had a material interest in a dormant company did not mean that his ability to serve Ward Evans was unimpaired by his interest. Mr Fox and Mr Phillips failed to act in the best interests of the company and their interest in the new company was a strong factor in their failure to do so.** It follows that a material interest in a dormant company does breach this type of clause. The defendants were not found to have induced the customer to leave Ward Evans, owing to the nature of the conversation between Mr Fox and the customer.
Dranez Anstalt v Zamir Hayek [2002] I BCLC 693 (Evans-Lombe J); [2003] FSR 32, CA	A doctor who invented a ventilator appealed against a judgment which enforced a covenant that he would not compete in the business of manufacturing and selling ventilators while the investors (the claimant) were conducting that business. The covenant had been incorporated in a side letter to the initial agreement.	**As the case concerned developments in medical science, it should be considered whether it was in the public interest to superimpose contractual restrictions on invention that went further than the statutory restraints. It was judged by the Court of Appeal not to be and the restriction was found to be unreasonably wide.** The judge had not considered whether the additional restrictions on the patent which exceeded those imposed by Parliament were justified as reasonable. On consideration, it was found that they were not reasonable.

Case name	Facts	Judgment
Arbuthnot Fund Managers Ltd v Rawlings [2003] EWCA Civ 518	The employee was a senior member of staff working for a fund management company. The employment contract held that for a twelve-month period he would not solicit or deal with any person or organization that had been a client of the firm within the twelve months prior to termination. Employment was terminated, and the employer applied for injunctive relief. This was granted and the employee appealed on the grounds that the restriction went against public policy.	**The court must construe the restraints on an interim application where it could properly do so. In doing so it should consider the object sought to be obtained by the provisions and in this case the object was set out in the opening words of the restraint clause, namely to 'protect the goodwill, confidential information, trade secrets and business connections of the company'. It should then bear in mind what the parties had meant in the circumstances in which the agreement had been made.** The restraint was upheld but with a narrower scope.
Axiom Business Computers v Frederick (Unreported, 20 November 2003)	The defendant, a technical support director for a software firm in Scotland, applied for a recall of an interim injunction given in a judgment in which the claimant had enforced two restrictions, the first from working for a competitor for six months and the second from transacting with the claimant's customers for eighteen months.	**The court recalled the restriction on working for competitors because there was no territorial restraint and no definition of the type of market Axiom operated in.** However, it found that the second restriction was enforceable because it protected Axiom's goodwill and was not compromised by the fact that it did not contain a territorial limit or a backstop.
Peninsula Business Ltd v Sweeney [2004] IRLR 49	The employee's wages were made up nearly entirely of commission. The rules of employment allowed for payment of commission only if he was in employment at the end of the calendar month when commission would normally be payable. The employee resigned at the beginning of the month and brought a claim for outstanding commission. The employee argued that the employer could only rely on the rule if it was fairly brought to the employee's attention first, that the term was contrary to the Unfair Contract Terms Act 1977 (UCTA 1977), and that the term amounted to a restraint of trade.	**A clause which disallowed payment if an employee was no longer in employment will not be unfair under UCTA 1977 or an unlawful restraint of trade.** The commission scheme had been validly incorporated into the contract. It set out his entitlement and the limits of his rights and accordingly did not breach UCTA 1977. His employment imposed no restraint on with whom he might work or what he might do after leaving the employer and therefore was not a restraint of trade.
Corporate Express v Day [2004] EWHC 2943	A sales executive for office supplies covenanted not to misuse confidential information by agreeing not to work with major named competitors, referred to as 'National Accounts' by the company. This was for a period of six months and an additional non-solicitation clause (which was not disputed) was for a period of twelve months.	**Corporate Express's need for protection outweighed the defendant employee's financial loss. By agreeing not to disclose trade secrets she was not restrained from using her skill, experience, know-how, and general experience acquired during her former employment.**

(Continued)

Continued

Case name	Facts	Judgment
		The court found that despite being banned from dealing with named competitors the defendant was still able to deal with a wide range of clients and the clause was reasonable for the protection of the Corporate Express's interests.
		However, in view of the short time remaining to run on the relevant covenant and the fact that the defendant employee would lose her job if she could not work the balance of the six months, the covenant would not be enforced.
Hydra plc v Anastasi and others [2005] EWHC 1559	The claimant, a reseller in the data networking and security markets, claimed that Mr Anastasi had poached the second defendant (Mr Marsh) and some of its customers in breach of a non-solicitation covenant in his compromise agreement. The defendant contended that the non-poaching restriction was too wide as it applied to all employees in the claimant's workforce.	**The covenant not to entice employees away or to solicit customers was not too wide as there were only twelve employees in the company and as such Hydra was entitled to protect the stability of his workforce.** Had the workforce been greater the covenant should have made a distinction between certain types of employees so as to remain enforceable.
TFS Derivatives Ltd v Morgan [2005] IRLR 246	The defendant was an equity derivatives broker, employed by TFS. He specialized in the DAX market. The defendant gave his notice and served most of that notice on garden leave. The claimant learned that the defendant had accepted employment with a competitor company, on that company's new DAX desk. The defendant's original employment contract included a number of non-compete covenants, including that the defendant was not directly or indirectly 'for six months [to] undertake, carry on or be employed, engaged or interested in any capacity in any business which is competitive with or similar to a relevant business within the territory . . .'. The claimant issued proceedings for injunctive relief to enforce that covenant.	**The court ruled that it was appropriate to grant injunctive relief enforcing the covenant, except that the words 'or similar to' would be deleted.** The covenant was necessary to protect the legitimate interests of the company which were found to be client connection and confidential information of TFS. With the words 'or similar to' removed, the covenant was narrow enough to protect the interests of the company and be enforceable.

Case name	Facts	Judgment
Dyson Technology Ltd v Ben Strutt [2005] EWHC 2814 (Ch)	The claimant was part of a group of companies which developed and sold vacuum cleaners of an innovative design. The claimant was in particular responsible for research and development within the group. The defendant was an engineer employed by the claimant. He left to join Black & Decker, which amongst other things developed and sold vacuum cleaners. An interim injunction application to enforce a twelve-month non-compete was settled by undertakings, and its enforceability and whether it was appropriate to grant an injunction went to be considered at speedy trial.	**At trial, following the approach in *TFS Derivatives v Morgan* (above), the twelve-month restriction was enforceable and it was appropriate to grant an injunction enforcing it.** The phrases 'business', 'similar to', and 'involved with' were considered. Discretion whether to grant an injunction also considered and *Insurance Co v Lloyd's Syndicate* [1995] 1 Lloyd's Reports 272 at 276–277 applied.
Allan Janes v Balraj Kaur Johal [2006] ICR 742, [2006] IRLR 599	A solicitor upon leaving a firm had solicited clients despite a one-year non-dealing covenant. The firm obtained an injunction pending a speedy trial while the solicitor claimed that the non-dealing clause was too wide, despite it being limited to certain defined areas within a 6-mile radius and the dealing was described in the clause as 'doing the work of a solicitor' as well as 'practise'.	**At trial the clause was wide, but when it was made it was within the contemplation of both parties that Ms Johal, with the potential to become a partner later on in the course of employment, would be introduced to a wide range of clients and so was reasonable on that basis. The application for an injunction was granted.** The court also considered whether solicitors were a special case for whom the restrictions operated differently and found that they are not.
Thomas v Farr plc [2007] ICR 932, [2007] IRLR 419	The claimant was the former managing director of the defendant. The defendant was a firm of insurance brokers in a niche market. The claimant sought (amongst other things) declaratory relief in relation to the enforceability of a twelve-month restraint on the claimant working for a competitor in the same geographic area in which he had worked for the defendant. This issue was tried as a preliminary issue. At first instance the judge upheld the restraint. The claimant appealed to the Court of Appeal.	**The Court of Appeal held that the appeal should be dismissed. The time for considering whether there was a protectable interest in terms of confidential information was at the date the contract was entered into. The fact that the confidential information may be difficult to particularize does not mean there is no protectable interest and may support the enforcement of a non-compete. The fact that there were confidentiality and non-solicit clauses did not mean the non-compete was too wide given the difficulty in policing such provisions. A clause which prevented him from working in the niche market he had been engaged in and which was for a period of twelve months was justifiable on the facts.**

(*Continued*)

Continued

Case name	Facts	Judgment
Intercall Conference services Ltd v Steer [2007] EWHC 519 (QB)	The claimant's business was to provide conference calling, audio, video, web, and event conferencing. The defendant was head of training and personnel development. The defendant was subject to a non-compete preventing him from joining certain named competitors for a period of six months after the termination of his employment. The defendant's new employer was one of those competitors. The claimant placed the defendant on one month's garden leave and then sought to uphold the non-compete on an interim basis alleging that the defendant had access to its trade secrets and other confidential information. The defendant offered undertakings in respect of the confidential information (while disputing the extent to which he had access to it) and alleged that the role he would fulfil at his new employer would not be competitive and so the restriction did not protect a legitimate interest. Further, just before the hearing he made an open offer to work for a subsidiary of the named competitor rather than the competitor itself and to not deal with customers or conferencing.	It was first necessary for the court to consider whether the information sought to be protected was confidential such as requires protection as a legitimate interest. It was. Secondly, it must be established that the employee was exposed to such confidential information in the course of his employment. He was. Thirdly, that he is likely to be able to remember sufficient parts of it so that he could be said to take it with him. His seniority and experience meant that he would and, fourthly, the court found there was a risk of breach of the duty of confidentiality. Fifthly, the court considered whether the clause was no wider than is reasonably necessary for the protection of the employer's legitimate interests. It found that it was even though it prevented the employee working for the competitor in a non-competitive role and even though it was worldwide in its extent, it was necessary to prevent disclosure of confidential information. Finally, it considered whether as a matter of discretion it was reasonable to grant an injunction having applied the balance of convenience and other appropriate tests as set out in *American Cyanamid* [1975] AC 396. It was and, accordingly, an interim injunction was granted to trial.
Beckett Investment Management Group Ltd v Hall [2007] ICR 1539, [2007] IRLR 793	The claimants are a financial services group operating through a number of companies. The defendants were senior employees of the claimant acting as independent financial advisers to its clients. The claimants sought to enforce a twelve-month restrictive covenant restraining dealings with clients in relation to certain prohibited services. Certain construction points were decided in the court below—in particular that the terms deal and client should be given a natural construction to mean 'do business with' and 'someone for	**In relation to the construction of the clause, the Court of Appeal found that the only sensible approach was a wide construction which meant that the clause did protect the group's clients.** To do otherwise would defeat the purpose of the clause, place too much emphasis on the lack of reference to subsidiary companies and ignore the reality of group companies and big business. **The client base was a protectable interest and a restraint on dealing was appropriate especially in a small market where former clients**

Case name	Facts	Judgment
	whom for the time being the professional person is in any contractual relationship under which he is to provide some service' respectively and this was not disputed in the Court of Appeal. However, the judge's finding that the restrictions as drafted did not protect the correct entity in the group, but rather the holding company which had no actual dealings with the clients was contested. Additionally, he considered the reasonableness of a twelve-month non-dealing restraint.	would naturally gravitate to those they knew. Nor was the twelve-month period too long; the length of the restraint will always be arbitrary but here a twelve-month period could be justified having specific regard to the defendants' seniority and importance, to the evidence about business patterns, to the logistics of replacing them, and to the uncontradicted evidence of an industry standard of twelve months. The Court of Appeal also considered the principles applicable to severance and applied the test in *Sadler v Imperial Life Assurance Co of Canada Ltd* [1988] IRLR 388.
Extec Screens and Crushers Ltd v Rice [2007] EWHC 1043 (QB)	The claimant manufactures screening and crushing equipment and manufactures and supplies spare parts for the same. The defendant, by the time he left their employment, was an after sales manager. He had a notice period of three months but contended that he had been constructively dismissed and joined a company which supplied spare parts for machinery including crushing and screening machinery during the notice period. That employment was stopped by a without notice injunction until speedy trial a few weeks later. The claimant sought to enforce at speedy trial the notice period by way of a garden leave injunction and post-termination restrictions preventing him from competing, dealing or soliciting clients, interfering with suppliers, or employing or soliciting employees for a period of eight months.	The defendant's case for constructive dismissal, which was based on the claimant's reaction to his resignation (refusing to accept it, sending lawyer's letters to remind him of his obligations, changing his duties) failed. The claimant wanted the employee to stay and their behaviour after his resignation was proper and reasonable and certainly not in breach of any implied or express term. It was accepted that the defendant had confidential information and customer connections. The main argument related to whether the defendant's new employer was a competitor; the judge found that it was. He also found that the restrictions would follow on after the period of garden leave, making a period of restriction of eleven months in total but that this was justifiable in the circumstances and accordingly he made the injunctions sought.

(Continued)

Continued

Case name	Facts	Judgment
EE & Brian Smith (1928) Ltd v Hodson and others [2007] EWCA Civ 1210	The claimant is in the business of sourcing fruit, fruit juice, and vegetable products. The first defendant was an employee of the claimant and latterly a director who resigned and went to work for the third defendant. The second defendant is a former employee of the claimant who left at the end of the previous year and set up the third defendant in the May prior to the proceedings. The third defendant is a competitor of the claimant. After the claimant became aware of the diversion of a major supplier and attempted diversion of three customers to the third defendant and that the first defendant was working for the third defendant it sought an interim injunction based on the restrictive covenants in the first and second defendants' contracts of employment, save that the period of restraint in relation to one supplier was reduced to three months for the second defendant. These were in identical form and comprised a non-solicit and non-employ of key employees, and a non-deal and non-solicit of clients, prospective clients, and suppliers, all of which were for a period of twelve months. The judge granted an injunction in the form of the restrictions but in doing so took four weeks to deliver his judgment and a further two weeks to give reasons. He refused permission to appeal but permission to appeal was granted by the Court of Appeal.	**The Court of Appeal held that the judge's delay was unacceptable.** Further, the order granted was too wide as it did not reflect the variation agreement reducing the restraint on the second defendant to a period of three months. Although this was corrected when reasons were given, it led to uncertainty for the second defendant. Additionally, the restraints relating to confidential information did not sufficiently particularize the confidential information, and the provisions relating to clients and suppliers prevented the third defendant from satisfying contracts which had come into existence between the hearing and the injunction. **Finally, the balance of convenience by the time the judge made the order (as opposed to at the time of the hearing) was against the making of an interim injunction pending speedy trial, and that was certainly the case by the time the matter came before the Court of Appeal.**
Mantis Surgical Ltd v Tregenza [2007] EWHC 1545 (QB); [2007] All ER (D) 387	The claimant was a distributor of surgical equipment. The defendant was latterly field sales manager for the south of the United Kingdom. She resigned to join a manufacturer of surgical equipment which had previously distributed its equipment through the claimant but was now going to distribute its products itself. The claimant sought to enforce restrictive covenants contained in an	**The court rejected the defendant's argument that her contract of employment was with a company other than the claimant. The test was what a reasonable person would have thought at the time of entering into the agreement and all the evidence pointed to the fact that the defendant thought she was entering into an agreement with the claimant. The court upheld the restrictions. The legitimate**

Case name	Facts	Judgment
	employment contract and obtained an interim injunction enforcing twelve-month restraints on competing with the claimant in the areas with which she had been concerned and soliciting away clients to her new employer with whom she had had dealings and an unlimited restraint on disclosing confidential information. There was a trial to consider whether the injunction should be continued or discharged.	interests of confidential information and customer connection were ones the claimant was entitled to protect especially as it was a 'people'-based sales business. A twelve-month period of restraint was not too long even though there was no regular contract renewal and nor in this case was it fatal to the enforceability of the confidentiality clause that it was unlimited in time. Finally, relief would not be refused on an equitable basis—although there had been some misrepresentation of the facts at the without notice application by the claimant it was not serious enough to prevent relief being granted.
Advantage Business Systems Ltd v Hopley [2007] EWHC 1783 (QB)	The claimant was a seller of IT related services and products including financial software. The defendant was a business consultant tasked with selling certain of these products on behalf of the claimant. The defendant had twelve-month no dealing with and solicitation of clients and prospective clients restrictions, who were defined by reference to the defendant's personal dealings with them. The contract also contained a liquidated damages clause which stated that £10,000 should be paid by the defendant to the claimant for each breach of the covenants. Prior to the defendant's resignation a lead was generated by the claimant for a potential customer. The defendant had no dealings with the potential customer but an appointment was made for him to visit them. Before he could do so the defendant resigned and joined a competitor. In his new employment he contacted the potential customer and had a meeting with them. The claimant's representative also turned up at the meeting and so he and the defendant presented jointly. The claimant alleged this was breach of the restrictive covenants and sought to enforce them.	The first issue considered by the court was whether in this case the lead could be considered a prospective customer for the purpose of the restrictions. The court found as a matter of fact that in this industry the parties considered prospective client meant a client or customer with whom there was a high degree of likelihood of winning business in the near future (although the judge would have been persuaded by a wider definition). On the facts the lead never satisfied the definition. This was backed up by the claimant's own internal paper work. The judge went on to consider (*obiter*) whether the claimant had a legitimate interest to protect and concluded that it did, which was the developing business contacts. He also held on the same basis that the covenants were reasonable.

(Continued)

691

Continued

Case name	Facts	Judgment
New ISG Ltd v Vernon and others [2008] ICR 319, [2008] IRLR 115	Interim hearing of applications by the claimant, a specialist recruitment company, to continue injunctions granted without notice to prevent the defendants from soliciting, canvassing, or dealing with any client, applicant, and/or temporary worker of the claimant. The claimant was in administration and the main point taken by the defendants was that their objection to their transfer to the claimant pursuant to regulation 4(7) of TUPE 2006 meant that they were not bound by any of the restrictive covenants. The claimant contended that the objection was not valid because of the timing of it (after the transfer) and whether it could be said to be a valid objection at all.	**Regulation 4(7) of TUPE 2006 should be given a purposive interpretation which means that an objection can occur before or after the transfer. In the alternative, the claimant was estopped from relying on the late objection because of its breach of its obligations in relation to the transfer. In this case** there was a valid objection and the defendants were not, therefore, bound by the restrictive covenants. In any case, the balance of convenience would not favour the continuation of the injunctions, one factor being taken into account being the delay of the claimant.
Greck v Henderson Asia Pacific Equity Partners (FP) LP and others [2008] CSOH 2; (2008) 15(6) ELA Briefing 95	The claimant was an employee of a fund management group based in Singapore. As part of those arrangements and in order for him to benefit from the profits on certain of the funds which he managed, he was also a partner in a limited partnership. On leaving, the claimant went to join another fund manager based in Australia. As a result he was declared a bad leaver under the terms of the limited partnership agreement and as a result his share of the profits from the fund was reduced to zero. The court was asked to consider whether under the arrangements the claimant was a bad leaver, including whether the bad leaver provisions were in restraint of trade.	The Court of Session held that the claimant was a bad leaver on a correct construction of the documents. It refused to consider the question of whether the bad leaver provision was in restraint of trade as the argument was raised late in the day and the defendants did not have proper opportunity to call evidence on the issue. **However, the judge indicated that the following would be relevant: one would need to consider whether the limited partnership agreement should be read with the contract of employment (which was not in evidence in this case) and treated as one transaction. This may give rise to difficulties where, as here, the parties to each of the documents are different; if the limited partnership agreement is looked at in isolation, the judge foresaw difficulties in simply severing the bad leaver provisions as other employees and investors were party to it and it would significantly alter the deal that had been done. Finally, the judge considered that application of the restraint of trade doctrine to a multi-party agreement was inappropriate—the different factual circumstances meant that a clause may be enforceable against one and not against the other which would not make commercial sense.**

Case name	Facts	Judgment
BFS v Fox [2008] All ER (d) 400	The claimant sought at the interim stage to enforce six-month nationwide restrictions on competition and solicitation of and dealing with clients against a salesperson. The legitimate interest it put forward was confidential information. The defendant contended that she would not be in competition and gave undertakings not to disclose confidential information.	**The court held that the defendant only had local confidential information and accordingly a nationwide provision preventing the defendant from working for a competitor could not be justified.** However, the court would require the undertaking in relation to confidential information already offered and further undertakings in respect of soliciting of and dealing with clients.
Duarte v Black & Decker Corp [2007] EWHC 2720 (QB), [2008] 1 All ER (Comm) 401	The claimant was a senior employee of the second defendant and resigned his employment on three months' notice to take up employment with a competitor. The defendants threatened an injunction to prevent him doing so based on restrictions of two years' duration contained in a long-term incentive plan which purported to prevent him from working for named competitors and inducing employees of the defendant group to leave their employ. The restrictions were subject to the law of Maryland in the United States. The claimant sought a declaration that the restrictions were unenforceable. The court considered the enforceability of the restrictions under English law as well as determining conflict of law issues relating to the choice of the law of Maryland to govern the restrictions (in relation to which see Chapter 7).	The judge decided under UK law (*obiter*—he also found the restrictions to be unenforceable under the law of Maryland) that although the claimant had access to confidential information and that was a sufficient legitimate interest to justify a non-compete restriction, in this case the restriction was not reasonable. **In particular the duration of the restriction was too long and other cases where a two-year restriction was upheld were not helpful.** The no poaching of employees restriction also sought to protect a legitimate business interest but was **too wide to be reasonable as the definition of employees included all 25,000 of the defendant group's employees, irrespective of where they were located, their role or seniority.** In neither case was it possible to sever any part of the provision to make it enforceable.
Wrn Ltd v Timothy Mark Ayris [2008] IRLR 889	The claimant, which provided services to the broadcasting industry, obtained an interim injunction by way of undertaking enforcing restrictions on solicitation and dealing with customers against the defendant who was at the termination date head of sales and marketing. The issues to be decided at trial were whether the restrictions were those contained in a leaving agreement or those in the original contract of employment signed in 1999 when the defendant was in a more junior position, and the reasonableness of those restrictions.	The court decided that the restrictions in the leaving agreement were not enforceable due to lack of consideration. **The enforceability of those contained in the original employment contract was to be considered by reference to the time they were entered into. Accordingly, the fact that the defendant had subsequently been promoted was irrelevant. The restrictions on dealing and solicitation were not enforceable solely on the basis that they were not limited to customers with whom the defendant had personal dealings.**

(Continued)

Continued

Case name	Facts	Judgment
Norbrook Laboratories (GB) Ltd v Adair and others [2008] IRLR 878	The claimant was a pharmaceutical company specialising in products for vets. The first defendant was employed as a salesperson with responsibility for the north west of England. The second defendant was a competitor of the claimant and the new employer of the first defendant. The claimant sought to enforce a confidentiality clause and post-termination restrictions consisting of a twelve-month non-compete and a twelve-month non-dealing with/solicitation of clients clause against the first defendant and to prevent the second defendant from inducing breach of the same. Relief had been granted on an interim basis and this was the hearing in relation to final relief.	**There was found to be a protectable interest in the form of the claimant's customer-related confidential information. However, the non-compete was found to go further than was reasonably necessary to protect that interest as it turned on an overlap between the products the first defendant had dealt with in the last five years and the products she would deal with when employed by the second defendant.** The non-solicit/non-deal provision was enforceable once its scope had been narrowed by the blue pencil. Final injunctions granted accordingly.
Basic Solutions v Sands [2008] EWHC 1388 (QB)	The claimant is a supplier of chemical based products and was in the process of tendering to Network Rail in relation to one of its products to deal with the 'leaves on the line' problem. The defendant resigned on six months' notice. The defendant worked three months of his notice and then went on sick leave. Two days before the expiry of his notice period he started work for a company which was also tendering to Network Rail in relation to a product designed to deal with leaves on the line. The claimant sought to enforce by way of injunction express terms in the contract in relation to working for an entity which dealt with similar products or services or dealing with and soliciting customers in relation to certain products for twelve months. Additionally it relied on the implied duty of confidentiality to prevent the defendant from going ahead with the tender process. The tendering process was such that the granting of an interim injunction was likely to be determinative of the issues between the parties.	The judge refused to uphold the restrictions as the definition of relevant products and services did not cover samples which were all that had been provided to Network Rail during the relevant time by the claimant. **He also held that the twelve-month period was too long notwithstanding the long lead time for tender processes such as this.** Further, he found that the defendant was not in breach of the duty of confidentiality. The defendant's product was on their unchallenged evidence based on different constituents and no confidential information had been passed to the chemist who created it. The defendants offered to allow the court to consider on a confidential basis a comparison of the two products but the claimant refused. The claimant's case was mainly based on assertion and was an attempt to stifle competition. There was no confidentiality in the tender process itself. **Further there was a public interest in ensuring that the leaves on the line problem was sorted in the most effective manner and this was not counterbalanced in this case by the legitimate interests of the claimant.** Injunctions refused.

Case name	Facts	Judgment
Kynixa v Hynes and others [2008] EWHC 1495 (QB)	The claimant was a company which provided rehabilitation services to victims of accidents. The first two defendants were senior employees who were bound by the terms of a shareholder agreement. The claimant sought to enforce the restrictive covenants in the shareholders' agreement against the first two defendants (in addition to various other claims against all the defendants). They consisted of a twelve-month non-compete drafted in wide terms and restrictions of the same length on the solicitation of clients and employees.	The court held that all the restrictive covenants were enforceable. **The claimant had a legitimate interest to protect its confidential information and despite the fact there were shorter, narrower restrictions in the employment contracts, and the fact that the clauses could be read to bind a very wide category of employee, even the putative cleaner, the court considered them enforceable.** Nor would the lesser restraints on solicitation mean the non-compete was unenforceable—the difficulties in policing such provisions meant that the non-compete was justified.
Personnel Hygiene Services Ltd v Mitchell [2009] EWCA Civ 1047	The claimant was the purchaser of shares from, amongst others, the defendant. Under the share purchase agreement, the defendant agreed to lengthy post-termination restrictions. A few weeks later his employment with the purchased company ended and he entered into a compromise agreement which also contained post-termination restrictions of a much shorter duration. It also contained an entire agreement clause. At first instance, the court held that the fact of the entire agreement clause meant that the claimant could only rely on the much shorter restrictions in the compromise agreement. The claimant appealed.	**The Court of Appeal held that taking into account the terms of the share purchase agreement, the compromise agreement and the service agreement of the defendant, which was not before the court below, the entire agreement clause did not apply to exclude the restrictions in the share purchase agreement.** The service agreement and share purchase agreement had existed together prior to the compromise agreement being executed and the compromise agreement made specific reference to the restrictive covenants in the service agreement being superseded but did not refer to those in the share purchase agreement. Further it could not have been intended that the compromise agreement would supersede all the terms of the share purchase agreement, some of which were plainly intended to continue.

(Continued)

Continued

Case name	Facts	Judgment
Swift Technical Group Holdings Ltd and others v Mulcahy [2009] EWHC 1485 (QB)	The first, second, and, third claimants were part of a group of companies whose business is sourcing and placing personnel in the oil and gas industries around the world. The fourth claimant was a major investor in the third defendant. The defendant was a shareholder in the group and also a director, initially in an executive role, but latterly non-executive involving only one day's work per month. The defendant also loaned the claimants some significant funds in 2008. He resigned his non-executive directorship in May 2009 but retained his shareholding and financial interest in the group. The defendant, during his directorship (and previous employment) with the knowledge of the claimant group, had an interest in and was a director of a non-competitive recruitment company which operated in Kazakhstan. In March 2009 it ceased to be non-competitive. In addition to alleging breaches of the defendant's duties as a director, the claimants sought an injunction based on a non-compete provision which was in an investment agreement relating to the defendant's shareholding and which applied for twelve months after the defendant ceased to be an employee of the claimant.	**The investment agreement was only intended to apply to executive employment (and the termination of the same) and not the termination of a non-executive directorship. Accordingly, the restriction in the investment agreement had expired as it was more than twelve months after the termination of the defendant's executive employment. In any case the restriction would be too wide and the balance of convenience was in favour of not granting the relief sought but the court did make an order restraining the defendant from disclosing the confidential information of the claimant.**
Thermascan v Norman [2009] EWHC 3694 (Ch)	The claimant company provided services to customers using infrared technology. 70 per cent of their business was repeat business. The claimant was an employee, director, and shareholder of the claimant. His contract of employment contained a restriction on the disclosure of information, a six-month restraint on the solicitation of customers and an obligation to deliver up all property of the company on termination. The defendant resigned his employment and his directorship to commence employment in a competitive role. Over the next few months the defendant solicited clients in a way that appeared to use the confidential	**As the contractual restraint on solicitation had expired, the claimant attempted to base its claim on the defendant's fiduciary duties as a director. The court dismissed its argument on the facts—there were no maturing business opportunities in this case. Further, the balance of convenience was against the granting of interim relief in the form sought. That restraint had previously expired four months previously. In the meantime the claimant had been taking steps to establish his new business. The balance had moved in favour of the defendant by the public interest in competition.**

Case name	Facts	Judgment
	information of the claimant (date of renewal, price for survey). The claimant applied for an injunction to restrain this solicitation of clients, the use of confidential information and for the defendant to deliver up the claimant's property together with an affidavit. At the first hearing the defendant gave undertakings in the form requested save that the solicitation restraint was only for a six-month period. Subsequently he delivered up some confidential information of the claimant, the restraint on solicitation expired and the defendant was made redundant. He was then attempting to set up his own business. The claimant applied for the continuation of the undertakings, including the non-solicitation restraint until trial. The defendant had offered to continue the restraint on the disclosure of confidential information.	
Keegan v Newcastle United Football Co Ltd [2010] IRLR 94	The claimant alleged constructive dismissal against the defendant and also sought an order that a clause limiting his damages claim under the contract should not apply. In particular, he alleged that as payment under the liquidated damages clause also restrained him for a period of six months from working for any Premier League club in any capacity, the restraint and the liquidated damages clause were in unlawful restraint of trade. He also alleged the liquidated damages clause was unenforceable as a penalty. The case was heard in private before the Premier League Manager's Arbitration Tribunal but the decision was published with the agreement of the parties.	The claimant's case for constructive dismissal was upheld. However, he was only entitled to the liquidated damages under the contract not an unlimited claim for damages. **The six-month restraint was not an unlawful restraint of trade. Even if the claimant joined another Premier League club in a capacity other than manager, he would be of value and it would be to the detriment of the defendant. He had information about the defendant which would also be useful to another Premier League team. The restriction was limited to UK Premier League teams, it was only for six months and it would not stop him *looking* for another job with a Premier League team. The clause was not unenforceable as a penalty. In this case it was almost impossible to come up with a genuine pre-estimate of loss and in so far as it was possible to do so, the clause was a reasonable pre-estimate.**

(Continued)

Continued

Case name	Facts	Judgment
Tullett Prebon plc and others v BGC Brokers LP and others [2010] IRLR 648	The claimant, an interdealer broker, sought and obtained springboard relief against the defendants, the relevant ones for the purposes of this summary being a competitor interdealer broker ('BGC'), and various brokers recruited by BGC to join it (the 'broker defendants'). Much of the trial concerned the claim of conspiracy against the BGC and two of its senior employees, and the constructive dismissal claims of the broker defendants but the court also considered the enforceability of restrictive covenants and clawback provisions in the claimant's employment contracts with the broker defendants. The restrictive covenants were restraints on competing with the business, soliciting, enticing, or inducing a client to transfer their business and soliciting or accepting business from a client all for a period of six months. The clawbacks were of retention payments and discretionary and performance bonuses and triggered by the broker resigning, ceasing to be actively performing his or her duties, working under notice of termination or if the employment of the broker was terminated by reason of his or her gross misconduct.	**The court held in relation to the restrictive covenant restraining competition that the fact that there was only a limited express provision for set off of garden leave did not affect its enforceability—any necessary adjustment between garden leave and the term of the restrictive covenants could be made by the court.** Further as non-solicit and non-deal clauses were notoriously difficult to police a non-compete was appropriate. A six-month period was no more than is reasonable in this business where broker/trader relationships were found to be very important. Subject to some small drafting points which were dealt with by the blue pencil, the non-solicit/non-deal provisions were also upheld. In particular the definition of client was held not to be too wide because it covered both clients for whom the broker was primarily responsible and also those clients for whom the broker provided cover. **The clawbacks were also upheld: they were not in restraint of trade, they did not affect the employees' ability to work after leaving. They were substantial sums paid to highly paid employees as a reward for loyalty. Nor were they penalties; the law relating to penalties was wholly inapplicable as they were not sums payable as a result of the employee's breach, rather repayment of sums paid to ensure loyalty.**
Phoenix Partners Group LLP v Maurice Asoyag [2010] EWHC 846 (QB)	The claimant provides broking services in a range of financial products including equity derivative products. The defendant was a broker in equity derivative products employed by the claimant. He resigned and gave three months' notice and was duly placed on garden leave during his notice period. He commenced work for a competitor broker the day after his garden leave expired, to broker an equity derivative product albeit not the one with which the claimant currently dealt. The claimant sought undertakings in the form of post-termination restrictions contained in the defendant's contract and the duty of confidentiality. The	**The main issue for the judge to determine was whether the defendant was competing, as the product which he was to broker was not one with which the claimant dealt at the time of the hearing. As a result of the defendant leaving, the claimant had only been able to do a negligible amount of trade in that product although it was trying to recruit a successor. The judge held that on the construction of these restrictive covenants, this meant the defendant was not in breach and so the injunction should be discharged.** Nor was the claimant able to establish a breach of the duty of confidence on the defendant's part. Although it was not

Case name	Facts	Judgment
	broker refused to give them so the claimant applied for injunctive relief which was granted. The claimant only had very short notice of the application. The restrictions consisted of a six-month non-compete and six-month restrictions on dealing and soliciting clients and prospective clients. The defendant applied to discharge the injunction with the period of garden leave to reduce the duration of the restrictions.	necessary for the purposes of his judgment, the judge found that the restrictions would probably be enforceable, but also that damages would have been an adequate remedy for the claimant, whereas if the injunction was discharged at trial the damage suffered by the defendant was far less easy to quantify.
Associated Foreign Exchange Ltd v (1) International Foreign Exchange (UK) Ltd, and (2) Abassi [2010] EWHC (Ch) 1178	The claimant's business was trading in foreign currencies. The second defendant was employed by the claimant as an account executive. The second defendant was placed on three months' garden leave by the claimant after some alleged impropriety with client funds. The second defendant was engaged to start work by the first defendant around the time of the expiry of his garden leave. The first defendant is a trade competitor of the claimant. The claimant sought an injunction to enforce the terms of the second defendant's post-termination restrictions which were a six-month non-dealing covenant and a twelve-month non-solicitation covenant. Undertakings were given in respect of the non-dealing covenant and the hearing concerned only the enforceability of the non-solicitation covenant.	**The judge considered the enforceability of the non-solicit covenant and found that a twelve-month period of restraint went beyond what was necessary to protect the legitimate interests of the claimant. In doing so he considered what was a reasonable time during which the claimant was entitled to protection and took into account the fast moving and competitive nature of the foreign exchange market, and found that anything more than a six-month restriction would be objectionable.** The second defendant was also found to be in breach of the post-termination restrictions prior to the hearing but there was not sufficient evidence to support a finding that the first defendant had procured the breach. However, the judge did state that if the non-solicitation covenant had been enforceable he would have been minded to grant a *quia timet* injunction against the first defendant.

INDEX